Database Marketing

Series Editor
Jehoshua Eliashberg
The Wharton School
University of Pennsylvania
Philadelphia, Pennsylvania USA

Books in the series
Blattberg, R., Kim, B., Neslin, S.
Database Marketing: Analyzing and Managing Customers

Ingene, C.A. and Parry, M.E.
Mathematical Models of Distribution Channels

Chakravarty, A. and Eliashberg, J.
Managing Business Interfaces: Marketing, Engineering, and Manufacturing
  Perspectives

Jorgensen, S. and Zaccour, G.
Differential Games in Marketing

Wind, Yoram (Jerry) and Green, Paul E.
Marketing Research and Modeling: Progress and Prospects

Erickson, Gary M.
Dynamic Models of Advertising Competition, 2nd Ed

Hanssens, D., Parsons, L., and Schultz, R.
Market Response Models: Econometric and Time Series Analysis, 2nd Ed

Mahajan, V., Muller, E. and Wind, Y.
New-Product Diffusion Models

Wierenga, B. and van Bruggen, G.
Marketing Management Support Systems: Principles, Tools, and Implementation

Leeflang, P., Wittink, D., Wedel, M. and Naert, P.
Building Models for Marketing Decisions

Wedel, M. and Kamakura, W.G.
Market Segmentation, 2nd Ed

Wedel, M. and Kamakura, W.G.
Market Segmentation

Nguyen, D.
Marketing Decisions Under Uncertainty

Laurent, G., Lilien, G.L., Pras, B.
Research Traditions in Marketing

Erickson, G.
Dynamic Models of Advertising Competition

McCann, J. and Gallagher, J.
Expert Systems for Scanner Data Environments

Hanssens, D., Parsons, L., and Schultz, R.
Market Response Models: Econometric and Time Series Analysis

Cooper, L. and Nakanishi, M.
Market Share Analysis

Robert C. Blattberg, Byung-Do Kim and Scott A. Neslin

Database Marketing

Analyzing and Managing Customers

 Springer

Robert C. Blattberg
Kellogg School of Management
Northwestern University
Evanston, Illinois, USA
and
Tepper School of Business
Carnegie-Mellon University
Pittsburgh, Pennsylvania, USA

Byung-Do Kim
Graduate School of Business
Seoul National University
Seoul, Korea

Scott A. Neslin
Tuck School of Business
Dartmouth College
Hanover, New Hampshire, USA

Series Editor:
Jehoshua Eliashberg
The Wharton School
University of Pennsylvania
Philadelphia, Pennsylvania, USA

Library of Congress Control Number: 2007936366

ISBN: 978–1–4419–0332–7 softcover
ISBN: 978–0–387–72578–9 hardcover
e-ISBN: 978–0–387–72579–6 ebook

Printed on acid-free paper.

To Our Spouses and Families

Preface

The confluence of more powerful information technology, advances in methodology, and management's demand for an approach to marketing that is both effective and accountable, has fueled explosive growth in the application of database marketing.

In order to position the field for future advances, we believe this is an opportune time to take stock of what we know about database marketing and identify where the knowledge gaps are. To do so, we have drawn on the rich and voluminous repository of research on database marketing.

Our emphasis on research – academic, practitioner, and joint research – is driven by three factors. First, as we hope the book demonstrates, research has produced a great deal of knowledge about database marketing, which until now has not been collected and examined in one volume. Second, research is fundamentally a search for truth, and to enable future advances in the field, we think it is crucial to separate what is known from what is conjectured. Third, the overlap between research and practice is particularly seamless in this field. Database marketing is a meritocracy – if a researcher can find a method that offers promise, a company can easily test it versus their current practice, and adopt the new method if it proves itself better.

We have thus attempted to produce a research-based synthesis of the field – a unified and comprehensive treatment of what research has taught us about the methods and tools of database marketing. Our goals are to enhance research, teaching, and the practice of database marketing. Accordingly, this book potentially serves several audiences:

Researchers: Researchers should be able to use the book to assess what is known about a particular topic, develop a list of research questions, and draw on previous research along with newly developed methods to answer these questions.

Teachers: Teachers should find this book useful to educate themselves about the field and decide what content they need to teach. We trust this book will enable teachers to keep one step ahead of their students!

Ph.D. Students: Ph.D. students should utilize this book to gain the required background needed to conduct thesis research in the field of database marketing.

Advanced Business Students: By "advanced" business students, we mean undergraduate and MBA students who need a resource book that goes into depth about a particular topic. We have found in teaching database marketing that it is very easy for the curious student to ask a question about topics such as predictive modeling, cross-selling, collaborative filtering, or churn management that takes them beyond the depth that can be covered in class. This book is intended to provide that depth.

Database Marketing Practitioners: This group encompasses those working in, working with, and managing marketing analytics groups in companies and consulting firms. An IT specialist needs to understand for what purpose the data are to be used. A retention manager needs to know what is "out there" in terms of methods for decreasing customer churn. A senior manager may need insights on how to allocate funds to acquisition versus retention of customers. A statistician may need to understand how to construct a database marketing model that can be used to develop a customer-personalized cross-selling effort. An analyst simply may need to understand what neural networks, Bayesian networks, and support vector machines are. We endeavor to provide answers to these and other relevant issues in this book.

While it is true that database marketing has experienced explosive growth in the last decade, we have no doubt that the forces that produced this growth – IT, methods and managerial imperatives – will continue. This book is based on the premise that research can contribute to this growth, and as a result, that database marketing's best days are ahead of it. We hope this book provides a platform that can be used to realize this potential.

One of the most important aspects of database marketing is the interplay between method and application. Our goal is to provide an in-depth treatment of both of these elements of database marketing. Accordingly, there is a natural sectioning of the book in terms of method and application. Parts II–IV are mostly methodological chapters; Parts I, V, and IV cover application. Specifically, we structure the book as follows:

Part I: Strategic Issues – We define the scope of the field and the process of conducting database marketing (Chapter 1). That process begins with a database marketing strategy, which in turn leads to the question, what is the purpose and role of database marketing (Chapter 2)? We discuss this question in depth as well as two crucial factors that provide the backdrop for successful DBM: organizational structure and customer privacy (Chapters 3 and 4).

Part II: Customer Lifetime Value (LTV) – Customer lifetime value is one of the pillars, along with predictive modeling and testing, upon which database marketing rests. We discuss methods for calculating LTV, including providing detailed coverage of the "thorny" issues such as cost accounting that are tempting to ignore, but whose resolution can have a crucial impact on practice (Chapters 5–7).

Part III: Database Marketing Tools: The Basics – DBM has one absolute requirement – customer data. We discuss the sources and types of customer data companies use (Chapter 8). We provide in-depth treatment of two other pillars of database marketing – testing and predictive modeling (Chapters 9–10).

Part IV: Database Marketing Tools: Statistical Techniques – Here we discuss the several statistical methods, both traditional and cutting edge, that are used to produce predictive models (Chapters 11–19). This is a valuable section for anyone wanting to know, "How is a decision tree produced," or "What are the detailed considerations in using logistic regression," or "Why is a neural net potentially better than a decision tree," or "What is machine learning all about?"

Part V: Customer Management – Here we focus our attention squarely on application. We review the conceptual issues, what is known about them, and the tools available to tackle customer management activities including acquisition, cross- and up-selling, churn management, frequency reward programs, customer tier programs, multichannel customer management, and acquisition and retention spending (Chapters 20–26).

Part VI: Managing the Marketing Mix – We concentrate on communications and pricing. We provide a thorough treatment of what we predict will be the hallmark of the next generation of database marketing, namely "optimal contact models," where the emphasis is on taking into account – *in quantitative fashion* – the future ramifications of current decisions, truly managing the long-term value of a customer (Chapter 28). We also discuss the design of DBM communications copy (Chapter 27) and several critical issues in pricing, including acquisition versus retention pricing, and the coordination of the two (Chapter 29).

Our initial outline for this book took shape at the beginning of the millennium, in May 2000. The irony of taking 7 years to write a book about techniques that often work in a matter of seconds does not escape us. Indeed, writing this book has been a matter of trying to hit a moving target. However, this effort has been the proverbial "labor of love," and its length and gestation period are products of the depth and scope we were aiming for. This book is the outcome of the debates we have had on issues such as how to treat fixed costs in calculating customer lifetime value, which methods merit our attention and how exactly do they work, and why the multichannel customer is a higher-value customer. Writing this book has truly been a *process*, as is database marketing.

Along the way, we have become indebted to numerous colleagues in both academia and business without whom this book would be a shadow of its current self. These people have provided working papers and references, exchanged e-mails with us, talked with us, and ultimately, taught us a great deal about various aspects of database marketing. Included are: Kusum

Ailawadi, Eric Anderson, Kenneth Baker, Anand Bodapati, Bruce Hardie,
Wai-Ki Ching, Kristoff Coussement, Preyas Desai, Ravi Dhar, Jehoshua
Eliashberg, Peter Fader, Doug Faherty, Helen Fanucci, Fred Feinberg, Edward
Fox, Frances Frei, Steve Fuller, Bikram Prak Ghosh, Scott Gillum, William
Greene, Abbie Griffin, John Hauser, Dick Hodges, Donna Hoffman, Eric J.
Johnson, Wagner Kamakura, Gary King, George Knox, Praveen Kopalle,
V. Kumar, Donald Lehmann, Peter Liberatore, Junxiang Lu, Charlotte Ma-
son, Carl Mela, Prasad Naik, Koen Pauwels, Margaret Peteraf, Phil Pfeifer,
Joseph Pych, Werner Reinartz, Richard Sansing, David Schmittlein, Robert
Shumsky, K. Sudhir, Baohong Sun, Anant Sundaram, Jacquelyn Thomas,
Glen Urban, Christophe Van den Bulte, Rajkumar Venkatesan, Julian Vil-
lanueva, Florian von Wangenheim, Michel Wedel, Birger Wernerfeldt, and
John Zhang.

We are extremely grateful for research assistance provided by Carmen
Maria Navarro (customer privacy practices), Jungho Bae and Ji Hong Min
(data analysis), Qing-Lin Zhu and Paul Wolfson (simulation programming),
and Karen Sluzenski (library references), and for manuscript preparation
support tirelessly provided by Mary Biathrow, Deborah Gibbs, Patricia Hunt,
and Carol Millay.

We benefited from two excellent reviews provided by Peter Verhoef and
Ed Malthouse, which supplied insights on both the forest *and* the trees that
significantly improved the final product.

The Springer publishing team was tremendously supportive, helpful, and
extremely patient with our final assembly of the book. We owe our deep
gratitude to Deborah Doherty, Josh Eliashberg, Gillian Greenough, and Nick
Philipson.

While people write and support the book, we also want to acknowledge
significant institutional support that provided us with funding, facilities, and
a stimulating environment in which to work. These include the Teradata
Center for CRM at Fuqua Business School, Duke University, which hosted
Scott Neslin during 2002, and our home institutions: the Kellogg School of
Management, Northwestern; Seoul National University; and the Tuck School
of Business, Dartmouth College.

Finally, we owe our profound and deepest gratitude simply to our *spouses
and families*, who provided the support, enduring patience, and companion-
ship without which this book would never have materialized. By showing us
that family is what really matters, they enabled us to survive the ups and
downs of putting together an effort of this magnitude. It is to our spouses
and families that we dedicate this book.

R. Blattberg
B. Kim
S. Neslin

Contents

Part III Database Marketing Tools: The Basics

Part IV Database Marketing Tools: Statistical Techniques

Part I
Strategic Issues

Chapter 1
Introduction

Abstract Database marketing is "the use of customer databases to enhance marketing productivity through more effective acquisition, retention, and development of customers." In this chapter we elaborate on this definition, provide an overview of why database marketing is becoming more important, and propose a framework for the "database marketing process." We conclude with a discussion of how we organize the book.

1.1 What Is Database Marketing?

The purpose of marketing is to enable the firm to enhance customer value. In today's competitive, information-intensive, ROI-oriented business environment, *database* marketing has emerged as an invaluable approach for achieving this purpose. The applications of database marketing are numerous and growing exponentially. Here are a few examples:

- "Internet Portal, Inc." determines which of its customers will be most receptive to targeted efforts to increase their usage of the portal. Perhaps more importantly, it determines which customers will *not* be receptive to these efforts.
- "XYZ Bank" decides which of its many financial products should be marketed to which of its current customers.
- "ABC Wireless" develops the ability to predict which customers are most likely to leave when their contract runs out, and designs a "churn management program" to encourage them to stay.
- UK Retailer Tesco develops thousands of customized promotion packages it mails to its 14 million customers (Rohwedder 2006).
- Best Buy has identified the major segments of customers who visit its stores. It then (1) tailors its store in a particular locality to fit the representation of the segments in that locality, and (2) trains its store personnel to recognize which segment a particular customer belongs to, so the customer can be serviced appropriately (Boyle 2006).

- Catalogers routinely use "predictive models" to decide which customers should receive which catalogs.
- "E-tailer Z" uses "recommendation engines" to customize which products it "cross-sells" to which customers.
- Dell Computer uses data analyses of prospects to improve its customer acquisition rate (Direct Marketing Association 2006).

These are but a few examples of database marketing in action. The common theme is that all of them are based on analyzing customer data and implementing the results.

1.1.1 Defining Database Marketing

While the above examples provide an idea as to what database marketing is about, it is useful to formally define the topic. The National Center for Database Marketing, quoted by Hughes (1996a, p. 4), defines database marketing as:

Managing a computerized relational database, in real time, of comprehensive, up-to-date, relevant data on customers, inquiries, prospects and suspects, to identify our most responsive customers for the purpose of developing a high quality, long-standing relationship of repeat business by developing predictive models which enable us to send desired messages at the right time in the right form to the right people – all with the result of pleasing our customers, increasing our response rate per marketing dollar, lowering our cost per order, building our business, and increasing our profits.

While perhaps a bit long-winded, this definition in our view captures the essentials of database marketing – analyzing customer data to enhance customer value. A more succinct definition, which we advocate, is:

Database marketing is the use of customer databases to enhance marketing productivity through more effective acquisition, retention, and development of customers.

Each phrase in this definition is carefully chosen. First, database marketing is fundamentally about using of *customer databases*. The "customer" can be either current customers or potential customers. Firms have data on their current customers' purchase behavior and demographic and psychographic information, as well as the firm's previous marketing efforts extended to these customers and their response to them. For potential customers – prospects – firms may be able to obtain data on customer demographics and psychographics, as well as purchase history data, although obviously not in the same depth as available for their current customers.

Second, database marketing is about *marketing productivity*. In today's results-oriented businesses, senior management often asks the simple question, "Do our marketing efforts pay off?" Database marketing attempts to quantify that effectiveness and improve it. It does this through effective targeting. The retail pioneer John Wannamaker is credited with saying, "I know half of my advertising doesn't work; I just don't know which half." Thinking more broadly, in terms of marketing rather than advertising, database marketing identifies which half of the firm's marketing efforts is wasted. It does this by learning which customers respond to marketing and which ones do not. The responsive customers are the ones who are then targeted.

Third, database marketing is about *managing customers*. Customers must be acquired, retained, and developed. Acquiring customers means getting an individual who currently does not do business with the company to start doing business with the company. Retention means ensuring the current customer keeps doing business with the company. Development means enhancing the volume of business the retained customer does with the company. A key concept in database marketing that captures these three factors is "customer equity" (Blattberg et al. 2001), which we investigate in detail when we discuss "Acquisition and Retention Management" in Chapter 26. For now, the important point is to recognize that database marketing is concerned with all three elements of customer equity. The Dell example above involves customer acquisition. The ABC Telecom example involves customer retention. The XYZ Bank, Tesco, and E-tailer Z examples involve customer development.

1.1.2 Database Marketing, Direct Marketing, and Customer Relationship Management

We can shed more light on the definition of database marketing by considering its close cousins, direct marketing and customer relationship management (CRM). Indeed, direct marketing and CRM overlap strongly with database marketing. While each of the three concepts has its own nuances, the key distinguishing characteristic of database marketing is its emphasis on the use of customer databases.

Customer relationship management emphasizes enhancing customer relationships. That certainly is part of the definition of database marketing (acquisition, retention, and development). However, firms can enhance customer relationships without using data. The local clothing store's salesperson gets to know individual customers through their repeated visits to the store. The salesperson learns how to treat each customer and what their tastes are. This produces and enhances a relationship between the store and the customer. There is no formal analysis of databases. Essentially, the "data" are the experiences remembered by the salesperson. Database marketing can be viewed as an approach for large companies to develop relationships with customers, because there are so many customers and so many salespersons

that it is impossible for every salesperson to really know each customer. Paradoxically, the software and computer systems for compiling the data needed
to implement database marketing to enhance customer relationships have
been marketed as *CRM* software or technology.

Direct marketing's emphasis is on "addressability," the ability to interact
with a customer one-to-one (Blattberg and Deighton 1991). Addressability
is certainly a key aspect of database marketing, since targeting is the key
way that database marketing enhances marketing productivity. But direct
marketing can directly address customers simply by purchasing lists that
"make sense," and sending customers on that list an offer. Note again, there
is no formal data analysis in this example. Database marketing emphasizes
the analysis of the data. In addition, while database marketing implementations often involve direct one-to-one contacts, this need not be always the
case. In the Best Buy example above, the first component of the application is that the analysis of customer data drives the design of the store.
This is not direct marketing but it is database marketing. The second component of the application, training salespeople to recognize particular market segments as they shop in the store, is more along the lines of direct
marketing.

In summary, database marketing, direct marketing, and customer relationship highly overlap. They differ in points of emphasis – database marketing emphasizes the analysis of customer data, direct marketing emphasizes
addressability, and customer relationship management emphasizes the customer relationship. However, many people who call themselves direct marketers certainly analyze customer data. And many CRM applications software companies emphasize customer data. So customer data analysis is not
the exclusive domain of database marketing – it's just database marketing's
specialty.

1.2 Why Is Database Marketing Becoming More Important?

It is difficult to find statistics that document the size of the database marketing industry. Some suggestive numbers are: (1) The market for "CRM
Software" is valued at $7.773 billion in 2005 and expected to grow to $10.940
billion by 2010 (Band 2006). (2) As of 2004, 100 of the top 376 companies
in the Fortune 500 list of US corporations are members of the Direct Marketing Association, the trade association for direct marketing (Direct Marketing Association 2004, pp. 22–23). (3) In 2004, 39.153 million US adults
bought products through the mail (Direct Marketing Association 2004, p. 29).
(4) Business-to-business direct marketing advertising expenditures totaled
$107 billion in 2003, and are expected to increase to $135 billion by 2007

(Direct Marketing Association 2004, p. 167). These numbers provide indications of the size of the industry, but do not include budgets for marketing analytics groups that analyze the data, for campaigns that implement database marketing programs, or for the multitude of service firms (advertising agencies, data compilers, and list management firms), that account for significant expenditures.

The indications are that the database marketing industry is huge and increasing. The question is, why? We hypothesize five major classes of reasons:

- *Information technology*: Companies now have the ability to store and manipulate terabytes of data. While the software to do so is expensive, the capabilities are dramatic.
- *Growth of the Internet*: The Internet is a data-collection "machine." Many companies that previously could not collect and organize data on their customers can now do so through the Internet.
- *Lower productivity of mass marketing*: While there are no good statistics on this, there is the belief that mass advertising and non-customized marketing efforts are eliciting poorer response, while costs are increasing and margins are declining. One can write the profitability of a marketing campaign as $\Pi = Npm - Nc$, where N is the number of customers reached by the campaign, p is the percentage that respond, m is the contribution margin when they respond, and c is the cost of contact per customer. For a campaign to be profitability, we need $p > c/m$. Unfortunately, all three of these terms are moving in the wrong direction. Response is lower (p), costs are higher (c), and margins are lower (m). Database marketing targets customers for whom response is maximal, helping the profit equation to remain in the black.
- *Marketing accountability*: Results-oriented senior managers are requiring all business functions to justify their existence, including marketing. No longer is it taken on faith that "marketing works" or "marketing is a cost of doing business." The demands of senior managers for proven results feed directly into database marketing's emphasis on analyzing data and measuring results.
- *Increasing interest in customer relationships*: Companies are more concerned than ever about their relationship with the customer. They see their products commoditizing and customer loyalty wilting away. Database marketing is a systematic way to improve customer relationships.
- *Establishing a competitive advantage*: Companies are always trying to determine what will be their source of competitive advantage. Perhaps that source lies in the data they have on their *own* customers, which allows them to service those customers better through database marketing.

We will discuss the marketing productivity, customer relationship, and competitive advantage issues in depth in Chapter 2, because they essentially define the database marketing strategy of the firm.

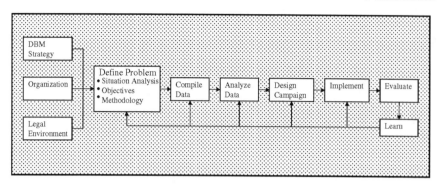

Fig. 1.1 The database marketing process.

1.3 The Database Marketing Process

Database marketing is implemented through a process depicted in Fig. 1.1. The process originates in an environment characterized by the firm's overall database marketing strategy, its organization, and legal issues (especially privacy). These factors determine the nature of problems the firm faces, and how they will be solved. The firm then needs to define the particular problem it wishes to address through database marketing. This entails a situation analysis, a statement of objectives, and an outline of the methodology that will solve the problem. For example, a firm whose DBM strategy emphasizes customer relationships may notice that it is losing too many customers. The objective may be to reduce the "churn rate" from 20% to 15% per year. The firm therefore decides to design a proactive churn management program (Chapter 24) with its attendant data requirements and statistical tools. Most of the work can be done internally because the company has the organizational capability in terms of information technology, marketing analytics, and campaign implementation. The company can then proceed to compile and analyze the data. The analysis yields a campaign design that is implemented and evaluated.

There are two key feedback loops in this process. First is the *learning* that takes place over time. After a program is evaluated, it provides guidance on what types of issues can be addressed successfully by database marketing, what data are most valuable for providing insights and for predicting customer behavior, how to analyze the data, and how to translate the analysis into program design and implementation. This learning and the expertise it breeds is one way in which database marketing can become a competitive advantage for the firm. The second feedback loop is that each database marketing campaign provides *data* for use in future analyses to solve future problems. For example, customer response to a catalog mailing is used to update "recency", "frequency", and "monetary" (RFM) variables for each customer. These become part of the database and are used to develop future targeting strategies.

Table 1.1 Database marketing activities

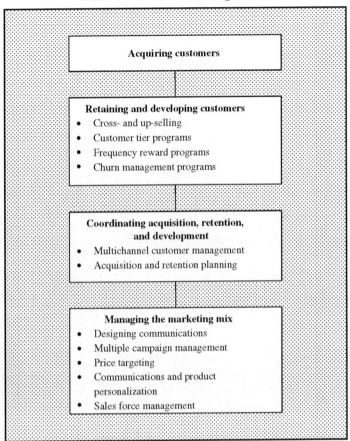

Table 1.1 provides a list of database marketing activities – essentially, a list of the marketing problems addressed by database marketing. These include acquiring customers, retaining and developing customers, coordinating acquisition, retention, and development, and managing the marketing mix. Several of the sub-issues within each of these merit their own chapter in this book. For example, we will devote full chapters to cross- and up-selling, multichannel customer management, etc. These are all very challenging problems and much work has been done on using database marketing to manage them more effectively.

Because of the focus on analyzing customer data, several data analysis techniques have emerged and been applied by database marketers. Table 1.2 lists these techniques. The two most basic analyses are lifetime value of the customer and predictive modeling. Lifetime value of the customer is the net present value of the incremental revenues and costs generated by an acquired customer. The reason LTV is so important is that it includes the long-term

Table 1.2 Database marketing analysis techniques

Lifetime value of the customer (LTV)

Predictive modeling

Statistical techniques
- Logistic regression
- Tobit models
- Hazard models
- RFM analysis
- Market basket analysis
- Collaborative filtering
- Cluster analysis
- Decision trees
- Neural networks
- Machine learning algorithms

Field tests

retention and development aspects of managing the customer. We devote three chapters to calculating and applying LTV. Predictive modeling is the most common form of analysis conducted by database marketers. It pertains to the use of statistical analysis to predict future customer behavior – will the customer churn, will the customer buy from this catalog, will the customer become more loyal if routed to the top-tier call center, will the customer be receptive to this recommended product? Predictive modeling is itself a process, and we devote a chapter to studying this process.

For the statistically oriented individual, "your ship has come in" when it comes to database marketing. Table 1.2 shows the multitude of methods used by database marketers. The reason why so many techniques have found application is partly due to the variety of problems to be addressed – e.g., collaborative filtering and market-basket analysis can be readily applied to cross-selling, hazard models are useful for predicting how long the customer will remain a customer; logistic regression, decision trees, and neural networks are all useful for predicting "0–1" behavior such as, will the customer respond, or will the customer churn?

However, in addition to the variety of problems stimulating the variety of techniques, the other reason for the plethora of statistical techniques that are applied by database marketers is the frantic race to achieve higher predictive accuracy. As we will see several times in this book, even a nominal increase in predictive accuracy can mean $100,000s in added profits for a single campaign. Each bit of information we can squeeze out of the data can be directly

Table 1.3 Organization of the book

Part 1: Strategic Issues

- Chapter 1: Introduction
- Chapter 2: Why Database Marketing?
- Chapter 3: Organizing for Database Marketing
- Chapter 4: Customer Privacy and Database Marketing

Part 2: Customer Lifetime Value (LTV)

- Chapter 5: Customer Lifetime Value – Fundamentals
- Chapter 6: Issues in Computing Customer Lifetime Value
- Chapter 7: Customer Lifetime Value Applications

Part 3: Database Marketing Tools: The Basics

- Chapter 8: Sources of Data
- Chapter 9: Test Design and Analysis
- Chapter 10: The Predictive Modeling Process

Part 4: Database Marketing Tools: Statistical Techniques

- Chapter 11: Statistical Issues in Predictive Modeling
- Chapter 12: RFM Analysis
- Chapter 13: Market Basket Analysis
- Chapter 14: Collaborative Filtering
- Chapter 15: Discrete Dependent Variable and Duration Models
- Chapter 16: Cluster Analysis
- Chapter 17: Decision Trees
- Chapter 18: Artificial Neural Networks
- Chapter 19: Machine Learning

Part 5: Customer Management

- Chapter 20: Acquiring Customers
- Chapter 21: Cross-Selling and Up-Selling
- Chapter 22: Frequency Reward Programs
- Chapter 23: Customer Tier Programs
- Chapter 24: Churn Management
- Chapter 25: Multichannel Customer Management
- Chapter 26: Acquisition and Retention Management

Part 6: Managing the Marketing Mix

- Chapter 27: Designing Database Marketing Communications
- Chapter 28: Multiple Campaign Management
- Chapter 29: Pricing

---

linked to marketing profitability and efficiency. For example, if a predictive model can increase response to a direct mail offer from 1% to 2%, this can literally make the difference between a huge loss and a huge gain. The reason is that while the percentage change is small, it is multiplied by 100,000s of customers, if not millions. In this way, the benefits of marginal increases in predictive accuracy add up, and we have a cornucopia of statistical techniques that compete for the title, "most accurate."

1.4 Organization of the Book

We have organized the book according to Table 1.3. Part I deals with the issues that shape the database marketing process – firm strategy, firm organization, and the legal environment. Chapter 2, "Why Database Marketing", relates to the firm's database marketing strategy, positing three fundamental reasons why companies might want to engage in database marketing: improving marketing productivity, improving customer relationships, or establishing competitive advantage. As discussed earlier, which of these reasons is the impetus for database marketing at a particular firm will influence the rest of the DBM process – which problems the firm attempts to solve, and how it tries to solve them. Chapter 3 deals with how to organize the firm's marketing function in order to implement database marketing. Chapter 4 represents the legal environment, in particular, the issue of customer privacy. This certainly determines the types of database marketing efforts the firm can undertake.

Parts II–IV of the book deal with database marketing tools – how to collect the data and do the analysis. Chapters 5–7 focus on the key concept of lifetime value of the customer (LTV). Chapters 8–10 focus on the basic tasks of compiling data, field testing, and predictive modeling. Chapters 11–19 cover the statistical methods used primarily in predictive modeling.

Parts V and VI focus on specific problems addressed by database marketing. They largely draw on the tools described in Parts II–IV. Part V covers customer management activities including Acquiring Customers (Chapter 20), Cross- and Up-selling (Chapter 21), Frequency Reward Programs (Chapter 22), Customer Tier Programs (Chapter 23), Churn management (Chapter 24), Multichannel Customer Management (Chapter 25), and Acquisition and Retention Management (Chapter 26). Part VI focuses on the marketing mix, particularly communications (Chapters 27 and 28) and Pricing (Chapter 29).

The result is intended to be a comprehensive treatment of the field of database marketing, including strategic issues, tools, and problem-solving.

Chapter 2
Why Database Marketing?

Abstract A basic yet crucial question is: why should the firm engage in database marketing? We discuss three fundamental motivations: enhancing marketing productivity, creating and enhancing customer relationships, and creating sustainable competitive advantage. We review the theoretical and empirical evidence in support of each of these motivations. Marketing productivity has the best support; there is some evidence for both customer relationships and competitive advantage as well, but further work is needed.

Perhaps the most fundamental question we can ask about any marketing activity is what is its *raison d'etre* – what purpose does it serve in enhancing firm performance? In this chapter, we propose and evaluate three reasons for database marketing:

- Enhancing marketing productivity
- Enabling the development of a customer/firm relationship
- Creating a sustainable competitive advantage

2.1 Enhancing Marketing Productivity

2.1.1 The Basic Argument

The pioneering retail entrepreneur, John Wannamaker, is said to have lamented about the inefficiency of his marketing efforts, "I know that half of my marketing is wasted; my problem is that I just don't know which half." The promise of database marketing is to identify which marketing efforts are wasted and which are productive, thereby allowing the firm to focus on the efforts that are productive. Database marketing does this by identifying customers for whom the marketing effort will pay off, and then targeting those customers. In this view, database marketing is fundamentally a segmentation and targeting tool for enhancing marketing productivity.

Table 2.1 The economics of database marketing: A prospecting example

- Untargeted Mailing

Number of offers mailed:	1,000,000
Profit contribution per response:	$80
Cost per mailing:	$0.70
Response rate:	1%

$$\text{Profit} = 1,000,000 \times 0.01 \times \$80 - 1,000,000 \times \$0.70$$
$$= \$800,000 - \$700,000$$
$$= \$100,000$$

- Targeted mailing

Decile	Number of prospects	Response rate (%)	Profit ($)	Cumulative Profit ($)
1	100,000	3.00%	170,000	170,000
2	100,000	2.00	90,000	260,000
3	100,000	1.40	42,000	302,000
4	100,000	1.15	22,000	324,000
5	100,000	1.00	10,000	334,000
6	100,000	0.60	−22,000	312,000
7	100,000	0.40	−38,000	274,000
8	100,000	0.30	−46,000	228,000
9	100,000	0.10	−62,000	166,000
10	100,000	0.05	−66,000	100,000
Total	1,000,000	1.00%	$100,000	

=> Target first five deciles (Profit = $334,000)

The power of this argument can be seen in the example shown in Table 2.1. The example depicts the economics of a direct marketing campaign whose goal is to profitably sell a new product to a list of 1,000,000 potential "prospects." Each prospect who "responds" to the offer generates $80 in profit. The cost to extend the offer is $0.70, including costs of mailing and printing of the mail piece. Assuming a 1% response rate – fairly typically for a large-scale mailing – profit would be:

$$\text{Profit} = 1,000,000 \times 1\% \text{ response} \times \$80/\text{response}$$
$$-1,000,000 \times \$0.70/\text{contact} = \$100,000$$

The mailing is profitable. However, the above calculation illustrates Wanna-maker's perspective taken to an extreme −99% of the marketing expenditures were wasted! Only 10,000 will respond to the offer, yet we are mailing to 1,000,000 customers to find those responders. This unfortunately is a typical outcome for many marketing expenditures. The cost is not only lost profits to the firm, but wasted "junk mail" and advertising clutter as well. If we could eliminate some of that waste, profits could be increased and perhaps society itself could be better served.

The lower portion of Table 2.1 shows how the results can be improved with database marketing. The prospect list is segmented into deciles, 100,000 in each decile, *prioritized by their likelihood of responding to the offer.*

The prioritization is determined by a process called predictive modeling (Chapter 10). Predictive modeling identifies a top decile of customers who have a response rate of 3%. The second decile has a response rate of 2%, etc., down to the 10th decile, which has a response rate of 0.05%. The profits from targeting the first decile would be 100,000 × 3% response × $80/response − 100,000 × $0.70/contact = $170,000. Targeting this decile alone would yield more profit than targeting the entire list. The key is that we are saving on the mailing costs – "only" 97%, not 99%, of the mail costs are wasted in this segment.

Going through the calculations for each decile, we see that it would be profitable to target the top 5 deciles, yielding a cumulative profit of $334,000, much higher than the $100,000 gained by targeting the full list.

Database marketing allows firms to segment their customers according to "lift tables" such as in Table 2.1, and then deliver the marketing effort to the customers whom the analysis predicts will be profitable. The key to the profit improvement is that the top deciles have substantially higher response rates than the lower deciles. The ratio of response rate in a decile to the average response rate is known as "lift." Note that a first-decile lift of 3 to 1 (3% response for that decile divided by 1% for the entire database) is enough to enhance profits significantly. The lift for the top 5 deciles is 1.71%/1% = 1.71. Lift levels of this magnitude are quite feasible given current statistical technology. This provides a fundamental reason for firms to employ database marketing – it increases the profits generated by marketing campaigns by targeting customers more effectively.

2.1.2 The Marketing Productivity Argument in Depth

The marketing productivity argument for database marketing follows from the recognition of three major forces: (a) a major problem of mass marketing (e.g., traditional electronic media such as television) is lack of targeting and database marketing provides the ability to target, (b) marketing needs to be accountable and database marketing provides accountability, and (c) mass marketing efforts are difficult to assess and adjust, whereas database marketing provides a process for learning how to target more effectively.

2.1.2.1 Database Marketing as a Solution to Targeting Inefficiencies of Mass Marketing

Beginning with Wannamaker's observation that half his advertising was wasted, marketers have long lamented their inability to target efforts effectively. For example, mass media advertising can be targeted only to a limited degree. Market research services identify demographic characteristics and product preferences associated with particular television shows, or geographic regions, but this produces nowhere near the desired level of individual targetability.

Blattberg and Deighton (1991) pioneered the notion that data technology can improve targeting in their concept of the "addressable consumer." Their main point was that database marketing could create a dialogue between the customer and the company, whereby the company would learn the responses of individual customers and respond to their needs. This was a radical departure from mass media. Deighton et al. (1994) elaborated on this theme: "At its most sophisticated, then, a transaction database is a record of the conversation between a firm and *each* [italics added] of its customers, in which the firm's offering evolves as the dialogue unfolds" (p. 60).

Coincident with the conceptual argument that data technology could improve targeting was the practical observation that the costs of maintaining and storing databases had decreased rapidly. Blattberg and Deighton (1991) maintained that "the cost of holding a consumer's name, address, and purchase history on line has fallen by a factor of a thousand since 1970 and is continuing to fall at this rate." Sheth and Sisodia (1995b) report that "Computing power that used to cost a million dollars can be had today for less than a dollar." Peppers and Rogers (1993, pp. 13–14) echo similar themes.

Second was the observation that the tools for extracting the necessary learning from the data (to construct the lift table in Table 2.1) were available and getting better. This led to an explosive growth in "data mining" (e.g., Peacock 1998). Peacock defines data mining as "the automated discovery of 'interesting,' nonobvious patterns hidden in a database that have a high potential for contributing to the bottom line . . . 'interesting' relationships are those that could have an impact on strategy or tactics and ultimately on an organization's objectives." He cites a few examples:

- Marriott's Vacation Club used data mining to cut the level of direct mail needed to accomplish a desired response level. This is a prime illustration of Table 2.1.
- Prudential Insurance tested the results of data mining for improved response rates among prospects, and found them to be doubled.
- American Express used data mining to "score" customers in terms of how likely they were to purchase various items. It then used these data to generate offers that match the products of its partners with the needs of its customers.

In summary, the recognition that targeting was the problem with mass marketing, that database marketing could theoretically improve targeting, that database costs were declining, and that data mining was effective in practice at developing the targeting plans, contributed mightily to the growth in database marketing as a tool for improving marketing productivity.

2.1.2.2 Marketing Accountability and the ROI Perspective

Emerging from the period of high inflation in the 1970s, senior management became very concerned with costs – production, labor, and materials. Webster (1981) (see also Lodish 1986) reported that by the early 1980s, CEO's had begun to focus on marketing. The fact that it was general managers – the CEO's – who were calling attention to marketing meant two things. First, the issue was broader than costs. It was productivity in the sense of Return on Investment (ROI), i.e., how much profit was being generated per marketing dollar. Second, marketing needed to be accountable, so that marketing productivity needed to be measured. Sheth and Sisodia (1995a) report that by the mid-1990s, "CEO's are demanding major cost savings and a higher level of accountability from marketing than ever before."

As illustrated in Table 2.1, database marketing fulfills the need to measure ROI. Rather than spending $700,000 to produce a profit of $100,000 (an "ROI" of 15%), database marketing would spend $350,000 to produce a profit of $334,000 (an ROI of 95%).[1] Expenditures have decreased and profits have increased. The key however is that the results are measurable. The entire database marketing mentality is based on measuring results. In Table 2.1, it is relatively simple since response can be measured and tabulated, and the costs can be calculated.

Costs, at least direct costs, are almost always easy to measure in a direct marketing context. Incremental revenues are sometimes difficult to measure, however, because it is not clear what response would have been without the marketing campaign. This is where the role of experimentation and learning comes in. For example, assume that in Table 2.1, it was possible that consumers could buy the product even without a direct mail campaign, e.g., through a different sales channel. The database marketer would then design an experiment by creating a control groups. Rather than mailing to all 100,000 prospects in Decile 1, he or she would mail to just 90,000, holding 10,000 aside as controls. The incremental gain from the campaign could then be calculated as the response rate for the 90,000 minus the "response" rate for the 10,000. The ease of conducting experiments plays a key role in measuring the results of database marketing, hence in making database marketing *accountable*.

While marketing ROI is naturally measured as profit generated per incremental expenditure divided by the investment, there are many other ways to measure it. Sheth and Sisodia (1995a, b) propose that marketing productivity be measured as a weighted average of customer acquisition productivity and customer retention productivity. Customer acquisition productivity would

---

[1] Note it is not clear that firms should maximize ROI rather than the absolute level of profits. ROI may be maximized at a lower level of expenditure than would maximize profits (see Table 2.1, where targeting just the first decile would maximize ROI, while targeting the first 5 deciles will maximize profits). (The authors thank Preyas Desai for these insights.)

consist of revenues generated by new customers divided by expenditures on acquiring new customers, "adjusted by a customer satisfaction index" (p. 11). The adjustment serves to quantify the long-run benefits of this acquisition. Customer retention productivity would consist of revenues from existing customers divided by expenditures for serving existing customers, adjusted by a "customer loyalty index," again to bring in the long-term value of the investment. There are several practical issues in constructing these measures, but the emphasis on acquisition and retention plays to the very definition of database marketing (the use of customer databases to increase the effectiveness of marketing in acquiring and retaining customers). We add that cross-selling or up-selling customers is also very important. Once a firm has a customer, the ability to sell additional products through database marketing provides the firm a significant advantage (Blattberg et al. 2001).

2.1.2.3 Database Marketing as a Learning System

Mass marketing efforts are difficult to assess and adjust. While marketing mix modeling has become very popular and generates useful results, a key limitation is the difficulty and cost in setting up controlled experiments. Database marketing is a learning marketing system because firms use both experimentation and data mining techniques to learn about the effectiveness of their marketing mix decisions and about their customers' behavior, and then adjusts these decisions accordingly. Experimentation is fundamental to database marketing. In its extreme database marketers test micro tactical decisions such as the color of the paper used in a direct marketing campaign or the greeting used in telemarketing. While very tactical, experimentation means that database marketers can learn from their "mistakes" – unsuccessful copy, pricing or offers – and can improve the effectiveness and efficiency of their marketing activities.

Traditional mass marketers in theory can set up experiments but they are prone to small sample sizes, difficulty creating controls and high costs. Tools such as IRI's Behavior Scan can be used in the consumer packaged goods industry to test advertising. However, for most products that can not be tracked with consumer panels, this option does not exist. Hence, database marketing has a significant advantage to firms because of the ability of the firm to experiment, learn, and adjust.

Database marketers such as Amazon now use more sophisticated targeting tools to learn about their customers' behavior and then use this to cross-sell other products. One technique used to analyze customer behavior and make product recommendations is called collaborative filtering (Chapter 14). This and similar techniques use purchase histories and other information to determine the likelihood a customer will purchase a related product. For example, Amazon uses a customer's book purchase history to make a recommendation of books the customer might be interested in purchasing.

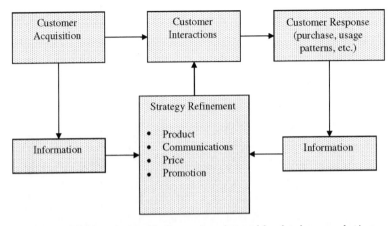

Fig. 2.1 The learning marketing system fostered by database marketing.

We call the process of implementing database marketing campaigns, learning, and adjusting a "learning marketing system". This system is depicted in Fig. 2.1. The figure shows that the firm uses information it collects in the process of acquiring and retaining customers to update its strategy for interacting with customers. This entails the product offering, communications, price, and promotion. The firm is able to target these elements more effectively because it has learned about consumer preferences and responsiveness.

A learning marketing system can also provide a competitive advantage to a firm because, if carefully crafted, it can provide better product recommendations and more targeted communications to the customer than if the customer switches companies and makes his or her first purchase from a competitor. That competitor does not have the information available to customize product recommendations and communications. Amazon should therefore have a significant advantage relative to Barnes & Noble and Borders because it has been tracking customer purchase much longer and offering recommendations throughout the customer's purchase experience with Amazon.

2.1.3 Evidence for the Marketing Productivity Argument

Table 2.1 suggests two crucial components to the marketing productivity argument for database marketing. First is that predictive modeling generates lift tables that separate customers who will respond from those who will not. Second is that these tables actually predict what will happen once the marketing campaign is launched.

There are several examples to demonstrate the feasibility of lift tables ("charts" when shown graphically). Figure 2.2 is from Ansari and Mela (2003)

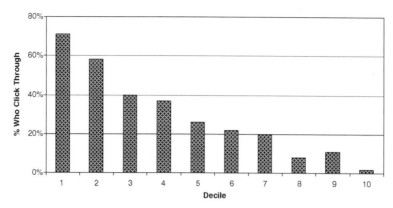

Fig. 2.2 Lift chart for an e-mail campaign (From Ansari and Mela 2003).

on targeted e-mail. The goal was to use e-mail to generate visits to an information-oriented website. As the figure shows, the average response rate was 20%. However, the authors were able to separate customers into deciles such that customers in the first 3 deciles had a response rate of 40%, a 2 to 1 lift. See Sheppard (1999) and Chapter 10 for a detailed discussion of lift tables.

Figure 2.3 shows a lift chart for predicting which credit card customers will close their accounts (i.e., "churn"). Predictions are based on customer behavior over the previous six months. As the chart shows, those in the top decile have a 7% chance of churning, compared to an average of less than 1% over the entire customer base. The top decile customers could be targeted with a customer retention program – perhaps a new offer, or simply a reminder of the favorable features of their credit card.

Figure 2.4 shows the predicted "next-product-to-buy" adoption of web banking for a retail bank (Knott et al. 2002). The most important variable for making these predictions was products currently owned by customers.

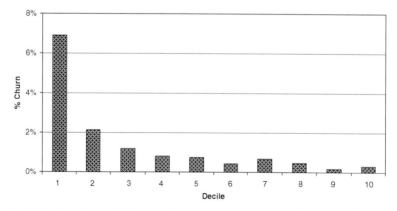

Fig. 2.3 Lift chart for predicting credit card customer attrition (Courtesy of ASA, Pittsburgh, PA, ModelMax Demonstration Data).

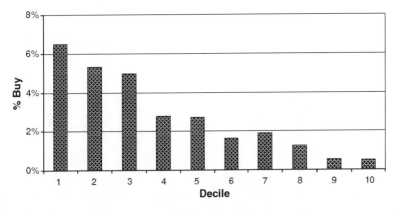

Fig. 2.4 Lift chart for predicting adoption of web banking using a next-product-to-buy (NPTB) model (From Knott et al. 2002).

The average adoption rate is 2.3%; the adoption rate in the top 3 deciles is 5%. These customers appear to be good prospects for a web banking direct mail piece.

In all three examples, the database marketer uses predictive models to separate customers in segments (deciles) in prioritized order of their partaking in some behavior – be it response to an e-mail, giving up a credit card, or adopting a new product. Different actions are called for depending on the decile in which a given customer falls.

These results are impressive and show customers can be segmented using predictive models. Note this is not the traditional form of segmentation used in marketing text books. It is segmentation based on the likelihood of buying determined from statistical models. A critical question is: does targeting implied by lift charts actually result in higher revenues and profits? Figure 2.5

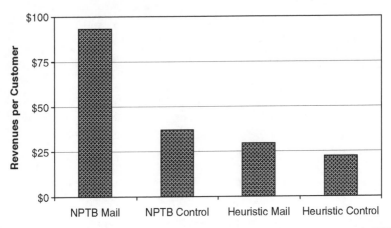

Fig. 2.5 Revenues from field-tested cross-selling campaign (From Knott et al. 2002).

shows one example from Knott et al. (2002). A predictive model was used to
prioritize customers according to their likelihood of purchasing a home equity loan. The top prospects were then targeted with a direct mail campaign.
Note that this tests the ability of the predictive model predictions to hold up
when the targeting actually occurs, subsequently to the modeling.

Figure 2.5 shows the targeted mailing generated revenues of \$93 per
mailed-to customer. However, customers could have obtained a loan through
other means, for example, simply by walking up to the bank and applying.
Did the mailing generated incremental revenue above what would have been
obtained through the usual marketing channel? To answer this, the authors
in advance set up a control group consisting of customers who were predicted
by the model to be top prospects, but were randomly selected not to receive
the direct mail piece. It turned out that some of these people did obtain
loans on their own, but revenues for this group were only \$37 per customer.
Finally, the question arises as to whether the model – based on a neural
net – worked better than a simple heuristic. In this case, the heuristic was
to target direct mail pieces for the loan to wealthier customers. As Fig. 2.5
shows, this heuristic barely produced any additional revenues compared to
its control group.

Knott et al. (2002) suggest three key findings. First, targeted campaigns
based on predictive models produce higher revenues. Second, the revenues
are incremental over what would have been achieved through existing marketing efforts. Third, the model outperforms a reasonable but non-statistical
heuristic. Overall, we see measurable improved performance from targeting.[2]
That is one of the promises of database marketing.

The above examples suggest that statistical methods can create beneficial
targeting efforts. One consideration is costs. As we saw earlier, the costs
include: compilation of a database, the lift chart capabilities generated by a
given investment, and average contact expenses with and without database
marketing. Industries that naturally maintain customer databases, such as
services and catalogs, obviously will find the database costs less expensive.

2.1.4 Assessment

The argument that database marketing's *raison d'etre* is to improve marketing productivity is compelling. It is based on (1) the recognition that effective targeting is crucial and that database marketing can deliver it, (2) that
modern marketers are accountable and that database marketing can measure ROI, and (3) that learning and refinement is key to effective marketing
and database marketing is indeed a learning process. These forces should

---

[2] The illustration in Fig. 2.5 is in terms of revenues, but Knott et al. (2002) show that
profits increase as well.

continue into the future. In addition, the targeting and ROI components of the argument have received direct empirical support.

While the marketing productivity argument is indeed powerful and undoubtedly has contributed to the growth of database marketing, the productivity argument is largely tactical. It focuses on the profitability of individual marketing campaigns. It leaves out two fundamental issues, developing customer relationships and establishing a competitive advantage. These two issues will be the focus of the next two sections of this chapter.

2.2 Creating and Enhancing Customer Relationships

2.2.1 The Basic Argument

The argument is that (1) strong customer relationships are good because they go hand-in-hand with brand loyalty, and (2) database marketing can be used to create and enhance customer relationships.

2.2.2 Customer Relationships and the Role of Database Marketing

2.2.2.1 The Emergence of Customer Relationships as an Area of Marketing Focus

Among the first researchers to articulate the CRM argument for database marketing was Berry (1983). Berry urged marketers to be "thinking of marketing in terms of having customers, not merely acquiring customers," (p. 25), and defined relationship marketing as "attracting, maintaining, and enhancing customer relationships in multi-service organizations." The importance of customer relationships was echoed by Webster (1992, p. 1): "Customer relationships will be seen as the key strategic resource of the business."

Berry outlined a number of relationship marketing strategies, including "customizing the relationship", which was an especially attractive strategy when "personal service capabilities are combined with electronic data processing capabilities." He describes examples at Xerox, American Express, and other companies where service capabilities were enhanced by customer data records. The key notion was that a customer service representative could cultivate a stronger relationship with the customer by having instant access to the customer's data file.

Berry's emphasis on relationships stemmed from the idea of enhancing customer service. Webster's emphasis on relationships stemmed from a desire to move the definition of marketing toward one based on social and economic *processes* rather than functional *tasks* (the 4 P's). More recently, the motivation for emphasizing customer relationships stems from the simple economics of lifetime value. The lifetime profits or "customer equity" delivered by a set of N customers can be written as (see Chapter 5):

$$Profits = N \sum_{t=0}^{\infty} \frac{(R - c - m)r^t}{(1 + \delta)^t} - Na \tag{2.1}$$

where:

N = Number of customers acquired.
a = Acquisition cost per customer.
R = Revenues per period per customer.
c = COGS per period per customer.
m = Ongoing marketing costs per period per customer.
δ = Discount rate.
r = Retention rate, i.e., the percentage of customers who are retained year to year.

Equation 2.1 can be re-written as:

$$Profits = N(R - c) \left(\frac{(1 + \delta)}{(1 + \delta - r)} \right) - Nm \left(\frac{(1 + \delta)}{(1 + \delta - r)} \right) - Na \tag{2.2}$$

where the first term is long-term profit contribution, the second term is long-term retention costs of marketing, and the third term is total acquisition costs. The emphasis on customer relationships is consistent with the fact that Equation 2.2 is a convex function of retention rate as opposed to a linear function of the number of acquired customers.

The convexity of long-term profits with respect to retention rate can be seen in Fig. 2.6. The implication is that an increase in retention rate by 20% increases profits more than increasing the number of customers (N) by 20%.

The benefits of customer retention have been reinforced by several researchers. Winer (2001) reports a McKinsey study that investigated how acquisition versus retention affects the market value of Internet firms. The study concluded that retention was far more powerful than acquisition. Reichheld (1996) found that small increases in retention have dramatic impact on total profits. Gupta et al. (2004a) reached similar conclusions.

A relationship management strategy is partly predicated on the belief that: (a) retaining customers is less expensive than acquiring new customers and (b) increasing retention is more valuable than increasing acquisition. The above discussion suggests a solid foundation for the revenue side. Unfortunately there is not a solid foundation for the cost side. It may be far more costly, or impossible, to increase retention rates from 80% to 90% than it is to increase acquisition rates from 1% to 5%. Generalizations about the costs of increasing intention rates have not been well documented. This is an empirical question and may be firm specific. See Chapter 26 for more discussion of acquisition versus retention strategies.

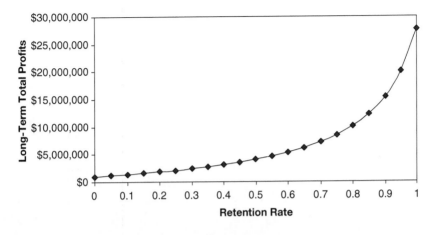

a=	$30	acquisition cost per customer
N=	100,000	number of customers
m=	10	ongoing marketing cost per customer
M=	100	revenues per customer
c=	50	COGS per customer
d=	0.15	discount rate

Fig. 2.6 Relationship between customer retention rate and total profits per customer (Equation 2.2).

Another impetus for the importance of relationships was research in the 1990s that showed a linkage from relationship strength to customer satisfaction to loyalty to firm performance. Several studies have investigated all or part of the satisfaction-loyalty-performance linkage. Anderson et al. (1994) used a three-equation model to describe the evolution of customer expectations, satisfaction, and return on assets. Their analysis was at the company level-77 Swedish firms across a wide variety of industries. The critical finding was a strong link between satisfaction and return-on-investment (ROA). They did not investigate brand loyalty per se but did hypothesize that one reason for a link between satisfaction and ROA is higher loyalty.

Rust and Zahorik (1993) model this more formally. They present a broad model that captures the relationship between satisfaction, retention, and market share. While they do not estimate the entire model, they provide an example where they predict retention likelihood for a retail bank as a function of satisfaction factors. The most important satisfaction factor influencing retention is "Warmth," which includes elements such as "friendliness," "how well the manager knows me," "listens to my needs," as well as "convenience to home." Most of these elements are basically indicators of the strength of the customer relationship.

Barnes (2000) studied 400 customers' relationships with companies from a variety of industries, including financial institutions, grocery stores, and telecommunications. He measured the closeness, strength, and emotional tone of the relationship, and found that closeness correlated strongly with satisfaction.

Bolton (1998) studied the effect of satisfaction on the length of the relationship. She found that prior cumulative satisfaction directly affects the length of the duration of the relationship. She also shows that the effect of transaction or service failures on duration times depends upon prior satisfaction. Her results show a direct relationship between customer satisfaction and the lifetime value of a customer.

Together, the above papers trace a relationship from the customer relationship to customer satisfaction to loyalty/retention to higher firm performance. They cement the argument that relationships are important because they increase retention, and retention is an attractive way to build firm performance.

2.2.2.2 The Role of Database Marketing in Establishing Customer Relationships

The previous discussion established the importance of customer relationships. What is needed next is to establish that database marketing is a way to establish relationships.

Fournier (1998) presented the conceptual foundation for customer-brand relationships, and provided exploratory evidence that relationships are a valid behavioral construct. Her conceptual foundation, based on the work of Hinde (1995), was that a relationship involves four aspects: (1) reciprocal exchange between the partners in the relationship, (2) purpose in that relationships satisfy goals of both participants, (3) multiplex in that they take on many different forms, and (4) a process, in that they evolve over time.

All four dimensions map to the capabilities of database marketing. The reciprocal exchange is that customers give firms data and firms give customers better products and service. The goals to be satisfied are profits for the firm and overall utility for the customer. The multiplex nature of relationships suggests that there must be several "touch points" where customers and firms interact, and all must be managed. Database marketing has the capability to manage these touch points. But the strongest fit between database marketing and relationships involves the notion that relationships are processes that evolve over time. The nature of database marketing is to collect data, take action, evaluate the action, collect more data, take more actions, etc. The customer data file and the conclusions one can draw from it evolve over time, as relationships should by their very nature.

Fournier's work suggests that database marketing and relationships bond at a conceptual level. Peppers and Rogers (1993, 1997) articulated that bond from a managerial perspective. Peppers and Rogers (1993) emphasized the importance of building relationships with a one-to-one mentality. They discussed critical relationship concepts such as "share of customer", "customer

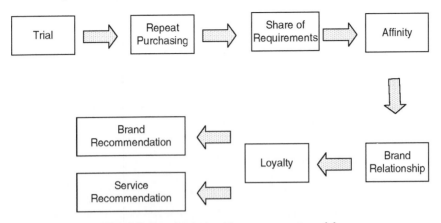

Fig. 2.7 Brand relationship management model.

driven," and "lifetime value." Peppers and Rogers (1997) emphasize that the way to manage these relationship concepts is through data. They state (p. 11), "the computer is now changing the actual character of the competitive model itself, supplanting it with a customer-driven model." The marketing mantra is now, "I know you. You tell me what you want. I make it. I remember next time."

Nebel and Blattberg (1999) developed the concept of Brand Relationship Management defined by them as, "An integrated effort to establish, maintain, and enhance relationships between a brand and its consumers, and to continuously strengthen these relationships through interactive, individualized and value-added contacts, and a mutual exchange and fulfillment of promises over a long period of time." Rather than concentrate on share of requirements (market share among the brand's customers) as the ultimate goal, they suggest that the end-state of brand relationship management is loyalty developed through affinity and the creation of a brand relationship. An example is Apple Computer who has created numerous customer interactions through their IPOD and Itunes and Apple Stores. These help build a brand relationship rather than simply a brand. The goal of a strong brand relationship is loyalty and recommendation of the product or service. Their framework is shown in Fig. 2.7.

Another example of brand relationship management is P&G's mother helpline. For a brand like Pampers (diaper) P&G provides an interactive helpline and website to answer mother's questions. Even if these questions are not directly related to diapers, this creates interactive, individualized, value-added contacts and hence a stronger brand relationship. The issues for academics are: (a) do these contacts strengthen brand loyalty and (b) does the enhanced loyalty create a brand relationship that leads to greater lifetime value.

Winer (2001) further strengthened the link between customer relationships and database marketing with his "framework for customer relationship management." This is a framework for implementing customer relationship management. The framework inter-twines data, data analysis, and relationship building, and consists of the following steps:

1. Creating a customer database
2. Analyzing the data
3. Selecting customers to target
4. Targeting customers with the appropriate vehicle
5. Developing relationship programs – reward programs, customized product, customer service, community building
6. Privacy considerations
7. Developing metrics to evaluate the process

Steps 5–6 involve the harnessing of database marketing specifically to develop relationships.

2.2.3 Evidence for the Argument that Database Marketing Enhances Customer Relationships

The evidence that database marketing exists to build customer relationships is not very strong. The issue is clouded by the faddish nature of "CRM" as the latest answer to company problems. CRM has indeed received less than favorable reviews from the business press. Most of this comes from company surveys of manager satisfaction with CRM initiatives.

- Insight Technology reported that 31% of companies believed they obtained no return on CRM, 38% got minor gains (Anonymous 2001).
- Gartner Group reported that 45% of CRM projects fail to improve customer interactions and 51% generate no positive returns in 3 years (Anonymous 2001).
- Meta Group reports that 75% of CRM initiatives fail to meet objectives (Anonymous 2001).
- "It is estimated that 60–80% of CRM projects do not achieve their goals, and 30–50% fail outright" (Sheth and Sisodia 2001).
- Mercer Management Consulting found that only 38% of companies are realizing expected returns from CRM tools, 26% are realizing expected returns from customer profitability tools (Jusko 2001).

These surveys do not pinpoint the source of the disappointment with CRM initiatives. It is not clear whether CRM initiatives have failed, or whether they are serving as a scapegoat for poor technological investments. In addition, the examples are from a particular time period – the "dot-com boom" – when companies had been over-investing in information technology. In any case, there are several possibilities as to why these initial efforts to integrate database marketing and customer relationship management may not have been successful:

- *Organizational Barriers*: Database marketing-based CRM requires organizational coordination. Companies have not been able to achieve this. Marketing quarrels with sales over who owns the customer (Boehm 2001). Marketing and finance quarrel about how deeply to go down the prioritized customer file in investing in the relationship. Marketing and IT do not share insights from the data mining (Gillet 1999). Management reward structures are too short term to encourage cultivating the customer. Peppers and Rogers (1997) argue that organization structures and compensation schemes must adapt to the customer-centric revolution. Srinivasan and Moorman (2002) show that a customer-focused reward system and strong interactions between marketing and IT encourage appropriate investment decisions that in turn breed customer satisfaction and better corporate performance. Reinartz et al. (2004) show that rewarding employees for cultivating relationships enhances the effectiveness of CRM efforts.

- *Acquisition versus Retention Costs*: While part of the attraction of CRM is the view that it is cheaper to increase retention than to increase acquisition, it this assumption may be incorrect. For example, part of the CRM strategy is to develop a "single view of the customer". This enables the firm to manage the customer as an entity, rather than focus on individual products. However, this may be very expensive to achieve. Gormley (1999) reports that 92% of companies think the single view of the customer is important, but 88% either "not really" or "not at all" have it today. So it may be that the IT costs associated with compiling the data needed to manage the customer are formidable.

- *Cultivating the Customer Side of Customer Relationship Management*: Fournier et al. (1998) argue that companies simply have not delivered reciprocal benefits that are a cornerstone of customer relationships (Fournier 1998). Companies make unrealistic demands on customers. They charge loyal customers higher prices rather than lower prices. They appear pre-occupied with their very best customers and under-occupied with their average customer. One of the supposed benefits of CRM is being able to identify best customers and focus on them (Peppers and Rogers 1993; Zeithaml et al. 2001). While this may be appropriate, it does not mean that average customers should be abandoned or relegated to automatic call-handling systems. Malthouse and Blattberg (2005) show that many of the future best customers come from customers who are currently average.

- *Relying on Technology to Solve What Essentially is An Issue of Corporate Culture*: The view of CRM as a database marketing activity is that databases are a tool for economies of scale. They allow large firms to know customers in the way that the corner drugstore used to know its customers (Swift 2001). However, this is only half the equation. The other part is that the proprietor of the corner drugstore truly cared about his/her customers. CRM is more than having the memory and database knowledge of consumer needs and wants. It requires a corporate culture oriented toward caring for individuals than the task-oriented corporate cultures that are

amenable to information technology (see Deshpandé et al. 1993). These
points have been raised by Sheth and Sisodia (2001) as well as Day (2000).

• *Companies Have Not Been Able to Balance Customer-Centricity and
  Product-Centricity*: CRM exhorts firms to become customer centric, that
  is, view their business as customer management rather than product
  management. Companies have perhaps come up against the financial
  problems in creating a single view of the customer, the organizational
  conflicts between CRM and product management and other groups, and
  the realization that their culture does not focus on the customer, and
  declared CRM to be a failure. Perhaps the answer is to view the solution
  along a continuum, from fully customer-centric to fully product-centric,
  and management's task is to find the right balance.

While the above paints a dim picture of database marketing as the basis
for CRM, the Conference Board (Bodenberg 2001) sampled 96 marketing
and sales executives, representing a cross-section of companies in terms of
manufacturing versus service, revenues, B2B versus B2C, and size of customer base. Eighty percent of respondents reported their CRM efforts either
somewhat or very successful. Companies who report very successful efforts are
more likely to warehouse their own data. This suggests a strong commitment
to CRM. The report finds that the factors that often lead to CRM success
are: corporate culture and leadership, process and technology improvement,
direct communications with the customer, and budgetary and cost savings.
There are also anecdotal testimonies to the success of CRM programs. These
include companies such as Harrah's Entertainment (Maselli 2002; Swift 2001)
and several others.

Two important empirical studies connect database marketing, customer
relationships, and firm performance. Zahay and Griffin (2004) surveyed 209
software and insurance managers. They measured: (1) personalization and
customization, i.e., using data to create individual-level products and communications, (2) customer information system (CIS) development, i.e., the
degree to which the firm can generate, remember, disseminate, and interpret
customer data, (3) customer performance, i.e., retention, LTV, and share-of-
wallet, and (4) business performance, i.e., self-reported growth and income.
The authors found that personalization and customization (i.e., the practice
of database marketing), related positively to the development of the CIS,
which in turn related positively to customer performance, which in turn related positively to firm performance (p. 186, fig. 2.5). In summary, database
marketing (developing a CIS and using it for personalization and customization), relationship development (customer performance), and business performance go together.

Reinartz et al. (2004) surveyed 211 executives to study the relationship
between CRM activities and firm performance. CRM activities consisted
of efforts to initiate, maintain, and terminate customer relationships. They
used several self-report scale items to measure these constructs. Items included "We use data from external sources for identifying potential high value

customers" (initiation), "We continuously track customer information in order to assess customer value" (maintenance), "We have formalized procedures for cross-selling" (maintenance), and "We have a formal system for identifying nonprofitable or lower-value customers" (termination). Performance was measured using both self-report, and for a subset of their sample, an objective measure (return on assets). The authors found that CRM efforts were positively associated with self-report and objective measures of performance. They also found organizational factors could enhance this association. Specifically, the degree of "organizational alignment," which entailed reward systems for employees who enhance customer relationships, and organizational capabilities to treat customers differently according to their profitability, interacted positively with the impact of CRM efforts on performance.

Interestingly, the authors found that investment in CRM technology, which included enhancements to the firm's ability to target 1-to-1 and to manage "real-time" customer information, was *negatively* related to the perceptual measures of performance. One interpretation of these results is that while having a good customer database enhances performance, it is all too easy to over-invest in sophisticated technology that does not pay out.

These two studies provide an initial set of evidence relating the compilation and utilization of customer data to customer relationships and to firm performance. The evidence is not definitive, and there are several avenues that need investigation. For example, Reinartz et al. (2004) do not isolate the role of customer data, treating it as a part of CRM efforts. In addition, the negative results for investment in CRM technology, which is often data-oriented, give pause to the "collect-all-possible-data" dictum, and need further research. The Zahay and Griffin (2004) study views CRM as the antecedent of customer data, whereas the causality may be the reverse, i.e., CIS enables CRM, which in turn enhances performance. In summary, future work should analyze different models with different measures in different industries before we can fully understand whether and under what conditions the collection and utilization of customer data enhances customer relationships and firm performance.

2.2.4 Assessment

Overall, the logic for database marketing as a tool for developing customer relationships is compelling. That retention has a bigger impact than acquisition is a mathematical truism. There is empirical work that says that strong relationships lead to better customer satisfaction, better retention, and hence better firm performance. One major question is: "Do retention investments have a higher payout than acquisition investments?" The literature on this question is almost non-existent. An exception is Reinartz et al. (2005) who find: (a) under-spending is more detrimental than over-spending; and (b) suboptimal allocation on retention has a greater effect than under-spending on acquisition. However, more research is needed to understand the allocation of resources between acquisition versus retention efficiencies and costs. Another question is whether database marketing can be used to create or improve customer relationships. There is evidence on both sides, including two empirical studies supporting a positive association among database marketing, CRM initiatives, and firm performance. But there is a critical need for more systematic research.

2.3 Creating Sustainable Competitive Advantage

2.3.1 The Basic Argument

Database marketing utilizes a customer information file, which by definition is owned by one company and not the other. The company can use its information to serve its customer better by identifying the correct services to offer, make product recommendations, or tailor promotions more effectively than its competition can do with this set of customers. This asymmetric information gives a company a potential sustainable competitive advantage. It is sustainable because it would cost the competition too much to obtain the same information – they would have to buy the company. In fact, increasingly the value of a company is determined by the value of its customer file (Gupta et al. 2004a).

This vision is compelling. Customer databases are proprietary and their advantage grows as the company learns from them and improves its customer offerings even more. However, this does not consider competition. In particular, will each competitor assemble its own database and allow a "live and let live" customer information environment, or will they compete more intensely to acquire the competitor's customers and retain their own customers? We investigate these issues as we trace the evolution of the sustainable competitive advantage argument.

2.3.2 Evolution of the Sustainable Competitive Advantage Argument

The argument that database marketing provides a sustainable competitive advantage has evolved in three steps. First was the emergence of "marketing orientation" as a source of competitive advantage. Marketing orientation involved the collection and utilization of customer information. However, customer information was defined broadly and not specifically as the customer information *file* used by database marketers. In the second step, Glazer (1991, 1999) and others sharpened the role of customer information files, and how they could provide companies with a competitive edge. In the third step, economists have developed formal models explaining how the customer information file could provide a sustainable increase in profits.

2.3.2.1 Marketing Orientation

Kohli and Jaworski (1990) defined marketing orientation as the "generation" of customer data, its "dissemination," within the organization, and the "responsiveness" of the organization to the information. A series of studies measured marketing orientation and related it to performance.

Jaworski and Kohli (1993) conducted executive surveys using two samples, of 145 and 136 strategic business units (SBU's) units respectively. (Also see Kohli et al. 1993). They defined market orientation similar to their 1990 paper, and measured it on a 32-item scale. The scale included items related to actions such as meeting with customers on a frequent basis, doing in-house market research, collecting industry information, etc. There was no explicit measurement of the use of customer information file.

The authors found that market orientation had a significant positive relationship with a judgmental business performance measure. However, market orientation had no relationship with an objective business performance measure-dollar market share. The antecedents of marketing orientation included top management emphasis, high interdepartmental connectedness and low conflict, decentralized organization, and a reward system orientation to executive compensation. This paper established that organizational factors create an environment for developing a marketing orientation. It did not however show that marketing orientation improves firm performance in terms of an objective business performance measure.

Moorman (1995) surveyed 92 marketing vice presidents and found that the mere collection and transmission of information had no effect on the firm's new product performance, but that "conceptual" and "instrumental" utilization were positively related. Conceptual utilization is the indirect use of information such as summarizing results, giving them meaning, etc. Instrumental utilization is the direct application of the information to evaluating projects and giving clear direction for implementation. Moorman's findings imply it takes more than the simple collection and dissemination of the information to create an advantage and the key is in making sense of the information and actually using it to guide policy.

Moorman and Rust (1999) surveyed two samples of managers, of sizes n = 330 and n = 128. They found that market orientation related to profitability and market performance but interestingly, not to customer relationship performance. Moorman and Rust's results imply that customer information can improve performance but not necessarily create loyal customers. It is as if the high market orientation firms use data to improve marketing productivity, but not necessarily to nurture customer relationships.

As described in Sect. 2.2.3, more recent work (Zahay and Griffin 2004; Reinartz et al. 2004) has specifically linked database marketing activities to firm performance. The information utilization constructs in these studies relate more directly to database marketing activities, and therefore extend the work relating marketing orientation to performance to the more specific realm of database marketing and firm performance.

Overall, the line of work linking database marketing to firm performance is growing although not yet definitive. Early work on marketing orientation finds some linkages, especially Moorman's (1995) study that it is the utilization, not the mere collection of data, which builds competitive advantage. This is reinforced by Zahay and Griffin (2004) as well as Reinartz et al. (2004). More work is needed, especially relating database marketing to *objective* performance measures.

2.3.2.2 The Customer Information File as a Firm Asset

Glazer (1991, 1999) presented the conceptual link between the general notion of customer information and the value of the *customer information file*. Glazer (1991) speaks of three types of information-based value creation: the information from upstream transactions with suppliers (V^s), the information from internal operations (V^f), and the information from downstream transactions with customers (V^c). Customer information is of interest to database marketers, and contributes in three ways: increased revenues from future transactions (e.g., through better targeting of the right products at the right price), reduced costs (e.g., through not having to mail every offer to every customer), and the sale of information itself (through say renting the customer list). These facets combine to determine the extent to which value generated by a product or service is due to customer information (V^f).

Glazer (1991) discusses that where the firm stands in terms of supplier, firm and customer information has important implications for the overall strategy of the firm. For example, it can determine whether the firm pursues a market share or market niche/targeting strategy. Market share strategies are based on economies of scale, high volume, and low cost, and require high supplier (V^s) and firm (V^f) information. High customer information tilts the firm toward targeting strategies, where the key is product differentiation and focus on a particular niche or target group. Glazer argues that if a firm can achieve high values on all three components, it can pursue a flexible manufacturing, mass customization strategy.

Rust et al. (2002) take a related but somewhat different perspective. They conceptualize the choice as between revenue expansion (focus on the customer), and cost reduction (focus on decreasing operations and organizational costs). Customer information supports the revenue expansion approach, whereas supplier and firm information supports the cost reduction

	Customer Characteristics	Responses to Firm Marketing	Purchase History	Profit Potential
Customer 1	Demographics	Offers and responses	Purchases	Lifetime value
Customer 2	Demographics	Offers and responses	Purchases	Lifetime value
Customer 3	Demographics	Offers and responses	Purchases	Lifetime value
Customer 4	Demographics	Offers and responses	Purchases	Lifetime value
Customer 5	Demographics	Offers and responses	Purchases	Lifetime value
Etc.				

Fig. 2.8 The customer information file (CIF) and marketing strategy (From Glazer 1999).

approach. They find that firms perform[3] better when they focus on revenue expansion, illustrating the importance of customer information, than when they focus on both revenue expansion and cost reduction. So it appears that companies in practice may have trouble achieving all three types of information-based value creation.

Glazer's 1991 paper set the stage for his 1999 paper, where he explicitly discusses the role of the customer information file (CIF), which is the source of V^c. He defines "smart markets" as markets where the stock of customer information changes frequently, and maintains that these markets are on the increase. He uses the customer information file as a framework to generate strategies for succeeding in smart markets.

The CIF is organized as in Fig. 2.8 and suggests three "generic" strategies: row management, column management, and row and column management ("whole file"). We will just cover "row" and "column" strategies. A column management strategy focuses on maximizing responses to a particular marketing program or product. This may involve tailoring the product to the customer (mass customization) or targeting appropriate prices to various buyers (yield management). Note that column management strategies are "product-centric". They start with a product, e.g., a credit card, and figure out how to tailor features, interest rates, and prices or fees to individual customers so as to maximize firm profits.

In contrast, row management strategies focus on each customer and ask what can the firm do to maximize profits from each or a particular set of customers. The focus is on interactive marketing communications designed to maximize the lifetime value of the customer. An example Glazer provides (p. 64) is American Express using a relationship-billing program with its commercial customers in which it first provides a given establishment demographic analysis of its customers and then uses this information to sell establishment advertising space in publications.

Glazer echoes Moorman's (1995) point that in smart markets (markets that are driven by customer information files), the ability to *process* information, not the information itself, is the scarce resource. Thus, the

---

[3] Performance is in terms of return on assets (ROA) and stock market returns.

source of competitive advantage to a firm is a combination of creating customer information files, processing of the information and then utilizing the information to drive superior marketing strategies.

2.3.2.3 Economic Theories of Customer Information as a Strategic Asset

The marketing orientation literature provided a conceptual and empirical basis for marketing information as a firm asset, and Glazer and others moved that literature toward a focus on the customer information file as the source of marketing advantage, and recent work suggests a link between customer data and firm performance. The economic modeling literature then analyzed the strategic implications of company's pursuit of competitive advantage through management of the customer information file.

There are several important phenomena we will discuss that have emerged from these efforts, but the central theme is that they focus on the goal of price discrimination, whereby the firms use customer information to identify and offer higher prices to their loyal customers and lower prices to switchers. The central question is: does an environment in which firms use customer data to target prices increase profits? Economists have investigated how this is influenced by competition, by the accuracy of the targeting, and by the strategic behavior of firms as well as customers.

Can Customer Information Be the Source of a Prisoner's Dilemma?

Shaffer and Zhang (1995) investigated whether company profits increase when customer preferences can be identified. Their customer behavior model arrayed customers along a continuum of preference for either Firm 1 or Firm 2 (the well-known Hotelling framework). Customers trade off their preference for the firm's product versus the price of that product to decide which firm to choose. The authors assumed that both firms have perfect information on customer preferences and on the relative weights customers place on preferences versus price.

Shaffer and Zhang's set-up is somewhat based on Catalina Marketing, a firm that targets coupons to customers based on their previous buying habits. The buying habits can be determined based on a full customer history, or simply on the product most recently purchased at the cash register. For example, if the customer buys Coke in a particular week, this suggests they prefer Coke. At that exact purchase occasion, Pepsi could target a coupon to the customer to induce a brand switch on the customer's next purchase occasion.

The initially surprising, and from the perspective of database marketing, dispiriting result was that in this scenario, firms engage in a "targeting war" in which profits are lower with customer information than without. The problem is that firms cannot practice price discrimination. They want to charge high prices to their loyal customers but cannot do so because the competing firm can attract these "loyals" with a steeply discounted coupon. As a result, prices for loyal customers are not high enough to effect price discrimination, and prices for switchers (customers in the middle of the Hotelling line) are very low as these customers are relatively indifferent between firms.

Shaffer and Zhang (1995) present a rather dismal view of database marketing simply as a vehicle for competing more intensively. Obviously, this does not match the real-world since more and more firms are using database marketing. This goes to the issue of model assumptions. One of the key assumptions in their model is that firms have perfect information on customer preferences. This is rarely the case. Firms typically know only a given set of customers (their own).

Imperfect Targetability

Chen et al. (2001), and Chen and Iyer (2002) both make a case that in a more realistic world of imperfect targetability, firm profits actually increase when they utilize customer databases. The reason is that firms are aware that their targeting is not perfect, and this cushions price competition compared to the targeting wars in the Shaffer and Zhang scenario. We will review these papers in detail because they are crucial for providing the case that database marketing can be a source of sustainable competitive advantage.

Chen et al. (2001) use Narasimhan's (1988) consumer model, assuming there are three types of consumers: loyal to Firm 1, loyal to Firm 2, and switchers, which occur with probabilities γ_1, γ_2, and χ respectively. Loyal customers will always buy from their preferred firm as long as its price is lower than their reservation price, anchored at $1 in the model. Switchers will buy the brand that is available at the lower cost to them, or will buy each brand with probability 0.50 if prices are equal. Note that this model is different than the Hotelling model used by Shaffer and Zhang, where customers were positioned along a continuum in terms of preference, and all were potentially vulnerable to low price discounts. The Chen et al. model is still realistic – there are customers loyal to Coke, McDonalds, Fleet Bank or Fidelity, who will continue to purchase these brands as long as their price does not become too high. We will examine how profits change in this scenario as targetability increases.

Chen et al. conceptualize "targetability" as the firm's ability to identify loyals and switchers. Chen et al. assume that a firm has information on its own loyal customers and switchers, but not on its competitors' loyals. It can target its own loyals, but not its competitors' loyals. Consider Fidelity Investments. The assumption Chen et al. make is that Fidelity has information on a given set of customers that they can classify as loyal to them (i.e., only buy financial services from them), or switchers (buy sometimes from Fidelity, but sometimes from Merrill Lynch), but they do not have information on customers who are loyal to Merrill Lynch. Chen et al. create a targetability index equal to 0 if the firm's ability to classify is no better than random and 1 if targeting is perfect.

In their first set of analyses, the targetability index for each firm is considered exogenous. The question is how profits change depending on this index. To answer this question, they identify three forces that depend on targetability. First is the *segmentation effect* which results when firms can correctly identify their loyals, leading to gains in profits because they can charge them appropriately high prices. Second is the *mistargeting effect*, whereby firms mis-identify switchers as loyals and hence charge them inappropriately high prices. Third is the *price competiton/share* effect, where firms correctly identify switchers and charge them low prices to gain share.

Chen et al.'s first result is that a firm that has targeting ability always attains higher profits if it competes with a firm that cannot target, and the profit advantage increases as targetability increases. The segmentation and price competition effects allow it to practice price discrimination without the concern of being undercut by the mass marketer, who cannot do so effectively because it does not know to whom to target. The mistargeting effect holds down the database marketers profits, but as this effect decreases due to better targetability, the database marketer's profits increase all the more. Interestingly, while the database marketer's profits are always higher than the mass marketer's profits, the mass marketer actually gains over its base profits when mistargeting is high. The reason is that when mistargeting is high, the database marketer charges overly high prices to mistargeted switchers, and the mass marketer gains some of these switchers without having to charge an excessively low price. In this way, the mass marketer can actually be better off than they would be if they were competing with a database marketer whose mistargeting costs are high.

This result says that database marketing provides a sustainable profit advantage if one firm practices it and another does not. However, a more likely scenario is that both firms have the ability to target. Chen et al. show that in this case, profits for both firms are always at least as high with imperfect targeting than without it, but the relationship between targetability and profits is an inverse U-shape, as in Fig. 2.9. Firm profits are maximized at intermediate values of targetability. At low levels of targetability, firms cannot practice price discrimination and hence profits are low. At intermediate levels of targetability, the segmentation effect enables firms to price discriminate and the mistargeting effect softens price undercutting. At high targetability, the price competition effect becomes important because both firms are identifying switchers, and the mistargeting benefit no longer cushions prices. The situation is similar to Shaffer and Zhang (1995). This yields lower profits.

Chen et al. develop a number of additional results. First, they find that Firm 1 has a profit advantage over Firm 2 if it has a larger number of

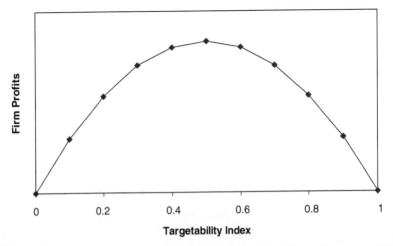

Fig. 2.9 Relationship between targetability and firm profits (From Chen et al. 2001).

accurately identified loyal users. Database marketing can become a sustainable competitive advantage especially for the firm with a strong customer base. The Chen et al. model is static in the sense that it does not consider the impact of targeting on future loyalty, if firms can use their targeting ability to nurture their loyal customers, which in turn can increase their ability to target (through more and better information revealed by these increasingly loyal customers), one can see how the firm can develop a *sustainable* advantage.

Chen et al. also consider the optimal levels that firms should invest in database marketing. They find that firms will decrease investment in database marketing if costs are high, although the firm with the larger loyal segment will invest more. When database marketing costs are low, both will invest in database marketing to the fullest extent possible. Keeping in mind Fig. 2.9, this implies that firms can "over invest" and end up on the right side of Fig. 2.9, where price competition becomes more intense, and the mistargeting effect is not strong enough to soften price competition. Chen et al. also find that even taking into account investment costs, if the firms have roughly the same number of loyal customers, profits for both firms are higher with targeting than without. So database marketing is a "win-win" for the industry. If the loyal segments are unbalanced, presumably it is the stronger firm that wins.

Chen and Iyer (2002) provide a different perspective on the role of imperfect targeting by changing the analysis in two ways. First, customers are located on a Hotelling line, similar to Shaffer and Zhang, and no firm commands absolute loyalty. Secondly, they provide a different definition of targetability. Their definition of targetability is the percentage of customers at each point on the line (preference level) who can be addressed by Firm I (a_i), where the assumption is that if the customer can be addressed, its preferences are known. Chen et al. assume all the firm's customers can be addressed, but that the firm is not sure whether the customers are loyals or switchers. Chen and Iyer assume that firms can perfectly identify the preferences of all customers it can reach, but that it cannot target all customers.

In Chen and Iyer's model, there are three main groups of consumers: Group 1 consists of customers that can be reached by Firm 1 but not by Firm 2 $(a_1(1-a_2))$. Group 2 consists of customers that can be reached by Firm 2 but not by Firm 1 $(a_2(1-a_1))$. Group 3 consists of customers that can be reached by both firms (a_1a_2). Firm 1 has monopoly power over Group 1, Firm 2 has monopoly power over Group 2, and both firms will compete for Group 3. Chen and Iyer call Group 1 and Group 2 the surplus extraction effect, because each firm can charge a high price and still acquire its customers. This is analogous to the segmentation effect in Chen et al. The Group 3 situation is called the "competitive" effect, since firms will compete strongly for this segment. This is analogous to the price competition effect in Chen et al.

Chen and Iyer capture the mistargeting effect in Chen et al. by assuming that Firm 1 knows what customers it can address but does not know what customers its competition can address. This assumption appears to make sense. Capital One knows what customers are in its database, but does not know which are also in its competitors' databases. More broadly, the assumption means that a firm knows its own marketing efforts for the customers on its list, but does not know the marketing efforts of other firms with these customers. As a result of this information asymmetry, each firm faces a trade-off in determining its prices. The firms want to price high for Groups 1 and 2, but need to price low in order to attract Group 3. Thus there is a trade-off between surplus extraction and price competition effects.

Chen and Iyer calculate equilibrium profits assuming given levels of a_1 and a_2. The profit for Firm 1 if these levels are roughly equal is:

$$Profit_1 = a_1(1-a_2)(r-t/2) + \frac{a_1(a_1+a_2)t}{2}\left[\frac{(a_2-a_1)r+a_1t}{(a_1+a_2)t}\right]^2 \quad (2.3)$$

where t is the per-unit distance disutility incurred by customers on the Hotelling line, and r is the reservation price for one unit of the good.

The first term represents the profits from Group 1 (of size $a_1(1-a_2)$) and represents the surplus extraction effect. The second term represents the profits from competing in the switching segment and represents the competitive effect. In the case where addressability is roughly equal, both these terms are important because Firm 1 realizes both Group 1 and Group 3 are sizable. So it tries to compete in both. If a_1 is much greater than a_2, Firm 1 realizes that Group 1 is the largest group, and does not bother to compete for Group 3 and profits just equal $a_1(1-a_2)(r-t/2)$. Firm 2 faces a similar situation if its addressability is much higher than Firm 1's.

One of Chen and Iyer's key results is that the equilibrium ratio of profits between Firms 1 and 2 will be proportional to their investments in database marketing. Therefore, the firm that invests more in database marketing has a competitive advantage. The advantage of having an addressability advantage is the ability to price high without having to worry about losing customers to the competitive firm (Group 3 is small). The database marketing leader is able to practice price discrimination along the Hotelling line, unfettered by worries about what its competitor might be doing.

Chen and Iyer also show that if addressability is high for both firms, the result is ruinous price competition for the switching segment. Both firms realize they have no monopoly power and must compete for switchers. This is analogous to the Chen et al. result that profits are lowest at very low or very high levels of targetability. Chen and Iyer show that if the costs of obtaining addressability are low, both firms will not invest in full addressability. One will choose $a_i = 1$ and the other will choose $a_j = 0.5$. The reason is that if Firm i has full addressability, Firm j realizes that to also achieve full addressability will precipitate targeting wars for the switching segment. Firm j is better off not investing fully in addressability. This creates a monopoly segment for Firm i, which in turn cushions Firm i's prices, since it now must trade off the surplus extraction and competition effects. Firm j makes less money than Firm i, but is better off than if invested fully in addressability. An important implication of this is that in the real world, where firms can invest sequentially, there is a first-mover advantage, and the smart company that is behind on database marketing should hold back investment to avoid the targeting war scenario of Shaffer and Zhang (1995).

Chen and Iyer explore two important assumptions regarding their analysis. First, concerns the segment $(1 - a_1)(1 - a_2)$ that is not addressable by either firm. Their model assumes these consumers are lost to the market, but they argue that if these customers can pay "posted prices" for the product, there still is the asymmetric equilibrium when addressability is low cost. Second, concerns the assumption that addressability is the same for all consumers, regardless of preferences. The authors find that if firms can choose addressability as a function of preference, they first will invest in being able to address customers who have high preference for their product. This makes sense, because then they can charge higher prices.

In summary, both Chen et al. (2001) and Chen and Iyer (2002) find that companies can obtain sustainable competitive advantages through investment in database marketing. Firms make more money when they have database marketing capabilities compared to when they do not. The key to this result is that there must be some mechanism that keeps firms from targeting wars as in Shaffer and Zhang. For Chen et al. that mechanism is that firms are not sure if a customer in their database is loyal to their firm or a switcher. Certainly this fits most situations. For Chen and Iyer, the mechanism is that firms do not know if their competitors can target their customers. This keeps firms from charging low prices because they realize that they may be "leaving money on the table" by charging low prices to customers who are not addressable by the competition. So the interesting conclusion is that an intermediate level of database marketing capability is best because it creates enough information to obtain the gains from targeting, but not too much as to spark targeting wars.

The Strategic Consumer

The Chen et al. and Chen and Iyer papers assume that firms are pre-
scient. They do not have perfect targeting information, but they are aware
of what they know and do not know, and consider the short and long-term
implications of their information set. The consumer, on the other hand, is
considered to be passive. However, what happens if the consumer realizes
that the underlying goal of the firms is to practice price discrimination, and
that by revealing their preferences, they may be the subject of price discrimination? In two important papers, Villas-Boas (1999, 2004) shows that
if consumers behave strategically, firms can be worse off if they can identify their customers. Villas-Boas (2004) is particularly important because
this is the monopolist case, and demonstrates that the disadvantage is not
due to a competitive targeting war as in Shaffer and Zhang. The problem
is that consumers hold out for lower prices because they realize that if they
do not reveal their preferences, firms will not be able to distinguish them
from brand switchers or customers new to the market and they will get low
prices.

Chen and Zhang (2002) acknowledge this possibility but argue that the
effect will be more than counter-balanced by the "price-for-information" effect. The effect arises as follows. Firms want to price discriminate but need
to identify customer preferences in order to do so. In a two-period model,
they are tempted to price low in the first period because they realize some
customers are holding out for cheaper two-period prices. However, they also
realize that by pricing high, they do not attract as many customers but the
customers they attract are clearly loyal to them, and they can use this information to charge appropriately high prices in the second period. In other
words, firms charge higher prices for the information they gain about customers that can be utilized in the long-term. This is the price-for-information
effect. Chen and Zhang show that even taking into account strategic customers, firms can be better off with database marketing than without. They
do have to lower their first-period prices to discourage their loyals from wait-
ing, but they do not need to lower them completely because they realize
they will gain in the long run from learning about the customers they do
attract.

The area of strategic consumers is a crucial one for the success of database
marketing. A very different venue where the effect shows up is a static rather
than a dynamic one. Feinberg et al. (2002) argue that customers can become
jealous of other customers who get better deals than them. They then may
refrain from purchasing from the firm according to their preferences. Essentially, the customer is taking into account prices available to other consumers
to assess its likelihood of buying from the firm. This may not be seen as
strictly rational (why should what someone else gets affect your utility for a
product), but Feinberg et al. show in experiments that the jealousy effect is
real. To the extent that this jealousy effect is large, it decreases the ability

of firms to price discriminate, which is the driving force behind the economic arguments to date for database marketing.

The economic models described above make a set of key assumptions which drive their results: (1) the only strategic variable is price, (2) the purpose of database marketing is to allow the firm to price discriminate, (3) firms can target their loyal customers, and 4) only two firms compete. Each of these assumptions is suspect in the real-world. These models assume the purpose of database marketing is price discrimination. There is no empirical evidence that this is the goal of database marketing. Database marketing goals are far broader than simply price discrimination, as Glazer (1999) discusses.

Glazer (1999) shows that firms can compete using different (row and column) strategies, some of which are different than price. Under column strategies, he provides examples, one of which is yield management (similar to price in the economic models), but discusses mass customization as another example. He also discusses row strategies in which firms use addressability to develop customer interaction strategies to increase their loyalty. Economic models (to date) do not consider customer interaction strategies to increase loyalty as a goal of database marketing.

Many firms do not have any information about their customer's loyalty. All they can observe is purchase behavior (and maybe demographic information). The assumption of all of these models is that the firm somehow knows the loyalty level of its customers and then targets based on it. For example, Fidelity Investments does not know if its customers have accounts with Merrill Lynch, T. Rowe Price or Vanguard. One of the few industries which might know its customer loyalty is credit card issuers in the USA because they have information about the number and usage of cards through credit bureaus. However, it is difficult to identify many other industries that know the loyalty level of their customers.

Some firms use customer behavioral data to price their *best* customers lower than the competition. Vanguard offers lower fees to its Admiral customers, determined by the size of balances they have within a given mutual fund. The higher balance customers receive lower fees as a percentage of money invested. This may be a form of competitive pricing but is not price discrimination as in the models reviewed above.

Firms may try to price discriminate (airlines) but can succeed because they use another strategic variable (level of service) as the basis for customers' willingness to stay loyal even though they may be paying a higher price. The database allows the firm to identify those customers to offer a better service.

The assumption that only two firms compete may also pose problems. If a new entrant cannot enter the industry because of the use of customer databases by incumbent firms, then there is a return to database marketing. Clearly in some industries, new entrants face an uphill battle because they cannot target. An important research area is to identify industries in which database marketing is an entry deterrent.

2.3.3 Assessment

The evidence to date regarding database marketing as a route to sustainable competitive advantage is built on the following arguments:

- Empirical studies find some, although not overwhelming, evidence that marketing orientation – the ability of firms to collect, process, and implement customer information – as well as undertaking database marketing activities, is positively related to firm performance.
- The customer information file – the firm's database of its customers – is the modern source of customer information. The file suggests two principle strategies – customer centric (row strategies), and product centric (column strategies). Strategic advantage is based on maintaining customer information and developing these strategies.
- Economic models develop theories under which firms using pricing-oriented column strategies can practice effective price discrimination. The main requirement is that targeting abilities need to be "moderately effective". Too little and there are not enough benefits of targeting; too much and firms engage in targeting wars.

The arguments are interesting but more is needed to make establish that database marketing is a long-term source of competitive advantage. The marketing orientation studies provide some empirical evidence, but they refer to customer information in general and not to database marketing *per se*. Zahay and Griffin (2004) and Reinartz et al. (2004) provide important evidence that database marketing itself – using the customer information file – can be associated with better performance. However, the performance measures in several of these studies are self-report. More studies with objective performance measures are needed. The conceptual arguments regarding the customer information file and row (customer-centric) versus column (product-centric) strategies are well-taken, but have not undergone empirical testing. Do row strategies really increase loyalty? Can they be implemented inexpensively enough to increase profits?

The economic models provide logic and some insights, but they have not been tested empirically. Empirical research along the lines of the marketing orientation literature is needed, with the focus on *targetability* through customer information, not customer information in general. In terms of column strategies, more work is needed to understand whether prices for loyal customers should be higher (price discrimination) or lower (pay the customer for their loyalty) (see Shaffer and Zhang 2000), or to keep the loyal customer from getting jealous as in Feinberg et al. (2002).

The theory also needs to be extended to non-price column strategies, e.g., cross-selling, and to row strategies, i.e., long-term management of customer value. The extension to non-price column strategies would be particularly interesting. Managers would certainly like to think that customer databases enable them to serve customers better by targeting appropriate services from their product line, or by tailoring their product line to the customer. It might be that this type of targeting is more sustainable because it is more difficult for a competitor to understand the details of a customer's preferences for various product attributes than it is to understand price response. Row strategies might also be a source of more sustainable advantage, because long-term relationships may create switching costs that bind the customer to the firm. This leads to the existence of database marketing as a tool for enhancing customer relationships.

2.4 Summary

In this chapter, we have proposed and reviewed three fundamental reasons for companies to practice database marketing: enhancing marketing productivity, enabling the enhancement of customer relationships, and establishing a sustainable competitive advantage.

The marketing productivity argument is based on the use of data and data mining tools to prioritize and target customers with appropriate products, services, and prices. There is good evidence that this can work. Data mining indeed can produce "lift charts" for predicting customer behavior that are much better than random, and therefore can identify the customers for whom marketing efforts would be wasted.

The enhancing relationship argument is based on the notion that enhanced customer relationships improve firm performance, and database marketing can enhance relationships. The first part of the equation is well-supported by the importance of customer retention in lifetime customer value, and empirical studies that link customer relationships, customer satisfaction, customer retention/loyalty, and firm performance. Regarding the second part of the equation, there is a host of articles in the managerial literature that raise questions about whether CRM *investments* lead to improved financial performance. However, systematic empirical studies are beginning to find that indeed these investments can pay off.

The competitive advantage argument is based on the notion that the customer data file is a company resource that is impossible for companies to duplicate, that the data enable firms to service customers better than competitors, and that the better-than-random yet imperfect nature of predictions that come from the model cushions price competition. This area has received the least empirical study although the concept is compelling.

There is significant academic research pertaining to the fundamental reasons firms should use database marketing but there is much more to do. Regarding the productivity argument, we need more field tests that show predictive models work, that they generate incremental profits beyond channel cannibalization and beyond what could be generated by simple management heuristics. Regarding the sustainable competitive advantage argument, we need survey-based research similar to the marketing orientation literature that links database marketing, as opposed to customer information in general, to firm profits. We need more economic theory on non-price targeting, high versus low prices for loyals, and the strategic consumer. We need empirical tests of the economic models, particularly the role of imperfect targeting.

Regarding the enhancing CRM argument, we need to establish the link from database marketing to enhanced relationships to satisfaction to retention to performance. The last four links have been investigated; the crucial link is that database marketing enhances relationships. We also need to investigate the cost side of database marketing, and in particular, whether acquisition costs are truly higher than marginal retention costs. More generally, we need to investigate if and under what conditions retention management is more cost-effective than customer acquisition strategies.

Chapter 3
Organizing for Database Marketing

Abstract Quantitative analysis is endemic to database marketing, but these analyses and their implementation are not conducted in an organizational vacuum. In this chapter, we discuss how companies organize to implement database marketing. The key concept is the "customer-centric" organization, whereby the organization is structured "around" the customer. We discuss key ingredients of a customer-centric organizational structure: customer management and knowledge management. We also discuss types of database marketing strategies that precede organizational structure, as well as employee compensation and incentive issues.

3.1 The Customer-Centric Organization

Successful implementation of database marketing certainly requires mastery of data management and modeling methodology. However, these tools are not applied in an organizational vacuum. In this chapter we discuss how to design organizations for implementing database marketing successfully.

A key concept to emerge in this context is that of the "customer-centric" organization. This means that the organization is structured "around" the customer – from the customer in, rather than from the product out. In the words of industry expert David Siegel as quoted by Stauffer (2001), "If you really care about customers...then you have to reorganize your entire company around customers." Stauffer then says, "It's not organizing the company to serve customers. It's letting customers determine how you organize." Galbraith (2005, p. 6), states customer-centricity as an imperative: "The need for customer-centricity is not going away, and it is up to each company to determine the level of application...required for success."

Fig. 3.1 Star model of the customer-centric organization (From Galbraith 2005).
* These concepts are used by Langerak and Verhoef (2003).

We will frame our discussion using the "Star" model developed by Galbraith (2002, 2005). The Star model emphasizes five ingredients for successful organizational design: strategy, structure, processes, rewards, and people (Galbraith 2005, p. 15). Strategy refers to the goals of the organization and the means by which it intends to achieve them. Structure refers to the organizational chart – what departments and positions need to be created, and how will they interact. Processes refer to the means by which information flows within the organization. Rewards refer to the compensation and incentives that ensure the employees of the organization perform effectively. People refers to the policies that ensure that employees have the right skills and "mind-set" to implement the organizational design.

Figure 3.1 shows the Star model applied to designing the customer-centric organization. Listed under each of the five components of the framework are the key issues that will be discussed in the following sections.

3.2 Database Marketing Strategy

The organization design for implementing database marketing emerges from the firm's database marketing strategy. The key issues are: (1) What is that strategy, and (2) How will the organizational design establish a competitive advantage?

3.2.1 Strategies for Implementing DBM

3.2.1.1 The Langerak/Verhoef Taxonomy

Langerak and Verhoef (2003) distinguish three types of CRM strategies: Customer Intimacy, Operational Efficiency, and Marketing Efficiency. Customer Intimacy means that the company's strategy truly is to deliver personal service to its customers, to know them on an intimate base and customize its products, services, and communications to them. Operational Efficiency employs CRM to reduce costs and utilize non-marketing resources efficiently. Marketing Efficiency uses customer data to improve marketing productivity, i.e., making marketing more effective at achieving less churn, more successful cross-selling, and in general, greater customer profitability.

Langerak and Verhoef argue that organization design should follow from which of the three strategies the company pursues. For example, they study a private investment banking firm whose strategy was Customer Intimacy, but the company approach to customer service was actually quite impersonal. The firm realized it needed to develop personal, intimate relationships with its customers. They grouped their customers into three need segments ("self-made man," "strategy maker," and "security seeker") and assigned a customer management team to each group. They created an organizational structure that best implemented their strategy.

Langerak and Verhoef also studied an insurance company that competed on operational excellence, i.e., "price, convenience, and speed." This meant that the company needed to keep operations costs as low as possible, and develop ways of interacting with customers that were as fast and efficient as possible. This strategy required a highly transactional relationship with customers. The company adopted an organizational structure based fundamentally on data management. The data management group fed information to the rest of the organization to help it be more efficient. It especially supported the firm's efforts on the Internet channel, where products could be personalized at low cost.

Finally, Langerak and Verhoef studied a holiday resort company whose marketing efforts were highly inefficient. They provided mass-mailing offers with very low response rates. They needed CRM to improve marketing efficiency. Accordingly, they set up a CRM department that focused on data mining, database management, and integrating database marketing and customer contact efforts. The system was in place only to increase the productivity of their marketing efforts.

The main point is that the three generic CRM strategies identified by Langerak and Verhoef each require different organizational designs and different levels of customer-centricity.

3.2.1.2 Galbraith's "Strategy Locator"

Galbraith (2005, pp. 32–33) also proposes that the desired degree of customer-centricity depends on the strategy of the company. He develops a "Strategy Locator", a measurement scale consisting of two dimensions: Scale and Scope, and Integration. Scale and Scope refers to the number and variety of products marketed by the company. Integration refers to the degree that the company's products must be packaged or bundled together to deliver satisfaction to the customer. According to Galbraith, the higher the company scores on this scale, i.e., the degree to which the company offers many varied products that must be integrated, determines the degree to which the firm must be customer-centric.

Galbraith describes a chemical company that only required "light-level" customer-centricity. The company had relatively few products that did not need to be integrated. It therefore rated low on the strategy locator. The organizational design did include some elements of customer-centricity – e.g., customer management teams – although the formal organizational structure centered on functions and geographic areas.

Galbraith then describes an investment bank that required a "medium-level" degree of customer-centricity. This company had a moderate number of banking products that required integration. It therefore rated medium on the strategy locator. The organizational design included not only customer managers, but formal processes to ensure that customer contacts were coordinated within the customer management team. Formal reward structures based on customer performance were implemented, and formal CRM training programs were put in place.

Galbraith uses IBM as an example of requiring a "complete-level" degree of customer-centricity. IBM has several different products, requiring a high degree of integration. IBM therefore rates high on the strategy locator. IBM's strategy focused on delivering customer "solutions", a highly customer-centric idea. The notion was to solve the customer's problem, whatever products and services were required. Given the complexity of problems, this required very high coordination among IBM management. IBM now has a solutions-oriented structure where Product managers work with the customer to deliver the right combination of IBM products and services to solve the customer's problem. Its processes help ensure that customer plans and priorities are shared easily among the relevant managers involved with the customer. The company still uses quotas to reward salespeople, a product-centric approach, but also formally assesses the "competencies" of its employees to make sure they match customer needs.

3.2.2 Generating a Competitive Advantage

Firms are constantly trying to establish a competitive advantage – a core competence that gives them a sustainable edge over its competition. One possibility is that the organizational design through which the company implements database marketing might be a source of competitive advantage.

Peteraf (1993), articulating the "resource-based view of the firm," defines four factors that determine whether a company's competences will translate into competitive advantage: heterogeneity, ex-post limits to competition, imperfect mobility, and ex-ante limits to competition.[1] Heterogeneity means that firms within the industry have different competencies. For example, one firm may develop a marketing analytics group that is different, and better, than the groups at other companies. Ex-post limits mean that the company's capabilities are difficult to replicate. For example, competitors may know which software package the firm uses for cross-selling, but because the firm has an organizational structure that emphasizes customer management, it knows its customers so well that no other firm can duplicate its success. Imperfect mobility means that the resources that give the firm its competitive advantage cannot be obtained by another firm. Competitors often try to hire away a firm's best managers. However, a customer manager might be effective because the scale of the firm permits frequent interaction with the marketing analytics group. So a firm cannot simply hire this manager away and expect the same success. Ex-ante limits refer to first-mover advantage. For example, a company that first uses CRM for operational efficiency may be "ahead of the curve" in terms of the organizational structure that best supports this strategy.

3.2.3 Summary

Strategy plays a pivotal role in determining the organizational structure for implementing database marketing. While "customer-centricity" has come into fashion, Langerak and Verhoef (2003) as well as Galbraith (2005) argue that not all organizations need to adopt the same degree of customer-centricity. Another major theme is that the goal is to wed the firm's database marketing strategy with an organizational design that creates a competitive advantage for the firm.

---

[1] The authors thank Professor Margaret Peteraf and Justin Engelland, Tuck MBA 2005, for helpful discussions on this topic.

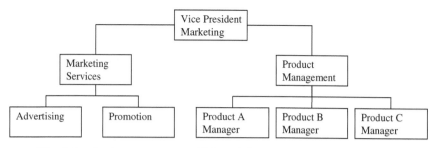

Fig. 3.2a Product management (Adapted from Peppers and Rogers 1993).

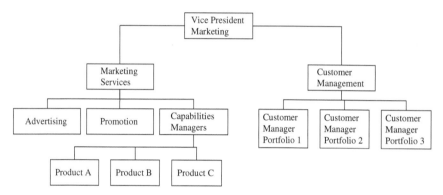

Fig. 3.2b Customer management (Adapted from Peppers and Rogers 1993).

3.3 Customer Management: The Structural Foundation of the Customer-Centric Organization

3.3.1 What Is Customer Management?

The customer management organization structure has been articulated by Peppers and Rogers (1993, pp. 175–206). Their idea is that the marketing efforts of the firm should be organized by customer groups or "portfolios", each portfolio managed by a customer manager. This is in stark contrast to the product management structure. Figure 3.2 illustrates. In the product management structure (Fig. 3.2a), product managers run their products as profit centers. They are responsible for generating sales and profits. They rely on the traditional "Four P's" (product, price, distribution, and promotion), draw on services provided by advertising and promotion departments, and work closely with production managers on product improvements and quality.

The customer management framework (Fig. 3.2b) clusters the firm's customers into portfolios. One possible clustering is by sales level – heavy, medium, and light user customer portfolios. Each customer would be assigned to one and only one portfolio. Each portfolio would be managed by a customer manager. The customer manager would draw support from advertising and promotion departments, and from "capabilities managers," the former product managers who would now be responsible for making sure the products performed up to the standards needed to serve customers. Customer managers would work with product managers on quality issues as well as new product features and other product development tasks.

The customer manager's goal is to increase the lifetime value of the customers in his or her portfolio. This emphasizes the long-term orientation of the customer manager. Peppers and Rogers define the customer manager's job as follows (1997, pp. 356–357): "... *someone* must be assigned the responsibility for managing *customers individually.* ... The customer manager's responsibility is to manage each customer relationship, supervising the firm's dialogue with each, finding products and services for each, and determining how best to customize to meet each customer's individual specifications. In short, the customer manager's job is to delve more and more deeply into each individual customer's needs in order to lock the customer in, make the firm more valuable to the customer, and increase the company's margin – with each customer."

3.3.2 The Motivation for Customer Management

The motivation for customer management rests on three assumptions: (1) Stronger customer relationships yield higher sales and profits. (2) The product management system is not effective at developing customer relationships. (3) The customer management system is effective at developing customer relationships.

The premise for the first assumption is that the customer is more powerful today than ever before. In a B2C context, customers in industries ranging from financial services to telecom to travel to retail face an ever-expanding array of choices and they make choices with more information (due to the Internet). In B2B industries, companies ranging from IBM to Xerox face the same sophisticated customer. Companies like P&G are becoming more like B2B companies – their customers are Wal-Mart and the newly consolidated supermarket companies. The assumption that better customer relationships feed firm performance has received some empirical support (Reinartz et al. 2004; Zahay and Griffin 2004; Day and Van den Bulte 2002; Chaston et al. 2003), although more work is needed.

The second assumption has not received empirical testing. The logic is that product management maximizes sales, not customer satisfaction. Each of the firm's product managers acts individually, with the result that customers are bombarded with offers and selling pitches. The customer is "turned off" by this marketing blitz, and perhaps most importantly, finds him or herself owning the wrong products. A good example would be financial services, where the customer becomes over-invested in retirement products like IRAs when he or she should be investing in college-funding instruments. In short, the firm spends too much money on marketing, many of its efforts cannibalize each other, and they don't yield better customer relationships.

The third assumption, that customer management is effective for developing customer relationships, has also not been tested directly. In Sect. 3.5, we discuss evidence that customer-oriented incentive systems produce more satisfied customers and better marketing performance. But this does not validate customer management *per se*. These incentives could be used for product managers as well as customer managers.

In summary, the motivation for customer management is that customer relationships are vital, product management is antithetical to this goal, and customer management will be successful at achieving this goal. This motivation has received some empirical support but much more evidence is needed.

3.3.3 Forming Customer Portfolios

A major challenge is how to define customer portfolios. Peppers and Rogers advocate that firms define portfolios based on customer needs. This allows the customer manager to specialize in serving the needs relevant to these customers. There are many ways to actualize this idea. One method is to group customers by volume. This is consistent with customer tier management (Chapter 23). An airline for example may have customer managers for its premium tier customers. While customer volume is a natural grouping scheme, there are many others. A financial services company may group customers by life-stage, e.g., young professionals, families, and retirees. A software company may group customers by line-of-business, e.g., education versus business, or by industry. In fact, a major challenge in customer management is to decide exactly how to form the customer portfolios, and how many portfolios should be defined. This is very much the perennial marketing issue of how a market should be segmented.

One challenge in defining customer portfolios is customer movement between portfolios. For example, the financial services customer manager for young professionals should be concerned with passing along good customers to the customer manager for young families. The customer manager for low-volume customers should be concerned with turning them into high value customers. The compensation system becomes key – it should be based not only the current profitability of the customer portfolio, but also on how many customers the customer manager converts to high volume customers, or the number and quality of young professionals the customer manager passes along to the young family customer manager. Referring back to the Star model (Fig. 3.1), this is an example where structure (the customer management system) interacts with compensation.

3.3.4 Is Customer Management the Wave of the Future?

To flesh out the key issues for firms deciding whether to pursue customer management organizational structures, in this section we discuss the pros and cons from an advocacy viewpoint.

3.3.4.1 Why Customer Management Is Inevitable

Customer management is inevitable and the firms that move first toward this system will achieve the highest rewards. The reasons for this are:

- *Customer satisfaction is the key to success and customer management will produce higher customer satisfaction than product management.* Customer management is truly focused on serving customer needs, whereas the product manager's goal is to sell product.
- *Customer management creates sustainable advantage.* Customer management encourages each company to know the needs of *its* customers better, and it is difficult for other firms to replicate this knowledge.
- *Product management is inherently short-term.* This is because it emphasizes current profits for one product. Customer managers are concerned with lifetime value of the customer, which is inherently long-term.
- *Modern Information technology enables customer management.* Until recently, firms did not have the data management systems nor the statistical tools required to pursue customer management activities such as cross-selling, lifetime value management, churn management, etc. These systems and tools are now in place.
- *Customer management may be revolutionary but it can be implemented in an evolutionary fashion.* For example, MacDonald (2001) reports that Nike Canada assigns "consumer champions" to specific customer groups. Customer champions do not have line responsibility as prescribed by a complete customer management structure, but they can change the conversation from "let's sell more basketball shoes" to "let's increases sales to teenage boys".

3.3.4.2 Why Customer Management Would Not Work

There are just too many practical, cultural, and structural reasons why customer management will be very difficult to implement. These include:

- *Product management is deeply ingrained in corporate culture.* Companies are product/sales/short-term oriented. Wall Street demands this, and it produces the most easily measured results. Customer management requires too much of a change in organizational culture.

- *Customer management will steer companies away from their distinctive competencies.* Most companies have distinctive competencies and cannot deliver the best product in each category. Customer managers may urge a financial services firm sell a mutual fund, but if this is not a high quality fund, this will produce dissatisfied clients in the long run.
- *Customer management will create even worse conflicts than those found among product managers.* Each customer manager will want more funds and will make competing demands on capabilities managers. For example, managers of the teen-age customers will demand certain features for the company credit card, while mangers of the 50+ customers will demand other features. Who has the authority to referee the demands of the customer managers for new product features versus the capabilities manager's view that these features are too expensive?
- *It is difficult to measure the key performance indexes for customer managers.* Performance indices for customer managers include share-of-wallet (SOW) and lifetime value (LTV). But SOW is difficult to measure because Firm A does not have data for how much business each customer does with Firms B and C. LTV calculations require many assumptions about retention rates, etc. It's impossible to design a reward system based on such fuzzy measurements.
- *It is not practical for many companies.* How can General Motors organize around Teens, Young Families, Young Professionals, Elderly, etc? How can General Mills organize around Families with Children, Singles, Elderly, etc? They just don't have direct access to customers on that basis.
- *Do customer managers have the expertise?* A customer manager must have the expertise to diagnose customer needs and prescribe the right products for each customer. In many industries, the product is so technical that no one manager can possibly understand all the products. IBM may try to address this through a team approach, but that requires a lot of coordination.
- *Customer management is expensive.* It adds a new layer of managers – the customer manager. It does not eliminate the product manager – it just changes his or her responsibilities. The result is higher personnel costs in salary and support.
- *Product management takes into account customer needs anyway.* Product managers are marketers – they develop products to fit the needs of a target group.

3.3.5 Acquisition and Retention Departmentalization

Until now, our focus has been on managing current customers, but what about the management of customer acquisition? An important aspect of the customer-centric organization is the division of efforts into acquisition and retention. These are two very different functions. For example, Del Rio (2002) describes a wireless phone company with separate departments for acquisition and retention. Publishers have traditionally employed acquisition editors, who sign up authors and books, and managing editors, who manage the editing, production, and marketing of the books.

The advantage of this departmentalization comes from the fact that acquisition and retention require two different mind-sets, involve different tools, and have different success measures. Acquisition is entrepreneurial. It is more straightforward to measure, reward, and motivate. It is short-term. Retention management is quite different. It is difficult to measure (i.e., it relies on lifetime value and share-of-wallet), and therefore difficult to reward. It is long term.

The disadvantage of acquisition/retention departmentalization is that the acquisition department may not acquire the right customers. For example, an acquisition manager might use price discounts to attract customers who are inherently deal prone churners; impossible to retain.

The key challenge therefore lies in coordination. Incentives could be used to make sure the acquirers attract the right customers. These might entail measures such as lifetime value. Ainslie and Pitt (1998) provide interesting evidence that it is possible to develop models that guide acquisition efforts according to long-term customer management goals. They model prospects in terms of their ultimate profitability, risk, and responsiveness to future modeling efforts. Then they prioritize customers in terms of an overall index of these three criteria. Thus it may be possible to use predictive models to facilitate coordination between acquisition and retention.

3.4 Processes for Managing Information: Knowledge Management

3.4.1 The Concept

Knowledge management is the systematic process of *creating, codifying, transferring, and using* knowledge to improve business performance. Knowledge management pertains to any type of knowledge generated by the organization, but in the context of database marketing, we are concerned with knowledge about the customer.

Davenport and Prusak (1998, pp. 1–6) distinguish among data, information, and knowledge. Knowledge management systems entail all three. Data is the raw, stored input, unanalyzed. Information is compiled data that "makes a difference" (Davenport and Prusak p. 3) in a decision. Knowledge is one step up from information. It is a mix of "experience, values, contextual information, and expert insight that provides a framework for evaluating and incorporating new experiences and information" (Davenport and Prusak p. 5).

For example, consider a cross-selling campaign for audio speakers that can be used with a computer. Each customer's response can be recorded. This is data. The data can be compiled to yield a response rate. This is information. It can be used to calculate profitability of the campaign. The data could be analyzed to determine that those who responded had bought a computer in the last 3 months. The insight, or knowledge, generated is that customers who have recently invested in computer hardware are "ripe" for peripherals. This suggests a particular target group as well as copy ("no new computer system is complete without the best speakers...").

Knowledge management draws on information technology, economics, organization behavior, human resource management, and marketing. Information technology underlies the data warehousing issues that are crucial for knowledge management. While we are not aware of formal economic analyses of knowledge management, Davenport and Prusak (1998) argue that the firm faces both an internal and external market for knowledge. There are buyers, sellers, and prices. Organizational behavior scholars have studied knowledge management under the label "organizational learning" (e.g., Argote 1999), focusing on how organizations learn, how they forget, how they remember, and how information is shared. Human resource management views knowledge management as a human capital issue, and is concerned with how to provide the skills for employees to learn and share their learning (Tapp 2002, p. 110).

Marketers have touched upon knowledge management in their study of "marketing orientation." In fact, Kohli and Jaworski (1990) define marketing orientation as the generation, dissemination, and utilization of information related to customer needs. This is very close to our definition of knowledge management.

3.4.2 Does Effective Knowledge Management Enhance Performance?

As just mentioned, the concept of marketing orientation is similar to knowledge management. Therefore, the evidence of a positive relationship between marketing orientation and firm performance (Jaworski and Kohli 1993; Moorman 1995; Moorman and Rust 1999) suggests knowledge management can pay off. The caveat, however, is that these studies focused on the general collection and utilization of customer information, and not on knowledge gained through database marketing.

Some research connects knowledge management with successful CRM. Chaston et al. (2003) surveyed 223 UK accounting firms. They measured knowledge management in terms of orientation toward acquiring knowledge from external sources, exploiting new knowledge, documenting carefully, making information available to all employees, and improving employee skills. They thus covered the create–codify–transfer–use dimensions of knowledge management (DiBella et al. 1996). They measured CRM orientation in terms of maintaining close contact with clients, regularly meeting with clients, gaining knowledge through building strong relationships, tailoring service toward clients, and gaining revenue mainly through repeat sales. The authors found a strong correlation between knowledge management and CRM. Firms that were above average in CRM orientation were above average in knowledge management. They were also above average in sales growth.

Croteau and Li (2003) surveyed 57 Canadian firms with greater than 250 employees, representing a variety of industries. Knowledge management was measured using scales such as "able to provide fast decision-making due to customer knowledge availability". The impact of CRM efforts was measured using company self-reported satisfaction with retention rates, loyalty, market share gains, innovative and convenient products. In a multi-equation structural model, knowledge management was found to be a significant predictor of CRM impact.

These studies suggest a connection between knowledge management and CRM. They help justify the view that data and CRM go hand-in-hand (O'Neill 2001; Swift 2001). However, they do not distinguish the type of knowledge being managed, i.e., whether it be data, information, or knowledge in Davenport and Prusak's framework. Further research is needed to sharpen our understanding of exactly what types of knowledge are most important for enhancing CRM efforts.

One potential benefit of knowledge management is that it provides continuity as employees move to other firms. In fact, employee turnover was arguably the prime stimulus for the emergence of knowledge management as a field (see Tapp 2002). Knowledge management can be viewed as a way of capturing the knowledge of current employees so if they physically leave, their wisdom still remains. However, studies are needed to investigate whether in fact this benefit materializes in the real world.

3.4.3 Creating Knowledge

The first step in the knowledge management process is creating knowledge, which can be categorized as internal versus external, and undirected versus directed.

Internal knowledge creation takes place as part of the process of analyzing data and making decisions (Davenport et al. 2001a). Gillett (1999, fig. 4) reinforces this point. Many lessons are learned each time a modeler builds a predictive model and a manager uses it to target. The result is a repertoire of experiences that creates knowledge about what works and doesn't work.

Knowledge can also be "created" externally, most obviously by hiring another firm's employees ("grafting" in the words of Huber 1991). At the micro level, grafting may be of individual employees (e.g., hiring the CRM manager from a rival company); at the macro level, grafting can occur by purchasing an entire company. For example, DoubleClick gained much knowledge of the list industry by purchasing Abacus.

Directed knowledge creation takes place when a company proactively focuses on a particular topic. For example, a service company may focus on customer satisfaction (DiBella et al. 1996). Davenport et al. (2001b) say that successful companies focus on learning about top customers, or customers most likely to provide future earnings. They cite FedEx and US West as examples. P&G focuses on understanding Wal-Mart. Microsoft began focusing on CIO's when it became clear that business customers were a prime source of future growth.

Undirected knowledge creation takes place as a "spin-off" benefit of the analysis/decision process. For example, a manager may want to design a frequency reward program. Upon tapping the firm's knowledge management system, the manager realizes that not much is known about the topic. The manager therefore conducts his or her own research, surveying other firms' programs and conducting survey research. Another form of undirected knowledge creation takes place as current employees mentor new employees. The new employee questions why something is done a certain way, and that forces the current employee to crystallize his or her knowledge.

Experiments are an effective way to create knowledge. They allow companies to test fundamental assumptions as opposed to marginal improvements (DiBella et al. 1996). The prevalence of experimentation in database marketing makes it particularly prone to this type of learning.

A final issue in knowledge creation is that it requires managers to have the *wherewithal* and *ability* to interpret data and information. For example, the most immediate use of a predictive model might be the prioritized list of customers. However, knowledge is created when the model-builder and the marketing manager sit down and review the important variables in the predictive model. Therefore, knowledge creation requires time, training, and often group work (Gillett 1999). Davenport et al. (2001a) report that most companies are not succeeding in turning data into knowledge, and are neglecting "the human realm of analyzing and interpreting data and then acting on the insights" (p. 118). They cite their own studies as well as two prime examples, supermarket scanner data in the grocery chain industry, and Web transaction data. The data certainly are being created, but managers simply do not have the time to generate information from the data, much less knowledge.

One response to this is to make more knowledge creation activities directed, or to require managers to record what they learned. Firms need to foster a work environment that allows time for reflection. This is a challenge for today's downsized companies.

3.4.4 Codifying Knowledge

Knowledge needs to be stored for two reasons. First, it enables more efficient transfer to other employees. Second, knowledge not recorded can be forgotten. Organization forgetting is a significant phenomenon (Argote 1999). It happens through employee turnover and through lack of repetition (e.g., "we once ran a campaign like this, but that was several years ago, and frankly, I forgot what happened").

The key issues in codifying knowledge are what to store and how to store it. Knowledge should be stored to the extent that is useful *and* necessary to sustain the firm's strategy. Obviously, companies whose strategy is to develop customer relationships must store all data, information, and knowledge related to customer relationships. However, there still may be a surfeit of knowledge to store and decisions need to be made as to what knowledge will truly be useful in the future.

The details of how to store the knowledge are the domain of information technology. Although expensive, it is *relatively* straightforward to compile and record customer data and information; that is what CRM information systems are designed to do. Insights, i.e., true knowledge, can be tougher to codify. This can be done by requiring key employees to write white papers. Expert systems are another possibility, as are knowledge maps (Davenport and Prusak 1998; Vail 1999).

Davenport et al. (2001b) emphasize the need to store both quantitative and qualitative data, and cite P&G as a company that tries to do both through either face-to-face meetings or "discussion databases" (p. 65). Sometimes, however, it will be very difficult to codify what is learned. Harley-Davidson and the Jeep division of DaimlerChrysler rely on ethnographic research to understand their customers. Consultants conduct the research, and communicate what they learn through discussions with managers, but this does not formally codify it.

Another issue is whether there should be one knowledge repository (the "enterprise warehouse") or several. Assuming cost is not an issue, the obvious preference is for one repository. This facilitates cross-referencing and equal access. However, perhaps due to costs, Davenport et al. (2001b) report that most firms do not store all their knowledge in one place. They cite Dell, who at the time of their paper, had not integrated their online data with data from the calling center.

Finally, knowledge is not only of the facts, but also of processes. It is perhaps even more important to codify processes. Davenport et al. (2001b) discuss Kraft's "3-Step Category Builder," a process for analyzing a product category and deciding how it can be grown.

3.4.5 Transferring Knowledge

There can be both formal and informal mechanisms to transfer knowledge to the appropriate people. The most common formal mechanism, especially for transferring data and information, is to train managers to access customer information housed in the data warehouse. Information also can be transferred automatically, e.g., a customer profile can appear on the screen when a catalog company representative is talking with the customer. Other formal forms of knowledge transfer are through in-house seminars and white papers.

Informal knowledge sharing is perhaps the most difficult to orchestrate. It involves installing a culture and a physical environment to facilitate conversation. For example, it would be a good idea to locate the model builders adjacent to the managers who make decisions based on the models, and to encourage mentoring whereby senior managers transfer their experiential knowledge to junior managers.

Huber (1991) summarizes the vast research from the organization behavior literature that describes the circumstances under which knowledge sharing will occur. Informant A may have to knowledge to transfer to Recipient B. Transfer is more likely if A views the information as relevant for B, A's costs of sharing are low, A's workload is low, A has incentives for sharing, and B has high power/status in the organization.

3.4.6 Using Knowledge

Using knowledge is probably the most critical component of the knowledge management system. What good is the knowledge if it's never used? If the first three steps – creation, codification, and transference – have been achieved correctly, usage should follow, because this means that insightful, relevant knowledge has been created, it's available in "the system", and it's easy for the manager to tap this knowledge base.

Consumer behavior researchers have established that individuals will use information to the extent that it is accessible and diagnostic (Feldman et al. 1988). Accessibility follows to the extent that the knowledge information system makes knowledge easily available, i.e., that knowledge transference is effective. Diagnosticity follows to the extent that the information is useful. Designers of knowledge management systems need to make sure that both these conditions hold. For example, in a study of a US health insurance company, Payton and Zahay (2003) found that "ease of use", i.e., accessibility, and "quality" of the data, i.e., diagnosticity, were the two key factors determining employee use of the corporate data warehouse. Top management support and training were also important factors.

The diagnosticity of information is difficult to judge, because it is subjective to establish whether the knowledge is truly useful. For example, a company's knowledge management system may contain information that says recent purchasers of computers are prime candidates for cross-selling external speakers. However, a new manager may believe these insights are not useful in today's marketing environment. The new manager may be of the opinion that it doesn't make sense to cross-sell external speakers to someone who has recently bought a computer system, because either the speakers would have been included in the purchase or if the customer wanted the speakers, he or she would have bought them then and there.

The difficulty is that the new manager might indeed be correct and the knowledge may not apply to today's marketing environment. It doesn't make sense to require the new manager to use the information. Perhaps the best tack is to make the information easily accessible, but allowing the new manager to make judgments as to whether the information is useful.

3.4.7 Designing a Knowledge Management System

Figure 3.3 suggests a process for designing a knowledge management system. The first step is to make sure the pre-requisites (the company's database marketing strategy, information technology infrastructure, skills, and organizational culture) are in place, (Davenport et al. 2001a). The strategy guides which knowledge gets created and stored. The information technology structure is essential because it defines the capability for housing the customer data as well as other forms of codified knowledge. Croteau and Li (2003), in their study of Canadian firms, found that technological "readiness" was an important precursor of successful knowledge management efforts. Employees need to have the skills to create, codify, transfer, and use knowledge. There needs to be an organizational culture that values knowledge.

The next phase is to design the core of the system: the content, creation activities, codification procedures, transference techniques, and usage mechanisms. Content decisions involve the topics and depth of knowledge that will be part of the system. Topics follow from the strategy and includes aspects of customer behavior, previous campaigns, strategies, etc. An important decision needs to be made regarding depth of knowledge – is this an information system or a knowledge system?

The various means of creating knowledge described in Sect. 3.4.3 need to be reviewed and prioritized. For example, how much will the knowledge management system rely on grafting? How will these activities be formalized? If there is to be a large emphasis on undirected proactive research, do managers have access to the tools they need to conduct that research? For example, if

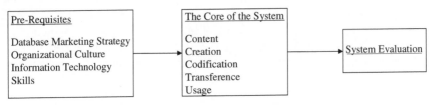

Fig. 3.3 Designing a knowledge management system.

a manager wants to learn about what types of customer tier programs work, does he or she have access to the customer data to conduct the investigation? Does he or she have access to the library resources one needs to learn vicariously about what other companies do and what academic researchers have learned?

Decisions need to be made on codification (Sect. 3.4.4). What will be required in terms of white papers and internal seminars? Is all the relevant information being captured and put into a usable computer format? A key decision here is on centralized versus decentralized repositories. As discussed earlier, centralized is attractive for cross-referencing and access, but may not be practical.

The issues discussed in Sects. 3.4.5 and 3.4.6 need to be addressed in order to make sure the knowledge will be transferred to those who need it, and in turn that the recipients will indeed use the knowledge. For example, decisions need be made that will ensure the system is *used* effectively. This includes the fine line between encouraging use and requiring it. On one extreme, the company can include a requirement that all proposals for marketing activities refer if possible to knowledge gleaned from the knowledge management system. On the other extreme, there can be no requirements.

A final step is to set up a mechanism for evaluating the system. Researchers have conducted cross-sectional studies showing that companies with more sophisticated knowledge management systems achieve better customer relationship outcomes (e.g., Chaston et al. 2003). However, to assess the value of the knowledge management system for a particular firm, a before–after type analysis is called for. This is difficult to execute because the knowledge management system's value would appear mostly in the long-term. One might find 2 years after implementing a knowledge management system that retention and loyalty have decreased. However, these indicators might have decreased even more if it weren't for the system. In some cases, competitive data might be available to serve as a cross-sectional benchmark.

Sharp (2003) describes one company's innovative approach to evaluating its knowledge management investment. The company was Shell International Exploration and Oil (SIEO). SIEO invested $6 million in a knowledge management system with a focus on enhancing knowledge transfer. SIEO measured ROI for this investment first by surveying disseminators of knowledge as to what types of questions were being asked. This provided them with a frequency distribution across all types of questions. SIEO then went to the users (engineers) and asked them to put a dollar figure on how much the information they received was worth for particular types of questions. These numbers were multiplied by the distribution of questionnaire frequency to determine ROI. SIEO calculated an ROI of 50, meaning that the $6 million investment had generated $300 million in financial benefit over a 3-year horizon.

The obvious concern with this methodology is whether users can self-report the value of the answers they receive. They may have a cognitive dissonance bias that inflates the value ("I decided to use this system; therefore, it must be valuable"). In addition, there is no benchmark. What would have happened if the knowledge management system had not been available? However, to its credit, SIEO made a reasonable effort to determine what they had gained from their investment.

3.4.8 Issues and Challenges

Knowledge management is clearly a crucial organizational process for implementing database marketing. The organizational learning literature provides a strong academic tradition in this area. But sorely needed are marketing-oriented studies on all aspects of knowledge creation, codification, transference, and usage, in a database marketing/CRM context. Among some of the key issues are:

- Which knowledge creation activities are most important?
- How important is *knowledge* management rather than *information* management? Is it worthwhile to generate, store, and disseminate insights that go beyond the narrow information typically available from compilations of customer data?
- How do we ensure that potential users will actually use the knowledge captured by the system (see Huber 1991)?
- How can companies evaluate their investment in a technology that is so broad in scope and so long-term in presumed effect?
- What in fact are the typical ROI's earned by investments in knowledge management systems, and what determines those ROI's?
- How important is organizational culture in the creation and use of knowledge? Perhaps cultures that emphasize teamwork and collectivism are more conducive to knowledge management effectiveness than cultures that emphasize entrepreneurship (see Deshpandé et al. 1993).
- Can knowledge management be a source of competitive advantage? It would appear that large-scale knowledge systems are imperfectly mobile, although there can be some leakage if managers switch firms and bring insights along with them.

3.5 Compensation and Incentives

Managers and employees in all organizations respond to incentives. For example, if the company needs to increase its acquisition rate, employees should be rewarded based on how many customers they acquire. Since database marketing allows managers to measure performance more accurately, developing appropriate incentives becomes even more relevant for successful implementation of database marketing. We will review some theoretical work in this area, and then discuss some empirical findings.

3.5.1 Theory

Hauser et al. (1994; "HSW") conduct an economic analysis to investigate how companies should use compensation incentives to reward employee-induced increases in customer satisfaction (long-term) versus employee-created immediate sales (short-term). In database marketing terms, this is the basic trade-off between acquisition and retention. The model uses a principal-agent framework where employees (agents) are not certain what will be the results of their efforts, and company management (principal) cannot perfectly observe the amount of employees' efforts. Companies compete on price and their compensation reward structure.

HSW construct a two-period model for two competing firms. Demand depends on prices and customer perceptions of quality. Employees can expend efforts to increase perceived quality, through efforts "a" that increase immediate first period sales, and efforts "b" that increase satisfaction in the first period and increase sales in the second period. The total employee effort is $a + b$. The firm cannot observe a or b directly, although first-period sales and satisfaction are indirect measures of these efforts. Employees cannot directly observe the impact of their efforts either, although they know what efforts they expended.

The focal firm and the competitor choose prices and compensation systems to maximize profits. The solution procedure assumes that the firms are Stackelberg leaders with respect to employees in that employees optimize efforts based on a set of prices and reward functions. Firms find optimal price based on a given reward function, and then find the optimal reward function, taking into account competitor as well as employee reactions. HSW show that the derived compensation (w_1 in period 1; w_2 in period 2) are linear functions of sales (q) and observed satisfaction (s):

$$w_1 = \alpha_1 + \beta_1 q_1 + \eta s \qquad (3.1a)$$
$$w_2 = \alpha_2 + \beta_2 q_2 \qquad (3.1b)$$

A key finding is that firms are better off rewarding employee-induced improvements in customer satisfaction ($\eta > 0$) as well as sales levels, no matter what its competitor does. The result is quite sensible. Even though the firm cannot observe employee efforts to create satisfaction, the firm knows that satisfaction is created through these efforts and satisfaction increases second-period sales. If customer satisfaction is not rewarded, the firm loses out on second period sales. HSW provide insights on how various factors influence the amount to which customer satisfaction should be rewarded:

- The firm should put more emphasis on rewarding satisfaction if employees are short-term oriented. If customers are not naturally long-term oriented, they need incentives to make them so.
- If satisfaction can be measured with greater precision, more emphasis should be placed on rewarding it. This makes sense in that if customer satisfaction is measured perfectly, the firm has a better measure of employee efforts.
- Satisfaction efforts should be rewarded more if they are targeted at customers who have low switching costs, i.e., are likely to churn without those efforts. This makes sense because these customers will churn unless they are satisfied.
- If a firm's baseline perceived quality level is larger, it should put more emphasis on rewarding satisfaction.[2] This is very important because it says that the gains from rewarding customer satisfaction are greater among top tier companies. This might be because the high quality firm can already count on short-term sales so can invest more in creating the satisfaction that will guarantee long-term sales.

HSW provide insightful results that generally support compensation schemes that reward employees who can create satisfied customers. One issue for further research is whether rewarding customer satisfaction increases total industry profits. Rewarding customer satisfaction could set off a "customer-satisfaction war" where firms compete to acquire customers because once these customers are acquired, they are locked in via customer satisfaction incentives.

Another area of reward compensation is for the statisticians who build predictive models. As has been repeatedly shown in this book, database marketing can have a direct and *demonstrable* impact on profits through better targeting. It might therefore make sense to compensate model-builders on the "lift" they generate from their models. A final area is how to compensate employees for knowledge management, especially creation, codification, and transference. It seems that incentives should especially encourage these activities, since these do not have immediate pay-offs.

3.5.2 Empirical Findings

There are systematic and anecdotal empirical studies that are building a case that compensation is a key ingredient to the success of database marketing or CRM efforts.

Reinartz et al. (2004) found evidence that compensating employees according to their success in cultivating relationships with high value cus-

---

[2] This result is stated and proven in a working paper version of the paper (Hauser et al. 1992).

tomers plays a role in improving company performance. The authors surveyed 211 managers and CRM experts in Austria, Germany, and Switzerland. They measured various aspects of CRM implementation along with market-based performance measures including customer satisfaction, retention, company image, and customer benefits. The authors found for example that "CRM-Compatible Organizational Alignment" enhanced company acquisition efforts in improving market performance. CRM-Compatible Organizational Alignment was a 4-scale item that included incentives to deliver the appropriate service to customers based on customer tier, i.e., "rewarding employees for building and deepening relationships with high value customers." Other items in the scale were less incentive specific (training, organized to respond optimally to different customer groups, etc.) so it isn't clear exactly what the incentive contribution is. However, incentives are definitely part of the picture.

Peppers and Rogers (1997, pp. 79–98) describe an interesting case involving the telecommunications firm MCI. Facing customer churn problems in the early 1990s, MCI instituted a Customer First retention program. The program focused on the top 5% of customers who generated 40% of revenues. MCI assigned customer managers to portfolios of these customers, and rewarded the customer managers based on retention-oriented metrics. According to Peppers and Rogers, the program was beginning to succeed. However, MCI's marketing group, which was compensated based on product-sales statistics, did not like this program because it took away their prime prospects for cross-selling and put them in the hands of the Sales and Services group.

Day and Van den Bulte (2002) surveyed 345 senior marketing, sales, and MIS executives in US companies. They identified potential factors related to CRM success, one of which they labeled "Configuration." Configuration involved "organization structures, incentives, and controls." Configuration turned out to be the most important factor underlying "customer relationship capability" (CRC), and CRC was strongly related to customer retention, sales growth, and profit. This provides further support that compensation incentives are important.[3]

Day (2003) reports that Siebel Systems ties 50% of management incentive compensation to customer satisfaction, and 25% of salesperson compensation to customer satisfaction. To link the employee efforts more directly to their impact on satisfaction, Siebel pays the bonus 1 year after the signing of a contract. Day also reports that Capital One allows a customer representative leeway in the packages he or she can offer a would-be churner to induce the churner to stay with Capital One. The representative is compensated based on his or her ability to retain the customer with as profitable a package as possible. In this way, Capital One rewards employees based on their ability to improve profitable retention.

---

[3] Note however that Configuration was measured on a single scale that did not refer directly to compensation.

Finally, Srinivasan and Moorman (2002) study the drivers of online retailer performance. They relate organization factors to customer-related investments, which in turn they relate to customer satisfaction, which in turn they relate to performance. They verify the satisfaction-performance relationship by linking BizRate.com customer ratings to executive-reported company cash flow. The most important customer-related investment is found to be expenditures on customer information systems. Having a customer-focused reward system was the second-most important determinant of information system expenditures (marketing/technology interactions were the most important). The implication is that setting up a CRM-related incentive system enhances performance by motivating the company to make the right early investments in customer information technology that in turn pay off in higher customer satisfaction and better company performance. Note this finding also reinforces the Star model (Fig. 3.1), which points out that the elements of organizational design (in this case compensation and knowledge management) all highly related.

3.5.3 Summary

There is good evidence that compensation incentive systems should and do play a role in successful implementation of database marketing. Most of this work is on the incentives–customer satisfaction–performance link. Hauser et al. (1994) provide the theoretical link, while Reinartz et al. (2004), Day and Van den Bulte (2002), and Srinivasan and Moorman (2002) provide the empirical links.

While these results are promising, one important topic for future work is coordinating the compensation schemes of various groups within the company. Hauser et al. (1994) propose that more incentives should relate most directly to the fruits of an employee's effort. For example, if employees focus on reducing churn, they should be compensated based on churn rate. Peppers and Rogers' (1997) MCI case, however, cites problems when one group being compensated based on acquisition and one on retention. In the MCI case, one group increased retention by "fencing in" the most profitable customers, essentially taking them away from the other group that wanted to sell these customers more products. Both groups were responding to the compensation incentive structure, but they were in conflict.

3.6 People

3.6.1 Providing Appropriate Support

Once the firm's strategy, structure, knowledge management process, and compensation are in place, employees need training and support. Training is especially important for knowledge management, particularly with regard to accessing and using the system (Payton and Zahay 2003). It is also important with regard to customer versus product management – these are two different mindsets. Finally, the organizational culture must reinforce what the rest of the organizational design is trying to accomplish. For example, using the culture types enunciated by Deshpandé et al. (1993), a "Clan" culture, which is characterized by interpersonal cohesion, teamwork, and mentoring, might be appropriate for a firm that wanted to put strong emphasis on the transference component of knowledge management. A "Market" culture, which emphasizes goal achievement and competitiveness, might be more appropriate for a firm that wanted to emphasize a highly results-oriented customer management system.

Another aspect of supporting people is the commitment of senior managers. Senior managers can articulate their support for the organizational design and reward individuals beyond the formal compensation plan. In addition, senior managers can contribute directly. For example, Senn (2006) reports a "Top Executive Relationship Process" at Siemens Information and Communications, in which top executives meet with Siemens' customers' top management on a regular, planned basis.

3.6.2 Intra-Firm Coordination

No matter what organization design emerges from the Star model (Fig. 3.1), it will only be successful to the extent that people work well with each other, i.e., they coordinate. Three potential sources of coordination problems include conflict, poor communication, and lack of education. Following is a list of different personnel who need to coordinate, and potential issues that may hinder coordination:

Groups	Coordination issue
Modelers and managers	Communication, education
Acquirers and retainers	Conflict
Customer managers and product managers	Conflict
Channel managers	Communication
Modelers and IT	Communication, education
Marketing managers and IT	Communication, education
Marketing and financial managers	Conflict
Database marketers and senior management	Communication, education

We discuss these issues in more depth in the following two sections.

3.6.2.1 Coordination Within the Marketing Function

Modelers and Managers: Gillett (1999) points out that the model builders and the managers who use modeling results need to coordinate effectively in order for database marketing to be successful. According to Gillett, this entails understanding each other's needs, managing expectations, and understanding each other's capabilities. These are largely communication and education issues. The model builder needs to be able to translate a business problem, e.g., how to cross-sell effectively, into a statistical analysis that solves the problem. The manager needs to have some idea what models can and cannot do. For example, predictive modeling is very good at prioritizing customers in terms of responsiveness, but not as good at drawing the line in terms of who should or should not be targeted. Managers also need to have realistic expectations on how fast models can be built and how accurate they can be. With today's emphasis on downsized staffing, it is very easy for managers to make unrealistic demands on model-builders. It is difficult for a manager to fathom why it takes a week to produce a predictive model, but these expectations need to be set appropriately.

Gillett (1999) recommends that data-mining should be a team effort, comprised of an IT specialist (for the data), a statistician (to do the data mining), and a manager (to make sure the effort fulfills a business need). The benefits of team play are (1) a result that's more likely to improve business performance, and (2) a set of insights that's more likely to increase the company's knowledge base long-term.

Acquirers and Retainers: One of the hallmarks of the customer-centric organization is separate management of acquisition and retention (Sect. 3.3.5). However, these functions have potentially conflicting mindsets. Acquirers are volume and short-term oriented, since their task is easily quantified. Retainers are customer relationship and long-term oriented. Problems occur when the acquirers attract customers who are difficult to retain. For example, a telecom company may find it easier to attract young users, but these are precisely the customers who innately are more difficult to retain. On the other hand, the customers who are easiest to retain might be the most difficult to acquire. For example, if older people are more naturally brand loyal, they are attractive for the retainers, but difficult for the acquirers to attract.

Customer managers and product managers: The conflict here is that customer managers may demand products that product managers can't produce. For example, the customer manager for teenagers may ask for a line of personal computers with high styling and large disk capacity. That sounds fine, but the product manager for personal computers may also be besieged with requests for other product features from the business customer manager, the educational institution customer manager, and the family customer manager.

Channel managers: Marketing can be organized by channel, and this raises coordination issues (Botwinik 2001). One problem is that in many companies, the online channel initially was set up as a separate profit center as a way to establish a company's web presence. Now companies have that presence, and they need to coordinate among the channels. Whereas originally there may have a conflict between channel managers in that they were seen as competing for the same customer, now the issue is more on communicating effectively so that the overall customer needs are addressed. As a simple example, a direct sales representative needs to have the customer's online purchase records easily on hand.

Different marketing functional managers: Botwinik (2001) argues that various marketing functions, e.g., marketing, sales, and service, view their domains as distinct and rarely coordinate. However, the customer views his or her relationship with the firm in terms of the overall experience. For example, the customer may have problems with Internet response time. The customer calls customer service, who may fix the immediate problem, but the real problem is that the customer has the wrong computer. Marketing can help identify that need. Then sales can help define the specs for the replacement computer. The three groups need to be communicating with each other so each of them can route customers seamlessly to the appropriate department.

3.6.2.2 Coordinating Outside the Marketing Function

Modelers and IT: While modelers and IT people are both technically oriented, it is not necessarily the case that these two groups communicate easily. Data managers are responsible for organizing so many different data entities that they have a hard time sitting down with an applied model-builder and helping to stipulate the database for a predictive modeling project. On the other hand, modelers may have little taste for defining the variables in the database – they're more interested in seeing what predictive power they can get for a given set of variables, and what statistical techniques work best. Put simply, the data managers need to take a course in statistics, and the data miners need to take a course in data management.

Marketing Managers and IT: IT departments typically handle data for the entire company, including finance and operations as well as marketing. As a result, the marketing department can wait an inordinate amount of time before the database it needs is assembled. The Directors of IT, Marketing, Finance, Operations, and Human Resources need to coordinate and set priorities. Coordination problems also occur when marketing managers want to access the data warehouse through queries, and can't easily translate their needs into a query the system can handle. Cunningham et al. (2006) describe an evaluation tool that can used to measure how well the system satisfies management needs. This should enhance coordination between IT and managers.

Marketing Managers and Financial Managers: This is an arena of potential conflict. The conflict stems from a classic tradeoff between Type I and Type II error (see Chapter 10). Type I error is not contacting a customer when contact would improve profits. Type II error is contacting a customer although this doesn't improve profits. The problem is that it is difficult to minimize both errors – there is an inherent conflict.

The problem is that marketing, i.e., customer managers, talk about investing in customers and producing long-term results. They feel that Type I is the worse error – nothing is worse than not increasing customer value when the opportunity is there. Financial managers however are more naturally concerned with Type II errors. The worse thing is to waste money on customers who are not worth it. Simply understanding each other's error priorities would go a long way for helping to resolve conflicts, but it appears that someone is needed to set the tone for which error is more important.

Database marketers and senior management: The issue here is one of communication and education, primarily on the part of senior management. Senior management needs to have a clear understanding of what database marketing can do, and database marketing needs to avoid over-selling what it can do. This is similar to the miscommunications that can occur between data miners and marketing managers, but on a more strategic scale.

Chapter 4
Customer Privacy and
Database Marketing

Abstract Probably the single most important aspect of the legal environment pertaining to database marketing is customer privacy. We examine this issue in depth. Privacy is a multidimensional issue for customers, and we begin by reviewing the nature and potential consequences of these several dimensions. We discuss the evidence regarding the impact of customers' concerns for privacy on their behavior – there is some although not definitive evidence for example that privacy concerns hinder e-commerce. We discuss current firm practices regarding privacy, as well as some of the major laws regarding customer privacy. We conclude with a review of potential solutions to privacy concerns, including regulation, permission-based marketing, and a strategic focus on trust.

4.1 Background

4.1.1 Customer Privacy Concerns and Their Consequences for Database Marketers

Customer privacy in database marketing pertains to the *customer's ability to control the collection, usage, and anonymity of his or her data*. The basic premise of database marketing is exchange: companies collect and analyze customer data, and in return provide customers with more appropriate products, services, and offers. However, this premise is muddled when customers become concerned about privacy. Figure 4.1 outlines these concerns and their ramifications.[1]

---

[1] See Smith et al's (1996) and Stewart and Segars (2002) for a formally developed measurement instrument of privacy concerns – the "Concern for Information Privacy" (CFIP) scale. This scale taps the security, third-party access, none-of-your-business, and fear of errors dimensions of information privacy discussed in this section.

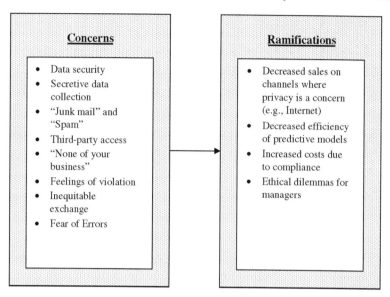

Fig. 4.1 Customers' privacy concerns and their ramifications for database marketers.

- *Data security*: Customers fear that computer hackers can gain access to their data. High-profile cases of "identity theft" fuel this fear. In one instance, ChoicePoint, a collector and seller of customer-level data available in the public domain, revealed that an identity-theft ring gained access to 145,000 records in its database (Perez 2005). The data included names, addresses, and social security numbers. Another well-known data company, Lexis-Nexis, revealed that criminals gained access to social security numbers, driver's license information, and addresses of 310,000 individuals (Timmons and Zeller Jr. 2005). These cases suggest to consumers that even if the companies collecting the data are well-meaning, these companies cannot protect the privacy of their data.

    Data security also pertains to access by persons within the organization. For example, a patient might be comfortable with a physician seeing his or her medical history, but not a medical student or a departmental administrator.
- *Secretive data collection* (George 2002): Customers suspect that companies collect data from them without their knowledge. The most conspicuous example is the use of cookies, a few lines of computer code inserted by an Internet website into the customer's computer that can then be used to track the customer over time (Turner and Dasgupta 2003). Cookies are usually inserted without the customer's permission. It is not the tracking *per se* that bothers customers, but the surreptitious nature of the data collection.
- *Junk mail and spam* (George 2002): Some customers fear that data collection leads to unwanted junk mail and emails. Good predictive models

should address this concern, as companies use these models only to target customers who will respond. But the best predictive models might boost a 1% response rate up to a 5–7% response rate. That can mean huge profits for the database marketers (Chapter 10), but the 93% who do not respond might view the solicitations as an invasion of privacy.

- *Third-party access* (Smith et al's 1996; Turner and Dasgupta 2003; George 2002): Customers realize that the company with whom they do business may sell the data it collects to unknown third parties euphemistically called "partners." Customers may not mind the company that collects the data using it, but want to control who else gets to use the data.
- *None of your business* (Smith et al's 1996; George 2002; Winer 2001): The customer may simply feel that it is none of the company's business to know what types of books, movies, electronic equipment, etc., that the customer prefers, or what areas of the country (or what countries) the customer calls on the telephone. These customers view their relationship with the company as purely transactional, and resent being classified as "mystery book readers" or "international callers".
- *Feelings of violation* (Winer 2001): Winer (2001) states this as, "How do they know that about me?" For example, a direct marketer may use a compiled database (Chapter 8) to learn that a customer reads *Newsweek* and recently purchased a high definition television. Even if the customer knows data are being collected and databases are being merged, when the company reveals what it knows to the customer, the overall data collection effort seems more invasive.
- *Inequitable exchange* (Fletcher 2003): While the premise of database marketing is for the customer to sacrifice some privacy in exchange for better service, prices, product, etc., some customers may not view this as an equitable exchange. Either they don't see the benefits of better targeting, or they view the costs of sacrificing privacy as too high. Either way, they view the database marketing exchange equation as an inequality, not favorably in their direction.
- *Fear of Errors* (Smith et al's 1996): Customers may fear that the data collected on them may include errors. The errors could occur through computer "glitches" or human mistakes. The end result is that the company may have an incorrect profile of the customer, without either the firm or the customer knowing it.

As Fig. 4.1 shows, there are four key ramifications of these privacy concerns. First, customer fears about privacy can decrease sales volume. Stewart and Segars (2002) found that consumers who were concerned with privacy intended to remove their names from mailing lists or were less likely to purchase products simply because of the manner in which the company used personal data. The issue is especially relevant for the Internet. Udo (2001) surveyed 158 online users and found that privacy and security concerns were the number one issue hampering more purchasing on the Internet. A Microsoft "Presspass" (Microsoft 2000) suggested, based on a Forrester Research study, that customer privacy concerns decreased Internet sales by $12.2 billion in 2000.

Second, privacy concerns may limit the data available to companies, therefore decreasing the precision and profitability of predictive modeling. Stewart and Segars (2002) found that consumers who were concerned with privacy were more likely to refuse to give information to companies. For existing customers, purchase history is typically the most important variable driving predictive model accuracy (e.g., Knott et al. 2002), and companies automatically collect those data. However, when acquiring new customers, the prospect has no purchase history with the company, so demographic and other customer characteristic data become very important. If cookies were outlawed, companies would not be able to track customers' Internet search preferences and behaviors – variables that are becoming important in predictive models. In the extreme, if companies were prohibited from using prior purchase histories to tailor campaigns, predictive modeling would virtually be brought to a standstill.

Third, privacy can increase costs. Turner (2001) notes that restrictions on access to external customer data could increase costs by 3.5–11%. This diminishes the efficiency of database marketing.

Fourth, managers may face difficult ethical questions if they find themselves collecting data the customer doesn't want them to collect. A good test of ethical behavior is, "Would I be embarrassed if the public knew my actions?" In the case of collecting and utilizing data that customers would prefer to remain private, the answer to that question may be "yes." This puts well-meaning managers in an ethical dilemma.

In summary, consumers have several concerns about privacy. The ramifications of these concerns are: (1) lower customer expenditures especially on the Internet, (2) less data available for predictive models, (3) higher costs for companies complying with various privacy rules, and (4) difficult ethical concerns for managers.

4.1.2 Historical Perspective

Concerns about customer privacy are not new. They probably emerged when customer data were first punched onto computer cards in the 1960s. One of the first uses of customer data was in the financial sector, where decisions needed to be made about customer credit-worthiness. Concerns about privacy led to the Fair Credit Reporting Act of 1970 and the Privacy Act of 1974, which delineated consumers' rights with regard to credit information (Turner and Dasgupta 2003). As technological sophistication increased and firms began to match and merge files and communicate information seamlessly, more legislation was passed – the Electronic Communications Privacy Act of 1986 and the Computer Matching and Privacy Protection Act of 1988 (Turner and Dasgupta 2003). Despite these steps, a 1992 survey found that

76% of consumers felt they had lost control over how information about them was collected and used by organizations (Turner and Dasgupta 2003).

A landmark privacy event of the Internet age was DoubleClick's purchase of Abacus in 1999 (Winer 2001). DoubleClick's specialty was the placement of Internet ads, and accordingly had cookie-based information on many consumers. Abacus was a customer-list exchange company that as a result had data on off-line purchase habits, as well as names and addresses, of millions of customers. DoubleClick's strategy was to merge their Internet data with Abacus' offline data. This would create a highly revealing portrait of millions of customers. The resounding negative publicity resulted in DoubleClick's declaring it would refrain from this plan. What DoubleClick was proposing was no different from many of the merge–purge operations that go on when various lists are combined. However, the magnitude of DoubleClick's endeavor, plus the involvement of the Internet, raised public awareness and kindled the fears raised above.

The Internet and rising privacy concerns in areas such as health care and the exploitation of children have given rise to a plethora of privacy laws; we will briefly review a few of these in Sect. 4.3.3. The fact that these regulations are part of a historical progression suggests that as technology develops and data collection and dissemination becomes more and more seamless, more legislation will be forthcoming.

4.2 Customer Attitudes Toward Privacy

While the above suggests the nature of the fears customers have regarding privacy, there has been some research that has measured customer attitudes and their impact on purchase behavior. In addition, segmentation schemes have been proposed for conceptualizing customer heterogeneity with respect to privacy.

4.2.1 Segmentation Schemes

Ackerman et al. (1999) surveyed web users and identified three segments with regard to privacy and the Internet. (a) Fundamentalists, who are very concerned about the use of data and do not want to provide any data through websites. (b) Pragmatists, who are concerned about privacy but whose fears could be allayed by laws, privacy policy statements, and the like. (c) Marginalists, who are only marginally concerned with the issue. The authors found that Fundamentalists comprised 17% of their sample, Pragmatists 56%, and Marginalists 27%. This suggests that extreme concerns about privacy are confined to a minority. However, if Fundamentalists publicize privacy concerns (e.g., the DoubleClick escapade) and if companies do not allay the concerns

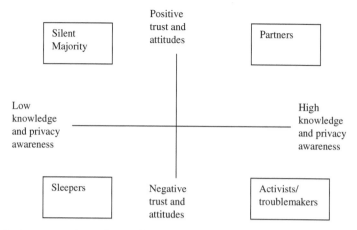

Fig. 4.2 A segmentation scheme of consumer attitudes toward privacy (From Fletcher 2003).

of the Pragmatists, these consumers could easily move to the Fundamentalist camp.

A follow-up study conducted in Germany (Grimm and Rossnagel 2000) similarly found 30% Fundamentalists and 24% Marginalists. The 45% Pragmatists were further subdivided into those concerned with identity (20%) versus profiling (25%). Identity would appear easier to deal with, because companies can use household ID's and contact individuals only after merging the ID's with the names/addresses/phone number file, which could be held by a third party or at least by a limited set of individuals in the organization. However, concerns about profiling seem endemic to what database marketing is all about. Predictive models essentially profile customers most likely to respond, most likely to churn, most likely to be profitable, etc.

Fletcher (2003) proposes a segmentation scheme depicted in Fig. 4.2. The scheme is based on two factors: attitudes toward and trust of the benefits of direct marketing, and knowledge and awareness with respect to privacy issues. Fletcher identifies four segments. (a) Silent majority, who have low knowledge awareness of privacy issues, but positive attitudes toward direct marketing. This group is cooperative but should be educated about the use of data and privacy issues, so they do not turn on companies if they see negative publicity. (b) Sleepers, who also have low knowledge and awareness of privacy issues, but are inherently hostile to direct marketing. There is little that can be done with this group in terms of bringing them into the CRM world. (c) Partners, who are highly aware of privacy issues but have positive views on direct marketing. These are the customers who "buy into" the database marketing exchange equation. (d) Activists, who are highly aware of privacy issues and have negative views on direct marketing. These are similar to the Fundamentalists. CRM companies need to try to educate these people on the value of direct marketing.

The above segmentation schemes are useful but need more testing and refinement. Complicating the picture is that segment sizes and intensity of feelings probably differ by product category (see Bart et al. 2005).

4.2.2 Impact of Attitudes on Database Marketing Behaviors

The key issue is how consumer attitudes toward privacy affect their attitudes toward various purchase behaviors in a database marketing environment. As mentioned earlier, Stewart and Segars found that consumers who were more concerned about privacy stated they would be more likely to request their names be removed from a mailing list, more likely to refuse to give information to a company, and more likely to refuse to buy a product because of the manner in which a company used personal information.

Verhoef et al. (2007) related customer attribute ratings of various sales channels (Internet, Catalog, Telephone) to their attitudes toward searching and purchasing on these channels. One attribute was the extent to which their privacy was guaranteed when purchasing on these channels. This attribute related negatively to purchasing on the Internet, significantly but less importantly to purchasing via catalog, and was not a significant determinant of purchasing in the store. These results make sense and highlight the privacy concerns evoked by the Internet. They also demonstrate that privacy concerns inhibit purchasing, and therefore slow down Internet commerce.

George (2002) studied the relationships among Internet experience, belief that one's data belong to oneself ("Property View"), trust in the privacy offered by the Internet, concerns with the security of buying on the Internet, Internet purchase intent, and Internet purchasing. The main results, based on a 1998 survey of Internet users, are depicted in Fig. 4.3.

The results show that Internet experience builds Internet trust, which begets favorable attitudes toward Internet security, which in turn increases

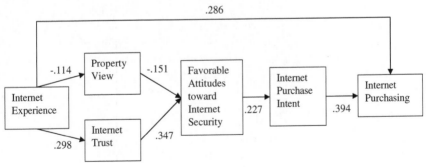

Fig. 4.3 The relationship between privacy attitudes and Internet purchasing (From George 2002).

Internet purchase intent and purchasing. Also, Internet experience is negatively associated with the property view of one's data, which in turn begets more favorable attitudes toward Internet security, and ultimately, higher Internet purchase intent and purchasing. In short, Internet experience induces favorable attitude changes that further enhance Internet usage.

George combines "trust" and "privacy" in his Internet Trust scale. Bart et al. (2005) separate the two. They measured trust as an overall belief that the website delivers on its promises and that the information on the website is believable. Privacy was measured in terms of the clarity of the privacy policy. They find that privacy affects trust, which in turn affects behavioral intent to use the Internet.

In a study reported by Peppers and Rogers (2004a), Intel and Urban found that levels of trust affected the number of software downloads from an Intel website. Privacy was not part of this study, but it reinforces the importance of trust in Internet marketing (see also Pepe 2005).

The emergence of trust as a key factor is very important. Trust is a broader issue than privacy – for example, it involves trusting the product recommendations made from the site, which is not a privacy issue – but it is not surprising that privacy concerns manifest themselves in a lack of trust. Note there may be reverse causality here. Surely privacy concerns undermine trust, but lack of trust could also trigger privacy concerns.

While the above studies clearly show that privacy concerns inhibit Internet purchasing Turner and Dasgupta (2003) suggest that consumers may be more willing to provide data than their attitudes indicate. Chain Store Age (2002) reports that 70% of US consumers report worrying about privacy, but only 40% bother to read privacy policies. On the other hand, Clampet (2005a) reports that 86% of consumers have asked to be removed from a mailing list, and 83% have refused to provide information because it was too personal.

4.2.3 International Differences in Privacy Concerns

An interesting question is whether privacy concerns differ across countries. Milberg et al. (1995) examined the inter-relationships among cultural values, regulatory environment, and information privacy concerns across nine countries. Cultural values included uncertainty avoidance index (UAI), power distance index (PDI), and individualism (IDV) (Hofstede 1980, 1991). UAI measures the degree to which society is averse to uncertainty. Milberg et al. hypothesized that consumers from countries with high UAI should have higher concerns for privacy. PDI measures the degree of inequality among various social classes. Milberg et al. hypothesized that consumers from high PDI countries will be more concerned about privacy, since high PDI countries are characterized by lower levels of trust. IDV measures the degree of independence encouraged in society. Milberg et al. hypothesized that consumers from high IDV countries would be associated with higher concerns for privacy.

For each of the nine countries, cultural values were measured using Hofstede's classifications. Regulatory levels were measured using the authors' judgments of the degree of regulation (low to high). The authors surveyed 900 members (IT professionals and financial auditors) of the Information Systems Audit and Control Association (ISACA) to measure the concern for privacy, using Smith et al's (1996) privacy measurement instrument.

The results were that (1) the level of concern for privacy differs across countries, (2) however, the prioritization of concerns for various privacy issues is the same, with secondary use first, improper access second, errors third, and collection fourth, (3) cultural values were not associated with privacy concerns, and (4) cultural values were associated with the degree of privacy regulation. Power distance and uncertainty avoidance were positively associated with the degree of regulation, and individuality was negatively associated with the degree of regulation.

These results are interesting and establish inter-country differences in privacy concerns. However, it is interesting that cultural values affected the degree of regulation while not apparently affecting concern for privacy. Milberg et al. (2000) conducted another survey of 595 ISACA members. They examined 19 countries rather than 9, and used partial least squares analysis rather than simple F-tests. In this study, they found that indeed, cultural values affected both the degree of regulation and the concern for privacy. PDI, IDV, and Masculinity (MASC) were positively associated with privacy concerns, whereas UAI was negatively associated with privacy concerns. Like their previous study, they found that UAI was positively associated with degree of regulation, and that IDV was negatively associated with regulation. They also found that MASC was negatively associated with degree of regulation. However, contrary to their previous study, they found that PDI was negatively associated with degree of regulation.

Bellman et al. (2004) surveyed 534 Internet users across 38 countries. Their research differs from the Milberg et al. studies in that Bellman et al. survey consumers. The authors examined three potential correlates of concern for information privacy: (1) cultural values (PDI, IND, UAI, and MASC), (2) current privacy regulatory structure, and (3) experience with using the Internet. Current privacy regulations were classified across countries as "No regulation or self help," "Sectoral" (meaning regulations specific to particular industries), and "Omnibus" (meaning general regulations that apply across industries).

The authors examined the role of regulatory approach as a mediator of the relationship between cultural values and concern for information privacy. Their results suggested that indeed regulatory approach mediated this relationship, in that the relationship between cultural values and overall concern for information privacy became insignificant when regulatory approach was added to the analysis.

However, there were relationships between cultural values and various sub-scales of the concern for information privacy measure. For example, respondents from cultures with lower IND indices indicated higher levels of concern for errors in the database; respondents from cultures with low PDI and low MASC had higher levels of concern about unauthorized secondary use; respondents from cultures with low PDI desired more privacy regulation and those from cultures with low MASC were more concerned about data security. In addition, online privacy concerns were negatively related to Internet experience.

Summarizing the Milberg et al. and Bellman et al. studies, concerns for privacy differ across countries. However, findings regarding the relationships between these concerns and cultural values, the desire for regulation, and regulatory environment have not been consistent. Milberg et al. (1995) find no relationship between cultural values and overall concern for privacy, whereas Milberg et al. (2000) find several results, and Bellman et al. (2004) find relationships between cultural values and particular subscales of the overall concern for privacy.

The studies differ in several ways. The Milberg et al. studies sample information system experts and financial auditors, whereas Bellman et al. sample consumers. Milberg et al. (1995) use simple statistical tests, Milberg et al. (2000) use partial least squares, and Bellman et al. use multivariate analysis of variance and mediation tests. An underlying issue here is to decide what is the underlying structural model?

One possible structure is shown in Fig. 4.4. In this model, the most straightforward path is that cultural values influence concern for privacy, which in turn influences desire for regulation, which in turn influences regulatory structure. However, cultural values might also have a direct impact on desire for regulation, which also influences regulatory structure, so concern for privacy might not play a role in determining regulatory structure. In addition, regulatory structure can influence concern for privacy as well as the desire for regulation. So there is also reverse causality in the model. Unraveling these relationships would be difficult but important. In addition, Bellman et al. show that consumers' Internet experience is associated with lower privacy concerns. Perhaps "Database Marketing Experience" should be added to the framework.

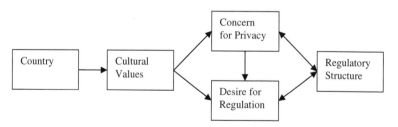

Fig. 4.4 Potential framework for analyzing country differences in concern for privacy and regulatory structure.

4.3 Current Practices Regarding Privacy

4.3.1 Privacy Policies

Companies – especially those selling through the Internet and catalogs – have adopted official privacy policies that they make available to consumers, typically on web-sites. There are three key components of these policies:

- *Opt-in vs. Opt-out*: "Opt-in" means that the customer has the opportunity *proactively* to agree to various uses of their data, where the "null" is that the data *will not* be used. Opt-out means that the customer can proactively assert that their data are not to be used, where the "null" is that the data *will* be used.
- *Internal vs. third-party usage*: Companies may use the data only for their own marketing efforts, or they may "partner" with other companies. They may sell the data to another company, e.g., a magazine may sell its subscription list to direct marketers, or the company might serve as an intermediary for transmitting offers to customers. For example, a cell-phone company might partner with an electronics company and offer a certain subset of its customers a deal on a DVD player.
- *Customer characteristic versus purchase history data*: Some companies only collect customer characteristic data such as age, gender, etc. Others, in fact most, also collect purchase history data.

These components suggest a taxonomy for privacy policies. For example, a company might be opt-in/only for internal use, for customer characteristic data, and opt-out/third-party use, for purchase history data. To gauge the prevalence of the various policies, we analyzed the privacy policies of the top 50 catalogers ranked by Catalog Age (2003). We visited each company website, read its privacy statement, and classified the policy accordingly.[2] The results are in Fig. 4.5. It was often difficult to interpret the various policies (this is an issue itself) and so these results should be taken as exploratory. However, the figure suggests some interesting findings:

- Opt-out is more prevalent than Opt-in. This is interesting, but begs the question of why opt-out is more popular. One hypothesis is that consumers make the choice that requires the least effort (see Bellman et al. and Sect. 4.4.3).
- Both personal characteristic and purchase history data are collected. This was sometimes difficult to gauge, especially regarding purchase history, and we classified nine companies as "don't say" regarding their use of purchase history data. But it appears that companies do inform customers that they are collecting both personal characteristic and purchase history data.

---

[2] The authors expressly thank Carmen-Maria Navarro for invaluable research assistance in this endeavor.

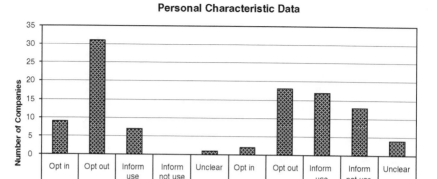

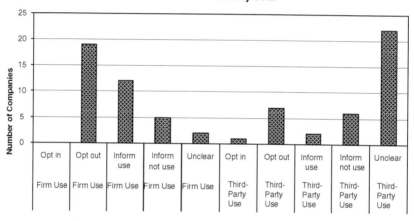

Fig. 4.5 Privacy statement practices among top 50 catalog companies in 2003.

- While opt-out is the most popular policy, there are a surprising number of instances where customers are simply informed of how the data are used and nothing stated about opting in or out.

Again, these results are exploratory, but they suggest a number of issues for further investigation in company use of privacy statements. First is that indeed, privacy statements are commonly made public but they are non-standardized and often difficult to interpret (see also Martin et al. 2000).

Second, companies seem to prefer opt-out. However, it isn't clear that this is the optimal policy. Since many customers do not read the privacy statements, they may not realize that their data is going to be used, possibly by third parties as well as the collecting firm. When they receive various offers that they then feel are an invasion of privacy, this only exacerbates the privacy problem and lowers response. It might be that if companies publicized their privacy statements better and utilized opt-in, privacy fears would be allayed and companies would be left with a highly responsive group. Opt-in might provide the first node in a decision tree predictive model in that those who do not op-in probably are less responsive.

Third, what is the optimum combination of policies for own versus third-party use, and for personal characteristics versus purchase history? Chen et al. (2001) use a game-theoretic analysis to show it may be of interest for a firm to sell its customer information to another firm (see Sect. 4.4.7). Another consideration in sharing information is whether to identify the partner with whom the information is shared. If that firm is prestigious, the customer may be more satisfied with the firm's sharing data with third parties and view it as an opportunity to form relationships with prestigious firms.

Fourth, exactly what it means to use or share data needs to be explained *thoroughly* to the customer. In the experience of the authors, a company would rarely provide their customers' complete purchase history data to a third party together with names and addresses. Instead, a third party might make a request, e.g., "extend this offer to customers who've bought a high definition television set over the last year". Serving as a conduit rather than actually giving the data to the third party might be perceived as less invasive by customers. In short, the black box of what it means to share customer information with third parties perhaps should be opened up for consumers.

4.3.2 Collecting Data

The manner in which companies collect data can increase privacy concerns. For example, companies often compile purchase histories directly from transactions. This is a seamless, unobtrusive way of collecting data. Internet companies, however, may want to collect data on customer search behavior. For this, they use cookies, thus potentially alarming the customer that their privacy is being invaded. Bricks-and-mortar stores have an even more challenging situation. It is often very difficult for them to "match-back" store purchases to the company's house file. Retailers therefore find themselves instituting a loyalty program, primarily for the purpose of collecting customer data! Registration for the card usually requires the customer to answer a few questions, at a minimum name and address, so it is easy to track customers who use their loyalty card.

Data on personal characteristics are collected in various ways: (1) upon registration at a web site or for a loyalty card, (2) from "complilers" such as Equifax, that collect as much publicly available information as possible on millions of individuals, (3) from purchasing lists (e.g., a company can purchase a list subscribers to a particular magazine), and (4) from data sharing (Stone and Condron 2002) and cooperative exchanges.

A well-known exchange forum in the catalog industry is run by Abacus. Companies contribute names to a database (perhaps with additional information such as whether the person has purchased in the last X months) and in turn withdraw names from the pool. Companies can specify certain competitors that cannot be allowed access to their names. In addition, sometimes companies exchange names directly. For example, company A and company B may provide each other access to 100,000 customers on their "12-month buyer" list. These exchanges can be a crucial way that companies acquire customers, and acquisition efforts arguably lower prices for the sought-after customers. In addition, the availability of list exchanges lowers the costs of customer acquisition, further driving down prices.

But should customers be informed of this practice? If informed, would so many customers opt out that this would cease to become a productive way of acquiring customers, driving up price? Chen et al. (2001) also would argue that information exchange could increase prices because it cushions price competition. How would customers react to this theory in terms of their attitudes toward sharing data?

4.3.3 The Legal Environment

A host of legislation has been enacted in the USA, Europe, and the rest of the world as well. Europe is known for its 1995 "Directive on Data Privacy," (http://europa.eu.int/eurlex/lex/Notice.do?val = 307229:cs&lang = en&list = 307229:cs,&pos = 1&page = 1&nbl = 1&pgs = 10&checktexte = checkbox&visu = #texte), which places the burden on organizations to seek permission before using personal information for any purpose (Turner and Dasgupta 2003). Specific provisions include:

- Data must be "collected for specified, explicit and legitimate purposes."
- The consumer ("data subject") must be told "the purposes of the processing for which the data are intended."
- "Personal data may be processed only if the data subject has unambiguously given his consent."
- The consumer must be informed of the "right of access to and the right to rectify the data concerning him . . . to guarantee fair processing in respect of the data subject."
- The company "controller" of the data must notify a "supervisory authority," a public authority for the correct administration of the law, "before carrying out . . . automatic processing . . . " of data.
- Data transfer to another country can take place only if "the third country in question ensures an adequate level of protection."

The directive pursues a full disclosure policy – the consumer will know what data are being processed for what purposes, will have access to the data, and can consent or not consent to particular analyses of the data. In addition, the directive sets up a public official to administer the law, and requires companies to report to this official.

The dictum that data transfer can take place only to a country that has an "adequate" level of protection raised concerns among US companies, since the USA does not offer as much protection as the European Directive. As a result, customer lists that flow freely within the USA might not flow from Europe to the USA. This would hamper direct marketing efforts of US companies in Europe, for example, US credit card companies seeking to acquire new customers. In 2000, negotiators created a "Safe Harbor" agreement, whereby American companies that ascribe to seven principles could do business without fear of European sanctions (Harvey and Verska 2001; Carlson 2001). Many American companies did not sign this agreement because it would still require full notification of customers whenever their data are being processed and for what purpose, and European customers could forbid specific analyses. However, in 2001, Microsoft signed onto Safe Harbor (Lucas 2001) and by 2005, 400 US companies had followed.

While the Safe Harbor system seems to be in place, as recently as 2005, the European Commission complained to the USA that its companies were not fully complying, and urged the US Department of Commerce to enforce the agreement fully (Swartz 2005). A complete description of the Safe Harbor agreement is available at http://www. export.gov/safeharbor/safeharbordocuments.htm. While it is a relaxation of the European Directive, it still has several strong requirements, including that (1) companies notify European consumers about the purposes for which it collects and uses their data, (2) if the company wishes to disclose data to a third party, consumers must have the right to opt out of any disclosure to a third party, or out of any use other than that originally notified, and (3) also must have access to the personal information companies hold on them (with the exception when the "expense of providing access would be disproportionate to the risks to the individual's privacy").

Clearly this is a regulatory issue in flux. There are many questions that will undoubtedly be resolved over the next few years. For example, if a cataloger obtains a list from a European company (assuming the consumer has consented), does the cataloger have to inform the consumer each time he or she is included in a predictive model?!? What are reasonable costs of providing consumers access to their data? If one division of a company obtains data, say the magazine division of AOL/Time Warner, would the magazine division need permission from the consumer in order for AOL to use the data? Finally, will the Safe Harbor agreement, or even its more highly regulatory European Directive parent, become law for transactions within the USA?

In addition to the European Directive and Safe Harbor agreement, there have been some specific laws passed in the USA pertaining to data privacy. Following is a brief summary of four significant laws (see

also Goldstein and Lee 2005; for a summary of additional laws, see
http://www.consumerprivacyguide.org/law/):

- The CAN-SPAM Act: This applies to commercial e-mail messages used for
  direct marketing (Dixon 2005). It requires that firms accurately identify
  the sender of the message, provide a clear mechanism for the customer
  to opt-out, and make clear that the message is an advertisement or a
  solicitation.
- Children's Online Privacy Protection Act (COPPA): Protects the privacy of children with regard to the Internet (http://www. consumerpri-
  vacyguide.org/law/). The law requires websites that cater to children 12
  and under to inform parents as to their information practices and obtain
  parent consent before collecting personal information from children. It also
  allows parents to review and correct information the website might have
  collected about their children.
- Gramm-Leach-Bliley Financial Modernization Act (GLB): Regulates the
  sharing of customer information in the domain of financial products and
  services (http://www.consumerprivacyguide.org/law/). It informs customers about the privacy policies of financial companies, and gives customers opt-out privileges over how financial companies share financial information.
- Health Insurance Portability and Accountability Act (HIPAA): The
  HIPAA Act of 1996 and subsequent regulations govern patient medical information, covering three main areas: privacy (e.g., when patient consent is
  needed to release medical records, when patients can access their records,
  etc.), security (protecting the confidentiality of data in electronic networks
  and transmissions, and transactions (standards for content and format of
  medical information when shared between health insurers, providers, and
  other health organizations) (Speers et al. 2004).

One can see elements of the European Directive incorporated in these laws.
For example, they emphasize clearly informing customers of privacy policies
(if not actual use of the data) and the right to opt-out and patient consent.

An additional regulatory step taken in the USA is the National
Do-Not-Call Registry (www.donotcall.gov). Citizens can sign up and as a
result cannot be called for many telemarketing purposes. There are some
obvious exceptions – calls that are for survey purposes, political campaigns,
and charities. In addition, the registry allows calls from companies with whom
the customer has an existing relationship. This would appear to favor large
companies, since they have more customers they could call. One might argue
this decreases competition. For example, if a customer has a cell-phone contract with Verizon, Verizon can call him or her to cross-sell services or adjust
the contract. This in turn gives Verizon more monopoly power over the customer, which enables higher prices. Whether this is in fact a consequence of
the do-not-call registry is of course conjecture, but it is an important consideration and illustrates the potentially subtle economic impact of all privacy
regulations.

4.4 Potential Solutions to Privacy Concerns

In this section, we review steps for addressing the privacy concerns listed in Fig. 4.1. Table 4.1 shows which steps might address each concern. We also discuss what the net effect of each step might be on the consequences of privacy concerns.

4.4.1 Software Solutions

A number of software solutions have been proposed to ensure customer privacy. Software is available that allows companies to take into account customer privacy preferences when marketing to their customers (Maselli et al. 2001). The software also allows sensitive data such as financial and credit information to be linked via a user ID but not to a specific name and address. As a result, very few people in the company would be able to associate a particular name with sensitive data. Software is also being developed to enable data mining of data owned by different organizations without the data actually having to be shared (Kantarcioglu and Clifton 2004).

A host of software solutions have been developed specifically for the Web and e-commerce (Turner and Dasgupta 2003). For example "anonymizers" provide customers with the ability shield their computer's IP address, or provide a new IP address each log in, so that the company cannot use cookies to record the customer's transactions. In fact, Hoffman et al. (1999) recommend that companies allow customers to be anonymous or "pseudo-anonymous", although they still need to be addressable in order to conduct database marketing. There are also tools the customer can use to block certain e-mails, counter the placement of cookies, or the customer can simply delete cookies.

In summary, software can address privacy concerns pertaining to data security, secretive data collection, third-party access, and fears of violation. One possible benefit is that ethical dilemmas can be avoiding by distancing managers from the data. For example, they would no longer have access to personally identifiable information. To the extent that companies use software to integrate customer privacy preferences with their marketing efforts, it can also diminish junk mail and spam and the "none-of-your-business" attitude. If customers interpret a company's use of sophisticated privacy software as a cue that the company cared about the customer, they might be more receptive to its marketing efforts. While these benefits are uncertain, it is certain that software and software maintenance is always expensive.

4.4.2 Regulation

Regulation can be thought of as a continuum from no regulation to self-regulation to government regulation (Milberg et al. 1995).

Table 4.1 Potential solutions to privacy concerns

	Potential solution							
Concerns	Software solutions	Government regulation	Self-regulation	Permission marketing	Customer data ownership	Engendering customer trust	Top management support	Privacy as profit maximization
Data security	√	√	√	–	√	√	√	–
Secretive data collection	√	√	√	–	√	√	√	–
Junk mail and spam	√	√	√	√	–	√	√	–
Third-party access	–	√	√	√	–	√	√	√
None-of-your-business	–	√	√	√	√	√	√	–
Violation of privacy	√	√	√	√	√	√	√	–
Inequitable exchange	–	–	–	√	√	√	√	–
Fear of data errors	√	–	–	–	–	–	√	–

A "√" means that the potential solution might address the corresponding concern.

4.4.2.1 Government Regulation

Regulations such as the European Directive and the other initiatives discussed in Sect. 4.3.3 can address many privacy concerns, including data security, secretive data collection, junk mail and spam, third-party access, and none-of-your-business attitudes. For example, the European Directive includes provisions on third-party access and informing customers what data are being collected. The CAN-SPAM Act curtails spam. The Gramm-Leach-Bliley Financial Modernization Act (GLB) regulates sharing of financial information among companies. The Do-Not-Call Registry alleviates concerns about unwanted telephone solicitations. Government regulation in the USA focuses especially on the privacy of truly sensitive data, such as medical information (HIPAA), financial data (GLB), and children's information (COPPA).

Government regulation provides an easy "out" on ethical issues, e.g., "What we did was legal under the Such-and-Such Act." However, government regulation is costly in that it often includes compliance monitoring, which can be expensive both for the government and for firms. Whether the benefits of regulation result in higher sales and profits depends on how customers interpret the regulations. If customers view regulations as addressing their fears so they can do business with companies and not be concerned about privacy, customers might be more receptive to firms' marketing efforts. The key unanswered question is, does government regulation increase trust (Turner and Dasgupta 2003)?

4.4.2.2 Self-Regulation

Self-regulation often consists of standards set by an industry trade organization and adhered to by its members. A prime example is the Direct Marketing Association's "Privacy Promise" (Direct Marketing Association 2007). This contains four key provisions: (1) provide annual notice of the customer's right to opt out of third-party information exchanges, (2) honor customer requests to opt out of these exchanges, (3) accept customer requests that they be added to in-house "suppression" files – lists of customers that are not to be contacted by the company, (4) use the DMA's Mail Preference, e-Mail Preference, and Telephone Preference Service lists to weed out prospects who do not wish to be contacted.

Another example of self-regulation is the Platform for Privacy Preferences (P3P) initiative. P3P was developed and recommended for company adoption by the World Wide Web Consortium (WC3) in 2002 (Computer and Internet Lawyer 2002). P3P offers the capability for the Internet customer to access the website's privacy policy in a standard format and compare to his or her own preferences (Matlis 2002; Grimm and Rossnagel 2000).

This type of self-regulation can allay the same customer fears that government regulation addresses. The problem however is whether customers perceive self-regulation to be as effective. For example, while all DMA member companies sign a statement agreeing to the Privacy Promise as part of their membership, identify a Privacy Promise contact person, and re-affirm compliance each year, customers may be concerned about whether the DMA monitors compliance. P3P has no compliance mechanism (Matlis 2002). As a result, self-regulation is less costly, but its effectiveness depends on whether customers are aware of it and believe it works.

4.4.3 Permission Marketing

Permission marketing (also called "permission-based marketing") refers to obtaining the customer's consent before initiating database marketing efforts (see Peppers and Rogers 2004b). The main benefit of permission marketing is to make clear the exchange proposition: the company wants to collect data on the customer and in return will use the data to personalize products and offers. Permission marketing should also address customer fears of secretive data collection, junk mail and spam, third-party access, and feelings of none-of-your-business and violation.

If permission marketing delivers on its promise, targeting can be more efficient. First, the customers who do not want to participate in permission marketing probably would be low responders anyway. Customers who directly permit database marketing messages probably are more apt to respond to them (Godin 1997). Second is that the customer presumably would allow the collection of a lot of data. Permission marketing is also ethical in that the customer has full information on the system, although it may increase costs in terms of gaining and recording the permission. A key question is whether sales and profits increase under permission marketing. To the extent that targeting efficiency is higher, profitability in the sense of ROI should increase. But whether absolute profits increase depends on how many customers agree to participate. It is quite possible that under permission marketing, the firm is left with a lucrative but small number of customers with whom it can undertake database marketing.

A central issue of permission marketing is the format of soliciting customers, i.e., how to "pop the question" of whether they wish to participate. There are two basic considerations in posing this question: (1) the framing of the request, which can be either positive "I wish to participate" or negative "I wish not to participate", and (2) the default action assumed, which can be "yes," "no", or neither. For example, if the question is framed, "I wish to participate" and a "yes" box is checked, the customer is participating unless he or she opts-out by checking the "no" box. Opt-in can therefore be defined as when the customer decides to participate either by default or by proactively saying yes. Opt-out can be defined as when the customer decides not to participate, either by default or by proactively saying no.

Bellman et al. (2001) investigated the premise that customers would respond in the direction that required the least effort, following the path of least resistance. They examined two factors in a controlled experiment: (1) positive versus negative framing of the solicitation ("I want to participate" versus "I do not want to participate") and (2) whether the default answer indicated participation, no participation, or neither.

The authors conducted two experiments. The first was to investigate just the framing. They asked 134 Internet users whether they wanted to receive surveys about health issues. The question was framed in two ways: (1) the statement "Notify me about more health surveys" appeared and the customer had to proactively check a box in order to participate (opt-in presentation); (2) the statement "Do not notify me about more health surveys" appeared and the customer had to proactively check a box in order not to participate (opt-out presentation). The authors found that 48.2% participated under the opt-in format, while 96.3% participated under the opt-out format.

In the second experiment, Bellman et al. combined question framing with default box-checking. There were two factors in the experiment: framing of the question and action requirements in terms of box-checking. The framing question was asked in two ways: "Notify me about future health surveys" (positive framing) or "Do not notify me about future health surveys" (negative framing). The box checking could either be so that the null was to participate, not participate, or neither (box not checked). So for example the statement "Notify me about future health surveys" with the "yes" box checked would be a positive frame with the default being opt-in.

The results, depicted in Fig. 4.6, showed that positive framing and the no-action default increased participation rates. Figure 4.6 shows that if the customer saw the statement "Notify me about more health surveys" and the "yes" box was checked rather than the "no" box, 89.2% would participate. That is, only 11.8% would uncheck the "yes" box and check "no." On the other extreme, if the wording was negative, "Do not notify me about more health surveys" and the "yes" box was checked, indicating the customer would have to press "no" in order to opt-in, only 44.2% opted in.

Bellman et al.'s work is important because it shows the format of how customers are solicited for permission marketing is crucial for how many customers sign up. Wording the question in a positive way ("I want to participate") and having a yes box checked, can double participation rates over wording the question in a negative way ("I don't want to participate") and having a yes box checked for that. Interestingly, with a positive frame, the default checking of the "yes" box does not seem crucial. As Fig. 4.6 shows, wording the question positively yields 88.5% participation even if no box is checked, whereas asking the same question and checking the "yes" box as a default adds only slightly, yielding a participation rate of 89.2%.

A crucial next question is whether "manipulating" the customer into participating influences further response to the direct marketing offers to follow. That is, perhaps positive wording with a yes default yields the most

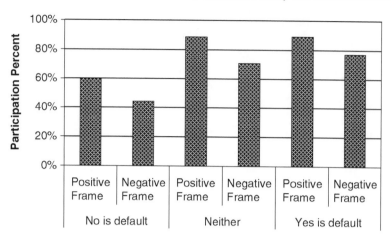

Fig. 4.6 Customer decisions to participate in permission marketing as a function of framing and default action. (**a**) Positive frame means the solicitation was worded "Notify me about more health surveys"; negative frame means the solicitation was worded "Do NOT notify me about more health surveys. (**b**) "No is default" means the box was checked that would indicate not to participate. "Yes is default" means the box was checked that would indicate participate. "Neither" means that neither box was checked (From Bellman et al. 2001).

customers, but many customers were essentially defaulted into participation, and they won't respond well to future direct marketing efforts. Whereas the customers who saw a negative wording with a default indicating non-participation had to take action in order to participate, and hence might be better responders further down the line. This is an important area for future investigation.

Another aspect of permission marketing is the need for companies to educate the customer – to spell out exactly what CRM is, and why the trade of privacy for database marketing is worth it. Customers seem to accept that financial institutions such as banks need to know their credit history. The view is that free flow of information lowers risk and keeps interest rates down. As a result, it helps the economy. The same argument needs to be made regarding other products – the free flow of information helps companies keep their marketing costs down, tailor appropriate services, and target price discounts. Customers need to "buy into" this notion and be willing to provide the data to make it happen – on a permission basis. In summary, in order for permission marketing to be profitable, it needs to be *marketed* to the customer.

4.4.4 Customer Data Ownership

The aim of customer data ownership is to grant the customer control of his or her data. There are two ways this can be done. First is to provide customers with access to their data and the right to change it (Zwick and Dholakia 2004). Cespedes and Smith (1993) early-on recommended consumer access to and control over their information. Zwick and Dholakia mention Amazon.com as a case in point, where customers can learn the reasons for recommendations Amazon makes, and update or add to their preference data in order to improve the quality of these recommendations. This essentially makes the customer an active participant in the estimation of predictive models-the data provided by the customer increase the accuracy of the recommendation engine used by Amazon. So this form of customer data ownership should result in higher response rates.

Another form of customer data ownership is to let customers house their data on their computers. Watson (2004) envisions a system of "Customer-Managed Interactions" (CMI) whereby customer compile their own data on preferences and behaviors regarding various product categories. They then submit their data to companies and ask for tailored offers. For example, the customer might maintain a database on his or her travel history, vacation preferences, etc. When it comes time to take a vacation, the customer sends the data to various travel agencies who then compile a product recommendation and offer for the customer. Essentially, this system brings the "request-for-proposal" (RFP) system used in government and B2B sectors to the realm of database marketing.

Data ownership addresses several concerns related to privacy. It addresses data security, secretive data collection, and none-of-your-business and violation attitudes. In addition, it makes the nature of the exchange-information for better service and more appropriate offers-more clear. One concern is that providing customers with ownership of their data can be costly. As with permission marketing, the question of whether it increases sales and profits depends on how many customers want to participate. It does appear to address the ethical concerns with database marketing, because customers know exactly what data are being housed in the company.

4.4.5 Focus on Trust

Bart et al. (2005) as well as other work discussed in Sect. 4.2 identify the intermingling of trust and privacy. How exactly to combine trust and privacy in a database marketing context is a fertile area for future research (e.g., see Peppers and Rogers 2005a). Trust addresses concerns about junk mail and spam, third-party access, data security, and fears of violation. However, its main promise is to define the DBM exchange equation – the customer trusts that by providing the company with better data, he or she will be better served. The result, as indicated by Bart et al.'s work, is higher sales levels. Customers who trust companies tend to buy more from them.

Cespedes and Smith (1993) suggest a three-faceted approach to engendering trust: (1) obtain clear and informed consent regarding the use of a customer's data, (2) acknowledge corporate responsibility for information accuracy and allow customers to access and edit their data, and (3) categorize customers based on behaviors rather than personal characteristics. The third recommendation is particularly interesting. Customers will perceive as fair a system that provides heavy users with special offers, but less likely to believe a system is fair if it provides customers of certain income groups with special offers. Perhaps the key theme of Cespedes and Smith is *transparency* – transparency in how the data are used, what data are collected, and access to the data.

Bart et al's (2005) rating scales for privacy involve transparency, reflected in phrases such as "easy to understand" and "clearly explains." The fact that this measure links so strongly to trust shows that transparency is crucial for establishing trust. Our review in Sect. 4.3.1 suggests current practice entails vaguely worded privacy policies. One possibility would be for companies to adopt a standard format for stating policies that makes clear where the company stands on the three crucial issues: what data are collected, do third parties have access to the data, and can the customer opt-out.

Additional recommendations for engendering trust include: make it part of the corporate culture; engender the attitude among the entire company that they need to do all that's possible, not merely all that is required, to ensure customer privacy (Peppers and Rogers 2005b); and publicize customer trust ratings obtained via surveys – e.g., a recent survey found eBay, P&G, Amazon, and HP among the most trusted companies (McClure 2004).

4.4.6 Top Management Support

The European Directive requires companies to create top management positions and empower the occupiers of these positions to ensure privacy within their company. It appears that more and more US companies are creating the position of Chief Privacy Officer (Clampet 2005b). For example, the CPO at Pfizer is needed simply to deal with the regulatory environment created by HIPAA (Corr 2004).

Top management support potentially can address all privacy concerns, because top management can enhance the implementation of software, compliance with government and self-regulation, permission marketing, data ownership, and taking the steps to engender trust. Milberg et al. (2000) measure "corporate privacy management environment" using a number of items, including "how important to the senior management of your organization is information privacy?" They find that the corporate privacy management environment is negatively associated with whether managers perceive privacy problems within the company. So at least company executives believe that top management support decreases privacy concerns. However, further research is needed to see whether customers see this link.

While the above suggests that top management support can address concerns, it is costly in that it increases personnel costs, and raises concerns about organizational bureaucracy. It hopefully would help resolve ethical dilemmas, because the CPO could make these issues more salient and more openly discussed within the company.

4.4.7 Privacy as Profit Maximization

One view is that the customer database is a competitive advantage for many companies, because it teaches them things about customers that no other companies know, and hence enables them to serve them better. It therefore behooves companies to protect this core competence by not sharing information.

Chen et al. (2001) present a more nuanced viewpoint, that a moderate level of sharing customer data may be a profitable equilibrium in a competitive environment. Chen et al. examine the case where companies vary in their abilities to target customers. Chen et al. express this as knowing brand preference and willingness to pay – their theory is about targeting in terms of price. But the general point is that an important industry capability is how much different companies know about different customers. A main finding of Chen et al. is that industry profits are maximized when targeting is imperfect, i.e., when companies do not know the preferences of all customers. Chen et al. show that when companies do not know much about customers, they should share information to increase profits. But at a certain point this becomes self-defeating because extensively shared customer information promotes price competition (see Fig. 4.2, p. 31 of Chen et al.).

In summary, Chen et al. alleviate the fear that firms will share information *without bounds*. However, they would advocate a balanced sharing of information because "when the achievable targetability in an industry is low, it is important to share customer information. However, it behooves firms in an industry to develop self-regulations at an early stage to protect customer privacy so as to ensure win-win competition in the industry" (pp. 36–37).

Another viewpoint of privacy as profit maximization is that privacy is a company attribute and rating higher on that attribute increases sales and loyalty. In the words of Peter Cullen, CPO of Royal Bank, quoted in Thibodeau (2002), privacy "is one of the key drivers of a customer's level of commitment and has a significant contribution to overall demand," and "plays a measurable part in how customers decide [to] purchase products and services from us. It brings us more share of the customer's wallet."

4.5 Summary and Avenues for Research

In this chapter we have reviewed the nature of the privacy "problem," the
consumer perspective on privacy, current industry practices, and potential
solutions to the problem. Some of our major conclusions are:

- *Privacy is multi-dimensional.* It ranges from customer feelings of violation
  to inequitable exchange to a reluctance to have their data transmitted
  to third parties. The implication is that any measurement of consumer
  perceptions of privacy needs to be multi-dimensional, and any solutions to
  privacy concerns must address several dimensions (see Table 4.1).
- *Negative consumer attitudes toward privacy appear to decrease sales.* The
  evidence comes from three studies: George (2002) found that privacy attitudes influenced Internet purchase intent, Verhoef et al. (2007) found
  that privacy attitudes decreased use of the Internet as a sales channel,
  and Bart et al. (2005) found that privacy concerns lead to lower trust and
  lower trust in turn leads to lower sales.
- *Companies communicate their privacy policies.* This communication takes
  place at least on the web, and policies vary in terms of opt-in/opt-out/no
  option for data collection, the type of data collected, and whether the data
  is shared with third parties. The statements are often difficult to interpret
  although there seems to be a clear tendency for opt-out rather than opt-in,
  and providing no option at all is more common than opt-in.
- *There is an active market for sharing customer data.* This occurs through
  the direct sale of lists, customer list exchanges, and third party collectors
  of customer data. Customer concerns regarding the sharing of data are
  well-founded.
- *There is a growing regulatory environment with respect to privacy.*
  Europe has taken the lead in adopting a strict, highly protective policy, and American companies have scrambled to comply with it. The USA
  is less regulated, but there are specific laws with regard to children, the
  financial industry, the health care industry, and e-mail marketing. The
  indications are that more laws will be forthcoming.
- *There are several potential ways to address customer privacy concerns.*
  Including software solutions, government and self-regulation, permission
  marketing, customer data ownership, focus on trust, top management support, and privacy as a profit-maximizing strategy. These solutions collectively can address all customer privacy concerns. They hence offer ways to
  improve sales levels and ensure efficient targeting, in an ethical way.

The chapter suggests several areas for further research:

- *Which privacy dimensions are most crucial?* How does this vary by industry and customer? Are there customer segments?
- *More evidence on how privacy concerns detract from commerce*: We do
  have some evidence summarized above that suggests privacy concerns

decrease economic activity, but we need new studies especially with regard to the Internet.

- *What is the impact of regulation?* Is regulation a friend or foe of database
  marketing? Which is more effective, government or self-regulation, and
  under what conditions? A fascinating question is whether the do-not-call
  registry has provided advantages to large firms with large customer bases.
- *What would be the impact of a more transparent information environment
  for the customer?* If customers knew exactly what data were collected, exactly how they were used, and what decisions were made as a result, would
  this enhance participation in database marketing or cause too many customers to opt out? This is a crucial issue because probably the underlying
  fear of many CRM executives is that complete transparency, coupled with
  opt-in, would result in very little opt-in.
- *Does customer experience with database marketing diminish or enhance
  concerns for information privacy?* This is a very important issue because if
  experience diminishes concern, the privacy issue might possibly melt away
  over time. This issue has been studied with respect to the Internet. The
  evidence seems to be that experience diminishes concerns (George 2002;
  Bellman et al. 2004). However, this issue warrants deeper investigation.
- *What is the effectiveness of the various solutions proposed for addressing privacy?* Are some of the customer data ownership proposals feasible? What would be their impact? Is permission marketing the ultimate
  solution? That is, make it clear what companies want to do, market or
  communicate the value of what they want to do, and see who signs up?
  How effective would this strategy be?

In conclusion, privacy is an issue in flux and difficult to research, but it gets
at the core of whether the database marketing premise of exchange – data
and some loss in privacy for better products/services/offers – is viable as a
long-term business model.

Part II
Customer Lifetime Value (LTV)

Chapter 5
Customer Lifetime Value: Fundamentals

Abstract Customer lifetime value (LTV) is one of the cornerstones of database marketing. It is the metric by which we quantify the customer's long-term value to the firm. This chapter focuses on the fundamental methods for calculating lifetime value, centering on "simple retention models" and "migration models." We present a general approach to calculating LTV using these models, and illustrate with specific examples. We also discuss the particular case of calculating LTV when customer attrition is unobserved.

5.1 Introduction

Marketing needs to develop key metrics if it wants to become more relevant to top management. The commonly used marketing metrics are sales and market share but these measures are "dated". They are aggregate "30,000 feet" measures and do not provide the level of insight modern executives need to manage their businesses. This chapter focuses on a relatively new metric: lifetime value of a customer (LTV).

LTV has two main applications: (1) to diagnose the health of a business and (2) to assist in making tactical decisions. LTV provides a longer-run economic view of the customer and generates diagnostics based on the parameters that determine it: retention rates, sales per customer, and costs. LTV, linked with customer acquisition rates and expenditures, quantifies the long-term profitability of the firm. A firm cannot reduce customer acquisition investment without a warning signal going off: the number of newly acquired customers multiplied by their LTV would decline, indicating a long-term decline in total company profit.

LTV's tactical applications include determining how much a firm can invest to acquire customers and deciding how much service to offer a given customer. For example, a bank might decide that high-LTV customers should receive better services (e.g., a personal representative and no service fees for bank checking accounts).

This chapter covers the fundamentals of calculating LTV. Chapter 6 covers challenging issues in computing LTV and Chapter 7 provides LTV applications.

5.1.1 Definition of Lifetime Value of a Customer

The definition we will use for the lifetime value of a customer (LTV) is:

The net present value of the profits linked to a specific customer once the customer has been acquired, after subtracting incremental costs associated with marketing, selling, production and servicing over the customer's lifetime.

There are a number of important issues implied in this definition. The firm needs to: (1) forecast future sales of a customer; (2) compute incremental costs per customer; and (3) determine the relevant discount rate to use in the present value calculation. Note also that we do not include acquisition costs as part of lifetime value. However, we often display customer acquisition cost alongside customer LTV. In this way, we gain insight on whether an unprofitable customer (for whom LTV minus acquisition cost is negative) is due to high acquisition cost or low LTV. Formally, we refer to LTV minus acquisition cost as "Customer Equity" (Blattberg et al. 2001).

5.1.2 A Simple Example of Calculating Customer Lifetime Value

Assume a firm spends $2.00 for mailing and printing a catalog which is sent to 1,000,000 prospects. The response rate to the mailing is 1%. Prospects who become customers spend $200 per year as long as they are still active customers. A customer has a probability of "attriting" ("churning")[1] each year of 20%. If a customer attrites, he or she ceases to be a customer and never returns. The firm also spends $20 per year in marketing (catalogs and service) to each active customer. The firm has a gross margin of 50% and uses a discount rate of 15%.

Table 5.1a shows the computations for the LTV of the customer just described along with the average acquisition cost per customer. We see that the acquisition cost is less than the LTV and so the firm should invest in acquiring this customer.

This example highlights some of the critical information required to compute LTV. Table 5.2 summarizes these issues and where they are covered.

---

[1] Throughout this chapter and book we will use attrite and churn interchangeably.

Table 5.1 Lifetime value and acquisition cost calculations: A simple example

Table 5.1a Lifetime value

Parameters	
Retention rate	80%
Revenues if still a customer	$200
Profit margin	50%
Gross profit if still a customer	$100
Marketing cost if still a customer	$20
Net annual profit if still a customer	$80
Discount rate	15%

Year	Survival rate[a]	Expected profit	Discount multiplier[b]	Net discounted profit
1	1.000	$80	1.000	$80
2	0.800	$64	0.870	$56
3	0.640	$51	0.756	$39
4	0.512	$41	0.658	$27
5	0.410	$33	0.572	$19
6	0.328	$26	0.497	$13
7	0.262	$21	0.432	$9
8	0.210	$17	0.376	$6
9	0.168	$13	0.327	$4
10	0.134	$11	0.284	$3

LTV = Total net discounted profit = $256

[a]The survival rate is the probability the customer is still a customer in a given year. In this case the survival rate in year t is 0.8^{t-1}. This is because the customer has a 0.2 probability of attriting each year; hence a retention rate of 0.8, and we assume the retention rate is constant over time.

[b]Discount multiplier $= 1/(1 + \text{discount rate})^{(\text{Year}-1)}$

Table 5.1b Acquisition cost

Mail cost per prospect	$2
Number of prospect mailings	1,000,000
Total mail costs	$2,000,000
Response rate	1%
Number of customers acquired	10,000
Cost per acquired customer	**$200**

Table 5.2 Information requirements for computing LTV

Parameter	Coverage
Retention rates	Section 3
Unobserved attrition	Section 4
Expected revenue per customer	Section 5
Relevant costs	Chapter 6
Appropriate discount rate	Chapter 6

5.2 Mathematical Formulation of LTV

Lifetime value can be stated as:

$$LTV = \sum_{t=1}^{\infty} \frac{E[\tilde{V}_t]}{(1+\delta)^{t-1}} \tag{5.1}$$

where:

$\tilde{V}_t$ = a random variable representing the customer's net profit contribution during time t.

δ = the discount rate per time unit t.

Profit contribution over time is uncertain; therefore LTV is the *expected* net present value of future profit contributions. The assumptions made in quantifying these uncertain returns determine LTV. For simplicity we do not include a customer subscript in Equation 5.1. Ideally, the calculation should be made at the customer level, but data might not be available to estimate the required parameters on a per customer basis. Therefore, LTV calculations are often made for the "average" customer using average parameters. However, calculating the LTV of a group of customers assuming an average retention rate will technically not yield the correct average LTV. The reason is that the mean of a function of a variable "X" does not equal the function evaluated at the mean of X (i.e., $E[f(X)] \neq f(E[X])$). The correct way to calculate the average LTV of a group of customers is to determine each customer's parameters (e.g., retention rate), use them to calculate each customer's LTV, and then average. For this reason, even if the firm only needed to compute LTV at the segment level, it is preferable to compute individual LTV values and then average at the segment level.

Larger discount factors result in future profit being less "important" to the firm. Despite the importance of the discount factor in the calculation of LTV, there is very little systematic work on what value to use. In practice, one sees annual discount factors varying between 10% ($\delta = 0.10$) and 20% ($\delta = 0.20$), usually with little justification. We cover this issue in depth in Chapter 6.

$E(\tilde{V}_t)$ can be decomposed into revenues and costs. Specifically, $\tilde{V}_t = \tilde{R}_t - C_t$ where $\tilde{R}_t$ is the revenue generated by the customer in period t and C_t includes costs of goods, marketing and servicing. Little has been written about how to compute relevant costs for LTV models. For example, one very important issue is how to treat "fixed" versus "variable" costs. This topic will be covered in Chapter 6. We assume future costs are known, but revenues are random, so to compute *expected* lifetime value, we need to compute $E(\tilde{R}_t)$, expected revenue. To do this, we multiply the probability the customer is retained through period t (the survival rate in Table 5.1a) times the expected revenue generated during the period, given the customer has survived. Formally, $E(\tilde{R}_t) = P(Survive\ until\ period\ t) \cdot E(\tilde{R}_t | Survive\ until\ period\ t) = S_t \cdot E(\tilde{D}_t)$ where

S_t is the probability the customer survives until period t, and $\tilde{D}_t$ is a random variable equal to the revenue the customer generates during period t, given the customer survives until then.

Hazard models can be used to estimate S_t, and regression models can be used to estimate $E(\tilde{D}_t)$. A significant challenge is to incorporate control variables such as pricing and marketing contacts. We discuss these issues in Chapters 6 and 28.

5.3 The Two Primary LTV Models: Simple Retention and Migration

There are two primary models used to calculate LTV – simple retention and migration (Dwyer 1989; Berger and Nasr 1998). Simple retention models assume once the customer has attrited, the customer is lost to the company. Table 5.1a assumes a simple retention model. Migration models acknowledge that customers might migrate in and out of being a customer during the normal course of their lifetimes. Simple retention models are more applicable for industries such as financial services, B2B businesses, magazine subscriptions, and pharmaceutical drugs. Migration models are more applicable for industries such as retailing, catalogs, and consumer packaged goods.

5.3.1 Simple Retention Models

5.3.1.1 Calculating the Retention Rate by Direct Observation

As Table 5.1a illustrates, one of the most important parameters for the simple retention model is the retention rate, the probability the customer remains with the company, given the customer has not yet left the company. The simplest way to calculate a retention rate is by direct observation. Using its customer base for year 1, the firm can determine what percentage of these customers remained with the company in year 2. The resulting retention rate is often assumed to apply for all periods. The computation can be made more detailed by segmenting customers based on how long they have been customers or by various other demographic or behavioral variables.

The method just described is perhaps the most common way that retention rates are calculated in the real world. The problem is that they assume retention rates from the past will hold up in the future. They also provide little flexibility to calculate the probability customer will still be with the firm $11/2$ years from now, or to calculate customer-level retention rates. Overcoming these deficiencies requires a model for which hazard models provide an ideal approach (see Chapter 15 for more detailed discussion of hazard models).

Table 5.3 LTV using a constant hazard rate

Example 1: Parameters
Hazard rate = 0.1
Revenue = $200
Cost = $100
Discount rate = 10%

LTV calculation:

Year	Hazard	Retention rate	Survival rate	Discount multiplier	Discounted expected profit
1	0	1	1.00	1.00	$100.00
2	0.1	0.9	0.90	0.91	$81.82
3	0.1	0.9	0.81	0.83	$66.94
4	0.1	0.9	0.73	0.75	$54.77
5	0.1	0.9	0.66	0.68	$44.81
6	0.1	0.9	0.59	0.62	$36.66
7	0.1	0.9	0.53	0.56	$30.00
8	0.1	0.9	0.48	0.51	$24.54
9	0.1	0.9	0.43	0.47	$20.08
10	0.1	0.9	0.39	0.42	$16.43

LTV after 10 years = $476.06
LTV over infinite horizon using Equation 5.2 = $550.00

Example 2: Parameters
Hazard rate = 0.2
Revenue = $200
Cost = $100
Discount rate = 10%

LTV calculation:

Year	Hazard	Retention rate	Survival rate	Discount multiplier	Discounted expected profit
1	0	1	1.00	1.00	$100.00
2	0.2	0.8	0.80	0.91	$72.73
3	0.2	0.8	0.64	0.83	$52.89
4	0.2	0.8	0.51	0.75	$38.47
5	0.2	0.8	0.41	0.68	$27.98
6	0.2	0.8	0.33	0.62	$20.35
7	0.2	0.8	0.26	0.56	$14.80
8	0.2	0.8	0.21	0.51	$10.76
9	0.2	0.8	0.17	0.47	$7.83
10	0.2	0.8	0.13	0.42	$5.69

LTV after 10 years = $351.49
LTV over infinite horizon using Equation 5.2 = $366.67

5.3.1.2 Using Hazard Models to Calculate LTV for a Simple Retention Model

Hazard models are used to compute S_t, the probability that a customer is still alive at (survived to) time t. Let $\tilde{T}$ be a random variable representing the time the customer attrites (dies) with probability density function $f(t)$. The probability of attrition is $P(\tilde{T} < t) = F(t)$, where $F(t)$ is the cumulative distribution function: $F(t) = \int_0^t f(x)dx$. The probability that a customer survives past time t is $S_t = P(\tilde{T} \geq t) = 1 - F(t) = \int_t^\infty f(x)dx$.

The hazard function is also very useful. It is the probability the customer attrites during the instantaneous period Δt *given the customer has remained with the firm up to period t*. It is defined as $h(t) = \frac{f(t)}{S(t)}$. The hazard functions can also be represented as $h(t) = \frac{d}{dx} \log S(t)$. Thus for a given survival function, there is a one-to-one relationship with a corresponding hazard function.

To show how the survival function is used in LTV calculations, we will begin with a very simple distribution for survival rates, the exponential distribution, where $f(t) = \lambda e^{-\lambda t}$. The survival function for the exponential distribution is $S_t = 1 - F(t) = e^{-\lambda t}$ and the hazard function is $h(t) = \frac{f(t)}{S(t)} = \lambda$. This means that if the lifetime of the customer follows an exponential distribution, the hazard is constant each period no matter how long the customer survives.

To make matters simpler, we will use the discrete version of the exponential distribution, the geometric distribution with parameter h. The hazard for the geometric distribution in any discrete time period is h and is constant. Let $r = 1 - h$ which is the retention rate. The survival function for τ periods after the initial period is r^τ. The value of a customer up to period τ is $\sum_{t=1}^\tau r^{t-1}(R_t - C_t)/(1+\delta)^{t-1}$ where R_t is revenue, δ is the discount rate and C_t is cost in period t.

Table 5.3 shows the computation of expected profit for the geometric assuming a hazard rate h per period and a retention rate each period of $r = 1 - h$. The table also shows the survival rate. The expected profit in each period is the survival rate times the discounted profit per period, which we assume to be known and constant. This case, where we assume constant retention rate and profit contribution, can be calculated using a simple formula:

$$LTV = (R - C)\frac{1+\delta}{1+\delta-r} \tag{5.2}$$

where δ is the discount rate, r is the retention rate, and R and C are the assumed known revenues and costs per period.[2]

---

[2] Assume revenues (R) and costs (C) are constant over time, and the discount factor is δ. Then

$$LTV = \sum_{t=1}^\infty \frac{(R-C)r^{t-1}}{(1-d)^{t-1}} = (R-C) + \frac{r(R-C)}{(1+\delta)} + \frac{r^2(R-C)}{(1+\delta)^2} \cdots$$

$$= (R-C) \times (1 + d + d^2 \cdots)$$

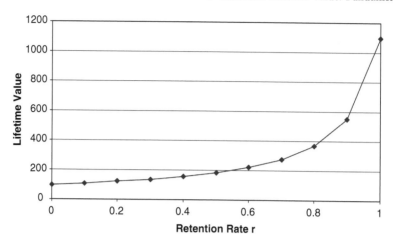

Fig. 5.1 Lifetime value as a function of retention rate − simple retention model.

Figure 5.1 shows the relationship between LTV and the retention rate using Equation 5.2. The relationship is convex and increases significantly as retention rate approaches one. This is the reason many authors argue small increases in the retention rates have a significant impact on LTV. What they do not include is the cost of changing the retention rate. It may be very costly to increase it from 0.90 to 0.95.

Other statistical distributions can be used to generate survival and hazard functions. For example, if one believes that customers have declining hazards, meaning that the longer the customers are with the firm, the lower the probability of attrition, then a Weibull distribution with specific parameters can be used. The Weibull distribution has a probability distribution function (p.d.f) of:

$$f(t) = \lambda \gamma (\lambda t)^{\gamma-1} e^{-(\lambda t)^{\gamma}} \tag{5.3}$$

The survival and hazard functions for the Weibull are respectively:

$$S(t) = e^{-(\lambda t)^{\gamma}} \tag{5.4a}$$

$$h(t) = \lambda \gamma (\lambda t)^{\gamma-1} \tag{5.4b}$$

The shape of the survival and hazard functions are determined by γ. If $\gamma < 1$, then the hazard function is decreasing over time, and if $\gamma > 1$, then it is increasing. If $\gamma = 1$, the Weibull become the exponential distribution with constant hazard λ. Figure 5.2 plots the hazard function for $\gamma = 0.7$ and $\gamma = 1.3$ (with $\lambda = 0.3$). The shape of the hazard is extremely useful for database marketers because it tells the decision maker whether the risk of customer attrition increases or decreases over time.

where $d = \frac{r}{(1+\delta)}$. Since $r < 1$ and $(1+\delta) > 1$, $d < 1$, we have an infinite geometric series. The sum of this series is $(R-C) \times \frac{1}{1-d} = (R-C) \times (\frac{1+\delta}{1+\delta-r})$.

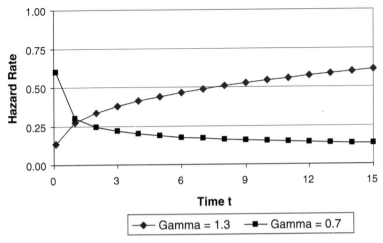

Fig. 5.2 Hazard function for Weibull with $\gamma = 0.7$ and 1.3 ($\lambda = 0.3$).

Researchers should try to explain the shape of the hazard function. For example, a decreasing hazard function may be due to heterogeneity across customers in their preference for the product and may not be due to changing hazard rates. Alternatively, as the customers uses the product or service, he or she increases preference or satisfaction or is locked in and that causes the decreasing hazard.

One can always transform continuous into discrete distributions.[3] Table 5.4 shows the results for a Weibull distribution with 10 years of data with $\gamma = 0.7$ and $\lambda = 0.3$. It shows a different pattern than one sees for a constant hazard rate model. For example in year 2 the retention rate increases to 0.81. In year 3 it is 0.84. The retention rate is the key statistic for computing LTV. By multiplying the retention rates over time, we compute the implied survival rate, i.e., the probability the customer is still active. Multiplying this times the $100 sales per year yields expected sales per year.

Hazard models are a powerful tool for calculating lifetime value. They can be used to calculate customer-specific LTV because they can be extended to incorporate customer-level information such as demographics and marketing variables (Chapter 15). They are flexible and can allow a constant or time-varying retention rate. Hazard models can be estimated using commonly available statistical packages. See Chapter 15, Seetharaman and Chintagunta (2003), and Lawless (2003) for more details.

A key issue that affects the use of hazard models for LTV computations is that we may not know when a customer attrites. For many non-subscription businesses, the firm cannot determine if the customer attrites. For example,

---

[3] It is often useful to use discrete distributions because continuous time distributions frequently require numerical integration to compute LTV. It is easier to think of revenue streams in discrete intervals as well.

Table 5.4 Transforming a continuous hazard into a discrete hazard

Weibull parameters:
    Gamma = 0.7
    Lambda = 0.3
Sales per customer per year = $100

Time	Survival	True hazard rate	Estimated hazard rate	Estimated retention rate	Estimated survival rate	Expected sales per year
0.1	0.92	0.60	–	–	–	–
1	0.65	0.30	0.34	0.66	0.66	$65.88
2	0.50	0.24	0.27	0.73	0.48	$48.27
3	0.39	0.22	0.23	0.77	0.37	$37.24
4	0.32	0.20	0.21	0.79	0.30	$29.55
5	0.26	0.19	0.19	0.81	0.24	$23.89
6	0.22	0.18	0.18	0.82	0.20	$19.58
7	0.19	0.17	0.17	0.83	0.16	$16.22
8	0.16	0.16	0.16	0.84	0.14	$13.56
9	0.13	0.16	0.16	0.84	0.11	$11.41
10	0.12	0.15	0.15	0.85	0.10	$9.67
11	0.10	0.15	0.15	0.85	0.08	$8.23
12	0.09	0.14	0.14	0.86	0.07	$7.04
13	0.07	0.14	0.14	0.86	0.06	$6.05
14	0.07	0.14	0.14	0.86	0.05	$5.21

Survival rates and Hazard rates are computed from Equations 5.4a, b. The estimated hazard is computed by taking the change in survival rate and dividing it by the average survival rate for a given row and the row above it. This can then be compared to the actual hazard rate computed from the model.

The estimated retention rate is simply 1 – hazard rate which is computed from the estimated hazard rate. The estimated survival rate is the estimated retention rates multiplied up to the given point in time for which the survival rate is computed.

The results show that the estimated hazard is very close to the actual hazard rate.

a catalog company does not know when a customer has attrited. If the time of attrition is not known, hazard models cannot be estimated. Later we will discuss ways to incorporate the "death" process to estimate the probability of attriting (Sect. 5.4).

5.3.2 Migration Models

5.3.2.1 The Basic Customer Migration Model for Calculating LTV

The second common model for measuring LTV is the migration model, which as we will see in the next section, models LTV as a Markov Chain. The term migration model is used because the model allows customers to "migrate" among different states. The most common way of defining states is in terms of how recently the customer has bought from the company. This model acknowledges, in contrast to the simple retention model, that the customer might not purchase from the firm each period, but can skip one or more periods and still come back to purchase.

To operationalize this model, we define "recency state j" to mean that the customer last bought from the company j periods ago. We assign customers to recency states at the conclusion of each period. So if at the end of period 15 the customer is in recency state 2, that means the customer did not buy in period 15 but bought in period 14. Recency state 1 would mean that the customer bought in period 15. The key parameters that drive the migration model are the "recency probabilities"[4]:

p_j = Probability the customer purchases in the current period, given that the customer last purchased j periods ago, i.e., that the customer is classified in recency state j at the end of the previous period ($NR \geq j \geq 1$).[5]

The migration model reduces to the simple retention model if $p_j = 0$ for $j > 1$ because then if the customer is not retained, he or she cannot purchase again. We assume the recency probabilities do not change over time, i.e., we have no time subscript for p_j. This assumption could be relaxed at the cost of added complexity.

Table 5.5 illustrates the calculation of LTV using a migration model. We have four recency states ($NR = 4$), labeled 1, 2, 3, and ≥ 4. The state "≥ 4" signifies that it has been four or more periods since the customer has purchased. In Table 5.5, this customer has no chance of purchasing again – in Markov chain terminology, state ≥ 4 is an absorbing state. We have acquired the customer in period 1. Therefore, the customer is classified in recency state 1 at the end of period 1. The probability the customer purchases in period 2 is $p_1 = 0.5$. With probability $1 - p_1 = 0.5$, the customer does not purchase and hence moves to recency state 2 at the end of period 2. To compute the probability the customer purchases in period 3, we calculate P(customer in state 1) $\times$ P(Purchase|state 1) + P(customer in state 2) $\times$ P(Purchase|state 2) = $0.5 \times 0.5 + 0.2 \times 0.5 = 0.35$. The general pattern is that the customer moves to recency state 1 if he or she purchases in that period, or slips one recency state if he or she does not. Note that for the absorbing state ≥ 4, we assume there is no chance the customer will purchase again so the customer stays in that state. So for period 5, the probability the customer is in state ≥ 4 is P(Customer is in state ≥ 4 in period 4) + P(Customer does not purchase|Customer is in state 3 in period 4) = $0.360 + (1 - 0.1) \times 0.200 = 0.540$.

---

[4] Note we generally follow the general development of Berger and Nasr in this section. See also also Dwyer (1989) and Calciu and Salerno (2002).

[5] Technically there is no upper limit to how many periods ago the customer might have purchased, but for computational purposes, we typically use an upper limit "NR". NR = "≥ 5" means that any customer who has not purchased in the past 5 or more periods would be classified in recency state ≥ 5.

Table 5.5 Migration model calculation

	Recency state (j)					Delta = 0.1		
$j =$	1	2	3	≥ 4				
$p_j =$	0.5	0.2	0.1	0	Purch$_t$	Profit contribution if purchase	Expected profit	Discounted expected profit
Period	1	2	3	≥ 4				
1	1.000	0.000	0.000	0.000	1.000	$100	$100.00	$100.00
2	0.500	0.500	0.000	0.000	0.500	$100	$50.00	$45.45
3	0.350	0.250	0.400	0.000	0.350	$100	$35.00	$28.93
4	0.265	0.175	0.200	0.360	0.265	$100	$26.50	$19.91
5	0.188	0.133	0.140	0.540	0.188	$100	$18.75	$12.81
6	0.134	0.094	0.106	0.666	0.134	$100	$13.43	$8.34
7	0.096	0.067	0.075	0.761	0.096	$100	$9.65	$5.45
8	0.069	0.048	0.054	0.829	0.069	$100	$6.92	$3.55
9	0.050	0.035	0.039	0.877	0.050	$100	$4.96	$2.31
10	0.036	0.025	0.028	0.912	0.036	$100	$3.56	$1.51
11	0.026	0.018	0.020	0.937	0.026	$100	$2.55	$0.98
12	0.018	0.013	0.014	0.955	0.018	$100	$1.83	$0.64
13	0.013	0.009	0.010	0.968	0.013	$100	$1.31	$0.42
14	0.009	0.007	0.007	0.977	0.009	$100	$0.94	$0.27
15	0.007	0.005	0.005	0.983	0.007	$100	$0.68	$0.18

LTV = Total = **$230.74**

If extend calculation 100 periods, **LTV = $231.08**

p_j = Probability customer buys in the current period, given the customer is in recency state j at the end of the previous period, i.e., last purchased j periods ago.
Delta = Discount factor = δ.
Purch$_t$ = Probability the customer buys in period t.

Table 5.5 shows that the sum of discounted expected profit after 15 periods is $230.74. One can see because of the declining values in later periods that this is close to the ultimate long-term LTV but not exact. Carrying out the calculation for 100 periods yields an LTV of $231.08.

Figure 5.3 shows sensitivity analyses based on the example in Table 5.5. The figure shows a convex relationship between recency probabilities p_2 and p_3 and LTV. These relationships could help a firm evaluate whether it would be worthwhile to attempt to induce customers who had not bought in say three periods to purchase this period.

Libai et al. (2002) describe a customer migration model for a European retailer. The models they use place customers into segments. Segment membership is dynamic. The authors argue that one way to increase customer equity is to increase the probability that a customer will move to a more profitable segment. By identifying key differences between segments, the firm can adjust the marketing and customer service mix for each segment. The concepts described by Libai et al. have the potential to link marketing mix actions to segment migration. The difficulty is creating the linkages. The authors do not describe the exact modeling methods they use. This becomes a research opportunity for academics and practitioners who have large customer databases and can develop the relevant methodology.

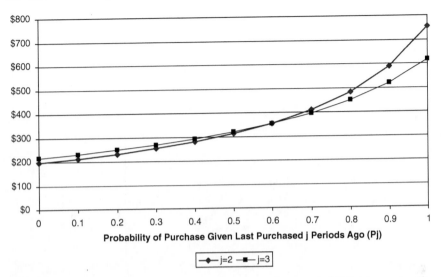

Fig. 5.3 Lifetime value as a function of recency purchase probabilities in a migration model.

5.3.2.2 Generalizing the Migration Model Using a Markov Chain Framework

Pfeifer and Carraway (2000) propose a Markov Chain framework that generalizes the calculations for the migration model. We use the same notation for p_j to signify the probability the customer purchases by the end of the current period, given the customer is in recency state j at the end of the previous period. We also label the recency states $R_1, R_2, \ldots, R_{NR}$. To simplify the exposition, we assume as in Pfeifer and Carraway that there are three possible (recency) states ($NR = 3$): bought last period (R_1), bought two periods ago (R_2), and bought three or more periods ago (R_3). The model of customer migration can be represented as a Markov chain with a 3×3 transition probability matrix, $\mathbf{P}$, as follows:

$$
\mathbf{P} = \text{Period t}\,
\begin{array}{c}
\\
R_1 \\
R_2 \\
R_3
\end{array}
\overset{\begin{array}{ccc} R_1 & R_2 & R_3 \end{array}}{\begin{bmatrix} p_1 & 1 - p_1 & 0 \\ p_2 & 0 & 1 - p_2 \\ p_3 & 0 & 1 - p_3 \end{bmatrix}}
\tag{5.5}
$$

$$\textbf{Period t} + 1$$

Each element of $\mathbf{P}$ represents the probability the customer migrates from one state to another in a single period. Consider a customer in state R_1. The customer will or will not purchase in the current period with probabilities p_1 and $1 - p_1$ respectively. If the customer purchases, he or she remains in R_1. If not, the customer moves to R_2. The customer in state R_2 will or will not purchase at the current period with probabilities p_2 and $1 - p_2$. Finally, the customer in state R_3 will or will not purchase at the current period with probabilities p_3 and $1 - p_3$. Some transitions have zero probability, such as R_2 to R_2. If a customer is in recency state R_2, he or she will either not purchase and go to recency state R_3 or purchase and go to R_1 but cannot stay in R_2.

Because of the property of the Markov Chain, we can easily calculate a t-step (t periods from now) transition matrix; that is, the matrix of probabilities of moving from one state to another after t periods. It is simply the matrix product of t one-step transition matrices, $\mathbf{P}^t$. The (i, j)th element of the matrix $\mathbf{P}^t$ is the probability that the customer who begins at the ith state and will be at the jth state t periods later.

Assume that the firm earns MC if a customer purchases, and the firm spends M for a customer to repurchase. The profit vector $\mathbf{G}$ can be written as:

$$\mathbf{G} = \begin{bmatrix} MC - M \\ -M \\ -M \end{bmatrix} \tag{5.6}$$

The first row of $\mathbf{G}$ represents the profit contribution if the customer is in state R_1 (just purchased), the second row represents the profit contribution if the customer is in state R_2 (the customer did not purchase but the firm spent M on marketing to the customer), etc. Let Π_1 = the profit after one period. Then,

$$\Pi_1 = \mathbf{PG} = \begin{bmatrix} p_1 MC - M \\ p_2 MC - M \\ p_3 MC - M \end{bmatrix} \tag{5.7}$$

The vector of the expected profit is $\mathbf{P}^2\mathbf{G}$ after two periods, and $\mathbf{P}^T\mathbf{G}$ after T periods. And the corresponding vector of the expected net present value that considers the discount factor d per period is $\mathbf{P}^1\mathbf{G}/(1+d)$ after one period, $\mathbf{P}^2\mathbf{G}/(1+d)^2$ after two periods, and $\mathbf{P}^T\mathbf{G}/(1+d)^T$ after T periods. Therefore, the vector of the total net present value from the period 0 to the period T is:

$$\mathbf{V}^T = \sum_{t=0}^{T} [(1 + d)^{-1}\mathbf{P}]^t \mathbf{G} \tag{5.8}$$

Hence the vector of the total net present value for the infinite time horizon becomes

$$\mathbf{V}^\infty = \lim_{T \to \infty} \mathbf{V}^T = [\mathbf{I} - (1 + d)^{-1}\mathbf{P}]^{-1}\mathbf{G} \tag{5.9}$$

where $\mathbf{I}$ is the identity matrix. The vector in Equation 5.9 is of particular interest because each element represents the expected lifetime value of a customer starting in state R_1, R_2, etc. The first element of $\mathbf{V}^\infty$ is of particular interest – it is the long-term value of a customer who starts out in state

R_1. This is the LTV of a just-acquired customer, because a just-acquired customer starts off in state R_1 (just purchased). The second element of $\mathbf{V}^\infty$ is the net present value of a customer who we currently observe to be in state R_2 (purchased two periods ago). In this way, we see that the Markov framework is a generalization of the migration model presented in the previous section.

To illustrate the connection between the "brute force" calculation in Table 5.5 and the matrix calculation, note the recency probabilities in Table 5.5 imply the following:

$$\mathbf{P} = \begin{bmatrix} .5 & .5 & 0 & 0 \\ .2 & 0 & .8 & 0 \\ .1 & 0 & 0 & .9 \\ 0 & 0 & 0 & 1 \end{bmatrix} \tag{5.10}$$

The matrix P is 4×4 because we have four states. The payoff matrix is simple:

$$\mathbf{G} = \begin{bmatrix} \$100 \\ \$0 \\ \$0 \\ \$0 \end{bmatrix} \tag{5.11}$$

The customer contributes $100 if he or she purchases; else contributes $0, and we are not considering any period-by-period marketing costs. To complete the model, note that the discount rate in Table 5.5 is 10%. From Equation 5.9, we therefore have:

$$\mathbf{V}^\infty = \left\{ \begin{bmatrix} 1 & 0 & 0 & 0 \\ 0 & 1 & 0 & 0 \\ 0 & 0 & 1 & 0 \\ 0 & 0 & 0 & 1 \end{bmatrix} - \left(\frac{1}{1+0.1} \right) \begin{bmatrix} .5 & .5 & 0 & 0 \\ .2 & 0 & .8 & 0 \\ .1 & 0 & 0 & .9 \\ 0 & 0 & 0 & 1 \end{bmatrix} \right\}^{-1} \begin{bmatrix} \$100 \\ \$0 \\ \$0 \\ \$0 \end{bmatrix}$$

$$= \begin{bmatrix} \$231.08 \\ \$57.29 \\ \$21.01 \\ \$0 \end{bmatrix} \tag{5.12}$$

The first element of $\mathbf{V}^\infty$ is the LTV of the customer. So LTV of the customer is $231.08, which is the number we obtain in Table 5.5 by extending the table to 100 periods ($\approx \infty$).

As another example, assume a customer generates $40 marginal contribution (MC) whenever a purchase is made, and the firm mails to the customer unless the customer lapse to state ≥ 4, in which case the firm knows the customer will not purchase no matter what, so doesn't bother to mail a catalog. The mailing costs are $4. The firm's discount rate is $d = 0.2$. The payoff matrix, $\mathbf{G}$, is then:

$$\mathbf{G} = \begin{bmatrix} MC - M \\ -M \\ -M \\ 0 \end{bmatrix} = \begin{bmatrix} 36 \\ -4 \\ -4 \\ 0 \end{bmatrix}$$

Next suppose the transition matrix is defined as

$$\mathbf{P} = \begin{bmatrix} .3 & .7 & 0 & 0 \\ .2 & 0 & .8 & 0 \\ .05 & 0 & 0 & .95 \\ 0 & 0 & 0 & 1 \end{bmatrix}$$

This transition matrix implies that if the customer is state R_1, he or she has a 0.3 chance of purchasing. If the customer is in state R_2, there is a 0.2 chance of a purchase but if the customer is in state R_4, the customer is the "absorbing" state "≥ 4" and has no chance of purchasing.

Suppose we want to study the behavior of a new customer (in state R_1) to determine how likely the customer is to be in state R_1 after four purchase occasions? We can multiply the transition matrix three times and see what the purchase pattern will be. For the period after the first purchase, we see that:

$$\mathbf{P}^2 = \begin{bmatrix} .23 & .21 & .56 & 0 \\ .10 & .14 & 0 & .76 \\ .015 & .035 & 0 & .95 \\ 0 & 0 & 0 & 1 \end{bmatrix}$$

and after the 4th period,

$$\mathbf{P}^4 = \begin{bmatrix} .0823 & .0973 & .1288 & .6916 \\ .037 & .0406 & .056 & .8664 \\ .0070 & .0080 & .0084 & .9766 \\ 0 & 0 & 0 & 1 \end{bmatrix}$$

The matrix shows that a customer who began in state R_1 has a 0.0823 probability of being in R_1 (having just made a purchase) 4 periods later.

Another question that can be answered using the method just described is that we can examine the expected present value for each initial state after 4 periods, which is:

$$\prod_4 = \sum_{i=0}^{4} \frac{P^i G}{(1+d)^i} = \begin{bmatrix} \$49.40 \\ \$2.69 \\ (\$1.98) \\ 0 \end{bmatrix} \text{ where } P^0 G = G$$

The interpretation of the 3rd row element of Π_4 is that a customer beginning in recency state 3 has a negative expected present value after 4 periods. The firm should not mail individuals in this cell because the value is negative at time 0.

Pfeifer and Carraway show that the states do not have to be defined in terms of recency. They can be defined in terms of recency plus frequency, for example. In this case, R_1 might represent a customer who just bought and has bought once over the last year. R_2 might represent a customer who just bought and has bought twice over the last year. If we have four recency states, each with four frequency states, the transition matrix will be a 16×16, but the same machinery as described in Equations 5.6–5.9 would be applicable. Particularly interesting would be to experiment with different marketing policies, which would change the values of the $\mathbf{G}$ vector. Pfeifer and Carraway show how this might be done in the context of a catalog manufacturer.

In summary Pfeifer and Carraway's formulation of migration models as a Markov chain is a valuable generalization. It provides a framework for extending the definition of customer states, and for experimenting with various marketing policies. Their contribution is very practical and hence of value to managers.

5.4 LTV Models that Include Unobserved Customer Attrition

A series of LTV models have been developed that incorporate unobserved attrition (Schmittlein et al. 1987; Fader et al. 2004, 2005). They derive results such as the expected future number of remaining purchases or the customer's expected remaining lifetime with the firm, given the customer's past purchase history. These models therefore can be used to value customers in terms of the future number of purchases, lifetime duration, or lifetime value.

A fundamental notion in these models is the concept of whether the customer is "alive" or "dead." Customer attrition (or churn) is an important concern for many companies (Chapter 24). In contractual settings, such as subscriptions in the telecom, magazine, or cable industries, it is easy to determine when customers have attrited – they do not renew their contract. However, in many industries the customer has no written contract with the company so attrition is unobserved. For example, catalog companies are known to keep sending catalogs to customers who have not purchased in several years. Perhaps those customers have attrited (churned) and sending them catalogs is a fruitless investment. This issue is of prime importance to non-contractual businesses such as travel services, restaurants, retail, health care providers, and catalogers.

Determining whether a customer is alive or dead would at first seem trivial – if the customer has not bought in a long time, he or she has attrited. However, what if the customer has an erratic, infrequent buying pattern? Perhaps there is a hiatus in the customer's purchase pattern (e.g., when a customer is on vacation or has changed jobs) and again will buy from the firm without any remedial action.

The models developed to date focus on four key phenomena:

- The number of purchases in a given time period.
- Heterogeneity in the parameters of the purchase rate model.

- Customer lifetime, i.e., how long the customer is alive.
- Heterogeneity in the parameters governing the lifetime model.

Table 5.6 shows how these phenomena are modeled. There are three main models developed to date. Schmittleim et al. (1987) (SCM) and Fader et al. (2005) (FHL) model purchases as a Poisson process, whereas Fader et al. (2004) (FHB) model it as a Bernouli process. SCM model customer lifetime as an exponential distribution, whereas FHL and FHB model it as a geometric process. We will concentrate our discussion on SCM and FHL.

SCM's propose the following:

- *Purchase rate*: While alive, each customer purchases according to a Poisson process with parameter λ.
- *Heterogeneity in purchase rate process*: The parameter λ is distributed across customers according to a gamma distribution with parameters r and α, so that the mean λ is r/α and the variance is r/α^2.
- *Lifetimes*: Each customer's lifetime follows an exponential distribution with parameter μ. μ is the "death rate," i.e., the mean of the lifetime distribution is $1/\mu$.
- *Heterogeneity in lifetimes*: The parameter μ is gamma distributed across customers with parameters s and β, so that the mean μ is s/β and the variance is s/β^2.

The most debatable assumptions are the Poisson purchase rates and exponential lifetimes. Both assumptions entail the memoryless property. For example the number of purchases by an alive *individual* customer with known parameters purchasing in the next t units of time is independent of how many purchases he or she made in any previous period of time. The implied exponential distribution between purchases (given the customer is alive) means that the customer is most likely to make another purchase directly after the previous purchase. This might hold in certain industries but not those where purchasing builds up customer inventory and the customer does not purchase again until the inventory is depleted. In addition, both the time between purchases and customer lifetimes have the property that the mean equals the variance, which is not intuitive and appears to be restrictive. The exponential lifetime assumption implies that the modal customer behavior is to leave the firm fairly soon after being acquired. This might be a good assumption in some non-contractual settings.

SCM derive two important metrics: (1) the probability the customer is alive and (2) the expected time a customer will purchase in a period of length T^*. SCM derive that for a customer who has made x purchases over T time periods, with the last purchase being at time t, the probability the customer is still alive can be expressed as[6]:

---

[6] This assumes $\alpha > \beta$. The authors derive other formulas for other cases.

Table 5.6 Comparison of stochastic models of unobserved customer attrition (From Schmittlein et al. 1987; Fader et al. 2004, 2005)

	Method		
	Pareto/NBD (P/NBD)	Beta geometric/NBD (BG/NBD)	Beta geometric/beta binomial (BG/BB)
	Schmittlein et al. (1987)	Fader et al. (2005)	Fader et al. (2004)
Phenomena			
Customer alive	τ = lifetime $\sim$ Exp(μ)	p = probability "die" after each purchase	q = probability "die" after each purchase
Heterogeneity	$\mu \sim$ gamma(s, β)	$p \sim$ Beta(a, b)	$q \sim$ Beta(γ, δ)
Purchase rate	x = number of purchases in time $t \sim$ Poisson (λ)	x = number of purchases in time $t \sim$ Poisson (λ)	p = probability of purchase in each period
Heterogeneity	$\lambda \sim$ gamma(r, α)	$\lambda \sim$ gamma(r, α)	$p \sim$ Beta(α, β)
Summary			
Liftetimes	Exponential	Geometric	Geometric
Purchases	Poisson	Poisson	Bernoulli
Interpurchase	Exponential	Exponential	Geometric

$$P(Customer\ Alive) = \left\{ 1 + \frac{s}{s+x+s} \left[\left(\frac{\alpha+T}{\alpha+t} \right)^{r+x} \left(\frac{\beta+T}{\alpha+t} \right)^s \right. \right.$$

$$\left. \left. \times F - \left(\frac{\beta+T}{\alpha+T} \right)^s F \right]^{-1} \right\} \qquad (5.13)$$

where F is the Gaussian hypergeometric function[7] (Schmittlein et al. 1987, p. 6) with four parameters related to the four parameters that govern the model: $a_1 = r+x+s$, $b_1 = s+1$, $c_1 = r+x+s+1$ and $z_1(T) = \frac{\alpha-b}{\alpha+y}$. The expected quantity purchased in a period of length T^* is:

$$E[X^*|T^*] = \frac{(r+x)(\beta+T)}{(\alpha+T)(s-1)} \left[1 - \left(\frac{\beta+T}{\beta+2T} \right)^{s-1} \right] \times P(Customer\ Alive)$$

$$(5.14)$$

Another important calculation is the expected remaining time that the customer stays with the company, calculated at time t. SCM show that after taking into account heterogeneity, the remaining lifetime for a customer (τ) follows a Pareto distribution:

$$f(\tau|s,\beta) = \frac{s}{\beta} \left[\frac{\beta}{(\beta+\tau)} \right]^{s+1} \qquad (5.15)$$

where s and β are the parameters of the gamma distribution of heterogeneity in death rate μ. The expected value of the Pareto distribution is

$$E[\tau|s,\beta] = \frac{\beta}{(s-1)} \qquad (5.16)$$

The authors point out that since the death rate and purchase rate are assumed independent, purchases made up to time T have no impact on the remaining time we expect the customer to live. However, if the customer is active at time T, we do need to update the β parameter to $\beta+T$. Therefore, given the customer is still active at time T, the remaining lifetime follows a Pareto distribution with parameters $\beta+T$ and s. So the expected remaining lifetime for a customer with purchase history $\{x,t,T\}$ is:

$$E[remaining\ lifetime|x,t,T,\alpha,t,\beta,s] = \frac{(\beta+T)}{(s-1)} P(customer\ alive)$$

$$(5.17)$$

where $P(customer\ alive)$ is calculated using Equation 5.13.

The above discussion centers on the "Paredo/NBD" model developed by Schmittlein et al. More recently, this model has been extended by

---

[7] See Fader et al. (2005) for a method to approximate the Gaussian hypergeometric function.

Fader et al. (2005) referred to as FHL. This extension retains the original ideas of the Paredo/NBD model but is much easier to estimate. In fact, the authors provide Excel spreadsheets for estimating the models.

FHL's model is called the Beta Geometric/NBD, or BG/NBD model. It models lifetime as a geometric distribution rather than an exponential distribution. The customer has a probability p of becoming inactive after any transaction, so:

$$P(become\ inactive\ after\ j^{th}\ transaction) = p(1-p)^{j-1} \qquad (5.18)$$

The parameter p is analogous to the death rate μ in the Pareto/NBD model, and also is modeled to be heterogeneous across customers, following a beta distribution. Fader et al. (2004) derive formulas for $P(Alive)$ and $E(Number\ of\ purchases)$ analogous to those for the Pareto/NBD model.

FHL assume a consumer follows a Poisson process for purchasing. Hence the interpurchase time is exponential. Specifically, let λ equal the purchase rate and t_j be the time the customer purchases for the jth time. Then,

$$f(t_j|t_{j-1}, \lambda) = \lambda e^{-\lambda(t_j - t_{j-1})} t_j > t_{j-1} \geq 0 \qquad (5.19)$$

As stated earlier, the probability an individual becomes inactive after the jth transaction is $p(1-p)^{j-1}$ where p is the probability the customer becomes inactive immediately after the jth purchase. These two equations then generate expressions of interest in computing LTV. The first is the *expected number of purchases* in a period of length t is:

$$E(X(t)|\lambda, p) = \frac{(1 - e^{-\lambda pt})}{p} \qquad (5.20)$$

and the *probability the customer is alive at time* τ is:

$$P(\tau > t) = e^{-\lambda pt} \qquad (5.21)$$

The critical parameters are λ and p. The higher p is, the fewer purchases and the less likely the customer is to be alive after t. This seems reasonable since the probability of dying should determine the number of purchases. In Equation 5.20 the limit as t goes to infinity is $1/p$ which is the expected number of purchases the customer will make over the long run. The probability the customer is alive decreases in p, which is also intuitively reasonable.

A potential problem is that as λ increases, the expected number of purchases increases because the numerator of Equation 5.20 increases. However, the expected time the customer remains alive declines as λ increases Equation 5.21. If a customer has a higher purchase rate, then he or she will have a lower probability of being alive at time τ. This follows from the assumption that the customer has probability p of dying after each purchase. FHL's model implicitly assumes the more times the customer purchases, the higher the probability the customer attrites. This is a questionable assumption.

Once FHL develop the individual customer model, they then study how heterogeneity in the purchase rate and probability of dying change the results. They use Gamma heterogeneity for λ and Beta heterogeneity for p.

$$f(\lambda|r,\alpha) = \frac{\alpha^r \lambda^{r-1} e^{-\lambda\alpha}}{\Gamma(\alpha)} \quad \text{for } \lambda > 0 \tag{5.22}$$

$\Gamma(\alpha)$ is the gamma function evaluated at α.

$$f(p|a,b) = \frac{p^{a-1}(1-p)^{b-1}}{B(a,b)} \quad 0 \le p < 1 \tag{5.23}$$

where $B(a,b)$ is the beta function which is equal to $\Gamma(a)\Gamma(b)/\Gamma(a+b)$.

The key expectations derived by FHL are:

$$E(X(t)|r,\alpha,a,b) = \frac{a+b-1}{a-1}\left[1 - \left(\frac{\alpha}{\alpha+t}\right)^r {}_2F_1\left(r,b;a+b-1;\left(\frac{t}{\alpha+t}\right)\right)\right]$$
$$\tag{5.24}$$

where ${}_2F_1(\bullet)$ is the Gaussian hypergeometric function. This is the expected number of purchases for the whole customer base over time. Obviously, the hypergeometric function makes it more difficult to understand the intuition behind the results.

The other expectation of interest is the expected number of transactions for an individual with a specific observed behavior characterized by the number of purchases made, x (frequency), the last time a purchase was made t_x (recency) and the length of the interval, T.

Let $E(Y(t)|X = x,t_x,T,r,\alpha,a,b)$ equal the expected number of transactions for a time period of length t given the number of prior purchases, the last observed purchase t_x and the end of the interval T. Then,

$$E(Y(t)|X = x,t_x,T,r,\alpha,a,b) =$$
$$\frac{\frac{a+b+x-1}{a-1}\left[1 - \left(\frac{\alpha+T}{\alpha+T+t}\right)^{r+x} {}_2F_1\left[\left(r+x,b+x;a+b+x-1;\left(\frac{t}{\alpha+T+t}\right)\right)\right]\right]}{1 + \delta_{>0}\frac{a}{b+x-1}\left(\frac{a+T}{a+t_x}\right)^{r+x}}$$
$$\tag{5.25}$$

While this expression appears to be complex, FHL argue that the Gausian hypergeometric function can be approximated using Excel. FHL test their model versus the Pareto/NBD and find it to be equivalent.

For a fixed future time interval, FHL's model will provide an estimate of LTV. They compute Equation 5.25 for a customer who makes x purchases with his or her last purchase at time t_x, with the end of the base period (period before computing future LTV) being T and the future period of length t, what is the expected number of purchases. This times the expected margin gives the undiscounted future LTV. To transform FHL (or SMC) into an LTV calculation with discounting requires setting the model up with discrete time intervals and creating conditional probabilities of staying alive (the hazard function) for their models.

To see how FHL's model behaves as a function of its parameters, we will provide a relatively simple version of their model by looking at one consumer and avoiding the complexity added by studying heterogeneity. The three key quantities that FHL (and SCM) provide and which are extremely useful in LTV modeling are:

$E[X(t)|\lambda, p]$ = the number of transactions in a period of length t,
$P(\tau > t|\lambda, p)$ = the probability the customer will be alive after period t, and
$E[Y(t)|x, t_x, T, \lambda, p]$ = the expected number of transactions in the period t to T, for an individual with observed behavior $X = x$, t_x, where t_x is the time of the last purchase in the interval $[0, t]$.

From above, λ is the purchase rate per period and p is the probability the customer attrites after a purchase. For the example, we will use several values of the parameters and time periods to show how the above quantities change. We will use the following formulas to compute the quantities described above:

$$E[X(t)|\lambda, p] = \frac{1 - e^{-\lambda pt}}{p} \tag{5.26a}$$

$$P(\tau > t|\lambda, p) = e^{-\lambda pt} \tag{5.26b}$$

$$E[Y(t)|X = x, t_x, T, \lambda, p)$$
$$= \frac{p^{-1}(1 - p)^x \lambda^x e^{-\lambda T} - p^{-1}(1 - p)^x \lambda^x e^{-\lambda(T + pt)}}{L(\lambda, p|X = x, t_x, T)} \tag{5.26c}$$

with

$$L(\lambda, p|X = x, t_x, T) = (1 - p)^x \lambda^x e^{-\lambda T} + \delta_{x>0}\, p(1 - p)^{x-1} \lambda^x e^{-\lambda t_x} \tag{5.26d}$$

The above expressions are easily computed in Excel. We will start with the expected number of purchases in given time interval t. We will use two values of λ and two values of p to contrast the expected number of purchases. Table 5.7a provides the values. It shows, as should be obvious, as p (the death probability) increases, the number of purchases decreases and as λ increases; so does the expected number of purchases. For a simple Poisson model with $\lambda = 0.1$, which represents .1 purchase per month and a time interval of 24 months, the expected number of purchases would be $\lambda t = 2.4$. For FHL, we see that the expected number of purchases is 2.13 purchases for $t = 24$ (24 months). As p increases, we see that the expected number of purchases decreases. For $p = 0.25$ and $\lambda = 0.1$, the expected value decreases to 1.8. Thus, the larger the value of p, the more the model diverges from a Poisson purchase rate model.

An interesting result is shown for the probability that a customer is alive which is displayed in Table 5.7b. It shows that as λ, the purchase rate,

Table 5.7 Calculating the expected number of purchases and the probability the customer is alive (From Fader et al. 2005)

	Death rate(p)	
	0.10	0.25
(a) Expected number of purchases over 24 periods ($t = 24$)		
Purchase rate (λ)		
0.10	2.13	1.80
0.25	4.51	3.10
(b) Probability customer is alive after 24 periods		
Purchase rate (λ)		
0.10	0.787	0.549
0.25	0.549	0.223
(c) Expected number of purchases over 24 periods, given past purchase history ($t = 24, t_x = 5, T = 10, x = 3$)		
Purchase rate (λ)		
0.10	1.80	1.16
0.25	3.25	1.43

(d) Expected number of purchases over 24 periods, varying recency (t_x)($t = 24, T = 10, x = 3, p = 0.1$)

	Purchase rate (λ)	
	0.10	0.30
Recency (t_x)		
3	1.74	2.69
5	1.80	3.42
7	1.85	4.03
9	1.90	4.46

increases, the probability of being alive decreases for fixed p. As discussed earlier, this is a counter-intuitive result.

Another result worth noting is the expected number of purchases in a given time interval, 24 months, *given past purchase behavior*. This is shown in Table 5.7c. This quantity is different than the expected number of purchases because it is conditional on the time of the last purchase. The table shows that the longer since the last purchase, the customer is expected to make fewer purchases. Intuitively, if a customer has a high purchase rate but does not purchase in a fixed interval, the likelihood increases that the customer has died. Hence, for a fixed number of purchases, x, the less recent t_x, the time of the last purchase is, the smaller the number of purchases. This makes intuitive sense and is consistent with the findings from recency modeling.

Table 5.7d shows that as λ increases, the impact of t_x is much greater. The change in the expected number of purchases has much greater differences from low to high values of t_x. Again this result makes intuitive sense.

In conclusion, the computations from FHL's model show that many of their results are reasonable except for the assumption that each time a customer makes a purchase, the probability of attriting is constant. This leads to counter-intuitive results regarding the probability of attriting as a function of the purchase rate. It may also lead to poor fits if their model is applied at the individual level rather than at the aggregate level after allowing for heterogeneity.

The next extension, due to Fader et al. (2004) (FHB) builds on the BG/NBD modeling the process entirely in discrete time. The key change is moving from a Poisson to a Bernoulli purchase process. In each period, the customer has the probability, p, of purchasing. Periods are independent and p is constant, analogous to the stationarity and independence assumptions of the Poisson. In fact, a Bernoulli process becomes a Poisson process as we move from discrete to continuous time. The parameter p is heterogeneous across customers according to a Beta distribution. The death process for the customer follows the same geometric distribution as FHL, but the unit is the time period, not the transaction. So each time period, the customer has a probability q of dying, and q is heterogeneous across customers according to a Beta distribution. The authors call this model the beta-geometric/beta-binomial (BG/BB) model. Again, they derive formulas for $P(Alive)$ and $E[Number of Purchases]$ as in the other cases.

In summary, the stochastic models developed by SCM, FHL, and FHB provide models of lifetime value when customer attrition is unobserved. These models can be used to calculate customer lifetime value estimates both on average (analogous to a simple retention model) and for individual customers with purchase histories (particularly the number of purchases and time of the last purchase). However, one needs to be careful when computing it for individuals because the amount of data per individual may be very small. The models are rich yet remarkably simple – Table 5.6 states all that is needed to define each model – and with the extensions of Fader et al. relatively easy to estimate.

There are two main areas for building on these models. The first is to allow for inter-relationships between the purchase and death processes, and especially between these processes and quantity purchased. Surely the parameters governing these processes should be correlated across customers. One would assume for example that customers with high purchase rates would have lower death rates.

The second extension is to incorporate marketing variables in these models. The parameters of the model could be made functions of marketing variables. This would require for example a hierarchical Bayesian framework, for example:

$$p \sim Beta(\alpha, \beta) \tag{5.27a}$$

$$\alpha \sim Normal(\mu, \sigma^2) \tag{5.27b}$$

$$\mu = f(marketing\ effort) \tag{5.27c}$$

The real complexity would come in predicting individual-level response in terms of purchase rates or *P[Alive]* as a function of marketing efforts. This endeavor, however, would be well worth it because it would turn what now is a *ceteris paribus* lifetime value model into a *potential* lifetime value model.

5.5 Estimating Revenues

The next major requirement in computing LTV is estimating revenues per customer per period. There are many possible ways to make these estimates.

5.5.1 Constant Revenue per Period Model

One computes the average revenue per customer for all periods and then uses this measure for revenue per customer per period. This is very easy to use but very naïve and likely to be unrealistic. It is often the case that revenue increases over time.

5.5.2 Trend Models

One can calculate the trend in revenue per period per customer from the initial customer acquisition period to the end of the customer's purchase series. We might use segments or aggregate across customers. The trend model then is used to capture the pattern of customer revenues over time. The trend can be modeled using a constant growth rate or a growth curve which asymptotes to a specific value or other shapes depending upon the revenue data pattern.

5.5.3 Causal Models

Revenue can be estimated using causal models in which the dependent variable is the log of spending (to avoid negative predictions) and the independent variables are causal variables such as price and other relevant variables that should predict spending. The decision maker or researcher can use historical values or patterns in causal variables to serve as the independent variables in the predictions. The problem with causal models is that while they fit may the data, they must predict future spending. To overcome this problem we can create scenarios to understand how different values of independent variables affect spending levels. Then the firm can decide upon which scenario(s) best fit likely firm behavior.

5.5.4 Stochastic Models of Purchase Rates and Volume

One could use the distribution of purchase volume across consumers to predict purchase volume for individual customers. The prediction will be a weighted average of the customer's historical purchase volume and the mean for all customers, the weights being determined by how many observations are available for the customer. (See Columbo and Jiang (1999) and the description of the model in Chapter 12.)

Chapter 6
Issues in Computing Customer Lifetime Value

Abstract This chapter addresses the challenging details in computing LTV that are all-too-easy to ignore. We focus particularly on the appropriate discount rate and appropriate costs. We draw from standard corporate finance and the CAPM model to derive the appropriate discount rate. We discuss the application of activity based costing (ABC) in computing costs. We advocate that the only costs appropriate for LTV calculations are those that change as a function of the number of customers within the particular application at hand (i.e., variable costs). We conclude with a discussion of incorporating marketing response and customer externalities in LTV calculations.

6.1 Introduction

This chapter discusses some of the major issues in computing LTV. Many of them have received little attention in the marketing literature. Yet, each is essential. Specifically, Sect. 6.2 addresses how to determine the appropriate discount rate for calculating LTV. Section 6.3 discusses customer portfolio management. We show that the firm reduces risk by constructing a portfolio of customers, but this comes at the cost of lower returns. We also discuss whether the firm should adjust the discount rate for the risk associated with individual customers or segments. Section 6.4 examines the relevant costs to include in LTV computations. Many firms allocate fixed costs when calculating LTV. We propose that for most database marketing decisions, such as targeting mailings to a specific set of customers, LTV should be calculated using just variable costs. Section 6.5 discusses incorporating response to marketing into LTV calculations. This is especially useful if the marketing environment is expected to change, or if the firm wants to determine long-term marketing policy using LTV. The chapter ends with a brief discussion of externalities (e.g., customer referrals) in the computation of LTV.

6.2 Discount Rate and Time Horizon

In the basic formula for LTV, LTV $= \sum_{t=1}^{\infty} \frac{E(\tilde{R}_t - C_t)}{(1+d)^{t-1}}$ where $\tilde{R}_t$ = revenue in period t, C_t = the cost in period t and d is the discount rate. We assume revenues are a random variable but costs are known.[1] A key parameter is the discount rate. A higher discount rate means that future profit streams $(\tilde{R}_t - C_t)$ are less valuable. Many firms solve the problem of setting the discount rate by limiting the length of the period over which LTV is computed. However, depending upon retention rates and the size of the revenue stream, revenue streams that accrue after the cutoff period may be significant.

  We discuss two approaches for determining d – opportunity cost of capital (Sect. 6.2.1), and source-of-risk (Sect. 6.2.2). Our goal in providing alternative methods is to spur further research in this area.

6.2.1 Opportunity Cost of Capital Approach

6.2.1.1 Basic Concepts

Capital budgeting theory in corporate finance tells us that the appropriate discount rate for evaluating the financial value of a proposed project equals the *opportunity cost of capital* for the firm's *investors*. By opportunity cost, we mean the rate of return investors can achieve on another investment of similar risk. In calculating LTV, we think of customers as investments or "projects" and hence use a discount rate equal to the rate of return investors could make on similar-risk investments, i.e., their opportunity cost of capital.

  There are three key concepts: (1) the link between the appropriate *discount rate* for LTV and *rate of return* investors could make on other investments, (2) what investors could expect to make on investments of similar *risk* as the customer projects undertaken by the firm, and (3) the definition of *investors*.[2]

  Rate of return and the discount rate are linked in that both represent the time value of money. If the investor can make a 10% return on investments, then the investor is indifferent between receiving $100,000 today and $110,000 tomorrow. So promising the investor $110,000 tomorrow is equivalent to giving the investor $100,000 today ($110,000/(1.10)). The rate of return (10%) and discount multiplier (1/1.10) are thus two sides of the same coin. If the investor can make 10% on alternative investments and the returns generated by a customer are not profitable when discounted by 10% per period, the investor would not want to invest in that customer. Hence if we want to use LTV to decide whether to undertake a marketing activity, the activity has to

---

[1] We implicitly are assuming costs are more predictable than revenues.

[2] See Hansen (2006) for a discussion of the cost-of-capital associated with LTV models. His discussion is somewhat different than ours but his work was helpful in framing the issues for us.

be profitable using a discount rate equal to what the investor could make on other projects.

The situation is amplified by the second key concept – risk. No investment is a sure bet, and so in calculating LTV, we need to use as a discount rate the rate of return the investor could make on a project *of similar risk* to the customer management project. For example, if the investor's opportunity cost of capital at a certain risk level is d, and the LTV of a customer is positive at that value for d, the investor still might not want to invest in that customer if the customer is considered more risky than other projects on which the investor can generate a return of d. A good portion of this section will be spent on how to determine the opportunity cost of capital (hence d) incorporating risk.

The third concept is the definition of "investor." For publicly owned companies, the investor is the shareholder. We say the manager makes the decision of whether to invest in the customer, but really the shareholder is making the decision because the manager represents the shareholder. For privately held companies, investor might be the owner who is funding the company from personal funds but has alternative uses of those funds.

6.2.1.2 Calculating the Opportunity Cost of Capital

With these concepts in mind, the first step is to calculate the opportunity cost of capital incorporating risk. A theory has been developed to do this for publicly owned companies. Brealey et al. (2004) state, "The cost of capital for corporate investment is set by the rates of return on investment opportunities in financial markets."[3] Hence, in its general form, the cost of capital represents the alternative investment a shareholder can make in financial markets that provides the same return and risk. It is computed as the weighted average cost of capital (WACC),[4]

$$WACC = \frac{D}{V} r_{debt} + \frac{E}{V} \cdot r_{equity} \qquad (6.1)$$

where:

D = amount of debt the firm has
E = amount of equity the firm has
$V = D + E$
r_{debt} = rate of return on the firm's debt
r_{equity} = rate of return on the firm's equity

To compute $WACC$ we need four key quantities: D, E, r_{debt} and r_{equity}. D and E are readily available from the firm's balance sheet. Usually, r_{debt} is

---

[3] Brealey et al. (2004), p. 40.
[4] Ibid, p. 325. Note Equation 6.1 is not adjusted for tax rates.

easy to compute because it is simply the marginal borrowing cost of the firm. The reason for using the marginal borrowing cost is that if debt is added to the firm, the cost of debt might increase because the risk increases.

Computing r_{equity} requires using another model. The formula for r_{equity} is:

$$r_{equity} = r_f + \beta(r_m - r_f) \qquad (6.2)$$

where:

$r_f =$ the risk free rate
$r_m =$ the market rate of return

r_f is usually the T-bill rate (treasury bills) for a long-bond (10- or 30-year treasury bond). The current rate of return for long-term treasury bonds is between 4% and 5%.[5] $r_m - r_f$ is the "risk premium" for stocks. Currently this is in the range of 4–5%.

The other unknown quantity is β ("beta"), which adjusts the risk premium based on how risky the firm (or investment) is. A market portfolio (e.g., an investment comprised of all the stocks in the S&P 500 or FTSE 100) will have a beta of one. Firms whose variability is greater than the market will have a beta higher than one and those with low variability relative to the market will have a beta of less than one. Beta is very important because the higher beta, the more the market wants to be compensated for the risk it is taking and hence the higher the weighted cost of capital.

Brealey et al. (2004) provide examples of betas from the period May 1997 to April 2002.[6] For example, Amazon.com had a beta of 3.3 and Pfizer had a beta of 0.57. We will use these and assume a specific corporate debt and equity structure and show how the weighted average cost of capital is computed. Assume Pfizer has 20% debt and 80% equity and Amazon has 30% debt and 70% equity. Also assume that Pfizer's borrowing rate is 6% and Amazon's is 7% because it is riskier. The market premium $(r_m - r_f)$ will be assumed to be 5% and risk free rate will be 4%.

The first step is to compute r_{equity} using Equation 6.2. For Pfizer it is $r_{equity}^{Pfizer} = 0.04 + 0.57(0.05) = 0.0685$ or 6.85% and for Amazon it is $r_{equity}^{Amazon} = 0.04 + 3.3(0.05) = 0.205$ or 20.5%. Thus, required expected return for Amazon is much higher than for Pfizer because it is much riskier. We can now compute WACC for each.

For Pfizer, $WACC^{Pfizer} = 0.2 \times 0.06 + 0.8 \times 0.0685 = 0.0688$ or 6.88% and for Amazon $WACC^{Amazon} = 0.3 \times 0.07 + 0.7 \times 0.205 = 0.1645$ or 16.45%. Clearly, Amazon has a much higher cost of capital than does Pfizer.

---

[5] www.Bloomberg.com for March 9, 2007 indicates the 10-year treasury bond yield is 4.59%.

[6] Brealey, et al. p. 296. Also see http://finance.yahoo.com/ to look up betas for specific stocks. Simply enter a stock's ticker symbol and then click on "Key Statistics" on the left-hand side of the page.

This will manifest itself in the types of projects for which Amazon can make investments to guarantee the rate of return its shareholders expect. Pfizer has much lower WACC and can invest in many more potential projects because it does not require as high a rate of return. In terms of LTV, Amazon should use a discount rate of 16.45%, whereas Pfizer needs only use 6.88%. Amazon will require higher returns and retention rates from its customers in order to generate positive LTV.

It is time to stop and digest the information just provided. The two critical elements in computing WACC are: (1) beta, reflecting the riskiness of the firm, and (2) the capital structure, namely, the amount of debt and equity.

The question now is whether weighted cost of capital is the appropriate measure for calculating LTV. The answer depends upon whether the LTV project the firm is undertaking is within the normal scope of business and similar to its normal investment strategy in terms of risk or it is not in the normal course of business. If it is, investors have assumed an appropriate cost of equity. The market has adjusted for this risk through r_{equity} and r_{debt}. Then WACC is the appropriate measure. If not, then a project-specific cost of capital should be used, which is discussed in the next section.

6.2.1.3 Project Weighted Average Cost of Capital

If the projects the firm is investing in are similar to those it has historically invested in, WACC is the appropriate discount rate. However, if a proposed project is significantly different, then there should be a project WACC because the risk is different than the market expects from the firm. Brealey et al. (2004) observe[7]:

The project cost of capital depends on the use to which that capital is put. Therefore, it depends on the risk of the project and not on the risk of the company. If a firm invests in a low-risk project, it should discount the cash flows at a correspondingly low cost of capital. If it invests in a high-risk project, those cash flows should be discounted at a high cost of capital.

Of course, every project has a different risk. However, only those projects with a substantially different risk level should have a project-specific cost of capital. For example, suppose Capital One is making an investment decision to solicit a segment of customers who are similar to those it targets for its typical credit cards. Then the firm's WACC is the appropriate discount rate. Now suppose Capital One decides to target the sub-prime market (poor credit quality customers), which we will assume it does not do currently. Is the risk the same as it is for its typical projects? Clearly it is much higher. Capital One should use a higher discount rate than its WACC for this project.

The major problem is determining an appropriate project-specific discount rate. The earnings for Capital One's sub-prime project are likely to have a

---

[7] Brealey et al. p. 309.

high beta because sub-prime customers are more vulnerable to downturns in the economy. The profit flows from sub-prime customers are more volatile than normal profit flows from investments Capital One usually makes. With a higher beta, the firm must use a higher cost of capital and hence a higher discount rate. To help understand how to determine the appropriate beta to use, it is helpful to understand what beta is and how it is computed.

6.2.1.4 Computing Beta and Project-Specific Discount Rates

Beta is computed several ways but we will concentrate on its definition:

$$\beta_i = \frac{\sigma_{im}}{\sigma_m^2} \tag{6.3}$$

where σ_{im} is the covariance between stock i's return and the market return and σ_m^2 is the variance of the market return. Thus, the more the stock co-varies with the market, the higher beta. In the case of no co-variation, beta is zero. Analysts typically obtain rates of return for a stock and the market, calculate the covariance and variance, and compute β.

Assume the firm determines there is a correlation of 0.5 between the profit flow from its customers and the overall stock market. Further, it finds that its variation in returns among its customers has a standard deviation of 0.1, which is the normal variability it sees in its annual returns. An analysis of the stock market shows that it has a 0.04 standard deviation in its returns. Noting that $\sigma_{im} = \rho_{im}\sigma_i\sigma_m$, we calculate $\beta_i = (0.5 \times 0.1 \times 0.04/0.04^2) = 1.25$. Obviously, the difficult part of the above computation is the linking of the returns from the market to returns from customers. Little has been published in marketing showing how to conduct these analyses and it would be useful to see real-world examples.

For a new project it is far more difficult to determine β because there are no data on cash flows for this project. Some firms develop general guidelines based on the type of project. Risky projects will have a significantly higher cost of capital than do standard projects. Some projects such as replacing a machine where the return is based on savings might have a very low discount rate because it is almost a guaranteed return (low σ_i).

While the notion of project-specific discount rates for calculating LTV is not particularly satisfying because it requires setting WACC subjectively, it is based on sound theory. It is important to understand the basic principles of how WACC is set and when to deviate. If the analyst is uncertain about the risk, he or she can always revert to using the firm's WACC.

6.2.1.5 Empirical Research on Calculating Customer-Specific Discount Rates

Wangenheim and Lentz (2004) applied the notion of project-specific discount rates to specific customers. The idea is that each customer is in a sense a different project, and hence has his or her own β. One deviation from theory in their application is that they calculated β relative to the returns from all customers, instead of relative to the returns from a financial market. Denote by "C" the returns from their entire customer base and "a" the firm's income stream customer a. They calculated:

$$\beta_a = \frac{Cov_{aC}}{\sigma_C^2} \tag{6.4}$$

Finance scholars would argue that one should use the market of all securities, not the firm's customer base, as the "market" from which to calculate the crucial covariance. The reason is that in a publicly owned company, managers supposedly are operating in the interest of investors who can invest in the entire securities market. Even in a privately held company, the owners of that company are investors who should be interested in the market as a whole.

Wangenheim and Lentz (2004) as well as Dhar and Glazer (2003) recommend ignoring the risk-free rate and just using $\beta_a \times R_m$ for the discount rate. This implicitly assumes the risk-free rate is zero for all customers and is a departure from finance theory. So theoretically this weakens the ties to the CAPM. However, pragmatically, customers with higher β's are assigned higher discount factors for the LTV calculation and those β's represent a measure of volatility relative to the portfolio of customers as a whole.

Wangenheim and Lentz (2004) calculate β_a for each customer in a European airline's customer base. They used revenue as the measure of returns, and used the revenues generated by all the company's customers as the market return. The sample included 26,776 customers over a 4-year period. The authors calculated an alternative measure of risk, the number of periods with no purchases (NIP) for each customer. These calculations were made for two separate periods, period 1-quarters 1–8, and period 2-quarters 9–16. The correlation matrix among the measures is shown in Table 6.1.

The results are quite clear: β_a is an unstable measure of customer risk. It is virtually uncorrelated between two separate time periods. On the other hand, the number of inactive periods, an *ad hoc* measure of risk but easier to calculate, is very stable over time. One could question whether NIP is a measure of risk or simply a measure of purchase frequency, but in any case, the

Table 6.1 Correlations between various measures of risk (From Wangenheim and Lentz 2004)

	β^a	β^b	NIP^a	NIP^b
β^a	1	–	–	–
β^b	0.087	1	–	–
NIP^a	−0.133	−0.157	1	–
NIP^c	−0.187	−0.067	0.613	1

[a] "1" and "2" refer to the data period.
[b] Is calculated by Wangenheim and Lenz using Equation 6.4.
[c] *NIP* stands for number of periods with no purchase.

instability of β is somewhat disappointing. It might be that there were not enough observations given that β was estimated with only eight observations, but this did not seem to hurt the stability of NIP. One alternative would have been to segment customers into groups based on demographics or some other variable. They could then create a β for each segment and determine its stability. It might have led to a higher correlation. In any case, this is an interesting but speculative investigation of β as a measure of customer-specific risk.

6.2.2 Discount Rate Based on the Source-of-Risk Approach

Many times the risk in a database marketing project may be attributable to a specific component. For example, in deciding whether to undertake an acquisition campaign, the acquisition rate may be very uncertain but the long-term customer income stream matches historical risk levels. One approach for handling this is to use a high discount rate for the component of lifetime value that is most risky (the acquisition rate), while using the firm's ordinary $WACC$ for discounting long-term income.

Consider the case of evaluating a customer acquisition program that requires an investment of $2,500,000 for a mailing of 1,000,000 pieces with an expected response rate of 2%. Once a customer responds to the mailing, he or she fits the traditional response patterns. Acquired customers generate $35 per year in net income and have a retention rate of 90%. However, the firm believes this is a very risky project because it is not certain about the acquisition rate. The firm therefore plans to use a 20% discount rate versus its normal rate of 10%.

Assume that the $2,500,000 acquisition investment is made at time $t = 0$, and revenues begin at time $t = 1$. We therefore begin discounting revenues at $t = 1$. In that case, the net present value of the investment is[8]:

$$NPV = N\alpha LTV - I = N\alpha m \left(\frac{1}{1 + d - r} \right) - 2{,}500{,}000 \qquad (6.5a)$$

where N = number of customer's mailed, m = margin per customer, α = response rate, r = retention rate, I = investment, and d = discount rate. For the example, $N = 1{,}000{,}000$, $m = \$35$, $\alpha = 0.02$, $r = 0.9$, $I = \$2{,}500{,}000$, and $d = 0.2$. Substituting into Equation 6.5a, the project has a net loss of $-\$167{,}667$. So using conventional NPV methods the firm should not invest in the acquisition project.

However, the abnormal risk is attributable only to the first-period returns. To account for this specific source of risk, one could find an appropriate

---

[8] Note LTV $= m/(1+d-r)$ rather than $m(1+d)/(1+d-r)$, which is the usual formula we use for a simple retention model LTV. The difference is because we assume the discounting begins in period 1.

discount rate for first-period revenues, then discount the ensuing revenues at the regular discount rate. We can arrive at an appropriate first-period discount rate by asking the manager to specify a certainty equivalent; that is, what amount of money would leave the manager indifferent between that amount and the expected first-period earnings. Then we could solve for the discount rate implied by the certainty equivalent, apply that discount rate to the first-period returns, and discount subsequent period returns by the company's $WACC$, which we assume to be 10%. The NPV of the project can be represented as follows:

$$\text{NPV} = \frac{Npm}{1+d_1} + \frac{Npmr}{(1+d_2)(1+d_2-r)} - I \qquad (6.5b)$$

The first term represents first-period returns, discounted by an amount d_1. The second term represents the discounted value of future returns beginning in period 2. These will be discounted by d_2, the firm's $WACC$ (10%). Given the parameters, $Npm = 1,000,000 \times 0.02 \times \$35 = \$700,000$. We then ask the manager, "What amount of money would leave you indifferent between that amount for sure and the $700,000 you expect to receive in period 1, given your uncertainty about the 2% response rate?" Say the manager answers, "$550,000". Then the manager has told us:

$$\$550,000 = \frac{\$700,000}{1+d_1}$$

or

$$d_1 = 27.3\% \qquad (6.5c)$$

Now we can substitute $d_1 = 0.273$ into Equation 6.5b, and use $d_2 = 0.10$. The NPV is now $606,818 and the project is profitable. Applying a 20% discount factor to the entire calculation over-penalized the lifetime value, making the investment appear unprofitable. When applying a high discount rate to the part of the calculation that was really uncertain (first-period revenues), the results changed and the project is profitable.

The "source-of-risk" approach appears to be a useful method when the project under consideration is abnormally risky. The approach has two benefits: (1) it requires the manager to think through why the project is abnormally risky, and (2) it computes a more realistic net present value, highly discounting the components of the project that are truly risky, while not penalizing the components that have normal risk. As we illustrated, the technique can change the decision. It relies on the manager stating a certainty equivalent, which would probably not be too difficult in the example we used. There may be other situations where it would be more difficult. Nevertheless, source-of-risk discounting appears worthy of consideration when a project and a customer's lifetime value is abnormally risky due to an attributable source.

6.3 Customer Portfolio Management

Finance theory has developed methods for dealing with risk. The CAPM model applies to the discount rate d and was discussed in Sect. 6.2. Modern portfolio theory (Sharpe 2000) applies to managing customers with different risks (variances) as well as expected returns (means). Marketers have barely scratched the surface in applying portfolio theory, which will be discussed in this section. Modern portfolio theory is concerned with what percentage of a firm's total investment should be allocated to the various investment opportunities available to it. The specification of these percentages creates the investment portfolio.

Consider two investments A and B. Each is characterized by an expected return, μ_A and μ_B, a standard deviation around that return, σ_A and σ_B and a correlation between these returns, ρ_{AB}. Let w_i be the fraction of investment placed in investment $i (i = A, B; \sum_i w_i = 1)$. The expected return and variance of that return for any set of w's are:

$$E[return] = \mu_p = w_1\mu_A + w_2\mu_B \tag{6.6}$$

$$Variance[return] = \sigma_p^2 = w_1^2\sigma_A^2 + w_2^2\sigma_B^2 + 2w_1w_2\sigma_A\sigma_B\rho_{AB} \tag{6.7}$$

The subscript p refers to the portfolio. A given specification of w's constitutes a portfolio with a specific expected return and risk (measured by the variance) calculated using Equations 6.6–6.7.

To see why a firm should invest in a portfolio rather than an individual security, suppose there are two stocks, both of which have the annual same rate of return, 10%. Each has a standard deviation of 2% and their returns have a correlation of 0.5. Consider the decision of whether to purchase 100 shares of stock 1 or purchasing 50 shares of each stock. If 100 shares of stock 1 is purchased, the expected return is 10% $(1 \times 10\%)$ and the variance is $1^2 \times 2^2 = 4$. If 50 shares of each stock are purchased, then the expected return is still $0.5 \times 10\% + 0.5 \times 10\% = 10\%$ but the variance is $0.5^2 \times 2^2 + 0.5^2 \times 2^2 + 2 \times 0.5 \times 0.5 \times 2 \times 2 \times 0.5 = 3$. This demonstrates a key principle – the lower the correlation between two securities, the greater the advantage is to creating a portfolio because for the same return, the portfolio will have lower variance. If the correlation between two securities is 1, then there is no diversification advantage in buying a weighted average of two securities.

For customer management, the same principle can apply. If a portfolio of two customers segments can be created, then it may have the same rate of return but lower variance than marketing to only one customer segment.

What does a portfolio of customers mean? It is the same concept as stocks except the factor determining the commonality between customers' rates of return may be related to economic factors (e.g., income level), or lifestyle differences.

Suppose a firm has two potential target segments – high and low income customers – and needs to decide whether to invest in both segments or one.

Table 6.2 Alternative customer portfolios

	Data	
	Segment 1 (high income)	**Segment 2 (low income)**
Mean return	10%	20%
Standard deviation	2%	10%
Correlation	0.75	

	Alternative portfolios		
	Portfolio 1	**Portfolio 2**	**Portfolio 3**
Weight for segment 1	0.9	0.7	0.5
Weight for segment 2	0.1	0.3	0.5
Expected portfolio return	11.00%	13.00%	15.00%
Standard deviation	2.06%	3.31%	5.10%

Assume the firm acquires 100,000 credit card customers per year from high-income prospects. The expected annual rate of return from these customers is 10% and the standard deviation is 2%.[9] The low-income customers have a higher expected rate of return, 20%, because they are charged a higher credit card interest rate, but they have a standard deviation of 10% because they are riskier. In some years, the rate of return from low-income customers is negative because of a higher default rate.[10]

The difference in the rates of return between the two segments are driven by two factors: the amount they borrow (called "revolving") and the degree to which they pay off their debt ("solvency" risk). The firm finds that the correlation between the returns of the two groups is 0.75.

The firm constructs three alternative portfolios. One contains 10% low-income and 90% high-income, the second has 30% low-income and 70% high-income and the third has 50% of each. The expected return and variance of each portfolio is computed using Equations 6.6 and 6.7. Table 6.2 shows the results.

The expected return for portfolio 1 is 11% with a standard deviation of 2.06%. For portfolio 2 it is 13% with a standard deviation of 3.31% and for portfolio 3 it is 15% with a standard deviation of 5.10%. The firm feels that portfolio 1 is far superior to its current strategy of targeting only high income customers (10% return with a standard deviation of 2%) because, for very little increase in risk (0.05%), it can increase its return to 11% versus 10%. However, portfolios 2 and 3 increase the risk beyond what it views as tolerable.

The concept of customer portfolios clearly has some benefits. The critical inputs the firm must determine are the relative rates of returns, the variability

---

[9] Note we are setting up this example in terms of expected annual returns, to follow finance theory as close as possible. However, we could also set up the problem in terms of LTV per customer segment, in which case we would want to use segment-specific discount rates.

[10] For example, homeowners from the lower income households are facing penalties and tougher credit causing default problems in the "subprime" market (see, Simon 2007).

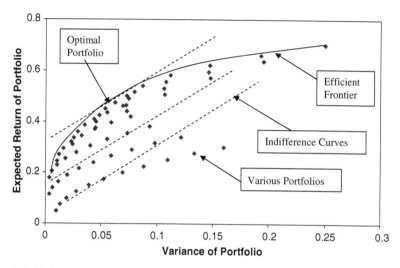

Fig. 6.1 Modern portfolio theory applied to managing a customer portfolio Assumptions:
3 customer segments (A, B, and C)

$\mu_A = 0.30(30\%)$
$\mu_B = 0.05$
$\mu_C = 0.70$
$\sigma_A = 0.4$
$\sigma_B = 0.1$
$\sigma_C = 0.5$
$Cov_{AB} = 0.02$
$Cov_{AC} = -0.06$
$Cov_{BC} = -0.04$

in returns and the correlation in returns. If these can be estimate adequately
by the firm, it can construct a portfolio of different segments of customers.

Figure 6.1 illustrates how these calculations could be used to find the "optimal" portfolio, the set of w's that is best for the investor. There are three
important steps:

1. Calculate and graph all the possible portfolios by considering all possible
   w's. (Note: Fig. 6.1 was constructed assuming three potential investments
   with characteristics shown in the notes to the figure.)
2. Identify the "efficient frontier" set of portfolios. This consists of the set of
   portfolios such that one cannot improve both the expected return and the
   risk by varying the w's. Figure 6.1 shows the efficient frontier as an upper
   envelope. Any portfolio within the envelope is not efficient because one
   can either increase return for the same risk or decrease risk and obtain the
   same return.
3. Place the investor's "indifference curves" on the graph and find the highest indifference curve that has a tangency to the efficient frontier. The
   portfolio at that tangency is the optimal portfolio. The indifference curves
   in Fig. 6.1 are based on a utility function of the form $U = b \times$ Expected

Return $- c \times$ Variance. This means that an indifference curve would be of the form Expected Return $= U/b + (c/b) \times$ Variance. The investor would be indifferent among any set of portfolios whose expected returns and variances satisfy this equation, since they all yield the same utility U. As one increases U, one gets higher indifference curves. So the point of tangency in Fig. 6.1 shows the portfolio that yields the highest utility.[11]

The above procedure can be used to decide how many customers of each risk/return profile to acquire in order achieve the firm's goal, which might be to create a portfolio of customers that generate high return at acceptable risk. The trade-offs between risk and return would be captured by the utility function. The w's would be the fractions of each type of customer to acquire.

In summary, the concept of customer segment portfolios is very important. Many firms use some variant of the concept but do it intuitively rather than systematically. In finance, a major breakthrough was creating stock portfolios to be on the efficient frontier. The opportunity exists for database marketers to apply the same concepts. Little work in database marketing has focused on customer portfolio management. However, it is a promising area of research.

6.4 Cost Accounting Issues

Whether in the context of LTV or any cost-related calculations of customer value, quantifying costs can be a severe challenge. Seppanen and Lyly-Yrjanainen (2002) make the useful distinction between product and customer costs. Product costs pertain to the cost of producing the product sold to the customer. Customer costs refer to the marketing and service costs incurred by the customer. Customer costs are particularly relevant for LTV calculations so we focus on them.

6.4.1 Activity-Based Costing (ABC)

Costs may vary significantly among customers, depending on variation in customer-specific marketing efforts, customer orders, and customer after-service calls. The challenge is to quantify these costs on a per customer basis. Searcy (2004) suggests activity-based costing (ABC) as a method for doing so. ABC attempts to link customer activities such as placing orders to the costs of executing those activities (Kaplan and Cooper 1998). Searcy suggests five steps to implement an ABC analysis:

---

[11] Sharpe(2000, part 1, chapter 4) shows how to formulate the identification of the efficient frontier and the selection of the optimal portfolio as a mathematical program.

1. List the "activities" which a customer might undertake (e.g., fulfilling an order).
2. Determine how much the organization spends on each activity in total.
3. Identify the organization's products, services, and customers.
4. Select "drivers" for each activity. A driver is the customer action that causes the activity to take place (e.g., placing an order).
5. Calculate the activity rates, i.e., the cost to fulfill one order.

Table 6.3 shows an example of an activity-based costing scheme for a hypothetical catalog company. The company identified five customer-related activities: catalog mailing, filling web orders, filling telephone orders, data maintenance, and after-sales support. It then listed the costs directly incurred in executing these activities – salaries, printing, shipping, and hardware/software. Then it listed the drivers of these costs, e.g., catalog mailing costs are incurred when catalogs are mailed, and the company mailed 1,000,000 catalogs in the year of consideration. The number of web orders drives the filling web orders activity. Next the company allocated these costs to each activity, using the cost drivers when possible. For example, the company spent $2,825,000 on salaries in the year under consideration. $1,875,000 was allocated to filling telephone orders. This is determined from telephone operators costing $22.50/h including benefits, time per order is 10 min per order and there are 500,000 orders totaling to $1,875,000. Other allocations such as printing and shipping costs can also be made accurately, whereas others were less scientific, e.g., salaries related to filling web orders.

Note that costs that could not be allocated directly to activities, but were considered part of customer-related costs, were classified as overhead. For example, there was $1,000,000 in hardware/software overhead, and $100,000 in salaries that were related to customers but not classifiable in any of the activities. The overhead was allocated to each activity proportionally to the subtotals of the direct costs for that activity. Allocating overhead is controversial and is discussed later.

An important and final step is then the calculation of cost per activity. The most expensive activity is after-sales support, because it absorbs typically as much as 30 min in service personnel time. Note the much lower cost of filling a web order compared to filling a telephone order. This comes about because of the salaries that must be paid to fill telephone orders, whereas the web requires almost no salaries.

Table 6.4 shows an application of the ABC-based costing scheme to evaluate the profitability of three customers. Customer A places only four orders, but they are all on the web and therefore do not cost much. This customer also only placed one after-sales call. The customer generated a profit of $58.91. Customer B places twice as many orders, but is actually less profitable. This is because the orders are placed on the telephone, and the customer demands significantly more after-sales support. Customer C is perhaps what management would like to do with Customer B. Customer C also places eight orders,

Table **6.3** Activity-based costing example for a hypothetical catalog company

Expense	Activity						
	Catalog mailing	Filling Web orders	Filling telephone orders	Data maintenance	After-sales	Overhead	Total
Salaries	$100,000	$50,000	$1,875,000	$200,000	$500,000	$100,000	$2,825,000
Printing	$500,000	–	–	–	–	$50,000	$550,000
Shipping	$400,000	$100,000	$500,000	–	–	$50,000	$1,050,000
Hardware/software	–	$50,000	–	$200,000	–	$1,000,000	$1,250,000
Total	$1,000,000	$200,000	$2,375,000	$400,000	$500,000	$1,200,000	$5,675,000
Overhead allocation	$268,156	$53,631	$636,872	$107,263	$134,078	$1,200,000	
Drivers	Catalogs mailed	Web orders	Telephone orders	Total orders	After-sales calls		
Number	1,000,000	100,000	500,000	600,000	50,000		
Cost per activity	$1.27	$2.54	$6.02	$0.85	$12.68		

Table 6.4 Customer profitability based on activity-based costing

	Catalogs mailed	Web orders	Telephone orders	Total orders	After-sales calls
Customer A					
Drivers	12	4	0	4	1
Costs	$15.22	$10.15	$0.00	$3.38	$12.68
Revenues	$200.00	(4 orders × $50/order)			
COGS	$100.00	(Revenues × 0.50)			
Customer costs	$41.43				
Total profit	$58.57				
Customer B					
Drivers	35	2	6	8	5
Costs	$44.39	$5.07	$36.14	$6.76	$63.41
Revenues	$400.00	(8 orders × $50/order)			
COGS	$200.00	(Revenues × 0.50)			
Customer costs	$155.77				
Total profit	$44.23				
Customer C					
Drivers	35	8	0	8	2
Costs	$44.39	$20.29	$0.00	$6.76	$25.36
Revenues	$400.00	(8 orders × $50/order)			
COGS	$200.00	(Revenues × 0.50)			
Customer costs	$96.80				
Total profit	$103.20				

but places them on the Web, and only makes two after-service calls. This customer's profit is more than double that of Customer B ($101.84 vs. $42.88).

Table 6.4 illustrates the value of the ABC approach. The analysis also raises important marketing issues. For example, it is clear that Customer B would be more profitable if the customer could be migrated to the Web and encouraged to use the Web for after-sales support. This makes sense from a cost perspective. However, the lack of human contact could weaken the customer's loyalty to the firm in the long run (Ansari et al. 2008). In any case, the analysis is valuable because it identifies potential cost savings, highlights differences among customers, and raises the broader issues of what happens to the customer when we cut costs.

6.4.2 Variable Costs and Allocating Fixed Overhead

An important issue in activity-based costing as well as in all cost calculations for LTV analysis is the allocation of fixed overhead. There are two schools of thought – full costing versus marginal costing. Full costing says that all fixed costs must be allocated. Table 6.4 shows that this "overhead" can be significant and its allocation a bit arbitrary. For example, why was so much hardware/software overhead allocated to telephone fulfillment? The arithmetic reason is that the allocations were proportional to the costs of that

Table 6.5 Firm profit statement before customer acquisition

Number of current customers	100,000
Sales per customer per year	$150
Gross margin percentage	40%
Administrative overhead costs	$3,000,000
Variable costs per customer	$10
Overhead per customer	$30
Sales	$15,000,000
Gross profit	$6,000,000
Variable customer costs	$1,000,000
Profit before overhead	$5,000,000
Administrative overhead costs	$3,000,000
Net profit after overhead costs	$2,000,000
Profitability per customer (excluding overhead)	$50
Profitability per customer (including overhead)	$20

activity. However, that may inflate the cost of filling orders via telephone, making telephone customers look more expensive and less profitable, and causing the company to migrate customers to the Web, which might not be good for loyalty.

Overhead allocations can saddle customers with huge costs that actually yield negative lifetime values. Consider a telecom firm that has just made a huge investment in infrastructure. If these costs are allocated per customer, it is easy for many customers to have negative LTV's, even though these customers contribute to profits and "firing" them would decrease profits.

The alternative is marginal (variable) costing where the only costs allocated to the customer are those that vary with the number of customers and are directly attributed to servicing or marketing to the customer. The view of the "marginal costers" is that the goal is to ascertain how much each customer contributes to fixed overhead and therefore to profit. To saddle the customer with arbitrarily allocated overhead costs hides the true value of the customer, and may convince the firm to "fire" a customer, leaving the firm with less profit, or not acquiring a customer and losing an opportunity to increase profit.

To understand why fixed overhead should *not* be included in LTV, suppose a firm has 100,000 customers who on average spend $150 per year with a gross margin of 40%. The firm has a fixed overhead cost of $3,000,000 which includes the office complex, top management's compensation and other fixed costs. Variable costs per customer (e.g., catalog mailings) are $10. Table 6.5 provides the income statement for the base case. The profitability of the customer is $50 without allocating overhead and $20 with overhead.

Suppose the firm is considering adding 10,000 new customers. Since we assume overhead is fixed, it does not increase when the 10,000 new customers are added. We can now construct an income statement with the new customers added. This is shown in Table 6.6. We see that profit increases by $500,000. This is $50 per customer, so the value of these new customers is $50 per customer, not $20.

Table 6.6 Firm profit statement after acquiring 10,000 customers

Number of current customers	100,000
Number of acquired customers	10,000
Sales per customer per year	$150
Gross margin percentage	40%
Administrative overhead costs	$3,000,000
Variable costs per customer	$10
Overhead per customer	$30
Sales	$16,500,000
Gross profit	$6,600,000
Variable customer costs	$1,100,000
Profit before overhead	$5,500,000
Administrative overhead costs	$3,000,000
Net profit after overhead costs	$2,500,000
Increase in net profits (cf. Table 6.5)	$500,000
Value added per acquired customer	$50

One might argue that the firm must allocate overhead because these costs must be "covered". True, for the firm to stay in business it must cover its overhead costs. But this is not relevant for making business decisions such as whether to add new customers. The firm can improve profits by adding customers that contribute *at the margin*. If the firm adds fixed overhead to the computation of the value of a customer, it will under-invest in adding new customers and will not maximize profits.

Many associate "overhead" with "fixed," but it is quite possible that overhead does vary with an increase in the number of customers. It is then a variable cost. Suppose that one could model these costs using an equation to capture how they change as the number of customers change. Assume the equation is $OH(N) = 2,500,000 + 5 \times N$ where N is the number of customers and $OH(N)$ is the overhead associated with N customers. To continue our example, $N = 100,000$ and $OH(100,000) = \$2,500,000 + \$5 \times N = \$3,000,000$. When the firm adds 10,000 customers, overhead increases by $50,000. Specifically, the marginal overhead cost for adding a new customer is $5 which is the coefficient in front of N. This cost should be subtracted from the profitability of a new customer and for our example the incremental profit would be lowered to $45.

How does the firm determine the coefficients for the equation above? One method is to run a regression in which the number of customers is the independent variable and the overhead expenses of the firm is the dependent variable. It is important to adjust these numbers for inflation because otherwise there is spurious correlation between the number of customers (usually increasing) and costs (also usually increasing).

Another important concept is that of "semi-variable" costs. Semi-variable costs vary with the number of customers according to a step-function. The complication this adds to the computation of LTV is that it makes costs a non-linear function of the number of customers.

To understand semi-variable costs, we begin with a firm that has 1,000,000 customers with average sales per year of $50, variable costs of $35 and a margin of $15. The firm incurs fixed costs of $2,000,000 per year including the costs of its call center. The average customer has a yearly retention rate of 85%. The acquisition cost per new customer is $50. The firm uses a discount rate of 15%. The LTV, given these assumptions and a simple retention lifetime value model, is $57.50.[12]

Assume that starting from its current situation, the next additional 200,000 customers require the firm to build another building, incurring a one-time cost of $500,000. The next 200,000 customers add $300,000 more, and each additional 200,000 customers after that adds $150,000. This traces out a step function. We call these *semi-variable* costs. More generally, customer center costs are nonlinear in the number of customers. The question is: "How does this affect the cost side of the LTV calculation?"

The answer depends upon the decision being made. Assume the decision is whether the firm should add 200,000 customers. Also assume for the first, simplest example, that the $500,000 is a one-time cost. The computation for the decision is then very straightforward. We have the acquisition cost of $50 per customer. The LTV calculated earlier is $57.50. The decision is to add 200,000 new customers comes with a one-time incremental cost of $500,000. The incremental profit from adding the customers is $200,000 \times ($57.50 - $50) - $500,000 = $1,000,000$. In this example the semi-variable cost is a one-time cost and so it is subtracted from the net profit at the time the decision is being made to add new customers. Table 6.7 shows the company's current year profit statement and the net gain in LTV. Note that current year profits decrease because of the investment in customer acquisition, but add $1,000,000 in the long term.

For our second example, suppose the same assumptions as above are used except instead of adding a building, the firm realizes if it adds 200,000 customers, the additional $500,000 will be *per year* due to adding supervisors and layers of management. It will have an incremental cost (above its current variable costs) of $2.50 per new customer ($500,000/200,000). How does the firm compute the LTV?

Thinking of lifetime value as the incremental benefits and costs associated with a customer, the solution is also straightforward. We add $2.50 to the variable costs for the new 200,000 customers. The total variable costs per new customer are now $35.00+$2.50 = $37.50, and profit contribution is now $12.50 per customer. LTV is now $47.92 rather than $57.50. The net impact of the acquisition is now $200,000 \times ($47.92 - $50) = -$416,667$ (Table 6.8). It is now unprofitable to add the new 200,000 customers.

The tricky part of this problem is that we are now assuming variable costs per the *new* customers are $37.50, different than $35.00 for existing customers. This is despite the fact that the new customers will use the call

---

[12] The formula for computing LTV for this example is $LTV = \frac{m}{1-k}$ where $k = r/(1+d)$, m is the margin, r is the retention rate, and d is the discount rate.

Table 6.7 Treatment of semi-variable costs: One-time expenditure

	Current year base	Current year proposed
Fixed costs	$2,000,000	$2,000,000
Semi-variable costs	$0	$500,000
Number of customers	1,000,000	1,200,000
Sales per customer	$50	$50
Variable costs per customer	$35	$35
Gross profit per customer	$15	$15
Acquisition cost per customer	$50	$50
Total acquisition costs	$0	$10,000,000
Total sales	$50,000,000	$60,000,000
Total variable costs	$35,000,000	$42,000,000
Gross profits	$15,000,000	$18,000,000
Profits after fixed and semi-variable costs	$13,000,000	$15,500,000
Profits after acquisition costs	$13,000,000	$5,500,000
Gross profit contribution per customer	$15	$15
Retention rate	0.85	0.85
Discount rate	0.15	0.15
LTV multiplier	3.83	3.83
Customer LTV	$57.50	$57.50
Total customer LTV	$57,500,000	$69,000,000
Total customer LTV after fixed, semi-variable, and acquisition costs	$55,500,000	$56,500,000
Net change in total LTV	–	$1,000,000

center no more or no less than current customers. However, this goes back to (1) linking the treatment of semi-variable costs to the decision at hand, and (2) thinking of LTV as incremental costs and benefits generated by customers. The decision is whether to add 200,000 more customers, and these customers force us to spend an additional $500,000 per year on the call center.

If we were to amortize the $500,000 among the 1,200,000 customers we would have after the acquisition of the 200,000 customers, it would amount to only $0.42 per customer. This would result in a profit contribution of $14.58 per customer, an LTV for the new customers of $55.89, and we would calculate the profits to be 200,000 × ($55.89 − $50) = $1,178,000, although Table 6.8 clearly shows the net result is lower profits.

For this example, the key point is that costs are non-linear, in this case a step function. The costs could also be concave or convex in the number of customers. The shape of the cost function is critical. Most articles about LTV assume a constant variable cost function, i.e., variable costs per customer are constant in the number of customers.

Our final example will cover a different decision. Suppose the firm wants to compute LTV after it has added the 200,000 new customers. However, we will change the parameters of the decision slightly to make the incremental customer profitable. We will use all of the same assumptions used earlier in this section except we will assume the 200,000 new customers add $0.50 (not $2.50) per customer due to supervisors and management personnel required

Table 6.8 Treatment of semi-variable costs: Yearly expenditure

	Current year base	Current year proposed
Fixed costs	$2,000,000	$2,000,000
Semi-variable costs	$0	$500,000
Number of customers	1,000,000	1,200,000
Sales per customer	$50	$50
Variable costs per current customer	$35	$35
Variable costs per acquired customer		$37.5
Gross profit per current customer	$15	$15
Grow profit per acquired customer		$12.5
Acquisition cost per customer	$50	$50
Total acquisition costs	$0	$10,000,000
Total sales	$50,000,000	$60,000,000
Total variable costs	$35,000,000	$42,500,000
Gross profits	$15,000,000	$17,500,000
Profits after fixed and semi-variable costs	$13,000,000	$15,500,000
Profits after acquisition costs	$13,000,000	$5,500,000
Gross profit contribution per current customer	$15	$15
Gross profit contribution per acquired customer	–	$12.5
Retention rate	0.85	0.85
Discount rate	0.15	0.15
LTV multiplier	3.83	3.83
Current customer LTV	$57.50	$57.50
Acquired customer LTV		$47.92
Total LTV among current customers	$57,500,000	$57,500,000
Total LTV among acquired customers	–	$9,583,333
Total customer LTV after fixed, semi-variable, and acquisition costs	$55,500,000	$55,083,333
Net change in total LTV	–	$-416,667$

to manage the additional customers. The profit contribution per customer is now $14.50 and the LTV for this segment of customers is $55.58 and Table 6.9 shows the acquisition is profitable.

Now suppose the 200,000 customers have been acquired and the firm wants to calculate LTV for planning purposes, e.g., to target certain customers for a loyalty program. If we know how much of each resource a customer uses, then customer-specific *variable* costs could be calculated using ABC costing. If the usage level is not known, we would simply use the average variable cost per customer. Total variable costs are now $35 \times 1,200,000 + \$100,000 = \$42,100,000$, or $42,000,000/1,200,000 = \$35.083$ per customer. Thus, the profit contribution per customer across their entire customer base is now $50 - \$35.083 = \$14.927$ and the average LTV per customer is now $57.18.

In summary, determining the costs to use in an LTV calculation can be the most difficult part of the calculation. The single most challenging issue is whether to include fixed or only variable (marginal) costs. Researchers can be found who advocate full costing (e.g., Searcy 2004; Foster et al. 1996, p. 11) as well as marginal costing (Mulhern 1999, p. 29; also see Gurau and

Table 6.9 Treatment of semi-variable costs: lower yearly expenditure

	Current year base	Current year proposed
Fixed costs	$2,000,000	$2,000,000
Semi-variable costs	$0	$100,000
Number of customers	1,000,000	1,200,000
Sales per customer	$50	$50
Variable costs per current customer	$35	$35
Variable costs per acquired customer	–	$35.5
Gross profit per current customer	$15	$15
Grow profit per acquired customer	–	$14.5
Acquisition cost per customer	$50	$50
Total acquisition costs	$0	$10,000,000
Total sales	$50,000,000	$60,000,000
Total variable costs	$35,000,000	$42,100,000
Gross profits	$15,000,000	$17,900,000
Profits after fixed and semi-variable costs	$13,000,000	$15,900,000
Profits after acquisition costs	$13,000,000	$5,900,000
Gross profit contribution per current customer	$15	$15
Gross profit contribution per acquired customer	–	$14.5
Retention rate	0.85	0.85
Discount rate	0.15	0.15
LTV multiplier	3.83	3.83
Current customer LTV	$57.50	$57.50
Acquired customer LTV	–	$55.58
Total LTV among current customers	$57,500,000	$57,500,000
Total LTV among acquired customers	–	$11,116,667
Total customer LTV after fixed, semi-variable, and acquisition costs	$55,500,000	$56,616,667
Net change in LTV	–	$1,116,667
Post-acquisition variable cost per customer	–	$35.08
Post-acquisition gross profit contribution per customer	–	$14.92
Post-acquisition LTV per customer	–	$57.18
Post-acquisition total LTV among current customers	–	$68,616,667
Post-acquisition total customer LTV	–	$56,616,667

Ranchhod 2002). Our recommendation is to link the determination of costs to the decision being made and recall that LTV is the net present value of *incremental* profits and costs. If the decision is to add customers, their LTV should be calculated using the costs they *add* to the company. Marketers are likely to skip over these elements of the calculation, but as the above discussion illustrates, they can be crucial in actual applications.

6.5 Incorporating Marketing Response

The LTV models reviewed so far do not take into account how customers respond to marketing efforts. These models view lifetime value as a *ceteris paribus* calculation: given the environment stays the same, what is the value of the customer? These calculations can be useful but including marketing response in the calculation of LTV can be very valuable (Berger et al. 2002; Calciu and Salerno 2002) for at least two reasons:

- Marketing efforts may in fact change so calculations that assume a constant marketing effort are erroneous;
- Incorporating market response allows firms to examine the impact of policy on customer value.

Note, however, that LTV is essentially a prediction of future customer value, discounted to the present. As a result, if incorporating marketing efforts requires the firm to predict future marketing efforts and these are difficult to predict, incorporating future marketing efforts might in fact diminish the accuracy of LTV.

Rust et al. (1995) were among the first to relate marketing expenditures to customer value. They model the following process:

Marketing => Objective => Perceived => Customer => Market =>
    Profit
Expense Quality Quality Retention Share

The authors do not measure LTV at the customer level, but rather aggregate up to market share and profit. Their market share and profit models are:

$$MS_t = \frac{rMS_{t-1}N_{t-1} + (1 - r' - c)(1 - MS_{t-1})N_{t-1} + A(cN_{t-1} + N_t - N_{t-1})}{N_t}$$

$$\text{(6.8a)}$$

$$Profit_t = Y \times MS_t \times N_t - X_t \tag{6.8b}$$

where:

r = retention rate
MS_t = market share in period t
N_t = number of customers in market, i.e., market size, in period t
r' = retention rate for competitors
c = rate at which customers leave the market
A = % of new customers who choose the brand, i.e., acquisition rate
Y = profit margin
X_t = Expenditure on quality improvement in period t

To complete the model, the authors assume that the retention rate r is a function of perceived quality, which in turn is a function of objective quality, which is a function of marketing expense, so essentially:

$$r = f(X_t) \tag{6.9}$$

In addition to the explicit link between marketing expense and retention rate in Equation 6.9, the authors include in Equation 6.8a the number of customers who switch to the firm, and the acquisition of new customers among the pool who either has left the market in the previous period (cN_{t-1}) or joined the market this period $(N_t - N_{t-1})$. Note that the authors focus on marketing's impact on retention rate, not on acquisition rate or the percentage of customers who leave the market. These would be obvious extensions to the model.

The challenge of course is to estimate Equation 6.8a. The authors suggest using market testing and discuss an application we review in Chapter 7. The authors also calculate the net present value of the profit stream as follows:

$$NPV = \sum_{k=1}^{P} \frac{Y \cdot MS_{t+k}(1+G)^k N_t - X_{t+k}}{(1+\delta)^{k-1}} \tag{6.10}$$

where

G = annual growth rate in the total number of customers in the market
δ = annual discount factor
NPV is the aggregate analog of LTV

Blattberg et al. (2001) and Blattberg and Thomas (2000) develop a "customer equity" model in which they model acquisition rate, retention rate, and future "add-on selling," as functions of marketing actions. Their customer equity model is at the customer segment level and is as follows:

$$CE_t = \sum_{i=1}^{I} \left[N_{it}\alpha_{it}(S_{it} - c_{it}) - N_{it}B_{iat} \right.$$

$$\left. + \sum_{k=1}^{\infty} \frac{N_{it}\alpha_{it} \left(\prod_{k=1}^{\infty} \rho_{j,t+k} \right) (S_{i,t+k} - c_{i,t+k} - B_{ir,t+k} - B_{i,AO,t+k})}{(1+\delta)^k} \right] \tag{6.11}$$

where:

N_{it} = Market "potential" in period t, i.e., the number of customers in segment i available to be acquired.
α_{it} = Acquisition rate for segment i in period t
S_{it} = Sales per customer in segment i in period t
c_{it} = Cost of goods sold for segment i in period t
B_{iat} = Acquisition expenditures per customer in segment i in period t
ρ_{it} = Retention rate for segment i in period t
$B_{ir,t}$ = Retention expenditures per customer in segment i in period t

$B_{i,AO,t}$ = Add-on sales expenditures per customer in segment i in period t
δ = Discount factor

Equation 6.11 traces the lifetime value of a firm's customer franchise starting from acquisition and proceeding over the customers' lifetimes. The analysis is at the segment level, which is practical in real-world applications. The model identifies three drivers of customer equity: acquisition, retention, and add-on sales. Add-on sales include cross-selling and up-selling sales. Blattberg et al. discuss strategies for increasing these quantities. Blattberg and Thomas suggest models that would link marketing expenditures to these three quantities, i.e.:

$$\alpha_{it} = k_a \left[1 - e^{-\sum_{j=1}^{J} \lambda_j B_{iatj}} \right] \tag{6.12a}$$

$$\rho_{it} = k_r \left[1 - e^{-\gamma B_{irt}} \right] \tag{6.12b}$$

$$S_{it} = \sum_{j=1}^{J_{it}} O_{ijt} r_{ijt} \tag{6.12c}$$

$$B_{i,AO,t} = \sum_{j=1}^{J_{it}} O_{ijt} C_{ijt} \tag{6.12d}$$

where:

B_{iatj} = Expenditures for acquisition activity j targeted at segment i in period t
O_{ijt} = Number of offers of type j made to segment i in period t
C_{ijt} = Unit cost of type j offers made to segment i in period t
r_{ijt} = Response rate and contribution from type j offers made to segment i in period t

Equations 6.12a–d are crucial for driving customer value over time and would have to be estimated through market testing.

Comparing the Rust et al. (1995) (RZK) and Blattberg et al. (2001) (BGT) models, both consider customer acquisition as well as retention. RZK is at the aggregate customer level whereas BGT is at the segment level, although RZK could easily formulate their model at the segment level (see Rust et al. 2000) in addition to Rust et al. (1995). RZK focus on retention rates and model the process from expenditure to objective quality to perceived quality/satisfaction to retention, whereas BGT model just the relationship between expenditures and behavior. BGT include acquisition and add-on selling impact as well as the impact on retention.

Both models could be used evaluate current versus alternative marketing efforts. The key relationships are between marketing effort and retention, and in BGT's case, acquisition and add-on selling as well. These relationships could be estimated using historical data, managerial judgment (see also

Blattberg and Deighton 1996), or market tests. For example, a firm could test an offer by extending it to each of its market segments and measuring the response rate r_{ijt}. Similar tests could be used to gauge the effectiveness of acquisition as well as retention efforts. With BGT's model, the firm would only have to measure customer behavior (i.e., how many customers were acquired, how many were retained, etc.) whereas the RZK model would require surveys to measure perceived quality/satisfaction. This would take more effort but provide rich diagnostics. Both models also require knowledge of the size of the market; i.e., how many potential customers are available in each time period. RZK model this explicitly through customers leaving the market (c) and customers defecting from competitors to the focal company (r'). RZK also explicitly model the growth of the market through the parameter G.

The next step is for these models to be estimated empirically and the links between marketing and LTV quantified. Another step would be to optimize marketing efforts over time. See Chapters 26, 28 and 29 for discussion along these lines.

6.6 Incorporating Externalities

Another measure of customer value is the externality generated by the customer. Externalities include word-of-mouth, which could be positive or negative, or the number of referrals generated by the customer.

A challenging circularity occurs in trying to incorporate customer referrals in lifetime value calculations. One could imagine including the expected revenue generated through referrals but that revenue is the lifetime value of the referred customer. In order to calculate that lifetime value, however, one must take into account that the new customers might refer customers, and these new customers have lifetime values. So one faces an infinite recursion and it is not clear how to incorporate it into lifetime value.

Another complication would be, if one wanted to value the entire customer database one customer at a time, one would have to be careful not to double-count. For example, customer i might have referred customer j, so customer i's LTV would include customer j's. So should customer j be treated as not having a separate LTV? In short, incorporating referral value of a customer in LTV calculations is a challenging area that needs to be addressed.

Hogan et al. (2003) conduct an analysis of word-of-mouth externalities in which they merge a lifetime value model and a Bass diffusion model to calculate the impact of a customer "disadopting" the category. An example of disadoption, analyzed by Hogan et al., is the decision not to continue with online banking after an initial trial. Note we do not mean that the customer is moving to another company's online banking service but that the customer has decided no longer to use online banking. This can produce a harmful effect to the entire industry due to a smaller customer base in the industry. For example, the Bass model can be stated as:

$$n(t) = \left(p + q \times \frac{N(t)}{m} \right) \times (m - N(t)) \tag{6.13}$$

where:

$n(t)$ = number of new adopters in period t
$N(t)$ = total adopters as of period t
m = marketing potential parameter
p = innovation parameter
q = imitation parameter

When customers leave the market, N(t) and m both decrease. Since N(t) > m, the impact of losing one customer is to decrease the ratio $\frac{N(t)}{m}$ and hence a smaller number gets multiplied by the imitation parameter. This slows the growth of the market and hence generates fewer sales for all firms.

In an empirical application to the online banking industry, Hogan et al. find that this indirect effect (on imitation) due to disadoption can be larger than the direct loss in revenues (in the case of online banking, cost savings), to the extent that the disadoption occurs earlier. Hogan et al. make two additional points. First is that a disadoption by a competitor also carries the indirect effect, so competitive disadoptions can hurt the firm. Second is that a disadoptor may in fact spread negative word of mouth and have a further negative impact on the firm. This is not explicitly incorporated in the Bass model ($m > 0$) but Hogan et al. use a simple assumption (one disadoptor causes another would-be adoptor to delay purchase by 5 years due to negative word-of-mouth) and show that the financial impact can be substantial.

In summary, customers can be valued by externalities in terms of word-of-mouth and in terms of the number of referrals. The referral issue needs empirical work to demonstrate its magnitude, and also conceptual work on how to incorporate it into lifetime value calculations. Word-of-mouth has been initially investigated by Hogan et al. (2003) but needs further work especially in estimating negative word-of-mouth from disadoption of the category.

Chapter 7
Customer Lifetime Value Applications

Abstract The prior two chapters have covered the technical aspects of Lifetime Value Modeling. But how is LTV applied in the real-world and what types of questions can LTV provide answers that traditional marketing analyses can not? This chapter will provide some answers to these questions. We will discuss how LTV models can be used in the real-world and describe some applications from the literature.

We begin this chapter with the basic analysis of customer acquisition, which has been one of the primary applications of LTV analysis. We will then study reactivation strategies in which the firm selects customers to target for reactivation based on their LTV. Next we will provide some examples of how LTV is used to segment the customer base and is then linked to specific market actions. We will end with the use of LTV models to value firm's customer bases and ultimately the value of the firm.

7.1 Using LTV to Target Customer Acquisition

Probably the earliest application of LTV modeling is for customer acquisition. It offers a very different approach than is commonly used in marketing analysis because it looks at the long-term value of a customer to determine if the firm should make the investment required to acquire the customer. By using an LTV metric for customer acquisition, the firm can determine which acquisition strategies provide the highest payouts or are above the hurdle rate.

Most marketing analysis would concentrate on marketing spending and its return (now called return on marketing investment – ROMI). The typical ROMI model does not separate acquisition from retention marketing spending and cannot see if investing in new customers pays out.

The method begins by determining how much is being spent on customer acquisition. This may be difficult to determine in some industries because it is not be possible to separate new from existing customer expenditures. For example, consumer packaged goods firms often do not know to whom their spending is targeted beyond certain demographic groups. To allocate their spending between acquisition versus retention spending is almost impossible. These firms have very little understanding of customer acquisition costs.

It is easiest to understand the steps if we use an example. Suppose a B2B firm wants to compute the cost of acquiring a customer. In our example, we will assume the firm makes 3 calls per prospect before it decides to cut off future sales calls if no progress is being made. Out of every three prospects, one on average becomes a lead – a prospect that provides some type of "buying signal". Each lead receives approximately 4 sales calls and 1 out of 2 leads become a customer. Thus, it takes on average 17 sales calls to generate one sale.

To cost a sales call the firm keeps records on the direct expenses of a sales person. The average sales person can make 4 calls per week and earns approximately $95,000 per year. Further, there are travel and direct support costs for the sales person which average $35,000 per year. Hence the direct costs associated with the sales person is $130,000 per year. A sales person makes approximately 200 sales calls per year (50×4). Thus the cost of a sales call is $650. If it takes 17 sales calls to close one customer, then the acquisition cost is $17 \times \$650 = \$11,050$.

The next step is to determine the lifetime value of the customer once acquired. For this example, the average new customer generates $8,000 incremental profit per year and the retention rate for the customer is 0.75. The firm's discount rate is 15%. Using the LTV formula for this set of assumptions (Chapter 5, Equation 5.2), we have LTV $= m(1+d)/(1+d-r)$, where $m =$ the incremental margin, $r =$ the retention rate and $d =$ the discount rate. This results in the LTV per customer of $23,000. This is greater than the acquisition costs of $11,050.

Suppose the firm could develop a segmentation strategy for its perspective customers. The firm has a segment of customers it estimates will have an incremental margin of $3,000 and the same retention rate as above. This yields LTV $= \$8,625$. The firm cannot afford these customers given the acquisition cost of $11,050.

If the firm can identify customers who have low potential sales, what methods can the firm use to acquire them that generates an LTV greater than the acquisition costs? The firm decided to use telemarketing to generate leads in which low potential firms (identified by firm size) were contacted by outbound telemarketing representatives. The average telemarketing representative makes 10 calls to generate a qualified lead and the estimated cost per call was $3. Through these calls the firm qualified a set of firms. It then sent a sales representative who on average made two direct sales calls and had approximately a 50% chance of closing the account. The acquisition costs for these customers are $30 (for telemarketing) $+\$650 \times 4 = \$2,630$ cost per customer acquired.

Assume the customers acquired through telemarketing contribute incremental profit of $3,000, a 0.75 retention rate and we use a discount rate of 15%. The LTV of these customers is therefore $\$3,000 \times (1 + 0.15)/(1 + 0.15 - 0.75) = \$8,625$, which is greater than the acquisition costs and makes it profitable to use telemarketing techniques to acquire lower-valued customers.

The lessons we have learned from using our LTV model for customer acquisition are: (1) LTV is a better metric for customer acquisition than initial year one profit because the firm is likely to lose money during the acquisition year which would result in not acquiring as many customers (or any customers) as is optimal; (2) comparing LTV to acquisition costs may allow the firm to design alternative acquisition strategies and tactics which can result in finding ways to acquire lower LTV customers.

7.2 Using LTV to Guide Customer Reactivation Strategies

In Chapter 6 we discussed some issues associated with customer reactivation which is a very important application of LTV modeling. We will discuss the generic reactivation problem and briefly mention several relevant articles.

According to Stauss and Friege (1999), regaining lost customers is important for several reasons. First, it helps to secure future sales and profits. Second, the acquisition costs associated with replacing lost customers can be reduced. Lastly, the negative effect of word-of-mouth can be controlled.

There are two metrics commonly used to assess the payback from reactivation: (1) the ex-customer's first-year profitability, and (2) the ex-customer's LTV. Stauss and Friege (1999) use Second Lifetime Value (SLTV) – the lifetime value of a recaptured customer – instead of LTV of the terminated relationship for calculating the value of a regained customer.

Griffin and Lowenstein (2001) build on the framework laid out by Stauss and Friege (1999). They propose a general outline for reacquiring lost customers. According to them, firms should segment lapsed customers on the basis of SLTV, and identify the reason why the customers defected.

Griffin and Lowenstein, using data from publishing firms, show that the SLTV decreases with the duration of a customer's lapse. In addition the way in which the customer was acquired also affects the SLTV. For example, the value of the customer is higher if the customer was recruited through a subscription card for that particular publication as opposed to a secondary subscription source that handles multiple subscriptions.

In a related study, Thomas et al. (2004a) looked at how firms should price customers when reacquiring them and how they should price them when they have been reacquired. The most interesting result shows that pricing affects reactivation tenure. An interesting and somewhat surprising result is that the higher the reactivation price, the longer the tenure of the reactivated customer. This finding can be explained by heterogeneity in price sensitivity with the more price sensitive customers being more likely to change their buying behavior due to price. They also hypothesized, contrary to Griffin and Lowenstein's result described above, that the longer lapse durations are positively related to second durations. Thomas et al. found, however, that the relationship was directionally negative although not statistically significant.

The area of customer reactivation strategies and SLTV is an under researched area. Because of addressability and knowledge of historical behavior, firms should be able to identify segments of lapsed customers who have high profit potential (SLTV). In order to determine lapsed customers profit potential, an understanding and analysis of the reliability of SLTV is needed. To date, no one has conducted such analyses.

7.3 Using SMC's Model to Value Customers

In Chapter 5 we discussed a model developed by Schmittlein et al. (1987) which we call the SMC model. The model provided estimates of how many active customers the firm has, the likelihood that each customer is "alive" and what expected number of purchases the customer will make over a given future time interval. For businesses in which there is no contractual relationship, using models provided by SMC or Fader et al. (2005) is essential for determining the customer's lifetime value. We will discuss a paper by Schmittlein and Peterson (1994) in which they applied the SMC model to an industrial firm to answer some of the questions discussed above. They also provided some empirical validation of the SMC model. We will not repeat the equations provide in Chapter 5 but will discuss the application and how SMC's model was used in an industrial setting.

Schmittlein and Peterson's (SP) application relates to an office products firm. The primary data SP obtained were order data, initial date on the file and amount spent per order. Because customers had no contractual obligation, determining when a customer was active was one of the primary modeling requirements.

SP show how SMC can be applied at the individual level. The key quantities needed are: (1) the probability the customer is alive within any time interval, (2) the number of orders to be made and (3) the average order quantity for the customer. In Table 4 of SP (1994, p. 57), which we summarize in Table 7.1,

Table 7.1 5-year predictions for illustrative customer accounts (From Schmittlein and Peterson 1994)

Customer #	Entry date	Most recent order	# of reorders observed	P(active)	Expected 5-year # reorders	Observed average reorder size ($)	Expected 5-year $ volume
1	Pre 3/86	4/89	15	0.99	21.0	70.81	1,521.88
2	Pre 3/86	6/89	2	0.18	0.7	42.50	45.98
3	6/86	2/89	1	0.99	2.8	210.50	424.32
4	8/86	5/87	2	0.38	1.7	59.00	125.48
5	10/86	11/88	6	0.95	10.3	113.00	1,148.68
6	12/86	None	0	0.15	0.3	97.00	24.61
7	12/87	1/89	4	0.91	11.1	54.25	703.49
8	3/87	None	0	0.16	0.3	124.00	29.71
9	5/87	6/87	1	0.05	0.2	79.50	15.52
10	Pre 3/86	10/86	2	0.91	3.9	86.00	350.33

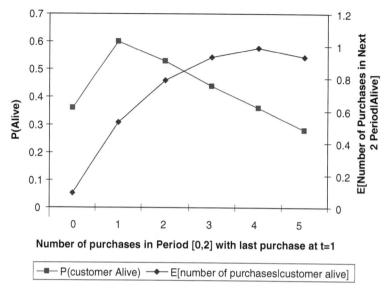

Fig. 7.1 Likelihood the customer is still alive and expected number of future purchases, as a function of number of recent purchases.
Assumptions:
  $R = 0.415$
  $\alpha = 0.415$
  $s = 2$
  $\beta = 4$

SP show the computations for a future 5-year period for ten customers. For each customer, they compute the probability the customer is active, the expected number of orders, the average order quantity and the expected dollar volume. Because of the nature of their model, they did not net present value the purchases. What is interesting in Table 7.1 is that customers have either a very high or very low probability of being alive. Only one customer has a probability of 0.38 while the other customer either have a probability of being alive of 0.9 or greater or 0.2 or less. This is an interesting result but may be caused by the choice of the ten customers for whom they displayed the data.

Another interesting insight to be gleaned from the model is the trade-off between the customer remaining active and the expected number of purchases in an upcoming period. Figure 7.1 graphs P(Alive) and E(number of purchases in next 2 periods) as a function of x, the number of purchases between time 0 and $T = 2$, with the last transaction at $t = 1$. Figure 7.1 shows that as the number of purchases increases, the expected number of purchases, *given the customer is alive*, increases. This is because if a customer has purchased a large number of times in [0,2], he or she probably has a high purchase rate, λ, even if the last purchase occurred in period 1. However, if the customer made a large number of purchases in [0,1] and did not purchase in period 2, there is a decent chance that customer has attrited. As a result P(active) follows an inverted U shape as the number of purchases increase. If the number of purchases is small and there have been no purchases in a while (x = 0), there is a good chance that customer is no longer alive. If the number of purchases is large but there have not been any purchases in a while, there is also a good chance the customer is no longer alive.

This has important ramifications for customer profitability analysis. The Schmittlein, Columbo, and Morrison method allows one to calculate the probability the customer is still alive, the expected remaining lifetime, and the expected number of purchases in a given time horizon, for each customer. The ideal customer will be one who is likely to be alive, has a long expected remaining lifetime, and has a high purchase rate. Figure 7.1 illustrates that there may be trade-offs among at least two of these quantities.

The other interesting aspect of their application is that they are one of the few authors who modeled the purchase dollar amount per order. Most applications merely assume the dollar amount per order is either the average for the population or for the individual. They used a weighted average estimate for the purchase dollar amount per order based on the information obtained from individual customers and the overall population average amount per order. This is a form of a shrinkage estimator and allows them to develop an individual dollar amount per order.

SP conduct a number of validation tests of the model. They show for example that the model predicts very accurately the number of customers who will make 0, 1, 2, etc., purchases over some future length of time. An important phenomenon the model attempts to capture, however, is the notion of the customer being "alive." To validate this, the authors classified each customer in their database into categories [0–10%], [10–20%], etc. Then they contacted 40 customers in each of these "deciles," and asked them whether they could report "active status." Figure 7.2 shows a clear monotonically increasing relationship between the predicted classification and the percentage who self-reported being alive. There may be some regression toward the mean, e.g., only 55% of those in the [90–100%] group reported being active, while 22% in the [0–10%] group reported being active. However, this could be a function of the way the "active" question was asked. In any case, the strong monotonically increasing relationship is clear and impressive.

SP's study is an excellent application of SCM's model. It shows how the model can be used to estimate individual LTV's and it also provides some model validation results. The other interesting element of their model is that it is applied in a business-to-business setting. Many of the applications of LTV models are better suited for industrial or business-to-business settings because the available databases are much better than for consumer product firms selling through channels of distribution.

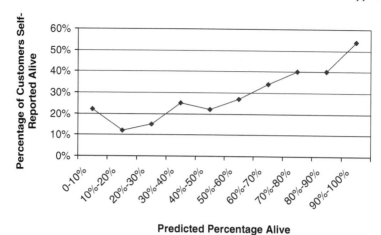

Fig. 7.2 Validation of P[alive] predictions (From Schmittlein and Peterson 1994).

7.4 A Case Example of Applying LTV Modeling

Van Raaij et al. (2003) report the first experience of a business-to-business company with incorporating customer value analysis into their marketing planning. The company, which we will call "DBM," was a multinational firm in the market for professional cleaning products. It sold directly to end-users such as in-flight caterers and professional cleaning services, as well as through distributors. It divided its market into sectors such as healthcare, lodging, or dairy. Sales and profits had been leveling off after years of growth and DBM was worried about new competitors. Further non-product costs (e.g., costs to service customers) had been increasing. The company desired to assign these costs to individual customers and calculate customer profit.

DBM undertook a six-stage process to calculate profit at the customer level and then develop strategies based on the results:

1. Select active customers
2. Design the customer profitability calculation model
3. Calculate customer profit
4. Interpret the results
5. Develop strategies
6. Establish an infrastructure for future applications.

Selecting active customers: The selection of active customers as a first step is quite interesting in view of the models we have reviewed for calculating whether in fact a customer is alive. DBM's approach was quite pragmatic: a customer was active if it had made at least one purchase in the period under consideration. Another issue facing DBM was whether to define the customer as end-users or distributors, or both. DBM decided on end-users because it wanted to develop its marketing efforts from the point of view of the end-user.

This made life difficult because sometimes DBM had to gather information on end-users through distributors, but DBM made the effort and excluded the revenues generated by distributors with whom it could gain agreement for them to supply information to DBM.

Designing the profitability model: The design of the profitability model centered on the assignment of costs. For this DBM used activity-based costing (ABC) (Chapter 6). DBM devised the following list of cost activities (the cost "pool") and cost drivers:

Cost activity	Cost driver
Logistics	Costs charged by logistics partner
Order processing	Number of orders placed by customer
Technical service	Service hours spent by mechanics at customer
Customer consultants	Consultant hours spent at customer
Equipment	Cost of equipment placed at customer

Much of the expense involved with each activity was labor costs, which prior to utilizing Activity Based Costing had simply been designated as overhead. Now with the ABC model, DBM could assign labor costs to the particular activities demanded by each customer, and hence calculate customer-specific costs. There were still overhead costs such as product development and non-activity specific sales and marketing costs, and these were allocated to each customer proportional to the customers' gross sales. These should not have been added to the value of the customer since they will distort future marketing costs (Chapter 6). Firm-level overhead such as office housing, etc., were not included in the cost calculations.

Calculating profitability: The calculation of profitability required data on revenues as well as costs, and these were assembled from various data sources within the company.

Interpreting the results: The most obvious initial finding was the great disparity in profitability across customers. While we often talk about the 80/20 rule, where 20% of customers accounts for 80% of revenues or profits, in this case, DBM found that 20% of customers accounted for 95% of profits. The customer "pyramid" is shown in Table 7.2.

Perhaps most interestingly, the top customers provided smaller per customer margins than the large customers. DBM reasoned that this was because

Table 7.2 Customer "pyramid" for DBM example

Customer type	% of customers	% of revenues	% of profits
Top	1	50	49
Large	4	23	25
Medium	15	20	21
Small	80	7	5

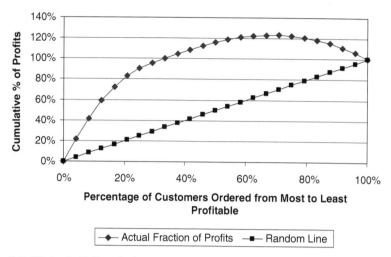

Fig. 7.3 "Stobachoff Curve" showing percentage of profits accounted for by customers ordered by profitability.

top customers had superior bargaining power and hence negotiated lower prices. They also required higher levels of support.

The company used the customer profit curve to plot what they called a "Stobachoff" curve (Storbacka 1997). This is simply the equivalent of a cumulative lift curve. It orders the customers according to profitability, and then plots the cumulative profit accounted for by these customers as one progresses from the highest to lowest profit. Figure 7.3 shows that in this example, 75% of the customers are profitable (the curve increases up to about that point) while 25% are unprofitable. Given that the top 75% of customers accounts for 120% of the profits, the remaining 25% really drag profits down. In this case there are a lot of profitable customers but they are subsidizing a relatively small number (at least a minority) of unprofitable customers. Note that by adding fixed costs through overhead, the firm may be distorting the true profitability of the remaining 25% of the customers. Some of these may be incrementally profitable.

DBM examined these Stobachoff curves for each of its 13 sectors. They classified each sector into one of four groups based on the number of profitable customers being relied on and how much they were subsidizing the unprofitable customers. The result is Fig. 7.4, which depicts four distinct cells. In the low dependence, low subsidizing cell, all customers are profitable and roughly equally so. In the low dependence, high subsidization cell, most customers are profitable but there are a few unprofitable customers who drag down total profits. In the high dependence, low subsidizing cell, there are only a few profitable customers and the rest of customers are unprofitable but not highly so. In perhaps the most dangerous case is the high dependence, high subsidization cell. In this case, there are a few highly profitable customers, and many highly unprofitable customers. This is dangerous because if those

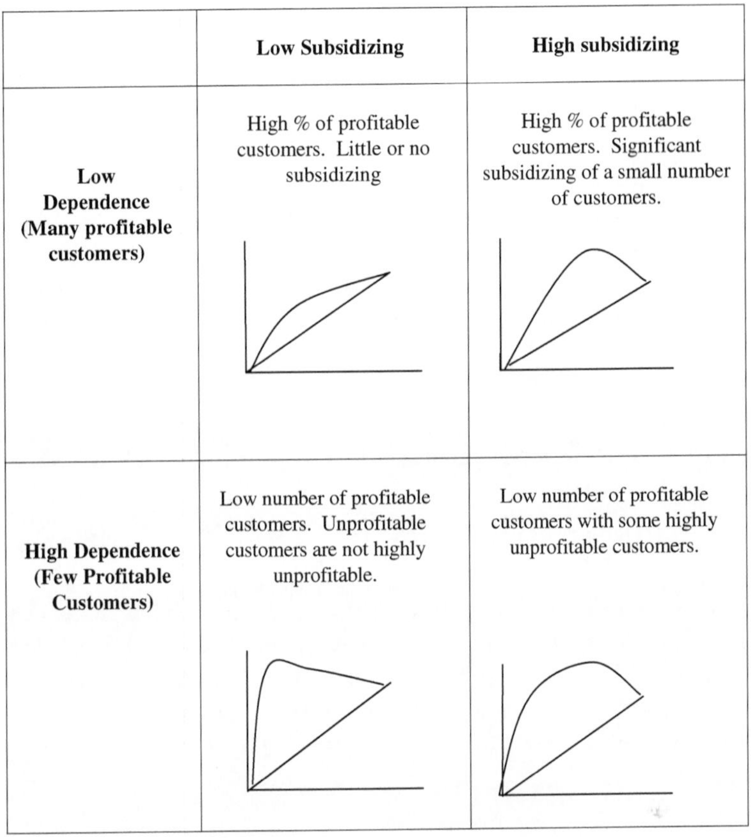

	Low Subsidizing	**High subsidizing**
Low Dependence (Many profitable customers)	High % of profitable customers. Little or no subsidizing	High % of profitable customers. Significant subsidizing of a small number of customers.
High Dependence (Few Profitable Customers)	Low number of profitable customers. Unprofitable customers are not highly unprofitable.	Low number of profitable customers with some highly unprofitable customers.

Fig. 7.4 Classification of Storbachoff curves.

few highly profitable customers should defect, the company would suddenly be losing a lot of money.

Develop Strategies: DBM analyzed its Stobachoff curves for each of its 13 sectors. Nine of them showed little subsidization. However, two sectors were in the low dependence, high subsidization cells, suggesting that the few customers dragging down profits should be dealt with individually. The remaining two sectors were in the high dependence, high subsidization cells, meaning the profitable customers had to be nurtured while the others either had to be "fired" or at least made marginally profitable.

In addition to the Stobachoff curve analysis, sector managers were provided with detailed profitability calculations for each customer. This allowed managers to focus on individual customers who were either extremely profitable or unprofitable. Often the unprofitable customers were consuming an inordinate amount of a particular cost activity, e.g., technical services. The manager could work with the customer to reduce these costs.

In summary, the customer profitability analysis (CPA) provided both sector-level and specific customer strategies that vastly improved the way DBM managed its customer base.

Establish infrastructure: DBM decided to perform the CPA every 6 months. The first major hurdle for this company was making sure it could assemble the cost information on a customer basis. Doing so enabled them to calculate individual customer profitability and went a long way in developing its customer strategy. DBM managers realized however that in the long-term, they needed to integrate marketing efforts and incorporate lifetime value and customer potential explicitly in the system.

7.5 Segmentation Methods Using Variants of LTV

7.5.1 Customer Pyramids

Probably the most common analysis of customer profitability data is to rank customers in terms of profit and classify them in a customer "pyramid" (Zeithaml et al. 2001). The pyramid shape occurs because usually a minority of customers account for the majority of profits. Figure 7.5 shows a hypothetical example of a customer pyramid. We saw a similar example in the DBM

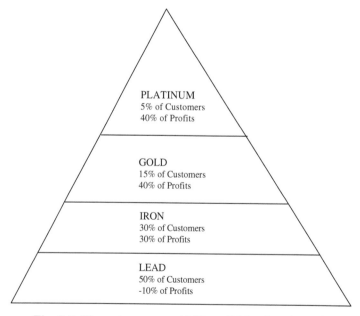

Fig. 7.5 The customer pyramid (From Zeithaml et al. 2001).

analysis above. Customer pyramids form the basis of customer tier programs, which are discussed in Chapter 23.

Figure 7.5 shows that the top 20% of customers account for 80% of profits, although this group can be sub-divided into Platinum and Gold segments, where the Platinum segment is only 5% of customers but accounts for 40% of profits, while the Gold segment is 15% of customers and accounts for 40% of profits. Clearly those in the Platinum segment are key customers. The Iron segment holds its own – it consists of 30% of customers and accounts for 30% of customers. The Lead segment, consisting of half the firm's customers, is unprofitable.

The customer pyramid is simply another way of displaying the Stobachoff curve used in the DBM example. However, the customer pyramid commonly displays the data in four segments and Zeithaml et al. discuss various ways to develop each of these segments. They discuss applications to the marketing research, real estate, and medical industries. Several aspects of creating and managing the customer pyramid are important.

- *Single-measure based*: The single measure can be profit, LTV, sales levels, or potentially even a combination of these. The advantage of a single measure is simplicity; the disadvantage of course is over-simplification. However, in actual applications, firms can look at several measures within each pyramid segment. For example, current period profit might be used to define the pyramid, but the firm could consider LTV as well as customer response to marketing when examining the customers within each pyramid.
- *Firing vs. ignoring vs. developing the customer*: A key decision in customer pyramid management is deciding when to develop a customer, when to leave a customer alone, and when to fire a customer. This corresponds to increasing marketing efforts, leaving marketing efforts as they are, and decreasing marketing efforts. The key questions are for example, "Can an 'iron-tier' customer be converted into gold, or should we avoid investing in this customer, make average profits, and invest in other customers?" These are difficult questions and depend of course on marketing response of the customer as well as competitive and firm resource issues.
- *The pyramid is only as good as the extent to which it differentiates customers*: Zeithaml et al. (2001) emphasize that while by definition the customer pyramid differentiates customers in terms of profitability, they should be differentiated in other key respects as well. For example, customers in different tiers should differ in their preferences for service levels and their willingness to pay for these levels. In addition, customers in each segment should be accessible, i.e., "addressable" in CRM terminology. The customer's potential LTV should be high in order to invest in converting at least some of these customers into higher tiers. Finally the firm should have the resources to be able to invest in potentially high-valued customers. Under these circumstances, customer pyramids are a valuable byproduct of customer value assessment.

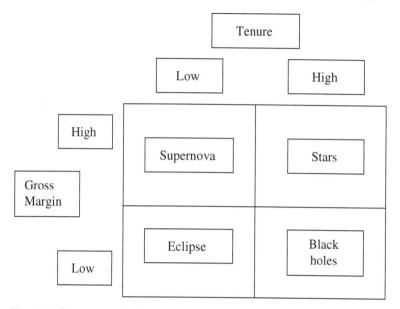

Fig. 7.6 Customer profitability mapping matrix (From Ang and Taylor 2005).

7.5.2 Creating Customer Portfolios Using LTV Measures

Ang and Taylor (2005) provide an interesting application of LTV measures to create a portfolio matrix of customers. They begin with two key measures that affect LTV, tenure and gross margin. Using these metrics they divide customers into four quadrants based on these metrics: low and high tenure and low and high margin. They then name these quadrants. Figure 7.6 below shows the matrix with the names used by Ang and Taylor.

The interesting element of their paper is that they then compute the size and customer profitability for each cell of the matrix. Figure 7.7 shows the results. Ang and Taylor show that 10% out of 14% (5/7) of the customers with low tenure and low profits are unprofitable and 20% out of 42% of the customer with high tenure but low profitability are unprofitable. The firm then has to decide what actions to take.

Ang and Taylor recommend certain actions for each cell. For low-tenure, high-margin customers encourage contracts by offering lower-priced service for entering a 12-month contract. For high-tenure, high-margin customers maintain high level of service and provide avenues for advocacy. For high-tenure, low-margin customers advertise benefits of high priced plans that come from additional features. Finally, for low-tenured, low-margin customers increase prices and reduce service.

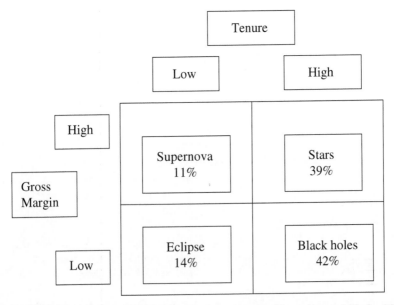

Fig. 7.7 Customer profitability mapping matrix – cell sizes (From Ang and Taylor 2005).

Applying the strategies above, Ang and Taylor described how 18% of the low-tenured, low margin customers were ultimately shifted to high margin customers. Thus, a combination of classifying customers and then applying different strategies, led to higher profits and longer tenure for some customers.

7.6 Drivers of the Components of LTV

In a two papers, Thomas et al. (2004b) and Reinart et al. (2005) discuss the drivers of two components of LTV – lifetime duration and cumulative profits – and the drivers of customer acquisition. Their study used a series of three linked models for duration, profits, and acquisition. Then by applying their model, they showed that many firms are either under or over investing in acquisition or retention marketing.

From the results provide in their papers, we have identified some of the key factors that determine acquisition rates. These are: (1) acquisition expenditure level, (2) demographics and (3) size of market. For duration, the key variables are: (1) retention expenditures, (2) customer usage rates, (3) cross-buying (how many categories purchased), and (4) share of wallet. For profitability, the key variables are: (1) acquisition and retention dollars (2) customer usage rates, (3) lifetime duration, (4) cross-buying, and (5) share of wallet.

Table 7.3 Potential gains from changing market spending (From Thomas et al. 2004b)

Company	How much more or less should be spent	How much profits would increase
B2B	−68.30%	41.52%
Pharmaceutical	31.40%	35.80%
Catalog retailer	−30.70%	28.90%

None of the results for acquisition rates is surprising but their method can be applied to any company's database to make a determination of what factors determine higher or lower acquisition rates. For lifetime duration and profitability, there are some interesting findings. Breadth of purchase and share of wallet are both intuitively appealing but not well-known in the real or academic world.

Thomas et al. (2004b) use their estimated equations for relationship duration, profit contribution, and acquisition likelihood to compute optimal marketing expenditures. They found that firms' spending is very far from "optimal". In Table 7.3 above, we show their key results. It shows that the lowest improvement is 28.9% in increased profitability. The conclusion we draw from their findings is that using models of key LTV components is likely to help firms improve their spending levels. No generalization can be made regarding whether firms over or under spend. However, if Thomas, Reinartz and Kumar's results are replicated across other firms, it appears there is a significant opportunity to increase profits through models of the type proposed in Thomas et al.

7.7 Forcasting Potential LTV

Employing traditional econometric models, Kim et al. (1999) provide a method of forecasting customer-level potential lifetime value for business customers in a telecommunication company. We formally define the potential lifetime value of customer i as:

$$PLV_i = \sum_{t=1}^{\infty} (R_{it} - C_{it})/(1 + \gamma)^{t-1} \qquad (7.1)$$

where PLV_i is the potential lifetime value of customer i, R_{it} is the revenue generated from customer i at time t, C_{it} is the cost or expenses incurred for customer i at time t, and γ is the discount rate. Depending on the firm's data collection interval, the time interval t above can be monthly, quarterly, or yearly. Similarly, the discount rate γ depends on the data interval t.

The firm's objective is to maximize the potential lifetime values of its customers. The firm should find the optimal C_{it} to maximize PLV_i for each time interval t. Hence, we need to solve a complex optimization problem since the revenue R_{it} is clearly a function of past and current costs/marketing expenditures (C_{it}). We need to specify the functional form of the revenue response curve with respect to the current and previous costs and estimate its parameters with appropriate data. Moreover, the costs consisted of several components such as cost of goods sold, service, and various marketing costs. Different allocation of total cost into these components may change PLV_i. Hence, we make an simplifying assumption that the firm incurs costs proportional to the corresponding revenue, $C_{it} = \beta R_{it}$. We also assume that β is constant over customer and/or time. With this proportionality assumption, Equation 7.1 becomes

$$PLV_i = \sum_{t=1}^{\infty} \frac{(1-\beta)}{(1+\gamma)^{t-1}} R_{it} \tag{7.2}$$

The problem of finding the potential lifetime value of customer i becomes the problem of forecasting his/her future revenue streams. The proportionality assumption allows us to easily calculate the PLV_i from forecasted future revenues. The appropriate specification of forecasting models (for future revenue streams) depends on several factors including data availability, industry characteristics, forecasting horizon, costs, ease of application, and so on Makridakis et al. (1983). So their forecasting model is somewhat customized for forecasting revenues of business customers in a telecommunications company. Compared to residential customers, business customers are better target markets for one-to-one marketing because their average revenues are large and their revenue distribution across business customers is highly skewed. In their study, the top 3% of its business customers account for 60% of total business revenues.

The revenue from customer i at time $t(R_{it})$ are decomposed into two parts and each component is estimated separately. That is, $R_{it} = Q_{it} \cdot CS_{it}$ where Q_{it} is the telecommunication demand of customer i at time t and CS_{it} is the firm's market/customer share. The econometric model for total telecommunication demand includes several independent variables such as the size of business, past telecommunication expenditures and growth rates. On the other hand, market share prediction is mainly based on a customer survey. Upon predicting future revenue streams for each customer, potential lifetime values are derived using the Equation 7.2. They also calculated the realized lifetime values for the corresponding customers that practitioners often use as its proxy. Figure 7.8 shows the relationship between the realized and the potential lifetime values. The correlation is about 0.4 and is statistically significant at $p = 0.05$. However, there are a number of customers whose potential lifetime values are fairly large but their realized lifetime values are small. They may be customers with high growth potentials. There are also some customers who have large realized lifetime values with relatively small potential lifetime values.

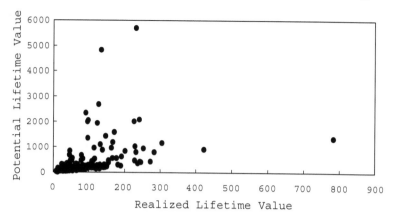

Fig. 7.8 Realized lifetime value versus potential lifetime value (From Kim et al. 1999).

7.8 Valuing a Firm's Customer Base

As mentioned at the beginning of this chapter, one of the important applications of customer valuation is to value the firm's customer base. This value should relate to the firm's stock market value, and hence be of significant interest to senior management. In addition, it helps other firms who might be interested in acquiring the company determine what would be a reasonable price.

Gupta et al. (2004a) applied a simple retention model of lifetime value to assess the value of five firms' customer bases. The analysis is conducted at the customer cohort level, where cohort 0 is the current customer base, cohort 1 is the customers to be acquired next year, cohort 2 is the customers to be acquired the year after, etc. The lifetime value of cohort 0 is:

$$LTV_0 = n_0 \sum_{t=0}^{\infty} m_t \frac{r^t}{(1+\delta)^t} - n_0 c_0 \tag{7.3}$$

where

LTV_0 = Lifetime value of the current customer base.
n_0 = The current number of customers.
m_t = The margin contributed by the average customer in the tth period of their lifetime.
r = Retention rate.
c_0 = Acquisition cost per customer among current customers.

Equation 7.3 is the standard simple retention model with acquisition costs subtracted to produce the net profit contribution of the cohort.

The authors recognize that an important contributor to the long-term value of the company (which supposedly is what the stock market and any acquirer should take into account) is the future set of customers to be acquired by the company.

In general, we have:

$$LTV_k = \frac{n_k}{(1+\delta)^k} \sum_{t=k}^{\infty} m_{t-k} \frac{r^{t-k}}{(1+\delta)^{t-k}} - \frac{n_k c_k}{(1+\delta)^k} \qquad (7.4)$$

where LTV_k is the net present value (in $t = 0$) of the lifetime value of the customer's to be acquired k periods from now. Summing Equation 7.4 over all cohorts $(k = 0, 1, \ldots, \infty)$ yields the total value of the customer database:

$$Customer Value = \sum_{k=0}^{\infty} \left\{ \frac{n_k}{(1+\delta)^k} \sum_{t=k}^{\infty} m_{t-k} \frac{r^{t-k}}{(1+\delta)^{t-k}} - \frac{n_k c_k}{(1+\delta)^k} \right\} \qquad (7.5)$$

The authors devote considerable time to estimating the key components of their model. To estimate n_k, the number of customers to be acquired k periods from the present, they obtain quarterly data on the size of each firm's customer base and estimate a diffusion-like growth model to project n_k into the future. This of course assumes the pattern of acquiring customers can be projected into the future, but the model is estimated on quarterly data over 5 years, fits well, and incorporates the notion of a peak and subsequent decline, so is realistic. To estimate contribution margin m, the authors use company annual reports and divide by the number of customers. We should note that they are using an average cost, not an incremental cost which will be important in businesses that have high fixed costs such as retailers or distribution businesses. They are able to calculate this number for the cohorts in their historical data, and find them to be fairly stable from cohort to cohort. In addition, they assume that the profit contribution for a given cohort does not change over time, given of course that the customer is still a customer.

The authors estimate acquisition costs by dividing the number of acquired customers by marketing costs. This is a fairly strong assumption, but four of the five firms they investigated were relatively new at the time of their study, so the assumption amounts to the majority of marketing expenditures going toward customer acquisition at least in the early periods. This assumption will break down in the future, but by that time the discount factor would make this not too bad an assumption. The authors estimate retention rate by consulting industry experts and other published data. The retention rates ranged from 70% for Amazon to 95% for Ameritrade. Finally, the authors used a discount rate of 12%.

The key results are shown in Fig. 7.9. The figure shows that customer valuation calculated via Equation 7.5 matches the stock's market value (share price times number of shares) very well for Ameritrade, Capital One, and E* Trade. Interestingly, the customer valuation strongly under-estimates the market value of Amazon.com and eBay.

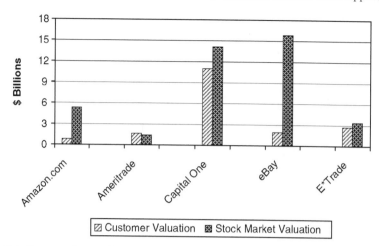

Fig. 7.9 Customer base valuation versus stock market value (From Gupta et al. 2004a).

The authors offer potential explanations, e.g., they cite reports that claim the market might be over-valuing eBay. Also, they discuss that the unique nature of eBay as a representative of buyers and sellers, makes it difficult to calculate the number of "customers."

The authors also raise the possibility that the model is not capturing all the phenomena the market is using the value the customer and hence the firm. For example, the simple retention model does not capture the value of word-of-mouth, which might be significant for Amazon and eBay. The market might also be thinking of extending the Amazon and eBay brand names into other industries. For example, Amazon started as a purveyor of books, and now sells DVD's, electronic equipment, etc. eBay started as a US company, but is now seeking to extend its reach to China. These issues would be factored into the lifetime value calculation by including add-on selling, or allowing margin contributions to increase over time, whereas Gupta et al. assumed they were constant.

There are technical issues in lifetime value calculation that might influence the accuracy of the simple lifetime value formula. First, if the customer base is highly heterogeneous in retention rates, using an average retention rates can underestimate lifetime value. Second, the authors are using a simple retention model on a quarterly basis and a migration model might be more appropriate, where customers could leave and then come back (Chapter 5). This might be accommodated indirectly by the model since the model calculates the number of additional customers each period, not distinguishing whether they are truly new to the firm or customers who are migrating back.

In any case, this is very promising and interesting work. It clearly demonstrates the potential to relate the value of a firm's *long-term* customer base with the market's assessment of the value of the firm. The three cases where the model predicts well show the potential of the approach; the two cases where the model does not predict well opens the door for future research.

Part III
Database Marketing Tools: The Basics

Chapter 8
Sources of Data

Abstract "Data" is the first word in database marketing with good reason – the quality, impact, and ultimately, ROI of database marketing programs depend on the availability of good data. We discuss the various types of customer data available, e.g., customer demographics, transactions, and marketing actions, and the sources that provide these data such as internal records, commercially processed numbers and segmentation schemes, externally available customer lists, and primary survey data.

8.1 Introduction

The customer information file (CIF) is the building block for database marketing. A customer-focused company always makes its decisions based on the analysis of customer data, and a detailed customer record is the prerequisite for useful analysis.

Customer information may include everything about customers, ranging from their names, addresses, phone numbers, their demographic and lifestyle information, transaction histories, and everything that can be derived from customer contacts. It is true that more detailed information leads to better decision-making. However, there is a trade-off between costs and benefits of collecting data. Therefore, it is a good idea to prioritize each data element once you list out the necessary data elements to be included in your customer information file.

The task of constructing the customer information file ideally begins with the objectives its users set. Hence, its size and specific data elements depend on the decision-making problems managers attempt to solve with the customer information file. Unfortunately, some companies have made mistakes, building their customer databases simply because their competitors have built one or because of some vague vision that it would be good to have all "the data" available. As a result, some companies have spent millions of dollars assembling data and have not seen a clear pay-off. The poor performance of these investments has given "CRM" a bad name in many companies. In these companies, CRM has become associated with huge information technology investment in assembling data, but no clear plan on how to use it productively.

Accordingly, we recommend the following process for constructing a customer database:

For example, in Step 1, a company's managers may stipulate their desire to focus on campaigns that reduce customer churn, and campaigns that increase cross-selling. In Step 2, they list customer product ownership, customer attrition, and previous campaign histories as the types of data they need to support these activities. In Step 3, they list the exact data they want and how they will obtain it. For example, they list the specific products for which customer ownership is needed and how they will obtain these data.

The rest of this chapter focuses on Steps 2 and 3, the types of customer data that are available, and the sources of these data. A fourth step not covered here but discussed to some extent in Chapters 10 and 25, is the financial evaluation of the data themselves. Many companies may find it is too expensive to compile a specific data field, even though the above process has determined it would be valuable. Sometimes, the company can purchase data from an outside source on a "trial basis," see how well it works in the predictive models that support its marketing activities, and if so, purchase the data for the long term.

8.2 Types of Data for Describing Customers

There are no standard ways of classifying the types of data elements included in customer information file. Moreover, the types of data elements are different across industries and companies. For our convenience, we classify them into (1) customer identification data, (2) demographic data, (3) psychographic or lifestyle data, (4) transaction data, (5) marketing action data, and (6) other types of data.[1] We focus on the common data elements that most companies have in their customer information file.

8.2.1 Customer Identification Data

Customer identification data is the most basic customer information, covering various classification data, the customer's contact addresses, and other useful customer-identification data. More specifically, they include customer's

---

[1] We did not include competitive data in our typology because most companies do not have them. However, in Section 8.3.3 we discuss the use of surveys to acquire competitive information for a small sample of customers and infer from that the competitive behavior of the rest of the customers.

name (first, middle, last, prefix and suffix), a unique id, home and business addresses, home, business and mobile telephone numbers, email addresses, date of birth, and so on. For business customer data, they may also include names of contacts, departments, fax numbers, etc.

Customer identification information is rarely used in building (statistical) response models partially because it is nominally scaled.[2] However, they are critical in maintaining the customer relationship because they provide the means to contact the customer. Catalogers can't send their catalogs to customers without customers' correct addresses. Telemarketers can't initiate selling activities without customer's phone numbers.

There are two customer identification fields worthwhile to mention in greater detail. The first is the customer ID that is uniquely assigned to each customer upon her first contact with the company. Later this customer id is used as a key field to link to other databases. Once the ID is assigned for a customer, the same ID will be used for her repeat visits/contacts. That is, in order to keep track of all customer interactions, we should have a system to identify who a customer is and then pull her customer ID or assign a new customer ID. It is relatively easy to keep track of purchases made by using store (credit) cards that have the ID number on the card. Similarly, online sellers will easily identify customers if they log in with their User IDs. But some customers may pay cash or by a new credit card. Many retailers have difficulty identifying customers without store cards. These retailers attempt to match repeat customers by name, address, phone number or their combination.

Second, identification fields such as address and phone number need to be regularly updated. More than 40 million Americans change their addresses annually. In a year, 17% of consumers move and 22% of businesses move. It is important to keep customers' addresses accurate and up-to-date. A fast and cheap way of updating address is to employ a NCOA (National Change of Address) supplier licensed by the United States Postal Service. To use this service, all customer names with their addresses are sent to the NCOA service provider. Then the data is typically standardized to confirm to the USPS requirements including ZIP+4 code. Next is to match the data against the NCOA file containing records of old and new addresses for people who moved during the last couple of years. The new addresses are provided for those matched customers. Even though it will not guarantee 100% coverage, it is far less expensive and faster than other address updating methods (e.g., correcting by customer survey).[3] Many companies regularly update their customer information file through this NCOA service once or twice a year.

---

[2] Date of birth and address can be converted to "age" and "location" and these factors can be important in predictive models. However, when they have been put in a usable form, we consider them demographic data.

[3] The standard fee is $3/M with an NCOA hit rate of 3% (Robinson 2002). However, some vendors charge a fee on a "hit per name" basis, generally less than 5 cents per name.

8.2.2 Demographic Data

Demographic data spans the kinds of data fields that US Census Bureau collects every 10 years. They include the age of head of household, family income, family size, occupation of head of household, marital status, presence of children, length of residence, education level, own or rent, type of dwelling, car ownership and its types, gender, race, and so on. For business customers, they may also include data ranging from the race of the CEO, to the number of employees, sales volume, years in business, and so on.

Demographic information is especially useful for targeting prospects. Marketing researchers have found that the best predictors for customers' future purchase behaviors are their historical purchase/transaction information. However, transactional data is mainly available for current customers. In order to target prospects without any transactions, we need to utilize their demographic (and/or psychographic) characteristics that are observable to marketers. For example, from current customers we could use a predictive model to identify what types of demographic characteristics a high-value customer has. Then we target prospects whose demographic profiles are similar to those of current high-value customers. And once prospects become customers, transaction data is collected to fine-tune targeting.

Most companies often do not have enough demographic information in their customer information files. It is especially true for companies that have built customer information files based on legacy databases scattered across various departments. As discussed later, those companies can enhance customer information files through overlaying demographic data provided by external data providers. Demographic data are available both at individual or geographical aggregate level. Individual level data are more accurate, but more expensive, and sometimes are not available. The aggregate data are the average demographic values of customers living in the same geographic boundary such as census tracts, ZIP codes, Zip + 4, and postal carrier routes. For example, customer income is usually not available on a customer basis, since IRS filings are private. In that case, income for individual customers may be assumed equal to the average for their census tract.

8.2.3 Psychographic or Lifestyle Data

Lifestyle is a way of life or style of living that reflects the attitudes and values of a consumer while psychographics are psychological characteristics of consumers such as attitudes, values, lifestyles, and opinions. Generally, lifestyles and psychographics are used interchangeably. Specific questions to measure lifestyles consist of three groups: *activities* on hobbies, vacation, entertainment, club membership, sports, etc.; *interests* in family, job, fashion, food, media, etc.; *opinions* on politics, business, economics, educations, products, culture, etc. (Plummer 1974).

Product usage or ownership can be classified as psychographic data since we can infer customers' attitude and behavior from their product usage. For example, Best Buy would like to know its customer's attitude toward technology, innovativeness, and market mavenism. Best Buy would also like to know its customer's use of various electronic products, as well as other products that may be complementary to electronic products. For example, hiking would be relevant information to know for Best Buy because they might be able to sell hikers electronic gizmos such as GPS locaters. Database marketers often purchase consumer "response lists" to collect these psychographic information. Consumer response lists are lists of individuals who have some identifiable product interest (e.g., martial art equipments or digital cameras) and have a proven willingness to buying by mail (Roberts and Berger 1999). There are several subcategories of consumer response lists. Buyer lists (those who have bought a product or service) and subscription lists (those subscribing to a publication) are most meaningful for database marketers. For example, the *Nordstrom Quality Women Apparel* (buyer) list includes about 500,000 purchasers of apparel from Nordstrom during the past 12 months.

Lifestyle research has grown out of the limitation of demographic variables to explain heterogeneous purchase behavior across consumers. Still few companies are collecting individual lifestyle data for their own database marketing use, partially because of large collection costs, even though they often purchase some lifestyle information from consumer response lists. However, database marketers should note that traditional marketing researchers have successfully used lifestyle data for targeting (or segmenting) prospects for a long time. It may be valuable to conduct a lifestyle survey for a sample of current customers and identify what types of lifestyle characteristics a high-value customer has. Then we might link those lifestyle characteristics to demographic or transaction data that we have available for all customers. Through the chain demographic/transaction data $\Rightarrow$ lifestyle $\Rightarrow$ customer value, we can target the customers we want.

The best-known lifestyle segmentation system is VALS, formerly known as the Values and Lifestyles Program, developed in 1978 by the Stanford Research Institute (SRI) and now owned and operated by SRI Consulting Business Intelligence (SRIC-BI). VALS was one of the first major consumer segmentation programs based on consumer lifestyle characteristics. It correlated people's values about social issues such as abortion rights and military spending with their product and media preferences. In 1989, VALS was revised. Psychological characteristics such as excitement-seeking were found to be more powerful predictors of consumer behavior and more stable over time than social values were. Over the years, many consumer product companies have used VALS for new product development, positioning and effective advertising.

VALS classifies American adults into eight distinctive groups: Innovators, Thinkers, Achievers, Experiencers, Believers, Strivers, Makers, and Survivors. The segments differ in terms of attitudes, decision making patterns, and purchases of products, services, and media. As shown in Fig. 8.1, the VALS segments are defined along two fundamental dimensions: primary motivation (horizontal dimension) and resources available, which is associated with innovative behavior (vertical dimension). VALS points out that people are driven by three powerful primary motivations: Ideals, Achievement, and Self-Expression. Resources refer to education, income, self-confidence, health, eagerness to buy things, and energy level. For example, Achievers have goal-oriented lifestyles and a deep commitment to career and family. They value consensus, predictability, and stability over risk, intimacy, and self-discovery. For more detailed descriptions on VALS, see http://www.sric-bi.com/VALS/types.shtml. GeoVALS estimates the percentage of the eight VALS types by DMA (designated metropolitan area) and zip code. Japan-VALS segments Japanese consumers.

8.2.4 Transaction Data

Transaction data are the most powerful data for predicting future customer purchase behavior. In fact, scanner data researchers for the last two decades have developed various models predicting consumer purchase behavior of packaged goods based on transaction histories. In addition, transaction data cannot typically be purchased outside.[4] Transaction-related data can be collected across various channels through which a company interacts with customers. In addition, valuable transaction information can internally be found in various departments such as customer service, fulfillment, billing, and accounting.

Generally, transaction data include purchase date, purchased items with their product categories, sizes, and prices, purchase amount, method of payment, discount, sales tax, return code, allowances, salesperson ID, and so on. Interpreting customer transactions more broadly, transactions are the outcomes of a process: attention, intention, desire, and action. Hence, we treat any transaction-related information before and/or after the purchase (e.g., product/service inquiry, Web clickstream data, customer complaints, customer satisfaction scores) as transaction data.

Because of data storage and maintenance costs, some companies only save some part of transaction data or its summary. For example, a typical telecommunication company has tens of million customers and each customer makes several calls a day. The size of calling data easily becomes terabytes in weeks.

---

[4] Transaction data defined here do not include product usage or ownership information that can be purchased through consumer response lists. That is, we limit our attention to the transaction-related information specific to the firm's product or service.

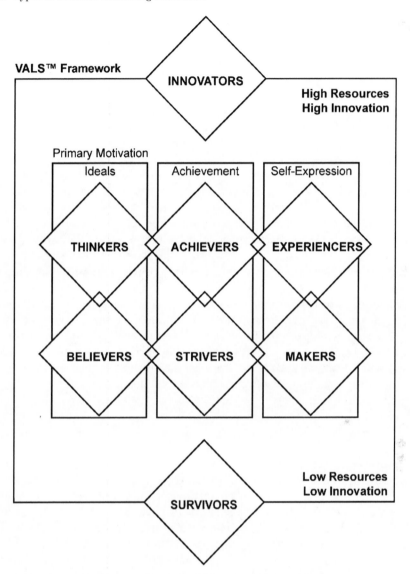

Fig. 8.1 Eight segments of VALS (From *The VALS Segments*, copyrighted graphic used with permission: SRI Consulting Business Intelligence, http://www.sric-bi.com/VALS/types.shtml).

Hence, instead of saving all calling data, the transaction data are recorded in summarized quantities (total number of calls made each day, the most frequently called numbers, etc.). As the data storage and access costs drop, we expect that more data will be stored in raw form.

:eting Action Data

ɔn data and transaction data may be the most important
r efficient marketing strategies and tactics. Marketing action
ɛrs all marketing efforts directing to customers and prospects
whereas transaction information is their responses to the marketing effects.
For example, if we send out a catalog and the customer responds, the mailing
of a catalog is marketing action data and the response or no response is
transaction data.

Remember that our ideal objective in database marketing is to find the
optimal set of marketing activities over time that will maximize the customer's long-run profit contribution. The control variables in our hands are
marketing activities. Should we send the catalog to a customer? Should the
salesperson visit the customer to cross-sell other products? We can make all
these marketing decisions efficiently if we have records on historical marketing activities and the corresponding customer responses or performances.
Hence, if possible, the two should be linked. Surprisingly, however, not many
companies record marketing action information partially because it is time-
consuming and cumbersome without an automatic recording system. And
it is sometimes difficult to link the marketing activities and the customer
response when the firm employs multiple channels. For example, customer
may receive a catalog and the catalog encourages the customer to buy on the
Internet. So is this purchase matched to the catalog or the Internet? This is
important for companies that want to evaluate their marketing efforts. (See
Chapter 25 for more discussion.)

Similar to the case of transaction data, marketing efforts are the outcome of
an ongoing interaction process with the customer. Accordingly, the gathering
of marketing action data is an ongoing process. Consider the case of the
life insurance industry. Marketing action data would include the number of
communications sent to customers (or prospects), the kinds of promotional
offers that were delivered, when the salesperson contacted the customer, when
thank you letters were mailed, and any follow-up conducted by the customer-
care department or by the sales representative.

Marketing data are also very diverse depending on the type of business.
The major marketing activity of a direct marketer is to select a group of
customers out of its house list and send mailing packages to them. The direct marketer should record customer lists of who received each mailing, the
content of mailings such as types of products and amount of discounts, date
of mailing, costs of mailing, etc. Marketing action data can be very complex
when the sources of selling products and services are diverse. For example,
an insurance company may sell its products through the Internet, in-house
or outside telemarketing agency, own sales force or brokers, or alliances with
other financial institutions. Marketing strategies differ across these various
channels, so the types of marketing action data differ as well. In addition,
the difficulty in collecting marketing action data is expected to differ across

various channels. Data collection is relatively easy with the Internet. It may be extremely difficult with brokers because sometimes their sales representatives do not record their selling activities or, even if they do, they are not willing to share this information with the insurance company.

8.2.6 Other Types of Data

Financial data are especially important for financial institutions and service providers who require monthly payments. Some external data providers supply customer-level financial data. For example, Fair Isaac Inc. has developed a credit score called a FICO score (Myers Internet 2005). A FICO score attempts to condense a customer's credit history (e.g., late payments, amount of time credit has been established, length of time at present residence, employment history) into a single number representing the financial risk of the customer. That is, a FICO score is the likelihood that credit users will pay their bills. There are actually three FICO scores computed by data provided by each of the three credit bureaus – Experian, Trans Union, and Equifax.

Some companies also include in their customer information files descriptors they calculate or infer about each customer. These are often derived from statistical models. Examples are lifetime value, values of RFM, credit score, up-selling score, cross-selling score, selling productivity, and so on. The actual score or a decile-ranking may be recorded.

8.3 Sources of Customer Information

Once customer information needs have been defined, we list the specific data fields required to achieve the information objective and determine how to collect them. The goal is to collect the most accurate or valuable information as cheaply as possible. Understandably, there is a tradeoff between the value of information and its acquisition costs.

Marketing researchers have classified marketing research data into primary and secondary data (Malhotra 1993). A researcher collects primary data for the specific purposes of addressing the problem at hand. Collecting primary data is expensive and time-consuming. On the other hand, secondary data are data that have already been collected for purposes other than the problem at hand. Secondary data are easier and faster to collect. Secondary data are classified into two types: internal and external. Internal data are those generated within the organization for which the research is being conducted, while external data are generated outside of the organization.

We use the same topology in classifying sources of customer information: internal (secondary) data, external (secondary) data, and primary data.

As explained, internal data are the cheapest to collect, followed by external data and primary data. In contrast, primary data are the most time-consuming to collect, followed by external and internal data. Hence, when we collect customer data, first we should look internally. If the data are there and its accuracy or quality is acceptable, we stop. But if not, we look for external data sources. And the final medium we rely upon is primary data.

8.3.1 Internal (Secondary) Data

Internal sources should be a starting point for the customer information file. Most companies have vast amounts of internal data, more than they expected to have. Data may have been collected and stored for other business purposes than marketing. For example, order processing or fulfillment system may have compiled order-taking channels, inventory availability, and delivery information. Billing and accounting computer systems may store information on pricing, sales volume, discounts, and net price paid. Contact management systems for the sales force often have valuable information on customer profiles, contact dates, types of promotions offered, and even the content of conversation. Providing information on customer complaints and satisfactions, the customer service department is another valuable internal data source. The marketing and/or sales department stores customer transaction histories and records for various marketing activities. An important but easily ignored source of data that marketing department may have is prospect data. They may come from participants of sweepstakes, names of the gift receivers, or names having called the 800 number.

Unfortunately, managers often do not know exactly where the internal data are stored. Or some of them are not in usable format. This is one of the reasons why the issue of data warehousing is important. A data warehouse is the process of assembling data from various sources, transforming and organizing it into a consistent form for decision-making and providing users with access to this information (Man 1996). That is, a data warehouse is a repository of data gathered from various departments for business decision making. A properly constructed data warehouse provides the company with a more precise understanding of its customer behaviors. For example, Victoria's Secret Stores, the US lingerie chain, used to spend too much time collecting information without thinking about using it (Goldberg and Vijayan 1996). Its data warehousing efforts allowed them to learn that its system of allocating merchandise to its 678 shops, based on a mathematical store average, was wrong. An average store sells equal numbers of black and ivory lingerie while stores in Miami sells ivory by a margin of 10 to 1.

In addition, a data warehouse helps the company to become more customer-centric since data from various functional areas are integrated around customers. With integrated customer databases, many banks such as

BankAmerica Corp. and Bank One Corp. can provide branch and customer service employees with comprehensive customer relationship information (Barthel 1995). As a result, they can improve customer services by satisfying inquiries about various accounts through a single point of contact. In addition, data integration allows banks to identify cross-selling possibilities more readily.

Typically thousands of users with different needs want to use a data warehouse. Hence it is not frequently efficient to meet the needs of all users with a single warehouse. The solution can be a "data mart" that is a kind of a departmental data warehouse. A data mart is a specialized system that stores the data needed for a specific department or purpose (e.g., marketing data mart). The (enterprise) data warehouse is the central repository for all company data with extensive data elements available while a data mart is considered as a subset of the data warehouse specializing in a narrow subject or functional area. For example, the Magazine division of AOL–Time Warner may have its own marketing data mart to satisfy its specific needs. The data mart is created and updated by tapping the enterprise data warehouse.

Compared to a data warehouse, the size of a marketing data mart is relatively small, hence the cost of building a marketing data mart is lower and only several months are required to build it. Recently, however, the size of many marketing databases is increasing rapidly. Several companies have reported that their marketing data marts are approaching the terabyte level (Stedman 1997). For example, Fleet Financial Group is building a 1 TB data warehouse and a 500 GB accompanying marketing database. MCI has 2.5 TB of sales and marketing information and Charles Schwab & Co. has built a customer data mart close to 1 TB. Experiencing performance degradation due to the size of their marketing data mart, they have negotiated with end users to include only critical information in the marketing data marts. Often, they separate the marketing database into even smaller pieces to increase query performance. For example, MCI has built 16 separate marketing data marts such that each is smaller than 100 GB.

8.3.2 External (Secondary) Data

Internal data do not always satisfy the data requirements specified by managers. Therefore, database marketers often purchase external data for two purposes. First, they may rent (targeted) customer lists for prospecting. Second, they may want to augment their customer information files by attaching various demographic and lifestyle characteristics. This is called data enhancement. To enhance your data, you would send your customer list (with identification information such as names and addresses) to a list enhancer and request that a couple of demographic characteristics (e.g., occupation) be attached to those customers. The list enhancer runs your list through its proprietary database by matching your names/addresses to theirs (Roberts and Berger 1999). Demographic information would be appended to those customers when your customers are on the list enhancer's customer list. The list enhancer returns back the enhanced data disk to you.

For marketing researchers, there are many external data sources including federal and state government, trade associations, commercial data providers, and marketing research firms (Malhotra 1993). In this section, we will limit our discussion on external data sources that are more relevant to database marketers.

8.3.2.1 US Census Data

US Census data are an easy and quick external source for enhancing your customer information file. The Census Bureau conducts a full census every 10 years and now the Census 2000 data is available (www.census.gov). In order to reduce the burden on citizens by asking too many questions, the Census Bureau introduced the long form along with the short form. Five out of six households get a short form containing only the basic demographic questions while the remaining household is asked to fill out the long form containing more than 100 questions about its lifestyles and backgrounds.

The US Census contains very useful information for database marketers. For example, variables in the census include household income, per capita income, education level, types of occupations, home values, rent or own, age of the head of the household, and so on. Individual-level census data are not available due to privacy concerns. However, geographical aggregate (average) information is made available to the public. The census data are available at zip code or block group levels. A block may have as few as 10–20 families in it, and their demographic characteristics in the same block are expected to be similar. Some data elements such as population and income are available at the block group level whereas others (e.g., place of birth by citizenship status, real estate taxes) are only available at the census track level.

Commercial data vendors use census data along with other data to make these data easier and more convenient for database marketers. Considering that the census is conducted every 10 years, they also provide the projected data for each year.

8.3.2.2 Mapping Data

Geocoding is the process of assigning latitude and longitude coordinates to a location. Geomarketing vendors provide geocoding services that can enhance your customer information files by assigning coordinates to each address, ZIP code, or ZIP + 4. Before assigning coordinates, they also verify whether the address is consistent with USPS standard.

Once the location coordinates are attached to the address records, mapping software can display the location on the map. Distances can be calculated between each customer and various store locations. The data can also be useful for presentations and overall understanding of the market from a spatial location perspective. And if it is integrated with marketing information (e.g., customer's demographic characteristics), it can be a valuable tool for both managers and analysts. For example, mapping can help retailers and banks to find a location for a new branch.

8.3.2.3 Individual Level Data

Several external data vendors provide list enhancement services at the individual customer level. For example, Donnelly Marketing, a subsidiary of InfoUSA, has various demographic and lifestyle information for over 225 million individuals and 100 million unique households. For each individual or household, it offers over 250 variables that can be appended to a client's customer information file. They include gender, age, estimated household income, home ownership, estimated home value, dwelling type, credit card information, mail order buyers, auto ownership, ethnicity, marital status, newlyweds, and so on (see http://www.infoUSA.com).

InfoUSA also provides list enhancement service for businesses. Extracted from various sources such as yellow pages, annual reports, leading business magazines and newspapers, and 17 million phone calls to verify information, its business database has over 14 million US businesses. Clients can enhance their business lists with more than 70 variables including type of business, sales volume, number of employees, the race of CEO, the establishment date, credit rating, phone number and fax number, and so on.

There are at least four major vendors competing in the list enhancement business: Acxiom, Experian, Equifax (previously R. L. Polk & Co.), and InfoUSA. Each vendor is slightly different in compiling its lists initially. For example, R. L. Polk & Co. complied its lists from the state motor vehicle registration information along with various public records. Hence, it has some automobile specialized information such as the make, model, and year of the automobile owned. Having sold its Consumer Information Solution group to Equifax, Polk now focuses on the automobile industry (http://www.polk.com). On the other hand, Donnelley Marketing originally compiled its lists through telephone and city directories. Now sources of its lists are expanded to mail order buyers and subscribers, magazine subscribers, credit information and other public sources. In 1999, Donnelley Marketing became the wholly owned subsidiary of InfoUSA, which was already a well-known provider of business databases.

An innovative way of collecting lifestyle data has been crafted by NDL (National Demographics and Lifestyles) in the 1970s.[5] NDL compiles its

---

[5] Afterwards, NDL has been acquired by R. L. Polk.

data by providing warranty card processing services to manufacturers and retailers. The manufacturer inserts warranty cards in its product packaging along with a lifestyle survey provided by NDL. NDL processes the data, provides the warranty information with some lifestyle data to the manufacture, but keeps adding all the information to its customer lifestyle database.

Even large compilers can not achieve 100% matches with a typical customer database. About 80–90% of a company's customer lists are covered by the large compilers (Roberts and Berger 1999). Moreover, for those lists of names matched, some data elements may not be available at the individual level. Compilers provide various geographic average values (e.g., ZIP, ZIP + 4 or block groups) for those data elements. Understandably, it costs more to enhance at the individual level. In addition, some data elements such as income are often the inferred values that are the outputs of a statistical model. For example, we can think of an income prediction model where the dependent variable is income and the independent variables may be the age of household head, automobile ownership, type and make of the car, home value, types of occupation, etc. The model is estimated on a group of individuals for whom individual-level income is available. The model can then be used to predict income for all households.

8.3.2.4 Pre-modeled or Cluster Data

Having applied customer analysis to customer (individual or geographic level) and business data, some external data providers segment the entire US population into several groups. Taking hundreds of demographic and lifestyle variables for each subject, a clustering algorithm attempts to find a number of clusters such that subjects in the same cluster are as homogeneous as possible and, at the same time, subjects in the different clusters are as heterogeneous as possible in terms of their characteristics. Once the plausible number of clusters is determined, each segment is characterized by the average values of its subjects' demographic, lifestyle, psychological, and media interest. See Chapter 16 for further discussion of "cluster analysis."

These segment codes can be said to be pre-modeled information in that they are the output of external data vendors' clustering algorithm. They can save your time and effort in modeling since it is already modeled. Once you have your customer lists cluster-coded, you can tell to which segment each customer belongs and enumerate his/her various characteristics based on the norms for that segment. Clustering information is sometimes criticized because it is too aggregated and/or demographic and lifestyle variables cannot explain the heterogeneity of purchase behavior among customers. For example, you wouldn't expect that the percentage of cat owners for one cluster would be significantly different than that for other clusters. However, clustering information is useful for targeting prospects at least.

Moreover, it helps you to develop appropriate advertising copy and media selections.

PRIZM is one of the first demographic and lifestyle based segmentation schemes (http://www.claritas.com). Developed by Claritas, PRIZM is based on the principle that "birds of a feather flock together." That is, people of similar demographic and lifestyle characteristics tend to live near each other. Applying a series of cluster and factor analyses to US Census data, it clusters census block groups with similar characteristics into 66 neighborhood types, listed in Table 8.1. With similar profiles in terms of demographic and lifestyle characteristics, each cluster has a unique name such as Blue Blood Estates, Furs & Station Wagons, Shotguns & Pickups, and Young Influentials. Once the customer information file of a client is PRIZM-coded, you can improve your targeting decision for prospects.

More recently, Looking Glass has developed a segmentation scheme called Cohorts. Unlike PRIZM, Cohorts is based on self-reported household level

Table 8.1 Brief descriptions of the 66 PRIZM-NE clusters (Courtesy of Claritas, Inc., accessed August 8, 2007. Available at http://www.claritas.com/MyBestSegments/Default. jsp?ID = 30&SubID = &pageName = Segment%2BLook-up)

Segment Name		Descriptions
GROUP U1: Urban uptown		
04	Young Digerati	With the boom in new computer and digital technology, this cluster represents the nation's tech-savvy singles and couples living in fashionable neighborhoods on the urban fringe
07	Money and Brains	The residents of Money & Brains seem to have it all: high incomes, advanced degrees and sophisticated tastes to match their credentials. Many of these city dwellers, predominantly white with a high concentration of Asian Americans, are married couples with few children who live in fashionable homes on small, manicured lots.
16	Bohemian Mix	A collection of young, mobile urbanites, Bohemian Mix represents the nation's most liberal lifestyles. Its residents are a progressive mix of young singles and couples, students and professionals, Hispanics, Asians, African-Americans and whites. In their funky rowhouses and apartments, Bohemian Mixers are the early adopters who are quick to check out the latest movie, nightclub, laptop and microbrew.
26	The Cosmopolitans	The continued gentrification of the nation's cities has resulted in the emergence of this segment-concentrated in America's fast-growing metros such as Las Vegas, Miami and Albuquerque. These households feature older homeowners, empty nesters and college graduates who enjoy leisure-intensive lifestyles.
29	American Dreams	American Dreams is a living example of how ethnically diverse the nation has become: more than half the residents are Hispanic, Asian or African-American. In these multilingual neighborhoods – one in ten speaks a language other than English – middle-aged immigrants and their children live in middle-class comfort.

(*continued*)

Table 8.1 (continued)

Segment	Name	Descriptions
GROUP U2: Midtown mix		
31	Urban Achievers	Concentrated in the nation's port cities, Urban Achievers is often the first stop for up-and-coming immigrants from Asia, South America and Europe. These young singles and couples are typically college-educated and ethnically diverse: about a third are foreign-born, and even more speak a language other than English.
40	Close-In Couples	Close-In Couples is a group of predominantly older, African-American couples living in older homes in the urban neighborhoods of mid-sized metros. High school educated and empty nesting, these 55-year-old-plus residents typically live in older city neighborhoods, enjoying secure and comfortable retirements.
54	Multi-Culti Mosaic	Capturing some of the growth of new immigrants to the USA – Hispanics now number 38 million people – this cluster is the urban home for a mixed populace of younger Hispanic, Asian and African-American singles and families. With nearly a quarter of the residents foreign born, Multi-Culti Mosaic is a mecca for first-generation Americans who are striving to improve their lower middle class status.
GROUP U3: Urban cores		
59	Urban Elders	For Urban Elders – a segment located in the downtown neighborhoods of such metros as New York, Chicago, Las Vegas and Miami – life is often an economic struggle. These communities have high concentrations of Hispanics and African-Americans, and tend to be downscale, with singles living in older apartment rentals.
61	City Roots	Found in urban neighborhoods, City Roots is a segment of lower-income retirees, typically living in older homes and duplexes they've owned for years. In these ethnically diverse neighborhoods – more than a third are African-American and Hispanic – residents are often widows and widowers living on fixed incomes and maintaining low-key lifestyles.
65	Big City Blues	With a population that's 50% Latino, Big City Blues has the highest concentration of Hispanic Americans in the nation. But it's also the multi-ethnic address for downscale Asian and African-American households occupying older inner-city apartments. Concentrated in a handful of major metros, these young singles and single-parent families face enormous challenges: low incomes, uncertain jobs and modest educations. More than 40% haven't finished high school.
66	Low-Rise Living	The most economically challenged urban segment, Low-Rise Living is known as a transient world for young, ethnically diverse singles and single parents. Home values are low – about half the national average – and even then less than a quarter of residents can afford to own real estate. Typically, the commercial base of Mom-and-Pop stores is struggling and in need of a renaissance.

(*continued*)

Table 8.1 (continued)

Segment	Name	Descriptions
GROUP S1: Elite suburbs		
01	Upper Crust	The nation's most exclusive address, Upper Crust is the wealthiest lifestyle in America – a haven for empty-nesting couples over 55 years old. No segment has a higher concentration of residents earning over $200,000 a year or possessing a postgraduate degree. And none has a more opulent standard of living.
02	Blue Blood Estates	Blue Blood Estates is a family portrait of suburban wealth, a place of million-dollar homes and manicured lawns, high-end cars and exclusive private clubs. As the nation's second-wealthiest lifestyle, it's characterized by married couples with children, college degrees, a significant percentage of Asian Americans and six-figure incomes earned by business executives, managers and professionals.
03	Movers & Shakers	Movers & Shakers is home to America's up-and-coming business class: a wealthy suburban world of dual-income couples who are highly educated, typically between the ages of 35 and 54 and often with children. Given its high percentage of executives and white-collar professionals, there's a decided business bent to this segment: Movers & Shakers rank number-one for owning a small business and having a home office.
06	Winner's Circle	Among the wealthy suburban lifestyles, Winner's Circle is the youngest, a collection of mostly 25- to 34-year-old couples with large families in new-money subdivisions. Surrounding their homes are the signs of upscale living: recreational parks, golf courses and upscale malls. With a median income of nearly $90,000, Winner's Circle residents are big spenders who like to travel, ski, go out to eat, shop at clothing boutiques and take in a show.
GROUP S2: The affluentials		
08	Executive Suites	Executive Suites consists of upper-middle-class singles and couples typically living just beyond the nation's beltways. Filled with significant numbers of Asian Americans and college graduates – both groups are represented at more than twice the national average – this segment is a haven for white-collar professionals drawn to comfortable homes and apartments within a manageable commute to downtown jobs, restaurants and entertainment.
14	New Empty Nests	With their grown-up children recently out of the house, New Empty Nests is composed of upscale older Americans who pursue active – and activist – lifestyles. Nearly three-quarters of residents are over 65 years old, but they show no interest in a rest-home retirement. This is the top-ranked segment for all-inclusive travel packages; the favorite destination is Italy.
15	Pools & Patios	Formed during the postwar Baby Boom, Pools & Patios has evolved from a segment of young suburban families to one for mature, empty-nesting couples. In these stable neighborhoods graced with backyard pools and patios – the highest proportion of homes were built in the 1960s – residents work as white-collar managers and professionals, and are now at the top of their careers.

(continued)

Table 8.1 (continued)

Segment	Name	Descriptions
17	Beltway Boomers	The nation's Baby Boomers are now in their forties and fifties, and this segment reflects one group of college-educated, upper-middle-class homeowners. Like many of their peers who married late and are still raising children, these Boomers live in comfortable suburban subdivisions and are still pursuing kid-centered lifestyles.
18	Kids & Cul-de-Sacs	Upscale, suburban, married couples with children – that's the skinny on Kids & Cul-de-Sacs, an enviable lifestyle of large families in recently built subdivisions. With a high rate of Hispanic and Asian Americans, this segment is a refuge for college-educated, white-collar professionals with administrative jobs and upper-middle-class incomes. Their nexus of education, affluence and children translates into large outlays for child-centered products and services.
19	Home Sweet Home	Widely scattered across the nation's suburbs, the residents of Home Sweet Home tend to be upper-middle-class married couples living in mid-sized homes with few children. The adults in the segment, mostly between the ages of 25 and 54, have gone to college and hold professional and white-collar jobs. With their upscale incomes and small families, these folks have fashioned comfortable lifestyles, filling their homes with toys, TV sets and pets.

Group S3: Middleburbs

Segment	Name	Descriptions
21	Gray Power	The steady rise of older, healthier Americans over the past decade has produced one important by-product: middle-class, home-owning suburbanites who are aging in place rather than moving to retirement communities. Gray Power reflects this trend, a segment of older, midscale singles and couples who live in quiet comfort.
22	Young Influentials	Once known as the home of the nation's yuppies, Young Influentials reflects the fading glow of acquisitive yuppiedom. Today, the segment is a common address for young, middle-class singles and couples who are more preoccupied with balancing work and leisure pursuits. Having recently left college dorms, they now live in apartment complexes surrounded by ball fields, health clubs and casual-dining restaurants.
30	Suburban Sprawl	Suburban Sprawl is an unusual American lifestyle: a collection of midscale, middle-aged singles and couples living in the heart of suburbia. Typically members of the Baby Boom generation, they hold decent jobs, own older homes and condos, and pursue cocooning versions of the American Dream. Among their favorite activities are jogging on treadmills, playing trivia games and renting videos.
36	Blue-Chip Blues	Blue-Chip Blues is known as a comfortable lifestyle for young, sprawling families with well-paying blue-collar jobs. Ethnically diverse – with a significant presence of Hispanics and African-Americans – the segment's aging neighborhoods feature compact, modestly priced homes surrounded by commercial centers that cater to child-filled households.

(*continued*)

Table 8.1 (continued)

Segment	Name	Descriptions
39	Domestic Duos	Domestic Duos represents a middle-class mix of mainly over 55 singles and married couples living in older suburban homes. With their high-school educations and fixed incomes, segment residents maintain an easy-going lifestyle. Residents like to socialize by going bowling, seeing a play, meeting at the local fraternal order or going out to eat.

GROUP S4: Inner suburbs

44	New Beginnings	Filled with young, single adults, New Beginnings is a magnet for adults in transition. Many of its residents are twentysomething singles and couples just starting out on their career paths – or starting over after recent divorces or company transfers. Ethnically diverse – with nearly half its residents Hispanic, Asian or African-American – New Beginnings households tend to have the modest living standards typical of transient apartment dwellers.
46	Old Glories	Old Glories are the nation's downscale suburban retirees, Americans aging in place in older apartment complexes. These racially mixed households often contain widows and widowers living on fixed incomes, and they tend to lead home-centered lifestyles. They're among the nation's most ardent television fans, watching game shows, soaps, talk shows and newsmagazines at high rates.
49	American Classics	They may be older, lower-middle class and retired, but the residents of American Classics are still living the American Dream of home ownership. Few segments rank higher in their percentage of home owners, and that fact alone reflects a more comfortable lifestyle for these predominantly white singles and couples with deep ties to their neighborhoods.
52	Suburban Pioneers	Suburban Pioneers represents one of the nation's eclectic lifestyles, a mix of young singles, the recently divorced and single parents who have moved into older, inner-ring suburbs. They live in aging homes and garden-style apartment buildings, where the jobs are blue-collar and the money is tight. But what unites these residents – a diverse mix of whites, Hispanics and African-Americans – is a working-class sensibility and an appreciation for their off-the-beaten-track neighborhoods.

GROUP C1: Second city society

10	Second City Elite	There's money to be found in the nation's smaller cities, and you're most likely to find it in Second City Elite. The residents of these satellite cities tend to be prosperous executives who decorate their $200,000 homes with multiple computers, large-screen TV sets and an impressive collection of wines. With more than half holding college degrees, Second City Elite residents enjoy cultural activities – from reading books to attending theater to dance productions.
12	Brite Lites, Li'l City	Not all of the America's chic sophisticates live in major metros. Brite Lights, Li'l City is a group of well-off, middle-aged couples who have settled in the nation's satellite cities. Residents of these typical DINK (double income, no kids) households have college educations, well-paying business and professional careers and swank homes filled with the latest technology.

(continued)

Table 8.1 (continued)

Segment	Name	Descriptions
13	Upward Bound	More than any other segment, Upward Bound appears to be the home of those legendary Soccer Moms and Dads. In these small satellite cities, upper-class families boast dual incomes, college degrees and new split-levels and colonials. Residents of Upward Bound tend to be kid-obsessed, with heavy purchases of computers, action figures, dolls, board games, bicycles and camping equipment.

GROUP C2: City centers

Segment	Name	Descriptions
24	Up-and-Comers	Up-and-Comers is a stopover for young, midscale singles before they marry, have families and establish more deskbound lifestyles. Found in second-tier cities, these mobile, twentysomethings include a disproportionate number of recent college graduates who are into athletic activities, the latest technology and nightlife entertainment.
27	Middleburg Managers	Middleburg Managers arose when empty-nesters settled in satellite communities that offered a lower cost of living and more relaxed pace. Today, segment residents tend to be middle-class and over 55 years old, with solid managerial jobs and comfortable retirements. In their older homes, they enjoy reading, playing musical instruments, indoor gardening and refinishing furniture.
34	White Picket Fences	Midpoint on the socioeconomic ladder, residents in White Picket Fences look a lot like the stereotypical American household of a generation ago: young, middle-class, married with children. But the current version is characterized by modest homes and ethnic diversity – including a disproportionate number of Hispanics and African-Americans.
35	Boomtown Singles	Affordable housing, abundant entry-level jobs and a thriving singles scene – all have given rise to the Boomtown Singles segment in fast-growing satellite cities. Young, single and working-class, these residents pursue active lifestyles amid sprawling apartment complexes, bars, convenience stores and laundromats.
41	Sunset City Blues	Scattered throughout the older neighborhoods of small cities, Sunset City Blues is a segment of lower-middle-class singles and couples who have retired or are getting closed to it. These empty-nesters tend to own their homes but have modest educations and incomes. They maintain a low-key lifestyle filled with newspapers and television by day, and family-style restaurants at night.

GROUP C3: Micro-city blues

Segment	Name	Descriptions
47	City Startups	In City Startups, young, multi-ethnic singles have settled in neighborhoods filled with cheap apartments and a commercial base of cafes, bars, laundromats and clubs that cater to twentysomethings. One of the youngest segments in America – with ten times as many college students as the national average – these neighborhoods feature low incomes and high concentrations of Hispanics and African-Americans.

(*continued*)

Table 8.1 (continued)

Segment	Name	Descriptions
53	Mobility Blues	Young singles and single parents make their way to Mobility Blues, a segment of working-class neighborhoods in America's satellite cities. Racially mixed and under 25 years old, these transient Americans tend to have modest lifestyles due to their lower-income blue-collar jobs. Surveys show they excel in going to movies, playing basketball and shooting pool.
60	Park Bench Seniors	Park Bench Seniors typically are retired singles who live in the racially mixed neighborhoods of the nation's satellite cities. With modest educations and incomes, these residents maintain low-key, sedentary lifestyles. Theirs is one of the top-ranked segments for TV viewing, especially daytime soaps and game shows.
62	Hometown Retired	With three-quarters of all residents over 65 years old, Hometown Retired is one of the oldest lifestyles. These racially mixed seniors tend to live in aging homes – half were built before 1958 – and typically get by on social security and modest pensions. Because most never made it beyond high school and spent their working lives at blue-collar jobs, their retirements are extremely modest.
63	Family Thrifts	The small-city cousin of inner-city districts, Family Thrifts contain young, ethnically diverse parents who have lots of children and work entry-level service jobs. In these apartment-filled neighborhoods, visitors find the streets jam-packed with babies and toddlers, tricycles and basketball hoops, Daewoos and Hyundais.

GROUP T1: Landed gentry

Segment	Name	Descriptions
05	Country Squires	The wealthiest residents in exurban America live in Country Squires, an oasis for affluent Baby Boomers who've fled the city for the charms of small-town living. In their bucolic communities noted for their recently built homes on sprawling properties, the families of executives live in six-figure comfort. Country Squires enjoy country club sports like golf, tennis and swimming as well as skiing, boating and biking.
09	Big Fish, Small Pond	Older, upper class, college-educated professionals, the members of Big Fish, Small Pond are often among the leading citizens of their small-town communities. These upscale, empty-nesting couples enjoy the trappings of success, belonging to country clubs, maintaining large investment portfolios and spending freely on computer technology.
11	God's Country	When city dwellers and suburbanites began moving to the country in the 1970s, God's Country emerged as the most affluent of the nation's exurban lifestyles. Today, wealthier communities exist in the hinterlands, but God's Country remains a haven for upper-income couples in spacious homes. Typically college-educated Baby Boomers, these Americans try to maintain a balanced lifestyle between high-power jobs and laid-back leisure.
20	Fast-Track Families	The migration of upscale city dwellers out to the countryside can be seen in the emergence of this exurban cluster. Fast-Track Families is filled with middle-aged parents who have the

(continued)

Table 8.1 (continued)

Segment	Name	Descriptions
		disposable income and educated sensibility for a granola-and-grits lifestyle: they fish, boat and shop over the Internet – all at high rates.
25	Country Casuals	There's a laid-back atmosphere in Country Casuals, a collection of middle-aged, upper-middle-class households that have started to empty-nest. Workers here – and most households boast two earners – have well-paying blue- or white collar jobs, or own small businesses. Today these Baby-Boom couples have the disposable income to enjoy traveling, owning timeshares and going out to eat.

GROUP T2: Country comfort

Segment	Name	Descriptions
23	Greenbelt Sports	A segment of middle-class exurban couples, Greenbelt Sports is known for its active lifestyle. Most of these middle-aged residents are married, college-educated and own new homes; about a third have children. And few segments have higher rates for pursuing outdoor activities such as skiing, canoeing, backpacking, boating and mountain biking.
28	Traditional Times	Traditional Times is the kind of lifestyle where small-town couples nearing retirement are beginning to enjoy their first empty-nest years. Typically in their fifties and sixties, these middle-class Americans pursue a kind of granola-and-grits lifestyle. On their coffee tables are magazines with titles ranging from *Country Living* and *Country Home* to *Gourmet* and *Forbes*. But they're big travelers, especially in recreational vehicles and campers.
32	New Home-steaders	Young, middle-class families seeking to escape suburban sprawl find refuge in New Homesteaders, a collection of small rustic townships filled with new ranches and Cape Cods. With decent-paying jobs in white-collar and service industries, these dual-income couples have fashioned comfortable, child-centered lifestyles, their driveways filled with campers and powerboats, their family rooms with PlayStations and Game Boys.
33	Big Sky Families	Scattered in placid towns across the American heartland, Big Sky Families is a segment of young rural families who have turned high school educations and blue-collar jobs into busy, middle-class lifestyles. Residents like to play baseball, basketball and volleyball, besides going fishing, hunting and horseback riding. To entertain their sprawling families, they buy virtually every piece of sporting equipment on the market.
37	Mayberry-ville	Like the old Andy Griffith show set in a quaint picturesque berg, Mayberry-ville harks back to an old-fashioned way of life. In these small towns, middle-class couples and families like to fish and hunt during the day, and stay home and watch TV at night. With lucrative blue-collar jobs and moderately priced housing, residents use their discretionary cash to purchase boats, campers, motorcycles and pickup trucks.

(continued)

Table 8.1 (continued)

Segment	Name	Descriptions
GROUP T3: Middle America		
38	Simple Pleasures	With more than two-thirds of its residents over 65 years old, Simple Pleasures is mostly a retirement lifestyle: a neighborhood of lower-middle-class singles and couples living in modestly priced homes. Many are high school-educated seniors who held blue-collar jobs before their retirement. And a disproportionate number served in the military; no segment has more members of veterans clubs.
42	Red, White & Blues	The residents of Red, White & Blues typically live in exurban towns rapidly morphing into bedroom suburbs. Their streets feature new fast-food restaurants, and locals have recently celebrated the arrival of chains like Wal-Mart, Radio Shack and Payless Shoes. Middle-aged, high school educated and lower-middle class, these folks tend to have solid, blue-collar jobs in manufacturing, milling and construction.
43	Heartlanders	America was once a land of small middle-class towns, which can still be found today among Heartlanders. This widespread segment consists of middle-aged couples with working-class jobs living in sturdy, unpretentious homes. In these communities of small families and empty-nesting couples, Heartlanders pursue a rustic lifestyle where hunting and fishing remain prime leisure activities along with cooking, sewing, camping and boating.
45	Blue Highways	On maps, blue highways are often two-lane roads that wind through remote stretches of the American landscape. Among lifestyles, Blue Highways is the standout for lower-middle-class couples and families who live in isolated towns and farmsteads. Here, Boomer men like to hunt and fish, the women enjoy sewing and crafts, and everyone looks forward to going out to a country music concert.
50	Kid Country, USA	Widely scattered throughout the nation's heartland, Kid Country, USA is a segment dominated by large families living in small towns. Predominantly white, with an above-average concentration of Hispanics, these young, these working-class households include homeowners, renters and military personnel living in base housing; about 20% of residents own mobile homes.
51	Shotguns & Pickups	The segment known as Shotguns & Pickups came by its moniker honestly: it scores near the top of all lifestyles for owning hunting rifles and pickup trucks. These Americans tend to be young, working-class couples with large families – more than half have two or more kids – living in small homes and manufactured housing. Nearly a third of residents live in mobile homes, more than anywhere else in the nation.
GROUP T4: Rustic living		
48	Young & Rustic	Like the soap opera that inspired its nickname, Young & Rustic is composed of young, restless singles. Unlike the glitzy soap denizens, however, these folks tend to be lower income, high school-educated and living in tiny apartments in the nation's exurban towns. With their service industry jobs and modest incomes, these folks still try to fashion fast-paced lifestyles centered on sports, cars and dating.

(continued)

Table 8.1 (continued)

Segment	Name	Descriptions
55	Golden Ponds	Golden Ponds is mostly a retirement lifestyle, dominated by downscale singles and couples over 65 years old. Found in small bucolic towns around the country, these high school-educated seniors live in small apartments on less than $25,000 a year; one in five resides in a nursing home. For these elderly residents, daily life is often a succession of sedentary activities such as reading, watching TV, playing bingo and doing craft projects.
56	Crossroads Villagers	With a population of middle-aged, blue-collar couples and families, Crossroads Villagers is a classic rural lifestyle. Residents are high school-educated, with lower-middle incomes and modest housing; one quarter live in mobile homes. And there's an air of self-reliance in these households as Crossroads Villagers help put food on the table through fishing, gardening and hunting.
57	Old Milltowns	With the shrinking of the nation's manufacturing sector, America's once-thriving factory towns have aged, as have their residents. Old Milltowns reflects the decline of these small industrial communities, now filled with retired singles and couples living quietly on fixed incomes. These home-centered residents make up one of the top segments for daytime television.
58	Back Country Folks	Strewn among remote farm communities across the nation, Back Country Folks are a long way away from economic paradise. The residents tend to be poor, over 55 years old and living in older, modest-sized homes and manufactured housing. Typically, life in this segment is a throwback to an earlier era when farming dominated the American landscape.
64	Bedrock America	Bedrock America consists of young, economically challenged families in small, isolated towns located throughout the nation's heartland. With modest educations, sprawling families and blue-collar jobs, many of these residents struggle to make ends meet. One quarter live in mobile homes. One in three haven't finished high school. Rich in scenery, Bedrock America is a haven for fishing, hunting, hiking and camping.

survey data rather than neighborhood aggregate data and, hence, it is expected to be more accurate in targeting households (http://www. cohorts.com). The source data are derived from two leading individual data providers, Experian and Equifax. Cohorts ends up with 30 clusters, each labeled with names such as Alex & Judith (affluent empty-nesters) and Chad & Tammie (young families) as summarized in Table 8.2.[6] So far more than 100 consumer marketers from various industries have employed Cohorts.

---

[6] Actually, there are 31 clusters in Cohorts. The last cluster named "Omegas" is formed from statistical anomalies that did not fit into 30 cohesive clusters.

Table 8.2 Brief description of the "2007 Cohorts Segments" (From *2007 Cohorts Segments*, Courtesy of: Looking Glass Inc. Accessed August 8, 2007. Available at: http://www.cohorts.com/pdf/2007_Briefs.pdf.)

Cohort segment name	Description	Median age	Median income
Married couples			
Alex & Judith	**Affluent Eempty-nesters** Dual-income, older couples who use their high discretionary incomes to enjoy all aspects of the good life.	61	$144,000
Jeffrey & Ellen	**Affluent couples with kids** Urban families who, despite having children at home, have sufficient financial resources to own the latest high-tech products and to lead very active recreational and cultural lifestyles.	43	$142,000
Barry & Kathleen	**Affluent professional couples** Educated, dual-income, childless couples who have connoisseur tastes and are focused on their careers, staying fit and investing.	46	$133,000
Stan & Carole	**Upscale middle-aged couples** Unburdened by children, these credit-worthy, dual-income couples divide their time between the great outdoors and domestic hobbies.	50	$75,000
Brett & Tracey	**Hyperactive newlyweds** Young, dual-income, childless couples whose energies are channeled into active sports, outdoor activities, careers and their home lives.	31	$65,000
Danny & Vickie	**Teen-dominated families** Middle-aged, middle-income families whose teen-dominated households keep busy with outdoor activities, computers and video games.	42	$59,000
Burt & Marilyn	**Mature couples** Comfortable, close-to-retirement homeowners who are active investors and who engage in charitable activities, travel, politics and their grandchildren.	67	$58,000
Todd & Wendy	**Back-to-school families** Families with mid-range incomes, pre-adolescent kids, pets, and lots of video, computer and outdoor activities to keep them occupied.	38	$57,000
Chad & Tammie	**Young families** Up-and-coming young families who curtail their lifestyle expenses through less-costly outdoors activities and working around the house.	31	$53,000
Frank & Shirley	**Older couples raising kids** Conservative grandparents, and older parents raising kids, whose home-oriented lifestyles include pets, home workshop, gardening, and sweepstakes.	60	$50,000
Ronnie & Debbie	**Working-class couples** Moderate-income couples with traditional interests including fishing, hunting, automotive work and crafts.	48	$38,000

(*continued*)

Table 8.2 (continued)

Cohort segment name	Description	Median age	Median income
Eric & Rachel	**Young, married starters** Young, childless renters whose lifestyle patterns include outdoor activities like camping, fishing and running, as well as automotive work and video games.	28	$20,000
Elwood & Willamae	**Modest-income grandparents** Retired couples with modest incomes who dote on their grandchildren and engage primarily in domestic pursuits.	72	$20,000

Single Females

Elizabeth	**Savvy career women** Affluent, working women with sophisticated tastes, very active lifestyles and good investing habits.	43	$182,000
Virginia	**Upscale mature women** Older women approaching or enjoying retirement, who travel and have upscale interests, including charitable causes and investments.	60	$72,000
Allison	**Educated working women** Childless, professional women building their careers, developing sophisticated tastes and staying fit.	32	$53,000
Andrea	**Single moms with careers** Successful, professional single mothers who balance their careers with the demands of raising their children.	40	$50,000
Bernice	**Active grandmothers** Home-oriented women who enjoy handicrafts, indoor gardening and their grandchildren.	62	$36,000
Penny	**Working-class women** Childless female office workers who are concerned with their appearance; enjoy music, pets and handicrafts; and add intrigue to their lives with the prospect of winning the big sweepstakes.	43	$18,000
Denise	**Single moms on a budget** Single mothers with modest incomes who indulge their kids with video games, movies, and music, and who try to find time for themselves.	36	$17,000
Megan	**Fit & stylish students** Young, fashion-conscious, career-minded female students who enjoy music, aerobic sports and the latest in high tech.	26	$16,000
Minnie	**Fixed-income grandmothers** Older single women who spend lots of time on their grandchildren, handicrafts and religious reading.	73	$11,000

Single males

Jonathan	**Elite single men** High-powered, career-driven men with sophisticated tastes, extensive investments, and the means to travel the world.	45	$186,000

(*continued*)

Table 8.2 (continued)

Cohort segment name	Description	Median age	Median income
Sean	**Affluent guys** Affluent, health- and fitness-minded men with investments and upscale interests.	46	$97,000
Harry	**Well-to-do gentlemen** Mature men who are savvy about their investments, travel and politics.	59	$49,000
Ryan	**Energetic young guys** Young, physically active men with strong career drives and upscale interests, including electronics and technology.	33	$48,000
Randy	**Single dads** Single fathers who enjoy outdoor activities, their home workshops and electronic entertainment with their kids.	38	$46,000
Jerry	**Working-class guys** Blue-collar men who spend their free time in the garage or outdoors.	48	$19,000
Jason	**Male students and grads** Physically active, technologically inclined young men finishing school or embarking on their first job.	26	$17,000
Elmer	**Sedentary men** Aging, sedentary men with fixed incomes and few interests beyond their grandchildren and their gardens.	73	$17,000

Households that defy classification

Omegas	Omegas are people who are impossible to classify distinctly. They may be married or single, homeowners or renters, 18–65 years old, have incomes that range from very low to six figures, and enjoy numerous and diverse interests.		

Clients have begun to criticize the nature of the clusters developed by the external data providers. Purchase behavior observed in financial services will be different from purchase behavior in groceries. Different industries will have different demographic and lifestyle drivers. In the 1980s, Pinpoint has developed FiNPiN, a consumer classification system designed for the financial service industry (Winters 1993). Several vendors have followed suit. For example, Claritas introduced its own industry-specific segmentation product called P$YCLE. Designed for financial institutions, P$YCLE segments US households into 42 clusters mainly in terms of their financial behavior. Claritas went one step further and develop a segmentation product named LifeP$YCLE for insurance marketers. Claritas gathers household data from a syndicated survey of 90,000 consumers about their use of financial services.

Finally, the segmentation vendors have actively incorporated databases from other specialty research firms. For example, by utilizing the data from Nielsen Marketing Research, Simmons Marketing Research Bureau, credit data, electoral rolls and additional customer survey, vendors can now report more extensive purchase behavior (e.g., usage pattern for particular products and services) for each segment.

8.3.2.5 List Rentals for Prospecting

Database marketers can increase the efficiency of their customer acquisition efforts significantly by carefully selecting the right mailing lists for prospecting. For example, a mail order company of women's petite sizes may want to target only short women (Hatch 1995). Driver's license data from state motor vehicle bureaus have information on drivers' heights and weights. This mail order company may seek and find a list that contains women and their heights and weights.

The list rental industry is very diverse. There is no standard way of categorizing the different types of lists. Roberts and Berger (1999) classify them into consumer and business lists first. Alternatively, lists can be categorized into house lists, response lists and compiled lists. A house list is the list of customers in the company's own customer information file, while (consumer) response lists are some other company's house list or "subscriber" list (Sect. 8.3.2.3). A compiled list is a list of customers compiled from public records, phone directories, or professional associations. The reason these lists are called compiled is that somebody has actually compiled the lists based on data available typically from various sources. Usually the compiled list has some common identifiable characteristics and its size is large with lower unit price. For example, InfoUSA is renting complied lists of 95 million ethnic individuals, 37 million homeowners, 8.4 million new movers, and so on. Hence, a compiled list is appropriate for wide market coverage. On the other hand, a response list is a list of customers who have either purchased or requested information from specific companies. Its mailing response rates are expected to be high since consumers in the response list have previously shown their interests to respond to the mailing. Moreover, there are a wide variety of response lists available, and customers in each response list often show interests on particular products and services. For example, subscribers of a cat magazine will have strong interests in cats. Cat food sellers may want to rent this subscriber list.

There are hundreds of thousands of list buyers and sellers. The "market" for lists is generally organized as follows:

The list buyer wishes to purchase a list say for prospecting. The buyer employs a list broker to find good lists. On the other side, there are owners of lists. This may be a list compiler as described above, or an individual company. Individual companies often employ list managers who are in charge of selling their customer list. For example, Best Buy may be interested in attracting customers to its stores with an offer for an Apple IPod. Crutchfield, an electronics cataloger, has a list of its recent customers. Best Buy's list broker and Crutchfield's list manager get together and negotiate terms by which Best Buy may rent Crutchfield's list. Crutchfield of course may decide not to rent to Best Buy if it thinks Best Buy will steal sales from them. But if Crutchfield is willing, the broker and list manager negotiate price, terms, etc. The list owner, in this case Crutchfield, then pays both the broker and the list manager a certain percentage. It is an interesting arrangement. Essentially, the list buyer does not pay *directly* for the services of the list broker or list manager. However, one might conjecture that the list buyer *indirectly* pays because undoubtedly the fact that the list owner pays both the broker and the list manager keeps prices relatively high.

For years, the list industry was relatively low-tech. Recently, however, computerized list search engines have appeared. These allow a broker, or the list buyer, to search directly for lists. One such search engine is Nextmark (http://www.nextmark.com). See Roberts and Berger (1999) for more detail about the list rental industry.

Another way to acquire a prospect list is through list exchange. This process is managed by companies such as Abacus (http://www.abacus-us.com). Abacus maintains what they call a cooperative database. Companies contribute names to the database, and in return can obtain new names from the database. List exchanges became more accepted during the cash crunch of the past few years. According to the 2004 *Catalog Age* Benchmark Report on Lists, 30% of all respondents have negotiated list exchanges (Del Franco 2004). They were more willing to exchange with non-competitors than competitors. Chen et al. (2001) showed that information sharing (or list exchange) can be profitable for two competing firms under reasonable conditions.

8.3.3 Primary Data

If the data elements are not available from internal or external sources, they need to be collected directly from a consumer survey. These are costly and time-consuming, but often worthwhile. We will not discuss various statistical issues on collecting primary data (survey, focus group and in-depth interview, observational data, etc.) since they are well documented in traditional marketing research textbooks. Instead, we provide a couple of real world examples how companies collect their primary data.

Traditionally packaged goods manufacturers are mass marketers. However, Quaker has seen the potential of one-to-one marketing. In order to create its own customer list, in 1990 Quaker mailed cents-off coupons, each of which had a unique household number. Analyzing who redeemed coupons and when they were redeemed, Quaker could learn customer-level purchase behavior for its product. Moreover, this information could be used to customize advertising and promotion to the unique needs of individual households (Mollie 1991).

Philip Morris gives another excellent example. Because of the increasing restrictions on tobacco advertising, it is necessary for Philip Morris to build its own customer information file and reach smokers directly. Customers fill out detailed questionnaires to get free shirts and sleeping bags (Berry 1994). With its 26 million smokers' names and addresses, Philip Morris sends targeted coupons and asks for grassroots support for their lobbying efforts. Similarly, Seagram has built its own customer information file and tracked consumers' names and addresses, the brands and types of alcohol they drink, their sex, birth date, income, and how many bottles they purchase in an average month (Berry 1994).

A strategic alliance with credit card companies or Internet portals often reduces costs of collecting primary data significantly. For example, GM offered GM credit card with MasterCard in 1992, and, as a result, could build a customer database with tens of millions of customers. More recently, several offline-based companies formed strategic alliances with online companies to target online customers and track online customer behaviors. For example, United Artists Theatre Circuit, one of the largest theater chains in the USA, made a long-term strategic alliance with AOL (Time Warner 1999). The alliance allows United Artists efficiently to reach the largest group of moviegoers in cyberspace.

Another important use of primary data, perhaps in its infancy, is to use surveys to gather competitive information (Kamakura and Wedel 2003; Du et al. 2005). For example, a company could survey its customers and ask them how often they purchase from a competitor, what competitive products they own, and what percentage of purchases are from a competitor ("share-of-wallet"). They would have these competitive data for just the sample, say 1,000 customers. The company would then run a predictive model to predict say share-of-wallet as a function of variables it has on all its customers. This model would then be used to score the rest of the customer file. So each customer would be scored in terms of their predicted share-of-wallet, i.e., what percentage of their business is with the company as opposed to the competition.

Du et al. (2005) noted that few firms were collecting competitive information. They suggested that the survey-based approach should be utilized to augment the company's interactions with its customers by adding the inferred competitive interactions. Their empirical analysis indicated that the volume customers transact within a firm has little correlation with the volume they transact with the firm's competitors. In addition, a small percentage of customers account for a large portion of all the competitive transactions, suggesting considerable potential to increase sales if these customers can be correctly identified and encouraged to switch.

8.4 The Destination Marketing Company

Competition among external data providers is getting stiffer as their products and services become less differentiated. In result, data-selling business has become a low margin business. To differentiate from others and increase value-added, external data vendors are beginning to integrate downstream and provide services such as predictive modeling, customer segmentation, cross-selling modeling, and other marketing consulting services. By providing selling and marketing research services, in addition to the data that drive these efforts, these vendors have taken one step further to increase their value share in the total value chain. We observe that a big marketing broker is emerging. We call it "Destination Marketing Company (DMC)." For example, Acxiom's business covers list-selling data enhancement, analytic and marketing services consulting, data quality assessment, and direct mail fulfillment service.

The essential role of the DMC is to connect sellers and buyers. The DMC is like a big marketing broker. A company can outsource its whole marketing function to the DMC. For example, a number of companies employ outside advertising agencies or marketing research companies to assist its marketing department. Similarly, a company may not need a marketing department by outsourcing all of its marketing function from the DMC. The DMC attempts to find potential customers for its products and services, sends communication messages, and closes the sales. The DMC may be compensated on a commission basis.

The DMC has two major resources: customer information and database marketing knowledge. That is, the DMC should have a huge customer information file that consists of individual and business customers, or at least be particularly astute at obtaining databases from external sources. The DMC is also knowledgeable in all aspects of database marketing techniques such as database management and predictive modeling. If a client company asks the DMC to sell its products, the DMC selects a group of customers from its customer information file to be predicted to have high probability of purchasing the product. In searching for the most efficient way of selling the product, the DMC also selects the best communication and sales channel for each customer. Once the sales are closed, the results are recorded back into the customer information file.

Can we find any empirical evidence of an emerging DMC? As discussed, some external data vendors such as Acxiom and Harte-Hanks are moving in this direction. Companies have been willing to outsource their advertising and marketing research function. And some companies use agencies and brokers to sell their products. However, you can argue that while companies may be willing to outsource some part of their marketing function, they should be responsible for the overall marketing strategy, including the target market and product positioning. Without a solid marketing strategy, products become commodities. For example, the profit margins for OEM manufacturers are very low. They may not have enough resources and capabilities to have their own one-to-one marketing infrastructure but outsource their marketing to the DMC. Therefore, while the Destination Marketing Company has its advantages, it can be a consequence, as well as a cause, of a poor marketing strategy. However, if the DMC is integrated into a firm's marketing group, and that group has a solid grasp of the big picture, the DMC can be extremely valuable.

Chapter 9
Test Design and Analysis

Abstract Another cornerstone of database marketing is testing. Testing provides transparent evidence of whether the program prescribed by sophisticated data analyses actually is successful in the marketplace. Much of the testing in database marketing is extremely simple – select 20,000 customers, randomly divide them in half, run the program for one group and not the other, compare results. However, there are several issues in designing and analyzing database marketing tests; we discuss these in this chapter.

9.1 The Importance of Testing

Capital One may be the one of the most successful credit card companies today (Cohen 2001). The secret to the success is its test-and-learn management philosophy that Capital One calls its Information Based Strategy (IBS). Capital One conducted 45,000 tests in the year 2000, which on average is 120 per day. For example, once Capital One comes up with an idea for a new product offering, it attempts to find a target population by testing the new product with various promotional campaigns to various samples of customers. Based on the test results, Capital One identifies what types of customers are most receptive to the new product and what should be the corresponding promotional campaign. It sometimes even conducts additional tests to fine-tune the strategy. Capital One always makes important marketing decisions (e.g., customized pricing, promotion, and packaging) through a series of tests.

Database marketers should not invest a large amount of company resources unless its expected benefit is greater than the costs. Frequently it may not be easy to calculate the expected benefit because the future is uncertain. Unless you are absolutely sure that it will succeed, you should conduct tests to make an informed decision. The objective of testing is to obtain more information before committing a large amount of resources and, hence, reduce the risk of possible failure. The field of database marketing is particularly amenable to tests because companies have addressable customer databases and hence can randomly assign its customers to various treatment conditions, and observe the results.

While Capital One is the acknowledged leader in database marketing tests and is known for extensive use of testing, most database marketers consider testing an integral part of the way they do business. Database marketers test various decisions including media choice, the development of promotional campaign, the selection of mailing lists, choice of message format, and so on. Moreover, the decision-making process is really "closed-loop." A campaign is revised based on a test, the modified campaign is tested, then implemented, and then the results are used to suggest further tests, and so on. That is, information learned from a test or from full-scale campaigns become inputs to the next tests, which in turn feed the next round of testing and full campaign roll-outs.

9.2 To Test or Not to Test

Probably the first question that should be asked before conducting a test is the most basic – should a test be conducted? As discussed, testing provides information to aid in making correct management decisions. However, information is usually obtained at a cost. Testing costs may include the cost of time delay as well as its administrative cost. For example, to assess the benefit of a loyalty program or a churn management program, one really should run the test for about a year. This is typically not practical. The database marketer must think through whether useful information can be gleaned from a 1 or 2-month test. Hence the decision to collect information or data can be analyzed to see if the expected benefit of the information exceeds its collection costs.

We discuss two approaches for deciding whether to run a test. The first is based on decision analysis and is called the "Value of Information." This potentially quantifies how much the database marketer should be willing to spend on a test. The second approach, "Assessing Mistargeting Costs," is more conceptual, but provides a framework for thinking about whether or not to conduct a test.

9.2.1 Value of Information

Testing provides information. In this section we discuss the fundamental concepts in quantifying the value of information. We first study a decision tree that is very useful for understanding complex decision-making problems. Using the decision tree, we show how to calculate the "value of perfect information" and then extend to the problem of computing the "value of imperfect information."

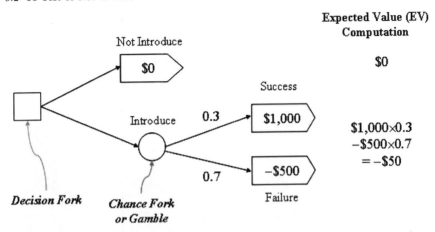

Fig. 9.1 Decision tree for calculating the expected value of a new product launch.

Consider a problem of a new product introduction. The average probability of new product success is known to be 30%. That is, without collecting any additional information on the new product, the success probability of the new product is 30%, and its failure probability is 70%. Suppose that a firm would make $1,000 if the new product succeeds and lose $500 if it fails. Should the firm introduce the new product? If the firm does not introduce the new product, the payoff is $0. On the other hand, if the firm decides to introduce the new product, it will succeed with probability 0.30 and gain a payoff of $1,000 and fail with probability 0.70 and obtain a payoff of −$500. As a result, the expected value or payoff for the new product introduction is −$50 (= $1,000 × 0.3 − $500 × 0.7). Therefore, the firm should not introduce the new product. The decision tree shown in Fig. 9.1 summarizes these calculations.

Decision trees are a graphical way to organize the probabilistic computations leading to the best decision. We draw the decision tree starting with a decision. Should the firm introduce the new product? The decision fork shown as the square box in Fig. 9.1 has two arrows (or alternatives) coming out: introduce or not introduce. We now evaluate the payoffs from each alternative. The outcome of the first alternative or "not introduce" is $0. The payoff from the second branch is more complicated to calculate. If the firm decides to introduce the new product, the payoffs will be determined by chance. We represent this as a circle – called the chance fork – distinguished from the decision fork. Two possible outcomes branching from "introduce" are "success" or "failure." The new product will succeed by 30% of the time and fail 70% of the time. The payoff given "success" is $1,000 and the payoff given "failure" is −$500. Hence the "expected value" or payoff from introducing the new product is −$50 (= $1,000 × 0.3 − $500 × 0.7). Since the expected payoff of "not introduce" ($0) is larger than that of "introduce" (−$50), the firm should not introduce the new product.

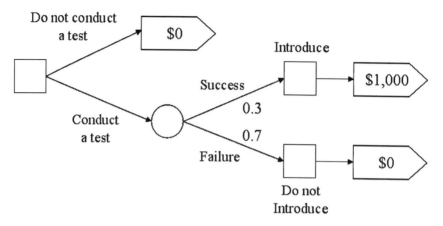

$$\text{Expected Value of Perfect Information}$$
$$= (0.3)(\$1,000) - (0.7)(\$0) = \$300$$

Fig. 9.2 Decision tree for assessing the value of perfect information.

9.2.1.1 Value of Perfect Information

We next consider a case of conducting a test to aid in making decision on introducing a new product. We first consider the value of the perfect test (or information). The perfect test can forecast with 100% accuracy whether the new product will succeed or fail. Figure 9.2 shows the decision tree to determine whether we conduct a test.

If we do not conduct the test, we will not introduce the new product (because the expected value of launching the product is −$50 as calculated above) so that the corresponding payoffs will be $0. However, if we decide to conduct a test, the payoffs will be determined by chance. There is a 30% chance that the new product will actually be a success and 70% chance it will be a failure. Assume the test can perfectly predict whether the new product will succeed or fail. If the new product is forecasted to succeed in the test, it will actually succeed. The firm should then introduce the new product and the resulting payoff will be $1,000. Alternatively, if the new product is predicted to fail in the test, it will actually fail. The firm should then not introduce the new product, and the corresponding payoff will be $0. Therefore, the expected payoff becomes $300(= $1,000 × 0.3 − $0 × 0.7). The value of perfect information (or the perfect test) is $300 since the payoff increases from $0 to $300 by conducting the test. In other words, the firm should conduct the perfect test unless its cost is greater than $300.

9.2.1.2 Value of Imperfect Information

Information provided by a test is rarely perfect. The test cannot provide perfect information for several reasons including small sample size, measurement errors, and so on. Going back to the problem of new product introduction, we assume that the test provides imperfect information. Assume the test correctly forecasts 90% of the time when the new product will actually succeed. So the test will say "failure" 10% of time for the would-be successful new product. In addition, if the new product will actually fail, the test is assumed to predict that the new product will fail 80% of the time, and wrongly forecast that it will succeed 20% of times. What is the value of information provided by this imperfect test?

Before we proceed into the decision tree for imperfect information, let us briefly calculate some important preliminary probabilities. We are able to calculate the joint probability of test results ("Success" or "Failure") *and* actual results (Success or Failure) by multiplying these two probabilities. For example, the (joint) probability that the test says "success" and the new product will actually succeed as P(Product is a Success & Test says "Success") $= P$(Success & "Success") $= P$(Product is a Success) $\times P$(Test says "Success," given that the product actually is a success) $= (0.3) \times (0.9) = 0.27$. Similarly, P(Product is a Success & Test says "Failure") is $(0.3) \times (0.1) = 0.03$ while P(Failure & "Success") $= 0.14$ and P(Failure & "Failure") $= 0.56$.

From these four joint probabilities, we can calculate the probability that the test says that the new product is a "success" or "failure." The probability the test says the product will succeed, P("Success"), equals P(Product is a Success & Tests says "Success") $+ P$ (Product is a Failure & Test says "Success") $= 0.27 + 0.14 = 0.41$. The test will say 41% of the time that the new product is a "Success." When the test says the new product will be a "Success," about 66% of the time $(= 0.27 \div 0.41)$ the product will actually succeed, but 34% of the time $(= 0.14 \div 0.41)$, it will fail. Similarly, P(Test says "Failure") is 0.59 $(= 0.03 + 0.56)$. The test will say 59% of the time that the new product is a "Failure." And when the test says "Failure," about 5% of the time $(= 0.03 \div 0.59)$ it will instead succeed and 95% of the time $(= 0.56 \div 0.59)$ it will fail.

Now we are ready to draw the decision tree for imperfect information. Similar to the case of perfect information, the firm has a decision making problem of whether to conduct a test. The payoffs will be $0 if the firm does not conduct a test. Note that the firm should not introduce the new product without additional information provided by the test. However, if the firm decides to conduct a test, the payoffs will be determined by chance. Figure 9.3 summarizes the decision tree to determine whether we conduct a test.

Given conducting a test, there is a chance fork where P("Success") $= 0.41$ and P("Failure") $= 0.59$. That is, the test will say 41% of times that the new

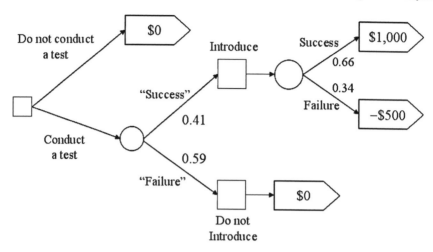

Expected Value of Imperfect Information
$$= (0.41)(\$1,000 \times 0.66 - \$550 \times 0.34) = \$200$$

Fig. 9.3 Decision tree for assessing the value of imperfect information.

product is a "Success" and 59% of times that the new product is a "Failure."
If the test predicts "Success," the firm will face another decision making problem of whether to introduce the new product or not. As computed before, if the test predicts "Success," there is a 66% $(= 0.27 \div 0.41)$ chance it will actually succeed, but a 34% $(= 0.14 \div 0.41)$ chance it will fail. The expected value of introducing the new product if the test says "Success" is $488 (= \$1,000 \times 0.66 - \$500 \times 0.34)$. As a result, the firm should introduce the new product when the test predicts "Success." Similarly, if the test predicts "Failure," the firm will face a decision making problem of whether to introduce the new product or not. If the test predicts "Failure," there is a 5% chance $(= 0.03 \div 0.59)$ it will instead succeed and a 95% chance $(= 0.56 \div 0.59)$ it will actually fail. Hence, the expected value of introducing the new product if the test says "Failure" is $-\$425 (= \$1,000 \times 0.05 - \$500 \times 0.95)$. As a result, the firm should not introduce the new product when the test predicts "Failure."

Combining the above results, if the test says "Success," the firm should introduce the new product and its expected profit is $488. Alternatively, if the test forecasts "Failure," the firm should not introduce the new product and its expected value is $0. In addition, P(Test says "Success") $= 0.41$ and P(Test says "Failure") $= 0.59$. Hence, the expected profit from conducting the imperfect test is $200 (= \$488 \times 0.41 + \$0 \times 0.59)$. That is, the payoff increases from $0 to $200 by conducting the imperfect test. Note that it is less than the value of perfect test ($300). The firm should conduct the imperfect test unless its cost is greater than $200.

The above illustrates a decision-theoretic technique for deciding whether the company should launch a product. The test might be a direct mail offer announcing the product, so this is very relevant to database marketing. The tree-approach is logical and provides a nice "picture" of the decision-making problem. However, it requires key inputs, for example, the probability that the test will say "Success" if indeed the product will succeed, etc. These probabilities typically must be assessed judgmentally. This may seem a bit disconcerting, but the decision-theoretic viewpoint is that managers internally weigh these chances anyway when deciding whether to conduct a test. The value of information approach merely asks the manager to write down those assumptions explicitly and then "play out" rigorously the implications of those assumptions on what the manager should decide.

9.2.2 Assessing Mistargeting Costs

Another way to view the question of whether to test is as follows: There is a correct or optimal decision to make. However, we may not make that optimal decision for two reasons: (1) We decide to conduct a test and the test involves wrong decisions for some or all of the customers involved in the test. This is called the mistargeting costs of the test, or MT_{test}. (2) We roll out what we think is the optimal action on our entire customer base and it turns out to be the wrong decision. This is what we call mistargeting costs of the rollout, or $MT_{rollout}$. We therefore have the following formula:

$$\Pi = Optimal\ Profit - DC_{test} - MT_{test} - MT_{rollout} \qquad (9.1)$$

where:

Π = Total profit
$Optimal\ Profit$ = Profit if the company takes the correct action
DC_{test} = Direct costs of the test
MT_{test} = Mistargeting costs of the test
$MT_{rollout}$ = Mistargeting costs of the rollout

For example, a company may need to decide whether to cross-sell Product A or Product B to its customers. There is a correct decision – Product A, B, or neither – but we don't know which is correct. The direct cost of a test would include administrative costs, the cost of delaying actions that may allow competitors to move faster, and the cost of contacting people for the test, etc. $MT_{rollout}$ would be the deviation we get from optimality because we cross-sell the wrong product or cross-sell when neither of the products are profitable. MT_{test} would be the cost we would incur by taking wrong actions during the test. For example, we might randomly select three groups of customers, each of sample size n, and cross-sell Product A to Group I, Product B to Group II, and neither to Group III. For one of these groups, we've made the right decision, but for two groups we have made the wrong decision. The mistargeting costs occur because for two of the groups, we've wasted resources and may not be able to cross-sell these customers again for this particular campaign (e.g., if you contact the customer for Product A, you can't go back to them later to cross-sell product B).[1]

The level of mistargeting costs will be lower if (1) we have good prior knowledge on the correct course of action, (2) there is low variation in the possible value of a response if the customer responds, and (3) there is low variation in the possible response rates that might be obtained. That is, if there are only a limited number of possible values for the value of response and the response rate, and we have a good prior on it anyway, mistargeting costs will be low. In addition, $MS_{rollout}$ will be lower to the extent that we've conducted a large test, i.e., have a large sample size, because then we're more likely to learn the correct action and won't mistarget on the test. We can summarize these thoughts in the following extension of Equation 9.1:

$$\Pi = Optimal\ Profits - DC_{test}(n) - f(Priors, \sigma_V, \sigma_p)$$
$$\times n - g(Priors, \sigma_V, \sigma_p, n) \times (N - n) \tag{9.2}$$

where:

$f(\bullet) =$ Mistargeting cost per participant in test
$g(\bullet) =$ Mistargeting cost per customer in rollout
$N =$ Total size of customer base
$n =$ Total number of customers participating in the test

Given our discussion above, $f(\bullet)$ and $g(\bullet)$ will both decline as a function of strong priors on the correct action, but increase if there is wide variation in the possible value of a response or the response rate itself.

Equation 9.2 provides the following insights:

- The purpose of a test is to transfer mistargeting costs from the full rollout to a test. The mistargeting costs in the test are incurred on a smaller subset of customers ($n << N$), but we learn from the test ($g(\bullet)$ is decreasing in

---

[1] We are implicitly assuming that the test "destroys" the experimental units. If the customers in a test could be included in the full rollout, MT_{test} would be much smaller. But this is often not the case. Consider a credit card test where Groups A and B are randomly selected to receive two different cards. The optimal credit card might turn out to be the Group B card. But to then go back to Group A and offer them that card would present problems. First, some of them would have signed up for the Group A card. Second, the Group B card may be perceived differently by the Group A customers because they saw the Group A card first. Third, the company may wish to avoid "cluttering" their customers, so may rule out tested customers from the full rollout.

n) so that mistargeting costs in the rollout are minimized, and these lower costs are multiplied by a large number $(N - n)$.

- If we have strong prior information on the right course of action, we need not test because we're pretty sure of the right answer. So why incur the direct costs of testing plus the mistargeting cost of taking the wrong action with one of our experimental groups in the test (MT_{test})?
- If there is wide variation in possible values of either the value of a response or the response rate, then we should test, because there is then a huge plus or minus around the mistargeting costs we could incur with a rollout.
- Too little testing (e.g., small n or not many treatment groups) can hurt because we don't learn enough from the test to decrease mistargeting costs for the rollout. On the other hand, too much testing (e.g., high n or too many treatment groups) can also hurt because we'll incur a lot of mistargeting costs on the test and even though we'll probably learn the correct course of action, we won't be able to apply the lower mistargeting costs on the rollout to enough customers ($N - n$ will not be large enough). So there is probably a middle-ground to be taken with regard to testing.

Hypothetically, Equation 9.2 could be quantified, but we see its value as a framework for providing guidance of whether or not to test. The above bullet points highlight the insights generated from the framework. Generally, a test should be run if (1) prior information on the correct course of action is not available or not reliable, (2) there is wide variation in the possible value of a response, (3) there is wide potential variation in the response rate, (4) the direct costs of running the test, in terms of time, administrative, and contact costs, are low, and (5) the number of customers and treatments needed to learn much from the test is not a significant fraction of our total customer base. For example, if our total customer base is 30,000 and we are thinking of response rates in the range of 1%, we may want to test three groups of 5,000. But that means 15,000 customers are involved in the test, and that is a significant proportion of our total customer base. We could calculate some scenarios depending on potential response value or response rate, but testing half a company's customer base means the direct costs are probably high, and we may only be able to apply our learning to the untested half of our customer base.

9.3 Sampling Techniques

Once we define the population and sampling units for a test, we draw one or more samples from the population. Broadly classifying, there are two types of sampling techniques: probability sampling and nonprobability sampling.

9.3.1 Probability Versus Nonprobability Sampling

A probability sample is where customers ("sampling units") are selected by chance, and, hence every customer in the population has a known chance of being selected for the sample (Boyd et al. 1981). A probability sample can be implemented objectively since customers are selected strictly at random. This probabilistic selection allows us to measure sampling error and consequently make statistical inferences based on the results.

On the other hand, a nonprobability sample is where samples are not selected randomly. Here one selects customers based on the researcher's judgment, convenience, or other nonrandom process. Since subjectivity is involved in the sampling process, we cannot determine the probability of each customer being included in the sample. As a result, we cannot measure sampling error and there is a high risk that statistical inference based on a nonprobability sample will be biased.

There are various types of nonprobability samples including convenience sampling, judgmental sampling, quota sampling, snowball sampling, etc. These samples are frequently used in survey research due to lower sampling costs and faster sample collection, even though they are statistically inferior to a probability sample. On the other hand, most database marketers use the probability samples. Typical database marketers have customer information files and, hence, are able to select random samples quickly and cheaply.

9.3.2 Simple Random Sampling

We focus now on the probability sample. Several kinds of probability samples are in common use. Varying in terms of efficiency, they include simple random sampling, systematic sampling, stratified sampling, cluster sampling and others. High efficiency means that, for the same sample size, a parameter is estimated more accurately, i.e., the standard error of its estimate is lower. Generally, sampling efficiency is positively related to sampling cost. Given the sampling budget, database marketers should select the most efficient sampling technique.

Simple random sampling is the most popular probability sampling technique. Most statistical inference assumes that observations are collected by simple random sampling. With an accurate list of all the firm's customers or prospects, it is cheap and easy to implement. In simple random sampling, every items/names has an equal chance of being included in the sample. That is, simple random sampling is similar to a lottery system. If we sample n items without replacement from the population of size N, this probability is n/N.

Let us explain how simple random sampling works from an illustration. Suppose a database marketer has 10 customers in her customer information file. She wants to select two customers by simple random sampling. To draw a simple random sample, each of ten customers (in the population) is assigned a unique identification number, one through ten for example. Next a random number (r_1) is generated from a 0–1 uniform distribution. If $0 \leq r_1 < 0.1$, then we select the first customer. We select the second customer for $0.1 \leq r_1 < 0.2$, the third for $0.2 \leq r_1 < 0.3$, and so on. After we select the first customer for the sample, another random number (r_2) is generated from a 0–1 uniform distribution. A customer is selected among the remaining nine customers. If $0 \leq r_2 < 1/9$, then we select the first customer. We select the second customer for $1/9 \leq r_2 < 2/9$, the third for $2/9 \leq r_2 < 3/9$, and so on.

Sample selection of size n from the population of size N can be similarly done. Fortunately to database marketers, most commercial software such as SAS have a built-in function of implementing simple random sampling. All database marketers need to do is specify a simple command for performing simple random sampling.

9.3.3 Systematic Random Sampling

Even though simple random sampling will be representative *on average*, there is still a chance it could yield an un-representative sample, especially if the sample size is small. Hence, many database marketers prefer employing other sampling techniques that provide higher statistical efficiency (without incurring not much additional costs) than simple random sampling. An alternative sampling technique frequently used by database marketers is systematic sampling. Systematic sampling provides an easy way to implement a simple random sampling. Moreover, it is often more efficient than simple random sampling, as explained below.

Let us illustrate systematic sampling by an example. Suppose we want to sample n out of the population size N. First, we determine the sampling interval (k) by rounding N/n to the nearest integer. Next, we randomly select a starting point and select every kth item successively in the target population. For example, if N is 1,000 and n is 100, then the sampling interval k should be 10.[2] Then an item between 1 and 10 is randomly selected. If this number is 8, the sample of 100 customers will consist of customer 8, 18, 28, and up to 998.

Systematic sampling is statistically more efficient than simple random sampling when the ordering of elements in target population is related to the variable of interest. For example, if the customer information file is ordered with respect to their cumulative purchase amounts, systematic sampling will evenly select customers with various purchase amounts. It increases the sample representativeness. On the other hand, a simple random sampling may be unrepresentative because it may sample only heavy users or

---

[2] Systematic sampling is often called a Nth name sampling in direct marketing applications. Here N represents a sampling interval k.

a disproportionate number of heavy users. However, if the population is ordered in a way unrelated to the variable of interest – for example, customers ordered alphabetically – systematic sampling will provide almost identical sampling error to simple random sampling (Malhotra 1993).

Systematic sampling yields a probability sample in that every element in the target population has a known and equal chance of being included in the sample. It is the most popular sampling technique among database marketers since it is frequently more efficient than simple random sampling without incurring additional costs.

9.3.4 Other Sampling Techniques

There are other probability sampling techniques such as cluster sampling, stratified sampling, area sampling, sequential sampling, etc. These are not very popular among database marketers, but among survey researchers.

Researchers often use cluster sampling rather than simple random sampling to save on survey costs. In cluster sampling, samples are selected in groups. For example, suppose a researcher needs a sample of 1,000 representative US customers for in-depth personal interviews. Simple random samples will provide 1,000 customers who live all over the country. It is not economically sensible to interview 3 customers in New York, 5 in Los Angeles, and so on. In cluster sampling, the USA is divided into several clusters or blocks – using zip codes, for example. And randomly select a manageable number of clusters, say 10, and select 100 customers for each of the selected cluster. Cluster sampling will significantly reduce the sampling costs by selecting a small number of clusters in the first stage, but there is a danger of sample misrepresentation. Customers in a block or a cluster tend to be similar in demographic characteristics. Hence, if clusters covering big metropolitan cities are only selected in the first stage, customers selected from those clusters in the second stage may not be representative of average US customers.

The goal of stratified sampling is to increase statistical efficiency by increasing the sample representativeness. Database marketers are beginning to use this sampling more frequently today. Stratified sampling first divides the target population into several segments with respect to one or more common characteristics and then randomly selects customers from each one of these segments. For example, the customer base might be segmented several groups based on profitability, a segment below $200, a segment of $200–300, and so on. Stratified sampling guarantees more representative samples with respect to the criterion used to segment the target population. Statistical efficiency will be greater when the customers within each segment are more homogeneous. There are several strategies of stratified sampling. The most popular is the proportional allocation which uses a sampling fraction in each of the strata proportional to that of the total population. For example, if the population consists of 70% in the female stratum and 30% in the male stratum, the relative size of the two samples should reflect this proportion. See Lehmann et al. (1998) for more details on stratified as well as cluster sampling.

9.4 Determining the Sample Size

Determining the test sample size is not an easy task. Marketers are interested in knowing the true parameter value (e.g., response rate for the direct mail offer) for the target population. Considering the cost of testing, they take small samples from the target population and attempt to estimate the true parameter. The larger the sample size, the closer the estimate will be to the true parameter value. However, the larger sample size increases the cost of testing (see Sect. 9.2.2). There is a trade-off between the accuracy of the test results and the cost of conducting tests.

In order to determine the optimal sample size, marketers need to consider various qualitative and quantitative factors including the cost/benefit of the correct decision-making, the level of prior knowledge for the true parameter value, the (expected) incident/response rates, the desired level of precision, etc. For example, larger sample size will be preferred if the benefit of correct decision-making is great.

Considering the complexity of determining the sample size, several authors have often provided some practical guidelines. For example, Schmid (1995) has suggested a rule of thumb, so-called the Rule of 100. It says that one should have a minimum of 100 responses for each cell. According to this rule, if you expect a 2% response, the sample size should be at least 5,000 to get 100 responses. Alternatively, Levin and Zahavi (1996) suggest that the sample size should be around 10% of the size of the population.

Although these heuristic rules are practically simple in determining the sample size, there is no compelling evidence on why these rules correctly yield an optimal sample size. In essence, these rules intentionally ignore various factors influencing the optimal sample size in order to provide a simple guidance to practitioners.

9.4.1 Statistical Approach

A more formal method to determine the sample size is based on traditional statistical inference. Most marketing research textbooks provide the statistical formula to determine the sample size required to achieve a given level of precision at a desired level of confidence (Tull and Hawkins 1993). The formula generally is provided in two forms: one for the estimation of means (e.g., mean order amount) and the other for proportions (e.g., response probability). The sample size for mean can be derived from the following:

$$z = (\overline{X} - \mu)/\sigma_{\overline{X}} = D/\sigma_{\overline{X}} = \frac{D}{\sigma/\sqrt{n}} \tag{9.3a}$$

where z is the "z-value" from the standard normal distribution corresponding to the desired level of confidence, $\overline{X}$ is the sample mean, μ is the population mean, $\sigma_{\overline{X}}$ is the standard error of the sample mean, σ is the population standard error, D is the level of precision, and n is the sample size. Similarly, in the case of proportions, we use the following formula:

$$z = (p - \pi)/\sigma_p = D/\sigma_p = \frac{D}{\sqrt{\pi(1 - \pi)/n}} \tag{9.3b}$$

where p is the sample proportion, π is the population proportion, and σ_p is the standard error of the sample proportion. From Equations 9.3a, b, we can solve for the sample size for the sample mean and the sample proportion to achieve a given level of precision (D) at a desired level of confidence (z):

$$\text{Sample size for estimating means: } n = \sigma^2 z^2/D^2 \tag{9.4a}$$
$$\text{Sample size for estimating proportions: } n = \pi(1 - \pi)z^2/D^2 \tag{9.4b}$$

For example, the population (or true) response rate for the catalog (π) is 1%. And the cataloger wants 95% confidence (hence, its z-value is 1.96) and allows the error (of the estimate) to be within 20% of the population response rate. Then, the optimal sample size should be about $\{(0.01)(0.99)(1.96)^2\}/\{(0.2)(0.01)\}^2 \approx 9,508.$[3]

If more than 10% of the population is included in the sample, the finite population corrections to the above formula are often applied. That is, the correction factor should be incorporated into Equations 9.3a, b as in the following.

$$z = \frac{D}{\sigma\sqrt{(N - n)/(N - 1)}/\sqrt{n}} \tag{9.5a}$$

$$z = \frac{D}{\sqrt{\pi(1 - \pi)}\sqrt{(N - n)/(N - 1)}/\sqrt{n}} \tag{9.5b}$$

where N is the size of the population. Solving Equations 9.5a, b with respect to n, we have:

$$n_c = \frac{nN}{N + n - 1} \tag{9.6}$$

---

[3] Note Equation 9.4b, the case of proportions, is somewhat paradoxical because it says we need to know the true response rate, π, in order to figure out the sample size we need to estimate π! However, often managers have some idea what to expect for a response rate. For example, if one were trying to estimate the response rate to a direct mailing, and management was willing to assume the response rate will be approximately 1%, the value $\pi^o = 0.01$ would be inserted in Equation 9.4b, where π^o is the a priori "guesstimate" of the true proportion π.

Table 9.1 Optimal sample sizes for the sample proportion p and the precision D

π^{oa}	$D = x \% \text{ of } \pi^{\mathrm{oa}}$			
	$x = 5\%$	$x = 10\%$	$x = 20\%$	$x = 30\%$
0.01	152,127[b]	38,031	9,508	4,226
0.05	29,196	7,299	1,825	811
0.10	13,830	3,457	864	384
0.20	6,147	1,537	384	171

[a] π^{o} represents an *a priori* estimate for the true proportion π, to be estimated by the sample proportion p.

[b] The samples sizes are calculated assuming $z = 1.96$, or 95% confidence.

where n_c is the adjusted sample size and n is the unadjusted sample size in Equations 9.3a, b. Note that the population size is very large, no correction is required since $n_c \approx n$.

One needs to determine three unknown values to determine the optimal sample size statistically: the population variance, the degree of confidence, and the desired level of precision. Estimates of the population variance, σ^2 or $\pi(1 - \pi)$, sometimes are available from similar previous studies (for the case of proportions, see footnote 3). If there is no secondary source, one may conduct a pilot study or simply rely on researcher's judgment. The two other unknowns are determined based on the researcher's subjective judgment. That is, we need to specify the level of precision (D) that is the maximum permissible difference between the sample mean/proportion and the population mean/proportion. We also need to specify the z value associated with the confidence level. For example, for a 95% confidence level, the probability that the difference between the population mean/proportion and the sample mean/proportion will be within the specified precision is 95%. The corresponding z value is 1.96. Table 9.1 shows the samples sizes required to estimate the population proportion π at a level of precision D.

In various database marketing applications, the level of confidence is typically assumed to be 95% (corresponding to $z = 1.96$). The true proportion π depends on application, but a response probability of 1% is not unusual in direct mail solicitations. The level of precision D may be acceptable if it is within 20% of the actual proportion. For example, given the true response rate of 10%, the estimated response rate of 8–12% is acceptable. Table 9.1 indicates that the optimal sample sizes for a typical database marketing application should be in the 1,000s, not 100s.

Summarizing, the statistical way of determining the sample size is theoretically sound. However, it is not very practical in that three unknown parameters should be specified quite subjectively to determine the sample size.

9.4.2 Decision Theoretic Approach

Considering both the statistical properties of the test samples and the economic factors, Pfeifer (1998) has proposed a practical method to determine the optimal sample size. His approach is decision-theoretic in that the optimal sample size is considered a business decision and, hence, the economic trade-offs should be carefully evaluated for the increase of sample size. Here we briefly describe Pfeifer's approach to determining the sample size. Even though Pfeifer applied the approach to a (direct) test-mailing problem, it can easily be applied to other database marketing situations.

9.4.2.1 Problem Definition

A direct marketer needs to decide the number of names to mail in a test (the sample size $= n$) from a total of N names (the size of population $= N$). The fixed cost for the test mailing is A and its unit variable cost is C. Let r be the number of responses from the test mailing and V be the net present value to the firm for a given response. Once r is observed, the direct marketer will decide whether to send the mail to the remaining $N - n$ names in the population. The fixed and variable cost for the rollout mailing is reasonably assumed to be the same as in the test mailing. Let r_R be the number of responses to the rollout mailing and V_R be the net present value to the firm for the corresponding rollout response.

9.4.2.2 Prior Response Probability

The key parameter of Pfeifer's model is the uncertain population response rate, π. The population response rate is the unknown probability that a randomly chosen name will respond to the offer. From her experience, the direct marketer is assumed to have a prior distribution for π. More specifically, Pfeifer assumes that the prior distribution of π follows a beta distribution with parameters $a = n_0 \pi_0$ and $b = n_0 (1 - \pi_0)$.

$$f(\pi) = \frac{\pi^{a-1}(1 - \pi)^{b-1}}{B(a,b)}, \quad 0 \le \pi \le 1, a > 0, b > 0 \qquad (9.7)$$

The parameters a and b, or n_0 and π_0, are the means by which the direct marketer expresses her prior knowledge on the population response rate π. These two parameters are the required inputs to determine the optimal sample size in Pfeifer's model. The parameter π_0 may be interpreted as the direct marketer's best guess for the population response rate and the parameter n_0 as the level of uncertainty in her guess.[4] The prior information incorporated in π_0 and n_0 is equivalent to the information that can be obtained from $\pi_0 n_0$ responses out of the (test) mailing to n_0 customers. For example, suppose

---

[4] The mean of a beta distribution is $a(a + b)^{-1} = \pi_0$. Hence, π_0 can be regarded as the direct marketer's best guess for the population response rate. Similarly, the variance of a beta distribution is $ab(a + b)^{-2}(a + b + 1)^{-1} = \pi_0 (1 - \pi_0)(n_0 + 1)^{-1}$. Hence, n_0 measures the level of uncertainty.

that 1,000 customers receive catalogs and 20 customers respond. Then the population response rate is estimated to be $\pi_0 = 0.05$ and the variance of π_0 is $\pi_o(1 - \pi_o)/n_o = (0.05)(0.95)/1,000$. Therefore, values of $\pi_0 = 0.05$ and $n_0 = 1,000$ would mean that the decision-maker was 95% confident the true response rate was somewhere within $\pm 1.96\sqrt{(0.05 \times 0.95)/1,000} = \pm 0.018$ of $\pi_0 = 0.05$.

Given the prior distribution on π, the direct marketer sends test mailings to n names and gets r responses. Observing the test mailing results, the direct marketer updates her estimate on π. Her updated probability forecast of π or the posterior distribution of π can be written as

$$f(\pi|n,r) = \frac{\pi^{r+a-1}(1 - \pi)^{n-r+b-1}}{B(r+a, n-r+b)} \tag{9.8}$$

9.4.2.3 Calculating the Expected Rollout Profit

The direct marketer will decide whether to roll out to the remaining $N - n$ names in the population after she gets the test mailing results. The profit from the rollout is

$$\text{Profit}_R = V_R r_R - (N - n)C \tag{9.9}^5$$

A risk-neutral marketer will roll out if the expected rollout profit, $E(\text{Profit}_R)$, is greater than zero. Hence, we compute the expected number of responses from the rollout mailing, $E(r_R)$. Noticing that r_R is distributed as a beta-binomial, its mean can be written as (Johnson and Kotz 1969)

$$E(r_R) = (N - n)\frac{r + a}{(r + a) + (n - r + b)} = (N - n)\frac{r + n_0\pi_0}{n_0 + n} \tag{9.10}$$

Therefore, the expected rollout profit is

$$E(\text{Profit}_R) = V_R E(r_R) - (N - n)C = (N - n)\left[V_R\frac{n_0\pi_0 + r}{n_0 + n} - C\right] \tag{9.11}$$

As mentioned, the direct marketer should roll out the population if $E(\text{Profit}_R) > 0$. Hence, the direct marketer should roll out the list if

$$r > C(N - n)(n_0 + n)[V_R(N - n)]^{-1} - n_0\pi_0 \tag{9.12}$$

Let r^* be the smallest integer that satisfies the Equation 9.11. Then the direct marketer should roll out if the number of responses from the test mailing is greater than and equal to r^* and should not if the number is less than r^*.

---

[5] Pfeifer (1998) included the fixed cost term for test mailing (A) in Equation 9.9. However, we delete it to simplify our exposition. Our key results do not change without the fixed cost. In addition, Pfeifer himself mentioned that fixed costs can be negligible if the test mailing is included as part of a regular mailing.

9.4.2.4 Selecting the Optimal Sample Size

In order to determine the optimal test sample size, let us consider the expected profit including both the test and the rollout mailing. If $r < r^*$ for the test mailing result, the direct marketer will not roll out and, hence, the profit (from the test) becomes $\text{Profit}_T = Vr - nC$. Alternatively, if $r \geq r^*$ for the test mailing result, the direct marketer will roll out. And the resulting profit (from both the test and the rollout) becomes $\text{Profit}_T + \text{Profit}_R = Vr - nC + V_R E(r_R) - (N - n)C$. That is, the total profit is a function of r. Since the probability distribution of r is the beta-binomial, the expected (total) profit becomes

$$
\begin{aligned}
& E(\text{Profit}_T + \text{Profit}_R | n) \\
&= \sum_{r=0}^{r^*-1} g(r|n)(Vr - nC) + \sum_{r=r^*}^{n} g(r|n)[Vr - nC + V_R E(r_R) - (N - n)C] \\
&= Vn\pi_0 - nC + \sum_{r=r^*}^{n} g(r|n)[V_R(N - n)(n_0\pi_0 + r)(n_0 + n)^{-1} - (N - n)C]
\end{aligned}
$$

$$(9.13)$$

where $g(r|n)$ is the beta-binomial density for r.

9.4.2.5 Illustrative Example

Given the test sample size n, the direct marketer can calculate the expected profit from Equation 9.13. To find the optimal sample size, the direct marketer evaluates Equation 9.12 for various candidate values of n and selects the one that maximizes the expected profit. Let us provide an illustrative example given by Pfeifer (1998). A house list consists of 50,000 customers and it costs $1 to mail. The direct marketer's best guess for the population response rate (π_0) is 2% and the corresponding level of uncertainty (n_0) is assumed to be 200. With this prior specification, Pfeifer implicitly assumes that the response rate of a given house list is a randomly drawn number from a beta distribution with $\pi_0 = 2\%$ and $n_0 = 200$. The responses to the mailing are worth $50 each. So mailing to all 50,000 customers in the list will result in $0 expected profit. It will cost $50,000 $(= \$1 \times 50,000)$ which is equal to the expected revenue of $50,000 $(= \$50 \times 2\% \times 50,000)$. Without a test mailing, the direct marketer will be indifferent between mailing to all 50,000 customers and doing nothing.

The values of the parameters in Equation 9.12 are all determined. The appropriate parameter values are: $N = 50,000, C = \$1, V = V_R = \$50, \pi_0 = 0.02$ and $n_0 = 200$. Figure 9.4 shows the plots of expected profits as a function of the test sample sizes n. It indicates that a test sample size of about 2,000 maximizes the expected profit. The expected profit with the test sample of

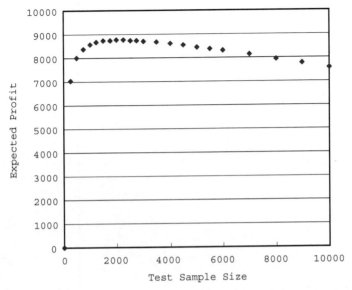

Fig. 9.4 Test sample size versus expected profit using Pfeifer (1998) Model (From Pfeifer 1998).

0 is $0, because the expected response rate of a house list is the breakeven response rate. Also, the expected profit is $0 if the test sample size $N = 50,000$, because there would then be no rollout and the expected profits for the test would just depend on the expected response rate which is at breakeven. For any test sample sizes between 0 to 50,000, we have the option of rolling it or not based on the sample information from the testing results. If the test indicates the full roll-out will not be unprofitable, the manager will lose money on the test but avoid the even larger loss of an incorrect roll-out. However, if the test indicates the full roll-out will be profitable, the manager makes money on the test and then makes even more on the full launch. That is, there is 50% chance that the test results suggest the full roll-out and 50% chance that the test results suggest no roll-out. But we lose some money when the test results are bad, whereas we can make big money when the test results are good. As a result, the manager on average makes money through testing, and the optimal test size is about 2,000 out of a population of 50,000, or 4%.

It also is important to note that the expected profit numbers that emerge from this analysis combine subjective and objective information. In a classical statistical sense, the expected profits could be a biased estimate of the true expected profits if the manager's prior for the response rate does not on average equal the true response rate. For example, if the manager's prior is overly optimistic, and overly confident in that prior, the test information will have little impact on the updated response rate and the expected profits will be overly optimistic. However, it can be argued that managers learn the *average* response rates across lists, and so their prior is not overly optimistic, and if they are not confident in the performance of the particular list to be tested, they can indicate low confidence through a small value for n_0.[6]

9.4.2.6 Extending Pfeifer's Model

This approach is very promising but could be extended in several ways. Foremost would be the incorporation of a control group. Note that the method assumes a rollout should occur if the expected profit from the rollout is greater than zero. However, this assumes that if no action is taken, no profit is generated. This may be the case for a direct marketer who is thinking of a program of contacting people who are not current customers, which is the orientation of Pfeifer's paper. But if the company has current customers, there will be profits from those customers even if the action is not taken. For example, if Product A is not cross-sold to the customer, the customer may buy it anyway through a different channel. These profits are uncertain as are the profits that might accrue from directly contacting the customer. Therefore there is uncertainty if the action is taken or not taken. This necessitates a control group. The question then becomes, what should be the size of the test group and the control group. Control groups are often used in testing and it seems the above approach could be extended to this situation.

Another extension would be to incorporate uncertainty in the value of the customer, V. If the decision is whether to send a catalog, V represents customer expenditure given the customer responds. This number will also be uncertain. An extension would be to incorporate priors on this quantity as well. Obviously, the more diffuse those priors are, the higher sample size will be needed.

In summary, Pfeifer's approach is a practical tool for deciding sample size, directly applicable to customer acquisition tests. Extending the method as discussed above would provide important and interesting avenues for future research. It also should be noted that the usefulness of the model hinges on the validity of the manager's prior. If the manager states a highly optimistic prior with great certainty, he or she is likely to calculate positive expected profits from a roll-out no matter what the test results, and lose money. The key point is that the expected profit calculations are a combination of objective evidence from the test and subjective judgment encompassed in the prior, and therefore essentially a subjective judgment of expected profits. Having noted this limitation, the model is still valuable because managers use judgments all the time in deciding whether to undertake a full roll-out. The model merely captures those judgments rigorously and calculates the implications for profitability.

---

[6] The authors thank Phil Pfeifer for helpful insights on presenting and discussing this model.

9.5 Test Designs

Experimental research generally consists of three phases: the experimental or planning phase, the design phase, and the analysis phase. In this section we focus our attention on the design phase and somewhat on the analysis phase. Once the objective of the research is set in the planning phase, the research problem should be expressed in terms of a testable hypothesis. For example, a cataloger would like to know whether the new catalog design increases the response rates among current customers. A mobile telecommunication service provider wants to know whether churn rates are higher among customers aged below 25. It is then time to design the experiment. In this section we study the test designs that are most popular among database marketers.

9.5.1 Single Factor Experiments

Single factor design is the simplest test design and is fundamental for understanding more complex designs. This section discusses single factor experiments in which no restrictions are placed on randomization. Randomization refers to the random assignment of sample units to experimental (or control) groups by using random numbers. Treatment conditions are also randomly assigned to experimental groups. For example, a credit card company is contemplating whether to make a promotional offer to increase card usage. It comes up with an idea of offering coupons on gas purchases. Ten randomly selected customers are given \$5 coupons and another ten randomly selected customers are offered \$10 coupon on gas purchase. It randomly selects an additional ten customers who do not receive any promotional offers. This is called a control group.[7] The card usages of 30 customers for a month after the experiment are shown in Table 9.2. Then single factor model becomes

$$Y_{ij} = \mu + \tau_j + \varepsilon_{ij} \tag{9.14}$$

where Y_{ij} represents the ith observation $(i = 1, 2, \ldots, n_j)$ on the jth treatment $(j = 1, 2, \ldots, k)$. For example, the third observation in control condition (Y_{31}) is 600 in Table 9.2. μ is a common effect for the whole experiment, τ_j is the treatment effect of jth condition, and ε_{ij} is a random error.

We usually assume that the error term ε_{ij} is distributed as $i.i.d.$ normal with zero mean and the common variance. That is, $\varepsilon_{ij} \sim N(0, \sigma^2)$. It is also assumed that the sum of all treatment effects is zero, or $\sum_{j=1}^{k} \tau_j = 0$. To

---

[7] In practice, a control group is defined as the group that receives the current level of marketing activity or receives no treatment at all. A control group is included to ascertain the true *incremental* effect of the treatments versus no treatment. For example, customers still use credit cards without promotional coupons. Hence, the true experimental effect of promotional coupon offers is the incremental card usage from the promotional coupon over the credit card usages among the control group customers.

Table 9.2 Credit card usage data for single factor experiment

Customer Id	Treatment conditions	Card usage
1	Control	$500
2	Control	$550
3	Control	$600
4	Control	$450
5	Control	$500
6	Control	$400
7	Control	$450
8	Control	$550
9	Control	$550
10	Control	$500
11	$5 coupon	$550
12	$5 coupon	$600
13	$5 coupon	$700
14	$5 coupon	$650
15	$5 coupon	$700
16	$5 coupon	$550
17	$5 coupon	$750
18	$5 coupon	$650
19	$5 coupon	$600
20	$5 coupon	$700
21	$10 coupon	$700
22	$10 coupon	$750
23	$10 coupon	$700
24	$10 coupon	$800
25	$10 coupon	$600
26	$10 coupon	$700
27	$10 coupon	$750
28	$10 coupon	$800
29	$10 coupon	$700
30	$10 coupon	$750

describe the basics of a one-way analysis of variance (ANOVA), we rewrite
Equation 9.14:

$$Y_{ij} = \mu + (\mu_{.j} - \mu) + (Y_{ij} - \mu_{.j}) \text{ or } Y_{ij} - \mu = (\mu_{.j} - \mu) + (Y_{ij} - \mu_{.j}) \quad (9.15)$$

where $\mu_{.j}$ is the expected value of Y_{ij} given the customer receives treatment
j. Comparing Equations 9.14 and 9.15, the jth treatment effect τ_j can be
represented by $\mu_{.j} - \mu$.

Since the means in Equation 9.15 are not known, they are estimated from
the n_j observations for each treatment condition j. These observations can be
used to estimate the grand mean μ and the treatment means $\mu_{.j}$. Restating
Equation 9.15 in terms of "sample means," we obtain:

$$Y_{ij} - \overline{Y}_{..} = (\overline{Y}_{.j} - \overline{Y}_{..}) + (Y_{ij} - \overline{Y}_{.j}) \quad (9.16)$$

where $\overline{Y}_{..}$ is the sample (grand) mean over all observations, $\overline{Y}_{.j}$ is the sample
mean over the observations with treatment condition j. The equation says

that the deviation of each observation from the overall mean consists of two parts: the deviation of the treatment mean from the overall mean and its deviation from its own treatment mean.

Taking squares and summations of Equation 9.16, we have:

$$\sum_{j=1}^{k}\sum_{i=1}^{n_j}(Y_{ij} - \overline{Y}_{..})^2 = \sum_{j=1}^{k}\sum_{i=1}^{n_j}(\overline{Y}_{.j} - \overline{Y}_{..})^2 + \sum_{j=1}^{k}\sum_{i=1}^{n_j}(Y_{ij} - \overline{Y}_{.j})^2 \quad (9.17)$$

The term in the left is called the total sum of squares while the first term in the right is called the between groups/treatments sum of squares and the second term is called the within groups sum of squares or the error sum of squares. Equation 9.17 says that the total sum of squares is equal to the between groups sum of squares plus the error sum of squares.

The main interest in single factor experiment is to test whether there are treatment effects. That is, we conduct a one-way analysis of variance test where the hypothesis to be tested is H_0: $\tau_j = 0$ for all j. If the hypothesis is accepted, we conclude that there are no treatment effects and all the variations in the dependent variable Y_{ij} are explained by the grand mean μ and the random error ε_{ij}.

Going back to the Equation 9.17, it can be shown that the between-group sum of squares divided by its degree of $(k-1)$, called mean squares, is distributed as chi-square. Similarly, the error sum of squares divided by its degree of freedom $\sum_{j=1}^{k}(n_j - 1) = (N - k)$ is also distributed as chi-square. And since these two chi-squares are independent, their ratio can be shown to be distributed as F with degrees of freedom, $(k - 1)$ and $(N - k)$. Therefore, if H_0 is true, we can test the hypothesis by evaluating the following quantity.

$$F_{k-1,N-k} = \frac{\sum_{j=1}^{k}\sum_{i=1}^{n_j}(\overline{Y}_{.j} - \overline{Y}_{..})^2/(k - 1)}{\sum_{j=1}^{k}\sum_{i=1}^{n_j}(Y_{ij} - \overline{Y}_{.j})^2/(N - k)} \quad (9.18)$$

The quantity in the numerator becomes larger when the deviations of the treatment means from the grand mean become larger. Hence, we reject the null hypothesis if the quantity in the Equation 9.18 is larger than the critical region $F_{1-\alpha}$, where α is the designated significance level.

An one-way analysis of variance is applied to the credit usage data in Table 9.2 and its results are summarized in Table 9.3. The test statistic for the hypothesis H_0: $\tau_j = 0$ for all $j = 1, 2, 3$ is $F^* = 124,000/3,916.7 \approx 31.7$ that is larger than the critical value $F_{2,27} = 5.45$ at the significant level $\alpha = 0.01$.[8] Hence, we reject the hypothesis and conclude that there are statistically

---

[8] Most of statistical software can handle an one-way analysis of variance and provide the ANOVA summary table similar to Table 9.3. See "PROC ANOVA" in SAS, "ANOVA Single" under Data Analysis & Tools in EXCEL, and "one-way ANOVA" under Compare Means & Statistics in SPSS.

Table 9.3 One-way ANOVA for credit card usage data

Source of variation	Degree of freedom	Sum of squares	Mean squares
Between groups	2	248,000	124,000
Within groups	27	105,750	3,916.7
Total	29	353,750	–

$F^* = 124,000/3,916.7 \approx 31.7 > F_{2,27} = 5.45$ at the significant level $\alpha = 0.01$

significant differences in credit card usages among different amount of coupon offers on gas purchases.

9.5.2 Multifactor Experiments: Full Factorials

Database marketers often need information on a wide variety of strategic issues. For example, a credit card company manager attempts to devise an optimal promotional package to increase credit card usages among current customers. She has more than one tactic of interest. For example, there might be three tactics, or three factors to test in the experiment: (1) the use of coupons for gas purchases, (2) the use of cash rebates, and (3) the use of "affinity" cards. The manager is interested in the impact of all three of these marketing strategies on credit card usage rate. One method is to hold all other factors constant except one and observe the effects over several levels of this chosen factor. Alternatively, one can perform a full-factorial experiment in which all levels of a given factor are combined with all levels of every other factor.

A full-factorial experiment is superior to the one-at-a-time experiment in several aspects (Hicks 1982). A factorial experiment will provide greater statistical efficiency since all data are used in computing the effect of each factor. In addition, we can evaluate interactions among factors with a factorial experiment. This design component is particularly important because we frequently observe synergistic effects among marketing variables.

To see how a full-factorial experiment works, let us again consider an example of a credit card company that is considering a promotional offer to increase the card usage. Now the manager wants to look at the effects of two promotional variables on card usage: coupons for gas purchases and a cash rebate for credit card usage. Three levels of coupon amount ($0, $5 and $10) and two levels of cash rebate (0% and 1%) are considered. That is, it is a 3×2 factorial experiment, yielding six possible combinations of coupon amount and rebate level. Five customers are randomly selected at each of these six treatment conditions. Table 9.4 shows the (monthly) credit card usage of these 30 customers after the experiment.

The mathematical model for this experiment can be written as

$$Y_{ijk} = \mu + \tau_{jk} + \varepsilon_{i(jk)} \tag{9.19}$$

Table 9.4 Credit card usage data for factorial experiment

Customer Id	1st treatment conditions	2nd treatment conditions	Card usage
1	Control	Control	$450
2	Control	Control	$500
3	Control	Control	$450
4	Control	Control	$400
5	Control	Control	$450
6	Control	$5 coupon	$500
7	Control	$5 coupon	$500
8	Control	$5 coupon	$600
9	Control	$5 coupon	$400
10	Control	$5 coupon	$500
11	Control	$10 coupon	$500
12	Control	$10 coupon	$550
13	Control	$10 coupon	$550
14	Control	$10 coupon	$500
15	Control	$10 coupon	$500
16	1% cash rebate	Control	$500
17	1% cash rebate	Control	$450
18	1% cash rebate	Control	$500
19	1% cash rebate	Control	$450
20	1% cash rebate	Control	$470
21	1% cash rebate	$5 coupon	$650
22	1% cash rebate	$5 coupon	$700
23	1% cash rebate	$5 coupon	$700
24	1% cash rebate	$5 coupon	$650
25	1% cash rebate	$5 coupon	$600
26	1% cash rebate	$10 coupon	$800
27	1% cash rebate	$10 coupon	$850
28	1% cash rebate	$10 coupon	$900
29	1% cash rebate	$10 coupon	$800
30	1% cash rebate	$10 coupon	$950

where the subscript $j(j = 1, 2, 3)$ represents the levels of coupon amounts, the subscript $k(k = 1, 2)$ represents the levels of cash rebates and the subscript $i(i = 1, 2, 3, 4, 5)$ represents the number of observations/customers for each treatment condition j and k. For example, Y_{422} is 650 in Table 9.4. Similar to the single-factor experiment, μ is the grand mean for the whole experiment, τ_{jk} is the treatment effect for jth coupon condition and kth rebate condition, and $\varepsilon_{i(jk)}$ is a random error.

Treating each treatment condition as unique, the model in Equation 9.19 does not consider the factorial or multifactor nature of the experiment. That is, we apply a one-way ANOVA to the data in Table 9.4 and summarize the results in Table 9.5a.

The test statistic for the hypothesis H_0: $\tau_{jk} = 0$ for all $j = 1, 2, 3$ and $k = 1, 2$ is $F^* \approx 54.0$ ($= 122,687.5/2,270.8$) that is statistically significant at the significance level of 1%. Hence, we reject the hypothesis and conclude that there are statistically significant differences in credit card usages among different coupon offers and cash rebates.

Table 9.5a One-way ANOVA for factorial data

Source of variation	Degree of freedom	Sum of squares	Mean squares
Between groups	5	613,437.5	122,687.5
Within groups	24	54,500	2,270.8
Total	29	353,750	–

We can slightly modify Equation 9.19 to represent the multi-factor nature of the factorial experiments. Decomposing τ_{jk} into the main effect of coupon treatment condition (C_j), the main effect of cash rebate treatment condition (R_k), and their interactions (CR_{jk}), Equation 9.19 can be rewritten as

$$Y_{ijk} = \mu + C_j + R_k + CR_{jk} + \varepsilon_{i(jk)} \qquad (9.20)$$

The two-way ANOVA is the appropriate tool to analyze the model in Equation 9.20, the general model for a two-way factorial experiment. The main interests in two-way factorial experiment are three tests: (1) whether there is a main treatment effect of coupon $(H_0 : C_j = 0$ for all $j = 1, 2, 3)$, (2) whether there is a main treatment effect of cash rebate $(H_0 : R_k = 0$ for all $k = 1, 2)$, and (3) whether there is an interaction effect between coupon and cash rebate $(H_0 : CR_{jk} = 0$ for all $j = 1, 2, 3$ and $k = 1, 2)$. If the hypothesis $H_0 : C_j = 0$ is accepted, we conclude that coupon amounts on gas purchase will not affect on credit card usage. Similar conclusions will be derived from other tests.

We apply a two-way ANOVA to the data in Table 9.4 and summarize the results in Table 9.5b.

The between group sum of squares in Table 9.5a (613,437.5) is now decomposed into three sums of squares in Table 9.5b: between coupons sum of squares (258,875), between rebates sum of squares (229,687.5) and the coupons × rebates interaction sum of squares (124,875). Table 9.5b also shows that each of the two main effects and the interaction effect are statistically significant at the 1% level.

The significant coupons × rebates interaction implies that a change in one factor produces a different change in the response variable at one level of the other factor than at the other levels of this factor. The interaction can be more clearly seen in Fig. 9.5 where the mean card usages (over each of five

Table 9.5b Two-way ANOVA for factorial data

Source of variation	Degree of freedom	Sum of squares	Mean squares	F
Between coupons	2	258,875	129,437.5	57.0
Between rebates	1	229,687.5	229,687.5	101.1
Coupons × rebates	2	124,875	62,437.5	27.5
Errors	24	54,500	2,270.8	–
Total	29	667,937.5	–	–

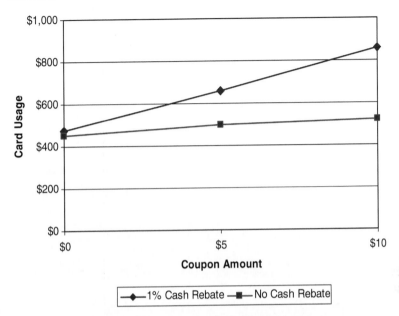

Fig. 9.5 Interaction in a factorial experiment.

customers) for each treatment condition are graphed. Given no cash rebates, the mean card usages are $450 for no coupons, $500 for $5 coupons, $520 for $10 coupons. On the other hand, with 1% cash rebates, the mean card usages are $475 for no coupons, $660 for $5 coupons, $860 for $10 coupons. That is, there exist positive synergies between coupons and cash rebates. Or coupons are more effective when they are used with 1% cash rebates. If there are no coupons × rebates interactions, the card usage plot of no cash rebates should be parallel to the card usage plot of 1% cash rebates.

9.5.3 Multifactor Experiments: Orthogonal Designs

A full-factorial experiment is very useful to database marketers since several factors are simultaneously considered and, hence, all interaction effects can be identified. However, as the number of factors considered in a factorial experiment increases, the number of treatment conditions increases very rapidly. For example, it is not unusual for database marketers to consider 5 factors where each factor has three levels. The number of treatment conditions for this factorial experiment is 245 ($= 3^5$). It is not economical – sometimes, it is not even feasible – to assign customers to each of 245 treatment conditions. In order to overcome this problem, researchers use "fractional factorial" designs, where only a fraction of all possible treatment combinations is selected for

Table 9.6 Orthogonal array for 2^9 factorial design

Combination	Factors and levels								
	A	B	C	D	E	F	G	H	I
1	1	1	1	1	1	1	1	1	1
2	1	1	1	1	2	2	1	2	2
3	1	1	1	2	1	2	2	1	2
4	1	1	1	2	2	1	2	2	1
5	1	2	2	1	1	1	1	2	2
6	1	2	2	1	2	2	1	1	1
7	1	2	2	2	1	2	2	2	1
8	1	2	2	2	2	1	2	1	2
9	2	1	2	1	1	1	2	1	2
10	2	1	2	1	2	2	2	2	1
11	2	1	2	2	1	2	1	1	1
12	2	1	2	2	2	1	1	2	2
13	2	2	1	1	1	1	2	2	1
14	2	2	1	1	2	2	2	1	2
15	2	2	1	2	1	2	1	2	2
16	2	2	1	2	2	1	1	1	1

testing (Hicks 1982). In fractional factorial designs one willingly gives up the measurement of all possible interaction effects and obtains a smaller number of treatment conditions.

A special class of fractional factorial designs, called orthogonal arrays, is a highly fractional design in which all main effects can be identified although all interaction effects are assumed to be negligible (Green 1974). Widely used in conjoint analysis experiments, orthogonal arrays are known to be the most parsimonious set of designs (in the sense of the lowest number of treatment conditions) available for estimating main-effect parameters. For example, we consider an experiment with 9 factors where each factor has two levels. Hence, the number of treatment conditions for the full factorial experiment is 512 (= 2^9). Table 9.6 shows an orthogonal array for this experiment that was provided by Addelman (1962). In the case of orthogonal arrays a necessary and sufficient condition for the main effects of any two factors be uncorrelated (unconfounded) is that each level of one factor occurs with each level of another factor with proportional frequency.

Assuming that all interaction effects can be neglected, we can reduce the number of treatment conditions from 512 to 16. With relatively few treatment combinations, orthogonal arrays allow us to estimate all main effects on an unconfounded basis for a dozen or more factors, each at two or three levels.

The concept of "confounding" is important in fractional designs and merits some elaboration. Assume we have a three-factor experiment where we want to test three treatments, each at two levels. Let's say the experiment is for a credit card and the factors are coupon (yes or no), rebate (yes or no), and

Table 9.7 Two potential fractional designs for a 2^3 experiment

Treatment	Design 1			Design 2		
	Coupon	Rebate	Affinity	Coupon	Rebate	Affinity
1	Yes	Yes	Yes	Yes	Yes	Yes
2	Yes	Yes	No	Yes	No	No
3	No	No	Yes	No	Yes	No
4	No	No	No	No	No	Yes

affinity card (yes or no). A full factorial experiment would have $2^3 = 8$ combinations. Let's assume eight combinations are impractical for the researcher so we want to design an experiment with just four combinations. Table 9.7 shows two possible designs. Which is the better design? Experiment 1 runs into the problem of "confounding." The confounding is between the Coupon and Rebate. With this experiment, we will not be able to differentiate the impact of the coupon from that of the rebate, because every treatment group that gets a coupon also gets a rebate, and every group that does not get a coupon does not get a rebate. If card usage is higher for groups 1 and 2, we don't know if it due to the coupon or the rebate. There is no way to differentiate these effects. In contrast, Experiment 2 has no confounds between any pairs of the three factors. If treatment groups 1 and 2 have higher usage rates, that can be interpreted as due to the coupon, because treatment groups 1 and 2 both always have coupons but sometimes have rebates or affinities and sometimes not. Similarly, groups 3 and 4 never have a coupon but sometimes have rebates or affinities and sometimes not. Experiment 2 is the preferred design.

Lists of orthogonal designs (e.g., Table 9.6) are provided by Plackett and Burman (1946) and Addelman (1962), making it easier to develop orthogonal arrays. SPSS also provides a routine for creating orthogonal arrays.

The price of the orthogonal array is that it assumes there are no interaction effects, whereas there may be interaction effects as we saw in the credit card example. Another way to state the assumption is that the orthogonal array cannot differentiate between a main effect and various interactions, so we just assume there are no interactions and that the main effects we estimate just reflect main effects and nothing else. This is somewhat troublesome but often main effects are clear and important, and interactions are indeed secondary. There are in fact intermediate-type fractional factorial designs where a fraction of all possible combinations are selected so that at least some of the interactions can be estimated (see Winer 1971 for a thorough treatment). These fractional factorials of course will require more treatments.

9.5.4 Quasi-Experiments

As the name implies, a quasi-experiment is almost a true experiment. A quasi-experiment is where we are unable to fully manipulate the scheduling or assignment of treatments to test units (Malhotra 1993). There are many types of quasi-experiments, but their common feature is that the assignment of treatments to customers is not controlled by the researcher.

Quasi-experiments are therefore used in database marketing when it is difficult to randomly assign customers to treatment conditions. For example, we may want to evaluate the impact of a customers' participation in a reward program on their purchase frequencies. We offer the reward program to all customers and let customers decide whether they participate the program or not. Suppose that 40% of customers participate and the rest do not. Monthly purchase dollars before and after launching the rewards program are measured. Program participants increase their purchase dollars from $100 to $120 as a result of the rewards program. Purchase dollars of non-participants are also increased from $90 to $100. Non-participants in this quasi-experiment serve as the control set. Hence, we may conclude that customers increase their purchase dollars by ($120–100) − ($100–90) = $10 due to their program participations. However, this conclusion is misleading since customers were not randomly assigned between program participants and non-participants. There could be a self-selection bias whereby the customers who self-selected into the rewards program were pre-disposed to buy from the company anyway (see Chapter 11, Statistical Issues in Predictive Modeling). A true experimental design would approach this situation by dividing customers randomly into participants and non-participants. The random assignment would eliminate concerns for selection bias.

One way of reducing the selection bias in quasi-experiments is to introduce covariates in analyzing the experimental effect. This is called the analysis of covariance (ANCOVA). ANCOVA tries to control statistically for factors that influence purchase frequency besides membership in a rewards program. One can also develop a formal selectivity model (see Chapter 11, Statistical Issues in Predictive Modeling).

In summary, quasi-experiments are in general less preferred because one loses the randomization of the true experiment. Randomization rules out other factors as causes (on average) and particularly addresses selection bias. However, in the real world, one may not have the luxury of randomizing. In that case, the researcher at a minimum should use an analysis of covariance framework, and consider formulating a formal selectivity model.

Chapter 10
The Predictive Modeling Process

Abstract The third cornerstone of database marketing (the other two being LTV and testing) is predictive modeling. Predictive modeling is the use of statistical methods to predict customer behavior – e.g., will the customer respond to this offer or catalog? Will the customer churn in the next 2 months? Which product in our product line would be most attractive to the customer? Which sales channel will the customer use if we send the customer an email? Predictive modeling first and foremost is a *process*, consisting of defining the problem, preparing the data, estimating the model, evaluating the model, and selecting customers to target. We discuss the process in depth, and conclude with a review of some important long-term considerations related to predictive modeling.

10.1 Predictive Modelling and the Quest for Marketing Productivity

Predictive modeling is the database marketer's primary tool for making marketing efforts more productive. Predictive modeling allows the firm to focus its marketing efforts on the customers for whom those efforts will be most effective.

Table 10.1 illustrates economic benefits of predictive modeling for a direct marketer. The company has a list of 1,000,000 potential customers purchased from a list vendor, and is planning to mail an offer for a compact DVD player. If the customer decides to purchase and responds to the offer, the profit contribution is $80. The cost of the mailing is $0.70 per mailed-to customer. Although this would not be known in advance, assume that a mailing to the entire list will generate 10,000 responses, a 1% response rate. If the company mails to the entire list, profit contribution is $1,000,000 \times 0.01 \times \$80 = \$800,000$, and costs are $1,000,000 \times \$0.70 = \$700,000$. The net profit is $\$800,000 - \$700,000 = \$100,000$, an ROI of $\$100,000/\$700,000 = 14.3\%$.

Table 10.1 Targeted versus mass marketing: The role of predictive modeling

• Parameters for a direct marketing campaign	
Number of prospects on list	1,000,000
Profit contribution per response	$80
Cost per mailing	$0.70
Response rate if mail to entire list	1%

• Mass marketing approach – contacting all 1,000,000 prospects

$$\text{Profit} = 1{,}000{,}000 \times 0.01 \times \$80 - 1{,}000{,}000 \times \$0.70$$
$$= \$800{,}000 - \$700{,}000$$
$$= \$100{,}000$$

• Targeted approach using predictive modeling – contacting the top five deciles

Decile	Number of prospects	Response rate (%)	Cumulative Profit ($)	Profit ($)
1	100,000	3.00	170,000	170,000
2	100,000	2.00	90,000	260,000
3	100,000	1.40	42,000	302,000
4	100,000	1.15	22,000	324,000
5	100,000	1.00	10,000	334,000
6	100,000	0.60	−22,000	312,000
7	100,000	0.40	−38,000	274,000
8	100,000	0.30	−46,000	228,000
9	100,000	0.10	−62,000	166,000
10	100,000	0.05	−66,000	100,000
⇒	Profit = $334,000 by targeting top five deciles			

The bottom portion of Table 10.1 shows how predictive modeling improves things considerably. Predictive modeling prioritizes the 1,000,000 prospects according to their likelihood of responding. We can then partition the prospects into 10 deciles ordered by likelihood of response. Those in the top decile have a 3.00% chance of responding; those in the bottom have only a 0.05% chance. The profit from mailing to the top decile is $100,000 \times 0.03 \times \$80 - 100,000 \times \$0.70 = \$170,000$. The top five deciles generate positive profit if mailed, whereas the bottom five deciles generate a loss. The decision is simple – mail to prospects in the top five deciles. The expected profit is $334,000 despite an investment of only $500,000 \times \$0.70 = \$350,000$. For only half the investment compared to a mass mailing, the predictive modeling approach yields more than three times the profit, for an ROI of $\$334,000/\$350,000 = 95.4\%$!

The key assumption is that the direct marketer is able to segment customers into deciles prioritized by likelihood of response. This is the job of predictive modeling.

The predictive model will be more successful to the extent that it can better separate responders from the non-responders. Table 10.2 shows that "small" improvements in this segmentation can have a dramatic impact on profits.

Table 10.2 shows three scenarios. Scenario 1 is the present situation, taken from Table 10.1. In Scenario 2, the predictive model is able to identify a

Table 10.2 The impact of more accurate predictive modeling[a]

Decile	Scenario 1 (Table 10.1)			Scenario 2			Scenario 3		
	Response rate	Profit	Cumulative profit	Response rate	Profit	Cumulative profit	Response rate	Profit	Cumulative profit
1	3.00%	$170,000	$170,000	3.50%	$210,000	$210,000	4.00%	$250,000	$250,000
2	2.00%	$90,000	$260,000	2.20%	$106,000	$316,000	2.80%	$154,000	$404,000
3	1.40%	$42,000	$302,000	1.50%	$50,000	$366,000	1.20%	$26,000	**$430,000**
4	1.15%	$22,000	$324,000	1.00%	$10,000	**$376,000**	0.80%	–$6,000	$424,000
5	1.00%	$10,000	**$334,000**	0.80%	–$6,000	$370,000	0.50%	–$30,000	$394,000
6	0.60%	–$22,000	$312,000	0.45%	–$34,000	$336,000	0.30%	–$46,000	$348,000
7	0.40%	–$38,000	$274,000	0.28%	–$47,600	$288,400	0.15%	–$58,000	$290,000
8	0.30%	–$46,000	$228,000	0.18%	–$56,000	$232,400	0.10%	–$62,400	$227,600
9	0.10%	–$62,000	$166,000	0.07%	–$64,400	$168,000	0.09%	–$63,200	$164,400
10	0.05%	–$66,000	$100,000	0.03%	–$68,000	$100,000	0.07%	–$64,400	$100,000
Average	1.00%			1.00%			1.00%		

[a]Numbers in bold are the profits earned by targeting the optimal number of deciles.

top decile that has a 3.5% response rate rather than a 3.00% response rate. The second and third deciles are also a little better (2.20% vs. 2.00% and 1.50% vs. 1.40%), while the lower deciles have lower response rates so that the average still comes to 1.00%, maintaining the assumption that 1.00% of the 1,000,000 prospects will respond. This slight increase in predictive ability means that if the direct marketer were to mail to the top five deciles, profits would be $370,000 rather than $334,000. Profits are maximized by mailing to the top four deciles, yielding $376,000 in profits. This is an increase of $42,000 and now ROI is $376,000/(400,000 × $0.70) = 134%. Scenario 3 continues this process, except now response rate in the top decile is 4.00% rather than 3.00%, etc. Optimal profits in this scenario are now $430,000, for an ROI of $430,000/(300,000 × $0.70) = 205%.

In short, predictive modeling allows dramatic increases in profits relative to mass mailing, and every "ounce" of additional predictive ability increases profits still further. An improvement from 3.0% response to 3.5% response doesn't seem that large. But multiplied through by the 100,000 customers in decile 1, and then by the $80 contribution, increases profit by 0.50 × $80 × 100,000 = $40,000.

Because of the above economics, predictive modeling has become a very competitive industry. While the basic process is straightforward, there are many subtleties and nuances. There is a continual race for the "latest and greatest" twist that produces a 3.5% top-decile response rather than 3.0%. Many of these details are described in Chapters 8 and 11 through 19, which cover the statistical methods and data sources that underlie the process. The purpose of this chapter is to focus on the process, to show how the methods and data combine to create the "lift table" shown in Table 10.1.

10.2 The Predictive Modeling Process: Overview

Figure 10.1 presents the predictive modeling process. It consists of four main steps – (1) Define the Problem, (2) Prepare the Data, (3) Estimate the Model, and (4) Select Customers to Target. Each of these consists of important sub-steps. Academic research often focuses on one sub-step at a time, e.g., comparing neural nets to logistic regression as a statistical model. However, as emphasized by Neslin et al. (2006a), *all* the steps are important in combination, and together constitute an *approach* to predictive modeling.

10.3 The Process in Detail

10.3.1 Define the Problem

Many managerial issues can be addressed by predictive modeling. For example, a financial services company may need to select prospects to target

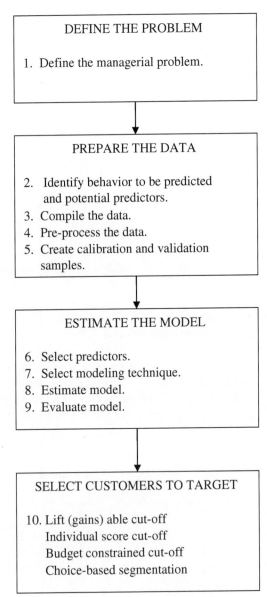

Fig. 10.1 The predictive modeling process.

for an acquisition campaign, identify current customers who are in danger of taking their business elsewhere ("churning"), decide which financial products to cross-sell to which customers, decide which customers should receive a new company-sponsored magazine, or decide which customers should be offered a free needs assessment by a financial advisor.

The Internet has generated many applications of predictive modeling, including: which customers should be serviced on the Internet versus a company representative, which products should be recommended to the customer as he or she navigates through the company website, which online ads should be "served" to which customers on which pages (Manchanda et al. 2006), which customers should receive which promotions as they purchase from an e-tailer website (Zhang and Krishnamurthi 2004), and which customers should receive e-mails with particular messages (Ansari and Mela 2003). Even as the Internet enters its mature stage as a marketing channel, answers to these questions are still not part of normal business routine.

10.3.2 Prepare the Data

Data preparation is perhaps the least exciting phase of the predictive modeling process, but it is the foundation upon which rests the success of the entire process. It involves a variety of tasks, ranging from conceptual to clerical.

10.3.2.1 Define the Behavior to Be Predicted and the Potential Predictors

The behavior to be predicted (the "dependent variable") follows directly from the definition of the problem. For example, if the problem is to identify would-be churners, the behavior to be predicted is customer churn.

The main categories of potential predictor variables include (see Chapter 8):

- *Customer characteristics* – demographics, lifestyle, psychographics, generally, variables that describe the customer and remain relatively constant over time.
- *Previous behavior* – previous purchases, previous product usage, and response to previous marketing efforts. Behavior is often described using "RFM" variables (recency, frequency, and monetary value), i.e., how recently did the customer purchase, how frequently has the customer purchased over the last x years, and what is the average expenditure when the customer makes a purchase.
- *Previous marketing* – previous marketing efforts targeted at the customer, including catalogs, e-mails, telemarketing, sales force visits, etc.

Table 10.3 depicts examples of managerial problems, the behavior of interest, and potential predictors. For example, in deciding which prospects to target for a customer acquisition campaign, the company may have conducted a test mailing. Response to that test is the behavior to be predicted. Potential predictors would be customer characteristics included in the prospect list, e.g., the customer's "FICO" score (a measure of financial risk developed by Fair Isaac, Inc. (Myers Internet, Inc. 2005).

Table 10.3 Illustrative managerial problems, behaviors to be modeled, and potential predictors

Managerial problem	Behavior to be modeled (dependent variable)	Potential predictors
Decide which prospects to target for acquisition campaign	Response to test mailing	Customer characteristics included in the prospect list (demographics, FICO score, etc.)
Identify would-be churners	Customer churn	Customer characteristics (demographics, location), previous behavior (usage rate, usage trend, complaints, etc.)
Decide what product to cross-sell to which customer	Product bought most recently	Customer characteristics (demographics, etc.), previous behavior (product ownership, cross-buying propensity, etc.)
Decide who should receive catalog	Response to test mailing of catalog	Customer characteristics (demographics, etc.), previous behavior (RFM variables), previous marketing (recency and frequency of catalogs previously sent; catalog "stock" variable)
Decide who should be invited to join customer tier program	Customer lifetime value	Customer characteristics (demographics, etc.), previous behavior (response to marketing efforts, RFM variables), previous marketing (# of contacts, etc.)

Sometimes the choices are not straightforward. For example, if the company has a particular product in mind for a cross-selling campaign, it can conduct a test and use response to the offer for this product as the dependent variable. However, the company might have several potential products to cross-sell and can't test each one. One possibility is to define the behavior to be predicted as the product most recently purchased. Important predictors would include the products the customer had bought previously to the most recent product (see Chapter 21, Knott et al. 2002).

Paradoxically, previous marketing efforts, and response to those efforts, often are the most difficult data to compile. This is partly due to poor record-keeping. For example, during the dot-com boom, companies e-mailed customers frantically without noting which customers received what. In contrast, previous purchase data are readily available because purchases are recorded by accounts receivable.

One category of data usually not used is competitive activity – marketing efforts received or competitive products purchased by current customers. This is due to the difficulty in collecting such data, and is endemic to database marketing.

10.3.2.2 Compile the Data

The behavior and predictors listed in the previous step must be quantified and assembled into a data file that can be accessed by statistical software. The data may be available from several sources:

- *The "house file"* – For example, for the next-product-to-buy application, the company should know from its current customer records the product most recently purchased and the products that were purchased before that one.
- *Purchased data* – For example, a financial services company may need a measure of financial risk such as a FICO score. It can purchase a list of individuals with their FICO scores, and merge it with its house file. This can also be done with variables such as product ownership, media usage, etc. The process is to find a list that has the desired variable and merge that with the house list. The parties that help do this are list brokers (who can find lists), list managers (who sell the lists), and service bureaus that merge purchased lists and house lists.
- *Test data* – Very often, a test provides the key source of data, especially the dependent variable. For example, a telecom company might test a churn management program on a group of 20,000 high-potential churners and observe which ones are "rescued" by the program. This provides the dependent variable – "rescue" – for a predictive model.
- *Surveys* – Surveys are useful for obtaining measures on two variables often missing from house data and difficult to purchase from a third party – consumer attitudes and competitive activity. The problem is that for a company with a million or so customers, it is impractical to survey all of them. However, one procedure is to survey a subset of customers and leverage the results to infer the attitudes of the rest of its customers, or infer the competitive activity of its customers (see Du et al. 2005).
- *Text Data* – The vast majority of data used for predictive modeling are metric – RFM, customer demographics, etc. However, text data such as the content of customer e-mails may be an important future source of data. See Coussement and Van den Poel (2007a) for a recent application to predicting customer churn.

Figure 10.2 illustrates schematically how predictive models can be used to leverage survey data on a subset of customers to infer data for the rest of the customer base (see also Chapter 16). The example is of a company using cluster analysis of survey responses to define market segments, estimating a predictive model to predict membership in those segments, and then applying that predictive model on its (non-surveyed) customers to predict their membership in the desired cluster.

The first step is to survey say 500 customers on their "attribute importances" (e.g., the importance of quality, reliability, durability, price, convenience). These data are then cluster analyzed to define market segments (in

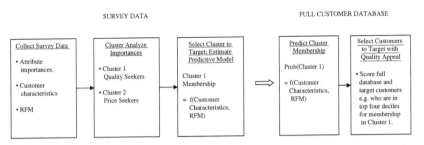

Fig. 10.2 Leveraging survey data for application to the complete customer database.

this case, Quality Seeker and Price Seeker segments). Then a predictive model is estimated to predict which customers in the survey are members of the desired segment. The predictors are customer characteristics and RFM variables collected from the survey respondents, but also available in the house data file.[1] The predictive model can then be applied to the full customer database to identify customers predicted to be in the desired cluster.

This procedure provides the potential to incorporate richer variables into a predictive modeling application. The spirit of the approach is similar to all predictive modeling, where a model estimated on a subset of customers is applied to the entire customer data file. However, the sample size for estimating the model is typically much lower (e.g., 500 rather than thousands) and the richness of the data being analyzed may make them more difficult to predict. Hence, companies should be cautious, using controlled tests before rolling out a full campaign based on this approach.

10.3.2.3 Pre-Process the Data

Once the data have been assembled in a data file, there is the often painstaking job of "pre-processing" the data. There are three main tasks – creating dummy variables, handling missing data, and creating composite variables.

Nominally scaled variables such as gender, country of residence, source of acquisition, etc., must be re-scaled as dummy variables. Some computer programs, e.g., ModelMax, distributed by ASA, Inc. (http://www.asacorp.com/index.jsp) do this automatically. SAS, SPSS, and Excel, can also be used to create dummy variables.

Composite variables are created by combining two or more of the original variables. For example, RFM variables are typically created from original variables. For example, recency is created by finding the date of the most recent purchase and calculating the time from that purchase to the time

---

[1] We assume the survey is anonymous so the customer characteristics and RFM variables have to be asked directly. If the survey were not anonymous, the firm could simply link the customer to the customer characteristics and RFM variables available in its house file, and just use the survey to collect the attitudinal data.

period when the dependent variable is observed; frequency is created by counting the number of purchases over a given period or since the acquisition of the customer; monetary value can be calculated as the average expenditure across all purchases ever made by the customer. RFM can be defined on marketing as well as purchase data. For example, RFM measures of outgoing customer contacts would include: when did the customer last receive a catalog (recency), how many catalogs did the customer receive over the last year (frequency), and what was the average size of the catalog received by a customer (monetary value).

Another composite variable is trend. For example, a telecom company may have data on the number of calls made each month over an 8-month period. The analyst may calculate a trend to indicate whether the number of calls is increasing or decreasing. This could be the compounded growth rate (geometric mean) over the 8-month period, or the trend coefficient from a regression of number of calls versus time.

Composite variables can quantify "massively categorical variables" such as zip code or state (Steenburgh et al. 2003). For example, there are 50 states in the USA. One can create 50 dummy variables to represent each state. But probably several states contribute equally to the dependent variable, so those states should be combined into one composite dummy variable (e.g., if State = CA, NH, ME, FA, or MA, then COMSTATE = 1; else COMSTATE = 0). The question is which states should be combined. There are algorithms for figuring this out, usually combining heuristics and statistical tests. States might be ordered in terms of response rates, and various breakpoints considered for grouping the states together. For each set of breakpoints, a statistical test can be used to decide whether the states grouped together by the breakpoints have equal response rates. These algorithms are employed by decision tree software (see Chapter 17) but are also available in software geared toward other statistical procedures (e.g., see the ModelMax program mentioned earlier, that "bins" variables such as state of residence into homogenous composite groups).

Another approach is due to Steenburgh et al. (2003). These authors create a hierarchical Bayes model for zip codes of the form:

$$Y_i = \sum_{j=1}^{J} \alpha_j X_{ij} + \beta_{z_i} + \varepsilon_i \tag{10.1}$$

$$\beta_z = \sum_{k=1}^{K} \gamma_k W_{kz} + \nu_z \tag{10.2}$$

where

Y_i = Value of the dependent variable (e.g., lifetime value) for customer i.
X_{ij} = Value of predictor variable j for customer i.
α_j = Parameter reflecting the importance of predictor variable j in predicting behavior.

β_z = Contribution of zip code z to predicting behavior.[2]

W_{kz} = Value of variable k associated with zip code z. For example, these variables might be the average income of all persons residing in zip code z, their average age, education, or the average home value of homes in zip code z.

γ_k = Importance of W_{kz} in determining the contribution of zip code z to predicting behavior. For example, a high value of γ_k for k = income would mean that zip codes with high income tend to have higher values of the dependent variable.

ε_i = Unobserved factors for customer i that influence this customer's behavior.

ν_z = Unobserved factors for zip code z that influence this zip code's contribution to customer behavior.

Rather than 10,000 zip code dummies, the idea is to model the contribution of zip code to behavior as a function of observed characteristics of the zip code. The authors estimate this model using Bayesian techniques, and show that it outperforms a more straightforward model that includes the characteristics of the zip code directly in the model. The authors find that if a lot of information is available for each zip code, the difference between the approaches is not as large.

The final phase of pre-processing the data is handling missing values. As described in Chapter 11, this can be done by eliminating customers with missing data (this is usually too wasteful), creating missing variable dummies, or imputing a value for the missing value. The simplest approach is to insert the mean for each missing variable, but this procedure can be highly inaccurate if the missing variable is highly correlated with other variables. For example, if income is highly correlated with education and income is missing, it would distort the results to impute the same income for both a highly educated and not highly educated customer. For that reason, missing variable dummies or more sophisticated methods of imputation, as described in Chapter 11, are preferred.

10.3.2.4 Create Calibration and Validation Samples

As described in Chapter 11, it is a good idea to estimate the predictive model on a "calibration" dataset, and test it on a "validation" dataset. This prevents model "over-fitting," i.e., finding statistical parameters that predict idiosyncratic characteristics of the calibration data that do not hold up in the real world.

The question arises as to what should be the sample size and percentage allocation of data to calibration versus validation. Usually, in database

---

[2] z is not indexed by i in Equation 10.2 because Equation 10.2 models the average contribution of zip code z to predicting behavior. In Equation 10.1, we would use the β for z_i, the zip code where customer i resides, to predict that individual's behavior.

marketing applications the sample sizes vary from 10,000 to 100,000s. Note this is the case even if all variables are observed for all millions of customers. The reason is that to estimate a model on say a million customers can use a lot of computer time, and sample sizes in the tens of thousands often are sufficient. If the sample size is relatively small (e.g., 10,000), intuitively the majority of the data should be allocated to the calibration data. In this case, Chapter 11 discusses a 2/3, 1/3 allocation to calibration and validation.

10.3.3 Estimate the Model

10.3.3.1 Select Predictors

In Chapter 11, we discuss various methods for selecting variables for inclusion in predictive models. These include:

- *Theory*: For example, customer satisfaction should predict customer churn.
- *Managerial Relevance*: For example, evaluating the call center may be on management's agenda, so including "number of calls to call center" may be an important variable to include in a churn model.
- *Stepwise Regression*: This method selects the subset of the variables that maximizes adjusted R^2. Adjusted R^2 penalizes the model if it uses too many variables to achieve a good level of fit. Stepwise procedures exclude variables that are correlated with the dependent variable, but also correlated with other predictors that are even more highly correlated with the dependent variable, and excludes variables that simply have low correlation with the dependent variable.
- *All-possible Subsets Regression*: This examines all models that can estimated given the set of predictors, and chooses the best one. This is an appealing idea but becomes impractical when there are even a moderate number of predictors.
- *Factor Analysis*: This groups together predictors that are highly correlated with each other to create a composite variable as a weighted sum of those variables.
- *Decision Trees*: Decision trees select variables that best separate responders from non-responders, among the customers left after previous subdivisions of the data.

There are no definitive studies on the best way to select variables for a predictive model. Data collected as part of a "churn modeling tournament" (Neslin et al. 2006a) provide some evidence for how commonly used various methods are, shown in Fig. 10.3. The churn modeling tournament invited academics and practitioners to predict customer churn using a database made available by the authors. There were 44 entries, divided roughly 50–50 between academics and practitioners. As shown in Fig. 10.3, the most commonly used

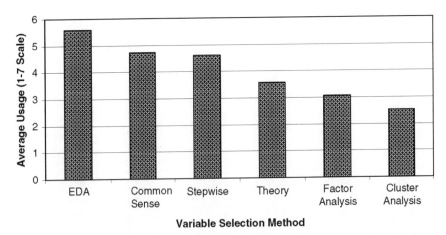

Fig. 10.3 Methods used to select variables for churn modeling tournament (Statistics provided by Neslin et al. 2006a).

methods for selecting variables were (1) exploratory data analysis (e.g., calculating correlations and examining the data), (2) "common sense," and (3) stepwise. Entrants also used, to a lesser degree, "theory," factor analysis, and cluster analysis. When confronted with a real problem, analysts apparently use relatively "low brow" methods to select variables, and among statistical techniques, stepwise regression dominates.

Another finding from the tournament is the number of variables included in the model. Figure 10.4 shows this distribution. There were approximately 75 predictors in the data provided. Participants could also create dummy variables and composite variables. Figure 10.4 shows that the clear majority of modelers included 40 or fewer variables, although a few included 100+.

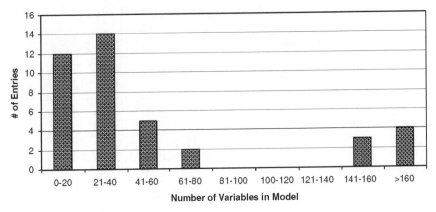

Fig. 10.4 Number of predictors used in predictive models for churn modeling tournament (Statistics provided by Neslin et al. 2006a).

These entrants used decision tree approaches that create several decision trees, each with a different set of variables. Therefore, the "norm" for a real-world application in this case was about 20–40.

10.3.3.2 Select the Statistical Modeling Technique

Statistical techniques that can be used for predictive models include:

- Regression
- Logistic regression (Chapter 15)
- Type I or Type II Tobit (Chapter 15)
- Decision trees (Chapter 17)
- Neural nets (Chapter 18)
- Machine learning algorithms (Chapter 19)

No one method is considered best in terms of predictive accuracy. Machine learning algorithms appear very promising, but they have not been applied often enough or compared enough to more traditional methods to make a definitive statement. It is noteworthy that the winning entry to the churn modeling tournament was a bagging and boosting decision tree algorithm, a machine learning method.

An important criterion in selecting a statistical model, besides predictive accuracy, is ease of interpretation, i.e., understanding and communicating what drives the behavior being modeled. Decision trees are especially strong here, and to a lesser degree logistic or regular regression. For example, the branches of a decision tree can easily be communicated to customer care center personnel so they can act accordingly (e.g., "if the customer is a heavy user, been a customer for at least 5 years, and has called before, route the customer to the...department"). Neural nets and machine learning algorithms are generally weaker on this criterion. Neural nets supposedly gain predictive accuracy because they are highly nonlinear and can capture interactions. However, to the authors' knowledge, most neural net programs do not clearly show these effects.

Another important issue is the nature of the dependent variable. If the dependent variable is continuous, regular regression is easy to use, whereas logistic regression is designed for the case of a 0–1 dependent variable (e.g., respond versus not respond). Multinomial logit can be used if the dependent variable is nominally scaled but contains several categories. Decision trees, neural nets, and machine learning algorithms can be used for both continuous and 0–1 dependent variables. Type I Tobits are designed for continuous variables that have a lower limit, such as customer expenditures, which are bounded below by zero. Type II Tobits are applicable when modeling a 0–1 *and* a continuous variable, such as whether the customer will respond, and if so, how much he or she will spend. Research is needed to compare Type II Tobits with using a regression model for expenditures, a logistic regression for response, and multiplying the results.

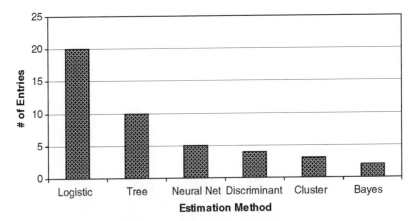

Fig. 10.5 Statistical models used for the churn modeling tournament (Statistics provided by Neslin et al. 2006a).

Figure 10.5 shows the methods that were used for the churn modeling tournament. Logistic regression was the most popular method, followed by decision trees and neural nets. Logistic regression is readily available on standard software, including SPSS and SAS. Decision trees require specialized software such as SPSS's AnswerTree. ASA's ModelMax (Sect. 10.3.2.3) is one alternative for developing neural nets.

10.3.3.3 Estimate the Model

As noted in Sect. 10.3.2.4, it is common to subdivide the data into calibration (estimation) and validation (holdout) samples. Sometimes a model is estimated on the calibration data, tested on the validation, and then re-estimated and re-tested as necessary, eventually arriving at the final model. Note this iterative process is *not* a validation test. In a validation test, the *final* model is used to predict for the validation sample. In the churn modeling tournament (Neslin et al. 2006a), more than three quarters of the submissions subdivided the data as part of estimation. In fact, neural net algorithms often use this tactic in employing "training" and "test" samples.

10.3.4 Evaluate the Model

10.3.4.1 Creating a Lift Table

Creating a lift table is a crucial first step in evaluating and then using a predictive model (Table 10.1). Consider the case of a catalog mailing. The

Table 10.4 Creating a lift table: RFM and response data for test mailing

Customer	Recency	Frequency	Monetary	Buy or no buy
1	0	5	$242	1
2	3	4	$221	1
3	1	6	$192	1
4	0	4	$182	0
5	1	4	$215	0
6	1	5	$244	1
7	1	6	$211	0
8	3	7	$180	0
9	4	6	$183	0
10	3	8	$210	0
11	2	8	$231	0
12	0	6	$182	0
13	2	5	$193	1
14	0	5	$214	0
15	0	7	$231	0
16	0	2	$168	0
17	4	10	$178	1
18	2	10	$191	1
19	3	12	$181	0
20	4	4	$227	1
21	1	5	$216	0
22	6	11	$244	0
23	1	4	$208	0
24	4	8	$202	0
25	1	5	$230	0
....	....	....	....	....
9,990	0	5	$240	1
9,991	1	11	$169	0
9,992	1	1	$172	0
9,993	1	6	$211	0
9,994	1	6	$179	0
9,995	0	4	$214	0
9,996	1	4	$220	1
9,997	2	11	$208	1
9,998	4	10	$215	0
9,999	2	5	$197	1
10,000	1	7	$229	0
Average	2.00	5.99	$200	0.261

company conducts a test on 10,000 customers and observes the responses shown in Table 10.4. It has measures of recency, frequency, and monetary value to use as predictors. For example, customer 1 bought last month and so has a recency of 0, bought 5 times over the last year and therefore has a frequency of 5, and the customer's average expenditure per purchase is $242. It turns out that the customer responded to the catalog and made a purchase. The responses were generating by simulating the following logistic regression model:

$$\text{Probability(Respond)} = \frac{1}{1 + e^{-(-7.5-0.15R+0.1F+0.03M)}} \qquad (10.3)$$

Response is negatively related to recency, and positively related to frequency and monetary value. It turns out, simulating this model, that 26.1% of all 10,000 customers responded to the catalog.

Using all 10,000 observations yields the following logistic regression:

$$\text{Probability(Respond)} = \frac{1}{1 + e^{-(-7.739-0.118R+0.092F+0.031M)}} \qquad (10.4)$$

Note this model is close to the true model, in Equation 10.3. The next step simply is to substitute each customer's values for R, F, and M into Equation 10.4 and calculate the predicted probability of response, yielding Table 10.5. We see that we predict a probability of 0.554 that customer 1 responds to the catalog.

Next we order the customers by predicted likelihood of response as shown in Table 10.6. Customer 7,672, with $R = 2, F = 11$, and $M = \$290$, has the highest predicted probability of response, 0.884. The top 25-ranked customers have high predicted response probabilities, and indeed, most of them responded. The bottom customers (#s 9,990–10,000) have low predicted probability of response, and none of them responded.

Now we are in a position to divide the data into n-tiles, in this case, deciles. The top decile includes customers ranked 1 through 1,000. Table 10.7 shows that the 1,000th customer has a predicted response probability 0.4588.[3] We would classify any new customer with a predicted probability between 0.4588 and 1 to be in the top decile. Note also that 54.2% of the customers in the top decile actually did purchase.

We can repeat this process for the 2nd, 3rd, etc. deciles. This produces the lift table shown in Table 10.8.[4] We can use Table 10.8 to calculate profit per decile as in Table 10.1. The model would then be applied to the company's 1,000,000 other customers. Each would be classified in the appropriate decile using the cut-offs in Table 10.8, and then mailed to if they were in a profitable decile. Note we would use the *actual* response rate, not the *predicted* response rate, in the profit calculations. In practice, there should not be too much difference between the two.[5]

Since we can view the 1,000 customers in each decile as a sample from all the company's customers, the actual response rate is a sample proportion. A 95% confidence interval therefore for the response rate for the

---

[3] We are assuming that there are no ties in predicted response probability, so we can isolate the single customer who is ranked 1,000th. Sometimes, especially with models with large samples but only a few predictor variables, it is possible to have ties in predicted response. In that case there could be an uneven number of customers in each n-tile.

[4] We describe the "lift" column of Table 10.8 in the next section.

[5] However, it is possible that the predicted response rate suffers from "rare event" bias (see Sect. 10.3.5.1 and Chapter 15, Sect. 15.1.3). Using the actual response rate is one way to avoid this problem.

Table 10.5 Creating a lift table – predicting response using estimated predictive model

$$\left[\text{Prob(Respond)} = \frac{1}{1 + e^{-(-7.739-0.118R+0.092F+0.031M)}}\right]$$

Customer	Recency	Frequency	Monetary	Buy or no buy	Predicted probability
1	0	5	$242	1	0.554
2	3	4	$221	1	0.293
3	1	6	$192	1	0.203
4	0	4	$182	0	0.151
5	1	4	$215	0	0.304
6	1	5	$244	1	0.543
7	1	6	$211	0	0.320
8	3	7	$180	0	0.133
9	4	6	$183	0	0.122
10	3	8	$210	0	0.299
11	2	8	$231	0	0.480
12	0	6	$182	0	0.178
13	2	5	$193	1	0.178
14	0	5	$214	0	0.343
15	0	7	$231	0	0.514
16	0	2	$168	0	0.087
17	4	10	$178	1	0.145
18	2	10	$191	1	0.245
19	3	12	$181	0	0.201
20	4	4	$227	1	0.310
21	1	5	$216	0	0.328
22	6	11	$244	0	0.529
23	1	4	$208	0	0.259
24	4	8	$202	0	0.229
25	1	5	$230	0	0.434
....	....	....	....	....	....
9,990	0	5	$240	1	0.538
9,991	1	11	$169	0	0.168
9,992	1	1	$172	0	0.081
9,993	1	6	$211	0	0.320
9,994	1	6	$179	0	0.147
9,995	0	4	$214	0	0.323
9,996	1	4	$220	1	0.337
9,997	2	11	$208	1	0.377
9,998	4	10	$215	0	0.350
9,999	2	5	$197	1	0.199
10,000	1	7	$229	0	0.475

kth decile is:

$$r_k \pm 1.96\sqrt{\frac{r_k(1 - r_k)}{n}} \tag{10.5}$$

where n in this case is the sample size in the kth decile, which in our case is 10,000. Therefore, the 95% confidence interval for the 54.2% response rate for the top decile is $.542 \pm 1.96\sqrt{\frac{.542(1-.542)}{1000}} = 54.2\% \pm 3.1\%$.

Table 10.6 Creating a lift table-data ordered by predicted probability of response

Rank	Customer	Recency	Frequency	Monetary	Buy or no buy	Predicted probability
1	7,672	2	11	$290	1	0.884
2	2,633	2	8	$296	1	0.874
3	1,887	2	8	$289	1	0.848
4	1,941	0	11	$270	1	0.837
5	3,330	2	10	$277	1	0.821
6	6,800	0	8	$273	1	0.814
7	1,972	2	13	$266	1	0.813
8	5,805	0	14	$255	1	0.809
9	9,686	0	10	$265	1	0.799
10	9,842	5	9	$286	1	0.795
11	4,842	2	4	$289	0	0.795
12	311	0	5	$277	1	0.789
13	9,258	1	7	$275	1	0.787
14	5,936	1	7	$275	1	0.786
15	635	2	3	$290	1	0.786
16	7,269	0	7	$270	1	0.781
17	7,230	3	5	$287	1	0.781
18	8,908	1	3	$285	0	0.778
19	8,590	0	5	$273	0	0.768
20	191	1	9	$265	1	0.767
21	251	0	6	$270	1	0.766
22	8,489	3	10	$268	1	0.758
23	8,096	1	9	$263	1	0.755
24	8,674	0	6	$268	1	0.753
25	4,592	2	7	$271	0	0.747
....	....	....	....	....	....	....
9,990	5,490	3	3	$132	0	0.023
9,991	5,152	5	1	$144	0	0.023
9,992	8,166	7	7	$134	0	0.022
9,993	5,944	6	4	$139	0	0.022
9,994	1,680	2	5	$119	0	0.021
9,995	481	5	7	$123	0	0.021
9,996	8,976	5	11	$111	0	0.020
9,997	5,892	4	2	$131	0	0.019
9,998	7,526	1	4	$112	0	0.018
9,999	95	1	3	$114	0	0.017
10,000	913	3	8	-$38	0	0.000

10.3.4.2 Calculating Lift

"Lift" is the most common measure of model performance (Chapter 11). This is because it is calculated directly from the gains or lift table in Table 10.1, and therefore relates directly to managerial decisions. Formally, we define lift for the nth n-tile as:

$$\lambda_k = \frac{r_k}{\bar{r}} \qquad (10.6)$$

Table 10.7 Creating a lift Table – deriving cut-offs and predicted probability for first decile

Rank	Customer	Recency	Frequency	Monetary	Buy or no buy	Predicted probability
1	7,672	2	11	$290	1	0.884
2	2,633	2	8	$296	1	0.874
3	1,887	2	8	$289	1	0.848
4	1,941	0	11	$270	1	0.837
5	3,330	2	10	$277	1	0.821
6	6,800	0	8	$273	1	0.814
7	1,972	2	13	$266	1	0.813
8	5,805	0	14	$255	1	0.809
9	9,686	0	10	$265	1	0.799
10	9,842	5	9	$286	1	0.795
11	4,842	2	4	$289	0	0.795
12	311	0	5	$277	1	0.789
13	9,258	1	7	$275	1	0.787
14	5,936	1	7	$275	1	0.786
15	635	2	3	$290	1	0.786
16	7,269	0	7	$270	1	0.781
17	7,230	3	5	$287	1	0.781
18	8,908	1	3	$285	0	0.778
19	8,590	0	5	$273	0	0.768
20	191	1	9	$265	1	0.767
....	....	....	....	....	....	....
990	2,090	5	9	$237	1	0.459
991	2,189	1	5	$233	0	0.459
992	731	1	3	$239	0	0.459
993	9,487	0	4	$232	1	0.459
994	5,273	2	10	$222	0	0.459
995	8,283	4	6	$242	0	0.459
996	1,985	2	4	$240	1	0.459
997	5,141	2	3	$243	0	0.459
998	3,274	2	6	$234	0	0.459
999	335	0	9	$218	0	0.459
1,000	7,111	2	4	$240	0	0.4588
1,001	1,882	1	9	$221	1	0.4585
					54.2%	55.1%

where:

λ_k = Lift for the kth tile.
r_k = Response rate for the kth tile.
$\bar{r}$ = Response rate across the entire sample.

In words, λ_k is how much more likely customers in n-tile k are to respond compared to the response rate for the entire sample. We want lift in the top tiles to be greater than 1, and lift in the lower tiles to be less than 1. Consider Table 10.9. The response rate across the entire sample – the "average" – is 1.60%. The response rate in the top decile is 6.00%. Therefore,

Table 10.8 Creating a lift table – the final table

Decile	Upper cut-off	Lower cut-off	Average predicted response probability	Average actual response rate	Lift
1	0.8845	0.4588	0.551	0.542	2.08
2	0.4585	0.3737	0.411	0.420	1.61
3	0.3736	0.3151	0.342	0.354	1.36
4	0.3151	0.2702	0.292	0.305	1.17
5	0.2702	0.2322	0.251	0.272	1.04
6	0.2322	0.1950	0.214	0.219	0.84
7	0.1949	0.1624	0.178	0.165	0.63
8	0.1623	0.1296	0.146	0.145	0.56
9	0.1296	0.0934	0.111	0.121	0.46
10	0.0933	0.0002	0.068	0.065	0.25
			Average $= 0.261$		

customers in the top decile are 3.75 times more likely to respond than average ($\lambda_1 = 6.00/1.60 = 3.75$). Top decile lift is 3.75 to 1.

Lift itself does not have direct managerial significance. What matters is the economics of profit, which are built off response rate, profit contribution, and cost, as in Table 10.1. However, higher lift makes a particular n-tile more profitable, since lift is directly proportional to response rate. Also, lift provides a common measure that can be used to compare models across applications and circumstances. For example, our experience is that top-decile lift typically is lies between 1.5 and 10.0, with 3–5 probably the norm.

There is a maximum achievable top-n-tile lift. Let $\bar{r}$ be the response rate across the entire sample; N is the sample size and n is the number of tiles. Then:

$$\text{Max Lift} = \begin{cases} n & \text{if } N \times \bar{r} \leq N/n \\ 1/\bar{r} & \text{if } N \times \bar{r} > N/n \end{cases} \tag{10.7}$$

The key is to account for whether there is a large enough sample in the top decile to accommodate all responders. Consider first the case that the number of responders ($N \times \bar{r}$) is less than the number of customers in the

Table 10.9 Calculating lift

Decile	Response rate	Lift
1	6.00%	3.75
2	3.50%	2.19
3	2.50%	1.56
4	1.50%	0.94
5	1.00%	0.63
6	0.65%	0.41
7	0.50%	0.31
8	0.19%	0.12
9	0.12%	0.08
10	0.04%	0.03
Average	1.60%	–

Table 10.10 Calculating cumulative lift

Decile	Response rate	Lift	Cumulative lift
1	6.00%	3.75	37.5%
2	3.50%	2.19	59.4%
3	2.50%	1.56	75.0%
4	1.50%	0.94	84.4%
5	1.00%	0.63	90.6%
6	0.65%	0.41	94.7%
7	0.50%	0.31	97.8%
8	0.19%	0.12	99.0%
9	0.12%	0.08	99.8%
10	0.04%	0.03	100.0%
Average	1.60%		

top tile (N/n).[6] Then the maximum response rate in that decile would be $\frac{N \times \bar{r}}{N/n} = n\bar{r}$ and maximum lift would be $n\bar{r}/\bar{r} = n$. Assuming this case holds for Table 10.9, the maximum top-decile lift is 10, so having achieved 3.75, we are about 37.5% of where we would be with a perfect model. If there are more responders than customers in the top tile, at best we can have all of customers in the top decile classified as responders, so top decile lift would be $1/\bar{r}$.

In Table 10.8, $\bar{r} = 0.261$, $n = 10$ and $N = 10,000$, so $N \times \bar{r} = 2,610 > 1,000$ and maximum top decile lift is $1/\bar{r} = 1/0.261 = 3.83$. Our top-decile lift of 2.08 means we have achieved 54.3% of what would be achieved with a perfect model.

10.3.4.3 Additional Ways of Evaluating the Model

Chapter 11 details other statistics for evaluating predictive models. One of the most common is the "cumulative lift chart," which tabulates cumulative response rates from the top n-tile down. Continuing the example in Table 10.9, Table 10.10 shows the calculation of cumulative lift.

The cumulative lift for the kth decile shows the percentage of all responders accounted for by the first k deciles. Table 10.10 says that the top 3 deciles account for 75.0% of all responders. Obviously, the higher the cumulative lift for a given decile, the better. Cumulative lift can be calculated by cumulatively summing the total number of responders in successive deciles, and dividing by the total number of respondents.[7]

As discussed in Chapter 11, another evaluation technique is to see how well the model predicts on a validation database. Assume 20,000, not 10,000

---

[6] We assume there are no ties in the top n-tile, so the exact number of customers in the top n-tile is N/n. See Footnote 3.

[7] One could also calculate lift by cumulating the lift column and dividing by the sum of all n lifts. However, that may not be exact if there are slightly different numbers of customers in each n-tile, due to ties. See Footnote 3. In Table 10.10, we are assuming this is not a problem.

customers, had been in the test, but the estimated predictive model (Equation 10.4) was based on the 10,000 calibration customers. That equation, and the corresponding cut-offs shown in Table 10.8, could be used to classify the validation customers, then we could calculate the actual percentage response rate among these customers. This rate should not differ appreciably from the actual response rates in Table 10.8. Another commonly used method of evaluation is to pit one model versus another, say the logistic regression model versus a neural net model, and compare them in terms of lift, cumulative lift, etc.

10.3.5 Select Customers to Target

There are four approaches to deciding which customers to target:

- Lift (gains) table cut-off (e.g., see Banslaben 1992)
- Individual score cut-off (e.g., see Bult and Wansbeek 1995)
- Budget constraint
- Choice-based segmentation (Gensch 1984; Gensch et al. 1990)

10.3.5.1 Lift (Gains) Table Cut-Off

There are four steps to using the lift table to decide which customers to target (see also Banslaben 1992):

- Finalize the lift table
- Score the rest of the data
- Place these customers into the appropriate n-tile
- Select n-tiles to target

Finalize the Lift Table

There are two issues here: (1) How many tiles to use? (2) Whether to use predicted response rates directly from the model, or the actual response rates for each decile? The number of tiles to use depends somewhat on the sample size. From Equation 10.5, the plus or minus around the predicted response rates for an n-tile depends on the sample size, which is N/n, where N is the total sample size and n is the number of tiles. This would favor fewer tiles. However, more tiles are beneficial if say the top decile is divided into a very high-responding group versus a less high-responding group. The trade-off is between added detail in looking at more tiles, and the smaller sample size available to quantify that detail. Our experience is that deciles are often used to evaluate models simply because deciles are a common benchmark.

However, more tiles, even centiles, are might be used to select the actual customers to target.

While it would be most logical to use the response probabilities calculated directly from the model to select customers, there are two arguments against this. First, nonlinear models such as logistic regression can under-estimate true response probabilities when response is relatively "rare." Chapter 15 discusses this as well as potential statistical corrections. But the simplest approach is to use the actual response rates in each n-tile as the prediction of response. Second, the calibration sample may intentionally be constructed to contain 50% responders and 50% non-responders. This is to provide more instances of response and hence the model can learn better how to profile responders. The result is that the predicted response rate certainly cannot be taken literally. However, the model could be used to rank a validation sample that reflects the true response rate for the population. Then we can group customers into deciles, observe the actual response rates, and use them as the predicted response probabilities.

Score the Rest of the Data

Most predictive models are estimated on a subset of all customers but decisions must be made for all customers. For example, in the example above, a test is conducted on 10,000 customers, the lift table is set up using this sample, and then predictions are made for the rest of the company's customers. This is referred to as "scoring" the database.

Place Customers into the Appropriate n-Tile

Once each customer is scored, he or she can be classified into the appropriate n-tile using the cut-offs shown for example in Table 10.8. This classification can be used to select customers for the immediate application at hand, or stored for use in future applications. For example, management might decide to take a particular action on customers who scored in the top decile for at least one of three catalog response models.

Select n-Tiles to Target

Once we have classified all customers in the appropriate tile, and decided what we will use for predicted response, customer selection is simple. We simply calculate the profit from each tile as in Table 10.1 and target customers who are in the profitable tiles. We saw in Table 10.1 how this targeting can vastly increase both profits and ROI compared to mass marketing. This is the heart of what database marketing is about.

10.3.5.2 Individual Score Cut-Off

Another approach to selecting customers to target is to use the predictive model to predict response for each customer, and select a cut-off point for these predictions so that all customers scoring above this point are targeted. The simplest way to implement this is first to calculate the breakeven response rate needed for the marketing effort to be profitable, and then select all customers whose predicted response likelihood is above that point. For example, if r is the response probability, w is the profit contribution per response, and c is the cost of contacting a customer, it is profitable to contact the customer as long as $rw - c > 0$, or $r > c/w$. So, the firm would target any customer whose predicted response rate is higher than the cut-off point c/w.

Bult and Wansbeek (1995) derive an optimal cut-off point so that the expected marginal contribution of mailing to customers above that point equals the marginal cost. Let customer i's score from a predictive model be n_i. Using a logistic predictive model and assuming a logistic distribution of the n_i's across customers, they obtain the following expression for the optimal fraction of customers to select:

$$q_{opt} = \frac{1}{1 + e^{\alpha\gamma}(w - 1)^{-\gamma}} \tag{10.8}$$

where

q_{opt} = Optimal fraction of customers to select for the direct marketing campaign.

γ = Parameter for the logistic distribution of the n_i's; higher γ means the n_i's are more concentrated, i.e., lower variance in predicted scores across customers.

α = Constant term in the logistic regression model.

w = Marginal contribution of a response, relative to the marginal cost. So, $w > 1$ means that the marginal response contributes more than the cost.

Equation 10.8 shows if the marginal contribution is higher, we can target more customers. If the constant in the logistic regression model is more positive, this means that the level of response is generally lower, and we will not want to target as many customers. The relation between γ and the optimal fraction to target is not monotonic (see Table 3 of Bult and Wansbeek).

Bult and Wansbeek compare their approach to the lift table approach using deciles and a linear probability model. They find their approach yields 8% higher profits. This happens for at least two reasons: (1) The authors use a logistic regression rather than a linear probability model, and the logistic regression could have been more accurate. (2) Separating into deciles was too coarse a segmentation for this application. The decile approach yielded 40% as the fraction to be mailed, whereas the proposed approach yielded 47% as the fraction to be mailed.

Bult and Wansbeek's approach is very promising. First, it realizes that dividing the population into tiles is only an approximation of the response rate as a function of the fraction invited. Second, it takes into account the uncertainty in predicting individual response rates, through its explicit accounting for the error term in the predictive model. However, the method makes assumptions not only with regard to the form of the predictive model (all predictive modelers do this) but also with respect to the distribution of predicted scores in the population. Future work is needed to make more detailed comparisons among (1) the Bult and Wansbeek method, (2) the lift-table cut-off method, and (3) the simple cut-off point method described at the beginning of this section.

10.3.5.3 Budget Constrained Cut-Off

Another approach to determining whom to target is to derive a budget-constrained cut-off. This is easy to do. If the contact cost per customer is c, and the budget is B, then the firm should contact the top B/c customers ranked by a predictive model. Companies may use this approach if they have decided on a marketing plan that specifies a total budget for direct marketing activities. Perhaps part of the plan is to spend $1 M on five direct marketing efforts, so the budget for each is $200,000.

An advantage of the budget approach is that it does not require the *level* of the prediction to be correct, just the *ordering* of the customers. This makes good sense. A predictive model may be estimated at time t and applied at time $t + x$, where x could be measured in months. During this time, competitive conditions, seasonality, the rest of the product's marketing mix, etc., could change the absolute level of response. However, it is less likely that the *ordering* of customers would change (unless there were interactions between the variables in the predictive model and the changes in the environment).

Of course the downside of the budget approach is that the budget may prevent the company from mailing to customers who might be profitable, or encourage the company to contact customers who will not respond profitably.

10.3.5.4 How Deeply to Go Down the List: Trading Off Mis-Targeting Errors

As just mentioned, there are two errors that can be made in selecting customers:

- "Type I Error" – Targeting a customer who really is not profitable.
- "Type II Error" – Not targeting a customer who would have been profitable.

Ideally a company would like the probability of *both* these errors small, but decreasing one tends to increase the other. For example, to prevent Type I

Table 10.11 Comparing companies that emphasize Type I vs. Type II error for deciding how deeply to go down the lift table in selecting customers to target[a]

Factor	Type I Error orientation	Type II Error orientation
Objective	ROI	Sales
View of contact	Clutter	Communication
Campaign budget	Small	Large
Future campaigns	Many	Few
Customer orientation	Transactional	Relationship
CRM Strategy	Tactical	Strategic

[a]Type 1 Error: Targeting a customer who turns out not to be profitable (e.g., does not respond).
Type II Error: Not targeting a customer who would have been profitable (e.g., would have responded).

Errors, the company would want to avoid contacting customers who are not profitable. That would "bias" the company not to mail as far down the list. As a result, the company would not contact several customers who would have been profitable. That means increased likelihood of Type II Errors. The same logic holds if we try to prevent Type II Errors. This would encourage the company to contact more customers, since the worst thing would be not to contact customers who were profitable. By giving the customers the benefit of the doubt and contacting more of them, undoubtedly several will be contacted who in fact are not profitable. This would increase the number of Type I Errors.

The root of these arguments is the classical statistics treatment of Type I and Type II Errors. The company essentially is trying to decide between two hypotheses – the customer is profitable versus the customer is not profitable. We have oriented the argument so that the null hypothesis is that the customer is not profitable. Under that definition, Type I Error is concluding the alternative (Profitable) is true even though the null (Unprofitable) is really true.

One possibility would be to formalize these issues in a decision-making framework by quantifying the costs of Type I and Type II Errors, as well as the firm utility function for these errors. We indeed recommend this as further research. We will instead focus on the strategic ramifications of Type I and Type II Error thinking.

A relevant question is under what circumstances a company would care more about Type I versus Type II Errors, and hence contact less aggressively or more aggressively, respectively. The following factors are important (see Table 10.11):

- *Objective*: Type I Error companies tend to care about ROI. This encourages them to make the denominator of ROI lower, i.e., not contacting as many. Type II companies tend to care more about sales. For sure, the steeper down the list one contacts, the more sales there will be.
- *View of contact*: Type I Error companies are concerned that contacts are clutter from the customer perspective, and don't want to bother the customer unless it's clear the contact will be profitable. Type II companies

view contacts as communication. Even if the customer doesn't respond, his or her awareness of the company has improved, and this can pay off later on.

- *Campaign budget*: Companies with a small budget for a campaign will by necessity be Type I Error oriented. Companies with large budgets can afford to be more concerned about not mailing to profitable customers (Type II Error).
- *Future campaigns*: The Type I Error company thinks of several campaigns. If the customer isn't profitable for the current campaign, hopefully he or she will be for a subsequent campaign. A company conducting only one campaign for the entire year has only one "shot," so might be concerned about Type II Error.
- *Customer orientation*: A company thinking of its relationship with the customer as transactional will be Type I Error oriented – if the contact pays off right now, do the contact; if not, don't contact. A more relationship-oriented company will be more Type II Error oriented – even if the contact doesn't pay off *now*, it is part of nourishing the long-term relationship with the customer.
- *CRM strategy*: Langerak and Verhoef (2003) distinguish "tactical" versus "strategic" CRM strategies. Tactical CRM views CRM strictly as a marketing efficiency tool. Companies with this view are more Type I Error oriented. Strategic CRM views CRM as a vehicle to cultivate the customer relationship and maximize lifetime value. Companies with this view care about Type II Error.

In summary, when expenditures are held accountable and the "warm and fuzzy" side of marketing is considered a luxury, companies will be Type I Error oriented. They will contact only the customers they know are good responders. The upside is high ROI. The downside, however, is catering only to customers who pay off in the short term and not developing marginal customers. Eventually, the company is left with a solid although relatively small group of loyal customers. The marginal customer has been allowed to drift away to competition. The company would have to conduct a reacquisition campaign to lure back these customers. It would contact deeply down its prioritized list, committing many Type I Errors, but avoiding the Type II Errors that got it into this mess.

While over-emphasis on Type I Errors can lead to trouble, so can over-emphasis on Type II Error. Such companies will contact a lot of customers, even if they are not profitable in the short-run. The problem is, they may not be profitable in the long-run either. The "warm and fuzzy" aspect of marketing may result in too much wasted effort spent on customers who turn out not to be profitable over any time horizon. Before we know it, the total marketing budget has mushroomed, marketing productivity is low, and even loyal customers are being flooded with unwanted contacts. Such a company may painfully have to pull in the reigns, not mail as deeply down the list, and reduce total expenditures. Sales may decrease, but ROI will increase.

Obviously one wants to balance Type I and Type II Errors in the long-run, and at a minimum, database marketers need to be aware of the two types of errors when deciding exactly where to draw the cut-off for implementing predictive modeling. It is a task for senior management as well as the specialist designing the campaign.

10.3.5.5 Choice-Based Segmentation

The lift table, individual score, and budget constrained methods for targeting customers are for situations where the predictive model has measured the probability of *response* or total sales volume that will result from a database marketing campaign. In some situations, however, the predictive model is measuring customer loyalty, i.e., the probability the customer will purchase in the absence of any marketing effort. In that case, the company may not want to target their 100% loyal customers, because these customers will purchase no matter what, and their chance of purchasing will not be enhanced by marketing efforts. At the other extreme, they do not want to target customers who cannot be swayed because their preference for the company is just too low. In this case, it may be better to target the customers "in the middle." This is known as "choice-based segmentation" (Gensch 1984; Gensch et al. 1990).

Gensch (1984) and Gench et al. (1990) illustrate choice-based segmentation using a multinomial logit model (Chapter 15):

$$P_{ik} = \frac{e^{V_{ik}}}{\sum_{j=1}^{J} e^{V_{ij}}} \tag{10.9a}$$

$$V_{ik} = \sum_{m=1}^{M} \beta_m X_{ikm} \tag{10.9b}$$

where:

P_{ik} = Probability customer i purchases from firm k.
V_{ik} = Customer i's preference for firm k.
X_{ikm} = Value of attribute m for firm k for customer i.
β_m = Importance of attribute m in determining preference.
M = Number of attributes used to evaluate firms.
J = Number of firms.

The model translates customer ratings of each firm along each of M attributes into the probability they will purchase from each firm. The data available for the model are each customer's attribute ratings and purchase choices. V_{ik} is not directly observed, but is calculated from Equation 10.9b and interpreted as preference, because higher V_{ik} translates into higher likelihood of purchase via Equation 10.9a.

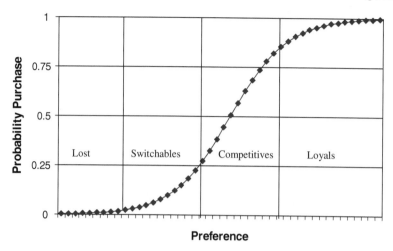

Fig. 10.6 Choice-based segmentation for selecting customers to target (From Gensch 1984).

Figure 10.6 shows a graph of probability of purchase as a function of preference. It identifies "Loyal," "Switchable," "Competitive," and "Lost" customers, depending on their preference value V_{ik}. Loyals have a very high likelihood of buying from the firm, and this probability will not change much even if V_{ik} changes a little bit. The customer's attribute ratings for the brand are so high that improving them a little bit, which will increase V_{ik}, will not appreciably change the likelihood of purchase. The same goes for the Lost customer. Their V_{ik} is so low that even if firm k were to improve on the attributes and V_{ik} changed a little bit, it wouldn't be enough to get them to purchase from the firm. In contrast are the Competitives and Switchables, whose V_{ik}'s are in the steeply increasing portion of the curve in Fig. 10.6. The Competitives lean toward firm k, but there are some to be gained, or more ominously, lost, if V_{ik} changes. The Switchables lean away from firm k, but if firm k can improve just a little bit, there is much to be gained in purchase probability.

One strategy is to target the Switchables and the Competitives because if the firm can improve itself a little bit on one or a few of the attributes, the resulting increase in preference will be significant. Gensch et al. (1990) illustrate the approach for a B2B firm, and demonstrate through a natural experiment that salespersons who focused on Switchables and Competitives outperformed salespersons who did not.

Choice-based segmentation is a rich way of selecting customers to target based on a predictive model. It stands out from the other customer selection methods because those methods focus on *response* as the dependent variable, whereas choice-based segmentation focuses on *probability of purchase* as the dependent variable. The responsiveness of the customer is inferred from their location on the graph in Fig. 10.6.

Table **10.12** Predictive modeling example[a]

Stage	Step	Result
Define the problem	1. What is the managerial problem?	Whom to target for holiday mailing of catalog?
Prepare the data	2. Identify behavior to be predicted and potential predictors	Behavior to be predicted is whether or not customer responds. Potential predictors are RFM and other previous behavior variables.
	3. Compile the data	Available from house data on results of previous year's catalog mailing.
	4. Pre-process the data	Nothing necessary – few missing values; only numeric variables.
	5. Create calibration and validation samples	$n = 30,000$ calibration; $n = 71,000$ validation
Estimate the model	6. Select predictors	Stepwise
	7. Select modeling technique	Logistic regression
	8. Estimate model	Use SPSS
	9. Evaluate the model	Lift tables – calibration and validation; interpretation
Implement the model	10. Set up the lift table	Use deciles
	11. Score the data	Use estimated logistic regression model
	12. Assign customers to n-tiles	Use cut-offs from lift table
	13. Select n-tiles to target	Assess profit assuming average expenditure per response and 40% profit margin. Contact cost = $1.00; fulfillment cost = $2.00 per order.

[a]The authors are grateful for the data provided by the Direct Marketing Educational Foundation for this example.

10.4 A Predictive Modeling Example

In this section, we briefly present an example of the predictive modeling process. Table 10.12 shows how each step in the process was implemented. Note this is just one possible actualization of the process, not necessarily the optimal process.

The example is based on data provided by the Direct Marketing Education Foundation (DMEF).[8] The situation is a gift catalog company that needs to decide which customers to mail catalogs to for the holiday season. The company has data from the 2002 holiday season, where it mailed catalogs

---

[8] We express our appreciation to the DMEF for allowing us to use the data for this example.

Table 10.13 Predictor and dependent variables available for catalog example[a]

1. Customer ID	MATCHOD
2. First Season Dollars	FORDSLS
3. First Season Orders	FORDORD
4. First Season Items	FORDITM
5. First Season Lines	FORDLNS
6. Latest Season Dollars	LORDSLS
7. Latest Season Orders	LORDORD
8. Latest Seasons Items	LORDITM
9. Latest Season Lines	LORDLNS
10. Orders This Year	ORDTYR
11. Dollars This Year	SLSTYR
12. Items This Year	ITMTYR
13. Lines This Year	LNSTYR
14. Orders Last Year	ORDLYR
15. Dollars Last Year	SLSLYR
16. Items Last Year	ITMLYR
17. Lines Last Year	LNSLYR
18. LTD Credit Card Orders	CHARGORD
19. LTD Credit Card Dollars	CHARGSLS
20. LTD AmerExp Card Orders	AMEXORD
21. LTD AmerExp Card Dollars	AMEXSLS
22. LTD MC&VISA Card Orders	MCVISORD
23. LTD MC&VISA Card Dollars	MCVISSLS
24. LTD Phone Orders	PHONORD
25. LTD Phone Dollars	PHONSLS
26. LTD Gift Orders	GIFTORD
27. LTD Gift Dollars	GIFTSLS
28. Orders 2 Years Ago	ORD2AGO
29. Dollars 2 Years Ago	SLS2AGO
30. Orders 3 Years Ago	ORD3AGO
31. Dollars 3 Years Ago	SLS3AGO
32. Orders 4 Years Ago	ORD4AGO
33. Dollars 4 Years Ago	SLS4AGO
34. LTD Spring Orders	SPRORD
35. LTD Fall Orders	FALORD
36. Seasons with Purchase	PURSEAS
37. Latest Purchase Year	LPURYEAR
38. Latest Purchase Season	LPURSEAS
39. Years with Purchase	PURYEAR
40. Purchased in Fall 2002	RESPONSE

[a]The authors are grateful for the data provided by the Direct Marketing Educational Foundation for this example.

to a large number of customers. The question is, which of these customers should be mailed a catalog this year, 2003.

The behavior to be modeled (the dependent variable) is whether the customer responded to last year's mailing. Potential predictors include the "typical" RFM variables as well as customer characteristics. In compiling the data, not many customer characteristics were available, so most of the assembled database consists of previous behavior variables. These are listed in

Table 10.13. Data include dollars spent, number of orders, number of items bought, and number of product lines purchased. Also, data on mode of payment (credit card as well as specific type of credit card, versus phone orders) are available, along with whether the purchase was for a gift (the orientation of the catalog is toward gifts, but customers can certainly buy for themselves). Variable 40 is the dependent variable, did the customer purchase in the Fall of 2002?

Many of the variables are highly related to each other. For example, First Season Dollars (FORDSLS) + Latest Season Dollars (LORDSLS) + Other Season Dollars (not quantified) = Dollars This Year (SLSLYR). As a result, FORDSLS, LORDSLS, and SLSLYR will be highly correlated.

No pre-processing was necessary for these data, as they are mostly continuous variables with very few missing. The 101,000 observations were divided into 30,000 for calibration and 71,000 for validation.

A stepwise logistic regression was estimated. Stepwise is particularly useful when there a lot of potential predictors with no particular theory as to which ones should be most useful (e.g., should first season or latest season orders be more predictive, and what even should be the sign of these variables?). Logistic regression is easy to estimate, in this case, on SPSS. The results of the estimation are shown in Table 10.14.

Table 10.14 shows this year's orders have a large impact on response, as do orders from last year, 2, 3, and 4 years ago, in diminishing degrees. Buying with a credit card (CHARGSLS) decreases response, but buying with American Express (AMEXSLS) or MasterCard/Visa (MCVISSLS) tends to increase response. This means American Express, Visa, and MasterCard customers have higher response, and implicitly that the other credit card

Table 10.14 Estimated logistic regression – catalog example[a]

Variable	Beta	S.E.	p-value	Exp(beta)
FORDLNS	−0.059	0.014	0.000	0.943
LORDSLS	−0.004	0.001	0.000	0.996
LORDORD	−2.970	0.359	0.000	0.051
LORDLNS	0.213	0.017	0.000	1.237
ORDTYR	1.175	0.058	0.000	3.238
LNSTYR	−0.054	0.023	0.018	0.947
ORDLYR	0.699	0.033	0.000	2.011
CHARGSLS	−0.595	0.208	0.004	0.552
AMEXSLS	0.595	0.208	0.004	1.814
MCVISSLS	0.596	0.208	0.004	1.815
PHONSLS	−0.002	0.000	0.000	0.998
ORD2AGO	0.429	0.034	0.000	1.536
ORD3AGO	0.307	0.036	0.000	1.359
ORD4AGO	0.297	0.037	0.000	1.346
Constant	−0.512	0.359	0.153	0.599

[a] The authors are grateful for the data provided by the Direct Marketing Educational Foundation for this example.

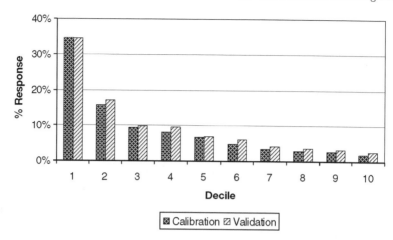

Deciles	Calibration Response	N	Validation Response	N
1	0.347	3051	0.345	7102
2	0.158	3051	0.172	7102
3	0.094	3048	0.098	7087
4	0.081	3053	0.096	7117
5	0.068	3052	0.070	7102
6	0.048	3053	0.060	7103
7	0.034	3050	0.041	7101
8	0.030	3051	0.036	7103
9	0.027	3075	0.033	7113
10	0.019	3027	0.026	7091
Total	0.091	30511	0.098	71021

Fig. 10.7 Lift charts and tables – Catalog example.*
*The authors are grateful for the data provided by the Direct Marketing Educational
Foundation for this example.

customers (e.g., Discover) have lower response. One counter-intuitive result
is that latest period number of lines ordered (LORDLNS) has a positive
coefficient, whereas first period number of lines ordered (FORDLNS) has a
negative coefficient. One would think both variables should have a positive
coefficient, or at least the same sign. Multicollinearity could be distorting
the signs. Stepwise should eliminate this because it tends to discard one of
two correlated variables. But this can't be guaranteed.

Figure 10.7 shows lift charts and tables for both the calibration and validation samples. The top-decile lift for the calibration sample is close to 4 to
1 (0.347/0.091 = 3.8). So the top decile customers are four times as likely to
respond as the average customer. Using Equation 10.7, we can calculate that
the maximum top-decile lift is 10. So the lift achieved by this model is 38%
of what maximally could have been achieved.

There is no fall-off in performance for the validation sample. This is not
rare. Large sample sizes coupled with relatively few predictors often spell

Table 10.15 Implementing the predictive model – deciding which deciles to target with catalog[a]

Decile	Predicted response rate	Predicted profit per customer
1	0.347	$5.59
2	0.158	$2.00
3	0.094	$0.79
4	0.081	$0.54
5	0.067	$0.27
6	0.049	−$0.07
7	0.034	−$0.35
8	0.030	−$0.43
9	0.027	−$0.49
10	0.019	−$0.64

Assumes:
Predicted profit = r*($60*0.40 − $5) − $1
where:
Average order size = $60
Contribution margin = 40%
Contact cost = $1
Fulfillment cost = $5
r = response rate from second column of lift table.

[a] The authors are grateful for the data provided by the Direct Marketing Educational Foundation for this example.

success for the validation sample. However that this does not mean the model will be perfectly accurate when implemented. All the data – calibration and validation – are from 2002. Things might have changed in 2003 that would render the model no longer accurate. This can only be assessed by implementing the model in 2003. It would be impractical to run a test because the holiday season is a short period.

Table 10.15 uses the decile cut-off approach to select customers to target. Average order size is assumed to be $60 with a contribution of 40%. A more thorough analysis would model order size as well as response and combine the two, but it is not unheard of to focus on response and assume an average purchase size (e.g., Bult and Wansbeek 1995). Contact cost is $1 per customer (printing and postage) and fulfillment cost (packing, packaging, and mail) is $5 per order. Therefore, the profit per customer for decile k is r_k × ($60 × 0.40 − $5) − $1. Table 10.12 predicts that deciles 1–5 are profitable. Decile 6 is marginally unprofitable. A Type II Error-oriented company might mail to decile 6 in addition to the top five deciles.

This example illustrates the full predictive modeling process, from problem definition to implementation plan. The case was a typical catalog example, where 0–1 response to the mailing was the prime behavior of interest, mostly RFM and previous behavior variables were used for predictors, and stepwise logistic regression was used to select variables and estimate the predictive model. The performance of the model appeared to be acceptably good (3.8

to 1 top-decile lift) with no fall-off on the validation sample. Implementation was a simple matter of using the decile cut-off approach.

10.5 Long-Term Considerations

While predictive modeling is of considerable use in targeting customers for particular marketing campaigns, there are important long-term issues in using these models. We discuss these issues in this section.

10.5.1 Preaching to the Choir

Repeated use of predictive models can affect the size of the company's loyal customer base. This happens as follows: The model classifies customers with favorable RFM scores in high deciles, and hence they are selected to be contacted. As a result, their RFM scores improve while those not contacted develop lower RFM scores. The next time the model is applied, the same customers score in the high deciles and the same customers in the low deciles, and the cycle continues. Over time, one group of customers receives a great deal of attention; another group receives little. The former group has become better customers, but the latter group has probably become worse.

The predicament can arise due to an over-emphasis on Type I Error. The answer strategically is occasionally to contact low-decile customers, even if they are not likely to respond to the current mailing. This contact is setting up the customer to respond to the next mailing. This is a Type II Error strategy. In more analytical terms, an optimal contact model is needed that takes into account the long-term management of the customer. The model needs to be forward looking – it needs to recognize that an investment may not pay off in the short run but will in the long term. See Chapter 28 for a discussion of optimal contact models.

10.5.2 Model Shelf Life and Selectivity Bias

A model has a "shelf-life," i.e., the number of applications for which its accuracy holds up. Accuracy may decline over time because of changing market conditions, especially competitive activity. The model therefore needs to be re-estimated. However, a problem can arise because only customers selected by the predictive model have received marketing efforts. For example, only 1,000,000 of the company's 10,000,000 customers may have received a special catalog. This targeting was based on a predictive model that is now possibly obsolete. Re-estimating the model is a good idea, but the catalog was only mailed to those who were predicted to respond in the first place. These customers provide the sample for the new predictive model. However, the results of a model estimated on these customers may not apply to the entire sample of customers.

This is an example of "selectivity bias." To understand the problem statistically, consider the case of estimating the relationship between wages and job training when only certain workers (e.g., ambitious or high aptitude) obtain training. If these variables are not included in the regression of wages versus job training, the result is a biased coefficient for the job training variable. Statistically, there are unobserved factors (ambition, aptitude) that affect both obtaining job training and the obtaining good wages:

$$\text{Wages} = f(\text{Job Training}) + \varepsilon \tag{10.10a}$$

$$\text{Job Training} = \varepsilon' \tag{10.10b}$$

Both ε's include worker ambition and aptitude and so are correlated. Since ε' is correlated with Job Training and ε' is correlated with ε, Job Training and ε are correlated and we have bias (Maddala 1983; Wooldridge 2002).

Our situation is similar but not identical. We measure *all* variables that determine receipt of the catalog, so if we include them in the re-estimated catalog response model, there should be no selectivity bias. However, the RFM predictor variables are "selectively" changed by who receives the catalog. In particular, since R and F are contingent on purchases, customers with high error terms end up with different values for R and F than those with low error terms. If the error terms are not correlated over time, this is just a one-period effect. However, if the errors are correlated over time, then R and F become correlated with these errors, setting up the potential for bias.

To explore this issue, we generated a simulation where we estimate an initial predictive model, repeatedly use it for targeting, and then re-estimate it at a later date. We assume response is generated by a probit model:

$$Z_{im}^* = \beta_0 + \beta_1 Recency_{im} + \beta_2 Frequency_{im}$$
$$+ \beta_3 Monetary\_Value_{im} + \varepsilon_{im} \tag{10.11a}$$

$$Response_{im} = \begin{cases} Yes & if\ Z_{im}^* > 0 \\ No & if\ Z_{im}^* \le 0 \end{cases} \tag{10.11b}$$

where

$Response_{im}$ = Signifies whether customer i responds to the mth mailing.
$Recency_{im}$ = Recency score for customer i at the time of the mth mailing.
$Frequency_{im}$ = Frequency score for customer i at the time of the mth mailing.
$Monetary\_Value_{im}$ = Monetary value score for customer i at the time of the mth mailing.

For the purpose of illustration, we assume the true response-generating process, governed by the β's, remains constant over time. The unobserved factors, ε, differ across individuals but are correlated over time for a given individual. The hypothesis is that if this correlation is nonzero, it will induce bias when we re-estimate the predictive model.

We assume the company has 1,000,000 customers and we randomly generate initial RFM values for each customer. Then we simulate a mailing to a random sample of 10,000 customers. We randomly generate response according to Equations 10.11 using $\beta_0 = -4.5$, $\beta_1 = -0.05$, $\beta_2 = 0.07$, and $\beta_3 = 0.01$. Therefore, the most likely responders have responded recently, frequently, and have high monetary value scores. We use the response to this mailing to estimate Equation 10.11a, and call this the "Initial Model." The coefficients of this model should on average equal the true coefficients. We then update the RFM variables for each customer, use the Initial Model to score all 1,000,000 customers, and select the top 200,000 for a mailing. Next we see who responds, update the RFM variables, re-score customers, and mail again. After this third mailing, we re-estimate the predictive model and call it the "Re-Estimated Model." Note the Re-Estimated Model uses as data the 200,000 customers who were most recently mailed. The reason is that, although it was not the case in our simulation, we want to see if the model has changed. We therefore want to use only recent data.

We then use both the Initial Model and the Re-Estimated model to target a fourth mailing. Our hypothesis is that the Re-Estimated model should be biased if the ε's are correlated over time. We also expect that as a result, the Re-Estimated model will generate poorer results on a fourth mailing.

Figure 10.8 shows the estimated results. As expected, the Initial Model's coefficients are unbiased, and the Re-Estimated Model's coefficients are unbiased if the correlation $\rho = 0.0$, but biased if $\rho = 0.4$, and even more biased if $\rho = 0.8$. These results show that if we re-estimate a model that has been used repeatedly to target customers, the new model has biased coefficients, even if the underlying process generating response has not changed. This nicely confirms our hypothesis.

However, Fig. 10.9 shows two surprising results if we apply the Initial and Re-Estimated Models to a fourth mailing: (1) Both models become more accurate as the correlation increases, i.e., they select customers with higher response rates. This may be due to the fact that the responders to a given mailing generally have higher ε's, and because they responded, they are more likely to have their R and F values favorably updated for the next mailing, where their high ε's persist. (2) The Re-Estimated model does not become worse as it becomes biased ($\rho = 0.4$ or 0.8). In fact, it becomes *better* than the Initial Model. We have an example where a biased model is more accurate than an unbiased model! The reason for this also lies in the selection of customers with high ε's. The Re-Estimated model indeed is biased, because the RFM variables become correlated with the error term over time. However, this information is incorporated in the biased coefficients, so although they are

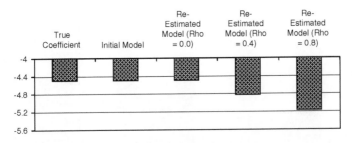

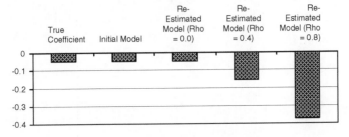

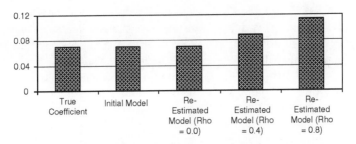

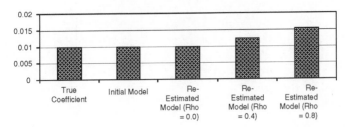

Fig. 10.8 Initial and re-estimated model coefficients depending on correlations between unobserved customer factors over time.

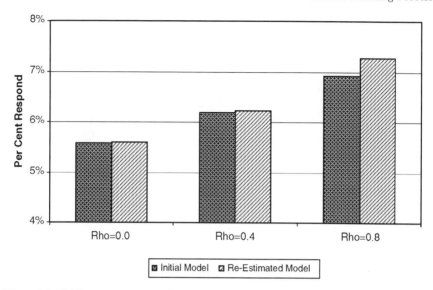

Fig. 10.9 Holdout response rates based on targeting with initial vs. re-estimated predictive models, depending on correlation between unobserved customer factors over time.

biased, they incorporate more information, the correlation between the error term and the RFM variables. Hence the Re-Estimated Model performs better.

This of course is a surprising result but in retrospect quite sensible. Essentially, the RFM variables become more informative as they become updated over time, singling out customers with higher ε's versus lower ε's. In fact, when we inspected the simulated ε's for the customers selected by the Re-Estimated model but not by the Initial Model, we found that the former selected customers with higher ε's on average. Obviously, this is an intriguing result that needs further investigation.

Managerially, the result exacerbates the "Preaching to the Choir" effect discussed earlier. Repeated use of a model identifies the best responders, and re-estimating the model identifies them even more accurately. The most straightforward remedy would be to conduct another test, randomly selecting 10,000 of the 1,000,000 customers, and re-estimating the model. Another possibility, needing further investigation, is whether two-stage least squares might generate consistent, albeit biased, results. Still another possibility would be to develop a selectivity-model in the same vein as described by Maddala (1983) or Wooldridge (2002).

10.5.3 Learning from the Interpretation
of Predictive Models

The role of predictive modeling emphasized in this chapter is efficient targeting. However, there is much to be *learned* from predictive models. For example, a churn model for a wireless phone company might not only predict churn but reveal that customers with older phones are most likely to churn. This suggests that company offer such customers special deals on new phones to keep them from churning (Chapter 24).

Sharing the interpretation of predictive models is important for several reasons: (1) Potential to employ the insights to improve marketing (as in the churn example above). (2) Assurance that the targeted customer is consistent with the overall marketing plan (e.g., the predictive model may find young people are more likely to respond to this particular campaign, but older people might be the firm's target group). (3) Assurance to senior managers that the model driving their business is credible. For example, it would be difficult to sell a model-based cross-selling campaign to senior management based on a model that is not interpretable.

Gillett (1999) recommends that predictive models should be implemented as part of a team effort involving analysts, database managers, CRM managers, and senior marketing managers. This way the insights are shared and credibility established, and all parties are able to do their jobs better.

10.5.4 Predictive Modeling Is a Process to Be Managed

It is common to think of predictive modeling as the statistical model – logistic regression, neural nets, machine learning, etc. But predictive modeling is a *process*; there are many choices along the way. As a result, there are various predictive modeling *approaches*, depending on these choices.

Neslin et al. (2006a) emphasize this in the analysis of their churn modeling tournament. They found that variables representing factors such as time spent on various tasks, the method used for selecting variables, as well as the statistical method, tended to be correlated. The authors factor analyzed these data and interpreted the factors in terms of five approaches to predictive modeling:

- "Logit": This entailed the use of logistic regression, and exploratory data analysis and stepwise for variable selection. Less time was spent on preparing files in comparison to selecting variables and estimating the model. Practitioners as opposed to academics were associated with this approach.
- "Tree": This was characterized by reliance on decision trees, low reliance on exploratory analysis or stepwise variable selection, and the use of estimation and test sub-samples of the calibration data. The approach involved a lot of time allocated for estimating the model, and entailed more time in total.
- "Practical": This approach did not emphasize any particular statistical model but placed strong emphasis on common sense in selecting variables. Users of this approach tended to allocate more time to downloading data,

although less time in total on the entire process, and did not sub-divide the data into estimation and test sub-samples. Practitioners were fairly strongly associated with this factor.

- "Discriminant": This approach relied heavily on discriminant analysis as the statistical model and cluster analysis for selecting variables. Users of this approach spent less time on data cleaning and more on estimation, and ended up using more variables than average in their models.
- "Explain": This approach was not associated with any particular statistical model, but was strongly associated with self-reported use of theory, factor analysis, and cluster analysis for variable selection. This suggests users of this approach were interested in understanding churn as well as (or as a means toward) predicting it. Users of this approach tended to use fewer variables in their final model, and explored several estimation techniques before selecting the final one.

The authors regressed each entry's prediction performance versus factor scores describing the degree to which each entry used each approach. They found the Logit and Tree approaches tended to perform best, Practical was a notch below, Explain was a notch below that, and Discrimant had the worst performance.

These particular results may not hold universally, but the analysis emphasizes that predictive modeling is a process, more than just a statistical technique. The implication is that various approaches can work but must be *managed*. For example, if a firm's analysts are using the Tree approach, they will require more time, especially on estimating their models. This means that investment in faster hardware may be worthwhile. Analysts using the Explain approach may not generate as accurate predictions, but these analysts should be tapped for the insights they are generating. If those insights are not forthcoming or illuminating enough, the analysts should be encouraged to use a Logit or Tree approach, which at least will gain accuracy if not as much insight.

10.6 Future Research

This chapter has several implications for future research. These include:

- *Appropriate sizes for calibration and validation samples*: Guidelines are needed for the best sample sizes in absolute as well as relative terms.
- *The relative importance of different types of variables in different types of predictive models*: Are customer characteristics worth the added expense of acquiring from list vendors? How important are competitive variables? How valuable are variables that measure previous marketing efforts and responses to those efforts?
- *New methods for variable selection*: New methods are needed to select variables for inclusion in predictive models. The ideal method would avoid

omitted variables bias that arises from using stepwise, and the effort involved with factor analysis, while coming up with a parsimonious model.

- *New methods for statistical models*: Machine learning algorithms (vector support machines, boosting and bagging, Bayesian Networks, etc.) need to be thoroughly investigated and compared with simpler techniques.
- *Use of Type II Tobit*: When predicting a 0–1 response and level of response, is a Type II Tobit better than a regression and logistic regression estimated separately and multiplied together?
- *Perfecting the n-tile cut-off approach*: We need better methods for determining how many n-tiles to use.
- *Optimal cut-off scores*: More work is needed to follow up on Bult and Wansbeek (1995), comparing their work with the n-tile cut-off approach.
- *Balancing Type I and Type II Errors*: Methods are needed that allow database marketers to quantify the costs of Type I and Type II Errors and determine an optimal cut-off score based on their consideration.
- *Optimal contact strategy models for determining cut-offs for successive campaigns*: There is promising work in this area (Chapter 28) but more is needed that takes into account wear-in, wear-out, and Type I and Type II Errors.
- *Selectivity and model wearout*: How should one re-estimate predictive models when the customers that provide data for those models have been selected to receive marketing efforts by previous marketing models?
- *Does model interpretation pay off?* Are firms that pay attention to the insights generated by predictive models able to translate those insights into long-run success? What organizational forms best encourage sharing of these insights? Does outsourcing the estimation or implementation phases of predictive modeling result in fewer shared insights, and lower long-term performance?
- *What are the approaches to the predictive modeling process and how can they be better managed?* Neslin et al. (2006a) show there are different approaches to predictive modeling, defined by the choices analysts make as they move through the process. Are there generic approaches that apply across all kinds of models, and if so, what are the costs and benefits of each, and how should these approaches be managed?

Part IV
Database Marketing Tools: Statistical Techniques

Chapter 11
Statistical Issues in Predictive Modeling

Abstract Whereas Chapter 10 describes the basic process of predictive modeling, this chapter goes into depth on three key issues: selection of variables, treatment of missing data, and evaluation of models. Topics covered include stepwise selection and principal components methods of variable selection; imputation methods, missing variable dummies, and data fusion techniques for missing data; and validation techniques and metrics for evaluating predictive models.

The word (scientific) "model" has several meanings. Here we focus on statistical models. A model is, in effect, a statement of reality or its approximation. Most phenomena in the social sciences are extremely complex. With a model we simplify the reality and focus on a manageable number of factors. For example, economists often assume a world where there are only two products available, apples and oranges, in order to understand the relationship between the price of an apple and the price of an orange. Economists know that the assumed world is far from the reality. However, they devise a model to allow them to answer the question of their interests within the assumed world. Once economists build knowledge from a simple world, they often extend their model to study more complex world that may be closer to the reality.

Managers build a statistical model to understand and predict variables of importance to their firms. Consider a manager in a bank who wants to determine to whom he or she should issue credit cards. Or the manager wants to know who will default and who will not. It is impossible to completely understand why consumers default and identify all the factors influencing customer's default behavior. Simplifying the reality, the bank manager sets up a statistical model that relates customer's default behavior to only two important factors, the income and the education. We know that this simple model is not very close to the reality. There surely are thousands of other variables that may influence customer's default behavior. The manager does not include them into the model because they are either minor factors or they are not available in the database. Hopefully, the manager could reduce the default rate by 80% with the help of this simple model.

This chapter describes the fundamentals of a statistical model building. We do not discuss statistical basics that can be found in other textbooks on statistics or marketing research. Instead, we focus on issues that are important to database marketers but are not well-treated in other books. We begin our discussion on the managerial justification for building a statistical model. Then we discuss three important statistical issues that are of prime importance to database marketers: model/variable selection, treatment of missing data, and evaluation of the model.

11.1 Economic Justification for Building a Statistical Model

Why do we want to build a statistical model? What is the economic benefit from building a model? Database marketers have often used the decile analysis to evaluate the economic value of a model. The concept may best be explained by an example. Suppose that a bank has budget available to issue 2,000 credit cards and needs to determine who should receive a card among 10,000 credit card applicants. It will lose $400 if a customer defaults and gain $100 if the customer does not default. And assume that the market average default probability is 11.5%. Without a statistical model, the bank does not know who will default and will not. Hence, it may randomly select 2,000 customers among 10,000 applicants and issue credit cards. Given the market (average) default probability of 11.5%, 230 (0.115 × 2,000) customers will default and 1,770 customers will not. Therefore, with randomly issuing credit cards to 2,000 applicants, the bank will collect total profits of $85,000 (1,770 × $100 − 230 × $400).

Now assume the bank develops a statistical model estimated using data from current customers. Based on the estimated model, it can predict the default probability for each of the 10,000 applicants. Customers are ranked in descending order in terms of their predicted default probabilities. The ranked customers are evenly divided into ten groups (or *deciles*), each with 1,000 customers as shown in Table 11.1. The second column in Table 11.1 represents the average of the predicted default probabilities over 1,000 customers. Instead of randomly selecting 2,000 customers to receive a credit card, it targets the 2,000 customers in decile 9 and 10, who are least likely to default.[1] The third column shows the percentage of actual defaulters. Eleven out of 1,000

---

[1] We could actually find the breakeven default rate to maximize the profit if we were not constrained to issue only 2,000 cards. The bank should issue the credit card if the expected profit is greater than zero. Therefore, the profit maximizing rule is "issue card if $100 × (1 − p) − $400 × p > 0$ where p is the default probability. Hence, the breakeven default probability is 0.2. That is, the bank should issue the credit card if the predicted

Table 11.1 Decile analysis demonstrating the economic value of a statistical model

Decile	Model predicted Default rate (%)	Actual Default rate (%)	Expected Profits ($)	Actual Profits ($)
1	25.5	26.7	−27,500	−33,500
2	21.4	22.3	−7,000	−11,500
3	18.0	17.8	10,000	11,000
4	13.3	12.9	33,500	35,500
5	12.6	12.5	37,000	37,500
6	10.8	10.4	46,000	48,000
7	8.1	7.6	59,500	62,000
8	3.7	3.3	81,500	83,500
9	1.2	1.1	94,000	94,500
10	0.1	0.1	99,500	99,500
Total	11.5	11.5	426,000	426,000

customers actually default in decile 9 while only one customer defaults in decile 10. The bank collects profits of $194,000 (1,988 × $100 − 12 × $400) by employing the statistical model. As a result, the bank can increase the profit from $85,000 to $194,000 with the model. Therefore, the economic benefit of the statistical model is $109,000.

The economic benefit of a statistical model can only be realized by building a good model that provides accurate predictions. The predictive model in Table 11.1 can be said to be a good model since its predicted default rates are very close to the corresponding actual default rates. However, we can easily think of more accurate model that perfectly forecasts who will default and who will not. In the following three sections, we discuss three key statistical (however, often ignored) issues that will help database marketers to develop more accurate models.

11.2 Selection of Variables and Models

11.2.1 Variable Selection

Most predictive models (e.g., regression, logistic regression, neural nets) can be stated in the following regression-type format:

$$Y = f(X_1, X_2, X_3, \ldots X_K) + \varepsilon \qquad (11.1)$$

where Y is the variable being predicted (customer response, customer value, etc.), the X's are the potential predictor variables, and ε are other (random) variables that have not been observed by researchers. Note that "K" is

---

default probability is less than 0.2. Applied to the data given in Table 11.1, credit cards should be issued to 8,000 applicants (from decile 3 to 10) to maximize its profits.

the number of potential predictor variables (including the intercept). In real-world applications, the value for K can be very high, easily in the hundreds if not in the thousands. This is because there are often many demographic variables and other customer characteristics available, several measures of previous customer behavior (RFM, etc.), and several previous contact variables (e.g., marketing contacts). There are several reasons why all K variables cannot be included in the model: (1) Computation time – for example, a neural net would take an enormous amount of time to run with 300 predictors. (2) Feasibility – in a decision-tree model, one would run out of observations if all 300 predictors were used. (3) Overfitting – there is a danger that using 300 variables will result in "overfitting," whereby the model is able to find a unique idiosyncratic combination of variables that can predict an individual observation, but the relationship implied by this combination does not hold up in general. (4) Interpretation – it is often difficult to interpret a model with 300 variables. As a result, the model cannot be easily communicated to upper level management, and hence is less likely to be trusted and used.

The ideal approach to selecting which variables should be in the model would be theory. To the extent that theory is available for why certain variables should be in the model, these variables should be included (e.g., if data on customer complaints are available, this variable should certainly be included in a model of customer churn). However, very often there is not good theory available that we would be confident in relying on. In this case, we should rely on statistical methods to select variables to be included in the model. There are several techniques available for this: (1) all-subset regression, (2) step-wise techniques, (3) principal components regression, and (4) other advanced techniques. We discuss these methods in this section.

11.2.1.1 All-Possible Subset Regression

All possible subset regression is frequently used to determine the optimal set of independent variables. This procedure first requires the fitting of all possible combinations among the available independent variables. For example, if three independent variables are available, we need to fit eight regression equations, $\varnothing$, $\{X_1\}$, $\{X_2\}$, $\{X_3\}$, $\{X_1, X_2\}$, $\{X_1, X_3\}$, $\{X_2, X_3\}$, and $\{X_1, X_2, X_3\}$. Next, select the best regression equation using some statistical criteria such as adjusted R^2, AIC (Akaike Information Criteria) or BIC (Bayesian Information Criteria):

$$\text{Adjusted } R^2 = 1 - \left[\frac{n-1}{n-k}\right]\left(1 - R^2\right) \tag{11.2a}$$

$$AIC = -2\log\hat{L} + 2k \tag{11.2b}$$

$$BIC = -2\log\hat{L} + k\log n \tag{11.2c}$$

where n is the number of observations, k is the number of predictors including the intercept and $\hat{L}$ is the value of the likelihood function achieved by the model. Different from R^2, these criteria penalize more complex models so that a simple model may often be chosen if the increase in fit by including additional variables is not large enough. We select the best model with the largest adjusted R^2 or the lowest AIC or BIC. The adjusted R^2 is used for linear regression models while AIC and BIC can be used for both linear and non-linear models. Assuming that the model errors (ε) are normally distributed, the AIC becomes $n \log \hat{\sigma}^2(k) + 2k$ where $\log \hat{\sigma}^2(k)$ is the variance of ε. AIC however still tends to select models that overfit the data. To overcome this difficulty, the BIC penalizes the number of estimated parameters, and hence the number of variables included in the model, more strongly (2 for AIC and $\log n$ for BIC) than the AIC (Schwarz 1978).

The major weakness of all-possible subset regression is that the method is not practical when there are a large number of independent variables. If there are 50 variables, we need to run $2^{50} = 1.16 \times 10^{15}$ regressions. Most of commercial statistical packages have all possible subset regressions but they cannot practically handle more than 30 independent variables.

11.2.1.2 Stepwise Selection

An alternative method to select an optimal set of independent variables is a stepwise selection method that combines "forward selection" and "backward elimination". The forward selection procedure begins with fitting a simple regression model for each of the $K - 1$ potential X variables. For each regression model, the F statistic for testing whether or not the slope is zero is obtained. The X variable with the largest F value is the candidate for first variable to be included. If this F value exceeds a predetermined level F_0, the X variable is added. Otherwise, the process terminates with no variables in the model. Suppose that X_1 is entered at step 1. Now the forward selection routine fits all regression models with two X variables, where X_1 is one of the two. For each such regression, we compute the partial F test statistic that will test whether or not $\beta_k = 0$ when X_1 and X_k are two variables in the model. The X variable with the largest partial F value is the candidate for addition. If this F value exceeds a predetermined level F_0, the second X variable is added. Otherwise, the process terminates. The forward selection continues until no further X variables can be added, at which point the routine terminates.

The backward elimination procedure is an attempt to achieve a similar conclusion working from the other direction. That is, it begins with the regression using all independent variables, and subsequently reduces the number of variables in the equation until a decision is reached on the equation to use. The order of deletion is determined by using the partial F value. The backward elimination begins with a regression containing all variables. The partial F value is calculated for every predictor variable treated as though it were the last variable to enter the regression equation. The variable for which this F value is the smallest is the candidate for deletion. If this F value is smaller than the predetermined level F_1, the variable is dropped from the model. Otherwise, the routine terminates. The backward elimination routine continues until no further X variables can be deleted, at which point the routine terminates.

The most popular stepwise selection procedure combines forward selection and backward elimination. It begins with the forward search procedure. And assume that X_1 is entered at step 1 and X_2 is entered at step 2. Now the backward elimination routine comes in to determine whether or not any of these two X variables already in the model (X_1 and X_2 in this case) should be dropped. If a variable's partial F is smaller than the predetermined level F_1, the variable is dropped; otherwise, it is retained. The stepwise selection routine continues until no further X variables can be added or deleted, at which point the search terminates. The stepwise selection allows an X variable to be added into the model at an earlier stage and to be dropped subsequently, if it is no longer useful in conjunction with variables added at later stages.

The stepwise selection is computationally very efficient since it does not need to evaluate the full factorial. However, because of its algorithmic characteristics (e.g., sequential search), the stepwise selection often leads to the sub-optimal solution. The relative merits and drawbacks of stepwise procedures, lower computational costs versus sub-optimality, have been mainly discussed within the linear regression context (Hocking 1976; Miller 1989).

An issue often raised in conjunction with stepwise selection (although it applies to all-possible subset regression as well) is the difficulty it can create in interpreting the results. Stepwise will tend to eliminate a variable if (1) it has little predictive power, or (2) it has predictive power but *is highly correlated with* a variable that has better predictive power. In this latter case is where difficulty in interpretation arises. For example, assume income predicts customer profitability well, but age predicts even better, and income and age are positively correlated. It is possible that stepwise regression will include age in the final model, and eliminate income. But as a result, the estimated coefficient for age picks up not only the impact of age but the impact of income as well – income is not in the model explicitly, so age serves as its representative. How should we interpret an age coefficient of say \$1,000? Taken literally, this means that every additional year of the customer's age makes her or him \$1,000 more profitable. But implicitly, it's the additional age *plus* the extra income that comes with age that makes the customer more profitable.

From a practical standpoint, researchers should always ask themselves – is this variable we've included in the model serving to represent certain other variables besides itself? If so, we need to be careful not to assume that changing that variable alone will induce the change in the dependent variable indicated by its coefficient. An important example of this is if data on catalogs and emails were available but stepwise selected only catalogs for the final model. The coefficient for catalogs would reflect the impact of catalogs *and* emails combined. If we just increase the number of catalogs without a concomitant increase in emails, we may not achieve the gain in sales predicted by the co-efficient for catalog. The careful researcher needs to be savvy in interpreting coefficients when stepwise selection has been used.

11.2.1.3 Principal Components Regression

Massy (1965) developed principal components regression by combining principal components analysis and regression analysis. We first review the method of principal components. Principal components analysis is a technique for combining a large number of variables into a smaller number of variables, while retaining as much information as possible in the original variables. Suppose we have an $n \times k$ matrix of $\mathbf{X}$ of n observations on k variables, and Σ is its variance–covariance matrix. The objective of principal components analysis is to find a linear transformation of $\mathbf{X}$ into a new set of data denoted by $\mathbf{P}$, where $\mathbf{P}$ is $n \times p$ and $p \leq k$. The p variables in $\mathbf{P}$ are called "factors" and the n observations for each factor are called factor scores. The data matrix $\mathbf{P}$ has certain desirable properties: (i) the p variables (columns) of $\mathbf{P}$ are uncorrelated with each other (orthogonality), and (ii) each variable in $\mathbf{P}$, progressing from P_1 to P_2, etc., accounts for as much of the combined variance of the X's as possible, consistent with being orthogonal to the preceding P's. The new variables correspond to the principal axes of the ellipsoid formed by the scatter of sample points in the n dimensional space having the elements of $\mathbf{X}$ as a basis. Hence, the principal components transformation is a rotation from the original X coordinate system to the system defined by the principal axes of this ellipsoid.[2] Specifically, the transformation to principal components is given by

$$\mathbf{P} = \mathbf{M'X} \tag{11.3}$$

To see how $\mathbf{M}$ $(p \times n)$ is determined, post-multiply Equation 11.3 by $\mathbf{P'}$. Then, $\mathbf{PP'} = \mathbf{M'XX'M}$. $\mathbf{XX'}$ is simply the variance–covariance matrix Σ. The variance–covariance matrix for principal components $\mathbf{PP'} = \Lambda$ should be diagonal by virtue of requirement (i) above. Hence, we have:

$$\Lambda = \mathbf{M'\Sigma M} \tag{11.4}$$

Equation 11.4 is an orthogonal similarity transformation diagonalizing the symmetric matrix Σ. The transformation matrix M has an orthonormal set of eigenvectors of Σ as its columns, and $\mathbf{PP'} = \Lambda$ has the eigenvalues of Σ as its diagonal elements. If the columns of $\mathbf{M}$ are ordered so that the first diagonal element of Λ contains the largest eigenvalue of Σ, the second the

---

[2] The principal axes spanned by the elements of $\mathbf{X}$ are not invariant to changes in the scales in which the variables are measured. Hence, $\mathbf{X}$ is usually standardized before the transformation to principal components.

next largest, etc., the principal components will be ordered as specified in requirement (ii).

Instead of fitting a linear regression $\mathbf{Y} = \mathbf{X}\beta + \varepsilon$, principal components regression fits the following regression:

$$\mathbf{Y} = \mathbf{P}\gamma + \varepsilon \tag{11.5}$$

where $\mathbf{P}$ is factor scores from Equation 11.3. Once the values of $\mathbf{P}$ are determined from principal components analysis, the parameters γ can be estimated by ordinary regression.

Massy (1965) suggested that only a few factors should be included – actually, data reduction is its main purpose – but did not provide formal guidelines to determine the number of factors. Marketers often employ heuristic methods. For example, a factor is selected if its eigenvalue is greater than one. Basilevsky (1994) proposed an alternative criterion to determine the number of factors using AIC, the Akaike's information criterion (Naik and Tsai 2004). Or the number of factors can be selected judgmentally according to which set of factors is easiest to interpret[3].

In summary, Principal Components Regression uses all the k original variables, but transforms them to a more manageable number of p factors. The value of this approach hinges on the interpretability of the p factors. Very often the factors generated by the transformation matrix $\boldsymbol{M}$ are difficult to interpret. It turns out however that $\boldsymbol{M}$ is not unique in that, for a given number of factors p, there are other "rotated" versions of $\boldsymbol{M}$ that can produce a factor score matrix $\boldsymbol{P}$ retaining the same amount of information as in the original $\boldsymbol{X}$ matrix (see Lehmann et al. 1998 for more discussion). Often, but not always, the rotated version of $\boldsymbol{M}$ produces factor scores that are easier to interpret. Hence, we recommend principal components regression only when the original independent variables are highly collinear with one another, when there are a great number of potential explanatory variables, and when the factors can be easily interpreted. Principal components regression can be implemented easily in SAS or SPSS by running the principal component analysis, interpreting the factors it yields, computing the factor scores, and then running a regression with these factor scores as independent variables.

11.2.1.4 Other Techniques

Recently, Naik et al. (2000) introduced a new reduction technique called sliced inverse regression to the marketing community. The method was originally developed by Li (1991). Similar to principal components regression, it attempts to extract important factors (a linear combination of all the original independent variables) to reduce dimension. But sliced inverse regression

---

[3] Principal components analysis generates a "loadings matrix," representing the correlation between each factor and each original X variable, that can be used to interpret the factors. See Lehmann et al. (1998) for more details.

provides simple tests for determining the number of factors to retain and for assessing the significance of factor-loading coefficients (the elements of M). The composition of factors is determined objectively on the basis of t-values. Naik et al. (2000) demonstrated that sliced inverse regression performs better than principal components regression using Monte Carlo experiments and two real-world applications. However, sliced inverse regression is also not free from the interpretation problems. So we only recommend its usage when the derived factors are meaningful.

Finally, the variable selection problem has attracted the interest of statisticians interested in applying newly developed Markov Chain Monte Carlo (MCMC) estimation methods. In the previous section, we discussed the relative merits and drawbacks of stepwise procedures, lower computational costs versus sub-optimality. George and McCulloch (1993) proposed a stochastic search variable selection model (SSVS) to overcome the problems of all-possible subset regression (computational costs) and the stepwise selection (sub-optimality). Their procedure uses probabilistic considerations for selecting promising subsets of X's. SSVS is based on embedding the entire regression setup in a hierarchical Bayes normal mixture model, where latent variables are used to identify subset choices. The promising subsets of independent variables can be identified as those with higher posterior probabilities. The computational burden is then alleviated by using the Gibbs sampler to indirectly sample from this multinomial posterior distribution on the set of possible subset choices. Those subsets with higher probability can then be identified by their more frequent appearance in the Gibbs sample.

11.2.2 Variable Transformations

One of the most popular models used among database marketers is the classical linear regression model. It is easy to apply and its interpretation is clear. However, the classical linear regression model assumes that the relationships between a dependent variable and several independent variables are linear. For example, consider the case that we are predicting customer value with a linear regression model:

$$Customer\ Value(i) = Y_i = \sum_{k=1}^{K} \beta_k X_{ik} + \varepsilon_i \qquad (11.6)$$

This linear regression assumes that the relationship between the customer value (Y_i) and the independent variables (X_{ik}) is linear. However, in many applications the straight-line assumption does not approximate the true relationship very well. For example, customer value will be minimal for small values of marketing contact (one of the X's), but once marketing expenditure passes a certain point, customer value increases dramatically. This is called a threshold effect. Or customer value increases rapidly at first with increased marketing investment, but then levels off. This is called a saturation effect.

However, the linearity assumption in classical linear regression is not as narrow as it might first appear. In the regression context, linearity refers to the manner in which the parameters and the disturbance enter the equation, not necessarily to the relationship between variables (Greene 1997). Specifically, we are able to write the linear regression model in a very general form. Let $\mathbf{X} = \{x_1, x_2, \ldots, x_k\}$ be a set of K independent variables and let f_1, $f_2, \ldots, f_M$ be M independent functions. And let $g(Y)$ be a function of Y. Then the linear regression model is:

$$\begin{aligned} g(Y) &= \beta_1 f_1(\mathbf{Z}) + \beta_2 f_2(\mathbf{Z}) + \ldots + \beta_M f_M(\mathbf{Z}) + \varepsilon \\ &= \beta_1 x_1 + \beta_2 x_2 + \ldots + \beta_M x_m + \varepsilon \end{aligned} \tag{11.7}$$

Hence, the original linear regression can be tailored to various modeling situations by using logarithms, exponentials, reciprocals, transcendental functions, polynomials, products, ratios, and so on for $f(\bullet)$ or $g(\bullet)$. For example, the relationship between X and Y might be hypothesized as:

$$Y = X_1^{\beta_1} X_2^{\beta_2} \ldots X_K^{\beta_K} e^\varepsilon = \prod_{k=1}^{K} X_k^{\beta_k} e^\varepsilon \tag{11.8a}$$

In logs,

$$\ln Y = \beta_1 \ln X_1 + \beta_2 \ln X_2 + \cdots + \beta_K \ln X_K + \varepsilon = \sum_{k=1}^{K} \beta_k \ln X_k + \varepsilon \tag{11.8b}$$

This model is known as a multiplicative model or log-linear model, where $f(\bullet) = g(\bullet) = \ln(\bullet)$. It is also known as the constant elasticity model since the elasticity of Y with respect to changes in X_k does not vary with X_k (note: $\eta_k = \partial \ln Y / \partial \ln X_k = \beta_k$). This model has been widely used for various marketing problems. We can estimate parameters of Equation 11.8 using a standard least squares procedure since its functional form belongs to the class of Equation 11.7.

Another popular model among marketers is an exponential model in which the relationship between X and Y is hypothesized as:

$$Y = e^{\beta_1 X_1 + \beta_2 X_2 + \beta_K X_K + \varepsilon} = e^{\sum_{k=1}^{K} \beta_k X_k + \varepsilon} \tag{11.9a}$$

In logs,

$$\ln Y = \beta_1 X_1 + \beta_2 X_2 + \cdots + \beta_K X_K + \varepsilon = \sum_{k=1}^{K} \beta_k X_k + \varepsilon \tag{11.9b}$$

Here we just apply the transformation $g(y) = \ln(y)$. This model is also known as a semi-log model in which the relationship between Y and X is not linear (but $\ln Y$ and X is linear). Again we can estimate parameters of Equation 11.9 using a standard least squares procedure since its functional form belongs to the class of Equation 11.7.

Another useful model is the Box-Cox model that embodies many models as special cases. Suppose we consider a form of the linear model $Y = \alpha + \beta g(x) + \varepsilon$ in which $g(x)$ is defined as:

$$g^{(\lambda)}(x) = \begin{cases} (x^\lambda - 1)/\lambda & \text{if } \lambda \neq 0 \\ \ln(x) & \text{if } \lambda = 0 \end{cases} \tag{11.10}$$

The linear model results if λ equals 1, whereas a log-linear or semi-log model (depending on how Y is measured) results if λ equals 0. If λ equals -1, then the equation will involve the reciprocal of x. That is, depending on the value of λ, we can explain various forms of relationship between Y and X. If λ is known, we simply transform x into $g(x)$ by inserting λ into Equation 11.9. But λ typically is unknown *a priori*. So we may try different values of λ's (e.g., $-1, 0, 1$) and compare the performance of models with different λ's. Alternatively, we can treat λ as an additional unknown parameter in the model that will provide us with a tremendous amount of flexibility. The cost of doing so is that the model becomes non-linear in its parameters. That is, the model does not belong to the class in Equation 11.7 so that we cannot use ordinary least square for its estimation. We would have to use nonlinear regression (available in SAS).

Finally, if we are ready to sacrifice the simplicity of the classical linear regression, we can employ nonparametric regression in which no *a priori* relationship is assumed. Simply assuming the relationship is smooth, nonparametric regression overcomes the highly restrictive structure of linear model and flexibly determines the shape of the relationship. It is data-driven method and, in result, its estimation is computationally intensive. However, because of the recent explosion in the size and speed of computers, several nonparametric procedures can be run on personal computers. For more on nonparametric regression, see Härdle and Turlach (1992), and Hastie and Tibshirani (1990).

11.3 Treatment of Missing Variables

Missing variables is a fact of life for DBM applications. For example, demographics such as income and marital status are often missing because customers do not wish to divulge this information. Previous marketing efforts may be available for some customers but not for others. The question is how to handle this situation. One extreme solution is to eliminate a variable from the analysis if it is missing for any customer. This is obviously wasteful. For example, income could be an important predictor. There would appear to be a huge opportunity cost for omitting this variable from the analysis just because it is missing for say 20% of customers. The following are methods that have been proposed and used for dealing with missing data.

11.3.1 Casewise Deletion

In casewise deletion, the observation is discarded if any one of the variables in the observation is missing. This method is simple but is not desirable if the entire sample size is small. It is especially undesirable when each record has a lot of variables and, hence, there is a high probability that at least one variable is missing. In addition, casewise deletion may lead to the biased results if the characteristics of the discarded records are different from those of the remaining records.

11.3.2 Pairwise Deletion

Pairwise deletion can be used as an alternative to casewise deletion in situations where different samples can be used for different calculations. For example, consider a case of calculating pairwise correlations. The correlation between variable 1 and 2 is calculated across the remaining observations after deleting observations in which variable 1 and/or 2 are missing. And the correlation between variable 1 and 3 is based on the observations after deleting observations in which variable 1 and/or 3 are missing. Each pairwise correlation is computed over different sets of observations. For example, several SAS procedures (in default) employ pairwise deletion. "PROC CORR" in SAS estimates a correlation by using all cases with non-missing values for the pair of variables.

This procedure is also not appropriate when the sample size is small. Moreover, if there is a systematic pattern in generating missing data, the correlation coefficient matrix may be seriously biased because each pairwise correlation is calculated over different subsets of cases.

11.3.3 Single Imputation

In single imputation, one substitutes a single value for each missing value. Once all missing values are substituted, standard statistical procedures are applied to the filled-in complete data set. The simplest form of the single imputation is "mean substitution", in which all missing values of a variable are replaced by the mean value for that variable (computed across observed values). Or the patterns in the complete (non-missing) data can be used to impute a suitable value for the missing response. For example, household income may be related to the value of the car owned and the value of the house owned. Hence, one estimates a regression model with household income as a dependent variable and the value of the car owned and the value of the house owned as two independent variables. The missing values for the household income can be predicted ("imputed") by the estimated regression.

A particular challenge in single imputation is when the analyst has available a variable at the aggregate level, but that variable is missing at the household level. Consider the case where the analyst has mean income for the census tract where the customer resides. It is common to use that mean income as the income value for that customer. However, Duan et al. (2007) show this leads to biased estimates of the income parameter in a predictive model if income is correlated with a variable observed at the individual level, e.g., age. Duan et al. then prescribe a Bayesian procedure for inferring an individual-level estimate of the income variable. The procedure relies on a survey or other source of data that contains individual-specific values of both age and income.

The most critical problem of the single imputation is that it ignores the uncertainty on the predictions of the unknown missing values. As a result, the variability in the variable for which observations are missing is misleadingly decreased in direct proportion to the number of missing data points.

11.3.4 Multiple Imputation

Multiple imputation is an advanced method of dealing with missing data that can solve the "over-certainty" problem of the single imputation method. Rather than replacing a single value for each missing data point, multiple imputation imputes multiple values. For example, we introduced the regression-based single imputation in which each missing value for the household income is predicted by the estimated regression. But we know that the predicted value is distributed as normal. In single imputation, we replace the missing value by the expected value of this normal distribution. In multiple imputation, we can impute the missing value several times by drawing from this normal distribution.

Statisticians have developed a general multiple imputation procedure that replaces each missing value by a *set* of plausible values to incorporate the uncertainty involved in imputing the missing value (Rubin 1987; Schafer 1997). The procedure consists of three steps. First, the missing data are generated m times, resulting in m sets of complete data. Second, each of the m complete data sets is analyzed using the predictive modeling technique being employed for this application. Finally, these intermediate results from the m complete data sets are combined to generate a final model.

There are several ways to implement the multiple imputation procedure. The choice depends on the type of missing data patterns. For monotone missing data patterns, either a regression method or propensity score method can be used. The data set is said to have monotone missing data pattern when a variable X_j is missing for the customer i implies that all subsequent variables $X_k(k > j)$ are all missing for the customer i. For an arbitrary missing data pattern, a Markov chain Monte Carlo (MCMC) method is used (Schafer 1997). We will discuss MCMC method since missing data patterns in database marketing are more likely to be arbitrary.

Let $\mathbf{X}$ be the $n \times p$ matrix of complete data, which is not fully observed. Let the observed part of $\mathbf{X}$ be $\mathbf{X}_{obs}$ and the missing part by $\mathbf{X}_{mis}$. Schafer's imputation method uses a Bayesian approach, in which information about unknown parameters is expressed in the form of a posterior probability distribution. MCMC has been applied as a method for deriving posterior distributions in Bayesian inference. In addition, we need to assume the data model or a probability model for the complete data. Multivariate normal models are usually used for normally distributed data while a log-linear model is assumed for categorical data. Without loss of generality, we assume that the complete data are from a multivariate normal distribution with the unknown parameters θ (i.e., mean vector and variance–covariance matrix). Our goal is to derive the joint posterior distribution of X_{mis} and θ given X_{obs} that is $h(X_{mis}, \theta | X_{obs})$. For multiple imputations for missing data, the following two steps are repeated.

1. *The Imputation Step:* Generate X_{mis} from $f(X_{mis} | X_{obs}, \theta)$. That is, given the estimated mean vector and variance–covariance matrix of the multivariate normal distribution (θ), the imputation step generates the missing values (X_{mis}) from a conditional distribution f.
2. *The Posterior Step:* Generate θ from $g(\theta | X_{mis}, X_{obs})$. The posterior step generates the posterior parameters (mean vector and variance–covariance matrix) for the multivariate normal distribution from a conditional distribution g. These new estimates will then be used in the imputation step.

The two steps are iterated long enough for the iterated values to converge to their stationary distribution. That is, at the tth iteration, the imputation step generates $X_{mis}^{(t+1)}$ given $\theta^{(t)}$ and the posterior step generates $\theta^{(t+1)}$ given $X_{mis}^{(t+1)}$. As a result, we have a Markov chain $\{X_{mis}^{(1)}, \theta^{(1)}\}$, $\{X_{mis}^{(2)}, \theta^{(2)}\}$, $\{X_{mis}^{(3)}, \theta^{(3)}\}\ldots$ which converges to $h(X_{mis}, \theta | X_{obs})$. In practice, 50 to 100 burn-in iterations are used to make the iterations converge to the stationary joint distribution before imputing missing values. Then a set of missing values are independently generated m times from this joint distribution.

When the imputation step is finished, each of the m complete data sets is in turn analyzed with the predictive model. This yields m different sets of the point and the variance estimates for the predictive model parameters. Let $\hat{Q}_i$ be the point estimate from the ith imputed data set and $\hat{U}_i$ be the corresponding variance estimate. That is, we have $\{\hat{Q}_1, \hat{U}_1\}, \{\hat{Q}_2, \hat{U}_2\}, \ldots, \{\hat{Q}_m, \hat{U}_m\}$ from m applications of the predictive model. Then the point estimate for Q from m complete data sets is the average of the point estimates from m different data sets.

$$\bar{Q} = \sum_{i=1}^{m} \hat{Q}_i / m \qquad (11.10a)$$

On the other hand, the variance estimate for $\bar{Q}$ should consider the between-imputation variance as well as the within-imputation variance.

$$Var(\bar{Q}) = \bar{U} + (1 + 1/m)B \tag{11.10b}$$

$$\bar{U} = \sum_{i=1}^{m} \bar{U}_i/m \text{ (within-imputation variance)}$$

$$B = \sum_{i=1}^{m} (\hat{Q}_i - \bar{Q})^2/(m-1)\text{(between-imputation variance)}$$

The total variance $Var(\bar{Q})$ is the weighted average of the within-imputation variance and the between-imputation variance. The within-imputation variance $\bar{U}$ is simply the average of the variance estimates from m different data sets. The between-imputation variance B is the key term which explains the uncertainty associated with missing values. Since single imputation does not consider this between-imputation variance for missing values, its variance estimates become underestimated.

Multiple imputation is becoming more popular in treating missing values among database marketers because of its theoretical attractiveness and the availability of commercial software. For example, SAS has a procedure PROC MI that can implement multiple imputations for an $n \times p$ matrix of incomplete data. Once the m complete data are generated and analyzed by using the predictive model of our choice, PROC MIANALYZE can be used to generate valid statistical inference (e.g., Equation 11.10) by combining results from the m applications of the predictive model.

11.3.5 Data Fusion

Kamakura and Wedel (1997) introduced a special type of missing data problem called data fusion. Figure 11.1 shows the structure of data set for data fusion. A marketing researcher conducts a survey and then attempts to relate its results to another survey conducted with a different sample of respondents. We conduct a survey to respondents in sample A to collect variables I and II, and conduct another survey to respondents in sample B to collect variable II and III. Combining these two survey responses, we have missing observations of variable III for sample A respondents and variable I for sample B respondents. The variables common to sample A and B can be demographic variables, whereas the variables unique to sample A or sample B can be brand choice behavior and media exposure, respectively.

It is not practical to apply the multiple imputation procedure to this type of data since there are too many missing variables to be imputed. Statisticians have traditionally developed a special technique called a file concatenation

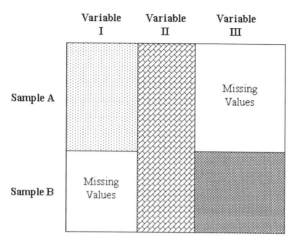

Fig. 11.1 Data structure for the data fusion problem (Modified from Kamakura and Wedel 1997).

method which is designed to combine data from two different sources. In a file concatenation approach, when a variable is missing from sample A (the recipient sample), its value is taken from sample B (the donor sample) to replace it (Ford 1983; Roberts 1994). Each recipient customer in sample A is linked to one or more donor customers in sample B on the basis of common variables. Similarity or distance between customers is measured in terms of common variables (e.g., demographic variables).

Kamakura and Wedel's data fusion method is different from previous file concatenation methods in several aspects. First, they assume the existence of a set of unobserved imputation groups in the combined sample of A and B. If some variables in sample A are missing, they can be replaced by values that are derived from the (mixture) model estimates obtained from customers from sample B belonging to that same latent imputation group. The fundamental idea is similar to the previous file concatenation methods. However, Kamakura and Wedel identify (latent) homogeneous groups based on statistical estimation, whereas the previous file concatenation methods identify similar customers in rather heuristic ways. Second, their procedure is specially tailored to discrete data and the problem of forming cross-classified tables with chi-square tests of significance among variables from independent studies obtained from separate samples. Third, previous methods concatenate two independent files by matching them on the basis of the information on the common variables (e.g., variable II in Fig. 11.1) only. In contrast, data fusion uses a mixture model that identifies homogeneous imputation groups on the basis of all information available from the two samples. Finally, their data fusion method overcomes problems of model selection encountered in previous approaches to modeling under missing data. Data fusion uses multiple imputations to provide an assessment of the uncertainty caused by the data-fusion process.

As mentioned, there are several ways to implement multiple imputation procedures. The choice depends on the type of missing data patterns. Data fusion is a special type of multiple imputation technique designed to combine data from multiple sources. Hence, the multiple imputation method in previous section may be appropriate for general missing variable problems encountered by database marketers. However, when database marketers attempt to combine customer data from various sources, data fusion can be a very efficient method.

11.3.6 Missing Variable Dummies

Another simple approach to treat missing variables is to create a missing variable dummy per covariate to signify that the variable is missing for a given customer (Van den Poel and Larivière 2003). The extra dummy takes on the value of 1 or 0 depending on whether a variable for a particular customer is missing or complete. For example, suppose that one of the independent variables is $INCOME$ that contains some missing values. We define:

$INCOMEM_i = 1$ if income is missing for customer i, and 0 if not missing

$INCOMEO_i =$ customer i's income if income is not missing, and 0 if missing

$Y_i =$ dependent variable to be predicted for customer i, e.g., customer value

The model is then $Y_i = \beta_0 + \beta_1 INCOMEM_i + \beta_2 INCOMEO_i + \varepsilon_i$. After estimation, we would have the following predictions:

$$\hat{Y}_i = \hat{\beta}_0 + \hat{\beta}_1 \text{ if income is missing for customer} i \tag{11.11a}$$

$$\hat{Y}_i = \hat{\beta}_0 + \hat{\beta}_2 INCOMEO_i \text{ if income is not missing for customer } i. \tag{11.11b}$$

This method allows us to learn about the relationship between income and customer value among the customers for whom we have such information. That relationship is quantified by $\hat{\beta}_2$. We also learn whether the fact that the customer has missing income data provides any insight on customer value. That insight is quantified by $\hat{\beta}_1$. For example, we might find $\hat{\beta}_1 > 0$ if wealthy people are reluctant to divulge their income. In summary, this method allows us to learn about the relationship between the missing variable and the dependent variable of interest, while at the same time providing information on the types of people for whom information is missing.

Missing variable dummies can actually be used after we impute missing observations from single or multiple imputations. The extra dummy takes on the value of 1 if the observation is imputed (previously missing) and 0 if the observation is complete. For example, we apply the above regression with two income variables: $INCOMEM_i = 1$ if income is imputed for customer i, and 0 if complete; $INCOMEO_i =$ customer i's income if income is not imputed, and customer i's imputed income if missing. If missing values occur randomly and our imputation procedure is unbiased, the coefficient associated with $INCOMEM$ will be estimated to be 0. If this coefficient is not zero and statistically significant, we conclude that our imputing method does not capture the pattern of missing data generation process appropriately.

11.4 Evaluation of Statistical Models

We often come up with several alternative models in a database marketing application. We then need to determine which one to use. This is the subject of model selection in statistics. In a typical database marketing application, we randomly partition the data into two mutually exclusive subsets, the estimation sample and the holdout (or test) sample. We estimate competing models on the estimation (also called calibration) sample, and test their predictive performance on the holdout (also called validation) sample.

The major drawback in comparing models in the estimation sample has been found to be the problem of overfitting (i.e., finding statistical parameters that predict idiosyncratic characteristics of the calibration data that do not hold up in the real world). For example, the estimation of classical regression model is designed to minimize its mean squared error (or sum of squared errors). As a result, a complex model is guaranteed to have a lower mean squared error (or higher R^2) than a simpler model. Taking an extreme case, using a polynomial of sufficiently high order, we can develop a regression model with zero mean squared error. However, this complex model may overfit the data by identifying random fluctuations as true patterns in the data. As mentioned in the section of all-possible subset regression, to overcome the problem of overfitting, statisticians have developed evaluation criteria such as adjusted R^2, AIC and BIC for model selection in the calibration sample. You select the model with the highest adjusted R^2 or the lowest AIC or BIC. Basically, these criteria avoid the problem of overfitting by panelizing the number of parameters to be estimated.

Even though model selection in the calibration sample has been widely studied in the statistical literature, database marketers rarely evaluate alternative models in the calibration sample. Hence, we limit our attention to model selection problems based on the validation sample. We first discuss various methods to divide the sample into calibration and validation samples, and then study evaluation criteria to compare alterative models in the validation sample.

11.4.1 Dividing the Sample into the Calibration and Validation Sample

How much of the data should be saved for the validation sample? The larger the calibration sample, the more accurate the model (hence, lower standard errors for the parameter estimates), although the returns would begin to diminish once the size of calibration data exceeds to a certain limit. And the larger the validation sample, the more discerning is the comparison between alternative models. There is a tradeoff.

11.4.1.1 The Holdout Method

The holdout method randomly partitions the data into two mutually exclusive subsets, the calibration sample and the validation (or holdout) sample. Models are estimated with the calibration sample and the prediction errors of the estimated models are compared using the validation sample.

The first important issue in the holdout method is what percentage of the data should be used for the calibration sample. More data in the calibration sample leads to more efficient estimates, while more in the validation sample leads to a more powerful validity test. That is, as more data are used for the calibration sample (so less data for the holdout sample), the model parameter estimates become more accurately estimated but the variance of the prediction errors for each competing model becomes larger. Alternatively, if you decrease the size of the calibration sample, the variance of the prediction errors becomes smaller but the parameter estimates become inaccurate.

In many database marketing applications, it is common to reserve one-third of the data for the holdout sample and use the remaining two-third for the estimation (Kohavi 1995). Steckel and Vanhonacker (1993) showed that the proportion of the sample optimally devoted to validation increases, levels off, and then decreases as the total sample size increases. Specifically, in small samples (e.g., $n < 100$), the one-quarter to one-third validation split was recommended. However, once the sample size gets larger, any reasonable split performed equally well. Hence, we may not need to worry about the optimal split between estimation and validation sample since the sample sizes in real database marketing applications are very large.[4]

A second issue in creating the calibration and holdout samples is the risk that the resulting calibration or holdout sample may not be representative despite the random partitioning. The overrepresented class in the calibration sample will be underrepresented in the holdout sample. For an example of credit scoring, suppose that the data have 50% of defaults and 50% of

---

[4] All the results from Steckel and Vanhonaker (1993) were based on a regression model containing two independent variables, which is a rather restrictive specification. Hence, more research may be required to generalize their results.

non-defaults. If the calibration sample happens to have more than 50% of defaults, then the percentage of defaults in the holdout sample will be less than 50%.

There are two ways of addressing this problem (Witten and Frank 2000). One is to employ stratification in partitioning the data. For the discrete dependent variable, a data is partitioned such that both the calibration and the holdout sample have the same proportion of each class. For the continuous dependent variable, the data are ranked in ascending order and is partitioned such that observations are evenly represented in both samples. An alternative way is to do random sub-sampling where the holdout method is repeated k times and the prediction error is derived by averaging the prediction errors from different iterations. Even though it is time consuming, random sub-sampling is a better way of minimizing the problem of sample misrepresentation.

A third issue is that selecting the best model from a single experiment (or partitioning) may be too naïve. The estimates of prediction errors are random variables so that they are expected to show random variations. Hence, in order to compare the true performances of alternative models, we require a set of prediction error estimates from multiple experiments. More specifically, we randomly divide our data into the calibration and the validation sample. Estimate two alternative models using the calibration sample, and derive the prediction errors of two models applied to the validation sample, $\{x_1, y_1\}$, where x_1 and y_1 are the prediction error estimate of the first model and the second model. We now repeat the procedure all over again. We divide the data, estimate models, and derive another set of prediction errors. This yields $\{x_2, y_2\}$. We repeat the same experiment k times resulting in k sets of prediction error estimates. Considering these k sets of estimates as a paired comparison data, we can design a formal statistical test for comparison, a paired t-test. The test statistic is $t = \bar{D}/\sqrt{\sigma_D^2/k}$ where $D_i = x_i - y_i$, $\bar{D}$ is the mean of D_i, and σ_D^2 is the variance of D_i. Given your choice of significance level, we reject or accept the null hypothesis that the performances of two models are the same.[5]

11.4.1.2 K-Fold Cross-Validation

As implied, the holdout method makes inefficient use of the data by reserving a large portion of the data for the validation sample. If the size of the data

---

[5] Once we find the best performing model, we are often interested in reporting its parameter estimates. Then we apply the best model to the entire sample and report its parameter estimates. This procedure is applied to the other calibration/validation methods such as k-fold cross-validation, leave-one-out and the bootstrap. That is, the goal of dividing the sample into the calibration and validation is to get accurate prediction error estimates in an efficient way. So if we are interested in parameter estimates, we do not need to divide the sample into two so that we can estimate the parameters more accurately.

is really big, this is not a significant problem. However, the size of your data in practice may often be smaller than you would like it to be. Database marketers frequently adopt K-fold cross-validation technique to use the data more efficiently.

In K-fold cross-validation, the data is randomly divided into K equal sized and mutually exclusive subsets (or folds). The model is estimated and validated k times; each subset in turn is reserved for the validation and the remaining data are used for estimation. The k prediction errors from different iterations are averaged to provide the overall prediction error estimate.

Similar to the holdout method, the problem of sample misrepresentation problem in K-fold cross-validation can be mitigated by stratification and/or repetition. If stratification is adopted to K-fold cross-validation, it is called stratified k-fold cross-validation. Repeating k-fold cross-validation multiple times using different partitions (or folds) and averaging the results will provide a better error estimate.

How many folds should be used? Various tests on a number of datasets have shown that ten is about the right number even though there are not any strong theoretical explanations as to why (Witten and Frank 2000). Kohavi (1995) has empirically shown that as k decreases (e.g., $k = 2$ and 5) and the estimation sample sizes get smaller, there is a variance due to the instability of the estimation sample, leading to an increase in variance. The k-fold cross-validation with 10 to 20 folds produced the best performance.

11.4.1.3 Leave-One-Out Method

Leave-one-out cross-validation is simply a type of k-fold cross-validation when k is equal to the size of the entire sample. Each observation in turn is reserved for validation and the remaining $(k - 1)$ observations are used for estimation. Upon estimation, the model is applied to the validation sample (consisted of one observation) and its prediction error is computed. The overall estimate of prediction error is the average of k error estimates from k iterations.

Leave-one-out cross-validation is an attractive method in using the data (Witten and Frank 2000). Since it uses a large amount of data for estimation, parameters are estimated more accurately. It is shown to work especially well when the dependent variable is continuous. However, it has not performed well for discrete dependent variable or for model selection problem (Shao 1993).

11.4.1.4 Bootstrap

Given a dataset of size n, the principle of the bootstrap is to select samples of size n with replacement from the original sample. Since the bootstrap samples are selected with replacement, some cases are typically sampled more than once. Originally introduced by Efron (1983), bootstrapping has been shown to work better than other cross-validation techniques, especially in small samples.

There are various bootstrap methods that can be used for estimating prediction error and confidence bounds (Efron and Tibshirani 1993). One of the simplest is the 0.632 bootstrap in which a dataset of n observations is selected (with replacement) from an original sample of size n. Since some cases are sampled more than once, there are cases that are not picked. Those observations not included in the bootstrap sample are used as validation samples. The probability of any given observation not being chosen in the original sample is $(1 - 1/n)^n \approx e^{-1} = 0.368$. Therefore, the expected number of distinct observations from the original dataset appearing in the calibration set is 63.2% of the sample size n. Accordingly, we expect that the size of the validation set will be 36.8% of the original sample size n for a reasonably large dataset. The 0.632 bootstrap has been improved to the popular 0.632+ bootstrap that performs very well for estimating prediction error with discrete dependent variables (Efron and Tibshirani 1993).

The estimate of prediction error for 0.632 bootstrap is derived by combining the error from the validation sample and the error from the calibration sample. Since the model is estimated on the sample containing only 63.2% of distinct cases, the prediction error applied to the validation sample may overestimate the true prediction error. On the other hand, the error in the calibration sample underestimate the true prediction error. Hence, the estimate is given by the linear combination of these two errors, given by 0.632 × (prediction error in validation sample) plus 0.368 × (error in calibration sample). Given a bootstrap sample, prediction errors for alternative models are calculated and compared to find the best model.

11.4.2 Evaluation Criteria

Here we describe several evaluation criteria frequently employed by database marketers to choose the best model. Several alternative measures are available to evaluate the performance of the model applied to the validation sample. All of them measure "goodness-of-fit", which refers to how well the model can predict the dependent variable. In other words, these measures all assess the distance between what really happened and what the model predicts to happen. But they differ in ways of quantifying the distance. Depending on the purpose of models, one criterion is preferred to another. There is no dominating criterion. Database marketers employ different performance measures depending on the nature of dependent variables. We first discuss various measures when the dependent variable is continuous (sales, market share, monthly shopping expenditure, etc.). Next we discuss discrete dependent variables (churn, response, etc.).

11.4.2.1 Continuous Dependent Variable

Suppose we have n observations for the validation sample on which we want to evaluate predictions. The actual values for the dependent variable are $Y_1, Y_2, \ldots, Y_n$ and the corresponding predicted values are $\hat{Y}_1, \hat{Y}_2, \ldots, \hat{Y}_n$. If the model predicts perfectly for the ith observation, $\hat{Y}_i$ should be the same as Y_i. There is no error. The distance between $\hat{Y}_i$ and Y_i indicates a prediction error. Table 11.2 summarizes the formulae of alternative performance measures frequently used for the continuous dependent variable. They are different in terms of defining this distance.

Mean squared error may be the most popular measure among statisticians partially because of its mathematical tractability. It is easier to make a statistical inference on the summation of the squared terms. An alternative measure is mean absolute error that measures the Euclidean distance between the predicted and the actual value. Mean squared error panelizes the larger errors more heavily by squaring them while mean absolue error treats all errors evenly. Hence, if your application accepts marginal prediction errors but tries to avoid large errors, you should employ mean squared error as the evaluation measure. On the other hand, note that mean absolute error is more robust to outliers than mean squared error.

Table 11.2 Various evaluation criteria for prediction error with a continuous dependent variable

Evaluation criteria	Formula
Mean squared error	$\sum\limits_{i=1}^{n} e_i^2/n = \sum\limits_{i=1}^{n} (Y_i - \hat{Y}_i)^2/n$
Mean absolute error	$\sum\limits_{i=1}^{n} |e_i|/n = \sum\limits_{i=1}^{n} |Y_i - \hat{Y}_i|/n$
Root mean squared error	$\sqrt{\sum\limits_{i=1}^{n} e_i^2/n} = \sqrt{\sum\limits_{i=1}^{n} (Y_i - \hat{Y}_i)^2/n}$
Mean absolute percentage error	$\left[\sum\limits_{i=1}^{n} \left|\frac{e_i}{Y_i}\right|/n\right] \times 100 = \left[\sum\limits_{i=1}^{n} \left|\frac{Y_i - \hat{Y}_i}{Y_i}\right|/n\right] \times 100$
Relative squared error	$\sum\limits_{i=1}^{n} e_i^2 / \sum\limits_{i=1}^{n} (Y_i - \bar{Y})^2 = \sum\limits_{i=1}^{n} (Y_i - \hat{Y}_i)^2 / \sum\limits_{i=1}^{n} (Y_i - \bar{Y})^2$
Relative absolute error	$\sum\limits_{i=1}^{n} |e_i| / \sum\limits_{i=1}^{n} |Y_i - \bar{Y}| = \sum\limits_{i=1}^{n} |Y_i - \hat{Y}_i| / \sum\limits_{i=1}^{n} |Y_i - \bar{Y}|$

e_i = the prediction error of the ith observation
Y_i = the actual value of the ith observation
$\hat{Y}_i$ = the (model) predicted value of the ith observation
$\bar{Y}$ = the mean of the actual values that is $\sum Y_i/n$

Sometimes it is more relevant to use a relative performance measure. Both mean squared error and mean absolute error are unit dependent. For example, we can increase or decrease mean squared error simply by multiplying our data by an arbitrary number (that is not zero). We cannot tell how good a model with mean squared error of 100 is. Relative squared error makes mean square error unit-free by normalization. Similar to R^2 in linear regression, total sum of squares is used for the normalizing factor. Similarly, relative absolute error normalizes mean absolute error. Mean absolute percentage error can also be interpreted as a kind of relative measure since it has normalization factor (actual value in the denominator) applied to each observation.

There is no dominant performance measure. As shown in the comparison between mean squared error and mean absolute error, each measure has its advantages and limitations. The choice will be determined after studying the research problem itself. For example, the cost associated with prediction errors helps us to select a prediction measure. But cost information is not always available. Hence, researchers report a number of measures to evaluate their model performance. Fortunately, a number of studies have shown that correlations among performance measures are strongly positive. We may not need to worry about much the selection among performance measures.

11.4.2.2 Discrete Dependent Variable

Hit Ratio

Different performance measures have been proposed when the dependent variable is discrete. We first describe two popular measures, the hit ratio and predictive log-likelihood, when the dependent variable takes on values of either 0 or 1. These measures can easily be generalized for the dependent variables with more than two discrete values. For a discrete dependent variable, the predictive value typically takes the form of probabilities. For example, suppose a bank wants to know who is going to default. Historical data includes both defaulters (coded 1) and no defaulters (coded 0) with their demographic characteristics. Upon estimation the model (e.g., logit) is applied to the test sample with n customers. With customer specific demographic information, the model provides the predictive default probability of each customer. If the probability is greater than a cut-off threshold 0.5, then we predict that she will default. Otherwise, she is predicted not to default. Hit ratio is calculated as

$$Hit\ ratio = \sum_{i=1}^{n} H_i/n \qquad (11.12)$$

where H_i is 1 if the prediction is correct and 0 if the prediction is wrong. That is, hit ratio is the percentage of correct predictions.

One may ask why we use the cut-off of 0.5 for the hit ratio. The answer is that if the prediction is higher than 0.5, the event is more likely to occur than not occur, and so we predict that it occurs. However, this is somewhat arbitrary and we will generalize this notion of hit rate, across all thresholds, when we discuss ROC curves.

Predicted Log-Likelihood

Hit ratio employs a 0/1 loss function. The loss is 0 if the prediction is correct and 1 if it is not. This loss function is intuitive and easy to understand. However, the hit ratio is a lexicographic type of measure. It treats the case with the predicted probability of 0.51 to be the same as the case with 0.99 when the customer actually defaults. It ignores the distance between the actual and the predicted once it passes the threshold (i.e., 0.5). Adopting a loss function with continuous form, the predictive log-likelihood overcomes the problem associated with the lexicographic loss function of the hit ratio. The predicted likelihood of observing the data can be expressed as:

$$\text{Predicted Likelihood} = \prod_{i=1}^{n} \left[\hat{P}_i^{Y_i} \times (1 - \hat{P})_i^{(1-Y_i)} \right] \tag{11.13a}$$

Taking logs of this equation, the formula for the predictive log-likelihood is

$$\text{Predictive log-likelihood} = \sum_{i=1}^{n} \left[Y_i \log \hat{P}_i + (1 - Y_i) \log(1 - \hat{P}_i) \right] \tag{11.13b}$$

where $\hat{P}_i$ is the predicted probability of default, and Y_i represents the actual default value taking 1 if customer defaults, 0 otherwise. The larger the log-likelihood, the better the model. The perfect model in which the model predicts 0 when the actual is 0 and 1 when the actual is 1 will have the log-likelihood of zero. Imperfect models will have negative log-likelihoods; the more negative the value, the worse the prediction.

ROC Sensitivity

The concept of ROC (Receiver Operating Characteristic) curve originated in the field of signal detection to measure the diagnostic power of a model (Swets 1988). In order to understand its concept, let us take a look at a two-by-two contingency table shown in Table 11.3. A diagnostic system (or model) looks for a particular "signal" and ignores other events called "noise." The event is considered to be "positive" or "negative," and the diagnosis made is correspondingly positive or negative. For example, there are customers who will respond to the mailing offer ("positive") and who will not ("negative").

Table 11.3 True event versus diagnosis (From Swets 1988)

		Event		
		Positive	Negative	
Diagnosis	Positive	True positive (a)	False positive (b)	$a + b$
	Negative	False negative (c)	True negative (d)	$c + d$
		$a + c$	$b + d$	$a + b + c +$ $d - N$

And using the predictive model we estimate customers' response probabilities, and assign them into responders or non-responders. There are two ways in which the actual event and the diagnosis can agree: "true-positive" and "true-negative" in Table 11.3. And there are two cases that diagnosis can be wrong: "false-positive" and "false-negative."

In a test of a diagnostic model, the true-positive proportion, $a/(a + c)$, and the false-positive proportion, $b/(b + d)$, can capture all of the relevant information on accuracy of the model. These two proportions are often called the proportion of "hits" and "false alarms." The true positive proportion is also called 'sensitivity' that is the probability of a randomly selected positive event being evaluated as positive by the model. In addition, the true negative proportion is often called specificity that is the probability of a randomly selected negative event being evaluated as negative by the model. Note that the false positive proportion is $(1 - \text{specificity})$. A good diagnostic model will provide many hits with few false alarms.

The ROC curve plots the proportion of hits versus false alarms for various settings of the decision criterion (see Fig. 11.2). Going back to the credit assessment example, we derived hit ratio based on the decision that if the predicted default probability of a customer is greater than a threshold value (e.g., 0.5), then we predict that she will default. Otherwise, she is predicted not to default. In an ROC curve, we initially set the threshold value high, say 0.9. We do not issue a credit card to a customer if her predicted default probability is higher than 0.9. We issue a credit card otherwise. Given the threshold, we can prepare the two-by-two contingency table. The proportions of hits and false alarms from the table will become a point of the ROC curve for the model. Now we set the threshold value a bit lower, say 0.8. And plot a point of the ROC curve. Changing the value of the threshold value to 0 will complete the ROC curve.

Note an ROC curve is generated for a particular model as a function of a critical decision criterion or parameter in the model, the cut-off threshold. The performance (or value) of the model is measured to be the area under the ROC curve. The area varies from 0.5 to 1. The major diagonal in Fig. 11.2 represents the case of the area equal to 0.5 when the proportions of hits and false alarms are the same. Random assignment will lead to the area of 0.5. On the other hand, a perfect model when the curve follows the left and upper axes has the area of 1. There are no false alarms with 100% hits. The realistic

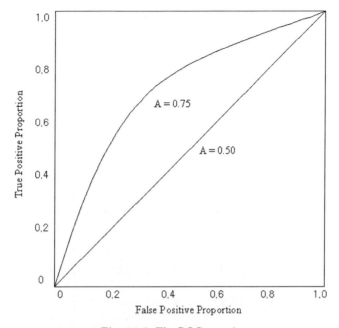

Fig. 11.2 The ROC curve*.

* "A" signifies the area under the ROC curve. The best model is the one that generates ROC curves with highest area (From Swets 1988).

model lies in between. The area under the curve increases as the model can increase more hits while reducing the number of false alarms. We want to select the model with the highest-area ROC curve, because this means that for a given threshold cut-off, it generates more true-positives relative to false-positives.

11.4.2.3 Evaluation Criteria to Assess Financial Performance

The evaluation criteria discussed so far measure the goodness-of-fit that refers to how well the model can predict the dependent variable. However, these evaluation criteria are not useful for assessing the financial performance of the predictive models. Models that do not fit well can still perform well (Malthouse 2002). There are several evaluation criteria to assess the financial performance of the models.

Lift (Gains) Chart

Direct marketers frequently evaluate their proposed models using a gains table (or chart) analysis. Gains table can be developed as follows (see Banslaben

Table 11.4 Gains and lift table

Decile	Response rate (%)	Lift	Cumulative lift (%)
1	6.00	3.75	37.5
2	3.50	2.19	59.4
3	2.50	2.56	75.0
4	1.50	0.94	84.4
5	1.00	0.63	90.6
6	0.65	0.41	94.7
7	0.50	0.31	97.8
8	0.19	0.12	99.0
9	0.12	0.08	99.8
10	0.04	0.03	100.0
Total	1.60	1.00	

(1992) and Chapter 10 more details). Once we estimate the response model, the model is applied to each customer in the validation sample to derive the corresponding response probability ($\hat{P}_i$). Then all customers in validation are ordered by their predicted response probabilities. In the final step, customers are sequentially divided in groups of equal size (usually ten groups), and the average actual response rate per group is calculated. The gains table describes the relationship between the ordered groups and the (cumulative) average response rate in these groups. Table 11.4 shows an example of gains table.

The response rate of the top decile is usually used to evaluate the performances of models. The response rate of the top decile in Table 11.4 is 6%, which is much higher than the overall response rate of 1.6%. The best performing model is the one which provides the highest response rate in the top decile. Alternatively, the variation among the response rates in each of 10 deciles can be used to evaluate the performances of competing models (Ratner 2002). The best model will show the greatest variation. That is, our goal here is to maximize the separation between top deciles and the bottom deciles.

Lift is a useful measure that can be calculated directly from the gains table, and also used to compare the performances among alternative models. Formally, we can define lift as $\lambda_k = r_k/\bar{r}$ where λ_k is lift for the kth tile, r_k is response rate for the kth tile and $\bar{r}$ is the average response rate across the entire sample. In words, λ_k is how much more likely customers in kth tile are to respond, compared to the average response rate for the entire sample. We want lift in the top tiles to be greater than 1, and correspondingly, lift in the lower tiles to be less than 1. For example, the average response rate across the entire sample is 1.60% while the response rate in the top decile 6.00%. Therefore, customers in the top decile are 3.75 times more likely to respond than average ($\lambda_k = 6.00/1.60 = 3.75$). We say, top decile lift is 3.75. Lift itself does not have direct managerial (or financial) significance. However, the extent to which top tiles have higher lifts makes them more profitable, since lift is directly proportional to response rate. In addition, it is easy to compare lift across models or different applications. See more discussion in Chapter 10.

Another evaluation criteria frequently used in database marketing is the cumulative lift chart, which tabulates cumulative response rates from the top n-tile down. Continuing our example in Table 11.4, the cumulative lift for the kth decile is defined by the percentage of all responders accounted for by the first k deciles. For example, the top 3 deciles account for 75.0% of all responders. Obviously, the higher the cumulative lift is for a given decile, the better the model.

Gini Coefficient

The Gini coefficient is essentially the area between the model's cumulative lift curve and the lift curve that would result from random prediction. It was originally developed by the Italian statistician Corrado Gini. To understand the general concept, we need to define the Lorenz curve and the perfect equality line. The Lorenz curve is a graph representing the cumulative distribution function of a probability distribution. For example, it is frequently used to represent income distribution of a country, where it shows for the top $x\%$ of its population, what percentage ($y\%$) of the total income they have. The percentage of the population is plotted on the x-axis, and the percentage of the total income on the y-axis. To draw the Lorenz curve, all the elements (or customers) of a distribution must be ordered from the largest to the smallest (in terms of their predicted response probabilities). Then, each element (customer) is plotted according to its cumulative percentage of x and y. The Lorenz curve is compared with the perfect equality line, which represents a linear relationship between x and y. For example, if all the people in the population earn the same income, the Lorenz curve becomes the perfect equality line.

In database marketing applications, we would plot the percentage of customers on the X-axis ordered by their predicted likelihood of responding, and the cumulative percentage of responders (i.e., the cumulative lift curve) on the Y-axis (see Fig. 11.3). The perfect equality line would represent a model where predictions are made randomly, since then each customer would have an equal chance of being predicted to be a responder. The higher this curve relative to the perfect equality line, the better the model because our model can account for a large percentage of the responders by targeting a relatively small percentage of cutomers.

The Gini coefficient is defined graphically as a ratio of the summation of all vertical deviations between the Lorenz curve and the perfect equality line (A) divided by the total area above the perfect inequality line (A + B).

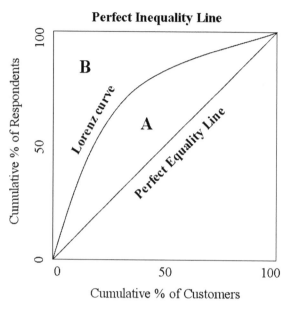

Fig. 11.3 Gini coefficient.

That is, the Gini coefficient is equal to A/(A + B) in Fig. 11.3. Its value lies between 0 and 1, where 0 corresponds to the perfect equality (i.e., everyone has the same income) and 1 corresponds to the perfect inequality (i.e., one person has all the income, while everyone else has zero income). In database marketing terms, a Gini coefficient of 0 means that the model is predicting no better than random, while a value of one corresponds to the (very rare case) that there is only one responder and that customer is identified as the customer with the highest probability of responding. In general, higher Gini Coefficients mean that more responders can be identified by targeting smaller numbers of customers.

The Gini coefficient for a given model can be calcualted as:

$$\text{Gini coefficient} = \sum_{i=1}^{N} (c_i - \hat{c}_i)/(1 - \hat{c}_i) \qquad (11.14)$$

where $\hat{c}_i$ is the proportion of the customers who have a predicted probability of response equal or greater than customer i's and c_i is the proportion of actual responders who are ranked equal or higher than customer i in their response probability. That is, $\hat{c}_i$ is the locus of the cumulative lift curve and c_i is the locus of the perfect equality line. We choose the model with the highest Gini coefficient, that is, the Gini coefficient closest to 1.

11.5 Concluding Note: Evolutionary Model-Building

The scientific method for predicting the future is based on the assumption that the future repeats the past. For many applications, this assumption is reasonable. Suppose we try to predict monthly sales of color television. We may build forecasting models, (whether they are time-series models or regression models) based on historical sales of color television, and isolate patterns from random variations. The predicted sales of a color TV are based on the estimated model (or identified patterns). However, the future can be very different from the past especially the market conditions are changing. The model becomes useless. This is why we need to keep updating models. Sometimes it may be enough to re-estimate the model with additional data. Sometimes we need to change the model itself. Remember that the model cannot be static. (See discussion of model "shelf life" in Chapter 10 (Sect. 10.5.2).)

Chapter 12
RFM Analysis

Abstract Recency (R), Frequency (F), and Monetary Value (M) are the most popular database marketing metrics used to quantify customer transaction history. Recency is how recently the customer has purchases; frequency is how often the customer purchases, and monetary value is the dollar value of the purchases. RFM analysis classifies customers into groups according to their RFM measures, and relates these classifications to behaviors such as the likelihood of responding to a catalog or other offer. RFM analysis was probably the first "predictive model" used in database marketing. This chapter discusses the RFM framework, how it can be used and various extensions.

12.1 Introduction

How do you select customers for target mailing? Or whom should you send your catalogs or direct mail offers to? The need to mail smarter is always among the top concerns of direct marketers. The direct mail promotion that results in sales to 2% of the mailed universe is considered a success. Identifying and targeting the customers who are most likely to respond are therefore of prime concern.

Because of the nature of their businesses, direct marketers including catalogers have been collecting customer data, analyzing them, and developing models for several decades to improve their business performance. One popular approach used to improve mailing efficiency is the RFM – Recency, Frequency, Monetary amount – model. The primitive form of the RFM model was used about 50 years ago by catalogers of general merchandise. For example, as early as 1961, George Cullinan promoted the use and understanding of RFM customer data analysis. Recognizing his contribution in advancing the direct marketing industry, the DMA (Direct Marketing Association) inducted him into the DMA Hall of Fame in 1989.

The core concept of the RFM model is based on the empirical evidence. Direct marketers have found that the response to a mailing offer is heterogeneous across customers. And they also found that customers who have responded well in the past are likely to respond in the future. More specifically, direct marketers have found that customers' purchase response can be predicted using their previous purchase histories. The three most important variables to summarize customers' purchase histories are recency (R), frequency (F), and monetary amount (M). That is, using RFM measures for each customer, one can predict his or her propensity to respond. Once identifying who is going to respond, the direct marketer sends catalogs to customers with high propensity.

This chapter first discusses the fundamental concepts of the RFM model. Second, using the notion of a breakeven point, we study how the model can be used to determine the number of customers to mail to, in order to maximize profits. In Sect. 12.2, highlighting the relationship of RFM model with other statistical tools, we criticize its current status and investigate the possibility of extending its potential. We conclude that while simple RFM analysis may provide a good starting point, statistical model-building using the raw customer data is the better option.

12.2 The Basics of the RFM Model

Suppose that a direct mail company has its house list with a million customers. Each season it decides to mail catalogs to a subset of customers from the house list. Sending catalogs to all customers will maximize its revenue or sales. But it may lose profits if the average response rate is too low. There are some customers who will not purchase the product whatever the company does. The company would like to select good customers who are likely to respond to the catalogs. The goal of an RFM analysis is to predict the response (or purchase) probability of each customer. Sending catalogs to only perhaps 20% of its customers based on these predictions (the good customers), the company can now make a profit.

12.2.1 Definition of Recency, Frequency, and Monetary Value

Based on their experience, direct marketers have found three important purchase-related variables that will influence the future purchase possibility of their customers. The first variable, recency (R), represents the last time the customer purchased from the company. It stands for the elapsed time (measured in days, weeks, months or years) since the last purchase. For example, suppose you randomly select 10,000 customers from a cataloger's house list. Your objective is to find the relationship between the recency and the response probability. You first choose a particular catalog mailing, say the June

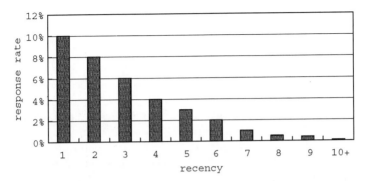

Fig. 12.1 The relationship between recency and the response probability.

catalog. You select 10,000 customers who received that mailing and record whether or not they responded. Then, you measure how many months had elapsed between receipt of the June catalog and the customer's previous purchase. That is the measure of recency. We summarize the results in Fig. 12.1.

Figure 12.1 shows that 350 of the 10,000 customers responded to the June catalog by placing an order. So the average response rate is 3.5%. And the decile analysis based on customers' recency values indicates a negative relationship between the recency and the response rate. Those customers who recently purchased from the company had the higher probability to purchase again when they received the June catalog. Many direct marketers believe that the negative relationship is a law. There may be various reasons why the response rates are decreasing with recency (Gönül et al. 2000). The initial order might serve as a trigger to encourage the customer to think about items that might complement that order. They thus place another soon after the initial order. Or a first time buyer may order a second item because of reduced uncertainty about the product and delivery quality with the arrival of the initial order.

However, the specific relationship between recency and purchase clearly depends on various factors such as the types of product categories and cataloger as well as catalog-specific factors. For example, Gönül et al. (2000) found a U-shaped relationship applied to household semi-durable items. Customers' response rates initially decrease with recency because of the reasons given above, but increase after a year or so because of an inventory effect. That is, customers may need to replace the old product after a year. It is also not hard to imagine a positive relationship between recency and purchase. Consider the customer who has just obtained a new credit card from Capital One. The customer probably would not be very receptive to an offer soon after that for another credit card – the customer just obtained a new credit card; why would he or she want another new one?

Summarizing, the important point is that we frequently find that there is some relationship between the recency and the response rate. It is most often assumed to be negative but it might be U-shaped or positive. Once we learn

the relationship, we can forecast response rate using recency calculated from
their historical purchase records. However, the exact shape of the relationship
is unknown to us before we look at the data.

The second variable, frequency (F), represents how often the customer
has purchased in a certain time period (Bult and Wansbeek 1995). It is
often measured as the number of purchase occasions since the first purchase.
Some direct marketers use the number of purchase occasions divided by the
duration of being the customer. Similar to recency, the exact relationship
between the frequency and response rates should be determined empirically.
But the relationship is often positive. Those customers who frequently bought
the product tend to have higher probability to respond.

Finally, response probabilities are related to monetary value (M) representing the dollar value of previous purchases. One might measure monetary
value as the amount of money spent during a certain time period (Bult and
Wansbeek 1995). Alternatively, one may use the total dollar amount divided
by the duration of being a customer, or simply the average expenditure per
order (Hughes 1996b). Similar to frequency, the monetary value tends to have
a positive relationship with the response probability.

You can see that in the case of frequency and monetary value, these variables can become confounded with the length of the customer relationship if
not expressed on a per-period or per-order basis. However, the length of the
relationship is probably an important predictor of future behavior. Therefore,
perhaps an RFML model would be more appropriate, with recency, frequency
per period, monetary value per order, and length of relationship (e.g., time
since first purchase). However, in the real world, RFM is used, and either F
or M are not often expressed on per period or per order basis, so that at least
one of these variables also captures the length of the relationship.

12.2.2 RFM for Segment-Level Prediction

Once the information on customer purchase histories is summarized in the
three RFM variables, direct marketers construct a model to predict the response propensity for each customer. Direct marketers transform the RFM
variables into discrete form in order to use them to predict response rates.
More specifically, three separate codes for each variable (RFM) are created.
For example, customers are sorted by their recency. A code of "5" is assigned
for the top 20% of customers in terms of their recency values. The next 20%
of customers are coded as "4", and so on. As a result, every customer has a
recency code of 5, 4, 3, 2, or 1. That is, we transform the continuous variable (recency) into five discrete variables (recency codes). As we will criticize
later, there is certainly information loss with this transformation. Similarly,
a frequency code and a monetary code are assigned to each customer. As a
result, each customer is now represented by three RFM codes.

Table 12.1 The predicted response probabilities from RFM model

Three codes R F M	Number mailed	Number responded	Percentage of response
5 5 5	100	15	15.0%
5 5 4	90	13	14.4%
5 5 3	100	13	13.0%
5 5 2	80	10	12.5%
5 5 1	70	7	10.0%
4 5 1	100	8	8.0%
–	–	–	–
–	–	–	–
1 1 2	70	1	0.01%
1 1 1	90	0	0.00%
Total	10,000	350	3.50%

The variable transformation from the original RFM to three RFM (discrete) codes allows us to segment customers into 125 $(5 \times 5 \times 5)$ groups. Every customer is represented by his or her RFM codes and classified into the one of the 125 groups. For example, suppose that a direct marketer randomly selects 10,000 customers out of the house list who received a recent direct mail offer. Responses to the offer are summarized in Table 12.1.[1]

The results in Table 12.1 essentially are a cross-tabulation of R by F by M by response, and become the RFM model for predicting a customer response rate. That is, we *model* the response probability as a function of three RFM codes. For example, if a customer has 5 for R, F, and M code, her response probability is predicted to be 15%. Once the predicted response probabilities are computed for all customers in the house list, one can select a group of customers for an upcoming mailing drop.

Reflecting the popularity of the RFM model, there are commercial packages available in the market to perform the above procedure in a fairly automatic way. Operated on a PC, they do everything necessary to code all customers in terms of RFM, select test groups, and provide reports so that the marketers can do the entire job themselves without any technical assistance. For example, one can get a demo program for "RFM for Windows" from http://www.dbmarketing.com.

12.3 Breakeven Analysis: Determining the Cutoff Point

If the number of direct mail offers to be sent has been dictated by budget considerations, we can easily select customers in the house list by rank-ordering

---

[1] Note that we only have on average $10,000/125 = 80$ customers per segment. With this small sample size, the segment-level response probabilities will be imprecisely estimated. For example, if the estimated response probability is 3.5% for a certain segment, its 95% confidence interval can be calculated to be $(-0.5\%, 7.5\%)$. In practice, more than 10,000 customers are often used to estimate the response probability of a single RFM segment.

them with respect to their predicted response probabilities. However, if we are not provided with this constraint, we cannot determine the number of customers to send direct mails by RFM model alone. We must determine the optimal number of direct mail offers to maximize profit.

12.3.1 Profit Maximizing Cutoff Response Probability

With cost information, the profit-maximizing rule for the mailing decision is rather simple. A firm should send the direct mail to a customer if the expected profit from the customer is greater than zero. That is, we send the direct mail if

$$m \times E(Z) \times \hat{r} - C > 0 \tag{12.1}$$

where m represents profit contribution margin, $E(Z)$ is the expected order amount (given that the customer responds to the mailing offer), $\hat{r}$ is the predicted response probability from the RFM model, and C is the unit mailing cost.

The unit cost of mailing a catalog (C) is reasonably treated to be the same across all customers. And only the variable costs such as printing, packaging and mailing should be included in the cost computation. Other costs such as overhead are not included since we assume the firm incurs no additional overhead for the marginal additional mailing.[2] On the other hand, both the expected order amount and the predicted response probability should be considered to be heterogeneous across customers. The RFM model can be employed to predict the response probability for each customer. As for the expected order amount, we will first assume that it is homogeneous across all customers. Specifically, we will predict the expected order amount for a customer to be the average of past orders across all customers. We will discuss the issue of estimating customer specific order amount later in this chapter.

Note that the Equation 12.1 can be rewritten as $\hat{r} > C/[mE(Z)]$. Given the same expected order amount across all customers, a firm should send the catalog only to customers whose predicted response probability is greater than the unit cost of mailing (C) divided by the expected net contribution dollar $(mE(Z))$. That is, $C/[mE(Z)]$ is the breakeven response probability. For example, suppose that the unit cost of mailing is $2.0, the profit contribution margin is 50%, and customers order $80 on average. Then,

---

[2] The allocation of overhead to database marketing campaigns is an important issue. See Chapter 6 for additional discussion. Also, see Schmid and Weber (1995), who have suggested that the cost computation should be varied depending on the nature of customers targeted. They claimed that only the variable costs should be considered for prospecting while all variable costs with overheads should be counted for old customers to be reactivated. Finally, all costs and some percentage of normal profits should be included for current customers.

the breakeven response probability is 0.05. Ranking its customers by their predicted response probabilities driven by the RFM model, direct marketers should send the mails to customers whose predicted response probabilities is greater than 0.05.

With the cost information, we can calculate the economic benefit of employing the RFM model. For example, again suppose that the unit cost of mailing is \$2, the profit contribution margin is 50%, and customers order \$80 on average. The direct marketer has one million customers and their average response probability is assumed to be 0.02. Hence, the breakeven response rate is $\$2/[(0.5)(\$80)] = 0.05$ or 5%.[3]

Without the RFM model, the direct marketer would not know who will respond and who will not. Hence, it randomly selects 200,000 customers for target mailing. (We would then expect to achieve the average response rate, 2%.) We expect that its net contribution dollar will be $\$160,000 (= \$80 \times 0.5 \times 0.02 \times 200,000)$ and the cost of mailing is $\$400,000 (= \$2 \times 200,000)$. So we have a \$240,000 net loss. Now the direct marketer employs the RFM model and calculates the predicted response probability for each customer. Assume only 20% of customers (or 200,000 customers) turn out to have the response probabilities greater than the breakeven point (0.05). So 200,000 mails are sent to those customers and 16,000 customers (assuming the average response rate of 8%) respond. The net contribution is $\$640,000 (= \$80 \times 0.5 \times 16,000)$ while the cost of mailings is $\$400,000 (= \$2 \times 200,000)$. So we have \$240,000 in net profit. As a result, this direct marketer can increase its profit from minus \$240,000 to \$240,000 by employing the RFM model.[4]

12.3.2 Heterogeneous Order Amounts

Now going back to the issue of the expected order amount, a simple way to predict the dollar amount of order for a customer is to take the average of past orders for each customer. This method is simple and still allows for utilizing a customer-level order amount. However, its prediction may be unreliable when the number of historical orders is small. As a result, we will observe the regression-to-the-mean effect. Consider a customer whose historical order amounts are relatively low. His or her next order will be greater than

---

[3] Practitioners often discount the predicted response rate based on the test market results (Hughes 1996a). This is because marketers often conduct an unfair test. They tend to use the first class mail and pick the best month for the test. As a result, the predicted response rate is biased upward. The discount of 10–15% is usually applied, meaning that the rollout response rate from any RFM cell is assumed to be only 85–90% of what the test response rate was.

[4] For illustration, the example in this section does not explicitly consider error in model predictions of response rates, nor long-term considerations that might influence how deeply down the list the direct marketer will want to mail. See Chapter 10 for further discussions.

this historical average (based on a small sample) because of the regression-to-the-mean effect. The opposite result is expected for those customers with historically high order amounts (Schmittlein and Peterson 1994). Recognizing this problem of the simple average approach, researchers have developed more sophisticated models (Schmittlein and Peterson 1994; Jen et al. 1996; Colombo and Jiang 1999).

Here we describe the model by Colombo and Jiang (1999) in more detail since their model makes perhaps the most reasonable distributional assumption. For a given customer, the dollar amount of order will vary from purchase occasion to occasion. And the amount cannot be negative. They use a gamma distribution with parameter u and θ to model the possible random variation of order amounts over time. [On the other hand, Schmittlein and Peterson (1994) and Jen et al. (1996) have proposed a normal distribution.] This gamma distribution has a mean of u/θ. In order to allow this mean to vary across customers, they keep u constant and allow θ to vary as another gamma distribution with parameters v and ϕ. The (unconditional) distribution for z, the observed dollar amount, is then given by

$$P(z|u, v, \phi) = \frac{\Gamma(u + v)}{\Gamma(u)\Gamma(v)} \left(\frac{z}{\phi + z} \right)^u \left(\frac{\phi}{\phi + z} \right)^v \frac{1}{z} \qquad (12.2)$$

The above equation can be used to estimate the parameters u, v and ϕ using maximum likelihood from the observed dollar amounts of orders.

Colombo and Jiang (1999) also derived the expected amount of order (w_i) for customer i, given that his/her average amount of order is $\bar{z}_i$ across the past x_i number of purchases. That is,

$$E(w_i) = \frac{u(x_i\bar{z}_i + \phi)}{(ux_i + v - 1)} = \left[\frac{v - 1}{ux_i + v - 1} \right] \frac{u\phi}{v - 1} + \left[\frac{ux_i}{ux_i + v - 1} \right] \bar{z}_i \qquad (12.3)$$

Equation 12.3 shows that individual customer-level expected amount of order is a weighted average of the expected order amount across all customers, $u\phi/(v - 1)$, and customer-level observed average amount of order, $\bar{z}_i$. As the number of transactions for customer i (x_i) increases, more weight will be assigned to his/her observed average amount of order. For example, Colombo and Jiang applied their model to the direct marketing data and estimated $u = 2.9, v = 2.5$, and $\phi = \$496$. Hence, the population mean, $u\phi/(v - 1)$, is calculated to be $953. Let us compare two customers, one with two transactions $(x_i = 2)$ and the other with 100 transactions $(x_i = 100)$. Assume that the average amount of order is $500 for both customers. Then the expected amount of order is $502 for the customer with 100 transactions and $592 for the customer with 2 transactions. As the number of historical transactions gets smaller, less weight is assigned to the observed average amount of order. As a result, its expected amount of order converges or "shrinks" more to the population mean.

12.4 Extending the RFM Model

Direct marketers have widely used the RFM model partly because it is easy to understand and it often predicts well. However, not many people know why it works and when it works. Recently researchers have criticized various aspects of the RFM model (Wheaton 1996; Yang 2004).

First, the coding of recency, frequency and monetary value is arbitrary. Quintiles (creating 5 recency, 5 frequency, and 5 monetary value divisions) are frequently used, and hence 125 segments are assumed. However, depending on budget, finer or cruder RFM coding may be employed (Hughes 1996a). Because of this *ad hoc* coding scheme, the resulting RFM cells often fail to generate response differences between segments. Yang (2004) has recently developed a more formal procedure to determine the number of RFM cells.

Second, direct marketers today are collecting additional customer-level information including their demographics and behavioral characteristics. Incorporating this information into the traditional RFM model would improve the predictive performance. However, it is cumbersome to add other variables to RFM models. Practitioners simply treat additional variables the same as RFM variables. For example, with a new variable, say gender (male or female), the number of RFMG cells becomes $2 \times 5 \times 5 \times 5 = 500$. As the number of additional variables increases, the number of cells will geometrically increase. It is unrealistic to estimate RFM model with more than two additional variables.

12.4.1 Treating the RFM Model as ANOVA

We formally evaluate the RFM model by formulating it as a formal statistical method. We then provide several suggestions on improving the traditional RFM model. Statistically speaking, the RFM model is simply a three-way ANOVA (analysis of variance) with all main effects and interactions. More specifically, consider a factorial experiment where we have three treatment conditions. Each of three treatments (recency, frequency, and monetary) has three levels (1, 2, and 3) and, hence, we need to estimate $3 \times 3 \times 3 = 27$ parameters if all interactions are allowed. The RFM model is identical to the full model for this factorial experiment.

Let us provide an example. Table 12.2 shows the results of $3 \times 3 \times 3$ RFM model applied to the response data for catalog mailing drops. Catalogs are mailed to 4,000 customers, and 325 of them responded. The overall response rate was 8.13%. The response rates widely varied across the 27 RFM cells, from 1.14% to 23.08%. Now we apply the three-way ANOVA with all main effects and interactions. Table 12.2 shows its results. Note that we estimate 27 parameters, which are the same as in RFM model. We can calculate the response probabilities of 27 RFM cells from these 27 parameter estimates.

Table 12.2 $3 \times 3 \times 3$ RFM model

Three codes R F M	Number mailed	Number responded	Percentage of response
1 1 1	455	26	5.71
1 1 2	354	38	10.73
1 1 3	239	24	10.04
1 2 1	50	5	10.00
1 2 2	50	8	16.00
1 2 3	33	6	18.18
1 3 1	52	12	23.08
1 3 2	167	32	19.16
1 3 3	303	58	19.14
2 1 1	277	12	4.33
2 1 2	196	10	5.10
2 1 3	134	6	4.48
2 2 1	39	3	7.69
2 2 2	27	2	7.41
2 2 3	27	2	7.41
2 3 1	37	3	8.11
2 3 2	84	11	13.10
2 3 3	178	17	9.55
3 1 1	351	4	1.14
3 1 2	269	12	4.46
3 1 3	168	6	3.57
3 2 1	29	1	3.45
3 2 2	39	2	5.13
3 2 3	27	1	3.70
3 3 1	45	4	8.89
3 3 2	149	8	5.37
3 3 3	221	12	5.43
Total	4,000	325	8.13

The three-way ANOVA with all main effects and interactions can be written as

$$\mu_{RFM} = \mu + \mu_R + \mu_F + \mu_M + \mu_{R*F} + \mu_{F*M} + \mu_{R*M} + \mu_{R*F*M} \quad (12.4)$$

where μ is the overall mean response rate (intercept), μ_R is the recency main effect, μ_F is the frequency main effect, μ_M is the monetary main effect, μ_{R*F} is the recency–frequency interaction effect, μ_{F*M} is the frequency–monetary interaction effect, μ_{R*M} is the recency–monetary interaction effect, and μ_{R*F*M} is the recency–frequency–monetary triple interaction effect. For example, the response rate of $(R = 1, F = 1, M = 1)$ cell is

$$0.054 - 0.019 + 0.035 - 0.072 - 0.059 + 0.005 - 0.024 = 0.057$$

which is identical to the response rate of cell (1,1,1) in Table 12.2.

Interpreting RFM model as ANOVA allows us to evaluate a traditional RFM model with formal statistical methodology. As a result, we are in a position to propose new types of RFM models. For example, Table 12.3

Table 12.3 ANOVA – Full Model

Degree of freedom	Type III sum of squared errors	Level			Estimate
Intercept					0.054[a]
R	2	3.59[a]	1		0.137[a]
			2		0.041
F	2	2.74[a]	1		−0.019
			2		−0.017
M	4	0.81	1		0.035
			2		−0.001
R*F	2	0.72[a]	1 1		−0.072[a]
			1 2		0.001
			2 1		−0.032
			2 2		−0.004
R*M	4	0.06	1 1		0.005
			1 2		0.001
			2 1		−0.049
			2 2		0.036
F*M	4	0.17	1 1		−0.059
			1 2		0.010
			2 1		−0.037
			2 2		0.015
R*F*M	8	0.29	1 1 1		−0.024
			1 1 2		−0.003
			1 2 1		−0.084
			1 2 2		−0.037
			2 1 1		0.072
			2 1 2		−0.039
			2 2 1		0.054
			2 2 2		−0.050

[a]Indicates statistically significant with $p = 0.05$

shows that among the main effects, only recency and frequency are statistically significant at the $p = 0.05$ level. Response rates are not different across customers with different monetary values. In addition, the recency–frequency interaction is the only significant interaction effect. Based on these statistical tests, we propose a simpler RFM model with a small number of parameters without losing predictive performance. Table 12.4 shows the estimation results of this simpler RFM model. The model takes two main effects (R and F) and an interaction term (R*F). As a result, the number of parameters estimated has been reduced to 9 from 27. Response rate for each of 9 cells can similarly be calculated. For example, the response rate of $(R = 1, F = 1)$ cell is $0.058 + 0.138 - 0.030 - 0.082 = 0.084$.

Another benefit from treating RFM model as ANOVA comes from the fact that it becomes easier to add other variables such as consumer demographics. We can incorporate additional variables into the RFM model by employing the concept of ANCOVA (analysis of covariance). ANCOVA is a technique that combines features of ANOVA and regression (Neter et al. 1985).

Table 12.4 ANOVA – Restricted model

Parameter	Degree of freedom	Type III sum of squared errors	Level	Estimate
Intercept				0.058^{a}
R	2	3.77^{a}	1	0.138^{a}
			2	0.046^{a}
F	2	3.47^{a}	1	-0.030
			2	-0.016
R*F	4	1.08^{a}	1 1	-0.082^{a}
			1 2	0.037
			2 1	-0.028
			2 2	-0.013

[a]Indicates statistically significant with $p = 0.05$

We can augment RFM model with several additional variables – also called concomitant variables – that are related to the response probability. These might include demographics and other customer characteristics. This augmentation will reduce the variance of error terms in the model and make the prediction more accurate.

12.4.2 Alternative Response Models Without Discretization

Although the RFM model has been used for decades, some researchers have criticized its heuristic nature and proposed alternative response models such as decision trees and logistic regression (Wheaton 1996). Using mail response data from the collectible industry, Levin and Zahavi (2001) compared the predictive performance of the RFM model to decision trees and logistic regression. They found that the RFM model was the worst, and logistic regression was slightly better than decision trees. However, as Levin and Zahavi (2001) themselves have point out, these results may be specific to the application. These studies empirically showed the inferiority of RFM model for a given data, but could not theoretically explain why RFM model worked or did not work.

Treating RFM model as ANOVA allows us theoretically to compare it with other popular response models. Since a main criticism given to RFM model is its discretization of recency, frequency and monetary values, as an alternative model, we propose a classical linear regression where the dependent variable is customer response (0 or 1) and independent variables are customers' original recency, frequency, and monetary values before transformed to discrete scores.[5] The regression model has two advantages over RFM model. First, the number of parameters estimated is significantly reduced. Only 4 parameters are required to estimate in regression model while 125 parameters (assumed $5 \times 5 \times 5$ model) are estimated in RFM model. Hence, we will get more accurate parameter estimates. Second, we may experience some information losses in the RFM model due to discretization. In contrast, there is no information loss with the regression model since it uses the original independent variables, Moreover, we can avoid the problem of arbitrarily determining the number of codes, say 5 levels for recency.

However, we can imagine situations where RFM model may perform better than the regression model. The relationship between the independent variables and the dependent variable may be highly nonlinear (especially, not monotonic). In this case, the discrete form of RFM model (or ANOVA) will work better. The linear regression model assumes that there is a linear relationship between the independent variables and the dependent variable. Similarly, the logistic regression assumes that there is a monotonic (consistently positive or negative) relationship between the independent variables and the dependent variable. On the other hand, the RFM model will well approximate the nonlinear relationship by discretizing the independent variables. Secondly, we expect that RFM model will work better than the linear or logistic regression model when there are significant interactions among independent variables. The regression model cannot include interactions among variables unless researchers explicitly incorporate them. On the other hands, the RFM model (or ANOVA) automatically considers and estimates interactions among variables.

Alternative response models to RFM model are decision trees such as CHAID and CART (Levin and Zahavi 2001). Decision trees overcome the limitations of the linear and logistic regression models even though they have their own weaknesses (see Chapter 17). The way of approximating the nonlinearity in the RFM model is based on variable discretization. The RFM model typically uses five codes with even percentiles. But the number of codes is arbitrary. For highly nonlinear relationship, you may need ten codes. In addition, even percentiles are also arbitrary. Decision trees can not only handle nonlinear relationship but also incorporate interactions among variables in a more formal and parsimonious way (see Chapter 17).

Finally, statisticians have recently developed nonlinear regression models such as kernel smoothing, radial-basis function neural nets, multilayer perceptron neural networks, additive models, that can fit highly nonlinear curves in formal and semi-automatic ways (Fahrmeir and Tutz 1994). Similarly, these modern regression models can incorporate interactions among indepen-

---

[5] If you are concerned about the discrete nature of the dependent variable, you can use the logit or probit model instead. Still, the independent variables are customers' recency, frequency, and monetary value.

dent variables. They are theoretically complex and not easy to understand. But many commercial packages with easy-to-use icons have become available so that database marketers can implement them without strong statistical training.

12.4.3 A Stochastic RFM Model by Colombo and Jiang (1999)

The RFM model simplifies the analysis of customer behavior by summarizing historical transaction data by three RFM variables. However, much information may be lost through summarization. This raises a possibility that without any summarization more comprehensive statistical models can be employed to analyze consumer purchase data in direct marketing. Moreover, it is not theoretically justified to use RFM variables in predicting future response.

Colombo and Jiang (1999) overcome these problems of the traditional RFM model by developing a formal model of buyer behavior rooted in well-established stochastic models. We describe their model for solicited transactions where consumers purchase in response to a specific offer such as a catalog.[6]

Suppose that customer i with a true unobserved response probability of π_i will respond r_i times to m_i solicitations. If the response probability is constant across all solicitations, then the distribution of the number of responses to m_i solicitations is given by the binomial distribution. That is,

$$P(r = r_i | m_i, \pi_i) = \binom{m_i}{r_i} \pi_i^{r_i} (1 - \pi_i)^{m_i - r_i} \tag{12.5}$$

Since the true response probability of π_i is heterogeneous across consumers, we assume that the π_i's have a beta distribution given by

$$f(\pi | \alpha, \beta) = \frac{\Gamma(\alpha + \beta)}{\Gamma(\alpha)\Gamma(\beta)} \pi^{\alpha-1} (1 - \pi)^{\beta-1} \tag{12.6}$$

The beta distribution has extensively been used to incorporate heterogeneity in consumer response in marketing (Lilien et al. 1992). Depending on the values of the parameters α and β, it can take a variety of shapes such as U-shape, J-shape, inverted U-shape, and so on.

From Equations 12.5 and 12.6, the observed number of responses (r_i) to m_i solicitations can be shown to follow a beta-binomial distribution:

---

[6] Colombo and Jiang (1999) also developed a model for unsolicited transactions where customers buy from a firm at any time rather than in response to a direct communications. We focus our attention on the case of solicited transactions because catalog industry has actively used traditional RFM models.

$$P(r = r_i|m_i, \alpha, \beta) = \int_0^1 \binom{m_i}{r_i} \pi_i^{r_i}(1 - \pi_i)^{m_i - r_i} d\pi$$

$$= \binom{m_i}{r_i} \frac{\Gamma(\alpha + \beta)}{\Gamma(\alpha)\Gamma(\beta)} \frac{\Gamma(m_i - r_i + \beta)}{\Gamma(\alpha + \beta + m_i)} \quad (12.7)$$

This distribution relates customer response behavior to the parameters of the beta distribution, α and β. Hence, their values can be estimated by maximum likelihood. Once α and β are estimated, we can easily calculate the expected response probability for customer i as

$$P(\pi_i|r_i, m_i, \alpha, \beta) = \frac{\alpha + r_i}{\alpha + \beta + m_i} \quad (12.8)$$

It is interesting to note that the only customer-level information Equation 12.8 requires is the number of solicitations (m_i) and the number of responses (r_i). That is, m_i and r_i are sufficient statistics for an individual customer's purchase history. This fact theoretically justifies the use of frequency in a traditional RFM model.

So far, we have assumed that all customers in the database are active. However, some customers may be inactive because they are unable or unwilling to purchase the product from the firm. Customers in a non-subscription setting do not usually give notice to the firm when they leave. Hence, the firm needs to infer the status of the customers from their transaction histories. For example, if a customer has not purchase for a long period of time, he or she can be considered to be inactive. Several researchers have studied models to estimate the probability that a customer is active given his or her transaction histories (Schmittlein and Peterson 1994; Schmittlein et al. 1987; Fader et al. 2005). We do not cover them in this chapter since these models are developed for unsolicited transactions where purchases are not directly solicited by the firm and they can occur at any time. See Chapter 5 for descriptions of these approaches.

Chapter 13
Market Basket Analysis

Abstract Market basket analysis scrutinizes the products customers tend to buy together, and uses the information to decide which products should be cross-sold or promoted together. The term arises from the shopping carts supermarket shoppers fill up during a shopping trip. The rise of the Internet has provided an entirely new venue for compiling and analyzing such data. This chapter discusses the key concepts of "confidence," "support," and "lift" as applied to market basket analysis, and how these concepts can be translated into actionable metrics and extended.

13.1 Introduction

Marketing researchers have been interested in studying product affinity for a long time. We have learned from the introductory economics or marketing course that coffee and sugar are complements while coffee and tea are substitutes. The price reduction of a product not only increases its own demand but also increases demand of its complementary product. That is, if two products are complements for each other, their demands tend to be positively associated. On the other hand, if two products are substitutes for each other, their demands tend to be negatively correlated since the price reduction of a product would decrease the demand of its substitute.

Marketing practitioners are interested in product affinities because they provide very useful information for designing various marketing strategies. It may not be surprising to a supermarket manager to see that coffee is purchased with coffee cream or sugar. In fact, an experienced manager may know lots of product pairs purchased together by consumers. However, considering that the typical supermarkets carry tens of thousands items, it is also likely that there are thousands of associated product pairs the manager may not have recognized. Maybe the best-known example in the data mining industry is that beers and diapers tend to be purchased together in the supermarket.[1] Whatever the reasons are, the beer–diaper association is not obvious to the manager. Market basket analysis is designed to find these types of product associations with minimal human interaction.

Typically the input to a market basket analysis is point-of-sale (POS) transaction data at the customer level. Market basket analysis extracts many interesting product associations from transaction data. Hence its output consists of a series of product association rules: for example, if customers buy product A they also tend to buy product B. Market basket analysis alleviates managerial effort and automates the process for finding which products are purchased together. Let the data speak for itself.

Market basket analysis was originally applied to supermarket transaction data. Actually it takes its name from the fact that consumers in a supermarket place all of their purchased items into the shopping cart or the market basket. Nowadays the application of market basket analysis is not limited to the supermarket. It can be applied to any industry selling multiple products such as banks, catalogers, direct marketers and so on, and to new sales channels, especially the Internet.

13.2 Benefits for Marketers

The output of a market basket analysis is a series of association rules. These rules are used to improve the efficiency of marketing strategies and tactics. We learn from the analysis which products/services are purchased at the same time or in a particular sequence. Hence the rules can be very useful and actionable for firms dealing with multiple products/services. Examples are retailers, financial institutions (e.g., credit cards company), catalog marketers, direct marketers, Internet merchants, and so on (Berry and Linoff 1997). Market basket analysis is especially popular among retailers because of their large number of SKUs. In a recent Aberdeen Group survey, 38% of the retailers polled said they used market basket analysis and felt it had a positive effect on their business (Nishi 2005).

Market basket provides valuable information for firms to develop various marketing strategies and tactics. First, association rules from a market basket analysis can be used for a supermarket to manage its shelf space. It may stock the associated items close together such that consumers would not forget to purchase both items. On the other hand, it may stock the associated items far apart such that consumers would spend more time browsing aisle by

---

[1] Thomas Blischok first discovered this interesting statistical pattern. As vice president of industry consulting for NCR, he did a study for Osco Drug in 1992 when he discovered dozens of correlations, including one connecting beer and diapers in transactions between 5 p.m. and 7 p.m. Blischok recounted the tale in a speech, and the story became the legend in data mining industry (Forbes 1998).

aisle (Chain Store Age 1998).[2] Other types of merchants such as retailers, catalogers and Internet may realize similar benefits.

Second, market basket analysis can be used for designing various promotional strategies. It will provide ideas on product bundling. In addition, it can be used to design a cross-coupon program where consumers purchasing an item A get the (discount) coupon for an item B.[3] Or it will help managers to select appropriate items to be loss leaders.

Third, market basket analysis with temporal components can be very useful to various marketers for selecting cross-selling items. For example, market basket analysis might indicate that customers who have purchased whole life insurance tend to purchase property insurance within 6 months. It suggests a cross-selling possibility – the insurance salesperson should contact his/her current customers with whole life insurance (within 6 months) and try to cross-sell the property insurance.

13.3 Deriving Market Basket Association Rules

Since the seminal paper by Agrawal et al. (1993), the problem of deriving association rules have been widely studied within the field of knowledge discovery (Agrawal and Srikant 1994; Mannila et al. 1994; Silverstein et al. 1998; Zhang 2000), and is often called the market basket problem. In this section, we study how a market basket analysis works and derives various association rules that are "interesting."

13.3.1 Setup of a Market Basket Problem

The input for a market basket analysis is customer-level transactions data, although it is not necessary that each customer be explicitly identified. For example, grocery stores record each customer's transaction data ("market basket") with their scanning device even though they do not know the customer's name, address, etc. For each transaction, the store knows the date, the casher number, items purchased, prices of each item, coupons redeemed, and so on. Table 13.1 shows the hypothetical transaction data from a grocery store. There are five transactions and each transaction consists of a set of

---

[2] As discussed later, market basket analysis is an exploratory data mining tool. Once an association between two products is identified, we should test two different shelf strategies (stocking two products adjacent or far apart) with control groups.

[3] Dhar and Raju (1998) have developed a model to study the effects of cross-ruff coupons on consumer choice behavior and derived conditions under which cross-ruff coupons can lead to higher sales and profits than other types of package coupons. However, they did not employ market basket analysis for their empirical application.

Table 13.1 Transaction data from a grocery store

Transactions	Items purchased (market basket)
1	Milk, orange juice, ice cream, beer, soap
2	Milk, ice cream, beer
3	Milk, orange juice, detergent
4	Milk, ice cream, pizza
5	Milk, orange juice, soap

items. The main focus of market basket analysis is the set of items purchased for each transaction. From this transaction data, market basket analysis provides a series of association rules where we infer which items are purchased together.

Each association rule consists of an antecedent and a consequent. For example, consider the association rule, "if a consumer purchases item A, s/he also tends to purchase item B." Here item A is the *antecedent* while item B is the *consequent*. Note that both antecedent and consequent can contain multiple items.

13.3.2 Deriving "Interesting" Association Rules

Let us intuitively derive a few association patterns from Table 13.1. At first glance, we can see that milk and orange juice are purchased together in three out of the five transactions. This observation may tell us that there is a cross-selling possibility between milk and orange juice. Anything else? Ice cream and beer are purchased together in two out of the five transactions. Again from this pattern, we may suggest an association rule like: "if a customer purchases ice cream, then s/he also purchases beer," or more compactly, "if ice cream then beer." Similarly, we can formulate an association rule between orange juice and soap.

We can generate many association rules from Table 13.1 but we are only interested in selecting "interesting" rules. That is, how managerially relevant are the rules we have generated? It is difficult to come up with a single metric quantifying the "interestingness" or "goodness" of an association rule (Bayardo and Agrawal 1999). Hence, researchers have proposed several different metrics. There are three most popular criteria evaluating the quality or the strength of an association rule: support, confidence and lift.

Support is the percentage of transactions containing a particular combination of items relative to the total number of transactions in the database. We can think of the support for an individual item A, which would just be the probability a transaction contains item A, or "P(A)". However, when we are interested in associations, we are concerned with multiple items, so the support for the combination A and B would be P(AB). For example, consider the association rule "if milk then beer" from Table 13.1. Support measures how often milk and beer are purchased together, as a percentage of the total number of transactions. They are purchased together two out of five transactions. Hence, support for the association rule is 40%.

Support for multiple items can be interpreted as a joint probability. It measures the probability that a randomly selected basket contains item A and item B together. Hence it is symmetric and does not hint at cause-and-effect. We know that the joint probability of A and B, $P(AB)$, is no different than the joint probability of B and A, $P(BA)$. For example, support for the association rule "if milk then beer" would be the same as the support for the association rule "if beer then milk."

Support has one critical disadvantage in evaluating the quality of an association rule. The example in Table 13.1 shows that the association rule "if beer then milk" has support of 40%. However, is the association rule "if beer then milk" an interesting rule? The answer is yes if this means that 40% of customers buy beer and milk together and no one buys milk without buying beer. However, Table 13.1 shows that all the transactions contain milk. All customers buy milk and only 40% of those buy beer. Hence, the association rule "if beer then milk" is not interesting even if its support is 40%. Milk is so popular in grocery shopping (by itself it has very high support) that the support for milk plus any other item can be large.

Confidence measures how much the consequent (item) is dependent on the antecedent (item). In other words, confidence is the conditional probability of the consequent given the antecedent, $P(B|A)$. For example, the confidence for the association rule "if ice cream then beer" is 66% since three transactions contain ice cream (the antecedent) and two among the three transactions also contain beer (the consequent). In other words, given that the baskets containing ice cream is selected, there is 66% chance that the same basket also contains beer. Different from support, confidence is asymmetric. For example, the confidence of "if beer then ice cream" is 100% while the confidence of "if ice cream then beer" is 66%.

The law of conditional probability states that $P(B|A) = P(AB)/P(A)$. That is, confidence is equal to the support of the association rule divided by the probability or the support of the antecedent. For example, the support of an association rule "if ice cream then beer" is 40% (two out of five transactions) while the support or the probability of ice cream is 60% (three out of five). Hence, its confidence is 66% (40%/60%).

Confidence surely is a good criterion for selecting interesting rules but is not a perfect criterion. Consider a rule "if ice cream then orange juice." Its confidence or $P(B|A)$ is 33% so you may think it is an interesting rule. However, there is 60% chance (e.g., $P(B) = 60\%$) that a randomly chosen transaction contains orange juice. Hence, ice cream is not a powerful antecedent for identifying an orange juice purchase – it has lower than a random chance of identifying an orange juice purchase. Thus there is no cross-selling opportunity.

Lift (also called improvement or impact) is a measure to overcome the problems with support and confidence. Consider an association rule "if A then B." The lift for the rule is defined as $P(B|A)/P(B)$ or $P(AB)/[P(A)P(B)]$. As shown in the formula, lift is symmetric in that the lift for "if A then B" is the same as the lift for "if B then A."

$P(B)$ is the probability that a randomly chosen transaction contains item B. In other words, it is an unconditional (or baseline) probability of purchasing item B regardless of other items purchased. Practitioners often use the term, "expected confidence" for $P(B)$ instead of unconditional probability.

Hence, lift is said to measure the difference – measured in ratio – between the confidence of a rule and the expected confidence. For example, the lift of an association rule "if ice cream then beer" is 1.67 because the expected confidence is 40% and the confidence is 67%. This means that consumers who purchase ice cream are 1.67 times more likely to purchase beer than randomly chosen customers. That is, larger lift means more interesting rules.

A lift of 1 has a special meaning. We know that $P(AB) = P(A)P(B)$ if A and B are independent. Therefore, lift equals one if the event A is independent of the event B. Lift greater than 1 indicates that the item A and the item B tend to occur together more often would be predicted by random chance. Similarly, lift smaller than 1 indicates that the item A and item B are purchased together less likely than would be predicted by random chance.

Lift has little practical value when the support for the antecedent item is very low. For example, suppose that $P(\text{mushroom pizza \& ice cream}) = 0.01$, $P(\text{mushroom pizza}) = 0.01$ and $P(\text{ice cream}) = 0.25$. The association rule "if mushroom pizza then ice cream looks like a good rule based on its lift of 4. However, only a small number of customers purchase mushroom pizza. A co-marketing program designed to encourage mushroom pizza buyers to purchase ice cream may not have a high impact. This problem can be partially resolved by taxonomies described in Sect. 13.4.1.

Summarizing, we have introduced three popular criteria for evaluating association rules in market basket analysis, defined as follows:

$$\text{Confidence} = P(B|A) \tag{13.1a}$$
$$\text{Support} = P(BA) \tag{13.1b}$$
$$\text{Lift} = P(B|A)/P(B) \tag{13.1c}$$

Each criterion has its advantages and disadvantages but in general we would like association rules that have high confidence, high support, and high lift. Association rules with high support are potentially interesting rules. Similarly, rules with high confidence would be interesting rules. Or you may look for association rules with very high or very low lift.[4] Practitioners generally

---

[4] The very low lift implies that the two products "repel" each other. Substitutes (e.g., Coke and Pepsi) tend not to be in the same basket. Knowing that two products "repel" each other can often suggest actionable recommendations. For example, Coke should not be promoted together with Pepsi.

employ all three together in generating a set of interesting association rules. They might set a threshold for each rule and let the market basket software choose rules to meet the condition (see Chapter 21 for further discussion). For example, practitioners might ask the software to find all associations so that support, confidence, and lift are all greater than some minimum threshold specification (e.g., see Yan et al. 2005).

13.3.3 Zhang (2000) Measures of Association and Dissociation

Other than three metrics discussed above, researchers have proposed a number of measures including chi-square value (Morishita 1998), entropy gain (Morimoto et al. 1998; Morishita 1998), gini (Morimoto et al. 1998) and laplace (Webb 1995). More recently, Zhang (2000) proposed a new metric that was theoretically shown to be better than traditional measures such as the confidence and/or the χ^2 test. He also applied his new measure (along with traditional measures) to a POS transaction data and a donation data, and showed that his measure could identify association patterns not discovered by traditional measures. Considering the importance of finding a good measure of association rules, we describe his measure with comparing others.

Zhang's point of departure is to recognize the difference between association and *disassociation*. If the probability of co-occurrence $P(A|B)$ for patterns A and B is larger than probability of no co-occurrence $P(A|\bar{B})$, then the relationship of A with B is association (attractive). Otherwise, the relationship is disassociation (repulsive). Association is described by $P_A(B \Rightarrow A) = 1 - P(A|\bar{B})/P(A|B)$ if $P(A|\bar{B}) < P(A|B)$. Disassociation is described by $P_D(B \Rightarrow A) = P(A|\bar{B})/P(A|B) - 1$ if $P(A|\bar{B}) \geq P(A|B)$. Combining the two formulas, we obtain

$$P(B \Rightarrow A) = \frac{P(A|B) - P(A|\bar{B})}{Max[P(A|B), P(A|\bar{B})]}$$

$$= \frac{P(AB) - P(A)P(B)}{Max[P(AB)(1 - P(B)), P(B)(1 - P(A))]} \quad (13.2)$$

where $B \Rightarrow A$ (e.g., B implies A) describes the association of A with B. For example, let us calculate $P(\text{beer} \Rightarrow \text{ice cream})$ in Table 13.1. Since $P(\text{ice cream}|\text{beer}) = 1$ is larger than $P(\text{ice cream}|\text{not beer}) = 1/3$, so the relationship of ice cream with beer is association. And $P(\text{beer} \Rightarrow \text{ice cream})$ is equal to 2/3.

The association metric in Equation 13.2 is asymmetric. That is, $P(B \Rightarrow A)$ can be different from $P(A \Rightarrow B)$. Zhang's metric has several other good properties. For example, consider three extreme cases: perfect association, perfect disassociation, and random or independent association. A good measure of association should yield a definitive result for each case. In other words, the result a measure of association should yield a constant number, independent of $P(A)$ and/or $P(B)$, for perfect association, perfect disassociation, or independent association.

The following table calculates the value for support, confidence, lift, and Zhang's measure for each of the three cases:

	Support	Confidence	Lift	Zhang
Perfect Association	$P(A)(=)P(B)$	1	$1/P(B)$	1
Perfect Dissociation	0	0	0	-1
Independence	$P(A)P(B)$	$P(B)$	1	0

The table shows that only Zhang's measure provides a unique number for all three cases. This means that Zhang's measure has a similar interpretation as a correlation coefficient: values close to 1 signify almost perfect positive association, values close to -1 signify almost perfect negative association, and values close to zero mean very little relationship. None of the other measures has this nice numerical interpretation.

13.4 Issues in Market Basket Analysis

13.4.1 Using Taxonomies to Overcome the Dimensionality Problem

The typical supermarket in the US carries about 30,000 items or SKUs (stock keeping units). It means that we need to evaluate about 4.5×10^8 potential association rules such as the ones "if A then B." Furthermore, as discussed later, you may be interested in association rules involved in more than two items. The "curse of dimensionality" comes into play unless we control the number of items to a manageable size.

Much research has focused on algorithms for computing all relevant associations (Agrawal et al. 1993; Agrawal and Srikant 1994; Hu et al. 2000; Yan et al. 2005). However, another way to overcome dimensionality problem is to aggregate items into some manageable number of categories. For example, Tropicana orange juices with various sizes can be grouped into the Tropicana orange juice category. Or different types of Tropicana juices such as orange and grape juice may be aggregated. More generalized categories such as the juice category (after aggregating all juices with different brands, sizes and types) can also be used as the input for market basket analysis.

There is another benefit from item aggregation. Unit sales of many SKUs in the original market basket data are so small. Hence, their supports are extremely low. As shown in the previous section, the presence of low-support items may make it difficult to find good association rules. For example, suppose that there is only one transaction including Brand A orange juice in the entire basket data. And the transaction containing Brand A orange juice also includes yogurt. The confidence of the association rule, "if Brand A orange juice then yogurt," for this basket data is 100%. But it is not an interesting association rule. We can easily avoid this problem through item aggregation.

Obviously, as we employ higher levels of aggregation, the computational burden for the market basket analysis is diminished. However, item aggregation often leads to the loss of transaction details useful for developing actionable marketing strategies. Suppose that the result of the market basket analysis suggests the cross-promotion opportunity between beer and orange juice. It is unusual for a supermarket to promote all items in the orange juice category together. Instead, they promote a particular brand of orange juice. The market basket data aggregated across brands does not allow the manager to select a brand for target promotion.

What is the right level of item aggregation for a market basket analysis? Practitioners often suggest aggregating items such that each of the resulting aggregates have roughly the same level of appearance or support in the market basket data (for example, see www.megaputer.com/html/mba.html). As a result, items with smaller unit sales will be grouped together so that we can avoid the problem of bad association rules due to the low support items. However, one should not apply this suggestion too strictly. The needs of the end user are more important in deciding the level of aggregation. For example, the marketing manager in a discount store will be more interested in selling a television than a DVD. That is, it may be more reasonable to aggregate cheap items than expensive items.

13.4.2 Association Rules for More than Two Items

So far, we have investigated association rules with two items – one antecedent and one consequent. However, managers might be interested in association rules involving more than two items. The idea behind market basket analysis with two items can be easily extended to the analysis of more than two items. For example, consider an association rule, "if A and B then C." The support of this association rule is $P(ABC)$ and its confidence is $P(C|AB)$. And $P(C|AB)/P(C)$ is its lift. Similar analysis can be performed for the sets of four items, five and so on.

As discussed above, the curse of dimensionality comes into play as the number of items considered simultaneously increases. The number of calculations to perform the market basket analysis increases exponentially with the number of items to be considered together. For example, going back to the supermarket with 30,000 items, we need to evaluate $_{30000}C_3 (\approx 4.5 \times 10^{12})$

potential association rules such as the ones "if A and B then C." And about 3.4×10^{16} calculations are required for the sets of four items.

Researchers have suggested various pruning methods to overcome the dimensionality problem associated with the market basket analysis of multiple items (Agrawal et al. 1993). One easy pruning method is to generate association rules that satisfy a given support constraint. In addition, is the pruning is performed iteratively so that the number of calculations can be minimized. For example, given the support constraint of 1%, any items less than this minimum support are first eliminated and only the remaining items are used for the analysis of two items. For association rules for three items, any pairs of items less than the support constraint are eliminated and only the remaining pairs of items are used as antecedents. Similar iterative pruning is applied for generating association rules involved with more than three items. Yan et al. (2005) assert that even simple pruning rules that use thresholds can result in too many calculations, and propose a genetic algorithm for producing interesting associations.

13.4.3 Adding Virtual Items to Enrich the Quality of the Market Basket Analysis

Market basket analysis has originally been developed to study association patterns among items sold in supermarket. However, it becomes a much more useful data mining tool when items considered are not restricted to real products. Virtual items are not real products sold in retail stores, but they are treated as items in the market basket analysis. For example, marketing managers may be interested in knowing which items are sold well with male customers. The market basket analysis can provide this information simply by adding one more virtual item (sex identifier: "male" or "female") to each transaction basket.

Practically, the number of virtual items can be unlimited. They may include customer demographic information such as income, household size, education and so on. Sometimes customer's purchase behavioral information – for example, the type of payment (e.g., cash or credit cards), the day of the week that the purchase is made, etc. – is used as virtual items. Or marketing variables such as the indicator for temporary price reductions and special display are often used as virtual items.

Creating relevant virtual items definitely enriches the quality of the market basket analysis. However, it does run into the curse of dimensionality problem described earlier. Therefore, before you decide to add the virtual items to the market basket data, you should have some idea or hypothesis on how the results of analysis associated with virtual items help marketing managers to solve their decision making problems. For example, supermarkets typically select a set of items every week and discount their prices significantly – called loss leaders – to increase the number of shoppers visiting their stores. Supermarket managers know that they lose money by selling loss leader items. But most of supermarkets employ this strategy since they expect that consumers would shop a lot of other (non-discounted) products. We can detect various issues associated with the loss leader strategy by adding the indicator of the loss leader item as virtual item.

13.4.4 Adding Temporal Component to the Market Basket Analysis

Market basket analysis was originally designed to analyze which products are purchased together at a given shopping trip. However, it can be applied to broader marketing problems if we incorporate a temporal component. This makes it more applicable to identifying cross-selling possibilities. For example, a segment of bank customers might open a savings account *after* they open checking accounts. Or customers who have purchased personal computers may tend to purchase printers within the next 3 months.

Researchers have attempted to accommodate a time-series component into market basket analysis to broaden its application domain (Agrawal and Srikant 1995; Chen et al. 1998; Ramaswamy et al. 1998). They have shown that temporal components can be incorporated into the existing association rule algorithm with minor modification. However, there is one big difference in terms of the data required. In particular, we need panel data whereby particular customers are identified and observed over time. Previously, each transaction was treated independently and there was no need to track *whose* transaction it is. To conduct a temporal analysis, a data-gathering system must track customer identification in order to relate transactions occurring at different times. For example, the traditional scanning device in the supermarket may provide transaction data with anonymous customer identity that is not appropriate for the market basket analysis with temporal component. To incorporate the temporal component, a customer identification device such as a store loyalty card is required where a cash register first scans the customer's store card and scans items purchased.

A temporal association rule can be considered a traditional association rule with some temporal relationships between items in the antecedent and the consequent. Theoretically, we need to consider all possible pairwise combinations among all transactions made by a given customer. As a result, we have all possible "before item(s)" (in the antecedent) and "after item(s)" (in the consequent) pairs. Because of this combinatorial nature of the problem, again the curse of dimensionality comes into play. For example, we need to consider $450(= {}_{100}C_2)$ paired combinations for a customer with 100 transactions.

Table 13.2 Association rules for two items (in tabular form)

Antecedent	Consequent	Support	Confidence	Lift
Orange juice	Soap	0.40	0.67	1.67
Orange juice	Detergent	0.20	0.33	1.67
Ice cream	Beer	0.40	0.67	1.67
Ice cream	Pizza	0.20	0.33	1.67
Beer	Ice cream	0.40	1.00	1.67
Soap	Orange juice	0.40	1.00	1.67
Detergent	Orange juice	0.20	1.00	1.67
Pizza	Ice cream	0.20	0.50	1.25
Beer	Soap	0.20	0.50	1.25

An easy way to reduce the number of paired combinations is to restrict the temporal space of interest. For example, we may focus on temporal association for the "next shopping trips" where we now consider 99 pairwise comparisons for a customer with 100 transactions. Or we may restrict our attention to the transactions "within 2 months" from the transaction date of the antecedent.

13.5 Conclusion

There are several commercially available data mining software packages for performing market basket analysis. Examples are Integral Solutions' Clementine (marketed by SPSS), Silicon Graphics' MineSet, etc. that provide market basket analysis as a differentiating feature from other data mining products. Marketing managers without much statistical expertise can perform market basket analysis by clicking icons and interpreting the output without much difficulty.

Most market basket analysis software presents its output or association rules either in tabular form or in plain English. Most software allows users to specify selection criteria and sort the resulting association rules by support, lift, confidence, antecedent or consequent. Table 13.2 shows the output example in compact tabular form. We have here applied market basket analysis to the transaction data given in Table 13.1, selected the association rules with lifts greater than one, and sorted them by lift. Also note that we have limited the association rules to two items.

Some software presents results in plain English. For example, the association rules in Table 13.2 might be presented as the following:

- When a customer buys **Orange Juice** then the customer also buys **Soap** in 67% of cases. This pattern is present in 40% of transactions.[5]

---

[5] This paragraph means that the confidence of the association 'if orange juice then beer' is 67% and its support is 40%.

- When a customer buys **Orange Juice** then the customer also buys **Detergent** in 33% of cases. This pattern is present in 20% of transactions.
- When a customer buys **Ice Cream** then the customer also buys **Beer** in 67% of cases. This pattern is present in 40% of transactions.

Market basket analysis is an attractive data mining tool for several reasons. First, relative to other data mining tools, it is computationally simple. Second, its outputs are easy to understand because they are expressed in the form of association rules. Third, it is actionable in that it is easy for marketing managers to turn the association rules into marketing strategies and tactics.

Market basket analysis is particularly well suited to the problems without well-defined marketing objectives. You simply have a large set of data (e.g., POS transaction data from a supermarket) and you do not have specific hypothesis to test because you do not have much experience analyzing them. That is, it is a good undirected data mining technique. Market basket analysis can also be used for directed data mining tasks (Zhang 2000). But we suggest other statistically sound techniques when you have clear hypothesis to test.

Chapter 14
Collaborative Filtering

Abstract Collaborative filtering is a relatively new technique to the database marketing field, gaining popularity with the advent of the Internet and the need for "recommendation engines." We discuss the two major forms of collaborative filtering: memory-based and model-based. The classic memory-based method is "nearest neighbor," where predictions of a target customer's preferences for a target product are based on customers who appear to have similar tastes to the target customer. A more recently used method is item-based collaborative filtering, which is model-based. In item-based collaborative filtering predictions of a target customer's preferences are based on whether customers who like the same products the target customer likes tend to like the target product. We discuss these and several other methods of collaborative filtering, as well as current issues and extensions.

14.1 Introduction

One day you rent a movie, "Independence Day," at a video rental store. You are surprised at the cash register to find that there are ten movie titles recommended on your receipt that happen to match your interests pretty well. An automatic collaborative filtering system in the store has a database storing the movie tastes of many other customers. It identifies customers in the database who like "Independence Day," finds out what other movies they liked, and recommends the ten most liked movie titles to you. It automatically recommends a set of movie titles as an expert, or more to the point, a *friend* would.

Collaborative filtering is a recently developed data mining technique. Its main concept originated from work in the area of information filtering and first introduced by Goldberg et al. (1992). Their email filtering system, called Tapestry, innovated the field of recommendation system even though it required users to evaluate items explicitly and respond to complex queries. Since then, the system has been improved to become automatic (Resnick

Table 14.1 Input data for collaborative filtering

	Movie 1	Movie 2	Movie 3	Movie 4	Movie 5
Amy	5	2	–	4	1
Joseph	1	–	1	2	–
Michael	–	4	3	–	5
Jim	3	1	–	1	2
Laura	5	3	4	–	1

et al. 1994) and the algorithm has been fine-tuned (Shardanand and Maes 1995). More recently, a number of websites including Amazon.com, CD-Now.com and MovieFinder.com have adopted collaborative filtering systems to provide personalized recommendations to their customers. Collaborative filtering is broadening its base of applications to include financial services, travel agencies, and so on.

Let us take an example of movie selection to understand the task applied to collaborative filtering. The objective of collaborative filtering is to select (and then recommend) a set of movies that each customer will like. The typical input data takes the form of preference ratings on each product/item evaluated by users. As shown on Table 14.1, it is the $n \times m$ user-item matrix (n users; m items) with each cell representing a user/consumer's preference rating on a specific item/product. Our main task is to predict the preference ratings for missing cells, based on other observed preference ratings. For example, Amy has rated Movies 1, 2, 4 and 5. Then what is Amy's predicted preference rating for Movie 3? Similarly, we wish to predict the missing preference ratings for all other customers. Once we have all the predicted movie ratings, we are ready to provide movie recommendations for each customer (e.g., suggest three highly rated movies for each customer).

14.2 Memory-Based Methods

There are a number of algorithms used in collaborative filtering, but they can be divided into two main categories, memory-based and model-based (Sarwar et al. 2001). Memory-based methods, also called neighborhood-based, user-based or heuristic methods, attempt to find a set of users that have similar preferences to the target user. Once a neighborhood of users is identified, memory-based methods combine their preferences to predict the preference of the target user. On the other hand, model-based methods first develop a model of user ratings. They usually take a probabilistic approach and calculate the expected preference for the target user. We first study memory-based methods in this section and describe model-based methods in the next section.

Memory-based methods predict the unobserved preferences of an active or target user based on the (observed) preferences of other users. Let $r_{i,j}$

be the preference rating of user i on item j (e.g., the value of cell in row i and column j in Table 14.1). The neighborhood-based method predicts the preference rating of an active user a for item j ($\hat{r}_{a,j}$) from the following equation.

$$\hat{r}_{a,j} = \bar{r}_a + \tau \sum_{i=1}^{n} s_{a,i}(r_{i,j} - \bar{r}_i) \tag{14.1}$$

where $\bar{r}_i$ is the mean preference rating of user i, $\bar{r}_a$ is the mean preference rating of the active user, $s_{a,i}$ is the similarity between user a and user i and τ is the normalizing constant such that the $\sum_{i=1}^{n} |s_{a,i}|$ becomes one. The mean preference rating is computed over the set of items that the user has evaluated. Note that the summation will only be applied to users whose preference ratings on item j are observed. For example, for predicting the preference of user a on "Independence Day" we incorporate only the ratings of users who have evaluated "Independence Day."

The predicted rating in Equation 14.1 consists of two components: the active user's own mean preference rating and the observed ratings of other users in the database. Without ratings from other users, the best guess for $\hat{r}_{a,j}$ is the mean of the user's previous preference ratings over other items. The beauty of collaborative filtering is the capability of improving the prediction accuracy by incorporating other users' opinions. The user i who experienced item j evaluates her preference rating for item j as $r_{i,j}$. So her relative preference is $(r_{i,j} - \bar{r}_i)$. This might suggest that the active user will also prefer movie j higher than her average. However, this depends on whether the active user and user i have similar tastes. This is measured by the similarity in tastes between the two users, $s_{a,i}$, which can be positive (the active user and user i tend to like the same movies) or negative (the active user and user i tend to have opposite tastes in movies).

The relative ratings of users who have rated on item j will be combined to predict $\hat{r}_{a,j}$, but the contribution of each user ($s_{a,i}$) will be different. If the other user is "similar" to the active user, a larger weight is assigned. If the other user is less similar to the active user, his or her opinions are not reflected heavily on the predicted preference rating of the active user. In sum, the predicted rating is her mean preference rating plus the weighted sum of other users' relative preferences. And the weights are determined by the similarity between each user and the active user.

The use of relative preference rather than absolute preference is based on the recognition that rating distributions are centered at different points for different users (Herlocker et al. 1999). Herlocker et al. show that the method using relative preference provides significantly better prediction accuracy than the method of using absolute preference. Some users may tend to use categories 3 to 5 on a five point rating scale while others may tend to use categories 1 to 3. If a user gives the same ratings for all items, her rating distribution will not provide any information for predicting the rating of the active user.

Going one step further, Herlocker et al. (1999) have also tried to incorporate the difference in spread between users' rating distributions. The original ratings are converted to z-scores with mean zero and variance one. However, this did not perform significantly better than relative preference approach. The authors conclude that the difference in variance among users' rating distributions does not influence the prediction performance, but the mean difference does.

14.2.1 Computing Similarity Between Users

Similarity between users, $s_{a,i}$, is the most important concept in the neighborhood-based collaborative filtering. Mainly based on the work of Breese et al. (1998) and Herlocker et al. (1999), this section reviews various similarity measures and their modifications used in collaborative filtering.

14.2.1.1 Similarity Measures

Researchers have proposed a number of different metrics that measure the similarity or the distance between users. We describe three similarity measures: Pearson correlation, Spearman rank correlation, and cosine vector similarity. Other similarity measures including the entropy-based uncertainty measure and mean-squared difference have been applied but found not to perform as well as Pearson correlation (Herlocker et al. 1999)

Pearson Correlation Coefficient

The most popular similarity measure may be Pearson correlation coefficient that GroupLens first introduced in its neighborhood-based algorithm (Resnick et al. 1994). The Pearson correlation coefficient between the active user a and the user i is given by

$$s_{a,i} = \frac{\sum_j (r_{a,j} - \overline{r}_a)(r_{i,j} - \overline{r}_i)}{\sqrt{\sum_j (r_{a,j} - \overline{r}_a)^2 \sum_j (r_{i,j} - \overline{r}_i)^2}} \tag{14.2}$$

Note that the above correlation is computed over the items that both users have evaluated. Hence, if there are only a few numbers of commonly rated items, these correlations may be unreliable.

Claiming its better performance, Shardanand and Maes (1995) have proposed the following constrained Pearson correlation coefficient as the similarity measure.

$$s_{a,i} = \frac{\sum_j (r_{a,j} - 4)(r_{i,j} - 4)}{\sqrt{\sum_j (r_{a,j} - \bar{r}_a)^2 \sum_j (r_{i,j} - \bar{r}_i)^2}} \qquad (14.3)$$

They use 4 because it is the midpoint of their seven-point rating scale. However, there are no theoretically convincing reasons why 4 is better than the mean ratings.

Spearman Rank Correlation Coefficient

Herlocker et al. (1999) criticized the rather restrictive data assumptions required for the Pearson correlation coefficient and proposed Spearman rank correlation coefficient as a similarity measure. The Pearson correlation coefficient can be cast in a regression framework that relies on several assumptions, including that the relationship is linear and the error distribution has a mean of 0 and constant variance. These assumptions are frequently violated in collaborative filtering data. Spearman rank correlation coefficient does not rely on these model assumptions. It is identical to Pearson except that it computes a measure of correlation between rank orders instead of rating values. There has not been any significant performance difference observed between Pearson and Spearman (Herlocker et al. 1999). However, these authors suggest using Spearman rank correlation for a rating scale with a small number of discrete values and Pearson correlation for the rating scale with continuous values.

(Cosine) Vector Similarity

Adopting the idea from information retrieval literature, Breese et al. (1998) have proposed the cosine vector similarity measure. In information retrieval, the vector of word frequencies characterizes each document and the angle between two vectors of word frequencies measures the similarity between two documents. Likewise, the similarity between the active user a and the other user i is defined as

$$s_{a,i} = \cos(\mathbf{r}_a, \mathbf{r}_i) = \frac{\mathbf{r}_a \cdot \mathbf{r}_i}{\|\mathbf{r}_a\| \, \|\mathbf{r}_i\|} \qquad (14.4)$$

where $\mathbf{r}_a = (r_{a,1}, r_{a,2}, \ldots, r_{a,J})$, $\mathbf{r}_i = (r_{i,1}, r_{i,2}, \ldots, r_{i,J})$, $\mathbf{r}_a \cdot \mathbf{r}_i = \sum_{j=1}^{J} r_{a,j} r_{i,j}$, $\|\mathbf{r}_a\| = \sqrt{\sum_{j=1}^{J} r_{a,j}^2}$, and $\|\mathbf{r}_i\| = \sqrt{\sum_{j=1}^{J} r_{i,j}^2}$. Note that the angle is calculated over items that both users have evaluated. Because of its origin in the field of information retrieval, ratings below zero as well as the unrated items receive zero rating values.

The cosine vector similarity is mathematically similar to Pearson correlation coefficient. However, Pearson correlation takes into account the differences in rating scale between different users (i.e., $\bar{r}_i$ and $\bar{r}_a$, see Equation 14.2).

The cosine vector does not. The cosine vector similarity has been shown to be successful in the field of information retrieval, but it does not perform well compared to the Pearson correlation coefficient in the area of collaborative filtering (Breese et al. 1998).

14.2.1.2 Significance Weighting

One critical problem that all similarity measures have in common is that they do not consider the significance (or confidence) of the similarity measure. Does the correlation of 0.9 between two users tell you that two users are very similar? It depends on the confidence attached to the correlation. If 0.9 is calculated based on 100 co-rated items, we will trust the correlation and conclude that preference structures of two users are very similar. However, if the correlation of 0.9 is based on five co-rated items, we may reserve our conclusion because we are not sure whether 0.9 is the true correlation or results from chance. That is, we need to recognize that the true similarity between users is an unknown parameter. Since the calculated correlation is the estimate of the true similarity, it is important to know the confidence of our estimate.

Herlocker et al. (1999) have found that some users who correlated highly with the active user did not perform well in predicting the preference ratings of the active user. Those high correlations (with terrible predicting performance) were frequently based on tiny sample sizes (often three to five co-rated items). In order to improve the prediction accuracy, a weighting factor has been proposed to add to the correlation such that the algorithm can discount the correlations based on small samples. More specifically, if two users had fewer than 50 co-rated items, Herlocker et al. multiplied the original correlation by a significance weight of $n/50$ where n is the number of co-rated items. For more than 50 co-rated items, a significance weight of 1 was uniformly used. The authors showed that applying significance weighting improved the prediction accuracy whether it is applied to Pearson or Spearman correlation (Herlocker et al. 1999). However, they did not provide any theoretically convincing reasons why they selected 50 as opposed to 10 or 100 as a cutoff.

14.2.1.3 Variance Weighting

Similarity measures discussed so far assume that all item ratings have the identical informational value in predicting the preference of the active user. However, researchers are beginning to recognize that preference ratings on certain items are more important than others in identifying similarities among users (Breese et al. 1998; Herlocker et al. 1999). For example, the item that all users rate highly or badly is not very a useful piece of information in differentiating users. On the other hand, the item that 50% of users rate very positively and the rest rate very negatively tells us a lot about similarities among users.

For treating the informational value of each item rating differently, Herlocker et al. (1999) have proposed to incorporate the item-variance weight factor into the calculation of the Pearson correlation coefficient. More specifically, first standardize each rating so that its mean is zero and its variance is one. Then Equation 14.2 can be written as

$$s_{a,i} = \sum_{j=1}^{J} z_{a,j} z_{i,j} \Big/ J \qquad (14.5)$$

where $z_{a,j} = (r_{a,j} - \bar{r}_a)/\sigma_a$, $z_{i,j} = (r_{i,j} - \bar{r}_i)/\sigma_i$ and J is the number of co-rated items. We now incorporate the item-variance weight factor into Equation 14.5, the standardized Pearson correlation.

$$s_{a,i} = \sum_{j=1}^{J} v_j z_{a,j} z_{i,j} \Big/ \sum_{j=1}^{J} v_j \qquad (14.6)$$

where $v_j = (\sigma_j^2 - \sigma_{min}^2)/\sigma_{max}^2$, $\sigma_j^2 = \sum_{i=1}^{n} (r_{i,j} - \bar{r}_j)^2/(n-1)$, σ_{min}^2 and σ_{max}^2 are the minimum and maximum variances over all items.

It intuitively makes sense to incorporate the variance weighting in the similarity computation. Unfortunately, however, employing the item-variance weighting factor did not show any significant gain in the prediction accuracy (Herlocker et al. 1999).

14.2.1.4 Selecting Neighborhoods

Shardanand and Maes (1995) have observed that selecting a subset of users instead of all possible users improved the prediction performance of collaborative filtering. Adding a large number of users with correlations (similarity) that were very low in magnitude seemed to increase the noise rather than providing additional information in predicting the ratings of the active user. Hence, they set an absolute correlation threshold so that only users with absolute correlations (with the active user) greater than the threshold are selected in computing Equation 14.1. An alternative way of selecting users with high informational values is to pick the n users that correlate most highly with the active user, where n is selected by the analyst (Herlocker et al. 1999).

How do you choose a specific value for the correlation threshold or the number n for the best n neighbors? Setting a high correlation threshold or a small n will allow you to limit users to those with high correlations. However, setting too high correlation threshold or too small n makes your predictions less accurate because you are not drawing on the opinions of enough neighbors. The magic number may have to be determined empirically for the given study. Herlocker et al. (1999) have compared the performance of various combinations of the correlation threshold and the best n neighborhood. They found the best n method (with n = 20) provided the best performance overall. Adding the feature of correlation threshold to the best n method does not improve the performance of the best n method.

14.2.2 Evaluation Metrics

Research in collaborative filtering evaluates the performance of each algorithm in terms of three metrics: coverage, statistical accuracy, and decision-support accuracy (Sarwar et al. 1998).

14.2.2.1 Coverage

Coverage measures the percentage of items for which a collaborative filtering algorithm can provide predictions. Since we evaluate algorithms of collaborative filtering, item predictions of an active user should be made using other users' ratings to be included in coverage counting. We do not expect 100% coverage because none of the users may rate certain items or similarities cannot be computed for some users who do not rate any items in common with the active user. As mentioned, applying the method of correlation thresholds or the best n correlates will reduce coverage.

14.2.2.2 Statistical Accuracy

Statistical accuracy measures the closeness between the predicted and the actual rating. Various metrics including mean absolute error, root mean squared error and Pearson correlation coefficient can be employed in measuring statistical accuracy. For more discussions on statistical accuracy, see Chapter 11.

14.2.2.3 Decision-Support Accuracy

Decision-support accuracy measures how effectively predictions enhance a user's ability to find items they like among the many choices in the full item set. The user's decision is a binary process in many instances. For example, a moviegoer will or will not watch the movie, *Matrix*. An Internet shopper will or will not purchase a book from Amazon. However, as shown in Table 14.1, the input data and the corresponding predictions are rating scores from 1 to 5. Hence, we need to convert the predicted rating scores into the binary variable (0/1). Suppose a moviegoer watches the movies scored greater than or equal to 4. Items with predicted scores of 4 or 5 are converted into the recommendation (1). Otherwise, items are converted into the recommendation (0). We study two important metrics for decision-support accuracy.

ROC Sensitivity

The concept of ROC (Receiver Operating Characteristic) curve originated in the field of signal detection to measure the diagnostic power of a model (Swets

Table 14.2 True event versus diagnosis – the basis for ROC curves (From Swets 1988)

		Event		
		Positive	Negative	
Diagnosis	Positive	True positive (a)	False positive (b)	$a + b$
	Negative	False negative (c)	True negative (d)	$c + d$
		$a + c$	$b + d$	$a + b + c + d - N$

1988; see also Chapter 11). In order to understand this concept, let us take a look at a two-by-two contingency table shown in Table 14.2. A diagnostic system (or model) looks for a particular "signal" and ignores other events called "noise." The event is considered to be "positive" or "negative," and the diagnosis made is correspondingly positive or negative. There are two ways in which diagnosis can be correct: "true-positive" and "true-negative" in Table 14.2. And there are two cases that diagnosis can be wrong: "false-positive" and "false-negative."

The true-positive proportion, $a/(a + c)$, and the false-positive proportion, $b/(b + d)$, captures all of the relevant information on accuracy of the model. These two proportions are often called the proportion of "hits" and "false alarms."[1] A good diagnostic model will provide many hits with few false alarms.

The ROC curve plots the proportion of hits versus false alarms for various settings of the decision criterion (see Fig. 14.1). Going back to the movie recommendation example, assume we set the rating threshold very high, say 4.9. We recommend the movie if the predicted preference rating is higher than 4.9. We do not recommend otherwise. Given the rating threshold, we can prepare the two-by-two contingency table after going through the filtering algorithm for the entire database. The proportions of hits and false alarms from the table will become a point of the ROC curve for the model. Now we set the rating threshold a bit lower, say 4.8. And plot a point of the ROC curve. Changing the value of the rating threshold to 0 will complete the ROC curve.

Note an ROC curve is generated for a particular model as a function of a critical decision criterion or parameter in the model, such as a cut-off. The performance (or value) of the model is measured to be the area under the ROC curve. The area varies from 0.5 to 1. The major diagonal in Fig. 14.1 represents the case of the area equal to 0.5 when the proportions of hits and false alarms are the same. Random assignment will lead to the area of 0.5. On the other hand, a perfect model when the curve follows the left and upper axes has the area of 1. There are no false alarms with 100% hits. The realistic model lies in between. The area under the curve increases as the model can increase more hits while reducing the number of false alarms.

---

[1] The true positive proportion is also called "sensitivity" that is the probability of a randomly selected positive event being evaluated as positive by the model. In addition, the true negative proportion is often called specificity that is the probability of a randomly selected negative event being evaluated as negative by the model. Note that the false positive proportion is (1 – specificity).

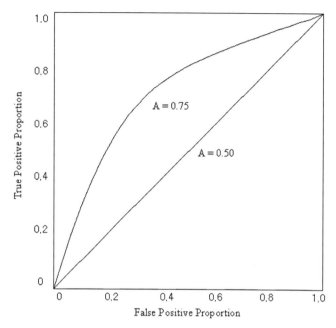

Fig. 14.1 The ROC curve (From Swets 1988).

PRC Sensitivity

Suppose that a movie prediction model recommends 100 titles and you like 50 of them, and another prediction model recommends 200 titles and you like 80 of them. Which movie prediction model is better? Researchers in information retrieval have developed decision-support accuracy measures called precision and recall to evaluate the model performance for cases as in this example.

Recall is the same as the true-positive proportion or the proportion of hits in the ROC (e.g., $a/(a + c)$ in Table 14.2). Precision is the number of true-positives divided by the total number of positives diagnosed by the model (e.g., $a/(a + b)$ in Table 14.2). Hence, precision indicates how selective the system is, and recall indicates how thorough it is in finding valuable information (Salton and McGill 1983). For example, suppose that the total number of movies in movie database a user will like is 500 (e.g., $a + c = 500$). Suppose a model recommends 100 movies and the user likes 50 of them (e.g., $a + b = 100$ and $a = 50$). Then $b = 50$ and $c = 450$. Hence, the precision is 0.5 ($= 50/100$) and the recall is 0.1 ($= 50/500$).

The PRC (precision-recall curve) plots recall versus precision for various settings of the decision criterion. Similar to drawing the ROC curve, we start with a very high rating threshold. Given the rating threshold, say 4.5, we create the resulting two-by-two contingency table, calculate recall and

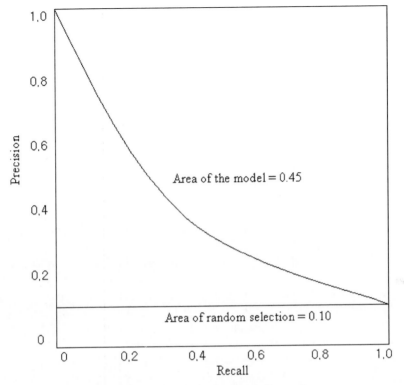

Fig. 14.2 The PRC (precision-recall curve).

precision, and plot it on the PRC graph. Decreasing the value of rating threshold gradually to zero, we can complete the locus of the PRC curve.

For a given level of recall, we would like the precision to be as high as possible. Therefore, the performance (or value) of the model is measured as the area under the PRC curve. Its shape is different from the ROC curve because of the different x-axis, as shown in Fig. 14.2. The area varies from 0 to 1. A perfect model with the area of one will have 100% precision for all recall values. The random selection will produce the horizontal line with its height determined by the proportion of actual positives in the entire samples. The area under the curve increases as the model can increase the precision for a given recall.

14.3 Model-Based Methods

Memory-based collaborative filtering has been widely used in practice because it is easy to implement. However, memory-based methods have several limitations (Ansari et al. 2000; Sarwar et al. 2001). First, when data are sparse, predictive accuracy becomes very poor. Many e-commerce sites such as Amazon.com carry a large number of products. Even heavy users in these sites may have purchased well under 1% of the products. Because of low coverage, similarities (or correlations) between users are unreliable, and sometimes cannot be computed. Second, memory-based methods require computations that grow with both the number of customers and the number of products. They will suffer serious scalability problem with millions of customers and/or products. Model-based methods attempt to overcome these limitations of memory-based methods.

14.3.1 The Cluster Model

Cluster models treat the recommendation problem as a classification task, and identify groups consisting of users who appear to have similar preferences (Iacobucci et al. 2000). The segments are created using a clustering algorithm in which the number of clustering variables is equal to the number of items. When the number of items is too large, it is often recommended to use only items that are rated (or purchased) by a minimum number of users (or buyers). Once the segments are determined, cluster models assign a target user to the segment containing the most similar users. Some clustering algorithms classify the target user into multiple segments and calculate the strength of each segment membership. Then the predicted preference for the target user can be made by averaging the preferences of the other users in the segment.

Cluster models overcome the scalability problem of memory-based methods because they compare the target user to a small number of segments rather than the entire customer base. However, cluster models provide less personal recommendations than memory-based methods. Hence, the quality of their predictions is often poor (Sarwar et al. 2001; Linden et al. 2003). Cluster models overcome the scalability problem by grouping numerous users into a small number of segments and treating all customers in the given segment as the same in predictions. Increasing the number of segments may improve the quality of prediction, but then the scalability problem comes in.

14.3.2 Item-Based Collaborative Filtering

Unlike the memory-based collaborative filtering method that matches the target user to similar users, item-based methods consider a set of items that the target user has rated, calculate how similar they are to the target item, and then combine those similar items into the prediction (Sarwar et al. 2001; Linden et al. 2003). That is, item-based methods proceed in two steps: item similarity computation and prediction computation.

The most critical step in item-based methods is to compute the similarity between items and select the most similar items to the target item. The similarity between item i and j ($s_{i,j}$) is calculated over the users who have rated both items. For the data provided in Table 14.1, item-based methods compute the similarity between movies (or columns) while memory-based methods compute the similarity between users (or rows). There are several ways to measure the similarity between items. Here we present two most popular metrics: the Pearson correlation coefficient and the cosine vector similarity.

$$s_{i,j} = \frac{\sum_{u \in U} (r_{u,i} - \bar{r}_i)(r_{u,j} - \bar{r}_j)}{\sqrt{\sum_{u \in U} (r_{u,i} - \bar{r}_i)^2 \sum_{u \in U} (r_{u,j} - \bar{r}_j)^2}} \tag{14.6a}$$

$$s_{i,j} = \cos(\mathbf{r}_i, \mathbf{r}_j) = \frac{\mathbf{r}_i \cdot \mathbf{r}_j}{\|\mathbf{r}_i\| \|\mathbf{r}_j\|} \tag{14.6b}$$

In Equation 14.6a, U indicates the set of users who both rated item i and j, $r_{u,i}$ is the rating of user u on item i and $\bar{r}_i$ is the mean rating of item i over users $u \in U$. In Equation 14.6b,

$$\mathbf{r}_i = (r_{1,i}, r_{2,i}, \ldots, r_{U,i}), \mathbf{r}_j = (r_{1,j}, r_{2,j}, \ldots, r_{U,j}), \mathbf{r}_i \cdot \mathbf{r}_j$$

$$= \sum_{u=1}^{U} r_{u,i} r_{u,j}, \|\mathbf{r}_i\| = \sqrt{\sum_{u=1}^{U} r_{u,i}^2}, \text{and } \|\mathbf{r}_j\| = \sqrt{\sum_{u=1}^{U} r_{u,j}^2}.$$

Once the similarity computations between items are completed, then the predicted rating of item j for a target user u is given by the weighted sum of ratings provided by the user on the items similar to the item j. And similarities between items i and j ($s_{i,j}$) will measured by the Pearson correlation coefficient or the cosine vector similarity. That is, the predicted rating of item j for a target user u ($\hat{r}_{u,i}$) can be written as

$$\hat{r}_{u,j} = \bar{r}_u + \sum_{i=1}^{I} w_{i,j}(r_{u,i} - \bar{r}_u) \tag{14.7}$$

In Equation 14.7, $\bar{r}_u$ is a target user u's average rating across all I products he or she has rated, and $w_{i,j} = s_{i,j}/|\sum_i s_{i,j}|$ is the weighted similarity of item i and item j. As a result, the user will receive a high prediction for item j if the other items the user has rated tend to have high predictions and be positively correlated with item j. In addition, similarities are scaled (e.g., $w_{i,j}$) by the absolute sum of the similarities to make sure that the predicted rating is within the predefined range.

Sarwar et al. (2001) showed that item-based methods provided better quality prediction than the memory-based algorithm across all sparsity levels even though the difference was not significantly large. In addition, since the item-similarity matrix is fairly static and can be created offline, their online recommendation is fast even for extremely large data sets. Their online speed of prediction does not depend on the total number of users, but depends only on how many items the target user has rated. In sum, item-based methods partially overcome the two challenging problems (data sparsity and scalability) that memory-based methods often face in online applications.

14.3.3 A Bayesian Mixture Model by Chien and George (1999)

Chien and George (1999) were the first to propose a model-based approach based on a Bayesian mixture model. They pointed out a limitation of memory-based methods that occurs when the number of co-rated items from a pair of users is very small (e.g., problem of sparse data). This can lead to high (but unreliable) similarity scores based on an extremely small number of co-rated items. Significance weighting schemes discussed earlier may alleviate this problem somewhat, but it is still heuristic. In addition, memory-based methods are not based on a statistical model so that we cannot statistically evaluate the uncertainty associated with the predicted values.

A Bayesian mixture model assumes that users who tend to give similar ratings can be modeled as having the same ratings probability distribution. That is, users can be partitioned into subgroups which are identified by common probability structure for the ratings. The prediction of a missing rating is based on the posterior distribution of the groupings and associated ratings probabilities. Markov Chain Monte Carlo (MCMC) methods with a hybrid search algorithm are used to estimate parameters and obtain predictions of the missing ratings. Chien and George (1999) show that their model outperforms memory-based methods both on two simulated data sets and a real data. We do not describe their model in detail here because a hierarchical Bayesian model in the next section overlaps with their model and is more practical.

14.3.4 A Hierarchical Bayesian Approach by Ansari et al. (2000)

Ansari et al. (2000) propose an effective hierarchical Bayesian model to predict missing ratings. They adopt a regression-based approach and model customer (or user) ratings as a function of product (or item) attributes, customer characteristics, and expert evaluations. Their model also accounts for unobserved sources of heterogeneity in customer preferences and product appeal structures. Specifically, customer i's rating on product j can be written as

$$r_{ij} = \mathbf{x}'_{ij}\mu + \mathbf{z}'_i\gamma_j + \mathbf{w}'_j\lambda_i + e_{ij}$$
$$e_{ij} \sim N(0, \sigma^2), \lambda_i \sim N(\mathbf{0}, \mathbf{\Lambda}), \gamma_j \sim N(\mathbf{0}, \mathbf{\Gamma})$$

(14.8)

In Equation 14.8, the vector $\mathbf{x}_{ij}$ contains all observed product attributes, customer characteristics, and their interactions. The vector $\mathbf{z}_i$ contains customer characteristics for customer i and the vector $\mathbf{w}_j$ represents product attributes for product j. The random effects λ_i account for unobserved sources of customer heterogeneity and appear in the model interactively with the observed product attributes. Similarly, the random effects γ_j represent unobserved sources of product attributes and appear in the model interactively with the observed customer characteristics. The variance-covariance matrices $\mathbf{\Lambda}$ and $\mathbf{\Gamma}$ provide the information about the extent of unobserved heterogeneity in customer characteristics and product attributes, respectively.

Ansari et al. (2000) applied their model to the EachMovie data, which is a popular movie rating database frequently used by collaborative filtering researchers. Model parameters are estimated by Markov Chain Monte Carlo. Their estimation results provided several interesting findings. First, they compare the full model in Equation 14.8, the model with customer heterogeneity only, the model with product heterogeneity, and the model without any heterogeneity at all. The full model outperforms all the other models on various comparison criteria. They conclude that it is important to consider both customer and product heterogeneity. In addition, accounting for customer heterogeneity is more important than accounting for product heterogeneity. Second, they compared their hierarchical Bayesian model with memory-based methods and showed that their model is substantially better in rating predictions.

The main contribution of Ansari et al.'s method in collaborative filtering research is to adopt a statistically formal approach. Unlike the memory-based approach, their model can provide information on how accurate their rating predictions are from the corresponding posterior distribution. In addition, their model can be used even when rating or preference data for an item does not exist. For example, it can provide the predicted ratings for a new movie, given data on its attributes and the characteristics of customers (x, z, and w in Equation 14.8). Their model also has some advantages over Chien and George's Bayesian mixture approach. Ansari et al.'s model explicitly incorporates explanatory variables (e.g., customer characteristics and item attributes) so that it can explain why customers like or dislike a product. Finally, Chien and George's Bayesian mixture assumes that all customers in a given segment have the same preference structure. This assumption can be restrictive in practice, and a large number of parameters are required to be estimated. On the other hand, Ansari et al.'s model employs continuous heterogeneity so that each customer has his/her unique set of preferences.

14.4 Current Issues in Collaborative Filtering

For the last 10 years, a number of researchers have improved the algorithm
of collaborative filtering significantly. In addition, it has been commercially
incorporated in several web sites for many years now. However, we still have
a number of practical and theoretical issues to be resolved.

14.4.1 Combining Content-Based Information Filtering with Collaborative Filtering

As shown, collaborative filtering is designed to solve the problem of making
accurate and efficient recommendations, that is, it is a recommendation "engine." There is an alternative method to approach the same problem: content-
based information filtering. Each method has its advantages and disadvantages. This section will briefly study the content-based information filtering
and introduce recently developed techniques combining it with collaborative
filtering.

14.4.1.1 Content-Based Information Filtering

Content-based information filtering recommends items for users by analyzing
the content of items that they liked in the past (Balabanovic and Shoham
1997). Its underlying assumption is that the content of an item is what determines the user's preference (Balabanovic 1997). We predict the item preferences of an active user from the observed preferences from other users in
collaborative filtering. In contrast, content-based filtering does not use the
preferences of other users. Instead, its prediction is solely based on the content of an item and the historical preference of the active user.[2]

Content-based methods have been widely used. E-mail filtering software
sorts e-mail into categories according to the sender and content of the title. New-product notification services advertise a new book or album by the
user's favorite author or artist (Schafer et al. 1999). Search engines such as
Yahoo recommend relevant documents on the basis of user-supplied keywords
(Ansari et al. 2000).

To show the main idea of the content-based filtering, let us define an item
as a vector $X = (x_1, \ldots, x_K)$ where each element x_i is the content or the
attribute of the item. For example, an item can be a movie *Matrix* and its

---

[2] The hierarchical Bayesian approach by Ansari et al. (2000) models customer ratings
as a function of product (or item) attributes. Hence, it can be considered as content-
based methods. However, customer ratings in their model not only depend on product
attributes but also customer characteristics and expert evaluations. It is a hybrid method
to combine content-based methods and collaborative filtering.

contents may be its genre, its main actor/actress, its director, etc. An active user has evaluated a set of items so that we observe their preference ratings with their content information. For each user, the set of evaluated items will be used as the estimation sample for the content-based filtering. That is, we run a regression model $r = f(x_1, \ldots, x_K)$ for each user where r is the item ratings. Once the model is estimated, we predict the preference ratings of missing items for the active user.

14.4.1.2 Combining Techniques

Content-based filtering is an effective recommendation tool for new items where rating information from other users does not exist. However, it also has several limitations (Sarwar et al. 1998; Good et al. 1999). First, it often provides bad recommendations since it only considers the pre-specified content of items. If two items have the same content, it will predict them to have the identical ratings. Second, it tends to restrict the scope of the recommendation to the similar items that consumers have already rated (Balabanovic and Shoham 1997).

In contrast, collaborative filtering overcomes the limitations of the content-based filtering by enabling consumers to share their opinions and experiences on items (Herlocker et al. 1999). It recommends items that similar consumers have liked. It automates the process of word-of-mouth communication among consumers. However, it also has its own limitations. First, collaborative filtering does not work very well when the number of evaluators/users is small relative to the volume of information in the system. That is, it is difficult to find similar users in predicting ratings for some unpopular items. Second, it has an early rater problem that occurs when a new product/item appears in the database. Note that the collaborative filtering cannot provide the predictive ratings for a new product until some consumers have evaluated it.

Recognizing that the content-based and the collaborative filtering systems both have their advantages and disadvantages in recommending products, researchers have recently attempted to develop a hybrid model to combine these two approaches (Balabanovic 1997; Balabanovic and Shoham 1997; Basu et al. 1998; Sarwar et al. 1998; Good et al. 1999; Herlocker et al. 1999; Kim and Kim 2001). Claiming that their models take advantage of the collaborative filtering approach without losing the benefit of the content-based approach, they have shown that their models performed better than the individual approach. We describe the hybrid model by Kim and Kim (2001).

14.4.1.3 Hybrid Model by Kim and Kim (2001)

Taking a statistically more formal approach than the other combining methods, Kim and Kim (2001) have developed a hybrid recommender system that combines the content-based and the collaborative filtering systems. Their point of departure is first to extract the content component of products/items by employing a regression and then to apply the collaborative filtering to the consumer's preference unexplained by this (content-based) regression. Specifically, the authors apply a simple regression to extract item attributes and then adjust upward or downward based on whether similar users have positive or negative errors associated with the regression-based prediction.

The Algorithm

The algorithm consists of six major steps. First, the system needs to determine a set of content features to characterize products/items. For the moviegoer example, key features may include the genre of the movie, the director, the producer, the main actors/actresses and so on.

The second step is to identify the relationship between item features and preference ratings. They use a simple regression applied to each user.

$$r_{aj} = \beta_{0a} + \beta_{1a}X_{1aj} + \ldots + \beta_{ai}X_{Kaj} + \varepsilon_{aj} \qquad (14.9)$$

where r_{aj} is the preference rating of the active user a for item j, K is the number of specified features and X_{1aj} is the value of the 1st feature for product j evaluated by the active user a. The parameters to be estimated (or β's) in the Equation 14.9 measure how important each feature is in determining the preference of the user. Upon estimation, the model can predict the active user a's preference on items not yet evaluated. For the moviegoer example in Table 14.1, we would apply the regression with Amy's observed movie preferences as a dependent variable and the corresponding movie features as independent variables. Given the features of Movie 3, the estimation model would be used to predict Amy's rating for Movie 3 that is not rated.

Steps 1 and 2 are nothing but a version of content-based filtering. Only the contents of items are utilized to predict the preferences of a user. Content-based filtering cannot explain anything beyond item features. For example, a user may provide different ratings for the two movies with identical features. Many other factors than the specified item features will influence the preference ratings. The unexplained portion of user ratings will be modeled in the following steps.

Steps 3 and 4 are required to derive the matrix of prediction errors. The prediction error ($\varepsilon_{aj} = r_{aj} - \hat{r}_{aj}$) is the difference between the actual preference and the predicted preference for user a, movie j. In other words, the prediction errors are the residuals in regression model or the preferences unexplained by the model. It is required to calculate the predicted ratings for both observed and missing items. But the prediction errors for missing items cannot be calculated. Hence, the data matrix of prediction errors consists of a series of prediction errors with a set of missing values.

Step 5 is to apply the collaborative filtering technique to the prediction error matrix. Kim and Kim (2001) have employed a typical neighborhood-based algorithm to calculate the values for missing cells. Hence, the predicted rating of an active user t on product j $(e_{t,j})$ can be calculated as

$$e_{a,j} = \bar{\varepsilon}_a + \tau \sum_{i=1}^{n} s_{a,i}(\varepsilon_{i,j} - \bar{\varepsilon}_i) \qquad (14.10)$$

where and n is the number of users in the prediction error matrix who have evaluated the item j. The weight $s_{a,i}$ is the (error) similarity between user i and the active user a. And τ is a normalizing factor such that the absolute values of the weights sum to one.

The final step is to sum the outputs from the third step and the fifth step. For the missing cells, the content-based filtering in step 3 provides $\hat{r}_{aj}$ while the collaborative filtering in step 5 produces e_{aj}. The predicted rating of item j for the active user a is the sum of these two numbers. Summarizing the algorithm,[3]

STEP 1: Determine a set of content features characterizing items.

STEP 2: Fit the (features) regression for each user.

STEP 3: Calculate the fitted preferences for all users and all items.

STEP 4: Derive a matrix of prediction errors.

STEP 5: Apply the collaborative filtering into the error matrix.

STEP 6: Sum the output from STEP 3 and STEP 5.

Performance of the Model

Kim and Kim's hybrid model is applied to the movie rating data. Four other competing models are also applied to the data. The baseline model that predicts the rating for each movie as the mean rating across users will benchmark the performance of the other personalized recommender systems. The second model is a content-based filtering method where the genres of the movie are used as the contents of the movie/item. A dummy variable is created for each of the ten genre variables including comedy, drama, action, art/foreign, classic, animation, family, romance, horror and thriller. A movie can be simultaneously classified into more than one of these genres. For each user, actual movie ratings are regressed on these ten genre dummies. The third is a collaborative filtering model using the neighborhood-based algorithm with similarities between users measured by Pearson correlation coefficients. In addition, twenty co-rated items are used as the cutoff for significance weighting, and the users with less than 0.01 correlations are not included as a set of neighborhood.

---

[3] A hybrid model by Kim and Kim (2001) has a same objective as a hierarchical Bayesian approach by Ansari et al. (2000) in combining content-based methods and collaborative filtering. Ansari et al.'s approach is statistically more rigorous. However, it is much easier to implement Kim and Kim's method.

Table 14.3 Predictive accuracy of various recommender models (From Kim and Kim 2001)

Type of Model	MAE	ROC
Baseline model	0.2238	0.7398
Content-based filtering	0.2103	0.7640
Collaborative filtering	0.1955	0.8058
Model by Kim and Kim (2001)	0.1832	0.8328

Table 14.3 shows the prediction accuracy for five models in the validation sample. Two performance measures are employed: the MAE and the ROC sensitivity measure. As expected, models incorporating some personalized components outperform the (aggregate) baseline model with respect to both MAE and ROC. In addition, the hybrid model is shown to outperform all other models for both prediction measures. With respect to the ROC, the hybrid model improves the predictive performance of the content-based and the collaborative filtering by 6.8% and 2.6%, respectively.

14.4.2 Implicit Ratings

So far we have limited our attention to case where we have preference rating data explicitly expressed by users on a discrete numerical scale. In the real world, however, explicit rating information is not always available. Often the data available are behavioral measures such as the user's web-browsing pattern, purchase history and so on. These data provide *implicit* ratings of products. GroupLens research shows that predictions based on reading time are nearly as accurate as predictions based on explicit numerical ratings in the news article recommendation (Konstan et al. 1997). However, Mild and Reutterer (2001) applied various versions of memory-based methods to actual purchase choices and found poor predictive performance. Considering its practical importance, the research on implicit ratings is relatively rare.

It is not obvious how to develop an implicit score from customers' purchase histories. One cannot simply assign one for an item purchased and zero for an item not purchased. A purchase of an item may imply that customer likes it.[4] But if an item has not been purchased, this might mean the customer dislikes it or the customer does not know its availability, or something else. Moreover, technically speaking, we cannot apply collaborative filtering to the data filled with either 1 or 0. You need 1's and 0's with missing cells that will be predicted.[5]

---

[4] Even this is debatable because purchase does not always imply the consumer liked the product. CDNOW allows customers later to go back and say *"own it but dislike it"* (Schafer et al. 1999).

[5] Sarwar et al. (2000) suggest that the frequency of purchases instead of purchase indicator (e.g., one) can be used for repeat purchase products.

An easy way of overcoming the problem is to use the default voting (Breese et al. 1998). The idea has been developed out of the observation that, when users only rate a small number of items, the correlation algorithm and neighbor-based collaborative filtering will not work well because it uses only ratings of the items both users have rated. The authors suggest that some default rating value is assigned for not-rated items such that the correlation is calculated over the union of the rated items. They also suggest that the same default value is assigned for some additional items k that neither user has rated. However, Breese et al. (1998) did not provide any justification on why some not-rated items should get default ratings and others should not. More research is definitely required.

Alternatively, Mild and Reutterer (2003) propose using the Jaccard or Tanimoto coefficient as the similarity measure to overcome the limited variance in similarities constructed for very sparse binary purchase data. The Tanimoto similarity between two users a and i ($s_{a,i}$) is defined as

$$s_{a,i} = \frac{\text{the number of items that both users purchased}}{\text{the number of items that either user } a \text{ or user } i \text{ purchased}}$$

That is, the Tanimoto similarity ignores the number of coinciding non-chosen items. Mild and Reutterer (2003) show that the Tanimoto similarity outperforms traditional similarity measures in the case of extremely asymmetric distributed or sparse data vectors (e.g., many zeros).

Another approach would be to calculate simple correlations between 0 and 1 data for the similarity measure for item-based collaborative filtering as in Sect. 14.3.2, Equation 14.7. That is, for each pair of items, we would calculate the correlation across users between 0 and 1 data of whether or not they purchased the product. That would provide the correlation needed in Equation 14.7. We would interpret a high correlation as meaning that customers who buy one product tend to buy the other. So if the active customer has purchased products that correlate positively with Product A, we would predict that the customer would be interested in purchasing Product A. This of course is a simple, brute force approach that avoids the fact that we do not know how to interpret the 0's and 1's (see Iacobucci et al. (2000) for a criticism of the use of correlations between 0 and 1 variables), but is worthy of future research because in all likelihood, the customer who has purchased a specific product tends to like it. Using this theme in an item-based collaborative filtering system would essentially just be an extension of market basket analysis (see Chapter 13), which looks at conditional probabilities of purchasing one product, given another product has been purchased. This is similar conceptually to the correlation that would be used in the item-based collaborative filtering system based on 0–1 data.

We may be able to increase the quality of data considerably by collecting implicit data that imply negative user preference. For example, information on returned products may indicate negative preference (Schafer et al. 1999). Or customer complaints on products/services can be incorporated. However, a really complex question on implicit negative preference may be how to code/rate them. If 1 is for purchase and 0 for non-purchase, then what number should be assigned to the implicit negative preference such as the product return? Without any theoretical development, researchers have empirically searched for the optimal value leading to the best prediction performance. The better approach may be to construct the unobserved distribution of customer preference on the product.

Another issue on implicit ratings is how to combine the explicit and the implicit rating. We might first derive the implicit preference ratings from purchase histories. The rating database will be revised once the explicit rating information is available. For example, Amazon.com users sometimes provide explicit ratings on books they bought. It is an interesting future research agenda to develop a concrete method of initializing ratings with implicit rating information and updating them with explicit rating information.

14.4.3 Selection Bias

Most collaborative filtering algorithms assume that the missing data is generated randomly. However, customers can evaluate only products that they have purchased. Or the set of movies rated by a moviegoer may be movies that she tends to like. We do not know all possible causes of the missing data pattern, but we know that most data employed in collaborative filtering research has non-ignorable missing data pattern.

If the missing evaluations are missing at random, we can safely assume that the missing data does not have any informational value in rating predictions. That is, the fact that the evaluation is missing does not depend on the value of that evaluation, when the missing evaluations are missing at random (Ying et al. 2006). But this assumption may be too restrictive in practice. Some customers do not provide ratings simply because they have not purchased the product in question. And the reason why they did not purchase the product may be that they did not like it. Failing to incorporate missing-data mechanism can lead to biased estimates unless the missing data is generated completely at random (Little and Rubin 1987). That is, our rating predictions can be suboptimal if we ignore missing-data mechanism.

Ying et al. (2006) account for non-random missing data by proposing a joint model for the latent processes underlying selection and prediction. In their model, the fact that a product is "selected" for evaluation influences the predicted rating of the product. More specifically, their selection and prediction model can be written as

$$U_s = \beta_s X_s + \varepsilon_s$$
$$U_p = \beta_p X_p + \varepsilon_p$$
$$(\varepsilon_s, \varepsilon_p) \sim N(0, 0, 1, 1, \rho)$$

(14.11)

Similar to Ansari et al. (2000), they view product evaluations (or recommendations) as a target customer's latent consumption utility. In Equation 14.11, the subscript s indicates the selection component while the subscript p indicates the prediction component. And X represents all covariates such as product or customer characteristics.

The selection equation in Equation 14.11 is the key to incorporate non-random missing data mechanism. The latent value U_s can be translated into the observed quantity by assuming that $P(Y_s = 1) = P(0 < U_s)$ where Y_s is the $0/1$ indicator representing whether the product is evaluated (see Chapter 11 for more discussion of selection models). The correlation ρ, representing the correlation between the error terms, is allowed to vary across customers captures the interrelation between the selection and the prediction processes.

We can interpret Equation 14.11 as a two-step rating process even though Ying et al. did not make any assumptions on temporal ordering of these two processes. First, a customer will make a decision on whether the item is evaluated (or purchased) according to the selection model. And then if the selection decision is affirmative, s/he will make the rating decision. If we ignore the selection model, the expected value for the prediction utility should be $E(U_p) = \beta_p X_p$. When the selection process is considered, it will change. For example, suppose that a customer has decided to evaluate (e.g., rating is not missing). Then the expected value for the prediction utility should be

$$E(U_p|U_s > 0) = \beta_p X_p + \rho\phi(\beta_s X_s)/\Phi(\beta_s X_s) \tag{14.12}$$

where $\phi(\cdot)$ and $\Phi(\cdot)$ are the density function and distribution function of the standard normal evaluated at $\beta_s X_s$. That is, incorporating the selection process changes the expected value for the prediction utility. It is also interesting to note the role of the correlation ρ. If the selection process is not correlated with the prediction process (e.g., $\rho = 0$), the expected value for the prediction utility in Equation 14.12 becomes $\beta_p X_p$ that is the same as the expected value without the selection model.

Applying their model into the EachMovie data, Ying et al. (2006) found that the correlation ρ is significantly different from zero. Hence, the missing-data generation process is not random. In addition, the inclusion of the selection model clearly improves the prediction accuracy for the item ratings.

14.4.4 Recommendations Across Categories

Current recommendation systems are designed to recommend a set of items from a single product category, whether their algorithms are based on collaborative filter, content-based filtering, or combining approach. For example, the recommendation system may select ten movies among thousands of movie titles. An interesting marketing issue may be the possibility of predicting item preference in one category based on the preference information from other product categories. For example, consider an Internet store selling books and CDs that attempts to develop a recommender system. One can construct two separate recommendation engines, one of book customers and the other for CD customers. This approach is somewhat limited in utilizing cross-category information. Alternatively, ignoring category differences and treating all items from books and CDs homogeneously, one may develop one recommendation system. Even though this approach maximizes the use of customer purchase information, it may lead to the prediction bias resulting from mixing apples and oranges. Finally, we can think of a method somewhere between these two extreme approaches. Acknowledging category differences, we can still use cross-category purchase information in predicting customer behavior.

One way of incorporating the category effect is to weight ratings differently in calculating similarities between customers and mean ratings. For example, suppose there are two categories, books and CDs. When we predict the preference ratings of books, we multiply the ratings of CDs by a factor α and apply the collaborative filtering algorithm. If α is equal to zero, then the approach becomes two separate recommendation engines. On the other hand, if α is equal to one, it becomes the approach of ignoring cross-category effects. If α is somewhere between, we are assuming that the importance of CD purchase information is α times as much as that of book purchase information in predicting the preference rating of books. Similarly, when we predict the preference ratings of CDs, we multiply the ratings of books by a factor β and apply the collaborative filtering algorithm. That is, we can allow for any asymmetric effect in providing information. That is, the purchase information on books may be valuable in predicting purchase preferences of the same customer for CDs. At the same time, the purchase information on CDs may not be very useful in predicting purchase preferences for books.

How do we determine the values of α and β? A simple approach may be to determine empirically. That is, try every possible value from 0 to 1, and choose the ones that would provide the best prediction performance.

Chapter 15
Discrete Dependent Variables and Duration Models

Abstract Probably the most common statistical technique in predictive modeling is the binary response, or logistic regression, model. This model is designed to predict either/or behavior such as "Will the customer buy?" or "Will the customer churn?" We discuss logistic regression and other discrete models such as discriminant analysis, multinomial logit, and count data methods. Duration models, the second part of this chapter, model the timing for an event to occur. One form of duration model, the hazard model, is particularly important because it can be used to predict how long the customer will remain as a current customer. It can also predict how long it will take before the customer decides to make another purchase, switch to an upgrade, etc. We discuss hazard models in depth.

Many database marketing phenomena we want to model are discrete. For example, consider predicting the brand of car a customer will choose in an upcoming car purchase. Or consider predicting which customers will respond to a direct mail offer. The brand choice or the response to the offer may be modeled to be a function of customer's demographic and purchase behavioral characteristics. However, the dependent variable is categorical (i.e., an identification of a brand or a response indicator). These are discrete dependent variables.

This chapter will discuss various statistical models that are designed to analyze discrete or what are also called qualitative dependent variables. We start with models for a binary response including the linear probability model, logit model (or logistic regression), probit model and discriminant analysis. In the next section, we introduce models for multinomial response that generalize the binary response models. Next, we briefly study models specially designed for count data, followed by the tobit model or censored regression. Finally, we discuss hazard models appropriate for analyzing duration data. The hazard model analyzes the time until an event occurs, so has both discrete and continuous aspects.

15.1 Binary Response Model

The dependent variable for the binary response model can take two different values. For example, a consumer responds to the promotional event ($Y = 1$) or will not ($Y = 0$). Or a customer purchases the firm's brand of car ($Y = 1$) or a competitor's brand ($Y = 0$). The specific values ($0/1$) assigned to each outcome of the dependent variable are arbitrary since all that matters is that we have a code for knowing which values of Y correspond to which outcomes. So we can assign $Y = 0$ for the response to the promotional event and $Y = 1$ for the non-response. Or it can be $Y =$ "Yes" for the response and $Y =$ "No" for the non-response.

In order to clarify the following discussion, consider a credit scoring model that has become a standard application for financial institutions deciding whether to grant credit to customers. The goal of the credit scoring model is to automate the credit-granting decision process by predicting the default probability for each credit applicant. The consumer's future response will be either default ($Y = 1$) or not default ($Y = 0$). Typically a customer's default behavior/response is modeled to be a function of her demographic and credit-related behavioral characteristics with a number of macro economic variables.

15.1.1 Linear Probability Model

Our goal is to model the default behavior of customer i. Let Y_i to be the default indicator variable for customer i that is assumed to be randomly drawn from a Bernoulli distribution with a mean of p_i. Hence, the probability that Y_i equals 1 is p_i while the probability that it equals 0 is $1 - p_i$. That is,

$$Y_i = \begin{cases} 1, \ P(Y_i = 1) = p_i \\ 0, \ P(Y_i = 0) = 1 - p_i \end{cases} \tag{15.1}$$

Our dependent variable Y_i will have a relationship with a set of independent variables by assuming that p_i is a function of the set of independent variables. That is, we assume that $p_i = F(\beta' \mathbf{X}_i)$ where $\mathbf{X}_i$ is a vector of independent variables for customer i (e.g., customer's credit-related variables) and β is a corresponding parameter vector. Then $E(Y_i) = (1)(p_i) + (0)(1 - p_i) = p_i = F(\beta' \mathbf{X}_i)$.

The key issue in a binary response model is the specification of the link function F. The simplest is to assume that F is linear, $p_i = F(\beta' \mathbf{X}_i) = \beta' \mathbf{X}_i$. Now since $E(Y_i | \mathbf{X}_i) = \beta' \mathbf{X}_i$, we can derive the following linear probability model.

$$Y_i = \beta' \mathbf{X}_i + \varepsilon_i \tag{15.2}$$

where ε_i is the error term of customer i. A linear probability model is a traditional regression model with a binary dependent variable Y_i and a set of independent variables $\mathbf{X}_i$. Consistent with the assumption for a classical linear regression, the expected value of the error term is 0, which can be seen in the following calculation:

$$
\begin{aligned}
E(\varepsilon_i) = E(Y_i - \beta'\mathbf{X}_i) &= p_i(1 - \beta'\mathbf{X}_i) + (1 - p_i)(0 - \beta'\mathbf{X}_i) \\
&= p_i - p_i\beta'\mathbf{X}_i - \beta'\mathbf{X}_i + p_i\beta'\mathbf{X}_i \\
&= p_i - \beta'\mathbf{X}_i \\
&= 0
\end{aligned}
$$

However, there are a number of shortcomings to the linear probability model. First, the error term in Equation 15.2 will violate the homoscedasticity assumption of classical linear regression model since Y_i is a binary discrete variable. Noting that ε_i can only take two values, $1 - \beta'\mathbf{X}_i$ with probability of p_i and $-\beta'\mathbf{X}_i$ with probability $1 - p_i$, we compute the variance of the error term as:

$$
Var(\varepsilon_i) = E(\varepsilon_i^2) = p_i(1 - \beta'\mathbf{X}_i)^2 + (1 - p_i)(-\beta'\mathbf{X}_i)^2 = \beta'\mathbf{X}_i(1 - \beta'\mathbf{X}_i)^2
$$

That is, the variance is not homoscedastic, but varies with the values of independent variables. The second problem associated with the linear probability model is more serious. We refer to it as the "unit interval" problem. Since p_i is the *probability* that $Y_i = 1$, its value should be bounded from 0 to 1. The predicted value of $\hat{p}_i = \hat{\beta}\mathbf{X}_i$ in the linear probability model is not guaranteed to be within the $[0, 1]$ range. As a result, predictions can be impossible to interpret as probabilities. In addition, the heteroscedasticity, if not corrected for, can increase prediction error. Because of these shortcomings, the linear probability model is becoming less frequently used in database marketing even though it is computationally simple to use.

Several researchers have discussed ways of overcoming the shortcomings of linear probability models (Judge et al. 1985; Greene 1997). For example, Goldberger (1964) suggested correcting the heteroscedasticity problem by employing GLS (generalized least squares) estimation. Judge et al. (1985) proposed an inequality-restricted least squares approach to overcome the unit interval problem, however their remedies are sample-dependent.

15.1.2 Binary Logit (or Logistic Regression) and Probit Models

A direct way to remedy the unit interval problem is to find a link function that satisfies the $[0, 1]$ constraint on p_i. One such function is a cumulative density function. The value of $p_i = F(\beta'\mathbf{X}_i)$ or the probability of $Y_i = 1$ approaches to 1 as the value of $\beta'\mathbf{X}_i$ goes to the plus infinity while it approaches to 0 as the value of $\beta'\mathbf{X}_i$ goes to the minus infinity (see Fig. 15.1). Even though

$F(\beta'X_i)$

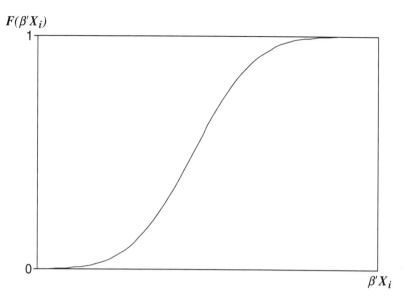

Fig. 15.1 Using a cumulative distribution function as the link function for a binary response model.

any cumulative distribution functions have this property, the following two cumulative density functions are most frequently used.

$$\text{Logistic cdf: } F(\beta'\mathbf{X}_i) = \frac{\exp(\beta'\mathbf{X}_i)}{1 + \exp(\beta'\mathbf{X}_i)} = \frac{1}{1 + \exp(-\beta'\mathbf{X}_i)} \quad (15.3\text{a})$$

$$\text{Standard normal cdf: } F(\beta'\mathbf{X}_i) = \int_{-\infty}^{\beta'\mathbf{X}_i} \phi(t)dt = \Phi(\beta'\mathbf{X}_i) \quad (15.3\text{b})$$

where $\phi(\cdot)$ is the density of a standard normal distribution and $\Phi(\cdot)$ is the corresponding cumulative density. The model is called a binary logit or logistic regression model when the link function F is logistic, and a probit model when F is the standard normal. The shape of the logistic distribution is very similar to that of the normal distribution except in the tails, which are heavier (Greene 1997). Hence, its estimation results are also similar. It is difficult to show that the logistic is better (or worse) than the standard cumulative normal on theoretical grounds. However, the binary logit model may be more frequently used because of its mathematical convenience – once the logistic regression has been estimated, Equation 15.3a provides a convenient formula for calculating predicted probabilities. In contrast, the probit model requires a table look-up of the normal distribution to calculate predicted probabilities, as shown in Equation 15.3b.

The binary logit and probit models are estimated using the method of maximum likelihood. Each observation is treated as an independent random draw from the identical Bernoulli distribution. Hence, the joint probability or the likelihood function of the binary response model with the sample size of n can be written as

$$L = \prod_{i=1}^{n} [F(\boldsymbol{\beta}'\mathbf{X}_i)]^{Y_i} [1 - F(\boldsymbol{\beta}'\mathbf{X}_i)]^{1-Y_i} \tag{15.4}$$

The estimation of the parameter vector $\boldsymbol{\beta}$ involves finding a set of parameters to maximize the likelihood function, Equation 15.4. It is difficult to derive an analytical solution for $\boldsymbol{\beta}$ because the likelihood function (except in the case of the linear probability model) is highly nonlinear. Therefore, the estimates $\boldsymbol{\beta}$ are found through an iterative search using Newton's BHHH method for the logit or probit model (Berndt et al. 1974).

Let us provide a simple example of the logistic regression model applied to credit scoring. Again our objective is to predict the prospect's default probability. For illustration, we assume that a customer's default likelihood is a function of her or his annual income and marital status, even though there are several other variables related to the default behavior. Annual income x_1 (measured in \$1,000) is a continuous variable while marital status x_2 is defined to be categorical ($x_2 = 1$ if the customer is single, divorced, or separated, and $x_2 = 0$ otherwise). The logistic regression model is applied to a sample of current customers whose default behaviors have been observed. We code $Y_i = 1$ if customer i defaults and $Y_i = 0$ if not. The following equation summarizes the estimation result.

$$P(Y_i = 1) = \frac{e^{0.5 - 0.01x_1 + 1.1x_2}}{1 + e^{0.5 - 0.01x_1 + 1.1x_2}} = \frac{1}{1 + e^{-(0.5 - 0.01x_1 + 1.1x_2)}} \tag{15.5}$$

Equation 15.5 indicates that there is a negative relationship between income (x_1) and default likelihood. A customer with higher income will have the lower chance of default. On the other hand, there is a positive relationship between marital status and the default probability. A customer who is single, divorced, or separated will have the higher probability of default. More specifically, the single customer with the income of \$40,000 ($x_1 = 40$ and $x_2 = 1$) is predicted to have a default probability of 0.08 while the married customer with the same income ($x_1 = 40$ and $x_2 = 0$) is predicted to have 0.03 probability of default. Hence, the marginal effect of the marital status x_2 (at $x_1 = 40$) is 0.05. This is the difference in default probabilities between a married customer and a single, divorced, or separated customer.

An intuitive way to interpret an individual logit parameter (β) is to consider the "odds ratio". First, the *odds* of a yes response ($Y_i = 1$) is defined to be $P(Y_i = 1)/P(Y_i = 0)$, i.e., the likelihood of the event happening relative to not happening. For example, an odds of "3", also known as "3 to 1 odds," means that the likelihood of defaulting is three times greater than the likelihood of not defaulting. Second, the *odds ratio* is the ratio of the odds when the independent variable equals $X_i + 1$ divided by the odds when the independent variable equals X_i. Hence the odds ratio shows by what factor the odds change when the independent variable increases by one unit.

It can be shown using simple algebra that for logistic regression, the odds ratio equals $exp(\beta)$ – the exponentiation of a logistic regression parameter tells us the factor by which the odds change per unit change in the corresponding independent variable. For example, the coefficient for marital status in Equation 15.5 is $\beta = 1.1$. Since $exp(1.1) = 3$, this tells us that the odds of defaulting change by a factor of 3, which means an increase of 200%, if the customer is single, divorced, or separated ($x_2 = 1$) versus married ($x_2 = 0$). The coefficient for income is $\beta = -0.01$. Since $exp(-0.01) = 0.99$, that means that the odds of defaulting change by a factor of 0.99, which means a *decrease* by 1% (($1 - 0.99) \times 100\% = -1\%$) per $1,000 increase in income.

In order to compare the impact of variables measured in different units, we can calculate the change in the odds per *standard deviation* change in the independent variable. Let σ = the standard deviations of the indendent variable of interest, then the odds ratio *per standard deviation change* can be shown to equal $exp(\beta\sigma)$. Hence if the standard deviation of income in our data is $15,000, we have $exp(-0.01 \times 15) = 0.86$, so a standard deviation increase in income on the odds of defaulting decreases the odds of defaulting by 14% (($1 - 0.86) \times 100\% = -14\%$).

15.1.3 Logistic Regression with Rare Events Data

Researchers have addressed problems in the statistical analysis of rare events data using logistic regression or binary probit. In the social and epidemiological sciences, there are dozens to thousands of times fewer ones (events) than zeros (non-events), for example in the analysis of wars, coups, presidential vetoes and infections by uncommon diseases. In database marketing, response rates below 1% are not unusual. When applied to rare events data, logistic regression or binary probit can *under-estimate* customer response probability.

Statistically, the problem emerges from the fact that the statistical properties of linear regression models are invariant to the (unconditional) mean of the dependent variable. But the same is not true for logistic regression or binary probit (King and Zeng 2001). In fact, King and Zeng show that for the logistic regression model, when the mean of a binary dependent variable, or the frequency of events in the data, is very small, parameter estimates of logistic regression become more biased and predicted response probabilities become too pessimistic. There are two intuitive explanations for this. (1) King and Zeng argue that in rare events data, there are plenty of values available for the independent variables to understand the circumstances that cause a non-event, however, there are far fewer to understand the circumstances that cause an event. Those few values do not fully cover the tail of the logistic distribution, and so the model infers that there are fewer circumstances under which the event will occur, resulting in an under-estimate of the probability the event occurs. King and Zeng show that the primary manifestation of this is downward bias in the constant term of the logistic regression.[1] (2) Parametric link functions such as those used for logit or probit lack flexibility. Logit and probit models assume specific shapes of the underlying link function (see Fig. 15.1), implying a given tail probability expression that remains invariant to observed data characteristics. As a result, these models cannot adjust for the case when there are not enough observations to fully span the range needed for estimating these link functions (see Kamakura et al. (2005) for further discussion).

The bias in logistic regression with rare events is potentially very important because it suggests that taking predicted logistic response probabilities literally under-estimates the actual likelihood of response. Too many customers will be deemed unprofitable and the firm will incur an opportunity loss by not contacting many customers who would have been profitable (a "Type II Error" as described in Chapter 10, Sect. 10.3.5.4).

Researchers have proposed three approaches to overcome the problem with using logistic regression (or probit) to analyze rare events data. These are all statistical approaches aimed at calculating unbiased individual-level predictions. When applying predictive models at the n-tile level, it is practical to use each n-tile's actual response rate as the prediction for customers in that n-tile (see Chapter 10, Sect. 10.3.5.1). Turning now to the statistical approaches to calculating unbiased individual-level predictions, the first is to adjust the coefficients and the predictions of the estimated logistic regression model. King and Zeng (2001, p. 147) describe how to adjust the maximum likelihood estimates of the logistic regression parameters to calculate "approximately unbiased" coefficients, $\tilde{\beta}$. When the $\tilde{\beta}$'s are inserted into the logistic equation for a given customer's set of independent variables, X_i, the resulting prediction is called $\tilde{\pi}_i$. King and Zeng then derive the following adjustment to predicting the probability of an event using logistic regression when events are rare:

$$P(Y_i = 1) = \tilde{\pi}_i + (0.5 - \tilde{\pi}_i)\tilde{\pi}_i(1 - \tilde{\pi}_i)X_i Var(\hat{\beta})X_i' \qquad (15.6)$$

where $Var(\hat{\beta})$ is the estimated variance/covariance matrix of the estimated coefficients. First, since we are dealing with rare events data, $\tilde{\pi}_i$ will be small and so predictions using Equation 15.6 are adjusted upwards. Second, to the extent that we have a very large sample size, we have more information, $Var(\hat{\beta})$ will be relatively small, and there is less need for adjustment.[2]

---

[1] King and Zeng note that logistic regression coefficients estimated using maximum likelihood are biased but consistent. However, the bias tends toward zero if observations are randomly sampled and the percentage of events approaches 50%. This makes sense given our intuitive explanation for the bias.

[2] Software for implementing these adjustments, called "Zelig," is available at Professor King's website, http://gking.harvard.edu/stats.shtml. We thank Professor King for his insights on this issue and for making his software available.

A second approach to addressing the bias issue is "choice-based sampling." In choice-based sampling, the sample is constructed based on the value of the dependent variable. For example, if we were constructing a predictive model for customer churn, we would gather all the churners and all the non-churners, then randomly select 10,000 churners and 10,000 non-churners. The intuitive appeal of choice-based sampling is that we now have an equal (or at least more well-balanced) number of churners and non-churners, so being a churner is no longer a rare event. The problem is that choice-based sampling may induce a selection bias regarding the independent variables because there may be unobserved factors that systematically produce different distributions of independent variables for churners and non-churners (King and Zeng 2001; Donkers et al. 2003).

As a result, choice-based sampling produces biased results and corrections must be undertaken. One of the popular ones is "Weighted Exogenous Sampling Maximum-Likelihood" (WESML), developed by Manski and Lerman (1977) (see Singh (2005) for an application). King and Zeng (2001) propose a simpler technique they find is equivalent to other econometric solutions, and show that it performs similarly to WESML, although acknowledge that WESML can be more effective with large samples and with functional form misspecification. The King and Zeng adjustment is only to adjust the constant term in the maximum-likelihood-estimated logistic regression model:

$$\hat{\beta}_{0,adj} = \hat{\beta}_0 - ln\left[\left(\frac{1-\tau}{\tau}\right)\left(\frac{\bar{y}}{1-\bar{y}}\right)\right] \qquad (15.7)$$

where $\hat{\beta}_{0,adj}$ is the adjusted constant term, $\hat{\beta}_0$ is the MLE estimate of the constant term, τ is the percentage of "1's" (i.e., churn, respond, etc.) in the population, and $\bar{y}$ is the fraction of 1's in the choice-based sample. For example, τ might equal 2% but $\bar{y}$ could equal 50%. One can see that since $\tau < \bar{y}$, the adjusted constant term will be smaller than the MLE-estimated constant term.

Donkers et al. (2003) investigated the similar issue and derived the adjustment factor to the constant term of the logistic regression. Their adjustment formula is identical to Equation 15.7 except that they did not consider the population (or prior) percentage. That is, $\hat{\beta}_{0,adj} = \hat{\beta}_0 - \ln[\bar{y}/(1-\bar{y})]$.

Research is needed to investigate WESML as well as King and Zeng's adjustment in a database marketing context, and to find the conditions under which random sampling (with King and Zeng's adjustment Equation 15.6) is preferred to choice-based sampling (with either King and Zeng's adjustment Equation 15.7 or WESML). See Ben-Akiva et al. (1997) for further discussion and cautions regarding choice-based sampling.

A third approach to addressing the rare-events problem is to relax the logit or probit parametric link assumptions, which can be too restrictive for rare events data (Bult and Wansbeek 1995; Naik and Tsai 2004). Naik and Tsai (2004) proposed an isotonic single-index model and developed an efficient algorithm for its estimation. Different from the logistic regression or probit model, its link function is flexible so that it encompasses all proper distribution functions and identifies the underlying distribution using information in the data rather than imposing a particular shape. More work is needed to investigate Naik and Tasi's method in a database marketing context.

15.1.4 Discriminant Analysis

Database marketers frequently use discriminant analysis as an alternative to logistic regression or probit in analyzing binary response data. Discriminant analysis is a multivariate technique identifying variables that explain the differences among several groups (e.g., respondents and non-respondents to mailing offers) and that classify new observations or customers into previously defined groups.

Discriminant analysis involves deriving linear combinations of the independent variables ($\beta'\mathbf{X}$) that will discriminate between *a priori* defined groups (e.g., responders and non-responders). The weights, called discriminant coefficients, are estimated in such a way that the misclassification error rates are minimized or the between-group variance relative to the within-group variance is maximized. Once the discriminant weights β are determined, the discriminant score ($\mathbf{y}_i = \beta'\mathbf{x}_i$) for each customer i can be obtained by multiplying the discriminant weight associated with each independent variable by the customer's value on the independent variable and then summing over the set of independent variables. The resulting score for each customer can be transformed into a posterior probability that gives the likelihood of the customer belonging to each group.

We apply the discriminant analysis into the credit scoring data in the previous section where a logistic regression was applied. The dependent variable is binary (i.e., $Y_i = 1$ if customer i defaults and $Y_i = 0$ if not). And there are two independent variables, annual income x_1 and marital status x_2. The discriminant function (d) is estimated to be $d = -0.02x_1 + 1.87x_2$. That is, the discriminant coefficient is -0.02 for x_1 and 1.87 for x_2. Among defaulters whose Y_i is equal to 1, the mean value of x_1 is 30 and the mean of x_2 is 0.7. Among non-defaulters whose Y_i is equal to 0, the mean value of x_1 is 50 and the mean of x_2 is 0.3. Hence, the average discriminant score of defaulters is $d_{defaulters} = (-0.02)(30) + (1.87)(0.7) = 1.249$ while the average discriminant score of non-defaulters is $d_{non-defaulters} = (-0.02)(50) + (1.87)(0.3) = 0.469$. A single customer with annual income of \$40,000 is classified as a defaulter because her or his discriminant score is $(-0.02)(40) + (1.87)(1) = 1.79$, which is greater than the midpoint of $d_{defaulters}$ and $d_{non-defaulters} (= 0.859)$.

There are many studies on the relative performance of logistic regression and discriminant analysis in the analysis of binary dependent variables. In terms of computational burden, discriminant analysis is better. Ordinary least squares can be used to estimate the coefficients of the linear discriminant function, while nonlinear optimization methods are required to estimate the coefficients of the logistic regression (Maddala 1983). However, computational simplicity is no longer an adequate criterion, considering the high-speed computers available now.

Amemiya and Powell (1983) found that if the independent variables are multivariate normal, the discriminant analysis estimator is the maximum-likelihood estimator and is asymptotically efficient. On the other hand, the discriminant analysis estimator is not consistent when the independent variables are not normal, but the logistic regression is and therefore more robust. Press and Wilson (1978) compared the performances of these two estimators in terms of the number of correct classification when the independent variables were dummy variables, and thus the assumption of normality was violated. They found that the logistic regression did slightly better than discriminant analysis.

15.2 Multinomial Response Model

Multinomial response models generalize binary response models to the situation of more than two possible outcomes or choice alternatives. Hence, the dependent variable for the multinomial response model takes more than two values. For example, consider a customer's choosing a brand of a car among J alternative brands. The consumer response will be the choice of the first brand ($Y = 1$), the second brand ($Y = 2$), or the Jth brand ($Y = J$).

It is much more complex to estimate multinomial response models than binary response models. However, the fundamental concepts, including the interpretation of results are identical. Marketers have frequently employed a multinomial logit model in analyzing multinomial response (or choice) data because it is mathematically more tractable. However, the multinomial logit fundamentally has a structural problem called the *IIA* (Independence of Irrelevant Alternatives) property (Maddala 1983; Hausman and McFadden 1984). The multinomial probit model avoids the *IIA* problem but it is computationally intense. More recently, McCulloch and Rossi (2000) proposed a simulation-based estimation technique called Gibbs sampling to overcome the computational problem of the multinomial probit model.

A multinomial logit is similar to a binomial logit, except that the number of choice (or response) alternatives is J. So we consider a consumer facing a choice problem among J alternatives. Then the probability of the consumer i's choosing alternative j can be written as:

$$P(Y_{ij} = j) = \exp(\boldsymbol{\beta}'\mathbf{x}_{ij} + \boldsymbol{\alpha}'_j\mathbf{z}_i)/\sum_{k=1}^{J}\exp(\boldsymbol{\beta}'\mathbf{x}_{ik} + \boldsymbol{\alpha}'_k\mathbf{z}_i) \qquad (15.8)$$

Table 15.1 Estimates of logit coefficients for electric utility customers (From Gensch et al. 1990)

Independent variables	Estimates of logit coefficients	t-value
Invoice price	3.45	1.45
Energy losses	7.45	3.29[a]
Appearance	4.32	2.11[a]
Availability of spare parts	2.45	0.99
Clarity of bid document	1.62	0.36
Knowledgeable salesmen	2.78	1.12
Maintenance requirements	2.64	1.31
Warranty	8.22	4.05[a]

[a]Significant at 0.05 level

where z_i represents a set of independent variables describing characteristics of customer i (e.g., consumer's income), x_{ij} are a set of independent variables representing the attributes of alternatives (e.g., price of brand j faced by the customer i), and β and α are parameters to be estimated. The alternative specific parameters α_j indicate that the effect of an independent variable is different across different alternatives.

Multinomial response models have rarely been employed in database marketing. The reason may be that database marketers do not usually have competitors' data (e.g., which competitor's brand to choose). They only observe whether customers do or do not purchase their products (or react/no react to their promotional offers). However, there are some database marketing problems in which a multinomial response model can be useful.

Gensch et al. (1990) used customer research and the multinomial logit model to understand the preferences and the decision-making processes of ABB Electric's customers. ABB sold medium-sized power transformers, breakers, switchgear, relays, etc., to electric utilities in the North American market, and its major competitors included General Electric, Westinghouse, McGraw–Edison, and so on. Gensch et al. identified 8 attributes that customers used to select among 7 alternative suppliers including ABB. The multinomial logit (Equation 15.8) was applied to evaluate which attributes were the most salient or key in determining the choice among 7 suppliers. Table 15.1 illustrates the output of the multinomial logit. It indicates that warranty, energy losses and appearance are the key variables in determining which supplier to purchase from. Gensch et al. also found that the salient attributes identified by the logit model are quite different from the attributes customers say are most important in their choice.

As mentioned, multinomial logit has not been used frequently in database marketing. However, we can think of several situations where the multinomial logit can be useful. Suppose that we classify current customers into J clusters (or segments) using cluster analysis. We can apply the multinomial logit with segment membership of each customer serving as the dependent variable. The estimated multinomial logit model can be used to identify the segment membership of potential customers. In addition, a multinomial logit model can be valuable when database marketers attempt to predict what products their customers will purchase. For example, insurance salesperson wants to know which products (e.g., term insurance, endowment insurance, and accident death benefits) the customer would be likely to buy when the salesperson needs to decide which products to cross-sell.

15.3 Models for Count Data

Some dependent variables are not categorical, but are discrete with an ordered metric. For example, the number of beers a consumer drinks in a week can be 0, 1, 2, and so on. Another example may be the number of mail orders a customer makes in a year. A multinomial logit model will not be appropriate because the dependent variable is ordered. One may apply a classical linear regression. But if there are many small numbers in the data, the discrete characteristic of the data will be prominent. As a result, the classical linear regression, which assumes a normal error term and hence a continuous dependent variable, may not work well either.

15.3.1 Poisson Regression

Let Y_i to be the value of the dependent variable for customer i. The Poisson regression model assumes that each $Y_i (i = 1, 2, \ldots, n)$ is a random variable independently drawn from a Poisson distribution with parameter λ_i. Its probability density function is

$$P(Y_i = y_i) = \lambda_i^{y_i} \exp(-\lambda_i)/y_i! \qquad y_i = 0, 1, 2, \ldots. \qquad (15.9)$$

The dependent variable Y_i will have a relationship with a set of independent variables specified by a link function. The log-linear link function is frequently used in Poisson regression. That is,

$$\ln \lambda_i = \beta' \mathbf{X}_i \qquad (15.10)$$

where $\mathbf{X}_i$ is a vector of independent variables for customer i and β is a corresponding parameter vector. It can be shown that the mean equals the variance for the Poisson distribution. That is:

$$E(Y_i|\mathbf{X}_i) = Var(Y_i|\mathbf{X}_i) = \lambda_i = \exp(\beta' \mathbf{X}_i)$$

The Poisson regression model is typically estimated by the method of maximum likelihood. Its log-likelihood function with the sample size of n can be written as

$$\ln L(\boldsymbol{\beta}|Y_i, X_i) = \sum_i (Y_i \ln \lambda_i - \lambda_i - \ln Y_i!) \propto \sum_i Y_i(\boldsymbol{\beta}'\mathbf{X}_i) - \sum_i \exp(\boldsymbol{\beta}'\mathbf{X}_i)$$

$$(15.11)$$

Parameters will be estimated by finding $\boldsymbol{\beta}$ maximizing the log-likelihood function in the Equation 15.11. Similar to the logit and probit, the log-likelihood function of the Poisson regression model is nonlinear and, hence, there is no analytical solution. An iterative search routine such as Gauss–Raphson can be applied to find the optimal solution.

15.3.2 Negative Binomial Regression

The Poisson regression model is often criticized because of its implicit assumption that the mean of the Poisson distribution is the same as its variance. There are a number of tests available (called tests for overdispersion) to determine whether this assumption is valid (Greene 1997). A number of researchers have found the assumption to be violated (Hausman et al. 1984; McCulloch and Nelder 1983). In that case, a more flexible model should be applied. A number of researchers have proposed several approaches to extend the Poisson regression model. We briefly discuss the most popular extension called a negative binomial regression.

Let the λ_i parameter of the Poisson distribution equal $\delta_i u_i$ where δ_i is the component observable to the researcher ($\ln \delta_i = \boldsymbol{\beta}'\mathbf{X}_i$) and u_i is the random error or the term for explaining unobserved cross-sectional heterogeneity, that is, differences between customers that are not explicitly measured by the researcher. Hence, $\ln \lambda_i = \ln \delta_i + \ln u_i = \boldsymbol{\beta}'\mathbf{X}_i + \ln u_i$. Then the conditional distribution of Y_i, given u_i, is Poisson with mean and variance of $\lambda_i = \delta_i u_i$. That is,

$$P(Y_i = y_i|u_i) = \lambda_i^{y_i} \exp(-\lambda_i)/y_i! = (\delta_i u_i)^{y_i} \exp(-\delta_i u_i)/y_i! \qquad (15.12)$$

The unconditional distribution is simply the expected value of the conditional distribution integrated over the conditioning variable u_i. That is,

$$P(Y_i = y_i) = \int_0^\infty [(\delta_i u_i)^{y_i} \exp(-\delta_i u_i)/y_i!]g(u_i)du_i \qquad (15.13a)$$

The choice of the density of u_i will determine the form of the unconditional distribution. For mathematical convenience, a gamma distribution is generally assumed for the density of u_i. Then the unconditional density of Y_i in Equation 15.13a becomes the density of the negative binomial distribution:

$$P(Y_i = y_i) = \frac{\Gamma(\theta + y_i)}{\Gamma(y_i + 1)\Gamma(\theta)} \left[\frac{\delta_i}{\delta_i + \theta}\right]^{y_i} \left[1 - \frac{\delta_i}{\delta_i + \theta}\right]^{\theta} \qquad (15.13b)$$

The negative binomial distribution in Equation 15.13b has a mean of δ_i and a variance of $\delta_i(1 + \delta_i/\theta)$. In contrast to the Poisson regression, the mean is different from the variance.

Models for count data have not been used in database marketing. However, there are situations in which they could be useful. Econometricians used count models for the number of accidents on a natural-gas pipeline, the number of patents issued and so on. Similar database marketing examples include the number of customer complaints, the number of returns, and the number of responses to direct marketing offers.

We can easily fit Poisson regression and the negative binomial regression models using the SAS GENMOD procedure.

15.4 Censored Regression (Tobit) Models and Extensions

The dependent variables of our interest in database marketing often are censored. As defined by Wooldridge (2002, p. 517), "censored regression models generally apply when the variable to be explained is partly continuous but has positive probability mass at one or more points." A simple example is monthly expenditures from a catalog firm's customers. Expenditures are continuous, but there will be several customers who spend no money during a particular month. Hence expenditures is a continuous dependent variable but has a positive probability mass at zero, and has no observations less than zero.

This can be modeled using a (Type I) Tobit model as follows: Define y_i^* as a latent variable that reflects customer i's propensity for spending money on the firm's product in a given time period. Consider a sample of size n, $(y_1^*, y_2^*, \ldots, y_n^*)$. Those observations of $y^* \leq c$ will be recorded as the value c (c is usually zero as in the case of expenditures). The resulting sample of observations $y_1, y_2, \ldots, y_n$ is said to be a censored sample. Note that $y_i = y_i^*$ if $y_i^* > c$ and $y_i = c$ otherwise.

One might proceed by estimating y_i as a function of various independent variables using OLS regression. However, Wooldridge (2002, pp. 524–525) shows that the resulting estimates will be inconsistent, whether we use all n observations or just those for which $y_i > 0$. The problem is that OLS does not account for the underlying censoring process. The regression model specially designed to analyze the censored sample is the censored regression (or Tobit) model can be written as:

$$y_i^* = \beta' \mathbf{x}_i + \varepsilon_i \tag{15.14a}$$

$$y_i = \begin{cases} 0 & \text{if } y_i^* \leq 0 \\ y_i^* & \text{if } y_i^* > 0 \end{cases} \tag{15.14b}$$

Equation 15.14a shows that a *latent* variable follows a usual regression model, with error term ε_i having mean zero and variance σ^2, while Equation 15.14b shows that the dependent variable we observe can only be non-negative. Our problem is to estimate β and σ^2 using n observations of y_i and x_i. This model is first studied by Tobin (1958). Because he related his study to the literature on the probit model, his model was nicknamed the Tobit model (Tobin's probit). If there are no censored observations, $E(y_i) = E(y_i^*) = \boldsymbol{\beta}'\mathbf{x}_i$ and a classical regression model can be applied. However, with censored observations, $E(y_i)$ is no longer equal to $\boldsymbol{\beta}'\mathbf{x}_i$. Restricting our attention to non-censored observations, we get

$$E(y_i|y_i > 0) = \boldsymbol{\beta}'\mathbf{x}_i + E(\varepsilon_i|\varepsilon_i > -\boldsymbol{\beta}'\mathbf{x}_i) = \boldsymbol{\beta}'\mathbf{x}_i + \sigma\frac{\phi_i}{\Phi_i} \qquad (15.15)$$

where ϕ_i and Φ_i are the density function and distribution function of the standard normal evaluated at $\boldsymbol{\beta}'\mathbf{x}_i/\sigma$. We can see that $\mathbf{x}_i$ is correlated with ϕ_i/Φ_i because ϕ_i and Φ_i are both functions of $\mathbf{x}_i$ and hence if we run an OLS regression as a function just of $\mathbf{x}_i$, we obtain biased and inconsistent results due to omitted variables bias. If we use all observations, we get

$$\begin{aligned} E(y_i) &= P(y_i > 0)E(y_i|y_i > 0) + P(y_i = 0)E(y_i|y_i = 0) \\ &= \Phi_i(\boldsymbol{\beta}'\mathbf{x}_i + \sigma\frac{\phi_i}{\Phi_i}) + (1 - \Phi_i)(0) = \Phi_i\boldsymbol{\beta}'\mathbf{x}_i + \sigma\phi_i \end{aligned} \qquad (15.16)$$

Still, an OLS regression will yield biased results because $\mathbf{x}_i$ is correlated with ϕ_i.

The Type I Tobit Model can be estimated using maximum likelihood (Wooldridge 2002, pp. 525–527). This can be done in SAS using Proc LIF-EREG or QLIM.

An important extension of the Type I Tobit is to model the *process* by which a customer purchases at the level c (0) or greater. For example, we may want to model which types of customers are likely to buy in a given month, and if so, how much do they spend. This can be formulated as follows:

$$y_i^* = \boldsymbol{\beta}'\mathbf{x}_i + \varepsilon_i \qquad (15.17a)$$

$$y_i = \begin{cases} 0 & \text{if } y_i^* \leq 0 \\ y_i^* & \text{if } y_i^* > 0 \end{cases} \qquad (15.17b)$$

$$z_i^* = \boldsymbol{\alpha}'w_i + u_i \qquad (15.17c)$$

$$z_i = \begin{cases} 1 & \text{if } z_i^* > 0 \\ 0 & \text{if } z_i^* \leq 0 \end{cases} \qquad (15.17d)$$

The probit model (Equations 15.17c and 15.17d) determines whether the customer buys in a given period, and if so, Equations 15.17a and 15.17b determine how much the customer spends. Note that expenditures are observed only if the customer buys, but we acknowledge through the Type I Tobit component that when a customer buys, he or she must spend at least \$0. Crucial to the formulation is that the error term u_i of the probit is correlated with the error term of the Type I Tobit (ε_i). This introduces additional "selectivity bias" into the estimation of Equation 15.17a if not accounted for.

This model is estimable in LIMDEP using a two-stage maximum likelihood procedure (Greene 2002, p. E23.18).

A variation of Equation 15.17 is not to include the censoring restriction 15.17b (e.g., see Greene 2002, p. 710). This might be applicable if the dependent variable can be positive or negative, such as the case if we are looking at customer profitability. Many authors refer to this as a Type II Tobit model (e.g., Wooldridge 2002, p. 562). This model can also be estimated within LIMDEP (Greene 2002, pp. E23-1–E23-5).

Another related model is where there is selectivity, but data are observed for all customers, so the selection variable can be an independent variable in the regression model. The example would be the case where we wanted to determine if Internet usage affects customer profitability, but wanted to recognize that only certain customers "self-select" into using the Internet. The model would be:

$$Y_i = \beta' X_i + \delta z_i + \varepsilon_i \tag{15.18a}$$

$$z_i^* = \alpha' w_i + u_i \tag{15.18b}$$

$$z_i = \begin{cases} 1 & \text{if } z_i^* > 0 \\ 0 & \text{if } z_i^* \leq 0 \end{cases} \tag{15.18c}$$

This is a recursive model (w determines whether the customer uses the Internet via Equations 15.18b and 15.18c, and then using the Internet determines customer profitability via Equation 15.18a. The only difference between this model and a standard linear recursive model is that whereas traditional recursive models consist of two or more linear equations, each one feeding into the next, the case here is a "mixed" recursive model, where one equation is a nonlinear discrete variable model, a probit, and the second equation is a linear model. OLS estimation of Equation 15.18a will be biased if ε and u are correlated, because that will set up a correlation between z and ε. Greene (2002, p. E23-14) describes this model and how to estimate it within LIMDEP.

The above models (Equations 15.16–15.18) are very relevant for database marketing, but there are few applications to date. An exception is the study by Reinartz et al. (2005) which is discussed in Chapter 26. They present a variation of Equation 15.17, where the probit model determines the acquisition (or selection) process and two (censored) regressions characterize relationship duration and customer profitability. They use their model to balance resources between customer acquisition and retention efforts.

15.5 Time Duration (Hazard) Models

What is the probability that a customer in a telecommunication company will remain as a customer after a year? Or what is the attrition probability of each customer in a month? Are attrition probabilities different depending on the customer's demographic characteristics? What is the expected duration of a customer's relationship with the firm? These questions can be addressed using time duration models, specifically the statistical technique called hazard modeling. We first discuss the characteristics of duration data. Then we discuss and criticize a traditional approach such as a logit model to analyze duration data. Finally, we introduce the hazard model specially designed to analyze duration data.

15.5.1 Characteristics of Duration Data

In order to understand the characteristics of duration data, let us consider an example of ABC newspaper. It has a database of its subscriber lists and keeps the records of subscribers who are or have been customers at least a month for the last 7 years. We randomly select 1,000 subscribers out of the database to study their purchase behavior. Figure 15.2 displays how long some of these customers have subscribed the ABC newspaper. We can exactly calculate the duration of subscription for some customers including Customers 1, 2 and 3 because they no longer subscribe the ABC newspaper. On the other hand, those customers such as Customers 4 and 1,000 still subscribe to the ABC newspaper. The duration information provided by these current customers is incomplete. We know when they began to subscribe, but we do not know when they stop. For example, we know that customer 4 has subscribed to the ABC newspaper for a year so far, but we do not exactly know how longer she will stay. The data are right-censored.

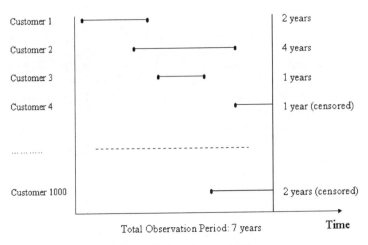

Fig. 15.2 Duration data for the ABC newspaper

The ABC newspaper recognizes that the concept of customer's lifetime value is important for its successful operations and customer retention is a critical component of customer's lifetime value. Hence, the ABC newspaper develops a model to understand factors determining a customer's subscription duration and forecasts how long each of the current and potential customers will stay. Based on this analysis, the ABC newspaper plans to develop various acquisition and retention strategies. The question is, what is the appropriate model?

15.5.2 Analysis of Duration Data Using a Classical Linear Regression

The classical regression model may be the simplest way to explain the relationship between the customer's subscription duration and her demographic characteristics (income, education, age, etc.). We might eliminate the incomplete (right-censored) observations – they are current customers – from the estimation because they will bias downward the mean duration since those observations actually have longer durations. Limiting our estimation sample only to non-current customers, we fit the regression model where the subscription duration of each customer is the dependent variable and the corresponding demographic characteristics are the independent or predictor variables.[3]

We apply the linear regression to the sample of previous customers with two customer characteristics, annual income (measured in thousand dollars) and sex (coded 1 if male and 0 if female customer). The estimated regression line is

$$\text{Subscription duration} = -1 + 0.2 \times \text{Income} + 0.5 \times \text{Sex} \qquad (15.19)$$

This regression line allows us to predict the expected subscription duration of a customer given his or her income and sex. The expected subscription duration for a female customer with the annual income of $20,000 is predicted to be 3 years $(= -1 + 0.2 \times 20 + 0.5 \times 0)$. On the other hand, a male customer with the annual income of $30,000 is predicted to maintain his subscription for 5.5 years $(= -1 + 0.2 \times 30 + 0.5 \times 1)$ on average. In addition, the regression line indicates that there is a positive relationship between subscription duration and annual income. With the same income, a male would stay longer than a female by $1/2$ year.

---

[3] The dataset of complete observations may result in sample selection bias when the characteristics of the complete observations are different from those of the right-censored observations. For example, current customers may be satisfied with the ABC newspaper, but previous customers may have switched to other newspapers. As a result, current customers may have longer subscription durations than previous customers.

The application of the regression line to current customers allows us to forecast how much longer they will remain with the ABC newspaper. Suppose that Customer 4 in Figure 15.2 is female with the annual income of $30,000. Her predicted duration is 5 years. Since she has subscribed for a year so far, we expect that she will remain four more years with the ABC newspaper. Moreover, we can use the results of the regression model to target potential customers. Computing the predicted duration for each of potential customers, we rank order them in terms of their subscription durations. Recognizing that a customer with the longer duration will generate bigger profits for the ABC newspaper, we only select customers with predicted duration greater than a specified cutoff.

However, a regression model has several limitations in analyzing duration data (Helsen and Schmittlein 1993). First, because of potential censoring bias, the regression model is not applied to all customers, but only those for whom we have observed their full lifespan. It will be problematic especially when the number of complete observations is small relative to the number of incomplete observations. Second, a regression model is very limited in helping marketers to manage the customer relationship. For example, marketers may want to know the attrition *probability* for each customer during the specified period of time. A bank prepares a special promotion to target customers who have high attrition probability during the upcoming month. A regression model cannot easily answer this question.[4] For more discussion on the limitation of a regression in the analysis of duration data, see Kalbfleisch and Prentice (1980) or Lawless (2003).

15.5.3 Hazard Models

Recently researchers from various disciplines have devoted considerable attention to the analysis of duration, survival time, lifetime, or failure time data. Engineers would like to know how long a light bulb lasts under various conditions. Medical researchers want to know how long an AIDS infected patient will live. Economists are interested in knowing the duration of unemployment. Subscription managers in newspaper want to know how long customers will subscribe to their newspapers. Customer managers at Verizon may have interest in knowing how long their customers will stay with Verizon before they switch to other carriers.

---

[4] We can partially overcome this limitation by dividing the observation period into even intervals. For each interval, a customer indicator (1 if a customer stays, and 0 if she does not) is used as a dependent variable. Because of its discrete nature, we now apply the binary logit or probit. However, the logit or probit has other shortcomings in modeling duration time such as arbitrarily determined time intervals. See Helsen and Schmittlein (1993) for more discussion.

Hazard models are specially designed to analyze duration data. Helsen and Schmittlein (1993) note several advantages over traditional tools such as a linear regression and discrete time probit or logistic regression in the analysis of duration data. Similar to the example given in the previous section, the variable of interest is the length of time that elapses from the beginning of an event either to the end of the event (for uncensored data) or the end of the observation period (for censored data). For the example in Fig. 15.2, we have observations, $t_1, t_2, \ldots, t_{1000}$ with $t_1 = 2, t_2 = 4, \ldots, t_{1000} = 2$. Note that the starting time of the event can be different across observations. Note also that we often have information on customer characteristics that will be related to the observed duration, $t_i (i = 1, \ldots, 1000)$. These characteristics are typically demographics such as family size, income and marital status, but hazard models can also include time-varying "covariates" such as purchase recency or the timing of previous marketing contacts.

Let us define T to be a random variable representing the duration time of interest (e.g., the time the customer stays with the company) and its (continuous) probability density function be $f(t)$, where t is a realization of T. Then its cumulative density function, or the probability the customer leaves the company before period t, is

$$F(t) = \int_0^t f(s)ds = P(T \leq t) \tag{15.20}$$

The survival function is defined as the probability that the length of the duration is at least t. That is, the survival function is $S(t) = 1 - F(t) = P(T > t)$. Researchers prefer directly to model the hazard function to the probability density function because of its mathematical convenience. The hazard rate is the probability that the event occurs at t, given that it has not occurred until t. That is, the hazard rate is a kind of a conditional probability. For an example in life insurance, the hazard rate measures the probability that a customer cancels the policy between periods t and $t + \Delta t$, where Δt is a short period of time, given that she maintains the policy for t years. Formally defined, the hazard rate is

$$h(t) = \lim_{\Delta t \to 0} \frac{P(t \leq T \leq t + \Delta t | T \geq t)}{\Delta t} = \lim_{\Delta t \to 0} \frac{P(t \leq T \leq t + \Delta t)/P(T \geq t)}{\Delta t}$$

$$= \lim_{\Delta t \to 0} \frac{[F(t + \Delta t) - F(t)]/S(t)}{\Delta t} = \frac{f(t)}{S(t)} \tag{15.21}$$

Note that $-d \ln S(t)/dt = -[dS(t)/dt]/S(t) = -[-f(t)]/S(t) = h(t)$. The term, $-\ln S(t) = \Lambda(t)$, is called the integrated hazard function. It equals $\int_0^t h(s)ds$ since $-d\Lambda(t)/dt = h(t)$. Then the survival function $S(t) = \exp[-\Lambda(t)]$.[5]

---

[5] This equation is useful to calculate the survival probability (up to T^*) for current customers once we have estimated the parameters of the hazard function.

Hazard rate

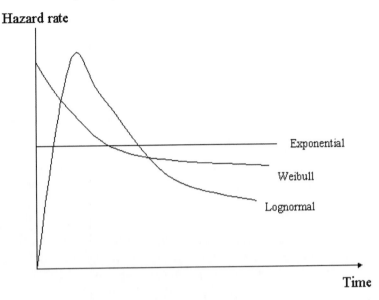

Fig. 15.3 Various hazard functions.

Hence, the density function $f(t)$ can be written as

$$f(t) = h(t)S(t) = h(t) \exp\left[-\int_0^t h(s)ds\right] \qquad (15.22)$$

How do we model the hazard rate $h(t)$? The simplest model may be to assume $h(t)$ is a constant h_0. This model implies that the hazard rate is constant as t increases as shown on Fig. 15.3. With a constant hazard rate, the probability that a customer cancels the insurance policy given she maintains the policy for 1 month is the same as the probability that a customer cancels the policy given she maintains the policy for 10 years. Substituting $h(t) = h_0$ into the Equation 15.22, we can derive $f(t)$ that equals to $h_0 e^{-h_0 t}$. That is, the probability density function corresponding to a constant hazard rate is an exponential distribution for duration time. The exponential distribution has a memoryless property that leads to the constant hazard rate.

For many applications, the constant hazard function is too restrictive. A natural extension allowing for monotonically increasing or decreasing hazard is to assume that $h(t) = \beta_0 + \beta_1 t$ where β_0 and β_1 are parameters to be estimated. If β_1 is zero, the model goes back to the constant hazard model. If β_1 is positive as shown in Fig. 15.3, the hazard rate is increasing with t. The case is said to have positive duration dependence. We occasionally find positive duration dependence in the analysis of shopping data. A shopper tends to have a low probability of repurchasing the product immediately after she buys it. The probability will increase as t increases because household inventory is depleting. On the other hand, if β_1 is negative, the hazard rate is monotonically decreasing with t. This negative duration dependence frequently occurs in the analysis of direct marketing data.

The exponential, Weibull, and log-logistic are the three most popular (parametric) hazard functions among researchers. Their probability density functions, hazard functions and survivor functions are:

	Probability density function: $f(t)$	Hazard function: $h(t)$	Survival function: $S(t)$
Exponential distribution	$\lambda \exp(-\lambda t)$	λ	$\exp(-\lambda t)$
Weibull distribution	$\lambda p(\lambda t)^{p-1} \exp[-(\lambda t)^p]$	$\lambda p(\lambda t)^{p-1}$	$\exp[(-\lambda t)^p]$
Log-logistic distribution	$\dfrac{\lambda p(\lambda t)^{p-1}}{[1+(\lambda t)^p]^2}$	$\dfrac{\lambda p(\lambda t)^{p-1}}{1+(\lambda t)^p}$	$\dfrac{1}{1+(\lambda t)^p}$

The shapes of these hazards are shown in Fig. 15.3. The exponential has a constant hazard while the Weibull can be monotonically increasing or decreasing function depending on the value of p. On the other hand, the log-logistic assumes that the hazard rate is monotonically increasing at the beginning and then decreasing later (Kalbfleisch and Prentice 1980).

The parameters of the hazard model can be estimated by maximum likelihood. Given the duration data of n samples, $t_1, t_2, \ldots, t_n$, the log-likelihood function can be written as

$$\ln L = \underbrace{\sum \ln f(t|\theta)}_{uncensored\ obs} + \underbrace{\sum \ln S(t|\theta)}_{censored\ obs} = \underbrace{\sum h(t|\theta)}_{uncensored\ obs} + \underbrace{\sum \ln S(t|\theta)}_{all\ obs} \quad (15.23)$$

Note that the only information available for the right-censored observations is the survivor rate. The above log-likelihood function is highly nonlinear so that an iterative search algorithm such as the BHHH method is used to find the optimal solution (Berndt et al. 1974). Hazard models can be estimated in SAS using either of two procedures. PROC PHREG may be more popular since it can handle time-varying covariates (e.g., marketing) and various forms of hazard functions. However, if the shapes of survival distribution and hazard function are known, PROC LIFEREG produces more efficient estimates with faster speed.

15.5.4 Incorporating Covariates into the Hazard Function

There are several approaches to incorporating independent variables in a hazard model. First, we can model the parameter of the parametric hazard rate $h(t)$ to be a function of independent variables. For example, the parameter λ of the exponential and the Weibull hazard is modeled as

$$\lambda_i = \exp(-\beta'\mathbf{X}_i) \quad (15.24)$$

Table 15.2 Parameter estimates and hazard rates of a customer churn model (Modified from Van den Poel and Lariviere (2004)

Independent variables	Estimates (β)	Relative hazard rate[a]
Interpurchase time	0.048	4.9
Product ownership	−6.856	99.9
Age	−0.022	2.2
Gender	0.879	140.8
Education level	−0.085	8.2
High social status	−0.593	44.7

[a]Relative hazard rate is calculated by $100 \times [\exp(\beta) - 1]$.

where $\mathbf{X}_i$ is the vector of independent variables for observation i and β is the corresponding parameter vector. Cox (1972) has proposed a more flexible method called the proportional hazard model. He defines the hazard rate of observation i, $h_i(t \,|\, \underline{X})$ as

$$h_i(t \,|\, \underline{X}) = h_0(t)\psi_i(\underline{X}) = h_0(t)\exp(-\beta'\mathbf{X}_i) \qquad (15.25)$$

where $h_0(t)$ is the baseline hazard rate and $\psi_i(\underline{X})$ incorporates covariates (or independent variables) that may be time-varying. The baseline hazard is the hazard rate that describes the relationship between the hazard rate and time duration, and can specified as constant, exponential, Weibul, etc., as discussed above (see also Seetharaman and Chintagunta 2003).

Going back to the example of ABC newspaper, we employ a proportional hazard model to the duration data with two independent variables, income and sex. Allowing for monotonically increasing or decreasing hazards, we estimated the hazard function incorporating independent variables as

$$h_i(t \,|\, \underline{X}) = h_0(t)\psi_i(\underline{X}) = h_0(t)\ \exp(-\beta_2 \times \text{Income} - \beta_3 \times \text{sex}) \qquad (15.26)$$

Upon estimation, we can evaluate from the β coefficients how each independent variable influences the hazard rate: $100 \times [\exp(\beta) - 1]$ measures the percentage change of the hazard rate with respect to the unit change of the independent variable (Tuma and Hannan 1984).

We conclude this section with a real application of the hazard model provided by Poel and Larivière (2004). They applied the proportional hazard model to data from a European financial services company that offers banking and insurance services towards customers. The data set consists of a random sample of 47,157 customers, of whom 47% churned (uncensored sample) and the rest are current customers (censored sample). They considered various categories of independent variable to explain retention (or churn), but we report some of their estimates for an expositional purpose in Table 15.2.

Table 15.2 shows that customers whose interpurchase time increases experience shorter duration time. Every additional year in the average interpurchase time is associated with a $100 \times [\exp(0.048) - 1] = 4.9\%$ higher probability to churn. The more products owned by a customer the more likely she is to stay with the company. An increase of one additional product lowers the switching probability with 99.9% (e.g., $100 \times [\exp(-6.856) - 1] = -99.9$). Older people are less inclined to leave the company. As a customer's age increases by one, her probability to leave decreases by 2.2%. Men (coded as 1) are 141% more likely to leave the company than females. More educated people have a somewhat (8.2%) lower attrition probability. Finally, customers with a high social status have a significantly lower attrition probability than customers who live in an area that is associated with a low social status.

Chapter 16
Cluster Analysis

Abstract Cluster analysis segments a customer database so that customers within segments are similar, and collectively different from customers in other segments. Similarity is in terms of the "clustering variables," which may be psychographics, demographics, or transaction measures such as RFM. The clusters often have rich interpretations with strong implications for which customers should be targeted with a particular offer or marketed to in a certain way. This chapter discusses the details of cluster analysis, including measures of similarity, the major cluster methods, and how to decide upon the number of clusters and their interpretation.

16.1 Introduction

Marketers have used cluster analysis to segment the market for a long time. It allows marketers to group their customers into several homogeneous clusters such that customers in the same cluster are similar in terms of their demographic and behavioral characteristics while customers across different clusters are different.

Cluster analysis is often confused with classification tasks. Both techniques segment subjects into several groups. But they are different in their goals. In classification we know the number of groups and the segment membership of each subject. The goal is to predict the segment membership of a new subject once a classification model is estimated. On the other hand, we do not have any predefined segments in clustering. Its objective is simply to group subjects into several homogeneous clusters. Using the terminology of machine learning, classification is a typical task of *directed* knowledge discovery while clustering is an example of *undirected* knowledge discovery.

In a classification task we have a dependent variable. For example, a bank wants to evaluate the credit risks of card applicants in order to decide whom to issue their credit cards. In order to develop the forecasting model, we first analyze the existing customer data for which each customer is already known to be either a defaulter or not. An appropriate model such as a discriminant analysis or logistic regression is applied to the data, taking customer's credit status (i.e., defaulter or not) as the dependent variable and his/her demographic and behavioral characteristics as the independent variables. Upon estimating model parameters, we can classify new card applicants into either defaulters or non-defaulters by obtaining information on their demographic and behavioral characteristics.

On the other hand, there are no pre-classified groups in clustering. We do not make any distinction between dependent and independent variables. Our goal is to group subjects into an arbitrary number of homogeneous segments in terms of their characteristics or variables. Because of the subjectivity involved in determining the number of clusters and selecting the clustering algorithm with a similarity measure, clustering is often considered as an exploratory data analytic technique.

Because of its exploratory nature, there is always the question of whether the cluster analysis has produced the "correct" segmentation scheme. A practical answer is that there are multiple ways to segment the market. The question is whether a given segmentation scheme is managerially useful. Certainly the interpretability of the segmentation scheme makes it more useful. But in a database marketing context, a crucial consideration is whether a given segmentation scheme can be used for targeting. We discuss this issue in Sect. 16.3.2. It is noteworthy that most of the clustering techniques are *algorithms* that try to group customers into groups so that customers within groups are similar to each other and collectively different from clusters in other groups. There is no underlying statistical model or theory that hypothesizes a true underlying grouping that needs to be discovered. This also clouds the issue of whether the obtained solution is "correct." With most clustering methods, sources of error and variation are not formally considered. Hence, clustering results will be sensitive to outliers or noise points. The exception to this is probabilistic clustering, which is described in Sect. 16.2.3.3.

16.2 The Clustering Process

Conducting a cluster analysis consists of several steps:

- Select variables on which to cluster
- Select a similarity measure and scale the variables
- Select a clustering method
- Determine the number of clusters
- Conduct the cluster analysis, interpret the results, and apply them

There are several methods that can be used for each of these steps, especially involving similarity measures and clustering methods. Choice of these methods is often subjective. For example, an analyst who has found a certain similarity measure, scaling procedure, and clustering method to be successful in the past will tend to use that approach again. It is often a good idea to try a few different approaches in one application, to see which yields the best results. The reader should recognize, however, that there are many methodological choices to be made with a cluster analysis, and no set of choices that all database marketers agree on as optimal. As mentioned above, often the choice of method hinges on the question – are the results useful?

16.2.1 Selecting Clustering Variables

The first question the analyst faces is what variables should form the basis for the clustering. That is, on which set of variables do we want to form homogeneous groups of customers? In typical applications, there are several variables available. These include:

- *Benefits sought:* These are measures of what benefits in a product or service customers deem to be important. They can be collected by asking customers directly in a survey (e.g., "How important is price to you?"), or via a conjoint analysis or other indirect measure of benefits sought.
- *Psychographics:* Attitudes and behaviors relevant to a particular product category. For example, if the product category is consumer electronics, customer self-report of whether they see themselves as innovators, opinion leaders, or "gadget freaks," are psychographics. Ownership and usage of various electronics products are also psychographics.
- *Demographics:* These include age, income, region, employment, etc.
- *Geo-demographics:* These include variables inferred by where the customer lives. For example, the US census makes publicly available average income, age, home ownership, etc., for fairly small geographic units such as "census blocks."
- *Behavior:* These include recency, frequency, and monetary value behaviors measured from the company's customer file. These can be measured by department (e.g., frequency of purchasing men's clothes, women's clothes, children's clothes, accessories). Behavior can also include sales channels through which the customer buys.
- *Competitive measures:* These include share of wallet, competitor preferences, etc.
- *Customer value:* These might include responsiveness to marketing, lifetime value, customer lifetime duration, customer risk, etc.

The choice of variables on which to cluster might depend on the application. For example, for a new product application, clustering on benefits sought might be most useful. For a cross-selling application, clustering on channel usage or RFM for various departments might be useful. For a customer tier program, clustering on customer value might be useful.

One strategy is to use one of the above sets of variables for the clustering variables, and then the other variables for the "discrimination variables."

These variables can aid in interpretation and in classifying new customers to clusters. The reason not to mix types of variables as clustering variables is the interpretation may become difficult, and also, different types of variables are most likely measured on different scales, which brings up a scaling problem (discussed in Sect. 16.2.2.3). In Sect. 16.3, we will show a hypothetical example to illustrate the roles of clustering and discrimination variables.

A practical question is, given we know the type of variables on which we want to cluster, how many variables should we use? This issue, the problem called "variable selection," has been well studied in classical regression. Omitting relevant variables results in biased parameter estimates while including irrelevant variables leads to overfitting the model (Greene 1997). However, the selection of clustering variables has rarely been studied. Technically speaking, one can cluster on any number of variables. However, often it is advantageous to keep the number of variables relatively small (say 5–15) to aid in interpretation.[1]

16.2.2 Similarity Measures

The goal of clustering is to group customers into several homogeneous clusters. Customers in the same cluster are supposed to be similar while subjects across different clusters are dissimilar. We need to be more precise. How do you define the similarity between customers?

Clustering begins with selecting a similarity measure and a set of variables regarding which the similarity is calculated. Care should be taken in selecting a similarity measure since different measures often lead to different clustering results. It is recommended to apply several different similarity measures and check the stability of clustering results. Unstable clustering results may imply that the clusters found do not provide a meaningful or usable segmentation scheme.

16.2.2.1 Distance-Type Similarity Measures

Broadly speaking, there are two types of similarity measures: distance type and matching type. Distance types of similarity measures are more appropriate when variables are measured on a common metric, so that the similarity between two customers can be measured as their distance in a metric space. For example, three customers are plotted in Fig. 16.1. Each customer is represented as a point in two-dimensional space. Expressed in matrix terminology,

---

[1] It is also recommended to study correlation structure among candidate clustering variables. Including highly correlated variables in a cluster analysis has the effect of weighting up an underlying dimension. Hence, if two variables are highly correlated, either one of them should be deleted.

Attribute 2

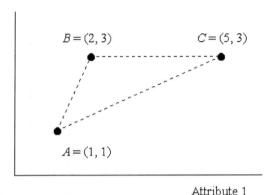

Fig. 16.1 Defining similarity*.
*Points A, B, and C represent customers, in particular their values for Attributes 1 and 2.

we have the 3×2 data matrix where there are three customers and two attributes describing each customer. The distance between Customers A and B is the shortest among all three pairwise inter-point distances. Hence, we may say that Customer A is similar to Customer B in terms of their attributes (e.g., income and age). We are implicitly using the distance between points or subjects as the similarity measure.

The most popular distance similarity measure is the Euclidean distance between points (Hair et al. 1992). The Euclidean distance between two p-dimensional subjects $\mathbf{x} = [x_1, \ldots, x_p]'$ and $\mathbf{y} = [y_1, \ldots, y_p]'$ is defined as

$$d(\mathbf{x}, \mathbf{y}) = [(x_1 - y_1)^2 + \ldots + (x_p - y_p)^2]^{1/2} = [(\mathbf{x} - \mathbf{y})'(\mathbf{x} - \mathbf{y})]^{1/2} \quad (16.1)$$

Each subject is represented in two-dimensional space ($p = 2$) in Fig. 16.1. Hence, the Euclidean distance between Customers A and B is $\sqrt{5} = [(1 - 2)^2 + (1 - 3)^2]^{1/2}$. Similarly, the distance between Customers A and C is $2\sqrt{5}$ and the distance between B and C is 3. The distance between Customers A and B is the shortest. So A and B are said to be the most similar.

The Minkowski metric generalizes the concept of the Euclidean distance. The Minkowski distance between two p-dimensional subjects is given by

$$d(\mathbf{x}, \mathbf{y}) = \left[\sum_{i=1}^{p} |x_i - y_i|^m \right]^{1/m} \quad (16.2)$$

where it becomes the Euclidean distance when m is equal to two. On the other hand, the Minkowski metric with $m = 1$ is called the city-block distance. For example, the city-block distance between Customers A and B in Fig. 16.1 is the sum of the horizontal and the vertical distance, which in this case would be 3 ($= 1 + 2$).

16.2.2.2 Matching-Type Similarity Measures

Geometric distance is not meaningful for categorical variables. Instead, we can use the degree of matching to measure the similarity between customers when they are represented by a set of categorical characteristics. For example, two customers are treated as similar if both of them are students.

More formally, we measure the similarity between two customers as the degree of matching, specifically, the ratio of the number of matching attributes to the total number of attributes considered. For a simple example, suppose that two customers are represented by the presence (coded as 1) or absence (coded as 0) of five attributes. If Customer A's attributes can be represented as $\mathbf{x} = [0, 0, 1, 1, 1]'$ and Customer B's as $\mathbf{y} = [1, 0, 1, 1, 0]'$, then there are three matches out of five attribute comparisons and, so the similarity between Customers A and B is 0.6.

There are some variants of matching-type similarity measures such as assigning differential weighting on matching from mismatching cases. For example, when there are an unusually large number of zeros in the data, we assign a large weight on the matches of ones. Similarly, when there are a lot of ones, a large weight is assigned on the matches of zeros. More sophisticated similarity measures are discussed in Chapter 14.

One question is what to do if some of the clustering variables are metric, in which case a distance type similarity measure would be appropriate, and some are categorical, in which case a matching metric may be appropriate. There is no clear answer here. One practical solution is to code the categorical variables as 0–1 and use them together with the metric variables and a distance-type similarity measure. This will "work" in that the distance measure can be calculated, but we would be mixing variables measured in different units and this raises a scaling problem (discussed in the next section). Another possibility is to use only one type of clustering variable (e.g., benefits sought), that are all scaled the same way (in this case, with a common metric), so the problem of mixing metric and categorical variables doesn't arise.

16.2.2.3 Scaling and Weighting

Even metric variables are frequently measured in different units, and this can distort the cluster analysis results. For an example, if we multiply one variable by a large number, say 100, then the similarity measure will be dominated by the value of the variable. Hence, it is advisable to rescale the variables such that a percentage change of one variable is not more significant than the same percentage change of another variable in similarity calculation.

The scaling problem essentially comes from the different variances measured in each variable. In order to avoid the scaling problem due to different units of measurement, one approach is to make the variances of all variables to be the same. There are two remedies commonly used in practice. The first approach is to rescale all the variables to range from zero to one. If X_i is the original variable and X_i^* is the scaled variable, $X_i^* = (X_i - X_{\min})/(X_{\max} - X_{\min})$ where $X_{\min}$ is the minimum and $X_{\max}$ is the maximum observed value for the original variable. Alternatively, we can standardize all the variables so that the rescaled variables have the common means of zero and the common variances of one. If X_i is the original variable, the rescaled variable $Z_i = (X_i - \bar{X})/\sigma_X$ where $\bar{X}$ is the mean of the original variable and σ_X is the corresponding standard deviation.[2]

While the above at first seems to solve the scaling problem, it may limit the results in important ways. For example, assume we have measured benefits sought on a 5-point scale. Further, assume that Price Importance has a mean of 3.0 and a standard deviation of 1.0. That suggests that customers vary considerably in the importance they attach to price. Now assume that Quality Importance also has a mean of 3.0 but a standard deviation of 0.5. This means that customers do not vary so much in the importance they attach to quality. If we standardize these variables, they will both have a variance of one, but we are losing important information, that in fact customers vary a lot on the importance of price, and not so much on the importance of quality. This example assumes the same units of measurement, but the same problem can arise when standardizing variables measured in different units. Let's say that we also include a measure of Service Importance based on the number of calls the customer has made to the call center. Let's say the mean of this variable is 10 with a standard deviation of 10. This means there is wide variation in this variable, and the variable is skewed to the right (since the number of calls cannot be less than zero). Standardizing this variable puts it on an equal footing with Quality Importance because both variables have the same variance. This obscures the fact that customers really all feel roughly the same about quality, but vary a lot in the importance they attach to service. This "true" variation on service importance could be an important factor in defining segments that we will miss out by equalizing the variance of all variables.

There are no easy answers to the re-scaling issue. One possibility is only to use as clustering variables that are scaled the same way, and not standardize (e.g., use measures of benefits sought measured on a 5-point scale). However, this is not always possible. For example, demographics are naturally measured on different scales (e.g., age and income). It is for this reason that cluster analysis truly is an exploratory technique. One can try various rescaling procedures, as well as distance measures, examine how it changes the nature and interpretation of the clusters, then make a decision of which clustering solution to use.

---

[2] Variables in database marketing (e.g., monetary value) are often highly skewed. And right skewed variables tend to produce many tiny clusters and a couple of big ones, which is not desirable. With skewed variables, it is recommended to take logs and then standardize the variables.

Another way to deal with the scaling issue, as well as take into account the managerial importance of different clustering variables, is to consider weighting each of the clustering variables. For example, if we believe that the income variable is much more important than the age of household head in deciding the similarities among households, it is reasonable to assign a large weight on the income variable by multiplying it by a large number (at least larger than one). However, in contrast to the objectivity of the scaling solution, finding the appropriate weights is a rather subjective task. We suggest that the weighting be considered only when you have a priori reasons based on previous studies or your own experience. In addition, if weighting is to be used, we suggest that a number of different weights (e.g., various multiples on the income variable) be tried and the corresponding clustering outcomes be compared in terms of interpretation and managerial relevance.

16.2.3 Clustering Methods

The goal of clustering is to group subjects into an arbitrary number of segments such that customers in the same segment are similar in their characteristics while customers across different segments are dissimilar. However, it is not a simple task to find the optimal clustering solution. For example, there exist millions of ways to cluster only 20 customers. There is one way to form one cluster with 20 customers. There are 524,287 ways to group 20 customers into two clusters! There are much more ways for three clusters, and so on.[3] A theoretical method of finding the optimal clustering solution may be to enumerate all possible clustering solutions and select the best one. However, it is practically impossible to list all possible solutions. Hence, researchers have developed heuristic methodologies that may not necessarily find the optimal solution (if indeed there is a single conclusion what could call optimal) but acceptable ones.

There are a number of algorithms available for clustering. As shown in Fig. 16.2, they are broadly classified into two groups: hierarchical and non-hierarchical clustering technique.

Hierarchical clustering develops a tree-like structure either by serially merging clusters (agglomerative method) or by successively dividing clusters (the divisive method). Given n customers, agglomerative hierarchical starts with the n cluster solution, where each customer is his or her own cluster. It then produces an $(n-1)$ cluster solution by combining the two most similar customers, an $(n-2)$ cluster solution, and so on. This merging is continued until all customers are classified into a single cluster. Divisive hierarchical clustering proceeds in the opposite direction. It starts with

---

[3] The number of ways of sorting n subjects into k nonempty groups can be computed by a Stirling number of the second kind that is given by $(1/k!)\sum_{x=0}^{k}(-1)^{k-x}{}_kC_x x^n$.

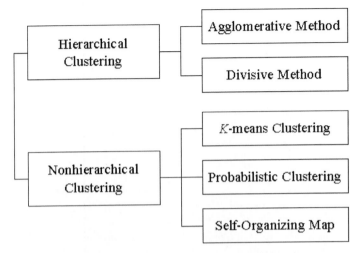

Fig. 16.2 Types of clustering methods.

the one-cluster solution consisting of all n customers, and then divides n customers into two clusters such that customers in one cluster are dissimilar to the customers in the other cluster. This division is continued until each customer becomes one cluster. We will cover agglomerative clustering in more detail in the next subsection. However, divisive method is not covered here since the algorithm is very similar to the decision trees described in Chapter 17.

More recently developed, nonhierarchical clustering techniques find the cluster solution given the number of clusters pre-specified by the user. Even though there are several methods that can be classified as nonhierarchical clustering, we will cover K-means clustering, probabilistic clustering and self-organizing map. K-means clustering starts with randomly assigning n customers into K clusters and successively improves the partitions by changing the cluster membership of each customer. Probabilistic clustering can be considered as a probabilistic version of K-means technique that overcomes its several limitations, at the cost of making various assumptions. Finally, self-organizing maps (SOM) is a special type of neural network model that can be useful in detecting clusters. It has several features that are similar to a typical neural network model and some other features that are similar to K-means clustering.

16.2.3.1 Agglomerative Clustering

Marketers have used agglomerative clustering algorithm for a long time in segmenting their customers. We describe the common algorithmic structure of agglomerative clustering even though there are a number of variants such

Table 16.1 Example of the agglomerative clustering algorithm

(a) 5-cluster solution						(b) 4-cluster solution				
	1	2	3	4	5		(12)	3	4	5
1	0					(12)	0			
2	2	0				3	5	0		
3	5	6	0			4	6	3	0	
4	6	7	3	0		5	10	8	7	0
5	10	11	8	7	0					

(c) 3-cluster solution				(d) 2-cluster solution		
	(12)	(34)	4		(1234)	5
(12)	0			(1234)	0	
(34)	5	0		5	7	0
4	10	7	0			

as linkage methods, variance methods and so on (Johnson and Wichern 1982). Agglomerative clustering starts with n clusters given n customers, that is, it considers each customer its own cluster, and then successively merges customers in terms of their similarities until all subjects are classified into a single cluster. The algorithm can best be understood by an example.

Suppose we have five customers and calculate pairwise similarities using one of the similarity definitions discussed in the previous section. The resulting similarity matrix is given in Table 16.1(a). Only the lower triangular of the matrix is shown because of its symmetric property (the similarity of Customer A to Customer B is the same thing as the similarity of Customer B to A). Table 16.1(a) shows that Customers 1 and 2 are the most similar (or the nearest) among all pairs. Hence, we merge these two customers into a cluster named (12). Now we have four clusters that consist of the cluster (12), the cluster (3), the cluster (4), and the cluster (5).

We update the similarity or distance matrix since a new cluster, cluster (12), has been created. The distances among the cluster (3), the cluster (4) and the cluster (5) stay the same. However, the distances between the new cluster (12) and the rest of the clusters should be recalculated. There are three different ways to define the distance between clusters: a simple linkage, the complete linkage and the average linkage. The simple linkage defines the distance as the shortest one among cluster members. For example, the cluster (12) has two customers. The distance between Customer 1 and the cluster (3) is 5 and the distance between Customer 2 and the cluster (3) is 6. Hence, the simple linkage distance between the cluster (12) and the cluster (3) is 5. The distances between the cluster (12) and the rest of the clusters can be similarly calculated. Table 16.1(b) shows the distance matrix of 4-cluster solution using a simple linkage method. On the other hand, a complete linkage selects the farthest distance. Hence, the distance between the cluster (12) and the cluster (3) is 6 by the complete linkage. Finally, an average linkage takes the average distance. If we use the average linkage, the distance between the cluster (12) and the cluster (3) is 5.5.

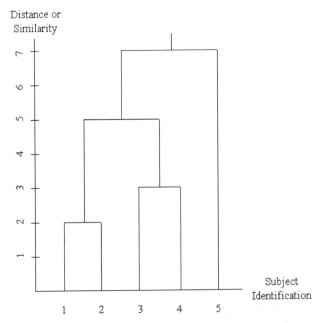

Fig. 16.3 Dendrogram for agglomerative clustering example.

From now on we limit our discussion to a simple linkage method. Table 16.1(**b**) suggests that the cluster (3) and the cluster (4) should be merged next since the distance between these two is the shortest among four clusters. Merging these two, we form the cluster (34), and now have three clusters: cluster (12), cluster (34) and cluster (5). Table 16.1(**c**) shows the updated distance matrix for the 3-cluster solution that indicates the next merging is between cluster (12) and cluster (34). The 2-cluster solution consists of cluster (1234) and cluster (5) and its updated distance matrix is shown in Table 16.1(**d**). Finally, merging these two clusters results in a single cluster including all five customers.

We often summarize the iterations from n-cluster solution to a single cluster by a tree-like diagram called dendrogram. The Greek word "dendron" means a tree. Figure 16.3 shows the dendrogram for the example with five customers. The x-axis in the dendrogram represents the identification of each customer while the y-axis shows the overall picture of cluster formation and distance information when merging. The dendrogram is often used as a tool for choosing the number of clusters relevant to the user. The distances at which clusters are combined can be calculated from the dendrogram. We choose the number of clusters at which the distance increase is suddenly large. However, as the number of customers becomes larger, the dendrogram becomes quite messy. Moreover, it is rather subjective to determine the number of clusters using the dendrogram. We discuss more formal procedures in determining the number of clusters in Sect. 16.2.4.

Agglomerative clustering is simple to apply and easy to understand. However, it has a critical limitation because of its tree-like structure. Also, once customers are incorrectly clustered in the earlier stage of the clustering process, the solution will be seriously biased, the error propagates through the rest of the tree, and re-clustering is not allowed.

16.2.3.2 K-Means Clustering

The K-means may be the most popular clustering method among data miners. Given the number of clusters k specified by the user, the algorithm starts with randomly choosing k points among n customers that become the initial cluster centers. Each of the remaining customers is assigned to the one of k cluster centers according to the Euclidean distance. Once all customers are grouped into k clusters, new cluster "centers" are calculated, typically as the mean values for each of the clustering variables for each cluster, and each subject is reassigned according to the distances to these new cluster centers. We stop iterations when no more reassignments occur.

We study the K-means algorithm in more detail by a simple example. Suppose we have four customers whose characteristics are represented in two attributes, say income and age. Table 16.2(a) shows the attribute values for each of these four customers. If we want to create two clusters (or $k = 2$), we randomly select two customers and their attribute values become the initial cluster centers. Suppose that Customers B and C be selected. Customer A is clustered into Customer C because its distance to Customer B is 10 and its distance to Customer C is $\sqrt{68} = 8.2$. Similarly, Customer D is merged into Customer B because its distance to Customer B is shorter than to Customer C. As a result, we have two clusters, the cluster (AC) and the cluster (BD), after the first iteration.

Once all subjects are assigned into two clusters, we calculate the "centers", or "centroids", of these two clusters shown in Fig. 16.2(b). Note that the centroid for a given cluster is simply the vector of mean characteristics across the cluster members. Now we check the possibility of reassignment by evaluating the distances between each subject and the new cluster centroids. Customer A should not be moved because his or her distance to the centroid of the cluster (AC) is $\sqrt{17} = 4.1$ while his or her distance to the centroid of the cluster (BD) is $\sqrt{122} = 11.0$. However, Customer C should be reassigned to cluster (BD) because his or her distance to the centroid of the cluster (BD) is $\sqrt{10} = 3.2$ that is shorter than the customer's distance to the centroid of the cluster (AC), $\sqrt{17} = 4.1$. Using the same method, Customers B and D are should stay in their current cluster. In result, we now have two new clusters, the cluster (A) and the cluster (BCD), after the second iteration.

Figure 16.2(c) shows the centroids of the new clusters. Given the new two clusters and their centroids, we again evaluate whether each customer should be moved or not. None of the customers should move. Hence, we stop the

Table 16.2 Example of the K-means algorithm

(a) Characteristics of four subjects		
Customers	x_1	x_2
A	13	3
B	3	3
C	5	1
D	1	1

(b) Clusters and their centroids for the first iteration		
Clusters	**Centroid (x_1)**	**Centroid (x_2)**
(AC)	9	2
(BD)	2	2

(c) Clusters and their centroids for the second iteration		
Clusters	**Centroid (x_1)**	**Centroid (x_2)**
(A)	13	3
(BCD)	3	1.7

algorithm at this iteration, and conclude that our final two-cluster solution is the cluster (A) and the cluster (BCD).

The K-means method is more appropriate than agglomerative clustering for large data application because it is computationally faster. The K-means is linear in the number of observations, while agglomerative is often cubic, depending on the dissimilarity measure. Moreover, it does not require a large amount of storage space in computer memory since its algorithm does not need to save the distance matrices. However, the final solution of the K-means clustering depends on its initial condition. In our example, we randomly selected k initial points or centroids.[4] Different initial centroids might result in a different final solution. Therefore, it is recommended to generate several starting points and compare the corresponding final solutions. Finally, K-means clustering algorithm implicitly assumes spherically shaped clusters with a common error variance. Hence, it tends to produce equal-sized clusters (Everitt 1993).

16.2.3.3 Probabilistic Clustering

Both agglomerative and K-means clustering have a critical limitation in assigning subjects into clusters. The models assume that each subject belongs to only one cluster. They do not allow any statements on the strength of a subject's cluster membership. Because of their deterministic nature, these methods are sensitive to outliers and do not perform well with overlapping clusters, i.e., when a customer is partially in one cluster and partially in

---

[4] Alternatively, we can randomly partition all subjects into k initial clusters. However, this method is not exempted from the same problem.

another. Attracting renewed attention from researchers, probabilistic clustering overcomes this problem by incorporating uncertainty about a customer's cluster membership. Another attractive aspect of probabilistic clustering is that it assumes there is a true underlying set of clusters, and the task is to uncover them. This is conceptually more pleasing than other methods that are really just common-sense algorithms for grouping customers together but can't guarantee the solution is unique or correct in any real sense.

Probabilistic clustering has other advantages as well. It does not require the scaling of variables. For example, when working with normal distributions with unknown variances, the results will be the same irrespective of whether the observed variables are normalized or not (Magidson and Vermunt 2002). In addition, it includes a more statistically justifiable way of determining the number of clusters and testing the validity of the clustering results. Probabilistic clustering is also called soft clustering, mixture-model clustering, model-based clustering, or latent class cluster analysis.

Probabilistic clustering assumes that the data to be clustered are generated from a finite mixture of underlying probability distributions in which each component distribution represents a cluster (Fraley and Raftery 1998). Let $\mathbf{x}_i$ be the vector of characteristics for Customer i. If Customer i is a member of cluster s, its conditional probability distribution or "density" is represented by $f_s(\mathbf{x}_i|\theta_s)$ where θ_s are the parameters that describe the conditional density. Then the unconditional probability distribution or density for the Customer $i(i = 1,\ldots,n)$ can be written as

$$g(\mathbf{x}_i|\theta) = \sum_{s=1}^{S} \pi_s f_s(\mathbf{x}_i|\theta_s) \tag{16.3}$$

where S is the number of clusters and π_s is the prior probability that the Customer i belongs to cluster s. Or π_s can be considered to be the size of the cluster s. Note that $\pi_s \geq 0$ for all s and $\sum_{s=1}^{S} \pi_s = 1$.

Most of studies on the specification of the Equation 16.3 assume that $f_s(\mathbf{x}_i|\theta_s)$ is multivariate normal (Banfield and Raftery 1993; Cheeseman and Stutz 1995; Dasgupta and Raftery 1998).[5] Hence, the parameters θ_s consist of a mean vector μ_s and a covariance matrix Σ_s. The most general model requires the estimation of means, variances, and covariances for all clusters. However, as the number of characteristics and/or clusters increase, the number of parameters to be estimated increases significantly. Hence, a number of researchers have proposed simpler models by restricting the potential values for the parameters in Σ_s.

An interesting restrictive model is the "local independence" model in which all within-cluster covariances are assumed to be zero, or Σ_s is assumed to be diagonal matrix. This model is not very restrictive as it sounds. The characteristics are (locally) independent within the given cluster. The observed

---

[5] On the other hand, latent class models assume that $f_s(\mathbf{x}_i|\theta_s)$ is Bernoulli or class-conditional distributions (Bartholomew 1987).

characteristics can still be correlated globally. Another interesting constraint is to assume that Σ_s is the same across all clusters (Banfield and Raftery 1993; Vermunt and Migidson 2000).

The estimation of the probability clustering is typically based on the EM algorithm (Dempster et al. 1977; Tanner 1993). The EM algorithm is a general approach to maximum likelihood in the presence of incomplete data. In probability clustering, the complete data for Customer i are considered to be $y_i = (\mathbf{x}_i, \mathbf{z}_i)$. The vector $\mathbf{z}_i = (z_{i1}, \ldots, z_{iS})$ represents the missing data, where z_{is} equals 1 if Customer i belongs to cluster s and 0 otherwise. Hence, the probability density of Customer i's data, $\mathbf{x}_i$, given $\mathbf{z}_i$ becomes $\prod_{s=1}^{S} f_s(\mathbf{x}_i|\theta_s)^{z_{is}}$. Each $\mathbf{z}_i$ is assumed to be independent and identically distributed as a multinomial distribution of one draw on S categories with probabilities $\pi_1, \ldots, \pi_S$. The resulting complete-data log-likelihood is

$$\ell(\theta_s, \pi_s, z_{is}|\mathbf{x}_i) = \sum_{i=1}^{n} \sum_{s=1}^{S} z_{is}[\log \pi_s f_s(\mathbf{x}_i|\theta_s)] \tag{16.4}$$

The complete-data log-likelihood represented by Equation 16.4 is maximized using an iterative EM algorithm. It iterates between an E-step in which values of $\hat{z}_{is} = E(z_{is}|\mathbf{x}_i, \theta_1, \ldots, \theta_S)$ are computed from the data with the current parameter values, and an M-step in which the complete-data log-likelihood, with each z_{is} replaced by its current conditional expectation $\hat{z}_{is}$, is maximized with respect to the parameters. The algorithm starts with initial guesses for $\hat{z}_{is}$. The E-step and the M-step are iterated until a convergence criterion of the researcher's choice is met.

As mentioned, probability clustering has several advantages over agglomerative or K-means clustering. However, it is not widely used among database marketers because of its computational difficulties. The optimization methods for probability clustering have storage and time requirements that grow at a faster than linear rate relative to the size of the initial partition (Fraley and Raftery 1998). Hence, it is not suitable for clustering a large number of customers.

The most popular commercial software implementing the probability clustering is included in the S-PLUS package as the function *mclust*. Several researchers have also improved the function *mclust* and written codes to interface with S-PLUS (e.g., see www.stat.washington.edu/fraley/mclust/soft.shtml). Alternative software to implement probability clustering is *Latent GOLD* by Statistical Innovations. It implements the probability clustering models assuming a mixture of normals, multinomials and others. It also estimates latent-class regression models.

16.2.3.4 Self-Organizing Maps (SOM)

There is a type of neural network model called the self-organizing map (SOM) that can be employed for a clustering task. Proposed by Tuevo Kohonen in

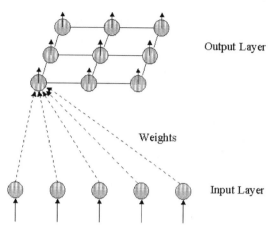

Fig. 16.4 Architecture of a self-organizing map.

1982 (Kohonen 1982), the SOM was originally used for image and sound, and recently applied to clustering people. Like other neural network models, the SOM has an input layer and an output layer (see Chapter 18). Each unit (or cluster) in the output layer is connected to units (or attributes) in the input layer and the strength of this connection is measured by a weight. However, the SOM is fundamentally different from other neural network models in that its goal is to identify no pre-specified "dependent variable" for the output layer. The SOM is looking for unknown patterns in the data. Using the terminology of machine learning, the SOM is developed for unsupervised learning. Hence, there are no training or pre-classified examples like other clustering algorithms.

Figure 16.4 shows the architecture of the SOM. Its input layer has five units, implying that each customer is represented by five attributes. Represented in a 3 × 3 two-dimensional grid, its output layer has nine units or clusters.[6] The output layers in the SOM are generally arranged in two-dimensional grid or lattice such as in Fig. 16.4. Each output unit is expected to become a prototype for a cluster of customers with one homogeneous class of input data vectors. The units in the output layers are not directly connected to each other. However, this grid-like structure allows output units to be related each other. Two adjacent units in the grid represent two similar clusters. If more nodes are in between two units (or clusters), they are meant to be more dissimilar.

Each unit in the output layer is connected to all units in the input layer even though we did not draw every line in Fig. 16.4. That is, the SOM can be

---

[6] Since the output layers in the SOM are typically arranged in 2-dimentional grid, the number of initial output units is restricted to certain numbers (e.g., 3 × 3 or 5 × 4). However, an SOM identifies fewer clusters than it has output units. Units with no hits or with very few hits are discarded. Hence, the final number of clusters chosen can be any numbers.

interpreted as a topology-preserving mapping from input space onto the two-dimensional grid of output units (Vesanto and Alhoniemi 2000). The number of data vectors available for training the SOM corresponds to the number of customers. In Fig. 16.4, each customer has been evaluated on five attributes. Each connection line has an associated weight, which is portrayed by a set of five lines, each with its own weight, connecting each output unit to each input variable.

The SOM computes the weights according to learning rules. The units in the output layer (through weight adjustments) get trained to learn about the patterns of the input data values. During the training each output unit (or cluster) competes to take "responsibility" for one particular observed input data vector. Only the winning output unit (and its neighbors) is allowed to learn by adjusting its weights for a given input data vector. Whether an output unit qualifies as the winner depends on the similarity of its current weight vector $\mathbf{w}$ and the data vector $\mathbf{x}$. More specifically, let the weight vector of output unit k be $\mathbf{w}_k = [w_{k1}, \ldots, w_{kJ}]$ where J is the number of attributes in the input layer. At each training iteration, a data vector $\mathbf{x}_i$ for customer i is randomly selected from the input data, and the similarity between the weight vector of the output unit k and the data vector is measured by their Euclidean distance.

$$\|\mathbf{x}_i - \mathbf{w}_k\| = \left[\sum_{j=1}^{J} (x_{ij} - w_{kj})^2 \right]^{1/2} \tag{16.5}$$

The distances between the data vector $\mathbf{x}_i$ and each of the units in the output layer are computed. The output unit with the smallest distance becomes the best-matching or winning unit for the given data vector $\mathbf{x}_i$.

Before the data vector is drawn, the weight vectors are initialized. At each iteration, a training data vector ($\mathbf{X}_i$) is randomly drawn from the input data, and the best-matching unit is determined by calculating the distances between the data vector and the weights for each of the units in the output layer (the $\mathbf{W}_i$'s). The weight vectors of the winning unit along with its neighboring units are updated to move closer to the data vector. As a result, each input data vector gradually belongs to one output unit as the weight updating repeats. More specifically, the weight vector of output unit i is updated according to the following rule.

$$w_{kj}(t+1) = \begin{cases} w_{kj}(t) + \lambda[x_{ij} - w_{kj}(t)] & \text{if } k \in N(k') \\ w_{kj}(t) & \text{otherwise} \end{cases} \tag{16.6}$$

where t is the iteration number, λ is the learning constant with $0 < \lambda < 1$, and $N(k')$ is the set of output units consisted of the winning unit k' and its neighbors (Kohonen 1994). Equation 16.6 implies that only the weights of the winning unit and its neighbors are adjusted. As a result, similar output units will be located closer to each other and similar data vectors occupy positions closer to each other than less similar ones. Even though there are many ways to specify the updating rule, Equation 16.6 is the simplest. For more sophisticated updating rules, see Kohonen (1995) or Vesanto and Alhoniemi (2000).

16.2.4 The Number of Clusters

Determining the appropriate number of clusters is one of the most difficult problems in clustering. Sometimes managerial judgment is critical in deciding the number of clusters even though this tends to be subjective. For example, the relative sizes of the clusters should be large enough to be managerially meaningful. The clusters with a couple of subjects may be treated as outliers and ignored. As another example, marketing managers often limit the number of clusters because the implementation cost may be beyond their budgets or the fine-tuned segmentation strategy may not be feasible.

We now focus our attention on more formal ways to determine the number of clusters. The methods for determining the number of clusters depend on the clustering algorithm being used and there are several criteria available. However, Milligan and Cooper (1985) showed that the procedure by Calinski and Harabasz (1974) performed the best among 30 different criteria. Calinski and Harabasz suggested the following criterion to determine the number of clusters:

$$G(k) = (n - k)(T - W)/(k - 1)W \tag{16.7}$$

where k is the number of clusters, n is the number of customers, W is the square sum of the distances of the customers to the center of its cluster, and T is the square sum of the differences of each customer to the average customer, essentially, the center of the full data. The optimal number of cluster can be determined by selecting k which returns the maximum value for $G(k)$, because in that case, W, or the distances between customers and the center of their clusters, is relatively small compared to T, the distances between customers and the center of the entire data.

For probabilistic clustering, there is a more formal way of determining the optimal number of clusters. Once we apply different numbers of clusters, we select the number of clusters that will minimize the BIC (Bayesian Information Criterion) proposed by Schwarz (1978). The BIC of the probabilistic clustering with s clusters can be written as

$$BIC_S = -2 \log l_s + m_s \log n \tag{16.8}$$

where m_s is the number of estimated parameters for the model with s clusters and $\log l_s$ is the corresponding log-likelihood. As the number of clusters increase, the log-likelihood will increase. However, the penalizing term m_s

increases at the same time. We choose the model with the optimal number of clusters that will minimize the *BIC*.

16.3 Applying Cluster Analysis

16.3.1 Interpreting the Results

The results of a cluster analysis are interpreted by examining the means for each cluster of the clustering variables, and also examining the means of any other variable, i.e., "discrimination variables," not included in the clustering routine. For example, we may cluster based on benefits sought but have a host of other variables, for example demographics, that we use for interpretation.

Table 16.3 shows a hypothetical example of a cluster analysis based on a survey of 500 customers in the personal home computer market. The clustering was based on benefits sought; all variables measured on a 7-point scale. In addition, there are several demographic and psychographic variables not used in the cluster analysis, but available as discrimination variables.

Interpreting the clusters is a subjective but interesting task that often adds insight into the nature of the market. In this case, customers in Cluster 1 are very concerned with "ease of use" and "technical support," and customers in this cluster are not very likely to own a home computer. This cluster might be called "Novices." Novices would be an attractive segment because they

Table 16.3 Hypothetical cluster analysis results for home computer market

	Means on clustering variables		
	Cluster 1 ("Novices")	Cluster 2 ("Family")	Cluster 3 ("Heavy Users")
Speed	2.4	3.4	5.4
Capacity	2.7	3.3	6.1
Ease of use	5.3	5.1	2.1
Aesthetics	1.2	5.7	2.3
Reliability	4.3	3.3	5.5
Technical Support	6.6	3.3	4.0
% of sample	30%	15%	55%
	Means on discrimination variables		
Age (years)	45.4	47.3	35.1
Children present (%)	10%	48%	29%
Income (K, in $)	45.2	50.1	35.2
Use for work	20%	10.1%	45.6%
Currently own computer	22%	56.1%	75.2%
Current Mac users	10%	11%	10%

do not own a computer but fit the age and income profile of a customer who could use a computer (e.g., comparing to Cluster 2). However, the Novices might be expensive to serve because they care about ease of use and technical support, so could end up calling the company's customer service center too often.

Customers in Cluster 2 care a lot about ease of use and aesthetics, and is dominated by families with children. We might call this the "Family" segment. Probably the children present leads to the importance of ease of use, and noting the slightly older age of customers in this cluster, perhaps those children are teenagers, where aesthetics of the computer could be important. The Family segment might be attractive for a company like Apple, a company that excels in aesthetics and design.

Customers in the third cluster cares a lot about speed, capacity, and reliability, and customers in this cluster use a computer at work as well as own their own computer. This might be called the "Heavy User" segment. This segment would be attractive to a company that can excel on technical specifications such as speed, and provide capacity and reliability at low cost. In addition, the cluster analysis classifies 55% of customers in this segment, so it is the largest segment. Also, the Heavy User segment might be expected to want to trade up their computer as often as possible to the latest, fastest, home computer available.

Note that the interpretations are subjective and make use of both the clustering and discrimination variables. Note also there are clear managerial implications in that companies with particular strengths could plausibly target one of these clusters, but probably not all of them (at least with the same product).

16.3.2 Targeting the Desired Cluster

Note that the cluster analysis was based on a survey of 500 consumers. Let's say the company decided to target the Family segment. The next task – the task of database marketing – would be to figure out how to reach these customers. The measurement of benefits sought is unique to the survey. There are probably no lists available of large numbers of consumers who have answered the same benefits sought questions. However, lists are available of customers that provide measures of the discrimination variables, since these are mostly demographics and usage behaviors. For example, to target the Family segment, one would compile a list of customers that contained most if not all of the discrimination variables. One might have to purchase different lists and merge them together, or have a company such as Vente (http://lists.venteinc.com/market) compile the list. One could next proceed in two ways. One would be to select from the list customers who tend to fit the profile on the discrimination variables for the Family segment. This could be done heuristically (e.g., select from the list households that own a home computer and have children present).

Another approach would be to estimate a predictive model based on the cluster analysis sample of 500, and apply it to the larger list for which the discrimination variables are available (see also Chapter 10). For example, one could use a logistic regression on the sample of 500 to determine whether or not the customer is in the Family segment, or use a multinomial logit to predict which of the three segments the customer is in. The dependent variable would be cluster membership. The independent variables would be the discrimination variables. Note this model would be estimated on the 500 customers because these are the customers for whom we know cluster membership. However, once we have the multinomial logit model, we can use it to "score" the entire customer list because we have the discrimination variables in that list. In this way, we could assign all 5,000,000 customers to benefits sought segments.

The above example shows how a rich set of measures obtained from a small sample can be used to identify and target customers among a larger set. The key to the success of this strategy is the existence of discrimination variables that are available for large numbers of customers. The small sample has available the clustering variables and the discrimination variables, while the compiled list has the discrimination variables. A predictive model or heuristic selection procedure allows the database marketer to infer the cluster membership of customers of the compiled list.

While this procedure is very valuable, it is possible that the clustering variables might be available for a large list and hence the above process might not be necessary. For example, consider the case of a company wanting to start a customer tier program. The company may cluster analyze its customers based on various measures of customer value (LTV, responsiveness to marketing, duration, RFM variables, etc.). It would be impractical to run the cluster analysis of all its 5,000,000 customers. So the analyst would run the cluster analysis on say 2000 customers. Then the rest of the customers could be assigned to a cluster by directly calculating its similarity to each cluster. This is obviously the most desirable situation. The small-sample – predictive model – compile list – score list approach obviously has more steps and relies on coming up with a good predictive model and being able to compile a list of many customers with data on the discrimination variables. However, many customer lists are available, and there are companies that specialize in list compilation, so especially for a customer acquisition scenario, the approach makes good sense.

The above illustrates how cluster analysis can be used to interpret segments, make a targeting decision, and then use database marketing to target potential members of the sought-after segment. The contribution of cluster analysis is extremely important to this process. It provides a rich portrait of how the market might be segmented, and often through the discrimination variables, how they might be reached. While as we've discussed in this chapter, there are many different methods we can use to form the clusters, the real "validation" of the technique is in the managerial value of interpreting the clusters, and the targetability and ultimately the profitability of the segments realized through list creation and predictive modeling.

Chapter 17
Decision Trees

Abstract Decision trees are a very intuitive, easy-to-implement predictive modeling technique. They literally can be depicted as a tree – a sequence of criteria for classifying customers according to a metric such as likelihood of response. The pictorial representation of the tree makes it easy to apply and communicate. This chapter discusses the methods for creating the branches of the tree, deciding how many branches the tree should have and further details in constructing decision trees.

17.1 Introduction

Decision trees have attracted considerable attention both from researchers and practitioners. For example, the survey paper on decision trees by Murthy (1998) cites more than 300 references from various disciplines including statistics, engineering, and decision science. Decision trees become the most popular data mining tool among managers because of their ability to generate rules that can easily be expressed visually and in plain English. A decision tree is often called a regression tree if the dependent variable is quantitative and a classification tree if it is qualitative.

The origin of decision trees goes back to the tree-based model called AID (Automatic Interaction Detection) developed by Morgan and Sonquist (1963). As the name implies, their original intention is to develop a model that efficiently identifies interactions among independent variables. In a predictive modeling context, an interaction exists when the effect of an independent (or predictor) variable on the dependent variable (customer response, customer value, etc.) depends on the level of other independent variables. When an interaction exists, the simple additive property of each independent variable in contributing the dependent variable no longer holds. For example, customer profitability may increase as a function of income among customers with lower level of education. However, the same variable may decrease as a function of income among customers with higher education. Statistically, it becomes a formidable task to incorporate all the interactions among independent variables as the number of independent variables increases. You need to consider all two-way interactions, three-ways, four-ways, and so on. For example, with real-world databases consisting of say 100 potential predictors, there would be $_{100}C_2 = (100)(99)/2 = 4,950$ potential two-way interactions and $_{100}C_3 = (100)(99)(98)/6 = 161,700$ potential three-way interactions! AID was designed to tackle this complex combinatorial problem in a heuristic way.

Hartigan (1975) later modified AID, employing a statistically more valid method of splitting the data into subsets. His model is called CHAID (Chi-Square Automatic Interaction Detection) because he used the chi-square test of statistical significance to split the data. Decision trees became even further popularized among statisticians since Breiman et al. (1984) developed their decision tree algorithm called CART (Classification and Regression Trees). Different from CHAID, CART intentionally grows oversized trees and then prunes some branches using a built-in cross validation procedure to avoid the possibility of overfitting. Finally, researchers in machine learning began to use decision trees. For example, Quinlan (1986) constructed his own tree-based model called C4.5.

17.2 Fundamentals of Decision Trees

A decision tree starts with the entire customer dataset and successively splits it into mutually exclusive discrete subsets, so that each customer is assigned to one subset or the other. There is exactly one *root node* that no edges enter. The root node is the entire dataset. This gets split into two or more *children nodes*. These children nodes are successively split until the algorithm decides the tree is complete. The final children nodes that define the end of the tree are called *terminal* (or *leaf*) *nodes*. All children nodes except the root and terminal nodes are called *internal nodes*.

All decision tree algorithms share several aspects in common. The goal is to build a tree that will allow us to predict the dependent variable (or in modern technical language, build a classification tree to assign a "class" for each observation) based on the values of attributes or independent variables. Starting from the root node, the decision tree model recursively partitions (splits) the attribute space into subsets, or children nodes, (e.g., $X_1 \geq a$ versus $X_1 < a$, where X_1 is an independent variable) such that the dependent variable becomes successively more homogeneous within each subset. After each split, we are left with two or more internal nodes. The algorithm then attempts to split these internal nodes into children nodes, using its own criterion function to find the best split. If the value of splitting an internal node is less than a pre-specified stopping threshold, the internal node will not split anymore and becomes a terminal node. The tree-growing proceeds until no

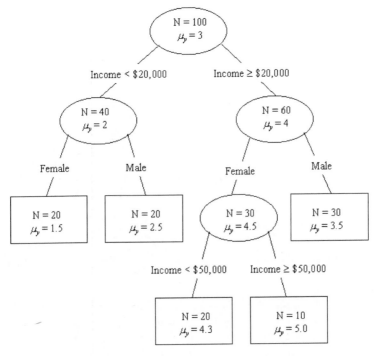

Fig. 17.1 Decision tree for brand preference.

more internal nodes are left in the tree that are worth splitting. The terminal
nodes of the tree correspond to distinct, mutually exclusive regions of the
attribute space and each observation can be assigned to one of the terminal
nodes.

Let us give a simple example of the decision tree applied to the prediction of customer's brand preference. We collect survey data from 100 customers regarding their brand satisfaction measured in five-point scale (y)
and two independent (predictor) variables, income (x_1) and sex (x_2). Income
is measured on a continuous scale while sex is a categorical variable (1 if the
customer is a male and 0 if she is a female). The decision tree attempts to
predict customer satisfaction by grouping customers according to their income and sex. The groups are represented in the tree-like structure shown in
Fig. 17.1.

The root node contains 100 customers with an average satisfaction of 3.2.
The first step is to decide the best way to split income if we are to use income
as the first variable for splitting the root node, and the best way to split sex
if we are to use sex as the first splitting variable. Sex is a categorical variable
with only two categories, so there is only one way to spit it (male versus
female). We therefore know without much thinking how we will split on sex
if we split the root node based on sex.

Finding the split value for income is nontrivial because it is a continuous variable and so there are many possible splits.[1] We first choose a split value say of $20,000, and assign the 100 customers into two segments: a segment with income lower than $20,000 and a segment with income higher than $20,000. Alternatively, you may choose a split value of $30,000, and assign 100 respondents into a group lower than $30,000 and a group higher than $30,000. The decision tree algorithm selects the best split value in the sense that the within group variation of Y's is minimized and the between group variations of Y's is maximized (see Sect. 17.3 for details). In other words, we divide 100 respondents into two groups using their income levels in such a way that brand satisfaction of customers within a group are as homogeneous as possible while being maximally different from those in the other group.

Now that we know the best way of splitting the root node if we use income as the splitting variable or sex, the next step is to decide which independent variable better predicts the dependent variable, customer satisfaction. This is similarly decided by calculating which variable does a better job of minimizing within group variation of Y's while also maximizing between group variation (see Sect. 17.3 for details). Because income is the better variable than sex, we start to draw the tree by splitting the root node into two children nodes, one with income broken down into two, say, lower than $20,000 and higher than $20,000.

We now branch out trees from each of these two internal nodes. Employing the same splitting rule, we find that the variable sex is the better feature to split both internal nodes. In the next tree branching stage, three out of four internal nodes are within the stopping threshold and, hence, become the terminal nodes. Finally, we split one of the four child nodes by income, leading to two more terminal nodes. The final tree has five terminal nodes.

The resulting tree is shown in Fig. 17.1. Each of the five terminal nodes corresponds to distinct regions of the attribute space. The first terminal node represents females with income less than $20,000. The second is for males with income less than $20,000. Other terminal nodes are interpreted similarly. The terminal nodes represent mutually exclusive and collectively exhaustive partitions of the original root node, so each respondents can be classified into the one and only one of these five terminal nodes. Moving from the root node to the terminal nodes allows us to predict the satisfaction rating. If a customer is identified to be female with income less than $20,000, she is assigned to the first terminal node, and her satisfaction is predicted to be 1.5. On the other hand, the satisfaction rating for a female with her income greater than $50,000 is predicted to be 5.0.

The tree in Fig. 17.1 demonstrates an interaction effect between the variable income and sex. Among respondents with the income less than $20,000,

---

[1] This would also be the case for a categorical variable with several categories. Any two-category variable, such as sex, is easy because there is only one way to split it.

the preference rating of a male is higher than a female. On the other hand, a female has the higher preference rating than a male, among respondents with the income greater than \$20,000. Depending on the level of income, the preference rating of a female will be higher or lower than a male.

17.3 Finding the Best Splitting Rule

The most important and widely researched issue in decision trees is to develop the best "splitting rule," that is, the method by which to decide on what value of the predictor variable should be split. In order to build a tree, it is necessary to apply at each internal node a testing measure for splitting the data into two children nodes.[2] Researchers have proposed a number of different splitting metrics. We here review some of the well-known splitting rules.

17.3.1 Gini Index of Diversity

The Gini index has been employed by CART (Breiman et al. 1984) and SLIQ (Mehta et al. 1996). Generally, a good splitting rule should partition the data at an internal node and make the data at the child nodes more "pure" or homogeneous (in the distribution of the dependent variable y). Breiman et al. (1984) proposed to define an impurity function $i(t)$ at every internal node t. Suppose that a potential split S will divide the internal node t into the two child nodes t_1 and t_2. And the total number of observations at the internal node is n, and n_1 observations go into t_1 and n_2 observations goes to t_2. The goodness of the split S is defined to be the decrease in impurity

$$\Delta i(S,t) = i(t) - (n_1/n)i(t_1) - (n_2/n)i(t_2) \qquad (17.1)$$

One will choose a split that maximizes $\Delta i(S,t)$ over all possible splits S at the internal node t.[3] Or choose a split that minimizes $(n_1/n)i(t_1) + (n_2/n)i(t_2)$. Breiman et al. (1984) suggest the Gini index of diversity as the impurity function.

$$i(t) = 1 - \sum_j p(j|t)^2 \qquad (17.2)$$

---

[2] We limit our attention to the decision tree design with a binary split. However, the binary split is not really a restriction because any ordered tree was shown to be uniquely transformed into an equivalent binary tree (Rounds 1980).

[3] In the sequence of values for continuous valued variables, the maximum number of possible splits is $(n-1)$ where n is the number of observations. Similarly, the number of possible splits for categorical variables is $(2^m - 1)$ where m is the number of distinct values.

Table 17.1 Responses to direct marketing offer

Customer ID	Response	Sex	Income
1	Yes	Male	$\geq$$50,000
2	Yes	Male	<$50,000
3	Yes	Female	$\geq$$50,000
4	Yes	Female	$\geq$$50,000
5	Yes	Female	$\geq$$50,000
6	No	Male	<$50,000
7	No	Male	<$50,000
8	No	Female	<$50,000
9	No	Female	$\geq$$50,000
10	No	Male	<$50,000

where $p(j|t)$ is the probability (or the relative frequency) a customer in node t is in "class" j (a class is a particular value of the dependent variable). The Gini index has the minimum value of 0 when all observations belong to one class and the maximum value of $(1 - 1/c)$ when observations are evenly distributed across all c classes. In other words, if the split is such that all customers in a given node t have the same value for the dependent variable, the customers are perfectly homogeneous and there is no impurity. However, say there are only two classes or values for the dependent variable, and $p(j|t) = 0.5$, that means the homogeneity of the customers in node t is no better than would be achieved based on random assignment, and impurity is maximal.

For illustration, consider the hypothetical data shown in Table 17.1. Suppose we develop a decision tree to predict the response probability to the direct mailing offer based on two independent variables, sex (male or female) and income ($\geq$ $50,000$ or $< 50,000$).

At the root node, the relative frequencies of response with "Yes" and "No" is $0.5(= 5/10)$. Hence, the Gini measure of impurity at the root node is $i(t) = 1 - 0.5^2 - 0.5^2 = 0.5$. To branch out the tree from the root node, we now have to know which variables would make the data more homogeneous at the children nodes. First, we calculate the impurity of a split with respect to sex. There are 10 observations ($n = 10$): 5 males ($n_1 = 5$) and 5 females ($n_2 = 5$). Its Gini measures of impurity at the child node are:

$$\text{Males: } i(t_1) = 1 - 0.4^2 - 0.6^2 = 0.48$$
$$\text{Females: } i(t_2) = 1 - 0.6^2 - 0.4^2 = 0.48$$

Hence, if we choose the split with respect to sex, the decrease in impurity is

$$\Delta i(sex, t) = i(t) - (n_1/n)i(t_1) - (n_2/n)i(t_2)$$
$$= 0.5 - (5/10)(0.48) - (5/10)(0.48) = 0.02$$

We similarly calculate the impurity of a split with respect to income. Again, there are 10 observations ($n = 10$): 5 high income ($n_1 = 5$) and 5 low income customers ($n_2 = 5$). The corresponding impurity measures at the child node are:

$$\geq\$50,000: i(t_1) = 1 - 0.8^2 - 0.2^2 = 0.32$$
$$<\$50,000: i(t_2) = 1 - 0.2^2 - 0.8^2 = 0.32$$

Hence, if we choose the split of income variable, the decrease in impurity will be

$$\Delta i(income, t) = 0.5 - (5/10)(0.32) - (5/10)(0.32) = 0.18$$

Since $\Delta i(income, t) = 0.18$ is greater than $\Delta i(sex, t) = 0.02$, we choose the split of income variable.

17.3.2 Entropy and Information Theoretic Measures

Uncertainty is at its maximum at the root node because a given customer could belong to any of the classes (values for the dependent variable). As we move from the root node through the internal nodes down to the terminal node, uncertainty is reduced because we become more certain of the customer's class. Hence, an objective function for a tree design could be to minimize uncertainty or maximize entropy reduction from each level to the next level (Suen and Wang 1984).

Shannon's entropy is frequently used among various entropy measures because of its strong additive property. The Shannon's entropy at node t can be defined as

$$\text{Entropy}(t) = -\sum_j p(j|t) \log p(j|t) \qquad (17.3)$$

where $p(j|t)$ is the probability or the relative frequency of class j at node t, (i.e., the probability a customer in node t has a dependent variable value of j). The entropy in Equation 17.3 will have the minimum of 0 when all observations belong to one class and the maximum value of $\log c$ when observations are evenly distributed across all c classes implying least information.[4]

Similar to the case of the Gini index, suppose that a potential split S will divide the internal node t into the two child nodes t_1 and t_2. And the total number of observations at the internal node t is n, and n_1 observations go into t_1 and n_2 observations goes to t_2. Then the information gain of splitting the node t can be defined as

$$\text{Gain}(t) = \text{Entropy}(t) - (n_1/n)\text{Entropy}(t_1) - (n_2/n)\text{Entropy}(t_2) \qquad (17.4)$$

---

[4] The logic is similar to that with the impurity index. If the split has perfect prediction, $p(j|t)$ will equal 1 for at least one classification, in which case $\log p(j|t) = 0$, and equal zero for all other classifications. The sum in Equation 17.3 will come out to be zero. If the split has random prediction, $p(j|t)$ will equal $1/c$ for all j, in which case Equation 17.3 will sum up to $\log c$.

Equation 17.4 measures the information gain or the reduction in entropy by splitting the node t. At the internal node t, you choose the split over all possible splits S maximizing Equation 17.4.

Using the hypothetical data shown in Table 17.1, let us demonstrate how to calculate the information gain measure and determine the best split. Remember that the relative frequencies of response $(p(j|t))$ with "Yes" and "No" is $0.5(= 5/10)$ at the root node. Hence, the Shannon's entropy at the root node is $\text{Entropy}(t) = -[(0.5)\log(0.5) + (0.5)\log(0.5)] = 0.3010$. Similar to the numerical example applied to the Gini measure, we have two candidate variables, sex and income, to branch out the tree from the root node. First, we calculate the entropy of a split with respect to sex. There are 10 observations ($n = 10$): 5 males ($n_1 = 5$) and 5 females ($n_2 = 5$). Its entropy measures at the child node are:

$$\text{Males: Entropy}(t_1) = -[(0.4)\log(0.4) + (0.6)\log(0.6)] = 0.2922$$
$$\text{Females: Entropy}(t_2) = -[(0.6)\log(0.6) + (0.4)\log(0.4)] = 0.2922$$

Therefore, if we choose the split with respect to sex, the information gain will be

$$\text{Gain}(t) = 0.3010 - (5/10)(0.2922) - (5/10)(0.2922) = 0.0088$$

Alternatively, if we choose the split of income variable, the corresponding entropy measures at the child node are:

$$\geq\$50{,}000\text{: Entropy}(t_1) = -[(0.8)\log(0.8) + (0.2)\log(0.2)] = 0.0930$$
$$<\$50{,}000\text{: Entropy}(t_2) = -[(0.2)\log(0.2) + (0.8)\log(0.8)] = 0.0930$$

Hence, the information gain for the split with income variable will be

$$\text{Gain}(t) = 0.3010 - (5/10)(0.0930) - (5/10)(0.0930) = 0.2080$$

The information gain of splitting with respect to income (0.2080) rather than sex (0.0930) is larger. So we choose the split of income variable.

The information theoretic measure has been employed by ID3 and C4.5 (Quinlan 1986). It tends to select splits that lead to so many partitions that the tree becomes unwieldy. Quinlan (1993) overcomes the overfitting problem by penalizing the number of partitions.

17.3.3 Chi-Square Test

The chi-square statistic may be the one of the oldest splitting rules that is still employed in CHAID (Hartigan 1975; Kass 1983). It is used to test the statistical significance of the observed association in a cross-tabulation. For the same example as before, suppose that a potential split S will divide the internal node t into two children nodes. Let N_{jk} be the number of customers in children node k that are in class j, and a dot $(\cdot)$ subscript designate the sum across nodes or classes as the case may be. The total number of observations at the internal node t is $N_{..}$ consisting of $N_{1.}$ observations of class 1, $N_{2.}$ observations of class 2, and finally $N_{c.}$ observations of class c. So $\sum_{j=1}^{c} N_{j.} = N_{..}$. Now the first child node has $N_{.1}$ observations consisting of N_{j1} for each class j. Similarly, the second child has $N_{.2}$ observations consisting of N_{j2} for each class j. Then the chi-square statistic is defined as

$$\chi^2 = \sum_{j=1}^{c} \frac{(N_{j1} - N_{j.}N_{.1}/N_{..})^2}{N_{j.}N_{.1}/N_{..}} + \sum_{j=1}^{c} \frac{(N_{j2} - N_{j.}N_{.2}/N_{..})^2}{N_{j.}N_{.2}/N_{..}} \qquad (17.5)$$

where $N_{..}(N_{j.}/N_{..})(N_{.1}/N_{..}) = N_{j.}N_{.1}/N_{..}$ and $N_{..}(N_{j.}/N_{..})(N_{.2})/N_{..}) = N_{j.}N_{.2}/N_{..}$ are the expected number of observations from class j in child nodes 1 and 2 respectively if the observations at the parent node t are randomly assigned to the two child nodes. Hence, a good split will produce the larger chi-square value.

Equation 17.5 is known to have the chi-square distribution with $(c - 1)$ degrees of freedom. We select the split with the largest chi-square value (or the lowest p-value) among all possible splits S. And we do not split the internal node t any more if its chi-square value of splitting is not statistically significant. Finally, an adjusted p-value using the Bonferroni multiplier is often used because the chi-square tests are sequentially done from the root node to the terminal nodes.

Using the hypothetical data shown in Table 17.1, let us demonstrate how to calculate the chi-square statistics for each independent variable and select the best split. For the sex variable we get

$$\chi^2 = \frac{(2 - 2.5)^2}{2.5} + \frac{(3 - 2.5)^2}{2.5} + \frac{(3 - 2.5)^2}{2.5} + \frac{(2 - 2.5)^2}{2.5} = 0.4$$

whereas for the income variable we get

$$\chi^2 = \frac{(4 - 2.5)^2}{2.5} + \frac{(1 - 2.5)^2}{2.5} + \frac{(1 - 2.5)^2}{2.5} + \frac{(4 - 2.5)^2}{2.5} = 3.6$$

That is, the chi-square value for the income split is much larger than for the sex split. So we choose the split of income variable.

Note that in this example, whether we use the impurity index, the entropy measure, or the chi-square measure, the conclusion is the same – split on the income variable. However, we cannot guarantee that this always will happen. There is no reason to prefer one measure over the other, because they all make good intuitive sense. The best solution is when possible, to try multiple splitting criteria and verify whether they all lead to the same tree. To the extent they do reinforces our confidence that the final tree captures real patterns in the data.

17.3.4 Other Splitting Rules

There are a number of other splitting rules including Bayes' classification rule (Buntine 1992) and activity-based measure (Moret et al. 1980). Ben-Bassat (1987) provides a useful taxonomy and Murthy (1998) provides lengthy lists of references on various splitting rules. So far no dominating splitting rule seems to emerge. The performance of each splitting rule seems to depend on various external factors such as the type of application area. However, Breiman et al. (1984) made an interesting comment that decision tree design is rather insensitive to a variety of splitting rules, and it is the stopping rule that is critical.

17.4 Finding the Right Sized Tree

Another important and widely researched issue in decision trees is when to stop growing the tree, i.e., when to stop adding branches. Breslow and Aha (1996) have surveyed the previous research on tree simplification. See also Murthy (1998) for references on finding the right sized trees. Here we review the most popular tree stopping criteria.

17.4.1 Pruning

Breiman et al. (1984) have proposed the pruning method to find the right sized tree and it became the most popular tree stopping method. Given the data, the strategy is to employ a greedy algorithm to grow a complete tree in which no more splitting would significantly improve the fitting criterion. The fully grown tree will have a misclassification error rate close to zero on the training, or calibration, data. However, its true error rate that should be measured on the test, or validation, data may be much higher. The fully grown tree may be overgrown because of the statistical exploitation of particular observations in the training data. The goal of pruning is to find a simpler tree that will provide the smallest true error rate. That is, pruning will generalize the tree and avoid the problem of overfitting.

In finding the right sized tree, it is often argued that pruning is better than a stopping threshold approach because it may partially solve the sub-optimality problem of greedy tree induction (Murthy 1998). For example, if there is a good node t_2 a couple of levels below a not-so-good node t_1, the stopping threshold method will stop growing the tree at node t_1. However, the pruning method will grow the complete tree and prune it back until node t_2.

The pruning proceeds in two steps: first generate a number of candidate sub-trees and select the one of these sub-trees based on their classification errors. In order to identify a set of candidate sub-trees, Breiman et al. (1984) introduce the concept of cost complexity that essentially adjusts the misclassification error rate for the complexity of the tree. That is why their pruning is called the cost complexity pruning method. The adjusted misclassification error rate is defined as

$$Adj\text{-}e(S) = e(S) + \alpha\lambda(S) \tag{17.6}$$

where $e(S)$ is the (original) misclassification error rate at the candidate tree S, α is the penalty parameter ($\alpha \geq 0$) imposed on the tree complexity or size, and $\lambda(S)$ is the number of terminal nodes (or "leaves") in the candidate tree S. The larger value assigned to α implies the heavier penalty imposed on a sizable tree. If α is zero, the fully grown tree will have the lowest adjusted misclassification error. Now the value of α is gradually increased. Given α_1, the adjusted error rates of all sub-trees are evaluated. If the adjusted error rate of a sub-tree is lower than that of the fully grown tree, the sub-tree becomes the candidate sub-tree α_1 and all branches that are not part of the sub-tree will be pruned. Then given $\alpha_2 > \alpha_1$, the adjusted error rates of all sub-trees of the tree α_1 are evaluated and the candidate sub-tree α_2 will be found. This sequence proceeds until the final sub-tree is the root node. As the value of α increases, the procedure will generate a set of candidate sub-trees α_1, α_2, and so on.

To illustrate, consider a hypothetical example shown in Fig. 17.2. If the terminal node contains customers belonging to only one class, it assumes to be allocated to the class. When the terminal node includes customers from several different classes, the customers at the terminal node are examined and the terminal node assumes to be allocated to the class which occurs most frequently. The tree has 4 terminal nodes: nodes 2, 5, 6, and 4. There are 28

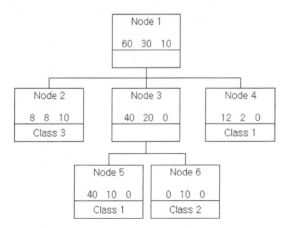

Fig. 17.2 Pruning decision trees.

customers in node 2. Eight are class 1 customers, 8 class 2 customers, and 10 class 3 customers. Hence, node 2 is predicted to be in class 2. Therefore, 16 out of 28 customers are wrongly classified. Similarly, node 5 is predicted to be in class 1, node 6 in class 2, and node 4 in class 1. Hence, 10 out of 50 customers in node 5 and 2 out of 14 customers in node 4 are misclassified. None of the 10 customers in node 6 is wrongly classified. Hence, the misclassification error rate (or $e(S)$) of the full tree (Tree I) is $28/100 = 0.28$ and its number of terminal nodes (or $\lambda(S)$) is 4. Next, consider the tree with node 5 and 6 pruned (Tree II). The resulting tree has 3 terminal nodes: node 2, 3 and 4. So its $\lambda(S)$ is 3. Node 2 is predicted to be in class 3, node 3 in class 1, and node 4 in class 1. Therefore, its misclassification error rate is $38/100 = 0.38$. Finally, consider the completely pruned tree only with node 1 (Tree III). Its $\lambda(S)$ is 1 and node 1 is predicted to be in class 1. Its misclassification error rate is $40/100 = 0.40$.

With $0 \leq \alpha < 0.04$, the $Adj\text{-}e(S)$ of Tree I is the smallest. With $0.04 \leq \alpha$, the $Adj\text{-}e(S)$ of Tree III is the smallest. Hence, a set of candidate sub-trees are Tree I and Tree III.

Once we determine the set of candidate (pruned) sub-trees, we select the sub-tree with the lowest misclassification error rate applied to the holdout sample. The holdout sample of the data is often a portion of the data that is set aside exclusively for pruning. It is typical to observe that the error rate initially decreases as the number of terminal nodes $\lambda(S)$, i.e., the tree complexity, increases. And beyond a certain point, the error rate increases as the tree complexity increases. That is, the best sub-tree is often in the middle, neither a naive simple tree nor an overly complex one.

The pruning method performs very well with the holdout sample. However, if the size of the data is limited, Breiman et al. (1984) suggest using a cross-validation that does not require reserving a portion of a training data for pruning. Pointing out some problems associated with the cross-validation, researchers have suggested alternative ways of using samples including a bootstrap method (Crawford 1989) and an efficient iterative tree growing and pruning (Gelfand et al. 1991).

17.4.2 Other Methods for Finding the Right Sized Tree

Several alternative techniques have been suggested for obtaining right sized trees even though pruning the most popular. The earliest method may be to restrict on minimum node size. A node is not split if it has smaller than k customers where k is a parameter to the tree induction algorithm. This strategy is known not to be robust (Friedman 1977). However, it may be managerially useful to set the minimum size for segments.

Another method of finding a right sized tree is to set a threshold stopping value on the value of splitting criterion. If the splitting criterion at the internal node t is greater (or smaller) than the specified threshold, the internal node becomes the terminal node. For example, if we are using the chi-squared splitting criterion, we can require that the chi-square p-value be less than 0.10 in order for there to be a split, and stop when the p-values at each terminal node are greater than 0.10. The problem, however, is that this does not guard against over-fitting, which is why pruning methods are popular. If the researcher does not want to use a formal pruning method, at a minimum, the predictive ability of the tree obtained using a threshold stopping rule should be tested on holdout data to make sure it doesn't decrease too much.

Thresholds can be imposed on local (i.e., individual node) goodness or on global (i.e., entire tree) goodness. The problem with the local threshold is that the value of most splitting criteria vary with the size of the calibration sample. Imposing a single threshold that is meaningful at all nodes in the tree is not easy and may not even be possible (Murthy 1998).

Finally, Mehta et al.'s (1996) SLIQ (Supervised Learning In Quest) employs an alternative pruning method called MDL (minimum description length) based on pruning that is essentially a generalization of Breiman's approach described in Equation 17.6. The MDL principle states that the best model for encoding the data is the one that minimizes the sum of the cost of describing the data using the model and the cost of describing the model. They define the total cost of description as

$$\text{Cost(Model, Data)} = \text{Cost(Data | Model)} + \text{Cost(Model)} \qquad (17.7)$$

That is, the total cost of description is the sum of the cost of describing a model and the cost of describing data that are exceptions to this model. The best model will be the one with the lowest description cost. In the case of decision trees, the alternative models may be viewed as the set of sub-trees made available as a result of pruning, and the data are the set of observations from which the full tree is initially built (Apte and Weiss 1997). SLIQ utilizes the classification error as the cost of describing the data for a given tree. The cost for describing the model (or a tree) is formulated as a recursive combination of the cost of creating a node and the cost of splitting that node. The total cost at each node in a fully grown tree is then used to prune the node back to a leaf node, or to prune its left sub-tree, or right sub-tree, or leave it unchanged.

17.5 Other Issues in Decision Trees

We briefly discuss some other issues in decision trees besides finding the best splitting rule and the right sized tree.

17.5.1 Multivariate Splits

All the decision trees discussed so far split the internal node into children nodes based on a single attribute. For example, suppose that X is the vector of predictors/features, $X = (x_1, x_2, \ldots, x_p)'$. For qualitative predictors, the splitting rule is based on the split value s, and assigns observations for which a single predictor $\{x_i > s\}$ or $\{x_i \leq s\}$ to the left or right child node respectively.[5] Now we extend the splitting rule into the multivariate case in which $\{h(X) > s\}$ is assigned to the left and $\{h(X) \leq s\}$ to the right child node.

Most of previous research on multivariate splits consider that $h(X)$ is (oblique) linear. Still the problem of finding an optimal linear split is much more difficult than that of finding a split with a single variable, since there is a much larger space of splits to be searched. In fact, finding optimal linear splits is known to be intractable for some tasks, so heuristic methods are required for finding good, albeit suboptimal, linear splits (Murthy 1998).[6] There are a number of methods available for finding an optimal linear combinations including linear discriminant analysis, hill climbing search, linear programming, and so on.

17.5.2 Cost Considerations

In real world application, the costs of misclassification vary from class to class, and the costs of collecting/measuring features are different across features. An easy way of incorporating the asymmetric misclassification costs is to use the prior probabilities or cost matrices (Breiman et al. 1984). That is, simply weight the error rate with the weights given by the cost of each misclassification. Alternatively, researchers suggest including a cost term into the feature evaluation criterion in order to incorporate attribute measurement costs.

17.5.3 Finding an Optimal Tree

The intrinsic difficulty in finding the "optimal" tree is that there are so many possible trees. The decision tree algorithms discussed in this chapter use a greedy approach. They grow a tree by sequentially creating nodes using splitting rules based on maximizing some fitting criterion, and then prune it

---

[5] Multivariate split should not be confused with higher-order splits for a single variable (e.g., for income, <\$30,000, \$30,000 to \$100,000, >\$100,000). Multivariate split is based on the splitting rule using more than two variables (e.g., sex = female and income >\$30,000).

[6] The problem of finding an optimal linear split should not be confused with the problem of finding optimal linear combinations of weights in discriminant analysis.

back to avoid over-fitting. This generates a sequence of trees each of which is an extension of the previous tree. Several authors pointed out the inadequacy of greedy algorithms since it may lead to sub-optimal solutions.

Several approaches have been proposed to improve upon the greedy algorithm. For example, researchers have incorporated a feature of partial or exhaustive look-ahead to improve the greedy tree induction (Chou 1991; Buntine 1992). However, they did not provide the convincing evidence that the look-ahead would outperform the greedy tree induction.

17.6 Application to a Direct Mail Offer

Decision trees have widely used among database marketers. For illustration, we summarize an application by Haughton and Oulabi (1997). Their goal is to identify prospects who are less likely to respond to a direct mail package in order to suppress their names from future mailings. The data consist of 316,068 customers: 3,319 respondents and 312,749 non-respondents. Independent variables included in the application are age, gender, total number of mailings, number of mailings in the last 6 months, number of consecutive mailings, and so on. For comparison, two types of decision trees (CHAID and CART) are applied to the same data.

Figure 17.3 represents the estimated CART tree and Fig. 17.4 represents the CHAID tree built on the same data. In the trees, GEO1 (% Spanish origin), GEO2 (% Oriental) and SGEO (median household income) denote three US census geodemographic variables. The variables MAIL6MNTHS (number of mailing in the last 6 months), MAILTOT (total number of mailings), and CONS MAIL (number of consecutive mailings) are related to mailing history. The variable SUMLIST is the number of lists a customer appears on. AGE IND is 1 if the actual age is on the file, 2 if the age was inferred, and 3 if the age is missing.

The trees are not identical by any means but there are similarities. In both trees, AGE is a strong predictor of response. They both attempt to split the less responsive age groups with a combination of geodemographic and mailing history variables. Both trees suggest interactions between AGE and the geodemographic and mailing history variables, and the CHAID tree implies a possible interaction between AGE and GENDER. However, the fact that the trees are different on several of the specifics shows that the specific algorithm makes a difference in the final tree.

Table 17.2 shows the (weighted) response rates per decile of the validation file, once the customers have been ordered from the most responsive to the least responsive. The gains tables constructed from the CART model and the CHAID model are remarkably similar. The response rate for the top decile is 1.77% (higher than 1.08% overall response rate) for both models. Coupled with the observation above that the trees themselves are different

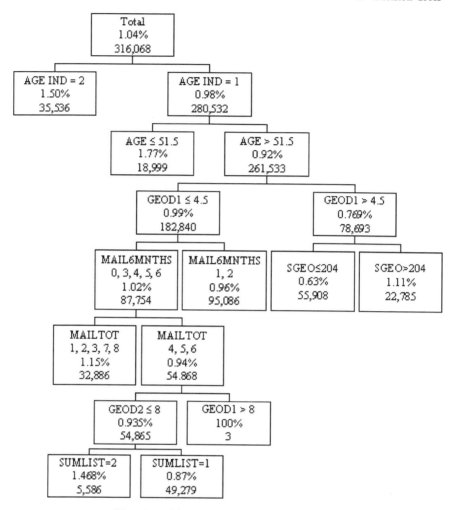

Fig. 17.3 CART tree for direct mailing drop.

on several specifics, perhaps these results illustrate that there may not be a single "optimal" tree, that several trees can produce more or less the same results. These trees will typically find similar most-important variables (e.g., age and mailing history) but may not split them the same way and may find different "moderate-importance" variables.

17.7 Strengths and Weaknesses of Decision Trees

Decision trees have been used successfully in many real-world problems. Their effectiveness has been compared widely to other data analytic techniques such

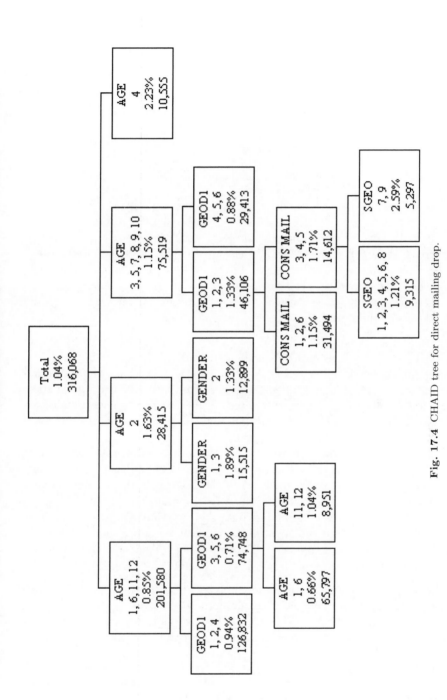

Fig. 17.4 CHAID tree for direct mailing drop.

Table 17.2 Gains table for direct mailing drop[a]

Decile	CART	CHAID
1	1.77	1.77
2	1.33	1.33
3	1.24	1.22
4	1.11	1.03
5	1.02	1.02
6	0.97	1.02
7	0.97	1.02
8	0.90	0.93
9	0.79	0.78
10	0.76	0.78

[a] Entries are the percentage of customers in
each decile that responded.

as neural networks, discriminant analysis, stepwise logistic regression and machine learning (Brown et al. 1993; see Murthy (1998) for more references). These research studies indicated that there were no dominant techniques in terms of predictive accuracy.[7]

Several advantages of decision trees have been pointed out (Berry and Linoff 1997; Murthy 1998).

1. Decision trees generate rules that can be easily expressed visually and in plain English. They are easy to understand. This is very important in obtaining senior management "buy-in," and in situations where discrimination based on age, gender, or race, is regulated and the role of these variables in targeting customers needs to be transparent. Because of decision trees are so transparent and simple, they became one of the most-loved data mining tools among managers.
2. Decision trees do not require a lot of assumptions on models and/or data. They are invariant to monotone transformation of predictor variables and robust to outliers of predictors. And they can easily handle interactions among independent variables. They are non-parametric in nature and can be applied to a wide range of data distributions. Moreover, they can handle multi-modal data in similar fashion to uni-modal data.
3. They are easy to implement. Extensive background in statistics is not required to build trees.

However, care should be taken in applying decision trees. Decision trees are essentially developed as an exploratory data mining tool. Still a lot of technical components associated with decision trees are heuristic. Researchers in decision trees often experiment several variations of the previous

---

[7] Researchers who have recently developed new techniques (e.g., support vector machines, bagging and boosting, and radial-basis function networks) often compared their approaches to traditional methods such as decision trees, and showed advantages of their methods in predictive performance. However, more objective comparisons in various situations are still required to conclude which one is better.

approach until they find a heuristic that works. Decision trees might be considered a starting point of the modeling process. A more formal statistical model would follow. In addition, there is a loss of information with decision trees in that people are grouped as homogeneous when they are not (e.g., all people with income >$50,000 might be grouped together) whereas in fact there is a linear relationship between income and the dependent variable.

Chapter 18
Artificial Neural Networks

Abstract Neural network models are intriguing because they are based on the intuitive notion of mimicking the structure of neurons that constitute the human brain. More importantly to database marketers, neural networks can provide great flexibility in handling non-linearities and variable-interactions that can be important in predictive modeling applications. We describe the neural net model, how it is estimated, and more advanced forms of neural networks.

18.1 Introduction

Artificial neural networks (ANN) are one of the most powerful tools in data mining. Based on a model analogous to the human brain, ANNs "learn" and generalize from external inputs. When exposed to "training observations", neural networks discover patterns and relationships. Their approach is fundamentally different from the way that traditional digital computers solve problems. Taking a top-down approach, computers solve problems as commanded by a series of instructions supplied by humans. In contrast, ANNs take a bottom-up approach, learning from examples and searching for patterns to infer important relationships.

18.1.1 Historical Remarks

Artificial neural networks have a long history. The basic idea dates to McCulloch and Pitts (1943) who developed a model to explain how biological neurons work. McCulloch was a neuroscientist and Pitts was a mathematician. Combining studies in neurophysiology and mathematical logic, they attempted to explain how the human brain works and described the logical calculus of neural networks (Berry and Linoff 1997; Haykin 1999).

Considered the founders of neural networks and artificial intelligence, Mc-Culloch and Pitts demonstrated that a network with a sufficient number of neurons and synaptic connections could compute any computable function. Hence, everything that can be done with a computer can be done with a neural network. Their model provided a new approach to solving various decision-making problems even though their original goal was to study how human brains worked.

There were not many applications of neural networks by the 1980s, partly because of limited computing power and a theoretical deficiency of the original neural network model noted by Minsky and Papert (1969). The recent growth in applying neural networks is generally agreed to be due to the paper by Hopfield (1982) and the book edited by Rumelhart and McClelland (1986). Using ideas from statistical physics, Hopfield overcame the theoretical weaknesses of McCulloch and Pitt's model. In addition, the well-known book, *Parallel Distributed Processing*, edited by Rumelhart and McClelland popularized the back-propagation algorithm that made neural networks practical.

18.1.2 ANN Applications in Database Marketing

The area of artificial neural networks is multidisciplinary. Researchers from neurophysiology, statistics, mathematics, computer science and engineering have contributed to the development of its concept and methodology. Accordingly, neural networks find applications in various fields including pattern recognition, signal processing and control, speech recognition, fraud detection, demand forecasting, and so on. By the 1990s, there were more than one hundred applications to business problems alone (Sharda 1994; Wong et al. 1995)

Since artificial neural networks comprise a class of general-purpose tools, there are many published applications to marketing. ANNs were compared to traditional econometric models in forecasting aggregate market demand (e.g., Hruschka 1993; Gruca et al. 1999). ANNs were also applied to market segmentation (Fish et al. 1995; Balakrishnan et al. 1996; Hruschka and Natter 1999), target mailing (Zahavi and Levin 1997) and other marketing problems (Yao et al. 1998; Knott et al. 2002; Kim et al. 2005).

ANNs can be applied to classification, prediction and clustering tasks that are all about what database marketing modelers do. For example, Balakrishnan et al. (1996) applied neural nets to market segmentation. The data employed in their study represent the brand switching probabilities on 18 different coffee brands for each of 207 households. They employed the neural net to cluster these 207 households represented by a vector of switching probabilities for 18 brands of coffee. Similarly, Hruschka and Natter (1999) employed neural networks to cluster 831 housewives. Each housewife was distinguished in her usage of household cleaner brands, demographic characteristics (age, household size, number of children, housewife's education, etc.) and her attitude variables (e.g., cleaning the household is cumbersome).

ANNs have also been applied to find target customers. Zahavi and Levin (1997) explored the feasibility of using neural networks as a means for targeting audiences for promotion through the mail, from a house list. Knott et al. (2002) applied neural nets to predict which product a customer was most likely to buy next, given the set of products the customer already owned. They applied the approach to a retail bank trying to identify customers who would be receptive to a certain type of loan. They found in a field test that the approach generated more profits than the heuristic approach the company was currently using. On the other hand, Kim et al. (2005) proposed an approach to employ ANNs guided by genetic algorithms for targeting households. They applied their procedure to a solicitation of 9,822 European households to buy insurance for recreational vehicles. Their model performed better than traditional logistic regression (with a principal component analysis) in targeting households interested in purchasing the insurance policy.

18.1.3 Strengths and Weaknesses

There are several driving forces contributing to the wide applications of ANNs for the last 2 decades. The broad availability of high-speed computing allows a sophisticated model like ANN to be handled within a reasonable amount of time. In addition, practitioners without strong statistical knowledge can implement ANNs due to the availability of off-the-shelf neural nets software.[1] More importantly, neural nets are no longer treated as black boxes. Statisticians have shown that ANNs are highly nonlinear regression models and a number of traditional statistical models such as linear and logistic regression are special cases of ANNs (White 1989, 1992). As a result, practitioners can be comfortable in employing ANNs because we know they are closely related to traditional statistical models.

Some commercial software vendors often mislead users by exaggerating the automatic features of their products. However, like the application of formal statistical techniques, successful applications of ANNs require deep understanding of neural net theory and their application domains. The user's subjective judgments will get involved in determining the network architecture and training parameters. Special care should be taken to check the

---

[1] Various neural network routines (e.g., multilayer perceptron and radial basis function) are available in SAS Enterprise Miner. Neural Connection from SPSS also delivers all the tools of neural network modeling for prediction, classification and time-series analysis. Advanced Software Applications (ASA) provides software called "ModelMax" particularly adapted to database marketing prediction applications.

performance of neural nets in the validation sample since ANN tends to overfit the training samples (see Chapter 11).

Several researchers compared ANNs with established statistical techniques such as clustering, logistic regression, discriminant analysis, time-series methods, decision trees etc. and found ANNs to be superior. For example, Fish et al. (1995) compared neural nets with discriminant analysis and logistic regression for industrial market segmentation. Neural nets were found to achieve higher hit ratios on the holdout sample than the other statistical techniques. Hruschka and Natter (1999) compared the clustering performance of ANNs to the K-means clustering technique and found that ANNs were better.[2] Time series forecasts produced by neural nets were compared with forecasts from six statistical time series methods (Hill et al. 1996). Across monthly and quarterly time series, the neural nets did significantly better than traditional time series methods. ANNs were particularly effective for discontinuous time series data.

On the other hand, other researchers have not been able to show the superiority of ANNs over traditional statistical techniques. For example, Zahavi and Levin (1997) compared neural nets with logistic regression for targeting customers for promotional mailing offers. Their results showed that the fit achieved for both methods was approximately the same but the interpretation was easier for logistic regression. Brown et al. (1993) compared back-propagation neural networks with decision trees on three problems that are known to be multi-modal. Their results suggested that there was not much difference between both methods. Comparing ANN (multilayer perceptrons) with decision trees (CART), Atlas et al. (1990) also found that there was not much difference in accuracy. Balakrishnan et al. (1996) compared neural nets with K-means algorithm and found that there was not much difference between two methods. However, a combination of the two methodologies, wherein the results of the neural nets are input as seeds to the K-means, provided more insightful segmentation schemes. More recently, Linder et al. (2004) compared neural nets with decision trees and logistic regression in simulated direct marketing data. ANNs outperformed the other two methods when the sample size was small, but decision trees and logistic regression yielded better results when sample size was large – with logistic regression being generally superior to decision trees. These results are rather surprising, because in other research simple models tend to outperform more complex models with small number of training examples or highly noisy data (Hastie et al. 2001).

Summarizing, we conclude that the relative performance of ANNs to traditional statistical methods depends on the types of data and applications. The main strength of ANNs lies in their ability to model highly nonlinear relationships and interactions with few a priori assumptions specified. Hence,

---

[2] Their neural net model is not the self-organizing maps described in Clustering chapter. They constructed a feed-forward artificial neural network specially designed in solving the problem of cluster-based market segmentation.

ANNs have been shown to outperform traditional statistical techniques when there exist highly nonlinear relationships and/or when there are significant interactions among independent variables (Rumelhart and McClelland 1986; Hill et al. 1996). If the true relationship is linear (or logistic), the linear (or logistic) regression will work better than an unnecessarily complex neural network because its linearity (or logistic) assumption functions like additional prior information. On the other hand, when the true relationship is complex, ANNs may outperform linear (or logistic) regression because the wrong assumption made in linear (logistic) regression will bias its result. More extensive research is required to find the areas of marketing problems in which ANNs can have unique advantages. From a practical standpoint, neural nets have certainly proven that belong in the "consideration set" of database marketers, especially under the conditions mentioned above. Our recommendation is the same as with the potential application of any statistical technique – apply the neural net and the incumbent method to the same data, and see which does better on the holdout data.

18.2 Models of Neurons

In this section we present a general model of an artificial neural network. In Sect. 18.3, we will focus on the most commonly used specific form, the multilayer perceptron. In Sect. 18.4, we describe another specific form, the radial-basis function network, which is currently less popular than the multilayer perceptron but has much potential.

Artificial neural networks are composed of basic units designed to mimic the behavior of biological neurons. ANN's are analogous to an organism's nervous system: stimuli or "inputs," if they are strong enough, cause neurons to fire off, in turn causing the organism to respond. In statistical terms, the inputs are the independent variables and response is the output or dependent variable. Neural nets can handle both categorical and continuous data, both for independent and dependent variables.[3] Output variables can involve just one response, or more than one (e.g., whether the customer will respond to a catalog, and if so, how much will the customer spend). As shown in Fig. 18.1, a neuron is an information-processing unit that translates input signals into

---

[3] Categorical data can be handled in two ways. The first is to treat each categorical feature as discrete, ordered value. For example, we assign 0.0 for brand A, 0.5 for brand B, and 1.0 for brand C for the brand choice variable with three brands. This method is somewhat problematic since the neural net will assume that the codes are ordered (i.e., brand A and C is far apart). The second way of handling categorical features, which is more popular, is to represent the categories by a set of dummy variables. For example, we create brand A, brand B and brand C dummies for the three-brand choice variable. Each brand dummy will take the value of 1.0 if the brand is chosen, and 0.0 otherwise. And for identification, one of the dummy variables is dropped before estimation.

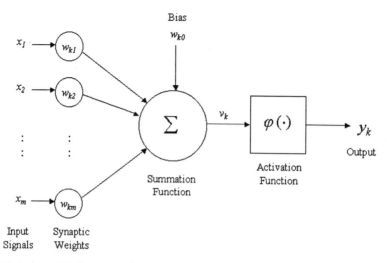

Fig. 18.1 A model of a neuron (adapted from Haykin, Simon, Neural Networks: A Comprehensive Foundation, 2nd Edition, (c) 1999, pg. 11. Reprinted by permission of Pearson Education, Inc., Upper Saddle River, NJ.).

outputs. There are three basic elements of any neural network model: synaptic weights, the summation function and the activation function.

Input x_j is connected to neuron k by a synaptic weight w_{kj}. Assigning different weights on each input implies that the importance or the strength of each input is different in producing an output. Input values with their weights are combined by a summation or combination function $\sum$. The most popular function is the linear combination function that can be written as

$$v_k = \sum_{j=0}^{m} w_{kj} x_j = w_{k0} x_0 + u_k \qquad (18.1)$$

where x_0 is set to be one. That is, the linear combination function is the weighted sum of all input values, where each weight is given by its synaptic weight. Note also that the above linear combination function contains a term $x_0 = 1$ with its associated weight of w_{k0}. The term w_{k0} plays a role of applying an affine transformation to the value of u_k (Haykin 1999). It has the effect of increasing or decreasing the net input of the activation function (u_k), depending on whether w_{k0} is positive or negative, respectively. In other words, its role is similar to that of the intercept term in linear regression.

Another important element in the neuronal model is the activation function that transforms the value from the combination function into the output. That is, $y_k = \varphi(v_k)$ where y_k is the output of the neuron k and $\varphi(\cdot)$ is the activation function. Its major role is to limit the amplitude of the output of a neuron. Typically, the range of the normalized amplitude for the output of a neuron is written as the closed unit interval [0, 1] or [-1, 1]. There are several types of activation functions: the linear, threshold, piecewise-linear, logistic

(a) Threshold Function

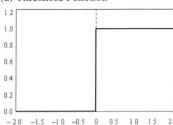

(d) Linear Function

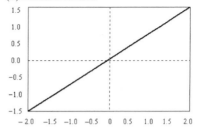

(b) Piecewise-linear Function

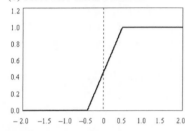

(e) Hyperbolic Tangent Function

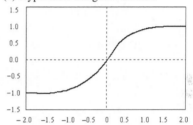

(c) Logistic Function

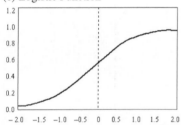

Fig. 18.2 Five types of activation functions.

and hyperbolic tangent (Berry and Linoff 1997; Haykin 1999). Figure 18.2 shows the shapes of these five activation functions.

For the threshold activation function, the output unit takes on the value of one if the value of v_k is nonnegative, and zero otherwise (see Fig. 18.2(a)). That is,

$$\varphi(v_k) = \begin{cases} 1 & if \ v_k \geq 0 \\ 0 & if \ v_k < 0 \end{cases} \tag{18.2}$$

The model by McCulloch and Pitts (1943) employed this threshold function. And the threshold function is commonly called as a Heaviside function (Haykin 1999).

Figure 18.2(**b**) shows the shape of the piecewise linear function that can algebraically be written as

$$\varphi(v_k) = \begin{cases} 1 & \text{if } v_k \geq 0.5 \\ v_k & \text{if } -0.5 < v_k < 0.5 \\ 0 & \text{if } v_k \leq -0.5 \end{cases} \qquad (18.3)$$

The piecewise linear function approximates the nonlinear logistic function in a linear form. The choice of the lower and the upper limit for the linear region (e.g., -0.5 and 0.5 in Fig. 18.2(**b**)) is up to the user. The piecewise linear function generalizes both the threshold and linear activation functions. It becomes the threshold function if we make the upper limit to be very close to the lower limit so that the linear region vanishes. Alternatively, if we do not specify the upper and lower saturation ranges, it will become the linear function shown in Fig. 18.2(**d**).

The S-shaped logistic function is the most frequently used activation function in ANNs. Its functional form shown in Fig. 18.2(**c**) is defined as

$$\varphi(v_k) = \frac{1}{1 + \exp(-\alpha v_k)} \qquad (18.4)$$

where α is the slope parameter of the logistic function. The logistic function exhibits linear behavior when the absolute value of v_k is small. However, as it gets larger, the logistic function gradually approaches either 0 or 1. This property of gradual saturation is a reasonable one in modeling various social (and natural) phenomena. Moreover, different from the piecewise linear, the logistic has an attractive mathematical property of differentiability.

Finally, the hyperbolic tangent function is different from the logistic function in that its range of the activation function is from -1 to 1 instead of 0 to 1. Shown in Fig. 18.2(**e**), the hyperbolic tangent is S-shaped similar to the logistic function, but the lower saturation is negative one rather than zero. The hyperbolic tangent function is defined as

$$\varphi(v_k) = a \tanh(bv_k) \qquad (18.5)$$

where a and b are the parameters controlling the shape of the hyperbolic tangent. With suitable values for a and b (e.g., $a = 1.7159$ and $b = 2/3$), the activation function becomes anti-symmetric, that is $\varphi(-v_k) = -\varphi(v_k)$. The logistic function does not have this property. ANNs can learn faster when the activation function is anti-symmetric (LeGun et al. 1991).

18.3 Multilayer Perceptrons

In this section we study the most commonly used class of artificial neural networks, multilayer feed-forward networks. This network is especially useful

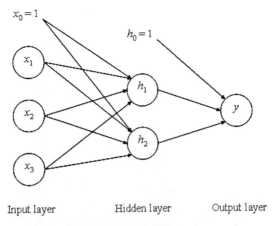

Fig. 18.3 Multilayer feed-forward network.

for prediction and classification tasks among others. We start our discussion with the "topology" or "architecture" of the multilayer perceptron, followed by its method of training, and the back-propagation algorithm. We then discuss more advanced issues in multilayer perceptrons: how to determine the number of neurons in the hidden layer, and the optimal value for learning rate and momentum parameters. This section also describes issues on transformation of input values and model validation.

18.3.1 Network Architecture

There are a number of different ways to classify network architectures. A primary differentiator is single-layer networks versus multilayer networks. Single-layer networks only consist of an input layer and an output layer, whereas multilayer networks have one or more hidden layers, as shown in Fig. 18.3. The networks can also be classified by the presence of at least one feedback loop. The networks without any feedback loop are called feed-forward networks where there is only one-way flow from input units to output units. Otherwise, they are called recurrent networks.

Figure 18.4 show an example of a recurrent network in which there are two inputs, two hidden neurons and an output. One feedback connection originates from the output and two feedbacks come out of hidden neurons. The presence of feedback loops can explain different learning capability of the network. For example, the feedback loops shown in Fig. 18.4 have the unit-delay term z^{-1} which incorporates dynamic learning behavior. The recurrent networks have typically been applied to (dynamic) time-series models such as adaptive equalization of communication channels, speech processing, plant control, and automobile engine diagnostics (Haykin 1999). Recurrent

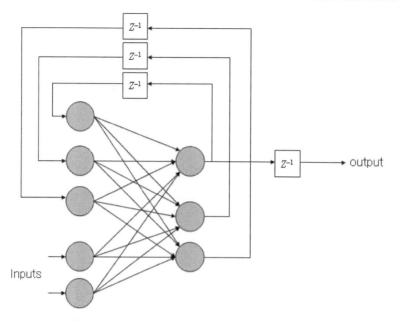

Fig. 18.4 Recurrent networks (From Haykin 1999).

networks have not been applied to database marketing problems, possibly because fewer dynamic models have been employed in database marketing applications. However, there are potential applications in areas such as multi-campaign management (see Chapter 28).

Returning now to the more commonly applied feed-forward multilayer neural network, also called the multilayer perceptron, Fig. 18.3 shows a typical structure. It consists of an input layer, one or more hidden layers, and an output layer. The multilayer perceptron in Fig. 18.3 has three input values (or independent variables in traditional regression models), one hidden layer, and one output value (or dependent variable). The hidden layer has two neurons. Hence, the multilayer perceptron in Fig. 18.3 is referred to as a 3-2-1 network. Finally, we say that the network is fully connected in that every node in each layer of the network is connected to every other node in the next or forward layer.

Positioned between the input and output layers, hidden layers translate the independent variables into a prediction of the dependent variables. Hidden layers are required for the ANN to model complicated interactions among input variables and other nonlinear relationships (Haykin 1999). As described above, a single-layer perceptron does not have hidden layers, but directly connects the input to the output layer.

Theoretically, a network can have any number of hidden layers. A network with a large number of hidden layers may be able to capture highly complicated relationships between inputs and outputs. However, a network with one hidden layer is frequently used for at least two reasons. First, a network with a large number of hidden layers may over fit the data and just capture random noise in the data. We want to make our model as simple as possible to avoid the problem of overfitting. More importantly, researchers employ the network with one hidden layer without hesitation because of the "universal approximation theorem". The theorem roughly states that a single hidden layer is sufficient for a multilayer perceptron to approximate any continuous relationship between inputs and outputs (Barron 1993; Haykin 1999).[4]

We now write the neural network in algebraic form for the discussion of back-propagation algorithm in the next section. To avoid notational complexity, we limit our discussion to the multilayer perceptron example in Fig. 18.3. Three input signals come into the input layer pass forward through the network, and produce an output signal at the end. Let a training sample of size N be denoted by $(\mathbf{x}_1, \mathbf{x}_2, \mathbf{x}_3, \mathbf{d})$. Three input vector $\mathbf{x}_1, \mathbf{x}_2$, and $\mathbf{x}_3$ represent the input layer and the output (response) vector $\mathbf{d}$ represents the output layer.

Neurons in the hidden layer perform two functions: combination and activation. Each neuron in the hidden layers receives the input values (x_1, x_2, x_3) from the input layer, applies the weighted summation and activation functions, and sends the resulting values (h_1, h_2) to the output layer. More specifically, neuron 1 in the hidden layer receives the input values (x_1, x_2, x_3) from the input layer and their associated weights are (w_{11}, w_{12}, w_{13}) respectively. Similarly, neuron 2 in the hidden layer receives the input values (x_1, x_2, x_3) from the input layer and their associated weights are (w_{21}, w_{22}, w_{23}) respectively. The combination function calculates the weighted sum of the input values. The resulting intermediate value $v_j (j = 1, 2)$ is written as

$$v_j = \sum_{i=0}^{3} w_{ji} x_i \tag{18.6}$$

where j labels the hidden layer neuron, $x_0 = 1$ and w_{j0} is intercept term. Applying the activation function, we have the output value for neuron j equal to $h_j = \varphi(v_j)$. For example, if a logistic activation function is applied, $h_j = 1/[1 + \exp(w_{j0} + w_{j1}x_1 + w_{j2}x_2 + w_{j3}x_3)]$. The resulting output values h_1 and h_2 become the input values to the output layer. Given a logistic activation function, the output value $y = \varphi(v_3) = 1/[1 + \exp(w_{30}h_0 + w_{31}h_1 + w_{32}h_2)]$ where $h_0 = 1, w_{30}$ is for intercept term, and v_3 represents the combination function relating the hidden layer to the output layer.

An interpretation of the above algebra is that we have two neurons; each has a probability h_j of firing off. Whether a given neuron fires off depends on the inputs or stimuli (x's) and how influential they are (w's). If enough neurons fire off, we get a response, i.e., the output, the dependent variable changes. This occurs through the function φ, which in turn depends

---

[4] However, the theorem does not say that the multilayer perceptron with a single hidden layer is the best. Interestingly, more hidden layers is often easier to implement and reduces learning time.

on whether the hidden layer neurons fire off (h's) and if they do, how influential they are in determining the response (represented by the w's).

18.3.2 Back-Propagation Algorithm

Training the network involves the process of finding the optimal weights (w_{ji}, where j indexes a node (either a hidden neuron or an output) and i the inputs that go into that node) to attach to the input values from the preceding layer. The process of neural net training is similar to the process of estimating parameters in nonlinear regression. The network searches for the optimal weights such that the predicted output value from the output layer is as close to the corresponding actual output value as possible.

The most well-known method of finding optimal weights for the multilayer perceptron is the back-propagation algorithm, which consists of two passes. We start with the calibration sample, also called the "training set." In the forward pass, for each observation in the training set, the values of the input variables in the input layer pass forward through the network, through the hidden layers, and produce predicted output values at the end. All the weights are fixed during the forward pass. That is, at each iteration, the predicted output values are calculated given the input values and the synaptic weights determined by the previous iteration. In the backward pass, the errors between the predicted output value and the corresponding actual output value are calculated. The errors are flowed backward through the network and the weights are adjusted to have smaller errors in the next iteration.

We more formally describe the back-propagation algorithm applied to the multilayer perceptron in Fig. 18.3. The error signal at the output for the nth training observation at iteration t, $e_n(t)(n = 1, \ldots, N)$ is defined by $e_n(t) = d_n(t) - y_n$ where y_n is the derived output value from the neural network for the nth training observation and $d_n(t)$ is the corresponding actual output (or response) value. We now define the total error at iteration t as

$$E(t) = \frac{1}{2} \sum_{n=1}^{N} e_n(t)^2 = \frac{1}{2} \sum_{n=1}^{N} [d_n(t) - y_n]^2 \qquad (18.7)$$

where N is the total number of training example. The scaling factor $1/2$ in Equation 18.7 is included to simplify matters in subsequent analysis (Haykin 1999). That is, differentiating Equation 18.7 with respect to $\mathbf{w}$, we have $\partial E(t)/\partial \mathbf{w} = \sum e_n(t)[\partial e_n(t)/\partial \mathbf{w}]$. Note also that the total error E is a function of all the free parameters (i.e., synaptic weights) of the network. For a given training set, E represents the cost function as a measure of learning performance. The objective of the learning process is to adjust the free parameters of the network to minimize E. That is, the synaptic weights are adjusted to make the actual response of the network move closer to the desired response in terms of squared error.

Rumelhart et al. (1986) have employed the generalized delta rule in adjusting weights that is similar to methods of nonlinear optimization employed in statistics. Hence, the goal of the algorithm is to find the optimal weights minimizing the total error E for a given training set. The optimal weights are found in an iterative way since the objective function is highly nonlinear. The generalized delta rule states the following adjustments for the synaptic weights at correction. The correction $\Delta w_{ji}(t)$ to the weight $w_{ji}(t)$ at iteration t is given by

$$\Delta w_{ji}(t) = \alpha \Delta w_{ji}(t-1) - \eta \frac{\partial E(t)}{\partial w_{ji}(t)} \qquad (18.8)$$

where α represents the momentum parameter, η is the learning-rate parameter, and $\partial E(t)/\partial w_{ji}(t)$ is the partial derivative of the total error (Equation 18.7) with respect to the weight $w_{ji}(t)$. The generalized delta rule becomes the delta rule when the momentum parameter α is set to zero.

In Equation 18.8, the partial derivative $\partial E(t)/\partial w_{ji}(t) = -\sum_{n=1}^{N} e_n(t)$ $[\partial y_n/\ \partial w_{ji}(t)]$ represents a sensitivity factor that determines the direction of search in weight space for the synaptic weight $w_{ji}(t)$. The minus sign (before η) ensures that the newly calculated weight will be in the opposite direction from which the partial derivative increases. That is, if the partial derivative is positive, that means that increasing the weight increases error. Hence we will want to change the weight in the negative direction, and the negative sign ensures this. The learning-rate parameter η controls the magnitude of the weight changes from iteration t to iteration $t+1$. A small value of η will lead to a large number of iterations, while too large a value of η will result in a network missing actual minima. The role of the momentum parameter α is to increase the rate of learning but avoid the possible problem of instability (Haykin 1999). Often restricted to $[0, 1)$ in practice, the momentum parameter measures how much the previous weight change influences the current weight change. Hence, a large value for α means the algorithm will tend to maintain the same direction of change as before, i.e., estimation with high momentum means the algorithm will respond slowly to training sample that suggest the reverse of weight change (Berry and Linoff 1997). In other words, assigning a large value for the momentum parameter will have a stabilizing effect in the direction in which weights are change, avoiding oscillations in the estimated parameter.

18.3.3 Application to Credit Scoring

In this section, we apply a multilayer feed-forward network to the credit scoring model. Kindly provided by Professor Fahrmeir, Institute of Statistics, University of Munich, Germany, the data set consists of credit behavior for 1,000 customers of a German bank. The data will be randomly divided into two equally sized groups, 500 customers for the estimation sample and 500

Table 18.1 Estimation results for multilayer perceptron (w_{ji}'s)

	First hidden neuron (w_{1i})	Second hidden neuron (w_{2i})	Output (DEFAULT) (w_{3i})
bias	5.65	9.23	
SEX	0.44	−12.78	
MARRIAGE	0.06	−18.39	
BAD	0.39	13.43	
GOOD	−12.48	0.96	
DURATION	−4.03	−2.68	
PAY	−8.02	−19.27	
PRIVATE	0.13	−15.99	
CREDIT	5.28	−16.37	
Bias-h			0.33
h_1			−0.99
h_2			−1.27

customers for the validation sample. The dependent variable (DEFAULT) measures creditworthiness of each customer that is coded 1 if s/he is not creditworthy and 0 if s/he is creditworthy. There are 8 independent variables. Two variables, SEX (female/male) and MARRIAGE (marital status), are customers' demographic characteristics. The rest of the variables represent previous customer behavior and credit characteristics: BAD (bad account), GOOD (good account), DURATION (duration of credit in months), PAY (payment of previous credits), PRIVATE (professional/private use) and CREDIT (line of credit). For more detailed description on variables, see Kim and Shin (1998).

The multilayer perceptron with a hidden layer is applied. The hidden layer has two neurons. In result, our multilayer perceptron is an 8-2-1 network. Using SAS Enterprise Miner, the weights are estimated by the back-propagation algorithm. The estimation results are summarized in Table 18.1.

Neuron 1 in the hidden layer receives 8 input values (plus a bias or an intercept term) from the input layer, and their associated weights are estimated to be the values in the second column in Table 18.1. Similarly, neuron 2 in the hidden layer receives the same input values from the input layer, and the corresponding weights are estimated to be the values in the third column in Table 18.1. Applying the combination and the (logistic) activation function into the input values with the associated weights, we have the output values of neuron 1 (h_1) and 2 (h_2). The resulting output values, h_1 and h_2, become the input values to the output layer. That is, an output neuron (DEFAULT) in the output layer receives two input values (plus an intercept term) in the hidden layer, and the corresponding weights are estimated to be the values in the fourth column in Table 18.1. As you can see, it is very difficult to interpret the weights directly. For example, the w's for few of the variables have opposite signs in the two neurons.

18.3.4 Optimal Number of Units in the Hidden Layer, Learning-Rate, and Momentum Parameters

ANNs are often criticized for their subjectivity in specifying network architecture and training parameters (Tam and Kiang 1992). Model selection has been the one of the most difficult problems in statistics. Similarly, selecting the best network architecture in ANN is not a trivial problem. The universal approximation theorem suggests that the multilayer perceptron with one hidden layer will perform satisfactorily. Still we need to determine the number of neurons in the hidden layer. Large numbers of hidden layers will be able to capture the sophisticated relationship between input and outputs. However, too many hidden layers will essentially memorize the training observations, leading to overfitting.

There are heuristic methods for determining the number of neurons in the hidden layer. In order to avoid over-fitting, they should not be more than twice the number of input variables in the input layer (Berry and Linoff 1997). Others use the square root of the number of input variables in the input layer as the number of neurons in the hidden layer (Kim et al. 2005).

The better way of finding the optimal number of units in the hidden layer is to find it empirically. We partition the data into the estimation and the validation samples. Then we train networks with different number of neurons in the hidden layer using the estimation sample and evaluate the trained networks in the validation sample. The network with the smallest SSE (or the highest hit-rate for the classification task, see Chapter 11) is chosen as the best network architecture that has the optimal number of units in the hidden layer.

We can also conduct a grid search to determine the optimal number of neurons in the hidden layer simultaneously with the optimal learning-rate and momentum parameters. For example, we may try out $\eta \in \{0.1, 0.4, 0.7, 0.9\}, \alpha \in \{0.0, 0.2, 0.6, 0.9\}$ and the number of neurons in the hidden layer $\in \{1, 2, 3, 4, 5\}$. Then you need to train $80 (= 4 \times 4 \times 5)$ different networks and compare their prediction performances.

18.3.5 Stopping Criteria

Similar to all nonlinear optimization problems, there are no clean-cut criteria for stopping the weight adjustments in the back-propagation algorithm. However, there are a couple of reasonable criteria. First, the objective function of the multilayer perceptron, Equation 18.7, will have a local or global minimum when the first-order partial derivatives $\partial E / \partial w_{ji}$ equal to zero for all i and j. Therefore, we can formulate a stopping rule with respect to the gradient vector of weights (Haykin 1999). We stop the iteration when the Euclidean norm of the gradient vector reaches a small gradient threshold specified by the user.

The limitations of the gradient method for the stopping rule are the length of running time with the requirement of computing the gradient vector. Alternatively, we can propose a stopping rule based on the rate of change in the objective function itself because it is stationary at the minimum (Haykin 1999). We stop the training iteration when the absolute rate of change in the objective function is sufficiently small.

Both these rules require subjectively determined thresholds, and undoubtedly the appropriate thresholds depend on the type of data being modeled. Researchers should try alternative values and settle on "default values" as they gain experience with their data.

18.3.6 Feature (Input Variable) Selection

Selecting relevant input variables is important in improving the performance of a neural network. The objective is to find the minimum subset of input variables that yield the highest accuracy. This problem, often called feature subset selection, is conceptually similar to the variable selection problem in a classical regression model (see Chapter 11). Interest in the feature selection problem is intensifying because the size of customer information file is increasing.

There are two types of approaches to finding an optimal feature subset in a neural network. The "filter" approach performs feature selection independently of the neural net learning algorithm. In contrast, the "wrapper" approach finds the optimal subset of features guided by the performance of the learning algorithm. The filter approach is computationally more efficient than the wrapper approach. However, many researchers have criticized the filtering model since it ignores the effect of the selected features on the performance of the neural network (Yang and Honavar 1998; Hsu et al. 2002). The wrapper model overcomes this problem of the filtering approach, but can be computationally expensive since each candidate feature subset must be evaluated in estimating the neural network.

Several algorithms have been proposed to speed up the computation in the wrapper approach. For example, Richeldi and Lanzi (1996) partitioned features into a number of groups (called factors) and employed a genetic algorithm to explore the feature space originated by the factors and determine the set of the most informative feature configurations. On the other hand, Setiono and Liu (1997) proposed a method that added a penalty term to the error function of the neural network and identified redundant network connections from those relevant ones by their small weights when the network training process was completed.

We briefly describe the wrapper approach proposed by Hsu et al. (2002). Their feature selection model, called the "artificial neural net input gain measurement approximation" (ANNIGMA), performed better than two benchmark wrapper models. They successfully applied their model to two real-world dataset, the one with 192 features and the other with 41 features. The ANNIGMA wrapper's method of finding an optimal feature subset is similar to that of a stepwise variable selection in a classical regression. It starts with a complete set of original features (or input variables) and removes features from candidate subsets during search. They presented three versions of their algorithm: (1) greedy backward elimination (BE), (2) backward elimination with backtracking (BEB), and (3) backward stepwise elimination (BSE). BE starts with estimating a neural net model of all features and obtains ANNIGMA scores of each feature measuring the relevance (or importance) of a feature to the performance of the neural net model. It repeatedly eliminates the next worst ANNIGMA ranked feature until the error rate of the neural net goes up. BEB allows for backtracking. That is, if the error rate goes up, the previous feature eliminated is restored and the next worst ranked feature is eliminated. The process is iterated until a performance-improving elimination is found for each size of feature subsets. Finally, BSE is designed to speed up feature selection for large databases. It eliminates a large number of seemingly irrelevant features in early cycles (i.e., employing BE) and adjusts the feature subset carefully in the subsequent cycles (i.e., employing BEB).

18.3.7 Assessing the Importance of the Input Variables

As we saw in Sect. 18.3.3, it is virtually impossible to interpret directly from the estimated w's how important each input variable is in its impact on the output variable. This is because the inputs influence several hidden neurons, and the signs can be in opposite directions. Even if the signs are the same, it is still difficult to compare one input variable to another based on the several estimated w's. For example, one variable may have a high w linking to one neuron, but a low value linking to another. Is this variable more important than one that has relatively moderate w's linking to each neuron?

There is no easy solution to this problem. A common approach to assessing variable importance is some form of sensitivity analysis (Berry and Linoff 1997). For example, to assess the importance of input variable X_1, one might fix the other variables at their means and then vary X_1 over its relevant range. One could graph the dependent variable or calculate a statistic to show how much the dependent variable changes. The problem with this approach is that nonlinearity of the neural net captures many interactions between the inputs, i.e., the impact of X_1 when the other variables are at their means may be very different than if the variables are at some different value.

Another approach is simply to graph the dependent variable as a function of the input, without doing any calculations from the neural net model. This can provide insight similar to a correlation, but as with sensitivity analysis, does not show the rich non-linearity and interactions that the neural net has derived. It also does not control, in the regression sense, for the other variables in the model.

Despite these difficulties, we recommend that the user examine at least some measure of relationship between the inputs and the output, whether it is calculated via sensitivity analysis or simply by graphing the independents against the dependent. This at least provides some idea as to the nature of the relationship that is in the data.

18.4 Radial-Basis Function Networks

The discipline of neural networks is broad, covering diverse classes of models. ANNs can be grouped into models for supervised learning (also called learning with a teacher) and for unsupervised learning (also called learning without a teacher). The most popular neural network models for the supervised learning tasks are the multilayer perceptron and a radial-basis function network while self-organizing map (SOM) may be the most well known neural net model for the unsupervised learning tasks. We cover the SOM in the Clustering chapter.

18.4.1 Background

In this section, we introduce one more neural net model for supervised learning called a radial-basis function (RBF) network that is recently attracting more attention (Poggio and Girosi 1990; Park and Sandberg 1991; Abdi 1994). After multilayer perceptrons, an RBF network is the most popular neural network model for supervised learning. Different from a multilayer perceptron, a radial-basis function network fundamentally views the design of a neural network as a curve-fitting approximation problem in multidimensional space. Its goal is to find the best multidimensional curve explaining the nonlinear relationship between inputs and outputs in the training data. A radial-basis function network can be said to have a more formal mathematical basis for the formulation of the network. As its name implies, a radial-basis function network adopts the theory on radial-basis functions in developing the foundation for the hidden layer. Originally introduced to solve the multivariate interpolation problem, radial-basis functions have become one of the main fields of study in numerical analysis (Light 1992).

A radial-basis function network has a similar architectural design as a multilayer perceptron. It consists of an input layer, a hidden layer and an output layer (see Fig. 18.3). The functions of the input layer are no different from those in a multilayer perceptron. However, two networks differ from each other in several important aspects (Haykin 1999). First, the activation function of each hidden unit in a radial-basis function network computes the Euclidean distance between the input vector and the center of that unit. In contrast, the activation function of each hidden unit in a multilayer perceptron computes the inner product of the input vector and the synaptic weight vector of that unit. Second, a radial-basis function network is allowed to have only one hidden layer while a multilayer perceptron can have one or more hidden layers. Finally, the hidden layer of a radial-basis function network is nonlinear while the output layer is only allowed to take the linear activation function. As explained later, the role of the hidden layer is quite different from the output layer in a radial-basis function network. However, the roles of the hidden and output layer in a multilayer perceptron are similar, and they are usually nonlinear.

Because of these differences, a radial-basis function network has the advantage of avoiding finding a set of parameters that only represents a local minimum. Applications of a multilayer perceptron often end up in a local minimum and their speed of convergence is sometimes problematic. In a radial-basis function network, the only parameters that are adjusted in the learning process are the linear mapping from the hidden layer to the output layer. Because of the linear activation function, the error surface of the radial-basis function network is quadratic, and hence has a single minimum.

18.4.2 A Curve-Fitting (Approximation) Problem

To fix ideas of radial-basis function network, let us consider a nonlinear regression problem where the value of the dependent variable for observation i ($i = 1, \ldots, N$) is d_i and the corresponding vector of the independent variables is $\mathbf{x}_i$. Then the general nonlinear relationship between the dependent variable and the vector of independent variables can be written as

$$d_i = f(\mathbf{x}_i) + \varepsilon_i \qquad (18.9)$$

where ε_i is the random error and $f(\mathbf{x}_i)$ is a smooth curve.

A radial-basis function network approximates the high-dimensional curve $f(\mathbf{x}_i)$ in the Equation 18.9 by $F(\mathbf{x})$.

$$F(\mathbf{x}) = \sum_{j=1}^{m} w_j \varphi_j(\mathbf{x}) \qquad (18.10)$$

where m is the number of neurons in the hidden layer and w_j represents the weight from the jth neuron of the hidden layer to the output. The number of neurons in the hidden layer or the number of basis function φ is generally less than the number of data points, $m < N$.

The mathematical justification of a nonlinear transformation followed by a linear transformation in the Equation 18.10 can be found in a number of studies (Cover 1965; Poggio and Girosi 1990). In general, a set of basis functions $\{\varphi_j(\mathbf{x}), i = 1, \ldots, m\}$ is assumed to be linearly independent, and each $\varphi_j(\mathbf{x})$ takes the form of a radial-basis function. That is,

$$\varphi_j(\mathbf{x}) = \varphi(\|\mathbf{x} - \mathbf{t}_j\|) \tag{18.11}$$

where $\|\cdot\|$ denotes an Euclidean norm and $\mathbf{t}_j$ is the center of the radial-basis function for neuron j. One of the most popular choices for the φ function is the Gaussian function.

$$\varphi_j(\mathbf{x}) = \exp\left[\frac{1}{2\sigma_j^2}\|\mathbf{x} - \mathbf{t}_j\|^2\right] \tag{18.12}$$

where σ_j^2 is the variance of the Gaussian distribution. The condition $\sigma_j^2 = \sigma^2$ for all j is often imposed for mathematical simplification. Different learning strategies can be adopted depending on how the centers of the radial-basis functions $(\mathbf{t}_j)$ are specified (Haykin 1999). The simplest approach is to choose the (fixed) locations of the centers randomly from the training dataset. A more sophisticated method is to utilize the k-means clustering algorithm which places the centers of the radial-basis functions in only those regions of the input space where significant data are present. Alternatively, the centers of the radial-basis functions (along with other parameters) can be treated as parameters to be estimated.

The role of the activation function of each hidden unit in a radial-basis function network $(\varphi_j(\mathbf{x}))$ is somewhat different from its role in a multilayer perceptron. The activation function in a radial-basis function network computes the distance from the input to each of the centers. Each cell of the hidden layer represents a center. On the other hand, the activation function of each hidden unit in a multilayer perceptron computes the inner product of the input vector and the synaptic weight vector of that unit.

Given the above specification, the estimation problem of the radial-basis function network is to determine a set of weights $\{w_j | j = 1, \ldots, m\}$ to minimize the following error function (Haykin 1999).

$$\mathrm{E} = \sum_{i=1}^{N} (d_i - F(\mathbf{x}_i))^2 + \lambda \|\mathbf{D}F(\mathbf{x})\|^2 \tag{18.13}$$

where $\mathbf{D}$ is a stabilizer and λ is the regularization parameter.

As seen in Equation 18.13, the error objective function for a radial-basis function network is different from that for a multilayer perceptron (e.g., backpropagation). The theory behind the derivation of Equation 18.13 is regularization theory by Tikhonov (1963). In order to solve an ill-posed hyper-surface reconstruction problem, he proposed to stabilize (or smooth) the solution by

Table 18.2 Estimation results for radial-basis function network

	First hidden neuron	Second hidden neuron
SEX	0.16	−1.44
MARRIAGE	−1.61	−0.64
BAD	0.80	1.58
GOOD	0.70	0.48
DURATION	−0.16	−0.30
PAY	0.11	−0.28
PRIVATE	0.23	0.88
CREDIT	0.78	−0.06

means of an auxiliary nonnegative functional that embeds prior information about the solution. That is, Equation 18.13, which is called the Tikhonov functional consists of two terms, the standard error term and the regularizing term. The standard error term or $\sum (d_i - F(\mathbf{x}_i))^2$ measures the error (or distance) between the actual response d_i and the estimated response $F(\mathbf{x}_i)$. The regularizing term or $\lambda ||\mathbf{D}F(\mathbf{x})||^2$ represents a model complexity-penalty function. The regularization parameter λ controls the balance between the importance of the training examples and the prior smoothness constraint. If λ is close to zero, the solution is mostly determined from training examples (i.e., less smoothing). As λ gets larger, training examples are more or less treated as unreliable. In addition, the stabilizer $\mathbf{D}$ represents prior information about the form of the solution.

18.4.3 Application Example

We apply a radial-basis function network to the same credit scoring data used in the example for the multilayer perceptron. We assume a hidden layer with two neurons and a Gaussian radial-basis function given by Equation 18.12. We also assume that $\sigma_j^2 = \sigma^2$. Using SAS Enterprise Miner, the center of the radial-basis function ($\mathbf{t}_j$) is determined and the results are summarized in Table 18.2.

The numbers in the second column of Table 18.2 are the centers of the Gaussian radial-basis function for the first hidden neuron. Similarly, the numbers in the third column are the centers of the Gaussian radial-basis function for the second hidden neuron. Similar to the results from multilayer perceptron, the training or estimation results are difficult to interpret.

We also applied the radial-basis function networks (along with multilayer perceptron and a logit model) to the validation sample of 500 customers. The hit ratio of the RBF networks is 79.2% (396/500) whereas the hit ratios of multilayer perceptron and a logit model are 79.6% (398/500) and 76.4% (= 382/500) respectively. We conclude that neural network models show slightly better prediction performances than a logit model. But there is no difference between the RBF networks and multilayer perceptron. There have been few researches that directly compared the RBF networks with multilayer perceptron. For example, Park et al. (2002) found that the RBF network is simpler to implement than multilayer perceptron, needs less computational memory, converges faster, provide slightly better predictions and global minimum convergence is achieved.

Chapter 19
Machine Learning

Abstract Traditionally there have been two paradigms of statistical analysis – classical and Bayesian. Machine learning is essentially a third paradigm, based on algorithms that rely heavily on the speed of modern computing to derive "decision rules" that predict customer behavior. We discuss several machine learning techniques, including covering algorithms, instance-based learning, genetic algorithms, Bayesian networks, support vector machines, and committee machine methods such as bagging and boosting.

19.1 Introduction

Machine learning encompasses a repertoire of data mining techniques that have mainly been developed in the field of computer science. Hence, its goal is no different from other data mining techniques: discover interesting patterns or information from data.

Historically, machine learning researchers have focused more on comprehensible patterns than on prediction *per se*. They have emphasized on understanding the structure of the data even though their techniques can be used for prediction and classification. They focused on explicitly representing knowledge so that decision makers know why the models work. In addition, researchers in machine learning have been more interested in the exploratory aspect of data analysis. Statistics has been more concerned with testing hypotheses whereas machine learning has been more concerned with formulating interesting hypotheses (Witten and Frank 2000). However, many techniques in machine learning have been significantly influenced by statistical concepts. Sometimes it is difficult to say whether a specific method is a machine learning technique or a statistical method.

Researchers in machine learning have developed a number of data analysis tools – they prefer the term "generalizations" – that can be used in prediction, classification, clustering, and uncovering associations. This chapter will focus on machine learning tools that are not covered in other chapters.

For example, constructing decision trees is one of the most important tools in machine learning, but it is extensively discussed in Chapter 17. Similarly, market basket analysis, a machine learning tool that discovers association rules, is covered in Chapter 13.

We first discuss three approaches to machine learning that may be unfamiliar to database marketing researchers: the 1-rule, rule-induction by covering algorithms, and instance-based learning. The 1-rule is a simple rule-induction algorithm that is often used as a baseline model for other machine learning algorithms. The 1-rule also provides insight for understanding other rule-induction algorithms. In the next section, we study two well-known covering algorithms for rule induction, PRISM and INDUCT. The PRISM algorithm constructs a set of "perfect" rules, assuming no "noise" in the data. The INDUCT algorithm overcomes this problem by introducing a probabilistic concept. In instance-based learning we describe the nearest-neighbor and k-nearest-neighbor methods, along with their extensions. We then discuss more recent machine learning techniques including genetic algorithms, Bayesian networks, support vector machines, and committee machines.

19.2 1-Rule

The 1-rule or $1R$ may be the simplest algorithm to generate a set of classification rules from training examples.[1] It is easy to understand and cheap to implement. The algorithm is conceptually similar to univariate profiling frequently used by database marketers. Each attribute (or independent variable) is considered one at a time, and a corresponding set of rules (i.e., relationships between the selected attribute and the dependent variable) is generated. The attribute with the smallest classification error is chosen and the corresponding set of rules becomes the final set of rules for the $1R$.

First introduced by Holte (1993), the 1-rule is often used as the baseline model to compare with a more sophisticated model. Because of its simplicity, the 1-rule has a critical problem in that the joint effect of multiple attributes on the response cannot be modeled because each attribute is considered one at a time. However, its classification performance in validation samples has been comparable to highly complex machine learning algorithms in various applications (Holte 1993).

To see how the 1-rule algorithm works, consider the promotional response data in Table 19.1. It is a typical classification task in which we would like to find target customers for a promotional offer. The data consist of a dependent variable indicating the response status to the promotional offer and

---

[1] Researchers in machine learning prefer the terms training example/instance (or training sample) to estimation sample in traditional statistics. Estimation samples are used to determine the values of parameters in statistical models. Similarly, we derive a set of rules (or patterns) from training instances or examples.

Table 19.1 Promotional response data

Response	Sex	Age	Contact channel
Yes	Male	Teen	E-mail
Yes	Male	Teen	DM
No	Male	Teen	TM
Yes	Male	20s	E-mail
No	Male	20s	DM
No	Male	20s	TM
No	Male	20s	E-mail
No	Male	30 plus	DM
Yes	Male	30 plus	TM
No	Male	30 plus	E-mail
Yes	Female	Teen	DM
No	Female	Teen	TM
Yes	Female	Teen	E-mail
Yes	Female	Teen	DM
No	Female	20s	TM
Yes	Female	20s	E-mail
Yes	Female	20s	DM
No	Female	30 plus	TM
Yes	Female	30 plus	E-mail
No	Female	30 plus	DM

three independent variables characterizing each respondent. For expositional purposes, all three independent variables are categorical in nature. We will extend the algorithm to numerical independent variables later.

We take each attribute in turn and develop a set of rules. For example, there are ten observations for males and ten for females. Among ten males, four respond and six do not. Hence for males, the most accurate rule we could generate would be, 'if male then do not respond' or 'male → no' in short. This rule accurately forecasts six out of ten cases and leads to the error rate of 40%. Similarly, we make a rule for female, 'female → no' that will lead to the same error rate. Therefore, if we apply the rules made by the attribute sex, we would erroneously forecast 8 out of 20 observations.

Applying the same procedure into the other two attributes, we summarize the result in Table 19.2. The number of errors for each rule is given, along with the total number of errors for the set of rules for each attribute. We

Table 19.2 $1R$ applied to promotional response data

Attributes	Rules	Errors	Total errors
Sex	Male → No	4/10	8/20
	Female → Yes	4/10	
Age	Teen → Yes	2/7	7/20
	20s → No	3/7	
	30 plus → No	2/6	
Contact channel	E-mail → Yes	2/7	6/20
	DM → Yes	3/7	
	TM → No	1/6	

now select the attribute that generates the set of rules with the smallest percentage of errors. In this case, that attribute is contact channel, and the set of rules is: If contact channel is through e-mail or DM, then the customer responds. If it is through TM, then she does not respond.

The 1-rule algorithm treats numeric attributes as continuous and uses a straightforward method to divide the range of values into several disjoint intervals. The method is similar to the partitioning technique employed in decision trees (see Chapter 17). Suppose that ages in Table 19.1 are provided in numeric values instead of three categories. We rearrange observations in ascending order according to age.

16	17	17	18	18	19	19	21	23	24	24	25	27	29	32	34	38	40	41	44
Y	Y	Y	Y	Y	N	N	Y	N	N	N	N	Y	Y	Y	N	N	N	N	Y

To partition the sequence wherever the response class changes, we need 6 breakpoints. That is, with 6 breakpoints of 18.5, 20, 22, 26, 33 and 42.5, we have a zero error rate on the training example. The corresponding rule is 'age $< 18.5 \rightarrow$ Yes,' '$18.5 \leq$ age $< 20 \rightarrow$ No,' '$20 \leq$ age $< 22 \rightarrow$ Yes,' '$22 \leq$ age $< 26 \rightarrow$ No,' '$26 \leq$ age $< 33 \rightarrow$ Yes,' '$33 \leq$ age $< 42.5 \rightarrow$ No,' and '$42.5 \leq$ age $\rightarrow$ Yes.'

There is a risk of over-fitting in generating rules for continuously valued attributes. As we can see in the age example, the $1R$ method will naturally create a large number of breakpoints and many of them may simply be due to chance. To avoid this problem, the $1R$ method requires each partition (except the rightmost) to contain a minimum number of examples for the majority response. Suppose that the minimum is set to be three. Then the second, the third, and the fourth partition in the above age example should be merged, and the result would be:

Age	16	17	17	18	18	19	19	21	23	24	24	25	27	29	32	34	38	40	41	44
Actual	Y	Y	Y	Y	Y	N	N	Y	N	N	N	N	Y	Y	Y	N	N	N	N	Y
Prediction	Y	Y	Y	Y	Y	N	N	N	N	N	N	N	Y	Y	Y	N	N	N	N	Y

The corresponding set of rules is 'age $< 18.5 \rightarrow$ Yes,' '$18.5 \leq$ age $< 26 \rightarrow$ No,' '$26 \leq$ age $< 33 \rightarrow$ Yes,' '$33 \leq$ age $< 42.5 \rightarrow$ No,' and 'age $\leq 42.5 \rightarrow$ Yes.' The error rate on the training sample would be 1 out of 20.

19.3 Rule Induction by Covering Algorithms

Rules are one of the most popular ways of representing knowledge that machine learning techniques use. There are hundreds of heuristics available to construct rules from a set of training examples. This section studies a class of rule-generating algorithms called covering algorithms that have been proven to be effective in a number of applications (Witten and Frank 2000)

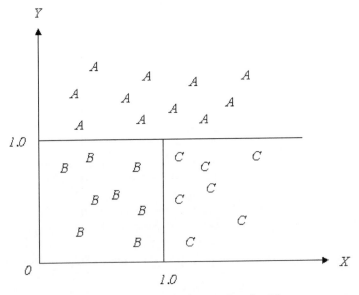

Fig. 19.1 The concept of a covering algorithm.

19.3.1 Covering Algorithms and Decision Trees

Trees and rules have some common features in representing knowledge. A set of rules directly can be constructed from a decision tree (even though the reverse is not always true). However, an important distinction is that decision trees are typically constructed using the principle of "divide and conquer." The decision tree algorithm works top-down, recursively. At each stage the algorithm selects the best attribute to separate examples into the known classes. The classification is refined as the process of branching is repeated.

On the other hand, the covering algorithm considers each class one at a time and attempts to construct a set of rules covering all examples (instances) of each class. That is, we select the rule such that it includes as many instances of a given class as possible and at the same time excludes as many instances of the other classes as possible (Witten and Frank 2000). The covering algorithm refines the selected rule by further restricting the number of instances. The process is repeated until the pre-specified condition for classification accuracy is met.

Figure 19.1 illustrates how the covering algorithm works. There are 26 training instances. Characterized in two attributes or dimensions, each instance is classified into one of three groups: A, B and C. First, let us construct a rule for class A. The horizontal line of $Y = 1$ will divide As from the other two classes. The rule for the class A should be: 'If $Y > 1$ then class $= A$.' Since all instances in the A class are covered by the rule, we construct a set of rules for class B. Restricting the attribute space by $Y \leq 1$

covers all instances in class B and C excluding all observations in class A. Adding $X \leq 1$ to the antecedent $Y \leq 1$, we can refine the rule to cover all instances in class B without including instances in class C. Hence, the rule for the class B should be: 'If $X \leq 1$ and $Y \leq 1$ then class = B.' Similarly, the rule for the class C is 'If $X > 1$ and $Y \leq 1$ then class = C.'

We could have applied a decision tree algorithm to the same example in Fig. 19.1. The tree will have the first split at $Y = 1$ and the second split at $X = 1$. Its result is similar to the covering algorithm. However, decision trees consider all classes in constructing trees while covering algorithms focus on one class (of response) at a time. Because of this difference in constructing rules, there are situations when the covering algorithm is much more effective in representing knowledge than decision trees.

Witten and Frank (2000) provide such case in which there are four attributes, w, x, y, and z and each attribute can take the value of 1, 2, or 3. Suppose that responses are 'Yes' if $x = 1$ and $y = 1$ (whatever the value of w and z), or if $w = 1$ and $z = 1$ (whatever the value of x and y). Otherwise, responses are 'No.' Rules derived from the covering algorithm are simple: 'If $x = 1$ and $y = 1$ then response = Yes,' 'if $w = 1$ and $z = 1$ then response = Yes,' and otherwise response = No. On the other hand, Fig. 19.2 shows the derived decision tree applied to the same training examples.[2] The solution provided by the decision trees is much more complicated than the rules by the covering algorithm. This is called the replicated sub-tree problem. The reason why rules from the covering algorithm are simple is that each rule (e.g., if $x = 1$ and $y = 1$ then response = Yes) represents an independent piece of knowledge. Hence, a new rule (e.g., if $w = 1$ and $z = 1$ then response = Yes) can be added to an existing rule without disturbing the previous set of rules. However, the whole tree needs to be reshaped if we want to add a new rule to an existing tree structure.

19.3.2 PRISM

A simple covering algorithm called PRISM has been proposed by Cendrowska (1987).[3] It is simple to implement and easy to understand. However, the method is known to overfit the training samples because it assumes no noise in the data.

To see how the PRISM algorithm works, we again consider the promotional response data in Table 19.1 introduced in the previous section. The promotional response consists of two classes: 'Yes' or 'No'. Applied to each class in turn, PRISM generates a set of rules for each of the two classes.

---

[2] Note that some sub-trees in the upper right of Fig. 19.2 are not drawn for simplification.

[3] Note: The PRISM algorithm is not to be confused with the PRISM market segmentation scheme derived from cluster analysis and discussed in Chapter 16.

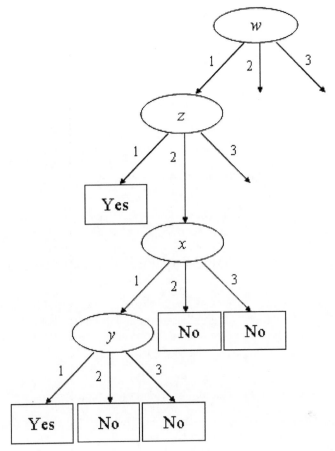

Fig. 19.2 The replicated sub-tree problem of decision trees (Modified from Witten and Frank 2000).

Let us first find a set of rules to identify the 'Yes' class. That is, we are seeking a rule taking the form like 'if X then response $=$ Yes' where X is the characteristic of an attribute. For example, consider a rule 'if sex $=$ male then response $=$ Yes.' There are ten males among the training examples, and four out of the ten respond 'Yes.' Hence, this rule can be said to have a classification accuracy of 40%. We generate potential rules considering all possible Xs in Table 19.1 and evaluate their classification accuracy.

If sex $=$ male then response $=$ Yes	4/10
If sex $=$ female then response $=$ Yes	6/10
If age $=$ teen then response $=$ Yes	5/7
If age $=$ 20s then response $=$ Yes	3/7
If age $=$ 30 plus then response $=$ Yes	2/6
If contact channel $=$ e-mail then response $=$ Yes	5/7
If contact channel $=$ DM then response $=$ Yes	4/7
If contact channel $=$ TM then response $=$ Yes	1/6

Among the above lists, the most accurate rules are when X is 'age = teen' or 'contact channel = e-mail.' Because they are tied with the accuracy of 5/7, we arbitrarily choose 'age = teen' and create a temporary rule:

'If age = teen then response = Yes'

Because this rule is not perfect (i.e., its predictive accuracy is less than 100%), we refine it by adding more terms in the antecedent. That is, we are now seeking a rule of the form 'if age = teen and Y then response = Yes' where Y is the characteristic of an attribute. Note that we restrict our search space into the observations with age = teen. There are seven respondents. We generate the refined rules considering all possible Ys and evaluate the corresponding classification accuracy.

If age = teen and sex = male then response = Yes   2/3
If age = teen and sex = female then response = Yes   3/4
If age = teen and contact channel = e-mail then response = Yes 2/2
If age = teen and contact channel = DM then response = Yes   3/3
If age = teen and contact channel = TM then response = Yes   0/2

The third and the fourth rules above both have perfect predictive accuracy. To select one of them, we apply the coverage heuristic where the rule with the greater coverage should be selected. We select the fourth since the third rule only covers two instances and the fourth covers three. We now have the final rule:

'If age = teen and contact channel = DM then response = Yes'

This is just one rule covering only three 'Yes' instances in the data. There are still seven other 'Yes' instances to be covered. Continuing the PRISM algorithm, we delete the three instances that are already covered. The resulting data are shown in Table 19.3, consisting of 17 observations.

    The same process is applied to the reduced data shown in Table 19.3. That is, consider a rule taking the form of 'if X then response = Yes.' Enumerating potential rules for all possible Xs with the corresponding classification accuracy:

If sex = male then response = Yes   3/9
If sex = female then response = Yes   4/8
If age = teen then response = Yes   2/4
If age = 20s then response = Yes   3/7
If age = 30 plus then response = Yes   2/6
If contact channel = e-mail then response = Yes   5/7
If contact channel = DM then response = Yes   1/4
If contact channel = TM then response = Yes   1/6

The most accurate rule is the sixth when X is 'contact channel = e-mail.' Hence, we create a temporary rule:

'If contact channel = e-mail then response = Yes'

Table 19.3 Promotional response data after the 1st iteration of the PRISM algorithm

Response	Sex	Age	Contact channel
Yes	Male	Teen	E-mail
No	Male	Teen	TM
Yes	Male	20s	E-mail
No	Male	20s	DM
No	Male	20s	TM
No	Male	20s	E-mail
No	Male	30 plus	DM
Yes	Male	30 plus	TM
No	Male	30 plus	E-mail
No	Female	Teen	TM
Yes	Female	Teen	E-mail
No	Female	20s	TM
Yes	Female	20s	E-mail
Yes	Female	20s	DM
No	Female	30 plus	TM
Yes	Female	30 plus	E-mail
No	Female	30 plus	DM

Again we refine this rule because it is not perfect. We consider a rule taking the form of 'if contact channel = e-mail and Y then response = Yes' where Y is the characteristic of an attribute. Enumerating potential rules for all possible Ys with the corresponding classification accuracy:

If contact channel = e-mail and sex = male then response = Yes   2/4
If contact channel = e-mail and sex = female then response = Yes   3/3
If contact channel = e-mail and age = teen then response = Yes   2/2
If contact channel = e-mail and age = 20s then response = Yes   2/3
If contact channel = e-mail and age = 30 plus then response = Yes   1/2

We find two perfect rules: the second and the third. Applying the principle of the greatest coverage, we select the second covering three instances and write another final rule:

'If contact channel = e-mail and sex = female then response = Yes'

We now cover 6 'Yes' instances out of 10 in the data. By the same process, we continue applying the PRISM algorithm in an effort to cover all 10 'Yes' instances. Summarizing all the final rules to identify the 'Yes' class:

'If age = teen and contact channel = DM then response = Yes'
'If contact channel = e-mail and sex = female then response = Yes'
'If contact channel = e-mail and age = teen then response = Yes'
'If age = 20s and sex = female and contact channel = DM then response = Yes'
'If sex = male and age = 30 plus and contact channel = TM then response = Yes'

As shown above, the first two rules cover three 'Yes' instances each. The remaining three rules cover one 'Yes' instance each. That is, the above five rules cover 9 out of 10 'Yes' instances – we could not cover all 10 'Yeses'. It is interesting to look at the instance that could not be covered by the PRISM algorithm. It is the fourth observation in Table 19.1. The trouble is that the seventh observation has the identical attributes with different response. We cannot cover both these observations using the three attributes in Table 19.1.

Once all the final rules are generated for the 'Yes' class, the PRISM algorithm is applied to the 'No' class. The same process is applied and a set of the final rules is constructed for the 'No' class.

19.3.3 A Probability Measure for Rule Evaluation and the INDUCT Algorithm

The accuracy ratio is the critical metric to construct a set of perfect rules in the PRISM rule-generating algorithm. It is defined as the ratio c/n where n is the total number of instances covered by a rule and c is the number of instances classified (or predicted) correctly by the rule. For example, the first rule of the five final rules for class Yes in the previous section, 'If age = teen and contact channel = DM then response = Yes,' covers three instances in Table 19.1 and correctly classifies all three. So the accuracy ratio of this rule is perfect.

However, the PRISM algorithm tends to overfit the training instances because it uses the accuracy ratio as a metric to select the best rules. A method of overcoming this problem is proposed by Gaines and Compton (1995) who introduced the concept of the quality of a rule. Their algorithm, called INDUCT, exploits the idea of statistical significance based on the binomial distribution.

The quality of a proposed rule can be evaluated by calculating the probability of the baseline rule providing equal or better classification accuracy to the proposed rule. Let N be the total number of instances covered by the baseline rule and C be the number of instances correctly classified by this rule. The baseline rule for the given class typically is the rule that can be made without knowing any attribute information. For the promotional response data in Table 19.1, the baseline rule of the response class 'Yes' (or 'No') is to say 'Yes' (or 'No') whatever the characteristics of an instance are. This baseline rule covers 20 instances ($N = 20$) of which 10 instances ($C = 10$) are correctly classified. Hence, the accuracy ratio of a proposed rule should be at least greater than $0.5 (= 10/20)$ if it has any value.

Given the baseline rule with N and C, assume the proposed rule covers n instances with c correct classifications. For example, one of the best rules for Yes class, 'If age = 20s and sex = female and contact channel = DM then recommend = Yes' is a perfect rule with $n = c = 1$. Then what is the probability that the baseline rule would correctly classify c instances when it is applied to n instances? This probability is known to follow a hypergeometric distribution. The problem is analogous to the well-known experiment of sampling without replacement in probability theory. That is, an urn contains N balls among which C balls are marked 'Yes' and the rest $N - C$ balls are marked 'No.' The experiment is to randomly draw n balls from the urn without replacement. The probability that the sample of n balls contains exactly c balls marked 'Yes' and the rest marked 'No' is given as a hypergeometric distribution.

$$P(c|N, C, n) = \frac{\binom{C}{c}\binom{N-C}{n-c}}{\binom{N}{n}} \tag{19.1}$$

We measure the quality of a proposed rule by the probability of the baseline rule providing equal or better classification accuracy to the proposed rule. Hence, going back to the urn example, it is the probability that the sample of n balls contains more than or equal to c balls marked 'Yes.' The quality of a proposed rule $q(R)$ is given by

$$q(R) = \sum_{i=c}^{n} P(i|N, C, n) \tag{19.2}$$

where $P(i|N, C, n)$ is the density of a hypergeometric distribution in Equation 19.1. Higher values of $q(R)$ mean that the proposed rule is not much better than the baseline rule, since the baseline rule has a high probability of achieving at least the same accuracy. For example, let us evaluate the quality of the proposed rule for class 'Yes': 'If age = 20s and sex = female and contact channel = DM then response = Yes'. It is a perfect rule with $n = c = 1$ and the corresponding baseline rule has $N = 20$ and $C = 10$. Employing Equation 19.2, the quality of the proposed rule $q(R)$ is calculated to be 0.5. That is, a random prediction baseline would have a 50% chance of predicting at least as well as the proposed rule. Now let us evaluate another perfect rule in the list. PRISM suggests 'If contact channel = e-mail and sex = female then recommend = Yes.' It is a first rule in the set of rules for class 'Yes.' It is a perfect rule with $n = c = 3$ and the corresponding baseline rule has $N = 20$ and $C = 10$. Its value of the quality is calculated to be 0.11. Hence, this proposed rule is better than the previously proposed rule because it is less likely the baseline rule could have generated the same or better accuracy as the new proposed rule.

We are ready to describe the covering algorithm of INDUCT (Gaines and Compton 1995). First, the PRISM algorithm is applied to construct the best perfect rules for each class. The perfect rules for class 'Yes' and 'No' are:

'If age = teen and contact channel = DM then response = Yes'

'If contact channel = e-mail and sex = female then response = Yes'

'If contact channel = e-mail and age = teen then response = Yes'

'If age = 20s and sex = female and contact channel = DM then response = Yes'

'If sex = male and age = 30 plus and contact channel = TM then response = Yes'

'If contact channel = TM and sex = female then response = No'

'If contact channel = TM and age = teen then response = No'

'If age = 30 plus and contact channel = DM then response = No'

'If sex = male and age = 20s and contact channel = TM then response = No'

'If sex = male and age = 20s and contact channel = DM then response = No'

'If sex = male and age = 30 plus and contact channel = e-mail then response = No'

Second, we use $q(R)$ to help us decide whether a given rule should be "pruned". Specifically, we compare each of the rules generated from the previous step with the corresponding rule before a further restriction is added. For example, consider one of the perfect rules in the above line, 'if contact channel = TM and sex = female then response = No.' This rule leads to 3 perfect classifications ($n = c = 3$) and the corresponding baseline rule has $N = 20$ and $C = 10$. The value of the rule ($q(R)$) is 0.11. In order to see whether pruning is appropriate, the preceding rule before adding the condition sex = female that is 'if contact channel = TM then response = No is considered.' This preceding rule is not perfect but $n = 6$ and $c = 5$. Its value is calculated to be 0.07, which is lower than the value of 0.11 calculated for the perfect rule. That is, cutting off the last term (sex = female) changes the accuracy ratio from 3/3 to 5/6 and improves the quality of the rule from 0.11 to 0.07. We continue this pruning process by removing the last term until the quality measure no longer improves. We apply this pruning process to each of 11 perfect rules above and summarize the results in Table 19.4.

Third, we select the rule with the smallest $q(R)$ among the set of pruned rules. There are 11 pruned rules in Table 19.4 and the rule 'if contact channel = TM' has the smallest $q(R)$ of 0.07.

Fourth, we delete the instances covered by the rule with the smallest $q(R)$ from the training examples and repeat the process of growing and pruning rules from step 1 to 3 for the remaining instances. We continue this procedure until no training examples remain.

The INDUCT covering algorithm elegantly avoids over-fitting by introducing a probabilistic metric of measuring the quality of a rule. However, the INDUCT does not guarantee the best rule generation partially because the evaluation of $q(R)$ is only made over the temporary rules generated by PRISM (Witten and Frank 2000). The ideal method of finding the best rule

Table 19.4 Pruning evaluation to PRISM rules

Consequent	Antecedent	$q(R)$	Status
Yes	Age = teen & contact channel = DM	0.11	Final
	Age = teen	0.21	
	Contact channel = e-mail & sex = female	0.11	Final
	Contact channel = e-mail	0.21	
	Contact channel = e-mail & age = teen	0.50	Prune
	Contact channel = e-mail	0.21	Final
	Age = 20s & sex = female & contact channel = DM	0.50	Prune
	Age = 20s & sex = female	0.50	Final
	Age = 20s	0.77	
	Sex = male & age = 30 plus & contact channel = TM	0.50	Final
	Sex = male & age = 30 plus	0.89	
No	Contact channel = TM & sex = female	0.11	Prune
	Contact channel = TM	0.07	Final
	Contact channel = TM & age = teen	0.50	Prune
	Contact channel = TM	0.07	Final
	Age = 30 plus & contact channel = DM	0.24	Final
	Age = 30 plus	0.34	
	Sex = male & age = 20s & contact channel = TM	0.50	Prune
	Sex = male & age = 20s	0.29	Final
	Sex = male	0.38	
	Sex = male & age = 20s & contact channel = DM	0.50	Prune
	Sex = male & age = 20s	0.29	Final
	Sex = male	0.38	
	Sex = male & age = 30 plus & contact channel = e-mail	0.50	Prune
	Sex = male & age = 30 plus	0.50	Prune
	Sex = male	0.38	Final

is to evaluate all possible rules exhaustively (e.g., all possible combinations of attributes), but this is too computationally burdensome. Recently a number of researchers have proposed alternative algorithms to search for the best rules without incurring too much computational time (Cohen 1995; Frank and Witten 1998).

19.4 Instance-Based Learning

Representing knowledge in the form of historical examples may be the simplest way of learning. People intentionally or unintentionally memorize a set of training instances. When a new instance comes up, memorized instances are searched to find the most similar one to the new instance. For example, when we first look at a person, we search our memory to find the person who has the most similar appearance. We judge the new person's personality based on this person whose personality is already known to us.

This section discusses a machine learning algorithm called instance-based learning or memory-based reasoning. Memory-based collaborative filtering discussed in Chapter 14 employs an instance-based learning algorithm to predict the preference of the target user. We here discuss instance-based learning in a broader context. Its original idea was developed by statisticians who employed the nearest-neighbor methods for prediction and classification tasks (Fix and Hodges 1951; Johns 1961). Aha (1992) provided techniques to handle noisy data in instance-based learning algorithms and popularized these methods among machine learning researchers.

19.4.1 Strengths and Limitations

Instance-based learning techniques have successfully been applied to various classification and prediction problems. Their broad appeal comes from several sources. Instance-based learning is simple to implement and its results are easy to understand. More importantly, it is very flexible in the required format of the input records (Berry and Linoff 1997). The algorithm only requires basic arithmetic operations in calculating similarities between instances. Hence, it can easily be applied to diverse data including images and text.

However, instance-based learning tends to be resource-intensive both in computation and storage space. We need to process all the historical instances to find the most similar instance and classify the new instance. Other data mining techniques such as neural networks spend much time analyzing the training examples and constructing models. Once a generalized model is constructed and saved, the classification of new instances is fast and easy. In contrast, instance-based learning takes a completely opposite approach. It is fast in the analysis of the training examples because it does not need to construct models or rules, but simply stores training examples for future use. Instance-based learning postpones major computations for later. It requires a great deal of computer memory for saving training examples that will be fetched when classifying new instances.

Results of instance-based learning are sensitive to the choice of distance function and the attribute-weighting scheme, the subset selection of the training samples, and the presence of outliers. As discussed later, a number of techniques have been developed to make the algorithm robust even though a single best algorithm does not exist.

19.4.2 A Brief Description of an Instance-Based Learning Algorithm

Suppose that we have N training instances in which we observe the classification membership of each instance with its attribute values. Let the category identification of instance i be y_i and the corresponding vector of attributes be $\mathbf{x}_i = (x_{i1}, \ldots, x_{im})$ where m represents the number of attributes. Our goal is to classify a new instance that has attributes $\mathbf{z} = (z_1, \ldots, z_m)$.

The nearest-neighbor method searches over the training instances and finds the most similar instance to the new instance. There are a number of ways to measure the similarity or the distance between two instances. Since the issue of similarity is extensively discussed in the chapter of collaborative filtering, here we simply use the Euclidean distance. That is, the distance between a new observation and instance i in the training set is

$$d(\mathbf{z}, \mathbf{x}_i) = \sqrt{(z_1 - x_{i1})^2 + \cdots + (z_m - x_{im})^2} \tag{19.3}$$

All attributes are transformed to have a range from zero to one so that each attribute is treated identically in distance contribution. Once the distances are calculated over all training instances, we find the training instance with the minimum distance. The class of the new instance is predicted to be the same as the category membership y of this closest training instance.

The nearest-neighbor method tends to be sensitive to few noisy instances. In order to reduce the effect of noisy instances on the results, we adopt the k-nearest-neighbor method where we select the k nearest training instances and use them together to predict the class of the new instance. One possibility is to take the majority class from the k nearest training instances as the predicted class of the new instance. Alternatively, each of the k nearest training instances can get differential weights in predicting the class of the new instance (Berry and Linoff 1997). The more similar to the new instance, the larger weight it is assigned. The inverse of the distance to the new instance is used for the weight assigned to each of the k nearest training instances.[4]

The suitable value of k should be determined empirically. That is, the k-nearest-neighbors method is applied with different values of k and performance in a validation sample is compared. In general, the optimal value of k increases with the amount of noise.

19.4.3 Selection of Exemplars

Instance-based learning easily becomes computationally intensive because all the training examples must be scanned to predict the class of a new instance. Hence, we want to limit the number of training examples used for classification to be as small as possible. We do not want to store a lot of redundant training examples. At the same time we do not want to exclude meaningful examples. Witten and Frank (2000) use the term "exemplars" to refer to the already-seen instances that are used for classification. We start with an exemplar randomly chosen from the calibration sample and classify each

---

[4] In order to avoid the problem of inversing zero distance, it is common to add one before taking the inverse.

new instance from the calibration sample with respect to the exemplar. If the new instance is misclassified, it is added to the exemplar database. Correctly classified instances (e.g., redundant instances) are discarded. Ideally, each exemplar in the exemplar database represents an important region of the instance space. However, this method of only storing misclassified instances will not work well when the data have a lot of noise. Noisy instances by definition cannot be explained by the model and should not be incorporated into the exemplar database. However, noisy instances are very likely to be misclassified and so saved into the exemplar database leading to low predictive accuracy. Our goal is to find interesting patterns (e.g., exemplars) without recording redundant patterns. We do not want to interpret statistical noise as meaningful patterns.

Aha (1992) proposed an instance-based learning algorithm to overcome the above problem of noisy instances, while minimizing the size of the exemplar database. It applies an accuracy filter that monitors the predictive performance of each instance and stores only those instances showing high classification accuracy. That is, it keeps track of the classification performance of each training instance (e.g., the ratio of the correctly classified to the total number of classifications). A test based on confidence intervals for proportions is employed to decide whether instances are acceptable, noisy or uncertain. The idea is to determine whether the instance predicts better than random. Therefore, a confidence interval is computed for both the instance's (cumulative) classification performance and its class's observed frequency. If the lower bound of the confidence interval for the instance's classification performance exceeds above the upper bound of the confidence interval for its class's observed frequency, the instance is acceptable for classification decision, and hence becomes the member of the exemplar set. In contrast, if the upper bound of the confidence interval for the instance's classification performance drops below the lower bound of the confidence interval for its class's observed frequency, the instance is indefinitely removed from the exemplar set. If the instance's performance is somewhere between acceptable and unacceptable, it is considered to be a member of the potential set. The instances in the potential set are not allowed to be used for prediction but their predictive performances are continually updated and eventually may be added to the exemplar set or indefinitely removed from the potential set.

For example, suppose that an exemplar has been used n_1 times to classify instances, and x_1 of these predictions have been correct. We can estimate the confidence interval for the true success rate of this exemplar.[5] Now, suppose the exemplar's class has occurred x_2 times out of a total number n_2 of training instances. From this, we can compute the confidence interval for the default (random) success rate (x_2/n_2), the probability of successfully classifying an

---

[5] This would be calculated using the confidence interval for proportions, $p \pm z_{\alpha/2} \sqrt{\frac{p(1-p)}{n}}$, where $p = x_1/n_1$ and $z_{\alpha/2}$ is the normal deviate from the standard normal distribution corresponding to a confidence level of $1 - \alpha$.

instance of this class without relying on the exemplar's information. The following table illustrates:

Method	Prediction	95% Conf. Int.	Comparison
Using exemplar	$x_1 = 250; n_1 = 500$	0.500 ± 0.044	Lower Bound = 0.456
Random prediction	$x_2 = 400; n_2 = 1,000$	0.400 ± 0.030	Upper Bound = 0.430

Since the lower bound of the 95% confidence interval for predictive accuracy using the exemplar is higher than the upper bound for predictive accuracy using random prediction, the exemplar is acceptable and would be added to the exemplar set.

Aha (1992) uses a high confidence level (5%) for acceptance and a lower confidence level (12.5%) for rejection. This makes it statistically easier for an instance to be dropped than to be accepted, and reduces the number of exemplars.

19.4.4 Attribute Weights

The accuracy of instance-based learning is sensitive to the type of distance function employed. The Euclidean distance in the Equation 19.3 performs reasonably well. However, it is intuitively unappealing to assume that all attributes should contribute equally in defining the distance or similarity between two instances. Hence, we generalize the Euclidean distance to accommodate unequal weightings,

$$d(\mathbf{z}, \mathbf{x}_i) = \sqrt{w_1(z_1 - x_{i1})^2 + \cdots + w_m(z_m - x_{im})^2} \qquad (19.4)$$

which becomes the Euclidean distance when all the weights are the same.

Aha (1992) suggests an algorithm to update attribute-specific weights dynamically. All weights are updated after we find the most similar exemplar to a new training instance. Given the new training instance $\mathbf{z}$ and the most similar exemplar $\mathbf{x}_i$, $|z_k - x_{ik}|$ is calculated for each attribute k. This is a measure of the contribution of attribute k to the classification decision. Attribute weight w_k is updated based on the size of $|z_k - x_{ik}|$ and whether the classification was indeed correct or not. If the new instance is classified correctly, the weight will be increased. If it is incorrect, the weight will decrease. And the difference $|z_k - x_{ik}|$ will determine the magnitude of this increase or decrease.

19.5 Genetic Algorithms

A genetic algorithm is a class of robust and efficient search techniques based on the concept of adaptation in natural organisms. The theory of evolution and survival of the fittest tells us that species (or individuals) well fitted to their environment survive over millions of years and their chromosomes or genome would be propagated one generation to the next. In a genetic algorithm, an individual (or candidate solution) is selected for reproduction based on how its fitness (predictive ability) compares to that of other individuals. Individuals are traditionally represented in binary as strings of 0s and 1s. The evolution begins with randomly generated individuals (solutions). In each generation, once the fitness of every individual is evaluated, less fit individuals do not survive and genomes of more fit individuals are propagated.

Genetic algorithms became popular after John Holland developed its solid theoretical foundation in the early 1970s (Holland 1975). They have been successfully applied to complex problems in diverse fields. Within marketing, Hurley et al. (1995) outlined 11 areas in which genetic algorithms have been applied. Gatarski (2002) employed a genetic algorithm to automatically design banner advertising. The resulting system created innovative banner designs that performed increasingly better than reference banners, improving the click-through rate from 0.68% for the standard banner to 3.1% without human intervention from the advertiser. Kim et al. (2005) used artificial neural networks guided by genetic algorithms to identify and profile customers who are most likely interested in a particular product or service. The genetic algorithm in their model plays a key role in selecting input features for an artificial neural network.

A simple example provided by Berry and Linoff (1997) will help us to understand the basic concepts of genetic algorithms. Suppose we try to find the integer value of p maximizing $f(p) = 31p - p^2$ where the integer p varies between 0 and 31. We first represent a *solution* (e.g., the parameter value p from 0 to 31) as an array of bits. Five bits are required to represent all solutions (e.g., 0 to 31). For example, $p = 1$ can be represented by {00001}. The fitness function, defined over the genetic representation, measures the quality of the solution. In this example, the fitness function is $f(p)$. Once we have the genetic representation and defined the fitness function, the genetic algorithm generates an initial set of solutions randomly, and then improves them through repetitive application of selection, crossover and mutation. Suppose that we randomly generate the initial set of solutions below. The average fitness of the initial solutions is 117.75.

Solution	p	Fitness
10110	22	176
00011	3	87
00010	2	58
11001	25	150

We now improve the fitness of the initial solutions through three "operators." The first operator selects solutions with higher fitness for successive generations. That is, the chance of a solution surviving to the next generation is proportional to its fitness value. Specifically, the total fitness value of the above four solutions is 471. The ratio of the fitness of each solution to the total fitness is 0.37, 0.19, 0.12 and 0.32, respectively. We now spin a roulette wheel four times in which each solution has an area of these four proportions. Each spin we select a solution (using sampling with replacement) to survive to the next generation. Below is the resulting set of solutions after selection through spinning a roulette wheel.

Solution	p	Fitness
10110	22	176
11001	25	150
00010	2	58
10110	22	176

Notice that the selection procedure results in more copies of the solutions with high fitness values and fewer for the less fit. One of the low fit solutions {00011} has not survived, but there are two copies of the solution with the highest fit {10110}. As a result, the average fitness value has increased from 117.25 to 140.

The second operator is crossover. This creates two new solutions (children) by selecting two existing ones (parents) and gluing pieces of each solution together. For example, suppose that two solutions {10110} and {00010} are selected from the selection process and a randomly chosen crossover position is between the second and the third position. Then the first two digits of the first solution (10) are replaced by the first two digits of the second solution (00). The resulting two children solutions – {00110} and {10010} – have a piece inherited from each of their parents solutions. The crossover probability of 0.5 is typically used. That is, once we select two solutions, we flip a coin to decide whether to apply the crossover operation to these two solutions.

The final operator is mutation. Its role is to prevent some valuable combinations from consideration in succeeding generations. Solutions generated by search and crossover depend on the initial set of solutions. Mutation provides an additional input not drawn from the initial set. Mutation therefore helps avoid premature convergence to a local optimum. The probability of a mutation is typically kept very small. When a mutation occurs, a bit changes from 0 to 1, or 1 to 0. For instance, if the mutation occurs in the solution {10010}, we randomly determine the position of mutation. If it is the third position, which is 0, it is changed to 1. The resulting solution becomes {10110}. Changes introduced by mutation may often decrease the average fitness value. But those mutated solution will not survive long.

Genetic algorithms improve the fitness of the population by selection, crossover and mutation as genes are passed from one generation to the next. The generational process continues until a termination condition (e.g., fixed number of generations) has been reached. Genetic algorithms do not guarantee the exact optimal solution, but they do a good job of getting close to the optimal solution quickly. See Chapter 27 for a detailed discussion of Gatarski (2002) use of a genetic algorithm to develop banner advertisements.

19.6 Bayesian Networks

Bayesian networks have made significant contributions in various fields such as software engineering, space navigation and medical diagnosis since Pearl (1988) published the first book on the topic (Haddawy 1999). Unlike traditional statistical models (e.g., logistic regression), Bayesian networks do not make any stringent assumptions on the types of data and their distributions (e.g., normality). In addition, they can effectively handle nonlinearity and take on any structure (Heckerman 1997; Cui et al. 2006).

Marketing researchers have begun to recognize Bayesian networks as an alternative to structural equations models. Cooper (2000) used Bayesian networks for strategic marketing planning of radically new products. The factors identified in an extensive situation analysis are woven into the economic webs surrounding the new product. The webs are mapped into Bayesian networks that can be updated as events unfold and used to simulate the impact that changes in assumptions underlying the web have on the prospects for the new product. Blodgett and Anderson (2000) applied a Bayesian network to the consumer complaint process. They generated several interesting findings. For example, the probability that a noncomplainer or a dissatisfied complainant will completely exit is quite low. On the other hand, the probability that a satisfied complainant will fully repatronize the retailer and engage in positive word of mouth is quite high. Finally, Cui et al. (2006) employed Bayesian networks (learned by evolutionary programming) to model consumer responses to direct marketing. They compared Bayesian networks with neural networks, decision trees (e.g., CART), and latent class regression, and found that Bayesian networks have advantages in accuracy of prediction,[6] transparency of procedures, interpretability of results, and explanatory insight.

The key feature of Bayesian networks is to provide a method of decomposing a complex joint probability distribution into a set of simple local distributions. Bayesian networks achieve this simplification through a directed acyclic graph. Nodes in the graph represent (random) variables and arcs represent the probabilistic correlation between the variables. Suppose we are interested in looking for relationships among a set of variables $\mathbf{X} = \{X_1, \ldots, X_n\}$. The Bayesian network is a graphical model that efficiently represents ("encodes") the joint distribution for $\mathbf{X}$. It consists of (1) a network structure S that encodes a set of conditional independence assumptions on variables in $\mathbf{X}$, and (2) a set P of local probability distributions associated with each variable (Herkerman 1997). The structure S is a directed acyclic graph whose nodes represent variables X_i's. If there is an arc from variable X_i to X_j, then variable X_j depends directly on X_i and X_i is called a parent of X_j. We denote $parents(X_i)$ to be the parents of variable X_i in S as well as the variables corresponding to those parents. Given a structure S, the joint probability

---

[6] In their tenfold cross-validation comparison, Bayesian networks provide the highest average lift in the top decile, followed by latent class regression, neural networks, and CART. In the second decile, however, the neural networks have the highest cumulative lift, followed by Bayesian networks, CART, and latent class regression.

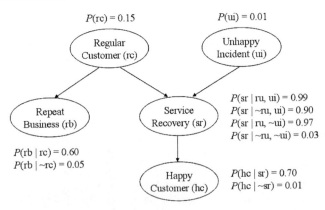

Fig. 19.3 A Bayesian network model for customer complaints (Reprinted by permission, from Cui, G., Wong, M.L., and Lui, H.K., "Machine Learning for Direct Marketing Response Models: Bayesian Networks with Evolutionary Programming", Management Science, Volume 52, Number 4 (April 2006), The Institute for Operations Research and the Management Sciences (INFORMS), 7240 Parkway Drive, Suite 310, Hanover, MD 21076 USA.)

distribution for **X** is

$$p(\mathbf{X}) = \prod_{i=1}^{n} p(X_i | parents(X_i)) \qquad (19.5)$$

The local probability distributions P are the distributions of $p(X_i | parents(X_i))$. As a result, the pair (S, P) encodes the joint distribution $p(\mathbf{X})$.

One advantage of a Bayesian network is that it is intuitively easier to understand its direct dependencies and local distributions than the joint distribution. For example, Fig. 19.3 shows a Bayesian network model for handling customer complaints provided by Cui et al. (2006). There are five binary variables: regular customer, unhappy incident, service recovery, repeat business and happy customer. The joint probability distribution table (without the Bayesian network structure) would have $2^5 - 1 = 31$ entries. However, a Bayesian network model in Fig. 19.3 has only 10 probability values.

The success of a Bayesian network mainly depends on a network structure S that encodes a set of conditional independence assertions about variables in **X**. In the model of customer complaints in Fig. 19.3, we have the conditional independencies

$$P(rc|ui) = P(rc)$$
$$P(rb|rc, ui) = P(rb|rc)$$
$$P(sr|rc, ui, rb) = P(sr|rc, ui)$$
$$P(hc|sr, rc, ui, rb) = P(hc|sr, rc, ui)$$

For example, the first relationship depicts the assertion that being a regular customer is unrelated to whether an unhappy incident occurs. Given the above four conditional independencies, we can obtain the model structure for the customer complaint model in Fig. 19.3.

Although the structure of a Bayesian network is formally defined as a set of conditional independence assertions about variables, it is often constructed using the notion of causal relationships (Heckerman 1997). In particular, we simply draw arcs from cause variables to their effect variables. For instance, given the assertion that *Regular Customer* is a direct cause of *Repeat Business* and *Service Recovery*, *Unhappy Incident* is a direct cause of *Service Recovery*, and *Service Recovery* is the direct cause of *Happy Customer*, we obtain the network structure in Fig. 19.3.

Once we estimate the Bayesian network model, we can make probabilistic inferences directly from the local probabilities $p(X_i|parents(X_i))$.[7] The inference is based on the direct causes as depicted in the model specification, without making any restrictive distributional assumptions on the local probabilities. For example, *Service Recovery* (sr) leads to *Happy Customer* (hc) in Fig. 19.3. Then

$$
\begin{aligned}
P(sr) &= P(sr|rc, ui)P(rc)P(ui) + P(sr| \sim rc, ui)P(\sim rc)P(ui) \\
&\quad + P(sr|rc, \sim ui)P(rc)P(\sim ui) + P(sr| \sim rc, \sim ui)P(\sim rc)P(\sim ui) \\
&= (.99)(.15)(.01) + (.90)(.85)(.01) + (.97)(.15)(.99) + (.03)(.85)(.99) \\
&= 0.1784 \\
P(hc) &= P(hc|sr)P(sr) + P(hc| \sim sr)P(\sim sr) = (.7)(.1784) + (.01)(.8216) \\
&= 0.1331
\end{aligned}
$$

We can also calculate the posterior probability of *Service Recovery* when the chosen customer is a *Happy Customer* by

$$
P(sr|hc) = P(hc|sr)P(sr)/P(hc) = (.7)(.1784)/(.1331) = 0.9383
$$

Blodgett and Anderson (2000) discuss the advantages of Bayesian networks over traditional causal models such as structural equation models. As mentioned, Bayesian networks are nonparametric so that no functional form or distributional assumptions are necessary for inference. In contrast, structural equation models are parametric in both distribution and function (e.g., normality, linearity and common factor theory). Another advantage of Bayesian networks is that both forward and backward inferences are possible. We can make predictions with forward inferences (e.g., $P(hc|sr)$) whereas backward inferences can address profile questions (e.g., $P(rc|hc)$). The main weaknesses of Bayesian networks are computational complexities and a relatively large sample size necessary for estimation.

19.7 Support Vector Machines

Support vector machines, pioneered by Vapnik and co-workers, originated from statistical learning theory (Boser et al. 1992; Vapnik 1995). In this

---

[7] Estimation of Bayesian networks is beyond the scope of this book. See Heckerman (1997) and Cui et al. (2006) for more discussions on estimation, and Haddawy (1999) for commercial software packages.

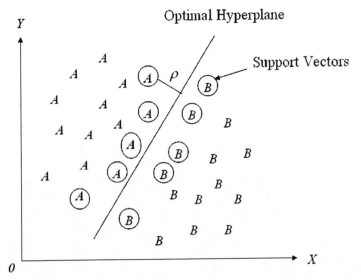

Fig. 19.4 Optimal hyperplane and support vectors in feature space.

section, we briefly describe the fundamental concepts of support vector machines and their advantages over traditional statistical methodologies since their complete treatment is mathematically demanding. See Burges (1998) for technical details of support vector machines and Cui and Curry (2005) for their marketing application.

In Chapter 15, we describe how discriminant analysis performs classification. Its key idea is to express the class as a linear combination of the independent variables (or attributes). For example, consider the training sample of size N, $\{\mathbf{x}_i, y_i\}$ where $\mathbf{x}_i$ is the vector of independent variables for observation i $(i = 1, \ldots, N)$ and y_i is the corresponding response. To simplify our exposition, we assume that the class represented by the subset $d_i = 1$ is linearly separable from the class of the subset $d_i = -1$. The hyperplane that linearly separates the two classes has the functional form $\beta'\mathbf{x} = \beta_0 x_0 + \beta_1 x_1 + \ldots + \beta_k x_k = 0$. That is, $\beta'\mathbf{x} > 0$ for $d_i = 1$ and $\beta'\mathbf{x} < 0$ for $d_i = -1$. The goal of support vector machine is to find the particular hyperplane (called the optimal hyperplane) which maximally separates two classes (Witten and Frank 2000; Flach 2001). Figure 19.4 illustrates the optimal hyperplane for 30 training instances with two independent variables.

Suppose weighting vector β_o defines the optimal hyperplane. That is, the optimal hyperplane is algebraically defined as $\beta'_o\mathbf{x} = 0$. The observations that are closest to the optimal hyperplane are called support vectors $\mathbf{x}_s$.[8] These vectors play a critical role in support vector machines. Since support

---

[8] We can derive the optimal weighting vector by solving a quadratic optimization problem. Support vectors can be derived once the optimal weighting vector is determined. For detailed discussion, see Cui and Curry (2005) or Haykin (1999).

vectors lie closest to the decision surface, they are the most difficult to classify. Support vectors reduce the number of instances (or observations) required to predict or classify a new instance. Figure 19.4 shows the scatter plot of 30 training instances with two attributes. All instances above the optimal hyperplane are class As while all instances below the hyperplane are class Bs. Only the instances circled – called support instances – are required to classify new instances. The rest of the instances play no role in predicting the class of new instances. As a result, we reduce the number of instances from 30 to 10. The set of support vectors uniquely defines the optimal hyperplane.

The biggest disadvantage of the linear hyperplane is that it can only represent linear boundaries between classes (Witten and Frank 2000). One way of overcoming this restriction is to transform the instance space into a new "feature" space with a nonlinear mapping. A straight line in feature space does not look straight in the original instance space. That is, a linear model constructed in feature space can represent a nonlinear boundary in the original space. For example, given two independent variables, the linear model is $Y = \beta_1 x_1 + \beta_2 x_2$. If we allow for all products with two factors, we have $Y = \alpha_1 x_1^2 + \alpha_2 x_1 x_2 + \alpha_3 x_2^2$. The original observations (or instances) x's are mapped into a feature space of z's (e.g., $z_1 = x_1^2$, $z_2 = x_1 x_2$ and $z_3 = x_2^2$). The model is nonlinear in the original space whereas it is linear in feature space. We can add more flexibility to the model by assuming polynomials of sufficiently high degree (instead of two factors).

The idea of support vector machines is based on two mathematical operations: (1) nonlinear mapping of the original instance space into a high-dimensional feature space, and (2) construction of an optimal hyperplane to separate the classes. In other words, we need to derive the optimal hyperplane defined as a linear function of vectors drawn from the feature space rather than the original instance space (Haykin 1999). We construct this hyperplane in accordance with the principle of structural risk minimization (Vapnik 1995).

Let $\mathbf{x}$ denote a vector of independent variables drawn from the input space, assumed to be of dimension K. Let $\varphi_m(\mathbf{x})$ denote a set of nonlinear transformations from the input space to the feature space where the dimension of the feature space is M. Define the feature vector $\varphi(\mathbf{x}) = [\varphi_0(\mathbf{x}), \varphi_1(\mathbf{x}), \ldots, \varphi_M(\mathbf{x})]'$ where $\varphi_0(\mathbf{x}) = 1$ for all $\mathbf{x}$. Similar to the linear hyperplane, we can define a hyperplane given a set of features:

$$\boldsymbol{\beta}' \varphi(\mathbf{x}) = 0 \tag{19.6}$$

We can now derive the weighting vector $\boldsymbol{\beta}_o$ that defines the hyperplane in feature space that optimally separates the classes (see Haykin (1999) for its detailed derivation):

$$\boldsymbol{\beta}_o = \sum_{i=1}^{I} \alpha_i d_i \varphi(\mathbf{x}_i) \tag{19.7}$$

where I is the number of support vectors, $\varphi(\mathbf{x}_i)$ denotes the feature vector corresponding to the input pattern $\mathbf{x}_i$ in the ith support vector, d_i is the response (or class) indicator (1 or -1) and α_i is the Lagrange multiplier. Substituting Equation 19.7 into 19.6, we have the optimal hyperplane.

$$\sum_{i=1}^{I} \alpha_i d_i \varphi'(\mathbf{x}_i)\varphi(\mathbf{x}) = \sum_{i=1}^{I} \alpha_i d_i K(\mathbf{x}_i, \mathbf{x}) = 0 \qquad (19.8)$$

The term in Equation 19.8 denoted by $K(\mathbf{x}_i, \mathbf{x}) = \varphi'(\mathbf{x}_i)\varphi(\mathbf{x}) = \sum_{m=0}^{M} \varphi_m(\mathbf{x})$ $\varphi_m(\mathbf{x}_i)$ is called the inner-product kernel. Note that M is the number of features plus the intercept. It represents the inner product of two vectors induced in the feature space by the input vector $\mathbf{x}$ and the input pattern $\mathbf{x}_i$ pertaining to the ith support vector. Various functions can be employed for the inner-product kernel. The most popular one may be a polynomial kernel where $K(\mathbf{x}_i, \mathbf{x}) = (\mathbf{x}'\mathbf{x}_i + 1)^p$ where power p is specified a priori by the user. A good way of choosing the value of p is to start with 1 (e.g., linear model) and increase the value until the errors cease to improve (Witten and Frank 2000). An alternative kernel function is the radial-basis function kernel where $K(\mathbf{x}_i, \mathbf{x}) = \exp(- \|\mathbf{x} - \mathbf{x}_i\|^2 / (2\sigma^2))$ where σ^2 is specified a priori by the user. The support vector machine with the radial-basis function kernel is simply a radial-basis function network that is a type of neural network specification (see Chapter 18). Finally, the support vector machine with the logistic kernel is a multilayer perceptron with no hidden layers which is another type of neural network. This is why support vector machines are often considered an extension of neural networks (Flach 2001). However, support vector machines offer a much more sophisticated mechanism to incorporate domain knowledge by means of kernels.

The support vector machine is an excellent semi-parametric technique that has great potential in prediction and classification. Cui and Curry (2005) introduced support vector machines to marketing, and showed it has significantly better predictive performance over the multinomial logit model in a simulation test. Its major drawbacks for database marketers may be that its implementation is mathematically complex and there is no off-the-shelf software available. However, we expect that in the near future database marketers will use support vector machines especially when the relationship between independent variables and the dependent variable is complex.

19.8 Combining Multiple Models: Committee Machines

When people make critical decisions, they usually consider opinions from several experts. In machine learning, each estimated model for a given set of training data constitutes an expert. We may be able to improve our decision (or prediction) if we combine the outputs from several different models. The combination of experts is said to constitute a "committee machine" (Haykin 1999). The original idea of a committee machine is traced back to Nilsson (1965), but was made popular by Breiman (1996). There are various ways of combining multiple models; they potentially perform better than a single

model. However, they all share a disadvantage of interpretation. It is difficult
to understand which factors are contributing to improved prediction (Witten
and Frank 2000).

Committee machines have received increasing attention in various disciplines (see Haykin (1999) and Lemmens and Croux (2006) for references).
In marketing, Lemmens and Croux (2006) applied the bagging and boosting
of binary logit to predicting churn in a wireless telecommunications company. They showed that both bagging and boosting significantly improved
prediction accuracy compared to a binary logit.

19.8.1 Bagging

A simple way of combining the predictions from multiple models into a
single prediction is to take a (weighted) vote for a classification task and
a (weighted) average for numeric prediction. Bagging adopts this simple approach. We denote the estimation (or calibration) sample as $\mathbf{Z} =
\{(\mathbf{x}_1, y_1), \ldots, (\mathbf{x}_N, y_N)\}$ where N is the total number of observations, $\mathbf{x}_i$ rep-
resents k predictors for observation i ($\mathbf{x}_i = (x_{i1}, \ldots, x_{iK})$), and y_i represents
the value of the dependent variable for observation i. From the original esti-
mation sample, we generate B bootstrap samples of size N, $\mathbf{Z}_1, \mathbf{Z}_2, \ldots, \mathbf{Z}_B$.
The term bagging actually stands for "bootstrap aggregating" (Breiman
1996). As we described in Chapter 11, each observation of size N in each
bootstrap sample is randomly drawn from the original estimation sample,
with replacement. Through this sampling procedure, each bootstrap sample
deletes and replicates some observations in the original sample. Once B bootstrap samples are constructed, a model (e.g., logistic regression or decision
trees) is applied to each bootstrap sample. Prediction is based on a vote for
classification from each estimated model and an average value for numeric
prediction.

The effect of bagging can be viewed through the statistical lens of bias-
variance decomposition (Witten and Frank 2000). Let $\mathbf{x}$ denote a set of independent variables not seen before and y denote the corresponding dependent
variable. That is, $\mathbf{x}$ and y are realizations of the random vector $\mathbf{X}$ and random variable Y. Let $F(\mathbf{x})$ denote the model predicting y. The expected mean
squared error of $F(\mathbf{x})$ with respect to $E[Y|\mathbf{X} = \mathbf{x}]$ can be decomposed into
the bias and the variance.

$$
\begin{aligned}
E[MSE] \\
&= E[\mathrm{Pr}\,edictd - Actual] \\
&= E[(F(\mathbf{x}) - E[Y|\mathbf{X} = \mathbf{x}])^2] \\
&= (E[F(\mathbf{x})] - E[Y|\mathbf{X} = \mathbf{x}])^2 + E[(F(\mathbf{x}) - E[F(\mathbf{x})])^2] \\
&= B[F(\mathbf{x})] + V[F(\mathbf{x})]
\end{aligned}
\tag{19.9}
$$

where $B[F(\mathbf{x})]$ is the bias squared and $V[F(\mathbf{x})]$ is the variance. The bias of the model is a systematic error that cannot be eliminated even by employing an infinite number of observations for estimation. However, the variance component comes from the particular estimation sample used, which is randomly selected from the true population and so is not perfectly representative. Bagging reduces the mean square error by decreasing the variance of the model (Haykin 1999). That is, bagging averages out the instability of a model applied to a particular estimation sample by constructing several bootstrap samples.

19.8.2 Boosting

Bagging will be effective when the model's estimated parameters change drastically over different bootstrap samples. That is, bagging addresses the instability of the model. Therefore, bagging does not work well with a robust model (e.g., linear model) in which predictions of the model change very little across bootstrap samples. Intuitively, it is only reasonable to combine multiple models with significantly different predictions (Witten and Frank 2000). That is, combining methods will be effective when models complement each other. Boosting exploits this insight by searching for models that complement each other.

Boosting is similar to bagging in combining predictions (votes or numerical values) of individual models. However, the main difference between boosting and bagging lies in the sampling scheme. Boosting sequentially estimates a model applied to adaptively re-weighted samples. More specifically, the boosting algorithm starts with assigning equal weight to all observations in the calibration sample. Once the model is estimated, we re-weight each observation according to the model's output. The weight of correctly classified observations is decreased, and that of misclassified ones is increased (Witten and Frank 2000). With this weighting scheme, we attempt to focus on classifying observations with high weights that are hard-to-classify (or misclassified) observations correctly. Such observations become more important because there is greater incentive to classify them correctly. By assigning weights to each observation, boosting provides an elegant way of generating a series of experts that complement one another. In the next iteration, the model is applied to the re-weighted calibration sample. There are several weighting schemes available, but we only introduce a widely used method called AdaBoost.M1 (Freund and Schapire 1996). For each iteration, the weights of all observations are updated as

$$w_{i,t+1} = w_{i,t}\{(1 - D_{i,t}) + D_{i,t}e_t/(1 - e_t)\} \qquad (19.10)$$

where $w_{i,t}$ represents the weight of observation i at iteration t, $D_{i,t}$ indicates whether the observation is correctly classified ($= 1$ if correctly classified, and

0 if misclassified), and e_t denotes the model's overall error (the percentage misclassified) for the tth re-weighted calibration sample. Since each successive sample is weighted more toward harder-to-classify observations, e_t tends to increase with t. We stop the iterations when classification becomes so difficult that e_t is worse than random prediction, i.e., greater than or equal to 0.5. So assuming $e_t \leq 0.5$ and using Equation 19.10, the weights do not change for misclassified observations while they decrease for correctly classified ones. After all weights have been updated, they are renormalized such that their sum at iteration $t + 1$ remains the same as the sum of weights at iteration t. For example, the renormalized weights of observation i at iteration t become $w_{i,t+1}^* = w_{i,t+1}(\sum_i w_{i,t} / \sum_i w_{i,t+1})$. As a result, the renormalized weights of the misclassified observations increase whereas those of the correctly classified ones decrease.

19.8.3 Other Committee Machines

Although bagging and boosting are popular, there are other methods to combine outputs from multiple models. For example, Breiman (2001) proposed a new classifier called a random forest which combines bagging by Breiman (1996) and the random subspace method by Ho (1998). Similar to bagging, a random forest combines the predictions from multiple (tree) models into a single prediction by generating multiple bootstrap samples and taking a weighted vote for a classification task. However, for each node of the tree, it randomly chooses m input variables (out of $M > m$ input variables) on which to base the decision at that node. That is, a random forest incorporates two types of randomness, one from training samples and the other from the input variables.

On the other hand, Wolpert (1992) has proposed another interesting committee machine called the stacked generalization (called "stacking"). Its main difference from bagging and boosting is its capability of combining multiple models of different types. Stacking can combine different models (e.g., logistic regression and decision trees) by introducing a "meta learner". The predictions of the base models (called level-0 models) become the input to the meta model (also called level-1 model). The meta model attempts to discover which base modes are the reliable ones and how to combine the predictions of the base models. Stacking has not been used as often as bagging and boosting, partially because it is analytically more demanding. For further materials on stacking, see Witten and Frank (2000), and Ting and Witten (1997).

Other techniques of combining multiple models include error-correcting output codes (Dieterich and Bakiri 1995) and mixture of experts (Haykin 1999).

Part V
Customer Management

Chapter 20
Acquiring Customers

Abstract All firms must build their customer base by acquiring customers. This chapter looks at the strategy and tactics for doing so. We start with the customer equity framework, which integrates customer acquisition, retention, and development. Key to that concept is the "acquisition curve," which relates expenditures on customer acquisition to the number of customers acquired. We discuss strategies for increasing acquisition rates suggested by the acquisition curve, and then present and elaborate on a framework for developing customer acquisition programs.

20.1 Introduction

A critical function of database marketing is to enhance the firm's ability to acquire customers. Blattberg et al. (2001) show that the total contribution of a customer to the firm, customer "equity", is the firm's cost of acquiring a customer relative to the future stream of customer value. As the dotcoms taught the market and database marketers, the cost of customer acquisition can sink a business. For example, Pet.com had an acquisition cost of $400 per customer. What is the revenue and profit potential of acquiring a pet food customer? Suppose the average customer spends $100 per purchase and the incremental profit margin is $20 since the purchases are likely to be heavily weighted to pet food, not the higher margin pet supplies. Then, it would take 20 purchases before the customer breaks even, and that assumes no costs associated with retaining customers. If there is a 75% chance on each purchase occasion the customer is retained, can the business model of Pet.com ever pay out? The answer is obvious. No. The value of that income stream, assuming no discounting, is $80 and the cost of acquisition is $400. Where is Pet.com today? Out of business.

What drove the willingness of dotcoms to go public with such a poor economic model? They believed that the acquisition cost would drop significantly and they would then earn profits from retained customers.

However, that belief was mistaken. Almost none of the dotcoms were able to drive down their acquisition costs to a level that made it feasible to make a profit.

This chapter discusses theories and methods for customer acquisition. Most of the marketing literature does not separate acquisition marketing from retention marketing or add-on selling. Exceptions can be found in the new product literature but most of this literature involves durable goods where diffusion of innovation and the Bass model are used. These products are not repeat purchased. There is a small literature on new non-durable goods marketing (see, e.g., Blattberg and Golanty (1978)) that separates trial (acquisition) from repeat (retention) but little has been written in recent years. Therefore, this chapter will have relatively few references. This should not be interpreted as lack of importance of the topic. Few academics have made a distinction between acquisition marketing and marketing in general. Yet the issues are different. Expectations play a very important role in acquisition, particularly with respect to product quality. Pricing and promotion are the lifeblood of acquisition marketing. It is more difficult to target acquisition efforts than to target retention efforts. The opportunity for academics is a wide open area of research.

We begin with a description of an overall framework for analyzing customer acquisition decisions. Then, we discuss drivers of customer acquisition. We next discuss the acquisition marketing mix, including methods for targeting customer acquisitions. We end with a brief discussion of relevant research issues.

20.2 The Fundamental Equation of Customer Equity

Throughout this chapter we will use the fundamental equation of customer equity as shown in Blattberg et al. (2001).

$$CE(t) = N_t \alpha_t (AS_t - c_t) - N_t B_{a,t} + \sum_{k=1}^{\infty} N_t \alpha_t \left(\prod_{j=1}^{k} \rho_{j,t+k} \right)$$

$$\times (RS_{t+k} - c_{t+k} - B_{r,t+k} - B_{AO,t+k}) \left(\frac{1}{1+d} \right)^k \qquad (20.1)$$

where

N_t = the number of prospective customers available at time t.
α_t = the acquisition probability at time t.
AS_t = acquisition sales at time t.
c_t = cost of goods sold at time t.
$B_{a,t}$ = acquisition marketing investment at time t.

$\rho_{j,t+k}$ = retention rate at time $t + k$ for customers acquired at time j.
RS_t = sales from retained customers at time t (including add-on sales).
$B_{r,t}$ = investment in retaining customers at time t.
$B_{AO,t}$ = investment in selling additional products to retained customers
   at time t.
d = the discount rate.

This equation describes three elements of customer equity. The first part of
the expression shows the acquisition costs and initial benefits; the second
represents customer retention, and the last part portrays how much is sold
to customers and the profit margins obtained. Specifically,

$$Acquistion(t) = N_t \alpha_t (AS_t - c_t) - N_t B_{a,t} \tag{20.2a}$$

$$Retention(t) = \sum_{k=1}^{\infty} N_t \alpha_t \left(\prod_{j=1}^{k} \rho_{j,t+k} \right) \tag{20.2b}$$

$$Retention\ Profit(t) = \sum_{k=1}^{\infty} N_t \alpha_t \left(\prod_{j=1}^{k} \rho_{j,t+k} \right)$$

$$\times (S_{t+k} - c_{t+k} - B_{r,t+k} - B_{AO,t+k}) \left(\frac{1}{1+d} \right)^k \tag{20.2c}$$

We will concentrate on acquisition. Equation 20.2a shows that the critical factors driving the contribution of acquisition to customer equity are:
(a) N, the market size, (b) α, the acquisition rate or probability of acquisition,
(c) B, the cost per customer contacted, and (d) $S - c$, the profit margin of
sales to the acquired customer. Below, we will describe strategies associated
with each of these factors.

20.3 Acquisition Costs

The cost of acquiring customers is at the heart of acquisition marketing. Sophisticated database marketing firms compute the cost of acquiring a customer and then trade it off versus the lifetime value of the customer. An example will be used to demonstrate how most firms compute
the cost of customer acquisition. Then, we will discuss the types of data
required.
   Suppose a cataloger is analyzing the cost of acquiring new customers. Assume the firm uses a two-step acquisition process in which the firm advertises
in a targeted publication to attract prospects and then mails the catalog to
those who respond. The process enables the firm to identify the names of
prospects, and then acquire (or "convert") them.

Table 20.1 Cost of acquiring a customer

Cost of advertisement	$50,000
Number of respondents to advertisement	100,000
Cost of mailing individual catalog	$2.00
Cost of catalog mailing	$200,000
Response rate from catalog mailing	5%
Number of customers acquired	5,000
Acquisition cost before sales to acquired customers	$250,000
Acquisition cost per customer before initial sale	$50.00
Initial purchase	$75.00
Initial margin	20%
Profit from purchase	$15.00
Acquisition cost per customer after including initial sale	$35.00

Table 20.1 shows the data. It costs the firm $50 to acquire a customer, or $35 if the initial sale is included. The critical metrics in customer acquisition are the response rate to the initial mailing(s) or communications (e.g., Internet ad), costs associated with acquiring the customer, the number of customers acquired, the profit from the initial sale and the future value of these customers.

Surprisingly, many firms do not know their cost of acquiring a new customer. Partly, this is because many firms do not track it and partly because some of the costs are difficult to allocate. For example, if this were a consumer packaged-good product such as Tide detergent, it would be very difficult to allocate media advertising between acquisition and retention marketing. However, while it is difficult, the firm could begin to analyze how important different types of advertising are for customer acquisition. Also, the firm could try to determine how much of its advertising is targeted to acquisition versus retention. Still, it is very difficult and hence why firms that use general media do not allocate it to acquisition versus retention marketing.

One must recognize that most customers are acquired at a loss, and only pay out if their long-term contribution is large enough. To be effective the firm should then try to determine how much it can afford to lose when acquiring a customer. Without this metric firms may either over or more likely under-invest in customer acquisition.

Because firms lose money when they are acquiring customers, when economic times are difficult, firms often decrease customer acquisition. A firm can then "milk" its existing customers and not acquire customers. This will increase short-term profitability but will cost profit growth in the long-run. Blattberg et al. (2001, Chapter 8) address this issue by recommending customer equity accounting statements so that firms are far less likely to under-invest in customer acquisition and milk short-term profits (see also the Customer Management Marketing Budget, Sect. 26.4.1, Chapter 26). The next section discusses the factors that increase customer acquisition rates, which as is obvious from the analysis of customer acquisition cost, is a critical parameter in decreasing the cost of acquisition.

20.4 Strategies for Increasing Number of Customers Acquired

20.4.1 Increasing Market Size

A critical driver in acquiring new customers is the number of potential customers in the market for the product or service. Obviously, the larger the number of prospective customers, the greater the market potential is. However, there is a trade-off. Marketers understand that increasing the size of the target market can be detrimental because the positioning of the product or service becomes amorphous and the product therefore fails to capture any share of the market. The firm can therefore try to increase the size of the potential number of customers (N) but in doing so, risks lowering the response rate (α).

What are some of the strategies used to increase the potential target market for a product or service? The first and most obvious is to suggest or develop new usage occasions. Examples abound, such as Arm & Hammer Baking Soda being used as a deodorizer and not just an ingredient in baking; cat litter being used to clean garage floors because of its absorbency; American Express using a variant of a gift card as a mechanism to provide cash to customers while they are overseas or on vacation. However, while we can give examples, firms often have difficulty finding new usage occasions for their products or services.

It is often easier to target new customer segments. This is a common acquisition strategy for firms. BMW introduced the 1 series; Johnny Walker introduced gold and blue versions of its Scotch whiskey brand. Costco began focusing on small businesses and then opened its warehouse club to individuals who were willing to pay an annual fee. Whole Foods began as an organic, natural grocery store but has expanded to "foodies" who enjoy higher quality products but also perceive the organic benefit as positive. USAA insurance opened its insurance to family members as well as military officers.

The major risk in trying to expand the size of the number of prospective customers is losing focus on the brand's positioning. Sometimes it can work as the above examples show but sometimes it does not. The consumer becomes confused about the positioning of the brand. As BMW expands the reach of its brand with lower-end offerings (1 series in Europe), it risks lack of exclusivity and damaging its image. Mercedes faces the same problem. The ultimate car example was Cadillac, which created the Cimarron in the late seventies. It was a "juiced-up" version of the Chevrolet Cavalier. It hurt the brand image of Cadillac because the consumer perceived Cadillac as no longer representing a luxury vehicle. While expanding the market through reaching new segments is obviously beneficial, the risks are significant. For every success story, there is a failure. Firms must be very careful how they approach this strategy.

Generally speaking, any time the firm expands the markets it is trying to reach, it jeopardizes reducing the acquisition rate (α). The broader the market is, the lower the acquisition rate. By having a lower acquisition rate, the cost of customer acquisition increases. While not necessarily problematic (if the customer generates enough immediate and long-term profit), it can lead to much lower return on invested capital and if the firm is not careful, profits can be negative.

20.4.2 Increasing Marketing Acquisition Expenditures

An obvious mechanism for increasing the number of customers acquired is to increase marketing expenditures on acquisition. The real issue is payout. However, before discussing payout, it is important to understand standard industry practice which is why this strategy becomes important. Several years ago, the Greater Chicago Food Depository, which is a food bank designed to feed the poor, decided to embark on a direct marketing campaign to raise funds through individual donations. The campaign was very successful. In fact, it was self funding: the acquisition expenditures were covered by the initial donations. However the Food Depository did not want to increase acquisition spending because it was above their allotted budget. This was a poor decision. However, it is symptomatic of many organizations.

Firms generally lose money on initial customer acquisition. They generally make up the loss on future purchases (dotcoms being a notable exception). The cost is recorded in the acquisition period and thus distorts the profit picture to make the acquisition period's profits look worse. Because of the short-term loss due to customer acquisitions, many firms under-invest in customer acquisition. This accounting "distortion" results in firms failing to capture the total potential of the future customer profit stream. In some businesses, firms are allowed to amortize customer acquisition over the "life" of the customer and those firms benefit because they can increase their customer acquisition investment relative to firms who face traditional accounting treatment of customer acquisition.

Another customer acquisition investment is general media advertising (not including direct marketing) to generate awareness of the product/service. By generating awareness, the newly aware potentially acquired consumer can seek out the product/service. This is becoming more common with the Internet. Firms can generate awareness, which leads to visits to websites and ultimately sales. Banner ads in which customers click through is an example. See Manchanda et al. (2006) for a study of the economic and sales impact of banner ads.

An important (and ostensibly free) source of awareness is word-of-mouth. Positive word-of-mouth also generates awareness as well as influences the consumer's intention to purchase. Factors affecting positive word-of-mouth include product/service quality, the value of the product/service, and relevant positioning of the product/service. Some firms rely exclusively on word-of-mouth such as USAA. Many small businesses rely on word-of-mouth as their primary source of new customers. Restaurants, movies and other entertainment services utilize word-of-mouth as a key source of customer acquisition. Some sophisticated marketing companies are using strategies to influence opinion leaders who provide credible word-of-mouth. One major consumer products company has identified teenage opinion leaders, uses direct marketing to reach and influence them, and then through word-of-mouth, the opinion leaders influence other teenagers. See Zhang (2006), who describes how word-of-mouth affects consumer learning, another important factor affecting the efficiency of acquisition spending.

20.4.3 Changing the Shape of the Acquisition Curve

The acquisition curve plots the probability of a customer being acquired as a function of total acquisition spending. The shape of the acquisition curve is critical to acquisition marketing. We have plotted two typical acquisition curves in Fig. 20.1. The steeper the slope of the line, meaning the higher the "elasticity" of response from additional spending, the more effective acquisition spending is. The reason the curve reaches an asymptote is that at some level of spending it is almost impossible to acquire new customers. The more important question is: how does a firm change the shape of the acquisition curve?

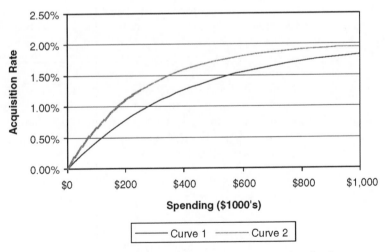

Fig. 20.1 Acquisition rates as a function of spending levels.

Table 20.2 Typical mailing response rates

List name	Number of names tested	Response rate	Size of name pool (000)
A	5,000	2.70%	250
B	10,000	2.50%	400
C	5,000	1.80%	750
D	10,000	1.60%	800
E	10,000	1.40%	1,300
F	5,000	1.10%	1,700
G	5,000	1.00%	230
H	10,000	0.90%	900
I	5,000	0.85%	600
J	15,000	0.60%	3,500
Breakeven cut-off:		1.5%	

The acquisition–spending curve is determined by how different segments of the market respond to acquisition marketing. As the firm spends more on acquisition in a given period (e.g., a year), it needs to dip deeper into the pool of potential segments it can target. We will use a simple example to highlight the issue.

Table 20.2 shows a typical response chart from a series of test mailings. Table 20.2 shows incremental change in response rates as spending increases while Fig. 20.1 shows the cumulative number of customers acquired. Figure 20.1 has decreasing returns. We have ranked the data from highest to lowest response as well as the size of the potential mailing to each list and the spending required for mailing the list. The table shows overall response rate. As the firm increases its acquisition mailings and spending, its overall response rate declines. The reason is simple. Firms target their best sources for acquisition first and then are forced to reach lower and lower into the pool of potential sources of names for acquisition as spending increases.

How then can a firm change the shape of its acquisition–spending curve? There are two answers. First, the firm can improve its targeting strategy. This is at the heart of database marketing. By finding better sources of names or identifying more responsive targets, the firm will increase its response rate for a fixed acquisition investment. Second, the firm can use various methods to drive up response rates such as using two-step communication strategies as described earlier[1] or investing in general media advertising to increase awareness and to position the product/service to increase the response rate.

Later in this chapter, we describe methods to improve the firm's targeting. However, improved targeting requires:

- A clear understanding of who the firm's target audiences are
- Testing and measurement

---

[1] An example of a two-step campaign begins with step 1 which might be an advertising in a magazine to generate prospects and step 2 using direct marketing to convert the leads into customers.

- Creative new ways to target consumers
- The use of new media

Using different marketing and communication vehicles to increase acquisition response rates requires testing and measurement. Surprisingly, few firms beyond database marketers are good at testing and measurement because of the discipline it requires. Some firms are disciplined but cannot easily track customer acquisition because they sell through intermediaries rather than direct.

Many of the ways that acquisition response rates are increased is through "acquisition enhancing vehicles". Firms must track and measure the impact of these vehicles. For example, a firm uses general advertising to generate awareness and create an overall positioning of its brand. Their general media advertising should then increase response rates to direct marketing communications or should generate some number of customers who seek out the firm's products/services. Without tracking it is impossible to determine if general media advertising is producing the desired result. This in turn makes it very difficult to measure the economic payout of the advertising campaign.

20.4.4 Using Lead Products

Another acquisition strategy is to identify lead products to acquire customers. Once the firm has acquired the customer, other products/services are sold to the customer. In the old days direct marketing insurance companies used a product called accidental death and dismemberment insurance. It was inexpensive since most people are rarely dismembered and accidental death (versus natural causes) was also relatively unlikely. Once the customer was acquired through this product, the firm then focused on selling other insurance products. Automobile companies sell "lower priced" products to bring the customer into the family of products and then over time hope to sell them more expensive ones. Grocery retailers use Coke and Pepsi to bring customers into the store with the goal of selling related products and building the size of the basket.
Lead products have certain characteristics:

- Broad appeal relative to other products/service in the firm's product line
- Entry level price points
- Consistency with the firm's image/positioning

Notice that high margin is not one of the characteristics. Some firms try to use expensive, high margin products to generate initial trial but this is likely to reduce, not increase acquisition rates. The goal is that once a customer makes an initial purchase, then the firm can sell the customer more expensive products/services. American Express acquires customers through its Green card in hopes of later selling them a Platinum card. BMW sells the 1 series in Europe in hopes of selling the 3, 5 and 7 series to the customer on the next purchase.

Obviously the use of lead products does not fit every business. How does Procter and Gamble use lead products? They instead use sampling or trial sizes to create initial trial and then hope to sell the larger sizes after the customer evaluates the product. Only firms that have extensive product lines they can cross-sell to the customer have the capability of using lead products as a customer acquisition vehicle.

20.4.5 Acquisition Pricing and Promotions

An obvious way to affect acquisition rates is through pricing and promotions. As the price decreases, acquisition rates almost always increase. The same with promotions, they can increase the acquisition rate. The caveat is that using price and promotions to acquire customers can affect future purchases. Part of the reason is that acquisition pricing and promotional discounts can influence the consumers overall reference price and image of the firm. If the firm offers a steep discount to acquire a customer, when the customer either renews the product/service or purchases another product/service he or she expects a discount and a low price. Customers develop expectations about the firm's pricing which is then used to evaluate future prices. The lower the introductory price or the more aggressive the introductory promotion, the lower will be the renewal rate unless the firm again offers an aggressive discount.

Acquisition pricing and promotion also influence which segments of customers are acquired. The lower the acquisition price or the more aggressive the promotion is, the more likely the consumers that are being attracted are price sensitive consumers. The pricing and promotional strategy for acquiring customers determines the pool of customers who will be available to either cross-sell and/or renew. Customer retention and cross-selling potentially depend upon the acquisition strategy being used.

Models can be developed that link acquisition and retention pricing. Thomas et al. (2004a) indirectly consider this issue in the context of a newspaper renewal. The focus of their paper is on renewal pricing, not acquisition pricing, but clearly both are related. Thomas (2001) shows how acquisition and retention can be jointly modeled using a Type II Tobit model. Feasibly, if acquisition price were included in the selection (acquisition) equation and retention price were included in the regression (retention) equation, the two prices could be optimized. Reinartz et al. (2005) extension of this model could also be used to optimize prices (see Chapter 26 for further discussion of these models).

Simple models of acquisition pricing, covered in more detail in Chapter 29, show that acquisition pricing depends upon the long-run value of the customer. The higher the long-run value of the customer, the lower the firm should make the acquisition price. The reason is obvious. The higher the firm's "backend" profits – profits after acquisition – the greater incentive the firm can offer to acquire customers. Similar arguments can be made for promotional discounting. Again the higher the firm's backend profits, the deeper the firm can discount to acquire customers.

There are two critical assumptions associated with the above argument. The first is that there is no relationship between the consumer's acquisition reservation price and retention reservation price. The literature on reference prices (see Briesch et al. 1997) makes this assumption tenuous. A potential model structure for considering how acquisition prices may affect retention price sensitivity coefficient is $\ln(\beta_r) = \beta_o + \delta \ ap_{t-1}$ where β_r = retention price coefficient and ap_t = acquisition price at time t and β_o is a constant influencing the overall price sensitivity. In words, the price last used to acquire customers influences retention price sensitivity. If the sign of δ is negative, higher acquisition prices get higher retention price sensitivity.

The second assumption is that the customers are homogeneous in price sensitivity. Clearly this assumption is violated. Direct marketers have long believed that as the firm lowers acquisition prices or as it uses deep discounts to acquire customers, price sensitive customers are then acquired. If retention prices are significantly higher than acquisition prices including the promotional discounts offered, price sensitive customers acquired will not renew. Because the firm loses money on acquiring customers, it can be very costly to acquire price sensitive customers because they will result in a net loss over their total lifetime which is likely to be only one purchase.

The above issues are covered in far more detail in the Chapter 29, which focuses on pricing. However, in designing an acquisition strategy, the firm must carefully consider the implications of its acquisition pricing strategy.

20.5 Developing a Customer Acquisition Program

20.5.1 Framework

To help understand customer acquisition, we present a schematic framework similar to those used in consumer behavior research. It highlights many of the issues in the design of customer acquisition strategies. We will briefly describe the model and its implications. The model draws on both the marketing literature and a previous descriptive model developed in Blattberg et al. (2001, Chapter 3).

Figure 20.2 presents the framework. The critical elements of this model are: (a) consumers develop expectations, partly influenced by the firm, which are then updated through their purchase experiences and the objective quality of the product/service; (b) consumers are heterogeneous and the firm must

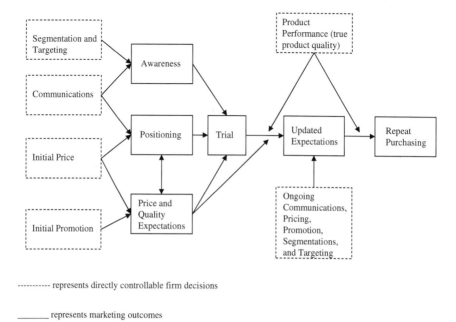

---------- represents directly controllable firm decisions

_____ represents marketing outcomes

Fig. 20.2 Customer acquisition process model.

select targets; (c) acquisition pricing and promotions influence price as well as quality expectations, which determine repeat buying rates; and (d) awareness is very important to the process and firms can use traditional media advertising to create awareness.

The firm directly controls (a) the true quality of the product/service, (b) marketing communications to create awareness and establish positioning, (c) segmentation and targeting of potential consumers, and (d) pricing and promotion.

Having discussed pricing and promotion earlier, we will focus the discussion on (1) segmentation, targeting and positioning, (2) product/service offering, (3) targeting methods, and media selection.

20.5.2 Segmentation, Targeting and Positioning (STP)

Interwoven in some of the examples used earlier is the identification of potentially viable segments to target. There are different methods of segmenting, many of which are covered in basic marketing texts (Kotler and Keller 2006, pp. 37, 310) and they will not be discussed here. It is important to recognize that the more finely the segments can be defined, the more precisely the firm can target. If the firm only uses broadly defined segments (e.g., women 18–49), it may be better for the firm to mass market.

Targeting is choosing the relevant segments whose customers the firm will invest its marketing resources to acquire. The ability to select the appropriate targets is extremely valuable. The greater the firm's ability to target, the higher the firm's acquisition response rate is. Better targeting does not necessarily mean that the firm should avoid going deeply into the acquisition file, because there may be customers who are unprofitable in the short term but profitable in the long term.

Positioning is critical. If the firm's positioning for a given product/service does not match the quality and benefits offered in the positioning statement, consumer's expectations are not matched when the product/service experience occurs. The likely outcome is lower repeat-purchasing rates. The difficult trade-off is designing an aggressive acquisition positioning statement to increase acquisition response rates while maintaining high repeat purchasing rates. When a firm over-promises about the merits of its product/service offering during acquisition marketing, it lowers its retention rates. Obviously, this is an important trade-off though there is very little research on the topic of how much retention declines because of over promising about the product/service offering during customer acquisition.

20.5.3 Product/Service Offering

The firm must understand the tangible and intangible attributes of the product/service being offered. This assessment must be objectively determined. It will ultimately be matched against the customer's expectations driven by marketing and other related contacts the customer has with the product/service. For example, the firm must realistically understand the quality of its product/service otherwise it will, in all likelihood, over-promise and under-deliver. Setting customer's expectations is critical to customer retention.

Examples abound of firms that over-promise and then have great difficulty with customer retention. The most notorious example is used-car salespersons. Used-car salespersons do anything to make the immediate sale but very few of their customers ever return. In the US Car Max and Auto Nation have tried to overcome this problem by offering warranties on used cars and by carefully evaluating and servicing the used (now called "pre-owned") cars sold to ensure they are less likely to have service and quality problems. Dealers now sell "authorized used cars" again to overcome this problem, where the cars are inspected and serviced to bring them up to a certain standard.

It is essential strategically that the firm understands its product/service quality and then targets the appropriate audience and position the product/service to set the appropriate expectations. A firm that has been very effective is Southwest Airlines. Its product/service is very basic. No first class, no frills, no fancy meals, no complex ticketing. They offer reliable, low-priced airline service. Southwest's advertising tag line was "We fly for Peanuts" which is a play on words. At one time, they only served peanuts as food on their flights. Flying for Peanuts also means flying for low fares. Thus, Southwest's delivers on its brand promise. Expectations meet actual customer experience. By managing expectations properly, Southwest was able to deliver no-frills service.

Target stores uses as its brand promise – "Expect more, pay less". It has been one of the few retailers able to compete effectively against Wal-Mart. By keeping its margins relatively low, Target is able to offer affordable fashion aimed at women. Instead of over-promising on being very chic as many department stores attempt to do, it recognizes its niche is affordable fashion.

20.5.4 Acquisition Targeting

Acquisition targeting and media strategies are the most well researched area in acquisition marketing. Numerous books cover how to target (see Hughes 2000; Sheppard 1999; Jackson and Wang 1994). The issue that needs to be addressed in acquisition targeting is: can the firm use various data and statistical methods to reach target segments more effectively than mass marketing? The general belief is that the firm can. The methods used by firms include finding relevant databases of target segments, testing, profiling and predictive modeling.

It is important to understand that sometimes it is better not to target and instead use general low-cost media for customer acquisition. One of the best examples is couponing. Assume the cost is $10 per thousand to distribute and produce the coupons. Suppose a firm distributes 50,000,000 FSI (free-standing inserts) coupons to acquire customers. Assume the response rate is approximately 3% which translates into 1,500,000 coupons redeemed. Of the 1,500,000 coupons redeemed, 5% are new customers to the brand. Thus, the firm acquired 75,000 customers. The cost of the coupon drop is $10.00 per thousand and the face value of the coupon is $0.50. This translates into a cost of $500,000 for the coupon drop and $750,000 for coupon redemption. The cost of acquiring each new customer is $16.67. Table 20.3 provides the calculations.

An alternative is for the firm to use targeted marketing to acquire customers. The firm, through a retailer's frequent shopper card, was able to send 3,000,000 coupons at a cost of $0.50 per coupon or $500 per thousand which is 50 times higher than the cost of an FSI.[2] However, the firm had a 6% response rate (higher than the 3% for the coupon) and of the 180,000 coupons redeemed 30% were new customers to the brand. The number of

---

[2] In the 1990s there were a number of firms who tried to market highly targeted coupons. Because of the high cost to reach customers, none was successful.

Table 20.3 Acquisition cost comparisons: Mass-marketed versus targeted coupons

Mass-marketed coupon	
Current HH penetration	
Number of coupons distributed	50,000,000
Cost per coupon distributed	$0.01
Response rate	3%
Redemption cost	$0.50
Incremental number of customers	5%
Number of new customers	75,000
Cost of coupon drop	$1,250,000
Cost per customer acquired	$16.67
Targeted coupon	
Number of coupons distributed	3,000,000
Cost per coupon distributed	$0.50
Response rate	6%
Redemption cost	$0.50
Incremental number of customers	30%
Number of new customers	54,000
Cost of coupon drop	$1,590,000
Cost per customer acquired	$29.44

new customers was 54,000. The total cost of the direct marketing campaign was $1,590,000. The cost to acquire a new customer was $29.44.

This is an illustrative example but it shows that the firm may be better off using an untargeted vehicle to acquire customers. It depends upon the financial structure of the two alternatives. Because the cost of targeting can be exceptionally high in certain industries (e.g., consumer packaged goods), it may be more efficient to use mass vehicles to acquire customers and then use targeting for customer retention. Alternatively, firms use two-step systems where mass media is used to qualify or identify prospects and direct marketing to the prospects is used to convert the prospects to customers.

Because the success of targeted acquisition is not guaranteed, one must follow a carefully orchestrated series of steps. The first step is to identify sources of prospective names. Different methods are available to identify potential sources of names and are discussed in the next section. Once the target segment(s) are determined, the firm must find a vehicle to reach them. List brokers can provide lists of addressable names within each target segment. Then the firm can test these lists.

An alternative form of acquisition has emerged that combines elements of targeted and mass marketed acquisition – the Internet; e.g., the firm can include a banner ad based on certain word searchers using a search engine (e.g., Google). This type of targeting allows prospects to self-select by searching for information using certain key words. As individuals search for a certain words, they are signaling their interest in the product or service. The firm then intervenes with an ad which hopefully leads to qualified prospects. This approach is mass marketing in the sense that ads are being placed in the equivalent of a magazine or television program, however, the placement is targeted based on interests the consumer implicitly reveals. Again the success of this type of prospecting depends upon the economic return. For example, Verhoef and Donkers (2005) find that the long-term value of a customer, measured by retention and cross-selling opportunities, are roughly average for Internet-acquired customers compared to other acquisition vehicles such as outbound telephone, TV/radio, and direct mail. (See Chapter 25 for further discussion of the value of alternative channels as acquisition tools.)

20.5.5 Targeting Methods for Customer Acquisition

There are several commonly used methods for targeting: profiling, predictive models using demographics or customer characteristics, random testing of prospect databases, and two-step acquisition programs. Each has benefits.

The basic rule is: it is difficult to develop accurate targeting methods for customer acquisition. Unlike targeting and managing existing customers, the data available for customer acquisition is very limited. Firms sell demographic or customer characteristic data (examples are Experian or Axciom) but these data are not very predictive of who will actual purchase. However, these data can be used for a test, followed by a predictive model used to forecast which customers on the list are most likely to respond (see Sect. 20.5.5.2).

20.5.5.1 Profiling

A very common method advocated by some direct marketers (Hughes 2000) is to profile the firm's existing customer base and then target customers based on the characteristics of current customers. The typical process is:

1. Take a sample of current customers,
2. Obtain and append to the customer record relevant demographic or customer characteristic information about these customers,
3. Cross-tab or use clustering of demographics to describe or "profile" current customers in terms of these characteristics,
4. Target customers with identical or similar profiles as the current customers.

There are two major issues in profiling analysis. First, how do we prioritize the variables that make up the profile? For example, the current customer profile might be older men. Which would be a more likely customer – a younger man or an older woman? Second, the firm only targets customers similar to its current customers, but these customers were acquired using previous targeting methods and advertising vehicles and so their profile was created by the process that acquired them. As a result, profiling may miss customers in other segments who would purchase if given the opportunity.

One solution to the first problem is to use techniques such as discriminant analysis, logistic regression, or decision trees. To do this, the firm must have a large list that includes non-customers. Logistic regression or discriminant analysis provide an equation that can be used to weight the several variables used in the profiling and derive a probability that the non-customer belongs in the customer group (see Chapter 15 on discrete dependent variable models). Alternatively, a decision tree method such as CHAID can be used to derive a tree-like structure showing the key variables that distinguish customers from non-customers (see Chapter 17). The end-nodes of the tree represent a particular customer profile, and calculate the probability the customers with this profile are current customers.

The second problem – the "self fulfilling prophecy" of targeting only individuals who are similar to current customers – is difficult to address. By targeting prospects with similar profiles, the firm never learns if it can attract other types of customers. To overcome this problem, firms should use random samples drawn from lists to see if those who respond have the same characteristics as current customers. If not, it opens the opportunity of adding new segments. However, the method requires more rigor than is generally applied to the problem. One must be careful because random responses that are not statistically reliable will cause the firm to target new segments that in fact do not prove fruitful.

20.5.5.2 Regression and Logistic Regression Modeling

Some firms find sources of names, often through list brokers, and then send a marketing communication including an offer to a random sample of these names. The names are appended with characteristics such as demographics. Then to identify responders the firm runs a regression or a logistic regression model (more appropriate) in which the dependent variable is buy or no-buy. The independent variables come from the characteristics appended to the database. The regression and logistic regression models can be stated as:

$$y_i = X_i\beta + \varepsilon_i \tag{20.3a}$$

$$p_i = \frac{1}{1 + e^{-X_i\beta}} \tag{20.3b}$$

where

$y_i = 1$ if a given prospect i purchases, otherwise it is 0
X_i = the explanatory variables used to characterize the prospect
p_i = the probability that prospect i purchases
ε_i = the error term
β = the coefficient weights for the explanatory variables

While in principle this type of approach sounds promising, its success hinges on the predictive power or "lift" provided by these models (see Chapter 10). While this approach can work in practice, its success is not guaranteed. The basic problem is that the explanatory variables available are typically demographic characteristics. Previously collected behavioral characteristics typically provide the most predictive power, but since we are attracting new customers, there are no data on previous behavior, at least with the acquiring firm.

20.5.5.3 Testing Several Lists

A very common acquisition method is to take a set of lists and then randomly mail to a subset of individuals on each list. Each list is then scored based on its response rate. Those lists that score above a specific cut-off are mailed in larger quantities. This method is as old as the direct marketing industry. The problem is that it has flaws. The main one is that unless the sample size is quite large, the test may not have the statistical power to identify truly profitable lists.

To demonstrate the problem, we have created 20 lists, each with a probability of response of 2%. A sample size of 5,000 per list is mailed and the response rates calculated. The firm has a cut-off of 2.3% as its breakeven point. Table 20.4 shows the results. It shows three lists are above the cutoff value.

Using a normal approximation to the binomial distribution with $n = 5,000$ and $p = 0.02$, the probability that at least 2 lists will be above the cutoff is

Table 20.4 Illustrative results from mailing using sample size of 5,000 for 20 lists, each with a true response rate of 2%

List number	Response rate
8	2.48%
1	2.36%
9	2.30%
15	2.28%
16	2.18%
6	2.16%
7	2.16%
14	2.12%
2	2.10%
17	2.02%
19	2.00%
4	1.96%
5	1.96%
20	1.96%
10	1.90%
11	1.82%
12	1.82%
18	1.82%
3	1.74%
13	1.68%
Cutoff response rate	2.30%

13.7%. The probability that at least one list will be above the cutoff is 37.6%. This is in spite of the fact that the cutoff is 2.3%. The problem is that the sample size of 5,000 does not provide enough precision in the estimate of the response rate to effectively discriminate between a 2% and a 2.3% response rate. In testing several lists, this problem multiplies, i.e., the 13.7% and 37.6% probabilities will become even higher the greater the number of lists that are tested. The 13.7% and 37.6% probabilities can easily be computed but most firms select lists to mail to that are above their cutoff. The implication is that if a firm does list testing, it is likely that some of the lists will be assumed to be better targeting vehicles than they actually are.

Therefore, some method or statistical model is needed to improve the firm's ability to test lists that adjusts for the fact that at random some lists are likely to be above the cutoff value, and this is more likely the more lists that are tested. Using classical statistical methods without adjusting for multiple list testing leads to a reasonable chance that rollouts of test lists above the cut-off will attenuate to the mean of all lists when re-tested or rolled out. One way to make the adjustment would be to require high levels of statistical confidence before concluding a particular list is profitable. This can be related to the number of lists tested using methods of multiple comparison (e.g., see classical statistics texts such as Lapin 1990).

Pfeifer (1998) proposes a Bayesian approach to deriving the optimal sample size to use for a test mailing. The approach takes into account the manager's "prior" expectation of the response rate, as well as the expected profits per response. Chapter 9 discusses the approach in detail.

20.5.5.4 Two-Step Acquisition Methods

The term two-step refers to the use of "self-selection" of prospective customers who respond to an initial, non-purchase communication and then receive a second communication which is an offer to purchase. This method is used because of the lack of precision in being able to identify prospective buyers using some of the methods discussed earlier in this chapter.

To make this more concrete, one often sees continuing education seminar series being offered in the *Wall Street Journal* or other publications (e.g., *The Economist*). The individual course is offered and is functioning as a lead product (Sect. 20.4.4), but when the individual responds to the seminar advertisement, he or she is also put on a mailing list. Then, future seminars are offered to the respondent through a catalog that can be mailed to the individual. The response rate from catalogs sent to first-step respondents is much higher than it would be if it were sent to the population at-large.

Catalog companies often use this method because of the high cost of sending catalogs through the mail. They advertise in relevant publications such as House and Garden to target a specific type of demographic or lifestyle segment group (e.g., women interested in gardening) and then those that respond are mailed a catalog. As importantly, they are kept on the mailing list so that even if they do not respond to the first catalog, they can be considered prospects for future mailings.

Two-step acquisition methods depend upon: (1) the cost structure of reaching specific audiences, and (2) the nature of the targeting. For example, it is very difficult to target on the basis of lifestyle even though firms recognize that it is important because lists rarely contain true lifestyle data. Therefore, using publications aimed at specific lifestyles (called "vertical publications") may be far more effective. Even when a publication sells its subscription list, it may be more cost effective to use a two-step acquisition method because of the lower cost of a mass advertisement to identify prospects.

20.6 Research Issues in Acquisition Marketing

In general, there is very little research on acquisition marketing. The traditional marketing literature does not separate the issue of acquiring customers from retaining customers. Positioning, segmentation, targeting is a generic concept. Research in advertising studies the general impact of communications but does not separate newly acquired customers from retained customers. Therefore, it is necessary to develop a new literature on the theory of customer acquisition. No doubt some of the existing studies can be modified to fit the issue of customer acquisition.

Important research questions that affect managerial practice are: (1) How do initial product/service expectations affect retention rates? (2) What theories can be used to predict the likely impact of expectations on retention rates? (3) How does the introductory price affect customer reference prices for future purchases? (4) What variables determine the shape and steepness of the acquisition response curve? (5) How does traditional advertising affect acquisition rates? (6) How is media advertising apportioned between acquisition and retention impact? (7) How do customers develop initial expectations about a product/service they have not purchased? (8) How does self-selection in acquisition targeting affect retention rates? (9) How does advertising frequency affect acquisition rates? (10) Can acquisition marketing techniques be used to create a brand image? (11) Can basic principles (or theories) of acquisition marketing be developed which help practitioners design acquisition programs?

No doubt there are many other issues that can be added to our list. However, as important as acquisition marketing is, researchers need to develop theories, principles and empirical generalizations that will help practitioners develop better acquisition marketing strategies and tactics.

Chapter 21
Cross-Selling and Up-Selling

Abstract Cross-selling and up-selling are fundamental database marketing activities for developing customers; that is, increasing customer expenditures with the firm. Cross-selling entails selling products in the firm's product line that the customer does not currently own. Up-selling entails selling "more" (higher volume, upgrades) of products they already are buying from the company. This chapter focuses on database marketing models for cross-selling and up-selling. Included are next-product-to-buy models, which predict which product the customer is likely to purchase next, and extensions using hazard models that predict *when* the customer will buy. We cover data envelope and stochastic frontier models for up-selling. We conclude with a framework for managing an on-going cross-selling effort.

21.1 The Strategy

Cross-selling and up-selling are important strategies for increasing revenues among current customers. Cross-selling is when the firm sells different products to its customers. For example, the customer uses Intuit's TurboTax software and the company tries to sell the customer Quicken. Up-selling is when the firm sells more of the same product to the customer. For example, a customer has $300,000 in term life insurance, and the company tries to sell the customer a $500,000 policy (Kim and Kim 2001).

There are three potential benefits of cross/up-selling, illustrated by the simple retention model of lifetime value:

$$LTV = \sum_{t=1}^{\infty} \frac{m_t r^{t-1}}{(1+\delta)^{t-1}} \qquad (21.1)$$

where m_t is the customer's profit contribution in period t, r is retention rate, and δ is discount rate. First, cross-selling can generate higher sales in the current period (m_1 is increased because this month, in addition to the normal

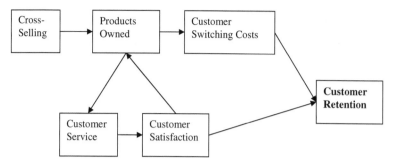

Fig. 21.1 Framework showing how cross-selling can increase customer retention.

monthly charge, the customer also has purchased a new phone). Second cross-selling can increase future revenue (higher m_t for $t > 1$). For example, a cell-phone company may cross-sell a feature, e.g., caller ID, which generates revenues in future periods because it is an additional monthly charge. Third and less obvious, cross-selling might increase retention rate (r).

Figure 21.1 shows why cross-selling might increase retention. Cross-selling results in the customer owning more of the company's products. The more products a customer owns, the better the customer can be serviced. This increases customer satisfaction and in turn, retention. In addition, the increased customer satisfaction encourages the customer to buy more products from the firm, reinforcing this cycle. Second, the more products the customer owns, the higher the customer's switching cost and this increases retention. For example, a customer who has checking, IRAs, CDs, and a mortgage with a bank incurs a large cost to switch even part of his or her business to a new bank, certainly compared to the customer who only has a checking account.

Kamakura et al. (2003) find a positive association between the number of products owned by the customer and their longevity with the firm. Of course causality may be mutual, but the association is as predicted. Kamakura et al. (2003) also provide evidence for the services-satisfaction-retention link in financial services. Recent studies reach different conclusions as to whether number of products owned enhances retention. Balachander and Ghosh (2006) and Van den Poel and Larivière (2004) find that cross-buying (owning more products) is associated with lower customer churn. Reinartz et al. (2005) find that cross-buying is associated with longer customer duration. However, Reinartz et al. (2006) use Granger causality tests to infer that cross-buying is caused by customer loyalty, rather than the reverse.

21.2 Cross-Selling Models

The key question is what products should the firm cross-sell to which customers at what time? Three types of predictive models have been developed to aid in this task: (1) Models that focus on *what* product the customer is likely to buy next ("next-product-to-buy" models). (2) Models that also consider *when* the product is likely to be bought. (3) Models that also consider how likely the customer is to *respond* to the cross-selling offer. The first two types infer what product the customer *needs*. The third type focuses on whether the customer will *respond* to cross-selling marketing efforts (Bodapati 2008). For example, a current iPod owner may "need" a car adaptor. However, the customer may not respond to a cross-selling offer.

21.2.1 Next-Product-to-Buy Models

The strategy behind next-product-to-buy models is to predict the product the customer is most likely to buy next, then cross-sell that product. However, if we predict the customer is going to buy this product next, why do we need to cross-sell it? The sale will happen naturally! The next-product-to-buy approach implicitly views this as a data problem. It would be ideal to survey Customer A and ask what product he or she needs. Since we do not have that data, we look at what products customers with similar profiles (current product ownership, personal characteristics) have bought next, and assume that is what Customer A needs (see Knott et al. 2002 for further discussion).

21.2.1.1 Market Basket Analysis and Collaborative Filtering Models

Market basket analysis and collaborative filtering are discussed in Chapters 13 and 14. These are the most basic cross-selling methods. Market basket analysis, in its simplest form, calculates Prob(Buy Product A | Bought Product B) across all "market baskets." This yields a large matrix where the ABth entry is Prob(Buy Product B | Bought Product A). P(B|A) is called "confidence." To apply this to cross-selling, one would isolate all the customers who bought Product A last, find the product B for which Prob(B|A) is maximal, and cross-sell that product to those customers.

There are several issues with using market basket analysis for cross-selling. First, is confidence, P(B|A), the right criterion? Consider the case that P(iPod Car Adaptor|iPod) = 0.2, and P(Video Game|iPod) = 0.4. On the basis of confidence, we would cross-sell the iPod buyer a video game. However, it may be that buying an iPod Car Adaptor is relatively uncommon, whereas buying a video game is quite common. That is, the unconditional probability, P(iPod Car Adaptor) = 0.1, while P(Buy Video Game) = 0.7. This means the "lift" is higher for the iPod Car Adaptor than for the video game (0.2/0.1 = 2 to 1, vs. 0.4/0.8 = 0.5 to 1). That is, customers are twice as likely to buy an iPod Car Adaptor if they've bought an iPod, *compared to the average customer*. Although the video game is the most likely product the customer will buy next, the argument in favor of the adaptor is that *if we want to sell iPod adapters*, we need to cross-sell it to iPod owners, because these are the only people who will buy the adapter.

A second issue is the time period over which to construct the $P(B|A)$ matrix. That is, during what period do we calculate $P(B|A)$? Often $P(B|A)$ is calculated based on data from a given store visit. However, if the cross-selling effort will take place after the current store visit, this may not be the correct calculation. What the customer buys in the same store visit, given he or she purchased product A, is not the same as what the customer might by say on the next store visit. The time period for calculating $P(B|A)$ should logically match up to the timing of the cross-selling effort.

A third issue is how many products to consider. Companies can have thousands and thousands of "SKU's," and to require the calculation of $P(B|A)$ for each of them may result in very low sample sizes (low "support," see Chapter 13). Companies may have to aggregate across SKU's. For example, an iPod accessory such as an iPod Cover may come in 25 varieties. The firm may think of "iPod Cover" as one product. However, this begs the question of which particular cover should be shown on the direct mail piece that targets the customers who are deemed likely to need a cover. Obviously, judgments have to be made when not every single SKU can be included in the $P(B|A)$ matrix.

Collaborative filtering is a "step up" from market basket analysis because it takes into account multiple antecedent products in a systematic way.[1] As discussed in Chapter 14, there are two types of collaborative filtering "engines," user-based and item-based. User-based systems find customers who have similar "tastes" as the target customer, and see whether these customers like the focal product. If so, that product is recommended to the target customer. Item-based systems start with the set of products the target customer has already bought. They then correlate, across all customers, the relationship between liking those products and liking the focal product. These correlations are then aggregated. The product most highly correlated with the set of products the customer has already bought is the one that is recommended.

Collaborative filtering has been the subject of much research (see Adomavicius 2005; Ansari et al. 2000). The emphasis of this research is on predicting preferences. We are not aware of assessments of these models in a field test to determine whether the customer bought the recommended product. Also, much of the collaborative filtering literature has assumed the data available are product ratings (see Mild and Reutterer 2003 for an exception). It is less clear how things should be handled if the data available are product purchases. These can be 0–1 coded and measures of association can be calculated, but the problem is how to interpret 0: 0 could mean the customer has considered the product and doesn't want it, or has never considered the

---

[1] Market basket analyses can calculate $P(A|BC)$, but data sparseness puts a limit on how many of these probabilities can be calculated.

product. We will later discuss an approach by Bodapati (2008) for addressing
this issue.

21.2.1.2 Structural Next-Product-to-Buy Models

Several next-product-to-buy models use a structural approach to predict
which product the customer will buy next. Structural means we assume an
underlying utility structure for the consumer, and the consumer is trying
to maximize utility. These models focus on the impact of previous product
ownership on next-product-to-buy.

A Latent Trait Model of Product Ownership: Kamakura et al. (1991) define
each customer by his or her financial "maturity," related to the customer's
financial goals and demographics. Products are "positioned" along this financial maturity dimension; a product is less likely to be owned if it is positioned
higher in financial maturity. These ideas are operationalized in a latent trait
model (see also Bawa and Srinivasan 1997):

$$P_{ij} = \frac{1}{\left\{1 + e^{[a_i(b_i - O_j)]}\right\}} \tag{21.2}$$

where:

P_{ij} = Probability customer j owns product i.
O_j = Financial maturity of customer j.
b_i = Positioning of product i on financial maturity dimension.
a_i = Slope parameter for product i.

The probability of owning any product increases as a function of the customer's financial maturity. However, ownership probability changes most
quickly for the product whose positioning b_i equals the customer's maturity
O_j. The slope parameter a_i regulates how strong that change is.

Kamakura et al. suggest cross-selling customers the product that they have
a high chance of owning but do not yet own. For example, checking accounts
have a small b_i parameter. If a particular customer has a fairly high maturity,
then $O_i > b_j$ and the customer will have a high probability of owning a
checking account. If he or she does not own it, it should be cross-sold.

Kamakura et al. estimate their model on 3,034 households, for 18 financial service products. Table 21.1 shows the hypothesized ordering of products
and categories according to financial maturity, and the corresponding estimated b_i's. The correspondence is excellent. It suggests that there is a logical
sequence by which customers purchase products as their financial maturity
grows, since only customers with high financial maturity tend to own the
high b_i products.

Kamakura et al. apply their procedure to a bank that recently added several products to its portfolio. The goal is to find which of these products to
target to which customers. Kamakura et al. first predict customer financial

Table 21.1 Model-predicted vs. hypothesized order of acquisition for financial products (Adapted from Kamakura et al. 1991)

Product	Hypothesized order	Estimated parameter (b_i)	Predicted order, given b_i
Foundation services			
Checking/savings/now	1	−1.84	1
Bank credit card	2	−1.52	2
Home mortgage	3	−1.30	3
Other loans	4	−0.87	4
Risk management/cash reserves			
Life insurance	5	−0.48	5
Pension plan	6	−0.24	6
IRA	7	−0.23	7
Money market	8	0.11	8
Growth to offset inflation	9	0.31	9
Corporate stocks	9	0.31	9
Cash management account	10	0.79	10
Mutual funds	11	1.13	11
Risky, tax protection assets			
Travel/entertainment card	12	1.24	14
Tax shelters	13	1.18	12
Corporate/government bonds	14	1.19	13
Real estate other than home	15	2.81	18
Current income/post retirement			
CDs/T-bills	16	1.44	15
Time deposits	17	1.87	16
Annuities	18	2.70	17

maturity as a function of demographics and the products the customers currently own. Then, using estimates of a_i and b_i, plus the predicted $O_{j,}$, they calculate predicted ownership probability for each customer. Following is a synopsis (see Table 21.4 in Kamakura et al. 1991):

Customer   **1**   **2**   **3**   **4**

Current product ownership (x => customer currently owns product)

Savings	x	x	x	x
Checking	x	x	x	x
Bank credit card	x	x	–	–
Mortgage	x	x	–	–
Loan	–	–	x	–
Etc.	–	–	–	–
=>Predicted O_j	0.7	0.9	−1.4	0.2

Probabilities of owning new products

Insurance	0.73	0.75	0.31	0.63
Stocks	0.72	0.74	0.23	0.59
Mutual Funds	0.38	0.42	0.03	0.21
Tax shelter	0.34	0.38	0.02	0.19

So for example, Customers 1 and 2 would be the best prospects for Insurance and Stocks, because they have the financial maturity consistent with owning this product.

Kamakura et al. pioneered the notion that there is a logical sequence of products that customers buy, and if we can model that sequence, we can target appropriately. However, as noted by the authors, the model has only one dimension, financial maturity. Estimated financial maturity will inherently be large for customers who own a lot of products. Thus the model will naturally try to target new products to customers who own a lot of products. Second, while the notion of purchase sequence is temporal, the model is estimated on cross-sectional data. We now examine time series models that predict next-purchase-to-buy.

Simple Time Series Models of Product Purchase

Knott et al. (2002) discuss simple models for predicting next-product-to-buy. They use data consisting of all customers who purchased a product in time t.[2] The product they bought becomes the dependent variable; product ownership and household variables as of time $t - 1$ are the predictors. The model is of the form:

$$PROB_{ijt} = f_j(OWNERSHIP_{ij,t-1}, HHCHAR_i) + \varepsilon_{ijt} \qquad (21.3)$$

where:

$PROB_{ijt}$ = Probability customer i purchases product j in time t.
$OWNERSHIP_{ij,t-1}$ = 0–1 indicator of whether customer i owned product j as of time $t - 1$.
$HHCHAR_i$ = Demographics or RFM measures for customer i.
ε_{ijt} = Unobserved factors that induce customer i to purchase product j in time t (the "error term").
f_j = Product-specific function that maps ownership and household characteristics into probability of purchase in time t.

The model can be estimated using neural networks, discriminant analysis, multinomial logit, or logistic regression. The logistic regression model is the simplest, as follows:

$$PROB_{ijt} = \cfrac{1}{1 + e^{-\left(\beta_{0j} + \sum\limits_{k=1}^{K} a_{kj} OWNERSHIP_{ik,t-1} + \sum\limits_{m=1}^{M} \beta_{mj} HHCHAR_{im}\right)}} \qquad (21.4)$$

where K is the number of products and M is the number of household characteristic variables. Note there is a separate logistic regression for each product

---

[2] The authors do not consider purchase timing in the base case of their model. They later append a hazard timing model, discussed in Sect. 21.2.2.

Table 21.2 Odds-ratios for next-product-to-buy (Adapted from Knott et al. 2002)

Product k	Base checking	No-fee checking	Base savings	No-fee savings	CDs
Base checking	2.16[a]	0.66[b]	2.29	0.73	0.36
No-fee checking	0.68	2.66	1.55	1.48	0.69
Base savings	1.67	1.09	0.83	0.96	1.36
No-fee savings	1.47	0.12	0.30	2.54	1.66
CDs	0.63	0.45	0.44	0.51	4.94

[a] To be read: Owning base checking increases the odds of next purchasing another base checking account by 116%.
[b] To be read: Owning base checking decreases the odds of next purchasing no-fee checking by 34% (1–0.66).

j, each yielding a different set of parameters $\{\beta_{0j}, a_{1j}, \ldots, a_{Kj}, \beta_{1j}, \ldots, \beta_{Mj}\}$. This procedure is extremely simple to implement. For each customer, we know whether the product they bought in time t was product j or not – that defines the dependent variable for the product j logistic regression. We have the customer's current product ownership and household characteristics as of time $t-1$. These define the independent variables. Time is typically measured on a monthly basis, so t might be October of 2002, and $t-1$ would be from September, 2002, back in time.

The product affinities, a_{kj}, shed light on the purchase sequence. Insight on this sequence is best obtained by calculating the odds ratio:

$$ODDSRATIO_{jk} = e^{a_{kj}} \tag{21.5}$$

For example, an odds ratio of 1.5 means that owning product k increases the odds of next purchasing product j by 50%. An odds ratio of 0.75 would mean that owning product k decreases the odds of next purchasing product j by 25%. Table 21.2 shows odds ratios for five financial products. The table reveals that most of the products are "self-reinforcing," i.e., owning it is the most powerful predictor of whether the customer will purchase it again. The effect is particularly strong with CDs.

Knott et al. investigate how various factors affect the accuracy of their model, measured as the percentage of times that the actual next product bought was either the first or second most likely product predicted by the model. The average accuracy across all manipulations was 49.9%. They compare statistical methods as well as the types of independent variables included in the model. They also consider whether the estimation sample represents the actual percentages of products bought (random sample), or ensures under-purchased products have relatively more observations (stratified sample; see discussion of choice-based sampling in Chapter 10).

A regression of predictive accuracy as a function of these factors is shown in Table 21.3. Perhaps the most striking finding in Table 21.3 is that data availability is at least as important as statistical method, particularly in the case

Table 21.3 Improvement in NPTB model predictive accuracy as a function of available data, sampling method, and statistical technique (Adapted from Knott et al. 2002)

Category	Variable	Regression coefficient
Available data	Product ownership	5.76*
	0–1 Coding of ownership	0.51
	Demographics	0.83*
	Account volume	1.83*
Sampling method	Random sample	5.98*
Statistical technique	Neural net	1.07*
	Logistic regression	0.41
	Multinomial logit	0.51

* Significant at 0.05 level.
The Available Data results can be interpreted as follows: Including product ownership variables increases predictive accuracy by 5.76 percentage points, versus not including product ownership data. The Sampling Method results can be interpreted as follows: Using a random sample increases predictive accuracy by 5.98 percentage points over stratified sample. The Statistical Technique results are interpreted relative to the left-out category – discriminant analysis. For example, using a neural net increases predictive accuracy by 1.07 percentage points over using discriminant analysis.

of product ownership variables. Including product ownership in the model increases predictive accuracy by 5.76 percentage points, whereas neural nets increase predictive accuracy by 1.07 percentage points over the worst statistical method, discriminant analysis. This reinforces previous that previous behavior is the best predictor of future behavior (Rossi et al. 1996), and suggests product ownership data provide the firm with a competitive advantage. It is also interesting that random sampling outperforms stratified sampling. This may be because stratification gets the base purchase rate wrong, so is not at determining the *most likely* product the customer is to buy next.

Knott et al. field test their approach with a retail bank that wished to increase sales of one of its loan products. Management had used a heuristic based on customer wealth to target customers in the past, but was willing to test an NPTB model. The model was estimated on 7,200 customers using a neural net. Nine products were considered, including the loan product. Predictor variables included current product ownership and customer variables such as total deposit and loan dollars, age, length in residence, income, and home ownership. Experimental groups were:

- *NPTB Mail Group*: Customers selected using the NPTB model. A customer was selected if the model predicted that the loan would be their first- or second-most likely next product to buy. This yielded 23,877 customers who were sent an offer for the loan ($n = 23{,}877$).
- *NPTB Control Group*: Customers selected using the model as described above, but not mailed an offer ($n = 1{,}209$).
- *Heuristic Mail Group*: Customers selected using managerial judgment based on wealth of the customer, and sent an offer for the loan ($n = 23{,}639$).

Table 21.4 Field test of the NPTB model – response and revenues (Adapted Knott et al. 2002)

Treatment group	Number of customers	Purchase rate	Revenues	Revenues/ purchaser	Revenues/ customer
NPTB mail	23,877	1.13%	$2,227,146	$8,249	$93.28
NPTB control	1,209	0.50%	$44,850	$7,475	$37.10
Heuristic mail	23,639	0.44%	$700,449	$6,735	$29.63
Heuristic control	1,186	0.42%	$26,346	$5,269	$22.21
Prospect mail	49,905	0.10%	$365,204	$7,453	$7.32
Prospect control	2,500	0.00%	NA	NA	NA

- *Heuristic Control Group*: Customers selected using managerial judgment but not mailed an offer ($n = 1{,}186$).
- *Prospect Mail Group*: Prospects who were not currently customers of the bank, and sent an offer for the loan ($n = 49{,}905$).
- *Prospect Control Group*: Prospective customers obtained from the list broker who were not sent an offer for the loan ($n = 2{,}500$).

Comparing the NPTB Mail Group to its control determines whether the loan offer generates incremental sales. That this effect will be positive is not a foregone conclusion. Customers could still obtain the loan directly from the bank, even if they were not mailed the offer. The same comparison is relevant between the Heuristic Mail Group and its control. The incremental sales for the NPTB and the Heuristic can then be compared to see which is superior. Both of these can then be compared to the Prospect Group. The results are shown in Table 21.4,[3] and suggest the following:

- *NPTB vs. Its Control*: The offer generates increases of 0.63%(1.13−0.50%) in purchase rate and $774 ($8,249–7,475) in revenue per purchaser. This yields a total gain of $56.18 in revenues per targeted customer. Targeting an offer to customers based on the NPTB model generates incremental sales compared to what would have been obtained had these customers not been targeted.
- *Heuristic vs. Its Control*: The offer generates increases of 0.02% (0.44–0.42%) in purchase rate and $1,466 ($6,735–5,269) in revenue per purchaser. This results in a total gain of $7.42 in revenues per targeted customer. Mailing to customers selected by the heuristic generates incremental revenues, but most comes from higher revenues given purchase, rather than a higher purchase rate.
- *NPTB vs. Heuristic*: The NPTB model outperforms the heuristic model in terms of incremental revenues per targeted customer ($56.18 vs. $7.42). The better performance of the NPTB model comes from incremental response (0.63% vs. 0.02% for the heuristic) rather than revenues per purchaser (gain of $774 vs. $1,466 for the heuristic).

---

[3] Please note the absolute levels of the numbers are disguised, but ratios are preserved.

Table 21.5 Field test of the NPTB model – profits[a] (Adapted from Knott et al. 2002)

Method	Incremental revenues	Gross profit contribution	Mail cost/mailee	Total mail cost	Total profit	ROI
NPTB	$1,341,362[a]	$36,485[b]	$0.2425	$5,790[c]	$30,695[d]	530.1%[e]
Heuristic	$175,342	$4,769	$0.2425	$5,732	−$963	−16.8%
Prospects	$365,204	$9,934	$0.2850	$14,223	−$4,289	−30.2%

[a] = $2,227,146 − 23,877 × 0.50% × $7,475 (23,877 × 0.50% × $7,475 is the revenues we would have expected to receive if the control group consisted of 23,877 customers as does the mail group; see Table 21.4).
[b] = $1,341,362 × 0.0272 (profit contribution %)
[c] = 23,877 × $0.2425 (prospect marketing cost includes another $0.0425 for list rental)
[d] = $36,485 − $5,790
[e] = $36,485/$5,790

- *Prospect Group*: As expected, none of the customers in the prospect control group obtained a loan. The purchase rate in the prospect mail group was 0.10%, with revenues per responder of $7,453. These are pure incremental sales, because no one from this group would have responded without the direct mail solicitation. The prospect mailing generated $7.32 incremental sales per targeted customer.
- *NPTB vs. Prospect*: The NPTB outperforms prospecting since it generates $56.18 incremental per targeted customer while the prospect mailing generates an additional $7.32 per targeted customer.
- *Heuristic vs. Prospect*: The heuristic performs about the same as prospecting, generating incremental sales of $7.42 per targeted customer, compared to $7.32 per targeted customer from the prospecting.

Table 21.5 shows profit and ROI of the different methods.[4] The first column shows incremental lift generated by the method, relative to its control group. The second column calculates gross profit contribution, assuming 272 basis points (0.0272) profit contribution per incremental lift. The third column shows mail cost/mailee. For NPTB and heuristic, this is simply the cost of mailing and printing. For prospects, this also includes list rental. Total mail costs are then calculated by multiplying the per-mailee cost times the total number mailed in Table 21.4. Subtracting this from gross profit contribution yields total profit; ROI is calculated by dividing profit by cost.

Table 21.5 shows that the NPTB model is the only method that pays out, with an ROI of 530.1%. The other two methods lose money. In defense of the prospecting approach, arguably these customers would generate additional revenues in the future. However, there could be some long-term benefits in terms of lifetime value for the NPTB and heuristic customers as well (e.g., higher retention).

Knott et al.'s approach is simple and easy to implement. However, the model could be improved. It focuses on what product the customer will

---

[4] Absolute levels of the numbers are disguised, but ratios are preserved.

purchase next, *given* that they will purchase. However, many customers will
not purchase anything in the next month or two. We want to target the
customer who is more likely to be in the market for a financial product in
the next month. An ideal model would include purchase timing. In addition,
the independent logistic models ignore cross-equation correlations and their
probabilities do not sum to one across equations. Finally, the approach does
not consider customer heterogeneity in its various parameters.

A Hierarchical Bayes Next-Product-to-Buy Model

Li et al. (2005) build on Kamakura et al. (1991) and Knott et al. (2002).
They model financial maturity (which they call "demand maturity") and
previous product ownership. Li et al. apply their model to financial services,
in particular, a retail bank. The model is:

$$U_{ijt} = \beta_i |O_j - DM_{i,t-1}| + \gamma_{1ij} COMPET_{ij} + \gamma_{2ij} OVERSAT_i$$
$$+ \gamma_{3ij} SWIT_{it} + \varepsilon_{ijt} \tag{21.6}$$

where:

U_{ijt} = Utility of customer i for product j at time t.
O_j = Position of product j along the demand maturity continuum.
$DM_{i,t-1}$ = The demand maturity of customer i at the end of period $t-1$.
$COMPET_{ij}$ = 1 if customer i has opened an account in the product category
    of product j with another bank within the last 6 months.
$OVERSAT_i$ = Customer i's overall satisfaction with the bank as measured
    in a customer satisfaction survey.
$SWIT_{it}$ = Customer i's "switching costs" at time t, equalling 1 if the cus-
    tomer is a white collar worker, the household as at least one child, and the
    household owns more than the average number of accounts with the bank.
ε_{ijt} = Unobserved factors influencing utility for product j at time t.

The model is a multivariate probit. The customer can choose any, all, or
none of the J products each period. Since it is possible that the customer
chooses no products in a given period, it incorporates purchase timing. Model
parameters are heterogeneous across customers and for *COMPET, OVER-
SAT,* and *SWIT,* also specific to the product. Heterogeneity is modeled as a
function of customer demographics. The error terms are allowed to correlate
across equations. This captures "coincidence" (Manchanda et al. 1999). The
term $|O_j - DM_{i,t-1}|$ captures the distance between the financial maturity of
the customer and the positioning of the product along the demand maturity
continuum. The O_j are product-specific constants to be estimated. Demand
maturity term is modeled as:

$$DM_{i,t-1} = \sum_{j=1}^{J} [O_j D_{ij,t-1} (\lambda_1 ACCTNBR_{ij,t-1} + \lambda_2 BAL_{ij,t-1}$$
$$+ \lambda_3 HOLDING_{ij,t-1})] \tag{21.7}$$

where

$D_{ij,t-1} = 1$ if customer i purchased product j in period $t - 1$.

$ACCTNBR_{ij,t-1}$ = Cumulative number of product j accounts purchased by customer i up to period $t - 1$.

$BAL_{ij,t-1}$ = Average monthly balance in product j accounts by customer i up to period $t - 1$.

$HOLDING_{ij,t-1}$ = Elapsed time since first opening of an account of type j, for customer i, up to period $t - 1$.

Assuming the λ's are positive, Equation 21.7 infers higher demand maturity for the customer who has bought a lot of products that are positioned high on the demand maturity continuum. The estimated model generates several important findings:

- The financial maturity parameter (β_i) is on average negative, meaning that the further away the product is from the customer's financial maturity, the less likely he or she is to purchase it.
- The financial maturity measure (O_j) orders financial products from low to high maturity as follows: checking, savings, debit card, credit card, installment loan, CD, money market account, brokerage account. This ordering has face validity and is consistent with Kamakura et al. (1991).
- Having recently bought a similar product in a competing bank ($COMPET = 1$) decreases likelihood of purchasing the product in the focal bank.
- Higher customer satisfaction ($OVERSAT$) makes it more likely the customer will purchase additional products from the bank.
- Higher switching costs (as measured by the $SWIT$ variable) are associated with higher likelihoods of purchasing additional products from the bank.

Li et al. (2005) show their model out-predicts a simple model of independent probits. It is a clear advance in structural models of next product to buy.

A Factor Analytic Model Combining Survey and Internal Record Data

Li et al.'s results suggest that ownership of products at competitive banks influences their likelihood of purchasing from the focal bank. Data on customers' product ownership at competitors are generally not available. A survey can be implemented for a random selection of customers, but a method is then needed to infer, for all the bank's customers, their likelihood of owning the product at a competitive bank.

Kamakura et al. (2003) propose a factor analysis model for this purpose, as follows:

$$E[Y_n|X_n] = h(\lambda' + X_n \Lambda') \tag{21.8}$$

where:

Y_n = Vector of ownership variables for customer n. There are J products.
For some customers, all product variables are observed via internal records
or survey. For most customers, only the variables obtainable via internal
records are observed.

X_n = Vector of P factor scores for customer n. P is less than J, consistent
with the notion of reducing the dimensionality of the data.

$\Lambda' = J \times P$ matrix of factor loadings, each element representing the correlation
between factor p and ownership variable j.

$\lambda' = J \times 1$ Vector of constant terms.

$h(\bullet)$ = Function that relates factor scores to each product ownership variable.

The key output of the estimation process are the factor loadings, Λ', which
can be graphed for interpretation. However, the model can also be used
to generate the factor scores, X_n, for each customer, and hence the probability distribution for ownership variables Y_n, whether they are observed
or not.

The authors apply their model to a commercial bank located in Brazil.
They have internal and survey data available for 5,500 customers. The internal data include product ownership at the focal bank, transaction volume,
and demographics. The survey data contain product ownership at competitive banks. They estimate the model on 1,387 customers, and use it to predict
competitive ownership for the remaining 4,163 customers. They can evaluate
their model on these customers since they know the actual competitive data
for these customers.

Figure 21.2 illustrates plots of factor loadings. The figure is not the authors' exact results but is illustrative. Looking first at the focal-bank loadings, car insurance and life insurance both load low on dimension 1 and high
on dimension 2. Because they have similar loadings, this means that ownership is driven by a similar process. Customers, if they own one of these
products, should own the other. If they don't, e.g., if a customer owns car
insurance with the bank but not life insurance, he or she would be a good
candidate for a cross-sell. Interestingly, credit card ownership at competitive banks has similar loadings as credit card ownership at the focal bank.
This means that customer ownership of credit cards is correlated across
banks. However, insurance ownership at the focal bank has different loadings than insurance ownership at the competitive bank. This means that if
the customer does not have car insurance at the focal bank, he or she probably has it with a competitive bank, and would not be a good cross-sell
prospect.

The authors use their model to predict competitive product ownership
for the 4,163 holdout customers. The prediction results are quite good. The
top decile predicted by the model accounts for a median of 35% of all the
customers who own the product at a competitive bank. The performance of
the model is thus very promising.

Ownership of Focal Bank Services

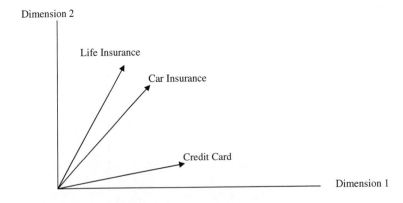

Ownership of Competitive Bank Services

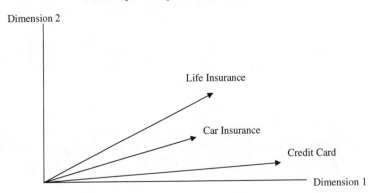

Fig. 21.2 Illustrative results of factor analysis model.
(Adapted from Kamakura et al. 2003).

21.2.2 Next-Product-to-Buy Models with Explicit Consideration of Purchase Timing

21.2.2.1 Hazard Models

Hazard models predict the next (or first) time an event will occur for a customer. To apply this to cross-selling, a hazard model can be used to calculate how soon each customer is likely to buy each product. Then we might cross-sell the product that is predicted to be the *soonest* next-product-to-buy for each customer.

There are many forms of hazard models. Perhaps the most common is the Cox proportional hazards model (see Cox 1972 and Chapter 15). The basic model is:

$$H(t) = H_0(t)e^{\beta X} \tag{21.9}$$

where:

$H(t)$ = The instantaneous probability the customer will purchase at time t, given it has been t time periods since the last purchase.

$H_0(t)$ = The "baseline" hazard, that portion of $H(t)$ due solely to the passage of time since the last purchase.

X = A vector of predictors ("covariates") for the customer, which could include ownership and household variables.

Hazard models differ in the functional form used for the baseline hazard (e.g., exponential) and in the covariates included for the customer. Given the hazard function, one can calculate the "survivor" function, $S(t)$, which is the probability the customer has not purchased by time t.

Harrison and Ansell (2002) apply a hazard model to predict when customers are likely to buy another insurance product. They estimate their model on 9,000 randomly selected customers. The "dependent variable" is the time between the previous purchase of any insurance product and the subsequent purchase of any insurance product. The covariates included marital status, age, gender, and categories derived from ACORN financial clusters (Chapter 8): financially sophisticated, financially involved, financially moderate, or financially inactive. The results were that married and separated customers had higher hazards than single, divorced, or widowed, and older males had higher hazards. As expected, financially sophisticated customers had the highest hazards, followed by financially involved, moderate, and inactive.

One way to apply the results is to score customers in terms of their hazard rates, and cross-sell to those with the highest hazard. However, this may depend on customer heterogeneity in hazard rates (see Jain and Vilcassim 1991). Consider Fig. 21.3. Customer A is likely to purchase sooner, so may be a good target. Customer B's hazard rate is highest in weeks 17–23. But what if the cross-selling campaign is scheduled for weeks 17–23? Should we target Customer B? Figure 21.3 would suggest "yes" but unfortunately the situation is a bit more complicated. It is possible that Customer A will purchase in weeks 3–7 and then return to the market by weeks 17–23. The hazard rate just depicts the likelihood of when the *next* purchase will occur. The question is whether Customer A will be in the market in weeks 17–23. This requires a more detailed calculation, conditioning on the number of purchases and the timing of them for a given customer. How to do this is an important area for future research.

Knott et al. (2002) integrate a hazard timing model with their next-product-to-buy model. They define the following events:

A = The customer buys some banking product in the next 3 months.
B = The customer will buy the focal product when he or she next buys.

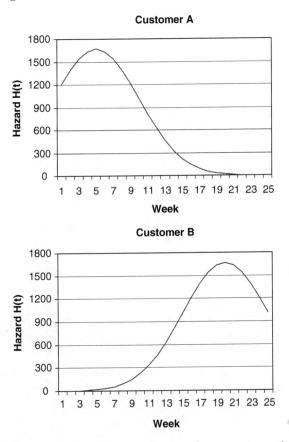

Fig. 21.3 Comparing hazard functions for two customers*.

*Hazard functions
Customer A: $H(t) = e^{[7.1+0.2(t-1)-0.04(t^2-1)/2]}$
Customer B: $H(t) = e^{[0.2+0.8(t-1)-0.04(t^2-1)/2]}$

They then calculate:

$$\text{Prob(A and B)} = \text{Prob(A)Prob(B|A)} \qquad (21.10)$$

The authors' original approach was to estimate Prob(B|A) via Equation 21.4 and target customers who have the highest Prob(B|A). But this may be a poor idea if the customer's probability of being in the market (Prob(A)) is small. It seems one should target the customer who is likely to be in the market *and* likely to buy the focal product.

Knott et al. estimate a hazard model for 271,000 customers (see Chintagunta and Prasad 1993; Haldar and Rao 1998; Helsen and Schmittlein 1993). The large sample is important because purchase frequency is very low. Once the model is estimated, customers are scored according to Equation 21.10, with the hazard model providing Prob(A), and the NPTB model providing

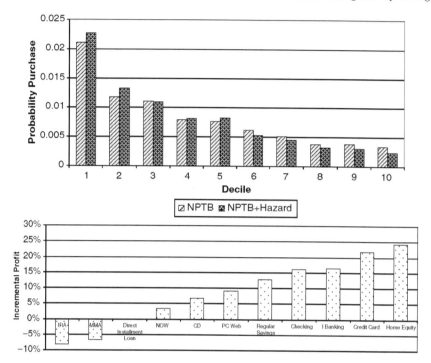

Fig. 21.4 NPTB logistic regression vs. NPTB logistic regression plus hazard purchase timing model. (**a**) Comparative lift charts. (**b**) Profit from targeting top two deciles: NPTB + hazard minus NPTB alone (Adapted from Knott et al. 2002).

Prob(B|A). Figure 21.4a shows that the NPTB + Hazard model provides somewhat better lift than the stand-alone NPTB model. Figure 21.4b shows that the NPTB + Hazard approach can generate significant additional profits. The gain isn't uniform, but certainly on average, these results suggest that a purchase incidence model (Prob(A)) is an important tool for cross-selling.

In summary, there are three ways to use hazard models for cross-selling:

- Predict how soon the customer is to buy any product and cross-sell to customers who are likely to purchase soon (Harrison and Ansell 2002).
- Predict how soon the customer will buy any product and combine with a prediction of which product will be bought, given the customer buys. Target the product the customer is most likely to buy soon (Knott et al. 2002).
- Estimate a hazard model for each product and target the product that a particular customer is likely to buy before the other products.

In addition, there is the question of whether to target customers who are predicted to buy soon or in a designated future time period. If the latter, the calculations are non-trivial because it is possible that a given customer might purchase more than once before the designated period.

21.2.2.2 A Hazard Model for New Product Cross-Selling

The models discussed so far have identified which *existing* product should be targeted to which customers. Kamakura et al. (2004) develop a model to identify the best prospects for cross-selling *new* products. The challenge is that there are no historical data for the new product. The authors develop a "split-hazard" model that takes into account (1) whether the customer will ever adopt the new product and (2) will the customer adopt the new product *soon*. Both phenomena are modeled using a factor structure – the "penetration space" for ever adopt, and the "innovation space" for whether the product will be adopted quickly. The penetration component of the model is:

$$\theta_{ij} = \frac{1}{1 + (\nu_j - w_i)'(\nu_j - w_i)} \qquad (21.11)$$

where

θ_{ij} = Probability customer i eventually will adopt product j.

ν_j = Location of product j in "penetration space." This is an M-dimensional set of factor scores. Each brand in the estimation data has scores on these dimensions, which represent attributes that drive eventual product adoption.

w_i = An M-dimensional vector representing the importance customer i attaches to each of the penetration dimensions.

Equation 21.11 is an ideal-point model. The probability of eventual adoption will be high to the extent that product j is located close to customer i's ideal point.

The innovation component measures the hazard rate, the likelihood the customer will adopt the product *now*. This is modeled as:

$$\ln(\lambda_{ij}) = \alpha_j + X_i\beta + \eta_j z_i \qquad (21.12)$$

where

λ_{ij} = Hazard rate that customer i will adopt product j at time t.

α_j = Baseline constant for product j.

X_i = Demographic variables describing customer i. β is the importance of each variable in determining adoption. A positive β increases the hazard rate and make it more likely the customer would adopt.

η_j = Vector of factor scores for product j, representing how that product is positioned on the factors that determine "innovation," i.e., how soon the product will be adopted.

z_i = Vector of customer-specific weights that represent the importance of the innovation factors in influencing adoption for customer i.

The authors combine the innovation and penetration models by multiplying θ_{ij} times λ_{ij} for each customer for a specific brand. The challenge, however, is that the values for the penetration (ν_j) and innovation (η_j) factors are not known for a new brand. The authors rely on expert judgment to provide subjective estimates of these values. The judgment is aided by the authors providing the positioning maps, both for penetration and innovation, which locate each of the existing products. This provides the ν_j's and η_j's needed to calculate the customer-specific $\theta_{ij} \times \lambda_{ij}$ index. Customers are then ranked by this index and the top customers would be targeted for the new product.

The authors apply their model to the pharmaceutical industry. The pharmaceutical company needed to decide whether a particular physician should be targeted for cross-selling a new drug. The authors estimate their model, use five experts to provide independent judgments of the penetration and innovation positioning, and compute cumulative lift charts to access how well the model forecasts physician adoption of the new drugs. They compare their model to a not-so-naïve model that ranks physicians according to how soon they adopted existing drugs in the database. The model does quite well. It achieves about a 2.5 to 1 top-quintile lift for four out of five drugs, and a 4 to 1 top-quintile lift for one drug. The model clearly out-predicts the naïve model, and all the experts do well and similarly to each other.

21.2.3 Next-Product-to-Buy with Timing and Response

The strategy for the models reviewed so far is to determine what the customer will do (what product they will buy next, when they will buy next) and use that information to target the right product to the right customer at the right time. Knott et al. (2002) field test demonstrates this can work. However, what we really need to know is how the customer will *respond* to a cross-selling offer, i.e., what *incremental* sales will be generated by cross-selling a product versus not cross-selling it. This is the model developed by Bodapati (2008).

Bodapati assumes customers go through two stages in deciding whether to buy a product. First they have to be aware of it. Second, given they are aware, they must decide whether they have a preference (or "satisfaction" in Bodapati's terms) for the product. If they are aware of the product and are satisfied with it, they will buy it. Bodapati's model assumes that if the firm recommends the product, it kindles awareness. This is where the incremental value of the recommendation comes in. The model is:

$$P(Y_{ui} = 1) = P(A_{ui}, S_{ui})$$
$$= P(A_{ui})P(S_{ui}|A_{ui})\text{(Un-aided purchase)} \quad (21.13a)$$
$$P(V_{ui} = 1) = P(A_{ui}, S_{ui})$$
$$= P(S_{ui}|A_{ui})\text{(Cross-sold purchase)} \quad (21.13b)$$

where:

$Y_{ui} = 1$ if customer u purchases product i on his or her own, without any specific cross-selling effort; 0 otherwise.

$V_{ui} = 1$ if customer u purchases product i as the result of a cross-selling recommendation; 0 otherwise.

A_{ui} = The event that customer u is aware of product i.

S_{ui} = The event that customer u prefers or is satisfied with product i and hence buys it.

Equation 21.13a shows that if the customer is not cross-sold the product, he or she has to develop awareness on his or her own. However, if the product is cross-sold (Equation 21.13b), awareness is automatically developed $(P(A_{ui}) = 1)$, so purchase depends only on whether the customer likes the product. The incremental impact of the cross-sell is Equation 21.13b minus Equation 21.13a.

Bodapati models awareness and satisfaction as logistic functions of an unobserved set of d attributes, denoted by the vector x_i, for product i. That is,

$$P(A_{ui}) = \frac{1}{1 + e^{\alpha'_u x_i}} \quad (21.14a)$$

$$P(S_{ui}|A_{ui}) = \frac{1}{1 + e^{\beta'_u x_i}} \quad (21.14b)$$

where α'_u is a customer-specific vector reflecting the importances of the d attributes in establishing awareness, and β'_u is a customer-specific vector reflecting the importances of the d attributes in establishing satisfaction, given awareness.

Bodapati creates a simple adjustment for purchase timing. If the product is recommended, awareness is automatically turned on, and if the customer is satisfied, purchase occurs immediately. If the product is not recommended, awareness is assumed to increase naturally on its own. Bodapati is then able to show that:

$$P(Y_{ui} = 1 \text{ during forecast period } f)$$
$$= \frac{T_f}{T_c} P(Y_{ui} = 1 \text{ during calibration period } c) \quad (21.15)$$

where T_f is the duration of the planning period ("forecast" period in Bodapati's terminology) and T_c is the duration of the period during which the model is estimated. The incremental impact of the recommendation, during the forecast period f, Δ_i, is therefore:

$$\Delta_i = P(S_{ui}|A_{ui}) - \frac{T_f}{T_c} P(S_{ui}|A_{ui})P(A_{ui}) \qquad (21.16)$$

The first term is the likelihood customer u will purchase product i as a result of the recommendation. The second term is the probability customer u would have purchased on his or her own, if the product had not been recommended. Equation 21.16 highlights the importance of the planning horizon. If the planning horizon is long, it is more likely that the customer would have purchased anyway and the recommendation will be less likely to generate an incremental sale.[5]

Bodapati estimates his model for an e-tailer. The data consist of 932 customers and 1,681 products. Bodapati conducts a predictive test on holdout data against two benchmark models: binary logit and collaborative filtering. Both these models do not distinguish between recommended and non-recommended products. There are total of 156,669 holdout observations. An observation is whether a customer bought a particular product during the holdout period; 149,269 of these observations are cases where the product was not recommended, i.e., there was no cross-sell; 7,400 of these observations are cases where the product was recommended, i.e., there was a cross-sell. For each observation, Bodapati calculates the probability of purchase and then observes whether in fact the product was purchased. The resultant lift charts are shown in Fig. 21.5. The figure shows that the proposed model achieves significantly better lift, both in cases where a product was and was not recommended.

Bodapati's model is the first to incorporate *which* product the customer is most likely to buy, *when* the customer is likely to buy, and how the customer is likely to *respond* to a cross-selling recommendation. The model makes some key assumptions, such as that a recommendation has a 100% chance of making the customer aware, and does not influence the likelihood of purchase, given awareness. In addition, the model does not take into account previous product ownership, a hallmark of the next-product-to-buy models reviewed earlier. The key to the model is incorporating response to previous recommendations. No other model to date has done this.

There may be simpler ways of incorporating data on previous recommendations, such as a binary logit where the dependent variable would be whether a product was bought, and the independent variables would be previous ownership and whether the product was recommended/cross-sold. The parameter for response to recommendation would be heterogeneous across customers, and this heterogeneity would be important in calculating the incremental

---

[5] Note there is an implicit assumption that $T_f < T_c$, that is, the planning horizon is shorter than the calibration period. This is usually reasonable, as a year's worth of data might be available for estimating the model, and the planning horizon for the cross-selling campaign might be one month.

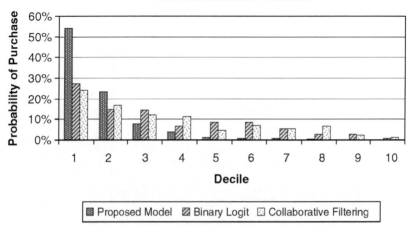

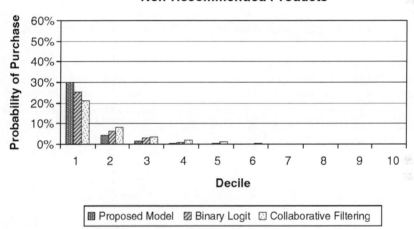

Fig. 21.5 Comparative lift charts for recommended vs. non-recommended products (From Bodapati 2008).

gain for each customer of recommending the product. Bodapati's significant contribution is showing that incorporating previous recommendation activity is crucial, and that this can be done with an insightful model.

21.3 Up-Selling

In up-selling, the decision is whether to try to sell the customer *more* life insurance, a bigger computer, a second cell-phone, or software upgrade (Pfeifer 1996). The natural question is what is the up-sell potential, i.e., how much more can we expect to sell to a given customer.

One way of approaching this is to measure share-of-wallet. Assume a customer buys \$30 worth of groceries from an online website per week. If \$30 represents 100% of the customer's total weekly expenditure on groceries, there is not much up-sell potential. If \$30 represents 40% of total weekly expenditure, there is obvious up-sell potential. However, share-of-wallet may not uncover all the potential for up-selling. Consider the customer who has a \$300,000 life insurance policy from Company A. Even if that is the only life insurance policy the customer owns, there still may be up-sell potential if the customer has funds to invest, etc.

21.3.1 A Data Envelope Analysis Model

A method for assessing up-selling potential, defined as the difference between maximum potential sales and actual sales, is data envelope analysis (DEA). Kamakura et al. (2002) use this to assess the upside potential of 162 branches of a large Brazilian bank. This illustrates the use of DEA to uncover under-performing case bank branches, but the application to customers is clear.

The approach is as follows. Find a linear combination of existing branches that could produce the same or greater output than the branch being evaluated, while using a fraction of the inputs. If that fraction is less than one, the branch is inefficient because a linear combination of other branches would produce more output using fewer resources. If the fraction is greater than one, the branch is efficient. The model is formulated as:

$$\min_{\tau_0,\alpha_{i0},\beta_{j0},\delta_{k0},\lambda_n} \left\{ \tau_0 + \sum_i \varepsilon\alpha_{i0} + \sum_j \varepsilon\beta_{j0} + \sum_k \varepsilon\delta_{k0} \right\} \qquad (21.17a)$$

such that:

$$x_{i0}\tau_0 = \alpha_{i0} + \sum_n \lambda_n x_{in} \qquad (21.17b)$$

$$z_{k0} = \delta_{k0} + \sum_n \lambda_n z_{kn} \qquad (21.17c)$$

$$y_{j0} = -\beta_{j0} + \sum_n \lambda_n y_{jn} \qquad (21.17d)$$

where:

x_{in} = Amount of controllable input i utilized by branch n.
z_{kn} = Amount of uncontrollable input k utilized by branch n.
y_{jn} = Amount of output j produced by branch n.
τ_0 = Efficiency of the branch to be evaluated.

Table 21.6 Efficiency of branch #154 with respect to customer satisfaction and retention(From Kamakura et al. 2002). (**a**) Customer satisfaction (From Kamakura et al. 2002); (**b**) Customer retention (From Kamakura et al. 2002)

(a) Efficiency = 0.495	Inputs				Outputs		
	Tellers	ATMs	Managers	Employees	Transact	Customers	Reco- mmended intent
Hypothetical	35.7	8.8	6.0	106.3	1,189.3	19,639.5	43.6
Branch #154	72.0	19.5	19.5	214.5	1,189.3	19,639.5	22.1
Slack	0.0	10.7	3.6	0.0	0.0	0.0	21.5

(b) Efficiency = 0.783	Input	Outputs		
	Recommended intent	Share of wallet	Years at branch	Account level
Hypothetical	17.3	58.5	25.8	12,229.6
Branch #154	22.1	49.3	25.8	12,229.6
Slack	0.0	9.2	0.0	0.0

λ_n = Weights used to create the most efficient branch, characterized by producing at least the same output using as few inputs as possible.

$\alpha_i, \beta_j, \delta_k$ = Slack variables for controllable input i, for output j, and uncontrollable input k., constrained to be >0. These represent how much the evaluated bank over-utilizes inputs and under-produces output j, relative to the best linear combination of banks.

ε = The "non-Archimedean infinitesimal," a very small ($\approx 10^{-6}$) number introduced to guarantee the solution is not at an extreme point (e.g., 0). See Chang and Guh (1991).

The linear program finds the λ's to create a hypothetical branch that utilizes no more than a fraction τ_0 of the controllable inputs (Equation 21.17b) yet uses no more uncontrollable inputs (Equation 21.17c) and produces at least as much output (Equation 21.17d) as the evaluated branch.

Kamakura et al. estimate two DEA models. The first takes the number of tellers, managers, and employees as controllable inputs and treats various measures of customer satisfaction as the outputs. The second takes one measure of customer satisfaction as a controllable input and treats customer retention as output.

The authors analyze 162 branches and create reports illustrated in Table 21.6. Example "a" shows that Branch #154 operates at 49.5% efficiency ($\tau = 0.495$) in creating customer satisfaction. A hypothetical branch consisting of a linear combination of four branches could produce at least as much output, using no more than 49.5% of the resources that Branch #154 uses. This branch would use only 45% of the ATM's and 30.8% of the employees that Branch #154 uses.

Example "b" shows that Branch #154 operates at 78.3% efficiency in translating customer satisfaction to retention. A hypothetical branch consisting of a linear combination of three branches would require only 78.3% of the satisfaction but produce at least as much retention as Branch #154. In fact, this hypothetical branch would produce 18.7% higher share of wallet than Branch #154.

To apply this method to customers, the inputs would be marketing efforts; the outputs would be purchase volume. Under-achieving customers might be targeted for up-selling efforts. Although this would not guarantee up-selling potential, the basic idea has merit and needs to be field tested.

There are also two methodological issues that merit attention. First is the assumed linear production function. This of course makes things easier, but in an application to cross-selling, one would be concerned about decreasing returns to marketing efforts. Second is that the model is deterministic – it does not explicitly take into account uncertainty.

21.3.2 A Stochastic Frontier Model

Kim and Kim (2001) construct a "stochastic frontier" model to estimate the extent to which inefficient marketing has kept the customer from realizing his or her true purchase potential. The model is as follows:

$$Sales_i = \beta_0 + \sum_{k=1}^{K} \beta_k X_{ik} + \nu_i - u_i \tag{21.18}$$

where

$Sales_i$ = Current sales/revenue level for customer i.

X_{ik} = Value for customer i on independent/predictor variable k.

ν_i = Unobserved factors influencing sales level for customer i, not related to marketing. Assume ν_i is normally distributed across the customer base, with a mean of 0.

u_i = Unobserved factors influencing sales level for customer i, related to marketing. Assume u_i is distributed to be truncated normal, truncated at 0 from below, so that $u_i \geq 0$.

Since $u_i \geq 0$, the maximum sales level for customer i is $Sales_i = \beta_0 + \sum_{k=1}^{K} \beta_k X_{ik} + \nu_i$. The goal is to estimate u_i for each customer. Kim and Kim (2001) show how this is done using stochastic frontier regression. This technique also yields estimates of the β's and ν_i's, which then can be used to calculate an estimated maximum sales level:

$$MaxSales_i = \hat{\beta}_0 + \sum_{k=1}^{K} \hat{\beta}_k X_{ik} + \hat{\nu}_i \tag{21.19}$$

One can then calculate a percentage marketing inefficiency as $\hat{u}_i/MaxSales_i$. Customers can then be rank ordered on this measure, where a higher value suggests more up-selling potential, and targeted for up-selling efforts accordingly.

Kim and Kim estimate their model using data from a life insurance company. The predictor variables include gender, age, employment, and various customer behavior variables such as whether the insured person is the policy owner, how long the customer has been a customer, payment method, and location at which the policy was purchased. Most of these variables turned out to be significant in predicting sales levels.

Customers are then rank ordered in terms of up-selling potential ($\hat{u}_i/MaxSales_i$). It turned out the distribution of potential was skewed to the right, suggesting a relatively small number of customers had significant up-selling potential and should be targeted for increased marketing efforts.

The stochastic frontier method shows much potential for identifying up-selling opportunities. It is relatively easy to implement and understand, and is not deterministic. It distinguishes between factors that are simply random and factors that detract systematically from sales levels. However, the technique needs field testing to show that the estimated $\hat{u}_i$'s are due to marketing inefficiencies, and not other factors that are beyond the firm's control.

21.4 Developing an Ongoing Cross-Selling Effort

21.4.1 Process Overview

Figure 21.6 depicts a process by which firms can develop an ongoing cross-selling effort. The steps involve: setting strategy, collecting data, developing the required marketing analytics, implementation, and evaluation.

21.4.2 Strategy

The first issue in setting strategy is to prioritize objectives: Immediate increase in sales, long-term increase in customer contribution, or increase in customer retention rate. We discussed these issues in Sect. 21.1.

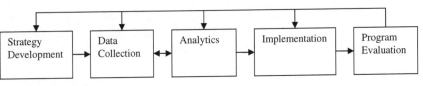

Fig. 21.6 Developing an ongoing cross-selling effort: Process overview.

Table 21.7 Product-centric versus customer-centric marketing using an NPTB model

Customer	Product A	Product B	Product C	Product D
1,000	0.1	0.1	0.6	0.2
1,001	0.2	0.1	0.6	0.1
1,002	0.1	**0.5**	0.1	**0.3**
1,003	0.2	0.2	0.1	0.3
1,004	0.1	0.3	0.2	0.4
1,005	0.3	0.3	0.2	0.2
1,006	0.5	0.1	0.1	0.3
1,007	0.1	0.6	0.1	0.2
1,008	0.5	0.2	0.2	0.1
1,009	0.7	0.1	0.1	0.1

Numbers are the predicted probability the customer will next buy the product in the particular column.

A second component of cross-selling strategy is the reliance on cross-selling versus up-selling. If the product line is limited, the company might want to rely on up-selling. Up-selling may also warrant emphasis if the goal is to increase long-term sales. For example, upgrading a cable customer's package to Premium increases sales not only this period but in future periods as well (m_t in Equation 21.1 increases permanently). If the emphasis is on long-term retention, it might be more appropriate to emphasize cross-selling, since the number of different products the customer owns *may* increase switching costs and enhance long-term retention rates.

Another component of cross-selling strategy is whether the efforts will be "product-centric" or "customer-centric." The entries in Table 21.7, which might be derived from one of the models reviewed in Sect. 21.2, represent the probability the customer will buy a particular product if it is cross-sold to that customer. There are two approaches to approaching the cross-selling efforts. In the product-centric approach, the firm finds say the top 40% of customers in terms of their likelihood of purchasing the product and targets them. In the customer-centric approach, the bank goes down the list customer by customer and targets the product they are most likely to buy next. These need not yield the same targeting plans. Table 21.7 shows that with the product-centric approach, customer 1,002 is targeted with product D. Under the customer-centric approach, customer 1,002 is targeted with product B.

In favor of the product-centric approach is that: (1) It allows the firm to target profitable products. (2) It avoids disappointing the customer with a product the firm can deliver but not with the highest quality. (3) It helps ensure economies of scale for all products. In favor of the customer-centric approach is that: (1) Customers will be more satisfied because they are being targeted with what they really want. (2) The overall program will maximize sales since it is not constrained by having to offer low-selling items. (3) It avoids over-burdening the customer with too many offers.

The issue is perhaps best resolved depending on whether the organizational structure is customer-centric or product-centric (Chapter 3). A company that

		Focal Bank		
		Own Product	Do Not Own Product	
			High Need	Low Need
Competitive Bank	High Likelihood of Ownership	Increase Share-of-Wallet	Risky Brand Switch	No Go
	Low Likelihood of Ownership	Potential Up-Sell	Highly Promising Cross-Sell	No Go

Fig. 21.7 Targeting cross-sell based on need and current product ownership: Integrating competition.

has powerful customer managers will urge a customer-centric approach to cross and up-selling. Note that the customer versus product-centric choice not a predictive modeling issue. The models in Sect. 21.2 can support either strategy. Also, an optimization model could be developed to maximize profits subject to product-centric as well as customer-centric constraints. For example, product-centric constraints would be a certain number of expected sales per product, while customer-centric constraints would include limits on how many cross-selling offers a customer can receive (to avoid wear-out).

Another strategic issue is competition. If the objective is market share or share of wallet, competition will respond. This will require models that infer customer ownership for competitive products (Kamakura et al. 2003). Figure 21.7 outlines the issues taking into account competition. It identifies the task, depending on what the customer currently owns, whether he or she owns it from the focal firm or the competition, and how likely the customer is to buy if cross-sold the product. Perhaps the toughest situation is when the customer owns the product, but with another company. Then either the focal company is trying to increase share-of-wallet or force a brand switch. Either way, the cross-selling effort will yield lower response rates, and potential competitive retaliation.

Another issue is whether the cross/up-sell efforts will be executed in real time or via campaigns (or some combination). An example of real-time cross/up-selling would be a Website recommendation system. By campaigns, we mean email, mail, or telemarketing campaigns that can be planned a month or more in advance. This relates to the firm's channel strategy. If the firm is trying to enhance its Web presence, it may emphasize real-time cross-selling on the Web. This has important implications for what data need to be collected and what models are feasible.

21.4.3 Data Collection

Cross-selling, especially customer-centric, may require a *two-dimensional* 360-degree view of the customer. The first dimension is that the firm may need to know what *products* the customer currently owns. The second dimension is the firm may need to know what *channels* the customer uses. The ideal database would include all products the customer has bought, from which channel, and what marketing efforts he or she has been targeted, on each channel. These data may be difficult to obtain (see Chapter 25).

Another issue is whether the company will collect competitive data, i.e., does the customer own the product with another company. If the strategy emphasizes competitive objectives, the company will have to invest in collecting competitive data or in inferring competitive ownership using a model (Kamakura et al. 2003).

Whether the strategy entails real-time or campaign-based cross/up-selling also influences data requirements. If the emphasis is on real-time, the data-requirements may be less, simply because it would be difficult to bring all previous activities and behaviors to bear in real time. If the emphasis is on campaigns, collecting more data – the full two-dimensional 360-degree view of the customer – may be worthwhile.

21.4.4 Analytics

At this stage, the firm must decide what predictive models it will use. We have reviewed several models in this chapter, summarized in Table 21.8 along several criteria. We classified a method as "high" on predictive accuracy if it has been tested versus other models and shown to be superior. Not surprisingly, the three models rated high on predictive accuracy are also rated "hard" on implementation. The only model to-date that tackles what, when, *and* response is Bodapati (2008). That model works well and provides interesting diagnostics, but is nontrivial to estimate. It would be interesting to see whether simpler forms of the model could capture what, when, and response without too much of a sacrifice in accuracy.

Another aspect of analytics is the application of optimization models. There are two areas where such models could be applied: (1) balancing cross-selling efforts between product-centric and customer-centric strategies, and (2) optimizing cross-selling efforts over time at the customer level. This is the domain of optimal contact models covered in Chapter 28. These

Table 21.8 Comparison of predictive models for use in cross/up-selling

	Market basket analysis	Collaborative filtering	Latent trait analysis (Kamakura et al. 1991)	Simple time-series next-product-to-buy (Knott et al. 2002)	Hierarchical Bayes next-product-to-buy (Li et al. 2003)	Factor-analytic model of product ownership (Kamakura et al. 2003)	Hazard model	New product hazard model (Kamakura et al. 2004)	Awareness and preference model (Bodapati 2008)	Stochastic frontier model (Kim and Kim 1999)	Data envelope analysis (Kamakura et al. 2002)
Time series approach	√[a]	–	–	√	√	–	√	√	√	–	–
Cross-sectional approach	√	√	√	–	–	√	–	–	–	√	√
Uses survey data	–	–	–	–	–	√	–	–	–	–	–
Models unobserved heterogeneity	–	–	–	–	√	√	–	√	√	–	–
Ease of implementation	Medium	Medium	Medium	Medium	Hard	Hard	Medium	Hard	Hard	Medium	Medium
Models what	√	√	√	√[b]	√	√	√[c]	√	√	√[d]	√[e]
Models when	–	–	–	–	√	–	√	√	√	–	–
Models response	–	–	–	–	–	–	–	–	√	–	–
Predictive accuracy	Medium	Medium	Medium	Medium	High	Medium	Medium	High	High	Medium	Medium

[a] Most naturally applied cross-sectionally, i.e., what was bought on the same trip.
[b] Can append a hazard timing model, which improves accuracy.
[c] Can be used to model when any purchase will be made, or when a particular product will be purchased.
[d] "What" in this case refers to how much more spending is feasible.
[e] "What" in this case refers to how much more spending is feasible.

models have focused on catalog mailings over time but not on cross-selling efforts over time. Similar issues would come into play in a cross-selling context, but the predictive models would have to include more dynamics, such as customer wear-out.

21.4.5 Implementation

Implementation requires organizational coordination, personnel training, and automation. Organization coordination is perhaps the toughest challenge. Coordination is needed between senior marketing management (to set the strategy), information technology (to provide the data), marketing analytics (to estimate the models that will drive the recommendations), service bureaus (to deliver the offers), and product, customer, and channel managers (to resolve which products and customers should receive priority, and through which channels should the offers be delivered). A working hypothesis would be that well-integrated organizations would be more successful at cross/up-selling, since it requires so much coordination.

Personnel training is also important. For example, a next-product-to-buy model can be used to generate a series of if/then rules for what a catalog phone representative should suggest as a cross-sell depending on the customer (Lau et al. 2004). However, the representative needs to know how to process these rules quickly. In-store personnel may need to be trained to recognize what to cross-sell to which customers

Another implementation issue is the actual creation and copy-writing of the offer. We discuss various creative approaches in Chapter 27. The point is that cross and up-selling can become very numbers-driven, and it is easy to forget that if the offer is confusing or doesn't catch the customer's eye, the campaign won't be successful.

A final implementation is automation. Ideally, the cross-selling system can be completely automated. For example, a market basket analysis can be used automatically to suggest additional products in a Web setting. However, it is difficult to program "common sense." For example, an important issue, easily automated once one is aware of it, is the need not to recommend a product the customer already owns. For example, a market basket analysis may tell a movie rental website to recommend Movie B to the customer, given the customer is renting Movie A, but the customer may already have rented Movie B.

21.4.6 Evaluation

Evaluation needs to be tied to the objectives stipulated at the beginning of the process. If the objective is just to increase short-term sales, simple control-group tests such as reported in Knott et al. 2002; Tables 21.4 and 21.5) can and should be designed. If however the objective is long-term increases in purchase volume or retention rate, tests need to run for longer periods of time (e.g., 6 months or more). In lieu of long-term experiments, the firm might survey customers and link measures such as purchase intentions and satisfaction to cross-selling efforts.

These evaluations may feed back to any previous step in the process. An unsuccessful campaign may be due to a variety of issues. For example, if the predictive model said the purchase rate among non-contacted customers would be 2%, and it turns out to be 5%, probably the predictive model is faulty, because these are customers in the control group who were not part of the cross-selling campaign.

21.5 Research Needs

Cross-selling and up-selling have received a fair amount of attention in the academic community. There are several models for predicting future customer product needs and converting those predictions to cross-selling plans. There is initial work on up-selling potential. Following are a few areas that warrant additional attention:

Cross-Selling Methods: Two opportunities for future research include (a) incorporating previous marketing efforts in the cross-selling model, and (b) comparing a broad set of models, both on holdout databases and in field tests.

Up-Selling Methods: The stochastic frontier approach is a promising tool for assessing up-selling potential. DEA is also promising, but has not been applied to up-selling. We need to compare the performance of stochastic frontier, DEA, and other potential approaches based on estimating unrealized potential.

Field Tests: While the field test described in Sect. 21.2 is a convincing and valuable test of at least one cross-selling model, we need many more such field tests so we can begin to compare methods and understand the circumstances under which cross-selling works and doesn't work.

The Value of Cross-Selling and Up-Selling: More work is needed to discern the relative impact of cross-selling on immediate sales, long-term contribution, or retention.

Coordinating Cross-Selling and Up-Selling: We need methods for coordinating cross-selling and up-selling activities across customers. We need the capability to decide when a customer should be cross-sold as opposed to be up-sold, and how cross-selling and up-selling activities should be balanced for the organization as a whole.

Chapter 22
Frequency Reward Programs

Abstract Frequency reward programs are customer development programs based on the theme, "Buy XXX, get a reward." "XXX" is usually a required purchase volume, and the reward can be free product, a cash rebate, or even "points" for another company's reward program. We discuss two ways that reward programs increase sales – points pressure and rewarded behavior – and the empirical evidence for each. We then review the rich economics literature that has endeavored to answer the question, "In a competitive environment, do reward programs increase firm profits?" We review several issues in designing reward programs, including the reward structure, and conclude with a review of reward programs offered by firms including Harrah's Entertainment and Hilton Hotels.

22.1 Definition and Motivation

Frequency reward programs attempt to increase customer value by rewarding customers proportional to their cumulative purchases, revenues, or profitability. Reward programs are used in a variety of industries such as hotels, car rentals, supermarkets, credit cards, office products, telecom, and gaming casinos. In fact, the airline industry's frequent flyer programs have in effect created a new currency in the "miles" travelers accumulate. In terms of the simple retention model of customer lifetime value,

$$LTV = \sum_{t=1}^{\infty} \frac{m_t r^{t-1}}{(1+\delta)^{t-1}} \tag{22.1}$$

frequency reward programs strive to increase both retention rate (r, the customer stays with the firm longer) and the amount purchased (m_t, the customer buys more to accumulate enough "points" to receive a reward).

We differentiate between frequency reward and customer tier programs (Chapter 23). Customer tier programs assign customers to segments or tiers and deliver different benefits to each tier. Frequency reward programs are a narrower promotional-oriented activity. They focus on the delivery of a single reward – a free flight, an upgrade, a coupon, etc. – based on accumulated points.

Both frequency reward and customer tier programs are often called "loyalty programs." We do not use that term because loyalty may be a *goal* of these programs, and they do increase purchase frequency. But whether they increase "loyalty", defined as "a favorable attitude toward a brand resulting in consistent purchase of the brand over time" (Assael 1995, p. 131) is another matter.

22.2 How Frequency Reward Programs Influence Customer Behavior

22.2.1 Mechanisms for Increasing Sales

There are three mechanisms by which the program can increase customer value: points pressure, rewarded behavior, and personalized marketing. Figure 22.1 illustrates.

The points pressure mechanism represents customers increasing their expenditures in order to earn the reward. The attractiveness of the reward obviously increases points pressure. Also, the reward program can create a switching cost for the customer, in that the customer who decides to purchase elsewhere forgoes the opportunity to accumulate points toward the reward (Taylor and Neslin 2005).

The points pressure effect should get stronger as the customer nears the requirements for a reward. First, the reward is subject to less discounting as it looms closer. Second, Kivetz et al. (2006) propose two psychological reasons for points pressure: (1) Goal-gradient hypothesis – this is a behaviorist

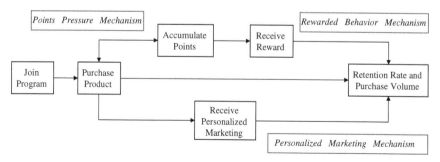

Fig. 22.1 Customer response to frequency reward programs: How reward programs influence retention and purchase volume.

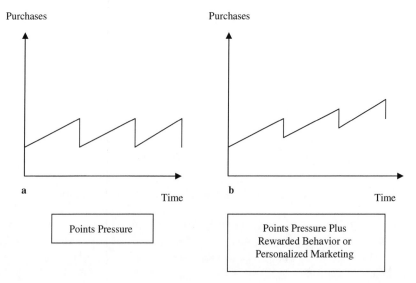

Fig. 22.2 Potential impact of frequency reward programs on purchase rates.

proposition originally due to Hull (1932) where organisms accelerate their efforts as they get closer to a goal. (2) Goal Distance Model – this is based on the psychophysical notion that humans make judgments relative to a benchmark. In the case of reward programs, the benchmark is the amount of effort (e.g., the number of purchases) to reach the goal (earn the reward). Consumers judge their progress by "calculating" the percentage of the distance they have covered toward receiving their reward. The authors hypothesize that motivation to reach the reward is an increasing function of this percentage.

The rewarded behavior mechanism is when customers increase their purchase rate *after* receiving the reward. Behavioral learning theory posits that "rewarded behavior is more likely to persist" (Blattberg and Neslin 1990, p. 22). Taylor and Neslin (2005) note that rewards can increase affect toward the firm, which subsequently translates into higher purchase rates. Whether the rewarded behavior effect is due to behavioral learning or increased affect is important for distinguishing whether rewards truly increase loyalty or just increase purchase inertia (Engel et al. 1995, p. 158).

The third mechanism for increasing retention and purchase volume is through the provision of personalized marketing efforts to members of the frequency reward program. These efforts include individually targeted promotions (for a retail store), cross-selling (for a gaming casino), or personalized customer service (for an airline). These efforts are not rewards *per se* but merely the company making use of what it learns about customer preferences through the customer's participation in the program.

Figure 22.2 illustrates the impact of the points pressure, rewarded behavior, and personalized marketing mechanisms on customer purchases (see Taylor and Neslin 2005). Figure 22.2a shows the build up in purchases due to the anticipation of the reward – the points pressure mechanism. Figure 22.2b shows an increase in purchasing above the previous baseline, due either to the rewarded behavior or personalized marketing.

22.2.2 What We Know About How Customers Respond to Reward Programs

22.2.2.1 Laboratory Experiments and Empirical Studies

Lal and Bell (2003) examined programs of the type "Spend $X over Y weeks and earn a reward". For example, one program awarded customers with a free ham if the customer spent $475 over a 6-week period. Lal and Bell grouped customers by baseline sales levels ("Worst," "Better," and "Best"). Their findings were important:

- The reward programs increased sales in the period leading up to the reward. This supports a points pressure effect.
- The points pressure effect was strongest among the Worst customers and weakest among the Best customers.
- The programs were generally profitable, due mainly to the increase in sales among the worst customers.
- There was a positive post-redemption impact, strongest among the Worst customer group. The authors had hypothesized that the post-redemption effect would be negative due to consumer stockpiling, so were surprised to find a positive effect. Our interpretation is that this was due to rewarded behavior.

Taylor and Neslin (2005) examine the same type of reward program as Lal and Bell (2003). Customers who purchased $500 worth of product over the 8-week period leading up to Thanksgiving were awarded a free turkey. Taylor and Neslin detect a points pressure effect in both years the program was run. In Year 1, sales per customer increase $2.44 per week on a customer baseline sales level of $37.91, a 6.1% increase, and $2.61 in Year 2 on a base of $41.02, a 6.4% increase. The authors calculate profits based on this points pressure effect and find the program to be profitable.

Taylor and Neslin (2005) also measure a rewarded behavior effect. The authors use a switching regression, where the first stage predicts whether a customer will redeem for a reward or not, and the second stage predicts post-redemption sales for redeemers versus non-redeemers. They find an average weekly post-redemption effect of $14, which on a baseline of $80, represents an increase of 17.5%. Taylor and Neslin also find that the rewarded behavior effect is strongest among customers with low current baselines, similar to Lal and Bell (2003).

Kivetz et al. (2006) examine the dynamics of points pressure in a series of field experiments. One involved a coffee shop, where the customer had to purchase 10 coffees in order to receive a free coffee. Another involved a music rating website, where visitors had to rate 51 songs in order to receive a gift certificate. The authors found that both programs induced points pressure. They found that the effect is gradual rather than a step function. This is consistent with the authors' goal-gradient and goal-distance theories. The authors found three additional and intriguing results:

- When the coffee shop offered a two-purchase credit to start off, acceleration toward the goal was faster. This supported the authors' goal-distance theory, because the percentage of the goal achieved was higher the more coffees that were bought.
- After the reward, respondents "reset" their purchase levels to the baseline levels before the promotion. This rules out stockpiling as a reason for the higher pre-reward purchase rates, but does not support rewarded behavior.
- Customers who were closer to their reward program goal were more receptive to promotions. This was investigated using a pencil and paper task, so is exploratory, but the implications for the third mechanism by which reward programs increase sales – targeted promotions – are obvious: Target promotions to customers who are approaching their goals.

Roehm et al. (2002) use laboratory experiments to investigate the impact of reward design on future loyalty, i.e., the rewarded behavior effect. The authors categorize rewards in terms of "cue compatibility" and "tangibility." A cue compatible reward is one that is consistent with what the brand stands for, e.g., a cue compatible reward for a supermarket might be a turkey. Tangibility refers to the directness of the incentive – newsletters and clubs are intangible, whereas price discounts are tangible. The authors hypothesize that an intangible cue-compatible reward would increase loyalty because the customer is encouraged to think about what the brand truly stands for. At the other extreme, a tangible cue-incompatible reward could hurt brand loyalty by encouraging customers to think just about the reward and not about the brand itself.

Roehm et al. create an experimental reward program and choice simulation for *Slice* soft drink. The cue-compatible, intangible reward was admission to a web-site featuring games and puzzles for "a refreshing change of pace" (p. 205). The cue-compatible, tangible incentive was a foam drink insulator. The cue-incompatible, intangible reward was admission to the *Slice* website featuring games and puzzles regarding fitness. The cue-incompatible, tangible reward was gym towels. The results showed that all four incentives were equally enticing in terms of brand choice. However, the impact on loyalty differed by type of reward, as follows:

Reward	Impact on low knowledge subjects	Impact on high knowledge subjects
Cue compatible, intangible	Increase	No change
Cue compatible, tangible	No change	Decrease
Cue incompatible, intangible	No change	No change
Cue incompatible, tangible	No change	Decrease

These results suggested a rewarded behavior effect only if the reward is cue compatible and not too tangible. Also, the impact is only on customers who are less familiar with the brand. Highly tangible rewards can decrease loyalty among customers highly familiar with the product, even if the reward is compatible with positioning.

Roehm et al.'s (2002) results are partially consistent with Lal and Bell (2003) and Taylor and Neslin (2005). In both those studies, the rewarded behavior effect was strongest among light users of the product. However, the rewards were tangible, which would work against finding a rewarded behavior effect. More work is needed to reconcile these findings.

Bolton et al. (2000) studied the impact of a reward program for a European credit card company. The authors collected data for 405 customers. They found that membership in the program did not directly affect customer retention or purchase volume. However, membership in the program decreased negative perceptions resulting from poor service encounters. This may be due to the reward distracting customers from evaluating poor service encounters.

Many reward programs require the consumer to decide whether to enroll in the program. A simple comparison of sales among enrollees versus non-enrollees will therefore be biased because it may be that currently loyal customers are pre-disposed to enroll. Leenheer et al. (2007) control for this in analyzing the impact of reward programs on share-of-wallet (SOW) for Dutch grocery stores. They model SOW as a function of program membership, and program membership as a function of store and household characteristics. The first relationship is estimated using two-stage least squares, since program membership is endogenous; the second relationship is measured using a selection model. The authors find (1) program membership increases SOW by on average 4.1 percentage points, and (2) this translates to a net revenue increase (net of program costs) of €163 per year. This analysis does not determine whether the gain in SOW is due to points pressure or rewarded behavior, but it has a firm footing in claiming a causal impact of reward program membership on firm revenues by controlling for the customer's decision of whether to join the program.

22.2.2.2 Dynamic Structural Models

Frequency reward programs "try to change the customer's choice process from operating in a spot market to operating in a multi-period, contractual relationship market" (Dowling and Uncles 1997). The customer realizes that purchasing from the company now has ramifications for *future* benefits, so needs to take into account not only the current benefits of purchasing, but future benefits as well. Dynamic structural models are designed to study consumer decision-making when customers take into account both current and future utility, especially when future utility depends on the decisions the customer makes now.

Characteristics of Dynamic Structural Models Relevant to Reward Programs

We first discuss the general structure of dynamic structural models so we do not need to repeat it for each model. The customer's task is to choose a set of decisions over a time period $\{t, \ldots T\}$ to maximize the net present value of their utility:

$$\underset{D_{ik\tau}, k \in C_{i\tau}}{Max} \sum_{\tau=t}^{T} \delta^{\tau-1} \sum_{k \in C_{i\tau}} U_{i\tau}(k) D_{ik\tau} \qquad (22.2)$$

where:

$D_{ikt} = 1$ if customer i chooses decision alternative k at time t.
$C_{it} = $ Set of decision alternatives available to customer i at period t. These alternatives might include whether or not to purchase from a particular firm; whether to "cash-in" points for a reward, etc.
$\delta = $ Discount factor; the degree to which the customer values future utility. Higher δ means the customer cares more about the future.
$U_{it}(k) = $ Utility customer i gains for choosing alternative k at time t.

This decision problem can be equivalently expressed using the principle of optimality, which says that the optimal decision for period t is that which maximizes current utility plus the expected value of future utility that results from the decision made in period t. This maximum utility is called the "Value Function", denoted by V. In particular:

$$V_{it}(S(T)) = \underset{D_{ikt}, k \in C_{it}}{Max} \{U_{it}(k) D_{ikt} + E\lfloor V_{i,t+1}(S(t+1)) | S(t), D_{ikt} \rfloor\} \quad (22.3)$$

where $S(t)$ are "state variables" at time t. State variables influence utility and change over time due either to a stochastic process or to the decision made at time t. A key state variable in frequency reward models is the number of points the customer has accumulated. The future values of state variables such as price are uncertain, so customers may form expectations of these variables (Erdem et al. 2003; Sun et al. 2003).

A Simple Model for Examining Competitive Equilibria

Kopalle and Neslin (2003) investigate competitive equilibria in reward programs. Their model is relatively simple. The customer decides each period which of two airlines to fly as well as whether to fly at all. The choice set is:

$$C_{it} = \begin{cases} 0 & \text{if customer } i \text{ flies neither airline in period } t \\ 1 & \text{if customer } i \text{ flies airline } ABC \text{ in period } t \\ 2 & \text{if customer } i \text{ flies airline } XYZ \text{ in period } t \end{cases} \quad (22.4)$$

The customer's utility function for each of these choices is as follows:

$$U_{it}(k) = \begin{cases} U_0 & \text{if } k = 0 \\ r_{i1t} - (1 - INV_{i1t})P_{1t} & \text{if } k = 1 \\ r_{i2t} - (1 - INV_{i2t})P_{2t} & \text{if } k = 2 \end{cases} \quad (22.5)$$

where:

U_0 = Utility for not flying, i.e., for the "outside category" (e.g., traveling by car).

r_{ijt} = Customer i's preference for Airline j in time t. r_{ijt} follows a logistic distribution with parameter a_j.

INV_{ijt} = The number of "points" customer i has applicable to airline j in time t:

$$INV_{ijt} = \begin{cases} 0 \text{ if } D_{ikt} = 1 & \text{for } k \neq j \\ 1 - INV_{ij,t-1} & \text{if } D_{ijt} = 1 \end{cases}$$

P_{jt} = The price of airline j in time t.

INV is defined as a zero–one variable. If the customer has no points accumulated for airline j and flies airline j, INV is set equal to 1. If the customer had one point accumulated for airline j and flies airline j, the flight is free (Equation 22.5). If the customer flies another airline or does not fly, INV is set to zero at time t, irrespective of whether the customer had accumulated points as of $t - 1$ or not. That is, customers build up a "credit" by flying a particular airline. They can cash in that credit for a free flight, but if they don't, they lose the credit. This is meant to model points expiration, a characteristic of some reward programs whereby customers lose points they do not cash in.

The state variables are INV_{ijt} and r_{ijt}. The customer is assumed to know the current values of r_{ijt} and the *probability distribution* of r_{ijt} for future periods. This means the customer knows his or her current preferences each airline, but is uncertain about future preferences because future flight requirements and schedules are not known.

Kopalle and Neslin derive insights from their model: (1) The value of the reward (the free trip) is increasing in δ, and hence a customer is more likely to repeat-fly an airline if the discount factor is large. This makes sense – if the customer cares more about the future, the accumulated points or credit will drive current purchase more strongly. (2) The value of the reward is increasing with the price charged by the airline. This is because the reward is a free flight. This means that expensive tickets are more valuable rewards. This is one reason why upgrades have become so popular. It is also why we often see frequency reward programs implemented by premium brands such as Hilton, Marriott, etc. (3) Reward programs expand the category if U_0 is large. If the outside category is not attractive, the market for Airlines ABC and XYZ will be large whether they have a reward program or not. However, if the outside category is attractive, category sales are currently low, but the program can grow the category.

A Model of an Online Retailer Frequency Reward Program

Lewis (2004) studied the frequency reward program of an online retailer. If the customer accumulated a threshold level of expenditures within a year, he or she would receive a reward (500 miles to be added to the customer's frequent flyer program). The reward is not free goods, but an *indirect* reward that can be applied to another good. We will discuss the question of whether to use direct or indirect rewards in Sect. 22.4.5. The choice set for Lewis' model is:

$$
C_{it} = \begin{cases}
0 & \text{if customer } i \text{ does not buy in period } t \\
1 & \text{if customer } i \text{ buys a small basket } (< \$50) \text{ in period } t \\
2 & \text{if customer } i \text{ buys a medium basket } (\geq \$50 \text{ and} \leq \$75) \quad (22.6) \\
& \text{in period } t \\
3 & \text{if customer } i \text{ buys a large basket } (\geq \$75) \text{ in period } t
\end{cases}
$$

Discretizing the amount bought makes the model easier to estimate. This is not a competitive model but there is an outside good, i.e., the customer may decide not to purchase at all from the website. The utility function is:

$$
U_{it}(k) = \begin{cases}
\beta_{i0} + \varepsilon_{i0t} & \text{if } k = 0 \\
\beta_{ik} + \beta_{ipk}P_t + \beta_{ick}C_{it} & \\
\quad + \sum_{h=1}^{4} \beta_{ihk}SH_{iht} + \sum_{g=1}^{G} \beta_{ig}Rcn_{igt} & (22.7) \\
\quad + \sum_{f=1}^{2} \beta_{ifk}FM_{ift} + \beta_{iL}L_{it} + \varepsilon_{ikt} & \text{if } k = 1, 2, 3
\end{cases}
$$

where:

P_t = Price index for the online retailer at time t.

C_{it} = Indicator variable of whether customer i received a coupon at time t.

SH_{iht} = Indicator variable of whether shipping charge schedule h was available to customer i at time t. The online firm used four different shipping charge schedules that they varied over time.

Rcn_{igt} = Indicator variable of whether customer i was in recency group g at time t. Recency is the time since the previous purchase.

Table 22.1 Frequency reward customer segments (From Lewis 2004)

	Segment 1	Segment 2
Percentage of sample	71%	29%
Mean annual # orders	8.7	14
Mean order size	$77	$42
Mean spending	$672	$586
Percentage earning reward	15%	1%
β_{iL}	0.75 (p < 0.01)	n.s.

FM_{ift} = Indicator variable of whether customer i was in cumulative purchase group f at time t. The expectation was that larger cumulative purchasing would mean the customer was learning to like the retailer so that the β's for this variable would be positive.

L_{it} = Value of reward customer i received in time t. The variable was coded as 0 (received no reward), 1 (received 500 frequent flyer miles for accumulating either $1,000 or $1,500 in expenditures), or 2 (received 1,000 frequent flyer miles for accumulating $2,000 in expenditures).

The parameter of most interest is β_{iL}, the utility of the reward. Lewis uses a latent structure formulation to capture customer heterogeneity in the utility parameters, thus yielding segments. Lewis includes an equation similar to the inventory accumulation used by Kopalle and Neslin to keep track of expenditures. If a given purchase will put the customer above a reward threshold, the L_{it} variable is set to 1 for that period. Assuming a positive β_{iL}, this provides an incentive for the customer to purchase.

Uncertainty in the model is incorporated via ε_{ikt} – the customer is uncertain before period t how much utility he or she will derive from decision k. Prices are also assumed uncertain and Lewis assumes customers form expectations for these prices. The state variables are the cumulative level of expenditures (i.e., the points inventory count), recency, frequency, price, couponing, and shipping. Lewis estimated the model and found two segments, as shown in Table 22.1.

The table shows that the majority of the sample derives extra utility from receiving the reward. This coincides with their generally higher level of spending, and the fact that 15% of them did earn a reward. This is in contrast to Segment 2, whose members derive no extra utility from the reward, and in fact, only 1% of them earned it.

The positive coefficient for the reward produces a points pressure effect. This is shown in Fig. 22.3 (based on fig. 2, p. 290 in Lewis' paper). It shows that if a customer has accumulated $900, the closer he or she gets to the end of the year, the more likely he or she is to purchase. Interestingly, if a customer has accumulated only $500, there is a *reverse* points pressure effect; the customer is discouraged from purchasing as time runs out. This is a fascinating finding. Remember the customer is working through a dynamic program. At the beginning of the year, achieving $1,000 in expenditures is a real possibility and this spurs sales. However, toward the end of the year,

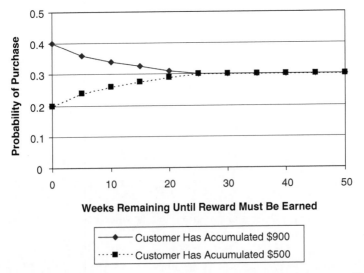

Fig. 22.3 Probability of purchase as time remaining to earn reward decreases (Adapted from Lewis 2004).

if the customer only has accumulated $500, the possibility is less real and *expected* future utility (V_{t+1} in Equation 22.3) is lower. This suggests one must be careful not to set reward thresholds too high. It might spur sales initially, but if many customers are not be able to make the threshold, they will become discouraged and sales will fall.

Lewis conducted simulations and determined that both the number of purchases and the average customer revenue increases when the reward program is in place versus when it is not, although the gain in revenues is only 2%. Perhaps the reward (500 frequent flyer miles) was not that highly valued, and in fact was not valued at all by 21% of the sample. Also, the threshold level ($1,000 for the first reward) was might have been set too high.

Modeling both Frequency Reward and Customer Tier Programs

Kopalle et al. (2006) develop a model of an airline's frequent flyer program. The model is distinct in modeling (1) the decision of whether to redeem miles for rewards, (2) the rewarded behavior effect, and (3) both a frequency reward program and a customer tier program. The choice set is defined as:

$$
C_{it} = \begin{cases}
0 & \text{if customer } i \text{ does not fly with this airline in time } t \\
1 & \text{if customer } i \text{ flies with airline in time } t \text{ but does not cash in} \\
2 & \text{if customer } i \text{ flies with airline in time } t \text{ and cashes in} \\
& \text{for level 1 reward} \\
3 & \text{if customer } i \text{ flies with airline in time } t \text{ and cashes in} \\
& \text{for level 2 reward}
\end{cases}
$$

(22.8)

The utility function is:

$$
U_{it}(k) = \begin{cases}
\varepsilon_{i0t} & \text{for } k = 0 \\
\alpha_{ik} + \sum_{s=1}^{S} \lambda_{is} E_{ist} + \beta_{i1} \sum_{l=2}^{3} D_{ilt-1} \\
\quad + \beta_{i2} \sum_{l=1}^{3} D_{ilt-1} + \varepsilon_{ikt} & \text{for } k = 1, 2, 3
\end{cases}
\tag{22.9}
$$

where E_{ist} is an indicator variable of whether customer i has accumulated enough miles to qualify for level s of the airline's customer tier program. If the customer does qualify, he or she automatically is a member of that level until either he or she accumulates more miles and hence qualifies for an even higher tier, or a year has gone by and the customer has not maintained the level of miles needed to remain in the tier.

Note that α_{i2} and α_{i3} reflect the immediate utility of a level 1 reward (upgrade) and a level 2 reward (free flight) respectively. The D_{ilt-1} terms equal 1 if the customer chose alternative 1, 2, or 3 in the previous period (indexed by l); 0 otherwise. Therefore, β_{i1} represents the rewarded behavior effect since it is added to the utility function only if the customer has cashed in for an upgrade or a free flight in the previous period. The β_{i2} term represents state dependence since it is added to the utility function as long as the customer flew with the airline last period, no matter whether it was a regular paid flight, an upgrade, or a free flight.

The state variables are the cumulative number of miles flown and the lagged decision variables. There are two sources of uncertainty. First, as in the other models reviewed in this section, overall utility for each decision is uncertain (the ε's). This uncertainty is resolved in the current period, but unknown for future periods. Second is the number of miles the customer will be awarded if he or she flies in some future period $t+x$. Kopalle et al. assume that customers are aware of the average number of miles they fly when they fly with this airline, and factor this in when considering the future.

The authors estimate their model on 200 customers and find two segments. The coefficients for the segments are as follows:

Parameter	Segment 1	Segment 2
Percentage of Sample	6.3%	93.7%
Base utility of flying (α_{i1})	0.62	0.75
Utility of upgrade (α_{i2})	1.56	−5.49
Utility of free flight (α_{i3})	1.77	−9.89
Utility of first customer tier (λ_{i1})	0.32	0.06
Utility of second customer tier (λ_{i2})	0.54	0.14
Utility of third customer tier (λ_{i3})	0.75	0.22
Rewarded behavior effect (β_{i1})	0.45	0.60
State dependence (β_{i2})	0.42	0.38

Segment 1, a distinct minority, has a positive utility for upgrades or free flights. Segment 2 has a negative utility. Since the upgrade and free flights parameters are a reduced form representations of the short-term gain minus the short-term cost of these rewards, this means that many customers find the benefits of cashing in for an upgrade of a free flight are not worth the hassle. This is consistent with many customers failing to cash in points they earn (Abu-Shalback Zid 2004a). This does not mean that Segment 2 will never cash in. First, there is positive carryover from cash-in, so the customer realizes that after they cash in, they will feel good about it. Second, random variation in ε can make cashing in the highest utility decision. For example, the customer's travel agent might notice the customer had a lot of accumulated miles and offer to arrange the cash-in. This is why, in the actual sample, Segment 1 averaged 1.5 cash-ins per year, while Segment 2 averaged 1.1 cash-ins.

The rewarded behavior effect is positive in both segments. The customer tier program provides significant utility for both segments. The results suggest the following interpretation of the segments. Segment 1 is "loyalty program enthusiasts" They like both the short-term "transaction utility" (Thaler 1985) cashing in for upgrades or free flights, as well as getting the more long-term customer tier reward. Segment 2 is more "customer tier focused." They like special treatment but have no need for upgrades or free flights.[1] Obviously, both frequency reward and customer tier programs have a place in the airline industry.

22.2.2.3 Summary: What We Know About How Frequency Reward Programs Affect Sales

The results from laboratory experiments, surveys, descriptive empirical analyses, and estimated dynamic rational models suggest the following:

- Frequency reward programs do increase sales. The level of increase is high enough to make these programs profitable.
- The points pressure effect is strongly confirmed (Lal and Bell 2003; Neslin and Taylor 2005; Lewis 2004; Kopalle et al. 2006) even to the level of detail that the effect is a gradual increase in sales leading toward the goal rather than a step increase (Kivetz et al. 2006; Lewis 2004; Kopalle et al. 2006).
- The majority of evidence supports a rewarded behavior effect (Lal and Bell 2003; Taylor and Neslin 2005; Kopalle et al. 2006; Bolton et al. 2000).[2] However, the evidence is not uniform (e.g., Kivetz et al. 2006) and may depend on the nature of the reward and the target group (Roehm et al. 2002).

---

[1] Note one cannot interpret differences in coefficient magnitudes between segments. Obviously, however, the signs of the coefficients can be interpreted and compared. All coefficients in the table are significantly different than zero.

[2] See also Leenheer et al. (2007), who find a causal relationship between supermarket frequency reward programs and share-of-wallet.

- Various market segments react differently to reward programs. Both the points pressure and rewarded behavior effects seems to be stronger among light users (Lal and Bell 2003; Taylor and Neslin 2005; Roehm et al. 2002). Dynamic structural models reveal two segments – one very much caught up in immediate rewards; the other segment less interested (Lewis 2004; Kopalle et al. 2006).

22.3 Do Frequency Reward Programs Increase Profits in a Competitive Environment?

An area that has received much attention by economists is whether reward programs produce higher profits in a competitive environment. The answer depends on various characteristics of consumer response and on the types of rewards used. We review the several studies on this issue in this section.

Klemperer (1987a, b) identified two forces that influence the profitability of frequency reward programs: (1) they create long-term monopoly power and hence can increase profits, but (2) short-term competition can decrease profits. The monopoly power stems from the points pressure mechanism, which means that customers with points inventory want to repurchase the product. The short-term competition develops because companies compete more strongly to induce customers to make that first purchase so that they begin to accumulate points. Klemperer (1987a) found that the net result of these two forces depended on the functional form of the demand function.

Beggs and Klemperer (1992) expanded this work by examining the impact of a reward program when customers enter and leave the market. They found that prices and profits uniformly increase in the presence of switching costs induced by reward programs. As enunciated by Klemperer (1995), the firm is faced with the question of either increasing prices to exploit the built-in loyalty of its previous customers who have accumulated points, or decreasing price in the battle for new customers so they can be exploited in the future. Klemperer maintains that current-period exploitation dominates because (1) the future benefits of getting customers is discounted by some factor less than 1, and (2) new customers are less price sensitive in the current period because they realize firms can increase prices in future periods.

One limitation of this work is that the existence of the reward program was exogenously specified; not a decision variable for the firm. Caminal and Matutes (1990) consider offering a reward program to be a strategic decision. The authors found that the profitability of reward programs depended on whether they were of the form of either a "coupon," promising a price discount but not specifying the future price, or a guaranteed future price, e.g., buy one, get one *free*. The authors found that the coupon reward program increases profits, but guaranteed future price decreases profits. The reason is that the coupon program allows the firm more latitude for increasing price later on. With a pre-committed price, firms lose latitude and this accentuates price competition. In addition, when firms *choose* between a coupon and a pre-committed price reward program, the result was that the pre-committed price was the equilibrium, implying that reward programs decrease profits.

Kim et al. (2001) examined the rationale for reward programs in the context of heavy users versus light users. The presence of the reward program, its form (efficient versus inefficient), and price were the decision variables. Efficient rewards are inexpensive compared to their value to the customer. For example, a free airline ticket costs the firm very little, but is worth the price of a ticket to the customer. Cash, however, is inefficient in that it is worth the same to the customer and the firm. The authors found that the light user segment can serve as the basis for a reward program. The light users pay higher prices and don't earn rewards. In effect, the light users are subsidizing the heavy users. This equilibrium is profitable unless the light user group is price sensitive, in which case firms compete too strongly for this group, driving down prices to the point that reward programs become unprofitable.

Kim et al. (2004) show how frequency reward programs can be profitable if they are used to manage excess capacity. Many firms face seasonal demand (e.g., hotels). Firms can let customers earn reward points during the high-season, to be redeemed during the off-season. This is an important argument since excess capacity is a chronic problem for so many companies. The strategy hinges on the effectiveness of the reward program, i.e., customers must be willing to earn points during the high season and redeem them during the off season. This may be how reward programs work in industries such as hotels, if rooms are only available as rewards during the off season.

Kopalle and Neslin (2003) study the impact of market expandability and consumer valuation of future benefits on the profitability of reward programs. They assume the consumer follows the decision-making process outlined by Equations 22.4–22.5 and that firms decide whether to use reward programs. The authors find that if the market is not expandable, reward programs are not profitable. The reason is that the power of the reward program is directed at stealing market share from competitors, and competitors react strongly. The competitive impact for a reward program is stronger than that of standard promotions because the reward program locks up customers for more than one period. This creates a higher stakes prisoner's dilemma. When the reward program serves to grow the market, it achieves the benefit of a powerful promotion without precipitating strong competitive response. The result is higher profits.

The authors show that frequent flyer programs appeared in the airline industry in 1981, coincident with the rapid entry of "low-frills" competitors. The authors interpret this as the major airlines using reward programs to enlarge *their* market. They also interpret supermarkets' use of reward programs as a way of protecting their market against mass merchandisers such as Wal-Mart (see Patton 2002). In both of these cases, the outside competitor is unable or unwilling to respond to the reward program. The low-frills airlines did not have the information system to offer reward programs. Wal-Mart, although it certainly has the information system, would find reward programs inconsistent with its positioning of everyday low pricing and simplicity.

Lal and Bell (2003) propose that reward programs eliminate competition between retailers due to cherry-picking. They assume a Hotelling model where two stores differ in which products are higher priced and which are lower priced. The cherry pickers, located roughly in the middle of the Hotelling line, buy the cheapest items at each store. This creates a transportation cost for the cherry pickers, as they are not always shopping at their closest store. If one store implements a reward program, prices generally increase enough to make the program profitable without turning off the cherry-pickers. However, if both stores implement programs the stores compete away these profits. If in addition there are high and low cost shoppers, and both stores offer frequency reward programs, profits can decrease depending on how much each store discounts its lower-priced items. Overall this presents a mixed view of frequency reward programs. If one store offers them and shoppers are not segmented in terms of shopping costs, the reward program can increase profits. But if both stores implement these programs, and if customers are segmented according to their shopping costs, profits can decrease.

Overall, the theoretical evidence is that reward programs can increase profits if they grow the market, "exploit" a price-insensitive light user group, enable firms to pre-commit to a price discount and not to a specific future price, manage excess capacity, or eliminate cherry picking. Certainly there are examples where these conditions are met. The airline industry may be one. Frequent flyer programs potentially exploit a large segment of light users, and might grow the market. Frequent flyer programs persist today even though the mass influx of new airlines has slackened, and even the lower tier airlines can and do offer reward programs (e.g., Goetzl 2000). However, it is possible that the frequent flyer programs are not growing the market in today's competitive environment, and in today's market the infrequent traveler might in fact be very price sensitive, in which case reward programs may be decreasing industry profits.

While empirical evidence has demonstrated that reward programs increase firm profits on a marginal basis (Lal and Bell 2003; Taylor and Neslin 2005; Leenheer et al. 2007), empirical work is needed to see if they increase profits in a competitive industry. Indeed, competitors' use of reward programs has been found to be one of the most important determinants of a firm's decision to adopt a reward program (Leenheer and Bijmolt 2003).

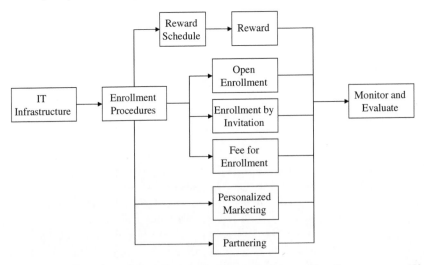

Fig. 22.4 Frequency reward program design considerations.

22.4 Frequency Reward Program Design

22.4.1 Design Decisions

Figure 22.4 depicts the design decisions involved with a frequency reward program. Infrastructure involves the information system for collecting data and awarding rewards. Enrollment procedures, reward schedules, and the reward are fundamental decisions that define the reward program. Partnering has also become a crucial element. Personalized marketing and partnering are potential add-ons. Finally, the program must be monitored and evaluated.

22.4.2 Infrastructure

A reward program must have an infrastructure for collecting customer data, determining which customers get which rewards, and then delivering the rewards. In a small shop this can be done by hand – the proprietor keeps a list of customers and updates their totals whenever the customer makes a purchase. However, when the customer counts reach into the thousands if not millions, major investments are needed in computer information systems.

These investments are not trivial. Even airlines, despite their large information systems, still need to make sure they avoid mishaps such as assigning top passengers to middle seats (Feldman 2002). Information system upgrades range from $5 to $10 million for airlines (Feldman 2002). Another company that one would expect to have ample information technology is American Express. However, the company cited higher costs to run loyalty programs as a cost factor that became a drag on earnings (Lee 2002).

22.4.3 Enrollment Procedures

The three alternatives are: (1) open enrollment, (2) fee for enrollment, and (3) enrollment only by invitation. Most frequency reward programs are open enrollment. Companies are eager to get customers onto their frequency reward program so they can reap the benefits of increased sales, etc. The obvious benefit of charging a fee is that it separates out the best from the worst customers, thus allowing the company to reward its best customers. The cost is the mixed message it gives customers: "We want to reward our best customers, so please pay us $25 and we'll reward you!"

Another way to separate out best from worst customers is to make the reward program available only by invitation. Viking Office Products, for example, will not reveal the criteria for being included in their program and does not promote their program (Miller 2001). The benefit of this approach is one can limit the size (and expense) of the program and use complex criteria (previous sales, future potential, etc.) to select members for the program. The downside is the limited opportunity for the reward program to attract new customers.

22.4.4 Reward Schedule

The reward schedule maps customer purchases to rewards. There are two dimensions that define reward schedules: linearity and continuity. Continuity refers to whether the customer earns rewards after each purchase or only after reaching a threshold. Linearity pertains to whether the relationship between purchases and rewards is the same no matter what the level of purchasing. Figure 22.5 illustrates.

The linear continuous schedule is very common. Many credit cards reward customers one frequent flyer mile for each dollar spent. The advantage of this schedule is its simplicity. It doesn't require the customer to "jump through hoops" to receive a reward, and today's consumers don't like to wait (Abu-Shalback Zid 2004b). Another advantage is that it continually rewards behavior, and behavioral learning suggests continual reinforcement is most effective (Rothschild and Gaidis 1981). However, linear continuous rewards do not create points pressure. Consider a credit card program that offers 1 mile per dollar spent. If a competitor has the same reward program, the customer does not lose anything by switching back and forth between the

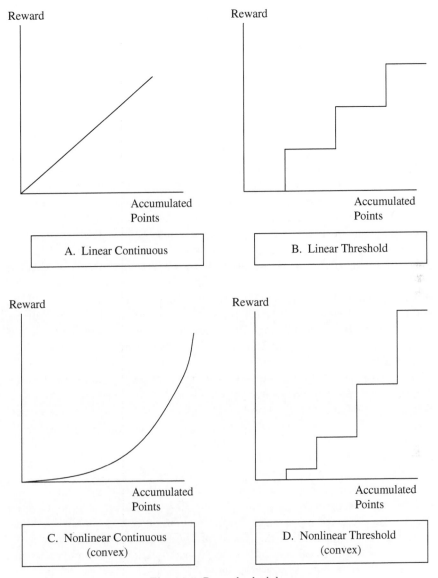

Fig. 22.5 Reward schedules.

credit cards. This nullifies points pressure. This might be addressed by using a continuous but convex reward schedule.

Yi and Jeon (2003) suggest that a linear continuous schedule may be better for low-involvement services. This makes sense as it would appear that high involvement is a necessary ingredient for customers to (implicitly) think through the dynamic rational model (Sect. 22.2.2.2) needed to make decisions under a nonlinear or threshold schedule. In addition, Keh and Lee (2006) find

Table 22.2 Convex (Schedule A) versus linear (Schedule B) frequency reward structures

Points requirement	Schedule A reward	Schedule B reward
25,000	$100	$100
50,000	$200	$200
75,000	$400	$300

that dissatisfied customers prefer constant rewarding, whereas satisfied customers prefer a delayed reward. In summary, despite their disadvantages, linear continuous reward schedules may work best for low involvement services or with dissatisfied customers.

Threshold reward structures set requirement levels at which point the customer receives a reward. For example, 25,000 miles of travel may be required for a free upgrade; a supermarket may reward a free turkey for customers who spend at least $500 over a 2-month period. The prime advantage of thresholds is they create points pressure. The customer with 24,000 miles on Airline ABC delays an upgrade by switching to Airline XYZ. The disadvantage of thresholds is that behavior is rewarded infrequently, and consumers may focus on the reward rather than on the brand itself. In addition, the design of the exact stepped structure is a challenge. The requirement levels should be set high enough to encourage more frequent purchasing, but not so stringent that customers don't see the reward as a real possibility.

The thresholds can be linear, concave, or convex. For example, Schedules A and B in Table 22.2 both have thresholds, but A is convex while Schedule B is linear. Which program is preferred would depend on customer response, which could be measured using a dynamic rational model. However, it would also depend on competition, so the complete analysis would involve firm's competing for dynamic rational customers using linear versus convex threshold reward schedules.

A related issue is whether points should ever expire. Expiration creates more point pressure (Kopalle and Neslin 2003) and can be used to price discriminate against light users (the infrequent flyer may finally build up enough miles to earn a free flight, but by the time he or she is ready to fly again, the reward has expired). However, expiration dates are more expensive to handle from a data processing perspective, and can cause considerable frustration and "turn-off" for customers.

Another aspect of the reward schedule is how clearly it should be stipulated to the customer. It seems that one would want to make the reward schedule clear. For example, Cunningham (2002), states, "the sheer complexity of points-based schemes can be a turn-off. Many people with loyalty cards do not take advantage of the offers because they do not have the time, or the will, to work out what they are entitled to". Complexity could decrease points pressure because the customer doesn't understand how much he or she needs to accumulate to get a reward. However, there may two potential benefits of complexity: First, the reward serves as a discrimination device, identifying those who really care about rewards (and will do the homework required to figure out the program). Second, complexity could increase the rewarded behavior effect: (1) The higher effort required to get the reward creates a cognitive dissonance that is resolved in favor of the brand – i.e., the customer asks, "Why did I go through so much trouble for this reward," and answers, "I must really like this brand" (Dodson et al. 1978). (2) If the customer is unclear of the reward structure, the reward may come as a surprise, surpassing customer expectations, and "delighting" the customer (Rust and Oliver 2000).

22.4.5 The Reward

There are several attributes of the reward that should be considered:

Immediacy: This pertains to the length of time between when the reward is earned and when it is delivered. Smart cards, for example, can let customers know immediately how many points they have accumulated, and the points can be cashed in instantly (Kuchinskas 2000; Lucas 2002; Pepe 2002). The advantage of immediacy is that coupling the reward with the correct behavior creates powerful reinforcement (Rothschild and Gaidis 1981), enhancing the rewarded-behavior effect. However, companies may decide to delay the reward, even if they have the capability to deliver it immediately (Kuchinskas 2000). Decoupling of the reward from the behavior might encourage the customer to focus on the brand experience instead of the reward.

Direct vs. Indirect: Direct rewards are the firm's product or a similar product. Indirect rewards are a different product or cash. Yi and Jeon (2003) found that for high involvement services (in their case, a hair salon) direct rewards were more effective than indirect rewards, whereas for low involvement services (in their case, a fried chicken restaurant), direct awards provided no advantage over indirect awards. One important form of indirect reward is cash. The advantage of cash is the flexibility it provides to the customer – the cash can be used in any way. Kim et al. (2001) advocate cash because it forces firms to commit to high prices. However, cash is expensive for the company. A cell-phone company can award a new cell-phone that is worth $200 to the customer because that is how much he or she would have to pay for it at retail. However, the company pays perhaps only $50. This is obviously less expensive than awarding $200 cash. In addition, non-cash indirect rewards provide utility in the form of pride or prestige. For example, the salesperson who has earned a unique sports jacket with an insignia can wear that jacket with pride and enjoy fielding questions from peers as to how he or she obtained it (Renk 2002).

Price Discount vs. Pre-Committed Price: As mentioned earlier, Caminal and Matutes (1990) conclude that price discount rewards are profitable, whereas pre-committed prices tie the hands of firms and increase competition. In their analysis, pre-committed prices were the equilibrium if firms could choose between the two, which suggests price discount rewards should be less prevalent than a pre-committed price. Indeed, the common buy-x-get-one-free nature of many programs would be a prime example of a pre-committed price. However, many retailer reward programs offer discount coupons. The key is to separate the reward from the price of the product. Premiums would do this just as well as a coupon, and are also common rewards.

Monetary Value: A key decision is the monetary value of the reward to the consumer. For example, a credit card offered one point for every dollar spent, and 5,000 points earned a $50 gift certificate (Polaniecki 2001). That amounts to a 1-cent reward for every dollar spent, a 1% discount. Southwest offered a free flight after 8 round trips (Goetzl 2000). That amounts to a 12.5% discount per flight. A high monetary reward coupled with a reasonably tough reward schedule (e.g., 8 flights for a free flight) can create a lot of points pressure. A higher reward might enhance the rewarded behavior mechanism, since a stronger reward should precipitate more affect toward the firm. However, if the reward is too strong, it becomes the "primary reinforcement" (Rothschild and Gaidis 1981; Rothschild 1987) and reinforces the use of reward programs rather than the use of the product.

Reward Attractiveness: This is similar to the question of monetary value of the reward, but applicable to premiums and other rewards that do not have clear monetary value. The same concern as with monetary rewards exists in that too strong a reward diverts attention from the brand. One has to be careful to anticipate the attractiveness of the reward in advance. Procter & Gamble offered Fisher-Price toys as a reward for frequent purchasers of its diapers. P&G under-estimated consumer response to the program, and months after the end of the program, it still hadn't been able to fulfill all the claims for the toys (Estell 2002a). This problem can be avoided with laboratory pre-testing such as the work by Roehm et al. (2002) and Kivetz and Simonson (2002).

Multiple vs. Single Rewards: The provision of a menu of rewards allows customers to select the reward they like the best, thereby increasing customer utility (Lucas 2002). The main disadvantage of multiple rewards is cost and complexity. For example, there is the question of whether the rewards should be of equal value to the firm or equal value to customers on average, or both. An airline may award a free seat (which costs nothing if it is available) or a travel bag (which has a cost). If too many customers select the travel bag, the reward program could be unprofitable.

Luxury vs. Utilitarian Rewards: Kivetz and Simonson (2002) found that consumers prefer luxurious rewards (facial massage, wine, jewelry, etc.) when program requirements are more stringent. Stringency assuages guilt customers might feel in receiving a luxurious reward. This suggests that if a company uses a convex, threshold reward structure, luxury products should be used for the higher thresholds, while utilitarian products can be used for the lower thresholds. The complication is customer heterogeneity. Customer A may consider eight flights to be an incredible effort, worthy of a luxury reward. While Customer B may average eight flights a month, so requires little effort. Still, the results suggest that if the program is targeting low-sales customers and sets up a high hurdle, it may be better to use a luxurious reward, since these customers have to work hard to achieve the reward.

Link to Brand Positioning: Roehm et al. (2002) suggest rewards should reinforce product positioning, and that the best way to do it is through intangible rather than tangible rewards. Access to a website with games and contests that reinforce the brand's positioning is better for loyalty than a premium that also reinforced the positioning but is more tangible. The problem with intangible rewards is that they may not create enough points pressure – the prospect of access to a website may not be a strong enough reward to create points pressure (although recall that in Roehm et al.'s experiment, all rewards created the same number of purchases). This means that the gains in retention from the program have to come entirely through the rewarded behavior effect. There are many examples of reward programs that link well to product associations. For example, AT&T Broadband, a television cable company, used premiums such as a Disney watch or a Showtime director's chair (Beeler 2000). Nantucket Nectars, a beverage company, capitalized on their bottle caps that contained clever sayings by using caps as points for the reward program (Estell 2002b).

22.4.6 Personalized Marketing

A major opportunity is to use reward programs to facilitate personalized marketing efforts, especially cross-selling. Cross-selling efforts work best when companies have data on customer purchase history (Knott et al. 2002), and such data are collected via reward programs. As mentioned earlier, Kivetz et al. (2006) found that customers were more receptive to special offers as they got closer to earning a reward. This finding was exploratory, but suggests how frequency reward programs and personalized marketing can be integrated.

It appears that personalized marketing is an under-utilized opportunity for reward programs. Many supermarkets collect purchase data through their frequent shopper programs, but few use those data to personalize marketing campaigns. There are at least three possible reasons for this. First, personalized marketing requires data analysis and supermarkets are not ready to undertake this task (see Leenheer and Bijmolt 2003). Second is privacy. Some shoppers do not want supermarkets scouring their purchase records, looking for "interesting" patterns (Weir 1999). In fact, laws have been proposed that would allow shoppers to forbid supermarkets from *collecting* data on their buying habits (Weir 1999). Third, supermarkets may be wary of customer dissatisfaction that could result from tailored marketing campaigns. This is because the personalized marketing would take the form of targeted price discounts. Customer A could become jealous if Customer B receives a coupon for a product Customer A wants to buy (Feinberg et al. 2002).

22.4.7 Partnering

An important trend in reward program design is partnering. Partnering takes two forms: "earn" partners and "burn" partners. If members of Company A's reward program can earn points by purchasing at Company B, Company B is Company A's earn partner. If Company A's customers can spend their points by getting discounted or free merchandise at Company B, Company B is Company A's burn partner. Obviously, Company B could be both an earn and a burn partner for Company A.

The advantage of partnering is that it makes the program more attractive to customers. To the extent that Company A has many earn partners, it is easier for customers to build up their point totals. To the extent that Company A has many burn partners, the rewards are more attractive. Firms have to be careful, however. Sharp and Sharp (1997) examine a program in Australia that involved several retail outlets that served as earn and burn partners for each other. They found that repeat purchasing did not increase at most of the retailers – so many stores were partners that customers did not have to change their purchase habits in order to earn many points.

Another noteworthy partnering arrangement was the AOL AAdvantage Reward Program (Direct Marketing 2000). In this partnership, AOL and American Airlines were earn and burn partners for each other (Regan 2000). AOL allowed its customers to earn miles when they shopped at AOL shopping affiliates, as well as when they flew on American Airlines. The miles could be spent on merchandise or free trips. The program was launched with much fanfare in 2000, but in January 2002, the program discontinued the key feature of allowing customers to earn miles when shopping with AOL affiliates. The burn feature of the program, redeeming miles for merchandise at affiliates, remained, but the earning miles feature has been dropped. What's more, the financial value of using miles for merchandise has been called to question. One report is that 50,000 AOL AAdvantage points could be used for \$187 in books, but those same miles could be used for a \$500 airplane flight (Drucker 2002).

Despite examples of mixed success, partnering has become a common feature of many reward programs. Many credit cards have programs with multiple burn partners, for example airlines, retailers, and travel agents (Polaniecki 2001).

22.4.8 Monitor and Evaluate

As with any marketing program, it is crucial to monitor and evaluate reward programs. This can be difficult because its desired impact is long-term. Statistical methods (e.g., Sect. 22.2.2.2 and Leenheer et al. 2007) are capable of measuring the points pressure and rewarded behavior mechanisms as well as the overall impact. Another way to evaluate reward programs is through surveys (Bolton et al. 2000), especially if they can be conducted on a before and after basis.

22.5 Frequency Reward Program Examples

22.5.1 Harrah's Entertainment[3]

Harrah's Entertainment has a highly successful reward program that includes both a frequency reward program and personalized marketing. Harrah's operates 21 gaming casinos across the USA, serving 19 million customers annually. Accordingly, Harrah's needs a large database to store customer information. The data are stored in a Patron Database (PDB) and a Marketing Work Bench (MWB). The PDB houses "raw" data and can be used for simple look-up. The MWB includes data in a form that can be analyzed for personalized marketing efforts. Total size of the databases is 300 GB, updated on a daily basis. The data are at the customer level, and include hotel stay, demographics, customer preferences, event attendance, games played, and marketing offers received and responded to. The data are integrated at the customer level across all Harrah's locations. This is truly a "single view of the customer" (Chapter 25).

Customers accumulate points by using Harrah's facilities, which can be cashed in for merchandise, rooms, food, and cash. This is implemented through the PDB database. Harrah's also uses the MWB database to design various personalized campaigns. These campaigns consist of offers, complimentary passes, etc. The campaigns can be targeted at individuals based on predictive modeling. For example, Harrah's identified consumers with high potential for increased visits based on their residence and gambling "velocity," (literally how fast they play the slot machines). These customers were then mailed offers for cash and food, and their visit frequency increased from 1.1 to 1.4 per month.

The Harrah's reward program is integrated with Harrah's customer tier program. Membership in the different tiers is based on accumulated points thresholds, and each tier has specific privileges such as priority reservations, seating, and check-in.

---

[3] Much of the material in this section is based on Watson and Volonino (2001). See also Watson and Eckerson (2000).

Overall, Harrah's estimates a 72% internal rate of return on their investment in information technology. They report strong increases in visit frequency, profit, and cross-market facility utilization. The Harrah's implementation is a well-publicized "success story" (Swift 2001; Davis 2001; Koller 2001; Rosen 2000; Heun 2000). Two aspects of the program are noteworthy. First, the data are very complete and provide a detailed profile of each customer. Second, the program employs points rewards *and* personalized marketing. The increase in customer profit undoubtedly comes through all three mechanisms in Fig. 22.1: points pressure, rewarded behavior, and personalized marketing.

22.5.2 The UK Supermarket Industry: Nectar Versus Clubcard

The UK supermarket industry has witnessed an intense "tit-for-tat" competition with reward programs. Tesco began the competition in 1995 (Gofton 1998). At the time it was second to Sainsbury's, and wished to retain customers and increase sales. Its "ClubCard" awarded 1 point per British pound spent, and 1 point was worth 1 pence in discounts at Tesco. This equates to a 1% discount. With profit margins of 5–7%, this represented a significant reduction in margin for Tesco (Croft 1995). The question is whether this paid off. Tesco claimed in 1995 to have overtaken Sainsbury's, and that the ClubCard was a major factor (Croft 1995).

There were two issues facing Tesco at this point. First was how Sainsbury's would respond. Indeed Sainsbury's did respond with its Saver Card, a frequency reward program with stepped rewards. The maximum number of points that could be accumulated on one card was 5,000, representing £2,000 purchases, which could be traded in for a discount of £50, a 2.5% savings. However, by 1998 they had also introduced an ongoing Reward Card that rivaled ClubCard (Marketing Week 1998). Second was whether Tesco would be able to utilize the data collected to develop personalized marketing programs that would earn additional profits. This was a crucial step. With a sacrifice of 1% margin on a base of 6% margin, Tesco would have to generate 20% additional revenues in order to break even.[4]

Indeed, Tesco set out to utilize the purchase data collected from its Club-Card members to tailor coupons and other discounts to shoppers. Each quarter ClubCard mailed a communication to members that including points totals, vouchers for redeeming points at Tesco, and targeted coupons. Tesco reportedly creates 100,000 personalized versions of these targeted coupons,

---

[4] Let R = base revenues, m = base margin (6%), and δ = incremental revenues. Baseline profits is therefore Rm, and profits under the reward program are $R(m-0.01)+R\delta(m-0.01)$. In order to break even, we must have $R(m-0.01)+R\delta(m-0.01) > Rm$, or $\delta > (m/(m-0.01)) - 1 = 0.20$, or 20%.

based on its analyses of purchase data (Gofton 1998). In 1998, Tesco reported a 1/3 increase in its loyal customer base. It also reported coupon redemption rates upwards of 30% (Gofton 1998). All indications are that the personalized marketing aspect of ClubCard has been highly successful, even in competing with Wal-Mart (Rohwedder 2006).

Over time, Tesco also expanded its card to bring in more earn and burn partners. By 2002, earn partners included Allders retail, Beefeater restaurants, H. Samuel jewelry, and several auto and tire centers. Burn partners included an almost bewildering array of recreation and travel opportunities, listed at the Tesco website (www.tesco.co.uk). Another recent burn partner is Air Miles, an air travel rewards program.

While Sainsbury's retained its own reward program during this period, it was not apparently as comprehensive as Tesco's. That changed in late 2002 with the launch of Nectar. Nectar is a reward program representing a consortium of four companies – Sainsbury's, BP gasoline, Debenhams retail stores, and Barclaycard credit card (Kleinman 2002). The earn partners consist of the four partners. The burn partners include Sainsbury's, McDonalds, Blockbuster, and additional companies. In 2002, Nectar claimed 12 million members, compared to 10 million for Tesco (Rogers 2002).

Two fascinating questions emerge: First, how will the programs evolve from this point? One intriguing possibility is that they will become branded products, each consisting of sets of earn and burn partners and various points schemes. Now, the main players in the UK market are Nectar, Air Miles (a frequent flyer program for which Tesco is an earn partner), Tesco's ClubCard, and Boots Advantage. There are other questions for the future. For example, will rewards increase above the 1% of revenues mark that has become more or less the standard?

Second and most importantly, will these programs raise profits for member companies? The sacrifice in margin requires either a substantial gain in revenues or an increase in profits through personalized marketing. Revenues could also increase if Tesco could raise prices. This would be the route to profits suggested by Klemperer and others. Also, heavy users build up more points and therefore have opportunities for burning their points with airlines and other partners that have minimum requirements. So we have the conditions in Kim et al. (2001) where the heavy user segment receives more benefits than the light user segment. As long as the light users are not price sensitive (see Kim and Rossi (1994) for an example where heavier users were more price sensitive than light users), the outcome could be profitable. The problem is that the light users may be price sensitive. First, they may be lower income individuals. Second they may be store-switchers. The important point is that Klemperer and his colleagues' theories are applicable toward thinking about and assessing the profitability of these reward programs.

In addition, the rewards at least for Tesco take the form of cash reductions (i.e., coupons) rather than guaranteed prices. Therefore Caminal and

Matutes' (1990) recommendations also apply. However, the market growth condition of Kopalle and Neslin (2003) would not appear to apply. The supermarket industry in the UK is relatively mature. The other route to profitability is personalized marketing. Tesco's reports suggest that this has been very helpful for them. In any case, the UK supermarket industry provides a fascinating glimpse of the evolution of reward program competition and the emergence of a reward program "industry."

22.5.3 Cingular Rollover Minutes

The wireless telephone industry is concerned about customer churn. Cingular created a reward program that allows customers to "roll over" unused minutes from the previous month into the current month (Thomaselli 2002). This is different from the standard reward program in that points accumulate based on *lower* usage.

Compete, Inc. reported that the program had strong short-term impact reducing churn (Business Wire 2002). However, the impact wore away quickly. Compete collects its data by observing web visit behavior. It measured potential churn as the percentage of a firm's current customers who investigate competitive offerings. Compete found that when Cingular launched its program, potential churn increased by 9–27% among Cingular's competitors, but remained level for Cingular. However, a month or so later, Cingular's potential churn increased by 11% while its competitors' improved. Compete does not have access to actual churn numbers, relying instead on customer search behavior as an indicator. The indication is that Cingular's program caused many competitors' customers to investigate Cingular, while retaining Cingular's current customers. However, things leveled off after the initial advertising campaign.

It is still possible of course that Rollover Minutes paid off. In any case, it is an interesting reward structure that could be used in various subscription services. However, perhaps Rollover Minutes was "merely" a promotion that had a positive short-term effect but little long-term impact. Part of the problem might be the lack of a true points-pressure effect. It seems self-defeating to motivate customers not to use the service now so they can use it more in the future. The points-pressure effect is to encourage *more* use now so customers can get a reward in the future.

22.5.4 Hilton Hotels

The hotel industry is a repeat-purchase business with chronic customer loyalty concerns. This makes it ripe for reward programs. Hilton Hotels offers

Hilton HHonors, open to anyone at no charge (Deighton 2000; Bell et al. 2002). Members earn points by staying at Hilton Hotels, but also through earn partners including various airlines, FTD Florists, and Mrs. Field's Cookies. The points can be used for upgrades and stays at Hilton Hotels, or burned at partners or converted to frequent flyer miles for free flights.

Points are earned at a rate of 10 points per dollar. The dollar value of the points depends on hotel and room availability. For example, 5,000 points could earn 50% off a $128 room at the Hilton Alburquerque. That equates to a 13% discount off a $500 investment. In contrast, 25,000 points could earn a free weekend night at a $239 Hilton Boston Back Bay hotel. That is a 9% discount off a $2,500 investment.

The program is integrated with Hilton's customer tier program: Blue, Silver, Gold, and Diamond. Membership is based on the number of stays in the most recent year. Benefits differ in terms of points earned per dollar and special upgrade offers. An interesting aspect of the Diamond tier is the lack of specificity in rewards. As reported by Deighton (2000), the strategy was to lower Diamond members' expectations and then "over-deliver" ("delight the customer" (Rust and Oliver 2000)).

Hilton also delivers personalized offers through HHonors (Orr 2000). For example, in any given month, the company has 80–130 potential messages/offers to be included in the customer's statement. The company selects about 14 of these messages based on variables such as previous stays, credit card usage, and demographics.

Hilton had specific motivations in starting HHonors. First was yield management. Hilton often has a pool of unsold rooms. The HHonors program provided the data that produced personalized offers for customers to fill the rooms. Second was to use partners to broaden the rewards it could provide to its customers. Third was to use it as an inducement for hotel owners to become Hilton franchisees – the benefit being access to reward program members who would want to burn points at the franchisee's hotel. Fourth was the more traditional motivation for reward programs – to build relationships with customers. For example, they can cross-sell travel opportunities, and provide better service by knowing customers' preferences for rooms, etc., when the customer checks in.

Its conjoint studies suggested that one in five stays by HHonors was due to membership in the program. These incremental stays are being given away at a steep discount, but travelers spend additional money besides the room when they stay at a hotel. Plus there are potential benefits due to rewarded-behavior and personalized marketing that might increase the visit frequency. Having said this, the company admitted that annual churn among HHonors Diamond members is 40% (Higley 2002). This does not say what churn would have been without the program, but this high number suggests that the industry is very competitive and reward programs do not completely lock in customers.

22.6 Research Needs

Reward programs are a popular form of customer management. There are a number of studies on reward programs but there is much more to be done. There are three basic areas: (1) How do customers respond to reward programs? (2) Are reward programs profitable? and (3) What are the best ways to design reward programs?

Regarding customer response, we have strong evidence that points pressure is a real phenomenon (Sect. 22.2.2), however, more work is needed to pinpoint the existence and impact of the rewarded behavior phenomenon, and the conditions under which it is most prevalent. In short, we need to know whether frequency reward programs, sometimes called loyalty programs, really create loyalty (see Shugan 2005).

We have good theories suggesting the conditions under which reward programs will be profitable in competitive equilibrium. However, these theories consider the points pressure mechanism (customers purchase more to receive the reward) and do not explicitly consider the rewarded behavior and personalized marketing mechanisms. In addition, we need empirical studies to discern the impact of reward programs on profits. The UK supermarket industry reviewed earlier would be a perfect venue.

Finally, there are several aspects of program design that need to be investigated. The overall need is to determine what types of designs work best under what circumstances. When should companies used continuous versus threshold rewards, or convex versus concave versus linear? How instantaneously should rewards be delivered? How transparent should the rules be for earning and burning points? How should earn and burn partners be selected, and what should be the financial arrangement between earn and burn partners? Is the best organizational set-up a company-run program with various earn and burn partners, or a consortium of companies banding together with the program managed by an outsider? Another fascinating issue is the frequent flyer points phenomenon. Frequent flyer points have become perhaps the most prevalent reward used by credit cards and even supermarket programs (see Tesco/Sainsbury example above). Research is needed to understand exactly what it is about this reward that makes it so attractive. A final issue is reward program branding – e.g., Tesco seems to have branded its ClubCard program. The methods to do this, and its benefits, need to be better understood.

Chapter 23
Customer Tier Programs

Abstract In today's highly competitive environment, many companies have made the strategic decision to protect and develop their most valuable customers. This strategy is implemented through customer tier programs, whereby customers are assigned to tiers – e.g., gold, silver, bronze – and accorded different levels of marketing and service depending on the tier to which they are assigned. We discuss various methods of defining the tiers and the fundamental allocation decisions firms must make in developing customers within a tier, possibly to the point where they can migrate to a higher tier. We conclude with a review of actual programs used by companies such as Bank One, Royal Bank of Canada, and Viking Office Products.

23.1 Definition and Motivation

Customer tier programs segment customers by their *actual or potential profitability* (Zeithaml et al. 2001) and provide different services or product depending on the tier to which they have been assigned. For example, a company might divide its customers into "Platinum," "Gold," "Silver," and "Bronze" segments or "tiers," and treat customers in each tier differently. The assumption is that segments defined in this manner will differ in their needs and responsiveness to various marketing programs.

Customer tier programs are related to frequency reward programs (Chapter 22), and the phrase "loyalty program" is often used for both of them. Indeed, customers may "earn" the right to be in a particular tier based on their accumulated purchases. However, customer tier programs and frequency reward programs differ in that frequency reward programs are narrower, focusing on a specific, typically one-time promotional reward such as free product. In contrast, customer tier programs provide customers with a long-term different level of service or a different product, based on their profitability.

Using the simple retention lifetime value formula, customer tier programs can be conceptualized as follows:

$$LTV_s = \sum_{t=1}^{\infty} \frac{m_{st} r_s^{t-1}}{(1+\delta)^{t-1}} \qquad (23.1)$$

where s is the segment (tier) index and m_{st} is the profit contribution of segment s in period t, and r_s is the retention rate of segment s. Customer tier programs try to manage profits and retention on a segment basis. This portrays customer tier programs as segment-based customer-management programs. However, firms can also acquire customers who qualify for particular tiers. In the fullest sense therefore, customer tier programs involve acquisition, retention, and development of customers.

There are several motivations for firms to employ customer tier programs:

- *Identifiability*: With more complete information systems (e.g., Rasmusson 1999), many firms are now able to calculate measures of profitability for each customer. This allows them to assign customers to profitability tiers.
- *Importance of Companies' Best Customers*: As Peppers and Rogers state it in their pioneering book, "Some customers are simply worth more than others" (Peppers and Rogers 1997, p. 37). Once companies started calculating customer-level profitability, they confirmed time after time the adage, "the top 20% of the customer base accounts for 80% of the profits." It is not always exactly 80–20, but the principle is the same. Hartfeil (1996) reports that the top 20% of customers account for 100% of Bank One's profits. Raider (1999) reports that Diet Coke "derives 80% of its sales from the top 13% of its customers," while for Taster's Choice coffee, the top 4% of customers account for 87% of sales. Storbacka (1994) reports that some banks have a profitability distribution more like 25–225, meaning that 25% of their top customers account for 225% of their profits (they are losing money on their least profitable customers).
- *Limited Resources*: Companies are under increased pressure to produce higher returns on investment (ROI) from a shrinking marketing investment. Given the relative ease in identifying a minority of its customers of paramount importance, it is logical to focus those limited resources on these customers to maximize ROI.
- *Refocus from Acquisition to Retention*: After an era in which the goal was to sign up new customers, more companies are turning to customer retention. Although not exclusively a customer retention strategy, the focus of most customer tier programs is on developing and retaining existing customers.
- *Profitability Segments Differ in Needs and Responsiveness*: In order for customer tier programs to make sense, segments in different tiers must differ in their needs and responsiveness. Research is finding that indeed this is the case. For example, Zeithaml et al. (2001) found that profitability segments of a major US bank differed in terms of age and income, their

perceptions of what defined service quality, what drove them to increase bank usage and volume, and the impact that changes in product quality would have on profits.

- *Competition*: Company A's *current* customers are Company B's *potential* customers. Hence, Company A faces pressure to insulate their best customers from competition. The strategy is to bestow these customers with Platinum status and provide them with services that increase their loyalty and are difficult for competitors to duplicate.
- *Desire to "Delight" the Customer*: Rust and Oliver (2000) define customer delight as very strong customer affect caused by exceeding customer expectations (see also Hatch 2002). Oliver et al. (1997) provide evidence that customer delight can lead to higher intentions and customer satisfaction. Customer tier programs capitalize on the delight phenomenon by placing their best customers in a high tier and *exceeding* their expectations. The downside, of course, is that those customers placed in the lower tiers may experience the opposite effect – their expectations for minimal service may not be met. However, to the extent that the best customers account for an overwhelming amount of profits, and that the market is highly competitive, delighting one's best customers may be a wise strategy.

23.2 Designing Customer Tier Programs

23.2.1 Overview

Figure 23.1 suggests steps required to develop a customer tier program. First is to review objectives. Next is to compile the database necessary for creating the segments. Then begins an iterative process of defining customer tiers, assessing the acquisition and development potential of each tier, allocating acquisition and development funds to each tier, and developing the specific

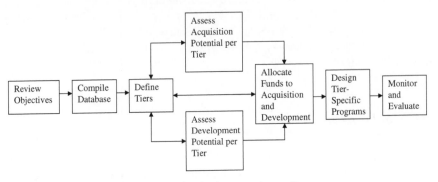

Fig. 23.1 Steps in developing a customer tier program.

services and marketing efforts that will be provided to the customers in each
tier. The final step is to implement and evaluate the program.

23.2.2 Review Objectives

Reviewing objectives is a crucial step as it guides tier definition and the
allocation of funds. Some key issues to review include:

- *Profits versus Revenues*: Is the company concerned about profits or revenues? Companies facing a huge debt from fixed cost investments (e.g.,
  telecom) may really be more concerned about generating immediate revenues than profits.
- *Growth versus Stability*: Is the company trying to grow its customer base?
  Customer tier programs can be managed to defend the company's core
  customers against competitive incursion, or used as an acquisition tool.
- *Customer Centric versus Product Centric*: Customer tier programs are
  primarily customer centric. The idea is to determine what members in each
  tier want or need, and deliver it. If a company is product centric, it might
  be better to segment customers on product ownership or psychographics,
  rather than profitability.

23.2.3 Create the Customer Database

Creating the customer database can become a "black hole" for investment. It
is very tempting to try to capture every possible piece of information about
every consumer. This is where the review of objectives is important. If the
objective emphasizes revenues, then the key data needs are product usage,
billing and payments, RFM, and demographics related to expenditures. If
the emphasis is on profits, the database needs to include costs. The easiest
costs to assemble are those associated with the delivery of the product, such
as costs-of-goods sold or mailing costs. Even these can require integration
of several databases for the multi-product company. Marketing costs (direct
mail offers, calls to the service center) and risks of payment default are more
difficult to compile.

23.2.4 Define Tiers

The task is to determine how many tiers to have, and what level of profitability will qualify each customer for each tier. The number of tiers and
profitability qualification may depend on the budget available. For example,

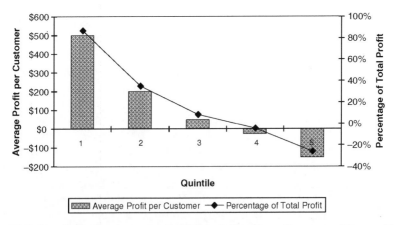

Fig. 23.2 Hypothetical customer profitability quintiles (From Peppers and Rogers 1997).

a company may define just two tiers, "VIP" and "All Others," and decide it can afford to provide 10% of its customers with the VIP treatment. The company would then rank order its customers by profitability and invite the top 10% to be members of their VIP program.

A more bottom-up approach is to rank order customers in terms of profitability, separate them into tiers, and determine the percentage of customers that are "crucial" for the company. A simple method for doing this is a decile or quintile analysis (Peppers and Rogers 1997, p. 39). Figure 23.2 shows a hypothetical quintile graph. The graph shows that the top 20% of customers accounts for 87% of profits, and that the company loses money on the lower 40% of its customers. This suggests that perhaps the top quintile (20%) should be included in the VIP program.

Two factors complicate this scenario. First is the difference between actual and *potential* profit. Customers can be assigned to tiers according to actual *or* potential profit. (Note the arrows in Fig. 23.1 between "Define Tiers" and "Assess Potential" run both ways.) Actual profit is much easier to calculate than potential, which requires assessing responsiveness to marketing actions (see Sect. 23.2.6). However, one could argue that potential profit is much more meaningful. Using actual profit, a firm might identify a segment that generates high profits, target special services at these customers, and have *no impact* on their behavior! A better way might be first to assess profit potential, then define tiers.

While potential profit is difficult to assess, actual profit can be a significant challenge as well. First is the question of profitability over what time period (Rasmusson 1999) – the past 5 years, 1 year, or projected over the remaining lifetime of the customer? Second is whether one can calculate profit or will rely on indicators. For example, actual profit cannot be calculated for potential customers to be acquired. This is why customer tiers can be defined using lifetime value, life event (e.g., recent retirees), demographics, stage of customer life cycle (newly acquired, growing, mature, declining) (Peppers and Rogers 1993, pp. 190–193), product usage (Zeithaml 2000), or loyalty (Reichheld 1993).

The basis for segmenting customers into tiers can depend on the industry. A large real estate company segmented customers based on the amount of time it takes the customer to decide on a new home, marketing costs, customer motivation/urgency to move, price sensitivity, likelihood of future purchases, and referral potential (Zeithaml et al. 2001). A marketing research firm defined customer tiers based on account size, willingness to plan research projects in advance, willingness to try new services and approaches, variety of methodologies employed, sales cost, referral potential, and loyalty (Zeithaml et al. 2001). A pharmaceutical company defined physician tiers based on prescription volume, prescription dollar value, sales and sample costs, and gross margins of prescriptions (Zeithaml et al. 2001).

The common thread is that defining customer tiers may require computation and integration of several measures of current customer value and future potential.

23.2.5 Determine Acquisition Potential for Each Tier

Customer tier programs are primarily customer development efforts. However, customer tier strategies shift the emphasis of the customer acquisition side of the business from "get customers" to "get the right customers." This is a challenge because it moves the company away from mass marketed acquisition efforts and toward targeted methods. Ideally, the company should be able to identify potential members each of its customer tiers in advance, and then acquire them.

A good example of developing an acquisition plan for a particular target group is presented by Ainslie and Pitt (1998) who analyze the customer acquisition efforts of a credit card company. Under their scheme, top tier customers are profitable, responsive to marketing efforts, and without a default risk. As a result, the probability the potential customer fits the top customer tier (P(Target)) can be expressed as:

$$P(\text{Target}) = P(\text{Responsive}) \times P(\text{Profitable}) \times P(\text{Not Risky}|\text{Profitable})$$

(23.2)

Ainslie and Pitt develop separate predictive models for Responsiveness, Profitability, and Risk, using a sample of approximately 3,000 current customers. Figure 23.3 shows how various predictors were associated with each of the responses. The researchers created variables that combined income and spending habits. Income could be low, medium, or high. Spending habits could either be "spenders" or "savers." Figure 23.3 shows that low-income spenders are more likely to be responders and more likely to be profitable on average.

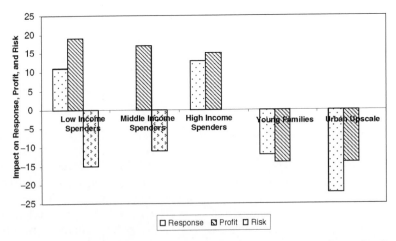

Fig. 23.3 Customer determinants of responsiveness, profit, and risk (From Ainslie and Pitt 1998).

However, they are more likely to be risky. This shows the trade-off between profitability and default risk, and why it is important to consider risk as another dimension of profitability. Middle income spenders are not different from average in terms of their responsiveness, but they are more likely to be profitable although risky. High-income spenders are more likely to be responders and more likely to be profitable, but not more likely to be risky than average. Undoubtedly this is because they have the financial resources to avoid default if they get overextended financially. In terms of demographics, young families are less responsive and less profitable, but no different from average in default risk. Urban upscale customers are far less responsive and also less profitable, but no different from average in terms of risk.

Ainslie and Pitt applied their model to identify potential new customers. While the models were estimated on the firm's own customers (because those are the customers for whom data were available), the models were used to score prospects from a national list. First, the authors scored the prospects in terms of their responsiveness. Second, they took the high-predicted responders from this list and scored them in terms of profit. Third, they took the profitable responders and scored them in terms of risk. The result yielded a set of prospects who were predicted to be profitable yet not risky responders, i.e., members of the top customer tier.

23.2.6 Determine Development Potential for Each Tier

This is perhaps the most difficult part of developing a customer tier program, but really the most crucial. The goal is to assess the responsiveness of the customers in a given tier to the services and marketing efforts that will be provided to that tier. It therefore plays the crucial role in allocating funds and designing programs.

There are two approaches to determining the relevant response functions, corresponding to whether the arrow runs from "Define Segments" to "Assess Potential" or from "Assess Potential" to "Define Segments" in Fig. 23.1.

The simpler approach is to define segments first. In this case, we segment customers based on their current profits, then measure responsiveness for customers in each segment. These response functions will govern how much is spent and what specific marketing efforts and services are used for each customer tier. The customer responses of interest are retention rate and revenues, since these determine lifetime value (Equation 23.1). The services and marketing efforts may include special call-center phone numbers, free shipping, easy check-in, free upgrades, up-selling, and cross-selling.

The second approach, more complicated but perhaps more preferred, is to measure the response functions at the customer level and then assign customers to tiers depending on their response functions. For example, the ideal customer to assign to the top tier would have high "baseline" profitability combined with high responsiveness to marketing efforts. Another factor to consider is the probability a customer can be "migrated" from one tier to another – i.e., what is the chance we can turn a "silver" customer into a "gold" customer based on marketing effort?

Examples of the types of response functions that are needed are found in the service quality literature (see Zeithaml 2000). These papers link service attributes to perceived service quality (Bolton and Drew 1991a, b), perceived service quality to customer satisfaction (Bolton and Drew 1991a, b; Rust et al. 1995), and customer satisfaction to increased retention (Bolton 1998) and usage (Bolton and Lemon 1999). Retention and usage (revenues) relate obviously to customer profitability (Rust et al. 1995). Rust et al. (2000) take a different approach, showing how service improvements improve three types of equity (value, brand, and retention), which figure directly into financial performance.

This research employs managerial judgment or customer surveys. We do not know of a field test of these approaches. This research has studied service attributes, which are definitely part of customer tier programs, but they have not studied the impact of cross-selling, direct marketing, or advertising. However, they provide the best illustrations of the types of response functions that are needed to show how the elements of a customer tier program translate into customer retention and revenues.

Wansink (2003) has conducted a provocative study comparing managerial perceptions of customer potential with actual potential. He defined three marketing programs, "low," "moderate," and "high," that could be applied to consumer packaged goods. The program definitions were as follows:

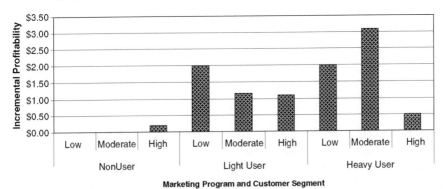

Fig. 23.4 Profitability of low, moderate, and high marketing programs targeted at different customer tiers (segments) (From Wansink 2003).

- Low: Quarterly one-page newsletter; $0.25 coupons included in the newsletter; Receive product line merchandise (e.g., coffee mug) with 20 proofs of purchase and $5.00 postage and handling fee.
- Moderate: Quarterly full-color booklet; $0.50 coupons included in the booklet; Receive product line merchandise with 20 proofs of purchase.
- High: Monthly full-color booklet; $1.00 coupons included in the booklet; Receive product line merchandise with 10 proofs of purchase.

Wansink then surveyed 132 packaged goods brand managers and asked them which program would be most effective for which segment: current nonuser, light user, and heavy user. The managers clearly responded that (1) in general, the High-level program would generate the most incremental sales and be most cost effective, (2) each program would be most effective (incremental sales and cost effectiveness) among heavy users, then light users, then nonusers. For example, not one of the brand managers thought the Low program would be effective among light users, whereas there was high agreement that the High program would be very effective among heavy users.

Wansink (2003) then tested these programs with consumers. He surveyed 643 consumers and randomly assigned each of them to a reward program – low, moderate, or high – as defined above. He tested three product lines (Kellogg's, Betty Crocker, and Land O'Lakes) with each consumer. For each consumer, he asked (1) their current level of purchasing, and (2) their anticipated level of purchasing over the next 12 months under the reward program to which they had been assigned. He used this to calculate the profitability of each type of program with each segment. The results are in Fig. 23.4.

Figure 23.4 suggests two startling results. First, the High program is generally not the most profitable. Second, the most profitable program for the heavy users is the Moderate program, the most profitable program for the light users is the Low program, and the most profitable program for the nonusers is the High program. The calculations showed that in absolute terms, the heavy users generated the most incremental sales under the High program. However, taking into account the costs of the program, the profit picture changed dramatically. For example, Wansink calculated that under the High program, heavy users would generate on average 2.4 more units purchased for a revenue gain of $7.20. However, these customers would be redeeming $6.70 worth of coupons, for a net gain of $0.50. Under the Moderate program, heavy users would generate on average 2.0 more units purchased for a revenue gain of $6.00, but the value of coupons redeemed would only be $2.90 ($0.50 versus $1.00 coupons for the High program) so the net gain was $3.10. Lavishing better treatment – $1.00 coupons – on the heavy users did generate more incremental units, but not enough to cover the costs.

This study challenges the conventional wisdom of defining customer tier programs to provide the most profitable customers (i.e., heavy users) with the most benefits (i.e., the High program). Of course the study itself could be challenged. Profit was calculated using consumer self-reported future purchasing. In addition, the study was in a product, not service, industry, and the rewards therefore were product and price oriented. However, the point is well taken, that profit *potential* is key to designing a customer tier program, and while heavy users may have the potential for the most incremental sales, this does not necessarily translate to the highest profits. It may not be profitable to lavish current loyal customers with extensive incentives.

Kopalle et al. (2006) developed a dynamic structural model to examine customer response to both frequency reward programs and customer tier programs. They estimated their model for an airline that offered both a frequent flyer program and a customer tier program consisting of three tiers. Customers were automatically placed in a particular tier if they achieved a certain number of miles within a year. We describe the model and findings in more detail in Chapter 22. The authors found that indeed customer tier programs increase customer utility, with the higher tier benefits providing more utility. Perhaps most important, the authors found two segments – "loyalty program enthusiasts" and "customer-tier focused." The loyalty program enthusiasts segment was smaller (about 6% of the sample) and cared about the benefits of both the frequency reward and customer tier programs. The customer-tier focused segment was much larger (about 94% of the sample) and actually disliked the frequency reward program. However, they gained utility from the customer tier program.

23.2.7 Allocate Funds to Tiers

Once we have assigned customers to tiers and understand the relationship between marketing efforts and customer acquisition and how customers in each tier will respond to marketing actions, we can allocate marketing funds to segments. We illustrate this process with two planning models. The first is simple and not dynamic. The second includes more complexities such as transitions between tiers and a period-by-period analysis. Both models are motivated by the work of Blattberg and Deighton (1996) and Rust et al. (1995), who consider trade-offs between acquisition and retention for single-segment customer franchises.

23.2.7.1 A Simple Fund Allocation Model for Customer Tiers

This model allocates funds between customer development and customer acquisition within each customer tier, subject to a budget constraint. The model is relatively simple and can be optimized. Following are the decision variables:

X_{ia} = Funds allocated to acquiring customers for tier i.
X_{id} = Funds allocated to retaining and developing customers in tier i.

The key response variables are:

A_i = Number of customers acquired for tier i.
LTV_i = Lifetime value of a customer in tier i.

We then assume the following response functions:

$$A_i = X_{ia}^{\delta_i} \tag{23.3}$$
$$LTV_i = \alpha_i + X_{id}^{\beta_i} \tag{23.4}$$

Equation 23.3 is the acquisition function. We would expect δ to be between zero and one – the number of customers acquired would increase as a function of acquisition expenditures, but at a decreasing rate – and would differ by tier. Also, Equation 23.3 assumes the company starts with no customers in either tier. The acquisition equation could be expanded by adding a constant term to Equation 23.3, indicating the initial number of customers in each tier.

Equation 23.4 summarizes how investments in each customer tier pay off in terms of customer lifetime value. The term α reflects baseline LTV, or the lifetime value of the customer if we do not allocate special marketing efforts to that tier. The parameter β represents how well marketing efforts increase LTV. Again we would expect β to be between zero and one, reflecting decreasing returns to scale. If we then define,

B = Marketing Budget
Π = Total profits,

the optimization problem is:

$$Max_{X_{ia},X_{id}} \Pi = \sum_i \{A_i LTV_i - X_{ia} - X_{id}\}$$

$$= \sum_i \{X_{ia}^{\delta_i}(\alpha_i + X_{id}^{\beta_i}) - X_{ia} - X_{id}\} \qquad (23.5)$$

$$s.t. \quad \sum_i (X_{ia} + X_{id}) = B \qquad (23.6)$$

This is a nonlinear program with $T \times 2$ decision variables, where T is the number of tiers Acquisition and development expenditures for each tier are the decision variables. The budget itself is not a decision variable. This assumption of course could be relaxed.

Table 23.1 illustrates an example of using the model. The top tier has a baseline LTV (α) of \$2,000, while the lower tier has a baseline LTV of \$300. Lower tier customers can be acquired more effectively ($\delta = 0.4$ versus 0.3) while higher tier customers respond more strongly to marketing efforts ($\beta = 0.7$ versus 0.6). The current budget allocates a lot of funds toward lower tier customers, however the company is losing money on these customers. Upper tier customers are profitable, but there aren't enough of them and there probably is potential for development. The scenario is not unlike many companies that in their early stages focus on increasing their customer base. If, after reviewing objectives, customer count is the objective, this is appropriate. However, if profits are the objective, Table 23.1 shows that the optimal allocation is to shift funds from lower tier customers to upper tier customers, even if it means fewer customers in total. This example is probably

Table 23.1 Example of optimal acquisition and development fund allocations for two customer tiers using simple allocation model (Equations 23.3–23.6)

Parameter values

Parameter	Description	Value
δ_1	Acquisition response Segment 1	0.30
δ_2	Acquisition response Segment 2	0.40
α_1	Baseline lifetime value Segment 1	\$2,000
α_2	Baseline lifetime value Segment 2	\$300
β_1	Lifetime value response Segment 1	0.70
β_2	Lifetime value response Segment 2	0.60
B	Budget	\$50,000

	Segment (tier)	Acquisition (\$)	Development (\$)	# Acquired customers	Profits
Current allocation	1	2,000	5,000	9.78	\$16.357
	2	28,000	15,000	60.10	−\$5717
Optimal allocation	1	21,720	14,932	20.00	\$20.059
	2	8,819	4,529	37.86	\$3,922

the quintessential motivation for customer tier segmentation – focus on the more valuable customers.

The above model illustrates the importance of knowing the response functions (β and δ) as opposed to just current profitability (represented by α). It is through this complete representation of both current and potential profitability that a company can sort through how funds should be allocated to customer tiers.

23.2.7.2 A Markov Allocation Model

We describe a Markovian model (Libai et al. 2002; Pfeifer and Carraway 2000) that allows customers to shift among three states – upper tier, lower tier, and not a customer – depending on marketing expenditures. The model is not optimized but can be used to evaluate alternative expenditure allocations on a *pro formal* basis. Figure 23.5 depicts the model. There are pools of potential

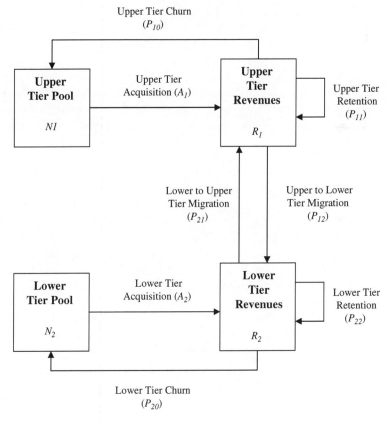

Fig. 23.5 Tier segmentation planning model allowing migration between tiers.

upper and lower tier customers who can be acquired. The decision variables are, as before:

X_{ia} = Amount spent on acquisition in tier i.
X_{id} = Amount spent on customer development in tier i.

We also have the following quantities:

N_i = Number of available customers for tier i.
A_i = Number of customers acquired for tier i.
R_i = Revenues in tier i.
P_{ij} = Probability move from tier i to tier j. i can equal 1 or 2, and j can equal 0, 1, or 2, where 0 stands for not a customer, 1 stands for the upper tier, and 2 stands for the lower tier. Thus P_{21} is the probability the customer will move from the lower tier to the upper tier.

All the above variables are indexed by time subscripts, which we do not include for easier exposition. Following are the response functions:

$$A_i = N_i(1 - e^{-\lambda_i X_{ia}}) \tag{23.7}$$

$$R_i = \alpha_i + X_{id}^{\beta_i} \tag{23.8}$$

$$P_{ij} = \frac{\phi_{ij} + X_{id}^{\gamma_{ij}}}{\sum\limits_{k=0}^{2} (\phi_{ik} + X_{id}^{\gamma_{ik}})} \tag{23.9}$$

Equation 23.7 is the acquisition response function. It exhibits decreasing returns to scale and assumes the company begins with zero customers in each tier. The term $(1 - e^{-\lambda_i X_{ia}})$ can be interpreted as the probability a customer moves from the not-a-customer state to either the upper $(i = 1)$ or lower $(i = 2)$ tier segment (P_{01} and P_{02}). Equation 23.8 is the same function we used for LTV in Equation 23.4. α is baseline revenues and β is the response of revenues to customer development expenditures.

Equation 23.9 is an attraction model representing the probability of transition between tiers, i.e., the likelihood customers turn from silver to gold, or regress from gold to silver. The ϕ's are baseline parameters representing whether a customer naturally moves from tier i ($i = 1$ or 2) to tier j ($j = 0, 1,$ or 2) each period. The γ's are the key parameters. For example, γ_{11} represents the impact of marketing expenditures on the customer staying in the top tier. γ_{21} is the impact of marketing expenditures on turning a lower tier customer into an upper tier customer. We would expect the retention parameter for the top tier, γ_{11}, to be positive and larger than γ_{12} and γ_{10}. For the lower tier, development funds would most likely serve to keep the customer in the lower tier (as opposed to churning) but a key parameter would be γ_{21}, the ability of development expenditures to turn lower tier into upper tier customers. So, we would expect $\gamma_{22} > \gamma_{21} > \gamma_{20}$, but the larger γ_{21} is, the better.

The γ's might depend on the design of the program. For example, if the customer tier program for the lower tier was highly price oriented (offering coupons, free giveaways, etc.), it might be less likely to move those customers into the top tier. However, a lower tier program that offered better services (e.g., dedicated phone representatives), might be more likely to move these customers to the upper tier.

There are two additional key assumptions. First is that the company is able to identify and target the customers that are in each tier. Formally, we assume the company knows when the customer's response function (Equation 23.8) changes from $i = 1$ to $i = 2$. This of course may be difficult and the firm might rely on a surrogate number such as previous-year profits, or create a hurdle value over which the customer is treated as if he or she is in a higher level tier. The model therefore does not incorporate the risk of misclassification. For example, the customer may be treated as a top tier customer, but might have the response function of a lower tier customer. Treating this customer as a higher tier customer would then be a mistake since the company would be assuming the wrong response function for this customer.

A second key assumption is that the costs of the program are linear in the number of customers within a tier. This might not hold if the higher tier involved very high service levels. For example, for an airline, the higher tier might have access to the airline's lounge available at the airport. The airline's ability to provide this service to all upper tier customers (as defined by their response functions) might be convex in the number of upper tier customers. That is, it would be nearly impossible to provide the top tier services to 90% of the firm's customers.

These two assumptions could be relaxed in a more sophisticated model. Now, however, we focus on the insights generated by the model at hand.

Figure 23.6 shows calculations using the above model, assuming a fixed budget ($2,000) for acquisition and retention each. The parameters show that the top tier segment is more difficult to acquire but has much higher baseline revenues. The top tier also responds better to development dollars in that these investments are more effective at retaining them and preventing them (negative sign) from leaving the company or regressing to the lower tier. Development funds can help move the lower tier customer to the upper tier ($\gamma = 0.05$) but the effect isn't very strong.

Figure 23.6a shows that assuming an equal distribution of acquisition dollars ($1,000 each to the top and lower tiers), it pays to allocate more of the retention budget to the upper tier segment (achieving profit maximization at around 85% allocation). This is undoubtedly because the upper tier has higher baseline revenues and equal response to marketing dollars. This would be the classic focus-on-the-best-customers result. Figure 23.6b shows that assuming an equal distribution of retention dollars ($1,000 each to the top and lower tiers) the acquisition budget should be completely allocated to the lower tier. This is also an interesting illustration. Given that it is cheaper to acquire lower tier customers ($\lambda_1 < \lambda_2$), and given that the company is spending money to develop customers in the lower tier ($1,000), it is more

Parameter	Description	Value
N_1	# of available upper tier customers	3,000,000
N_2	# of Available lower tier customers	3,000,000
λ_1	Acquisition response for upper tier	0.5×10^{-9}
λ_2	Acquisition response for lower tier	1.0×10^{-8}
α_1	Baseline revenues – upper tier	$500
α_2	Baseline revenues – lower tier	$50
β_1	Revenue response – upper tier	0.4
β_2	Revenue response – lower tier	0.4
γ_{21}	Move up response – lower tier	0.05
γ_{22}	Retention response – lower tier	0.2
γ_{20}	Churn response – lower tier	−0.05
γ_{11}	Retention response – upper tier	0.30
γ_{12}	Move down response – upper tier	−0.01
γ_{10}	Churn response – upper tier	−0.05
ϕ_{21}	Baseline move up – lower tier	0.1
ϕ_{22}	Baseline retention – lower tier	0.5
ϕ_{20}	Baseline churn – lower tier	0.4
ϕ_{11}	Baseline retention – upper tier	0.5
ϕ_{12}	Baseline move down – upper tier	0.1
ϕ_{10}	Baseline churn – upper tier	0.4
δ	Discount factor	10%
B_A	Acquisition budget	$2,000
B_R	Retention budget	$2,000

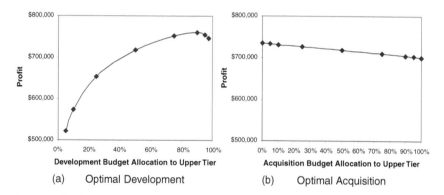

(a)   Optimal Development   (b)   Optimal Acquisition

Fig. 23.6 Profit as a function of acquisition and development allocations based on flow allocation model (Equations 23.7–23.9). (a) Optimal development[a]; (b) Optimal acquisition[b]
[a] Assumes the $2,000 acquisition budget is divided equally between the upper and lower tiers.
[b] Assumes the $2,000 retention budget is divided equally between the upper and lower tiers.

efficient to acquire lower tier customers and convert them to upper tier than acquire upper tier customers directly.

These examples are just illustrations. Different parameter values could easily tilt things in the other direction. For example, if retention dollars were relatively ineffective for the upper tier, but had a strong effect on moving customers from the lower to the upper tier, it would be worthwhile to allocate most retention funds to the lower tier, not so much for helping that tier as to convert these customers into upper tier customers.

23.2.8 Design Tier-Specific Programs

Once the tiers are defined and funds have been allocated, one must design the specific service and marketing programs for each tier. This often involves enhanced service levels – special call lines, special attention to deliveries, etc. More broadly, it could involve special products developed for upper tier customers based on their needs.

A key design issue is how to develop programs that convert lower tier to upper tier customers.[1] Zeithaml et al. (2001) describe the efforts of Home Depot in this regard. Home Depot noticed that many of its lower tier customers were being underserved because Home Depot was selling them materials for home remodeling but was not helping them to manage the entire process. Home Depot therefore opened Home Depot Expo stores targeted to current lower tier customers who have the financial wherewithal to purchase a full process-managed service for remodeling their home. While this is a good example of designing a program to move customers up the "pyramid," it is not a highly targeted product – the store is open for everyone. There are undoubtedly customers who investigate Expo but really are not suited for it (see http://www.consumeraffairs.com/homeowners/home_depot_expo.htm).

Another interesting aspect of designing a customer tier program is shrinking the size of the lower tier segment. One way this can be done is to cut acquisition funds for this segment. However, if acquisition funds cannot be targeted at upper versus lower tier customers, lower tier customers may inadvertently be recruited. The task then becomes to encourage those customers to leave (Zeithaml et al. 2001). Most commonly this is done through high prices and low service levels. However, this can create a backlash (since many of these customers may have been recruited through special deals provided in the hopes of attracting top tier customers), and generate negative word-of-mouth.

Another interesting issue in customer tier program design is the extent of public recognition to extend to top tier customers (Shugan 2005). For example, airlines often make announcements such as "XYZ Airlines Platinum customers may board now." This public recognition might enhance the loyalty of top tier customers by increasing their sense of identity as an XYZ Airline customer. However, the public recognition may ask the lower tier customers to ask, "Am I not special?", and as a result, diminish any positive feelings they had toward the company.

---

[1] This assumes of course the company wants to create more upper tier customers. For cost reasons, the company may not be able to afford to provide enough customers with the special services accorded to members of the upper tier.

In fact, a major design consideration is whether indeed the customer should even *know* what tier he or she is in. In addition to the recognition factor, the advantage to the customer knowing is that this can provide an incentive to purchase more, i.e., to earn the right to be a Platinum customer (Kopalle et al. 2006). This especially works well if the company is using a transparent method to assign customers to tiers, e.g., previous year's purchase volume. However, it might be better under certain circumstances for the company just to keep track of tier membership internally. For example, a catalog company may still offer its high RFM customers special catalogs and services, but without the "Platinum" appellation attached. The advantage of customers not knowing their status is that purchase volume or marketing responsiveness can change over time, and the company may decide it wants to change the customer's status without alienating the customer. This is a crucial issue in customer tier design – public recognition, customer awareness of status – and needs careful research.

A final note is that while from a marketing standpoint, we think of customer tier development programs as enhancing customer value, sometimes these programs are guided by cost reduction objectives. Cost reductions may have a negative impact on revenues and retention. For example, an automated call center to serve the lower tier may save money compared to having company personnel answer inquiries, but revenues and retention can decrease because of the lower service level. This makes it difficult for these call centers to pay out.

23.2.9 Implement and Evaluate

An important and easily overlooked implementation issue is organizational. Does the company need to restructure its organization in order to implement a customer tier approach? Peppers and Rogers (1993, pp. 173–206) argue that rather than product managers, effective customer management requires customer managers (Chapter 3). For many companies, this means an entirely different way of doing business. The value of the customer management system is part of the ongoing customer centric versus product centric debate.

Another crucial issue is the management of customer transitions between tiers. If the company is using the profitability-first approach to creating tiers, then classifying customers in tiers is a simple matter. Managers would wait until the end of the year, calculate the profits generated by the customer, and then assign the customer to a new tier as appropriate. For example, a lower tier customer who generated higher than average profits might be assigned to the top tier. This would take the form of a formal invitation to the customer. One danger in managing this way is the customer's *response* function might be that of the typical top tier customer, resulting in a mis-allocation of funds (see Sect. 23.2.7.1). Another danger is that the top tier may become too large (e.g., the airline's lounge becomes too crowded), and so the Platinum treatment "isn't what it used to be." and the customer development impact of Platinum membership diminishes.

If the company is using a response-function-first approach to creating tiers, individual response functions would be estimated at the end of each year. The customer would be re-assigned if necessary according to his or her current response function. In practice, the company might run a test among current lower tier customers, the test being designed to measure these customers' response to some of the "perks" provided in the upper tier. Alternatively, the company might survey a sample of lower and upper tier customers, asking them to self-report their responsiveness to various upper tier perks (e.g., "Would you buy more from us if you had a dedicated customer service number that guaranteed no more than a five-minute wait for service?"). The goal would be to determine whether a customer seemed to be responding like the customers in the tier to which he or she had currently been assigned, or like customers in a different tier.

In general the best way to monitor and evaluate the program is by setting up control groups. Otherwise we can compile statistics such as "revenues in the upper tier group grew by 40% after we initiated the program." However, we don't know what the growth would have been without the program, or what growth would have been in the lower tier group if equal dollars had been spent on that group.

23.3 Examples of Customer Tier Programs

23.3.1 Bank One (Hartfeil 1996)

Hartfeil (1996) reports the efforts made by Bank One to implement a customer tier segmentation strategy. It started with the belief that 20% of a bank's customers account for *more than* 100% of their profits. Faced with limited resources, the company focused its marketing efforts on that top tier. For example, branch sales forces re-allocated their time toward top tier customers.

Hartfeil describes the important details of implementing a customer tier program. First is the calculation of profitability. Bank One took into account revenues, risk, and cost on a customer basis in defining profitability, and ironed out difficult issues involving the timing of profit. For example, if a customer has an installment loan and is in the last stages of paying back that loan, he or she is not generating as much profit as one who has just taken out the loan. One solution would be simply to calculate profit generated by the loan in total. That would depict both customers as equally profitable. But currently, it's the newer customer who's generating the profit. Bank One resolved this by calculating two measures of installment loan profit – essentially the current profit and the total profit – and incorporating both into defining their top tier customers. Interestingly, Bank One shied away from using formal lifetime value calculations because (1) they did not have enough historical information, (2) it would be difficult to apply a projection to customers on an individual basis, and (3) short-term profit was very relevant and could be more easily calculated.

23.3.2 Royal Bank of Canada (Rasmusson 1999)

Rasmusson (1999) describes the customer tier program at Royal Bank of Canada. The motivation for the program was to improve customer retention. They segmented customers into A, B, and C levels based on profitability. Tier A customers were assigned account managers and were contacted two or more times annually with cross-selling offers. Rasmusson reports that profit per Tier A customer grew by 268% over a 2-year horizon, and the number of Tier A customers grew by 292%. Aside from the increase in marketing costs, there was a large investment in data warehousing required to calculate profitability and conduct the segmentation.

23.3.3 Thomas Cook Travel (Rasmusson 1999)

Rasmusson (1999) also describes the customer tier program at Thomas Cook Travel. The company divided customers into A, B, and C tiers based on annual revenues. The key differentiating feature in the program was the level of service provided to each tier. The most challenging aspect of this program was that travel agents had to decrease their service levels to certain clients (C customers) whereas the mentality of the company had traditionally been to provide all customers with superior service. Thomas Cook provides the information agents need to identify A, B, or C clients, and agents receive detailed records of the A clients so they can tailor sales pitches to these customers' particular tastes and needs.

23.3.4 Canadian Grocery Store Chain (Grant and Schlesinger 1995)

Grant and Schlesinger (1995) discuss the potential for customer tier segmentation at a Canadian grocery chain. They emphasize three aspects of customer value: how many customers the company has, what their behavior is, and how long they stay with the company. These are the elements of the total lifetime value of the firm's customers. The chain segmented the customer base for a typical store into three tiers based on "share of wallet": primary shoppers (>80%), secondary shoppers (10–50%), and non-shoppers. They then calculated the profit margin impact of changes in the behavior of these groups. Due to the nature of the business with high fixed cost and small operating margins, relatively minor changes in these customer tiers could produce huge increases in profitability. For example, expanding the primary shopper segment by 2% would increase profitability by 45%. Moving 200 secondary shoppers to primary status would increase profits by more than 20%. Decreasing the churn rate from current 20% per year to 10% would double customer lifetime (and hence approximately double lifetime value).

This example points out the need to focus on all customer tiers as a source of profits, and the value of viewing lower tiers as a source of upper tier customers, rather than as customers to be "fired."

23.3.5 Major US Bank (Rust et al. 2000)

Rust et al. (2000, pp. 195–202) describe a customer tier example based on a major US bank that utilized in-house profitability information merged with survey data. The profitability information served to form the segments, while the survey data served to understand the needs of each segments and how they would respond to various marketing programs. Rust et al. divided the customers into two pools based on profitability: the top 20% (Gold) and the bottom 80% (Iron).

The tiers differed significantly in profitability – the Gold tier had an average account balance that was 5 times bigger than a member of the Iron tier, and average profit that was 18 times bigger. The tiers differed in terms of demographics (Gold being older with higher annual income). Most intriguing were the very different perspectives of customers in each tier on defining quality and on profitability drivers. The Gold tier defined quality in terms of personal respect, reliability, and speed. The Iron tier did not think of reliability as part of quality. This makes sense since as less frequent users of the bank, reliability would be less salient to them. The authors analyzed the propensity of each tier to adopt new products offered by the bank ("incidence"), and the volume of the new business ("volume"). They found that for the Gold tier, incidence was driven by speed whereas for the Iron tier, incidence was driven by personal attention. The implications for differing marketing programs are obvious. In addition, the authors found that the Gold tier was more responsive to changes in service improvements than the Iron tier (essentially, $\beta_{Gold} > \beta_{Iron}$ in terms of Equations 23.4 or 23.8).

The implication of this analysis was that the company should focus its retention budget on improving speed of service for the Gold group. Speed drives incidence and volume for this group, and this group responds more strongly to changes in service than the Iron group. Of course, these implications could be analyzed more extensively using one of the planning models described above.

This example points out the benefits of integrating in-house and survey data. The in-house data are necessary for defining the segments, because these data are available for each customer and include the required detail for profitability calculations. The survey data can be collected for a sample within each tier. These data provide information on tier differences that provide guidance on how to design marketing programs for each tier. In addition, through regressions such as Volume = f(speed, personal respect, reliability), one has guidance on where various improvements will pay off. What is needed still is a translation from expenditures to changes in attributes. For example, Speed = f(expenditures), etc. This would provide the response parameters needed to make budget decisions. See Rust et al. (1995, Fig. 23.6) for a discussion of how one might derive these functions.

23.3.6 Viking Office Products (Miller 2001)

Viking Office Products is an office product catalog company whose customer tier program has three levels – platinum (consisting of 500 of the best customers), gold, and silver. Membership in these tiers is based on *current and future* potential spending. The benefit line-up illustrates the extent to which services can be tailored to various segments. These benefits, which differ from tier to tier, include specialized phone lines for placing orders, free shipping, lifetime guarantees, special pricing, free samples and gifts, personalized order pads, and access to the best, most experienced phone representatives.

23.3.7 Swedbank (Storbacka and Luukinen 1994, see also Storbacka 1993)

Sparbanken Sverige AB (Swedbank) was formed as the merger of 12 regional banks in Scandinavia. Swedbank did not design different marketing programs for different tiers. Instead, Swedbank implemented changes in bank-wide policies that affected various tiers differently.

Upon completion of the merger, Swedbank decided that it would adopt a two-pronged strategy: (1) focus on existing customers, and (2) create efficiencies such as pricing proportional to usage. The first step was an analysis of 214,000 customers from 32 branches. Swedbank found that volume (dollar value of deposits, etc.) and profitability were not highly correlated. In fact higher volume was associated with much more dispersion in profitability. Swedbank also found that more than 50% of its customers were unprofitable, and that profit was highly concentrated among the best customers: the top 3% of customers accounted for 54% of profits, 6% accounted for 98%, and 32% accounted for 205% of profits. The bank found that the key differentiators in profits, even after controlling for volume, were reliance on checks (as opposed to a bankcard) and tellers (as opposed to an ATM). The reliance on checks was especially unprofitable.

Swedbank then instituted changes, perhaps the most dramatic of which was to charge for checks, although the charge was reduced for customers who had profitable behavior (e.g., use of ATMs). A new high interest account was developed for high-volume investments, and the bankcard was made easier to use. In addition, Swedbank undertook marketing communications to explain the changes and emphasize the wastefulness of checks. The changes were communicated to employees (who themselves were often unprofitable customers) and employees contacted best customers personally to explain the changes.

The result was an 84% reduction in the use of checks, which is not surprising. More striking was the disproportionate number of defections among unprofitable customers. For example, of the defections that ensued, fewer than 1% were from the most profitable customers, and 80% were from low volume, unprofitable customers. The example shows that customer tier segmentation can be used to guide decisions that affect the tiers differentially, without explicitly different policies for each tier.

23.4 Risks in Implementing Customer Tier Programs

Customer tier segmentation has gained popularity for many firms that are concerned about competing for customers, and at the same time, pressured for marketing funds. The concept is compelling – focus your limited funds on your best customers. While this is strong logic, there are certain risks to customer tier programs, as follows:

- *Under-serving the lower tier*: While hypothetically it is possible that customer tier programs should allocate more money to the lower tiers, most applications and the managerial mindset is to focus dollars on the upper tiers. The result could be profit losses in the lower tier segments that have to be offset by the gains in the upper tier. This of course is a natural consequence of shifting funds from one asset to another. However, there are factors that could make the losses from the lower tiers worse than expected (Scherreik 2002; Mazur 1999). First, there is some evidence that automated service systems result in lower loyalty than personal service (Selnes and Hansen 2001; Ariely et al. 2002). Ariely et al. found in a lab experiment

that customers interacting with a computer-generated advisor were less re-
silient to market crashes. The group that interacted with a human advisor
recovered to its pre-crash level, while the group that interacted with the
computer advisor suffered a permanent downswing in usage. Selnes and
Hansen (2001) found that customers who had personal interactions with a
bank were more likely to form social bonds with the bank, and this in turn
resulted in higher loyalty. Also, self-service interactions improved bonding
if personal-service interactions were also high. These studies suggest that
routing the lower tier customers to automated services may make them
even less profitable than if they are accorded personal service. Second,
Feinberg et al. (2002) demonstrate the betrayal effect, whereby customers
will decrease their preferences for their favorite company if that company
offers special deals to other customers. The case here is a little different –
the question is whether a firm's bottom tier customers will feel betrayed if
the firm gives special treatment to its top tier customers. However, it would
be important to examine the betrayal effect for customer tier programs.
It may depend in subtle ways on how the tiers are defined. For example,
I may be completely loyal to Airline A although I don't take many trips.
Under Airline A's customer tier program, I may not make the "Gold" tier
and therefore receive poor service, yet I perceive that I deserve better.

- *Over-serving the higher tier*: Funds should be allocated proportional
  to the marginal benefit generated by additional allocation. Recalling
  the planning models above, where revenues or $LTV = \alpha + X^\beta$. A key
  factor in deciding on allocating development funds is β, the marginal
  productivity of funds. As a result, firms that define tiers solely based on
  current profitability (basically α) and allocate most marketing funds to
  the segments with high α's, may be wasting money.

- *Confusing current profit level with responsiveness*: Over-serving the higher
  tier segment is part of the general problem of confusing level and response.
  The problem is that measures on α are more readily available than β.
  α can be approximated by current profitability, whereas β requires a
  statistical model, survey, or difficult judgments on the productivity of
  marketing funds (Rust et al. 1995). In fact, customer tiers should really
  be defined based on Fig. 23.7. Figure 23.7 depicts 4 groups according to
  the current profit level (α) and responsiveness (β). The high level/high
  response group is called the "Develop" group, since this group merits
  significant investment. The high level/low response group is called the
  "Cash Cow" group, since this group requires little investment. The low
  level/high response group is called the "Move Up" group, since this group
  can possibly be moved to top tier with appropriate investment. The low
  level/low response group is called the "Fire" group, since these customers
  are not valuable and can't be changed.

The problem is that companies define customer tiers based on levels
and then think of all high-level customers as Develop, and all low level
customers as Fire. They can be wasting significant funds on the Cash Cow

		Current Profit Level	
		Low	High
Responsiveness	Low	*Fire*	*Cash Cow*
	High	*Move Up*	*Develop*

Fig. 23.7 Combining current profit level and responsiveness in developing customer tier management strategy

group, and missing out on important opportunities with the Move Up group. Of course the problem here is one of measurement – it is very difficult to obtain the segment-level β's. However, managers need to be aware of these issues and researchers need to develop effective ways of estimating the segment-level β's. This is why Rust et al. work (2000) is so important.

- *Mis-Classifying customers in tiers*: As in any segmentation scheme, companies can mistakenly classify customers in the wrong tiers. This is especially an issue for acquisition (anticipating in advance whether a customer will be a top tier customer), if multiple measures are used for classification, and if not all required data are available from all customers. The acquisition issue is a key one, since companies do not want to abandon acquisition efforts altogether. But acquiring the wrong customers actually can result in lower profits. Ainslie and Pitt's approach for UniBank is an important contribution here. The idea is to create a predictive model that identifies top tier customers by predicting scores as a function of predictors available in acquisition lists. Obviously not a lot of data are available in these lists, but Ainslie and Pitt (1998) found that demographic and credit data were valuable predictors. The problem with using multiple measures is that some customers may be put into the high tier group since they are like top tier customers on say 3 out of 5 measures. But those 2 measures in which they are unlike top tier customers may make them non-receptive to the customer tier program. A customer may have the income but not the age level to be placed in a company's top tier. As a result the customer will not be receptive to the appeals designed for higher income, older people. The missing data issue is also crucial. An obvious example is missing data on responsiveness, as discussed above. Another example would be missing data on share-of-wallet. A high profit level customer with a low share of wallet obviously should be treated differently than a high profit level customer with a high share of wallet.

23.5 Future Research Requirements

Research is needed on all aspects of customer tier programs, and can be organized around the steps in designing these programs shown in Fig. 23.1.

- *Review objectives*: For which types of objectives are customer tier programs best suited? How do different objectives (e.g., emphasis on customer count and revenues versus emphasis on profitable growth of a stable customer base) influence the design of programs?
- *Creating databases*: How do the information technology costs compare with the profitability gains from customer tier segmentation?
- *Create segments:* What are the best variables for defining customer tiers? How do we integrate both level and response measures?
- *Determine acquisition potential for each tier*: How do we develop segment-level acquisition functions? How can we identify segment members in advance of acquisition?
- *Determine development potential within tier*: How do we develop the response functions for revenues and retention that are the core of what makes customer tier programs work? While there is some work that suggests customers respond to tier programs (Wansink 2003; Kopalle et al. 2006), there is much more work to be done in this area.
- *Allocate funds to segments*: We need to enhance the planning models proposed in Sect. 23.2.7, and show that they can be used to improve customer tier strategy performance. Can managerial judgment be used to guide these models (see Blattberg and Deighton 1996; Rust et al. 1995)?
- *Design programs*: What types of programs are the best for developing high tier segments? What programs work for moving customers up? To what extent should customers be aware of their tier status, and if made aware, how extensively should this publicly acknowledged?
- *Implement and evaluate*: Can product-centric organization structures implement customer tier programs successfully? What is a reasonable ROI for a customer tier program, including IT and marketing costs?

In addition, more research is needed on the competitive implications of customer tier programs. If customer tier programs entail lower prices for the upper tiers, where do the increased profits come from? They could come from selling additional products to those customers. But if the market size is finite, haven't the same number of firms simply divided the market up at lower prices and possibly higher costs? For example, the airline industry lavishes a lot of service on its upper tier – that costs money. What would be the profit implications of dropping the program? Would costs increase? Why? Is customer tier management simply a prisoner's dilemma whereby firms spend extra money and offer lower prices to retain their best customers? Or perhaps the entire movement really isn't a marketing strategy as much as a cost management strategy.

Most importantly, we need convincing controlled field experiments that demonstrate customer tier programs work. The examples cited above report sales and profit increases, but they do not report baselines of what would have occurred without the program. To our knowledge, there is no example of systematically investigating in a controlled setting the profitability of treating an upper tier much better than it was treated before, and the potential losses from treating a lower tier much worse than it was treated before.

Chapter 24
Churn Management

Abstract While database marketing activities such as cross-selling, up-selling, frequency reward, and customer tier programs focus on developing the customer, there is always the fear that in the midst of these efforts, the customer will decide to leave the company, i.e., "churn." We discuss the approaches that can be used to control customer churn, focusing on proactive churn management, where the customer is contacted ahead of when he or she is predicted to churn, and provided a service or incentive designed to prevent the customer from churning. We review predictive modeling of customer churn, and present a framework for developing a proactive churn management program.

24.1 The Problem

Using a simple retention model, the lifetime value of a customer is:

$$LTV = \sum_{t=1}^{\infty} \frac{m_t r^{t-1}}{(1+\delta)^{t-1}} \qquad (24.1)$$

Customer churn management focuses on the retention component, r. At the customer level, churn refers to the probability the customer leaves the firm in a given time period. At the firm level, churn is the percentage of the firm's customer base that leaves in a given time period. Churn is therefore one minus the retention rate:

$$\text{Churn} = c = 1 - \text{Retention Rate} = 1 - r \qquad (24.2)$$

High customer churn is a concern for any industry where a simple retention lifetime value model is applicable, i.e., where customers can leave and not naturally return without a significant re-acquisition effort. This includes many services such as magazine and newsletter publishing, investment services, insurance, electric utilities, health care providers, credit card providers, banking, Internet service providers, telephone service providers, online services, and cable service providers.

There are two major types of customer churn: "voluntary" and "involuntary." Involuntary churn refers to the *company* deciding to terminate the relationship with the company, typically because of poor payment history. Voluntary churn refers to the *customer* deciding to terminate the relationship with the company. Hadden et al. (2006) further distinguish between "deliberate" voluntary churn, where the customer is dissatisfied or has received a better competitive offer, and "incidental" voluntary churn, where the customer cancels service because he or she no longer needs the product or has moved to a location where the company does not offer service.

Table 24.1 displays reported total churn rates for various industries and companies. The table shows it is not uncommon for between 20% and 50% of the customers who begin the year with a company to leave by the end of the year.[1] Table 24.1 suggests two observations: (1) Churn seems to be decreasing in the US wireless telecom industry.[2] This could be due to industry consolidation as well as better service. (2) Nascent industries such as digital services have high churn rates. This could be due to competition, poor service, or using steep promotions to acquire customers.

A few calculations illustrate the importance of churn rates of the magnitude reported in Table 24.1. First, consider the expected lifetime of the customer, that is, how long the customer stays with the company. This can be shown to equal the reciprocal of the churn rate (Appendix 24.1), i.e.,

$$\text{Expected Lifetime of Customer} = \frac{1}{c} \qquad (24.3)$$

Figure 24.1 graphs expected lifetime as a function of the churn rate. The figure shows that if the annual churn rate is 50%, the average customer is with the company for 2 years. At a 40% churn rate, this becomes 2.5 years; at 30% it's 3.3 years; and at 20% churn, it's 5 years. So within the range of the data reported in Table 24.1, a company with a relatively low churn rate keeps its customers for roughly 2 1/2 additional years compared to a company with a relatively high churn rate. What's more, the function is convex: The 20% churn company starts with a customer lifetime of 5 years, but can move to 6.6 years by decreasing its churn rate by just 5 percentage points, to 15%. If it can decrease churn all the way to 10%, average customer lifetime doubles, to 10 years.

Second, we can look at the lifetime value of the customer. Restating Equation 24.1 in terms of churn rather than retention, and assuming constant profit

---

[1] Note that one can extrapolate the monthly churn rates to annual churn rates by calculating $1 - (1 - c)^{12}$. This calculation assumes that the customer base on which the monthly churn rate is calculated retains that same churn rate for 12 consecutive months.

[2] The latest statistics are for "post-paid" customers, who typically have lower churn levels than "pre-paid" customers. But post-paid customers are the dominant customer type. In addition, Prudential Equity Group (2006) reports that the *post-paid* churn rate among the top four wireless carriers has on average steadily declined since 2002.

Table 24.1 Churn rates reported in the trade press

Industry	Year	Company/industry	Annual churn (%)	Reference
Internet service	2001	America Online	21	Kolko (2002)
Internet service	2001	Earthlink	34	Kolko (2002)
Internet service	2001	AT&T WorldNet	36	Kolko (2002)
Internet service	2001	NetZero/Juno	46	Kolko (2002)
Internet service	2001	MSN	57	Kolko (2002)
Internet service	2001	Industry range	38.7–63.2[a]	Pierce (2001)
Internet service	2000	Earthlink	47	Pierce (2001)
Internet service	2002	Industry range	31–39[a]	Yang (2002)
Wireless telephone	2000	Industry average	26.2[a]	Davidor (2000)
Wireless telephone	4Q1999	Industry med.	23.4[a]	Young (2000)
Wireless telephone	2001	Industry range	23.4–28.7[a]	Pierce (2001)
Wireless telepone	3Q2001	Verizon	31[a]	Fitchard (2002)
Wireless telephone	3Q2001	Cingular	34[a]	Fitchard (2002)
Wireless telephone	3Q2001	AT&T	37[a]	Fitchard (2002)
Wireless telphone	3Q2001	Sprint PCS	31[a]	Fitchard (2002)
Wireless telphone	3Q2001	VoiceStream	46[a]	Fitchard (2002)
Wireless telephone	3Q2001	Nextel	28[a]	Fitchard (2002)
Wireless telephone	1Q06	Verizon	10[a,b]	Prudential Equity Group, LLC (2006)
Wireless telephone	1Q06	Cingular/ATT	18[a,b]	Prudential Equity Group, LLC (2006)
Wireless telephone	1Q06	Sprint/Nextel	22[a,b]	Prudential Equity Group, LLC (2006)
Wireless telephone	1Q06	T-Mobile	22[a,b]	Prudential Equity Group, LLC (2006)
Satellite TV	1999	Pegasus Com.	17	Henderson (1999)
Satellite radio	2002	XM Satellite	20[a]	Wachovia Capital Markets, LLC (2006)
	2003	XM Satellite	19[a]	Wachovia Capital Markets, LLC (2006)
	2004	XM Satellite	29[a]	Wachovia Capital Markets, LLC (2006)
	2005	XM Satellite	28[a]	Wachovia Capital Markets, LLC (2006)
Financial services	1996	UK industry average	6	Supply Management (1998)
Financial services	1997	UK industry average	9	Supply Management (1998)
Financial services	2001	UK industry average	20–30	Fisher (2001)
Digital services	2005	Audible, Inc.	46[a]	Kaufman Bros (2005)
Digital services	2005	Netflix	39[a]	Needham & Company, LLC (2006)
Digital services	2005	HouseValues, Inc.	52[a]	Thomas Weisel Partners (2005)

[a] Numbers were provided on a monthly basis. Annual churn calculated as $1 - (1 - c)^{12}$. (See Footnote 1).

[b] Churn among "post-paid" as opposed to "pre-paid" customers.

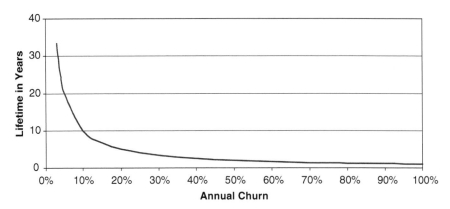

Fig. 24.1 Expected lifetime as function of churn rate (Equation 24.3).

contribution, yields:

$$LTV = \sum_{t=0}^{\infty} \frac{m(1-c)^{t-1}}{(1+\delta)^{t-1}} = \frac{m(1+\delta)}{(\delta+c)} \qquad (24.4)$$

where:

m = Annual profit contribution per customer.
c = Annual churn rate.
δ = Annual discount rate.

Figure 24.2 shows lifetime value as a function of churn rate assuming $m =$ $500 per year and $\delta = 14\%$. The firm with a 50% churn rate has a lifetime value of $891 per customer. The 40% churn firm has LTV = $1,056; 30% translates to LTV = $1,295; and 20% churn implies LTV = $1,676. Assume acquisition costs in the wireless telephone or ISP industry of roughly $300–400

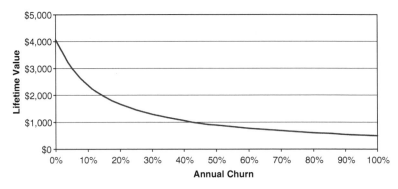

Fig. 24.2 Lifetime value of customer as function of churn rate (Equation 24.4)*.
* Assumes $\delta = 0.14$ and m = $500.

per customer (Fitchard 2002; Pierce 2001). Companies then would be making money, but the 20% churn company has an ROI of ($1,676–$400)/$400 = 319%, while the 50% churn company has an ROI of ($891–$400)/$400 = 123%, which is quite different.

Figure 24.2 shows a convex relationship between churn rate and lifetime value – firms enjoy increasing returns with respect to decreasing churn. A telecom company with 20% annual churn starts with an LTV of $1,676, but can increase it to $1,966 by reducing churn to 15%. On a base of 5,000,000 subscribers, that's $1.45 billion in additional profits!

Of course it is difficult to decrease churn and it costs money, but one sees the opportunity for increased profits by managing churn effectively, and conversely, the threat to company viability if churn escalates.

24.2 Factors that Cause Churn

The first step toward predicting and remedying churn is to understand the factors that cause or alleviate it. Table 24.2 provides a categorization of these factors: customer satisfaction, switching costs, customer characteristics, marketing efforts, and competition.

More satisfied customers should be less likely to churn, i.e., have higher lifetime durations (Anderson and Sullivan 1993; Hallowell 1996; Bolton 1998). In fact, Anderson and Sullivan (1993) found that companies with higher satisfaction levels enjoy lower elasticities of retention with respect to quality, i.e., these firms are insulated from short-term negative deviations in quality. There is some evidence that gross measures of overall satisfaction may not be perfectly predictive of churn (Kon 2004). Therefore, satisfaction should be measured with respect to particular components of the product, e.g., perceived service quality, whether the product is meeting expectations, how well the product fits customer needs, and price. Service quality and expectations are of course fundamental issues in services marketing (Anderson and Sullivan 1993).

"Fit-to-needs" is another important issue in customer satisfaction. For example, when companies use strong promotional incentives for acquisition, it succeeds in acquiring the customers, but acquires the wrong customers, i.e., customers for whom this is not really their best choice. Another point regarding fit-to-needs is the belief that the one-size-fits-all approach to services marketing often leads to lack of fit and results in lower satisfaction and churn. Companies in online retailing, Internet service provision, satellite TV, telecommunications, news and information, banking, and shipping are trying to customize their products to the customer to prevent this lack of fit problem and create customer satisfaction (Verton 2001; Kreitter 2000; Kleinman 2000; Bitner et al. 2000).

Table 24.2 Factors hypothesized to cause or alleviate churn

- Customer satisfaction

  o Service quality
  o Fit-to-needs
  o Meeting expectations
  o Price

- Switching costs

  o Physical
  o Psychological

- Customer characteristics

  o Risk aversion
  o Variety seeking
  o Deal proneness
  o Mavenism

- Marketing

  o Reward programs
  o Promotions
  o Price
  o Customized products

- Competition

  o Within category
  o Between category

Keaveney and Parthasarathy (2001) find intriguing evidence that the information source customers use to choose a particular service influences churn. This is consistent with evidence that acquisition channel is related to customer retention (Verhoef and Donkers 2005). Keaveney and Parthasarathy attribute their finding to the influence that information source has on customer expectations and perceived fit-to-needs. They find that customers are less likely to churn if they use external or experiential information in making their choices. This information leads to more accurate expectations, more knowledgeable choice, and a potential bias to confirm the positive "priors" set up by the information. However, information from peers was associated with more churn, since the information provided there is vicarious and less convincing.

Unfortunately, rarely does the database marketer have direct measures of customer satisfaction. For this reason, prior purchase and usage behavior variables, which are usually measurable, often serve as surrogates for satisfaction. Reinartz and Kumar (2003) find that sales volume and cross-buying are negatively associated with churn,[3] while returns and focused buying are positively associated. Purchase frequency has a U-shaped relationship with

---

[3] Note cross-buying might also create switching costs, making it less likely the customer will churn.

churn, with very light and very heavy users having higher churn likelihood. The light user might be clearly unhappy with the service, while the heavy users might be so involved in the product that they are more demanding, hence less satisfied and always on the look-out for a better alternative. Li (1995) also finds that cross-buying is negatively related to churn but finds sales volume is positively related.

As additional indicators of satisfaction, companies sometimes measure previous customer contacts with the call center, or complaints and objective measures of customer quality. Hadden et al. (2006) include these variables in a predictive churn model, and we will discuss the results in Sect. 24.3.1. Coussement and Van den Poel (2007b) find that the "emotionality" displayed in customer e-mails to the company can be measured and improve churn prediction.

Switching costs, or the lack of them, are another reason for churn. Switching costs can take two forms – psychological and physical – but both have the same theme: If it does not cost the customer much to switch to a competitor, the customer is more likely to churn. Psychological switching costs include psychological barriers to switching such as inertia, brand pull, familiarity, and perceptions of a relationship with the current company. Physical switching costs include real inconveniences due to switching. Consider for example Internet portals. The customer might have invested much effort in customizing the home page of their chosen portal (e.g., AOL). Switching to a new portal would require those efforts to be repeated Kolko 2002).

An interesting natural experiment regarding physical switching costs occurred in the wireless telephone industry, regarding "number portability." Before the fall of 2003 customers who switched carriers would have to change their telephone numbers as well. As of fall of 2003, customers were allowed to retain their old numbers. The wireless industry braced for a huge increase in churn (La Monica 2003). This was supported by a Forrester study (Golvin 2002), which found that 22% of cell-phone users were interested in switching carriers if they could retain their current phone number, while only 9% were interested in churning if they could not keep this number. Interestingly, they found that high volume callers would be the most likely to switch under number portability. This makes sense in that these customers are spending much money and looking for a better deal, but without portability, the cost of switching is enormous because they would have many people to notify of their new number.

Figure 24.3 displays customer churn for the six major carriers during the period when number portability was instituted (November 2003). The results reveal, quite surprisingly, that churn did not generally increase. The possible exception is ATT (perhaps not unexpectedly, ATT was later to merge with Cingular). But besides ATT, the major carriers experienced virtually no increase in churn.

There are several possible reasons for the lack of churn experienced after number portability. First, there still may have been switching costs because the customer would have to purchase a new phone and the new phone would

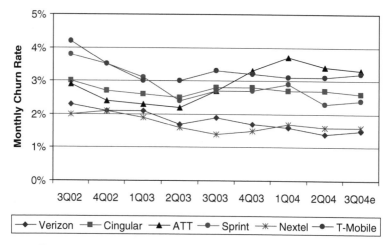

Fig. 24.3 Customer churn in the wireless telephone industry before and after the implementation of number portability (November 2003) (From Jefferies Equity Research 2004).

need the old number programmed into it. Second, when all is said and done, customers by November 2003 were not really so dissatisfied with their service that they wanted to churn (intentions do not always translate into behavior (Morwitz 1997)). Third, companies may have increased marketing efforts during this period (e.g., see The Economist (2007)).

Customer characteristics also play a role in churn. Risk takers, variety seekers, innovators, shopping mavens, and deal prone consumers might be more likely to churn. Keaveney and Parthasarathy (2001) found that risk taking was positively related to churn, and churn was also higher for lower income and lower levels of education. Reinartz and Kumar (2003) found that rural and higher income customers were less likely to churn. Li (1995) found that married and higher income customers were less likely to churn, and car owners and frequent movers were more likely to churn. Hallowell (1996) also found that higher income customers were less likely to churn. The higher loyalty from higher income customers may be due to lower price sensitivity.

Company marketing efforts ideally should have an impact on churn. This includes special services, loyalty programs, and price. Reinartz and Kumar (2003) found marketing efforts and loyalty programs associated with lower churn, although Reinartz and Kumar (2000) found that catalog mailing costs relative to total sales were not different between long and short lifetime customers. Li (1995) found that discount programs were associated with less churn. One common assumption is that matching the customer to the right pricing plan (e.g., for telecom) is associated with less churn. However, Lambrecht and Skiera (2006) find that customers have a systematic bias toward selecting a flat rate plan over a pay-per-use plan, even if they would save money on the pay-for-use plan. What's more, they find that using the flat fee plan (the "wrong" plan in terms of dollars spent) is not associated with higher churn. The authors attribute this to an "insurance effect" desired by customers. These results caution companies to be careful in encouraging customers to adopt new pricing plans to head off churn.

Competition is the fifth major category of causes for churn. Competition can come from both within and outside the product category. For example, dial-up ISP providers need to worry other dial-up providers as well as broadband (Kolko 2002). Online bankers have to worry about regular banking (Ensor 2002). The conventional wisdom is that competitive offers and opportunities are a major cause of churn (Elstrom 2002; Whiting 2001), but there has been little empirical verification on this, perhaps due to the fact that a given company often has little direct information on competitive offers.

In any given situation, all five factors above may be at work. Consider for example the Internet Service market. Many companies in this business relied on ubiquitous promotions and deals to sign up subscribers. Customer satisfaction and fit-to-needs were not always high, but high switching costs prevented churn. Many of the first ISP's used dial-up service, which did not satisfy needs for speed and convenience. So when a competitive category (broadband) offered better service, these ISP's developed a significant churn problem (Yang 2002). Forrester Research hypothesized that the "savviest" users (the market mavens) were most likely to churn (Kolko 2001). This churn problem continued despite ample marketing efforts to arrest it.

24.3 Predicting Customer Churn

A key step in proactive churn management is to predict which customers are most likely to churn. While predictive models can be developed for this purpose, their accuracy is hampered by lack of access to direct measures of the causes for churn. Companies therefore use behavioral measures such as recency, frequency, and monetary value as surrogates. They may also have records on customer complaints or previous offers extended to customers, as well as current prices paid, previous retention efforts, or acquisition source. They might have good measures of physical switching costs such as number of products used by the customer. They typically would not have good data on customer psychographics such as risk-taking, but they often have demographic measures that can link well to psychographics (e.g., Ailawadi et al. 2001). Finally, they typically have no data on competitive activity.

There are two types of churn prediction models, "Single Future Period" and "Time Series." In Single Future Period models, predictors are available for one or several time periods before the "churn period," where we observe whether or not the customer churned. For example, predictors might be measured for February and March, and those data are used to predict whether the customer churns in April. Often a month is skipped between the predictor and churn periods because it will take a month for the analyst to predict would-be churners and then contact the would-be churners with an offer to prevent the customer from churning in the subsequent month.

Time Series models are based on data where we observe predictors and churn simultaneously as they occur period to period. So, each customer would be observed for several periods. Each period potential predictors would be collected, as well as whether or not the customer churned. Obviously, one still must use data from period $t - 1, t - 2$, etc., to predict for period t or later, but the major difference is that churn is observed over time rather than in a single future period.

24.3.1 Single Future Period Models

An excellent example of a single future period churn model is from the credit card industry, provided by Advanced Software Applications as a demo for their ModelMax software.[4] This software uses an exploratory/stepwise procedure to select predictors, and then estimates a neural net to predict the dependent variable. Predictors were collected for 6 months prior to the target month when churn was observed. Predictors included demographics (age, occupation, credit rating), current product ownership (various other services offered by the bank), and product usage variables (RFM measures such as number of purchases, credit card balance, purchase amounts, etc.). The usage variables were calculated for each of the 6 months prior to the churn month. For example, "Credit card balance in month 6" refers to the customer's credit card balance in the month before the churn month. In all, there were 105 potential predictors. The model selected six predictors:

- *Credit card balance in month 6*: Users with low balances are more likely to churn. It may be difficult for those with high balances to transfer those balances to a new credit card (a switching cost).
- *Interest charged in month 3*: Customers with low interest charges, but not zero, are more likely to churn. This may be because such customers view interest as nuisance charges.
- *Purchase level in month 6*: Customers with low purchase levels are more likely to churn. This makes sense as these customers are probably less satisfied with the card, or have in fact adopted a new card and are phasing out the old one.
- *Household age*: Younger customers are more likely to churn. This may be due to the venturesome nature of younger people in credit card market, since it is relatively new to them. They are not set in their ways. They are also more likely to be courted by competitors.
- *Payment year-to-date month 2*: This is an overall measure of monetary value. The finding is that customers in the mid-range are more likely to churn. It might be that high-monetary value customers are satisfied with

---

[4] The authors are grateful to Advanced Software Applications for allowing us to use this example.

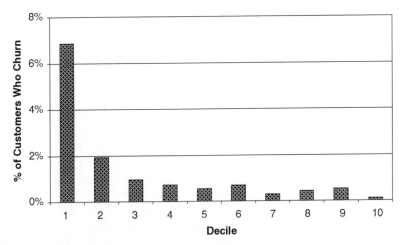

Fig. 24.4 Calibration data lift chart for neural net churn model – credit card company*.
* This example provided courtesy of Advanced Software Applications. Model estimated
using ModelMax software.

the card, which is why they use it so much, while it is not worth it for
low-monetary value customers to switch because there is little at stake
(e.g., a low interest rate would not save them much money because their
spending level is low).

- *Cash advances month 4*: Customers who do not use this feature are more
  likely to churn. Customers who use the feature may be more satisfied
  with their card, or would have a higher switching cost to switch cards
  since they'd have to learn how to use the cash advance feature with their
  new card.

Figure 24.4 shows the lift chart for this model. It is very strong, with 5.3
to 1 top-decile lift for the 40,000-customer calibration data. There was no
appreciable degradation in prediction on the 10,000-customer validation data.
This performance is much better for example than for the wireless telephone
churn models reported by Neslin et al. (2006a) and discussed later in this
section. There can be a variety of reasons. One could be the relative maturity
of the credit card category, so behaviors are stable and easier to predict.
Obviously, the reason why churn model accuracy differs by category, and
indeed why predictive model accuracy differs by category, is an important
topic for future research.

Lemmens and Croux (2006) investigate the use of boosting and bagging
(Chapter 19) in predicting churn. They use the same data as those used in
the Teradata Churn Prediction Tournament described subsequently in this
section (Neslin et al. 2006a). The authors show that both boosting and bagging of a decision tree model improve performance significantly over logistic
regression. Since the true churn rate was approximately 2% for these data
(i.e., churn is a "rare event", see Chapter 10; Donkers et al. 2003), the authors use choice-based sampling to create a balanced calibration dataset. The

authors investigate ways to adjust for this when the calibration data model is applied to holdout data, which reflects the true proportion of churners (2%). They find a simple intercept correction performs best. The authors find that how long the customer has owned his or her handset is the most important predictor of churn. This makes sense. Given the rapid changes in handset technology and features, customers who have owned the same handset for a long time are ripe for a competitive offer featuring a new handset if they switch.

Wei and Chiu (2002) also address the issue of rare events in modeling customer churn. In their data, the average monthly churn rate is 1.5–2%. The authors develop a "multi-classifier class-combiner" approach to address this issue. Say 1:X is the ratio of churners in the sample, i.e., with a 2% churn rate, 1:X = 1:50. The researcher desires a ratio of 1:Y, where Y = 1 means a 50–50 split between churners and non-churners. The researcher creates X/Y databases as follows. Each database contains all available churners and $N/(X/Y)$ non-churners. The same churners are used in each sub-database, while the non-churners are evenly divided among the sub-databases. A model is estimated for each sub-database. Assume that n_{c_1} models predict the customer will churn, while n_{c_2} models predict the customer will not churn. We predict the customer is a churner if $wn_{c_1} > (1 - w)n_{c_2}$, where w is a weight such that $w \in [0, 1]$. If $w = 0.5$, the customer is classified as a churner according to majority rule. If $w > 0.5$, churn predictions are given heavier weight, and we are more likely to predict the customer is a churner.

The authors test various sub-database ratios (1:2, 1:4, 1:8, and 1:16) and compare the false alarm and miss rates for these ratios to a single sample, for all w's between 0 and 1 in 0.01 increments. The authors find of course that as w increases, the multi-classifier class-combiner approach has fewer false alarms (Prob(Not churn | Predict Churn) decreases) but the miss rate is much higher (Prob(Churn | Predict Not Churn) increases). This is because a high w "biases" the method to predict more non-churners. Most importantly, the multi-classifier class-combiner approach is superior to the single-sample approach for all sub-database ratios tested. The authors prefer the 1:2 ratio because it provides a greater spread in miss rates as w varies, giving the analyst more leeway as to where to establish a cut-off. The comparison to the single-sample approach is shown in Table 24.3. The results show that for a given miss rate, the multi-classifier class-combiner yields a lower false alarm

Table 24.3 Performance of multi-classifier class combiner in predicting customer churn (From Wei and Chieu 2002, adapted from Figure 1, p. 108)

Method	False alarm rate (%)	Miss rate (%)
Single sample	21	48
Multi-classifier class combiner (Miss rate = miss Rate for single sample)	15	48
Multi-classifier class combiner (false alarm rate = false alarm rate for single sample)	21	40

rate, or for a given false alarm rate, it yields a lower miss rate. Depending on the value of w, the multi-classifier class-combiner method can be superior in terms of false alarms and miss rates (see the authors' graph on p. 108).

Hadden et al. (2006) demonstrate the use of predictors that, while not direct measures of satisfaction, are very good surrogates. In particular, the authors had 24 variables representing "Complaints" (type, number, etc.), "Repairs" (type of problem, how long it took make the repair, etc.), and "Provisions" (appointments broken before making the repair, days after the promised date that the repair was resolved, etc.). The authors do not identify the industry but state that the company was "one of the largest in the world in its domain," (p. 105), which explains why the company kept such careful data.

The authors compare neural nets with Bayesian architecture (Li and Wen 2005; Yu and Dayan 2005), neural nets with feed-forward back propagation, decision trees, and linear regression. The neural nets used all 24 variables ("inputs" in neural net parlance) along with two hidden layers (see Chapter 18). The decision tree method used was CART ("classification and regression tree," see Chapter 17) and while all 24 variables were made available, the final tree utilized only seven variables. To select variables for the regression model, the authors calculated the standard error rate (total number of errors divided by total number of classifications) for each of the 24 variables, and decided to retain 14.

The authors find that the models differ in accuracy. In their validation data, 30% of customers were churners; 70% were non-churners. They use a cut-off for each model's prediction (0.70) to classify customers and the results are in Table 24.4.

The NN–Bayesian model achieved a "lift" of $70/30 = 2.33$ (the customers it predicted to churn were more than twice as likely to churn as average). However, the NN–Bayesian method did little better than average in predicting a customer was not going to churn, i.e., the lift would be $75/70 = 1.07$. Regression and decision trees appear to balance the two errors the best.

While, clearly, Complaints, Repairs, and Provisions data are quite useful in predicting churn, similar to what we observed earlier, there was little overlap across models in the variables determined to be most important. For example, neural networks found that "resolution time" was among the seven most important variables; none of the other methods found this to be in the top seven.

Table 24.4 Performance of alternative methods for predicting churn (From Hadden et al. 2006)

Method	P(Churn | predict churn) (%)	P(No churn | predict no Churn) (%)	Overall accuracy (%)
NN–Bayesian	70	75	74
NN–standard	55	79	72
Decision tree	66	88	82
Regression	51	94	81

This may be because the predictors are highly correlated and in that context, we might not expect the top seven of 24 variables to have much overlap.

Hadden et al.'s study is important because it shows that data very "close" to customer satisfaction – complaints, repairs, and repair provisions – have predictive power. Consistent with this observation, Coussement and Van den Poel (2007b) find that measures of customer emotionality in e-mails they send to the firm provide additional predictive power to predicting churn for newspaper subscriptions. More work is needed to show the incremental contribution of these data over usage history variables typically also used as surrogates of customer satisfaction.

Coussement and Van den Poel (2008) compare the accuracy of support vector machines (SVM), random forests (Breiman 2001; a form of bagging, see Chapter 19), and logistic regression in predicting churn for a Belgian newspaper. Their predictor variables include measures of client–company interactions such as complaint behavior; renewal variables such as whether the last subscription was renewed before it expired; customer characteristics, and previous purchase and usage behavior variables such as length of the current subscription. The authors use two approaches for estimating the SVM, each differing in the criterion used for a grid search – one is based on percentage correctly classified (PCC) using a threshold; the other is based on the area under the ROC (receiver operating characteristic curve; see Chapter 11), which they call AUC. The authors find that random forests perform the best. The differences do not appear markedly different (top-decile lifts were 4.48 for logistic, 4.75 for random forests, 4.21 for SVM_{PCC}, and 4.49 for SVM_{AUC}). However, as we will see in Sect. 24.4.2, differences in lift on the order of a tenth of a point can have an important impact on the profitability of churn management programs.

Neslin et al. (2006a) conducted a "churn modeling tournament" to investigate the best ways to predict churn. They made available data from a wireless service provider to anyone interested in participating in the tournament. The data consisted of a 100,000-customer calibration dataset including 171 predictors including customer characteristics, previous cell phone usage, and previous contact variables (calls to the customer care group, etc.). The data were of the typical single future period format – the predictors were collected over a 3-month period, then 1 month was skipped, and then churn was observed in the fifth period. There were two holdout datasets – one compiled at the same time as the calibration dataset ("current" validation data); the other compiled roughly 3 months later ("future" validation data).

The tournament attracted 44 entries from 33 participants. Roughly half were academics; half were practitioners. The top-decile lift results for the two validation databases were as follows:

Validation data	Mean	Std. Dev	Minimum	Maximum
Current	2.14	0.53	1.07	2.90
Future	2.13	0.53	1.19	3.01

There are two very important conclusions from the above results: (1) There is wide variation in achieved lift (from roughly 1–3). This means that method matters – not every entry achieved the same lift. We will show how to calculate the importance of lift in financial terms in Sect. 24.4.2. (2) There is very little fall-off between the current and future validation databases. This means that the shelf life of a churn prediction model is at least 3 months.

Perhaps most important is the authors' analysis of the methods used to make the predictions. As discussed in Chapter 10, they use factor analysis to uncover five general approaches to modeling churn:

1. *Logit*: These entrants used logistic regression as the statistical model, exploratory data analysis (EDA) and stepwise regression for variable selection, and allocated relatively less time to preparing the final prediction files. Practitioners tended to be more highly associated with this approach.
2. *Decision Tree*: These entrants heavily relied on decision trees as the statistical model. They were far less likely to use EDA and stepwise procedures, but allocated a lot of their time to estimation. This is quite consistent with the decision tree method, which requires careful pruning, etc., of the decision tree. Users of this approach spent more time in general on the task and subdivided the calibration data into estimation and holdout samples.
3. *Practical*: These entrants did not favor any particular statistical model. They relied heavily on common sense in selecting variables and allocated more time than average on downloading data but less time on average on the entire task. They did not subdivide the data as the Decision Tree entrants did. Users of this approach tended to be practitioners.
4. *Discriminant*: These entrants used discriminant analysis as their statistical technique. They allowed less time to data cleaning and more time to estimation, and tended to use many variables in the final model.
5. *Explain:* These entrants did not favor any particular statistical model and tended to explore several statistical techniques. They reported that they relied on theory, factor analysis, and cluster analysis to selecting variables, and tended to use fewer variables in their final models. Although the following is subjective, by their reliance on theory, factor analysis, and cluster analysis, it is as if these entrants were trying to come up with a parsimonious explanation of churn as well as trying to predict it.

The authors found that the Logit and Decision Tree approaches predicted most accurately, followed by Practical and Explain, with Discriminant lagging behind. But their major message is that predicting churn, as well as predictive modeling in general, is about much more than the statistical technique. It entails allocation of time, methods for selecting variables, and details such as subdividing the calibration data into estimation and holdout samples. For researchers, this is important because it suggests the importance of topics such as variable selection and holdout samples, but also the need to study predictive modeling holistically rather than as a statistical model. For practitioners, the implications are that logistic and decision tree-based approaches can both work well, but require different management. Decision tree approaches require much time for estimation; hence managers need to make sure their analysts have sufficient, in fact, more than sufficient, computing power. Logistic tree approaches will probably entail stepwise, so managers need to question analysts as to what variables were omitted and how this might affect the interpretation of the results.

This tournament is exciting in its use of a contest to find the best ways to predict churn, and its drawing on both academics and practitioners. However, the study has important limitations that suggest future research. First, there was not ample representation of machine learning techniques. It turns out that the winning entry was a machine learning version of decision trees, but there were not many entries like this and no entries of support vector machines and genetic algorithms, etc. Second, the data were so highly correlated that the authors could not tease out the individual contribution of statistical model, time allocation, etc. These variables tended to clump together to form "approaches," and this is instructive. Still, it would be nice to know the individual contributions of the components of the approaches. Third, other details such as treatment of missing data could not be explored in depth.

In summary, the message of Neslin et al. (2006a) is that churn modeling requires an *approach*, not just a statistical technique, and that while different approaches can be successful, not all approaches are successful.

24.3.2 Time Series Models

Hazard models provide a particularly attractive method of predicting churn using time series data (see Chapter 15). Lu (2001) employs a hazard model estimated using the LIFEREG routine in SAS.[5] The model does not allow for time-varying covariates but the user can assume a parametric baseline hazard function. This permits a closed form expression for survival probabilities, which in this case are the probability a customer does not churn up to a certain number of months from the origin of the data. In this application, Lu assumed a log-normal distribution for the baseline hazard function.

Lu collected data on 41,374 customers who were active as of August 2000 and observed over time whether each one churned. Predictors included demographics, internal customer data (RFM type data on call behavior, plus data on plan type, customer segmentation code, ownership of other company products, billing disputes, late fee charges, etc.), and customer contact data (inbound calls to the company's call center and outbound mail contacts with the customer). These 212 variables were narrowed to 29 by first omitting variables that did not significantly correlate with churn, and then using a stepwise procedure.

---

[5] See also Van den Poel and Larivière (2004) for an application of hazard models to predicting churn for a financial services company.

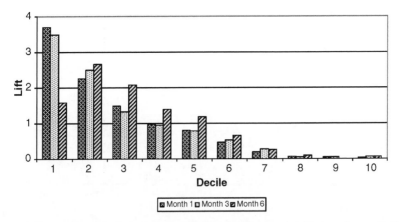

Fig. 24.5 Lift charts for hazard churn model depending on time horizon for prediction. Base churn probabilities were not available, but decile-by-decile lift could be calculated from cumulative gains charts that were provided. (From Lu 2001)

Survival probabilities were calculated to create lift charts, shown in Fig. 24.5. The figure shows the lift for predicting the probability that a customer will churn in a given future month – month 1, 3, or 6. There are two interesting findings in Lu's lift charts. First, the top decile lift is the highest for month 1, next highest for month 3, and noticeably lower for month 6. This may be because the author did not use time varying covariates (the covariates were defined as of time zero and did not change), and it is inherently more difficult to predict churn 6 months out than 1 or 3 months out.[6] Second, the top decile lift in month 3 is 3.5 to 1, which is better than most of the entries in the Teradata Churn Prediction Tournament described in the previous section (Neslin et al. 2006a), which predicted for month 2. This better performance may of course be due to the fact that these are different data. Or it could be due to the hazard model, which makes use of the time series nature of the data.[7]

Yan et al. (2001) propose an interesting approach to time series data that (1) combines several consecutive windows of data, and (2) can be used even if the dependent variable is not available for some observations. We discuss the first feature in more detail since it is more relevant to most churn modeling situations.

Assume the company has $T+1$ "windows" available, e.g., January–March for predictors; April to observe churn would be one window, February–April for predictors; May to observe churn would be the next, etc. This is essentially a time series of observations divided into $T+1$ databases. A predictive model

---

[6] Note the 2nd, 3rd, and other deciles look better for the 6-month predictions, but that's because fewer churners were grouped into the first decile, so they were more likely to be in other deciles.

[7] Even though in this case the author did not use time-varying predictors, his hazard model is inherently dynamic due to the log-normal hazard function.

could be estimated for each window, as in the Single Future Period approach. The prediction works as follows:

$$P[c|x_i] = \sum_{t=0}^{-T} w(t)P_t[c|x_i] \tag{24.5}$$

where:

x_i = Vector of attributes for customer i applicable at the prediction period.
$P[c|x_i]$ = Predicted probability customer i churns during the prediction period, given x_i.
$P_t[c|x_i]$ = Predicted probability customer i churns using the model estimated for the tth window, $t = 0, \ldots, -T$, where $t = 0$ signifies the most recent window, and $t = -T$ is the oldest model.
$w(t)$ = Set of weights.

and:

$$w(t) = \frac{e^{-\sigma_{t-1}}}{Z} \tag{24.6}$$

where:

σ_{t-1} = Mean square error using the model $t - 1$ to predict for model 0's dataset.
Z = Normalization constant so that the w's sum to 1.

The prediction of whether the customer will churn in the current period is a weighted average of predictive models estimated from previous data windows, where the weights are proportional to a model's ability to predict the most recent data window. One would expect the weights to decline as we move back in time, but the weights are determined empirically by σ. Note this is very similar to the multi-classifier class-combiner approach of Wei and Chiu (2002) discussed above. The windows are the sub-samples, and Equations 24.5 and 24.6 describe how the different predictions are combined.

The authors compare three models: (1) the proposed "Combined" model based on three windows, (2) a single model using all the data from four periods before the prediction period, and (3) a single model based on one period before the prediction period. Model 2 is similar to a time series model since customers may churn in each period. Model 3 is similar to the Single Future Period approach since there is only one period when the customer might churn. The models are based on between 67,278 and 72,431 customers per window, and 71 potential predictors (customer credit classifications, location, use of various services, monthly service charges, monthly usage rate of various services, monthly number of dropped calls, and monthly number of customer service calls, etc.) were derived to predict churn for a 2-month period during which churn was roughly 6%. All the estimated models were neural nets with 71 inputs, one hidden layer, and 10 hidden nodes.

The results were that the Combined model and Model 2 predicted equally well, and together, both performed better than Model 3. The authors advocate their Combined model over Model 2 because the Combined model has smaller data requirements per model and is easier to estimate and utilize. This of course depends on the model used for Model 2. It isn't clear that a Combined model using neural nets for each model would be easier, or superior, to a hazard model. In any case, Yan et al.'s approach is very interesting and shows the potential of combining models into a single prediction, a theme that runs throughout the machine learning literature (Chapter 19).

Bonfrer et al. (2007) propose a Brownian motion model for predicting customer churn and apply it to a telecom company. The model assumes that weekly usage rate for customer $i(x_{it})$ follows a first-order Markov process. Future usage can be predicted from (1) usage in the previous period, (2) a drift parameter μ_i related to the mean of the process, and (3) a volatility parameter σ_i related to the standard deviation of the process. Customers are assumed to churn if they hit zero consumption. If weekly usage follows a normal distribution, and $x_{it} > 0$, then the time until the customer churns follows an inverse-Gaussian distribution, and the cumulative distribution, or the probability the customer churns within time τ of the current time t can be written as:

$$F(\tau | x_{it}, \mu_i, \sigma_i) = 1 - \Phi\left(\frac{\mu_i t + x_{it}}{\sigma_i \sqrt{t}}\right) + \exp\left(\frac{-2x_{it}\mu_i}{\sigma_i^2}\right) \Phi\left(\frac{\mu_i t - x_{it}}{\sigma_i \sqrt{t}}\right)$$

$$(24.7)$$

where Φ is the cumulative standard normal distribution. The probability of churning is increasing in the drift parameter (μ) and decreasing in recent consumption (x). A customer with negative drift and low recent consumption is a churn candidate. Higher volatility generally signals trouble for a customer with positive drift, but can actually lessen the chances of churn if drift is negative. These results make sense.

Since the model only has two parameters – drift and volatility – it can be estimated at the individual customer level. This makes the model easy to implement and avoids heterogeneity assumptions. The authors test their model and find it achieves roughly 2 to 1 top-decile lift in holdout data, similar to the predictive accuracy found in the churn modeling tournament discussed in Sect. 24.3.1. Overall, the simplicity and interpretability of the Brownian motion model makes it a promising method for future application and development.

24.4 Managerial Approaches to Reducing Churn

24.4.1 Overview

Approaches to reducing churn can be first categorized as targeted or untargeted. Untargeted approaches try to increase customer satisfaction or increase customer-switching costs by improving the product, advertising, or using loyalty programs. Targeted approaches, in contrast, identify customers most likely to churn and attempt to "rescue that customer." The key difference between targeted and untargeted approaches is that the targeted approaches identify potential churners and take action, whereas the untargeted approaches do not single out potential churners.

There are two types of targeted approaches: reactive and proactive. Reactive approaches wait for the customer to identify him/herself as a likely churner, usually when the customer calls to cancel service. A proactive approach identifies, in advance, customers most likely to churn, diagnoses the reason for the potential churn, and targets an appropriate action or incentive to induce the customer to stay.

Reactive churn management programs have the advantage of perfect prediction, or at least near-perfect. The customer has called and is about to cancel service, and then corrective action is taken. Because of the perfect prediction, the company can afford a significant incentive to keep the customer. However, at this point a strong incentive is *necessary*, and the company is basically bribing the customer to stay. This costs a lot in the short term and also may "train" the customer to call whenever he or she has an attractive competitive offer, expecting the company to match or exceed that offer.

Proactive churn management programs use predictive models to identify would-be churners, and hence have imperfect predictive accuracy – the accuracy depends on the quality of the churn model. Even with a 5 to 1 lift ratio, if the overall churn rate is 2%, only 10% of customers in the high churn segment are real churners. As a result, the company can't spend as much money per incentive as in a reactive program, since some of it may be wasted. On the other hand, the company may not need to spend as much, because things haven't gotten so bad yet that the customer is walking out the door.

Another potential concern for proactive churn management programs is that they might stimulate non-would-be churners to contemplate churning. Perhaps the customer is identified to be at risk for churning based on a predictive model, but really wasn't going to churn. However, the proactive contact and accompanying offer might stimulate "need recognition" (Engel et al. 1995, Chapter 5) and set in motion the customer's decision process for deciding whether to churn. Another way of looking at it is that the customer had a "latent need" to churn that was identified by the predictive model, but it took the proactive contact to enable the customer to recognize that need. This idea is advanced by Berson et al. (2000, pp. 282–295), who describe a UK telecom company case where indeed, the apparent result of a proactive program was to reduce churn among customers who responded to an offer designed to reduce churn, but increase churn among those who did not respond.[8]

---

[8] The authors are indebted to Professor Charlotte Mason of University of North Carolina for bringing this example to their attention.

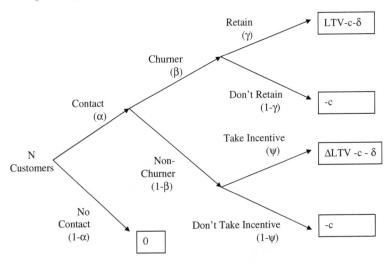

Fig. 24.6 Profitability framework for proactive targeted churn management program.

24.4.2 A Framework for Proactive Churn Management

The above discussion identifies some of the trade-offs inherent in a proactive churn management program, e.g., the predictive accuracy of the model, the effectiveness of the offer, and the potential wastage of offers made to customers who weren't going to churn. These issues can be quantified using the model portrayed in Fig. 24.6, which uses the following quantities:

N = Total number of customers.

α = The probability a customer is contacted as part of the churn management program. For example, if the program is to contact all customers in the top decile identified by a churn predictive model, then $\alpha = 0.10$.

β = The probability the customer is a churner, given the customer is contacted. For example, if all customers in the top decile are contacted and 15% of them are churners, then $\beta = 0.15$.

γ = The probability the customer is rescued, given he or she is a churner. This is the effectiveness of the incentive. For example, if a would-be churner has a 50% chance of being rescued by the offer, $\gamma = 0.50$.

ψ = The probability a non-churner takes the incentive. That is, a customer who isn't going to churn may take the incentive, e.g., if it is a price reduction or a free gift, ψ could be quite large, possibly 100%.

Δ = Percentage increase in lifetime value among non-churners who take the incentive. Although a non-churner has not been prevented from churning, having received an incentive could increase their retention probability or their purchase level of the company's services. This could be interpreted as a "delight the customer" effect (Rust and Oliver 2000; Hatch 2002).

The free offer is an unexpected surprise, one that enhances the customer's satisfaction with the company.

c = Contact cost, i.e., the cost of contacting a customer with a churn management offer. This might be \$0.50 if contact is made by mail.

δ = Cost of the incentive. If for example the incentive is a free cell phone, δ would equal the out-of-pocket cost of the cell phone.

LTV = Lifetime value of the customer. This differs of course by customer.

Given these definitions, one can calculate the total profit for a proactive churn management program by summing the appropriate probabilities times payoffs in Fig. 24.6. The result is:

$$\Pi = N\{\alpha\beta\gamma(LVC - c - \delta) + \alpha\beta(1 - \gamma)(-c) + \alpha(1 - \beta)\psi(\Delta LVC - c - \delta)$$
$$+ \alpha(1 - \beta)(1 - \psi)(-c)\}$$
$$= N\alpha\{(\beta\gamma + (1 - \beta)\psi\Delta)LVC - \delta(\beta\gamma + (1 - \beta)\psi) - c\} \qquad (24.8)$$

Equation 24.8 has a simple interpretation. The $\beta\gamma$ and $(1 - \beta)\psi\Delta$ terms within the {} brackets represent the incremental profits of the program. The $\beta\gamma$ term is due to the rescued churners; the $(1 - \beta)\psi\Delta$ term is due to delighted non-churners. The $\delta(\beta\gamma + (1 - \beta)\psi)$ and c terms represent the incremental costs of the program. The $\delta(\beta\gamma + (1 - \beta)\psi)$ term represents incentive costs, first among churners, then among non-churners. The c term represents contact costs, which are incurred among all α customers who are contacted.[9]

Equation 24.8 shows how key factors come together to determine the profitability of a churn management campaign. Note for example that if a customer's lifetime value is small, Equation 24.8 can easily turn out to be negative. Similarly, if the rescue probability (γ) is small and we can't assume any delight effect (Δ), the campaign may not be worth it.

The total investment in the program is $\alpha(\delta(\beta\gamma + (1 - \beta)\psi)) - c)$, the third and fourth terms in Equation 24.8. Equation 24.8 divided by investment therefore is ROI for the program. One can then set an ROI requirement, say ROI $> \rho$ and solve for the incentive value δ. This yields the maximum the firm could spend on an incentive, namely:

$$\delta < \frac{(\beta\gamma + (1 - \beta)\psi\Delta)LTV - c(1 + \rho)}{(1 + \rho)(\beta\gamma + \psi(1 - \beta))} \qquad (24.9)$$

Figure 24.7 graphs maximum allowable incentive (δ) as a function of predictive accuracy (β) for two different values of incentive effectiveness (γ), assuming c = \$0.50, LTV = \$2,000, required ROI = ρ = 15%, non-churner

---

[9] Note we are assuming that the only cost among non-churners who do not accept the offer is the contact cost. If as in the UK telecom case described by Berson et al. (2000), churn rates actually increase among this group, the cost will be higher than the contact cost. Importantly, Fig. 24.6 provides a framework that with some extension could be used to analyze the impact of this possibility.

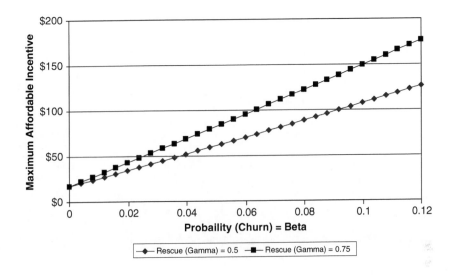

Fig. 24.7 Maximum possible incentive as function of churn model accuracy (β) and retention (Rescue) effectiveness (γ).
Calculations based on Equation 24.9 with $c = \$0.50$, $LTV = \$2,000$, $\rho = 0.15$, $\Delta = 0.01$, and $\psi = 100\%$.

acceptance rate $\psi = 100\%$, and delight effect $\Delta = 1\%$. The figure shows that given these parameters, one can spend more money on incentives to the extent that the churn model is more accurate and that would-be churners respond to the incentive.

For example, if, 5% of the customers in the targeted group were churners ($\beta = 0.05$), and the rescue rate from the program is 50% ($\gamma = 0.50$), the company could afford to spend $61.03 per customer in a churn management program. Even though the lifetime value of the customer is $2,000, the company can only afford to spend much less than that per customer, because of low predictive accuracy and because only half the churners will be swayed by the incentive. Of course, the rescue parameter γ is really a function of δ, and one could incorporate this explicitly as well.

Interestingly, the positive relationship between predictive accuracy and profit in Fig. 24.7 does not hold in general. For example, taking the derivative of Equation 24.8 with respect to predictive accuracy β yields $(\gamma - \psi\Delta) > 0$ as a necessary condition for increased accuracy to improve profits. If many non-churners take the incentive, and doing so delights them, we are better off targeting non-churners with the incentive, i.e., having poor predictive accuracy. This highlights the importance of the delight phenomenon and the need to understand its magnitude in a churn management context.

Neslin et al. (2006a) show how the framework also allows one to calculate the financial value of predictive accuracy. For simplicity and to be conservative, they assume $\psi = 1$ (i.e., all contacted customers accept the incentive) and $\Delta = 0$ (there is no delight effect). Then, they express predictive accuracy β as a function of lift (Chapter 10) as follows: Let β_0 be the base churn rate in the data, and λ be the lift among the customers contacted by the churn management program. Then $\beta = \lambda\beta_0$. Substituting this into Equation 24.8 and re-arranging terms, they obtain:

$$\Pi = N\alpha\{[\gamma LTV + \delta(1 - \gamma)]\beta_0\lambda - \delta - c\} \qquad (24.10)$$

The terms in front of the lift parameter (λ) are the slope of profits with respect to predictive accuracy. That is,

$$GAIN = N\alpha\{[\gamma LTV + \delta(1 - \gamma)]\beta_0\} \qquad (24.11)$$

represents the impact on profits of increasing lift by one unit. For example, consider a campaign with the following parameters:

$N = 5,000,000$ customers
$\alpha = 0.10$ (10% of the customer base is to be contacted)
$LTV = \$500$ (lifetime value of rescued customer)
$\gamma = 0.10$ (10% of contacted would-be churners stay with the company)
$\delta = \$50$ (incentive cost)
$\beta_0 = 0.018$ (base monthly churn rate)

Then, the gain in the profitability of a single churn management campaign, per *half* unit increase in lift (e.g., from 2.5 to 3.0; note 0.5 is the standard deviation in performance among the entries in Neslin et al.'s churn modeling tournament), is $5,000,000 \times 0.10 \times \{[0.10 \times \$500 + \$50 \times (1 - 0.10)] \times 0.018 = \$427,500$. As we see, the framework can illustrate the profit impact of better churn prediction, and in this example, we see that the impact can be substantial.

The framework integrates key concepts of churn predictive accuracy, incentive effectiveness, delight effects, lifetime value, and costs into an expression for the profitability of a proactive churn management program. The model provides diagnostics regarding the maximum a company could spend on an incentive, which increases as:

- Predictive accuracy (β) increases (as long as $(\gamma - \psi\Delta) > 0$; see above).
- Incentive effectiveness (γ) increases.
- Lifetime value of customers (LTV) increases.
- The impact of the incentive on churners (the delight factor Δ) increases.
- Contact costs (c) decrease.
- Required ROI from the program decreases.

In addition, the framework can be used to calculate the benefits of improved churn prediction. This is important for a firm that needs to decide whether to invest in expanding its churn analytics department or purchasing additional data.

An important limitation of the framework is that it is a single-campaign model. It does not explicitly answer questions such as how soon before the customer is predicted to churn should the customer be contacted, or how many times to contact a customer.

24.4.3 Implementing a Proactive Churn Management Program

Implementing a proactive churn management program consists of four steps: (1) identifying potential churners, (2) understanding why they might churn, (3) designing an appropriate contact/offer strategy for the churners, and (4) monitoring and evaluating results.

The first two steps can be accomplished by a predictive model. The predictive model identifies the customers most likely to churn, and provides diagnostics for why they might churn. The third step requires creativity to consider the various incentives that one might implement. Inevitably this will entail costs, and the framework in Fig. 24.6 can help identify the upper bound of how much one can spend on incentives. As Equation 24.9 shows, one will spend more for higher lifetime value customers. Another consideration here is that the incentive should be such that it does not stimulate "need recognition" among those who do not accept the offer (Berson et al. 2000).

Another important challenge is to decide how many customers to contact, i.e., what should be the value of α? This could be decided in two ways. First would be to use a budget. If \$X are allocated to the campaign and we anticipate the values for rescue (γ), predictive ability (β), contact cost (c), and non-churner acceptance (ψ), total expenditures are $N\alpha\{(\beta\delta + (1-\beta)\psi) + c\}$. One can adjust α so that the total expenditure is within budget. Second would be to quantify the relationship between α and β: β is the percentage of contacted customers who are would-be churners, and will naturally decrease as a function of the number of customers contacted (since we are using a predictive model to identify churners and ordering customers in terms of their likelihood of churning). One could then calculate profits of the campaign for different combinations of α and β and choose the combination that maximizes profits.

Evaluating a churn management program is best accomplished using a field test. For example, estimating the rescue rate γ is challenging because rescued churners cannot be identified with certainty. Following is how a field test based on the framework in Fig. 24.6 could be used for this purpose. Let

A = Group that receives the churn offer (treatment group).
B = Group that does not receive the offer (control group).
N = Number of customers assigned to each group (assumed equal).

R_g = Churn rate in group g during the churn management campaign (either A or B).

O = Number of offers accepted in the treatment group.

LTV_g = Average lifetime value per customer in group g calculated a reasonable amount of time after the campaign is finished.

The impact of the program would be estimated by $N(LTV_A - LTV_B)$. To estimate the rescue rate, we express the churn rates in each group as:

$$R_A = \beta(1 - \gamma) \tag{24.12a}$$
$$R_B = \beta \tag{24.12b}$$

Using β from the control group, we can solve Equation 24.12a for the rescue rate γ. Also, the total number of offers accepted in the treatment group equals the number of would-be churners who accept plus the number of non-would-be churners who accept. This yields:

$$O = N\{\beta\gamma + (1 - \beta)\psi\} \tag{24.12c}$$

Since we know N, β and γ, we can solve for ψ.

This illustrates how a field test can be used to provide an overall evaluation of a churn management campaign. In addition, the test provides estimates for key parameters such as the rescue rate to be used for future planning. Providing an overall evaluation is crucial; one cannot take for granted that the churn management program will work. As discussed earlier regarding the UK telecom case (Berson et al. 2000), it is even possible for $N(LTV_A - LTV_B)$ to be negative!

Another issue in implementing a proactive churn program is how early to intervene.[10] This may require a trade-off between churn model accuracy (β) and rescue effectiveness (γ). Earlier intervention may rescue more would-be churners (higher γ), but predictive accuracy will be lower (see discussion of Lu 2001 in Sect. 24.3.2). Intervening later might benefit from higher model accuracy, but a rescue offer may be less effective or have to be more costly to achieve a desired rescue level (γ). The point is, the question is not only *what* the churn management offer should be, but *when* it should be delivered.

A final issue is the single campaign versus multiple contact approach. For example, consider the customer who receives an offer in March and does not churn, but appears in the top decile risk group in May. Should that customer receive a second incentive in May? There may be a chronically high churn risk group for the company, and under this policy, they will be receiving offers every few months. This could erode their profitability, or at least their loyalty, as we train them that they can always expect new offers and deals from the company. One way investigate this would be to include previous churn rescue offers in the predictive churn model. This would

---

[10] The authors benefited from discussions with Wagner Kamakura and Carl Mela (both at Duke University) on this issue.

tell managers whether previous offers enhance or diminish long-term loyalty. Another approach would be to formulate and implement an optimal contact model (Chapter 28). In this model, the current period decision to offer an incentive to a would-be churner would take into account the future impact of that offer.

24.5 Future Research

We have discussed the churn problem, its causes, how predictive models can identify churners and diagnose the reasons they churn, and how companies can manage churn. There are many exciting findings and methods developed to address this topic, but there are several avenues for future research on churn, as follows:

- *Predicting churn*: What are the key variables? Which models work best? How high a lift is feasible and how does it vary by product category?
- *Churn programs*: We need field tests to show that churn management programs can work.
- *Profitability framework*: We need parameter estimates of the framework in Fig. 24.6 so that we can understand the factors that feed into churn program profitability, and how they vary by program and product category.
- *Dynamic optimization*: We need a optimal contact model to decide which customers should be contacted when, on an ongoing basis, to minimize churn. This would take into account the impact of current incentives on future responsiveness, lifetime value, and churn likelihood. This would be a substantial contribution to the literature and to the practice of effective churn management.

Chapter 25
Multichannel Customer Management

Abstract Nowhere is the potential – and challenge – for database marketing more acute than in the "brave new world" of multichannel customer management. Whereas many companies historically interacted with their customers through one channel – the bricks-and-mortar retail store, the bank branch, the company catalog, the financial advisor – today almost all companies are multichannel. This gives rise to several key questions and management issues; for example, "Is the multichannel customer a better customer?" "If so, why?" "Should we encourage our customers to be multichannel?" We have just begun to understand questions such as these, and this chapter reviews what we know and do not know. We discuss the multichannel customer in depth, including the association between multichannel usage and sales volume. We also discuss the factors that influence customers' channel choices, the phenomenon of research shopping and the impact of channel introductions on firm revenues. We present a framework for developing multichannel customer strategies, and conclude with industry examples of multichannel customer management.

One of the most promising applications for database marketing is the management of customers over multiple marketing channels. These channels include the Internet, call centers, sales forces, catalogs, retail stores, and in the near-future, interactive television. Neslin et al. (2006b, p. 96) define multichannel customer management as "the design, deployment, and evaluation of channels to enhance customer value through effective customer acquisition, retention, and development." As Neslin et al. note, marketers have always considered channel management to be a fundamental component of the marketing mix (e.g., Stern and El- Ansary 1972; Webster 1991). However, while traditional channel management has taken the perspective of the firm (Rangaswamy and Van Bruggen 2005), multichannel *customer* management centers on the customer, on the creation of customer value as a means to increase firm value (Payne and Frow 2005; Boulding et al. 2005).

25.1 The Emergence of Multichannel Customer Management

25.1.1 The Push Toward Multichannel

Company adoption of multichannel customer strategies has been driven by company, customer, and competitive forces. Companies have developed enhanced technological capabilities, particularly in data management and the Internet. The Internet has created an entirely new channel; one that naturally links to other channels. For example, customers can research products on the Internet and purchase them in the store (see Sect. 25.2.5).

Customers have rapidly expanded their channel experiences beyond the traditional store or sales call. They are also comfortable with catalogs, the Internet, ATM's, and call centers. They therefore expect companies to have a presence in all these channels.

Lastly is the impact of competition. Driven by company and customer factors, Company A initiates a multichannel strategy, and Company B has to follow suit. Whether this precipitates a Prisoner's Dilemma is a major issue (see Sect. 25.3.3.1).

25.1.2 The Pull of Multichannel

Companies have also been *pulled* toward multichannel management by potential improvements in loyalty, sales growth, and efficiency. Loyalty may benefit from increased satisfaction or higher switching costs. Sales may grow simply because the brand is more available. See Sect. 25.2.2.2 on sales growth and Sect. 25.2.7 on loyalty.

The promise of improved efficiency is driven by the Internet and call centers (see Sect. 25.3.4.1). Both channels are highly automated and may seem antithetical to enhancing customer relationships. However, the choice may not be between personal and automated contact, but rather, between automated or no contact. The customer's *need* for company contact has risen dramatically. Consider the multitude of features that now accompany a cell phone. These stimulate customers to contact the company, to inquire about a feature or determine why it isn't working. The challenge is to develop effective yet low-cost channels for dealing with this skyrocketing demand for service.

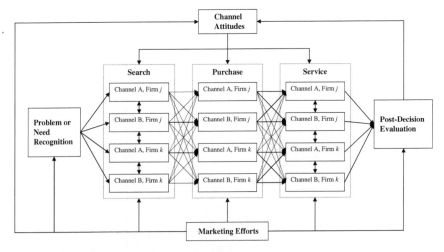

Fig. 25.1 A general model of customer channel choice.

25.2 The Multichannel Customer

25.2.1 A Framework for Studying the Customer's Channel Choice Decision

Figure 25.1 presents a framework for studying the customer channel choice decision. The framework weds the customer's decision process (Engel et al. 1995; Peterson et al. 1997) with the firm's marketing efforts (see also Neslin et al. 2006b). The customer recognizes a need, searches for information for a product that addresses the need, purchases the product, and then seeks after-sales service. Along the way, the customer can access various channels at various companies. The process is guided by the customer's attitudes toward the various channels, by the firms' marketing efforts, and by the outcomes of previous stages in the process. Finally, the customer evaluates the experience and updates his/her attitudes.

For example, stimulated by a Sony advertisement, a customer realizes he/she might want a high-definition television (HDTV). The customer requires information, and accesses Circuit City's and Best Buy's websites. Now the customer can talk intelligently to an expert. The customer decides to visit a store to gather more information, and chooses Best Buy because the store is closest. Now the customer knows what kind of HDTV he or she wants. Having recently seen a Wal-Mart ad claiming brand-name HDTVs at lower prices, the customer goes to Wal-Mart and purchases the product. After purchasing the HDTV, the customer has trouble installing it and goes back to Wal-Mart for help. Finally, the HDTV is successfully installed and the customer evaluates the process. One sees in this example the complexity

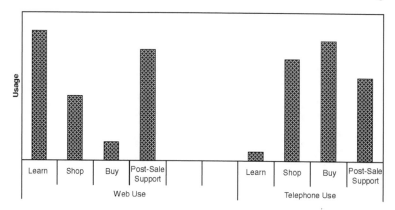

Fig. 25.2 Customer self-reported use of marketing channels (From IOMA 2002).

of the process, the choice between channel and firm, and the dynamics of search ⇒ purchase ⇒ after-sales.

Figure 25.2 compares B2B customer preference for the Internet versus telephone for various stages of the buying process (IOMA 2002). The search stage is divided into "learning" and "shopping." Learning is gathering information about general product attributes. Shopping is specifying exactly what product is wanted at what price. The Internet excels on learning and after-sales; the telephone is preferred for shopping and actual purchase. The figure is clear evidence that customers prefer different channels for different stages of the decision process (see also Verhoef et al. 2007).

25.2.2 Characteristics of Multichannel Customers

25.2.2.1 Demographic and Psychographic Characteristics

Individual difference variables have been shown to describe customers who use multiple rather than single channels. Ansari et al. (2008) found the multichannel shopper to be younger and higher income. Kumar and Venkatesan (2005) found that customer size and annual sales, purchase frequency, tenure as a customer, number of customer-initiated contacts, and the level of cross-buying were positively associated with multichannel usage. In addition, the number of returns had an inverse U-shaped relationship to multichannel usage. These findings show that multichannel shoppers have different personal characteristics than single-channel shoppers.

25.2.2.2 Purchase Volume and Profitability

An emerging generalization in multichannel research is that multichannel shoppers purchase higher volumes (Neslin et al. 2006b). Figure 25.3 shows

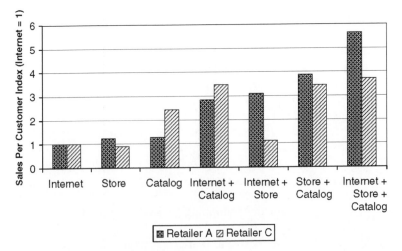

Fig. 25.3 Channel usage and purchase volume (From Retailer A: DoubleClick 2004a; Retailer C: Thomas and Sullivan 2005a).

the evidence for two US retailers. Note, it may not be that every multi-channel combination exceeds every single channel, but the customer who purchases from channels A *and* B purchases more than the customer who purchases only from channel A *or* B. Further evidence on the association between multichannel buying and purchase volume can be found in Kumar and Venkatesan (2005), Myers et al. (2004, p. 1), Kushwaha and Shankar (2005), and Ansari et al. (2008). One interesting exception to this generalization is the work of Campbell and Frei (2006). These authors find that adoption of online banking is associated with higher transaction volume, but a net decrease in revenues, which they conjecture may be due to customers managing their balances more effectively and avoiding various fees.

There are three reasons why the multichannel customer might buy more: (1) loyalty, (2) self-selection, and (3) marketing. Identifying which of these explanations applies is very important because of the implications for whether companies should encourage customers to be multichannel.

The loyalty explanation is that purchasing from multiple channels increases customer service and satisfaction, resulting in higher loyalty to the firm and therefore higher sales volume. Another possibility is that the multichannel customer purchases more products from the company and hence would incur higher switching costs for leaving. If higher loyalty is indeed a natural consequence of multichannel usage, this would favor companies encouraging customers to become multichannel.

The self-selection explanation is that high volume customers have more complex needs and more purchase occasions, so naturally use more channels. Self-selection says that multichannel does not grow the business – it simply allows high-volume customers to purchase from more convenient outlets.

Self-selected multichannel shopping may still increase profits if it decreases costs, e.g., as customers spend more time on the Internet.

The marketing explanation works in three ways: First, multichannel customers may receive more marketing because they are higher volume and hence targeted with more marketing. If this is the case, whether multichannel should be encouraged depends on customer response to marketing. Second, the multichannel customer may be exposed to more marketing *as a consequence* of being multichannel. The customer who only uses the firm's retail store is exposed to in-store merchandising, whereas the customer who uses the firm's store and catalog is also exposed to the advertising value of the catalogs. Third, multichannel is a form of increased distribution and hence makes the company's products more easily available. If increased marketing occurs as a consequence of multichannel shopping or availability, then multichannel shopping should be encouraged.

Ansari et al. (2008) support the marketing explanation. They find that multichannel customers receive more marketing and are more responsive to it. They find that using the Internet is associated with lower, not higher, purchase frequency in the long run. They also find that at the beginning of their data, the customer group that eventually became multichannel was equal in purchase volume to the group that stayed single channel. These results tend to refute the loyalty and self-selection hypotheses. Hitt and Frei (2002), however, support the self-selection hypothesis. They find that while customers who adopt online banking (and presumably are multichannel) acquire new products at a faster rate, the magnitude is only about 10% of the overall difference between online and offline customers (p. 746). The authors conjecture that self-selection therefore plays a large roll in differences between on and offline customers.

A related issue is the relationship between multichannel behavior and customer profitability. Three studies have investigated this.

Venkatesan et al. (2007) use a two-equation model where the first equation regresses current period customer profits versus lagged multichannel purchasing. The second equation regresses the probability of being a multichannel shopper versus lagged multichannel purchasing. Their results are that the coefficient for *lagged* multichannel shopping in the first equation is statistically significant and positive.

Hitt and Frei (2002) and Campbell and Frei (2006) analyze the impact of adoption of online banking services. Hitt and Frei (2002) use cross-sectional analyses to infer that online customers are more profitable than their offline counterparts. Campbell and Frei (2006) analyze per-period data of banking customers over an 18-month period. They find that online customers increase the number of transactions after adoption. These customers substitute online transactions for ATM and automated as well as human call-center transactions, but slightly increase their usage of the bank branch. The net increase in transactions, however, results in increased costs. The authors then find that revenues actually decrease, as reported earlier. The net result is a decrease in profits. However, the authors find that online adoption leads to higher retention rates, so the net result may be higher customer lifetime value.

Clearly more work is needed to sort out why the multichannel shopper is higher volume, and ultimately, whether adoption of new channels yields more profitable customers. There are challenging methodological issues (Sect. 25.2.4.3), and we need to gather more empirical evidence to generalize the initial findings reviewed above.

25.2.3 Determinants of Channel Choice

25.2.3.1 Overview

Much work has been conducted on the determinants of channel choice. Figure 25.4 draws on Neslin et al. (2006b) to list six major determinants: (1) marketing, (2) channel attributes, (3) social influence, (4) channel integration (5) situational factors, and (6) individual differences. We review what is known about these determinants.

25.2.3.2 Individual Differences

As reported by Neslin et al. (2006b), several individual difference variables are associated with channel choice, including age, gender, education, income, family size, and region (Ansari et al. 2008; Gupta et al. 2004b; Inman et al. 2004; Kushwaha and Shankar 2005; Verhoef et al. 2007). Interestingly, Thomas and Sullivan (2005b) find that stage in the customer lifecycle determines channel choice.

Another important individual-difference variable is channel experience. Montoya-Weiss et al. (2003), Inman et al. (2004), and Ansari et al. (2008) find that experience in using a particular channel makes it more likely the customer will use that channel in the future. Whether this is due to mindless inertia or to cognitive learning has not been explored.

Ward (2001) provides a theory for the role of channel experience. He proposes that customers make human capital investments in learning to use particular channels. If the skills gained through these investments "spillover" to other channels, customers can become multichannel users. For example, a skill in using a catalog is the ability to determine the best product without actually touching it. This skill spills over to using the Internet, and as a result, the catalog and Internet become substitutes.

To measure spillover, Ward obtains data on customer purchases, by channel, in several product categories. The author estimates an equation of the customer's propensity to purchase a category in each channel as a function of channel-specific and category-specific dummies. The residuals from these

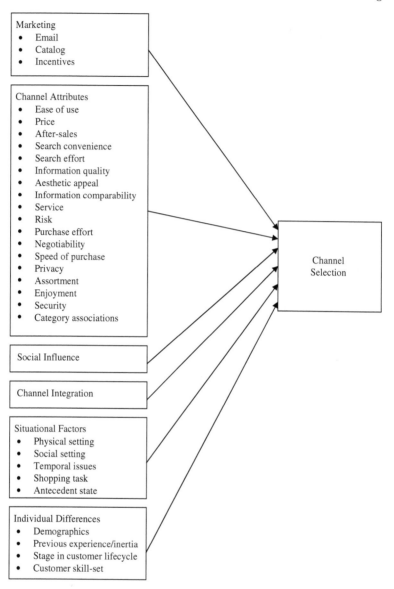

Fig. 25.4 Determinants of customer channel selection (From Neslin et al. 2006b).

regressions represent effects that cause deviations from which channel we would expect the customer to use on average. By correlating these residuals between channels, the author estimates spillover.

The results suggest that the spillover effects are largest between online and direct marketing. The spillover between retail and direct or between retail and online is lower. However, there is somewhat more spillover between retail and direct than retail and online. Overall, Ward's work is quite interesting because it provides theory as to why certain channels might be substitutes for each other.

25.2.3.3 Situational Factors

Neslin et al. (2006b) cite five situational factors suggested by Nicholson et al. (2002): (1) physical setting (e.g., weather), (2) social setting, (3) temporal issues (time of day, urgency of the purchase, (4) task definition (e.g., type of product), and (5) antecedent state (e.g., mood). Neslin et al. note that particular attention has been devoted to task definition, hypothesizing for example that experience goods are more likely to be purchased at a store, while search goods are more likely to be bought on the Internet (Mathwick et al. 2002), and customizable products are more likely to be purchased on the Internet (Mahajan et al. 2002).

25.2.3.4 Channel Integration

Integrated channels make it easy for the customer to choose whichever channel is more convenient under the circumstances. Companies can enhance this effect through incentives and their design of the channels. Neslin et al. (2006b) cite the case where the Internet includes store locators and in-store pick-up that allow the customer to search on the Internet but make the purchase at the store.

   Bendoly et al. (2005) survey customers regarding their perceptions of whether channels were integrated, and their use of the Internet and the retail store. They identify two types of integration – information integration, such as advertising local stores on the Internet, and physical integration, such as purchases made via the Internet being returnable at the store. The authors found these dimensions interacted with perceived product availability. For example, if the product was perceived as available at the store, *and* the store and Internet were perceived as being integrated, the customer was more likely to purchase the product on the Internet. These results suggest that to the extent channels are integrated, they are perceived as equally desirable for purchase. This shows how integrated channels breed multichannel shopping.

25.2.3.5 Social Influence

The theory of reasoned action (e.g., Fishbein and Azjen 1975; Sheppard et al. 1988) suggests that consumers make decisions based not only on their own perceptions of the decision, but their perceptions of whether peers, friends, spouses, etc. perceive the decision is a good one, and whether these others' opinions matter to the decision-maker. Accordingly, one would expect that channel usage would depend on the influence of significant others.

This has been verified. Keen et al. (2004) utilized "Norm" as a factor in a conjoint analysis of channel choice. Norm was defined at two levels ("85% of people important to you have made an online purchase like this," and "5% ..."). The authors found that Norm was an important factor in channel choice, although channel format and price were most important. Verhoef et al. (2007) modeled customers' channel preferences as a function of several attributes, including "Clientele" – the belief that the customer's acquaintances used the channel. The authors found that Clientele particularly influenced customers' choice of the Internet. This makes sense in that the Internet is a new channel and one would expect consumers to model their behavior after peers when they personally have less experience. It also could relate to the "community" concept behind the Internet. Nicholson et al. (2002) found in an ethnographic study that a mother decided to purchase a gift for her child at a store rather than the Internet because the effort in using the store was consistent with the mother's devotion to her child.

25.2.3.6 Channel Attributes

As Fig. 25.4 shows, perceived channel attributes play an important role in channel choice. This follows from the theory of reasoned action. Neslin et al. (2006b) cite several papers that investigate these attributes, including Keen et al. (2004), Nicholson et al. (2002), Burke (2002), Montoya-Weiss et al. (2003), Kacen et al. (2003), Teerling and Huzingh (2005), Jing and Rosenbloom (2005), Thomas and Sullivan (2005b), Ancarani and Shankar (2004), Tang and Xing (2001), Morton et al. (2001), Pan et al. (2002a), Gupta et al. (2004b), Inman et al. (2004), Kushwaha and Shankar (2005), and Verhoef et al. (2007) (see also Teerling 2007). As Fig. 25.4 shows, the list of potential attributes is long and varied.

Figure 25.5, from Verhoef et al. (2007), shows how the Internet, Store, and Catalog are "positioned" in terms of customer perceptions of 15 attributes. The store is strong on lack of risk, service, assortment, and after-sales support. It is also strongly positioned on privacy. The Internet excels on search convenience and information comparison, but lags on service, privacy, after-sales support, and risk. The catalog is similar to the Internet, not as convenient but without the privacy concerns. The privacy result is interesting. The catalog is not anonymous, especially when used for purchase. However, the lack of privacy is transparent. The catalog buyer knows the firm knows who they are; with the Internet, there is no telling who is monitoring one's actions.

Figure 25.6 shows attribute importances inferred by Verhoef et al. by a regression of overall attitude versus attribute perceptions. Attributes differ markedly in their importance and importance differs by channel. Purchase risk, after-sales support, assortment, and enjoyment are important

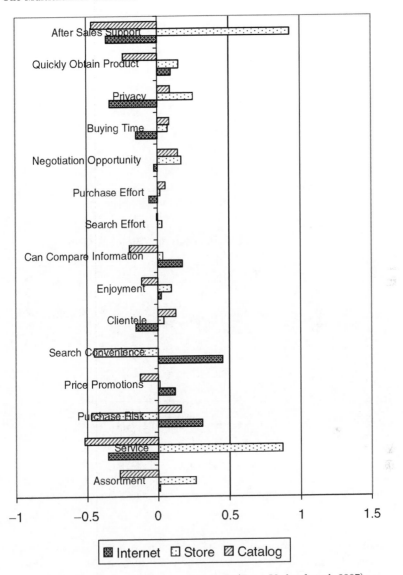

Fig. 25.5 Attribute positioning of channels (From Verhoef et al. 2007).

determinants of attitudes toward using the Internet for purchase, whereas negotiation opportunity and purchase effort are less important. Privacy is an important attribute for using the Internet for purchase, but less so for the catalog and of no concern for the store. The Internet and catalog are more "attribute-driven" than the store. In Verhoef et al.'s sample, customers had uniformly high attitudes toward the store, perhaps due to an experience "halo".

Impact of Attributes on Channel Choice for Search

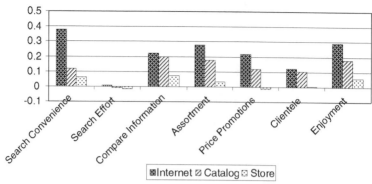

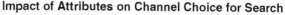

Impact of Attributes on Channel Choice for Purchase

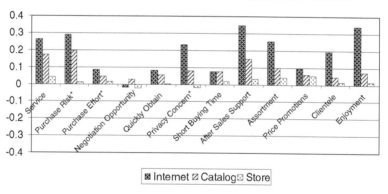

Fig. 25.6 Attribute importances for search and purchase (From Verhoef et al. 2007).
* Signifies that the attribute is reverse-coded. That is, purchase risk has a negative impact on channel choice, as does purchase effort. Privacy concern has a negative impact for Internet and catalog; the impact for store is nominally positive, but was not statistically significant.

In summary, channels are "positioned" much in the way products are. An extension of the Verhoef et al.'s research would be to create a positioning map for each channel, for each decision stage, for each *firm*.

25.2.3.7 Marketing

Recent work has verified that marketing can drive channel choice. Thomas and Sullivan (2005a) found that direct marketing influenced choice of store, catalog, or Internet. They found two segments. For one segment, direct marketing expenditures migrated customers to the Internet at the expense of the store. For the other segment, direct marketing expenditures moved customers to the store rather than the Internet. The main finding is that marketing determines migration, and segments respond differently, even in opposite directions. Ansari et al. (2008) reach the same conclusion.

Venkatesan et al. (2007) studied the time it took customers to adopt new channels, given they had bought earlier from another channel. They found that marketing communications (direct mail and e-mail) had an inverse U-shaped relationship with the timing of new channel adoption. Up to a point, increasing communications would shorten the time till adoption; however, after that threshold, increasing communications would actually lengthen the time till adoption.

Ansari et al. (2008) found that e-mails were strongly associated with choice of the Internet. This makes sense – e-mails and the Internet are basically the same technology, and the availability of a click-through URL in an e-mail would encourage movement to the Internet. This is supported by Knox (2005), who found that newly acquired customers evolve toward online, offline, and multichannel segments. The online segment was highly responsive to e-mails and this appeared to guide them toward the Internet.

In summary, marketing efforts influence channel choice, and the influence is heterogeneous across customers. Ansari et al. (2008), and Knox (2005), have also found that marketing influences purchase incidence. As a result, marketing influences sales volume as well as the channel that produces that volume. Avenues for future work include: (1) Is there a "channel/marketing congruency," whereby marketing and channels link well if they use similar technology (e.g., e-mails and the Internet)? (2) How effective are direct incentives in influencing channel choice? For example, how effective is free shipping in getting customers to buy online? (3) Much more needs to be learned about customer heterogeneity. What types of customers respond to marketing by moving to one channel versus the other?

25.2.4 Models of Customer Channel Migration

Researchers have begun to model the customer channel "migration" process. Migration can be thought of simply as channel choice, but we use it to convey choices over time. This is particularly important to managers who wish to route customers to different channels over time, or learn how to create multichannel customers.

25.2.4.1 Integrating Channel Choice with Purchase Frequency and Order Size

Models developed for consumer scanner data are being adapted to study customer channel migration. Analogous to the brand choice/purchase incidence/purchase quantity (e.g., Bell et al. 1999), we now have channel choice/

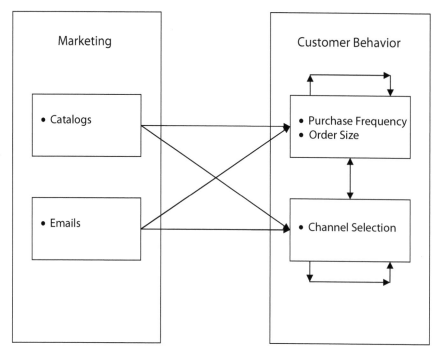

Fig. 25.7 Impact of marketing on channel migration (From Ansari et al. 2008).

purchase frequency/order size. Since data are available typically for a given firm, brand choice cannot be modeled. Purchase frequency therefore entails purchase of the focal firm's products. Order size is the amount spent on the firm's products, given incidence.

The advantages of studying purchase frequency/order size/channel choice holistically are twofold: First, we learn not only the factors that determine migration, but explicitly link that migration to sales volume. Second, some researchers (Keane 1997; Sun et al. 2003) suggest that stand-alone choice models can mis-estimate choice effects: The impact of marketing on choice construed by a stand-alone choice model might also represent the impact on purchase incidence.

Ansari et al. (2008) use the framework depicted in Fig. 25.7. Marketing communications determine customer behavior, in the form of channel selection (choice), purchase frequency, and order size. These behaviors are related contemporaneously and reinforced over time through "experience effects." The authors utilize a type-2 tobit model of purchase frequency and order size, and integrate it with a binary probit model of choice between catalog and Internet. The model is as follows:

$$b_{it} = \begin{cases} Purchase & if\ b_{it}^* > 0 \\ No\ Purchase & Otherwise \end{cases} \qquad (25.1a)$$

$$q_{it} = \begin{cases} e^{q_{it}^*} & if \; b_{it}^* > 0 \\ 0 & otherwise \end{cases} \tag{25.1b}$$

$$w_{it} = \begin{cases} Use \; catalog & if \; w_{it}^* > 0 \; and \; b_{it}^* > 0 \\ Use \; Internet & if \; w_{it}^* \leq 0 \; and \; b_{it}^* > 0 \end{cases} \tag{25.1c}$$

The un-starred variables (b, q, and w) are observations of whether the customer purchases from the firm in period t (b_{it}), if so, how much is spent (q_{it}), and which channel is chosen (w_{it}). The starred variables (b^*, q^*, and w^*), are customers' latent utilities that drive the observed data. These are linear functions of customer characteristics, previous behavior or experience, marketing, and seasonality/trend:

$$b_{it}^* = Customer \; Characteristics_{bi} + Experience_{bit} + Marketing_{bit}$$
$$+ Time \; Effects_{bt} + e_{bit}$$
$$q_{it}^* = Customer \; Characteristics_{qi} + Experience_{qit} + Marketing_{qit}$$
$$+ Time \; Effects_{qt} + e_{qit}$$
$$w_{it}^* = Customer \; Characteristics_{wi} + Experience_{wit} + Marketing_{wit}$$
$$+ Time \; Effects_{wt} + e_{wit} \tag{25.2}$$

Customer characteristics include demographics, etc., that remain constant over time. Experience effects include variables such as expenditures in the previous period, channel choice in the previous period, etc. The authors also include cumulative Web usage – since the Internet was new at the time, they wanted to investigate permanent learning that might occur. Marketing includes catalogs and e-mails, modeled as stock variables and interactions described in Chapter 28. Time effects include seasonality and trend.

The error terms are assumed to follow a multivariate normal distribution, correlated across equations. The correlations are considered during the estimation process, which means that selectivity effects driven by unobserved variables influencing two or more of the three dependent variables are controlled for.

The authors found that catalog choice exhibited strong inertia, i.e., spending a lot of money on a catalog in the previous month increased the likelihood the catalog will be chosen if a purchase were made this month. E-mails were associated with choosing the Internet, although with decreasing returns to scale. Catalogs did not influence catalog choice at low levels, although did so at high levels. The authors found several significant effects in their purchase frequency model, while they find very few significant parameters in the order size equation. This is quite interesting, suggesting that purchase frequency is malleable, whereas order size is stable. Perhaps most importantly, the authors found a negative association between cumulative use of the Internet and purchase incidence, suggesting that Internet purchasing may undermine customer retention.

Knox (2005) developed a similar model to capture purchase frequency, order size, and choice. He used a nested logit to capture incidence and channel choice. The main focus of Knox's work, however, is on modeling the process whereby consumers evolve to form three channel usage segments: Online-oriented, Off-line oriented, and Multichannel. We discuss this in Sect. 25.2.4.2.

While we mentioned that estimating stand-alone choice models may be problematic when variables in the model might also affect purchase incidence, this needs more study and replication before one can say that stand-alone choice models are taboo! An example of a very interesting stand-alone logit model of channel choice is by Thomas and Sullivan (2005a), discussed earlier. These authors model the choice among the bricks-and-mortar store, the catalog, and Internet. The authors include channel-specific effects of all the independent variables and find that marketing can affect the choice of Channel A vs. B differently than it affects the choice of Channel A vs. C. This is an important notion – that marketing can affect various channel migrations differently.

25.2.4.2 Channel Adoption Models

An important issue is the *process* by which customers become loyal to certain channels, or choose to adopt certain channels. Knox models channel adoption as a hidden Markov process. The customer is assumed to be in an (unobserved) segment at any point in time. The possible segments include the initial or "learning" segment, as well as the ultimate online, offline, and multichannel segments. The transition matrix assumed to govern migration between segments is shown in Table 25.1. Knox assumes that offline, online, and multichannel are absorbing states – once customers evolve to one of those segments, they stay there. This of course is debatable, but useful to study the initial evolution of segments. The probabilities of migrating from the learning segment (the P's) depend on marketing (m). This is modeled using a Dirichlet distribution for each marketing instrument combination (received catalog, received e-mail, received both, received neither). This captures heterogeneity in transition likelihood across customers depending on what if any marketing communications are received. Knox finds that customers migrate to one of the three segments, that marketing influences the migration probabilities, and that the multichannel segment accounts for the highest sales volume.

Table 25.1 Tansition matrix governing migration between customer segments (From Knox 2005)

		State (Segment) at time $t+1$			
		Learning	Offline	Online	Multichannel
State (Segment) at time t	Learning	$P_{11}(m)$	$P_{12}(m)$	$P_{13}(m)$	$P_{14}(m)$
	Offline	0	1	0	0
	Online	0	0	1	0
	Multichannel	0	0	0	1

Venkatesan et al. (2007) model the time until the adoption of a second channel, given the customer is initially using one channel, and then the time until the adoption of a third channel, given the customer is using two channels. The authors consider a retailer using a full-priced store, discount-priced store, and the Internet. The authors define t_{ij}, where j equals either 2 or 3, as the time taken to adopt the second or third channel. The authors formulate a hazard model of t_{ij} as follows:

$$h(t_{ij}, X_{ij}^*) = h_0(t_{ij}) \bullet \psi(X_{ij}^*, \beta) \bullet w_i \qquad (25.3)$$

where:

X_{ij}^* = A set of variables including customer characteristics, customer behavior, and marketing variables for customer i, that occur between the adoption of the $j - 1$th and jth channel.

$h(t_{ij}, X_{ij}^*)$ = The instantaneous "hazard" probability that customer i will adopt his or her jth channel at time t_{ij} since the adoption of the $j - 1$th channel ($j = 2, 3$).

$h_0(t_{ij})$ = Baseline hazard rate, i.e., that part of the hazard probability that is influenced only by the passage of time. The authors use a flexible Weibul distribution to capture this influence.

$\psi(X_{ij}^*, \beta)$ = The impact of the X variables on the hazard probability.

w_i = "Shared Frailty" impact on the hazard probability for customer i. This picks up unobserved but stable heterogeneity across customers in their time to adopting the next channel.

The authors find that marketing encourages faster channel adoption, although with decreasing returns. The authors find that cross-buying and purchase frequency shortens the time of channel adoption, presumably because these customers need more channels. Note this supports the self-selection hypothesis (Sect. 25.2.2.2) that high-volume shoppers seek out more channels. The authors find the number of returns especially increases the length of time to adopt the third channel. Once customers are using two channels, they have to be shopping at least at one type of store, so their returns needs are satisfied. Another finding involves the baseline hazard – all else equal, customers adopt their second channel less quickly than their third. This suggests that once the customer learns to adopt a second channel, they have acquired the skill to shift channels (cf. Ward 2001).

25.2.4.3 Challenges in Modeling Customer Channel Migration

There are several challenges in modeling channel migration. Selectivity bias (Chapter 15) can arise regarding the level of marketing received or regarding channel usage. With respect to marketing, Ansari et al. (2008) include e-mails as an independent variable in their channel choice equation. However, there may be unobserved variables, e.g., "Internet orientation," that generate the receipt of e-mails, and these same variables generate channel choice. The result would be a biased estimate of the e-mail $\Rightarrow$ channel choice coefficient. We use Ansari et al. as an example, but this problem could occur in any customer migration model.

With regard to channel usage, customers may select channels due to unobserved factors – e.g., customer involvement with the category – that drive both channel usage and total revenues or profits. An observed relationship between channel usage and profits may be spurious, due not to channel usage but to these unobserved factors.

There are two ways to address selectivity. First is to include all variables that generate marketing contacts or channel usage. For example, companies use RFM variables to target catalogs; if those variables are included in the model, this helps to address selectivity in the form of marketing received. Ansari et al. include several "experience" variables that implicitly measure RFM. A second alternative is statistical. One might specify a formal selection model (Chapter 15; Wooldridge 2002; Maddala 1983) or use instrumental variables or two-stage least squares to purge the endogenous channel selection or marketing variables of their endogeneity.

Ansari et al. (2008), and Knox (2005), control for selectivity in channel usage by allowing the error terms for purchase, order size, and channel selection equations to be correlated and incorporate that in estimation. Including an unobserved heterogeneity intercept does not control for selectivity bias because the term is still unobserved and could be correlated with the receipt of marketing, thus the results would still be biased unless this information is incorporated in the estimation (Chamberlain 1980).

Gönül et al. (2000) address selectivity bias due to marketing, and Campbell and Frei (2006) address selectivity in channel choice, using instrumental variables. They find in both cases that the use of this technique does not change their results. However, these are just two instances and more work is needed.

Other methodological challenges in modeling channel migration include (1) the use of single-equation choice models that do not incorporate purchase incidence (see Sect. 25.2.3.1) and (2) detail in specifying the marketing variables ("catalogs sent" is a very gross measure, given that firms send so many different kinds of catalogs (Ansari et al. 2008). A final challenge is to model the research $\Rightarrow$ purchase $\Rightarrow$ service process. Verhoef et al. (2007) investigate this, but their model is cross-sectional. A dynamic model is needed since the process is temporal.

25.2.5 Research Shopping

Research shopping is the propensity of consumers to gather information (search) on one channel but purchase on another. Kelley (2002) reports roughly half of online shoppers search on the Internet and then purchase "offline." This is particularly common in consumer electronics, computer hardware, toys, books, and automobiles. Figure 25.8 reports a DoubleClick

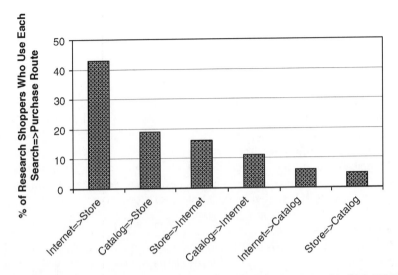

Fig. 25.8 Frequency of various types of research shopping (From DoubleClick 2004b).

(2004b) study documenting the extent of various types of research shopping. The study shows that Internet $\Rightarrow$ Store is the most common form (see Ward and Morganosky 2002, and Farag et al. 2005).

Research shopping has strategic implications because the customer can search at competitors' channels yet buy from Firm A. The probability a customer buys from Firm A is:

$$\text{Prob(BuyA)} = \text{Prob(BuyA|Search A only)} \bullet \text{Prob(Search A only)}$$
$$+\text{Prob(Buy A|Search competitors only)} \bullet \text{Prob(Search competitors only)}$$
$$+\text{Prob(Buy A|Search A and competitors)} \bullet \text{Prob(Search A and competitors)}$$
$$(25.4)$$

The first term represents a loyal customer, i.e., the customer searched for the product at one of Firm A's channels and purchased from Firm A.[1] The last two terms represent customers who bought from Firm A despite searching at other firms. Kelley (2002) shows these quantities differ significantly by retailer. For example, Wal-Mart does a good job of attracting the research shopper, especially in consumer electronics, computer hardware, computer software, and small appliances. In books, Barnes and Noble does the best, whereas Best Buy is best in CD's. Inside 1 to 1 (2003) reports that Coach, Neiman Marcus, and J. Crew are particularly successful with the first term in Equation 25.4, i.e., they are particularly successful of directing their Internet researcher to purchase from their store.

Verhoef et al. (2007) propose three mechanisms that enable research shopping: attribute advantage, channel lock-in, and cross-channel synergy. At-

---

[1] For simplicity, we do not specify channel in Equation 25.4. However, as Fig. 24.1 indicates, the full equation would include terms such as B_{A1}, meaning purchase from retailer A, channel 1, and S_{A2}, meaning search at Retailer A, channel 2.

tribute advantage is the perceived advantage of one channel over another in
terms of attributes related to search or purchase. For example, the Internet
may be superior to the store in "search convenience," but inferior in "service."
This suggests Internet ⇒ Store research shopping. Channel lock-in pertains
to the intrinsic ability of a channel to hold onto its customer. Stores have high
channel lock-in because a sales person courts the customer and the customer
pays a high switching cost to walk out of one store and go to another. The Internet has low lock-in, because there is little to prevent "cart abandonment."
Low lock-in encourages research shopping. Cross-channel synergy pertains to
the benefit searching on Channel A has for purchasing at Channel B. The
catalog may be a good search channel because it gets the customer 90%
through the decision of what product to buy. This sets the customer up to
interact effectively with in-store personnel. Cross-channel synergy encourages
research shopping.

Verhoef et al. measure attribute advantage, channel lock-in, and cross-
channel synergy using a cross-customer model of the research and purchase
channel choice decisions. Table 25.2 summarizes their results. The authors
find that the Internet has an attribute advantage over the store for search,
while the store has an attribute advantage over the Internet for purchase. As
expected, the Internet has low lock in. The authors find a marginally significant cross-channel synergy between searching on the Internet and purchasing
in the store. As a result, attribute advantage, lack of lock-in, and cross-
channel synergy are all at work and Internet ⇒ Store was the most common
form of research shopping they observed, collaborating the DoubleClick study.

The above shows that research shopping is a real phenomenon that can
be managed. Research is needed on exactly how to do this. The phenomenon
needs to be studied at the firm-channel level rather than just the channel level.
In this way the components of Equation 25.4 could be quantified. Finally,
the competitive ramifications of research shopping need to be examined (see
Balasubramanian 1998).

Table 25.2 The determinants of research shopping as applied to various research shopping patterns (Verhoef et al. 2007)

	Determinant of research shopping					
Research shopping pattern	Attribute differences					
Search channel	Purchase channel	Search channel advantage	Purchase channel advantage	Search channel lock-in	Cross-channel synergy	Observed research shopping
Internet	Store	√	√+	Low	Positive	50%
Catalog	Store	No	√+	High	No	34%
Catalog	Internet	No	No	High	Positive	7%
Store	Internet	√	No	High	No	6%
Store	Catalog	√	No	High	Negative	2%
Internet	Catalog	√	No	Low	No	1%

25.2.6 Channel Usage and Customer Loyalty

In Sect. 25.2.2.2 we noted that one possible explanation for multichannel customers being higher volume is that multichannel shopping breeds higher loyalty. Neslin et al. (2006b) report the evidence on this is mixed but leaning positive. Wright (2002, p. 90), in referring to the banking industry, states that new technologies had "loosened the banker–customer relationship." However, Shankar et al. (2003) find that Internet usage is associated with higher loyalty, as do Hitt and Frei (2002) and Campbell and Frei (2006). Danaher et al. (2003) find that Internet usage enhances the loyalty enjoyed by high-share brands. Wallace et al. (2004) find that multichannel usage is associated with enhanced attitudes toward the firm's product. However, as mentioned earlier, Ansari et al. (2008) find that repeated use of the Internet is associated with lower purchase frequency.

Much of the question hinges on the impact of the Internet. The potential problems with the Internet are: (1) Switching costs are low – the mildly dissatisfied customer can easily switch to another website. (2) The Internet is inherently transaction-oriented with little human contact. Ariely et al. (2002) find in a lab experiment that customers who used the Internet but thought they were interacting with a human "on the other side" developed higher loyalty to the website than those who thought they were interacting with a computer-generated recommendation engine.

Managers can take steps to combat both problems. They can increase switching costs by storing important information (e.g., credit card number) so the customer is disadvantaged by switching to another site. Managers can also humanize their website through the use of "shopping advisors" – sales representatives who engage in an "Instant-messenger" type conversation with the online shopper. Perhaps even the use of pictures of people on a website can humanize it. The humanization of the Internet is an important area for future research, because the evidence is mixed as to whether the Internet currently enhances loyalty. Ironically, many of the changes one might propose to enhance the website increase its cost, and for some companies, the attractiveness of the Internet is lower cost.

25.2.7 The Impact of Acquisition Channel on Customer Behavior

The key issues in the use of channels for customer acquisition are cost per acquired customer and quality of acquired customer. Acquisition cost should obviously vary by channel. That the quality of customer acquired would differ is less obvious. It is on this topic that we are beginning to learn more.

Villanueva et al. (2003) use a vector autoregression (VAR) to compare the return on investment for various channels used for customer acquisition.

		Level of Contact	
		Personal	**Broadcast**
Level of Intrusiveness	**High**	Direct Marketing Catalogs E-Mail Telemarketing	Advertising Television Radio Print Online
	Low	Word of Mouth Among Friends From Search Engines	Public Relations Print Articles Online Articles

a

			Level of Contact	
			Personal	**Broadcast**
Level of Intrusiveness	**High**		Direct Marketing	Advertising
		Increased Logins	9.22	30.51
		Acquisition \$/Customer+	\$27	\$323
		Logins/\$	0.34	0.09
	Low		Word of Mouth	Public Relations
		Increased Logins	14.03	16.58
		Acquisition \$/Customer+	*	\$82
		Logins/\$	*	0.20

+ These numbers were obtained by the authors from a third-party source; see Table 4 of Villenueva et al (2003).	* Could not be directly calculated. Breakeven Acquisition Cost is \$149 vs. advertising, \$41 versus direct marketing, and \$69 versus public relations

b

Fig. 25.9 Classification of acquisition channels and ROI per channel (From Villanueva et al. 2003). (a) Classifications (From Villanueva et al. 2003); (b) ROI (From Villanueva et al. 2003)

They classify acquisition channels into the matrix shown in Fig. 25.9a. The two dimensions are level of contact (personal versus mass-market broadcast) and level of intrusiveness (high versus low). The authors use data from a website-hosting company that had asked acquired customers to reveal the channel through which they had been acquired. This yielded a time series of number of acquisitions per channel. The company also kept track of subsequent contribution from each acquired customer, measured as the number of subsequent logins to the website. This is an appropriate measure because it relates to advertising revenue that can be generated by the firm.

The results showed that each acquisition channel contributed differently. Figure 25.9b shows contribution (short-term plus long-term increase in logins), acquisition cost, as well as increased logins per acquisition dollar

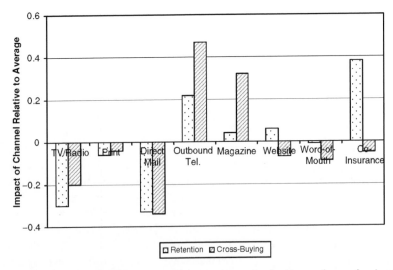

Fig. 25.10 Relationship between acquisition source and retention and cross-buying rate (From Verhoef and Donkers 2005).

(ROI). Broadcast advertising (AD) acquires the most valuable customers, but its cost per acquisition is so high that ROI is the lowest. Conversely, direct marketing (DM) attracts the least valuable customers, but its acquisition cost is so low that its ROI is quite high. Villanueva et al. (2008) expand on these results and find that customers acquired through marketing efforts tend to add more short-term value compared to word-of-mouth, but customers acquired through word-of-mouth add more long-term value.

Verhoef and Donkers (2005) study the impact of acquisition channel on customer quality in the insurance industry. They model retention and cross-buying as a function of acquisition channel as well as several control variables such as customer characteristics. Figure 25.10 displays the logit coefficients for each channel relative to the average coefficient across channels. Retention and cross-buying differ appreciably by acquisition channel, *after* controlling for customer characteristics. Direct Mail and TV/Radio perform poorly on both retention and cross-buying. Outbound telephone is good for both retention and cross-buying. Co-insurance (where customers obtain the insurance through their employer) is very good for retention, but less so for cross-buying. The Internet is a little better on average for retention, and a little below average for cross-selling.

25.2.8 The Impact of Channel Introduction on Firm Performance

As the competition to provide multiple channels heats up, a fundamental question is, what is the impact of adding channels on firm revenues and performance?

Biyalogorsky and Naik (2003) estimate a time series model using data from Tower Records, which had introduced an Internet channel. The authors find that current Web purchases encouraged future Web purchases. They also find the point estimate for cannibalization of store sales was only $0.89 and only marginally significant (t = 1.2). However, store sales were autoregressive – the lagged store sales coefficient was 0.95 in the store sales equation. To illustrate, if we take the point estimate for cannibalization as "true," the total impact of the Internet would be $0.89/(1 − 0.95) = $17.80, suggesting that of the average Web purchase of $32.06, roughly half is taken from current and future store sales. Again, this is just an exploratory calculation since the statistical significance of the cannibalization effect is marginal, but illustrates the importance of short and long-term cannibalization effects.

Deleersnyder et al. (2002) use time series analysis to analyze the performance of British and Dutch newspapers during the time in which they introduced a website version. They analyze both the *level* and *trend* in performance of two measures – circulation and advertising revenue. They find that the introduction of the website had a nominally negative impact on circulation trend for 35 newspapers, but the result was statistically significant in only five instances. The authors found a nominally positive impact of website on circulation trend for 32 newspapers, 10 of which were statistically significant. Results were similar for advertising, as well as for *levels* as opposed to trends. Overall, the predominant effect seems to be that the introduction of a website did not influence newspaper circulation or advertising, although for a minority of cases the effect can be either positive or negative.

Pauwels and Dans (2001) examine the impact of the regular print newspaper on visits to the newspaper website. Newspapers with larger print readership obviously experience greater website visit levels, but also, newspapers whose demographic profile matches that of the Internet-browsing public also experience greater website visits. This reinforces the impact that individual characteristics have on Web usage.

In a time series analysis of 106 firms during 1992–2000, Lee and Grewal (2004) found that early adoption of the Internet as a *communications* channel improved stock market performance as measured by Tobin's q, but adoption as a *sales* channel had no impact. This could due to the market perceiving synergies due to communications but potential inter-channel cannibalization from another sales channel (at least in the early days of the Internet). Consistent with this, Geyskens et al. (2002), in an event analysis of firms in the newspaper industry, found that the stock market reacted positively to Internet introductions on average, especially for firms that did not currently have a strong direct market channel presence.

Coelho et al. (2003) examined 62 UK financial services companies. They find multichannel companies have higher levels of customer acquisition, market share, and sales growth, but lower levels of customer retention, profit, service, and cost control. The retention results are consistent with Ansari et al. (2008).

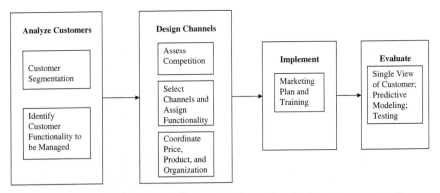

Fig. 25.11 Multichannel design process (drawn heavily form Rangan 1994).

Most recently, Pauwels and Neslin (2007) study the impact of introducing a retail store channel on total company revenues and on revenues from the company's catalog and website. They find that the store channel increases total company sales, mostly through increasing customer purchase frequency. Pauwels and Neslin hypothesized and found that the stores cannibalized the catalog somewhat, but had virtually no impact on website sales.

In summary, we have just begun to learn the impact of channel additions on total firm performance. Most of the work has been on the impact of adding the Internet channel. Obviously more work is needed to flesh out the complete cross-impact matrix showing the impact of adding Channel A on Channel B, C, D, etc.

25.3 Developing Multichannel Strategies

25.3.1 Framework for the Multichannel Design Process

A multichannel customer strategy entails the selection of channels, the assignment of channels to functions and customers, implementation of the strategy, and evaluation. Figure 25.11 proposes a framework for this process, drawing heavily on Rangan (1994).

25.3.2 Analyze Customers

25.3.2.1 Customer Segmentation

The goal is to segment customers with an eye toward possibly serving each segment with different channels. Bases for segmentation include customer profitability and customer channel preferences. Highly profitable customers

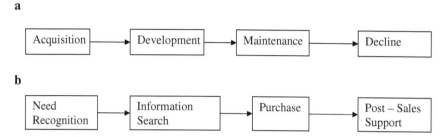

Fig. 25.12 Alternative definitions for customer functionality to be managed. (a) Custome-life-cycle; (b) Custome decision process.

might be given access to personal service channels or routed to more sophisticated call-centers.

Companies can use surveys and then predictive models to measure preferences and "assign" customers to channels. Keen et al. (2004) use the part-worths from a conjoint analysis, followed by a cluster analysis, to derive four segments: "generalists," who care about all issues, "formatters," who have a particular channel preference, "price sensitives," who care about price and find the channel with the lowest price, and "experiencers," who are creatures of habit, selecting the channel they used last. Konus et al. (2007) use survey results to derive three segments: "enthusiastic multi-channel shoppers, unenthusiastic multi-channel shoppers, and store shoppers. Segmentation based on channel preference is therefore feasible, although Knox (2005) suggests these preferences evolve over time.

Note the key issue is not the *current* level of profits or channel preferences, but how the customer will *respond* to using a particular channel – will it enhance customer value? This is where purchase frequency/order size/channel choice models would be useful for segmentation (Sect. 25.2.4).

25.3.2.2 Identifying Customer Functionalities to Be Managed

This stage identifies the functions or customer needs that channels must serve. Figure 25.12 displays two models for identifying these functions (see also Urban 2004, pp. 119–120). Figure 25.12a is based on stage in the customer life-cycle: acquisition, development, maintenance, and decline. Figure 25.13b is based on the customer decision process: need recognition, information search, purchase, and after-sales.

Customer life-cycle and customer decision functionality could be combined. For example, one could primarily define functions as acquisition, development, maintenance, and decline, and then *within* each of these functions, subdivide into search, purchase, and after-sales. Customers in the development stage might be encouraged to use a certain set of channels for search, purchase, and after-sales, while customers in the decline stage might be encouraged to use a different set of channels.

25.3.3 Design Channels

25.3.3.1 Assess Competition

Competitive effects are particularly salient for multichannel design. The mantra of "We must have a Web presence" was spurred by competition. Neslin et al. (2006b) question whether competitive multichannel strategies may just be a form of Prisoner's dilemma, as follows:

		Firm B	
		Single channel	Multiple channel
Firm A	Single channel	$100, $100	$60, $120
	Multiple channel	$120, $60	$80, $80 or $120, $120?

If both firms pursue the single-channel status quo, they each earn $100. If Firm A adds a channel while Firm B stands pat, Firm A earns $120 while Firm B decreases to $60. If Firm B matches Firm A, the result is the lower-right cell. Here there are two crucial possibilities: (1) competition is exacerbated because the firms compete on several fronts. Prices decline but the market does not grow, and both firms are left with lower profits. (2) Multi-channel engenders loyalty, or grows the market (e.g., it is quite possible that opening stores in shopping malls helped grow the market for cell phones). In this case, both firms benefit.

How this competition plays out in the real world is a crucial question. Chu et al. (2007) shed light on it. They study the personal computer market and develop a logit demand model with a no-purchase option. This enables the market to grow depending on prices as well as the channels available. The authors model equilibrium pricing by considering competition among manufacturers as well as downstream pricing of indirect channels, i.e., retailers. The authors use their model to calculate the profits for various channel configurations. They find through policy simulation that Dell, for example, made the correct decision to exit the retail channel in 1994. That is, in equilibrium, they made higher profits by exiting the retail channel.

Chu et al.'s (2007) work is a significant step forward. The work can be expanded in several ways. First would be to incorporate the channel decision as a strategic variable-equilibria could change if the channel decision were made endogenous. Second would be to consider the impact of market segmentation. Third would be to consider channel functionality, either via the customer life-cycle or the customer decision process. These are exciting areas for future work.

Price competition between multichannel (MC) and single channel (PP for "pure play") retailers has received particular attention. Tang and Xing (2001) find that Internet prices are higher for MC than PP DVD retailers, and that price dispersion is lower among PP retailers. Pan et al. (2002a) find that customers perceive MC Internet prices to be higher than PP Internet prices. They develop a Hotelling model and find that a bricks-and-mortar retailer should launch an online presence and charge higher prices, *if* that online store can be superior to pure play online retailers. This may work if the multichannel retailer can use the Internet and the bricks-and-mortar store *in combination* to provide a superior customer experience.

As a follow-up, Pan et al. (2002b) study *actual* prices and find that prices are lower for PP Internet compared to MC Internet for CD's, DVD's, desktop computers, and laptop computers, while they are similar for PDA's and electronics. Interestingly, they found prices are higher for PP Internet for books and software.

Ancarani and Shankar (2004) compare MC Internet, PP Internet, and PP Store prices. They find that PP Store prices are the highest, followed by MC Internet and PP Internet. However, when shipping and handling is figured in, the order is MC Internet > PP Internet > PP Store. This differs from Brynjolfsson and Smith (2000), who find Internet prices net of shipping are generally lower than in bricks-and-mortar stores. They however did not break out the results by pure play versus multichannel.

In summary, it appears that MC Internet prices are greater than PP Internet prices. Perhaps multichannel Internet retailers leverage their bricks-and-mortar store to create monopoly power. Ancarani and Shankar (2004) find two instances – books and software – where MC Internet < PP Internet. Perhaps these pure play Internet retailers have built monopoly power through higher customer loyalty (e.g., Amazon). Indeed, in an important review paper, Pan et al. (2004) find that price dispersion, i.e., differences in prices across retailers, is often higher on the Internet than off-line. This suggests that Internet retailers have been able to differentiate themselves.

25.3.3.2 Select Channels and Assign Functionality

This stage is a mix-and-match process of assigning channels to segments and functionalities. Figure 25.13 suggests three strategies. Figure 25.13a is the "Multi-Contact Strategy." This does not emphasize segmentation or functional assignment – all channels are available to all customers. The question of which channels the firm should use would be dictated by competitive considerations and cost and revenue impact.

Figure 25.13b shows a "Functional Strategy," where customer segmentation is still not considered, but channels are assigned to specific functionalities. A wireless phone company might use outbound telemarketing to stimulate customer awareness of new features. Customers may then be directed to the company's website to learn about the specifics and "design" their optimal phone. Purchase may be made through the Internet or the company's store. Post-sales support would be provided by a company representative reachable through the call center.

Figure 25.13c shows the "Segmentation Strategy." This involves assigning segments to different channels for different functions. For example, Segment 1 may be low value and hence assigned to the Internet for all functions. An e-mail may stimulate need recognition and encourage the customer to click

Need recognition	Information search	Purchase	Post-sales support	
		(a) Multi-contact strategy		
X	X	X	X	Internet
X	X	X	X	Call center
X	X	X	X	Catalog
X	X	X	X	Store
X	X	X	X	Representative
		(b) Functional strategy		
–	X	X	–	Internet
X	–	–	–	Call center
–	–	–	–	Catalog
–	–	X	–	Store
–	–	–	X	Representative
		(c) Segmentation strategy		
Segment 1	Segments 1, 3	Segments 1, 3	Segment 1	Internet
–	–	–	Segment 2	Call center
Segment 2	Segment 2	–	–	Catalog
–	–	Segment 2	–	Store
Segment 3	–	–	Segment 3	Representative

Fig. 25.13 Matching functionality with segments: Three generic strategies.

through to the website, design their optimal telephone, purchase it, and receive after-sales support. Segment 3 might consist of high value customers. They would be contacted by a company representative who would carefully explain the new services. The customers would be invited to seek further information, design their telephone, and purchase it over the Internet, because the visuals provided online make things easier for the customer. The particular website for these customers would include an "instant-messenger" type facility for interacting with a company representative if desired. After the purchase, the same representative would contact the customer for after-sales support.

Zettelmeyer (2000) analyzes competitive equilibria in channel functionality and prices when customers are heterogeneous in their preferences (i.e., there are segments) and online and offline channels can be used for search and/or purchase. He finds that information provision is one way that firms can differentiate. For example, if a medium number of customers prefers the Internet for purchase, firms differentiate themselves in terms of the information they provide as well as price. This is very promising work that supports the segmentation strategy to multichannel design.

The functionality/segment assignment decision lends itself to an optimization. The decision variables would be what channel to assign to what segment for what function. Required of course would be customer response to these assignments. Knox (2005), Thomas and Sullivan (2005a), or Ansari et al. (2008) would be useful in this regard. While optimizing the entire decision might be too ambitious, one could isolate one stage. Villanueva et al. (2003) formulate a model to allocate financial resources to different channels for customer acquisition, as follows:

$$Max_{x_k} \Pi = \sum_k m_k n_k(x_k) - B \qquad (25.5a)$$

$$\text{s.t.} \sum_k x_k \leq B \qquad (25.5b)$$

where:

Π = Profits.
x_k = Dollar expenditures allocated to channel k for customer acquisition.
m_k = Profit contribution per customer acquired through channel k.
n_k = Number of customers acquired through channel k. This is a function of the dollar expenditures allocated to channel k.
B = Acquisition budget.

Profit contribution (m_k) would be available from results such as those shown in Fig. 25.9. The authors propose a particular function for n_k that could be estimated judgmentally, through testing, or through regression models.

25.3.3.3 Channel Coordination

Consider Fig. 25.2, which shows customer preferences for the Internet vs. Telephone. If we use a functional strategy and assign the Internet to be our search channel, the telephone to be our purchase/after-sales channel, *and* provide easy links from the Internet to the telephone (e.g., 800 numbers prominently displayed on the Internet), we have covered the customer decision process and coordinated the two channels.

However, there are many other details to be coordinated among channels, including marketing mix, research shopping, and organization. There is even a question of whether channels *should* be coordinated? Neslin et al. (2006b) list advantages as: (1) economies of scale, (2) ability to assign channels to the functions for which they are efficient and make sense competitively (see Zettelmeyer 2000; Achabal et al. 2005; Sect. 25.3.3.2), (3) Better customer data (Stone et al. 2002), (4) avoidance of channel conflict, (5) improved communications within the firm, (6) stronger customer relationships through better service (Sousa and Voss 2004; Stone et al. 2002; Bendoly et al. 2005), and (7) barriers to entry – an entrant must enter on multiple channels *and* coordinate them. The disadvantages include: (1) loss of flexibility – one cannot opportunistically use a particular channel to solve a problem without re-coordinating all the channels, (2) large investment (see Sect. 25.3.3.1; Sousa and Voss 2004), (3) decreased motivation for non-owned intermediaries who do not see a benefit from channel coordination, and (4) increased skill-requirements for channel mangers.

Assume the firm decides to coordinate its channels. Consider coordination of product assortment. The problem is that carrying the same products in each channel creates channel conflict if some of the channels are non-owned intermediaries. For example, financial services agents (who sell products from several companies) may become less devoted to the firm if the same products are available over the Internet.

One solution, supported by Bergen et al. (1996) is to use "branded variants," where the firm distributes minor variations of its products across channels. This increases customer search costs because customers have to compare more details to decide which product to buy. This creates more monopoly power for each channel. For example, a consumer electronics firm may distribute Model 446G through Best Buy, but Model 446Gb through Wal-Mart. The differences may be minor, but the customer finds it difficult to compare them. Hence, the customer shops only at one channel and focuses on what that channel can offer. Branded variants are a potential way to avoid conflicts between channels. However, there still may be conflicts if various channels vie for the best variants! For example, Wal-Mart may demand that Model 446Gb be the model with extra features, whereas Best Buy would want the model with the extra features.

When channels are owned by the firm, product coordination becomes an issue of targeting. For example, Best-Buy may know that its Internet customers are less quality sensitive and more price sensitive, so may carry a lower tier product line on its website.

Another area of coordination is price. As Neslin et al. (2006b) note, a compelling reason to offer different prices across channels is price discrimination. Lynch and Ariely (2000) and Shankar et al. (2001) suggest that price sensitivity is lower for online customers. Assuming this to be true, prices online should be higher than prices offline. However, the online shopper can learn that the same product can be bought less expensively at the retail store. This has several negative implications. First, the profits from price discrimination are lost. Second, the customer feels cheated and loses trust in the company. Third, more traffic is driven to the store, which is the higher cost channel. Fourth, one solution is branded variants, but this adds costs and confuses customers who expect the Internet and the retail store of the same company to be in sync.

Two ways to charge different prices are price promotions and channel surcharges. The regular price of the same product may be the same at the Internet and the store, but the store can temporarily discount the product. Surcharges are another way to increase prices, particularly on the Internet. For example, the price of the product may be identical on the Web and in the store, but the shipping charges may be significantly higher than needed to cover the marginal shipping cost to the firm. This effectively increases price on the Web (and sets up a strong promotion – free shipping!).

A third area of channel coordination is communications. The argument for coordination is that it reinforces positioning and creates a stronger customer relationship. However, if the firm is using a segmentation strategy (Fig. 25.13c), communications perhaps should differ by channel. For example, the website design might highlight low prices if the target group is price sensitive, while retail store communications should emphasize product quality and service if it is targeting the quality-sensitive customer.

Another aspect of communications is how much to spend on communicating through each channel. Berger et al. (2006) develop an analytical model that differentiates three cases: (1) "separation," where the channels are managed as separate entities, (2) "partial integration," where one channel may be considered a separate entity but the firm may be willing to pay some of its costs, and (3) "full integration," in which the firm manages all its channels collectively to maximize total profits. The authors find that the optimal communications expenditures yield highest profit under the full integration strategy. This is a good argument for holistic management of the firm's channels, at least the channels the firm owns.

An important coordination issue is managing the research shopper so as to prevent the customer from searching on Firm A's website but purchasing at Firm B's store. One way to prevent research shopping is to improve purchase attributes of the Internet or increase Internet channel lock-in (Verhoef et al. 2007). However, the customer may still want to research shop. The key then is to make sure the shopping is at Firm A's store and not Firm B's. Actions Firm A can take include: (1) provide store locators on the Internet, (2) offer a coupon on the Web for purchases at the store, (3) offer free product pickup if the product is ordered on the Web but picked up at the store.

A final channel coordination issue is organizational. One example is when a predictive model is used to identify the best customer prospects, say for an insurance company. The most cost-efficient approach might be to send a direct-mail piece to these customers. However, this bypasses the financial agents, who are always looking for prospects. The solution is to divide the top prospects in half and solicit half of them through direct mail, and provide the other half to the financial agents for their own prospecting efforts. This may be less profitable in the short term, but more profitable in the long term because the financial agents' loyalty to the firm is increased.

Another important organizational issue is whether channels should be managed as independent profit centers or one entity. When the Internet channel emerged, many firms set up separate Internet operations and let Internet channel managers "run their own show." However, this does not necessarily maximize total firm profits (cf. Berger et al. 2006). Firms must achieve a balance so that channel managers have the flexibility to pursue opportunities that other channels aren't ready to pursue, while coordinating efforts so for example channel managers don't fight over the same customers.

25.3.4 Implementation

There are several tasks in implementing a multichannel strategy. One of course is the physical design of the channels – i.e., the website design, the store layout, etc. These details are beyond our scope. However, there are two issues – "right channeling" and employee management – that warrant our attention.

25.3.4.1 Right-Channeling

Right-channeling means making sure that the right customers utilize the right channels. This is a crucial part of implementing a Segmentation strategy (Fig. 25.13 c). Right-channeling might occur naturally if customer segments self-select into the channels they prefer. However, this may not be the most profitable arrangement for the company. Companies can therefore use a variety of incentives (targeted promotions, etc.), dedicated websites or firm agents, etc., to ensure the right customer uses the right channel.

A particular challenge in right-channeling customers is managing call centers. Companies can provide different levels of service within a call center, making the call center a collection of separate channels. The question is which customers should be routed to which center? This has an impact on immediate as well as future profits.

Sun and Li (2005) develop a dynamic optimization model for deciding whether customer inquiries should be directed to an "on-shore" or "off-shore" call center. The off-shore call center is less expensive; the on-shore call center generates higher satisfaction levels. In addition, there are different types of calls – *transactional* questions involve billing, product news, and product services; *technical* questions involve service, software or installation problems.

Sun and Li (2005) model call duration and customer retention. Duration is a function of previous duration, the type of call, and the call center. Retention depends on previous call duration and variables such as promotions that might have been offered to retain the customer. These models are inserted into an optimization that decides which call center customer i should be routed to at time t for call type k in order to maximize long-term profits. The optimization captures trade-offs such as: the customer prefers on-shore call centers, but the customer tends to take a long time when making an inquiry. This suggests the customer be allocated to the off-shore call center. However, if the consumer is averse to off-shore call centers, the customer might churn and the company will lose its monthly subscription fee. In addition, customer-level parameters are not known in advance, so must be learned over time. This is done by estimating the descriptive models using a latent class approach, and re-classifying each customer in one segment or another after each transaction.

The authors find two segments: Customers in Segment 1 are time-sensitive and dislike off-shore call centers. Customers in Segment 2 are less time-sensitive and less averse to off-shore call center. The optimization therefore tends to allocate Segment 2 customers to the off-shore call center. Policy simulations show that the proposed optimization improves both retention and profits, and the degree of improvement increases over time as the model learns which segment the customer is in.

Sun and Li's research is important because it shows that right-channeling can be achieved through predictive modeling coupled with forward looking optimization. It implements the Segmentation Strategy in Fig. 25.13c with respect to after-sales support. While in this situation, the customer was *assigned* to a channel, the model could be expanded to include which channel the customer should be *encouraged* to use, and if so, whether an incentive is needed to get the customer to use the "right channel."

25.3.4.2 Employee Training and Incentives

Employees are key participants in the multichannel strategy. A retailer may want high value customers to use the store and receive special service. Sales personnel need to be trained to recognize a high value customer, and how to service him or her. A catalog company may recognize that its catalog customers who order by phone seek service and conversation, as opposed to its Internet customers, who are more efficiency minded. Accordingly, phone personnel must be trained as sales representatives, not order takers.

Employee incentives can encourage the right employee behavior. For example, rewarding store personnel based on whether the customer cites them at checkout is one technique. The call center representative for the on-shore call center can be rewarded for the brevity of service times, assuming the query is satisfactorily resolved.

25.3.5 Evaluation

25.3.5.1 Single View of the Customer?

Using more channels makes it difficult for the firm to assemble a complete database of the customer's interactions with the company. There are three dimensions to the data picture: (1) channels, (2) stages of the decision process, and (3) competitive information. A true *single view of the customer* would mean the firm knows about the interaction of its customers with all its channels at all stages of the customer decision process, with the firm and with its competitors. Interactions with competitors are extremely difficult to obtain, although recent work by Du et al. (2005) and Kamakura et al. (2003) propose statistical procedures for inferring customer competitive activity.

Given the difficulty in obtaining competitive data, we focus only on decision process and channel. For a three-channel firm, the possible combinations

Table 25.3 Possible data to be assembled by a multichannel firm

Channel	Search	Purchase	Aftersales	S + P	S + A	P + A	S + P + A
			Decision process				
Web (W)	Moderate	Easy	Moderate	Moderate	Moderate	Moderate	Moderate
Store (S)	Difficult	Moderate	Difficult	Difficult	Difficult	Difficult	Difficult
Catalog (C)	Difficult	Easy	Easy	Difficult	Difficult	Easy	Difficult
W + S	Difficult	Moderate	Difficult	Difficult	Difficult	Difficult	Difficult
W + C	Difficult	Easy	Moderate	Difficult	Difficult	Moderate	Difficult
S + C	Difficult	Moderate	Difficult	Difficult	Difficult	Difficult	Difficult
W + S + C	Difficult	Moderate	Difficult	Difficult	Difficult	Difficult	Difficult

of data to be assembled are shown in Table 25.3. The table shows our judgments of how easy it is for firms to assemble each combination. The bottom-right cell signifies a single view of the customer across all channels and all decision stages. It is very difficult to assemble these data. Catalog information is easy to assemble for purchase and after-sales. This is why single-channel catalog companies were the first to apply database marketing. Purchase data are also easy to collect from the Web, because the customer must provide a name and billing address. It is therefore easy to merge these data with the catalog information and create a catalog/Web integrated database of purchase behavior. However, it is not as easy to collect after-sales usage on the Web, because customers may just use the Web for information and not identify themselves. Search behavior is very difficult to obtain for the catalog and store, although a little easier for the Web, since customers may register or have a cookie on their computers if they have previously done business with the firm.

Table 25.3 shows the myriad of information required for a single view of the customer. It is for this reason that a firm might be content to consider single view of the customer as obtaining *purchase* information across all channels. Even this is challenging because store purchase data is moderately difficult to obtain unless the customer is a member of the firm's loyalty program and diligently uses his or her loyalty card.

Illustrating the challenges in implementing a single view of the customer (Yates 2001) found that roughly half of 50 retailers they surveyed had learned "nothing" about cross-channel shoppers. Zornes (2004) reports more recently on these challenges and potential solutions. For example, he finds that many firms use "homegrown" customer data integration (CDI) solutions; more than 68% of IT and business professionals he surveyed were planning to evaluate commercial CDI software.

The question then becomes, how much should the firm invest in acquiring a single view of its customers? Neslin et al. (2006b) present a formal model in which the benefits of the percentage of customers for which it has a single view are a concave function of this percentage, and the costs are convex. The benefits of single view are concave because once the company has a single view for a critical mass of customers, it can use predictive modeling to score the rest of its customers for cross-selling programs, churn management, etc. The costs are convex because the costs of tracking down the customer for every single store purchase become astronomical once the "easy" customers, i.e., those who use a loyalty card, are monitored. The result is that a middle range percentage of customers with single view is optimal. Ridgby and Leidingham (2005) reinforce this conclusion in their discussion of the banking industry.

One important study that suggests CDI may pay off is by Zahay and Griffin (2004). These authors survey 209 B2B executives and measure "CIS Development" – the quality and specificity of information available to the company, as well as how easily that data are shared among executives. The authors do not measure data integration *per se*, but companies that self-report high CIS development probably are more likely to have a single view of its customers. Importantly, the research finds a positive relationship between CIS Development and better performance measures related to customer retention, lifetime value, etc., and in turn, these measures relate positively to business growth. This is the most promising indication we have so far that the quality of the data collected leads to improved performance. Obviously, more work is needed that specifically hones in on the performance impact of data integration across channels.

25.3.5.2 Predictive Modeling Implications

The challenge of predictive modeling in a multichannel environment is articulated nicely by Hansotia and Rukstales (2002). Consider the case of a direct mail offer that asks customers to respond via an 800 telephone number. Response is measured through this single channel. However, the predictive model based on these data may be misleading. First, "non-responders" may have bought on another channel. Second, responders possibly would have bought on another channel even if they had not received the offer. The solution is to: (1) assemble data on customer purchases across all channels. (2) include customers who received as well as did not receive the offer. Only then can the predictive model be used to forecast *incremental* sales per customer.

Consider the case (Hansotia and Rukstales 2002) that a company delivers an offer to a subset of its customers (the "treatment group") but not to a "control group." Assume the company has a single view of its customers. Following is a hypothetical decision tree analysis based on the predictor variable X, split on the value "A."

	Split 1	Split 2
Predictor variable X	$\leq A$	$\geq A$
Treatment group purchase rate	4%	3%
Unadjusted difference in purchase rate due to X	1.0%	
Control group purchase rate	1.5%	1%
Incremental purchase rate for each split	2.5%	2%
Adjusted "Incremental" difference in purchase rate due to X	0.5%	

For X ≤ A, 4% of the treatment group purchased from the company in a given time period, across all channels. This compares to 3% for X ≥ A. The apparent, "unadjusted" increase in purchase rate due to X is 1%. However, a portion of the treatment group customers might have bought without the offer. Consider the control group that did not receive the offer. For X ≤ A, 1.5% of these customers purchased across all channels. That means that only 2.5% (4 − 1.5) of the customers with X ≤ A incrementally purchased as a result of the offer. For X ≥ A, the incremental response was 2.0% (3 − 1). In conclusion, the true incremental difference in purchase rate between X ≤ A and X ≥ A is the adjusted 0.5%, not the unadjusted 1%.

Hansotia and Rukstales (2002) discuss a tree-modeling procedure for analyzing incremental response. This can also be accomplished with a regression model:

$$\text{Response} = \beta_0 + \beta_1 X + \beta_2 D \tag{25.6a}$$

$$\beta_1 = \delta_0 + \delta_1 D \tag{25.6b}$$

$$\Rightarrow \text{Response} = \beta_0 + (\delta_0 + \delta_1 D)X + \beta_2 D$$
$$= \beta_0 + \delta_0 X + \delta_1 DX + \beta_2 D \tag{25.6c}$$

where Response is customer purchases across all channels, X indicates whether the customer received the offer, and D is a set of predictors. The term $\delta_0 + \delta_1 D$ measures the extent to which response to the offer is incremental. The term $\beta_0 + \beta_2 D$ represents baseline sales among customers with demographic profile D. If $\beta_0 = \beta_2 = 0$, baseline sales equal zero, i.e., customers would not have bought had they not received the offer, and we could run a traditional predictive model only among customers who received the offer. However if β_0 or $\beta_2 \neq 0$, Response (among those who receive the offer) $= \beta_0 + \delta_0 + \delta_1 D + \beta_2 D = (\beta_0 + \delta_0) + (\delta_1 + \beta_2)D$. This estimated equation would be used to score customers, but the resultant rank ordering will be inaccurate because it will confuse incremental response (δ_0 and δ_1) and baseline response (β_0 and β_2).

In summary, in a multichannel environment, traditional predictive models may not predict *incremental* response. One needs multichannel data and data that include customers who received and did not receive the offer. This issue can occur in subtle ways even in a single channel company. A catalog company sends out several catalogs, which are essentially different channels. The typical predictive model includes only those who received Catalog A and considers response only to Catalog A. This may not represent incremental sales generated by Catalog A, since customers might have bought from other catalogs even if they had not received Catalog A.

25.4 Industry Examples

25.4.1 Retail "Best Practice" (Crawford 2002)

Crawford (2002) cites Sears and REI as exemplars of successful multichannel retailers. Sears emphasizes a single "face" to the Sears brand in all channels – Web, catalog, or retail store. Sears coordinates its website and store by allowing customers to order on the Web and pick up the product at the store. This is achieved because Sears has an integrated database between the website and store, so when the customer places an order on the Web, the store sees that order. This linkage pays off because 21% of customers who pick up at the store buy additional product in the store. In addition, Sears has reinforced the centrality of their bricks-and-mortar stores by crediting stores with any purchase picked up at the store, even if "purchased" via the catalog or the Web.[2]

REI specializes in outdoor sporting products, positioned around the expertise and enthusiasm of it store representatives. Similar to Sears, this makes the store the central focus of multichannel management, and the goal is to move customers from the catalog or website to the store. REI does this by emphasizing the stores at the website. REI has an easy-to-use store locator and a "stores and events" tab that promotes special store activities. REI thought at first that the website would replace the catalog, but they found that catalog customers resisted changing their shopping habits to frequent the Web. The entire coordination of catalog, Web, and store is facilitated by data integration – REI has a single view of 80% of its individual customers across channels. It uses this information to target marketing efforts such as e-mails.

25.4.2 Waters Corporation (CRM ROI Review 2003)

CRM ROI Review (2003) reports the experiences of the Waters Corporation, a large chemical company in the liquid chromatography business. The privately held company traditionally emphasized customer relationships, a simple task when the direct sales force was the only channel, and reps could develop relationships and collect all the data needed to monitor that relationship. However, as the company began to rely on additional channels, Waters made a significant investment in information technology to achieve the information integration they desired. They purchased the mySAP system (see Urban 2004), which integrated their customer data. In addition,

---

[2] Note there are compensation issues and measurement issues that can ensue because the catalog or Internet may be instrumental in generating the sale, yet they are not "credited" with the sale. Over time, the importance of these channels is less salient and the firm may under-invest in them.

they took the next step to use the data to target marketing efforts more efficiently.

For example, the chemistry group used to implement 15 direct mail campaigns per year targeting 40,000 names, and the HPLC and mass spectrometry groups each implemented 5–6 campaigns targeting 28,000 customers. The first mundane but crucial task was to understand the level of duplication among these separate efforts. Now, the chemistry group mails to 32,000 customers while the HPLC and mass spectrometry groups mail to 25,000 customers, and response rates have risen by 50%. With the savings in marketing budget, the chemistry group implements three additional campaigns per year, yielding an additional $120,000 in revenue.

Data integration is especially important at the acquisition stage. Lead follow-up is more efficient now. No matter how the lead enters the system, the sales rep has access to the data and can follow-up. Service efficiency has improved dramatically because service personnel have complete data on the customer at each service call.

CRM ROI Review (2003) calculates an internal rate of return of 35% on the $5.1 million investment, including benefits of $250,000 from lead follow-up, $3 million in revenue from online sales (net of channel switching), and $750,000 in additional telesales and increased response rates due to better-targeted direct marketing campaigns.

25.4.3 The Pharmaceutical Industry (Boehm 2002)

The pharmaceutical industry has traditionally relied on physicians, retail pharmacies, and managed care organizations to sell its product. It now wishes to add channels such as the Web, mail-order, and call centers. One potential barrier is patients' privacy concerns. While privacy certainly is an issue among many patients, a surprising number of patients support targeted marketing efforts. Boehm (2002) finds that in certain treatment categories (mental health, asthma, gastrointestinal problems), more than 70% of patients would value personalized disease information, more than 50% would share personal information with a drug company to learn more about treatment approaches, and more than 50% do not mind drug marketing as long as it is personalized.

Boehm (2002) emphasizes that the pharmaceutical industry must coordinate its channel efforts across the phases of the patient decision process, including awareness, consideration, physician contact, filling the prescription, and persistence and compliance (loyalty). For example, advertising may be best for generating awareness, while the Web and call centers may work well for facilitating consideration. These channels need to funnel patients to their physicians, where traditional detailing can ensure that the physician is equipped to answer patient questions and prescribe the drug if it suits the patient. Then the Web or e-mail can be used to ensure patient compliance and persistence, i.e., that the patient takes medications as prescribed, and fills prescriptions when they run out. This is an example of a Functional channel strategy (Fig. 25.13b).

25.4.4 Circuit City (Smith 2006; Wolf 2006)

Circuit City faces a highly competitive business in retail consumer electronics. However, they recently have improved results dramatically through upgrades in their retail stores and Internet channel, and coordination between the two. In the words of Phil Schoonover, chairman of Circuit City Stores, "Our multichannel marketing efforts drove improved traffic trends in all channels, and we saw an increase in Web-originated sales picked up in our stores." Indeed, not only were online sales up 85% during the first quarter of 2006 versus a year ago, but more than half of all items ordered online were picked up at the store. This of course enabled the customer to obtain the product immediately, and allowed Circuit City staff to cross-sell as appropriate. In fact, a major part of the multichannel strategy was increasing training for store personnel.

25.4.5 Summary

The above industry examples illustrate the importance of channel coordination. Sears, REI and Waters integrate data across channels. This seems to pay off in two ways. First is through better targeted marketing campaigns (Waters). Second is through the ability to offer better services (Sears and REI) such as store pick-up of items ordered on the Web.

In addition, we see in the Circuit City case that right-channeling allows the firm to retain research shoppers. Right-channeling was achieved by encouraging store pick-up of Web orders. This case involves a Functional channel strategy with segmentation occurring on a self-selection basis (e.g., half of Circuit City's Web orders were not picked up at the store). The pharmaceutical industry would like to move in this direction, and there appear to be promising opportunities despite concerns about privacy and the highly traditional ways of doing business in that industry.

Chapter 26
Acquisition and Retention Management

Abstract While customer acquisition and retention programs are important in their own right, the firm needs to manage acquisition and retention in a coordinated fashion. This chapter addresses how companies should allocate their efforts to acquisition and retention. We discuss the models that are relevant to this task, and then optimize several of them to demonstrate their value and gain insights on when the company should allocate more resources to either acquisition or retention. We show for example that the adage, "It's cheaper to retain than acquire a customer, so we should spend more on acquisition," needs to be sharpened considerably before it can be used to guide acquisition and retention spending. We conclude by introducing the "Customer Management Marketing Budget," a tool for planning acquisition and retention expenditures over time.

26.1 Introduction

Customer acquisition and retention are the means by which a company manages the size and profitability of its customer base. This chapter is about coordinating these two efforts. We examine the following questions:

- How can we model the roles of acquisition and retention expenditures in developing the size and profitability of the customer base?
- How can the firm decide how much to spend on acquisition or retention?
- Under what conditions is it better to emphasize acquisition versus retention?
- How can firms organize acquisition and retention spending in a planning budget?
- How can firms develop an overall strategy for acquisition and retention?

It seems that acquisition and retention go in and out of "vogue" in terms of popularity. During the 90's, with the advent of new consumer services such as the Internet and cellular telephones, as well as deregulation of industries such as financial services, the emphasis was on acquisition. Later, as these industries matured and mantras such as "it costs less to retain than to acquire a customer" prevailed, retention became crucial. AOL presents a good example. During the 1990s, the firm focused almost solely on customer acquisition, blanketing the USA with computer CD disks that promoted customer trial. Then, as AOL saw its total customer base drop from 23.4 million in June 2004 to 20.8 million in June 2005 (Cohen et al. 2005), and faced a maturing market, it focused on customer retention (Bold 2003). As another example, Citibank decided to "cut top acquisition job in retention refocus" (*Marketing* 2003). On the other hand, in a survey of business-to-business managers 28.4% reported that customer acquisition would be their primary goal for 2005; only 7.7% named customer retention (Maddox and Krol 2004).

In short, companies are facing real, difficult decisions regarding acquisition and retention, and this is the focus of this chapter. Our emphasis is on allocation – how much money should be invested in acquisition and retention – rather than the tactics of how to efficiently acquire customers or retain them. These specifics are covered in earlier chapters on customer acquisition, churn, and multichannel management.

26.2 Modeling Acquisition and Retention

26.2.1 The Blattberg and Deighton (1996) Model

Blattberg and Deighton (1996) presented the seminal treatment of acquisition and retention by (1) articulating the objective function as "customer equity," and (2) showing how customer equity could be modeled. By customer equity, Blattberg and Deighton mean the profit generated through the firm's acquisition and retention efforts. While lifetime value of the customer (LTV) is the profit of the customer once acquired, customer equity combines acquisition and subsequent LTV. Blattberg and Deighton consider the case of a firm investing \$A in acquiring customers at some point in time, and the long-term pay-out of that investment. Their fundamental equation can be stated as[1]:

$$\Pi = a\,(M - R)\left(\frac{1+d}{1+d-r}\right) - A \tag{26.1}$$

where:

Π = Profit per prospect.
a = The fraction of prospects that is acquired.

---

[1] This equation differs from Blattberg and Deighton (1996, p. 142) due to the assumed timing of when retention expenditures are made and have their effect. We assume that firms acquire customers in a given year and spend \$R per customer during that year to

M = The profit contribution per year per acquired customer (assumed constant over time).

r = The fraction of acquired customers that is retained each year.

R = Expenditures per year per customer on customer retention.

A = Expenditures per prospect on customer acquisition.

d = Annual discount rate.

The above formulation assumes a simple retention LTV model with constant retention rate (Chapter 5), and customers contribute $M-R$ per year. It therefore can be written as:

$$\Pi = aLTV - A \tag{26.2}$$

Equation 26.1 and the simplified Equation 26.2 captured for the first time the coordination of acquisition and retention. Profits will be high to the extent that the firm is able to convert a high percentage of its prospects (a) into high-value customers (LTV) at low cost (A).

Acquisition and retention expenditures $(A\&R)$ are the firm's decision variables, and acquisition rate, retention rate, and customer contribution $(a, r,$ and $M)$ are the key outcome variables. Blattberg and Deighton modeled acquisition rate as follows:

$$a = c_a\left(1 - e^{-k_a A}\right) \tag{26.3}$$

where

c_a = The acquisition ceiling, i.e., the percentage of prospects that could be acquired with an infinitely high acquisition budget.

k_a = Acquisition efficiency, i.e., how fast the acquisition rate approaches the ceiling as the firm increases its acquisition expenditures.

Figure 26.1 shows acquisition response curves for various parameter values. The model assumes customers do not naturally start buying from the company, e.g., through word-of-mouth. Therefore, we see that with $0 spent on acquisition, no customers are acquired. It would be easy to add a constant term to Equation 26.3 to represent this baseline acquisition rate. However, the zero-zero assumption seems realistic for most situations. The other important assumption is decreasing returns to scale – the gains from additional expenditures get smaller and smaller as more money is spent.

---

retain them. The total contribution from an acquired customer is therefore $(M - R) + (M-R)\times(r/(1+d))+(M-R)\times(r/(1+d))^2+\ldots = (M-R)\times(1+d)/(1+d-r))$. Blattberg and Deighton assume the money to retain customers acquired in Period 1 is spent in Period 2, so have R/r in their equation to "discount" retention expenditures back one period. That is, if there are 1,000 customers in Period 1 and a 70% retention rate, there are 700 in period 2. The firm spends $R \times (700/r)$ on retention in period 2, so R/r per customer *retained* in period 2. We find our formulation a bit more straightforward, e.g., a company acquires 1,000 customers during Year 1 and spends $R per customer during that year (on service, renewal forms, etc.), to retain the customer for Year 2.

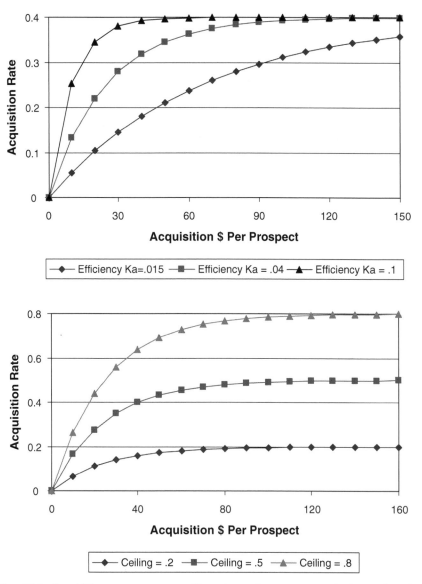

Fig. 26.1 Acquisition response curves: Percentage of prospects acquired as a function of expenditures per prospect using Blattberg and Deighton (1996) model. (a) Different efficiency coefficients (k_a) assuming $c_a = 0.4$; (b) Different ceiling coefficients (c_a) assuming $k_a = 0.04$.

Pfeifer (2005) provides some important insights on the model's implication for *average acquisition costs* and *marginal acquisition costs*. Average acquisition cost answers the following question: Given the firm has spent $\$A$ on acquisition and acquires $a\%$ of its prospects, what is its average cost per acquired customer? The answer is simply A/a. Average acquisition cost is easy to calculate – without any model – simply by dividing total acquisition expenditures by the number of acquired customers. On the other hand, marginal acquisition cost answers the following question: Given the firms is spending $\$A$ and acquires $a\%$ of its prospects, what would be the cost of acquiring an additional prospect?

Average and marginal acquisition costs are profoundly different in the information they convey. Average acquisition cost summarizes what it currently costs to acquire customers. Marginal acquisition cost tells what it would cost to add *more* customers. We draw on Pfeifer (2005) to derive expressions for average and marginal acquisition cost. Pfeifer solves the acquisition response curve for expenditure A as a function of acquisition rate a:

$$\text{Number of Customers Acquired} = A = -\frac{1}{k_a} \ln\left(\frac{(c_a - a)}{c_a}\right) \qquad (26.4)$$

from which it follows:

$$\text{Average Acquisition Cost} = \frac{A}{a} = -\frac{1}{ak_a} \ln\left(\frac{(c_a - a)}{c_a}\right) \qquad (26.5)$$

$$\text{Marginal Acquisition Cost} = \frac{\partial A}{\partial a} = \frac{1}{k_a(c_a - a)} \qquad (26.6)$$

The equations imply three things. First, both costs sensibly decrease if acquisition is more efficient (higher k_a). Second, both costs decrease if the ceiling is higher (higher c_a). For average costs, this follows because a higher ceiling means more customers are acquired for a given expenditure. For marginal costs, Fig. 26.1b shows that with a higher ceiling, the slope of the curve is less positive for a given acquisition expenditure.

Third, higher acquisition expenditures imply higher average as well as higher marginal costs. This is a consequence of decreasing returns. Figure 26.2 captures the relationship. On the x-axis is the amount spent per prospect. On the y-axis are average acquisition cost, marginal acquisition cost, and the acquisition rate. Note that marginal costs increase quite rapidly at high expenditure levels. This is because at high expenditure levels, the acquisition rate curve is almost at its ceiling. Additional expenditures bring only minor increases in acquisition rate, so the cost of bringing in another "marginal" customer becomes very expensive.

The Blattberg and Deighton model includes a retention response function analogous to the acquisition function. Accordingly, we have, as derived by Pfeifer:

$$\text{Retention Rate} = r = c_r(1 - e^{-k_r R}) \qquad (26.7)$$

$$\text{Average Retention Cost} = \frac{R}{r} = -\frac{1}{rk_r} \ln\left(\frac{(c_r - r)}{c_r}\right) \qquad (26.8)$$

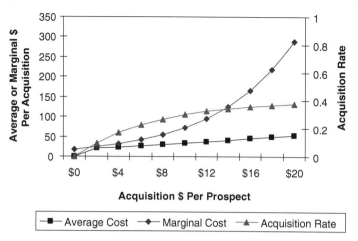

Fig. 26.2 Average and marginal acquisition costs using Blattberg and Deighton (1996) model.

$$\text{Marginal Retention Cost} = \frac{\partial R}{\partial r} = \frac{1}{k_r(c_r - r)} \qquad (26.9)$$

Equation 26.7 means that if we spend R per customer in Year 1, we retain $r\%$ of them in Year 2. Therefore, our average retention cost per Year 1 customer is simply $R = -\frac{1}{k_r} ln(\frac{(c_r - r)}{c_r})$. Average cost per *retained* customer is given by Equation 26.8.

Figure 26.3 graphs retention response functions and Fig. 26.4 graphs average and marginal cost curves. Note similar to the case of acquisition, the

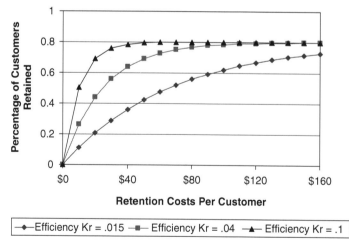

Fig. 26.3 Retention response curve: Percentage of customers retained as function of expenditures per customer using the Blattberg and Deighton (1996) model.

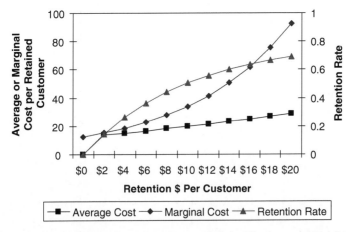

Fig. 26.4 Average and marginal retention costs using the Blattberg and Deighton (1996) model.

model assumes that if nothing is spent on retention, the retention rate would be zero. This might not hold in practice. For example, a cable provider might spend virtually zero on customer retention yet have very high retention rates because of the absence of strong competition.

Blattberg et al. (2001) extend the basic Blattberg/Deighton model in three important ways. First, they stipulate different segments with different acquisition rates, retention rates, and contributions. Second, they do not rely on the simple retention model, which is assumed in Equation 26.1. Third they distinguish between retention expenses and "add-on" selling, which includes up-selling and cross-selling. The resulting equation for the long-term profitability of acquisition efforts made in period t is:

$$\Pi_t = \sum_{i=1}^{I} \left[N_{it} a_{it} (S_{it} - C_{it}) - N_{it} A_{it} + \sum_{k=1}^{\infty} N_{it} a_{it} \left(\prod_{j=1}^{k} r_{i,t+j} \right) \right.$$
$$\left. \times \; (S_{i,t+k} - C_{i,t+k} - R_{i,t+k} - R_{i,t+k}^{ao}) \left(\frac{1}{1+d} \right)^{k} \right] \qquad (26.10)$$

where:

N_{it} = Number of prospects in segment i available in period t.
a_{it} = Acquisition rate of prospects from segment i in period t.
S_{it} = Sales per customer in segment i in period t.
C_{it} = Costs of goods sold per customer in segment i in period t.
A_{it} = Acquisition costs per prospect in segment i in period t.
$r_{i,t+j}$ = Retention rate, i.e., the percentage of segment i customers who are customers in period $t + j - 1$ who will still be customers in period $t + j$.
R_{it} = Retention costs per customer in period t for customers in segment i.

R_{it}^{ao} = Add-on selling costs per customer in period t for customers in segment i.

d = Discount factor.

Blattberg et al. (2001) discuss different ways to make the acquisition, retention, and add-on selling efforts more productive (i.e., higher ceiling and efficiency coefficients in terms of the Blattberg/Deighton model).

26.2.2 Cohort Models

At any point in time, the customer base consists of customers acquired at various times in the past, i.e., different cohorts. Equations 26.1 or 26.10 could form the basis for such a cohort model, since they model the cohort acquired in period t. Gupta et al. (2004a) develop their own cohort-specific model[2]:

$$LTV_k = \frac{n_k}{(1+\delta)^k} \sum_{t=k}^{\infty} m_{t-k} \frac{r^{t-k}}{(1+\delta)^{t-k}} - \frac{n_k c_k}{(1+\delta)^k} \qquad (26.11)$$

where:

LTV_k = Lifetime value of cohort k, the customers who will be acquired k periods in the future. k is numbered from 0 to ∞.

n_k = The initial number of customers in cohort k.

m_{t-k} = The profit contribution of cohort k in period t. Note that for a given k, t goes from k to ∞, so $t - k$ goes from 0 to ∞.

r^{t-k} = Percentage of cohort k that is still a customer in period t. Note this is based on the simple retention model.

c_k = Average acquisition costs per customer in cohort k.

δ = Discount factor.

The model does not include a specific term for retention spending. This however could be easily added – the profit contribution term m_{t-k} could be expressed as $(m_{t-k} - R_{t-k})$. One would also require a retention response model $r = \mathrm{f}(R)$. We will optimize a similar model in Sect. 26.3.4.

26.2.3 Type II Tobit Models

Thomas (2001) introduced Type II Tobit models to modeling acquisition and retention, consisting of a "selection" equation governing whether the

---

[2] See Chapter 7 for a discussion of the application of this model to customer base valuation.

customer is acquired, and a "regression" equation for lifetime duration. Her acquisition model is:

$$z_i^* = \alpha_s' v_i + \mu_{is} \tag{26.12a}$$

$$\begin{cases} z_i = 1 & \text{if } z_i^* > 0 \\ z_i = 0 & \text{if } z_i^* \leq 0 \end{cases} \tag{26.12b}$$

The term z_i denotes whether or not prospect i is acquired. This depends on the value of the "latent" variable z_i^*. Equations 26.12a–b define a probit model of whether or not a prospect will be acquired. The independent variables v_i include prospect characteristics and firm's marketing efforts. Thomas allows the response parameters α_s to vary by customer segment.

The customer's lifetime duration is modeled as:

$$y_i^* = \beta_s' x_i + \varepsilon_{is} \tag{26.13a}$$

$$\begin{cases} y_i = c_i & \text{if } y_i^* \geq c_i \\ y_i = y_i^* & \text{if } y_i^* < c_i \end{cases} \tag{26.13b}$$

Customer lifetime, y_i, is observed only if the customer is acquired. Equation 26.13b accounts for data censoring, that is, several customers are still customers when the data collection period ends (c_i periods after the customer is acquired). The x_i's in Equation 26.13a include customer characteristics and retention efforts expended after the customer has been acquired. Note that response to these variables depends on the market segment s, so β_s is subscripted by s.

The final piece is the behavior of the error terms in Equations 26.12a and 26.13a. These are assumed to follow a bivariate normal distribution:

$$\{\varepsilon_{is}, \mu_{is}\} \sim BVN\{\bar{0}, \Sigma\} \tag{26.14a}$$

$$\Sigma = \begin{Bmatrix} \sigma_{\varepsilon s}^2 & \rho_s \\ \rho_s & 1 \end{Bmatrix} \tag{26.14b}$$

The non-zero correlation between acquisition and retention error terms allows unobserved variables determining acquisition and duration to be correlated. For example, a variable such as customer preference would not be measured, but would drive both acquisition and retention.

Because of the correlation between the error terms, it is necessary to estimate the model jointly (Wooldridge 2002). This is analogous to the need to estimate recursive regression models jointly if their error terms are correlated. In summary, Thomas' model captures the following key phenomena:

- Different drivers (v_i and x_i) govern acquisition and retention.
- There are segments of customers; each responds differently to the various drivers.

- Data for customer lifetime duration may be right-censored because many customers may still be customers at the end of the data collection period.
- Acquisition and retention are linked in two ways: First, the same drivers may govern these processes, albeit with different effect (α_s and β_s may differ for the same variable), and second, unobserved variables may be correlated between equations.

Thomas (2001) applied her model to a sample of 2,300 customers who were members of a service organization serving airplane pilots. Customers must renew their membership each year, and Thomas uses the acquisition equation to describe whether or not the customer renews. Thomas used several variables to describe the renewal (acquisition) process and the lifetime process (how long the customer remained a customer). These include customer characteristics (level of pilot certificate earned by the pilot), and marketing variables (purchase of fee-based products offered by the organization; free products and services used, such as credit card; and free premiums and rewards received by the members).

Thomas found two segments and that different variables drove acquisition and lifetime of each segment. Segment 1 was responsive to credit cards, premiums, and legal advice in sustaining their lifetime, whereas Segment 2 was only responsive to premiums. Customer renewal was influenced by type of pilot certificate, with commercially-licensed pilots more likely to be renewed in Segment 1. Thomas then used her model to evaluate the financial impact of various marketing tactics used by the organization, using the marketing variables v and x in Equations 26.12 and 26.13. She found that special services and add-on selling had a positive impact on profits, whereas rewards had a negative impact.

Thomas' (2001) model was extended by Reinartz et al. (2005) who added a profit equation. Their model can be expressed as:

Acquisition:

$$z_i^* = \alpha_s' v_i + \mu_{is} \tag{26.15a}$$

$$\begin{cases} z_i = 1 & \text{if } z_i^* > 0 \\ z_i = 0 & \text{if } z_i^* \le 0 \end{cases} \tag{26.15b}$$

Lifetime:

$$y_{Di} = \begin{cases} \beta_{Ds}' x_{Di} + \varepsilon_{Dis} & \text{if } z_i = 1 \\ 0 & \text{otherwise} \end{cases} \tag{26.16}$$

Profitability:

$$y_{Li} = \begin{cases} \beta_{Ls}' x_{Li} + \gamma_s' y_{Di} + \varepsilon_{Lis} & \text{if } z_i = 1 \\ 0 & \text{otherwise} \end{cases} \tag{26.17}$$

Error Terms:

$$\{\varepsilon_{Lis}\varepsilon_{Dis}\mu_{is}\} \sim IID\ MVN\ \{0, \Sigma\}$$

$$\Sigma = \left\{ \begin{array}{ccc} \sigma_L^2 & \rho_{LD} & \rho_{LA} \\ \rho_{LD} & \sigma_D^2 & \rho_{DA} \\ \rho_{LA} & \rho_{DA} & 1 \end{array} \right\} \tag{26.18}$$

Equations 26.15 and 26.16, capturing acquisition and lifetime, are a standard Type II Tobit (Wooldridge 2002). Equation 26.17 is the key addition, representing customer profitability. Note that customer lifetime duration is used as a driver of customer profitability. The profitability equation, along with the selection and lifetime equations, also have their own drivers (x_L, v, and x_D). Since the application is to a non-contractural setting, there is no formal way to know whether the relationship is still active. However, the authors used an approach proposed by Allenby et al. (1999), which computes the expected time until the next purchase. If that time exceeds the actual time elapsed, the customer is still considered active. If a purchase has not occurred by the expected time, the relationship is considered to have terminated at the last purchase.

Reinartz et al. (2005) apply the model to a "large, multinational, B-to-B high-tech manufacturer." Data were available for 12,024 prospects, and of those, 2,908 were acquired. The independent variables included the type and number of contacts made through face-to-face sales calls, telephone, e-mail, and Internet. These variables applied both to prospecting (Equation 26.15) and the two customer performance equations (26.16 and 26.17). In addition, the authors considered the total amount of dollars spent on acquisition and retention for each customer. These variables could be computed for a given set of contacts, although the same acquisition and retention dollars could map to a different profile of contacts. It was for this reason that both variables are included in the same model equations. The authors also had measures of customer-initiated contacts, the degree of cross-buying, transaction frequency, and customer share-of-wallet. Finally, the authors considered variables characterizing the customer's firm, such as industry type, annual sales revenue, and size of the firm.

The authors estimated their model and found several results:

- *Acquisition dollars increase acquisition rate (Equation 26.15) with decreasing returns* (a linear term had a positive sign while a quadratic term had a negative sign). This supports the Blattberg and Deighton model.
- *Retention dollars increase customer duration (Equation 26.16) with decreasing returns* (a linear term had a positive sign while a quadratic term had a negative sign). This also supports the Blattberg and Deighton model.
- *Acquisition and retention dollars increase customer profitability (Equation 26.17), again at decreasing rates.* Note this is apart from

their effect on acquisition and lifetime. This is a very interesting result, suggesting that spending more money to acquire and retain customers has an impact on profits beyond the mere act of acquiring and retaining them. This might occur through larger expenditure levels and greater propensity to cross-buy.

- *All contacts (face-to-face, telephone, e-mail, and Internet) had positive impact on acquisition, lifetime duration, and profits.* This is as expected. In addition, there were some positive interactions between contacts. For example, there was positive synergy between e-mail and telephone as well as face-to-face contacts.

- *Cross-buying enhances customer duration.* The more products the customer buys from the firm, the longer the customer stays with the firm. This is an important confirmation of the role of cross-selling in enhancing lifetime (see Chapters 21, 29).

The Reinartz et al. (2005) model is an important extension of Thomas (2001) because it links acquisition, retention (in the form of lifetime duration), and profits. It suggests several rich extensions. First is the method of handling duration in a non-contractual setting. The authors follow a methodology by Allenby et al. (1999), but further research would be useful. Second, the authors include both acquisition /retention dollars and contact strategy in the same equation, even though acquisition/retention dollars follow by definition from the contact strategy. Econometrically, this should have induced perfect collinearity because the acquisition or retention dollars would be linear combinations of the contact variables. But evidently this was not a problem, perhaps because not all acquisition and retention dollars were accounted for. Third, the authors measure the impact of duration on profitability, but another approach would be to model duration and expenditures separately and then combine them to obtain lifetime value. Finally, the model does not trace out the dynamics by which expenditures and purchases occur over time. This might be useful for period-by-period optimization for acquisition and retention.

One model that might address the last two issues would be as follows:

Acquisition:

$$z_i^* = \beta' x_{ai} + \mu_i \tag{26.19a}$$

$$z_i = \begin{cases} 1 & if \ z_i^* \geq 0 \\ 0 & if \ z_i^* < 0 \end{cases} \tag{26.19b}$$

Purchase Incidence:

$$w_{it}^* = \gamma' x_{pit} + \varepsilon_i + \eta_{it} \tag{26.20a}$$

$$w_{it} = \begin{cases} 1 & if \ w_{it}^* \geq 0 \ and \ z_i^* \geq 0 \\ 0 & otherwise \end{cases} \tag{26.20b}$$

Expenditure:

$$y_{it}^* = \delta' x_{eit} + \omega_i + \kappa_{it} \tag{26.21a}$$

$$y_{it} = \begin{cases} y_{it}^* & if \ w_{it} = 1 \\ 0 & otherwise \end{cases} \tag{26.21b}$$

Error Structure:

$$\{\mu_i \ \varepsilon_i \ \omega_i\} \sim IID \ MVN \ \{0, \Sigma\}$$

$$\Sigma = \begin{Bmatrix} \sigma_a^2 & \rho_{ap} & \rho_{ae} \\ \rho_{ap} & \sigma_p^2 & \rho_{pe} \\ \rho_{ae} & \rho_{oe} & 1 \end{Bmatrix} \tag{26.22a}$$

$$\{\eta_{it} \ \kappa_{it}\} \sim IID \ BVN \ \{0, \Sigma_T\}$$

$$\Sigma_T = \begin{Bmatrix} \sigma_{Tp}^2 & \rho_{Tpe} \\ \rho_{Tpe} & \sigma_{Te}^2 \end{Bmatrix} \tag{26.22b}$$

The lifetime value of the customer could be written as:

$$LTV = \sum_{t=1}^{\infty} \frac{w_{it} y_{it}}{(1+d)^{t-1}} \tag{26.23}$$

Equation 26.19 could be used to calculate whether the customer is acquired. This could be used to compute customer equity $aLTV - A$. Finally, retention costs could be explicitly included and either LTV or customer equity could be optimized over time. This just sketches the approach; obviously there is a need to develop and test this model. Its potential is to provide (1) estimates of the drivers of acquisition, retention, and expenditure, and (2) a platform for optimizing expenditures over time.

26.2.4 Competitive Models

The acquisition and retention models reviewed so far omit explicit consideration of competition. This is because most firms do not have data on their competitors' customer behavior nor do they have data on competitor's marketing activity. Fruchter and Zhang (2004) developed a model of acquisition and retention that includes competition. Their purpose was to develop insights on theoretical equilibrium levels of acquisition and retention spending. The model represents a firm's share as that arising from retained customers plus that arising from acquired customers. Marketing expenditures serve to retain customers or acquire them. These expenditures can be viewed as defensive or offensive.[3] The market share equations

---

[3] In fact, this is how Fruchter and Zhang (2004) view them. We view them as retention and acquisition expenditures, and redefine notation to reflect this – using "a" for acquisition rather than "o" for offensive, and "r" for retention rather than "d" for defensive.

are as follows:

$$x_{k_r}(t) = \text{firm } k\text{'s share due to retained customers.} \qquad (26.24a)$$

$$x_{k_a}(t) = \text{firm } k\text{'s share due to acquired customers.} \qquad (26.24b)$$

$$x_k(t) = x_{k_r}(t) + x_{k_a}(t) = \text{firm } k\text{'s market share} \qquad (26.24c)$$

The term k signifies the firm, and Fruchter and Zhang (2004) assume two firms ($k = 1, 2$). The role of marketing in determining these shares is expressed as follows:

$$\rho_k^r \left(\delta_k^r(t) x_{k_r}(t) \right)^{(1/2)} = \text{effectiveness of firm } k\text{'s actions in retaining}$$
$$\text{customers} = E_k^r(t). \qquad (26.25a)$$

$$\rho_k^a \left(\delta_k^a(t) x_{k_a}(t) \right)^{(1/2)} = \text{effectiveness of firm } k\text{'s actions in attracting}$$
$$\text{customers} = E_k^a(t). \qquad (26.25b)$$

$$f_{kj}^{ar}(t) = E_k^a(t) - E_j^r(t) = \text{firm } k\text{'s advantage in marketing effectiveness}$$
$$\text{in acquiring customers from firm } j. \qquad (26.25c)$$

$$f_{jk}^{ar}(t) = E_j^a(t) - E_k^r(t) = \text{firm } j\text{'s advantage in marketing effectiveness}$$
$$\text{in acquiring customers from firm } k. \qquad (26.25d)$$

where:

$\delta(t)$ = acquisition (a) or retention (r) expenditures per customer for firm k in period t. Therefore, $\delta(t) \times x(t)$ = total acquisition or retention expenditures. The authors assume decreasing returns (the $1/2$ exponent).
ρ = effectiveness of firm k's acquisition or retention expenditures.

Firm k's advantage in acquiring customers from firm j (f_{kj}^{ar}) will be higher to the extent that firm k spends a lot on acquisition (δx), that the spending is effective (ρ), and firm j spends little on retention and what it does spend is ineffective. The authors model the change in market share over time as follows:

$$\dot{x}_{k_r}(t) = f_{kj}^{ar}(t)[x_k(t) - x_{k_r}(t)] - f_{jk}^{ar}(t) x_{k_r}(t) \qquad (26.26a)$$

$$\dot{x}_{k_a}(t) = f_{kj}^{ar}(t)[x_j(t) - x_{k_a}(t)] - f_{jk}^{ar}(t) x_{k_a}(t) \qquad (26.26b)$$

Note that $\dot{x}$ stands for the derivative of market share with respect to time, or the change in market share over time. Equation 26.26a describes how share due to retained customers evolves; Equation 26.26b shows how share due to acquired customers evolves. Equation 26.26a is reasoned as follows: Firm k's share among retained customers increases if they can convert newly acquired customers to repeat customers (first term) and prevent losses among current customers by overcoming firm j's acquisition efforts (second term). Equation 26.26b is reasoned as follows: Firm k's share from acquired customers increases if its acquisition efforts are successful among the pool of potential switchers (the first term) and if it can prevent firm j from acquiring its recently acquired customers (second term). Equations 26.26a and 26.26b add up to the following intuitive result:

$$\dot{x}_k(t) = f_{kj}^{ar}(t)\left[1 - x_k(t)\right] - f_{jk}^{ar}\left[x_k(t)\right] \qquad (26.27)$$

Equation 26.27 says that firm k's share grows to the extent that it has an acquisition marketing superiority over its competitor j and firm j has a higher share (there are many customers available) and to the extent that firm j has weak acquisition efforts so that it cannot acquire firm k's current customers.

Fruchter and Zhang (2004) assume customers contribute on average q_k and that each firm attempts to maximize its profits by optimizing its acquisition and retention expenditures over time. The authors solve the resulting model as an optimal control problem. Their main findings are:

- *Acquisition and retention spending as defined by the δ's depend on the effectiveness of firm k's spending relative to firm j.*
- *Retention spending increases as the value of customers, captured by q_k increases.*
- *Large share firms should spend more on retention and small share firms should spend more on acquisition.* This is an intuitive result but shows that not all firms should have the same acquisition and retention strategy, and market share is a key determinant of that strategy.

One can think of obvious improvements in the Fruchter/Zhang analysis. For example, customer contribution q_k could be a function of marketing expenditures. Also, including a "lock-in" term, namely a constant in the retention marketing equation, might result in less competition, since it becomes more difficult to acquire a competitor's customers. Finally, the model assumes a finite pool of customers, whereas in many markets the customer base is growing over time.

Fruchter and Zhang (2004) offer a unique perspective on the competitive determinants of acquisition and retention expenditures. They show that market share is a key determinant of these expenditures, and that acquisition and retention expenditure decisions should consider expected competitive expenditures. Future research needs to expand upon and estimate the model to learn how these forces play out in practice.

26.2.5 Summary: Lessons on How to Model Acquisition and Retention

We have examined four types of acquisition/retention models: (1) the Blattberg/Deighton customer equity model, (2) the Thomas Type II Tobit model, (3) cohort models, and (4) competitive models. This examination suggests the essential phenomena to include when modeling acquisition and retention:

- *Acquisition and retention rates are fundamental.* The key quantities to be modeled are the percentage of the firm's prospects that is acquired, and what percentage of its current customers is retained.
- *Acquisition and retention rates are functions of marketing.* Marketing expenditures influence acquisition and retention rates. There is evidence the impact of these expenditures has decreasing returns (Reinartz et al. 2005).
- *Acquisition and retention are integrated.* The relationship is quantified by the equation, Customer Equity $= aLTV - A$. LTV depends on the retention rate which in turn is a function of retention marketing expenditures. Statistically, the need to integrate the phenomena comes through correlations between acquisition and retention rates due to correlations between unobserved variables. This says that selectivity-type models are important for empirically estimating acquisition/retention models (e.g., Thomas 2001; Reinartz et al. 2005).
- *Retention consists of two components – will the customer stay with the company and how much will the customer spend.* The "staying" aspect has received much more attention than the spending aspect, but they both need to be modeled.
- *Customer segments exist.* This is brought out by the Thomas' (2001) Type II Tobit model.
- *The customer base evolves over time.* This is seen most directly by the customer equity (Equation 26.10) and cohort models (Equation 26.11). The customer base evolves for several reasons: First, the pool of available prospects change over time. Second, customers are never 100% retained, so firms are constantly losing customers. Third, retention rates may change over time due either to retention expenditures. We will see how this can be optimized in the next section.
- *Competition plays a role in acquisition and retention strategy.* Typical empirical models of acquisition and retention ignore competition. However, the empirically observed acquisition and retention expenditures of the firm are the result of a competitive interaction where acquisition and retention expenditures are the main weapons. Accordingly, to ignore competition can create an endogeneity problem in acquisition and retention expenditures.

26.3 Optimal Acquisition and Retention Spending

In this section we use various models of acquisition and retention to derive optimal spending levels. We consider the Blattberg/Deighton model first. This leads to insights regarding the notion that since it "costs less" to retain a customer than acquire one, more money should be put into customer retention. We then investigate a multi-period optimization based on the Blattberg/Deighton model. Finally, we discuss the optimization of the Reinartz et al. (2005) model.

26.3.1 Optimizing the Blattberg/Deighton Model with No Budget Constraint

To optimize the Blattberg/Deighton model, we assume the firm has current customers and prospects. The optimization therefore takes the following form:

$$
\underset{A,R}{Max}\Pi = N_p \left[a\left(M - R\right)\left(\frac{1+d}{1+d-r}\right) - A \right] + N_c \left[\left(M - R\right)\left(\frac{1+d}{1+d-r}\right) \right]
$$

$$(26.28a)$$

such that:

$$
a = c_a(1 - e^{-k_a A}) \tag{26.28b}
$$

$$
r = c_r(1 - e^{-k_r R}) \tag{26.28c}
$$

where:

N_p = Number of prospects available to the firm.
N_c = Number of current customers for the firm.

The other terms are defined in Sect. 26.2.1. The decision variables are how much to spend on acquisition and retention $(A\&R)$. These expenditures drive the acquisition and retention rates through the marketing efficiency Equations 26.28b and 26.28c.

Table 26.1 presents illustrative results. The example assumes the company has 1,000,000 prospects and 10,000 current customers. Acquisition and retention spending efficiency is about the same ($k_a = 0.1$ and $k_r = 0.08$) but the acquisition ceiling is much lower than the retention ceiling ($c_a = 0.1$ and $c_r = 0.7$). Profit contribution per customer, gross of retention expenditures, is $200, and the discount rate is 10% per year.

The optimal solution[4] yields $21,083,762 in profits by spending $14.14 per prospect on acquisition and $38.01 per customer on retention. The result is an acquisition rate of 7.6% and a retention rate of 66.7%. The optimal acquisition rate is 76% of the ceiling (7.6%/10.0%) and the optimal retention rate is 95% of the ceiling (66.7%/70%). The optimal solution prescribes acquisition and retention rates lower than their ceilings due to decreasing returns with respect to spending on these efforts.

While spending per prospect is $14.14, average acquisition cost is $186.81 per acquired customer. This is higher than the average retention cost, which is $38.01. Using Equations 26.6 and 26.9, one can compute the marginal costs of

---

[4] This is a nonlinear optimization obtained using the Solver add-in for Excel.

Table 26.1 Optimal advertising and retention expenditures: Blattberg and Deighton model (Equations 26.1 and 26.28)

Parameters	
Number of prospects $= N_p =$	1,000,000
Number of current customers $= N_c =$	10,000
Acquisition ceiling $= c_a =$	0.1
Acquisition efficiency $= k_a =$	0.1
Retention ceiling $= c_r =$	0.7
Retention efficiency $= k_r =$	0.08
Margin $= M =$	$200
Discount rate $= d =$	0.1

Optimal solution	
Acquisition spending per prospect $= A^* =$	$14.14
Retention spending per customer $= R^* =$	$38.01
Acquisition rate $= 0.1(1 - e^{-0.1(14.14)}) =$	7.6%
Retention rate $= 0.7(1 - e^{-0.08(38.01)}) =$	66.7%
Number prospects acquired $= 1,000,000 \times 7.6\% =$	75,674
Total number of customers $= 10,000 + 75,674 =$	85,674
Average acquisition cost per acquired customer $=$ ($14.14 \times$ 1,000,000)/75,674 $=$	$186.81
Average retention cost per customer $= \$38.01$	$38.01
Total acquisition cost $= \$14.14 \times 1,000,000 =$	$14,136,357.89
Total retention cost $= \$38.01 \times 85,674 =$	$3,256,791.55
Marginal acquisition cost $= 1/(k_a(c_a - a)) = 1/(0.1(0.1 - 0.076)) =$	$411.09
Marginal retention cost $= 1/(k_r(c_r - r)) = 1/(0.08(0.7 - 0.667)) =$	$373.72
$LTV = M \times \frac{1+d}{1+d-r} = 200 \times \frac{1+.1}{1+.1-.667} =$	$411.09
Total profits	$21,083,762

acquiring or retaining customers at the optimal spending levels. The marginal acquisition cost turns out to be $411.09 and the marginal retention cost turns out to be $373.72. Note that at optimal spending, the lifetime value of the customer is $411.09. As we shall show rigorously, it is no coincidence that at optimal spending, optimal marginal acquisition cost $= LTV$, and optimal marginal retention cost $= LTV/(1 + d)$.

Figures 26.5 and 26.6 show how optimal acquisition and retention spending change as a function of the acquisition and retention response equations. Figure 26.5 shows that as the acquisition ceiling increases, optimal acquisition expenditures (A) increase at a decreasing rate, optimal retention expenditures (R) remain the same, and profits increase. These results make sense. First, as the ceiling increases, the marginal cost of acquiring a customer decreases for a given level of expenditure, hence more money can be spent on acquisition and more customers will be acquired. Second, this has no impact on retention spending because the optimal lifetime value of a customer, and hence the optimal retention spending level, is independent of how many customers are acquired (note we are not in a budgeted situation).

Figure 26.5b shows that as acquisition efficiency increases, profits increase, and acquisition dollars increase to a point, and then decrease. The reason for this presumably is that when acquisition spending becomes highly efficient,

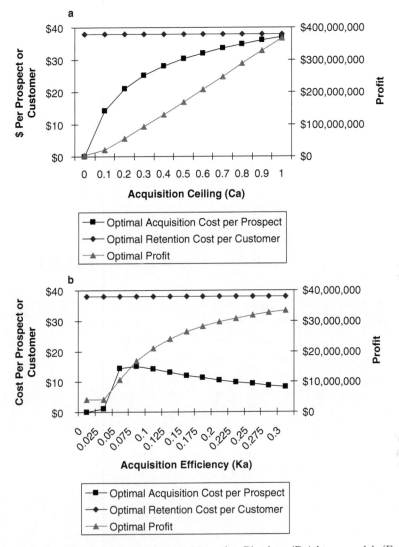

Fig. 26.5 Sensitivity analysis of optimizing the Blattberg/Deighton model (Equation 26.28): Acquisition function parameters. (a) Sensitivity to acquisition ceiling c_a; (b) Sensitivity to acquisition efficiency k_a.

one reaches the acquisition ceiling, or very close to it, with less and less acquisition expenditure, so that at high efficiency, one can spend less on acquisition and still have a huge acquisition rate.

Figure 26.6a shows that as the retention ceiling increases, more is spent on retention *and* on acquisition. That more is spent on retention is certainly no surprise. But it is interesting that more is also spent on acquisition. This is because with a higher retention ceiling and more spent on retention, *LTV* increases, and thus it is worthwhile to invest in acquisition because higher *LTV* allows the higher acquisition costs to pay out.

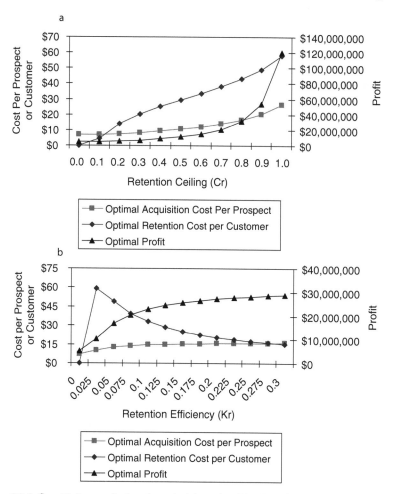

Fig. 26.6 Sensitivity analysis of optimizing the Blattberg/Deighton model (Equation 26.28): Retention function parameters. (a) Sensitivity to retention ceiling c_r; (b) Sensitivity to retention efficiency k_r.

Figure 26.6b shows that as retention efficiency increases, retention costs first increase and then decrease. The decrease occurs for similar reasons as in the case of acquisition – the increased efficiency allows the firm to attain very high retention rates at low levels of spending. Therefore it is not necessary to spend as much on retention. Acquisition spending goes up because at higher retention efficiency, retention rates are high, so LTV is higher, so higher levels of acquisition pay out.

Perhaps the most interesting insight from the above analysis is the asymmetric relationship between acquisition and retention expenditures. If acquisition response improves, either through a higher ceiling or greater efficiency, acquisition spending changes but retention spending is unaffected. However, if retention response improves, retention spending changes and so does acquisition spending. This is because as will be formalized in the next section, acquisition costs are optimal when the marginal cost of acquisition equals the lifetime value of the customer. If the acquisition response curve improves, it makes it worthwhile to change acquisition expenditures to keep this equality in balance. However, the optimal retention rate is not affected by how many customers are acquired, so the optimal retention expenditure remains the same. In contrast, when retention response changes, LTV changes, and so acquisition costs must adjust to re-equilibrate the relationship between acquisition spending and LTV.

26.3.2 The Relationship Among Acquisition and Retention Costs, LTV, and Optimal Spending: If Acquisition "Costs" Exceed Retention "Costs", Should the Firm Focus on Retention?

Often companies do not explicitly measure acquisition and retention response curves, and so cannot formally optimize expenditures. They look for rules of thumb for guiding these expenditures. One of the more common such heuristics is that since it costs more to acquire than retain a customer, firms should focus on retention. Pfeifer (2005) makes three crucial points: (1) One must define more rigorously what is meant by costs – average costs or marginal costs. (2) Marginal costs, not average costs, are key to determining how much should be spent on either acquisition or retention. (3) Acquisition spending should be at a level such that the marginal cost of acquisition equals the lifetime value of the customer, and retention spending should also be at a level such that the marginal cost of retention should equal the lifetime value of the customer.[5]

Point (1) simply emphasizes that we need to be precise in defining costs, as in all managerial situations. As we have seen earlier, average costs and marginal costs vary differently as the response curves change. Point (2) is the most crucial. Average costs reflect what the firm is currently spending. But we want to determine whether that current spending is optimal or not. What matters therefore is how much it would cost to *change* the acquisition or retention rate. This is the domain of marginal cost, i.e., the crucial question is, what would it cost to acquire *an additional customer*, or retain *an additional customer*. Once we are thinking in terms of marginal costs, Point (3) follows intuitively. In terms of acquisition, if we can acquire an additional customer for an $200 (marginal cost equals $200) and the LTV is $300, we should spend

---

[5] Note that our actual result will differ because of the assumed timing of expenditures (see Footnote 1), and therefore, we will find the optimal $R = LTV/(1 + d)$ rather than $R = LTV$ (see Equations 26.30 and 26.31).

Table 26.2 Does lower average retention cost per customer mean the firm should spend more on retention?

		Current	Optimal
Acquisition	# Prospects	1,000,000	1,000,000
	$/Prospect	$8.00	$14.14
	Total acquisition ($)	8,000,000	14,136,358
	Acquisition rate	5.51%	7.57%
	# Acquired	55,067	75,674
	Average acquisition $/customer	145.28	186.81
Retention	# Initial customers	10,000	10,000
	# Acquired customers	55,067	75,674
	Total customers	65,067	85,674
	Average retention $/customer	38.01	38.01
	Retention rate	66.66%	66.66%
	Total retention ($)	2,473,200	3,256,791
Profit	Margin per customer	$200	$200
	Total profits	$18,748,270	$21,083,262
Marginals	*LTV*	$411.09	$411.09
	Marginal acquisition cost/customer	$222.55	$411.09
	Marginal retention cost/customer	$373.72	$373.72
	LTV discounted one period	$373.72	$373.72

that $200. In fact, we should spend until the marginal cost equals *LTV*. The same logic follows for marginal retention costs, although when we derive the result formally, we will differ by a factor of $(1 + d)$ because of the timing of the benefits of additional retention.

We illustrate the above principles in Table 26.2, which assumes the same parameters as in Table 26.1. However, it assumes that at the current time, the company is spending $8.00 per prospect and $38.01 per customer. This results in an average acquisition cost of $145.28 per acquired customer and retention cost of $38.01 per customer. Note (average) acquisition costs exceed (average) retention costs, so it is tempting to recommend spending more on retention per customer. However, we see that the *LTV* is $411.09, which is much higher than the marginal cost ($222.55) of acquiring another customer. It costs us $222.55 to acquire another customer, and that customer is worth $411.09. We should put money into acquisition, which is reflected in the "Optimal" column, which is the same result as Table 26.1. In fact, we can formalize these arguments and prove the following:

Proposition: *For the Blattberg/Deighton model without a budget constraint, optimal acquisition spending is determined at the point where marginal acquisition cost equals LTV, and optimal retention spending is determined at the point where marginal retention costs = LTV/$(1 + d)$.*

Proof: The objective function is:

$$\Pi = N_p \left[a\,(M - R) \left(\frac{1 + d}{1 + d - r} \right) - A \right] + N_c \left[(M - R) \left(\frac{1 + d}{1 + d - r} \right) \right] \tag{26.29}$$

To prove the acquisition part of the proposition, we take the derivative of profit with respect to acquisition expenditure A and solve for the optimal A. This yields:

$$\frac{\partial \Pi}{\partial A} = N_p \left(M - R\right) \left(\frac{1+d}{1+d-r}\right) \frac{\partial a}{\partial A} - N_p$$

$$set = 0 \Rightarrow \left(M - R\right) \left(\frac{1+d}{1+d-r}\right) \frac{\partial a}{\partial A} - 1 = 0 \Rightarrow LTV \frac{\partial a}{\partial A} - 1 = 0$$

$$\Rightarrow \frac{\partial A}{\partial a} = marginal\ acquisition\ cost = LTV \qquad (26.30)$$

The result shows that at optimality the marginal cost of acquiring an additional customer equals the lifetime value of the customer.

To prove the retention part of the proposition, we take the derivative of profit with respect to retention expenditure R and solve for the optimal R. This yields:

$$\frac{\partial \Pi}{\partial R} = N_p a \left(\frac{1+d}{1+d-r}\right)(-1) + N_p a \left(M - R\right) \left(\frac{(1+d)(-1)}{(1+d-r)^2}\right)(-1)\frac{\partial r}{\partial R}$$

$$+ N_c \left(\frac{1+d}{1+d-r}\right)(-1) + N_c \left(M - R\right) \left(\frac{(1+d)(-1)}{(1+d-r)^2}\right)(-1)\frac{\partial r}{\partial R}$$

$$set = 0 \Rightarrow -N_p a \left(1 + d\right) + N_p a \left(M - R\right) \left(\frac{1+d}{1+d-r}\right) \frac{\partial r}{\partial R}$$

$$-N_c \left(1 + d\right) + N_c \left(M - R\right) \left(\frac{1+d}{1+d-r}\right) \frac{\partial r}{\partial R} = 0$$

$$\Rightarrow -\left(N_p a + N_c\right) \left(1 + d\right) + \left(N_p a + N_c\right) \left(M - R\right) \left(\frac{1+d}{1+d-r}\right) \frac{\partial r}{\partial R} = 0$$

$$\Rightarrow -\left(1 + d\right) + LTV \frac{\partial r}{\partial R} = 0$$

$$\Rightarrow \frac{\partial R}{\partial r} = marginal\ retention\ cost = \frac{LTV}{(1+d)} \qquad (26.31)$$

At optimality, the marginal cost of retaining another customer should equal $LTV/(1+d)$. The reason for the $(1+d)$ term in the denominator is that in our formulation of the Blattberg/Deighton model, the benefit of retaining an additional customer occurs in the next period, i.e., the benefit of a higher retention expenditure is that we are more likely to retain the customer in the *next* period. This is why in Tables 26.1 and 26.2, at optimality, the marginal retention cost = $373.72 = LTV/(1+d) = $411.09/(1+0.1)$.

In conclusion, the lessons from this exercise are:

- Marginal costs, not average costs, are relevant to guiding optimal acquisition and retention spending. Average costs provide information acquisition and retention spending only to the extent that under some circumstances, average costs may equal marginal costs within the range of actions being considered.

- In an unconstrained budget, static setting, marginal acquisition costs should equal LTV, and marginal retention costs should equal $LTV/(1+d)$.

Note the proviso that we assume an unconstrained budget. We also have not considered potential interactions between acquisition and retention over time. We consider these issues in Sects. 26.3.3–26.3.5. Meanwhile, the proposition provides a well-grounded "first-cut" at optimal expenditures, and strongly suggests that it is inappropriate to use average costs as a basis for setting acquisition and retention expenditures.

In practice, implementing the proposition is hampered because companies often do not know their *marginal* costs, because this requires acquisition and retention curves. Without knowledge of the acquisition response curve, the company might assume that for a given acquisition channel, average cost = marginal cost. For example, if the firm distributes 1,000,000 CD's at a cost of $100,000 and acquires 1,000 customers, its average acquisition cost is $100. It *may* be reasonable to assume that if it distributed 500,000 additional CD's, it would acquire customers at the same rate, i.e., 500 more customers. The cost would be $50,000, so the marginal acquisition cost would be $100 per customer. Note, however, that this assumes we have not reached the decreasing returns portion of the acquisition response curve.

While we might see some justification for using average acquisition cost as a proxy for marginal cost, extrapolating average *retention* costs in this way would be more tenuous. Additional retention costs are being spent on the same customer, so most certainly will be subject to decreasing returns. In the acquisition case, we are simply reaching 1,500,000 prospects rather than 1,000,000. In the retention case, we are spending more on our 10,000 current customers. We can't simply extrapolate as we did in the acquisition case because it will be the same customers who are the subject of the additional expenditure. The company needs to estimate a retention response curve or conduct market tests to gauge the impact of additional retention spending.

26.3.3 Optimizing the Budget-Constrained Blattberg/Deighton Model

Companies often operate under budget constraints.[6] Formally, the situation is:

$$
\underset{A,R}{Max\Pi} = N_p\left[a\left(M-R\right)\left(\frac{1+d}{1+d-r}\right) - A\right] + N_c\left[(M-R)\left(\frac{1+d}{1+d-r}\right)\right]
$$

$$(26.32a)$$

---

[6] See also Berger and Bechwati (2001) for budget-constrained optimization of the Blattberg/Deighton model.

such that:

$$a = c_a(1 - e^{-k_a A}) \tag{26.32b}$$

$$r = c_r(1 - e^{-k_r R}) \tag{26.32c}$$

$$A + R = B \tag{26.32d}$$

Equation 26.32d is the budget constraint. Table 26.3 shows the optimal solution using the same parameters as in Table 26.1, except now with a budget constraint of $10,000,000. The table shows that optimal spending is now $7.78 per prospect in acquisition costs, and $34.63 per customer in retention costs. These numbers are lower than the optimal spending without budget constraints. Total A&R spending was $14,136,358 + $3,256,792 = $17,393,150 in the unconstrained case. In the constrained case total A&R spending is $7,781,287 + $2,218,713 = $10,000,000.

Profits have decreased from $21,083,762 to $18,478,670. This makes sense because if a $10,000,000 budget yielded the highest profit, we would have found this out in the unconstrained optimization. Figure 26.7 illustrates this

Table 26.3 Optimal acquisition and retention for budgeted Blattberg and Deighton model (Equation 26.32)

Parameters	
Acquisition ceiling = c_a =	0.1
Acquisition efficiency = k_a =	0.1
Retention ceiling = c_r =	0.7
Retention efficiency = k_r =	0.08
Margin = M =	200
Number of prospects = N_p =	1,000,000
Number of current customers = N_c =	10,000
Budget	$10,000,000
Discount rate = d =	0.1

Optimal solution	
Optimal acquisition spending per prospect = A^* =	$7.78
Optimal retention spending per customer = R^* =	$34.63
Acquisition rate = $0.1(1 - e^{-0.1(7.78)})$ =	0.054
Retention rate = $0.7(1 - e^{-0.08(34.63)})$	0.656
Optimal profit =	$18,478,670
Total acquisition spending = $1,000,000 \times \$7.78$ =	$7,781,287
Total retention spending = $\$34.63 \times (10,000 + 0.054 \times 1,000,000)$ =	$2,218,713
Total spending = $\$7,781,287 + \$2,218,713$ =	$10,000,000
LTV = $M \times \frac{1+d}{1+d-r} = \$200 \times \frac{1+.1}{1+.1-.656}$ =	$409.84
Marginal acquisition cost = $\frac{1}{k_a(c_a-a)} = \frac{1}{0.1(0.1-0.054)}$ =	$217.74
Marginal retention cost = $\frac{1}{k_r(c_r-r)} = \frac{1}{0.08(0.7-0.656)}$ =	$285.04
Average acquisition ($) = $\frac{\$7,781,287}{1,000,000 \times 0.054}$ =	$143.90
Average retention ($) = $\frac{\$2,218,713}{1,000,000 \times 0.054 + 10,000}$ =	$34.63

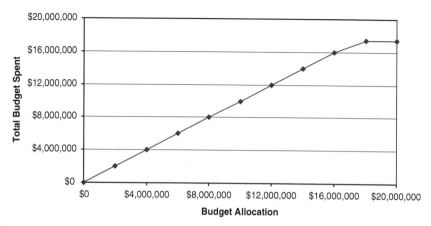

Fig. 26.7 Budgeted Blattberg and Deighton model: Optimal budget spent vs. budget allocated.

by graphing the budget constraint on the x-axis versus the total budget spent. One sees that the amount spent on acquisition and retention increases with larger budgets, up to the point where we reach the unconstrained optimal spending ($17,393,150). So, quite sensibly, as budgets increase, firms will spend more on acquisition and retention, up to the optimal level of spending as would be determined from the unconstrained case.

Figure 26.8a shows how optimal acquisition spending per prospect and optimal retention costs per customer change as budgets increase. As the budget increases, these costs increase until we reach the optimal budget, $17,393,150. Figure 26.8b shows how marginal costs at optimal spending change as a function of the budget. At the optimal budget the marginal acquisition cost equals lifetime value of the customer, and marginal retention cost is somewhat lower (by a factor of $1 + d$). Before we reach the optimal budget, both marginal acquisition marginal retention costs increase convexly. LTV hardly increases at all once it reaches about $400. It seems that in this case, retention gets first priority and the amount is spent that increases retention rate so that LTV is about at its optimal maximum. Then as the budget increases, it is used disproportionately to acquire more customers. This result may due to a function of the higher ceiling for retention rates. This encourages the company to spend scarce resources on retention, since they rapidly increase LTV. Then, once the firm runs into steeply increasing marginal retention costs, it spends money on acquiring customers.

In summary, we have learned the following regarding optimal acquisition and retention expenditures in a budgeted situation:

- *Budgets are sub-optimal in that they constrain spending so that the firm does not achieve the optimal marginal cost/LTV relationship derived in the proposition.*

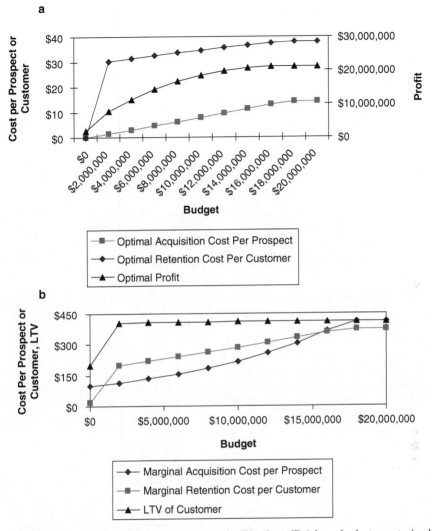

Fig. 26.8 Sensitivity analysis of optimizing the Blattberg/Deighton budget-constrained model (Equation 26.32): Impact of budget. (a) Optimal acquisition and retention spending; (b) Marginal costs and *LTV*.

- *As budgets are increased, the firm will not overspend.* It will spend up to the point where the marginal cost/*LTV* relationships are achieved.
- *As budgets increase, acquisition and retention expenditures increase in different proportions.* It may be optimal to focus first on retention, although this may be due to the fact that it has a higher ceiling. Further work is needed on "which should come first" as budgets increase.

26.3.4 Optimizing a Multi-Period, Budget-Constrained Cohort Model

We derive optimal acquisition and retention spending for the budgeted case in a multi-period setting. The model is as follows:

$$\underset{A_t R_t}{Max} \left\{ \sum_{t=1}^{T} \frac{\Pi_t}{(1+d)^{(t-1)}} \right\} \tag{26.33a}$$

such that:

$$\Pi_t = (N_{ct} + N_{at}) \times M_t - A_t - R_t \tag{26.33b}$$

$$N_{ct} = \begin{cases} N_{c1} & t = 1 \\ (N_{c,t-1} + N_{a,t-1}) \times r_{t-1} & t = 2, \ldots, T \end{cases} \tag{26.33c}$$

$$N_{at} = N_{pt} \times a_t \tag{26.33d}$$

$$a_t = c_a(1 - e^{-k_a A_t}) \tag{26.33e}$$

$$r_t = c_f + c_r(1 - e^{-k_r R_t}) \tag{26.33f}$$

$$A_t + R_t = B \tag{26.33g}$$

Equation 26.33a is the objective function. Note the finite horizon T. In these situations, it is common to find "end game" solutions, which in this case could mean no spending on retention in period T because its benefits are not felt until period $T + 1$. We therefore will optimize the model for $T = 4$ but report the results for $t = 1, 2,$ and 3, in the spirit of deriving a 3-year marketing plan.

Equation 26.33b is the per-period profit equation. Note that each period we begin with N_{ct} current customers and acquire N_{at} new customers. We assume that these customers contribute on average M_t and the *total* costs of acquiring N_{at} customers is A_t and the amount spent on customer retention is R_t.

Equations 26.33c and 26.33d keep track of how many customers we have in each period. We start off with N_{c1} customers and acquire N_{a1} customers in period 1 (via Equation 26.34d; N_{pt} is the number of prospects). Our total profit contribution in period 1 is therefore $(N_{c1} + N_{a1}) \times M_1$ via Equation 26.34b. The second part of Equation 26.34c shows how many customers we retain for the beginning of the next period.

Equations 26.33e and 26.33f are our familiar acquisition and retention response functions. We add a floor effect for retention response. Even if the firm spends \$0 on retention, it will retain a fraction c_f of its customers in the next period. In the optimization, we assume $c_f = c_a = k_a = k_r = 0.1$, and the retention ceiling is $c_r = 0.8$. So if the firm spends an infinite amount on retention, its retention rate would be $0.1 + 0.8 = 0.9$. If it spends nothing on retention, it would still retain $0.10 = 10\%$ of its customers. We assume contribution margin, M_t, is \$200, and the discount rate d is 10%. The budget (B) is \$10,000,000.

Table 26.4 shows the results. The company starts off with 50,000 customers (N_{c1}) and 1,000,000 prospects (N_{p1}). It spends \$7.36 per prospect, for a total

Table 26.4 Optimal acquisition and retention spending for cohort model (Equation 26.33)

		Year 1	Year 2	Year 3
Customers	Initial customers	50,000	85,744	111,791
	Prospects	1,000,000	1,000,000	1,000,000
	Acquired customers	52,080	48,908	47,814
	Total customers	102,080	134,652	159,605
	Customers lost	16,337	22,861	30,241
	Customer retained	85,744	111,791	129,364
Budget	Acquisition (\$)/prospect	7.36	6.72	6.50
	Retention (\$)/customer	25.90	24.39	21.91
	Total acquisition costs	\$7,356,458	\$6,715,427	\$6,503,605
	Total retention costs	\$2,643,542	\$3,284,573	\$3,496,395
	Total spent	\$10,000,000	\$10,000,000	\$10,000,000
	Marginal acquisition cost	\$209	\$196	\$192
	Marginal retention cost	\$167	\$143	\$112
Profits	Contribution per customer	400	400	400
	Total contribution	\$40,832,164	\$53,860,754	\$63,842,132
	Total profit	\$30,832,164	\$43,860,754	\$53,842,132
	Discounted total profit	\$30,832,164	\$39,873,412	\$44,497,630
	Total discounted profit	\$115,203,189		
	LTV	\$1,692	\$1,631	\$1,520

of \$7,356,458 in acquisition costs, and \$25.90 per customer in retention costs, for a total of \$2,643,542. This adds up to the budget constraint of \$10,000,000. The optimal spending results in an $85,744/102,080 = 84\%$ retention rate and a $52,080/1,000,000 = 5.2\%$ acquisition rate.

Note that over time, the company is building up its customer base, 50,000 at the beginning of Year 1, to 111,791 at the beginning of Year 3. It will enter Year 4 with 129,364 customers. Interestingly, however, the amount spent on acquisition decreases over time. One reason is that when the firm acquires customers in Year 1, this increases the number of customers retained and then subject to retention efforts in Year 2. This necessitates higher retention spending and hence lower acquisition spending. This illustrates the multi-period interaction between acquisition and retention. Expenditures on acquisition in period 1 increase the "retention burden" in period 2, requiring more retention dollars in total and less spent on acquisition. The optimization finds a "happy median" whereby retention rates are maintained relatively high yet money is still available for the ample pool of prospects. Retention rates go from 84% (Year 1) to 83% (Year 2) to 81% (Year 3), so they are maintained at pretty high levels.

The marginal acquisition and retention costs are way below the customer LTV of \$1,692. The budget is clearly constraining what would be a higher optimal spending level. However, an additional factor is the finite horizon. Given the relatively high retention rate (80%+), the customer's full lifetime lies outside the time horizon of the optimization. This is perhaps realistic for companies that have a 3-year planning horizon. They are sub-optimizing in the sense that an infinite budget and infinite time horizon will yield higher discounted

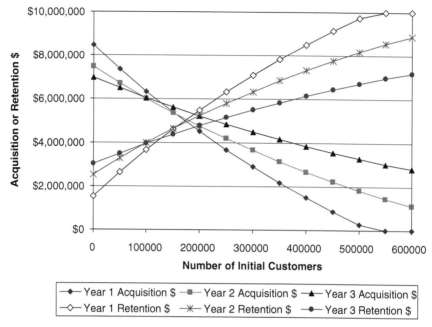

Fig. 26.9 Sensitivity analysis for optimizing the cohort model (Equation 26.33): Impact of initial number of customers on acquisition and retention expenditures by year.

profits, but the company has limited available funds so that it must resort to budgeting. In addition, it cannot take on too long a planning horizon because there is no guarantee the company will exist 4 years from now!

Figure 26.9 shows the impact on Year 1, 2, and 3 spending as the number of initial customers increases. In general, the larger the number of initial customers, the greater the amount spent on retention. This is reminiscent of the Fruchter and Zhang (2004) result that higher share companies should spend more on retention. But in the case of Fig. 26.9, the emphasis on current customers is because acquisition and retention are roughly equal in efficiency yet retention has a higher ceiling, so the more customers on hand, the more it pays to spend money on retaining them. Note that when the number of initial customers is low, retention spending increases over time as in Table 26.4. But when the number of initial customers is large, the company invests a lot in them initially but then decreases that expenditure over time. This may be because as more customers are acquired and the retention burden becomes higher, it becomes harder to devote the money to maintain high retention rates, so the firm lets up a little on retention spending and allocates more to acquisition spending.

In summary, this example shows the following:

- *Multi-period acquisition and planning models can be set up using the basic Blattberg/Deighton's framework incorporated in a cohort model. The result is a planning tool that can be used to derive a realistic limited horizon marketing plan.*

- *Acquisition and retention interact over time.* Heavy acquisition spending in early periods can impose a *retention burden* that forces the firm to spend more on retention in future periods. The opposite can also occur: Early high retention spending levels can be difficult to maintain because even at high spending, customers leave the company, so acquisition eventually becomes important.

- *Marginal acquisition and retention costs do not correspond to customer LTV as we derived for the long-term, infinite budget case.* The reasons are: (1) the limited budget means that these marginal costs typically are lower than *LTV*, and (2) the finite horizon means that the long-term value of customers is not fully considered.

26.3.5 Optimizing the Reinartz et al. (2005) Tobit Model

Reinartz et al. used their model to derive an optimal spending strategy for the company that provided their data. The case is analogous to the un-budgeted Blattberg/Deighton optimization in Sect. 26.3.1. The difference is the model (Type II Tobit rather than the Blattberg/Deighton response functions) and the fact that the decision variables are how much to spend on specific vehicles (telephone, face-to-face, Internet, and e-mail), as well as acquisition and retention in total. The authors optimized their model using the Solver add-on for Excel, yielding several interesting findings:

- The optimal solution called for 21.1% of marketing to be spent on acquisition and 78.9% to be spent on retention. Interestingly, the company was actually spending these percentages. However, the *level* of spending in total was much higher than the optimal level. This suggests that managers overspend on marketing, but allocate the proportions correctly. The reason for the overspending could be that the managers are risk-averse in the sense that they are afraid of losing their customers, or that they are taking into account competitive spending, which the Reinartz et al. model (similar to most other empirical models) does not take into account.

- E-mail dominates the marketing effort, although it isn't particularly effective on a per-e-mail basis. The reason is that it is inexpensive. One way to account for e-mail "costs" would be to include quadratic terms to represent wearout, which would suggest an optimal pulsing strategy (Chapter 28). Interestingly, however, the authors' results suggested positive interactions with telephone and face-to-face communications.

- Under-spending on retention is generally more costly in lost profits than under-spending on acquisition, although it is particularly costly to under-spend on both.

- Over-spending on retention or acquisition does not hurt profits much. This may suggest one reason why managers were indeed over-spending.
- While a small departure from the optimal spending does not hurt profits much on a percentage basis, the total amount of lost profits can be large because of the large number of customers. For example, Reinartz et al. (p. 75) report that when the acquisition budget is 90% of optimal and the retention budget is optimal, profits per customer are reduced by 0.03%. However, the authors calculate across all customers, this can mean a loss of $39.3 million in long-term profits.

The above results show the richness of the Reinartz et al. approach. It is particularly attractive in its linking of particular marketing instruments (e-mail, Internet, etc.) to acquisition and retention, and it ties together acquisition and retention in a rich way as described earlier in Sect. 26.2.3. Further extensions could consider optimal expenditures over time using a cohort approach (Sect. 26.3.4).

26.3.6 Summary: When Should We Spend More on Acquisition or Retention?

The optimizations discussed in this section suggest guidelines on when the firm should spend more on acquisition or retention. These are just guidelines because in only one case did we actually prove one of them, and that was for a single-period model with an unconstrained budget. Further work is needed to generalize these findings:

- *The acquisition and retention response curves are key drivers of relative and absolute spending.* There are two components to these curves, (1) the ceiling effect, i.e., the highest possible acquisition or retention rate, and (2) efficiency, i.e., how fast we approach the ceiling by increasing spending. To the extent that say acquisition is more responsive than the retention (through either higher ceiling, higher efficiency, or both), more money will be spent on acquisition. But there are four key parameters (efficiency and ceiling for both acquisition and retention), and how these play out is difficult to predict and needs to be analyzed using optimization.

  Two additional points should be noted. First, the emphasis in the literature has been on acquisition and retention rates, but customer expenditures (contribution), is also important. There is a response curve for expenditures and this should be considered as well. Second, the parameters of the response curve (efficiency and ceiling) can be influenced by policy. For example, the objective of a loyalty program may be to improve the retention response curve, i.e., make it more efficient or have a higher ceiling. Another way to think of it is that different marketing activities have different response curves. So, how the firm allocates its acquisition or retention money across various marketing instruments determines its aggregate acquisition or retention response curve. Aggregate response curves drive allocation, but these curves can be determined by marketing decisions.

- *Marginal cost, not average cost, should guide investments.* This is because average costs simply measure what we have achieved with expenditures to date, whereas the question of whether we should spend more or less depends on the *change* in acquired or retained customers per unit increase or decrease in spending. This is the concept of marginal cost. Unfortunately, marginal costs are usually more difficult to determine than average costs. Average costs can be obtained from an A&R budget. Marginal costs require a response model or controlled tests of additional investments.

- *In a single period, unlimited budget setting, increase spending on acquisition until the marginal acquisition cost equals the lifetime value of the customer.* We derived this result analytically and stated it as a proposition (Sect. 26.3.2). We saw however that in multiple-period, limited budget settings, the optimal spending level may yield marginal acquisition and retention costs lower than *LTV*.

- *In a single period, unlimited budget setting, increase spending on retention until the marginal cost of retaining another customer equals the lifetime value of the customer, divided by one plus the discount rate.* The logic behind this is the same as with acquisition. We should spend more on retaining customers if the marginal cost of retaining another customer is less than the (discounted) value that customer will provide in the future. Again, however, this result may not hold in a limited budget, multiple period setting.

- *In a single-period, unlimited budget setting, improvements in acquisition response affect acquisition investment but not retention investment.* This is because improvements in acquisition response determine how much the firm must spend before the marginal cost of acquisition equals *LTV*, but does not affect *LTV* itself.

- *In a single-period, unlimited budget setting, improvements in retention response affect both retention and acquisition investment.* This is because better retention response yields higher retention rates and higher *LTV*. This in turn increases the amount one is willing to invest in acquisition, since marginal acquisition costs are increasing in acquisition spending, but we now have a higher *LTV* so can afford higher marginal acquisition costs.

- *Spend more as budgets increase, but monitor marginal costs to make sure you don't overspend.* Generally, as budgets increase, the firm should spend more on acquisition and retention, the exact ratio determined by the response curves as well as period-to-period interactions between acquisition and retention – such as increasing future retention burdens. However, with decreasing returns to expenditures, there eventually is a limit on how much should be spent.

- *Budgeting results in "locally" sub-optimal spending.* Budgets yield lower profits than unlimited budgets. However, there are reasons why companies use budgets. They serve as a management control mechanism and take into account the efforts of the entire company, not just the product line being considered by the optimization.

- *"Retention burden" can hold back acquisition spending in a multi-period, limited budget setting.* In a multi-period setting, there are interactions between actions taken in year t and actions taken in year $t + x$. One of these is "retention burden." If a lot is spent on customer acquisition in a given year, this increases the number of customers that "demand" retention expenditures in future years. If initial acquisition is too high, and if we have a limited budget, we may not be able to spend enough on retaining customers in subsequent periods. An alternative may be to spend less on acquisition initially, so that the customers who are acquired can be retained effectively.
- *Companies with a larger installed customer base should spend more on retention, although perhaps decrease these expenditures over time.* Current customers typically have high retention rates, so at first it pays to invest in these customers. However, over time, more current customers eventually churn, and attention shifts to acquisition.

Again, the above are just a set of guidelines based on the analyses in this section. The most important theme is to illustrate the practicality of using optimization to guide acquisition and retention spending, and to emphasize the need for companies need to invest in learning response functions.

26.4 Acquisition and Retention Budget Planning

In this section we reinforce the "Customer Management Marketing Budget" (CMMB), implicitly introduced in Table 26.4, as a planning tool.

26.4.1 The Customer Management Marketing Budget (CMMB)

Table 26.5 portrays a template for the CMMB. This multi-period planning tool consisting of three sections: Customers, *A&R* Spending, and Profit. This contrasts to a more typical marketing budget, which would consist of expenditures and profits. The key contribution of the CMMB is that it keeps track of the firm's customer base and shows where the marketing expenditures are going – for acquisition or retention.

The Customer section of the CMMB keeps count of current, lost, retained, and acquired customers each year, along with prospects. It also tabulates retention and acquisition rates. At a glance, the manager can examine the growth or decline in the firm's customer base and its reasons. For example,

Table 26.5 Template for the customer management marketing budget (CMMB)

	Year 1	Year 2	Year 3	Year 4
Customers				
Current	100,000	170,000	219,000	253,300
Lost	30,000	51,000	65,700	75,990
Retained	70,000	119,000	153,300	177,310
Prospects	1,000,000	1,000,000	1,000,000	1,000,000
Acquired	100,000	100,000	100,000	100,000
Total end of year	170,000	219,000	253,300	277,310
Retention rate	0.7	0.7	0.7	0.7
Acquisition rate	0.1	0.1	0.1	0.1
A&R Spending				
Average ($)/prospect	5	5	5	5
Average ($)/current	10	10	10	10
Total acquisition ($)	5,000,000	5,000,000	5,000,000	5,000,000
Total retention ($)	2,000,000	2,700,000	3,190,000	3,533,000
Total A&R budget	$7,000,000	$7,700,000	$8,190,000	$8,533,000
Average ($) per acquisition	50	50	50	50
Profit				
Sales ($) per customer	600	600	600	600
Total sales	$102,000,000	$131,400,000	$151,980,000	$166,386,000
COGS	$20,400,000	$26,280,000	$30,396,000	$33,277,200
GS&A	$30,000,000	$30,000,000	$30,000,000	$30,000,000
Total profit	$51,600,000	$75,120,000	$91,584,000	$103,108,800
LTV	$1,320	$1,320	$1,320	$1,320
Discounted profits	$273,047,333	–	–	–

a declining customer base could be the result of decreasing retention rates, decreasing acquisition rates, or fewer prospects. The CMMB Spending section shows acquisition and retention expenditures, and average expenditures per acquisition or retention. In the case of Table 26.5, the total amount spent on A&R is increasing. This is because the customer base is increasing, thus the retention burden is increasing, but the company is continuing to spend the same amount per prospect and per current customer. The final section, Profits, shows sales per customer, total sales, COGS, GS&A (other than A&R), and total profits.

The various entries in the CMMB can be linked to acquisition and response functions, as they are in Table 26.4, which drew on Equations 26.33. However, even without these underlying models, the simple layout of CMMB provides a valuable portrait of the state of the firm from a CRM vantage point.

26.4.2 Implementation Issues

A challenge in implementing a CMMB is the calculation of acquisition and retention costs. For example, is mass advertising part of acquisition or

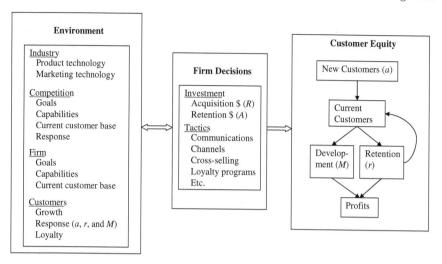

Fig. 26.10 Acquisition and retention strategy: An overview.

retention? Probably both, and the firm would want to make an allocation, either using a relatively *ad hoc* method based say on the number of customers acquired and retained, or using acquisition and retention response curves that show which aspect – acquisition or retention – is influenced by mass advertising. While some marketing activities will be difficult to allocate, others will be easy. For example, contacts of prospects are clearly acquisition costs; contacts of current customers are clearly retention costs.

Another issue of course is the allocation of overhead. Should for example the salaries of the marketing staff be allocated to the A&R portion of the budget or to GS&A? This is a debatable issue, relating to the variable versus fixed-costing debate discussed in Chapter 6. Our stance is toward variable costing, so we would enter only variable costs in the A&R Spending section, or at least separate variable from fixed costs. Obviously the A&R section can be made more specific, listing various vehicles such as e-mail, direct mail, and various costs such as product fulfillment and variable salary costs. We would not however allocate other GS&A costs that are expected to be stable over time, or are not a function of the number of customers. Activity-based costing such as discussed in Chapter 5 might be of help in determining the relevant costs.

26.5 Acquisition and Retention Strategy: An Overall Framework

In closing this chapter, we step back from detailed optimizations and modeling and examine an overall framework for developing acquisition and retention strategy. Figure 26.10 provides this framework.

Figure 26.10 shows three components: the environment, firm decisions, and customer equity. The environment includes industry factors, competition, the firm's goals and capabilities, and current and potential customers. Firm decisions are both at the level of monetary expenditures on acquisition and retention, and how that money should be allocated to various tactics (similar to the Reinartz et al. and Blattberg et al. approaches). Note that the environment determines these decisions, but that the decisions also determine the environment. For example, growth in potential customers may cause the firm to spend more on acquisition, but over time this decreases the level of potential customers, and this feeds back probably to an emphasis on retention.

Firm decisions have a direct impact on customer equity – the net long-term profitability of the firm's customer base. There are three key parameters that govern this equity: the acquisition rate a, the retention rate r, and the contribution level M. The firm's investment and tactical decisions have to be designed to influence at least one of these three quantities. We have seen throughout this chapter how the relationships between these three quantities and marketing efforts (the firm decisions) can be modeled and optimized. We have also seen how the A&R budget can keep track of customer equity by charting the customer base, A&R expenditures, and profits over time.

In summary, acquisition and retention can be attacked at a strategic level, only considering aggregate expenditures over a long-term time horizon, or at a tactical level, considering issues such as which particular marketing instruments to use for acquisition, retention, or profit contribution, and how much to spend on them. In any case, the topic is challenging, both for the researcher attempting to model and optimize this process, and the manager attempting to develop and implement acquisition and retention decisions.

Part VI
Managing the Marketing Mix

Chapter 27
Designing Database Marketing Communications

Abstract When all the LTV calculations, predictive modeling, and acquisition and retention planning have been done, the firm ultimately must *communicate* with the customer. In this chapter, we discuss how to design database marketing communications. We discuss the planning process for designing communications, and devote most of the discussion to copy development and media selection. We pay special attention to "personalization," or individualizing the message that is communicated to each customer.

27.1 The Planning Process

Figure 27.1 presents a planning process for designing database marketing communication campaigns. The focus might be on a single campaign or a program consisting of multiple campaigns. The four major steps are: Set the Overall Plan, Develop Copy, Select and Schedule Media, and Evaluate Results. We discuss the overall plan, copy, vehicle selection, and evaluation in this chapter, and scheduling, particularly for multiple campaigns, in Chapter 28.

The process in Fig. 27.1 could apply to mass marketing as well as database marketing. However, database marketing campaigns differ from mass marketing in their emphasis on field testing and personalization. Each of the copy and media steps can be tested and personalized to individual customers. Even the evaluation can be conducted using a test. We will see illustrations of testing and personalization in this chapter.

The personalization aspect of database marketing communications is part of a broader theme: 1-to-1 marketing. That term was coined by Peppers and Rogers (1993; 1997), who applied it to creating specific products for individual customers. Hess et al. (2007) define 1-to-1 marketing more broadly, as "tailoring one or more elements of the marketing mix to each customer." Hess et al. distinguish two types of 1-to-1 marketing: "personalization" and "customization." Personalization is when firms use customer data to individualize

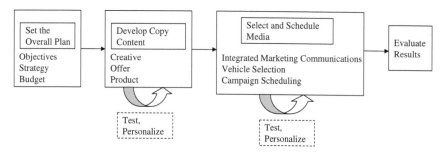

Fig. 27.1 Communication planning process for database marketing.

one or elements of the marketing mix – products, channels, prices, communications – for each customer. Customization is when the customer takes
the lead, typically in the product arena, designing the product he or she
most prefers. A prime example of customization is Dell's website that allows
the customer to specify the product. Examples of personalization include
the Amazon website's recommendations or Tesco's personalized promotion
system (Chapter 22). Throughout this book, we have emphasized personalization, since it is based directly on customer databases. In this chapter, we
emphasize the personalized design of communications.[1]

27.2 Setting the Overall Plan

27.2.1 Objectives

The overall plan consists of objectives, a strategy for achieving the objectives,
and a budget. Objectives usually include specific goals such as 'increase sales
by 10%," "acquire 20,000 customers," or "reduce churn by 5%." Campaign
objectives are usually action oriented, similar to sales promotion objectives
(Blattberg and Neslin 1990).

It is useful to make "qualitative" as well as quantitative considerations part
of the objective. For example, the objective of a direct marketing campaign
for an electronics device manufacturer might be, "Achieve a 1% response rate
while *reinforcing product positioning on quality and reliability.*" The objectives of an offer for an upscale retailer's customers to join a reward program
might be "induce 20% of current customers to sign up for the reward campaign by *emphasizing our quality and service.*"

Qualitative goals are important for three reasons: First, database marketing campaigns often play a dual role as promotions and advertising

---

[1] See Murthi and Sarkar (2003) for an excellent review of product personalization.

(e.g., Smith and Berger 1998). Promotions are most directly concerned with changing behavior, while advertising is often concerned with changing attitudes. Overly focusing on the promotion aspect of the communication can preoccupy the customer with the "deal" rather than the merits of the product.[2] Second, since database marketing campaigns are amenable to evaluation in terms of quantitative criteria such as sales, profits, ROI, etc., it is easy to lose sight of overall marketing strategy. Third, while qualitative objectives are difficult to evaluate, they guide the creative, offer, product, and copy elements of the campaign.

27.2.2 Strategy

Following Nash (2000, p. 36), we consider communications strategy to encompass: (1) Creative, (2) Offer, (3) Product, and (4) Media. Creative refers to overall tone and approach of the communication, as well execution in terms of artwork, type font, layout, etc. The offer refers to price, promotions, financial terms, shipping charges, etc. The product refers to the specific product (or service) contained in the offer, and how it is described (positioned). Media refers to the choice of media and how they will be scheduled. These aspects of the campaign can be stated in general terms when setting the overall plan, but the details are worked out as the planning process progresses. We discuss these details in subsequent sections of this chapter.

27.2.3 Budget

Budgets can be set in three ways: (1) based on last year's budget, (2) derived from objectives and strategy, or (3) derived from an optimization. From a purely scientific point of view, budgets should be derived from an optimization. However, while optimization models provide a good starting point and can help managers think "out-of-the-box," they omit strategic and organization issues that play an important role in determining the budget. Roberts and Berger (1999) discuss the role of last year's budget in determining this year's budget. If last year's results were acceptable, a small adjustment from last year might be appropriate. Also, if the objectives are for marginal growth, or emphasize ROI rather than absolute sales or profits, using last year's budget as a benchmark might be useful.

Deriving the budget from objectives and strategy involves a direct determination of what it will cost to achieve the desired objectives using the

---

[2] This is known as transaction versus acquisition utility. See Neslin (2002) for discussion.

prescribed strategy. For example, the plan might be to acquire 200,000 customers using direct mail. We might assume that the cost of acquiring these 200,000 additional customers via direct mail will be $20 per acquisition. This implies a $4,000,000 budget. Note we use the *marginal*, not average cost per acquisition (Chapter 26). The distinction is important. While last year the firm might have averaged $20 per acquisition, it may cost much more than that to acquire 200,000 *additional* customers this year. While deriving budget from objectives is attractive, one must be very careful to distinguish marginal from average costs.

In summary, optimization, last year's budget, or a calculation of what is required to meet objectives, all have their plusses and minuses as budgeting techniques. It is advisable to use at least two of the three techniques and check consistency.

27.2.4 Summary

The first step in developing a communications program is to develop objectives, strategy, and a budget. Objectives are almost always quantitative in a database marketing context although can contain qualitative considerations as well, even if they are difficult to measure. Strategy consists of creative, offer, product, and media plans. Budget may be derived from last year's budget, from the objectives and strategy, or from an optimization. Consider an acquisition campaign for a consumer electronics company:

Objectives:

Acquire 200,000 customers while not compromising on price.

Strategy:

Creative: Emphasize informational approach, professional tone.
Offer: Maintain standard price; perhaps offer free delivery or easy payment terms.
Product: Include three products from our product line in the offer, personalized for each customer using predictive model derived from tests.
Media: Direct mail

Budget:

Direct mail historically acquires customers at a cost of $20 per customer, so the budget is 200,000 × $20 = $4,000,000. However, money is very tight this year and our hope is through personalization we can lower that cost. Cost savings will go toward R&D for various product lines.

27.3 Developing Copy

27.3.1 Creative Strategy

As discussed earlier, the creative strategy represents the overall tone or approach to the communications piece, as well as the particular executions in terms of artwork, layout, etc. Various creative approaches include:

- *Informational*: Emphasizes the provision of information. This might be appropriate for a B2B product or a "serious" product such as a pharmaceutical.
- *Humorous*: Humor might be appropriate for a gift-oriented catalog.
- *Testimonial*: Emphasizes testimonials by satisfied customers. This would be appropriate for a high-risk product such as consumer electronics.
- *Deal-oriented*: Emphasizes price and getting a good deal. This might be appropriate when the target group is price sensitive or for a sale catalog.
- *Authoritarian*: Relies on an authoritarian figure such as an expert. For example, a campaign designed to enhance drug compliance might use a physician as a spokesperson.
- *Glossy*: Emphasizes an expensive look. This would be appropriate for a high-end cataloger.
- *Personal*: Oriented toward the individual's needs. This would be appropriate for a cross-sell appeal.
- *Comparative*: Compares the company's product to a competitor's.

There are several other possibilities. Nash (2000, chapter 9, p. 217) thinks of the creative strategy as consisting of three major elements: the product (what does it deliver), the customer (how does it make the customer feel emotionally), and company credibility (does the company have the credibility to deliver what it claims). Nash suggests that a relatively small company selling risky products might "allocate" most of its creative effort toward establishing product credibility. This might be accomplished through a testimonial, authoritarian, or comparative approach.

Lewis (1999) distinguishes among "romantic," "sedate," and "flat" approaches to devising copy for direct marketing pieces. Romantic approaches emphasize an idealistic, dreamy tone. An example for cookware would be (Lewis 1999, p. 57):

C'est Merveilleuse! Bourgeat Copper Cookware from France! One of the world's greatest chefs cooks with the world's best copperware. Now you can too.... This master chef's solid copper gourmet cookware ensemble cooks as beautifully as it looks.

A sedate approach emphasizes the benefits of the product but in an informative, expository style. For example (Lewis 1999, p. 57):

All-Clad Copper Cookware. No other material spreads heat faster or more evenly than copper, which is why you'll find a gleaming battery of copper pots in every famous restaurant.

All-Clad lines their copper cookware in stainless steel, making them easy to clean, impervious to scratches, and non-reactive with food.

A flat approach lays out the bare facts. Following is an example (Lewis 1999, p. 58):

Five-piece place setting in 18/10 stainless steel with pearlized resin handles. Choose lime, yellow, blue, or clear. Silver-plated connectors. Imported.

The flat approach emphasizes just the facts. It might be appropriate for a business-to-business communication or in any case where the customer is an expert and just needs to know the facts to make a purchase decision.

Fiore and Yu (2001) compare "imagery" and "descriptive" approaches (analogous to romantic versus sedate) in designing a clothing catalog. They conduct an experiment in which one catalog used just descriptive ads (communicating the benefits of the product but in a factual way) while another included both the descriptive and imagery approaches (also adding a romantic story about wearing the clothing on an adventurous vacation, etc.). The authors found there was no difference in respondent attitudes or intentions to buy between the two catalogs. This may be due to (1) heterogeneity in the target group, i.e., some resonate with the romantic approach while some are turned off, or (2) the combination of descriptive and imagery diluted their individual contributions.

Creative approaches should harmonize with the positioning of the product. An upscale cataloger should use a glossy approach. A price-oriented catalog should adopt a deal-oriented approach. A cross-sell by a local bank might utilize the personal approach (e.g., "As part of our continued efforts to attend to your personal banking needs, we thought you might be interested in our IRA transfer service"). Casual experience suggests this may not always be the case. Credit card solicitations often are deal-oriented ("Get 5% APR and bonus miles when you sign up for the ABC credit card") rather than informational ("The ABC credit card is accepted nearly everywhere and rewards you with airline miles for every dollar spent – as a special introductory offer, you get a 5% APR and bonus miles when you sign up"). See Schlosser et al. (1999) for a discussion of Internet shopper preferences for various creative approaches.

Comparative advertising has received much attention in the advertising literature. Database marketing provides a particularly attractive venue for comparative advertising, because appropriate comparisons can be targeted to the right customers. The general benefits of comparative advertising are increased attention and more effective communication of information, while its pitfalls include competitive response, customer confusion, and even customer sympathy for the "attacked" brand (Assael 1995, pp. 439–441; 726–728). While the evidence is somewhat mixed, it appears that comparative advertising can produce higher sales when the source of the information is credible, or when the target product is new or lower share (Assael 1995, pp. 439–441; 726–728; Engel et al. 1995, pp. 569–570).

Smith and Burger (1998) investigated comparative advertising in the context of a direct mail offer for a new video camera. The authors found using a laboratory experiment that the effectiveness of comparative advertising depended on what was being compared (price, product attributes, or product experiences) and the target customer (highly knowledgeable about the category, medium knowledge, or low knowledge). The results also depended on whether the dependent variable was purchase intentions for a single product or choice between two side-by-side products. In terms of purchase intentions (most relevant for direct marketers), price comparisons increased purchase intentions for low and high knowledge customers. Attribute comparisons were effective for low knowledge customers, while experience comparisons were effective for high knowledge customers. When choosing between products (as in retail shopping), experience comparisons were effective for low-knowledge customers.

This study highlights that comparative advertising may be an appropriate creative approach for database marketing provided the appropriate comparisons can be targeted based on product knowledge. Database marketers may therefore find it advantageous to test various comparative advertising executions. However, the potential pitfalls of comparative advertising (sympathy and hence sales for the competitive brand, and competitive retaliation) are difficult to measure in a test. More research is needed to gauge these effects in a database marketing context.

While the above discussion pertains to the overall creative appeal, there are several execution details that need to be worked out. These include everything from the type font to specific colors to the wording of sentences (length, use of active verbs, etc.) to the placement of larger pictures on the bottom versus the top of a catalog page. Usually these decisions on the basis of judgment; sometimes specific elements might be tested if deemed important enough.

Gatarski (2002) presents a method for developing over time the optimal creative for an Internet banner ad. A crucial measure of success for an online ad is its click-through rate (CTR). CTR is defined as the number of click-throughs divided by the number of exposures. Gatarski describes the use of a genetic algorithm to design online advertising copy as factorial combinations of ad attributes. The genetic algorithm systematically weeds out under-performing ads over time when it creates a new "generation" of ads. A given ad may generate a high CTR and therefore replicate itself in succeeding generations. However, as its CTR decreases perhaps due to wear out, it is less likely to replicate itself and it dies out, replaced by another ad whose CTR is higher.

Gatarski applied the method to a Compact Disk retail website. The author selected a particular artist and tested the ability of the algorithm to create banner ads that would maximize CTR for the artist's CD. Ads were created as factorial combinations of ad attributes called "genes." Each gene consisted of a number of levels (as in a conjoint analysis) called "alleles." For example, one gene (attribute) was the artist's picture, of which there were four alleles (versions). Other genes included the product picture and use of action phrases such as "Click to Play." A collection of genes with their specific alleles would constitute a particular ad, called a "chromosome." The algorithm to create and evolve chromosomes was as follows:

1. Start with 20 randomly generated banners. This is the first "generation" of chromosomes.
2. Place those banners on the website (the algorithm does not optimize the placement of ads, just the ad copy).
3. Observe response (click-throughs) to the banners.
4. After a period of time, generate the next generation of banners:
    a. Calculate click-through rate for each banner (chromosome).
    b. Calculate the "Fitness" for each chromosome, proportional to its CTR. Fitness represents the probability each chromosome will be selected as "parents" for the next generation.
    c. Select two chromosomes randomly but proportional to fitness.
    d. Randomly select the "cross-over point" gene.
    e. Generate a new child that has the genes of one parent from the left side of the cross-over point, and of the other parent to the right side of the cross-over. (The genes for each chromosome are displayed in a sequence, so one can think of the left or right side of the cross-over gene.)
    f. "Mutate" the child by randomly changing a few of its genes.
    g. Return the parents to the "pool" of prospective parents.
    h. Repeat steps c–g 19 more times, generating a total of 20 children, the next generation of banner ads.
    i. Repeat steps 2–4 for as many generations as desirable.

The algorithm ensures that the more successful a banner is at generating click-throughs, the more likely it is to be selected as a parent for the next generation of banners. Twenty children are created each generation, and each is generated by two randomly selected parents. As a parent, the banner gets to pass on its genes (a randomly generated amount depending on the cross-over point). The mutation step represents the key step in evolution whereby potentially valuable new banner characteristics become part of the banner population. If these mutations are not effective, the chromosome is less likely to be selected as a parent and the mutation dies out. In general, the chromosomes with valuable genes replicate and their genes are perpetuated as long as they are effective.

It is interesting to note the genes that flourished. Use of a click-through sign became more and more prevalent over time. A close-up of the artist's face also became prevalent, as did "Click to Play." Figure 27.2 shows the average click-through rate achieved for the successive generations. The average CTR starts at about 1% and grows to 1.66% by the 16th generation. There are some "lapses," possibly caused by mutations that didn't work or by wear out. The average CTR for the standard banner used by the company was 0.68% over the course of the experiment, and the CTR for the first generation of

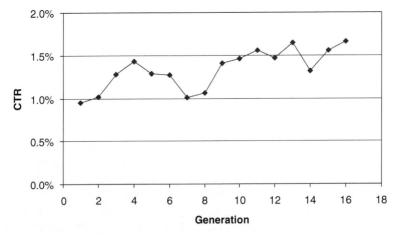

Fig. 27.2 Click through rates for 16 generations of optimally designed banner ads (From Gatarski 2002).

banners when they are not allowed to change over time averaged 1.00%. The genetically engineered banners outperform both these benchmarks.

This example presents promising evidence that the creative details of advertising copy can be optimally generated and adjusted over time. The adjustment is driven by customer data in the form of click-through rate. Ads would have to be quantifiable as factorial combinations of attributes, which may not always be possible. However, Gatarski's work suggests the practicality of the approach for banner advertising.

27.3.2 The Offer

Price is often a critical component of a database marketing offer. Research has investigated how to communicate price in a catalog or direct mail offer, particularly the use of end-nine prices and Sales signs.

Simester and Anderson (2003) investigate the use of end-nine prices by conducting a field experiment with three catalogs. The control catalog contained 50 items whose price ended in a nine. In the two treatment catalogs, prices of these items were either increased or decreased by $1. The three catalogs were each mailed to 20,000 customers. The authors found that after controlling for the popularity of specific items, price *per se* had insignificant impact on sales within the plus-or-minus $2 range in which it was manipulated. However, an end-nine price generated on average 35% higher sales. That is, if an item was presented at $58, $59, or $60, the $59 version would generate 35% higher sales than either the $60 or $58 version! They conducted a second test where prices were varied in a broader range, and the incremental sales due to end-nine was about 15%. In addition, the authors found that the end-nine effect was particularly pronounced for new items.

In another test, the authors manipulated the use of a "Sale" cue along with the price. They found that the use of the Sale cue decreased the end-nine effect. For example, an end-nine price would increase sales of a new item by 8.5%, but if a "Sale" message is already included, the incremental gain is only 3.9%.

The authors posit two explanations for the end-nine effect. The drop-off explanation is that customers round down, process left to right, or just process the left-most digit because of the cognitive cost of processing all digits. If they round down, then $59 is the same as $50. Similarly, if they process left to right, $55 will look different from $45 but the same as $59. The information explanation is that customers use an end-nine as a cue that the item is specially priced or on sale. They may have been conditioned by previous promotional pricing that used end-nine prices.

In a *post hoc* analysis, Simester and Anderson find support for the information explanation and not the drop-off explanation. They use a regression analysis of sales to show that the tens and ones digits of a price are equally important. That is, on a per dollar basis, a change in the tens digit of the price is equally important as a change in the ones digit. Moreover, the end-nine and Sale effects remain significant in this analysis.

If indeed the end-nine effect is due to the information it conveys, one would naturally be concerned about over-using end-nines. If the customer reacts positively to end-nines because he/she infers the product is specially priced or on sale, one cannot use all end-nine prices because it is doubtful that all items could be on sale.

The authors follow this line of reasoning in their investigation of the use of Sale signs in catalogs (Anderson and Simester 2001). They find in a regression analysis that the impact of a Sale sign on sales of a particular catalog item is smaller if more items on the page have Sale signs. Similarly, in a field experiment, they create a control and a treatment catalog. In the control catalog, three items on four pages are depicted as on sale and the remaining five items are not depicted as on sale. In the test catalog, all eight items are depicted as on sale. The results showed that sales decreased for the three items on sale in both catalogs when the other five items are put on sale.

There are three possible explanations for the results: substitution, attention, and credibility. Substitution means that Sale signs become less effective because items on sale cannibalize each other. Attention says that consumers pay less attention to the Sale sign when more brands have them. Credibility says that consumers do pay attention, but don't believe the Sale sign because it is not plausible that so many items could have a reduced price at the same time.

The authors discriminate between substitution and credibility/attention effects by noting the impact of Sales signs on total category demand. The substitution argument would predict category demand to be constant no matter how many Sale signs the catalog has. However, the credibility and attention arguments would suggest that category sales will increase up to a certain point and then decrease when there are too many Sale signs that are either ignored or not believed. In a study of packaged goods, the authors indeed find an inverted-U relationship between the number of Sale signs and category sales, supporting the credibility/attention arguments.

To discriminate between attention and credibility explanations, the authors run a laboratory experiment in which they vary the number of items on a catalog page that contain Sale signs. They find that when an item is on sale and additional products are also on sale, subjects think it more likely that the item will be on sale next period and that the average future price will be lower. This implies they pay attention to the Sale sign in that it influences their perception of future prices. However, they don't believe the current price is "special" in that the item is more likely to be on "sale" next period. That is, Sale signs lose their credibility as signaling a special price the more they are used.

The authors conclude that the credibility effect is the best explanation for Sale signs becoming less effective the more items use them. One avenue for future research is to investigate the substitution effect in a catalog environment rather than packaged goods. Packaged goods are purchased in a supermarket, and category effects may dominate since most of these products can be stored in household inventory (see Van Heerde et al. 2004). In buying from a catalog, shoppers may focus on which computer to buy, or which dress to buy, so substitution would dominate.

In summary, a key tactical issue in copy design for database marketing is how to communicate price. The evidence is that (1) end-nine prices increase sales, (2) the end-nine effect is particularly strong for new items, (3) Sale signs decrease the impact of end-nine prices, (4) Sale signs increase sales of particular items until too many items have Sale signs, at which point its effectiveness per item actually decreases. The reason for the end-nine effect appears to be the information conveyed that the item is at a special price. The reason for the Sale-sign-saturation effect seems to be a loss in credibility. While no research has investigated the loss of credibility for end-nine prices, this is an obvious avenue for future study. The above conclusions are based on two excellent, carefully researched studies, but only two. The results need replication and extension.

The implication is that database marketers should use end-nine and Sale signs albeit judiciously, in designing their offer. In the case of a catalog, the database marketer can make sure he or she does not overuse end-nine prices or Sale signs. However, in designing a single offer, the decision is either/or, not how many. The individual database marketer may feel he or she is not overusing this tactic, but if all database marketers behave the same way, the result is a collective saturation of the impact – customers grow weary of so many end-nine prices and Sale signs. It would be valuable to see this issue explored further.

27.3.3 The Product

27.3.3.1 Deciding Which Products to Feature in Communications

Often the product to be included in the communication is known beforehand. For example, a B2B electric generator company knows the set of products it will include in its catalog. There may still be issues such as which product(s) to promote. Lin and Hong (2008) use market basket analysis (Chapter 13) to select various bundles of products to promote in an electronic catalog. They utilize the "support" (P(AB), see Chapter 13) for various combinations of products to create the bundles and provide evidence that this method increased catalog sales.

Database marketing provides the capability to personalize the firm's product to be offered. For example, a fundamental tenet for Capital One's credit card business is that the particular credit card to be included in a direct mail offer is determined by test mailings. Financial services routinely decide which products to cross-sell to which customers (Knott et al. 2002).

Ansari and Mela (2003) develop a model and optimization for deciding which URL links to include in customer-specific e-mails. The setting is a news/information website that sends e-mails to its users to entice them to the site. The company wishes to gain "readership," thereby increasing its advertising revenues. The website has 12 content areas (products) and it must decide which k content areas to feature in the e-mail ($k \leq 12$) and in which order. The content areas are featured by providing a URL link to the page in the company's website that includes this content. The authors collect data on response to previous e-mails, and estimate the following model:

$$U_{ijk} = X'_{ijk}\mu + Z'_{jk}\lambda_i + W'_{ik}\theta_j + \gamma_k + e_{ijk} \qquad (27.1)$$

where:

U_{ijk} = Utility of customer i for content link k in e-mail j.

X'_{ijk} = Vector of attributes describing e-mail j with content link k seen by customer i. These include for example the content area, the position of the content link (1st, 2nd, 3rd, etc., on the list), the number of content area links featured on the e-mail, whether the e-mail was text or HTML, the length of time since customer i last clicked through an e-mail, etc. These represent "fixed effects" in that μ is the average response to these variables.

Z'_{jk} = A subset of the X variables that vary across content areas or e-mails, for which response is assumed to be heterogeneous across customers. Customer response to content link, number of content areas in the e-mail, and position was assumed heterogeneous, captured by λ_i.

W'_{ik} = A subset of the X variables that vary across customer or content-area levels, whose effect could be heterogeneous across e-mails. This could include position as well as dummy variables for the content area. For example, it might be that two e-mails featuring the same content area might differ in the response they elicit (due to unobserved factors such as season, etc.). The degree that the effects of these variables varies across e-mails is reflected in θ_j.

γ_k = Unobserved factors specific to content area k.

e_{ijk} = Unobserved factors specific to customer i, e-mail j, content area k.

The authors estimate Equation 27.1 using Bayesian techniques and experiment with various ways to capture heterogeneity. Some of their key results are: (1) Few content areas are universally preferred by all customers. (2) There is ample heterogeneity in content preferences across customers. (3) The lower the position of a content area in an e-mail, the less likely it is to be clicked through. (4) The number of content areas featured in an e-mail had no effect *on average* across customers, but there was some heterogeneity across customers.

The estimation generated individual-level response coefficients to content areas featured, position of a particular content area in the e-mail, and number of content areas featured in the e-mail. The authors then develop an optimization model to design each customer's e-mail. They considered two objectives – maximizing the expected number of clicks per e-mail, or maximizing the likelihood of at least one click through. We show the formulation for the latter objective, because it is unlikely the customer would come back to the e-mail after clicking through one of the content area URL's.

To make the optimization easier, the authors undertake a two-phase approach where for a fixed number of items in the e-mail (k), they find the best content areas to include in which position. They vary k from 1 to 12 (since there are 12 content areas, $k \leq 12 \equiv n$). For a given customer and a given number of items, the optimization is:

$$\underset{x_{ij}}{Maximize} \sum_{i=1}^{n} \sum_{j=1}^{k} \left[1 - \prod_{i=1}^{n} \prod_{j=1}^{k} (1 - p_{ijk})^{x_{ij}} \right]$$

$$\Rightarrow \underset{x_{ij}}{Minimize} \sum_{i=1}^{n} \sum_{j=1}^{k} [x_{ij} \log(1 - p_{ijk})] \qquad (27.2)$$

subject to:

x_{ij} = 1 if content area i is include in the e-mail in position j. There are $n = 12$ content areas and k possible positions, with $k \leq n$.

p_{ijk} = Probability the customer clicks through content area i if it is in position j when the total number of content areas included is k.

The optimization is performed for all 12 values of k for the 100 customers in the sample. The authors then test their predictions on a holdout sample using three approaches: (1) the optimization described above, (2) an ordering algorithm which took takes each e-mail in the holdout and re-orders the content areas according to the customer's model-inferred preferences. Whether

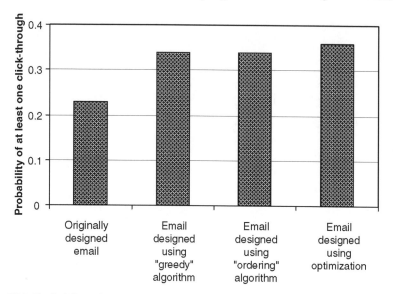

Fig. 27.3 Probability of at least one click-through in a personalized e-mail (From Ansari and Mela 2003).

the most preferred was placed on top or bottom depended on the sign of the position variable (a positive sign implies the customer has higher utility if the content link is toward the bottom of the set of links, i.e., the customer is a bottom-up processor, while a negative sign implies the customer is a top-down processor), and (3) a greedy algorithm that kept the number of content areas the same, i.e., k, but included the k highest-preferred content areas for each customer and inserted them in the e-mail in order of preference. The results are shown in Fig. 27.3.

All three algorithms improve significantly over the baseline click-through rate: the rate in the holdout data using the e-mails as they were originally designed. The strong performance of the ordering and greedy algorithms, which took the number of links in the e-mail as given, is probably due to the fact that the number-of-items variable turned out not to be crucial – its coefficient on average was not different than zero, and although there was customer heterogeneity on this coefficient, it was not enough to make a big difference. However, the success of the ordering and greedy algorithms shows that the customer-level content preference and top-down versus bottom-up processing measures (reflected by the position variable) were important.

Ansari and Mela's work is very important because it shows how to personalize a communication to include the products most relevant to a customer. The model could be extended to include creative and offer variables as well (in fact, the authors included one creative detail – text versus html – in their model). Two avenues for future research building on this work would apply it to multi-campaign scheduling – i.e., scheduling several e-mails over time (see Chapter 28), and scaling the heterogeneity up to a company's full house list. One approach would be to use latent class segmentation and calculate posterior probabilities of segment membership using Bayes theorem.

27.3.3.2 Allocating Catalog Space to Various Departments

Single Catalog

Squeezed by mailing costs that limit the size of catalogs coupled with expanded product lines, allocating catalog space to departments or product lines has become a challenging issue for catalogers. The problem is somewhat similar to the space allocation problem in bricks-and-mortar retail stores. However, as Desmet (1993) points out, the space decision is fixed for the duration of a catalog whereas it is flexible in a store. In addition, catalog space allocations draw the customer into the catalog, whereas shelf space allocations in stores influence the customer who has already decided on a shopping trip. Of additional interest to database marketers is that catalogs can be tailored to individual customers, which cannot happen in a bricks-and-mortar store.

While from a database marketing perspective, personalization is the ultimate goal, it is useful to examine first the situation of a single mass-marketed catalog. Rao and Simon (1983) pioneered this case. They derive the simple rule that under certain assumptions, the optimal allocation of space is such that the profit per square inch of allocated space is equal for all departments. Their decision problem is as follows:

$$Max_{x_i} \ Z = \sum_i m_i S_i(x_i) - \sum_i C_i(x_i) \tag{27.3}$$

$$\text{subject to:} \ \sum_i x_i = P \tag{27.4}$$

where:

m_i = Profit margin for category i.
S_i = Sales of department i.
x_i = Space allocated to department i.
C_i = Cost function for department i.
P = Total page limit for catalog.

This can be solved using Lagrange multipliers. The most important implication is that the space allocation should be such that the marginal profit contributions for all departments is the same. If at a given allocation, the marginal contribution of one department is higher than the others, we would add more space to that department and reduce space for the others. That is, we are not at an "equilibrium" allocation until all the marginal contributions are equal.

Rao and Simon (1983) show that if sales response is a simple power function, $S_i = \alpha_i x_i^{\beta_i}$ with all β_i's less than 1,[3] and if the β_i's are equal for all departments, then the optimal allocation is:

$$x_i^* = \frac{P m_i S_i}{\sum_j m_j S_j} \tag{27.5}$$

or,

$$\frac{m_i S_i}{x_i^*} = \frac{\sum_j m_j S_j}{P} \tag{27.6}$$

Equation 27.6 says that at the optimal allocation, all departments will generate the same profit per square inch (or other unit of area) of allocated space. This is a very usable rule of thumb since profit per square inch is easily calculated. If the space response elasticities are not all equal, Equations 27.5 and 27.6 are modified so that $\beta_i m_i$ replaces m_i, and $\beta_j m_j$ replaces m_j. Equation 27.6 then becomes:

$$\frac{m_i S_i}{x_i^*} = \frac{\sum_j \beta_j m_j S_j}{\beta_i P} \tag{27.7}$$

Equation 27.7 implies that profit per square inch for a given department is inversely proportional to its elasticity. The reason for this is that as elasticity increases, we tend to allocate more space to the department, but the increase in profits has diminishing returns (since $\beta_i < 1$). As a result, the profit per square inch decreases with higher elasticity.

An important assumption is the absence of cross-department effects.[4] There could be complementarity or substitution effects, which would make the allocation more complicated. The objective would still be the same as Equation 27.3, except there would probably not be a closed-form solution. Corstjens and Doyle (1981) or Bultez and Naert (1988) solve similar problems in a retail store environment.

A critical empirical question for the above analysis is, what is the space response elasticity (β)? Equation 27.6 for example is predicated on the assumption that elasticities are all less than one and equal to each other across departments. Equation 27.7 abandons the equality assumption but still assumes concave returns.

---

[3] This assumption means diminishing returns to space allocation, or concave returns. If space elasticities are >1, the optimal allocation is to devote all possible space to the highest elasticity department.

[4] See Hofacker and Murphy (2000) for a discussion of banner ad cannibalization in the context of Internet Web page design.

The evidence is limited in scope but it appears to be that elasticities are less than one. Desmet (1995) found that space elasticities for a book catalog were 0.43 for new books and 0.43 for old books. Sokolick and Hartung (1969) found an elasticity of 0.56. Desmet (1993) found an elasticity of 1.18 for clothing, although suspects that this is over-stated. Desmet (1993) finds managerial judgments of elasticities range from 0.55 to 0.77. This work is suggestive, but much more work is needed to measure own and cross-department elasticities. To obtain these estimates, managers must be willing to vary space allocation systematically in a field test. See Seaver and Simpson (1995) for an experiment to study catalog design.

Personalized Catalogs

Of keen interest to the database marketer is how to personalize catalog space for individual customers. We present an illustration of how this might be done. We assume there are J market segments, each with a different response function. The goal is to design a catalog tailored to each segment by allocating the number of pages from each of D departments to each of the J catalogs. Note the number of catalogs equal the number of customer segments, so J is both the total number of segments and the total number of catalogs to be specified. The problem can be expressed as:

$$\max_{\vec{x}_j} \sum_j m\delta_j S_j(\vec{x}_j) \tag{27.8}$$

subject to:

$$\sum_i x_{ij} = P \qquad \forall j \tag{27.8a}$$

$$CL_i \le x_{ij} \le CU_i \qquad \forall i,j \tag{27.8b}$$

$$DL_i \le \sum_j x_{ij} \le DU_i \qquad \forall i \tag{27.8c}$$

$$x_{ij} \ge 0 \qquad \forall i,j \tag{27.8d}$$

$$x_{ij} \quad integer \qquad \forall i,j \tag{27.8e}$$

where:

$\vec{x}_j = \{x_{ij}\} = (x_{1j}, x_{2j}, \ldots, x_{Dj})$, where x_{ij} is the number of pages for department i allocated to catalog j. D is the number of departments.

S_j = Sales per customer in catalog j as a function of the allocation $\vec{x}_j$. The sales response function differs for each catalog because each catalog represents a different market segment.

δ_j = Percentage of customer base represented by segment $j (\sum_j \delta_j = 1)$.

m = Profit margin, assumed to be equal across departments.

P = Number of pages to be allocated to each catalog.

Table 27.1 Parameters and optimal solution for catalog customization

Response functions				
	Constant	Dept A elasticity	Dept B elasticity	Dept C elasticity	Segment percentage
Segment 1	0.01	0.4	0.5	0.2	30%
Segment 2	0.015	0.3	0.1	0.7	50%
Segment 3	0.0325	0.3	0.7	0.8	20%

Catalog page constraints				
	Within catalog Lower bound	Upper bound	Across catalogs Lower bound	Upper bound
Department A	10	40	30	120
Department B	10	40	30	120
Department C	10	40	30	120

Other parameters	
Profit margin	30%
Number of customers	100,000
Page limit per catalog	50

Optimal number of pages allocated				
	Dept A	Dept B	Dept C	Sales/customer
Segment 1	18	22	10	$0.236
Segment 2	12	10	28	$0.410
Segment 3	10	19	21	$5.818
			Profit/customer	$0.431
			Total profit	$43,186

Constraint 27.8a ensures that each catalog has P pages. Constraints 27.8b and 27.8c are departmental exposure requirements that arise because the firm wants to make sure that each department gets at least minimum exposure, but is not over-emphasized. This reflects long-term considerations in the positioning of the catalog and inventory management. Constraint 27.8b ensures that each catalog contains at least a minimum number of pages from each department, and no more than a maximum. Constraint 27.8c ensures that each department has minimum and maximum representation across all catalogs. Constraints 27.8d and 27.8e require that page allocations take on integer values greater than zero. Therefore, this is an integer programming problem.

Note this is a joint optimization does not maximize profits from each segment separately. Therefore, there is the possibility that one of the generated catalogs, say j', generates more profit in segment j than the catalog generated for segment j! This is because the catalogs are being generated to satisfy departmental representation constraints (27.8b and 27.8c) so segment j's catalog may contain a large number of pages from department i, not because this maximizes sales from segment j but because segment j has the best response to department i and we need a minimum representation of department i among the J catalogs.

Table 27.1 summarizes the parameters for an illustrative analysis of the model. We have three segments so there will be three catalogs ($J = 3$). There are three departments ($D = 3$). Each catalog consists of 50 pages, and must contain between 10 and 40 pages of each department (given the 50-page total, the effective upper bound is 30 for each department). Across all catalogs, we must have between 30 and 120 pages for each department. The space response function is:

$$S_j = \alpha_j \prod_{i=1}^{D} x_{ij}^{\beta_{ij}} \qquad (27.9)$$

This is a multiplicative response function with constant elasticities shown in Table 27.1. The elasticities and segment percentages show that Segment 2 is the largest segment and is particularly responsive to Department C space. Segment 3 is the smallest and likes Departments B and C. Segment 1 is mid-sized and likes Departments A and B.

The bottom of Table 27.1 shows the optimal allocation of pages. The allocations are intuitive. Segments generally are allocated pages proportional to their elasticities. For example, Segment 3 gets pages mostly from Departments B and C and has the minimal amount required for Department A. Segment 2 receives 2 more pages than the minimum for Department A even though its elasticity is the same as Segment 3's. This is because Segment 2 has a very low elasticity for Department B. None of the across-catalog departmental representation constraints is binding, although the within-catalog requirements sometimes are binding on the low side. Clearly it isn't optimal for Segment 2 taken in isolation to receive 10 pages of Department B, since its elasticity is only 0.1. However, long-term considerations dictate the minimum requirement. Finally, note that Segment 3, although it is smallest in terms of percentage of customers, has a high constant term so contributes the most to overall profit.

Figure 27.4 shows how the optimal solution changes as elasticity increases. In particular, we vary Segment 2's elasticity for Department B. The results are predictable. As elasticity increases, the pages allocated to Department B for Segment 2 increases. Since we have a 50-page limit, something has to give. The optimal solution takes away pages from both departments. After the allocation to Department A hits its lower bound, more pages are taken from Department C. Profits increase exponentially after elasticity becomes greater than 1, because then we have a convex demand function. While not shown in Fig. 27.4, the allocations to the other segments remain about the same.

Figure 27.5 shows how the optimal solution changes as a lower bound constraint increases. In particular, we vary the across-catalog minimum for Department B. This minimum is currently at 30 while the current solution allocates 51 pages. So the constraint is non-binding and the optimal solution does not change until the constraint moves above 50 pages. At 60 pages, the model has to allocate an additional 9 pages, and allocates them to Segment 1's catalog. As the constraint increases, it allocates next to Segment 2's

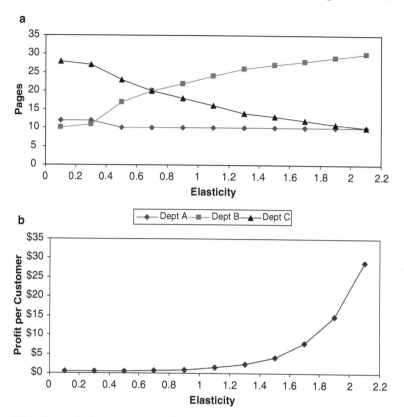

Fig. 27.4 Optimal allocation and profits as a function of elasticity. (**a**) Page allocations as a function of Department B, Segment 2 elasticity; (**b**) Catalog profit as function of Department B, Segment 2 elasticity.

catalog, and finally to Segment 3's.[5] The reason for this order of allocation is that Segment 1 has a fairly high elasticity for Department B, so we can take away pages from the other departments in Segment 1's catalog without too much sacrifice. Next the model allocates additional pages to Segment 2's catalog although this is a low elasticity department for this segment. The reason is that although we will have to take away from Department C, which is popular with this segment, the segment does not influence total profits as much. Finally, the model allocates more Department B pages to Segment 3's catalog. This severely diminishes profit because Segment 3 represents the majority of firm profits and we are using a sub-optimal catalog for that segment in order to fulfill the lower bound requirement.

---

[5] As noted above, while the explicit upper bound is 40 pages per catalog per department, the effective constraint is 30 because the other departments have to have at least 10 pages and the total catalog has 50 pages.

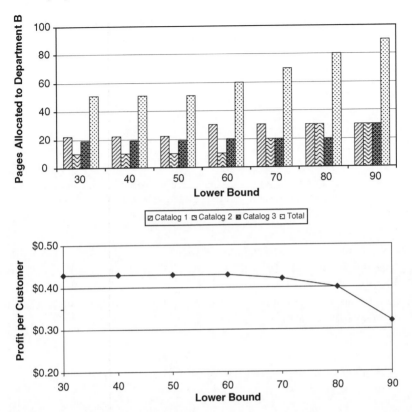

Fig. 27.5 Optimal allocation and profits as function of lower bound page requirement. (**a**) Page allocation as a function of Department B lower bound; (**b**) Profit per customer as function of Department B lower bound.

The example illustrates that pages are allocated roughly proportional to elasticities, but minimum and maximum requirements create distortions that reverberate across as well as within segments. One might therefore question why we have these constraints. The reason is that catalogers wish to maintain a presence in several departments, they may have plans to grow various departments in the future, and they need to make up for the fixed costs of running a particular department.

While the above demonstrates that the optimization in Equation 27.8 is quite rich, it does not contain explicit cross elasticities between departments. The demand function is for the catalog as a whole, not individual departments. Extensions of this model would include departmental level demand functions with cross-elasticities.

Another extension would be to apply the model to the customer level, where segments now correspond to individual customers. With 1,000,000 customers (N = 1,000,000), we could have 1,000,000 different catalogs. This would be Equation 27.8 with J = 1,000,000. Another possibility would be to specify J < N: We might have 1,000,000 customers with 1,000,000 different response functions, but only have say 10 catalogs (J = 10). This would be a more difficult problem because the objective function would have to distinguish between catalogs and customers. It would be:

$$\max_{\vec{x}_j, M_{cj}} \sum_c \sum_j m S_{cj}(\vec{x}_j) M_{cj} \qquad (27.10)$$

where:

$S_{cj}(\vec{x}_j)$ = Sales for customer c if mailed catalog j and catalog j has page allocation $\vec{x}_j$.

$M_{cj} = 1$ if catalog j is mailed to customer c; 0 if not. We require of course that only one catalog can be mailed to each customer, and all customers must receive a catalog.

This would be a more complicated optimization because we have two decision variables, the page allocation to creating each catalog, and the decision of what catalog to mail to each customer. In the problem analyzed in this section, catalogs corresponded to segments, which made the allocation and mailing decision the same.

27.3.4 Personalizing Multiple Components of the Communication

Ansari and Mela (2003) focused on personalizing the product(s) featured to the customer, but their model also contained creative elements (their "Text" variable). It also could have included aspects of the offer such as price (see Rossi et al. (1996) for a price-personalization model, and Chapter 29). Therefore, if a customer response model contains variables representing creative, product, and offer components, it can be used to personalize communications in terms of all these elements.

Customer-level response models are attractive for personalizing communications. However, they rely on a fair amount of data per customer and the optimization can become complex when tailoring more components. Another approach is to use machine learning tools to personalize communications. One domain where there has been initial work on this is in personalizing websites.

Ardissono and Goy (2000; see also Ardissono et al. 2002) describe "SETA", a system that personalizes the products featured, the use of graphics, and the length and terminology of product descriptions on an e-tailing website. A demonstration can be found at http://www.di.unito.it/~seta/seta.htm. SETA employs a user-based collaborative filtering system that associates each user with a "stereotype," then predicts preferences for product attributes, styles of presentation, etc., based on the probability the user belongs to each stereotype (see also Kohrs and Merialdo 2001). The probability is based on how well the available information for the user matches each stereotype. The more information available for the user the more accurate this probability distribution is, and hence the predictions are more accurate. If the user registers at the website, the information can be stored and grows over time. If the user does not register, the system starts with a generic presentation and then learns more about the customer as the customer navigates through the site.

Between customer-response models and machine learning systems, there is great potential for personalizing all aspects of a database marketing communication. More work is needed both to develop and test these methods.

27.4 Selecting Media

27.4.1 Optimization

Database marketers have a plethora of outlets through which to communicate with customers, including direct mail, e-mail, telephone, the Internet, and catalogs (Tellis 1998). Selecting which media vehicle(s) to use is amenable to the same approaches that have been used for vehicle selection in mass marketing (see Tellis, Chapter 16; Lilien et al. 1992, Chapter 6). The basic requirements are response functions for each medium, and the degree of overlap between media. For example, if a database marketer purchases 1,000,000 Internet impressions, and e-mails a list of 1,000,000 addresses, what would be the net number of individuals exposed to the campaign? To our knowledge, no research has yet investigated this issue or the general problem of vehicle selection in a database marketing context. To formulate the problem, let

E = Number of times customer is exposed to the offer.
X_i = Number of insertions of the offer in vehicle i.
$i = 1, \ldots, N$ where N is the total number of vehicles.
$P(E|X_1, X_2, \ldots, X_N)$ = Probability a randomly selected customer will be exposed to the offer E times, given the vehicle selection strategy $X_1, X_2, \ldots, X_N$.
λ = Parameter depicting decreasing returns to multiple exposures.
$(1 - e^{-\lambda E})$ = Probability a randomly selected customer will respond to an offer, given he or she is exposed to it E times.
C_i = Cost per insertion in vehicle i.
B = Budget.

Then the optimization problem is:

$$\underset{X_1 X_2 \ldots X_N}{Max} \sum_{E=1}^{N} (1 - e^{-\lambda E}) P(E | X_1 X_2 \ldots X_N) \qquad (27.11)$$

such that

$$\sum_{i=1}^{N} C_i X_i = B \qquad (27.12)$$

Equation 27.11 shows the goal is to select media $\{X_1, X_2, \ldots, X_N\}$ to maximize average response rate (equivalent to maximizing the total number of responses). The average response rate is the sum of the customer response rates for each number of possible exposures, weighted by the probability the customer receives that number of exposures. The optimal vehicle selection also must satisfy the budget constraint (Equation 27.12).

The key parameters are the response parameter λ and the exposure probability function P. λ could be estimated judgmentally or through testing. The exposure probability function is a frequency distribution estimated for example by Rice (1988) or Rust et al. (1986) in the context of mass media.

The approach can easily be made more complex, and potentially more effective. First is that individual customers may differ in their response rates. We would have λ_c, where c labels the customer. Second, λ may depend on vehicle, so that we have λ_i. Finally, λ could depend both on customer and vehicle, λ_{ci}.

The importance of adjusting λ by vehicle is illustrated by Sherman and Deighton (2001). They consider the problem of selecting websites on the Internet for a banner advertising campaign. The goal of the campaign was to induce web surfers to visit the drugstore.com website. The task was to identify the websites on which drugstore.com should place banner ads in order to maximize visits to its website. The approach was to estimate a predictive model predicting visits to the drugstore.com website as a function of visits to other websites. The results yielded an "affinity" between the websites and drugstore.com. Then a cluster analysis was used to group websites by various website attributes, and the affinity for each cluster was then calculated. This enabled the researchers to identify clusters, and hence websites, that had particular affinities for drugstore.com. These websites were then targeted with banner ads.

The results were quite favorable. The high-affinity sites generated 10 times the purchases per impression as were generated by the low-affinity sites. One site generated 43% of all orders using just 32% of the overall budget.

Sherman and Deighton show that response rates differ across websites and hence should be incorporated in Equations 27.11 and 27.12. The study also shows that predictive modeling can be used to increase website visits. The study focuses only on the response of individual sites and does not consider decreasing returns to repetition as in Equation 27.11. It could be that placing ads on several websites within an affinity cluster creates duplication. This means that it may have been possible to improve the allocation. However, the example shows clearly that starting with a relatively simple approach can generate important gains.

27.4.2 Integrated Marketing Communications

The analysis in Sect. 27.4.1 assumes media vehicles have to be selected to distribute a given offer. The more general case is that different messages might be distributed in different vehicles. For example, mass television advertising may be used to create awareness for the product, and the Internet may be used to extend a promotional offer. The "ads" themselves would be different. However, the concept of "integrated marketing communications" (IMC) posits that the content of these ads should be coordinated. The basic tenet of IMC is that the firm benefits by consistency, or at least complementarity, in its advertising messages.

IMC is especially important in database marketing because the modern database marketer sends out many different communications. Sheehan and Doherty (2001) discuss IMC in a database marketing context. They measure the degree of coordination in advertising messages between print and online advertising for 186 companies. They collected their data by first finding a print ad; then going to the company website to assess the consistency between the ads. The authors find a higher degree of coordination in certain aspects of the advertising but not in others. For example, in 82.8% of cases, the same logo could be found on both the website and the print ad. However, the "promise or single most important message of the print advertisement" was easily found on the website only 38.6% of the time. It was found albeit with difficulty 33.9% of the time, and not found at all 27.5% of the time.

Sheehan and Doherty show that companies do not necessarily coordinate their communication strategy across advertising vehicles. The next step is to assess empirically the importance of coordination in a database marketing context.

27.5 Evaluating Communications Programs

Four methods for evaluating a communications program are: (1) calculation of profits, (2) *post hoc* statistical analysis, (3) embedded testing, and (4) surveys.

Often a database marketing communications campaign can be evaluated directly by calculating profits. For a direct marketing campaign, the general form of the calculation is:

$$\Pi = NrM - Nc \qquad (27.13)$$

where

Π = Profits
N = Number of contacts (e.g., number of pieces mailed)
r = Response rate
M = Profit margin per response
c = Contact cost

Another important measure is return on investment or ROI:

$$ROI = \frac{NrM - Nc}{Nc} = \frac{rM - c}{c} \qquad (27.14)$$

ROI is the profits earned by the program divided by its cost. It has become popular to talk about "marketing ROI," and the strong advantage of the concept is that it is comparable across programs, companies, and industries. It also has high face validity: "For every dollar invested, we made [ROI] dollars in profit." However, one problem is that ROI is oblivious to scale. Is it better to make $2,000,000 on a $1,000,000 investment or $200,000 on a $10,000 investment (ROI = $2 per dollar versus $20 per dollar)? As discussed in Chapter 10, "Type I error" decision-making – where the goal is to avoid investments that would not have paid out, rather than avoid not making investments that would have paid out – emphasizes ROI. Shrinking the denominator of Equation 27.14 may inherently increase ROI, because the smaller investment is made on the customers who are sure to pay out. However, the total profits may not be impressive.

Another important issue with both Equations 27.13 and 27.14 is they typically are single channel, not multiple channel calculations. The multichannel company runs the risk that a marketing effort in Channel A takes away from Channel B. For example, a bank conducting a direct mail campaign to sell credit cards may take away from credit card sales in the its branch offices. Communications evaluation in a multichannel context requires data on *total* sales, not just those generated through the channel through which the communication was distributed.

Statistical analysis to evaluate communications falls under the rubric of "marketing mix modeling." These analyses take the form of regression models such as:

$$Sales_t = \beta_0 + \beta_1 \ Marketing_t + \beta_2 \ Seasonality_t + \varepsilon_t \qquad (27.15)$$

The coefficient β_1 measures the increase in sales per dollar increase in marketing expenditure. To calculate total profits, one would multiply the total marketing expenditure during the period of interest times β_1 to yield total sales generated, and then apply the margin percentage to calculate total profits or ROI. Equation 27.15 is an outline of a marketing mix model. There are several other variables that might be included (e.g., other marketing efforts besides the campaign being evaluated, competitive marketing efforts, and carryover effects of marketing). The reader is referred to Leeflang et al. (2000) for a thorough discussion (also see Dean 2006).

Equation 27.15 can be estimated for each of the company's channels. For a retail bank, there would be equations for mail-order and branch sales of credit cards. It is possible that β_1 would be positive in the mail-order equation but negative in the branch equation, signifying cross-channel cannibalization. This provides important learning as well as the "bottom line" profits of the campaign.

In practice, regression modeling can become quite complex and one is never sure that all possible influencers of sales during the period of interest have been included. Therefore, a good practice is to embed a "control group" within the full launch of the campaign to provide an experimental test of the campaign. That is, the full credit card campaign might have been mailed to 1,000,000 customers, but an additional 10,000 were not mailed the campaign to provide a control. Profit is calculated by comparing sales, and hence profit, per customer in the campaign group versus the control group.

A few issues are important in using embedded tests. First, sales data need to be collected for all customers across all channels. In the banking example, the control group will be of no use if the bank cannot compile credit card sales for *all* its customers across *both* direct mail and in-branch channels. Second, the control group must be randomly selected from the group *eligible* for the campaign. For example, the customers selected to receive the direct mail credit card piece might have scored in the top four deciles as classified from a predictive model (Chapter 10). The 10,000 control customers must be selected from that group, not from the bottom six deciles. This means that the company is incurring an opportunity cost in not mailing to the control group, since they are prime prospects for the campaign (Chapter 9). That is why the sample size for the control group in an embedded test should be much smaller than the full mailing.

Testing plays a crucial role both in campaign design *and* evaluation. In the banking example, a test mailing to 30,000 customers could provide data for a predictive model. That model would be used to score the company's 1,000,000 customers, 400,000 of whom might fall in the top four deciles that are profitable. Of those 400,000 customers, the mailing might go to 390,000, with 10,000 held out as a control. The first test is crucial for targeting the campaign; the second test is crucial for evaluating it.

Customer surveys are especially important for evaluating qualitative aspects of the campaign such as reinforcing product positioning. The company may survey a subgroup (e.g., 500–1,000) of its customers after the campaign to make sure the product and company is being perceived according to plan. The time and expense of conducting surveys may preclude evaluating every communication using a survey. However, periodic use of surveys can be an important way to ensure a firm's database marketing efforts are not leading the company astray from its desired positioning and target group.

In summary, communications campaigns can be evaluated using direct calculations, *post hoc* statistical analysis, embedded tests, and surveys. Direct calculations are the easiest when there are no "externalities" to worry about, such as cross-channel cannibalization. Embedded tests are easy to "read" and the opportunity cost is worth the clean calculation of profits. However, testing may not always be practical. For example, a direct response television campaign cannot be randomly targeted to some customers within a given locale and not targeted to others. *Post hoc* statistical analyses become essential (Tellis et al. 2000). Surveys are especially useful for evaluating the qualitative objectives of a campaign, and can be an important source of insight for the database marketing firm that can easily get caught up with the immediate "bottom line" while losing sight of the long term.

Chapter 28
Multiple Campaign Management

Abstract Many database marketing programs are constructed as one-shot efforts – they determine the best campaign to implement *now*. However, more recently, academics and companies have recognized that the actions we take now influence what actions we will be compelled to take in the future, and if the current actions are not managed correctly, these future actions will not be successful. The key is to manage the series of communications holistically, taking into account the future as we design the current campaign, and to do so at the customer level. This chapter discusses "optimal contact models" for managing a series of campaigns. Many of the examples we draw on involve the catalog industry, although we also discuss examples involving e-mails, product magazines, promotional discounts, and even online survey panel management.

28.1 Overview

Managing multiple campaigns is an emerging issue in database marketing due to the confluence of two forces: First, optimizing a single contact using a predictive model has become commonplace – we know how to do this and can do it well. Second, there is concern that customers are becoming cluttered with direct marketing communications such as catalogs, e-mails, online advertising, etc.

Multiple campaigns can be managed by "optimal contact models." These models specify the number and/or schedule of communications including catalogs, e-mails, online advertising, even requests for online panelists to participate in surveys, at the customer level. Two factors make this a challenging task. First is dynamic customer response. Customer response to a contact changes over time, depending on the customer's previous contact and response history. Second, because of response dynamics, a natural way to optimize the *schedule* of contacts over time is to be "forward looking," i.e., recommend decisions for period t taking into account the impact this has on customer response and hence future profits in period $t + 1$, $t + 2$, etc. In Section 28.2 we discuss dynamic response. In Section 28.3 we discuss optimal contact models.

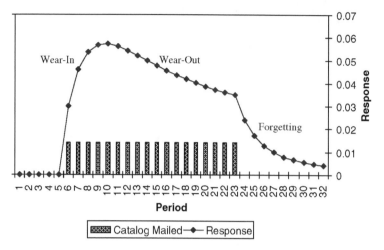

Fig. 28.1 Wear-in, wear-out, and forgetting.

28.2 Dynamic Response Phenomena

28.2.1 Wear-in, Wear-out, and Forgetting

These phenomena were first identified in the advertising literature (see Little 1979) but we explain them in the context of mailing catalogs to customers. Wear-in means it takes several mailed catalogs before the customer responds – it takes several mailings before we fully capture the customer's attention. Wear-out means that once a critical number of mailings is reached, subsequent catalogs produce lower response rates. The customer may no longer be paying attention to the catalog. Forgetting means that once mailings are halted, response does not instantly go to zero but decays gradually. This is because the customer still has the previous catalog(s) on hand, although eventually discards them. Figure 28.1 shows the three phenomena.

While wear-out is explained most easily by a lack of attention, there are three additional possibilities. First is that too much information confuses customers to the point that they make incorrect decisions (Assael 1995, pp. 231–232; Jacoby et al. 1974), or to make more mistakes in evaluating brands (Hutchinson and Alba 1991). A second explanation is that the customer gets angry at the constant "harassment" and refuses to buy. Third, the customer's needs could have been satiated by earlier catalogs.

Wear-in and forgetting can be modeled with a stock variable:

$$Stock_t = \lambda Stock_{t-1} + \beta C_t \qquad (28.1)$$

C_t is an indicator variable (0–1) of whether a catalog was mailed to the customer in period t. The parameters $\lambda (0 < \lambda < 1)$ and $\beta (\beta > 0)$ refer to

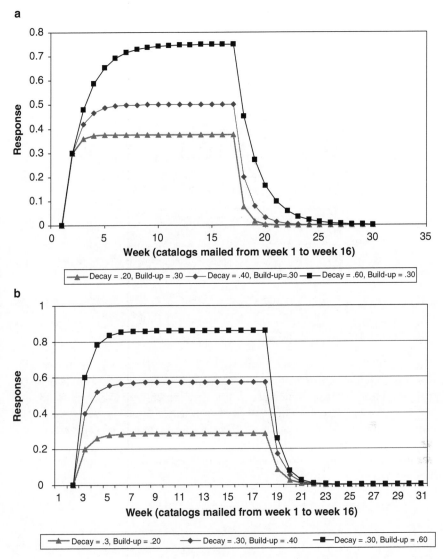

Fig. 28.2 Dynamic wear-in and forgetting generated from a stock model (Equation 28.1).

decay and build-up of catalog stock (see Fig. 28.2). λ controls the rate of wear-in and forgetting – large λ means faster wear-in and slower forgetting. Both β and λ determine the peak stock level:

$$\text{Peak Stock Level} = \frac{\beta}{(1 - \lambda)} \qquad (28.2)$$

The stock model includes wear-in and forgetting but not wear-out. Simon (1982) devised a simple way to accommodate wear-out and forgetting, as

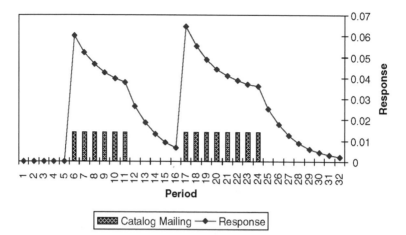

Fig. 28.3 Simon's (1982) model of wear-out and forgetting (Equation 28.3.)*
*$\mathrm{Prob(Buy)_t} = 0.7\mathrm{Stock_{t-1}} + 0.01\mathrm{C_t} + 0.05\max(0, \mathrm{C_t} - \mathrm{C_{t-1}})$

follows:

$$Stock_t = \lambda Stock_{t-1} + \beta C_t + \delta max(0, C_t - C_{t-1}) \qquad (28.3)$$

The term $C_t - C_{t-1}$ creates an immediate increase ("shock") in stock whenever a catalog is mailed in the current period after not being mailed in the previous period. High values for δ boost stock higher than its maximum ($\beta/(1-\lambda)$). As more catalogs are mailed, stock declines (wears out) to this value. Figure 28.3 shows Equation 28.3 for specific values of the parameters. Wear-out and forgetting are clearly visible in the figure.

An even more flexible model that includes wear-in, wear-out, and forgetting is:

$$Stock_t = \lambda Stock_{t-1} + \beta_t C_t + \delta ShockStock_t \qquad (28.4a)$$

$$ShockStock_t = \lambda' ShockStock_{t-1} + \beta' Max(0, C_t - C_{t-1}) \qquad (28.4b)$$

$$\beta_t = \lambda'' \beta_{t-1} + \beta'' C_t \qquad (28.4c)$$

Equation 28.4b smoothes the $Max(0, C_t - C_{t-1})$ shock variable. It peaks immediately at β' and then decays by a factor λ'. Equation 28.4c grows the immediate impact of catalog mailings up to a maximum $\beta^* = (\beta''/(1-\lambda''))$. The net result is that the maximum induced by the $C_t - C_{t-1}$ shock is not realized until some delay, creating a wear-in effect. Once we reach that maximum, we have wear-out down to the level $\beta^*/(1-\lambda)$, and then forgetting by the factor λ once the mailing stops (see Fig. 28.4).

One can graph the number of communications made over several periods versus response aggregated over several customers. This "aggregate response function" can take on several shapes depending on the degree of wear-in, wear-out, and forgetting occurring at the micro level (see Fig. 28.5).

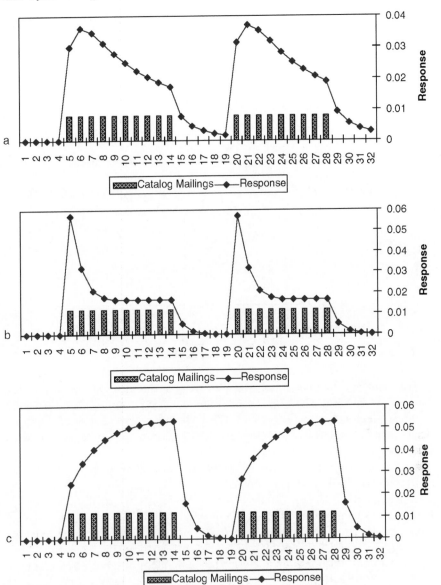

Fig. 28.4 A stock model including wear-in, wear-out, and forgetting (Equation 28.4)*.
(a) Wear-in, wear-out, forgetting; (b) No wear-in, wear-out, forgetting; (c) Wear-in, no
wear-out, forgetting;

*Parameter values (see Equations 28.4a–c)

	Scenario 1	Scenario 2	Scenario 3
λ	0.3	0.3	0.3
δ	0.05	0.05	0.01
λ'	0.8	0.1	0.3
β'	0.5	1	1
λ''	0.4	0.4	0.6
β''	0.005	0.007	0.015

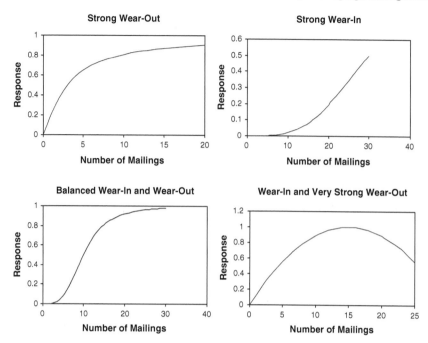

Fig. 28.5 Aggregate response functions depending on degree of wear-in and wear-out.

Wear-out is an especially crucial phenomenon because it provides a non-cost reason to limit the number of contacts. Fewer mailings may actually produce more sales (see Fig. 28.6). With 20 consecutive weeks of catalogs, response peaks relatively soon and then starts to wear out. However, with catalog "pulsing," the wear-out effect is mitigated and the total expected response increases. This is why aggregate response as a function of contacts can be inverse U-shaped as in Fig. 28.5d.

Ansari et al. (2008) estimate λ's ranging from 0.04 to 0.14 for e-mails and catalogs using weekly data, implying fast wear-in as well as forgetting.[1] Gönül et al. (2000) include time since the last catalog was received in a catalog response model. Its estimated coefficient was negative, consistent with forgetting. The authors also include the cumulative number of catalogs received after the last purchase and find a negative relationship. This supports wear-out. Campbell et al. (2001) report wear-out regarding net returns as a function of "advertising expenditure."

Eastlick et al. (1993) asked catalog buyers how many catalogs they received in the past 12 months, and how much they purchased during that time. The researchers fit a regression across buyers and find an inverse U-shaped relationship between catalogs and expenditures. This is consistent with very

---

[1] Note that estimates of λ can be biased upward when data are temporally aggregated, e.g., to the monthly or quarterly levels (see Leeflang et al. 2000, pp. 85–91. Estimating on the weekly level is therefore advisable.

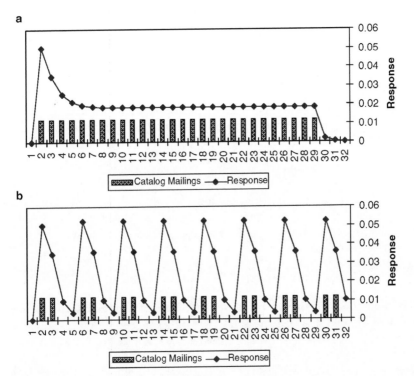

Fig. 28.6 With high wear-out, pulsing produces more responses than constant mailing, even with fewer total mailings. (a) Constant mailing strategy (total response = 0.580); (b) Pulsing mailing strategy (total response = 0.810)

Note: Model used to generate graphs based on Equations 28.4a–28.4c parameterized as follows:

$$\text{Stock}_t = 0.1 * \text{Stock}_{t-1} + \beta_t * C_t + 0.05 * \text{ShockStock}_t$$
$$\text{ShockStock}_t = 0.4 * \text{ShockStock}_{t-1} + 0.8 * \text{Max}(0, C_t - C_{t-1})$$
$$\beta_t = 0.4 * \beta_{t-1} + 0.01 * C_t$$

We also assume that stock translates linearly into response, whether it be response rate, revenues, etc. One could in general assume Response = f(Stock$_t$), where "f" is a nonlinear function.

strong wear-out as in Fig. 28.5. Ganzach and Ben-Or (1996) note the authors did not distinguish between strong wear-out and very strong wear-out. Feinberg et al. (1996) reply that the wear-out is visible in the data. However, they note that only a "low number of subjects" received more than the estimated overload point.

28.2.2 Overlap

The database marketer contacts its customers with different communications. For example, L.L. Bean has a male clothing catalog, a women's catalog, etc.

The degree of content overlap between communications might moderate the wear-in, wear-out, and forgetting phenomena. For example, Equation 28.1 might be extended as follows:

$$Stock_t = (\lambda + \lambda_s Sim)^* Stock_{t-1} + (\beta + \beta_s Sim)^* C_t \qquad (28.5)$$

where Sim is the similarity between the current and previous catalogs. Campbell et al. (2001) include overlap in a model of catalog profits as follows[2]:

$$Profit = R_p(1 - S_{qp}) + R_q(1 - S_{pq}) \qquad (28.6)$$

where $R_{p(q)}$ is the profit from catalog $p(q)$, and S_{AB} is the "saturative" effect of catalog A on catalog B. $S_{pq} = 0.05$ means that catalog q's profits are reduced by 5% when catalog p is also mailed. The authors model the saturative effect as:

$$S_{AB} = [time\ index\ (A, B)]^*[similarity\ index\ (A, B)] \qquad (28.7)$$

Both indices are between 0 and 1. The similarity index captures content overlap – if A and B are the same catalogs, similarity equals 1. The time index captures proximity of mail dates. If the catalogs are mailed at exactly the same time, the time index equals 1. So the greater the content overlap between closely mailed catalogs, the more saturation. The authors indeed find cannibalization between catalogs mailed close to each other.

28.2.3 Purchase Acceleration, Loyalty, and Price Sensitivity Effects

Database marketing communications often entail promotions. Catalogs contain descriptive information, but they are similar to weekly store circulars in that they list products and prices. E-mails as well as online advertising are also similar to feature advertising. In addition, all these communications often offer price discounts.

Database marketing communications therefore can produce the same long-term effects as do promotions. These include accelerating forward in time sales that would have occurred anyway (Blattberg et al. 1981; Neslin et al. 1985; Macé and Neslin 2004), changing brand loyalty (Guadagni and Little 1983; Gedenk and Neslin 1999; Seetharaman 2004), and increasing price sensitivity (Mela et al. 1997; Jedidi et al. 1999).

---

[2] Note this differs a little bit from equation 1 in Campbell et al. (2001, p. 89), but is consistent with their definition of saturation on page 81.

Findings of a negative impact of recency (the more recently the customer has purchased, the less likely the customer is to purchase now) suggest purchase acceleration, assuming the recent purchase was stimulated by communication. Ansari et al. (2008) and Gönül et al. (2000) find evidence of negative recency effects.

Anderson and Simester (2004) studied the long-term impact of promotion depth. Each of three experiments included a "control" and "promotion" catalog. Both catalogs had the same number of promotional prices, clearly communicated as "Regular Price $X, Sale $Y," but Y was smaller for the promotion catalog. Purchasers were followed for at least 24 months, and all purchasers, whether in the control or promotion group, received the same catalogs during this period. In all three tests, the promotions clearly increased sales. But the key question was, what happened in the long term?

The authors investigate acceleration, repeat purchasing, and price-sensitivity effects. They also determine whether promotions draw a different group of customers. They find evidence for all these effects. For example, promotion purchasers bought fewer units in months 1–12 after purchasing from a promotional catalog than they did in months 13–24. This is suggestive of acceleration.

They also found that promotion purchasers bought fewer units after the purchase compared to non-promotion purchasers. This effect however vanished when the authors controlled for selection, i.e., they found that the promotion catalog drew a lower RFM customer and after controlling for this, the number of units purchased in the future was unaffected by promotion (see Neslin and Shoemaker 1989). The authors found that customers who were infrequent, not recent purchasers bought additional units in the future, whereas the number of units subsequently purchased by higher RF groups was unaffected. This suggests that inexperienced, low RF customers learned about the positive aspects of the product due to the purchase experience induced by the promotion. Finally, the authors found that customers who had historically paid high prices purchased at lower prices after purchasing on a steep promotion, whereas customers who had historically paid low prices continued to do so. This is consistent with sensitizing heretofore not-price-sensitive customers to buying on deal.

Overall, there is some evidence, mostly through Anderson and Simester's study, that database marketing communications can act like promotions and induce the same long-term effects observed in the promotions literature (see Neslin 2002). More empirical work is needed to measure these effects in other settings (e.g., e-mail communications, non-promotional catalogs, etc.), but the evidence suggests that optimal contact models need to consider these issues. For example, a communication may accelerate a purchase, so it would not make sense to communicate again until sufficient time had elapsed for the customer to need the product again.

28.2.4 Including Wear-in, Wear-out, Forgetting, Overlap, Acceleration, and Loyalty

Ansari et al. (2008) develop a model to study customer channel migration that includes wear-in, wear-out, forgetting, acceleration, and loyalty. They refer to the first four phenomena as "communication effects," while the last two they call "experience effects." The communications model is:

$$Communication\ Effect_{it} = Direct\ Effect_{it} + Interaction\ Effects_{it}$$

(28.8)

The communication effect includes the impact of all communications currently and previously received by customer i on that consumer's decisions at time t.

The direct effect is each communication's impact in isolation and allows the model to capture wear-in and forgetting. The interactions are between communications and allow the model to capture wear-out and overlap. Specifically,

$$Direct\ Effect_{it} = \sum_{c \in C} \beta_{ic} \lambda_c^{\tau_{ict}} d_{ict} \qquad (28.9a)$$

$$Interaction\ Effects_{it} = \sum_{c,c' \in C} \delta_{icc'} \lambda_c^{\tau_{ict}} \lambda_{c'}^{\tau_{ic't}} d_{ict} d_{ic't} \qquad (28.9b)$$

where

C = Set of all communications distributed by the firm. Particular communications are denoted by c or c'.

β_{ic} = Direct response of customer i to communication c.

λ_c = Decay parameter for communication c.

τ_{ict} = Time since customer i received communication c, as of period t.

d_{ict} = Step indicator equal to 1 if customer i received communication c on or before period t; 0 otherwise. The indicator turns on once the customer has received the communication, and remains on thereafter.

$\delta_{icc'}$ = Interaction response of customer i between communications c and c'.

The model does not measure overlap explicitly, but the authors model the δ's, as well as the β's and λ's, as functions of communication attributes. The attributes could include content (e.g., men vs. women's catalogs, etc.) as well as vehicle types (catalog vs. e-mails). Indeed they find that the interaction terms between like vehicles (catalogs and catalogs; e-mails and e-mails) are generally stronger than between different vehicles (catalogs and e-mails). This suggests an overlap effect due to vehicle overlap.

That the direct effects determine wear-in and forgetting is shown in Fig. 28.7a. In that figure, all the interactions (δ) are set equal to zero. We see that over the course of four communications, response builds toward a maximum, then declines to zero, although not instantly, once the communications end. Figure 28.7**b** demonstrates that with negative interactions, the model produces wear-out. In this example, the first two communications have a stronger interaction than any other pair. The effect is so strong that response declines when the second communication is delivered. This could be due to strong overlap between the first two communications.

Equation 28.9b captures the timing effects suggested by Campbell et al. (2001). Wear-out/overlap effects will be strongest when communications are delivered consecutively (because the λ terms for both communications will be relatively large).

Ansari et al. capture repeat purchase and acceleration effects through lagged incidence, order size, or channel choice variables. For example, they include a variable called "Wuse" equal to log(1+ the cumulative number of purchases made on the Internet). They find this variable has a negative average coefficient in their purchase incidence model, suggesting that purchasing on the Internet decreases future purchase incidence. They include a recency variable, "since," equal to the time since the previous purchase. The coefficient for this variable was positive on average, meaning that it is less likely the customer will purchase in the current period if the customer has purchased last period. Since the marketing variables being studied – catalogs and e-mails – made it more likely that a purchase took place, this suggests purchase acceleration.

28.3 Optimal Contact Models

Optimal contact models determine the number and/or schedule of communications to be delivered to each customer in a given time frame. These models consist of a response model and an optimization. The response model predicts how the customer will respond to a particular "contact." This depends on the "state" the customer is in at a given point in time, for example, how long it has been since the customer was last contacted. Response is probabilistic – there is uncertainty as to whether the customer will respond. The optimization is often forward looking because actions the firm takes in the current period may influence the actions it should take in future periods. For example, if we contact the customer now, we may need to wait a few periods before it becomes worthwhile to contact the customer again. The probabilistic and forward looking aspects suggest that optimal contact models be formulated as a stochastic dynamic program (Ross 1983; Bertsekas 1995). This technique is designed to handle optimizations where the outcomes of firm decisions are probabilistic and there are dynamics in the response to these decisions. For example, the first optimal

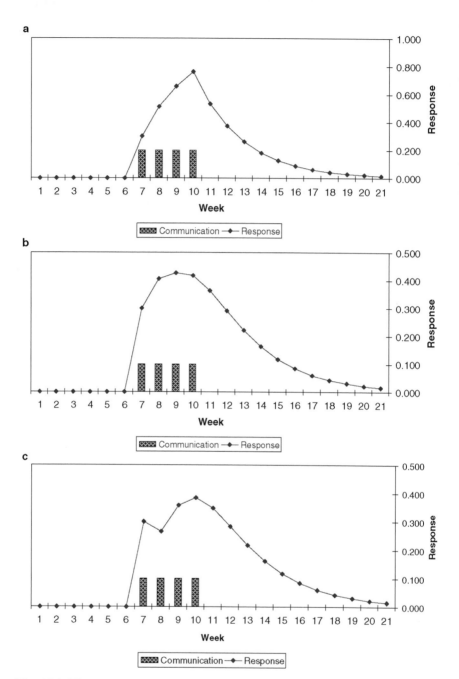

Fig. 28.7 Phenomena captured by Ansari et al. (2008) model Equations 28.8–28.9. (a)*
Wear-in and forgetting: Communications in Periods 7–10; (b)+ Wear-in, wear-out, forgetting, and overlap: Communications in Periods 7–10; (c)^ Wear-in, wear-out, forgetting, and overlap: Communications in Periods 7–10 – stronger overlap between communications 1 and 2 than between others (From Ansari et al. 2008)

* $\beta = 0.3, \lambda = 0.7, \delta = 0$
+ $\beta = 0.3, \lambda = 0.7, \delta = -0.15$ for all pairs of communications
^ $\beta = 0.3, \lambda = 0.7, \delta = -0.35$ between 1st and 2nd communications, $\delta = -0.15$ for other communication pairs.

contact model we discuss (Ching et al. 2004) makes direct use of this methodology.

28.3.1 A Promotions Model (Ching et al. 2004)

28.3.1.1 Response Model

Ching et al. (2004) develop a stochastic dynamic program to decide when to offer a promotion to customers of a computer services company. Customers are assigned to one of four states depending on their usage in the previous week: (1) 0 min, (2) 1–20 min, (3) 21–40 min, (4) > 40 min. Using historical data, the authors estimate $P_{ik}{}^j$, the probability the customer moves from state i to k, if the customer receives promotion j. Both i and k take on values 1, 2, 3, or 4; j can equal 1 (promotion), or 2 (no promotion). The authors calculate c_i^j, the expected revenue from a customer in state i who receives promotion j. The state definitions, "transition probabilities" P_{ik}^j, and revenues c_i^j are the ingredients for a stochastic dynamic program.

28.3.1.2 Optimization Model

In each period, the firm can observe what state the customer is in. The question is whether to promote or not to promote to this customer. This problem can be formulated as the following recursion:

$$v_i(t) = \operatorname*{Max}_{j=1,2} \left\{ c_i^j - d_j + \delta \sum_{k=1}^{4} p_{ik}^j v_k(t-1) \right\} \qquad (28.10)$$

where:

$v_i(t)$ = The expected optimal revenue given the customer is in state i and there are t periods remaining in the planning horizon.

d_j = Cost of implementing promotion j ($j = 1$ or 2).

δ = Discount rate applied to future profits.

The $c_i^j - d_j$ term represents expected profits in period t depending on whether the firm promotes ($j = 1$) or not ($j = 2$). The $\delta \sum_{k=1}^{4} p_{ik}^j v_k(t-1)$ term represents the discounted expected profit for the remaining $t - 1$ periods after the current period. Depending on whether the firm promotes or not in the current period, the customer progresses with probability p_{ik}^j to state k in the next period, and if so, expected optimal revenues are $v_k(t-1)$. The expression of the optimization in this recursive form is a fundamental "principle of optimality" in dynamic programming. It says that the optimal solution can be determined by deciding what to do in the current period, taking into account the repercussions for future periods. Appropriately, $v_i(t)$ is called the "value function."

Equation 28.10 assumes a finite time horizon. In this case the optimal solution will prescribe what action to take if the customer is found to be in state i at time t. The authors also consider the infinite horizon problem, which assumes the firm is maximizing over an infinite period. This may sound a bit unrealistic (will the firm be in existence forever!), but the discount factor effectively limits the time horizon, and makes the model an optimization of lifetime value. When considering an infinite horizon, the stochastic dynamic program prescribes what action should be taken in "steady state," i.e., for any arbitrary period, the optimal action is determined solely by what state the customer is in.

Steady state solutions can be obtained using various techniques, including successive approximations, policy improvement, and linear programming (Ross 1983, pp. 35–42). Finite horizon solutions can be obtained by solving Equation 28.10 using backward induction. Ching et al. solve the infinite horizon version of their model using linear programming and the finite horizon version using backward induction. They include computer programs in Excel that illustrate. Their application finds, intuitively, that if promotion costs (d) are large, they should only be used for inactive customers (state 1). However, if the cost is small, the promotion should be used for light users (state 2). In the finite horizon case, the authors also impose the constraint that a maximum of four promotions can be administered. They find (for low promotion costs), that promotions should be administered to inactive customers as soon as possible, while generally speaking the light users should receive their promotions as late as possible. The first result is intuitive, while the latter may be due to the particular p_{ik}^j's.

The Ching et al. model is a straightforward yet powerful example of deriving an optimal contact strategy from a stochastic dynamic program. Many optimal contact models either embellish the state definitions, the response function, or the optimization requirements. However, these can be nontrivial improvements, both managerially and technically.

28.3.2 Using a Decision Tree Response Model (Simester et al. 2006)

28.3.2.1 Response Model

Simester et al. (2006) design an optimal contact model for a single catalog. Their approach is particularly rich in its use of a decision tree for the response model (Chapter 17). Customer states are defined based on which end node of the tree the customer is classified in at a given point in time. The authors' decision tree method is distinctive in two respects: (1) the dependent variable is a measure of long-term potential, not response to a single catalog;

(2) they develop a decision tree algorithm for handling this continuous dependent variable. The end nodes of the decision tree define customer states. This is an innovative approach. The alternative would be to use a decision tree with 0–1 response as the dependent variable. However, the authors use both response and expenditure, and the long term rather than the short term, to define their dependent variable and derive their customer states.

28.3.2.2 Optimization Model

The stochastic dynamic program is set up as follows:

$$V^{\pi}(s) = E_{r,T,s'}[r_{s,\pi(s)} + \delta^T V^{\pi}(s')|s, \pi(s)] \qquad (28.11)$$

where:

$\pi(s)$ = Mailing policy; a decision rule of whether or not to mail a catalog to the customer who is in state s.

$V^{\pi}(s)$ = Expected long-term profits for the customer in state s under mailing policy π.

$r_{s,\pi(s)}$ = Immediate period profits for the customer in state s under mailing policy π.

δ^T = Discount factor given time T between catalog mailings.

The random elements taken into account in the expected value are the short-term response r, the time T between mailings, and the future states s' that customer may enter as a result of the mailing policy. Equation 28.11 is a value function. It says that the expected long-term profits for the customer in state s under policy π is the sum of the current period optimal profits plus expected future optimal profits.

The authors calculate that their method significantly increases profits over the current policy used by the firm they study, especially if the future is not highly discounted. This is sensible because the states are defined in terms using long-term potential as the dependent variable. Their policy mails more catalogs to customers who have not recently received catalogs, and few catalogs to customers who have recently received catalogs. The authors find that profits increase with more states. However, this may simply be taking advantage of chance variation. Indeed, in a holdout test, profits are independent of the number of states (although still greater than under the current policy).

The authors field test their approach over a 6-month period. They test three customer groups (low, moderate, and high value), and two methods (model versus current). They find the model improves profit for low and moderate value customers, but decreases it for high value customers. The model under-mails these customers relative to the current method, but by the end of the test, the gap tightens. The authors diagnose the problem was that the historical data were skewed toward mailing many catalogs to high value customers. In prescribing fewer catalogs for these customers, the model was going out of the range of the data. The lesson is that the historical data for optimal contact models need to include ample variation in contacts. Elsner et al. (2003, 2004) use field tests to generate the data to estimate their response models.

28.3.3 Using a Hazard Response Model (Gönül et al. 2000)

28.3.3.1 Response Model

Gönül et al. (2000) develop a catalog optimal contact model based on a proportional hazard response model (Cox 1972). The response model is:

$$h_i(t|X) = h_{0i}(t)\psi_i(X) \tag{28.12}$$

where:

t = Time since the last purchase.
$h_i(t|X)$ = The likelihood that customer i purchases at time t.
$h_{0i}(t)$ = The baseline hazard for customer i, due only to the passage of time t.
$\psi_i(X)$ = The proportional covariate adjustment for customer i – due to covariates that vary across customers or over time.

The authors operationalize Equation 28.12 as follows:

$$h_i(t|X) = exp(\gamma_{0i} + \gamma_{1i}t + \gamma_{2i}ln(t) + \gamma_{3i}t^2) \tag{28.13a}$$

$$\psi_i(X) = exp(\beta_1 MALE_i + \beta_2 AVG\_CONSUMP_i + \alpha_{1i}PROM\_REST_i$$
$$+ \alpha_{2i}WEAROUT_i) \tag{28.13b}$$

The baseline hazard model captures recency, since t is the time since the last purchase. Equation 28.13a can capture many monotonic and non-monotonic relationships. The covariate adjustment consists of several multipliers. The MALE variable allows for gender to influence response. AVG_CONSUMP is defined as the average daily expenditure of the household. It combines frequency and monetary value.

PROM_REST is the number of periods since the last catalog was mailed to the customer. The authors hypothesize that α_{1i} should be negative to reflect forgetting. The impact of a catalog in the current period is implied by setting PROM_REST to 0. WEAROUT is defined as the number of catalogs since the last response. If α_{2i} is negative the likelihood of responding in the current period decreases if a large number of catalogs have been mailed since the last purchase. This can be interpreted as wear-out. Note however that if α_{2i} is positive, that could be interpreted as wear-in.

The model includes heterogeneous response in the baseline hazard (γ's) and mailing response parameters (α's). The authors use a latent class approach (Kamakura and Russell 1989) to model heterogeneity, yielding different parameters for each segment ($i = 1, \ldots, S$). The authors account for endogeneity of the catalog mailing variables (PROM_REST and WEAROUT) using instrumental variables. They use a logistic regression of catalogs mailed as a function of RFM variables and use the predictions from this model to calculate PROM_REST and WEAROUT. Interestingly, they do not find much impact of this procedure on their estimated parameters.

The authors estimate their model for 979 customers. They find a two-segment model fits best ($S = 2$). The product category is a durable good, so the customer typically would not need to re-order until a long time had elapsed since purchase. Accordingly, the authors find the baseline hazard is monotonically increasing for Segment 1. However, it is U-shaped for the second. Perhaps these customers order another product to augment the first immediately after purchase, but baseline hazard then decreases and rises again as the customer needs to replace the product(s).

The authors find that males are less likely to respond ($\beta_1 < 0$) and that heavy users are more likely to respond ($\beta_2 > 0$). They also find in both segments that a response is less likely if there has been a longer the time since the last catalog was mailed ($\alpha_{i1} < 0$). This indicates forgetting is a real phenomenon in catalog mailing. They find a significantly negative WEAROUT coefficient in one segment ($\alpha_{i2} < 0$), suggesting wear-out.

28.3.3.2 Optimization Model

The optimal policy considers each customer at time t and recommends a mailing at that time if expected profit over the period $t + x$ is greater with a mailing than without, where x is the time horizon. They find that the qualitative findings for different x's do not vary for $x \in [1, 12]$ and use $x = 3$. Profit for customer i is:

$$\pi_i(D_i) = mE(A_i)[D_i P_i^c - (1 - D_i)P_i^n] - cD_i \qquad (28.14)$$

where:

$D_i = 1$ if mail to customer i at time t; 0 if not.

$\pi_i(D_i)$ = Profit earned on customer i over next x months depending on whether or not the customer is mailed a catalog.

m = Profit margin per response.

$E(A_i)$ = Expected expenditure level for customer i over next x months if the customer purchases.

P_i^c, or P_i^n = Probability that customer i purchases ("responds") over the next x months depending on whether he or she receives a catalog at time t ("c") or does not receive a catalog ("n").

c = Cost of mailing catalog (production plus mail cost).

Table 28.1 Optimal versus actual mailing policy for Gönül et al. model (From Gönül et al. 2000)

		Actual		
		Send	Do not send	Total
Optimal	Send	16	92	108
	Do not send	92	779	871
	Total	108	871	979

The hazard response model provides the response probability estimates. Note P_i^n does not equal zero because the customer has been mailed catalogs before and could order from those catalogs. The variables that change when the customer receives a catalog are WEAROUT (increases by 1) and PROM_REST (resets to 0). Gönül et al. (2000) decision rule is to mail to customer i if:

$$\Delta\pi_i = \pi_i(D_i = 1) - \pi_i(D_i = 0) > 0 \qquad (28.15)$$

The authors apply their method to a durable household products catalog. Table 28.1 compares the optimal and actual policies. Out of 108 customers actually sent catalogs, 16 should have been sent the catalog. However 92 of them (close to 90%) should not have been sent catalogs. The total expected profit is \$6,327 under the optimal policy compared to \$5,968 under the actual policy.

These findings suggest the cataloger is mis-targeting catalogs. The authors speculate this may be due to management not understanding the wear-out and forgetting phenomena captured by the hazard model, or are not considering heterogeneity.

The Gönül et al. (2000) approach is a rigorous, practical approach to catalog mailing. The model is not a dynamic program in that it only optimizes one mailing at a time. Gönül and Ter Hofstede (2006) extend the approach to address this by considering a finite decision period of length P periods, and evaluate 2^P possible mailing schedules. They evaluate each schedule in terms of the utility of the firm, using risk-neutral as well as risk-neutral profit functions. They also use simulation to "integrate out" the uncertainty in customer parameter values. The method evaluates each of the 2^P schedules separately. For a 52-week schedule, this could get prohibitive in terms of computer resources. However, the authors show that $P = 6$ improves over a myopic ($P = 1$) optimization, so practically speaking, the model promises improvements over non-forward looking mail decisions.

28.3.4 Using a Hierarchical Bayes Model (Rust and Verhoef 2005)

28.3.4.1 Response Model

Rust and Verhoef (2005) use a hierarchical Bayes model to estimate customer response to two marketing mix interventions – direct mail and a relationship magazine. The setting is a Dutch insurance company that must decide how many direct mail pieces and how many "relationship magazines" to send to each customer in the coming year. The response model is as follows:

$$\Delta R_{i,(t-1)\to t} = [ln(\overrightarrow{M}_i + 1)]\beta_i + \varepsilon_i \qquad (28.16a)$$

$$\beta_i = \overrightarrow{Z}_i \alpha + \delta_i \qquad (28.16b)$$

where:

$\Delta R_{i,(t-1)\to t}$ = Change in profits (gross of marketing costs) for customer i between previous and current year.

$\overrightarrow{M}_i = \{M_{i1}, M_{i2}\}$, where M_{i1} is the number of direct mail pieces sent to customer i, and M_{i2} is the number of relationship magazines sent to customer i, in the current year.

$\beta_i = \{\beta_{i1}, \beta_{i2}\}$, customer i's responsiveness to direct mail and relationship magazines respectively.

$\overrightarrow{Z}_i$ = Vector of behavioral and demographic variables for customer i, such as lifetime duration, number of products purchased, gender, etc.

$\alpha = \{\alpha_1, \alpha_2\}$ Impact of behavioral and demographic variables on customer i's responsiveness to direct mail and relationship magazines, respectively.

ε_i, δ_i = Unobserved factors influencing customer i's change in profits in the current year and responsiveness to marketing, respectively.

Equation 28.16a reflects diminishing returns to marketing efforts through the log transformation (the "1" is to avoid having to take the log of zero). Equation 28.16a represents the impact of behavioral and demographic variables on customer response to marketing. For example, the authors hypothesized that in general, loyal customers would be more receptive to the relationship magazine and less receptive to direct mail.

The model was estimated for 1,580 customers using MCMC methods implemented in WinBugs. The dependent variable is *change* in profits over a 1-year horizon. The authors found several interesting results, generally supportive of their hypothesis regarding loyalty. For example, cumulative number of purchases had a negative impact on responsiveness to direct mail, whereas had no impact on responsiveness to the relationship magazine. Membership in the company's loyalty program had a stronger effect on response to the magazine than it did to response to direct mail.

28.3.4.2 Optimization Model

The objective is to maximize each customer's change in profits in the coming year:

$$\Pi_{i,(t-1)\to t} = \Delta R_{i,(t-1)\to t} - \overrightarrow{M}_i \overrightarrow{C} \qquad (28.17)$$

where $\vec{C} = \{C_1, C_2\}$ is the per unit cost per customer of direct mail and re-lationship magazines, respectively. Given this formulation and the response function, the optimal level of marketing instrument k (k = direct mail, rela-tionship magazine) for customer i can be obtained using simple calculus:

$$M_{ik}^* = \frac{\beta_{ik}}{C_k} - 1 \qquad (28.18)$$

Equation 28.18 says that more of marketing instrument k should be allocated to customer i if customer i is more responsive to that instrument, and mar-keting instrument k is less expensive. Since responsiveness is the only factor that varies across customers, it is the key measure, and it is provided by the estimation of Equations 28.16.

The authors calculate the optimal level of marketing for each customer and find it is quite heterogeneous due to heterogeneity in the response mea-sures (β). They compare their model to three others: segmentation based on demographics, segmentation based on RFM variables, and latent structure segmentation. They find that their model fits better than the other two, and that the predicted profits generated by their model are higher than those generated by the competitive models. In particular, they find:

Model	Mean square Error (Fit)	Projected average Profit (Guilders)
Demographic	12.98	14.46
RFM	13.44	8.61
Latent class	23.49	3.12
Hierarchical	12.42	23.12

Profits under the marketing plan currently used by the company generated 10.57 guilders, so the hierarchical model outperformed both the other models and current practice.[3]

The Rust and Verhoef model is a very practical yet rigorous approach to deciding customer-specific investments in the intermediate term. Like Gönül et al., it is not a dynamic optimization – it does not take into account the investments made in the coming year have on long-term retention rates and lifetime value. It does not explicitly model wear-in, wear-out, and forgetting, and so could not be used to *schedule* marketing activities within the year. However, the model does include decreasing returns on an aggregate basis, so it implicitly accounts for these factors for the 1-year time horizon. The model depends heavily on the customer-specific response parameters estimated on the calibration sample of 1,580 customers. A challenge would be to infer the coefficients for the rest of the firm's customers.

---

[3] Note the authors use the hierarchical model to project profits for both their model and the other models. The justification is that the hierarchical model predicted best, so would make the most accurate projection.

28.3.5 Incorporating Customer and Firm Dynamic Rationality (Gönül and Shi 1998)

28.3.5.1 Response Model

Many optimal contact models assume that the firm is forward looking, i.e., "dynamically rational." However, there is growing evidence that customers are also dynamically rational – they consider the impact of their current purchase on future costs and benefits. For example, consumers have been shown to take into account the likelihood of future promotions in deciding whether to purchase in period t (Gönül and Srinivasan 1996; Sun et al. 2003).[4]

Gönül and Shi's (1998) optimal contact model takes into account that *both* the customer and the firm may be forward looking. The customer's utility function is:

$$u_{it} = \alpha + \beta_m m_{it} + \beta_{1r} r_{it} + \beta_{2r} r_{it}^2 + \beta_{1f} f_{it} + \beta_{2f} f_{it}^2 + \varepsilon_{it} \qquad (28.19)$$

where:

u_{it} = Utility for customer i of making a purchase in period t; = 0 if the customer does not make a purchase.

m_{it} = 1 if customer i receives a catalog in period t; 0 if not.

r_{it} = Recency, the number of periods since the last purchase.

f_{it} = Frequency, the number of purchases made by the customer since the beginning of the data.

Utility is considered quadratic functions of both recency and frequency for flexibility.

The customer is assumed to maximize his or her long-term utility of making a purchase in period t, taking into account the future impact of a current purchase on his or her recency and frequency variables. Recency and frequency are the state variables in the customer's dynamic program, summarized by $S_{it} = \{r_{it}, f_{it}\}$. Each period, the customer decides whether to buy ($d_{it} = 1$) or not buy ($d_{it} = 0$) by considering the following:

$$V_{it}(S_{it}) = \begin{cases} u_{it} + \delta_c E[V_{i,t+1}(S_{i,t+1}|d_{it} = 1)] & \text{if } d_{it} = 1 \\ 0 + \delta_c E[V_{i,t+1}(S_{i,t+1}|d_{it} = 0)] & \text{if } d_{it} = 0 \end{cases} \qquad (28.20)$$

Customers realize that purchasing or not purchasing changes recency and frequency, and that will affect future utility depending on the parameter values in Equation 28.19. Gönül and Shi (1998) estimate Equation 28.19 by maximum likelihood (see also Keane and Wolpin 1994).

---

[4] Note that competitive economic models in the database marketing literatures have considered the case that both firms and customers are forward looking. See Chapter 2 for discussion.

Gönül and Shi (1998) find the dynamic model fits better than a static model. This suggests customers consider the future when deciding whether to buy now. The mail variable has a positive coefficient as expected. Both recency and frequency have U-shaped impacts. The recency result means that the customer is most likely to buy right after the previous purchase or after a significant lapse of time. The frequency result implies that customers who have bought the product very frequently or very infrequently have more need for the product in the current period.

Gönül and Shi's response model does not take into account wear-in, wear-out, and forgetting. However, this could be done through lagged mailing variables as in Gönül et al. (2000). The model includes a "structural model" of acceleration in the sense that the customer will purchase earlier if he or she realizes that this will increase his or her future utility. See Li et al. (2005) for an extension of the Gönül and Shi model optimizing two elements of the marketing mix (messages and price).

28.3.5.2 Optimization Model

The firm's problem is to decide whether to mail to a customer each period depending on which state the customer is in. The current period profit for the firm is:

$$\pi_{it}(S_{it}, m_{it}) = R \, Prob_{it}(d_{it} = 1 | S_{it}, m_{it}) - cm_{it} \tag{28.21}$$

where:

$\pi_{it}(S_{it}, m_{it})$ = Profit for customer i in period t, given the customer is in state S_{it} and a decision to mail or not mail.
$m_{it} = 1$ if mail to customer i in period t; 0 otherwise.
R = Revenues from customer i if the customer purchases.
$d_{it} = 1$ if customer purchases; 0 otherwise.
c = Cost to mail to customer i.

The recency/frequency state (S_{it}) is the state variable for the dynamic program. The firm decides on the mailing policy that maximizes long-term profits:

$$P_{it}(S_{it}) = \sum_{j=t}^{\infty} \delta_f^{j-t} \pi_{it}(S_{it}, m_{it}^*(S_{it})) \tag{28.22}$$

where:

$P_{it}(S_{it})$ = Maximum expected profits to be gained through an optimal mailing policy for customer i who starts period t in state S_{it}.

By the principle of optimality, long-term profits equal the profits from maximizing current period profits plus the maximal profits to be earned from period $t + 1$ onward, i.e.,:

$$P_{it}(S_{it}) = max\left\{\pi_{it}(S_{it}, m_{it}) + P_{it+1}(S_{it+1})\right\}$$
$$= \max_{m_{it}}\left\{\pi_{it}(S_{it}, m_{it}) + \delta_f[Prob_{it}(d_{it} = 1|S_{it}, m_{it})P_{it+1}(S_{it+1}|d_{it} = 1)\right.$$
$$\left. + Prob_{it}(d_{it} = 0|S_{it}, m_{it})P_{it+1}(S_{it+1}|d_{it} = 0)]\right\} \qquad (28.23)$$

Gönül and Shi (1998) calculate the steady state optimal mail decision using successive approximation (Ross 1983). The authors maximize the firm's future profits taking into account the customer's forward looking response to the mailing decision. They apply their model to a durable product. The authors find that if recency is low, the firm does not mail, but if recency is medium or high, the firm does mail. The reason for this is that if recency is low, the customer is likely to buy anyway (recall the U-shaped finding for recency) so mailing is unnecessary. If recency is medium, response probability is low without a mailing so the mailing is needed. When recency is high, customers are likely to buy on their own, but it pays to mail to these customers anyway to make sure they purchase and push up frequency to a higher level where the customer will buy on his/her own.

Gönül and Shi (1998) calculate that profits using their model would have been 16% higher than what the firm actually earned during the data period. They also note that if one just considers the short term, the firm would probably not do any mailing. This is because the break-even incremental response probability to justify a single period mailing is 9.37%, and the incremental response probability from a mailing is typically less than that. However, from a long-term perspective, a mailing in the current period boosts consumers to profitable recency and frequency states.

In summary, the Gönül and Shi approach embeds a dynamic rational customer response model within a dynamic firm optimization. While no other mail policy will increase firm profits, other mail policies might increase customer utility. This is similar to a Stackelberg game where the leader is the firm and the follower is the customer. The customer is assumed to know the mailing schedule. Indeed, many customers probably do learn how often they receive catalogs from a given company. However, it would be interesting to include customer catalog mailing expectations in the model.

28.3.6 Incorporating Inventory Management (Bitran and Mondschein 1996)

28.3.6.1 Response Model

Bitran and Mondschein (1996) use an RFM model (Chapter 12) as follows:

S_i = Market segment or "state" i, defined by specific values of recency, frequency, and monetary value.

$p_{s_i,s_j,k}$ = Probability that a customer moves from state S_i to S_j when he or she receives k mailings in a given time period.

Recency is defined as the number of periods since the last purchase. Frequency is defined as 1 if the customer has bought once and 2 if more than once. Monetary value is defined as two values, $55 and $80. This makes for a total of $7 \times 2 \times 2 = 28$ RFM states. The authors estimate the response probabilities using historical data available from the catalog company with whom they applied their model.

28.3.6.2 Optimization Model

Bitran and Mondschein's (1996) optimization considers (1) how many catalogs to mail to house list *and* rental list customers each season, and (2) how much the firm should invest in inventory, subject to a budget. The model takes into account firm-level constraints; it does not "simply" optimize individual customers. The optimization is a stochastic dynamic program, but because the model is at the firm level, the states are numerous and continuous. They include the *number* of customers in each RFM state, plus the budget available and inventory levels. The model is not easily solved because of the "curse of dimensionality" – there are too many state variables and each of them takes on too many values. That is, if there are 27 RFM states, there are 27 number-of-customers variables plus a budget variable plus an inventory variable, resulting in 29 continuous state variables. This compares to just four states for the Ching et al. (2004) model.

To simplify, the authors first calculate the number of catalogs to mail to a customer to maximize lifetime value, assuming no budget restrictions or inventory costs. Second, they calculate optimal inventory re-ordering to maximize one-period profit. Third, they incorporate their lifetime value and inventory calculations to derive the optimal mailing policy across all customers. The lifetime value optimization is:

$$LF(s_i) = \underset{k}{Max} \begin{cases} \bar{b}_{s_i k} + \beta \sum_{s_j} p_{s_i s_j k} LF(s_j) & k = 1 \ldots K \\ \beta \sum_{s_j} p_{s_i s_j 0} LF(s_j) & k = 0 \end{cases} \qquad (28.24)$$

where:

$s_i =$ RFM state i, defined by particular values of RFM.
$LF(s_i) =$ Lifetime value of a customer in state s_i.
$k =$ Number of catalogs mailed under optimal policy (this will differ for each s_i). K is the maximum number of catalogs to be mailed.
$p_{s_i s_j k} =$ Probability customer in state s_i migrates to state s_j if mailed k catalogs.
$\beta =$ Discount factor.
$\bar{b}_{s_i k} =$ Current period profit if customer in state s_i mailed k catalogs.

$$= \sum (d_{s_i s_j}(1 - g) - c_1) p_{s_i s_j k} - k c_h \qquad (28.25)$$

where:

$d_{s_i s_j}$ = Amount of money spent by customer who migrates from s_i to s_j.
g = Cost of goods sold as percentage of revenue.
c_1 = Cost of filling order.
c_h = Cost of mailing to member of house list.

The inventory optimization calculates the amount of inventory to order to maximize one-period profit, assuming the firm enters period t with a certain level of inventory. The authors find the optimal amount to invest in inventory is:

$$Z_t = \sigma_t a + \mu_t - I_t \tag{28.26}$$

where:

Z_t = Amount to invest in inventory at the beginning of period t.
μ_t = Expected demand during period t.
σ_t = Standard deviation of demand in period t.
I_t = Inventory value at beginning of period t.
a = Solution to the following equation:

$$F_y(a) = \frac{1 + c_2 - g}{1 + c_2 + c_3 - \beta g} \tag{28.27}$$

where:

$F_y(a)$ = The cumulative standard normal distribution.
c_2 = Penalty cost for unfulfilled demand.
c_3 = Inventory holding cost.

From Equation 28.26, it follows immediately that the amount to order is increasing in average demand and decreasing in inventory. From Equation 28.27, it can be shown that the firm should order more if the penalty costs for unfulfilled demand are higher, less if it costs more to hold inventory, and order less if COGS is high.

Note that the inventory investment depends on demand, which depends on the mailing policy and response. Likewise, the amount spent on inventory influences the number of mailings because it limits cash availability. Bitran and Mondschein make a major contribution by combining marketing and operations decisions. The optimal firm-level mailing policy is derived by the following linear program:

$$max \sum_{s_i} \sum_k LF(s_i k) d(s_i, k) + \sum_j LF(j) d(j) \tag{28.28}$$

subject to:

$$\sum_{s_i} \sum_k k c_h d(s_i, k) + \sum_j c_m d(j) \leq Y_t + a_t \tag{28.29a}$$

$$\sum_{s_i} d(s_i, k) \le N_{s_i t} \qquad \forall s_i \qquad\qquad (28.29\text{b})$$

$$d(j) \le L_{jt} \qquad\qquad \forall j \qquad\qquad (28.29\text{c})$$

where:

$LF(s_i k)$ = Lifetime value of customer in state s_i assuming mail k catalogs in current time period, and the optimal number thereafter according to Equation 28.24. j refers to customers on rental list j.

$d(s_i, k)$ = Number of customers in RFM state s_i who receive k catalogs in current period.

$d(j)$ = Number of catalogs mailed to rental list j in current time period.

Y_t = Available funds after mailing and inventory investment.

a_t = Exogenously provided funding from corporate level in time t.

$N_{s_i t}$ = Number of customers in state s_i in period t.

L_{jt} = Number of customers available from rental list j in period t.

The decision variables are $d(s_i, k)$ and $d(j)$. The first constraint says that the firm cannot spend more on mailings than available funds. Equations 28.29b–c ensure that the total number of customers who receive catalogs does not exceed the sum of individuals who are in each RFM group or on each rental list.

The authors implement the optimization by calculating the optimal mailing plan via Equations 28.28–28.29, calculating the optimal re-order implied by that plan (via Equation 28.26), then checking to make sure the re-order plus mailing costs are within the cash constraint. If not, the lowest lifetime value segment (determined by Equation 28.24) is dropped. The process iterates until the cash constraint is satisfied.

The authors apply their model using data from a catalog company, and compare simulated profits generated from their method to a theoretical upper bound. They find their method does well compared to the upper bound, usually capturing more than 95% of the upper bound profits. The authors generate several insights based on their simulations. For example, when constrained by cash availability, it is better mail to more customers than mail more often to a smaller set of customers. This is to prevent the not-mailed-to customer's recency from becoming so high that they effectively exit the house list. Also, start-up catalogs should use multiple mailings early to build up frequency so that the customer becomes firmly entrenched in the house list. This is the intuitive notion that new companies should emphasize acquisition over retention (see Chapter 26).

28.3.7 Incorporating a Variety of Catalogs (Campbell et al. 2001)

28.3.7.1 Response Model

Campbell et al. (2001) describe the methodology implemented by Fingerhut, a cataloger that was mailing more than 340,000,000 catalogs to 7,000,000

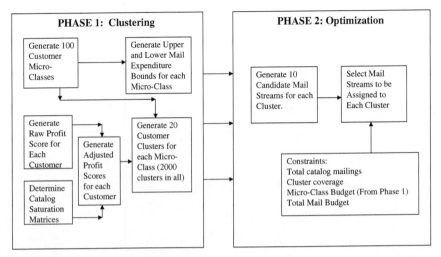

Fig. 28.8 Catalog mail stream optimization system (From Campbell et al. 2001).

customers annually. The problem is to generate a *set* of catalogs (a "mail stream") to send to each customer over the planning horizon. Catalogs differ in terms of their content and when they are to be sent. The method consists of two steps, "Clustering" and "Optimization," as shown in Fig. 28.8. The Clustering phase measures response, while the Optimization phase determines which mail stream to send to which cluster.

The Clustering phase first produces 100 micro classes homogeneous with respect to customer value, lifetime duration, and catalog productivity. This is used to set mailing budgets per class. A second stage produces 20 clusters within each micro class that are homogeneous with respect to predicted response to the catalogs under consideration. Mail streams are then tailored to each of the resulting 2,000 (100 × 20) clusters.

28.3.7.2 Optimization Model

The customer-level optimization problem can be stated as:

$$MAX \ Profit = \Pi = \sum_i \sum_p [G_p^i - F_p^i] X_p^i - \sum_i \sum_p \sum_{p'} G_p^i S_{p,p'} X_p^i X_{p'}^i$$

$$(28.30a)$$

such that:

$$\sum_i \sum_p F_p^i X_p^i \leq B \qquad (28.30b)$$

where:

G_p^i = Gross profit from mailing catalog p to customer i.
F_p^i = Cost to mail catalog p to customer i.

$X_p^i = 1$ if mail catalog p to customer i; 0 otherwise.
$S_{p,p'}$ = Saturative effect between catalogs p and p' (Sect. 28.2.2)
B = Mailing budget constraint.

The saturative effects provide interesting dynamics. However, the authors cannot maximize the above because there are 7,000,000 customers times 40 potential catalogs, or 280,000,000 decision variables. That is simply too large to solve directly.

　　Accordingly, Campbell et al. simplify by dividing customers into the 2,000 clusters described above. They then conduct the optimization in two steps. First they generate 10 candidate mail streams for each cluster. Next they decide which mail streams to use for each cluster. The individual cluster optimization is virtually the same as Equations 28.30a–b, and is described by Campbell et al. (2001) as follows:

$$MAX\ Z = \sum_p [R_p - E_p]Y_p - \sum_p \sum_{p'} R_p S_{p,p'} Y_p Y_{p'} \qquad (28.31a)$$

$$\text{such that}: \sum_p E_p Y_p \le B \qquad (28.31b)$$

where:

R_p = Gross profit from mailing catalog p to the cluster.
E_p = Cost to mail catalog p to the cluster.
Y_p = 1 if mail catalog p to the cluster; 0 otherwise.

The difference between Equations 28.31a–b and Equations 28.30a–b is dropping the i subscript for individuals. Optimization 28.31a–b is solved for 2,000 different customer clusters. For each optimization, there are 40 decision variables corresponding to 40 catalogs, and a budget constraint. The optimization is solved using a range of 10 values for the budget constraint, so 10 candidate mail streams are generated for each cluster.

　　A crucial output from this stage is the expected profit per customer for mailing mail stream m to cluster j within micro-class k, G_m^{kj}. This quantity drives the objective function for the global optimization that maximizes profits across clusters:

$$Max \sum_k \sum_j \sum_m G_m^{kj} X_m^{kj} \qquad (28.32)$$

subject to:

$$Q_p \le \sum_k \sum_j \sum_m C_{pm}^{kj} X_m^{kj} \le \bar{Q}_p \quad \forall p \qquad (28.33a)$$

$$A^k \le \sum_m \sum_j F_m^{kj} X_m^{kj} \le \bar{A}^k \qquad \forall k \qquad (28.33b)$$

$$\sum_m X_m^{kj} = V^{kj} \qquad\qquad \forall j, k \qquad\qquad (28.33\text{c})$$

$$T \le \sum_k \sum_j \sum_m F_m^{kj} X_m^{kj} \le \bar{T} \qquad\qquad (28.33\text{d})$$

where:

G_m^{kj} = Profit per customer for mailing mail stream m to cluster j within micro-class k (from stage 1 optimization).

X_m^{kj} = Number of customers in cluster j, micro-class k, who receive mail stream m.

$Q_p, \bar{Q}_p$ = Lower and upper bounds for number of catalogs of type p that can be distributed.

C_{pm}^{kj} = 1 if catalog p is included in mail stream m, for cluster j, micro-class k.

$A^k, \bar{A}^k$ = Lower and upper bounds for catalog mailing budget for micro-class k.

F_m^{kj} = Cost of mailing mail stream m to cluster j in micro-class k.

V^{kj} = Total number of customers in cluster j in micro-class k.

$T, \bar{T}$ = Lower and Upper bounds for total mailing costs.

The decision variable is the number of customers within a given cluster who receive a particular mail stream. There are 20,000 decision variables since there are 2,000 clusters and 10 potential mail streams per cluster. Equations 28.33a–d represent 2,141 constraints. The first (Equation 28.33a) is that each catalog has an upper and lower bound for the total number of mailings. These cover catalog development costs and maintain firm positioning. There are 40 such constraints, one for each catalog.

The second constraint (Equation 28.33b) is that each of the 100 micro-classes has a minimum and maximum level of catalog mailing investment. There are 100 such constraints. The bounds are generated in the first phase of the system. This ensures that customer segments receive minimum levels of investment while avoiding wear-out. The third constraint (Equation 28.33c) is that all customers in each cluster must receive a mail stream. There are thus 2,000 such constraints. The final constraint (Equation 28.33d) requires that the total mailing investment must be between upper and lower bounds.

In summary, Campbell et al. (2001) replace an optimization over 280,000,000 decision variables with one constraint by two optimizations – one with 40 decision variables and one constraint that is solved 2,000 times, and another that has 20,000 decision variables and 2,140 constraints.

Campbell et al. (2001) report a field test consisting of 700,000 test and 700,000 control customers. The goal was to see if the system could generate incremental profit by lowering mailing costs. Indeed, the system reduced mailing costs by 6%, and as a result, revenues fell by 1.5%. However, the net impact was a profit gain of 2%. The effects were particularly strong for customers who had not bought recently from Fingerhut. Campbell et al. (2001)

report that the system is "directly responsible for a \$3.5 million annual profit gain," and that the "project paid for itself within the first year" (p. 86).

The system is very innovative in its use of saturation interactions (Sect. 28.2.2). The formation of clusters assumes customers within cluster have homogeneous response to mail streams, but the clustering is based not on response to mail streams, but to individual catalogs and aggregate measures of mailing response. On the optimization side, it is not clear how much is lost by optimizing in two stages rather than one. In conclusion, Campbell et al's (2001) method is innovative in its response function, practical in its optimization, has demonstrated value in the real world, and provides ample opportunities for future research.

28.3.8 Multiple Catalog Mailings (Elsner et al. 2003, 2004)

28.3.8.1 Response Model

Elsner et al. (2003, 2004) develop a "dynamic multilevel model" (DMLM) for optimizing the targeting of a single catalog, and a "dynamic multidimensional model" (DMDM) to target different catalogs. We focus on the DMLM model and then discuss how it is extended to DMDM. DMLM consists of three steps or levels, each of which requires its own response function analysis:

1. Determine how many catalog campaigns to conduct during the next 12 months, what should be the timing between campaigns, and on what day to mail the catalogs for a given campaign. Let n_{opt} be the optimal number of campaigns.
2. Determine which customer segments should receive the n_{opt} campaigns.
3. Conduct an additional segmentation analysis that determines which customers are "inactive" and hence should receive a "reactivation package" and which if any should receive the normal catalog mailing

In the first step, the authors conduct field tests that provide data for regressions that relate response rates and order sizes to the number of catalogs distributed, the day of which customers received catalogs, and the time between mailings. An interesting finding is that Saturday is the optimal day to deliver a catalog. This makes sense in that Saturday begins the weekend, when customers have more time to read through catalogs.

In Step 2, the authors divide customers into three segments based on recency. They then estimate the response rate for each segment per catalog. The authors assume that for a given segment, the response rates do not change from campaign to campaign. They can then forecast how customers will migrate between recency segments, similar to Bitran and Mondschein

(1996). They then calculate profits if a segment participates in n_{opt} campaigns and hence whether it is profitable receive n_{opt} campaigns. An important output of this step is a breakeven cut-off s^*. If a given segment's expected sales rate is less then s^*, that segment does not receive the n_{opt} campaigns.

Step 3 looks at a complete array of RFM and other variables and determines whether a customer segment will achieve the critical breakeven point or not. If not, further analysis is conducted to determine if it is worthwhile to send the customers in that segment a special "reactivation" package.

Note that the authors assume in step 2 that response rates for a given segment are constant over time and do not depend on the frequency or timing of catalogs. It thus appears that this model does not take into account wear-in, wear-out, and forgetting. However, as in the Rust and Verhoef (2005) model, step 1 implicitly does, since it regresses at an aggregate level total response and order size as a function of frequency and timing.

28.3.8.2 Optimization Model

They authors find in Step 1 that 25 bimonthly catalog campaigns, spaced 14 days apart, and delivered on Saturdays is optimal (Elsner et al. 2003; Fig. 28.4). The authors then divide their customer base into three recency segments (e.g., recency < 12 months, 12 < recency < 24, and recency > 24). Given the response rate and order size for each segment, as determined in Step 2, they derive expressions for the expected number of customers in each segment and hence its profitability, if that segment receives n_{opt} catalogs. They take into account that customers may be acquired or leave the database entirely by moving without a forwarding address, etc. In summary, these expressions calculate the total profit as a function of the customer migrations that occur between recency states depending on whether a customer receives and responds to a given catalog. Using these expressions, they calculate s^*. If a given segment j's s_j = response rate × order size is greater than s^*, the segment receives the n_{opt} catalogs.

Step 3 provides a predictive model that identifies more specifically (on the basis of more than just recency variables) which customers will have $s_j < s^*$. For those customers, the authors conduct additional analysis, scrutinizing their response rates, etc., to determine if it is worthwhile to send them a "reactivation package."

The authors apply their procedure to a German catalog company, Rhenania, and report improvements in sales and the size of the customer base. Profit starts increasing a year later. The company does so well that they acquire another catalog company, Akzente, and apply the model to that company. Similar to the results for Rhenania, the number of active customers, sales growth, and even profit immediately start to increase after 2–3 years of decline.

The authors attribute the success to: (1) a forward-looking optimization rather than optimizing one mailing at a time; (2) the use of segmentation to help decide what minimum number of expected sales was required in order to mail to the segment, and (3) further segmentation to identify active versus inactive customers, and using a reactivation campaign selectively on customers considered most likely to respond profitably.

The authors found that after acquiring additional direct mail companies, a new model was needed, DMDM, to optimize customer contacts across three different types of catalogs. The authors follow generally the same three steps as in DMLM, however, for example in Step 1, they also consider response to the total number of mailings, across the three catalogs. Implicitly included is the cross-correlation between response to catalogs for the different brands. In applying this model (Elsner et al. 2004), they find for example there is more cross-buying of products from different catalogs.

28.3.9 Increasing Response to Online Panel Surveys (Neslin et al. 2007)

28.3.9.1 Response Model

Neslin et al. (2007) develop a model to increase response rates for online survey panels. Online survey panels have become an important source of survey data. Nearly 80% of consumer goods and 74% of B2B companies use online panels (Thornton 2005). Online panels provide fast turnaround, lower operations costs (compared to mail surveys or personal interviews), and more specialized sample frames. To increase response rates, the online panel manager might increase participation incentives or recruit more panelists. Either way this increases costs. Another alternative is to use an optimal contact model. This identifies panelists who are likely to respond and uses them judiciously over time to maximize response rates.

Neslin et al. use a decision tree to model response to previous survey solicitations. They consider several potential predictors; their final model contains the following four:

- Days between the previous invitation or joining the panel and the current invitation (INVJOIN): Lower INVJOIN was associated with higher response.
- E-mail response confirmation (CONFIRM): The firm had sent an e-mail to panelists asking whether they were still interested in participating. Possible responses were "Yes," "No," and "No response." Those who said yes were most likely to respond to mailings, while those who said no were unlikely to response. No-response customers fell in the middle.
- Response to previous invitation (PREVRESP): Respondents might have responded to the previous invitation, not responded, or never been invited

before. Responders were obviously more likely to respond to subsequent invitations, non-responders were least likely, and never-invited were in the middle.

- Gender: Females were somewhat more likely to respond than males.

The decision tree includes two variables that change over time, INVJOIN and PREVRESP. The authors found no evidence of wear-out. This may be due to the range of the data. Very few panelists in the data had been invited to more than two studies.

As in Simester et al. (2006), the decision tree end nodes divide customers into states. Customers migrate from state to state. For example, if the cut-off for being in the low INVJOIN state is 61 days, then after 61 days, the customer migrates to the INVJOIN > 61 state, where response rates are generally lower. Similarly, since PREVRESP is a predictor, panelists migrate to different states depending on whether they respond to a given invitation. This customer migration plays a critical role in the optimization, as it does for several of the other models reviewed in this chapter.

28.3.9.2 Optimization Model

The optimization model is forward looking over a finite horizon the authors chose to be the next four studies. The decision is how many customers in state j to invite to participate in a given study. The optimization takes into account that new panelists may be added to the database over time. It also takes into account that given studies may require demographic balance, for example, an equal number of males and females.

Specifically, the authors formulate their optimization as a linear program:

$$\underset{X_{js}}{Minimize} \sum_{s=1}^{S} \sum_{j=1}^{N} X_{js} \tag{28.34}$$

subject to:

$$X_{js} \leq A_{js} \quad j = 1, \ldots, N; s = 1, \ldots, S \tag{28.35a}$$

$$\sum_{j \in M_g} r_j X_{jt} \geq Q_{sg} \quad g = 1, \ldots, G; s = 1, \ldots, S \tag{28.35b}$$

$$A_{ks} = \sum_{j=1}^{N} p_{jk} X_{j,s-1} + \sum_{j=1}^{N} q_{jk}(A_{j,s-1} - X_{j,s-1})$$
$$+ R_{ks} \quad k = 1, \ldots, N; s = 2, \ldots, S \tag{28.35c}$$

where:

$X_{js} =$ Number of panelists in state j invited to participate in study s.
$A_{js} =$ Number of panelists in state j available to participate in study s.

r_j = Response rate for panelists in state j.

Q_{sg} = Number of respondents desired from demographic group g for study s.

p_{sj} = Probability panelist in state j migrates to state k if invited to participate in a given study.

q_{jk} = Probability panelist in state j migrates to state k if invited to participate in a given study.

R_{ks} = Number of newly recruited panelists joining state k in time for study s.

The objective is to minimize the number of invites over the horizon. Since the model includes constraints on the desired number of respondents for each study, this is equivalent to maximizing average response rate. Constraint 28.32a ensures the solution can not invite more panelists from a given state to participate in a given study than are available. Constraint 28.32b states the required number of respondents from each demographic group; M_g is the set of states that contain panelists from demographic group g. Constraint 28.32c keeps track of panelists available for each state, for each study. The number of panelists in state k equals the number of responding panelists who migrate to state k plus the number of non-responding panelists who migrate to state k, plus the number of newly recruited panelists who enter state k. The migration is governed by the migration probabilities p and q. These in turn are derived by the definition of states as determined by the end nodes of the decision tree, and to the schedule of studies.

The authors use a rolling horizon implementation. Rolling horizons are used frequently in operations management (Baker 1977; Chand et al. 2002) as a pragmatic way to implement models when uncertainty is involved. In the authors' context, the approach is: (1) Find the optimal solution for Studies 1, 2, 3, and 4. This solution is based on *expected* panelist migration calculated using Equation 28.35c. (2) Implement the solution for Study 1. (3) Observe who actually responds or does not, thus calculating the *actual* numbers of customers in each state as of Study 2. (4) Find the optimal solution for Studies 2, 3, 4, and 5. (5) Implement the solution for Study 2, etc.

The authors field test the model and compare it to random selection and the firm's current heuristic for selecting panelists. Figure 28.9 shows the model outperforms both alternatives. The reason the optimization distinguishes itself particularly for the last three studies is that for the first study, there were not many panelists available in what the predictive model identified as high-responding states. However, in the first study, the model solicits panelists to discern whether they were in the high-responding group or not. For example customers with low INVJOIN and PREVRESP = "respond" are high response panelists. However, there were not any of these available for Study 1. By inviting high INVJOIN previous responders, the model could create a pool of low INVJOIN previous responders for Study 2 who would be highly likely to respond to that study. This strategy evidently worked well.

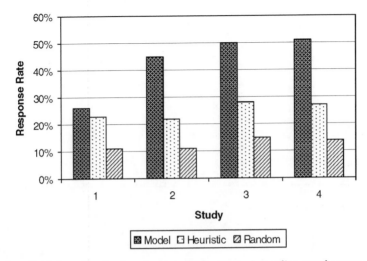

Fig. 28.9 Field test of optimal contact model for increasing online panel response rates (From Neslin et al. 2007).

28.4 Summary

Table 28.4 summarizes the various features contained in the optimal contact models discussed in this section. All but one of the models is applied to direct mailings or promotions. Neslin et al. (2007) show that the method is more broadly applicable (see also Sun and Li 2005, Chapter 25, for an application to call centers). Other potential applications include e-mails, online advertising, and multi-channel promotions. Most of the methods focus on one type of communication, e.g., a single catalog, rather than a selection of catalogs. Campbell et al. (2001), Rust and Verhoef (2005) and the extension of the basic model in Elsner et al. (2003, 2004) are important exceptions. Considering a selection of communications raises the issue of communication overlap, which Campbell et al. model in an innovative way.

Optimization methods range from simple profit cut-offs (Gönül et al. 2000) and linear programs (Neslin et al. 2007) to multi-stage optimizations (Campbell et al. 2001; Elsner et al. 2003, 2004). In both these multi-stage optimizations, the first consideration is the schedule of catalogs, while the second is which customer segment should receive which schedule. This approach may be a necessary simplification when there are different types of communications under consideration.

Most of the models assume the firm is forward looking. Rust and Verhoef (2005) are one exception. They focus on the aggregate level of marketing effort to expend on each customer within a year, without worrying about several years or the schedule within a year. The detailed scheduling of marketing effort is what creates a complex dynamic optimization. It would be very

Table 28.2 Comparing optimal catalog mailing procedures

		Bitran and Mondschein (1996)	Gönül and Shi (1998)	Gönül et al. (2000)	Campbell et al. (2001)	Elsner et al. (2003)	Ching et al. (2004)	Rust and Verhoef (2005)	Simester et al. (2006)	Neslin, Novak, Baker, and Hoffman (2007)
Decisions	Catalog mailing	√	√	√	√	√	("Promotions")	(Direct mail; magazine)	√	√ [a]
	Catalog diversity	–	–	–	√	b	–	√	–	–
Optimization	Method	Dynamic program	Dynamic Stackelberg	Short-term profit cut-off	Integer and linear programs	Calculus	Dynamic program	Calculus	Dynamic program	Dynamic Linear Program
	Decision variable	# of catalogs to mail to segments each season[c]	Mail catalog to customer i at time t	Mail catalog to customer i at time t	Use mailstream m for segment j.	Timing and # of catalogs – which segment receives these catalogs	Whether to promote to a given customer	Number of direct mail pieces and magazines during 1 year	Mail to customer in segment s.	# of panelists in segment j to invite for study s
	Customer growth	√	–	–	–	√	–	–	–	√
	Budget	√	√ (Firm and customer)	–	√	√	–	–	–	d
	Forward looking	√	–	–	√	√	√	–	√	√
	Optimal solution	Steady state	Steady state	Steady state	Steady state	Steady state	Steady state and finite horizon	Single-period calculus-derived	Steady state	Rolling horizon

Costs	Mailing	√	√	√	√	√	√	√	√	–
	Inventory	√	–	–	–	–	–	–	–	NA
	Out-of-stock	√	–	–	–	–	–	–	–	NA
	COGS	√	√	√	√	√	√	√	√	NA
	Order processing	√	–	–	–	–	–	–	–	–
Response model	Type	RFM	Dynamic rational	Hazard	Regression	Regression, R and RFM	Response = f(customer volume)	Hierarchical Bayes' Regression (Profit)	Decision tree	Decision tree
Response phenomena in model	Response rate	√	√	√	√	√	√	–	√	√
	Order size	Implicit	–	–	√	√	√	–	√	√
	Wear-out	Implicit	–	√	√	Implicit	–	Implicit	√	√
	Wear-in	Implicit	√	–	–	Implicit	–	Implicit	√	–
	Forgetting	Implicit	√	√	–	Implicit	–	Implicit	–	√
	Overlap	–	–	–	√	–	–	–	–	–

[a] Determine the schedule of invitations to an online survey panel to maximize average response rate.

[b] Extension of base model considers different catalogs and correlation between responses to different catalogs.

[c] Also decide how much to invest in inventory each season.

[d] No explicit monetary budget; budget takes form of required number of respondents per study.

interesting to compare the aggregate approach with an *ad hoc* scheduling rule to a true dynamic optimization.

Gönül and Shi (1998) are unique in allowing the customer also to be forward looking. Gönül and Shi are also unique in considering potential endogeneity of the mailing decision in the data they use to estimate the predictive model. That they do not find this to be an issue is re-assuring, but there is need to investigate this more fully (see Ansari et al. 2008).

Most of the models devise a steady state decision rule, as in "if the customer is in this RFM state at time t, mail a catalog to the consumer" (e.g., Simester et al. 2006). One exception is Neslin et al. (2007), who use a rolling schedule approach so there is no general decision rule.

Bitran and Mondschein (1996) are unique in their treatment of a broader class of decisions, particularly dealing with the operations side of the business. They consider "back door" inventory and ordering costs, which are vital to a catalog organization.

The methods also use a variety of response models, including RFM, hazard models, and decision trees. The RFM and decision tree models divide customers into segments; membership in these segments changes over time, allowing for dynamics in the optimization. Another important, practical aspect considered by Bitran and Mondschein (1996), Campbell et al. (2001), and Elsner et al. (2003, 2004) is to consider both whether the customer responds, and if so, how much does the customer spend. Finally, a key issue uncovered by Simester et al. (2006) is that it is important that the data used to estimate the response functions represent a broad range of mailing histories. The point is very important. Optimization models do not explicitly consider the quality of the data that drive them. Simester et al. point out that in practice, ample data variation is crucial.

A final note is that while the collection of models summarized in this chapter collectively show that optimal contact models can be constructed and implemented, more work is needed to demonstrate they improve over current practice or simpler models (e.g., myopic models as mentioned above) in actual field tests. Campbell et al. (2001) and Neslin et al. (2007) demonstrate successes in controlled field tests, Elsner et al. (2003, 2004) provide quasi-experimental evidence of success, and Simester et al. 2006) demonstrate mixed results. More field testing is needed. Given the complexity of customer-specific multi-campaign scheduling, it is crucial to understand where the simplifications can be made, and which issues need to be confronted head on without any simplification.

Chapter 29
Pricing

Abstract The database marketing environment presents many challenges involving pricing. How should we coordinate acquisition pricing and retention pricing? How should we price when we want to re-activate customers? How should we use database marketing to price discriminate? This chapter reviews models and methods for providing insights on these questions. We point out that pricing cannot be considered in a vacuum; for example, that customer quality expectations play a key role in acquisition pricing.

Pricing is a critical area in customer management. There is a vast literature, primarily in economics, about pricing products and services. Yet, very little has been written about pricing over the lifetime of customers. This chapter will examine basic pricing theories that have applicability to pricing for individual customers over time as well as offering different customers different prices (price discrimination). A major theme is our emphasis on customer-based as opposed to product-based pricing. Customer-based pricing maximizes total customer profitability, across the several products the customer might buy, whereas product-based pricing takes the vantage point of maximizing profits for a given product. Customer-based pricing is particularly appropriate for database marketing where the focus is on managing customers.

29.1 Overview – Customer-based Pricing

Most firms price products individually. Product pricing optimizes the price of a given product/service without regard to optimizing the pricing of the total bundle of products/services the customer purchases over his or her lifetime.

Suppose a customer is more likely to buy a second product if the customer already purchased another product from the firm. Then, the firm must jointly optimize the profits based on the profitability of the two products, not each separately. An example is a financial service firm selling mortgages. Assume that the customer is more likely to purchase a mortgage if the customer has previously purchased a fee-based credit card. Hence the pricing of the fee-based credit card should reflect the purchase of future products.

Mathematically, we can set up the problem as a two-stage optimization in which the first purchase affects the probability of a second purchase. Later in the chapter we will study this structure for customer-based pricing. A related but more complex issue, not addressed currently in the marketing literature, is if the firm has two products and each could be purchased as the lead product (first product purchased), what is the optimal product-line pricing? Intuitively, both products should be priced lower.

Most of the marketing literature on acquisition pricing focuses on the pricing of durable goods with learning on the cost side and diffusion on the demand side. The issue this literature addresses is how should the firm price a new durable good overtime? Each customer is "acquired" because there is no repeat purchasing. Also, the prices for the "early adopters" affect the future price of the product through the cost side.

If the firm does not have repeat purchasing, then one commonly used solution to acquisition pricing is skim pricing – pricing high at first and then lower overtime. This is covered extensively in the literature beginning with Robinson and Lakhani (1975) and continuing to Nair (2007). Skim pricing is driven, in part, due to experience curves, if the firm has a monopoly position and customers exhibit innovator/adopter behavior. If marginal costs decline as a function of cumulative volume, then, ceteris paribus, the firm should "skim" price. If consumer tastes are different (heterogeneous) and the monopolist firm can price differentially over time, then, ceteris paribus the firm can execute a skim pricing strategy. If the discount rate for product consumption is high, then, ceteris paribus, the firm should skim price. However, if the customer is willing to wait, and the firm has a high discount rate, it may be better to price uniformly overtime or lower price. Lazear (1986) described how it is optimal to price high at the beginning of the fashion season to attract price insensitive fashion-forward consumers and then lower prices overtime to price discriminate to reach the more price sensitive customers.

Kalish (1983) examined different diffusion model assumptions. For the consumer side of the model he uses a Bass curve and for the cost side he assumes there is learning through producing. Kalish's key finding is that depending upon different assumptions, different price paths are possible. Production learning curves result in marginal costs declining over time, which always causes prices to decline. Diffusion works in the other direction causing the firm to price low to increase the number of innovators who in turn increase the number of adopters. Because diffusion and production learning curves are working in the opposite direction, the price path can decrease or increase depending upon the relative importance of the diffusion process relative to learning curves.

Numerous other articles have been written about Bass model pricing (see Bass 2004). We will not use these models in this chapter because they focus on diffusion behavior of customers. We will not assume any diffusion effects in the customer-based pricing models we will consider. Researchers may see an opportunity to incorporate diffusion in the types of customer-based pricing we will study but to do so, it would be necessary to show that there is diffusion for standard products/services that are already in the market place. We will briefly mention acquisition learning curves because many dot.com firms believed that as more customers were acquired, the cost of acquisition would decline because the firm would learn how to be more efficient in customer acquisition. However, while acquisition learning cost reductions probably exist, the dot-coms were overly optimistic. There is no documented literature showing the magnitude of these effects.

The remainder of this chapter will focus on customer-based pricing. The objective will be to maximize the long-term profitability of the customer. The reason is that customers are assets (see Blattberg et al. 2001), not simply transactions, and profit maximization must be over their long-term purchase behavior. Customer-based pricing can be broken into three components: acquisition, retention and "add-on selling" pricing. In this chapter we will focus on all three. The reason one needs to separate acquisition from retention pricing is that the price that a customer is acquired influences retention rates. Therefore, the prices are not independent. This will be discussed in detail later in the chapter. Also, because the customer's behavior is dynamic (changes over time), it is necessary to make certain assumptions about the customer's price sensitivity over time.

When one considers customer-based pricing, there are two different directions to take: (1) pricing products/services that are "one-shot" purchases but the customer purchases multiple products from the firm (e.g., electronics from Sony) and (2) pricing a repeat purchase product in which the customer purchases the same product/service multiple times. We will consider both cases in this chapter.

This chapter will be organized with Sect. 29.2 addressing customer-based pricing when customers purchase multiple one-time products from the firm; Sect. 29.3 studies pricing products/services to customers over two periods; Sect. 29.4 utilizes the customer equity model to determine acquisition and retention prices; Sect. 29.5 studies pricing to recapture customers; Sect. 29.6 addresses pricing of add-on sales; and Sect. 29.7 covers the use of price discrimination and how to value the information the firm has available to price differentially.

29.2 Customer Pricing when Customers Can Purchase Multiple One-Time Products from the Firm

Database marketers often are able to offer a "lead" product to acquire a customer. Examples include checking accounts for financial services companies, low-cost low-featured automobiles (e.g., Mercedes 1 series) for car companies, or accessories for clothing retailers. Pricing lead products is tricky because if the price is too low and repeat purchasing through other product lines is low, then the firm loses money. On the other hand, if its pricing is too high and the product quality is high, the firm may under-invest in customer acquisition.

In the model provided in this section, we will not assume the firm is price discriminating. While this is often discussed in the marketing and database marketing literature, it may be more difficult to execute in practice. Later in the chapter in the section titled Price Discrimination through Targeting Models, we cover an article by Feinberg et al. (2002) which shows some of the problems with trying to price discriminate when customers can learn about other customers' prices. The relevance of this section to database marketers is that it teaches the firm how to price "lead" products for customer acquisition. Database marketers have a major advantage in using these methods, because through their databases, they can learn which are the "lead" or first products a customer purchases.

We will begin by assuming there is a relationship between the purchase of several products because once the customer purchases one of the firm's products/services, the customer is more likely to purchase another. The products do not have to be complements. The pricing strategy and pricing levels are different than if the customer just purchased one product. For example, Dell historically sold computers but now sells printers and flat screen televisions. After purchasing one of Dell's products, its quality influences the probability of purchasing another from Dell. This should affect Dell's pricing of products that customers tend to acquire on their first purchase occasion. Dell, through its databases, can learn which are the first products customers purchase, and then consider how best to price those products recognizing their pricing affects the number of customers Dell acquires. Another example is a financial service firms that uses mortgages as its lead product and then sells traditional banking products such as checking and deposit products as second and third products.

When the products are not complements but the customer purchases multiple products from some firm, we will call these brand-linked purchases. Why is there a link? Customers learn about the brand's quality through the use of the first product. Customers have higher awareness of the brand after the initial purchase. Customers receive targeted communications from the firm. Because of the link, the firm should use customer-based pricing, not product-based pricing.

As a first example of customer-based lead product pricing, we will use a model adapted from Shapiro (1983). We will consider two products (1, 2). The firm has already set the price of product 2. The issue is: how should it price product 1 given that the probability the customer purchases product 2 depends upon the purchase and quality of product 1?

We will use an example to help make this section concrete. Suppose a firm sells two products. Product 2 is a flat screen TV, product 1 is a computer.

The firm sets the price of the flat screen television at \$2,000 and makes a margin 20% or \$400. The question is how to price the computer. The firm's cost is \$2,000. Since both products are made by the same firm, the customer estimates the quality of the flat screen television based on the quality of the computer. Both have the same brand name.

The key to this analysis is to price product 1 taking into account that after purchasing that product, the customer will revise his or her quality estimate of product 2. The assumption to be used in the model is that customers revise their quality estimate upward, although one could investigate the other case as well.

We will make the following assumptions. The firm is a monopolist who chooses product quality, q_i, for product i, which is given and not subject to change. We will use a constant cost (c_i) for the ith product. Consumers are indexed by their taste for quality for product i, θ_i, which represents the dollar value consumer of type θ_i places on product i's quality, q_i. Note that in different product categories customers may have a different preference for quality. θ_i is bounded between 0 and 1. θ_i is basically the importance of quality to the customer. A consumer of type θ_i who pays p_i for the product of quality q_i enjoys consumer surplus of $\theta_i q_i - p_i$ for $i = 1, 2$.

Consumers have an expectation about the quality of the seller's products, $R_i > 0 (i = 1, 2)$. R_i is a point expectation (not a distribution). The value of R_i is based on the firm's reputation. It does not depend upon marketing activities but could easily be related to advertising and positioning decisions by the firm.

A consumer of type θ_i will purchase initially if and only if $\theta_i R_i > p_i$ which implies $\theta_i > p_i/R_i$. Consumer diversity is captured through the distribution of θ_i across customers, denoted by $f(\theta_i)$. Then the fraction of consumers with taste parameter greater than θ_i is:

$$1 - F(\theta_i) = \int_{\theta_i}^{1} f(t)dt$$

with

$$(29.1)$$

$$F(\theta_i) = \int_{0}^{\theta_i} f(t)dt$$

Demand for the initial product is given by:

$$s(p_1) = 1 - F(p_1/R_1) \qquad (29.2)$$

As R_1 increases, demand increases and as p_1 increases, demand decreases. Thus, initially, if the firm could control R_1, it would try to set it as high as possible.

We will continue with our example. Suppose we assume the value of R_1 is 5,000 and θ_1 follows a uniform distribution. The firm sets a price for its computers of \$3,000. Then, the fraction of customers who will purchase the product is those for whom $\theta_1 > p_1/R_1 = 1 - (3,000/5,000) = 0.4$. Suppose the price were raised to \$4,000. Then the fraction of customers purchasing the product is $s(4,000/5,000) = (1 - F(.8)) = (1 - 0.8) = 0.2$.

We will consider two cases. Case 1: The consumer only purchases product 1. Case 2: The consumer purchases product 1 and then based on the purchase of product 1, updates the expected quality of product 2 to q_2 from R_2. The price of product 2, p_2, is set. The estimate of the quality of product 1 is R_1 and is less than the true quality q_1. However, after using product 1, the consumer updates his or her estimate of quality from R_2 to q_2.

29.2.1 Case 1: Only Product 1 Is Purchased

The customer has a purchase probability for product 1 of

$$\text{Prob(Purchase Product1)} = 1 - F\left(\frac{p_1}{R_1}\right) \tag{29.3}$$

and the profit function is:

$$\pi_1 = N\left[1 - F\left(\frac{p_1}{R_1}\right)\right](p_1 - c_1) \tag{29.4}$$

where N is the size of the market. We will assume a uniform distribution for θ_1. Then, $F(\frac{p_1}{R_1}) = \frac{p_1}{R_1}$.

Differentiating with respect to p_1 and setting the derivative equal to zero gives:

$$\frac{d\pi_1}{dp_1} = \left(1 + \frac{c_1}{R_1}\right) - \frac{2p_1}{R_1} = 0 \ or$$

$$p_1 = \frac{R_1 + c_1}{2} \tag{29.5}$$

The above is based on a uniform distribution, which is tractable and shows the results clearly. Shapiro (1983) shows more general results than we show here.

Continuing with our example, let $c_1 = \$2,000$ and remembering that $R_1 = 5,000$, we have $p_1 = (5,000 + 2,000)/2 = \$3,500$. We will contrast this result to the two product purchase case.

29.2.2 Case 2: Two Product Purchase Model with Lead Product 1

In Case 2 we assume the customer purchases a second product based on his or her experience with product 1. After purchasing product 1, the customer updates his or her expectations about the quality of the firm's brand and expected quality goes from R_2 to q_2 where $q_2 > R_2$. One could also assume $R_2 > q_2$ and analyze that case. However, we will analyze the case in which consumers' expectations are below the true quality for product 2 and the consumer uses product 1 to update their expectations about the true quality of product 2, q_2.

The probability of purchasing is $1 - F(\frac{p_i}{R_i})$ for both products. Then the number of customers purchasing over both periods is:

$$S = N \left\{ \left[1 - F\left(\frac{p_1}{R_1}\right) \right] + \left[1 - F\left(\frac{p_2}{q_2}\right) \right] \right\} \qquad (29.6)$$

The q_2 in the second part of the equation is due to the assumption that the customer learns the true quality of product 2 after the initial purchase of product 1. Profit, π, is:

$$\pi = N \left[1 - F\left(\frac{p_1}{R_1}\right) \right] \times \left\{ (p_1 - c_1) + \left[1 - F\left(\frac{p_2}{q_2}\right) \right] \times (p_2 - c_2) \right\} \qquad (29.7)$$

Let $[1 - F(\frac{p_2}{q_2})] \times (p_2 - c_2)] = k$. Again, assuming a uniform distribution for θ_1, we can optimize with respect to p_1, assuming p_2 is given. The optimal price is

$$p_1 = \frac{R_1 + (c_1 - k)}{2} \qquad (29.8)$$

Because $k > 0$, the optimal price to charge for product 1 is lowered based on the additional profit to be made on product 2.

Continuing with our example, let $c_2 = \$1,000, p_2 = \$1,500$ and $q_2 = 3,000$. Then, using Equations 29.7 and 29.8 above, we have $k = (1 - F(1,500/3,000)) \times (1,500 - 1,000) = 250$. Next we substitute k into Equation 29.8 and we have $p_1 = (5,000 + (2,000 - 250))/2 = \$3,375$.

The result from the two product case shows that the profit from future purchases enters into the pricing of the first product and lowers the price when the true quality is higher than the expected quality. Thus, the firm induces more customers to sample product 1 because of its lower price which then impacts the purchase level of product 2 because the customers update their expectations about the quality of product 2. If customers do not use product 1 to update their expectations about the quality of product 2, then the firm should use the myopic price (Equation 29.5).

Obviously there are many issues associated with this model and example:

1. Why is the mean expectation for product 2 different than the true quality? When this is true, rational expectations assumptions are violated but in the real-world firms may know their product quality is greater than consumers' perceptions (through marketing research) and can influence future purchasing by using lower prices for the lead product.

2. How can a firm estimate the difference between expected quality for product 2 (R_2) and actual quality for product 2 (q_2)? This is marketing research question and can be determined by using research to ascertain the actual quality versus consumer expectations of quality. The other related issue is that once a consumer samples product 1, the firm can determine if that consumer updates his or her estimate of product 2.

3. Why is this example relevant to database marketing? Database marketers have the capability to determine which are lead products (product purchased first by customers) and can also develop targeted programs for selling the second product. Traditional marketers may also be able to use this type of pricing when products are introduced sequentially but database marketers can use their data to determine which products naturally are the lead products ever if both products are in the market.

The conclusions from analyzing these two cases are:

- Even if the lead product is a low-priced product, the firm should be very careful about its product quality because lead product quality impacts pricing and profits from future products its customers purchase firm.
- Firms need to develop mechanisms for estimating lead products and understanding how their quality levels match future products purchased by the customers.
- Firms should develop pricing policies based on the quality of its products and the purchase sequence used by customers.

29.3 Pricing the Same Products/Services to Customers over Two Periods

We now consider the case where the same product may be purchased over time, but customers do not know initial quality. The question is: should a database marketing company use a higher (lower) introductory price to acquire customers and then lower (raise) its price after acquiring the customer?

We use the same "machinery" as in Sect. 29.2. Customers are indexed by their taste for quality, θ, which represents the dollar value consumers of type θ places of the product of quality q. θ is bounded between 0 and 1. A consumer of type θ who pays p for a product of quality q enjoys consumer surplus of $\theta q - p$. Consumers have an expected quality of the seller's product, $R > 0$. R is a point expectation. The value of R is based on the firm's reputation.

A consumer of type θ will purchase initially if and only if $\theta R > p$ which implies $\theta > p/R$. Consumer diversity is captured through the distribution of θ which is denoted by $f(\theta)$. Then the number of consumers with taste parameter greater than θ is:

$$1 - F(\theta) = \int_\theta^1 f(t)dt$$

or   (29.9)

$$F(\theta) = 1 - \int_\theta^1 f(t)dt$$

Initial demand is given by:

$$s(p) = 1 - F(p/R) \qquad (29.10)$$

As R increases, demand increases. Thus, initially, if the firm could control R, it would try to set it as high as possible. However, in future periods, all consumers who learn the true quality and for whom R is greater than q, will stop buying.

Demand for the product if the quality were known (fully informed consumers) would be:

$$s(p) = 1 - F(p/q). \qquad (29.11)$$

where q is substituted for R because the consumer knows the true quality. We will assume that learning occurs through personal experience and is complete and immediate.

29.3.1 Pessimistic Case: $R < q$ – Expectations of Quality are Less than Actual Quality

The pessimistic case assumes customers have initial expectations about quality (R) below the true quality level (q). The customer, after trying the product/service learns the true quality is q. We will assume that the firm sets the introductory price (p_1) to attract customers and sets the future price for subsequent purchases (p_2).[1] We will assume a two-period model. The first-period profit function is $\pi_1 = 1 - F(\frac{p_1}{R}) \times (p_1 - c)$. Customers who try the product/service learn the true quality q. The two-period profit function is

$$\pi = \left[1 - F\left(\frac{p_1}{R}\right)\right](p_1 - c) + \left[1 - F\left(\frac{p_1}{R}\right)\right](p_2 - c) \qquad (29.12)$$

The number of acquired customers is $1 - F(\frac{p_1}{R})$. All of the customers who purchased in the first period will be willing to continue purchasing if $p_2/q < \theta$. The condition for these customers to purchase in the first period was $p_1/R < \theta$. Therefore all customers will be retained if $p_1/R = p_2/q$. Since $q > R$, we can make $p_2 > p_1$. Hence, because the true quality is higher than the estimated quality, the firm will raise its price in period 2.

---

[1] Note the subscript is now indicating period 1 versus 2, not product 1 versus product 2 as in Sect. 29.2.

Table 29.1 Comparison between two-period and one-period acquisition model

Cost (c)	Expected Actual price (R) quality (q)		Ratio of q/R	Price in period 1 (p_1)	Price in period 2 (p_2)	Myopic price	Ratio of myopic to optimal
2	3	5	1.67	$2.25	$3.75	$2.50	1.11
3	4	6	1.50	$3.20	$4.80	$3.50	1.09

To determine the optimal introductory price, the firm optimizes Equation 29.12 with respect to p_1 with $p_2 = p_1(q/R)$. It can be shown that the optimal first period price is:

$$p_1 = \frac{R}{2} + \frac{c}{1 + q/R} \tag{29.13}$$

To the extent that expected quality underestimates true quality ($q > R$), we price lower in period 1 but then adjust upwards in period 2. We can contrast this with the myopic solution (one-period) which is $p_1 = (c + R)/2$ (Equation 29.5). Table 29.1 shows some results for various values of q, R and c. The two-period model chooses a lower initial than second-period price, and the myopic price is between these two.

The pricing model offered by Shapiro can be expanded to include other assumptions. For example, one can add retention to the model and discount future sales quite easily. The optimal first-period price will depend upon the level of future profits. The higher the future profits, the lower will be the price in the first period.

29.3.2 Optimistic Case: R > q – Expectations of Quality are Greater than Actual Quality

When customers under estimate the true quality (pessimistic case), price should be low in the introductory period and higher in future periods. The opposite occurs when customer expectations are higher than the true quality. In this case the optimal pricing path is to charge a higher price in the introductory period and skim off those customers who incorrectly perceive quality. Then the price is reduced in the second period after the customer observes the true quality.

29.3.3 Research Issues

The work of Shapiro provides a wide variety of research questions. First, if the same price has to be offered to existing and new customers, the pricing decision becomes more complex. Database marketing potentially solves this problem because it can offer different prices to different customers. Non-database marketers have significantly greater difficulty price discriminating between new and existing purchasers.

Second, what is the impact of competition on the pricing strategy? The problem with incorporating competition is that most models assume it is a duopoly. However, in the real-world there are often many competitors and the firm is differentiated. Then, what is the impact of competition? This raises the question if it is better to assume a monopolistic model and derive the relevant pricing strategies or use a duopolist model with its attendant limitations.

A third issue for many database marketing firms is that there are many prices to be set, not just one. This is similar to a retailer's pricing problem. How does the firm develop a customer pricing strategy when it has multiple products being sold to a new customer?

A fourth issue is learning. When customers purchase a new product or service, they often are learning about the firm. Further, the firm is learning about the customer. Some papers in the economic literature on new product pricing assume the firm and/or the customer learn. Initially, the papers studied monopolistic behavior but recently have studied duopolistic behavior. See, for example, Bergemann and Valimaki (1997, 2000).

29.4 Acquisition and Retention Pricing Using the Customer Equity Model

An alternative approach to customer-based pricing is to use a customer equity model (e.g., Blattberg et al. 2001) and optimize it with respect to both acquisition and retention pricing. The Blattberg et al. (BGT) model is divided into acquisition and retention. N_t customers are available to be acquired and $N_t \alpha_t$ are actually acquired. Then, in the first period ρ_{t+1} customers are retained; in period 2 $\rho_{t+1} \times \rho_{t+2}$ customers are retained and so on. The basic model is:

$$CE(t) = \{(P_{a,t} - C_{a,t}) \times N_t \alpha_t - N_t B_{a,t}\} + \sum_{k=1}^{\infty} \left[\left\{ (P_{r,t+k} - C_{r,t+k}) \right. \right.$$
$$\left. \left. \times N_t \alpha_t \times r_{t+k}^k - B_{r,t+k} \times N_t \alpha_t r_{t+k-1}^k \right\} \left(\frac{1}{1+d} \right)^k \right] \qquad (29.14)$$

where

$$r_{t+k}^k = \prod_{i=1}^{k} \rho_{t+i}$$

and

$CE(t) =$ Customer equity for customers acquired at time t.
$P_{a,t} =$ Introductory price offered at time t.
$P_{r,t} =$ Retention price offered at time t.
$C_{a,t} =$ Average product cost in the acquisition period per customer at time t.
$C_{r,t} =$ Average product costs in the retention period per customer at time t.
$\alpha_t =$ The acquisition rate at time t.
$\rho_t =$ The retention rate at time t.
$r^k_{t+k} =$ The survival rate at time $t + k$.
$B_{a,t} =$ The acquisition marketing expenditures per prospect at time t.
$B_{r,t} =$ Retention marketing expenditures per existing customer at time t.
$d =$ Discount factor
$N_t =$ Number of prospects at time t.

The survival rate in the second term of Equation 29.14 (r^k_{t+k-1}) is lagged one period because the retention marketing expenditures are assumed to occur at the beginning of the period. We will assume that $\rho_{t+k} = \rho_t$ for all k, meaning a constant retention rate. We also will assume that the retention period price ($P_{r,t+k}$) and cost ($C_{r,t+k}$) are constant over time. These assumptions make the derivations tractable.

Pricing enters the equation through several variables in the model: acquisition and retention rates, and sales for acquisition and retention. Thus, in developing "optimal pricing," it is critical to understand the impact of price on each of these factors.

The objective function is:

$$
\underset{P_a, P_r}{MAX} \ CE(t) =
\left[
\begin{array}{l}
\{(P_a - C_a) \times (N_t \times \alpha(P_a)) - N_t \times B_a\} + \left\{ \sum_{k=1}^{\infty} \{(P_r - C_r) \right. \\
\times (N_t \times \alpha(P_a) \times \rho(P_a))^k - B_r \times N_t \times \alpha(P_a) \times \rho(P_r))^{k-1} \big\} \\
\times \left(\frac{1}{1+d} \right)^k
\end{array}
\right]
$$

(29.15)

Rearranging terms in Equation 29.15 and dropping N_t yields:

$$
\begin{aligned}
\underset{P_a P_r}{MAX} \ CE(t) &=
\left[
\begin{array}{l}
\{(P_a - C_a)(\alpha(P_a)) - B_a\} + \sum_{k=1}^{\infty} \left[\{(P_r - C_r)\alpha(P_a) \right. \\
\times \rho(P_r)^k - B_a \alpha(P_a)\rho(P_r)^{k-1} \big\} \left(\frac{1}{1+d} \right)^k \big]
\end{array}
\right] \\
&= \left[\{(P_a - C_a)(\alpha(P_a)) - B_a\} + \phi\alpha(P_a) \sum_{k=1}^{\infty} \rho(P_r)^k \left(\frac{1}{1+d} \right)^k \right] \\
&= \{(P_a - C_a)(\alpha(P_a)) - B_a\} + \alpha(P_a)\phi\theta
\end{aligned}
$$

(29.16)

where

$$\phi = \frac{(\rho(P_r)(P_r - C_r) - B_r)}{1 + d}, \theta = \frac{1}{1 - \rho(P_r) \times r} \text{ and } r = \frac{1}{1 + d}.$$

Note that $\phi\theta$ is increasing in retention rate and retention price; it therefore represents future profits after acquisition. Optimizing yields the following equations.

$$\frac{\partial CE(t)}{\partial P_a} = (P_a - C_a) \times \frac{\partial\alpha(P_a)}{\partial P_a} + \alpha(P_a) + \frac{\partial\alpha(P_a)}{\partial P_a} \times \phi\theta = 0 \qquad (29.17)$$

and

$$\frac{\partial CE(t)}{\partial P_r} = \theta\frac{\partial\phi}{\partial P_r} + \phi\frac{\partial\theta}{\partial P_r} = 0$$

$$=> \theta\left[(P_r - C_r)\frac{\partial\rho(P_r)}{\partial P_r} + \rho(P_r)\right] + \phi\left[\frac{r}{(1 - \rho(P_r)r)^2}\frac{\partial\rho(P_r)}{\partial P_r}\right] = 0$$

$$(29.18)$$

Solving Equation 29.17 for P_a reveals that the optimal acquisition price does depend upon the firm's retention tactics (i.e., retention price and marketing expenditures) and profitability. Specifically[2]:

$$P_a = \frac{E^\alpha_{P_a}}{1 + E^\alpha_{P_a}}C_a - \frac{E^\alpha_{P_a}}{1 + E^\alpha_{P_a}}\phi\theta$$

$$= P_m - \frac{E^\alpha_{P_a}}{1 + E^\alpha_{P_a}}\phi\theta$$

$$(29.19)$$

where

P_m = The myopic monopolist price.

$E^\alpha_{P_a} = \frac{\partial\alpha(P_a)}{\partial P_a} \times \frac{P_a}{\alpha(P_a)}$ = Price elasticity of the acquisition probability.

Equation 29.19 suggests two insights concerning optimal introductory pricing:

- As future profits, represented by $\phi\theta$, become higher, the optimal acquisition price decreases.
- As future profits, represented by $\phi\theta$ approach zero, the optimal acquisition price increases towards the myopic price.

Thus customers who become more profitable over time (e.g., customers who purchase add-ons, become less costly to serve, have a strong positive influence on other customers, or have higher retention rates) should be offered a lower

---

[2] In a monopoly in which the firm is maximizing current period profits (i.e., behaving myopically), the optimal price for the firm to charge would be $\frac{E^\alpha_{P_a}}{1 + E^\alpha_{P_a}} \times C_a$ (Pindyck and Rubinfeld 2004). Thus P_m is referred to as the myopic monopolist's price.

Table 29.2 Impact of retention price sensitivity on retention pricing

Retention spending per customer	$0.10	–	–
Acquisition probability	10%	–	–
Discount rate	20%	–	–
Marginal cost of product	$3.00	–	–
Model parameters	–	–	–
Exponent	1.5	–	–
Price sensitivity parameter (lambda)	0.01	0.02	0.03
Optimal retention price	$9.53	$7.31	$6.39
Optimal retention rate	63.6%	54.2%	47.0%

introductory price than customers who are not as profitable in future periods. Therefore the firm should price discriminate based on the future value of a customer. This result suggests that an optimal acquisition pricing policy should be based on expected future profits because myopic pricing may not generate the optimal number of customers.[3]

Implicitly solving for the optimal retention price from the differential in Equation 29.18 is more difficult. Unlike the optimal acquisition price, the optimal retention price can not be isolated on one side of the equation and must be written as a function of the other retention parameters. The optimal retention price can be studied only through numerical examples.

We use a numerical example that depends upon the choice of the retention price model. Assume:

$$\rho(P_r) = \frac{e^{-\lambda P_r^\gamma}}{2(1 + e^{-\lambda P_r^\gamma})} \tag{29.20}$$

λ was varied over three values and then an optimization routine was run to find the optimal retention price. The results are given in Table 29.2. It shows that as λ increases, making the retention rate more price sensitive, the optimal retention price decreases. The difficult practical issue is being able to determine the model's parameters. Field testing could provide data points to estimate the model.

29.5 Pricing to Recapture Customers

A related problem to acquisition and retention pricing is pricing to recapture customers. Alternative theories exist. One implies that pricing to recapture customers is based on the previous price paid, which becomes the reference price. Another states that increasing price generates a "loss" and reducing

---

[3] In some industries (e.g. telecommunications), this is called "sling-shot pricing." Firms price low to acquire customers, losing significant money in the first period, and then make profits through high retention rates. It is called "sling-shot pricing" because profits explode in later periods.

price is a "gain"; hence there should be asymmetry in response. The simplest hypothesis is that there is no connection between prices and reacquisition prices.

Thomas et al. (2004a) investigate various hypotheses about what affects pricing when recapturing customers. The methodology used is a split hazard model. The process begins when the customer is reacquired by the firm and ends when the customer terminates the subsequent relationship. A split hazard formulation is comprised of separate reacquisition and duration components. The reacquisition component measures the probability of recapturing a lapsed customer while the duration component predicts the length of the second tenure given the customer has been successfully recaptured.

For customer i ($i = 1 \ldots C$) the reacquisition component is specified as a binomial probit with observation equation:

$$Z_i = \begin{cases} 1 & \text{if } Z_i^* > 0 \\ 0 & \text{otherwise} \end{cases} \tag{29.21}$$

The latent dependent variable $z_i{}^*$ is modeled

$$z_i{}^* = w_i g + n_i \tag{29.22}$$

where $w_i g$ is the deterministic component and n_i is the stochastic component; w_i is the customer's vector of predictors and g is the associated parameter vector.

Modeling of the second tenure is complicated by the firm's propensity to change the offer price during the relationship. Each consumer's second tenure consists of one or more subspells that differ only in the offer price. Assuming the termination of the relationship is independent of the current duration allows the authors to assume the duration of a subspell does not depend on the length of prior subspells. For some observations, the customer has not terminated and hence tenure is right-censored.

The model is as follows:

$$y_{is_i} = \begin{cases} y_{is_i}^* & \text{if } y_{is_i} < c_{is_i} \\ c_{is_i} & \text{otherwise} \end{cases} \tag{29.23}$$

y_{is_i} is the observed duration of the relationship and c_{is_i} is the censoring value, the length that a price is offered. If the customer terminates the relationship before the price changes, then $y_{is_i} = y_{is_i}^*$. Otherwise the duration of the subspell is right censored. Latent duration $y_{is_i}^*$ is modeled as:

$$\ln(y_{is_i}^*) = X_{is_i} \beta + \varepsilon_{is_i} \tag{29.24}$$

where $X_{is_i} \beta$ is the deterministic component, ε_{is_i} is the stochastic component; X_{is_i} is the customers' vector of predictors during subspell s_i, and β is the parameter vector. Variance components are used to link acquisition and retention behavior. Customer heterogeneity is also modeled. See Thomas et al. for the specific variance structure and Chib (1993) for the estimation method.

The conclusions from Thomas et al. are:

1. Customers are more likely to be reacquired if the reacquisition price is lower.
2. The absolute effect of price is much more important than the effect of price relative to the last price paid in the prior relationship. Reacquisition strategies emphasizing decreasing price relative to the prior relationship are not likely to be effective. The most effective method for winning back lapsed customers is to offer a lower price. Also, customers who were acquired with low prices will not be enticed with significantly lower prices (in other words, relative price is not the critical factor).
3. Price increases have no effect on second tenure duration and price decreases relative to the prior price leads to a longer second tenure.
4. Higher retention prices lead to longer relationship duration. This result is different from Reinartz (2000) finding that long-life customers pay lower average prices than short-life customers. An alternative explanation is heterogeneity in reservation prices (similar to the model used by Shapiro 1983). Basically, usage allows the customer to tell true quality, which then implies a willingness to pay higher prices. Thus, the customer will pay a higher price when the customer recognizes the quality is superior through usage.

29.6 Pricing Add-on Sales

The Customer Equity model given in Equation 29.14 will be the basis for a discussion of pricing add-on sales with an additional variable added to the model.

$$
\begin{aligned}
CE(t) = \{ (P_{a,t} - C_{a,t}) * N_t \alpha_t - N_t * B_{a,t} \} + \\
\sum_{k=1}^{\infty} \left[\begin{cases} (P_{r,t+k} - C_{r,t+k}) * N_t \alpha_t {}^* \rho_{t+k}^k (\sum_{j=1}^{k-1} X_j) - B_{r,t+k} * N_t \alpha_t \\ + N_t \alpha_t {}^* \left[\rho_{t+k}^k (\sum_{j=1}^{k-1} X_j) \right] X_k (P_{ao}) m_{ao} \end{cases} \left(\frac{1}{1+d} \right)^k \right]
\end{aligned}
$$

$$(29.25)$$

where

$$
X_k = \begin{cases} 1 & \text{if an add-on purchase is made} \\ 0 & \text{otherwise} \end{cases}
$$

m_{ao} is the margin for add-on sales.

Note that X_k depends upon the price of add-on sales but as importantly, the retention rate, ρ, depends upon the number of add-on purchases the customer makes. The model assumes that the greater the number of purchases made, the higher the retention rate. This is consistent with RFM models. In the banking industry it is believed that if the firm can sell multiple products to the customer (e.g., a mortgage, checking and savings account), the customer has more difficulty changing relationships and therefore there is greater retention. The problem is distinguishing the number of purchases (relationships) from customer heterogeneity. Many studies show that the more purchases from the firm, the greater the probability of buying. However, is this due to consumer preference for the firm's products and satisfaction with the firm or is it due to the number of purchases the customer makes?

The implications of these two possibilities are quite different. If it is the number of purchases that increases retention, then the optimal price to charge for "add-on" selling will be lower. If the cause of the higher retention rates being correlated with the number of purchases is heterogeneity in preference and satisfaction, then the firm should not lower prices when selling additional products/services.

While pricing add-on sales is a critical customer-based pricing issue, there is very little literature on the topic. One research paper that investigates a related issue is Israel (2005), who examined the relationship between recency and retention rate. Through the clever use of an automobile insurance database, Israel (2005) was able to investigate whether retention rates were affected by recency or due to unobserved heterogeneity in customer preferences. Using the auto insurance data he found evidence for both effects but concluded that the role of unobserved heterogeneity was much more important. A recent study by Reinartz et al. (2006) uses Granger causality tests to investigate whether cross-buying determines loyalty or loyalty determines cross-buying. For two firms, they conclude that loyalty causes cross-buying. If the findings from the Israel and Reinartz et al. studies were generalized, one would conclude that many of the recommendations that the number of products is a very good predictor of retention rates might in fact simply be related to consumer preference for the service. This is a crucial area for future research, and see Chapter21 for further discussion.

29.7 Price Discrimination Through Database Targeting Models

There is a vast literature in marketing and economics on price discriminating among customers. We will review several articles including one of the seminal articles on this topic by Rossi et al. (1996).

Any basic micro economics textbook discusses the conditions under which a firm can price discriminate. We will focus on how does database marketing help a firm price discriminate and can customer databases always be used to price discriminate?

We begin with an article by Rossi et al. (1996) which addresses the issue of the value of purchase history data for targeting. They compare the use of demographic data, which many marketing firms believe should serve as the basis for selecting market segments, and purchase history data.

The basic proposition of Rossi et al. is that information sets are used to draw inferences about household preferences and household-specific parameters such as price sensitivity measures. These household-specific preferences and price elasticities can be used to target promotions and prices at the individual level.

Rossi et al. compare decisions with information from the household with decisions in which there is no relevant information (causal or demographic information). The value of the information is determined by assessing how much the firm's profit increases when it uses the specific types of information versus when it does not.

The authors conclude that demographic data explains very little of the variation in price sensitivity (only 7%). Their results are consistent with other studies that find demographic information explain even less of the variability (Bucklin and Gupta (1992) and Gupta and Chintagunta (1994)). This finding is consistent with predictive models that often find demographic data have limited value in targeting. Of course, this will vary by product category and there may be instances in which demographic data could provide insights into price sensitivity (e.g., expensive durable goods).

The other conclusion Rossi et al. draw is that purchase histories have significant value even if the purchase histories are short. This is reassuring because many database marketers have limited causal data (promotional histories) captured in their databases.

The most important contribution of Rossi et al. is providing a methodology for determining the value of information to a database marketer. The methodology can be applied to situations in which the firm wants to determine the value of keeping its promotional histories for targeting. Do long purchase history data or solicitation data provide enough value to justify the cost of keeping the data?

An article by Zhang and Krishnamurthi (2004) considers the issues of when to offer promotions and how much to discount to individual customers. They use a purchase incidence, purchase timing, brand choice model which allows for inertia/variety seeking behavior and consumer heterogeneity to address these questions. Their major modeling contribution is that their model can continuously update the model's parameters by individual and then determine the optimal timing of promotions. Using their model they then evaluate different promotional strategies. Their finding is that by varying the timing of promotions based on continuously updating the model, profits can increase.

One issue Zhang and Krishnamurthi raise is consumers anticipating promotions (consumer expectations). Others such as Erdem et al. (2003) and Hendel and Nevo (2002) have developed models that include consumers' expectations about prices. This is a critical issue and was discussed earlier in this chapter. If consumers anticipate price changes, then the models need to be altered to take into account how changes in promotional or price strategies lead to changes in consumers' expectations which then change consumers' purchase patterns. This phenomenon is well understood for durable goods (particularly electronics and computers) where consumers know that prices will drop in the future. For database marketers, as pricing strategies become dynamic, consumer expectations may also be dynamic and understanding the implications of having both changing at once becomes an important modeling challenge. Research has just scratched the surface of this issue.

In another paper, Zhang and Wedel (2007) ask the question about what level of personalized promotions work in different environments. They consider two types of retailers – bricks and mortar (offline) and online – and three levels of promotions – mass market, segment level and individual-level. They build a similar model to that of Zhang and Krishnamurthi which includes a purchase incidence, choice and quantity model and allows for heterogeneity.

One interesting finding by Zhang and Wedel (2007) is that the gains in profits from mass market to segment to individual-level optimization are not that large, especially in off-line environments, while there is a substantial gain in moving from current managerial practice to mass market optimization. This is a provocative result. One factor driving their results is the retailer's cost structure. For offline retailers the ability to reach its customers through mass-communications may be more cost-effective than it is for online retailers because they have the store environment to communicate promotions, which is very low cost. Also, the cost of offering promotions through tools such as Catalina Marketing Systems is low for offline retailers. Hence the gains from personalization are offset by the low delivery costs. Another factor is that both offline and online retailers have data on their customer's behavior with *their* business, but not with competitors. This might add significant measurement error to individual-level and even segment-level price elasticity estimates (see Park and Fader 2004).

Zhang and Wedel do indicate that individual level databases do have the potential to provide significant economic returns in the correct environment. However, for a database marketer when the costs of mass promotions are very low, the payouts from having an extensive customer database may also be very low. This is exemplified by the struggles offline grocery retailers worldwide are having with the use of their customer databases. With the exception of a few retailers such as Tesco (UK) or CVS (USA), very few have been able to generate a significant payout from frequent shopper programs. This may be caused by the fact that mass promotions are more cost effective.

One final issue associated with price discrimination is do consumers/ customers care if others are receiving a lower price than they do? Feinberg et al. (2002) address this issue using laboratory experiments. Their basic premise is that consumer preference for a firm's products is affected not just by the price the consumer pays but the prices that other consumers are paying.

To test this premise, they design a series of laboratory experiments in combination with various models to answer the question above. They find two effects beyond traditional economic rationality: (1) consumers feel *betrayed* if their favored firm offers promotions to switchers; and (2) consumers are *jealous* if another firm offers a price decrease to its own loyal customers and the favored firm does not.

These findings are in a laboratory setting in which the authors can manipulate the information each consumer receives. In the real-world, it is not clear how much of this information is available to customers. However, regarding finding one above, consumers can often tell if a firm is offering lower prices to new customers. Mobile phone firms offer lower prices to new customers; credit card companies offer low teaser rates to prospective new customers. This type of offer may lead to a sense of betrayal and therefore affect the ability of the firm to offer low prices to new customers and then raise their prices over time. The findings of Feinberg et al. are provocative and should lead to additional research, particularly understanding in the real-world the prevalence of consumers' knowledge about what others pay and what their reaction is to that information (see Krishna et al. (2004) for an interesting follow-up paper on whether betrayal and jealousy effects exist when firms target price *increases* selectively).

References

Abdi, H. (1994). A Neural Network Primer. *Journal of Biological Systems*, 2(3), 247–283.

Abu-Shalback Zid, L. (2004a). Why Wait. *Marketing Management*, 13(6), 6.

Abu-Shalback Zid, L. (2004b). Loyalty Doesn't Always Pay. *Marketing Management*, 13(3), 4.

Achabal, D.D., Badgett, M., Chu, J., and Kalyanam, K. (2005). *Cross-channel Optimization*. Somers, NY: IBM Institute for Business Value, IBM Global Services.

Ackerman, M., Cranor, L., and Reagle, J. (1999). Privacy in E-Commerce: Examining User Scenarios and Privacy Preferences, *ACM Conference on E-Commerce*. Denver, CO.

Addelman, S. (1962). Orthogonal Main-effect Plans for Asymmetric Factorial Experiments. *Technometrics*, 4(1), 21–46.

Adomavicius, G. (2005). Toward the Next Generation of Recommender Systems: A Survey of the State-of-the-Art and Possible Extensions. *IEEE Transactions on Knowledge and Data Engineering*, 17(6), 734–749.

Agrawal, R. and Srikant, R. (1994). Fast Algorithms for Mining Association Rules in Large Databases, *Proceedings of the 20th International Conference on Very Large Data Bases*, pp. 487–499.

Agrawal, R. and Srikant, R. (1995). Mining Sequential Patterns, *International Conference on Data Engineering*. Taipei, Taiwan.

Agrawal, R., Imielinski, T., and Swami, A. (1993). Mining Association Rules Between Sets of Items in Large Databases, *Proceedings of the ACM SIGMOD International Conference on the Management of Data*, pp. 207–216.

Aha, D. (1992). Tolerating Noisy, Irrelevant, and Novel Attributes in Instance-based Learning Algorithms. *International Journal of Man–Machine Studies*, 36(2), 267–287.

Ailawadi, K.L., Neslin, S.A., and Gedenk, K. (2001). Pursuing the Value-conscious Consumer: Store Brands Versus National Brand Promotions. *Journal of Marketing*, 65(1), 71–89.

Ainslie, A. and Pitt, L. (1998). Unibank and the Analysis of the Excursion Card Customer Database: A Practical Application of Statistical Techniques in Database Marketing. *Journal of Interactive Marketing*, 12(3), 57–66.

Allenby, G.M., Leone, R.P., and Lichung, J. (1999). A Dynamic Model of Purchase Timing with Application to Direct Marketing. *Journal of American Statistical Association*, 94(6), 265–374.

Amemiya, T. and Powell, J. (1983). *A Comparison of the Logit Model and Normal Discriminant Analysis When Independent Variables Are Binary* in Studies in Econometrics, Time Series, and Multivariate Statistics, S. Karlin, T. Amemiya and L. Goodman (Eds.). New York: Academic Press.

Ancarani, F. and Shankar, V. (2004). Price Levels and Price Dispersion Within and Across Multiple Retailer Types: Further Evidence and Extension. *Journal of the Academy of Marketing Science*, 32(2), 176–187.

Anderson, E.T. and Simester, D.I. (2001). Are Sale Signs Less Effective When More Products Have Them? *Marketing Science*, 20(2), 121–142.

Anderson, E.T. and Simester, D.I. (2004). Long-run Effects of Promotion Depth on New Versus Established Customers: Three Field Studies. *Marketing Science*, 23(1), 4–20.

Anderson, E.W. and Sullivan, M.W. (1993). The Antecedents and Consequences of Customer Satisfaction for Firms. *Marketing Science*, 12(2), 125–143.

Anderson, E.W., Fornell, C., and Lehmann, D.R. (1994). Customer Satisfaction, Market Share, and Profitability: Findings from Sweden. *Journal of Marketing*, 58(3), 53–66.

Ang, L. and Taylor, B. (2005). Managing Customer Profitability Using Portfolio Matricies. *Database Marketing and Customer Strategy Management*, 12(4), 298–304.

Anonymous (2001). Does CRM Pay? *Journal of Business Strategy*, 22(6), 3.

Ansari, A. and Mela, C.F. (2003). E-Customization. *Journal of Marketing Research*, 40(2), 131–145.

Ansari, A., Essegaier, S., and Kohli, R. (2000). Internet Recommendation Systems. *Journal of Marketing Research*, 37(3), 363–375.

Ansari, A., Mela, C.F., and Neslin, S.N. (2008). Customer Channel Migration. *Journal of Marketing Research*, Forthcoming.

Apte, C. and Weiss, S. (1997). *Data Mining with Decision Trees and Decision Rules*, Research Report. IBM Research Division.

Ardissono, L. and Goy, A. (2000). Tailoring the Interaction with Users in Web Stores. *User Modeling and User-adapted Interaction*, 10(4), 251–203.

Ardissono, L., Goy, A., Petrone, G., and Signan, M. (2002). Personalization in Business-to-Customer Interaction. *Communications of the ACM*, 45(5), 52–53.

Argote, L. (1999). *Organizational Learning: Creating, Retaining and Transferring Knowledge*. Norwell, MA: Kluwer.

Ariely, D., Lynch, J.G., and Moon, Y. (2002). Taking Advice from Smart Agents: The Advice Likelihood Model, *Marketing Science Institute, Duke Joint Conference on Customer Relationship Management*. Durham, NC.

Assael, H. (1995). *Consumer Behavior and Marketing Action, 5th Edition*. Cincinnati, OH: South-Western College.

Atlas, L., Cole, R., Muthuswamy, Y., Lipman, A., Connor, J., Park, D., el-Sharkawi, M., and Mark, R. (1990). A Performance Comparison of Trained Multilayer Perceptrons and Trained Classification Trees. *Proceedings of the IEEE*, 78(10), 1614–1619.

Baker, K.R. (1997). An Experimental Study of the Effectiveness of Rolling Schedules in Production Planning. *Decision Sciences*, 8(1), 19–27.

Balabanovic, M. (1997). An Adaptive Web Page Recommendation Service, *First International Conference on Autonomous Agents*.

Balabanovic, M. and Shoham, Y. (1997). Fab: Content-based, Collaborative Recommendation. *Communication of the ACM*, 40(3), 66–72.

Balachander, S. and Ghosh, B. (2006). *Cross-buying and Customer Churning Behavior*, Working Paper. West Lafayette, IN: Krannert Graduate School of Mangement, Purdue University.

Balakrishnan, P., Cooper, M., Jacob, V., and Lewis, P. (1996). Comparative Performance of the FSCL Neural Net and K-means Algorithm for Market Segmentation. *European Journal of Operational Research*, 93(10), 346–357.

Balasubramanian, S. (1998). Mail Versus Mall; A Strategic Analysis of Competition Between Direct Marketers and Conventional Retailers. *Marketing Science*, 17(3), 181–195.

Band, W. (2006). *CRM Market Size and Forecast: 2006 to 2010, with Andrew Bartels and Mary Ann Rogan*. Cambridge, MA: Forrester Research.

Banfield, J.D. and Raftery, A.E. (1993). Model-based Gaussian and Non-Gaussian Clustering. *Biometrics*, 49(3), 803–821.

Banslaben, J. (1992). Predictive Modeling. In E. Nash (Ed.), *The Direct Marketing Handbook*. New York: McGraw-Hill.

Barnes, J.G. (2000). Closeness in Customer Relationships: Examining the Payback from Getting Closer to the Customer. In T. Hennig-Thurau and U. Hansen (Eds.), *Relationship Marketing: Gaining Competitive Advantage Through Customer Satisfaction and Customer Retention*, pp. 90–106. New York: Springer.

Barron, A. (1993). Universal Approximation Bounds for Superpositions of a Sigmoidal Function. *IEEE Transactions on Information Theory*, 39(3), 930–945.

Bart, I.Y., Shankar, V., Sultan, F., and Urban, G.L. (2005). Are the Drivers and Role of Online Trust the Same for all Web Sites and Consumers? A Large Scale Exploratory Empirical Study. *Journal of Marketing*, 69(4), 133–152.

Barthel, M. (1995). The Relational Data Base: A Survival Kit for Banks. *American Banker*, 160(184), 10A–11A.

Bartholomew, D. (1987). *Latent Variable Models and Factor Analysis.* New York: Oxford University Press.

Basilevsky, A. (1994). *Statistical Factor Analysis and Related Methods.* New York: Wiley.

Bass, F.M. (2004). Comments on "A New Product Growth Model for Consumer Durables". *Management Science,* 50(December Supplement), 1833–1840.

Basu, C., Hirsh, H., and Cohen, W. (1998). Recommendation as Classification: Using Social and Content-based Information in Recommendations, *Proceedings of the 1998 Workshop on Recommender Systems,* pp. 11–15. AAAI.

Bayardo, R. and Agrawal, R. (1999). Mining the Most Interesting Rules, *Proceedings of the Fifth ACM SIGKDD International Conference on Knowledge Discovery and Data Mining,* pp. 145–154.

Beeler, A. (2000). Loyalty Efforts Score Points with Cable TV. *Advertising Age,* 71(9), 65–66.

Beggs, A. and Klemperer, P. (1992). Multi-period Competition with Switching Costs. *Econometrica,* 60(3), 651–666.

Bell, D.R., Chiang, J., and Padmanabhan, V. (1999). The Decomposition of Promotional Response: An Empirical Generalization. *Marketing Science,* 18(4), 504–526.

Bell, D.R., Deighton, J., Reinartz, W.J., Rust, R.T., and Swartz, G. (2002). Seven Barriers to Customer Equity Management. *Journal of Service Research,* 5(1), 77–85.

Bellman, S., Johnson, E.J., and Lohse, G.L. (2001). To Opt-in or Opt-out? It Depends on the Question. *Communications of the ACM,* 44(2), 25–27.

Bellman, S., Johnson, E.J., Kobrin, S.J., and Lohse, G.L. (2004). International Differences in Information Privacy Concerns: A Global Survey of Consumers. *The Information Society,* 20(5), 313–324.

Ben-Akiva, M., McFadden, D., Abe, M., Bockenholt, U., Bolduc, D., Gopinath, D., Morikawa, T., Ramaswamy, V., Rao, V., Revelt, D., and Steinberg, D. (1997). Modeling Methods for Discrete Choice Analysis. *Marketing Letters,* 8(3), 273–286.

Ben-Bassat, M. (1987). Use of Distance Measures, Information Measures and Error Bounds on Feature Evaluation. In P.R. Krishnaiah and L.N. Kanal (Eds.), *Classification, Pattern Recognition and Reduction of Dimensionality, Volume 2 of Handbook of Statistics,* pp. 773–791. Amsterdam: North-Holland.

Bendoly, E., Blocher, J.D., Bretthauer, K.M., Krishman, S., and Venkataramanan, M.A. (2005). Online/In-store Integration and Customer Retention. *Journal of Service Research,* 7(4), 313–327.

Bergemann, D and J Valimaki, (1997), Market Diffusion with Two-Sided Learning, *Rand Journal of Economics,* Vol 28, No. 4, pp. 773–795.

Bergemann, D and J Valimaki, (2000), Experimentation in Markets, *Review of Economic Studies,* Vol. 67, p. 213–234.

Bergen, M., Dutta, S., and Shugan, S.M. (1996). Branded Variants: A Retail Perspective. *Journal of Marketing Research*, 38(1), 9–19.

Berger, P.D. and Bechwati, N.N. (2001). The Allocation of Promotion Budget to Maximize Customer Equity. *Omega*, 29(1), 49–61.

Berger, P.D. and Nasr, N.I. (1998). Customer Lifetime Value: Marketing Models and Applications. *Journal of Interactive Marketing*, 12(1), 17–30.

Berger, P.D., Bolton, R.N., Bowman, D., Briggs, E., Kumar, V., Parasuraman, A., and Terry, C. (2002). Marketing Actions and the Value of Customer Assets: A Framework for Customer Asset Management. *Journal of Service Research*, 5(1), 39–54.

Berger, P.D., Lee, J., and Weinberg, B.D. (2006). Optimal Cooperative Advertising Integration Strategy for Organizations Adding a Direct Online Channel. *Journal of the Operational Research Society*, 57(8), 920–927.

Berndt, E., Hall, B., Hall, R., and Hausman, J. (1974 October). Estimation and Inference in Nonlinear Structural Models. *Annals of Economic and Social Measurement*, 3/4(10), 653–665.

Berry, J. (1994). A Potent New Tool for Selling: Database Marketing. *Business Week*(September 5), 56–62.

Berry, L.L. (1983). Relationship Marketing. In L.L. Berry, G.L. Shostack, and G. Upah (Eds.), *Emerging Perspectives in Services Marketing*, pp. 25–28. Chicago, IL: American Marketing Association.

Berry, M. and Linoff, G. (1997). *Data Mining Techniques for Marketing Sales, and Customer Support*. New York: Wiley.

Berson, A., Smith, S., and Thearling, K. (2000). *Building Data Mining Applications for CRM*. New York: McGraw-Hill.

Bertsekas, D.P. (1995). *Dynamic Programming and Optimal Control*. Belmont, MA: Athena.

Bitner, M.J., Brown, S.W., and Meuter, M.L. (2000). Technology Infusion in Service Encounters. *Journal of the Academy of Marketing Science*, 28(1), 138–149.

Bitran, G.R. and Mondschein, S.V. (1996). Mailing Decisions in the Catalog Industry. *Management Science*, 42(9), 1364–1381.

Biyalogorsky, E. and Naik, P.A. (2003). Clicks and Mortar: The Effect of On-line Activities on Off-line Sales. *Marketing Letters*, 14(1), 21–32.

Blattberg, R.C. and Deighton, J. (1991). Interactive Marketing: Exploiting the Age of Addressability. *Sloan Management Review*, 33(1), 5–14.

Blattberg, R.C. and Deighton, J. (1996). Manage Marketing by the Customer Equity Test. *Harvard Business Review*, 17(4), 136–144.

Blattberg, R. and Golanty, J. (1978). Tracker: An Early Test Market Forecasting and Diagnostic Model for New Product Planning. *Journal of Marketing Research*, 15(2), 192–202.

Blattberg, R.C. and Neslin, S.A. (1990). *Sales Promotion: Concepts, Methods, and Strategies*. Englewood Cliffs, NJ: Prentice-Hall.

Blattberg, R.C. and Thomas, J.S. (2000). Valuing, Analyzing and Managing the Marketing Function Using Customer Equity Principles. In D. Iacobucci (Ed.), *Kellogg on Marketing*. New York: Wiley.

Blattberg, R.C., Eppen, G.D., and Lieberman, J. (1981). A Theoretical and Empirical Evaluation of Price Deals for Consumer Nondurables. *Journal of Marketing*, 45(1), 116–129.

Blattberg, R.C., Getz, G., and Thomas, J.S. (2001). *Customer Equity: Building and Managing Relationships as Valuable Assets*. Boston, MA: Harvard Business School.

Blodgett, J. and Anderson, R.D. (2000). A Bayesian Network Model of the Consumer Complaint Process. *Journal of Service Research*, 2(4), 321–338.

Bodapati, A.V. (2008). Recommendation Systems with Purchase Data, *Journal of Marketing Research*, forthcoming.

Bodenberg, T. (2001). Customer Relationship Management: New Ways of Keeping the Customer Satisfied, *Research Report R-1299-01-RR*. New York: The Conference Board.

Boehm, E.W. (2001). *Pharma Must Bridge the Sales and Marketing Chasm*. Cambridge, MA: Forrester Research.

Boehm, E.W. (2002). Right-channeling Consumer Drug Marketing, *The Tech Strategy Report*. Cambridge, MA: Forrester Research.

Bold, B. (2003). AOL Hires Senior Duo to Aid Customer Retention. *Marketing*, June 19, 2003, 10.

Bolton, R.N. (1998). A Dynamic Model of the Duration of the Customer's Relationship with a Continuous Service Provider: The Role of Satisfaction. *Marketing Science*, 17(1), 45–65.

Bolton, R.N. and Drew, J.H. (1991a). A Longitudinal Analysis of the Impact of Services Changes on Customer Attitudes. *Journal of Marketing*, 55(1), 1–9.

Bolton, R.N. and Drew, J.H. (1991b). A Multistage Model of Customers' Assessment of Service Quality and Value. *Journal of Consumer Research*, 17(March), 375–384.

Bolton, R.N. and Lemon, K.N. (1999). A Dynamic Model of Customers Usage of Services: Usage as an Antecedent and Consequence of Satisfaction. *Journal of Marketing Research*, 36(2), 171–186.

Bolton, R.N., Kannan, P.K., and Bramlett, M.D. (2000). Implications of Loyalty Program Membership and Service Experiences for Customer Retention and Value. *Journal of the Academy of Marketing Science*, 28(1), 95–108.

Bonfrer, A., Knox, G., Eliashberg, J., and Chiang, J. (2007). *Diagnosing and Predicting Individual Customer Defection in a Contractual Setting*, Working Paper. Philadelphia, PA: The Wharton School.

Borna, C. (2000). Combating Customer Churn. *Telecommunications*, 34(3), 83–85.

Boser, B., Guyon, I., and Vapnik, V. (1992). A Training Algorithm for Optimal Margin Classifiers, *Fifth Annual Workshop on Computational Learning Theory*, pp. 144–152. San Mateo, CA: Morgan Kaufmann.

Botwinik, S.L. (2001). *Organizing to Get CRM Right*. Cambridge, MA: Forester Research.

Boulding, W., Staelin, R., Ehret, M., and Johnston, W.J. (2005). A Customer Relationship Management Roadmap: What Is Known, Potential Pitfalls, and Where to Go. *Journal of Marketing*, 69(4), 155–166.

Boyd, H., Westfall, R., and Stasch, S. (1981). *Marketing Research: Text and Cases – 5th Edition*. Homewood, IL: Richard D. Irwin.

Boyle, M. (2006). Best Buy's Giant Gamble. *Fortune*, 153(6), 68.

Brealey, R.A., Myers, S.C., and Marcus, A.J. (2004). *Fundamentals of Corporate Finance*. New York: McGraw-Hill/Irwin.

Breese, J., Heckerman, D., and Kadie, C. (1998). Empirical Analysis of Predictive Algorithms for Collaborative Filtering, *Proceedings of the Fourteenth Conference on Uncertainty in Artifical Intelligence*. Madison, WI.

Breiman, L. (1996). Bagging Predictors. *Machine Learning*, 24(2), 123–140.

Breiman, L. (2001). Random Forests. *Machine Learning*, 45(1), 5–32.

Breiman, L., Friedman, J., Olshen, R., and Stone, C. (1984). *Classification and Regression Trees*. Monterery, CA: Wadsworth and Brooks/Cole.

Breslow, L. and Aha, D. (1996). *Simplifying Decision Trees: A Survey*: Navy Center for Applied Research in Artificial Intelligence, Naval Research Lab.

Briesch, R., Krishnamurthi, L., Mazumdar, T., and Raj, S.P. (1997). A Comparative Analysis of Reference Price. *Journal of Marketing Research*, 24(3), 202–214.

Brown, D., Corruble, V., and Pittard, C. (1993). A Comparison of Decision Tree Classifiers with Back-propagation Neural Networks for Multimodal Classification Problems. *Pattern Recognition*, 26(6), 953–961.

Brynjolfsson, E. and Smith, M.D. (2000). Frictionless Commerce? A Comparison of Internet and Conventional Retailers. *Management Science*, 46(4), 563–585.

Bucklin, R. and Gupta, S. (1992). Brand Choice, Purchase Incidence and Segmentation: An Integrated Approach. *Journal of Marketing Research*, 29(2), 201–215.

Bult, J.R. and Wansbeek, T. (1995). Optimal Selection for Direct Mail. *Marketing Science*, 14(4), 378–394.

Bultez, A. and Naert, P.A. (1988). SH.A.R.P.: Shelf Allocation for Retailers' Profit. *Marketing Science*, 7(3), 211–231.

Buntine, W. (1992). Learning Classification Trees. *Statistics and Computing*, 2(2), 63–73.

Burges, C. (1998). A Tutorial on Support Vector Machines for Pattern Recognition. *Data Mining and Knowledge Discovery*, 2(2), 121–167.

Burke, R.R. (2002). Technology and the Customer Interface: What Consumers Want in the Physical and Virtual Store. *Journal of the Academy of Marketing Science*, 30(4), 411–432.

Business Wire (2002). Cingular Rollover Minutes Campaign Sparked Consumer Interest and Reduced Potential Churn – But Not for Long. Boston, MA: Business Wire.

Calciu, M. and Salerno, F. (2002). Customer Value Modelling: Synthesis and Extension Proposals. *Journal of Targeting, Measurement and Analysis for Marketing*, 11(2), 124–147.

Calinski, T. and Habarasz, J. (1974). A Dendrite Method for Cluster Analysis. *Communications in Statistics*, 3(1), 1–17.

Caminal, R. and Matutes, C. (1990). Endogenous Switching Costs in a Duoply Model. *International Journal of Industrial Organization*, 8(3), 353–373.

Campbell, D., Erdahl, R., Johnson, D., Bibelnieks, E., Haydock, M., Bullock, M., and Crowder, H. (2001). Optimizing Customer Mail Streams at Fingerhut. *Interfaces*, 31(1), 77–90.

Campbell, D. and Frei, F.X. (2006). *The Cost Structure, Customer Profitability, and Retention Implications of Self-service Distribution Channels: Evidence from Customer Behavior in an Online Banking Channel*, Working Paper. Cambridge, MA: Harvard Business School.

Carlson, C. (2001). US Firms Find No Haven in Safe Harbor. *EWeek*, 37(March 19).

Catalog Age (2003). The Catalog Age 100. http://multichannelmerchant. com/catalogage/2003_CatalogAge100.pdf. Accessed July 27, 2007.

Cendrowska, J. (1987). PRISM: An Algorithm for Inducing Modular Rules. *International Journal of Man–Machine Studies*, 27(4), 349–370.

Cespedes, F.V. and Smith, H.J. (1993). Database Marketing: New Rules for Policy and Practice. *Sloan Management Review*, 34(4), 7–22.

Chain Store Age (1998). Data Mining is More than Beer and Diapers. *Chain Store Age*, 74(6), 64.

Chain Store Age (2002). Privacy Worries Aren't Acted On. *Chain Store Age*, 78(7), 62.

Chamberlain, G. (1980). Analysis of Covariance with Qualitative Data. *Review of Economic Studies*, 47(146), 225–238.

Chand, S., Hsu, V.N., and Sethi, S. (2002). Forecast, Solution and Rolling Horizons in Operations Management Problems. *Manufacturing and Services Operations Management*, 4(1), 25–43.

Chang, K.P. and Guh, Y.Y. (1991). Linear Production Functions and the Data Envelopment Analysis. *European Journal of Operations Research*, 52(2), 215–223.

Chaston, I., Badger, B., Mangles, T., and Sadler-Smith, E. (2003). Relationship Marketing, Knowledge Management Systems and E-Commerce Operations in Small UK Accountancy Practices. *Journal of Marketing Management*, 19(112), 109–129.

Cheeseman, P. and Stutz, J. (1995). Bayesian Classification (Autoclass): Theory and Results . In U. Fayyad, G. Piatetsky-Shapiro, P. Smyth, and R. Uthurusamy (Eds.), *Advances in Knowledge Discovery and Data Mining*. Menlo Park, CA: AAAI.

Chen, X., Petrounias, I., and Heathfield, H. (1998). Discovering Temporal Association Rules in Temporal Databases, *Proceedings of International*

Workshop on Issues and Applications of Database Technology, pp. 312–319. Berlin.

Chen, Y. and Iyer, G. (2002). Consumer Addressability and Customized Pricing. *Marketing Science*, 21(2), 197–208.

Chen, Y. and Zhang, Z.J. (2002). *Price-for-information Effect and Benefit of Behavior-based Targeted Pricing*, Working Paper. New York: Stern School of Business, New York University.

Chen, Y., Narasimhan, C. and Zhang, Z.J. (2001). Individual Marketing with Imperfect Targetability. *Marketing Science*, 20(1), 23–41.

Chib, S. (1993). Bayes Inference in the Tobit Censored Regression Model. *Journal of Econometrics*, 51(1/2), 79–99.

Chien, Y. and George, E.I. (1999). A Bayesian Model for Collaborative Filtering, *Proceedings of the Seventh International Workshop on Artificial Intelligence and Statistics*. San Francisco, CA.

Ching, W., Ng, M., Wong, K., and Altman, E. (2004). Customer Lifetime Value: Stochastic Optimization Approach. *Journal of the Operational Research Society*, 55(8), 860–868.

Chintagunta, P.K. and Prasad, A.R. (1993). An Empirical Investigation of the Dynamic McFadden Model of Purchase Timing and Brand Choice: Implications for Market Structure. *Journal of Business and Economic Statistics*, 16(1), 2–12.

Chou, P. (1991). Optimal Partitioning for Classification and Regression Trees. *IEEE Transactions on Pattern Analysis and Machine Intelligence*, 13(4), 340–354.

Chu, J., Chintagunta, P.K., and Vilcassim, N.J. (2007). Assessing the Economic Value of Distribution Channels: An Application to the Personal Computer Industry. *Journal of Marketing Research*, 44(1), 29–41.

Clampet, E. (2005a). New Laws Could Spell Privacy's Future. *Inside 1 to 1: Privacy*. Norwalk, CT: Peppers and Rogers Group, May 12, 2005.

Clampet, E. (2005b). Privacy Works Its Way into the Boardroom at IBM. *Inside 1 to 1: Privacy*. Norwalk CT: Peppers and Rogers Group, April 14, 2005.

Coelho, F., Easingwood, C., and Coelho, A. (2003). Exploratory Evidence of Channel Performance in Single vs. Multiple Channel Strategies. *International Journal of Retail and Distribution Management*, 31(11), 561–573.

Cohen, A., Metz, C., Steinhart, M.J., Broida, R., and Pike, S. (2005). AOL. *PC Magazine*, 24(17), 124.

Cohen, J. (2001). Growth Formula. *Computerworld*, 35(27), 36–37.

Cohen, W. (1995). Fast Effective Rule Induction. In A. Prieditis and S. Russell (Eds.), *Proceedings of Twelfth International Conference on Machine Learning*, pp. 115–123. San Francisco, CA: Morgan Kaufmann.

Columbo, R. and Jiang, W. (1999). A Stochastic RFM Model. *Journal of Interactive Marketing*, 13(3), 2–12.

Computer and Internet Lawyer (2002). World Wide Web Consortium Recommends P3P. *Computer and Internet Lawyer*, 19(7), 33–34.

Conley, C. (1998). Loyalty Cards Are Missing the Point. *Marketing Week, London*, 21(16), 21–22.

Cooper, L. (2000). Strategic Marketing Planning for Radically New Products. *Journal of Marketing Research*, 64(1), 1–16.

Corr, A. (2004). Hepp Holds Pfizer Pharmacia Merger Together. *Inside 1 to 1: Privacy*. Norwalk, CT: Peppers and Rogers Group, July 8, 2004.

Corstjens, M. and Doyle, P. (1981). A Model for Optimizing Retail Space Allocation. *Management Science*, 27(7), 822–833.

Coussement, K. and Van den Poel, D. (2007a). *Integrating the Voice of Customers through Call Center Emails into a Decision Support System for Churn Prediction*, Working Paper. Ghent, Belgium: Ghent University, Faculty of Economics and Business Administration, Department of Marketing.

Coussement, K. and Van den Poel, D. (2007b). *Improving Customer Churn Prediction Using Emotionality Indicators in Emails as Additional Features*, Working Paper. Ghent, Belgium: Faculty of Economics and Business.

Coussement, K. and Van den Poel, D. (2008). Churn Prediction in Subscription Services: An Application of Support Vector Machines while Comparing Two Parameter-selection Techniques. *Expert Systems with Applications*, 34(2), forthcoming.

Cover, T. (1965). Geometrical and Statistical Properties of Systems of Linear Inequalities with Applications in Pattern Recognition. *IEEE Transactions on Electronic Computers*, EC-14(3), 326–334.

Cox, D.R. (1972). Regression Models and Life-tables. *Journal of the Royal Statistical Society*, Series B(34), 187–200.

Crawford, J. (2002). Multichannel Best Practices: Sears and REI, *TechStrategy Report*. Cambridge, MA: Forrester Research.

Crawford, S. (1989). Extensions to the CART Algorithm. *International Journal of Man–Machine Studies*, 31(2), 197–217.

CRM ROI Review (2003). *Using Technology to Leverage Loyalty and Ignite the Bottom Line*. Norwalk, CT: Peppers and Rogers Group, June 2003.

Croft, M. (1995). Retention Seekers. *Marketing Week*, 18(7), 27–33.

Croteau, A. and Li, P. (2003). Critical Success Factors of CRM Technological Initiatives. *Canadian Journal of Administrative Sciences*, 20(1), 21–34.

Cui, G. and Curry, D. (2005). Prediction in Marketing Using the Support Vector Machine. *Marketing Science*, 24(4), 595–615.

Cui, G., Wong, M., and Lui, H. (2006). Machine Learning for Direct Marketing Response Models: Bayesian Networks with Evolutionary Programming. *Management Science*, 54(4), 597–612.

Cunningham, C., Song, I., and Chen, P. (2006). Data Warehouse Design to Support Customer Relationship Analyses. *Journal of Database Management*, 17(2), 62–84.

Cunningham, S. (2002). Where The Loyalty Really Lies, *The Observer*. http://money.guardian.co.uk/print//0.,4543225102272.00.html: Accessed July 26, 2007.

Danaher, P.J., Wilson, I.W., and Davis, R.A. (2003). A Comparison of Online and Offline Consumer Brand Loyalty. *Marketing Science*, 22(4), 461–476.

Dasgupta, A. and Raftery, A. (1998). Detecting Features in Spatial Point Process with Clutter Via Model-based Clustering. *Journal of the American Statistical Association*, 93(441), 294–302.

Davenport, T. and Prusak, L. (1998). *Working Knowledge: How Organizations Manage What They Know*. Boston, MA: Harvard Business School.

Davenport, T., Harris, J., DeLong, D., and Jacobson, A. (2001a). Data to Knowledge to Results: Building an Analytic Capability. *California Management Review*, 43(2), 117–138.

Davenport, T., Harris, J., and Kohli, A.K. (2001b). How Do They Know Their Customers So Well? *Sloan Management Review*, 42(Winter), 63–73.

Davidor, Y. (2000). Winning the Wireless War. *Telephony*, 238(23), 296–300.

Davis, L. (2001). It's in the Cards: Harrah's Trumps Competitors with a Winning CRM Hand. *Teradata Magazine*, 23(11), 51–54.

Day, G.S. (2000). Managing Market Relationships. *Journal of the Academy of Marketing Science*, 28(1), 24–30.

Day, G.S. (2003). Creating a Superior Customer-relating Capability. *Sloan Management Review*, 44(3), 77–82.

Day, G.S. and Van den Bulte, C. (2002). *Superiority in Customer Relationship Management: Consequences for Competitive Advantage and Performance*, Report No. 02–123. Cambridge, MA: Marketing Science Institute.

Dean, B. (2006). Online Exclusive: Quantifying Advertising's Impact on Business Results: DM News.

Deighton, J. (2000). Hilton Honors Worldwide: Loyalty Wars, Case Study No. 9-501-010. Boston, MA: Harvard Business School.

Deighton, J., Peppers, D., and Rogers, M. (1994). Consumer Transaction Databases: Present Status and Prospects. In R. Blattberg, R. Glazer, and J. Little (Eds.), *The Marketing Information Revolution*. Boston, MA: Harvard Business School.

Del Franco, M. (2004). The Dos and Don'ts of List Exchanges. *Catalog Age*, 21(8), 23.

Del Rio, E. (2002). Cell2Cell: The Churn Game, "Case for Classroom Discussion". Durham, NC: Teradata Center for CRM, Fuqua School of Business, Duke University.

Deleersnyder, B., Geyskens, I., Gielens, K., and Dekimpe, M.G. (2002). How Cannibalistic is the Internet Channel. *International Journal of Research in Marketing*, 19(4), 337–348.

Dempster, A.P., Laird, N.M., and Rubin, D.B. (1977). Maximum Likelihood for Incomplete Data Via the EM Algorithm. *Journal of the Royal Statistical Society Society*, 39(Series B), 1–38.

Deshpandé, R., Farley, J.U., and Webster, F. E, Jr. (1993). Corporate Culture, Customer Orientation and Innovativeness in Japanese Firms: A Quadrad Analysis. *Journal of Marketing*, 57(1), 23–37.

Desmet, P. (1993). Catalog Space Allocation at the Department Level. *Journal of Direct Marketing*, 7(2), 7–18.

Desmet, P. (1995). Merchandising and the Life Cycle of Books Sold by Mail. *Journal of Direct Marketing*, 9(3), 61–71.

Dhar, R. and Glazer, R. (2003). Hedging Customers. *Harvard Business Review*, 81(5), 86–92.

Dhar, S.K. and Raju, J.S. (1998). The Effects of Cross-Ruff Coupons on Sales and Profits. *Management Science, Part 1 of 2*, 44(11), 1501–1515.

DiBella, A.J., Nevis, E.G., and Gould, J.M. (1996). Understanding Organizational Learning Capability. *Journal of Management Studies*, 33(3), 361–379.

Dietterich, T. and Bakiri, G. (1995). Solving Multiclass Learning Problems via Error-collecting Output Codes. *Journal of Artificial Intelligence Research*, 2, 263–286.

Direct Marketing (2000). AOL and American Airlines Create Largest Online Customer Loyalty Program. *Direct Marketing*, 63(1), 10.

Direct Marketing Association (2004). *Statistical Fact Book*. New York: The Direct Marketing Association.

Direct Marketing Association (2006). 2006 NCDM Database Excellence Award Campaigns Demonstrate Originality and Success. http://www.the-dma.org/cgi/dispannouncements?article = 630 + + + + + +. Accessed July 30, 2007.

Direct Marketing Association (2007). Privacy Promise: Member Compliance Guide. *The Direct Marketing Association, New York*. http://www.the-dma.org/privacy/privacy_promise.pdf. Accessed July 27, 2007.

Dixon, J.H. (2005). Privacy Laws and Doing Business Online. *Intellectual Property and Technology Law Journal*, 17(2), 11–20.

Dodson, J.A., Tybout, A.M., and Stenthal, B. (1978). Impact of Deals and Deal Retraction on Brand Switching. *Journal of Marketing Research*, 15(1), 72–81.

Donkers, B., Franses, P.H., and Verhoef, P.C. (2003). Selective Sampling for Binary Choice Models. *Journal of Marketing Research*, 40(4), 492–497.

DoubleClick (2004a). Retail Details: Best Practices in Multi-channel Integration. New York: DoubleClick, March.

DoubleClick (2004b). Multi-channel Shopping Study – Holiday 2003. New York: DoubleClick.

Dowling, G.R. and Uncles, M. (1997). Do customer Loyalty Programs Really Work? *Sloan Management Review*, 38(71), 82.

Drucker, J. (2002). Takeoffs & Landings, *Wall Street Journal* (p. W12, February 08). New York.

Du, R.Y., Kamakura, W.A., and Mela, C.F. (2005). *Size and Share of Customer Wallet*, Working Paper. Athens, GA: Terry College of Business, University of Georgia.

Duan, J., Sancheti, S., and Sudhir, K. (2007). *Beating the Average with Conditional Averages: Target Selection Using Geo-Demographic Joint*

Distributions, Working paper. New Haven, CT: Yale School of Management, Yale University.

Dwyer, F.R. (1989). Customer Lifetime Valuation to Support Marketing Decision Making. *Journal of Direct Marketing*, 3(4), 8–15.

Eastlick, M.A., Feinberg, R.A., and Trappey, C.V. (1993). Information Overload in Mail Catalog Shopping. *Journal of Direct Marketing*, 7(4), 14–19.

Efron, B. (1983). Estimating the Error Rate of a Prediction Rule: Improvement on Cross-validation. *Journal of the American Statistical Association*, 78(382), 316–331.

Efron, B. and Tibshirani, R. (1993). *An Introduction to the Bootstrap*. London: Chapman & Hall.

Elsner, R., Krafft, M., and Huchzermeir, A. (2003). Optimizing Rhenania's Mail-order Business Through Dynamic Multilevel Modeling (DMLM). *Interfaces*, 33(1), 50–66.

Elsner, R., Krafft, M., and Huchzermeir, A. (2004). Optimizing Rhenania's Direct Marketing Business Through Dynamic Multilevel Modeling (DMLM) in a Multicatalog-Brand Environment. *Marketing Science*, 23(2), 192–206.

Elstrom, P. (2002). What Ails Wireless? *Business Week* (April 1), 60.

Engel, J.F., Blackwell, R.D., and Miniard, P.W. (1995). *Consumer Behavior, 8th edition*. Fort Worth, TX: Dryden.

Ensor, B. (2002). Why Online Banking Users give Up. *Forrester Technographics: Consumer Technographics North America Brief*, May 23.

Erdem, T., Imai, S., and Keane, M.P. (2003). A Model of Consumer Brand and Quantity Choice Dynamics Under Price Uncertainty. *Quantitative Marketing and Economics*, 1(1), 5–64.

Estell, L. (2002a). Diaper Mess. *Incentive*, 176(5), 12.

Estell, L. (2002b). Loyalty Lessons. *Incentive*, 176(11), 38–41.

Everitt, B. (1993). *Cluster Analysis, 3rd Edition*. London: Edward Arnold.

Fader, P.S., Hardie, B.G.S., and Berger, P.S. (2004). *Customer-based Analysis with Discrete-Time Transaction Analysis*, Working Paper. Philadelphia, PA: Wharton School of Management.

Fader, P.S., Hardie, B.G.S., and Lee, K.L. (2005). Counting Your Customers the Easy Way: An Alternative to the Pareto/NBD Model. *Marketing Science*, 24(2), 275–284.

Fahrmeir, L. and Tutz, G. (1994). *Multivariate Statistical Modelling Based on Generalized Linear Model*. New York: Springer.

Farag, S., Schwanen, T., and Dijst, M. (2005). *Shopping Online and/or In-store? A Structural Equation Model for the Relationships between E-Shopping and In-store Shopping*, Working Paper. Utrecht, NE: Urban and Regional Research Centre Utrecht, Faculty of Geographical Sciences, Utrecht University.

Feinberg, F.M., Krishna, A., and Zhang, Z.J. (2002). Do We Care What Others Get? A Behaviorist Approach to Targeted Promotions. *Journal of Marketing Research*, 39(3), 277–291.

Feinberg, R.A., Eastlick, M.A., and Trappey, C.V. (1996). Using Information Overload or Decreasing Marginal Responsiveness to Determine 'How Many Catalogs Are Too Many?': It Really Makes a Difference – Reply to Ganzach and Or. *Journal of Direct Marketing*, 10(2), 10–12.

Feldman, J., M. and Lynch, J.G. (1988). Self-generated Validity and Other Effects of Measurement on Belief, Attitude, Intention and Behavior. *Journal of Applied Psychology*, 73(August), 421–435.

Feldman, J. M. (2002). CRM is Back. *Air Transport World*, 39(6), 52–55.

Fiore, A.M. and Yu, H. (2001). Effects of Imagery Copy and Product Samples on Responses. *Journal of Interactive Marketing*, 15(2), 36–46.

Fish, K., Barnes, J.H., and Aiken, M. (1995). Artificial Neural Networks: A New Methodology for Industrial Market Segmentation. *Industrial Marketing Management*, 24(5), 431–438.

Fishbein, M. and Ajzen, I. (1975). *Belief, Attitude, Intention, and Behavior: An Introduction to Theory and Research*. Reading, MA: Addison-Wesley.

Fisher, A. (2001). Winning the Battle for Customers. *Journal of Financial Services Marketing*, 6(1), 77–83.

Fitchard, K. (2002). Standing by Your Carrier. *Telephony Online*, 242(11), 36.

Fix, E. and Hodges, J. (1951). Discriminatory Analysis; Non-parametric Discrimination Consistency Properties, *Technical Report*. Randolph Field, TX: USAF School of Aviation Medicine.

Flach, P. (2001). On the State of the Art in Machine Learning: A Personal Review. *Artificial Intelligence*, 131(1–2), 199–222.

Fletcher, K. (2003). Consumer Power and Privacy: The Changing Nature of CRM. *International Journal of Advertising*, 22(2), 249–272.

Forbes (1998). Birth of a Legend. *Forbes*. http://www.forbes.com/forbes/1998/0406/6107128sl.html. Accessed July 31, 2007.

Ford, B. (1983). An Overview of Hot-deck Procedures. In W.G. Madow, I. Nisselson, I. Olkin, and D.B. Rubin (Eds.), *Incomplete Data in Sample Surveys*, Volume II, Part 2: *Theory and Bibliographies*, pp. 185–207. New York: Academic.

Foster, G., Mahendra, G., and Sjoblom, L. (1996). Customer Profitability Analysis: Challenges and New Directions. *Cost Management*, 10(1), 5–15.

Fournier, S. (1998). Consumers and Their Brands: Developing Relationship Theory in Consumer Research. *Journal of Consumer Research*, 24(March), 343–373.

Fournier, S., Dobscha, S., and Mick, D.G. (1998). Preventing the Premature Death of Relationship Marketing. *Harvard Business Review*, 76(1), 42–51.

Fraley, C. and Raftery, A. (1998). How Many Clusters? Which Clustering Methods? Answers Via Model-based Cluster Analysis. *Computer Journal*, 41(8), 578–588.

Frank, E. and Witten, H. (1998). Generating Accurate Rule Sets Without Global Optimization. In J. Shavlik (Ed.), *Fifteenth International*

Conference on Machine Learning, pp. 144–151. San Francisco, CA: Morgan Kaufmann.

Freund, Y. and Schapire, R. (1996). Experiments with a New Boosting Algorithm. In L. Saitta (Ed.), *Thirteenth International Conference on Machine Learning*, pp. 148–156. Bari, Italy: Morgan Kaufmann.

Friedman, J. (1977). A Recursive Partitioning Decision Rule for Nonparametric Classifiers. *IEEE Transactions on Computers*, C-26(4), 404–408.

Fruchter, G.E. and Zhang, Z.J. (2004). Dynamic Targeted Promotions: A Customer Retention and Acquisition Perspective. *Journal of Service Research*, 7(1), 3–19.

Gaines, B. and Compton, P. (1995). Induction of Ripple-down Rules Applied to Modeling Large Data Bases. *Journal of Intelligent Information Systems*, 5(3), 211–228.

Galbraith, J. (2002). *Designing Organizations*. San Francisco, CA: Jossey-Bass.

Galbraith, J. (2005). *Designing the Customer-centric Organization*. San Francisco, CA: Jossey-Bass.

Ganzach, Y. and Ben-Or, P. (1996). Information Overload, Decreasing Marginal Responsiveness, and the Estimation of Nonmonotonic Relationships in Direct Marketing. *Direct of Direct Marketing*, 10(2), 7–9.

Gatarski, R. (2002). Breed Better Banners: Design Automation through On-line Interaction. *Journal of Interactive Marketing*, 16(1), 2–13.

Gedenk, K. and Neslin, S.A. (1999). The Role of Retail Promotion in Determining Future Brand Loyalty: Its Effect on Purchase Event Feedback. *Journal of Retailing*, 75(4), 433–459.

Gelfand, S., Ravishankar, C., and Delp, E. (1991). An Iterative Growing and Pruning Algorithm for Classification Tree Design. *IEEE Transactions on Pattern Analysis and Machine Intelligence*, 13(2), 163–174.

Gensch, D. (1984). Targeting the Switchable Industrial Customer. *Marketing Science*, 3(1), 41–54.

Gensch, D., Aversa, N., and Moore, S.P. (1990). A Choice-modeling Market Information System That Enabled ABB Electric to Expand Its Market. *Interfaces*, 20(1), 6–25.

George, E.I. and McCulloch, R. (1993). Variable Selection Via Gibbs Sampling. *Journal of the American Statistical Association*, 88(423), 881–889.

George, J.F. (2002). Influences on the Intent to Make Internet Purchases. *Internet Research*, 12(2), 165–180.

Geyskens, I., Gielens, K., and Dekimpe, M.G. (2002). The Market Valuation of Internet Channel Additions. *Journal of Marketing*, 66(2), 102–119.

Gillet, F. (1999). *Business-centered Data Mining, with Ted Schadler, Christine, S. Overby, Amanda, J. Ciardelli and Joshua Walker*. Cambridge, MA: Forrester Research.

Glazer, R. (1991). Marketing in an Information-intensive Environment: Strategic Implications of Knowledge as an Asset. *Journal of Marketing*, 55(4), 1–19.

Glazer, R. (1999). Winning in Smart Markets. *Sloan Management Review*, 40(4), 59–69.

Godin, S. (1997). Permission Key to Successful Marketing: Turning Prospects into Customers Demands Commitment from Both. *Advertising Age (Midwest Region Edition)*, 68(45), S31.

Goetzl, D. (2000). JetBlue's Growth Strategy: Low Prices and High Loyalty. *Advertising Age*, 71(44), 4.

Gofton, K. (1998). Best Uses of a Customer Database. *Marketing*, The Marketing Awards for Relationship Marketing, p. 19.

Goldberg, D., Nicholas, D., Oki, B., and Terry, D. (1992). Using Collaborative Filtering to Weave an Information Tapestry. *Communications of the ACM*, 35(12), 61–70.

Goldberg, M. and Vijayan, J. (1996). Data Warehouse Gains. *Computerworld*, 30(15), 1–2.

Goldberger, A. (1964). *Econometric Theory*. New York: Wiley.

Goldstein, D. and Lee, Y. (2005). The Rise of Right-time Marketing. *Database Marketing and Customer Strategy Management*, 12(3), 212–225.

Golvin, C.S. (2002). Number Portability: A Prescription for Churn. *Forrester Technographics: Consumer Technolographics North America Brief*, October 24.

Gönül, F. and Shi, M. (1998). Optimal Mailing of Catalogs: A New Methodology Using Estimable Structural Dynamic Programming Models. *Management Science*, 44(9), 1249–1262.

Gönül, F. and Srinivasan, K. (1996). Impact of Consumer Expectations of Coupons on Purchase Behavior. *Marketing Science*, 15(3), 262–279.

Gönül, F. and Ter Hofstede, F. (2006). How to Compute Optimal Catalog Mailing Decisions. *Marketing Science*, 25(1), 65–74.

Gönül, F., Kim, B., and Shi, M. (2000). Mailing Smarter to Catalog Customers. *Journal of Interactive Marketing*, 14(2), 2–16.

Good, N., Schafer, J., Konstan, J., Borchers, A., Sarwar, B., Herlocker, J., and Riedl, J. (1999). Combining Collaborative Filtering with Personal Agents for Better Recommendation, *Proceedings of the 1999 Conference of the American Association ofArtificial Intelligence (AAAI–99)*, pp. 439–446.

Gormley, J.T., III (1999). *The Demise of CRM*. Cambridge, MA: Forrester Research, June.

Grant, A.W.H. and Schlesinger, L.A. (1995). Realize Your Customers' Full Profit Potential. *Harvard Business Review*, 73(September–October), 59–72.

Green, P. (1974). On the Design of Choice Experiments Involving Multifactor Alternatives. *Journal of Consumer Research*, 1(2), 61–68.

Greene, W.H. (1997). *Econometric Analysis*. Upper Saddle River, NJ: Prentice-Hall.

Greene, W.H. (2002). *LIMDEP Version 8.0, Econometric Modeling Guide, Volume 2*. Plainview, NY: Econometric Software.

Griffin, J. and Lowenstein, M.W. (2001). *Customer Winback: How to Recapture Lost Customers – And Keep Them Loyal.* San Francisco, CA: Jossey-Bass.

Grimm, R. and Rossnagel, A. (2000). Can P3P Help to Protect Privacy Worldwide?, *2000 ACM Workshops on Multimedia, International Multimedia Conference*, pp. 157–160. Los Angeles, CA.

Gruca, T., Klemz, B., and Petersen, E. (1999). Mining Sales Data Using a Neural Network Model of Market Response. *ACM SIGKDD*, 1(1), 39–43.

Guadagni, P.M. and Little, J.D.C. (1983). A Logit Model of Brand Choice Calibrated on Scanner Data. *Marketing Science*, 2(3), 203–238.

Gupta, A., Su, B., and Walter, Z. (2004b). An Empirical Study of Consumer Switching from Traditional to Electronic Channels: A Purchase-decision Process Perspective. *International Journal of Electronic Commerce*, 8(3), 131–161.

Gupta, S. and Chintagunta, P.K. (1994). On Using Demographic Variables to Determine Segment Membership in Logit Mixture Models. *Journal of Marketing Research*, 31(1), 128–136.

Gupta, S., Lehmann, D.R., and Stuart, J.A. (2004a). Valuing Customers. *Journal of Marketing Research*, 41(1), 7–18.

Gurau, C. and Ranchhod, A. (2002). How to Calculate the Value of a Customer – Measuring Customer Satisfaction: A Platform for Calculating, Predicting and Increasing Customer Profitability. *Journal of Targeting, Measurement and Analysis for Marketing*, 10(3), 203–219.

Haddawy, P. (1999). An Overview of Some Recent Developments in Bayesian Problem Solving Techniques. *AI Magazine*, 20(2), 11–19.

Hadden, J., Tiwari, A., Roy, R., and Ruta, D. (2006). Churn Prediction: Does Technology Matter. *International Journal of Intelligent Technology*, 1(2), 104–110.

Hair, J., Anderson, R.E., Tatham, R., and Black, W. (1992). *Multivariate Data Analysis with Readings, 3rd Edition.* New York: Macmillan.

Haldar, S. and Rao, V.R. (1998). A Micro-analytic Threshold Model for the Timing of First Purchases of Durable Goods. *Applied Economics*, 30(7), 959–974.

Hallowell, R. (1996). The Relationship of Customer Satisfaction, Customer Loyalty, and Profitability: An Empirical Study. *International Journal of Service Industry Management*, 7(4), 27–42.

Hansen, W. (2006). *Risky Customers: Choosing the Discount Rate for Lifetime Value Calculations: Stanford Institute for Economic Policy Research*, Working Paper. Palo Alto, CA: Stanford University, July 2006.

Hansotia, B.J. and Rukstales, B. (2002). Direct Marketing for Multichannel Retailers: Issues, Challenges, and Solutions. *Journal of Database Marketing*, 9(3), 259–266.

Härdle, W. and Turlach, B. (1992). Nonparametric Approaches to Generalized Linear Models. *Springer Lecture Notes*, 78, 213–225.

Harrison, T. and Ansell, J. (2002). Customer Retention in the Insurance Industry: Using Survival Analysis to Predict Cross-selling Opportunities. *Journal of Financial Services Marketing*, 6(3), 229–239.

Hartfeil, G. (1996). Bank One Measures Profitability of Customers, not Just Products. *Journal of Retail Banking Services*, 18(2), 23–29.

Hartigan, J. (1975). *Clustering algorithms*. New York: Wiley.

Harvey, J.A. and Verska, K.A. (2001). U.S. Firms Weigh Their Options on EU Data Privacy Obligations. *The Computer and Internet Lawyer*, 18(4), 17–20.

Hastie, T. and Tibshirani, R. (1990). *Generalized Additive Models, Monographs on Statistics and Applied Probability 43*. London: Chapman & Hall.

Hastie, T., Tibshirani, R., and Friedman, J. (2001). The Elements of Statistical Learning: Data Mining, Inference, and Prediction, *Springer Series in Statistics*. New York: Springer.

Hatch, D. (1995). Dumbing Down What We Know. *Target Marketing*, 18(10), 24–26.

Hatch, D. (2002). Delight Your Customers. *Target Marketing*, 25(4), 32–39.

Haughton, D. and Oulabi, S. (1997). Direct Marketing Modeling with CART and CHAID. *Journal of Direct Marketing*, 11(4), 42–52.

Hauser, J.R., Simester, D.I., and Wernerfelt, B. (1992). *Customer-satisfaction Based Incentive Systems*, Working Paper. Cambridge, MA: International Center for Research on the Management of Technology, Sloan School of Management, MIT.

Hauser, J.R., Simester, D.I., and Wernerfelt, B. (1994). Customer Satisfaction Incentives. *Marketing Science*, 13(4), 327–350.

Hausman, J. and McFadden, D. (1984). A Specification Test for the Multinomial Logit Model. *Econometrica*, 52(5), 1219–1240.

Hausman, J., Hall, B.H., and Griliches, Z. (1984). Economic Models for Count Data with an Application to the Patents – R&D Relationship. *Econometrica*, 52(4), 1219–1240.

Haykin, S. (1999). *Neural Networks: A Comprehensive Foundation, 2nd Edition*. Upper Saddle River, NJ: Prentice-Hall.

Heckerman, D. (1997). Bayesian Networks for Data Mining. *Data Mining Knowledge Discovery*, 1(1), 79–119.

Helsen, K. and Schmittlein, D.C. (1993). Analyzing Duration Times in Marketing: Evidence for the Effectiveness of Hazard Rate Models. *Marketing Science*, 11(4), 395–414.

Hendel, I. and Nevo, A. (2002). *Sales and Consumer Inventory*, Working Paper 9048. Cambridge, MA: National Bureau of Economic Research.

Henderson, B. (1999). Pegasus's Plight. *Barron's*, 79(25), 28.

Herlocker, J., Konstan, J., and Riedl, J. (1999). An Algorithmic Framework for Performing Collaborative Filtering, *Proceedings of ACM SIGIR 1999*, pp. 230–237.

Hess, J.D., Neslin, S.A., Syam, N., Zhang, Z.J., Arora, N., Ghose, A., Dreze, X., Iyengar, R., Jing, B., Joshi, Y., Kumar, V., Lurie, N.H., Sajeesh,

S., Meng, S., and Thomas, J.S. (2007). One-to-one Marketing and Choice, *Seventh Annual Triennial Invitational Choice Symposium*. Philadelphia, PA: The Wharton School, University of Pennsylvania.

Heun, C.T. (2000). Harrah's Bets on IT to Understand Its Customers. *Information Week*, December 11(816), RB10-RB12.

Hicks, C. (1982). *Fundamental Concepts in the Design of Experiments*. New York: CBS College.

Higley, J. (2002). Hilton Shifts Focus to Frequent-guest Recognition Efforts. *Hotel and Motel Management*, 217(3), 4.

Hill, T., O'Connor, M., and Remus, W. (1996). Neural Network Models for Time Series Forecasts. *Management Science*, 42(7), 1082–1092.

Hinde, R.A. (1995). A Suggested Structure for a Science of Relationships. *Personal Relationships*, 2(1), 1–15.

Hitt, L.M. and Frei, F.X. (2002). Do Better Customers Utilize Electronic Distribution Channels? The Case of PC Banking. *Management Science*, 48(6), 732–748.

Ho, T. (1998). The Random Subspace Method for Construcing Decision Forests. *IEEE Transactions on Pattern Analysis and Machine Intelligence*, 20(8), 832–844.

Hocking, R. (1976). The Analysis and Selection of Variables in Linear Regression. *Biometrics*, 32(1), 1–49.

Hofacker, C.F. and Murphy, J. (2000). Clickable World Wide Web Banner Ads and Content Sites. *Journal of Interactive Marketing*, 14(1), 49–59.

Hoffman, D.L., Novak, T.P., and Peralta, M.A. (1999). Building Consumer Trust Online. *Communications of the ACM*, 42(4), 80–85.

Hofstede, G. (1980). *Culture's Consequences: International Differences in Work Related Values*. Beverly Hills, CA: Sage.

Hofstede, G. (1991). *Cultures and Organizations: Software of the Mind*. New York: McGraw-Hill.

Hogan, J.E., Lemon, K., and Libai, B. (2003). What is the True Value of a Lost Customer? *Journal of Service Research*, 5(3), 196–208.

Holland, J. (1975). *Adaptation in Natural and Artificial Systems*. Ann Arbor, MI: University of Michigan Press.

Holte, R. (1993). Very Simple Classification Rules Perform Well on Most Commonly Used Datasets. *Machine Learning*, 11(1), 63–91.

Hopfield, J. (1982). Neural Networks and Physical Systems with Emergent Collective Computational Properties Like Those of Two-state Neurons. *Proceedings of the National Academy of Sciences*, 84, 8429–8433.

Hruschka, H. (1993). Determining Marketing Response Functions by Neural Network Modeling: A Comparison to Econometric Techniques. *European Journal of Operational Research*, 66(1), 22–35.

Hruschka, H. and Natter, M. (1999). Comparing Performance of Feedforward Neural Nets and K-means for Market Segmentation. *European Journal of Operational Research*, 114(2), 346–353.

Hsu, C., Huang, H., and Schuschel, D. (2002). The ANNIGMA-Wrapper Approach to Fast Feature Selection for Neural Nets. *IEEE Transactions on Systems, Man, and Cybernetics – Part B: Cybernetics*, 32(2), 207–212.

Hu, Z., Chin, W., and Takeich, M. (2000). Calculating a New Data Mining Algorithm for Market Basket Analysis, *Second International Workshop on Practical Aspects of Declarative Languages*, pp. 169–184.

Huber, G.P. (1991). Organizational Learning: The Contributing Processes and the Literatures. *Organization Science*, 2(1), 88–115.

Hughes, A.M. (1996a). *The Complete Database Marketer: Second Generation Strategies and Techniques for Tapping the Power of Your Customer Database.* Chicago, IL: Irwin.

Hughes, A.M. (1996b). Boosting Response with RFM. *Marketing Tools*, 3(3), 4–5.

Hughes, A.M. (2000). *Strategic Database Marketing, 2nd Edition.* New York: McGraw-Hill.

Hull, C.L. (1932). The Goal-Gradient Hypothesis and Maze Learning. *Psychological Review*, 39(1), 25–43.

Hurley, S., Mouthino, L., and Stephens, N. (1995). Solving Marketing Optimization Problems Using Genetic Algorithms. *European Journal of Marketing*, 29(4), 39–56.

Hutchinson, J.W. and Alba, J.W. (1991). Ignoring Irrelevant Information: Situational Determinants of Consumer Learning. *Journal of Consumer Research*, 18(December), 326–345.

Iacobucci, D., Arabie, P., and Bodapati, A. (2000). Recommendation Agents on the Internet. *Journal of Interactive Marketing*, 14(3), 2–11.

Inman, J.J., Shankar, V., and Ferraro, R. (2004). The Roles of Channel-Category Associations and Geodemographics in Channel Patronage Decision. *Journal of Marketing*, 68(2), 51–71.

Inside 1 to 1 (2003). *High-end Retailers Top the Multi-channel List.* Norwalk, CT: Peppers and Rogers Group, February 3.

IOMA (2002). Multi-channel Integration Makes the Best Use of All Your CRM Contact Points. *IOMA's Report on Customer Relationship Management*, 2002(12), 1.

Israel, M. (2005). Tenure Dependence in Consumer–Firm Relationships: An Empirical Analysis of Consumer Departures from Automobile Insurance Firms. *Rand Journal of Economics*, 36(Spring), 165–192.

Jackson, R. and Wang, P. (1994). *Strategic Database Marketing.* Lincolnwood, IL: NTC.

Jacoby, J., Speller, D.E., and Kohn, C.A. (1974). Brand Choice Behavior as a Function of Information Load. *Journal of Marketing Research*, 11(1), 63–69.

Jain, D. and Vilcassim, N.J. (1991). Investigating Household Purchase Timing Decisions: A Conditional Hazard Function Approach. *Marketing Science*, 10(4), 1–23.

Jaworski, B.J. and Kohli, A.K. (1993). Market Orientation: Antecedents and Consequences. *Journal of Marketing*, 57(3), 53–70.

Jedidi, K., Mela, C.F., and Gupta, S. (1999). Managing Advertising and Promotions for Long-run Profitability. *Marketing Science*, 18(1), 1–22.

Jefferies Equity Research (2004). *Telecommunications Services Third Quarter 2004 Preview*. New York: Jefferies Equity Research, Jefferies.

Jen, L., Allenby, G.M., and Leone, R.P. (1996). *Customer Valuation: A Hierarchical Bayes Approach for Estimating Recency, Frequency and Monetary Value in Direct Marketing*, Working Paper Series 96–1. Columbus, OH: Max M. Fisher College of Business, The Ohio State University.

Jing, P. and Rosenbloom, B. (2005). Customer Intention to Return Online Price Perception, Attribute-level Performance, and Satisfaction Unfolding Over Time. *European Journal of Marketing*, 39(1/2), 150–174.

Johns, M. (1961). *An Empirical Bayes Approach to Non-parametric Two-way Classification*. Palo Alto, CA: Stanford University Press.

Johnson, N. and Kotz, S. (1969). *Discrete Distribution, Distribution in Statistics*. New York: Wiley.

Johnson, R. and Wichern, D. (1982). *Applied Multivariate Statistical Analysis*. Englewood Cliffs, NJ: Prentice-Hall.

Judge, G.G., Griffiths, W.E., Hill, R.C., Kütkepohl, H., and Lee, T.C. (1985). *The Theory and Practice of Econometrics*. New York: Wiley.

Jusko, J. (2001). Digital Investments Disappoint. *Industry Week*, 250(10), 12.

Kacen, J.J., Hess, J.D., and Chiang, W.K. (2003). *Bricks or Clicks? Consumer Attitudes Toward Traditional Stores and Online Stores*, Working Paper. Champaign, IL: Department of Business, University of Illinois.

Kalbfleisch, J. and Prentice, R. (1980). *The Statistical Analysis of Failure Time Data*. New York: Wiley.

Kalish, S. (1983). Monopolistic Pricing and Dynamic Demand and Production Cost. *Marketing Science*, 2(2), 135–160.

Kamakura, W.A. and Russell, G.J. (1989). A Probabilistic Choice Model for Market Segmentation and Elasticity Structure. *Journal of Marketing Research*, 26(4), 379–390.

Kamakura, W.A. and Wedel, M. (1997). Statistical Data Fusion for Cross-tabulation. *Journal of Marketing Research*, 34(4), 485–498.

Kamakura, W.A. and Wedel, M. (2003). List Augmentation with Model-based Multiple Imputation: A Case Study Using a Mixed-outcome Factor Model. *Statistica Neerlandica*, 57(1), 46–57.

Kamakura, W.A., Ramaswami, S.N., and Srivastava, R.K. (1991). Applying Latent Trait Analysis in the Evaluation of Prospects for Cross-selling of Financial Services. *International Journal of Research in Marketing*, 8(4), 329–349.

Kamakura, W.A., Mittal, V., de Rosa, F., and Mazzon, J.A. (2002). Assessing the Service – Profit Chain. *Marketing Science*, 21(3), 294–317.

Kamakura, W.A., Wedel, M., de Rosa, F., and Mazzon, J.A. (2003). Cross-selling Through Database Marketing: A Mixed Data Factor Analyzer for

Data Augmentation and Prediction. *International Journal of Research in Marketing*, 20(1), 45–65.

Kamakura, W.A., Kossar, B.S., and Wedel, M. (2004). Identifying Innovators for the Cross-selling of New Products. *Management Science*, 50(8), 1120–1133.

Kamakura, W.A., Mela, C.F., Ansari, A., Bodapati, A., Fader, P., Iyengar, R., Naik, P.A., Neslin, S.A., Sun, P.C., Verhoef, P.C., Wedel, M., and Wilcox, R.T. (2005). Choice Models and Customer Relationship Management. *Marketing Letters*, 16(3/4), 279–291.

Kantarcioglu, M. and Clifton, C. (2004). Privacy-preserving Distributed Mining of Association Rules on Horizontally Partitioned Data. *IEEE Transactions on Knowledge and Data Engineering*, 16(9), 1026–1037.

Kaplan, R.S. and Cooper, R. (1998). *Cost and Effect: Using Integrated Cost Systems to Drive Profitability and Performance*. Boston, MA: Harvard Business School.

Kass, G. (1983). An Exploratory Technique for Investigating Large Quantities of Categorical Data. *Applied Statistics*, 29(2), 119–127.

Kaufman Bros. Equity Research (2005). *Company Note: Audible*. Kaufman Bros. Equity Research, October 5.

Keane, M.P. (1997). Current Issues in Discrete Choice Modeling. *Marketing Letters*, 8(3), 307–322.

Keane, M.P. and Wolpin, K.J. (1994). The Solution and Estimation of Discrete Choice Dynamic Programming Models by Simulation and Interpolation: Monte Carlo Evidence. *Review of Economics and Statistics*, 76(4), 648–672.

Keaveney, S.M. and Parthasarathy, M. (2001). Customer Switching Behavior in Online Services: An Exploratory Study of the Role of Selected Attitudinal, Behavioral, and Demographic Factors. *Journal of the Academy of Marketing Science*, 29(4), 374–390.

Keen, C., Wetzels, M.,de Ruyter, K., and Feinberg, R.A. (2004). E-Tailers versus Retailers. Which Factors Determine Consumers Preferences. *Journal of Business Research*, 57(7), 685–695.

Keh, H.T. and Lee, Y.H. (2006). Do Reward Programs Build Loyalty for Services? The Moderting Effect of Satisfaction on Type and Timing of Rewards. *Journal of Retailing*, 82(2), 127–136.

Kelley, D. (2002). Capturing Cross-channel Dollars, *The Technographics Report*. Cambridge, MA: Forrester Research.

Kim, B. and Kim, S. (2001). A New Recommender System to Combine Content-based and Collaborative Filtering System. *Journal of Database marketing*, 8(3), 244–252.

Kim, B. and Rossi, P.E. (1994). Purchase Frequency, Sample Selection, and Price Sensitivity: The Heavy-user Bias. *Marketing Letters*, 5(1), 57–67.

Kim, B. and Shin, J. (1998). Maximizing the Value of Credit Card Customers: Credit Scoring, Revenue Scoring, or Both? *Journal of Database Marketing*, 6(2), 164–173.

Kim, B., Min, S., and Shin, J. (2000). Calculating Lifetime Values of Business Customers for Telecommunications Company, *Journal of Database Marketing*, 7(3), 254–264.

Kim, B., Shi, M., and Srinivasan, K. (2001). Reward Programs and Tacit Collusion. *Marketing Science*, 20(2), 99–120.

Kim, B., Shi, M., and Srinivasan, K. (2004). Managing Capacity Through Reward Programs. *Management Science*, 50(4), 503–520.

Kim, Y., Street, W., Russell, G.J., and Menczer, F. (2005). Customer Targeting: A Neural Network Approach Guided by Genetic Algorithm. *Management Science*, 51(2), 264–276.

King, G. and Zeng, L. (2001). Logistic Regression in Rare Events Data. *Political Analysis*, 9(2), 137–163.

Kivetz, R. and Simonson, I. (2002). Earning the Right to Indulge: Effort as a Determinant of Customer Preferences Toward Frequency Program Rewards. *Journal of Marketing Research*, 39(2), 155–170.

Kivetz, R., Urmininsky, O., and Zheng, Y. (2006). The Goal-Gradient Hypothesis Resurrected: Purchase Acceleration, Illusionary Goal Progress, and Customer Retention. *Journal of Marketing Research*, 43(1), 39–58.

Kleinman, M. (2000). SkyDigital Personalises Mailings to Subscribers. *Marketing* (August 31, 2000), 9.

Kleinman, M. (2002). Nectar to Replace Top Loyalty Brands. *Marketing* (June 6), 1.

Klemperer, P. (1987a). Markets with Consumer Switching Costs. *The Quarterly Journal of Economics*, 102(2), 375–394.

Klemperer, P. (1987b). The Competitiveness of Markets with Switching Costs. *Rand Journal of Economics*, 18(1), 138–150.

Klemperer, P. (1995). Competition When Consumers Have Switching Costs: An Overview with Applications to Industrial Organization, Macroeconomics, and International Trade. *Review of Economic Studies*, 62(213), 515–539.

Knott, A., Hayes, A., and Neslin, S.A. (2002). Next-product-to-buy Models for Cross-selling Applications. *Journal of Interactive Marketing*, 16(3), 59–75.

Knox, G. (2005). *Modeling and Managing Customers in a Multichannel Setting*, Working Paper. Tilburg, The Netherlands: University of Tilburg.

Kohavi, R. (1995). A Study of Cross-validation and Bootstrap for Accuracy Estimation and Model Selection, In *The Proceedings of the Fourteenth International Joint Conference on Artificial Intelligence*, pp. 1137–1143. Montreal, Canada and San Francisco, CA: Morgan Kaufmann.

Kohli, A.K. and Jaworski, B.J. (1990). Market Orientation: The Construct, Research Propositions, and Managerial Implications. *Journal of Marketing*, 54(2), 1–18.

Kohli, A.K., Jaworski, B., and Kumar, A. (1993). MARKOR: A Measure of Market Orientation. *Journal of Marketing Research*, 30(4), 467–477.

Kohonen, T. (1982). Self-organized Formation of Topologically Correct Feature Maps. *Biological Cybernetics*, 43(1), 59–69.

Kohonen, T. (1994). *Self-organizing and Associative Memory*. New York: Springer.

Kohonen, T. (1995). *Self-organizing Maps*. Berlin: Springer.

Kohrs, A. and Merialdo, B. (2001). Creating User-adapted Websites by the Use of Collaborative Filtering. *Interacting with Computers*, 13(6), 695–716.

Kolko, J. (2001). ISP Loyalty Starts to Crumble. *Forrester Technographics: Consumer Technolographics North America Report*, January.

Kolko, J. (2002). AOL Isn't Hemorrhaging Subscribers. *Forrester Technographics: Consumer Technographics North America Brief*, June 13.

Koller, M. (2001). Harrah's Rewards Gamblers. *InternetWeek*, October 8(881), 10–11.

Kon, M. (2004). Customer Churn: Stop It Before It Starts. *Mercer Managemnt Journal*, 17(6), 54–60.

Konstan, J., Miller, B., Maltz, D., Herlocker, J., Gordon, L., and Riedl, J. (1997). GroupLens: Applying Collaborative Filtering to Usernet News. *Communications of the ACM*, 40(3), 77–87.

Konus, U., Verhoef, P.C., and Neslin, S.A. (2007). *Identifying Multi-channel Shopper Segments and Their Antecedents*, Working Paper. Groningen, The Netherlands: University of Groningen, Faculty of Economics.

Kopalle, P.K. and Neslin, S.A. (2003). The Economic Viability of Frequency Reward Programs in a Strategic Competitive Environment. *Review of Marketing Science*, 1 (Article 1). http://www.bepress.com/romsjournal/. Accessed August 1, 2007.

Kopalle, P.K., Neslin, S.A., Sun, B., Sun, Y., and Swaminathan, V. (2006). *A Dynamic Structural Model of the Impact of Airline Reward Programs on Frequent Flier Behavior*, Working Paper. Hanover, NH: Tuck School of Business, Dartmouth College.

Kotler, P. and Keller, K.L. (2006). *Marketing Management*. Upper Saddle River, NJ: Prentice-Hall.

Kreitter, D. (2000). Controlling ISP Churn: Borrowing from the Telco Model. *Telecommunications*, 34(11), 73–74.

Krishna, A., Zhang, Z.J., and Feinberg, F.M. (2004). *Should Price Increases be Targeted? – Pricing Power and Selective Versus Across-the-board Price Increases*, Working Paper. Ann Arbor, MI: University of Michigan Business School.

Kuchinskas, S. (2000). Netcentive Aids Amex with Rewards Program. *AdWeek, Eastern Edition*, 41(4), 81.

Kumar, V. and Venkatesan, R. (2005). Who Are Multichannel Shoppers and How Do They Perform? Correlates of Multichannel Shopping Behavior. *Journal of Interactive Marketing*, 19(2), 44–61.

Kushwaha, T.L. and Shankar, V. (2005). *Multichannel Shopping Behavior: Antecedents and Implications for Channel and Customer Equity*, Working Paper. College Station, TX: Texas A&M University.

La Monica, P.R. (2003). Get Ready for a Wireless War. *CNNMoney. com,* September 5, 2003. http://money.cnn.com/2003/2009/2004/technology/ techinvestor/lamonica/index/htm?cnn = yes. Accessed July 26, 2007.

Lal, R.B. and Bell, D.E. (2003). The Impact of Frequent Shopper Programs in Grocery Retailing. *Quantitative Marketing and Economics,* 1(2), 179–202.

Lambrecht, A. and Skiera, B. (2006). Paying Too Much and Being Happy About It: Existence, Causes, and Consequences of Tariff-choice Biases. *Journal of Marketing Research,* 43(2), 212–223.

Langerak, F. and Verhoef, P.C. (2003). Strategically Embedding CRM. *Business Strategy Review,* 14(4), 73–80.

Lapin, L.L. (1990). *Statistics for Modern Business Decisions, 5th Edition.* San Diego, CA: Harcourt Brace Jovanovich.

Lau, K., Chow, H., and Liu, C. (2004). A Database Approach to Cross Selling in the Banking Industry: Practices, Strategies and Challenges. *Database Marketing and Customer Strategy Management,* 11(3), 216–234.

Lawless, J. (2003). *Statistical Models and Methods for Lifetime Data, 2nd Edition.* New York: Wiley.

Lazear, E. (1986). Retail Pricing and Clearance Sales. *American Economic Review,* 76(1), 14–32.

Lee, R.P. and Grewal, R. (2004). Strategic Responses to New Technologies and Their Impact on Firm Performance. *Journal of Marketing,* 68(4), 157–171.

Lee, W.A. (2002). In Brief: American Express Quadruples Earnings. *American Banker,* 167(139), 19.

Leeflang, P.S.H., Wittink, D.R., Wedel, M., and Naert, P.A. (2000). *Building Models for Marketing Decisions.* Boston, MA: Kluwer.

Leenheer, J. and Bijmolt, T.H.A. (2003). *Adoption and Effectiveness of Loyalty Programs: The Retailer's Perspective,* Working Paper 03–124. Cambridge MA: Marketing Science Institute.

Leenheer, J., Van Heerde, H.J. Bijmolt, T.H.A., and Smidts, A. (2007). Do Loyalty Programs Really Enhance Behavioral Loyalty? An Empirical Analysis Accounting for Self-selecting Members. *International Journal of Research in Marketing,* 24(1), 31–47.

LeGun, Y., Kanter, I., and Solla, S. (1991). Second Order Properties of Error Surfaces: Learning Time and Generalization, *Advances in Neural Information Processing Systems,* pp. 918–924. Cambridge, MA: MIT.

Lehmann, D.R., Gupta, S., and Steckel, J.H. (1998). *Marketing Research.* Reading, MA: Addison-Wesley.

Lemmens, A. and Croux, C. (2006). Bagging and Boosting Classification Trees to Predict Churn. *Journal of Marketing Research,* 43(2), 276–286.

Levin, N. and Zahavi, J. (1996). Segmentation Analysis with Managerial Judgment. *Journal of Direct Marketing,* 10(3), 28–47.

Levin, N. and Zahavi, J. (2001). Predictive Modeling Using Segmentation. *Journal of Interactive Marketing,* 15(2), 2–22.

Lewis, H.G. (1999). The Three Faces of Copy. *Catalog Management Handbook, 2nd Edition.* Stamford, CT: Primedia.

Lewis, M. (2004). The Influence of Loyalty Programs and Short-term Promotions on Customer Retention. *Journal of Marketing Research*, 41(3), 281–292.

Li, C., Xu, Y., and Li, H. (2005). An Empirical Study of Dynamic Customer Relationship Management. *Journal of Retailing and Consumer Services*, 12(6), 431–441.

Li, K. (1991). Sliced Inverse Regression for Dimension Reduction. *Journal of American Statistical Association*, 86(414), 316–342.

Li, S. (1995). Survival Analysis. *Marketing Research*, 7(4), 16–23.

Li, S., Sun, B., and Wilcox, R.T. (2005). Cross-selling Sequentially Ordered Products: An Application to Consumer Banking Services. *Journal of Marketing Research*, 42(2), 233–239.

Li, Y. and Wen, P. (2005). Bayesian Model for Brain Computation. In J. Wu and K. Ito (Eds.), *First International Conference on Complex Medical Engineering (CME 2005)*, pp. 683–686. Takamatsu, Japan: Institute of Complex Medical Engineering.

Libai, B., Narayandas, D., and Humby, C. (2002). Toward an Individual Customer Profitability Model: A Segment-based Approach. *Journal of Service Research*, 5(1), 69–76.

Light, W. (1992). Ridge Functions, Sigmoidal Functions and Neural Networks. In C.C.E. Cheney and L. Schumaker (Eds.), *Approximation Theory VII*, pp. 163–190. Boston, MA: Kluwer.

Lilien, G., Kotler, P., and Moorthy, S. (1992). *Marketing Models.* Englewood Cliffs, NJ: Prentice-Hall.

Lin, C. and Hong, C. (2008). Using Customer Knowledge in Designing Electronic Catalog. *Expert Systems with Applications*, 34(1), 119–127.

Linden, G., Smith, B., and York, J. (2003). Amazon.com Recommendation: Item-to-item Collaborative Filtering. *IEEE Internet Computing*, 7(1), 76–80.

Linder, R., Geier, J., and Kölliker, M. (2004). Artificial Neural Networks, Classification Trees and Regression: Which Methods for Which Customer Base? *Database Marketing & Customer Strategy Management*, 11(4), 344–356.

Little, J.D.C. (1979). Aggregate Advertising Models: The State of the Art. *Operations Research*, 27(4), 629–667.

Little, R. and Rubin, D.B. (1987). *Statistical Analysis with Missing Data.* New York: Wiley.

Lodish, L.M. (1986). Are You Wasting Your Advertising Money. *Chief Executive*, 37(Autumn), 20–23.

Lu, J. (2001). Predicting Customer Churn in the Telecommunications Industry – An Application of Survival Analysis Modeling Using SAS, *SAS User Group International (SUGI) Online Proceedings.* http://www/sas/com/usergrups/sugi/proceedings/.

Lucas, M. (2001). Microsoft Agrees to Sign Safe Harbor Privacy Pact. *Computerworld*, 35(21), 18.

Lucas, P. (2002). A Big Lift for Loyalty. *Credit Card Management*, 15(3), 26–31.

Lynch, J.G. and Ariely, D. (2000). Wine Online: Search Costs Affect Competition on Price, Quality, and Distribution. *Marketing Science*, 19(1), 83–103.

MacDonald, J. (2001). Nike Does It Here. *Marketing Magazine*, 106(12), 9.

Macé, S. and Neslin, S.A. (2004). The Determinants of Pre- and Postpromotion Dips in Frequently Purchased Goods. *Journal of Marketing Research*, 41(3), 324–338.

Maddala, G.S. (1983). *Limited-dependent and Qualitative Variables in Econometrics.* Cambridge, UK: Cambridge University Press.

Maddox, K. and Krol, C. (2004). Marketers to Stress Customer Acquisition in 2005. *B to B*, 89(15), 1.

Magidson, J. and Vermunt, J. (2002). Latent Class Models for Clustering: A Comparison with K-means. *Canadian Journal of Marketing Research*, 20, 37–44.

Mahajan, V., Srinivasan, R., and Wind, J. (2002). The Dot.com Retail Failures of 2000: Were There Any Winners? *Journal of the Academy of Marketing Science*, 30(4), 474–486.

Makridakis, S., Wheelwright, S., and McGee, V. (1983). *Forecasting: Methods and Applications.* New York: Wiley.

Malhotra, N. (1993). *Marketing Research: An Applied Orientation.* Englewood Cliffs, NJ: Prentice-Hall.

Malthouse, E. (2002). Performance-based Variable Selection for Scoring Models. *Journal of Interactive Marketing*, 16(4), 37–50.

Malthouse, E.C. and Blattberg, R.C. (2005). Can We Predict Customer Lifetime Value? *Journal of Interactive Marketing*, 19(1), 2–16.

Man, D. (1996). Answering Some Common Data Warehousing Questions. *Direct Marketing*, 59(8), 12–14.

Manchanda, P., Ansari, A., and Gupta, S. (1999). The 'Shopping Basket': A Model for Multicategory Purchase Incidence Decisions. *Marketing Science*, 18(2), 95–114.

Manchanda, P., Dubé, J., Goh, K.Y., and Chintagunta, P. (2006). The Effect of Banner Advertising on Internet Purchasing. *Journal of Marketing Research*, 43(1), 98–108.

Mannila, H., Toivonen, H., and Verkamo, A. (1994). Efficient Algorithms for Discovering Association Rules, *Proceedings of the AAAI Workshop on Knowledge Discovery in Databases*, pp. 144–155.

Manski, C.F. and Lerman, S.R. (1977). The Estimation of Choice Probabilities from Choice Based Samples. *Econometrica*, 87(3), 624–638.

Marketing (2003). Citibank Cuts Top Acquisition Job in Retention Refocus. *Marketing*, June 26, 2003, 4.

Marketing Week (1998). Sainsbury's Emerges as Leader in Card War, Claims Consumer Survey. *Marketing Week*, 20(41), 8.

Martin, D., Smith, R., Brittain, M., and Fetch, I. (2000). The Privacy Practices of Web Browser Extensions. *Communications of the ACM* (February), 45–50.

Maselli, J. (2002). Customer Focus Is Strong, But CRM Vendor's Sales Slip. *Informationweek* (873), 24.

Maselli, J., Whiting, R., and Rosen, C. (2001). CRM Plus Privacy Protection Equals Smart Business. *Informationweek* (832), 34.

Massy, W. (1965). Principal Components Regression in Exploratory Statistical Research. *Journal of the American Statistical Association*, 60(3), 234–256.

Mathwick, C., Malhotra, N.K., and Rigdon, E. (2002). The Effect of Dynamic Retail Experiences on Experiential Perceptions of Value: An Internet and Catalog Comparison. *Journal of Retailng*, 78(1), 51–60.

Matlis, J. (2002). P3P. *Computerworld*, 36(44), 28.

Mazur, L. (1999). Elite Focus Risks Alienating the Up and Coming. *Marketing* (June 3), 18.

McClure, M. (2004). eBay Wins New Privacy Commitment Survey. *Inside 1 to 1: Privacy*. Norwalk, CT: Peppers and Rogers Group, July 8, 2004.

McCulloch, P. and Nelder, J. (1983). *Generalized Linear Models*. New York: Chapman & Hall.

McCulloch, R. and Rossi, P.E. (2000). A Bayesian Analysis of the Multinomial Probit Model with Fully Identified Parameters. *Journal of Econometrics*, 99(1), 173–193.

McCulloch, W. and Pitts, W. (1943). A Logical Calculus of the Ideas Immanent in Nervous Activity. *Bulletin of Mathematical Biology*, 5(4), 115–133.

Mehta, M., Agrawal, R., and Rissanen, J. (1996). SLIQ: A Fast Scalable Classifier for Data Mining, *Proceedings of the Fifth International Conference on Extending Database Technology*.

Mela, C.F., Gupta, S., and Lehmann, D.R. (1997). The Long-term Impact of Promotions on Consumer Stockpiling Behavior. *Journal of Marketing Research*, 35(2), 250–262.

Microsoft (2000). Privacy Concerns Limit Growth of Online Commerce. *Microsoft PressPass – Information for Journalists*. http://www.microsoft.com/presspass/features/2000/Dec00/12–08forrester.asp., December 8. Accessed July 27, 2007.

Milberg, S.J., Burke, S.J., Smith, H.J., and Kallman, E.A. (1995). Values, Personal Information Privacy, and Regulatory Approaches. *Communications of the ACM*, 38(December), 65–74.

Milberg, S.J., Smith, H.J., and Burke, S.J. (2000). Information Privacy: Corporate Management and National Regulation. *Organization Science*, 11(1), 35–57.

Mild, A. and Reutterer, T. (2001). Collaborative Filtering Methods for Binary Market Basket Data Analysis, *Active Media Technology, Lecture Notes in Computer Science*, pp. 302–313. Berlin: Springer.

Mild, A. and Reutterer, T. (2003). An Improved Collaborative Filtering Approach for Predicting Cross-category Purchases Based on Binary Market Basket Data. *Journal of Retailing and Consumer Services*, 10(3), 123–133.

Miller, A. (1989). *Subset Selection in Regression*. London: Chapman & Hall.

Miller, P. (2001). Case Study: Viking Office Products. *Catalog Age*, 18(6), 84–86.

Milligan, G. and Cooper, M. (1985). An Examination of Procedures for Determining the Number of Clusters in a Dataset. *Psychometrika*, 50(2), 159–179.

Minsky, M. and Papert, S. (1969). *Perceptrons*. Cambridge, MA: MIT.

Mollie, N. (1991). Quaker's Direct Hit. *Direct Marketing*, January 1. http://www.allbusiness.com/marketing/direct-marketing-direct-mail/151342-1.html. Accessed August 3, 2007.

Montoya-Weiss, M.M., Voss, G.B., and Grewal, D. (2003). Determinants of Provider. *Journal of the Academy of Marketing Science*, 31(4), 448–458.

Moorman, C. (1995). Organizational Market Information Process: Cultural Antecedents and New Product Outcomes. *Journal of Marketing Research*, 32(3), 318–335.

Moorman, C. and Rust, R.T. (1999). The Role of Marketing. *Journal of Marketing*, 63(Special Issue), 180–197.

Moret, B., Thomason, M., and Gonzales, R. (1980). The Activity of an Variable and Its Relation to Decision Trees. *ACM Transactions on Programming Language Systems*, 2(4), 580–595.

Morgan, J. and Sonquist, J. (1963). Problems in the Analysis of Survey Data, and a Proposal. *Journal of the American Statistical Association*, 58(302), 415–434.

Morimoto, Y., Fukuda, T., Matsuzawa, T., and Yoda, K. (1998). Algorithms for Mining Association Rules for Binary Segmentations of Huge Categorical Databases, *Proceedings of the 24th Very Large Data Bases Conference*, pp. 380–391.

Morishita, S. (1998). On Classification and Regression.*Proceedings of the First International Conference on Discovery Science – Lecture Notes in Artificial Intelligence*, pp. 40–57.

Morton, F.S., Zettelmeyer, F., and Silva-Risso, J. (2001). Internet Car Retailing. *Journal of Industrial Economics*, 49(4), 501–519.

Morwitz, V.G. (1997). Why Consumers Don't Always Accurately Predict Their Own Future Behavior. *Marketing Letters*, 8(1), 57–70.

Mulhern, F.J. (1999). Customer Profitability Analysis: Measurement, Concentration, and Research Directions. *Journal of Interactive Marketing*, 13(1), 25–40.

Murthi, B.P.S. and Sarkar, S. (2003). The Role of the Management Sciences in Research on Personalization. *Management Science*, 49(10), 1344–1362.

Murthy, S. (1998). Automatic Construction of Decision Trees from Data: A Multi-disciplinary Survey. *Data Mining and Knowledge Discovery*, 2(4), 345–389.

Myers Internet (2005). What Is a FICO Score? http://www.mtg-net.com/sfaq/faq/fico.htm: Accessed July 31, 2007.

Myers, J., Van Metre, E., and Pickersgill, A. (2004). Steering Customers to the Right Channels. *The McKinsey Quarterly: McKinsey on Marketing* (October).

Naik, P.A. and Tsai, C. (2004). Isotonic Single-index Model for High-dimensional Database Marketing. *Computational Statistics & Data Analysis*, 47(4), 775–790.

Naik, P.A., Hagerty, M.R., and Tsai, C. (2000). A New Dimension Reduction Approach for Data-rich Marketing Environments: Sliced Inverse Regression. *Journal of Marketing Research*, 37(1), 88–101.

Nair, H. (2007). *Intertemporal Price Discrimination with Forward-looking Consumers: Application to the US Market for Console Video-games*, Working Paper. Stanford, Palo Alto, CA: Graduate School of Business, Stanford University.

Narasimhan, C. (1988). Competitive Promotional Strategies. *Journal of Business*, 61(4), 427–449.

Nash, E. (2000). *Direct Marketing: Strategy, Planning, Execution*. New York: McGraw-Hill.

Nebel, J.F. and Blattberg, R. (1999). Brand Relationship Management: A New Approach for the Third Millennium, *Montgomery Research, CRM Project*.

Needham & Company (2006). *Internet Services and Digital Media*. Netflix. Needham, May 30.

Neslin, S.A. (2002). *Sales Promotion*. Cambridge, MA: Marketing Science Institute.

Neslin, S.A. and Shoemaker, R.W. (1989). An Alternative Explanation for Lower Repeat Rates After Promotion Purchases. *Journal of Marketing Research*, 26(2), 205–213.

Neslin, S.A., Henderson, C., and Quelch, J. (1985). Consumer Promotions and the Acceleration of Product Purchases. *Marketing Science*, 4(2), 147–165.

Neslin, S.A., Gupta, S., Kamakura, W.A., Lu, J., and Mason, C.H. (2006a). Defection Detection: Measuring and Understanding the Predictive Accuracy of Customer Churn Models. *Journal of Marketing Research*, 43(2), 204–211.

Neslin, S.A., Grewal, D. Leghorn, R., Shankar, V., Teerling, M.L., Thomas, J.S., and Verhoef, P.C. (2006b). Challenges and Opportunities in Multi-channel Customer Management. *Journal of Service Research*, 9(2), 95–112.

Neslin, S.A., Novak, T.P., Baker, K.R., and Hoffman, D.L. (2007). *An Optimal Contact Model for Maximizing Online Panel Response Rates*, Working Paper. Hanover, NH: Tuck School of Business.

Neter, J., Wasserman, W., and Kutner, M. (1985). *Applied Linear Statistical Models: Regression, Anlaysis of Variance, and Experimental Designs*. Homewood, IL: Richard D. Irwin.

Nicholson, M., Clarke, I., and Blakemore, M. (2002). One Brand, Three Ways to Shop: Situational Variables and Multichannel Consumer Behavior. *The International Review of Retail, Distribution and Consumer Research*, 12(2), 131–148.

Nilsson, N. (1965). *Learning Machines: Foundations of Trainable Pattern – Classifying Systems*. New York: McGraw-Hill.

Nishi, D. (2005). Market-basket Mystery. *Retail Technology Quarterly* (12A).

Oliver, R.L., Rust, R.T., and Varki, S. (1997). Customer Delight: Foundations, Findings, and Managerial Insight. *Journal of Retaiilng*, 73(3), 311–336.

O'Neill, S. (2001). Courting the Customer. *Knowledge Management* (May), 20–23.

Orr, A. (2000). How Hilton Honors Its Loyal Customers. *Target Marketing*, 23(11), 51–54.

Pan, X., Shankar, V., and Ratchford, B.T. (2002a). Price Competition between Pure Play vs. Bricks-and-Clicks E-Tailers: Analytical Model and Empirical Analysis. *Advances in Microeconomics: Economics of the Internet and e-Commerce*, 11, 29–62.

Pan, X., Ratchford, B.T., and Shankar, V. (2002b). Can Price Dispersion in Online Markets Be Explained by Differences in E-Tailer Service Quality. *Journal of the Academy of Marketing Science*, 30(4), 433–445.

Pan, X., Ratchford, B.T., and Shankar, V. (2004). Price Dispersion on the Internet: A Review and Directions for Future Research. *Journal of Interactive Marketing*, 18(4), 116–135.

Park, I. and Sandberg, I. (1991). Universal Approximation Using Radial-basis Function Networks. *Neural Computation*, 3(2), 246–257.

Park, J., Harley, R., and Venayagamoorthy, G. (2002). Comparison of MLP and RBF Neural Networks Using Deviation Signals for On-line Identification of a Synchronous Generator, *Proceedings of the 2002 International Joint Conference on Neural Networks*, pp. 919–924. Honolulu, HI.

Park, Y. and Fader, P.S. (2004). Modeling Browsing Behavior at Multiple Websites. *Marketing Science*, 23(3), 280–303.

Patton, S. (2002). Food Fight, As They Struggle for Survival Against Discounters Like Wal-Mart, Supermarkets Turn to IT to Make Shopping Easier, Cheaper and More Profitable for Them. *CIO*, 16(2), 86–92.

Pauwels, K. and Dans, E. (2001). Internet Marketing the News: Leveraging Brand Equity from Marketplace to Marketspace. *Brand Management*, 8(4–5), 303–314.

Pauwels, K. and Neslin, S.A. (2007). *Building with Bricks and Mortar: The Revenue Impact of Opening Physical Stores in a Multichannel Environment*, Working Paper. Hanover, NH: Tuck School of Business, Dartmouth College.

Payne, A. and Frow, P. (2005). A Strategic Framework for Customer Relationship Management. *Journal of Marketing*, 69(4), 167–176.

Payton, F.C. and Zahay, D. (2003). Understanding Why Marketing Does Not Use the Corporate Data Warehouse for CRM Applications. *Journal of Database Marketing*, 10(4), 315–326.

Peacock, P.R. (1998). Data Mining in Marketing: Part 1. *Marketing Management*, 6(4), 8–18.

Pearl, J. (1988). *Probabilistic Reasoning in Inelligent Systems*. San Mateo, CA: Morgan Kaufmann.

Pepe, A. (2005). Online Banking Success Hinges on Trust. *Inside 1 to 1: Privacy*. Norwalk CT: Peppers and Rogers.

Pepe, M. (2002). Smart Cards Go to Front of the Line. *CRM*, 989, 45.

Peppers, D. and Rogers, M. (1993). *The One to One Future: Building Relationships One Customer at a Time*. New York: Doubleday.

Peppers, D. and Rogers, M. (1997). *Enterprise One to One: Tools for Competing in the Interactive Age*. New York: Doubleday.

Peppers, D. and Rogers, M. (2004a). Intel Measures Trust to Grow Its Business. *Inside 1 to 1*. Norwalk, CT: Peppers and Rogers Group, October 11, 2004.

Peppers, D. and Rogers, M. (2004b). *Managing Customer Relationships: A Strategic Framework*. Hoboken, NJ: Wiley.

Peppers, D. and Rogers, M. (2005a). Return on Customer: The Privacy Perspective. *Inside 1 to 1: Privacy*. Norwalk, CT: Peppers and Rogers Group, June 9, 2005.

Peppers, D. and Rogers, M. (2005b). Privacy Success: The CPO Can't Do It Alone. *Inside 1 to 1: Privacy*. Norwalk, CT: Peppers and Rogers Group, April 14, 2005.

Perez, E. (2005). ChoicePoint Is Pressed to Explain Database Breach, *Wall Street Journal* (Eastern Edition) (p. A6, February 25, 2005).

Peteraf, M.A. (1993). The Cornerstones of Competitive Advantage: A Resource-based View. *Strategic Management Journal*, 14(3), 179–191.

Peterson, R.A., Balasubramanian, S., and Bronnenberg, B.J. (1997). Exploring the Implications of the Internet for Consumer Marketing. *Journal of the Academy of Marketing Science*, 25(4), 329–346.

Pfeifer, P.E. (1996). Intuit: QuickBooks Upgrade. Case UVA-M-0496. Charlottesville, VA: University of Virginia Darden School Foundation.

Pfeifer, P.E. (1998). The Economic Selection of Sample Sizes for List Testing. *Journal of Interactive Marketing*, 12(3), 5–20.

Pfeifer, P.E. (2005). The Optimal Ratio of Acquisition and Retention Costs. *Journal of Targeting, Measurement, and Analysis for Marketing*, 13(2), 179–188.

Pfeifer, P.E. and Carraway, R.L. (2000). Modeling Customer Relationships as Markov Chains. *Journal of Interactive Marketing*, 14(2), 43–55.

Pierce, L. (2001). What the Cost of Customer Churn Means to You. *Network World*, 18(46), 43.

Pindyck, R. and Rubenfeld, D. (2004). *Microeconomics*. Englewood-Cliffs, NJ: Prentice-Hall.

Plackett, R. and Burman, J. (1946). The Design of Optimum Multi-factorial Experiments. *Biometrika*, 33(4), 305–325.

Plummer, J. (1974). The Concept and Application of Life Style Segmentation. *Journal of Marketing*, 38(1), 33–37.

Poggio, T. and Girosi, F. (1990). Networks for Approximation and Learning. *Proceedings of the IEEE*, 78(9), 1481–1497.

Polaniecki, R. (2001). Credit Cards: How Rewarding. *Credit Union Management*, 24(4), 30–36.

Press, S. and Wilson, S. (1978). Choosing between Logistic Regression and Discriminant Analysis. *Journal of the American Statistical Association*, 73(364), 699–705.

Prudential Equity Group (2006). *Industry Overview: Telecom Services.* Prudential Equity Group, LLC, July 20, 2006.

Quinlan, J. (1986). Induction of Decision Trees. *Machine Learning*, 1(1), 81–106.

Quinlan, J. (1993). *C4.5: Programs for Machine Laerning.* San Mateo, CA: Morgan Kaufmann.

Raider, A.M. (1999). Pointing to Customer Needs and Retailers' Profits. *Progressive Grocer*, 78(6), 17.

Ramaswamy, S., Mahajan, S., and Silberschatz, A. (1998). On the Discovery of Interesting Patterns in Association rules, *Proceedings of 24th VLDB Conference*, pp. 368–379. New York.

Rangan, F. and Kastiri, V. (1994). *Designing Channels of Distribution.* Note 9–594–116. Boston MA: Harvard Business School.

Rangaswamy, A. and Van Bruggen, G. (2005). Opportunities and Challenges in Multichannel Marketing: An Introduction to the Special Issue. *Journal of Interactive Marketing*, 19(2), 5–11.

Rao, V. and Simon, J.L. (1983). Optimal Allocation of Space in Retail Advertisements and Mail-order Catalogues: Theory and a First-approximation Decision Rule. *International Journal of Advertising*, 2(2), 123–129.

Rasmusson, E. (1999). Wanted: Profitable Customers. *Sales and Marketing Management*, 151(5), 28–34.

Ratner, B. (2002). Rapid Statistical Calculations for Determining the Success of Marketing Campaigns. *Journal of Targeting, Measurement and Analysis for Marketing*, 10(4), 385–390.

Regan, K. (2000). AOL Trumps Amazon with Air Miles Plan. *E-Commerce Times*, October 2, 2000. http://www/ecommercetimes.com/per//story/4439.html. Accessed July 26, 2007.

Reichheld, F.F. (1993). Loyalty-based Management. *Harvard Business Review*, 7(2), 64–73.

Reichheld, F.F. (1996). Learning from Customer Defections. *Harvard Business Review*, 74(2), 56–69.

Reinartz, W.J. and Kumar, V. (2000). On the Profitability of Long-life Customers in a Noncontractual Setting: An Empirical Investigation and Implications for Marketing. *Journal of Marketing*, 64(4), 17–35.

Reinartz, W.J. and Kumar, V. (2003). The Impact of Customer Relationship Characteristics on Profitable Lifetime Duration. *Journal of Marketing*, 67(1), 77–99.

Reinartz, W.J., Krafft, M., and Hoyer, W.D. (2004). The Customer Relationship Management Process: Its Measurement and Impact on Performance. *Journal of Marketing Research*, 41(3), 293–305.

Reinartz, W.J., Thomas, J.S., and Kumar, V. (2005). Balancing Acquistion and Retention Resources to Maximize Customer Profitability. *Journal of Marketing*, 69(1), 63–79.

Reinartz, W.J., Thomas, J.S., and Bascoul, G. (2006). *Investigating Cross-buying and Customer Loyalty*, Working Paper. Fontainebleau, France: INSEAD.

Renk, K. (2002). The Age-old Question: Cash vs. Merchandise? *Occupational Health and Safety*, 71(9), 60.

Resnick, P., Iacovou, N., Suchak, M., Bergstrom, P., and Riedl, J. (1994). Grouplens: An Open Architecturer for Collaborative Filtering of Netnews, *Proceedings of the ACM 1994 Conference on Computer Supported Cooperative Work*, pp. 175–186. New York: ACM.

Rice, M.D. (1988). Estimating the Reach and Frequency of Mixed Media Advertising Schedules. *Journal of the Market Research Society*, 30(4), 439–452.

Richeldi, M. and Lanzi, P.L. (1996). Performing Effective Feature Selection by Investigating the Deep Structure of the Data. In E. Simoudis, J. Han, and U.M. Fayyad (Eds.), *Proceedings of the Second International Conference on Knowledge Discovery and Data Mining*. AAAI.

Ridgby, D.K. and Leidingham, D. (2005). CRM Done Right. *Harvard Business Review*, 82(11), 118–129.

Roberts, A. (1994). Media Exposure and Consumer Purchasing: An Improved Data Fusion Technique. *Marketing and Research Today*, 22(3), 159–172.

Roberts, M.L. and Berger, P.D. (1999). *Direct Marketing Management, 2nd edition*. Upper Saddle River, NJ: Prentice-Hall.

Robinson, B. and Lakhani, C. (1975). Dynamic Pricing Models for New Product Planning. *Management Science*, 21(10), 1113–1122.

Robinson, M. (2002). Will NCOA Save You Money? *Target Marketing*, 25(3), 16.

Roehm, M.L., Pullins, E.B., and Roehm, Jr. H.A. (2002). Designing Loyalty – Building Programs for Packaged Goods Brands. *Journal of Marketing Research*, 39(2), 202–213.

Rogers, D. (2002). The Ultimate Loyalty Scheme. *Marketing*(June 6), 17.

Rohwedder, C. (2006). Stores of Knowledge: No. 1 Retailer in Britain Uses 'Clubcard' to Thwart Wal-Mart; Data From Loyalty Program Help Tesco Tailor Products As It Resists US Invader – Ms. Fiala Changes Detergent, *Wall Street Journal* (Eastern Edition) (p. A1, June 6).

Rosen, C. (2000). Harrah's Bets on Loyalty Program. *Information Week*, October 30(810), 153.

Ross, S.M. (1983). *Introduction to Stochastic Dynamic Programming*. New York: Academic.

Rossi, P.E., McCulloch, R., and Allenby, G. (1996). The Value of Purchase History Data in Target Marketing. *Marketing Science*, 15(4), 321–340.

Rothschild, M.L. (1987). A Behavioral View of Promotions Effects on Brand Loyalty. In A. Wallendorf and P. Anderson (Eds.), *Advances in Consumer Research, Volume XIV*, pp. 119–120. Provo, UT: Association for Consumer Research.

Rothschild, M.L. and Gaidis, W.C. (1981). Behavioral Learning Theory: Its Relevance to Marketing and Promotions. *Journal of Marketing*, 45(2), 70–78.

Rounds, E. (1980). A Combined Non-parametric Approach to Feature Selection and Binary Decision Tree Design. *Pattern Recognition*, 12(5), 313–317.

Rubin, D.B. (1987). *Multiple Imputation for Nonresponse in Surveys*. New York: Wiley.

Rumelhart, D. and McClelland, J. (1986). *Parallel Distributed Processing: Explorations in the Microstructures of Cognition*. Cambridge, MA: MIT.

Rumelhart, D., Hinton, G., and Williams, R. (1986). Learning Representations of Back-propagation Errors. *Letters to Nature*, 323, 533–536.

Rust, R.T. and Oliver, R.L. (2000). Should We Delight the Customer. *Journal of the Academy of Marketing Science*, 28(1), 86–94.

Rust, R.T. and Verhoef, P.C. (2005). Optimizing the Marketing Interventions Mix in Intermediate-term CRM. *Marketing Science*, 24(3), 477–489.

Rust, R.T. and Zahorik, A.J. (1993). Customer Satisfaction, Customer Retention and Market Share. *Journal of Retailing*, 69(2), 193–215.

Rust, R.T., Zimmer, M.R., and Leone, R.P. (1986). Estimating the Duplicated Audience of Media Vehicles in National Advertising. *Journal of Advertising*, 15(3), 30–38.

Rust, R.T., Zahorik, A.J., and Keiningham, T.L. (1995). Return on Quality (ROQ): Making Service Quality Financially Accountable. *Journal of Marketing*, 59(2), 58–70.

Rust, R.T., Zeithaml, V.A., and Lemon, K.N. (2000). *Driving Customer Equity: How Customer Lifetime Value is Reshaping Corporate Strategy*. New York: Free Press.

Rust, R.T., Moorman, C., and Dickson, P.R. (2002). Getting Return on Quality: Revenue Expansion, Cost Reduction, or Both? *Journal of Marketing*, 66(4), 7–24.

Salton, G. and McGill, M. (1983). *Introduction to Modern Information Retrieval*. New York: McGraw-Hill.

Sarwar, B., Konstan, J., Borchers, A., Herlocker, J., Miller, B., and Riedl, J. (1998). Using Filtering Agents to Improve Prediction Quality in the GroupLens Research Collaborative Filtering System, *Proceedings of 1998 Conference on Computer Supported Collaborative Work*.

Sarwar, B., Karypis, G., Konstan, J., and Riedl, J. (2000). Analysis of Recommendation Algorithms for E-Commerce, *Proceedings of the ACM EC'00 Conference*, pp. 158–167. Minneapolis, MN.

Sarwar, B., Karypis, G., Konstan, J., and Riedl, J. (2001). Item-based Collaborative Filtering Recommendation Algorithms, *10th International World Wide Web Conference* pp. 285– 295: ACM Press.

Schafer, B., Konstan, J., and Riedl, J. (1999). Recommender Systems in E-Commerce, *Proceedings of ACM Electronic Commerce 1999 Conference*.

Schafer, J. (1997). *Analysis of Incomplete Multivariate Data*. New York: Chapman & Hall.

Scherreik, S. (2002). Is Your Broker Leaving You Out in the Cold: The New Focus on High-end Clients Means Less Service for Many, *Business Week*, pp. 102–104, February 1–18.

Schlosser, A.E., Shavitt, S., and Kanfer, A. (1999). Survey of Internet Users' Attitudes Toward Internet Advertising. *Journal of Interactive Marketing*, 13(3), 34–54.

Schmid, J. (1995). Six Mistakes Catalogs Make. *Target Marketing*, 18(5), 32–34.

Schmid, J. and Weber, A. (1995). Catalog Database Marketing Done Right, *Target Marketing*, 18(10), 34–37.

Schmid, J. and Weber, A. (1998). *Desktop Database Marketing*. Chicago, IL: NTC.

Schmittlein, D.C., Morrison, D.G., and Colombo, R. (1987). Counting Your Customers: Who Are They and What Will They Do Next. *Management Science*, 33(1), 1–24.

Schmittlein, D.C. and Peterson, R.A. (1994). Customer Base Analysis: An Industrial Purchase Process Application. *Marketing Science*, 13(1), 41–65.

Schwarz, G. (1978). Estimating the Dimension of the Model. *Annals of Statistics*, 6(2), 461–464.

Searcy, D.L. (2004). Using Activity-based Costing to Access Channel/Customer Profitability. *Management Accounting Quarterly*, 5(2), 51–60.

Seaver, B. and Simipson, E. (1995). Mail Order Catalog Design and Consumer Response Behavior: Experimentation and Analysis. *Journal of Direct Marketing*, 9(3), 8–20.

Seetharaman, P.B. (2004). Modeling Multiple Sources of State Dependence in Random Utility Models: A Distributed Lag Approach. *Marketing Science*, 23(2), 263–271.

Seetharaman, P.B. and Chintagunta, P.K. (2003). The Proportional Hazard Model for Purchase Timing: A Comparison of Alternative Specifications. *Journal of Business and Economic Statistics*, 21(3), 368–382.

Selnes, F. and Hansen, H. (2001). The Potential Hazard of Self- service in Developing Customer Loyalty. *Journal of Service Research*, 4(2), 79–80.

Senn, C. (2006). The Executive Growth Factor: How Siemens Invigorated Its Customer Relationships. *Journal of Business Strategy*, 27(1), 27–34.

Seppanen, M. and Lyly-Yrjanainen, J. (2002). Vague Boundaries of Product and Customer Costs. *2002 AACE International Transactions, Risk 12,* RI121–RI126.

Setiono, R. and Liu, H. (1997). Neural-Network Feature Selector. *IEEE Transactions on Neural Netwoks,* 8(3), 654–662.

Shaffer, G. and Zhang, Z.J. (1995). Competitive Coupon Targeting. *Marketing Science,* 14(4), 395–416.

Shaffer, G. and Zhang, Z.J. (2000). Pay to Switch or Pay to Stay: Preference-based Price Discrimination in Markets with Switching Costs. *Journal of Economics and Management Strategy,* 9(3), 397–424.

Shankar, V., Rangaswamy, A., and Pusateri, M. (2001). *The Online Medium and Customer Price Sensitivity,* Working Paper. University Park, PA: Pennsylvania State University.

Shankar, V., Smith, A.K., and Rangaswamy, A. (2003). The Relationship between Customer Satisfaction and Loyalty in Online and Offline Environments. *International Journal of Research in Marketing,* 20(2), 153–175.

Shao, J. (1993). Linear Model Selection by Cross-validation. *Journal of the American Statistical Association,* 88(422), 486–494.

Shapiro, C. (1983). Optimal Pricing of Experience Goods. *The Bell Journal of Economics,* 14(2), 116–130.

Sharda, R. (1994). Neural Networks for the MS/OR Analyst: An Application Bibliography. *Interfaces,* 24(2), 116–130.

Shardanand, U. and Maes, P. (1995). Social Information Filtering: Algorithms for Automating Word of Mouth, *Proceedings of ACM CHI'95 Conference on Human Factors in Computing Systems,* pp. 210–217.

Sharp, B. and Sharp, A. (1997). Loyalty Programs and Their Impact on Repeat-purchase Loyalty Patterns. *International Journal of Research in Marketing,* 14(5), 473–486.

Sharp, D. (2003). Knowledge Management Today: Challenges and Opportunities. *Information Systems Mangement,* 20(2), 32–37.

Sharpe, W.F. (2000). *Portfolio Theory and Capital Markets.* New York: McGraw-Hill.

Sheehan, K.B. and Doherty, C. (2001). Re-weaving the Web: Integrating Print and Online Communications. *Journal of Interactive Marketing,* 15(2), 47–59.

Sheppard, B.H., Hartwick, J., and Warshaw, P.R. (1988). The Theory of Reasoned Action: A Meta-analysis of Past Research with Recommendations for Modifications and Future Research. *Journal of Consumer Research,* 15(3), 325–343.

Sheppard, D. (1999). *The New Direct Marketing.* New York: McGraw Hill.

Sherman, L. and Deighton, J. (2001). Banner Advertising: Measuring Effectiveness and Optimizing Placement. *Journal of Interactive Marketing,* 15(2), 60–64.

Sheth, J.N. and Sisodia, R.S. (1995a). Feeling the Heat – Part 1. *Marketing Management,* 4(3), 8–23.

Sheth, J.N. and Sisodia, R.S. (1995b). Feeling the Heat – Part 2. *Marketing Management*, 4(3), 19–33.

Sheth, J.N. and Sisodia, R.S. (2001). High Performance Marketing. *Marketing Management*, 10(3), 18–23.

Shugan, S.M. (2005). Brand Loyalty Programs: Are They Shams? *Marketing Science*, 24(2), 185–193.

Silverstein, C., Brin, S., and Motwani, R. (1998). Beyond Market Basket: Generalizing Association Rules to Dependence Rules. *Data Mining and Knowledge Discovery*, 2(1), 39–68.

Simester, D.I. and Anderson, E.T. (2003). Effects of $9 Price Endings on Retail Sales: Evidence from Field Experiments. *Quantitative Marketing and Economics*, 1(1), 93–110.

Simester, D.I., Sun, P., and Tsitsiklis, J.N. (2006). Dynamic Catalog Mailing Policies. *Management Science*, 52(5), 683–696.

Simon, H. (1982). ADPULS: An Advertising Model with Wearout and Pulsation. *Journal of Marketing Research*, 19(3), 352– 363.

Simon, K. (2007). Mortgage Refinancing Gets Tougher: As Adjustable Loans Resert at Higher Rates, Homeowners Find Themselves Stuck Due to Prepayment Penalties, Tighter Credit. *Wall Street Journal* (Eastern Edition), D1.

Singh, J. (2005). Collaborative Networks as Determinants of Knowledge Diffusion Patterns. *Management Science*, 51(5), 756–770.

Smith, G.E. and Berger, P.D. (1998). Different Message-framing for Different Direct Response Marketing Goals: Choice Versus Attitude Formation. *Journal of Interactive Marketing*, 12(2), 33–48.

Smith, H.J., Millberg, S.J., and Burke, S.J. (1996). Information Privacy: Measuring Individuals' Concerns about Organizational Practices. *MIS Quarterly*, 20(2), 167–196.

Smith, S. (2006). Circuit City Posts Profit, Sales Gains in Quarter. *Twice: This Week in Consumer Electronics*, 21(14), 4.

Sokolick, W. and Hartung, P. (1969). Catalog Advertising Allocation. *Management Science*, 15(10), B521–529.

Sousa, R. and Voss, C.A. (2004). *Service Quality in Multi-channel Services Employing Virtual Channels*, Working Paper. London: London Business School.

Speers, T., Wilcox, S., and Brown, B. (2004). The Privacy Rule, Security Rule, and Transaction Standards: Three Sides of the Same Coin. *Journal of Health Care Compliance*, (January– February 2004).

Srinivasan, R. and Moorman, C. (2002). Analysis of Customer Satisfaction Among Online Retailers, *Customer Relationship Management: Customer Behavior, Organizational Challenges, and Economic Models*. Durham NC: Marketing Science Institute and the Teradata Center for Customer Relationship Management at Duke University, January 31–February 2, 2002.

Stauffer, D. (2001). What Customer-centric Really Means: Seven Key Insights. *Harvard Management Update*, 6(8), 1–3.

Stauss, B. and Friege, C. (1999). Regaining Service Customers. *Journal of Service Research*, 1(4), 347–361.

Steckel, J.H. and Vanhonacker, W. (1993). Cross-validation Regression Models in Marketing Research. *Marketing Science*, 12(4), 415–442.

Stedman, C. (1997). Marketing Megamarts on the Rise. *Computerworld*, 31(38), 65–66.

Steenburgh, T.J., Ainslie, A., and Engebretson, P. (2003). Massively Categorical Variables: Revealing the Information in Zip codes. *Marketing Science*, 22(1), 40–57.

Stern, L.W. and El-Ansary, A.I. (1972). *Marketing Channels*. Englewood Cliffs, NJ: Pretice-Hall.

Stewart, K. and Segars, A.H. (2002). An Empirical Examination of the Concern for Information Privacy Instrument. *Information Systems Research*, 13(1), 36–49.

Stone, M. and Condron, K. (2002). Sharing Customer Data in the Value Chain. *Journal of Database Marketing*, 9(2), 119– 131.

Stone, M., Hobbs, M., and Khaleeli, M. (2002). Multichannel Customer Management: The Benefits and Challenges. *Journal of Database Marketing*, 10(1), 39–52.

Storbacka, K. (1993). *Customer Relationship Profitability in Retail Banking*, Research Report #29. Helsinki, Finland: Swedish School of Economics and Business Administration.

Storbacka, K. (1994). Customer Relationship Profitabilty – Propositions for Analysis of Relationships and Customer Bases. In J.N. Sheth and A. Parvatiyar (Eds.), *Relationship Marketing: Theory, Methods and Applications*. Atlanta, GA: Roberto C. Goizueta Business School, Emory University.

Storbacka, K. (1997). Segmentation Based on Customer Profitability – Retrospective Analysis of Retail Bank Customer Bases. *Journal of Marketing Management*, 13(5), 479–492.

Storbacka, K. and Luukinen, A. (1994). Managing Customer Relationship Profitability – Case Swedbank, *Banking and Insurance: From Recession to Recovery*, pp. 79–93. Amsterdam: ESOMAR.

Suen, C. and Wang, Q. (1984). ISOETRP: An Interactive Clustering Algorithm with New Objectives. *Pattern Recognition*, 17(2), 211–219.

Sun, B. and Li, S. (2005). *Adaptively Learning about Customers and Dynamic Service Matching – An Empirical Investigation of Service Allocation with Off-shore Centers*, Working Paper. Pittsburgh, PA: Tepper School of Business, Carnegie Mellon University.

Sun, B., Neslin, S.A., and Srinivasan, K. (2003). Measuring the Impact of Promotions on Brand Switching When Consumers Are Forward Looking. *Journal of Marketing Research*, 40(4), 389–405.

Supply Management (1998). Customer Loyalty Set to Wane. *Supply Management*, 3(16), 17.

Swartz, N. (2005). U.S. Companies Not Complying with E.U. Safe Harbor Rules. *Information Management Journal*, 39(1), 12.

Swets, J.A. (1988). Measuring the Accuracy of Diagnostic Systems. *Science*, 240(4857), 1285–1289.

Swift, R.S. (2001). *Accelerating Customer Relationships: Using CRM and Relationship Technologies*. Upper Saddle River, NJ: Prentice-Hall.

Tam, K. and Kiang, M. (1992). Managerial Applications of Neural Networks: The Case of Bank Failure Predictions. *Management Science*, 38(7), 926–947.

Tang, F. and Xing, X. (2001). Will the Growth of Multi-channel Retailing Diminish the Pricing Efficiency of the Web? *Journal of Retailing*, 77(3), 319–333.

Tanner, M. (1993). *Tools for Statistical Inference*. New York: Springer.

Tapp, A. (2002). The Strategic Value of Direct Marketing: Expanding Its Role Within the Company, Paper 2. *Journal of Database Marketing*, 9(2), 105–112.

Taylor, G.A. and Neslin, S.A. (2005). The Current and Future Sales Impact of A Retail Frequency Reward Program. *Journal of Retaiilng*, 81(4), 293–305.

Teerling, M.L. (2007). Determining the Cross-channel Effects of Informational Web Sites, Ph.D. Dissertation, Research School, Systems, Organisations, and Management. Ridderkerk, The Netherlands: University of Groningen.

Teerling, M.L. and Huizingh, E.K.R.E. (2005). *The Complementarity Between Online and Offline Consumer Attitudes and Behaviour*, Working Paper. Ridderkerk, The Netherlands: University of Groningen.

Tellis, G.J. (1998). *Advertising and Sales Promotion Strategy*. Reading, MA: Addison-Wesley.

Tellis, G.J., Chandy, R.K., and Thaivanich, P. (2000). Which Ad Works, When, Where and How? Modeling the Effects of Direct Television Advertising. *Journal of Marketing Research*, 37(1), 32–46.

Thaler, R. (1985). Mental Accounting and Consumer Choice. *Marketing Science*, 4(3), 199–214.

The Economist (2007). Change is in the Air. *The Economist*, 383(8512), 78.

Thibodeau, P. (2002). Profitable Privacy. *Computerworld*, 36(8), 46–47.

Thomas, J.S. (2001). A Methodology for Linking Customer Acquisition to Customer Retention. *Journal of Marketing Research*, 38(2), 262–268.

Thomas, J.S. and Sullivan, U.Y. (2005a). Managing Marketing Communications with Multichannel Customers. *Journal of Marketing*, 69(4), 239–251.

Thomas, J.S. and Sullivan, U.Y. (2005b). *Investigating Best Customers in a Multi-channel Setting*, Working Paper. Evanston, IL: Medill School, Northwestern University.

Thomas, J.S., Blattberg, R.C., and Fox, E.J. (2004a). Recapturing Lost Customers. *Journal of Marketing Research*, 4(1), 31–45.

Thomas, J.S., Reinartz, W.J., and Kumar, V. (2004b). Getting the Most Out of All Your Customers. *Harvard Business Review*, 82(11), 117–123.

Thomas Weisel Partners (2005). HouseValues: A Look at the Churn Issue: November 29, Thomas Weisel Partners.

Thornton, R. (2005). Online Panels: The New Frontier of B2B Research, *Cial GmbHBIG Annual Conference.*

Thomaselli, R. (2002). Cingular Focuses on Loyalty. *Advertising Age* (Midwest region edition), 73(33), 4.

Tikhonov, A. (1963). On Solving Incorrectly Posed Problems and Method of Regularization. *Doklady Akademii Nauk USSR,* 151, 501–504.

Time Warner (1999). American Online and United Artists Theatre Circuit Announce Multi-year Strategic Alliance. *Time Warner Press Releases* (November 2). http://www.timewarner.com/corp/newsroom/pr/2000,20812,666397,666300.html. Accessed July 31, 2007.

Timmons, H. and Zeller Jr. T. (2005). Security Breach at LexisNexis Now Appears Larger, *New York Times (Late Edition – East Coast),* pp. C.7, April 13. New York.

Ting, K. and Witten, I. (1997). Stacked Generalization: When Does It Work?, *Fifteenth International Joint Conference on Artificial Intelligence,* pp. 866–871. Nagoya, Japan: Morgan Kauffmann.

Tobin, J. (1958). Estimation of Relationships for Limited Dependent Variables. *Econometrica,* 26(1), 24–36.

Tomaselli, R. and Elkin, T. (2002). Cingular Focuses on Loyalty. *Advertising Age,* 73(33), 4.

Tull, D. and Hawkins, D. (1993). *Marketing Research: Measurement & Methods.* New York: Macmillan.

Tuma, N. and Hannan, M. (1984). *Social Dynamics: Models and Methods.* Orlando, FL: Academic.

Turner, E.C. and Dasgupta, S. (2003). Privacy on the Web: An Examination of User Concerns, Technology, and Implications for Business Organizations and Individuals. *Information Systems Mangement,* 20(1), 8–18.

Turner, M. (2001). *The Impact of Data Restrictions on Consumer Distance Shopping,* White Paper, March. New York: Direct Marketing Association.

Udo, G.J. (2001). Privacy and Security Concerns as Major Barriers for E-Commerce: A Survey Study. *Information Management and Computer Security,* 9(4), 165–174.

Urban, G.L. (2004). *Digital Marketing Strategy.* Upper Saddle River, NJ: Pearson Prentice-Hall.

Vail, E.F. III (1999). Knowledge Mapping: Getting Started with Knowledge Management. *Information Systems Mangement,* 16(4), 1–8.

Van den Poel, D. and Larivière, B. (2004). Customer Attrition Analysis for Financial Services Using Proportional Hazard Models. *European Journal of Operational Research,* 157(1), 196– 217.

Van Heerde, H.J., Leeflang, P.S.H., and Wittink, D.R. (2004). Decomposing the Sales Promotion Bump with Store Data. *Marketing Science,* 23(3), 317–334.

Van Raaij, E.M., Vernooij, M.J.A., and Van Triest, S. (2003). The Implementation of Customer Profitability Analysis: A Case Study. *Industrial Marketing Management,* 32(7), 573–583.

Vapnik, V. (1995). *The Nature of Statistical Learning Theory*. New York: Springer.

Venkatesan, R., Kumar, V., and Ravishanker, N. (2007). Multi-channel Shopping: Causes and Consequences. *Journal of Marketing*, 71(2), 114–132.

Verhoef, P.C. and Donkers, B. (2005). The Effect of Acquisition Channels on Customer Loyalty and Cross-buying. *Journal of Interactive Marketing*, 19(2), 31–43.

Verhoef, P.C., Neslin, S.A., and Vroomen, B. (2007). Multi- channel Customer Management: Understanding the Research Shopper Phenomenon. *International Journal of Research in Marketing*, 24(2), 129–148.

Vermunt, J. and Magidson, J. (2000). Latent Class Cluster Analysis. In J.A. Hagenaars and A.L. McCutcheon (Eds.), *Advances in Latent Class Models*. Cambridge, UK: Cambridge University Press.

Verton, D. (2001). Churn. *Computerworld*, 35(6), 50.

Vesanto, J. and Alhoniemi, E. (2000). Clustering of the Self- organizing Map. *IEEE Transactions on Neural Netwoks*, 11(3), 1–38.

Villanueva, J., Yoo, S., and Hanssens, D.M. (2003). *The Impact of Acquisition Channels on Customer Equity*, Working Paper. Los Angeles, CA: The Anderson School at UCLA.

Villaneva, J., Yoo, S., and Hanssens, D.M. (2008). The Impact of Marketing-Induced vs. Word-of-Mouth Customer Acquisition on Customer Equity Growth. *Journal of Marketing Research*, Forthcoming.

Villas-Boas, J.M. (1999). Dynamic Competition with Customer Recognition. *Rand Journal of Economics*, 30, 604–631.

Villas-Boas, J.M. (2004). Price Cycles in Markets with Customer Recognition. *RAND Journal of Economics*, 35(3), 486–501.

Wachovia Capital Markets (2006). Equity Research Department: Meeting Packet, February 17: Wachovia Capital Markets.

Wallace, D.W., Giese, J.L., and Johnson, J.L. (2004). Customer Retailer Loyalty in the Context of Multiple Channel Strategies. *Journal of Retailng*, 80(4), 249–263.

Wangenheim, F.V. and Lentz, P. (2004). *Understanding Your Customer Portfolio: A Simple Approach to Customer Segmentation According to Lifecycle Dynamics*, Working Paper. Dortmund, Germany: University of Dortmund.

Wansink, B. (2003). Developing a Cost-effective Brand Loyalty Program. *Journal of Advertising Research*, 43(3), 301–309.

Ward, M.R. (2001). Will Online Shopping Compete More with Traditional Retailing or Catalog Retailing. *Netnomics*, 3(2), 103–117.

Ward, M.R. and Morganosky, M. (2002). Consumer Acquisition of Production Information and Subsequent Purchase Channel Decisions. In M.R. Baye (Ed.), *Advances in Applied Microeconomics: The Economics of the Internet and E-Commerce, Volume 11*. Boston, MA: JAL.

Watson, H.J. and Eckerson, W. (2000). Harrah's, *Harnessing Customer Information for Strategic Advantage: Technical Challenges and Business Solutions*. Seattle, WA: The Data Warehousing Institute.

Watson, H.J. and Volomino, L. (2001). Harrah's High Payoff from Customer Information. http://text.usg.edu:8080/tt/www.terry.uga.edu/~hwatson/ (Harrah's.doc). Accessed August 7, 2007.

Watson, R.T. (2004). I Am My Own Database. *Harvard Business Review*, 82(11), 18–19.

Webb, G. (1995). OPUS: An Efficient Admissible Algorithm for Unordered Search. *Journal of Artificial Intelligence Research*, 3, 431–465.

Webster, F.E. Jr. (1981). Top Management's Concerns About Marketing: Issues for the 1980's. *Journal of Marketing*, 45(3), 9–16.

Webster, F.E. Jr. (1991). *Industrial Marketing Strategy, 3rd Edition*. New York: Wiley.

Webster, F.E. Jr. (1992). The Changing Role of Marketing in the Corporation. *Journal of Marketing*, 56(4), 1–17.

Wei, C. and Chieu, I. (2002). Turning Telecommunications Call Details to Churn Prediction: A Data Mining Approach. *Expert Systems with Applications*, 23(2), 103–112.

Weir, T. (1999). Customer Loyalty and Personal Privacy: A Conflict? *Supermarket Business*, 54(9), 1.

Wheaton, J. (1996). The Superiority of Tree Analysis over RFM: How it enhances regression. *DM News*, 21–23.

White, H. (1989). Learning in Artificial Neural Networks: A Statistical Perspective. *Neural Computation*, 1, 425–464.

White, H. (1992). *Artificial Neural Networks: Approximation and Learning Theory*. Cambridge, MA: Blackwell.

Whiting, R. (2001). Managing Customer Churn. *Information Week, Manhasset, NY*, May 14, 2001(837), 71.

Winer, B.J. (1971). *Statistical Principles in Experimental Design*. New York: McGraw-Hill.

Winer, R.S. (2001). A Framework for Customer Relationship Management. *California Management Review*, 43(4), 89–105.

Winters, P. (1993). Masses of Census Opportunities. *Marketing* (April 1), 23.

Witten, I. and Frank, E. (2000). *Data Mining: Practical Machine Learning Tools and Techniques with Java Implementations*. San Francisco, CA: Morgan Kaufmann.

Wolf, A. (2006). Seeds of Change Bearing Fruit for Chain. *Twice: This Week in Consumer Electronics*, 21(14), 4.

Wolpert, D. (1992). Stacked Generalization. *Neural Networks*, 5(2), 241–259.

Wong, B., Bodnovich, T., and Selvi, Y. (1995). A Bibliography of Neural Network Business Applications Research: 1988–September 1994. *Expert Systems: The International Journal of Knowledge Engineering*, 12(3), 253–262.

Wooldridge, J. (2002). *Econometric Analysis of Cross Section and Panel Data*. Cambridge, MA: MIT.

Wright, A. (2002). Technology as an Enabler of the Global Branding of Retail Services. *Journal of International Marketing*, 10(2), 83–98.

Yan, L., Miller, D.J., Mozer, M.C., and Wolniewicz, R. (2001). Improving Prediction of Customer Behavior in Nonstationary Environments, *UCNN 01 International Joint Conference*, pp. 2258–2260: Neural Networks.

Yan, X., Zhang, C., and Zhang, S. (2005). ARMGA: Identifying Interesting Association Rules with Genetic Algorithms. *Applied Artificial Intelligence*, 19(7), 677–689.

Yang, A. (2004). How to Develop New Approaches to RFM Segmentation. *Journal of Targeting, Measurement and Analysis for Marketing*, 13(1), 50–60.

Yang, C. (2002). AOL Is Relearning Its ABCs. *Business Week*(October 14), 52.

Yang, J. and Honavar, V. (1998). Feature Subset Selection Using a Genetic Algorithm. In H.M.a.H. Liu (Ed.), *Feature Extraction, Construction and Subset Selection: A Data Mining Perspective*. (p. Chapter 8). Norwell, MA: Kluwer.

Yao, J., Teng, N., Poh, T., and Tan, C. (1998). Forecasting and Analysis of Marketing Data Using Neural Networks. *Journal of Information Science and Engineering*, 14(4), 843–862.

Yates, S. (2001). *Integrating Financial Channels*. Cambridge, MA: The Forrester Report, Forrester Research.

Yi, Y. and Jeon, H. (2003). Effects of Loyalty Programs on Value Perception, Program Loyalty, and Brand Loyalty. *Journal of the Academy of Marketing Science*, 31(3), 229–240.

Ying, Y., Feinberg, F.M., and Wedel, M. (2006). Leveraging Missing Ratings to Improve Online Recommendation Systems. *Journal of Marketing Research*, 43(3), 355–365.

Young, D. (2000). They Love Me, They Love Me Not. *Wireless Review*, 17(21), 38–42.

Yu, A.J. and Dayan, P. (2005). Inference, Attention, and Decision in a Bayesian Neural Architecture. In L.K. Saul, Y. Weiss, and L. Bottou (Eds.), *Advances in Neural Information Processing Systems 17*. Cambridge, MA: MIT.

Zahavi, J. and Levin, N. (1997). Applying Neural Computing to Target Marketing. *Journal of Direct Marketing*, 11(1), 5–22.

Zahay, D. and Griffin, A. (2004). Customer Learning Processes, Strategy, Selection, and Performance in Business-to-Business Service Firms. *Decision Sciences*, 35(2), 169–203.

Zeithaml., V.A. (2000). Service Quality, Profitability, and the Economic Worth of Customers: What We Know and What We Need to Learn. *Journal of the Academy of Marketing Science*, 28(1), 67–85.

Zeithaml, V.A., Rust, R.T., and Lemon, K.N. (2001). The Customer Pyramid: Creating and Serving Profitable Customers. *California Management Review*, 43(4), 118–142.

Zettelmeyer, F. (2000). Expanding to the Internet: Pricing and Communications Strategies When Firms Compete on Multiple Channels. *Journal of Marketing Research*, 37(8), 292–308.

Zhang, J. and Krishnamurthi, L. (2004). Customizing Promotions in Online Stores. *Marketing Science*, 23(4), 561–578.

Zhang, J. and Wedel, M. (2007). *The Effectiveness of Customized Promotions in Online and Offline Stores*, Working Paper: College Park, MD: Robert H. Smith School of Business, University of Maryland.

Zhang, J. (2006). *The Sound of Silence – Evidence of Observational Learning from the U.S. Kidney Market*, Working Paper. Cambridge, MA: MIT Sloan School.

Zhang, T. (2000). Association Rules, *Proceedings of 4th Pacific-Asia Conference, PADKK*, pp. 245–256. Kyoto, Japan.

Zornes, A. (2004). Customer Data Integration: Market Review and Forecast for 2005–2006. http://www.dmreview.com/editorial/newsletter_archive. dfm?nl = bireport&issueid = 20160. Accessed July 27, 2007.

Zwick, D. and Dholakia, N. (2004). Whose Identity Is It Anyway? Consumer Representation in the Age of Database Marketing. *Journal of Macromarketing*, 24(1), 31–43.

Author Index

Subject Index